Communications in Computer and Information Science 3019

Rationale

The CCIS series is devoted to the publication of proceedings of computer science conferences. Its aim is to efficiently disseminate original research results in informatics in printed and electronic form. While the focus is on publication of peer-reviewed full papers presenting mature work, inclusion of reviewed short papers reporting on work in progress is welcome, too. Besides globally relevant meetings with internationally representative program committees guaranteeing a strict peer-reviewing and paper selection process, conferences run by societies or of high regional or national relevance are also considered for publication.

Topics

The topical scope of CCIS spans the entire spectrum of informatics ranging from foundational topics in the theory of computing to information and communications science and technology and a broad variety of interdisciplinary application fields.

Information for Volume Editors and Authors

Publication in CCIS is free of charge. No royalties are paid, however, we offer registered conference participants temporary free access to the online version of the conference proceedings on SpringerLink (http://link.springer.com) by means of an http referrer from the conference website and/or a number of complimentary printed copies, as specified in the official acceptance email of the event.

CCIS proceedings can be published in time for distribution at conferences or as post-proceedings, and delivered in the form of printed books and/or electronically as USBs and/or e-content licenses for accessing proceedings at SpringerLink. Furthermore, CCIS proceedings are included in the CCIS electronic book series hosted in the SpringerLink digital library at http://link.springer.com/bookseries/7899. Conferences publishing in CCIS are allowed to use our online conference service (Meteor) for managing the whole proceedings lifecycle (from submission and reviewing to preparing for publication) free of charge.

Publication process

The language of publication is exclusively English. Authors publishing in CCIS have to sign the Springer CCIS copyright transfer form, however, they are free to use their material published in CCIS for substantially changed, more elaborate subsequent publications elsewhere. For the preparation of the camera-ready papers/files, authors have to strictly adhere to the Springer CCIS Authors' Instructions and are strongly encouraged to use the CCIS LaTeX style files or templates.

Abstracting/Indexing

CCIS is abstracted/indexed in DBLP, Google Scholar, EI-Compendex, Mathematical Reviews, SCImago, Scopus. CCIS volumes are also submitted for the inclusion in ISI Proceedings.

How to start

To start the evaluation of your proposal for inclusion in the CCIS series, please send an e-mail to ccis@springer.com

Barbara Vantaggi · Giulianella Coletti ·
Thierry Denoeux · Anne Laurent ·
Davide Petturiti · Enrique Miranda ·
Jesús Medina · Bernadette Bouchon-Meunier ·
Ronald R. Yager
Editors

Information Processing and Management of Uncertainty in Knowledge-Based Systems

21st International Conference, IPMU 2026
Rome, Italy, June 15–19, 2026
Proceedings, Part I

Springer

Editors
Barbara Vantaggi
Sapienza University of Rome
Rome, Italy

Giulianella Coletti
University of Perugia
Perugia, Italy

Thierry Denoeux
Université de Technologie de Compiègne
Compiègne, France

Anne Laurent
LIRMM Université de Montpellier
Montpellier, France

Davide Petturiti
Sapienza University of Rome
Rome, Italy

Enrique Miranda
University of Oviedo
Oviedo, Spain

Jesús Medina
University of Cádiz
Cádiz, Spain

Bernadette Bouchon-Meunier
Sorbonne Université
Paris, France

Ronald R. Yager
Iona College
New Rochelle, NY, USA

ISSN 1865-0929 ISSN 1865-0937 (electronic)
Communications in Computer and Information Science
ISBN 978-3-032-28993-3 ISBN 978-3-032-28994-0 (eBook)
https://doi.org/10.1007/978-3-032-28994-0

This Springer imprint is published by the registered company Springer Nature Switzerland AG
The registered company address is: Gewerbestrasse 11, 6330 Cham, Switzerland

Preface

We are very pleased to present the proceedings of the 21st International Conference on Information Processing and Management of Uncertainty in Knowledge-Based Systems (IPMU 2026). The conference was held on June 15–19, 2026, at the Faculty of Economics of Sapienza University of Rome in Rome, Italy.

The IPMU conference is held every two years and aims to bring together scientists working on methods for the management of uncertainty and aggregation of information in intelligent systems. Since 1986, the IPMU conference has been providing a forum for the exchange of ideas between theoreticians and practitioners working in these areas and related fields.

In addition to many contributed scientific papers, the conference has attracted prominent plenary speakers, including Nobel Prize winners Kenneth Arrow, Daniel Kahneman, and Ilya Prigogine. A very important feature of the conference is the presentation of the Kampé de Fériet Award for outstanding contributions to the management of uncertain and imprecise information. Past winners of this prestigious award include Lotfi A. Zadeh (1992), Ilya Prigogine (1994), Toshiro Terano (1996), Kenneth Arrow (1998), Richard Jeffrey (2000), Arthur Dempster (2002), Janos Aczel (2004), Daniel Kahneman (2006), Enric Trillas (2008), James Bezdek (2010), Michio Sugeno (2012), Vladimir N. Vapnik (2014), Joseph Halpern (2016), Glenn Shafer (2018), Barbara Tversky (2020), Tomaso Poggio (2022), and Judea Pearl (2024). In this 2026 edition, the recipient of the Kampé de Fériet Award was Robert Kowalski (Imperial College London, UK) for his seminal work on human-oriented models of computing and computational models of human thinking. We warmly congratulate him.

The IPMU 2026 conference offered a rich and comprehensive scientific program. It featured four plenary talks delivered, in addition to Robert Kowalski, by Luc De Raedt (KU Leuven, Belgium and Örebro University, Sweden), María Ángeles Gil (University of Oviedo, Spain), and Marco Zaffalon (IDSIA, Switzerland).

The 2026 edition of IPMU celebrated the 40th anniversary of the first edition of the conference, which took place in Paris, France. Rome was a particularly fitting choice for this special occasion, as Rome and Paris have been exclusively and reciprocally twinned since April 1956.

The IPMU 2026 program consisted of 183 presentations divided into 22 special sessions and a general track, authored by researchers from more than 25 countries.

For IPMU 2026, the authors had the option to submit either regular papers or short papers. These three proceedings volumes contain 111 accepted regular papers. All accepted papers underwent a thorough single-blind review process and were evaluated by at least two reviewers, and in most cases by three. Furthermore, all papers were examined by the program chairs. The reviewing process respected the usual conflict-of-interest standards, so that all papers received multiple independent evaluations.

Organizing a conference would not be possible without the assistance, dedication, and support of many people and institutions, and IPMU 2026 was no exception. We are particularly grateful to the organizers of special sessions. Such sessions, dedicated to a variety of topics and organized by experts, have always been a characteristic feature of IPMU conferences.

We would like to acknowledge all members of the IPMU 2026 Program Committee, as well as the additional reviewers who played an essential role in the reviewing process, ensuring a high-quality conference. We thank them sincerely for their work and commitment. We gratefully acknowledge the technical co-sponsorship of the IEEE Computational Intelligence Society and the European Society for Fuzzy Logic and Technology (EUSFLAT).

We also acknowledge the support from Sapienza University of Rome, and in particular from the Faculty of Economics and the Department of Methods and Models for Economics, Territory and Finance; from the Rome Technopole Foundation; and from the Springer team who managed the publication of these proceedings. We want to thank EUSFLAT for funding five student grants; the *International Journal of Approximate Reasoning* (– Elsevier) for funding a best paper award; and Springer for funding a best paper award. Our very special and greatest gratitude goes to the authors who submitted the results of their work and presented them at the conference. Without them, this conference would not have been possible.

We hope that these proceedings provide readers with multiple ideas leading to numerous research activities, significant publications, and stimulating presentations at future IPMU conferences.

Barbara Vantaggi
Giulianella Coletti
Thierry Denoeux
Anne Laurent
Davide Petturiti
Enrique Miranda
Jesús Medina
Bernadette Bouchon-Meunier
Ronald R. Yager

Organization

General Chair

Barbara Vantaggi	Sapienza University of Rome, Italy

Program Committee Chairs

Giulanella Coletti	University of Perugia, Italy
Thierry Denoeux	Université de Tecnologie de Compiègne, France
Anne Laurent	LIRMM, Université de Montpellier, France
Davide Petturiti	Sapienza University of Rome, Italy

Publication Chair

Enrique Miranda	University of Oviedo, Spain

Special Session Chair

Jesús Medina	University of Cádiz, Spain

Social Media Chairs

Andrea Cinfrignini	University of Siena, Italy
Silvia Lorenzini	University of Perugia, Italy

Advisory Board

João Paulo Carvalho	Instituto Superior Técnico, Universidade de Lisboa, Portugal
Davide Ciucci	University of Milano-Bicocca, Italy
Giulianella Coletti	University of Perugia, Italy
Miguel Delgado	University of Granada, Spain
Mario Fedrizzi	University of Trento, Italy

Laurent Foulloy	Université de Savoie, France
Salvatore Greco	University of Catania, Italy
Julio Gutierrez-Rios	Polytechnic University of Madrid, Spain
Eyke Hüllermeier	Ludwig Maximilians University, Germany
Uzay Kaymak	Eindhoven University of Technology, The Netherlands
Anne Laurent	LIRMM, Université de Montpellier, France
Marie-Jeanne Lesot	Sorbonne University, France
Luis Magdalena	Polytechnic University of Madrid, Spain
Christophe Marsala	Sorbonne University, France
Benedetto Matarazzo	University of Catania, Italy
Jesús Medina Moreno	University of Cádiz, Spain
Manuel Ojeda-Aciego	University of Granada, Spain
Maria Rifqi	Université Panthéon-Assas, France
Lorenza Saitta	University of Eastern Piedmont, Italy
Olivier Strauss	LIRMM, Université de Montpellier, France
Enric Trillas	University of Oviedo, Spain
Llorenç Valverde	University of the Balearic Islands, Spain
José Luis Verdegay	University of Granada, Spain
Maria-Amparo Vila	University of Granada, Spain

Executive Directors

Bernadette Bouchon-Meunier	Sorbonne Université-CNRS, France
Ronald Yager	Iona University, USA

Program Committee

Rui Jorge Almeida	Maastricht University, The Netherlands
Nahla Ben Amor	Institut Supérieur de Gestion de Tunis, Tunisia
Isabelle Bloch	Sorbonne Université, France
Ulrich Bodenhofer	University of Applied Sciences Upper Austria, Austria
Gloria Bordogna	CNR, Italy
Andrea Capotorti	University of Perugia, Italy
Christer Carlsson	Åbo Akademi University, Finland
João Paulo Carvalho	Instituto Superior Técnico, Universidade de Lisboa, Portugal
Davide Ciucci	Università di Milano-Bicocca, Italy
Oscar Cordón	University of Granada, Spain

Maria Eugenia Cornejo Piñero	University of Cádiz, Spain
Keeley Crockett	Manchester Metropolitan University, UK
Bernard De Baets	Ghent University, Belgium
Marzieh Derakhshannia	University of Toulouse, France
Sébastien Destercke	Université de Technologie de Compiègne, France
Antonio Di Nola	University of Salerno, Italy
Scott Dick	University of Alberta, Canada
Ivana Dragovic	University of Belgrade, Serbia
Krzysztof Dyczkowski	Adam Mickiewicz University, Poland
Zied Elouedi	Institut Supérieur de Gestion de Tunis, Tunisia
Juan Carlos Figueroa-García	Universidad Distrital Francisco José de Caldas, Colombia
Lluis Godo	Artificial Intelligence Research Institute, Spain
Fernando Gomide	University of Campinas, Brasil
Uzay Kaymak	Eindhoven University of Technology, The Netherlands
Laszlo T. Koczy	Budapest University of Technology and Economics, Hungary
Rudolf Kruse	University of Magdeburg, Germany
Marie-Jeanne Lesot	Sorbonne University, France
Christophe Marsala	Sorbonne University, France
Trevor Martin	University of Bristol, UK
Jerry Mendel	University of Southern California, USA
Radko Mesiar	Slovak University of Technology in Bratislava, Slovak Republic
Javier Montero	Complutense University of Madrid, Spain
Ignacio Montes	University of Oviedo, Spain
Jacky Montmain	IMT Mines Alès, France
Serafín Moral	University of Granada, Spain
Amira Mouakher	University of Budapest, Hungary
Vilém Novák	University of Ostrava, Czech Republic
Hannu Nurmi	University of Turku, Finland
Dickson Owuor	Strathmore University, Kenya
David Pelta	University of Granada, Spain
Irina Perfilieva	University of Ostrava, Czech Republic
Frédéric Pichon	Université d'Artois, France
Olivier Pivert	IRISA-ENSSAT, France
Henri Prade	IRIT - CNRS
Raúl Pérez-Fernández	University of Oviedo, Spain
Barbara Pekala	University of Rzeszów, Poland
Benjamin Quost	University of Technology of Compiègne, France
Eloisa Ramírez Poussa	University of Cádiz, Spain

Marek Reformat	University of Alberta, Canada
Maria Rifqi	Université Panthéon-Assas, France
M. Dolores Ruiz	University of Cádiz, Spain
Thomas A. Runkler	Siemens AG, Germany
Daniel Sanchez	University of Granada, Spain
Giuseppe Sanfilippo	University of Palermo, Italy
Grégory Smits	IMT Atlantique, France
Martin Stepnicka	University of Ostrava, Czech Republic
Eulalia Szmidt	Polish Academy of Sciences, Poland
Andreja Tepavcevic	University of Novi Sad, Serbia
Matthias Troffaes	Durham University, UK
José Luis Verdegay	University of Granada, Spain
Paolo Vicig	University of Trieste, Italy
Susana Vieira	Universidade de Lisboa, Portugal

Additional Reviewers

Stefano Aguzzoli
Roberto G. Aragón
Sally Giuseppe Arcidiacono
Michal Baczynski
Paolo Baldi
David Barilla
Juan Baz
Akram Bensalem
Matteo Bianchi
Maria del Mar Bibiloni-Femenias
Henri Bollaert
Jana Borzová
Agustina Bouchet
Matteo Brunelli
Vittoria Bruni
Humberto Bustince
Marco Calautti
Antonio Calcagni
Andrés Cano
Andrea Campagner
Catrin Campbell-Moore
Giuseppe Caristi
Davide Cazzorla
Martine Ceberio
Fernando Chacón
William D. Chicaiza
Tiziana Ciano
Salvatore Corrente
Esther Anna Corsi
Anderson Cruz
Martina Dankova
Rocío de Andrés Calle
Wannes de Maeyer
Pasquale de Meo
Laura de Miguel
José Angel Díaz García
Francesco DiFatta
Anton Dolhopolov
Paweł Drygaś
Phuc Do
Jorge Elorza
Alexander Erreygers
Juan Manuel Escaño
Javier Fernández
Carlos Fernandez Basso
Raquel Fernández Peralta
Massimiliano Ferrara
Giuseppe Filippone
Tomasso Flaminio
Alberto Gaetano Valerio
Diego García Gil
Ramón García

Salvatore Greco
Przemyslaw Grzegorzewski
Zuzana Haniková
Piotr Helbin
Ondrej Hutník
Simon James
Gabriel Jaume Martin
Balasubramaniam Jayaram
Enol Junquera
Katarzyna Kaczmarek-Majer
Martin Kalina
Vladik Kreinovich
Konrad Kułakowksi
Gianmarco La Rosa
Dominique Laurent
David Lobo
Victor Lopes de Sousa
Salvador López Joya
Miguel López Pérez
Manuel Mancini
Brice Mayag
Jiri Mazurek
Arnau Mir Fuentes
Yacine Mokhtari
Samuel Molina Ruiz
Serafín Moral García
Andrea Morales Garzón
Kavit Nanavati
Serena Nicolazzo
David Nieto-Barba
Francisco José Ocaña
Manuel Ojeda-Hernández
Jonathan Okz
Bartolomé Ortiz
Bruno Antonio Pansera
José M. Pavía
Banu Pazar Varol
Graçaliz Pereira Dimuro
Boris Pérez Cañedo
Francisco Pérez Gámez
Sandro Preto
Nageswara Rao Vemuri
José María Rivas
Umberto Rivieccio
Jesús Rodríguez López
Maciej Romaniuk
Aleksandra Rutkowska
Mikel A. Serra-Moll
Luca Spada
Nik Stopar
Umberto Straccia
Marco Elio Tabacchi
Zdenko Takáč
Osamu Takahashi
Menelaos Tasiou
José Antonio Torné Zambrano
Leonardo Valera
Arthur Van Camp
Amanda Vidal
Binbin Xu
Nicolás Zumelzu

Web Chair

Domenico Vitulano — Sapienza University of Rome, Italy

Webmaster

Massimiliano Coppola — Sapienza University of Rome, Italy

Contents

Aggregation Theory

Aggregation Theory

Two-Sample Goodness-of-Fit Tests to a Location-Scale Family Using OWA-Based Skewness Coefficients

Marina Iturrate-Bobes(✉), Ignacio Montes, and Raúl Pérez-Fernández

Department of Statistics and O.R. and M.D., University of Oviedo, Oviedo, Spain
{iturratemarina,imontes,perezfernandez}@uniovi.es

Abstract. Aggregation theory offers different tools for combining multiple sources of information into a single summary measure. Among these, Ordered Weighted Averaging (OWA) functions have recently been employed to define skewness coefficients, which quantify the degree of asymmetry of a random variable. Because skewness coefficients are location-scale invariant, the proposed OWA-based skewness coefficients can be used to conduct two-sample tests of goodness-of-fit to both a known and unknown location-scale family. In this contribution, we introduce the corresponding test statistics, derive their asymptotic distribution, and evaluate the performance of the associated tests through Monte Carlo simulation.

Keywords: Skewness coefficient · OWA function · Goodness-of-fit · Location-scale family

1 Introduction

In the field of statistics, *goodness-of-fit* tests aim to assess whether a random variable follows a specific distribution based on a random sample drawn from it. Some prominent examples include goodness-of-fit tests to a fully specified distribution and goodness-of-fit tests to a location-scale family (such as tests of normality). This problem has been extended to two-sample goodness-of-fit tests, where the goal is to determine whether two random samples drawn from two (typically independent) random variables follow the same distribution. In this context, two-sample versions of the Anderson-Darling [13] and Kolmogorov-Smirnov [10,16] tests can be found in the literature.

From a seemingly different perspective, several authors, such as Oja [11], have studied *skewness coefficients*, which are used to quantify the degree of asymmetry of a random variable. Interestingly, these skewness coefficients may also be used to conduct goodness-of-fit tests to a location-scale family [3]. This approach has already been followed in [7], where goodness-of-fit tests to a location-scale family using a skewness coefficient based on OWA functions [18] were proposed. The present work extends this line of research to the two-sample case, where

B. Vantaggi et al. (Eds.): IPMU 2026, CCIS 3019, pp. 3–16, 2026.
https://doi.org/10.1007/978-3-032-28994-0_1

we address two different problems: (i) goodness-of-fit to a *known* location-scale family, and (ii) goodness-of-fit to an *unknown* location-scale family.

The rest of the contribution is organised as follows. After presenting some preliminaries in Sect. 2, we extend in Sect. 3 the one-sample goodness-of-fit tests to a location-scale family based on an OWA-based skewness coefficient [7] to the two-sample case, considering both cases in which the location-scale family is known and unknown. The performance of the presented tests is analysed in Sect. 4, where we carry out some experiments to evaluate their powers. Finally, we end with some conclusions in Sect. 5.

2 Preliminaries

Let $\mathcal{L}(\Omega, \mathcal{A}, P)$ be the set of real-valued random variables on a probability space $(\Omega, \mathcal{A}, P)$, $\mathcal{L}_1(\Omega, \mathcal{A}, P)$ be the set of absolutely continuous random variables on $(\Omega, \mathcal{A}, P)$, and $\mathcal{L}_2(\Omega, \mathcal{A}, P)$ be the set of absolutely continuous random variables on $(\Omega, \mathcal{A}, P)$ with strictly increasing cumulative distribution function on the preimage of the interval $]0,1[$ and twice differentiable. A random variable $X \in \mathcal{L}(\Omega, \mathcal{A}, P)$ is said to be symmetric with respect to a point of symmetry $t \in \mathbb{R}$ (which coincides with the mean and the median if the former exists and the latter is unique) if it holds that $P(X \geq t + x) = P(X \leq t - x)$ for any $x \in \mathbb{R}$. To quantify the degree of asymmetry of $X \in \mathcal{L}(\Omega, \mathcal{A}, P)$, the so-called *skewness coefficients* are used. These coefficients are real-valued functions on $\mathcal{L}(\Omega, \mathcal{A}, P)$ that fulfil the following axiomatic definition introduced by Oja [11].

Definition 1 **([11]).** *A function $\gamma : \mathcal{L}(\Omega, \mathcal{A}, P) \to \mathbb{R}$ is called a skewness coefficient if it satisfies the following axioms:*

O1. *$\gamma(X) = 0$ if X is symmetric.*
O2. *$\gamma(cX + d) = \gamma(X)$ for any $c, d \in \mathbb{R}$ with $c > 0$.*
O3. *$\gamma(-X) = -\gamma(X)$.*
O4. *$\gamma(X) \leq \gamma(Y)$ if $X \precsim Y$, meaning that X precedes Y in the convex transform order [15],* i.e., *$G^{-1}(F(x))$ is convex for any x in the support of X, where F and G are the cumulative distribution functions of X and Y, respectively.*

A positive value of γ identifies a right-skewed random variable, whereas a negative value indicates a left-skewed one. Moreover, axioms O2 and O3 imply O1, though the latter is stated separately to emphasize that any symmetric random variable has zero skewness.

In [5], Hinkley proposed a family of skewness coefficients based on the aggregation of population quantiles. For any $p \in]0, 0.5[$, this family is defined in terms of the quantiles $C_p(X), C_{0.5}(X)$ and $C_{1-p}(X)$ as follows $\gamma_p(X) = \frac{(C_{1-p}(X) - C_{0.5}(X)) - (C_{0.5}(X) - C_p(X))}{C_{1-p}(X) - C_p(X)}$. Within this family, prominent examples include Bowley's skewness coefficient [1], also known as *quartile skewness*, and the *octile skewness* [2], corresponding to $p = 1/4$ and $p = 1/8$, respectively. Moreover, a new family of skewness coefficients in which $k \in \mathbb{N}$ population quantiles are aggregated (taking as reference Hinkley's family) was proposed in a recent paper [7], as presented below.

Definition 2 ([7, Def.2]). *The function $\gamma : \mathcal{L}_1(\Omega, \mathcal{A}, P) \to \mathbb{R}$ is defined, for any $X \in \mathcal{L}_1(\Omega, \mathcal{A}, P)$, by:*

$$\gamma(X) = \frac{(\mathbf{v} - 2\mathbf{w} + \mathbf{v}^{\mathrm{r}})^T \mathbf{C_p}(X)}{(\mathbf{v} - \mathbf{v}^{\mathrm{r}})^T \mathbf{C_p}(X)} = \frac{\mathbf{a}^T \mathbf{C_p}(X)}{\mathbf{b}^T \mathbf{C_p}(X)},$$

where $\mathbf{C_p}(X)$ is a vector containing $k \in \mathbb{N}$ (with k odd) increasingly-ordered population quantiles of X, verifying that if $C_p(X) \in \mathbf{C_p}(X)$ for a given $p \in]0,1[$, then $C_{1-p}(X) \in \mathbf{C_p}(X)$ and $\mathbf{v}, \mathbf{v}^{\mathrm{r}}, \mathbf{w} \in \mathbb{R}^k$ are real-valued weight vectors such that:

- $\mathbf{v}$ *satisfies* $\mathbf{v}_i = 0$ *for any* $i \in \{1, \dots, \lceil k/2 \rceil\}$.
- $\mathbf{v}^{\mathrm{r}}$ *is the reversed vector of* $\mathbf{v}$, i.e., $\mathbf{v}^{\mathrm{r}}_i = \mathbf{v}_{k-i+1}$ *for all* $i \in \{1, \dots, k\}$.
- $\mathbf{w}$ *satisfies* $\mathbf{w}_{\lceil \frac{k}{2} \rceil} = 1$ *and* $\mathbf{w}_i = 0$ *for any* $i \neq \lceil k/2 \rceil$.

The family of coefficients introduced in Definition 2 is well-defined for any absolutely continuous random variable X (see [7, Prop. 1]). It is worth noting that this well-definedness result holds under a more general choice of weight vectors $\mathbf{v}, \mathbf{v}^{\mathrm{r}}, \mathbf{w}$ and $\mathbf{C_p}(X)$. In particular, it remains valid when the vector $\mathbf{v}$ is not symmetric, provided that its reverse $\mathbf{v}^{\mathrm{r}}$ dominates $\mathbf{v}$, *i.e.*, $\sum_{i=1}^{\ell} \mathbf{v}_i \leq \sum_{i=1}^{\ell} \mathbf{v}^{\mathrm{r}}_i$ for all $\ell \in \{1, \dots, \lfloor k/2 \rfloor\}$ and the vector $\mathbf{w}$ is symmetric, without requiring k to be odd.

It is shown in [7, Prop. 2] that γ in Definition 2 restricted to $\mathcal{L}_2(\Omega, \mathcal{A}, P)$ satisfies the axioms of Oja introduced in Definition 1 and, thus, defines a family of skewness coefficients. Given a random sample $\mathbf{X} = (\mathbf{X}_1, \dots, \mathbf{X}_n)^T$ of size $n \in \mathbb{N}$ drawn from $X \in \mathcal{L}_1(\Omega, \mathcal{A}, P)$, we may compute the sample version of the coefficient as $\hat{\gamma}(\mathbf{X}) = \frac{\mathbf{a}^T \widehat{\mathbf{C_p}}(\mathbf{X})}{\mathbf{b}^T \widehat{\mathbf{C_p}}(\mathbf{X})}$, where $\widehat{\mathbf{C_p}}(\mathbf{X})$ is the sample estimation of $\mathbf{C_p}(X)$ in terms of the order statistics $\widehat{\mathbf{C}_{\mathbf{p}_i}}(\mathbf{X}) = \mathbf{X}_{(\lceil n\mathbf{p}_i \rceil)}$ for any $i \in \{1, \dots, k\}$. Observe that $\hat{\gamma}(\mathbf{X})$ can be interpreted as a ratio of the sum of three OWA functions to the difference of two of these OWA functions, resulting in an OWA-based skewness coefficient. Note that a sufficient condition for the (almost sure) well-definedness of the sample version of the skewness coefficient [7, Prop. 2] is that the sample size $n \in \mathbb{N}$ satisfies $n \geq (\min_{i=1,\dots,k-1} \mathbf{p}_{i+1} - \mathbf{p}_i)^{-1}$. Moreover, it is shown in [7, Thm. 1] that, restricted to $\mathcal{L}_2(\Omega, \mathcal{A}, P)$, the sample version $\hat{\gamma}$ is asymptotically normal with known variance and it is both asymptotically unbiased and consistent. In particular, if f denotes the probability density function of $X \in \mathcal{L}_2(\Omega, \mathcal{A}, P)$, it holds that $T_{X,n} := \frac{\sqrt{n}\left(\hat{\gamma}(\mathbf{X}) - \gamma(X)\right)}{\tau_X} \xrightarrow{\mathcal{D}} \mathcal{N}(0,1)$, where $\xrightarrow{\mathcal{D}}$ indicates convergence in distribution and

$$\begin{aligned}\tau_X^2 = & \frac{4}{\left[(\mathbf{v}^T - \mathbf{v}^{\mathrm{r}^T})\mathbf{C_p}(X)\right]^4} \sum_{j=1}^{k} \sum_{i=1}^{k} \sigma_X^{ij} \big[\mathbf{v}_i(\mathbf{w}^T - \mathbf{v}^{\mathrm{r}^T}) + \mathbf{v}^{\mathrm{r}}_i(\mathbf{v}^T - \mathbf{w}^T) \\ & + \mathbf{w}_i(\mathbf{v}^{\mathrm{r}^T} - \mathbf{v}^T)\big]\mathbf{C_p}(X) \cdot \big[\mathbf{v}_j(\mathbf{w}^T - \mathbf{v}^{\mathrm{r}^T}) + \mathbf{v}^{\mathrm{r}}_j(\mathbf{v}^T - \mathbf{w}^T) \\ & + \mathbf{w}_j(\mathbf{v}^{\mathrm{r}^T} - \mathbf{v}^T)\big]\mathbf{C_p}(X), \end{aligned} \tag{1}$$

for any $i, j \in \{1, \dots, k\}$ with $\sigma_X^{ij} = \frac{\min\{\mathbf{p}_i, \mathbf{p}_j\}(1 - \max\{\mathbf{p}_i, \mathbf{p}_j\})}{f(\mathbf{C}_{\mathbf{p}_i}(X)) f(\mathbf{C}_{\mathbf{p}_j}(X))}$.

3 Two Sample Goodness-of-Fit Tests to a Location-Scale Family

Given a random sample $\mathbf{X} = (\mathbf{X}_1, \ldots, \mathbf{X}_n)^T$ of size $n \in \mathbb{N}$ drawn from X and a random sample $\mathbf{Y} = (\mathbf{Y}_1, \ldots, \mathbf{Y}_m)^T$ of size $m \in \mathbb{N}$ drawn from Y, where $X, Y \in \mathcal{L}_2(\Omega, \mathcal{A}, P)$, a two-sample goodness-of-fit test can be used to assess whether the distributions of X and Y coincide. A location-scale family is a set of random variables closed under location and scale transformations. In particular, for any $X, Y \in \mathcal{L}_1(\Omega, \mathcal{A}, P)$ within the same location-scale family, it holds that $f_Y(x) = \frac{1}{d} f_X\left(\frac{x-c}{d}\right)$ for any $x \in \mathbb{R}$ where $c \in \mathbb{R}$ is the location parameter, $d \in \mathbb{R}^+$ is the scale parameter and f_X, f_Y are the corresponding density functions of X and Y, respectively. As a consequence, any location-scale family can be generated from a single density function (typically denoted as *standard distribution*) via location and scale transformations. Skewness coefficients are invariant within a location-scale family (see axiom O2 in Definition 1). Building on this idea, and extending the skewness-based one-sample goodness-of-fit test to a location-scale family proposed in [7], we introduce in the following a skewness-based two-sample goodness-of-fit test to location-scale families. With this objective in mind, we present a theorem showing the asymptotic distribution of an expression that combines two sample versions of skewness coefficients of the family introduced in Definition 2. From now on, we assume that $n = g(m)$ with $g : \mathbb{N} \to \mathbb{N}$ an increasing function such that $\lim_{m\to\infty} \frac{m}{g(m)} = \lambda \in]0, \infty[$. This simply means that both sample sizes grow to infinity at comparable rates.

Theorem 1. *Let $\mathbf{X} = (\mathbf{X}_1, \ldots, \mathbf{X}_n)^T$ and $\mathbf{Y} = (\mathbf{Y}_1, \ldots, \mathbf{Y}_m)^T$ be two independent random samples drawn from two independent random variables $X, Y \in \mathcal{L}_2(\Omega, \mathcal{A}, P)$. It holds that:*

$$\frac{(\hat{\gamma}(\mathbf{X}) - \gamma(X)) \pm (\hat{\gamma}(\mathbf{Y}) - \gamma(Y))}{\sqrt{\frac{\tau_X^2}{n} + \frac{\tau_Y^2}{m}}} \xrightarrow{\mathcal{D}} \mathcal{N}(0,1)\ ,$$

where τ_X^2 and τ_Y^2 are defined as in Eq. (1).

Sketch of Proof. Using the connection between $n = g(m)$ and m, it holds that

$$\frac{(\hat{\gamma}(\mathbf{X}) - \gamma(X)) \pm (\hat{\gamma}(\mathbf{Y}) - \gamma(Y))}{\sqrt{\frac{\tau_X^2}{n} + \frac{\tau_Y^2}{m}}} = \frac{(\hat{\gamma}(\mathbf{X}) - \gamma(X)) \pm (\hat{\gamma}(\mathbf{Y}) - \gamma(Y))}{\sqrt{\frac{\tau_X^2}{g(m)} + \frac{\tau_Y^2}{m}}} =: T_m\ ,$$

which depends on m, and can be rewritten as

$$T_m = \frac{\tau_X}{\sqrt{\tau_X^2 + \tau_Y^2 \frac{g(m)}{m}}} T_{X,g(m)} \pm \frac{\tau_Y}{\sqrt{\tau_X^2 \frac{m}{g(m)} + \tau_Y^2}} T_{Y,m}\ . \tag{2}$$

From [7, Thm. 1], *it follows that $T_{X,g(m)}, T_{Y,m} \xrightarrow{\mathcal{D}} \mathcal{N}(0,1)$. Moreover, it holds that $\sqrt{\tau_X^2 + \tau_Y^2 \frac{g(m)}{m}} \xrightarrow[m]{P} \sqrt{\tau_X^2 + \frac{\tau_Y^2}{\lambda}}$ and $\sqrt{\tau_X^2 \frac{m}{g(m)} + \tau_Y^2} \xrightarrow[m]{P} \sqrt{\lambda \tau_X^2 + \tau_Y^2}$,* *where* $\xrightarrow{P}$ *denotes convergence in probability. Therefore, applying* [17, Lemma 2.8] *(known as Slutsky's theorem) to both addends in Eq.* (2), *it holds that*

$$\frac{\tau_X\, T_{X,g(m)}}{\sqrt{\tau_X^2+\tau_Y^2\,\frac{g(m)}{m}}} \xrightarrow[m]{\mathcal{D}} \mathcal{N}\left(0, \frac{\tau_X}{\sqrt{\tau_X^2+\frac{\tau_Y^2}{\lambda}}}\right) \text{ and } \frac{\tau_Y\, T_{Y,m}}{\sqrt{\tau_X^2\,\frac{m}{g(m)}+\tau_Y^2}} \xrightarrow[m]{\mathcal{D}} \mathcal{N}\left(0, \frac{\tau_Y}{\sqrt{\lambda\tau_X^2+\tau_Y^2}}\right),$$

and given the independence of X and Y, we obtain the desired result. ■

The previous result not only shows the asymptotic normality of the sum or difference of the sample version of $\hat{\gamma}(\mathbf{X})\pm\hat{\gamma}(\mathbf{Y})$, but also indicates the asymptotic expected value is $\gamma(X) \pm \gamma(Y)$. The result above provides the foundation for constructing test statistics, as detailed in the upcoming subsections.

3.1 Goodness-of-Fit Test to a Known Location-Scale Family

Throughout this subsection, we aim to test the following hypotheses:

$$\begin{cases} H_0 : X \text{ and } Y \text{ belong to the same known location-scale family } \mathcal{F}_0\,, \\ H_1 : X \text{ and } Y \text{ do not belong to the same known location-scale family } \mathcal{F}_0\,. \end{cases} \tag{3}$$

With the aim of testing the hypotheses above, we need to define a test statistic that, ideally, has a completely specified distribution under the null hypothesis. Building on Theorem 1, we derive the following result, where we propose a test statistic which is distributed under the null hypothesis of Eq. (3) as a standard normal.

Theorem 2. *Let* $\mathbf{X} = (\mathbf{X}_1,\ldots,\mathbf{X}_n)^T$ *and* $\mathbf{Y} = (\mathbf{Y}_1,\ldots,\mathbf{Y}_m)^T$ *be two independent random samples drawn from two independent random variables* $X, Y \in \mathcal{L}_2(\Omega,\mathcal{A},P)$. *The test statistic* $\frac{\sqrt{n\,m}}{\sqrt{n+m}}\frac{\left(\hat{\gamma}(\mathbf{X})+\hat{\gamma}(\mathbf{Y})-2\,\gamma_{\mathcal{F}_0}\right)}{\tau_{\mathcal{F}_0}}$ *asymptotically follows a standard normal distribution under the null hypothesis of Eq.* (3), *where the asymptotic variance* $\tau^2_{\mathcal{F}_0}$ *coincides for any distribution belonging to the location-scale family* $\mathcal{F}_0$.

Sketch of Proof. Under the null hypothesis of Eq. (3), it holds that $\mathcal{F}_X = \mathcal{F}_Y = \mathcal{F}_0$. Consequently, due to the location-scale invariance property of the skewness coefficient γ, it follows that $\gamma(X) + \gamma(Y) = \gamma_{\mathcal{F}_0} + \gamma_{\mathcal{F}_0} = 2\,\gamma_{\mathcal{F}_0}$. Therefore, Theorem 1 applied to the sum yields the following asymptotic behaviour for the test statistic: $\frac{\hat{\gamma}(\mathbf{X})+\hat{\gamma}(\mathbf{Y})-2\,\gamma_{\mathcal{F}_0}}{\sqrt{\frac{\tau_X^2}{n}+\frac{\tau_Y^2}{m}}} \xrightarrow{\mathcal{D}} \mathcal{N}(0,1)$. Moreover, using again the location-scale invariance property of the skewness coefficient γ (see O2 in Definition 1) as well as of its sample version $\hat{\gamma}$, and the uniqueness of the convergence in Theorem 1, it directly follows that $\tau^2_{\mathcal{F}_0} = \tau^2_Z$ for any $Z \in \mathcal{F}_0$ under the null hypothesis in Eq. (3). In particular, it holds that $\tau_X = \tau_Y = \tau_{\mathcal{F}_0}$ under the null hypothesis and, thus,

$$\sqrt{\frac{\tau_X^2}{n}+\frac{\tau_Y^2}{m}} = \sqrt{\frac{\tau^2_{\mathcal{F}_0}}{n}+\frac{\tau^2_{\mathcal{F}_0}}{m}} = \sqrt{\frac{m\,\tau^2_{\mathcal{F}_0}+n\,\tau^2_{\mathcal{F}_0}}{n\,m}} = \tau_{\mathcal{F}_0}\sqrt{\frac{n+m}{n\,m}},$$

which leads to the desired result. ■

According to the previous result, we may construct the rejection region of the two sample goodness-of-fit test to a known location-scale family $\mathcal{F}_0$ for two independent random variables at a significance level $\alpha \in]0,1[$ as follows:

$$\text{R.R.} = \left\{ (\mathbf{x}, \mathbf{y}) \in \mathbb{R}^{n+m} \;\middle|\; |\hat{\gamma}(\mathbf{x}) + \hat{\gamma}(\mathbf{y}) - 2\,\tau_{\mathcal{F}_0}| > \tau_{\mathcal{F}_0} \sqrt{\frac{n+m}{n\,m}} z_{1-\alpha/2} \right\},$$

where $z_{1-\alpha/2}$ is the $1 - \frac{\alpha}{2}$ quantile of the standard normal distribution.

3.2 Goodness-of-Fit Test to an Unknown Location-Scale Family

We may also perform goodness-of-fit tests to check whether two samples belong to the same location-scale family, even when it is unknown. In such case, we are not interested in testing whether the underlying location-scale family of two samples is a specific one, but to assess whether both samples are drawn from the same location-scale family. In that case, the hypotheses are similar to those stated before, but no information about the location-scale family is available:

$$\begin{cases} H_0 : X \text{ and } Y \text{ belong to the same location-scale family}, \\ H_1 : X \text{ and } Y \text{ do not belong to the same location-scale family}. \end{cases} \tag{4}$$

As a consequence of the lack of information about the location-scale family under the null hypothesis, a new test statistic is required. Taking Theorem 1 as a baseline again, it must be noted that $\mathcal{F}$ is unknown now and, thus, τ_X and τ_Y cannot be computed. To address this issue, given a random sample $\mathbf{X}$ of size $n \in \mathbb{N}$ drawn from a random variable X, we may estimate τ_X^2 as follows:

$$\begin{aligned} \hat{\tau}^2(\mathbf{X}) = {} & \frac{4}{\left[(\mathbf{v}^T - \mathbf{v}^{\mathrm{r}^T})\widehat{\mathbf{C}_{\mathbf{p}}}(\mathbf{X})\right]^4} \sum_{j=1}^{k} \sum_{i=1}^{k} \hat{\sigma}^{ij} \left[\mathbf{v}_i(\mathbf{w}^T - \mathbf{v}^{\mathrm{r}^T}) + \mathbf{v}_i^{\mathrm{r}}(\mathbf{v}^T - \mathbf{w}^T)\right. \\ & \left. + \mathbf{w}_i(\mathbf{v}^{\mathrm{r}^T} - \mathbf{v}^T)\right]\widehat{\mathbf{C}_{\mathbf{p}}}(\mathbf{X}) \cdot \left[\mathbf{v}_j(\mathbf{w}^T - \mathbf{v}^{\mathrm{r}^T}) + \mathbf{v}_j^{\mathrm{r}}(\mathbf{v}^T - \mathbf{w}^T)\right. \\ & \left. + \mathbf{w}_j(\mathbf{v}^{\mathrm{r}^T} - \mathbf{v}^T)\right]\widehat{\mathbf{C}_{\mathbf{p}}}(\mathbf{X}), \end{aligned} \tag{5}$$

where $\hat{\sigma}^{ij} = \frac{\min\{\mathbf{p}_i, \mathbf{p}_j\}(1 - \max\{\mathbf{p}_i, \mathbf{p}_j\})}{f_n(\widehat{\mathbf{C}_{\mathbf{p}_i}}(\mathbf{X})) f_n(\widehat{\mathbf{C}_{\mathbf{p}_j}}(\mathbf{X}))}$ for any $i, j \in \{1, \ldots, k\}$, with f_n the kernel-density estimation [4,12,14] of the probability density function f of X, being pointwisely estimated for any $x \in \mathbb{R}$ as $f_n(x) = \frac{1}{n\,h(n)} \sum_{i=1}^{n} K\left(\frac{x - \mathbf{x}_i}{h(n)}\right)$, with $K : \mathbb{R} \to \mathbb{R}$ and $h : \mathbb{N} \to \mathbb{R}$ chosen so that the estimator f_n is consistent and asymptotically unbiased[1]. Given a random sample $\mathbf{Y}$ of size $m \in \mathbb{N}$ drawn from Y, τ_Y^2 may be estimated analogously.

Next, we present a theorem concerning the distribution of the test statistic when performing the two-sample goodness-of-fit test to an unknown location-scale family. Note that substituting $\tau_{\mathcal{F}}$ by its corresponding estimation in the test

[1] Throughout this work, the Gaussian kernel K and the rule-of-thumb h bandwidth will be chosen.

statistic introduced in Theorem 2 is not enough for defining a test statistic for the two sample goodness-of-fit test to an unknown location-scale family, since $2\gamma_{\mathcal{F}}$ is unknown in that case. Therefore, the following theorem considers an alternative approach to defining the test statistic.

Theorem 3. *Let* $\mathbf{X} = (\mathbf{X}_1, \dots, \mathbf{X}_n)^T$ *and* $\mathbf{Y} = (\mathbf{Y}_1, \dots, \mathbf{Y}_m)^T$ *be two independent random samples drawn from two independent random variables* $X, Y \in \mathcal{L}_2(\Omega, \mathcal{A}, P)$*. The test statistic* $\frac{\hat{\gamma}(\mathbf{X})-\hat{\gamma}(\mathbf{Y})}{\sqrt{\frac{m\,\hat{\tau}^2(\mathbf{X})+n\,\hat{\tau}^2(\mathbf{Y})}{n\,m}}}$ *asymptotically follows a standard normal distribution under the null hypothesis of Eq.* (4).

Sketch of Proof. Following the same steps as in the proof of Theorem 1, it holds that $\frac{(\hat{\gamma}(\mathbf{X})-\gamma(X))\pm(\hat{\gamma}(\mathbf{Y})-\gamma(Y))}{\sqrt{\frac{\hat{\tau}^2(\mathbf{X})}{n}+\frac{\hat{\tau}^2(\mathbf{Y})}{m}}} = \frac{(\hat{\gamma}(\mathbf{X})-\gamma(X))\pm(\hat{\gamma}(\mathbf{Y})-\gamma(Y))}{\sqrt{\frac{\hat{\tau}^2(\mathbf{X})}{g(m)}+\frac{\hat{\tau}^2(\mathbf{Y})}{m}}}$ asymptotically follows a standard normal distribution by taking into account that $\hat{\tau}^2(\mathbf{X}) \xrightarrow[m]{P} \tau_X^2$ and, similarly, $\hat{\tau}^2(\mathbf{Y}) \xrightarrow[m]{P} \tau_Y^2$ (see the proof of [6, Thm. 3]). Consequently, the desired result holds under the null hypothesis of Eq. (4) by taking the difference and noting that $\gamma(X) = \gamma(Y)$ under the null hypothesis. ∎

As a consequence of the previous result, we may construct the rejection region of the two sample goodness-of-fit test to an unknown location-scale family for two independent random variables at a significance level $\alpha \in]0, 1[$ as follows:

$$\text{R.R.} = \left\{ (\mathbf{x}, \mathbf{y}) \in \mathbb{R}^{n+m} \;\middle|\; \left| \frac{\hat{\gamma}(\mathbf{x}) - \hat{\gamma}(\mathbf{y})}{\sqrt{m\,\hat{\tau}^2(\mathbf{x}) + n\,\hat{\tau}^2(\mathbf{y})}} \right| > \frac{z_{1-\alpha/2}}{\sqrt{n\,m}} \right\}.$$

4 Experimental Study

In the following, we present the results of the experimental study carried out to analyse the performance of the two-sample goodness-of-fit tests introduced in Eq. (2) based on the family of skewness coefficients. For this purpose, we analyse the power of the tests, which is computed using Monte Carlo simulation with 10^5 repetitions and significance level $\alpha = 0.05$. In Subsect. 4.1, we tackle the issue when the location-scale family $\mathcal{F}_0$ under the null hypothesis is known, whereas in Subsect. 4.2 we tackle the issue when no prior information on this family is available. In both scenarios, we fix $\mathbf{w} = (0, 0, 1, 0, 0)^T$ while we explore five choices for $\mathbf{v}$ (referred to as $\mathbf{v}^1$, $\mathbf{v}^2$, $\mathbf{v}^3$, $\mathbf{v}^4$ and $\mathbf{v}^5$, respectively), which are defined as $\mathbf{v} = \lambda\,(0, 0, 0, 1, 0)^T + (1-\lambda)\,(0, 0, 0, 0, 1)^T$, where $\lambda \in \{0, 1/4, 1/2, 3/4, 1\}$. We report the results of the power computation in Figs. 1–4, which are all organised as a 4×4 grid of subfigures, with the subfigure corresponding to the scenario(s) under the null hypothesis highlighted in light green. In these layouts, the rows and columns are associated with the normal, uniform, (shifted) exponential and

Cauchy distributions on their standard form[2]. The rows correspond to the underlying distribution of the sample $\mathbf{X}$ drawn from X while the columns correspond to that of $\mathbf{Y}$ drawn from Y. The sample size of $\mathbf{X}$ is fixed at $n = 100$ whereas the sample size of $\mathbf{Y}$ is varied over $m \in \{10, 20, 100, 200\}$, for which different colours and sizes of the points are used. Moreover, the black horizontal line represents the significance level $\alpha = 0.05$ at which the tests are expected to remain under the null hypothesis.

4.1 Goodness-of Fit Test to a Known Location-Scale Family

Throughout this subsection, we explore the performance of the goodness-of-fit tests when the location-scale family under the null hypothesis is known (see Eq. (3)). In particular, we test for normality, uniformity and (shifted) exponential distribution under the scenarios detailed above.

Goodness-of-Fit to the Normal Distribution. Given $\mathcal{F}_0$ the normal location-scale family, it is expected that the two-sample goodness-of-fit tests exhibit low powers when both samples $\mathbf{X}$ and $\mathbf{Y}$ are drawn from the normal distribution. Otherwise, large values for the powers should be obtained. Figure 1 shows the results of the experiments when testing for normality, in which we observe that powers on the subfigure at the first row and first column (in which $\mathbf{X}$ and $\mathbf{Y}$ are both drawn from the normal distribution) are close to the significance level $\alpha = 0.05$ as expected. Nevertheless, a similar behaviour is observed when the samples involved in the tests are drawn from all two-distribution combinations of normal, uniform and Cauchy distributions, except for the situation in which $\mathbf{X}$ and $\mathbf{Y}$ are both drawn from the Cauchy distribution. This is due to the fact that the three distributions are symmetric, leading to a value of all skewness coefficients of zero (axiom O1 in Definition 1). It must be noted that, in other cases, powers tend to increase as the sample size m increases, which is consistent with the asymptotic distribution of the test statistic detailed in Theorem 2. Moreover, if we compare the performance of the tests in terms of the weight vector $\mathbf{v}$, we observe that the tests exhibit increasing power from $\mathbf{v}^1$ to $\mathbf{v}^5$ in general. Concerning the exponential distribution (third row and third column), we observe large powers, attaining the highest values when both samples are drawn from the exponential distribution since the values of both skewness coefficients are different from that of the distribution under the null hypothesis. Lastly, one should note that the tests exhibit a remarkable behaviour when both samples are drawn from the Cauchy distribution, as there is no consistent increase in power with the sample size and the performance of the test is rather similar across the five choices of $\mathbf{v}$. Furthermore, interchanging $\mathbf{X}$ and $\mathbf{Y}$ generally yields a similar behaviour.

[2] The parameters of the distributions are irrelevant, as they are associated with location and scale and skewness coefficients are invariant under such transformations.

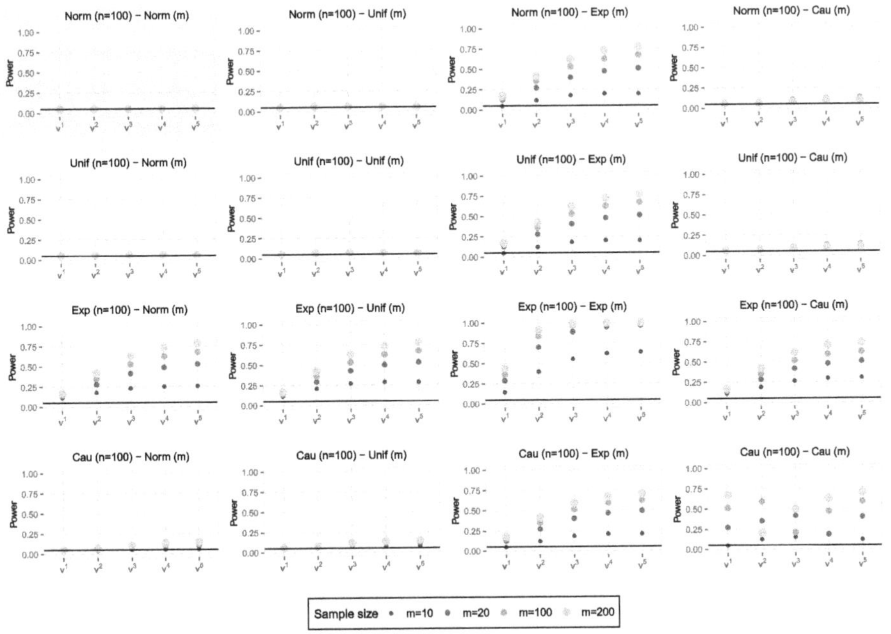

Fig. 1. Power of the two-sample goodness-of-fit tests to the normal distribution.

Goodness-of-Fit to the Uniform Distribution. Let $\mathcal{F}_0$ be now the uniform location-scale family. It is expected that powers remain close to the significance level $\alpha = 0.05$ whenever both samples $\mathbf{X}$ and $\mathbf{Y}$ are drawn from the uniform distribution, *i.e.*, in the subfigure at the second row and second column. However, after a quick glance at Fig. 1 (where normality tests are conducted) and Fig. 2 (where goodness-of-fit tests to the uniform distribution are conducted), the similarity between them stands out clearly, including the observed symmetry with respect to the exchange of $\mathbf{X}$ and $\mathbf{Y}$. More specifically, it is easy to see that the tests do not only exhibit low powers under the null hypothesis (as expected), but also under the alternative hypothesis (not expected) whenever the samples $\mathbf{X}$ and $\mathbf{Y}$ are drawn from normal, uniform and Cauchy distributions (except the case where both are drawn from the Cauchy distribution).

Goodness-of-Fit to the (Shifted) Exponential Distribution. Lastly, we take $\mathcal{F}_0$ as the (shifted) exponential location-scale family and present the results of these experiments in Fig. 3, where we observe a more favourable performance of the tests compared to that when testing for normality or uniformity. This is due to the fact that the (shifted) exponential distribution is the only distribution among those considered (normal, uniform and Cauchy distributions) for which the skewness coefficient is nonzero. In particular, powers remain close to the significance level $\alpha = 0.05$ only when the null hypothesis holds, *i.e.*, when both samples $\mathbf{X}$ and $\mathbf{Y}$ are drawn from the (shifted) exponential distribution, corre-

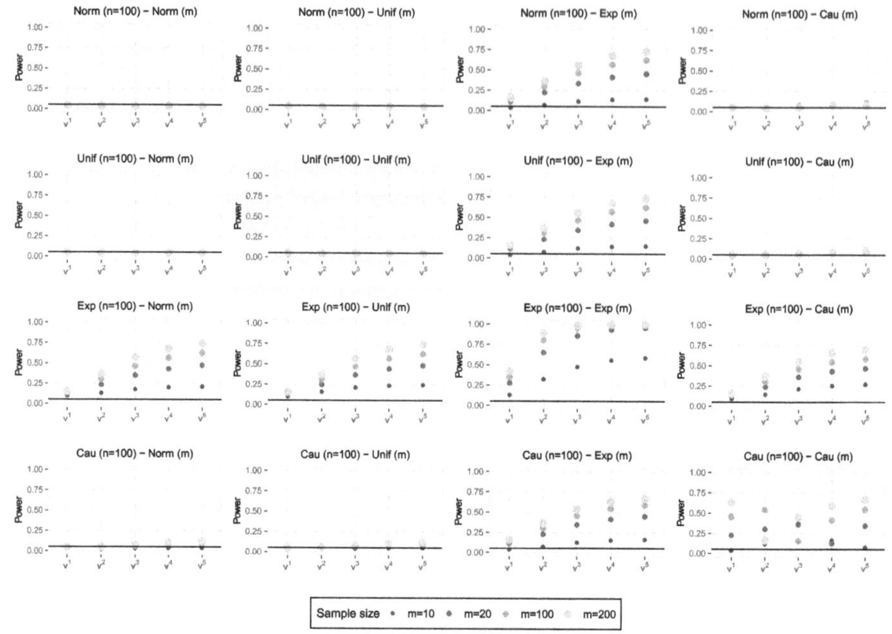

Fig. 2. Power of the two-sample goodness-of-fit tests to the uniform distribution.

sponding to the subfigure at the third row and third column. Otherwise, the tests exhibit large powers as expected, increasing with larger sample size m and when more weight of $\mathbf{v}$ is assigned to the extreme values. Also, under the alternative hypothesis, it must be noted that lower powers are observed when the (shifted) exponential distribution is involved in the generation of any of the samples $\mathbf{X}$ or $\mathbf{Y}$, *i.e.*, any subfigure at the third row or at the third column; whereas the powers at the first, second and fourth rows are comparable, except the case in which both samples $\mathbf{X}$ and $\mathbf{Y}$ are drawn from the Cauchy distribution, which exhibits an extraordinary performance again.

4.2 Goodness-of-Fit Test to an Unknown Location-Scale Family

In the subsequent subsection, we aim to analyse the performance of the goodness-of-fit tests with the hypotheses stated in Eq. (4), *i.e.*, when no location-scale family under the null hypothesis is specified. In that case, low powers are expected when both samples $\mathbf{X}$ and $\mathbf{Y}$ are drawn from the same location-scale family, regardless of the distribution itself. On the one side, the results presented in Fig. 4 support this fact, as we can observe from the subfigures highlighted in light green. However, besides these four subfigures, we also observe low powers when the two samples involved come from random variables for which the skewness coefficient takes the same value but are not necessarily drawn from the same distribution *i.e.*, when both $\mathbf{X}$ and $\mathbf{Y}$ are drawn from either the normal, uniform

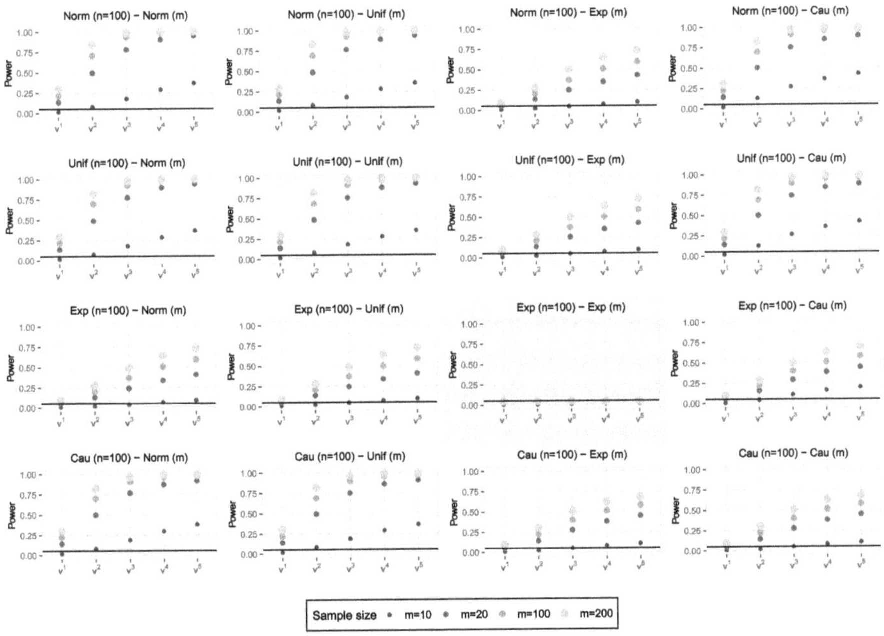

Fig. 3. Power of the two-sample goodness-of-fit tests to the (shifted) exponential distribution.

or Cauchy distributions. This is specially noticeable when dealing with samples from the normal and uniform distributions, where powers remain close to the significance level α for all sample sizes m and weight vectors $\mathbf{v}$. On the other side, whenever exactly one of $\mathbf{X}$ or $\mathbf{Y}$ is drawn from the exponential distribution, the tests exhibit higher powers, increasing as the sample size m grows and as more weight of $\mathbf{v}$ is assigned to the extreme values. Moreover, as mentioned earlier, we can observe a certain symmetry with respect to the exchange of $\mathbf{X}$ and $\mathbf{Y}$, except for the combination of the Cauchy and exponential distributions, where lower powers are obtained when $\mathbf{X}$ is drawn from the Cauchy distribution.

4.3 Discussion

Based on the presented results, we conclude that the tests successfully maintain the significance level $\alpha = 0.05$ under the null hypothesis for any sample size m and weight vector $\mathbf{v}$ when assessing goodness-of-fit to both a known and unknown location-scale family. Unfortunately, in both scenarios, the tests have difficulty distinguishing location-scale families whenever the skewness coefficient takes the same value, *e.g.*, for the symmetric distributions in which the skewness coefficient is zero. For this reason, the performance of the tests when testing for normality and for uniformity is rather similar, due to the symmetry of both normal and uniform distributions, which makes the test statistic in Theorem 2 differ only in the asymptotic variance of $\frac{\sqrt{n\,m}}{\sqrt{n+m}}\left(\hat{\gamma}(\mathbf{X}) + \hat{\gamma}\,(\mathbf{Y})\right)$. However, as shown in

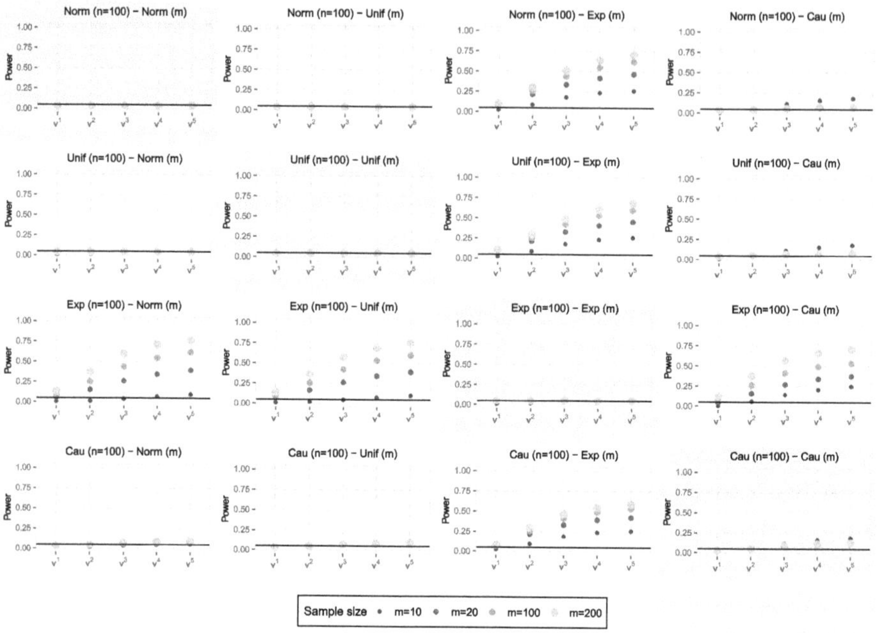

Fig. 4. Power of the two-sample goodness-of-fit tests to an unknown location-scale family.

Table 1, this difference is minor for all the considered choices of $\mathbf{v}$. Also, the performance of the tests is rather similar for the normal, uniform and Cauchy distributions when testing for the (shifted) exponential distribution (leading to a good behaviour in this setting since the tests exhibit large powers) or for an unknown location-scale family. A possible approach to solve this issue would involve combining skewness with additional statistical measures such as kurtosis, as proposed by Jarque and Bera for normality testing [8,9]. This approach would allow distributions with identical skewness (*e.g.*, symmetric distributions) to be easily distinguished. On the contrary, when the location-scale family under the null hypothesis and the samples involved in the tests differ in their skewness coefficient, the performance of the tests is more accurate under the alternative hypothesis as it can be observed when testing for the (shifted) exponential distribution or whenever a sample from this distribution for all three other cases. With regard to the Cauchy distribution (for which the tests exhibit an extraor-

Table 1. Asymptotic standard deviation $\tau_{\mathcal{F}}$ for different location-scale families.

Distribution	$\mathbf{v} = \mathbf{v}^1$	$\mathbf{v} = \mathbf{v}^2$	$\mathbf{v} = \mathbf{v}^3$	$\mathbf{v} = \mathbf{v}^4$	$\mathbf{v} = \mathbf{v}^5$
Normal	1.6958	1.3316	1.1911	1.1486	1.1481
Uniform	1.7321	1.4283	1.2910	1.2372	1.2247

dinary performance), it should be noted that (i) its first and second moments are not defined and (ii) as mentioned in [6], the uniform discretization employed by the `density()` function in the statistical software R to estimate the probability density function may lead to erroneous results, since the Cauchy distribution typically exhibits highly dispersed values. These factors may partially explain the observed performance of the tests in this setting.

Regarding the choice of the weight vector $\mathbf{v}$, although it is practically irrelevant under the null hypothesis, it must be noted that the more weight is concentrated in the extreme, the better the performance of the test is under the alternative hypothesis, as it more easily detects differences in symmetry and, thus, in distribution. Moreover, an evident better performance of the test is observed when dealing with samples with large sample size, in accordance with the asymptotic distribution of the test statistics detailed in Theorems 2 and 3.

5 Conclusions

In this contribution, we have taken as reference the family of skewness coefficients introduced in [6], which is based on Hinkley's class of coefficients [5] and compliant with the axiomatic definition of Oja for a measure of skewness [11], to construct several statistical tests. In particular, we have addressed two-sample goodness-of-fit tests to a location-scale family using two different approaches: when the null hypothesis specifies the location-scale family, and when it does not. For this purpose, we began by presenting in Theorem 1 the asymptotic distribution of the sum and difference of the sample version of the skewness coefficients computed on two independent samples. Afterwards, we used this result for defining the test statistics for performing goodness-of-fit tests in case the location-scale family is known (see Theorem 2) and unknown (see Theorem 3). The conducted experiments show that the powers of the tests remain at the significance level α under the null hypothesis, however they fail at distinguishing location-scale families when both have the same value of the skewness coefficient. Moreover, regarding the choice of $\mathbf{v}$, we suggest using weight vectors in which the weight is placed on the right extreme, as they show the greater power under the alternative hypothesis.

As future work, we plan to introduce a statistical measure that allows us to distinguish between random variables with the same value of skewness. For instance, following Jarque and Bera [8,9], we propose to incorporate a measure of kurtosis into the test statistics for goodness-of-fit.

Acknowledgments. This contribution is part of grant PID2022-140585NB-I00 funded by MICIU/AEI/10.13039/501100011033 and "FEDER/UE".

Disclosure of Interests. The authors have no competing interests to declare that are relevant to the content of this article.

References

1. Bowley, A.L.: Elements of Statistics, 4th edn. Scribner (1920)
2. Brys, G., Hubert, M., Struyf, A.: A comparison of some new measures of skewness. In: Developments in Robust Statistics, pp. 98–113 (2003)
3. Brys, G., Hubert, M., Struyf, A.: A robust measure of skewness. J. Comput. Graph. Stat. **13**(4), 996–1017 (2004)
4. Fix, E., Hodges, J.L.: Nonparametric discrimination: Consistency properties. Tech. Rep. Report 11, USAF School of Aviation Medicine, Randolph Field, Texas (1951)
5. Hinkley, D.V.: On power transformations to symmetry. Biometrika **62**, 101–111 (1975)
6. Iturrate-Bobes, M., Montes, I., Pérez-Fernández, R.: Skewness coefficients based on L-statistics with applications in tests of symmetry. Submitted
7. Iturrate-Bobes, M., Montes, I., Pérez-Fernández, R.: Goodness-of-fit tests to location-scale families based on OWA functions. In: Baczyński, M., De Baets, B., Holčapek, M., Kreinovich, V., Medina, J. (eds.) Advances in Fuzzy Logic and Technology, pp. 53–65. Springer, Switzerland (2025)
8. Jarque, C.M., Bera, A.K.: Efficient tests for normality, homoscedasticity and serial independence of regression residuals. Econ. Lett. **6**(3), 255–259 (1980)
9. Jarque, C.M., Bera, A.K.: A test for normality of observations and regression residuals. Int. Stat. Rev. **55**(2), 163–172 (1980)
10. Kolmogorov, A.: Sulla determinazione empirica di una legge di distribuzione. Giornale dell'Istituto Italiano degli Attuari **4**, 83–91 (1933)
11. Oja, H.: On location, scale, skewness and kurtosis of univariate distributions. Scand. J. Stat. **8**, 154–168 (1981)
12. Parzen, E.: On estimation of a probability density function and mode. Ann. Math. Stat. **33**(3), 1065–1076 (1962)
13. Pettitt, A.N.: A two-sample Anderson-Darling rank statistic. Biometrika **63**(1), 161–168 (1976)
14. Rosenblatt, M.: Estimation of a probability density-function and mode. Ann. Math. Stat. **27**, 832–837 (1956)
15. Shaked, M., Shanthikumar, J.: Stochastic Orders. Springer, New York (2007)
16. Smirnov, N.: Table for estimating the goodness of fit of empirical distributions. Ann. Math. Stat. **19**(2), 279–281 (1948)
17. Van der Vaart, A.W.: Asymptotic statistics, vol. 3. Cambridge University Press (2000)
18. Yager, R.R.: On ordered weighted averaging aggregation operators in multicriteria decision making. IEEE Trans. Syst. Man Cybern. **18**(1), 183–190 (1988)

Asymptotic Confidence Intervals for a Skewness Parameter by Using OWA Functions

Marina Iturrate-Bobes(✉), Ignacio Montes, and Raúl Pérez-Fernández

Department of Statistics and O.R. and M.D., University of Oviedo, Oviedo, Spain
{iturratemarina,imontes,perezfernandez}@uniovi.es

Abstract. Ordered Weighted Averaging (OWA) functions are a prominent tool in aggregation theory and decision making for selecting a representative of a given list of values to be aggregated. From an apparently different field, skewness coefficients are often used in probability and statistics for quantifying the asymmetry of a probability distribution. Recently, a connection between both constructs has been made explicit by using OWA functions to define a family of skewness coefficients. In this work, we use this OWA-based family of skewness coefficients to develop a new method for constructing asymptotic confidence intervals for a skewness parameter within a location–scale–skewness family. The method is illustrated through a comprehensive case study for the (shifted) Weibull distribution. Theoretical results for this distribution together with an empirical study via Monte Carlo simulation are provided.

Keywords: OWA function · Skewness coefficient · Confidence interval · Weibull distribution

1 Introduction

Data analysts typically rely on a variety of descriptive measures such as measures of location, dispersion, skewness, and kurtosis to characterize different aspects of a probability distribution. In this work, we concentrate on measures of skewness, which quantify the extent to which a probability distribution departs from symmetry. Many classical authors, including Pearson [16], Charlier and Edgeworth [4,6], Yule [21], and Bowley [2], have introduced different skewness coefficients aimed at assessing and comparing the degree to which random variables are not symmetric. More recent works such as those by Hinkley [10] and by Brys, Hubert and Struyf [3] have proposed robust skewness coefficients. Other approaches propose to construct skewness coefficients by incorporating popular tools such as expectiles [5], L-moments [11] and OWA functions [12].

In the present work, we follow the latter approach and use OWA functions [20], which are an old acquaintance of aggregation theory [8], to build asymptotic confidence intervals for a skewness parameter within a location-scale-skewness family. This type of family of probability distributions was introduced by Oja [14] and accommodates several well-known distributions, being

B. Vantaggi et al. (Eds.): IPMU 2026, CCIS 3019, pp. 17–30, 2026.
https://doi.org/10.1007/978-3-032-28994-0_2

the (shifted) Weibull distribution one of the most prominent ones. Interestingly, within a location-scale-skewness family all distributions are comparable in terms of their skewness and, even more, most of the existing skewness orderings coincide (see, e.g., [1] and [13]).

The remainder of the paper is structured as follows. Firstly, some preliminaries are presented in Sect. 2. Next, the main results concerning how to construct confidence intervals for a skewness parameter within a location-scale-skewness family are developed in Sect. 3. We provide a case study for the Weibull distribution in Sect. 4, divided into a theoretical part (Subsect. 4.1) in which the necessary results concerning the Weibull distribution are presented and an empirical part (Subsect. 4.2) in which an experimental study via Monte Carlo simulation is carried out. We end with some conclusions and open problems in Sect. 5.

2 Preliminaries

Given a probability space $(\Omega, \mathcal{A}, P)$, we denote by $\mathcal{L}(\Omega, \mathcal{A}, P)$ the set of (real-valued) random variables on $(\Omega, \mathcal{A}, P)$ and by $\mathcal{L}'(\Omega, \mathcal{A}, P)$ the subset of random variables in $\mathcal{L}(\Omega, \mathcal{A}, P)$ that are absolutely continuous and whose cumulative distribution function is strictly increasing on the preimage of the interval $]0,1[$ and twice differentiable. Given $X \in \mathcal{L}(\Omega, \mathcal{A}, P)$, we denote by F_X and Q_X its cumulative distribution function and quantile function, respectively, and we use the notation $C_p(X)$ for the p quantile of X, that is, for $Q_X(p)$. Moreover, whenever X is absolutely continuous, f_X denotes its probability density function; when no confusion can occur, we will omit the subscript for the sake of simplicity. For any two random variables $X, Y \in \mathcal{L}(\Omega, \mathcal{A}, P)$, the convex order of van Zwet [19] intuitively represents whether X is not more strongly skew to the right than Y, denoted $X \precsim Y$, and is defined by $Q_Y(F_X(x))$ is convex on the support of X. An equivalent definition of $X \precsim Y$ is that, for any $a, b \in \mathbb{R}$ with $a > 0$, $F_X(x) - F_Y(ax+b)$ changes of sign (ignoring zeros) at most twice with the sequence of signs being positive to negative to positive [13].

The notion of skewness coefficient [14] allows us to quantify the skewness of a random variable and its associated probability distribution.

Definition 1 ([14]). *A skewness coefficient is a function* $\gamma : \mathcal{L}(\Omega, \mathcal{A}, P) \to \mathbb{R}$ *satisfying the following properties for all* $X, Y \in \mathcal{L}(\Omega, \mathcal{A}, P)$*:*

O1. $\gamma(X) = 0$ *if* X *is a symmetric random variable;*
O2. γ *is location scale invariant:* $\gamma(cX + d) = \gamma(X)$ *for any* $c \in \mathbb{R}^+$ *and* $d \in \mathbb{R}$*;*
O3. $\gamma(-X) = -\gamma(X)$*;*
O4. γ *preserves the convex transform order:* $\gamma(X) \leq \gamma(Y)$ *whenever* $X \precsim Y$*.*

Note that property O1 follows directly from properties O2 and O3, but it is kept within the definition to emphasize that any symmetric random variable X satisfies $\gamma(X) = 0$, as well as for historical reasons.

Many skewness coefficients have been studied in the literature. Here, we consider the following family of skewness coefficients, which as shown in [12,

Prop.1] is well-defined and, according to [12, Prop.2], fulfills the axioms of Oja when restricted to $\mathcal{L}'(\Omega, \mathcal{A}, P)$:

$$\gamma(X) := \frac{\mathbf{a}^T \mathbf{C_p}(X)}{\mathbf{b}^T \mathbf{C_p}(X)} = \frac{(\mathbf{v} - 2\mathbf{w} + \mathbf{v}^{\mathrm{r}})^T \mathbf{C_p}(X)}{(\mathbf{v} - \mathbf{v}^{\mathrm{r}})^T \mathbf{C_p}(X)}, \tag{1}$$

where $m \in \mathbb{N}$ is odd and

- $\mathbf{a} = \mathbf{v} - 2\mathbf{w} + \mathbf{v}^{\mathrm{r}}$ and $\mathbf{b} = \mathbf{v} - \mathbf{v}^{\mathrm{r}}$ with $\mathbf{v}$, $\mathbf{v}^{\mathrm{r}}$ and $\mathbf{w}$ are three m-dimensional weight vectors verifying that $\mathbf{v}_i = 0$ for any $i \in \{1, \ldots, \lceil m/2 \rceil\}$, $\mathbf{v}^{\mathrm{r}}$ the vector where the elements are arranged in the opposite order than $\mathbf{v}$, and $\mathbf{w}_{\lceil \frac{m}{2} \rceil} = 1$, and $\mathbf{w}_i = 0$ for any $i \neq \lceil m/2 \rceil$.
- $\mathbf{C_p}(X)$ is a vector containing m increasingly-ordered population quantiles of X verifying that if $C_p(X) \in \mathbf{C_p}(X)$ for a given $p \in]0, 1[$, then $C_{1-p}(X) \in \mathbf{C_p}(X)$.

Let $\mathbf{X} = (\mathbf{X}_1, \mathbf{X}_2, \ldots, \mathbf{X}_n)^T$ be a random sample of size $n \in \mathbb{N}$ from a random variable $X \in \mathcal{L}'(\Omega, \mathcal{A}, P)$. The sample version of any skewness coefficient within the family introduced in Eq. (1) is the function $\hat{\gamma} : \mathbb{R}^n \to \mathbb{R}$ given by:

$$\hat{\gamma}(\mathbf{X}) := \frac{\mathbf{a}^T \widehat{\mathbf{C_p}}(\mathbf{X})}{\mathbf{b}^T \widehat{\mathbf{C_p}}(\mathbf{X})} = \frac{(\mathbf{v} - 2\mathbf{w} + \mathbf{v}^{\mathrm{r}})^T \widehat{\mathbf{C_p}}(\mathbf{X})}{(\mathbf{v} - \mathbf{v}^{\mathrm{r}})^T \widehat{\mathbf{C_p}}(\mathbf{X})},$$

where $\widehat{\mathbf{C_p}}(\mathbf{X}) = \left(\widehat{\mathbf{C}_{\mathbf{p}_1}}(\mathbf{X}), \ldots, \widehat{\mathbf{C}_{\mathbf{p}_m}}(\mathbf{X})\right)^T$ is the sample estimate of $\mathbf{C_p}(X)$ by means of the order statistic $\widehat{\mathbf{C}_{\mathbf{p}_i}}(\mathbf{X}) = \mathbf{X}_{(\lceil n\mathbf{p}_i \rceil)}$ for any $i \in \{1, \ldots, m\}$. Note that the sample version of the skewness coefficient $\hat{\gamma}(\mathbf{X})$ can be seen as a ratio of the addition of three OWA functions to the difference of two of these OWA functions, then resulting in an OWA-based skewness coefficient. Moreover, it is proven in [12] that $\hat{\gamma}(\mathbf{X})$ is well-defined almost surely if the sample size $n \in \mathbb{N}$ verifies

$$n \geq \left(\min_{i=1,\ldots,m-1} (\mathbf{p}_{i+1} - \mathbf{p}_i) \right)^{-1},$$

where $\min_{i=1,\ldots,m-1}(\mathbf{p}_{i+1} - \mathbf{p}_i)$ is the smallest difference between the order of two consecutive quantiles of the vector $\mathbf{C_p}(X)$. Moreover, it holds that:

$$\sqrt{n}(\hat{\gamma}(\mathbf{X}) - \gamma(X)) \xrightarrow{\mathcal{D}} \mathcal{N}(0, \tau), \tag{2}$$

where $\xrightarrow{\mathcal{D}}$ indicates convergence in distribution and

$$\begin{aligned}\tau^2 =& \frac{4}{\left[(\mathbf{v}^T - \mathbf{v}^{\mathrm{r}^T})\mathbf{C_p}(X)\right]^4} \sum_{j=1}^{m} \sum_{i=1}^{m} \sigma^{ij} \big[\mathbf{v}_i(\mathbf{w}^T - \mathbf{v}^{\mathrm{r}^T}) + \mathbf{v}_i^{\mathrm{r}}(\mathbf{v}^T - \mathbf{w}^T) \\ &+ \mathbf{w}_i(\mathbf{v}^{\mathrm{r}^T} - \mathbf{v}^T)\big]\mathbf{C_p}(X) \cdot \big[\mathbf{v}_j(\mathbf{w}^T - \mathbf{v}^{\mathrm{r}^T}) + \mathbf{v}_j^{\mathrm{r}}(\mathbf{v}^T - \mathbf{w}^T) \\ &+ \mathbf{w}_j(\mathbf{v}^{\mathrm{r}^T} - \mathbf{v}^T)\big]\mathbf{C_p}(X),\end{aligned}$$

for any $i, j \in \{1, \ldots, m\}$ with

$$\sigma^{ij} = \frac{\min\{\mathbf{p}_i, \mathbf{p}_j\}(1 - \max\{\mathbf{p}_i, \mathbf{p}_j\})}{f(\mathbf{C}_{\mathbf{p}_i}(X)) f(\mathbf{C}_{\mathbf{p}_j}(X))}.$$

3 Confidence Intervals for the Skewness Parameter of a Location-Scale-Skewness Family

As introduced by Oja [14], a location-scale-skewness family is a family of random variables that is closed under transformations of location and scale and for which any two distributions within the family are comparable in terms of their skewness.

Definition 2. *A location-scale-skewness family is a family* $\mathcal{F} \subseteq \mathcal{L}'(\Omega, \mathcal{A}, P)$ *of random variables for which:*

- *For any* $X \in \mathcal{F}$, $c \in \mathbb{R}^+$ *and* $d \in \mathbb{R}$, *it holds that* $cX + d \in \mathcal{F}$.
- *For any* $X, Y \in \mathcal{F}$, *it either holds that* $Q_Y(F_X(x))$ *is a convex or concave*[1] *function on the support of* X.

Interestingly, due to property O4 of a skewness coefficient, all skewness coefficients necessarily agree on how to order any two random variables within a location-scale-skewness family. Most importantly, many orders related to skewness which are generally weaker than the convex order turn out to be equivalent (see [14, Theorem 5.2]) within a location-scale-skewness family. For instance, assuming expected values μ_X, μ_Y and standard deviations σ_X, σ_Y exist, $X \lesssim Y$ becomes equivalent to the standardized distributions $F_X(\mu_X + \sigma_X x)$ and $F_Y(\mu_Y + \sigma_Y x)$ crossing each other exactly once on each side of $x = 0$ with $F_X(\mu_X) \leq F_Y(\mu_Y)$ (see [13]).

From here on, we devote our attention to location-scale-skewness families parametrized by means of a location parameter $\mu \in \mathbb{R}$, a scale parameter $\sigma \in \mathbb{R}^+$ and a skewness parameter $\delta \in \mathbb{D} \subseteq \mathbb{R}$. With regard to the skewness parameter, we require that the family is of any of the two following types:

Type A: $Q_{\mu',\sigma',\delta'}(F_{\mu,\sigma,\delta}(x))$ is convex on the support of the random variable with distribution $F_{\mu,\sigma,\delta}(x)$, for any $\mu, \mu', \sigma, \sigma', \delta, \delta'$ with $\delta \leq \delta'$;
Type B: $Q_{\mu',\sigma',\delta'}(F_{\mu,\sigma,\delta}(x))$ is concave on the support of the random variable with distribution $F_{\mu,\sigma,\delta}(x)$, for any $\mu, \mu', \sigma, \sigma', \delta, \delta'$ with $\delta \leq \delta'$.

Note that both conditions above hold independently of the values of $\mu, \mu', \sigma, \sigma'$ since the convexity/concavity of $Q_{\mu',\sigma',\delta'}(F_{\mu,\sigma,\delta}(x))$ does not depend on changes of location and scale. For both types, property O2 of a skewness coefficient guarantees that any two random variables X and Y with cumulative distribution functions $F_{\mu,\sigma,\delta}$ and $F_{\mu',\sigma',\delta}$ verify $\gamma(X) = \gamma(Y)$, and, thus, the skewness coefficient can be seen as a function $\gamma(\delta) := \gamma(X)$ of δ. Actually, due to property O4 of a skewness coefficient, in a location-scale-skewness family of Type A the function γ is assured to be increasing and is denoted by $\phi := \gamma$, whereas in a location-scale-skewness family of Type B the function γ is assured to be decreasing and is denoted by $\varphi := \gamma$. Ideally, ϕ and φ are continuous and, most importantly,

[1] As discussed in [14], $Q_Y(F_X(x))$ is a concave function on the support of X if and only if $Q_X(F_Y(x))$ is a convex function on the support of Y.

strictly monotone so that they are invertible; otherwise, we will deal with the lower and upper generalized inverses, which are defined for increasing functions as $\phi_{\downarrow}^{-1}(x) = \inf\{\delta \in \mathbb{D} \mid \phi(\delta) \geq x\}$ and $\phi_{\uparrow}^{-1}(x) = \sup\{\delta \in \mathbb{D} \mid \phi(\delta) \leq x\}$ and for decreasing functions as $\varphi_{\downarrow}^{-1}(x) = \inf\{\delta \in \mathbb{D} \mid \varphi(\delta) \leq x\}$ and $\varphi_{\uparrow}^{-1}(x) = \sup\{\delta \in \mathbb{D} \mid \varphi(\delta) \geq x\}$. By convention, when the sets over which the infimum and the supremum are taken are empty, the infimum and the supremum are defined to be those of the set $\mathbb{D}$. Also, we recall that, for a strictly monotone function, the lower and upper generalized inverse functions coincide with the usual inverse function.

Under the assumptions above, we can construct a confidence interval for the skewness parameter of a location-scale-skewness family.

Theorem 1. *Consider a location-scale-skewness family $\mathcal{F} \subseteq \mathcal{L}'(\Omega, \mathcal{A}, P)$ of Type A or Type B. Given a random sample $\mathbf{X}^T = (\mathbf{X}_1, \mathbf{X}_2, \ldots, \mathbf{X}_n)$ from a random variable $X \in \mathcal{F}$, an asymptotic confidence interval for δ with confidence level $1 - \alpha$ is:*

$$\textbf{Type A: } \left[\phi_{\downarrow}^{-1}\left(\hat{\gamma}(\mathbf{X}) - \frac{\hat{\tau}(\mathbf{X})\, z_{1-\alpha_2}}{\sqrt{n}}\right), \phi_{\uparrow}^{-1}\left(\hat{\gamma}(\mathbf{X}) - \frac{\hat{\tau}(\mathbf{X})\, z_{\alpha_1}}{\sqrt{n}}\right)\right],$$
$$\textbf{Type B: } \left[\varphi_{\downarrow}^{-1}\left(\hat{\gamma}(\mathbf{X}) - \frac{\hat{\tau}(\mathbf{X})\, z_{\alpha_1}}{\sqrt{n}}\right), \varphi_{\uparrow}^{-1}\left(\hat{\gamma}(\mathbf{X}) - \frac{\hat{\tau}(\mathbf{X})\, z_{1-\alpha_2}}{\sqrt{n}}\right)\right],$$

where the endpoints of the confidence interval are taken to be open whenever they are infinite, $\alpha_1, \alpha_2 \in [0, \alpha]$ are such that $\alpha_1 + \alpha_2 = \alpha$, z_p is the quantile of order p of the standard normal distribution, and $\hat{\tau}(\mathbf{X})$ is given by:

$$\begin{aligned}\hat{\tau}^2(\mathbf{X}) = & \frac{4}{\left[(\mathbf{v}^T - \mathbf{v}^{\mathrm{r}^T})\widehat{\mathbf{C}_{\mathbf{p}}}(\mathbf{X})\right]^4} \sum_{j=1}^{m}\sum_{i=1}^{m} \hat{\sigma}^{ij} \left[\mathbf{v}_i(\mathbf{w}^T - \mathbf{v}^{\mathrm{r}^T}) + \mathbf{v}_i^{\mathrm{r}}(\mathbf{v}^T - \mathbf{w}^T)\right. \\ & \left. + \mathbf{w}_i(\mathbf{v}^{\mathrm{r}^T} - \mathbf{v}^T)\right]\widehat{\mathbf{C}_{\mathbf{p}}}(\mathbf{X}) \cdot \left[\mathbf{v}_j(\mathbf{w}^T - \mathbf{v}^{\mathrm{r}^T}) + \mathbf{v}_j^{\mathrm{r}}(\mathbf{v}^T - \mathbf{w}^T)\right. \\ & \left. + \mathbf{w}_j(\mathbf{v}^{\mathrm{r}^T} - \mathbf{v}^T)\right]\widehat{\mathbf{C}_{\mathbf{p}}}(\mathbf{X}),\end{aligned}$$

with $\hat{\sigma}^{ij} = \frac{\min\{\mathbf{p}_i,\mathbf{p}_j\}(1-\max\{\mathbf{p}_i,\mathbf{p}_j\})}{f_n(\widehat{\mathbf{C}_{\mathbf{p}_i}}(\mathbf{X}))f_n(\widehat{\mathbf{C}_{\mathbf{p}_j}}(\mathbf{X}))}$ for any $i, j \in \{1, \ldots, m\}$, $\widehat{\mathbf{C}_{\mathbf{p}}}(\mathbf{X}) = \mathbf{X}_{(\lceil n\mathbf{p}\rceil)}$, and f_n the kernel-density estimation[2] of the density function f of X.

Proof. Consider the set $D = \{\mathbf{z} \in \mathbb{R}^m \mid \mathbf{z}_1 < \mathbf{z}_2 < \ldots < \mathbf{z}_m\}$ and the function $\Psi : D \times (\mathbb{R}^+)^m$ defined as

$$\begin{aligned}\Psi(\mathbf{z}_1, \ldots, \mathbf{z}_m, \mathbf{t}_1, \ldots, \mathbf{t}_m) = & \frac{4}{\left[(\mathbf{v}^T - \mathbf{v}^{\mathrm{r}^T})\mathbf{z}\right]^4} \sum_{j=1}^{m}\sum_{i=1}^{m} \frac{\min\{\mathbf{p}_i, \mathbf{p}_j\}(1 - \max\{\mathbf{p}_i, \mathbf{p}_j\})}{\mathbf{t}_i\, \mathbf{t}_j} \\ & \cdot \left[\mathbf{v}_i(\mathbf{w}^T - \mathbf{v}^{\mathrm{r}^T}) + \mathbf{v}_i^{\mathrm{r}}(\mathbf{v}^T - \mathbf{w}^T) + \mathbf{w}_i(\mathbf{v}^{\mathrm{r}^T} - \mathbf{v}^T)\right]\mathbf{z} \\ & \cdot \left[\mathbf{v}_j(\mathbf{w}^T - \mathbf{v}^{\mathrm{r}^T}) + \mathbf{v}_j^{\mathrm{r}}(\mathbf{v}^T - \mathbf{w}^T) + \mathbf{w}_j(\mathbf{v}^{\mathrm{r}^T} - \mathbf{v}^T)\right]\mathbf{z}\,.\end{aligned}$$

[2] The kernel-density estimation of a probability density function f is the pointwise estimation of $f(x)$, for any $x \in \mathbb{R}$, as $f_n(x) = \frac{1}{n\, h(n)} \sum_{i=1}^{n} K\left(\frac{x - \mathbf{x}_i}{h(n)}\right)$, with the kernel function $K : \mathbb{R} \to \mathbb{R}$ and the bandwith $h : \mathbb{N} \to \mathbb{R}$ appropriately chosen so that the estimator f_n is consistent and asymptotically unbiased. For more details, we refer to [7,15,17].

Note that $\Psi\left(\mathbf{C_p}(X), \mathbf{f}\left(\mathbf{C_p}(X)\right)\right) = \tau^2$ and $\Psi\left(\widehat{\mathbf{C_p}}(\mathbf{X}), \mathbf{f}_n\left(\widehat{\mathbf{C_p}}(\mathbf{X})\right)\right) = \hat{\tau}^2(\mathbf{X})$, where $\mathbf{f}, \mathbf{f_n} : \mathbb{R}^m \to \mathbb{R}^m$ denote the functions obtained by applying f and f_n componentwisely, respectively. By construction $\mathbf{C_p}(X) \in D$ and $\widehat{\mathbf{C_p}}(\mathbf{X}) \in D$ (almost surely) for any realization with large sample size. In addition, $f\left(\mathbf{C_{p_i}}(X)\right) > 0$ since $X \in \mathcal{L}'(\Omega, \mathcal{A}, P)$ and $f_n\left(\widehat{\mathbf{C_{p_i}}}(\mathbf{X})\right) > 0$ for all $i \in \{1, \ldots, m\}$ by construction. Thus, since $\left(\widehat{\mathbf{C_p}}(\mathbf{X}), \mathbf{f_n}\left(\widehat{\mathbf{C_p}}(\mathbf{X})\right)\right)$ converges in probability to $\left(\mathbf{C_p}(X), \mathbf{f}\left(\mathbf{C_p}(X)\right)\right)$ and Ψ is a well-defined and continuous function, it follows from [18, Thm. 2.3] that $\hat{\tau}^2(\mathbf{X}) = \Psi\left(\widehat{\mathbf{C_p}}(\mathbf{X}), \mathbf{f_n}\left(\widehat{\mathbf{C_p}}(\mathbf{X})\right)\right)$ converges in probability to $\tau^2 = \Psi\left(\mathbf{C_p}(X), \mathbf{f}\left(\mathbf{C_p}(X)\right)\right)$. This latter fact and the asymptotic normality of the statistic in Eq. (2) may be put together so direct application of Slutsky's Theorem [18, Lemma 2.8] shows that:

$$\sqrt{n}\frac{\hat{\gamma}(\mathbf{X}) - \gamma(X)}{\hat{\tau}(\mathbf{X})} \xrightarrow{\mathcal{D}} \mathcal{N}(0, 1)\,. \tag{3}$$

For a location-scale-skewness family of Type A, the result follows from the following (asymptotic) equalities:

$$\begin{aligned}
1 - \alpha &= P\left(z_{\alpha_1} \leq \sqrt{n}\frac{\hat{\gamma}(\mathbf{X}) - \phi(\delta)}{\hat{\tau}(\mathbf{X})} \leq z_{1-\alpha_2}\right) \\
&= P\left(\frac{\hat{\tau}(\mathbf{X})\, z_{\alpha_1}}{\sqrt{n}} \leq \hat{\gamma}(\mathbf{X}) - \phi(\delta) \leq \frac{\hat{\tau}(\mathbf{X})\, z_{1-\alpha_2}}{\sqrt{n}}\right) \\
&= P\left(\hat{\gamma}(\mathbf{X}) - \frac{\hat{\tau}(\mathbf{X})\, z_{1-\alpha_2}}{\sqrt{n}} \leq \phi(\delta) \leq \hat{\gamma}(\mathbf{X}) - \frac{\hat{\tau}(\mathbf{X})\, z_{\alpha_1}}{\sqrt{n}}\right) \\
&= P\left(\hat{\gamma}(\mathbf{X}) - \frac{\hat{\tau}(\mathbf{X})\, z_{1-\alpha_2}}{\sqrt{n}} \leq \phi(\delta) \,\wedge\, \phi(\delta) \leq \hat{\gamma}(\mathbf{X}) - \frac{\hat{\tau}(\mathbf{X})\, z_{\alpha_1}}{\sqrt{n}}\right) \\
&\leq P\left(\phi_{\downarrow}^{-1}\left(\hat{\gamma}(\mathbf{X}) - \frac{\hat{\tau}(\mathbf{X})\, z_{1-\alpha_2}}{\sqrt{n}}\right) \leq \phi_{\downarrow}^{-1}(\phi(\delta))\right. \\
&\qquad\qquad \left.\wedge\ \ \phi_{\uparrow}^{-1}(\phi(\delta)) \leq \phi_{\uparrow}^{-1}\left(\hat{\gamma}(\mathbf{X}) - \frac{\hat{\tau}(\mathbf{X})\, z_{\alpha_1}}{\sqrt{n}}\right)\right) \\
&\leq P\left(\phi_{\downarrow}^{-1}\left(\hat{\gamma}(\mathbf{X}) - \frac{\hat{\tau}(\mathbf{X})\, z_{1-\alpha_2}}{\sqrt{n}}\right) \leq \delta \wedge \delta \leq \phi_{\uparrow}^{-1}\left(\hat{\gamma}(\mathbf{X}) - \frac{\hat{\tau}(\mathbf{X})\, z_{\alpha_1}}{\sqrt{n}}\right)\right) \\
&= P\left(\phi_{\downarrow}^{-1}\left(\hat{\gamma}(\mathbf{X}) - \frac{\hat{\tau}(\mathbf{X})\, z_{1-\alpha_2}}{\sqrt{n}}\right) \leq \delta \leq \phi_{\uparrow}^{-1}\left(\hat{\gamma}(\mathbf{X}) - \frac{\hat{\tau}(\mathbf{X})\, z_{\alpha_1}}{\sqrt{n}}\right)\right),
\end{aligned}$$

where the first inequality follows from the fact that $\phi_{\downarrow}^{-1}$ and $\phi_{\uparrow}^{-1}$ are increasing since ϕ is increasing, and the second inequality follows from the properties $\phi_{\downarrow}^{-1}(\phi(\delta)) \leq \delta \leq \phi_{\uparrow}^{-1}(\phi(\delta))$.

Similarly, for a location-scale-skewness family of Type B, the result follows from the following (asymptotic) equalities:

$$\begin{aligned}
1-\alpha &= P\left(z_{\alpha_1} \leq \sqrt{n}\frac{\hat{\gamma}(\mathbf{X})+\varphi(\delta)}{\hat{\tau}(\mathbf{X})} \leq z_{1-\alpha_2}\right) \\
&= P\left(\frac{\hat{\tau}(\mathbf{X})\, z_{\alpha_1}}{\sqrt{n}} \leq \hat{\gamma}(\mathbf{X})-\varphi(\delta) \leq \frac{\hat{\tau}(\mathbf{X})\, z_{1-\alpha_2}}{\sqrt{n}}\right) \\
&= P\left(\hat{\gamma}(\mathbf{X}) - \frac{\hat{\tau}(\mathbf{X})\, z_{1-\alpha_2}}{\sqrt{n}} \leq \varphi(\delta) \leq \hat{\gamma}(\mathbf{X}) - \frac{\hat{\tau}(\mathbf{X})\, z_{\alpha_1}}{\sqrt{n}}\right) \\
&= P\left(\hat{\gamma}(\mathbf{X}) - \frac{\hat{\tau}(\mathbf{X})\, z_{1-\alpha_2}}{\sqrt{n}} \leq \varphi(\delta) \,\wedge\, \varphi(\delta) \leq \hat{\gamma}(\mathbf{X}) - \frac{\hat{\tau}(\mathbf{X})\, z_{\alpha_1}}{\sqrt{n}}\right) \\
&\leq P\left(\varphi_{\uparrow}^{-1}\left(\hat{\gamma}(\mathbf{X}) - \frac{\hat{\tau}(\mathbf{X})\, z_{1-\alpha_2}}{\sqrt{n}}\right) \geq \varphi_{\uparrow}^{-1}(\varphi(\delta))\right. \\
&\qquad\qquad \left. \wedge \;\; \varphi_{\downarrow}^{-1}(\varphi(\delta)) \geq \varphi_{\downarrow}^{-1}\left(\hat{\gamma}(\mathbf{X}) - \frac{\hat{\tau}(\mathbf{X})\, z_{\alpha_1}}{\sqrt{n}}\right)\right) \\
&\leq P\left(\varphi_{\uparrow}^{-1}\left(\hat{\gamma}(\mathbf{X}) - \frac{\hat{\tau}(\mathbf{X})\, z_{1-\alpha_2}}{\sqrt{n}}\right) \geq \delta \wedge \delta \geq \varphi_{\downarrow}^{-1}\left(\hat{\gamma}(\mathbf{X}) - \frac{\hat{\tau}(\mathbf{X})\, z_{\alpha_1}}{\sqrt{n}}\right)\right) \\
&= P\left(\varphi_{\downarrow}^{-1}\left(\hat{\gamma}(\mathbf{X}) - \frac{\hat{\tau}(\mathbf{X})\, z_{\alpha_1}}{\sqrt{n}}\right) \leq \delta \leq \varphi_{\uparrow}^{-1}\left(\hat{\gamma}(\mathbf{X}) - \frac{\hat{\tau}(\mathbf{X})\, z_{1-\alpha_2}}{\sqrt{n}}\right)\right),
\end{aligned}$$

where the first inequality follows from the fact that $\varphi_{\downarrow}^{-1}$ and $\varphi_{\uparrow}^{-1}$ are decreasing since φ is decreasing, and the second inequality follows from the properties $\varphi_{\downarrow}^{-1}(\varphi(\delta)) \leq \delta \leq \varphi_{\uparrow}^{-1}(\varphi(\delta))$. ∎

4 Case Study: the (shifted) Weibull Distribution

4.1 Theoretical Development

The Weibull distribution is a popular probability distribution in reliability analysis. Technically, in its most common form, the Weibull distribution is only parametrized with respect to a scale and a shape parameter so it does not form a location-scale-skewness family; however it is straightforward to define the shifted Weibull distribution which indeed is a location-scale-skewness family. The probability density function of this distribution is the following:

$$f(x) = \frac{\delta}{\beta}\left(\frac{x-\theta}{\beta}\right)^{\delta-1} e^{-\left(\frac{x-\theta}{\beta}\right)^{\delta}}\, \mathbb{1}(x \geq \theta),$$

where $\theta \in \mathbb{R}$ is the location parameter, $\beta \in \mathbb{R}^+$ is the scale parameter and $\delta \in \mathbb{D} = \mathbb{R}^+$ is the shape parameter. We denote the fact that a random variable X has a shifted Weibull distribution with location parameter θ, scale parameter β and shape parameter δ by $X \rightsquigarrow \mathcal{W}(\theta, \beta, \delta)$. Note that the shape parameter δ of a (shifted) Weibull distribution is known to be a skewness parameter within a location-scale-skewness family (see [9,13]).

The cumulative distribution function of a random variable $X \rightsquigarrow \mathcal{W}(\theta, \beta, \delta)$ is given by:

$$F(x) = \left(1 - e^{-\left(\frac{x-\theta}{\beta}\right)^\delta}\right) \mathbb{1}(x \geq \theta) = \begin{cases} 1 - e^{-\left(\frac{x-\theta}{\beta}\right)^\delta}, & x \geq \theta, \\ 0, & x < \theta, \end{cases}$$

whereas the quantile function is given by:

$$Q(p) = \theta + \beta(-\ln(1-p))^{1/\delta},$$

for any $0 < p < 1$. Note that if $X \rightsquigarrow \mathcal{W}(\theta, \beta, \delta)$ and $Y \rightsquigarrow \mathcal{W}(\theta', \beta', \delta')$, it follows that

$$Q_Y(F_X(x)) = \theta' + \beta' \left(\frac{x-\theta}{\beta}\right)^{\delta/\delta'}.$$

for any $x \in [\theta, +\infty[$. This function is convex if and only if $\delta \geq \delta'$ or, equivalently, is concave if and only if $\delta \leq \delta'$. Therefore, the shifted Weibull distribution is a location-scale-skewness family of Type B and, thus,

$$\varphi(\delta) = \gamma(X) = \frac{\mathbf{a}^T \mathbf{C}_\mathbf{p}(X)}{\mathbf{b}^T \mathbf{C}_\mathbf{p}(X)} = \frac{(\mathbf{v} - 2\mathbf{w} + \mathbf{v}^\mathrm{r})^T \left(-\ln(\mathbf{1} - \mathbf{p})\right)^{1/\delta}}{(\mathbf{v} - \mathbf{v}^\mathrm{r})^T \left(-\ln(\mathbf{1} - \mathbf{p})\right)^{1/\delta}}$$

is decreasing. Actually, φ is strictly decreasing. This fact can be proven similarly to Proposition 2 in [12] but noting that, in the last case ($i < \lceil m/2 \rceil < j$) the inequality $\frac{\mathbf{C}_{\mathbf{p}_i}(Y)}{\mathbf{C}_{\mathbf{p}_i}(X)} \leq \frac{\mathbf{C}_{\mathbf{p}_j}(Y)}{\mathbf{C}_{\mathbf{p}_j}(X)}$ is strict for $X \rightsquigarrow \mathcal{W}(\theta, \beta, \delta)$ and $Y \rightsquigarrow \mathcal{W}(\theta', \beta', \delta')$ with $\delta > \delta'$ and $\mathrm{Me}(X) = \theta + \beta(\ln 2)^{1/\delta} = 0 = \theta' + \beta'(\ln 2)^{1/\delta'} = \mathrm{Me}(Y)$; this is due to the fact that

$$h(x) = \frac{Q_Y(F_X(x))}{x} = \frac{-\beta'(\ln 2)^{1/\delta'} + \beta' \beta^{-\delta/\delta'} \left(x + \beta(\ln 2)^{1/\delta}\right)^{\delta/\delta'}}{x},$$

defined for any $x > \theta = -\beta(\ln 2)^{1/\delta}$, is strictly increasing as long as $\delta > \delta'$. Also, $2\mathbf{v}_j \mathbf{v}_i^\mathrm{r} > 0$ for at least one (i, j) with $i < \lceil m/2 \rceil < j$. Putting both things together in the proof of Proposition 2 in [12], we conclude that all addends are non-positive with at least one being negative. Additionally, as proven in Proposition 1 in [12] the denominator is strictly positive for random variables in $\mathcal{L}'(\Omega, \mathcal{A}, P)$, and, thus, φ is continuous.

Figure 1 illustrates φ for different choices of weight vectors $\mathbf{v}$ and $\mathbf{w}$. More precisely, we consider $\mathbf{w}^T = (0, 0, 1, 0, 0)$ to be the weight vector associated with the median, and $\mathbf{v}^T = \lambda\,(0, 0, 0, 1, 0) + (1 - \lambda)\,(0, 0, 0, 0, 1)$, with $\lambda \in \{0, 1/4, 1/2, 3/4, 1\}$. The considered vector of increasing probabilities is restricted to $\mathbf{p}^T = (1/6, 2/6, 3/6, 4/6, 5/6)$.

It can be seen that in all cases the function is continuous and strictly decreasing, therefore invertible.

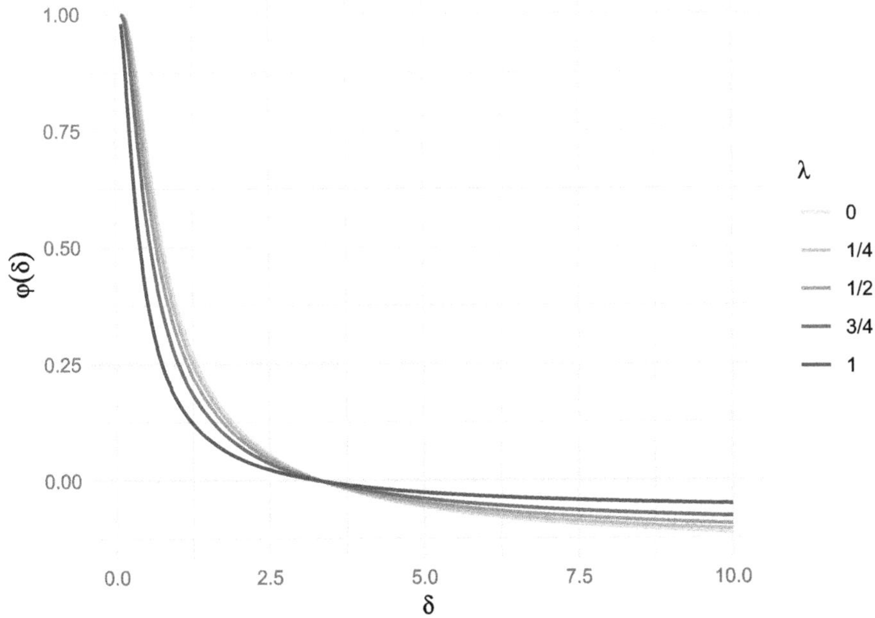

Fig. 1. Illustration of φ for different choices of weight vector $\mathbf{v}$ (dependent on λ).

4.2 Empirical Study at the (Shifted) Weibull Distribution

The present section presents an empirical study of the proposed methodology for the (shifted) Weibull distribution via Monte Carlo simulation for two different settings: (i) $\alpha_1 = \alpha_2 = \alpha/2$; and (ii) $\alpha_1 = 0$ and $\alpha_2 = \alpha$. The second setting is chosen in order to minimize the probability of obtaining an unbounded confidence interval, something that can only happen on the right-end since $\mathbb{D} = \mathbb{R}^+$ for the Weibull distribution. We consider 10^5 replications for estimating the coverage of the confidence interval presented in Theorem 1 for the shape parameter δ of the (shifted) Weibull distribution at significance level $1-\alpha = 0.95$ (see Table 1 for the setting $\alpha_1 = \alpha_2 = \alpha/2$ and Table 3 for the setting $\alpha_1 = 0$ and $\alpha_2 = \alpha$). Moreover, we also present the proportion of unbounded confidence intervals (see Tables 2 and 4). We consider $\mathbf{w}^T = (0, 0, 1, 0, 0)$, $\mathbf{v}^T = \lambda (0, 0, 0, 1, 0) + (1 - \lambda) (0, 0, 0, 0, 1)$ with $\lambda \in \{0, 1/4, 1/2, 3/4, 1\}$, and $\mathbf{p}^T = (1/6, 2/6, 3/6, 4/6, 5/6)$. Different sample sizes ($n \in \{10, 50, 100, 200\}$) and values of the shape parameter ($\delta \in \{0.5, 1, 1.5, \ldots, 6\}$) are considered. It must be noted that although values around $1-\alpha = 0.95$ are expected for the empirical coverage, any higher value would also indicate that the confidence intervals are valid. For this reason, the one-sided confidence interval at confidence level 0.95 for the parameter of the Bernoulli distribution for samples of size 10^5 and mean 0.95, *i.e.*, the interval $[0.94887, 1]$, is taken as a reference to indicate whether the confidence intervals succeed at maintaining the significance level or not. Values within the aforementioned interval are highlighted in green in Tables 1 and 3.

Table 1. Empirical coverage of the confidence interval for the parameter δ at significance level $1-\alpha = 0.95$ with $\alpha_1 = \alpha_2 = \alpha/2$ for different weight vectors $\mathbf{v}$ with associated λ, sample sizes n and true values of the shape parameter δ.

		δ											
λ	n	0.5	1	1.5	2	2.5	3	3.5	4	4.5	5	5.5	6
0	25	0.94784	0.94905	0.95191	0.95356	0.95628	0.95579	0.95874	0.95845	0.96028	0.95992	0.96224	0.96240
	50	0.93511	0.93738	0.94617	0.94863	0.94919	0.95085	0.95109	0.95154	0.95313	0.95339	0.95387	0.95527
	100	0.92069	0.93802	0.94628	0.94971	0.95030	0.95160	0.95077	0.95288	0.95269	0.95261	0.95420	0.95483
	200	0.92017	0.94122	0.94971	0.95166	0.95294	0.95214	0.95473	0.95363	0.95371	0.95363	0.95491	0.95475
$1/4$	25	0.94468	0.95311	0.95516	0.95675	0.95684	0.95910	0.95912	0.96085	0.96204	0.96186	0.96337	0.96391
	50	0.94458	0.94534	0.94784	0.95012	0.95101	0.94983	0.95207	0.95165	0.95057	0.95312	0.95312	0.95352
	100	0.92791	0.94417	0.95077	0.95219	0.95241	0.95356	0.95357	0.95418	0.95348	0.95456	0.95455	0.95476
	200	0.90451	0.94391	0.95151	0.95417	0.95301	0.95287	0.95286	0.95424	0.95339	0.95304	0.95395	0.95468
$1/2$	25	0.94301	0.95480	0.95779	0.95816	0.95809	0.96006	0.96065	0.96200	0.96391	0.96357	0.96401	0.96476
	50	0.94263	0.94732	0.94930	0.95031	0.95080	0.94991	0.95220	0.95108	0.95205	0.95234	0.95243	0.95365
	100	0.92263	0.94525	0.95188	0.95364	0.95364	0.95319	0.95370	0.95346	0.95347	0.95421	0.95421	0.95377
	200	0.87378	0.93789	0.95065	0.95352	0.95402	0.95382	0.95379	0.95269	0.95295	0.95318	0.95176	0.95213
$3/4$	25	0.89915	0.95670	0.96657	0.97014	0.97173	0.97264	0.97312	0.97378	0.97411	0.97394	0.97505	0.97572
	50	0.86912	0.94780	0.95794	0.95933	0.95879	0.95666	0.95564	0.95490	0.95429	0.95343	0.95437	0.95206
	100	0.71962	0.91265	0.95087	0.95833	0.95866	0.95923	0.95679	0.95514	0.95511	0.95415	0.95225	0.95112
	200	0.40843	0.81688	0.92450	0.95024	0.95569	0.95686	0.95368	0.95136	0.95102	0.94785	0.94553	0.94408
1	25	0.84235	0.95324	0.97489	0.97999	0.98233	0.98349	0.98333	0.98461	0.98400	0.98448	0.98493	0.98484
	50	0.74577	0.92888	0.96128	0.96700	0.96624	0.96556	0.96386	0.96216	0.96025	0.95897	0.95653	0.95760
	100	0.44053	0.84885	0.94113	0.95931	0.96306	0.96307	0.96184	0.95987	0.95611	0.95480	0.95116	0.95128
	200	0.10767	0.66755	0.88962	0.94275	0.95536	0.95775	0.95619	0.95253	0.94876	0.94444	0.94232	0.93756

First Setting: $\boldsymbol{\alpha_1 = \alpha_2 = \frac{\alpha}{2}}$. From Eq. (3), it follows that the sample version of the skewness coefficient γ introduced in Eq. (1), when τ is estimated via kernel-density estimation is asymptotically normally distributed and, thus, symmetric. Consequently, when constructing the asymptotic confidence interval for δ with confidence level $1-\alpha$, it may feel natural to set $\alpha_1 = \alpha_2 = \alpha/2$. In Table 1, we report the empirical coverage under this setting. It can be readily seen that most values lie within the expected interval $[0.94887, 1]$. Moreover, the coverage tends to decrease as both the sample size n and the parameter λ increase. Regarding the parameter δ, the confidence intervals exhibit their best performance for intermediate values, namely when δ is around 2.5 and 4, for which the empirical coverage remains within the expected interval for all considered values of λ and for any sample size n. Note that for small values such as $\delta = 0.5$, the coverage is substantially lower, reaching values as small as 0.10767, whereas for large values such as $\delta = 6$, the lowest observed value is 0.93756.

According to the discussion above, the coverage is generally as expected, especially for large sample sizes and intermediate values of δ. Nevertheless, as reported in Table 2, a large proportion of the constructed intervals is unbounded. This is due to the fact that applying $\varphi_{\uparrow}^{-1}$ to $\hat{\gamma}(\mathbf{X}) - \frac{\hat{\tau}(\mathbf{X})\, z_{1-\alpha_2}}{\sqrt{n}}$ typically leads to the computation of the supremum of an empty set under the setting considered

Table 2. Empirical proportion of unbounded confidence intervals for the parameter δ at significance level $1-\alpha = 0.95$ with $\alpha_1 = \alpha_2 = \alpha/2$ for different weight vectors $\mathbf{v}$ with associated λ, sample sizes n and true values of the shape parameter δ.

		δ											
λ	n	0.5	1	1.5	2	2.5	3	3.5	4	4.5	5	5.5	6
0	25	0.07035	0.44289	0.69915	0.81197	0.86821	0.89765	0.91911	0.92908	0.93847	0.94216	0.94864	0.95132
	50	0.00118	0.11282	0.38110	0.58678	0.71246	0.78468	0.82971	0.85984	0.87867	0.89226	0.90502	0.91321
	100	0.00000	0.00713	0.11635	0.32431	0.50497	0.63165	0.71810	0.77741	0.81403	0.84240	0.86347	0.88023
	200	0.00000	0.00001	0.00867	0.08275	0.23448	0.39063	0.51751	0.61837	0.68835	0.73896	0.77913	0.80915
$1/4$	25	0.08570	0.47333	0.71431	0.82070	0.87630	0.90328	0.91983	0.93024	0.93928	0.94356	0.94839	0.95167
	50	0.00260	0.13439	0.39906	0.59472	0.71215	0.77966	0.82268	0.85112	0.86988	0.88677	0.89604	0.90539
	100	0.00001	0.01217	0.14168	0.34752	0.51882	0.63598	0.71583	0.76895	0.80685	0.83476	0.85444	0.87210
	200	0.00000	0.00006	0.01409	0.10061	0.24522	0.39201	0.51131	0.60314	0.67080	0.72250	0.75889	0.78925
$1/2$	25	0.09474	0.49024	0.72588	0.82829	0.87789	0.90558	0.92111	0.93233	0.93792	0.94363	0.94884	0.95188
	50	0.00301	0.14435	0.41500	0.60392	0.71684	0.78140	0.82049	0.84804	0.87070	0.88352	0.89288	0.90359
	100	0.00000	0.01591	0.15562	0.36452	0.52868	0.64282	0.71872	0.76947	0.80456	0.83277	0.85053	0.86762
	200	0.00000	0.00011	0.01697	0.11137	0.25614	0.40255	0.51760	0.60813	0.66905	0.71988	0.75305	0.78452
$3/4$	25	0.23641	0.66661	0.82496	0.88801	0.91716	0.93264	0.94131	0.94860	0.95311	0.95766	0.95975	0.96202
	50	0.02157	0.30907	0.56827	0.70138	0.77506	0.81547	0.84121	0.86145	0.87526	0.88405	0.89350	0.89889
	100	0.00062	0.10414	0.35453	0.53856	0.65233	0.71945	0.76858	0.79879	0.82148	0.83831	0.85245	0.86199
	200	0.00000	0.00801	0.11268	0.27442	0.42162	0.52811	0.60341	0.65987	0.69861	0.73016	0.75426	0.77389
1	25	0.64001	0.84238	0.91230	0.93901	0.95311	0.95975	0.96371	0.96776	0.96996	0.97206	0.97360	0.97463
	50	0.23491	0.58834	0.74680	0.81331	0.84897	0.86895	0.88491	0.89226	0.89986	0.90498	0.90933	0.91340
	100	0.07178	0.42881	0.63916	0.73546	0.78552	0.81527	0.83683	0.85174	0.85974	0.86801	0.87296	0.88116
	200	0.00372	0.18126	0.41255	0.55717	0.63503	0.68752	0.72280	0.74821	0.76733	0.78371	0.79566	0.80094

here. By convention, in those cases, one takes the supremum of the set $\mathbb{D}$, which is unbounded from above in the case of the (shifted) Weibull distribution where $\mathbb{D} = \mathbb{R}^+$. Therefore, $\varphi_\dagger^{-1}\left(\hat{\gamma}(\mathbf{X}) - \frac{\hat{\tau}(\mathbf{X})\, z_{1-\alpha_2}}{\sqrt{n}}\right) = +\infty$ and the confidence intervals are unbounded from above in those cases. Note that this situation is more frequently observed for small sample sizes and large values of the parameter λ. Moreover, the proportion of unbounded intervals increases with δ. For instance, when $\delta = 6$ and $n = 25$, the proportion of unbounded intervals remains around 0.96 for all considered values of λ, whereas for $\delta = 0.5$ and $\lambda \in \{0, 1/4, 1/2\}$, this proportion is below 0.10 for all sample sizes.

Second Setting: $\alpha_2 = \alpha$. The results presented in Table 2 suggest that constructing one-sided confidence intervals by considering different values for α_1 and α_2 might be more appropriate. More specifically, based on the discussion above, it may be suitable to set $\alpha_1 = 0$ and $\alpha_2 = \alpha$, so that the resulting confidence intervals tend to be bounded from above with a larger probability. This setting is considered in Table 3 where we present the empirical coverage of the confidence intervals. The obtained coverage values are smaller than those observed in the previous setting (see Table 1), although they remain close to the nominal level of $1 - \alpha = 0.95$. As a positive counterpart, the empirical proportion of unbounded confidence intervals reported in Table 4 is substantially smaller across all combi-

Table 3. Empirical coverage of the one-sided confidence interval for the parameter δ at significance level $1 - \alpha = 0.95$ with $\alpha_2 = \alpha$ for different weight vectors $\mathbf{v}$ with associated λ, sample sizes n and true values of the shape parameter δ.

		δ											
λ	n	0.5	1	1.5	2	2.5	3	3.5	4	4.5	5	5.5	6
0	25	0.95643	0.94887	0.95320	0.95308	0.95310	0.95521	0.95480	0.95459	0.95474	0.95506	0.95534	0.95571
	50	0.92350	0.91925	0.92846	0.93213	0.93583	0.93506	0.93710	0.93904	0.93751	0.93889	0.93900	0.93932
	100	0.90276	0.91844	0.93202	0.93508	0.93971	0.94212	0.94200	0.94305	0.94324	0.94466	0.94567	0.94462
	200	0.91371	0.92850	0.93908	0.94253	0.94470	0.94519	0.94559	0.94527	0.94618	0.94626	0.94760	0.94743
$1/4$	25	0.95627	0.95020	0.95239	0.95339	0.95286	0.95523	0.95376	0.95548	0.95513	0.95492	0.95685	0.95377
	50	0.92265	0.91903	0.92863	0.93350	0.93509	0.93704	0.93860	0.93741	0.93805	0.93861	0.93883	0.93831
	100	0.90309	0.91863	0.93131	0.93522	0.93943	0.94035	0.94274	0.94241	0.94381	0.94328	0.94460	0.94409
	200	0.91317	0.92845	0.93771	0.94242	0.94352	0.94454	0.94524	0.94632	0.94637	0.94851	0.94656	0.94806
$1/2$	25	0.95771	0.95085	0.95186	0.95377	0.95407	0.95442	0.95425	0.95492	0.95595	0.95546	0.95599	0.95435
	50	0.92387	0.92064	0.92953	0.93256	0.93417	0.93614	0.93635	0.93866	0.93905	0.93904	0.93943	0.94005
	100	0.90197	0.91628	0.92967	0.93556	0.93909	0.93970	0.94194	0.94296	0.94322	0.94529	0.94438	0.94487
	200	0.91447	0.92788	0.93881	0.94280	0.94322	0.94583	0.94542	0.94640	0.94644	0.94637	0.94682	0.94612
$3/4$	25	0.95704	0.94960	0.95238	0.95394	0.95399	0.95435	0.95486	0.95602	0.95496	0.95413	0.95528	0.95512
	50	0.92331	0.92047	0.92689	0.93262	0.93294	0.93569	0.93749	0.93756	0.93903	0.93978	0.93865	0.94010
	100	0.90507	0.91674	0.93004	0.93514	0.93799	0.94186	0.94182	0.94339	0.94442	0.94371	0.94435	0.94539
	200	0.91349	0.92821	0.93894	0.94148	0.94485	0.94448	0.94545	0.94568	0.94641	0.94720	0.94659	0.94677
1	25	0.95838	0.94907	0.95133	0.95321	0.95329	0.95500	0.95481	0.95540	0.95501	0.95561	0.95653	0.95604
	50	0.92297	0.91848	0.92676	0.93297	0.93561	0.93571	0.93897	0.93789	0.93873	0.93963	0.93999	0.93860
	100	0.90439	0.91628	0.93168	0.93555	0.93911	0.94112	0.94388	0.94197	0.94374	0.94448	0.94376	0.94465
	200	0.91392	0.92911	0.93882	0.94231	0.94445	0.94526	0.94580	0.94720	0.94609	0.94678	0.94656	0.94689

nations of n and δ. Moreover, the parameter λ appears to have little impact on the proportion of unbounded confidence intervals, as similar results are obtained for all values of λ, given any combination of n and δ.

Discussion. Based on the obtained results, we conclude that the method employed to construct confidence intervals for the skewness parameter δ of a (shifted) Weibull distribution with confidence level $1 - \alpha$ performs as expected, but depending on the choice of α_1 and α_2 the method may lead to unbounded confidence intervals with a large probability. In particular, applying Theorem 1 with $\alpha_1 = 0$ and $\alpha_2 = \alpha$ yields confidence intervals with coverage slightly below the nominal level. By contrast, setting $\alpha_1 = \alpha_2 = \alpha/2$ typically results in slightly higher coverage, at the cost of a higher probability of producing unbounded confidence intervals, especially for larger values of δ. The small effect of λ indicates that the position at which the weights are placed in the weight vector $\mathbf{v}$ is not very significant with regard to the confidence level, as the results are very similar across all considered values of λ.

Table 4. Empirical proportion of unbounded confidence intervals for the parameter δ at significance level $1 - \alpha = 0.95$ with $\alpha_2 = \alpha$ for different weight vectors $\mathbf{v}$ with associated λ, sample sizes n and true values of the shape parameter δ.

		δ											
λ	n	0.5	1	1.5	2	2.5	3	3.5	4	4.5	5	5.5	6
0	25	0.04323	0.34390	0.59523	0.72565	0.79500	0.83681	0.86009	0.87945	0.89125	0.89977	0.90575	0.91351
	50	0.00046	0.06814	0.27555	0.46459	0.59808	0.67919	0.73794	0.77697	0.80147	0.82258	0.83898	0.85155
	100	0.00000	0.00307	0.06709	0.21916	0.38353	0.50665	0.60092	0.66782	0.71704	0.75384	0.78261	0.80287
	200	0.00000	0.00000	0.00339	0.04296	0.14674	0.27505	0.38831	0.48683	0.56131	0.62163	0.67146	0.70826
1/4	25	0.04347	0.34649	0.59250	0.72672	0.79431	0.83809	0.85919	0.88009	0.89106	0.90042	0.90808	0.91133
	50	0.00055	0.06868	0.27334	0.46812	0.59563	0.68170	0.73660	0.77681	0.80518	0.82350	0.83972	0.85095
	100	0.00000	0.00276	0.06669	0.21894	0.38158	0.50909	0.59865	0.66812	0.71728	0.75305	0.77947	0.80199
	200	0.00000	0.00000	0.00312	0.04374	0.14696	0.27477	0.39136	0.48471	0.56279	0.62381	0.66961	0.71033
1/2	25	0.04465	0.34364	0.59437	0.72558	0.79642	0.83629	0.86221	0.87796	0.89231	0.90147	0.90778	0.91209
	50	0.00065	0.06685	0.27390	0.46826	0.59827	0.67999	0.73636	0.77567	0.80443	0.82317	0.84026	0.85367
	100	0.00000	0.00297	0.06555	0.22037	0.38292	0.50755	0.60225	0.66850	0.71689	0.75499	0.78170	0.80067
	200	0.00000	0.00000	0.00323	0.04437	0.14367	0.27125	0.39142	0.48852	0.56559	0.62480	0.67076	0.70790
3/4	25	0.04356	0.34629	0.59363	0.72549	0.79541	0.83684	0.86216	0.87998	0.89036	0.89868	0.90687	0.91310
	50	0.00062	0.06704	0.27315	0.46493	0.59400	0.68027	0.73482	0.77495	0.80353	0.82578	0.83904	0.85236
	100	0.00000	0.00281	0.06564	0.21857	0.38054	0.50763	0.60282	0.66944	0.71636	0.75261	0.78029	0.80250
	200	0.00000	0.00000	0.00332	0.04534	0.14651	0.26920	0.38818	0.48711	0.56099	0.62530	0.66985	0.70909
1	25	0.04496	0.34528	0.59287	0.72572	0.79495	0.83541	0.86192	0.87802	0.89087	0.90038	0.90962	0.91379
	50	0.00057	0.06728	0.27647	0.46779	0.59584	0.68066	0.73789	0.77533	0.80308	0.82349	0.84039	0.85193
	100	0.00000	0.00302	0.06616	0.22056	0.37842	0.51020	0.60304	0.66777	0.71746	0.75244	0.78099	0.80157
	200	0.00000	0.00000	0.00379	0.04656	0.14727	0.26943	0.39435	0.48524	0.56513	0.62289	0.66872	0.70737

5 Conclusions

The present work has studied how to use OWA-based skewness coefficients for constructing asymptotic confidence intervals for the skewness parameter of a location-scale-skewness family. The experiments carried out on the (shifted) Weibull distribution illustrate the method and show that it succeeds at constructing confidence intervals with the desired coverage probability, regardless of the chosen weight vector $\mathbf{v}$. Furthermore, it is shown that the method performs well for all sample sizes and all the considered values of δ. A trade-off between maximizing empirical coverage and minimizing the probability of obtaining unbounded confidence intervals must be carefully managed by the user.

Future work aims at exploring different location-scale-skewness families. It is also interesting to explore how a similar methodology could be developed for constructing asymptotic confidence intervals for the kurtosis parameter of a location-scale-kurtosis family (see [14]).

Acknowledgments. This contribution is part of grant PID2022-140585NB-I00 funded by MICIU/AEI/10.13039/501100011033 and "FEDER/UE".

Disclosure of Interests. The authors have no competing interests to declare that are relevant to the content of this article.

References

1. Arnold, B.C., Groeneveld, R.A.: Skewness and kurtosis orderings: an introduction. Lecture Notes-Monograph Series, pp. 17–24 (1992)
2. Bowley, A.L.: Elements of Statistics (4th ed.). Scribner (1920)
3. Brys, G., Hubert, M., Struyf, A.: A robust measure of skewness. J. Comput. Graph. Stat. **13**(4), 996–1017 (2003)
4. Charlier, C.V.L.: Über das fehlergesetz. Arkiv för Matematik, Astronomi och Fysik **2**(20), 1–35 (1905)
5. Eberl, A., Klar, B.: Expectile-based measures of skewness. Scand. J. Stat. **49**(1), 373–399 (2021)
6. Edgeworth, F.Y.: The law of error. Trans. Cambridge Philosophical Soc. **20**, 36–65 and 113–114 (1904)
7. Fix, E., Hodges, J.L.: Nonparametric discrimination: Consistency properties. Tech. Rep. Report 11, USAF School of Aviation Medicine, Randolph Field, Texas (1951)
8. Grabisch, M., Marichal, J.L., Mesiar, R., Pap, E.: Aggregation Functions. Cambridge University Press, Cambridge (2009)
9. Groeneveld, R.A.: Skewness for the Weibull family. Stat. Neerl. **40**(3), 135–140 (1986)
10. Hinkley, D.V.: On power transformations to symmetry. Biometrika **62**, 101–111 (1975)
11. Hosking, J.R.M.: L-moments: analysis and estimation of distributions using linear combinations of order statistics. J. Roy. Stat. Soc.: Ser. B (Methodol.) **52**(1), 105–124 (1990)
12. Iturrate-Bobes, M., Montes, I., Perez-Fernandez, R.: Goodness-of-fit tests to location-scale families based on OWA functions. In: Baczyński, M., De Baets, B., Holčapek, M., Kreinovich, V., Medina, J. (eds.) Advances in Fuzzy Logic and Technology, pp. 53–65. Springer Nature Switzerland (2025)
13. MacGillivray, H.L.: Skewness and asymmetry: measures and orderings. The Annals of Statistics, pp. 994–1011 (1986)
14. Oja, H.: On location, scale, skewness and kurtosis of univariate distributions. Scand. J. Stat. **8**, 154–168 (1981)
15. Parzen, E.: On estimation of a probability density function and mode. Ann. Math. Stat. **33**(3), 1065–1076 (1962)
16. Pearson, K.: Contributions to the mathematical theory of evolution. II. Skew variation in homogeneous material. Philosophical Transactions of the Royal Society of London. Series A **186**, 343–414 (1895)
17. Rosenblatt, M.: Estimation of a probability density-function and mode. Ann. Math. Stat. **27**, 832–837 (1956)
18. Van der Vaart, A.W.: Asymptotic statistics, vol. 3. Cambridge University Press (2000)
19. van Zwet, W.R.: Convex Transformations of Random Variables. Mathematisch Centrum, Amsterdam (1964)
20. Yager, R.R.: On ordered weighted averaging aggregation operators in multicriteria decision making. IEEE Trans. Syst. Man Cybern. **18**(1), 183–190 (1988)
21. Yule, G.U.: An Introduction to the Theory of Statistics, 2nd edn. Griffin, London (1912)

Derivative for Discrete Sugeno Integral

Yasuo Narukawa[1], Zuzana Ontkovičová[2(✉)], and Vicenç Torra[3]

[1] Tamagawa University, 6-1-1 Tamagawagakuen, Machida, Tokyo 194-8610, Japan
nrkwy@eng.tamagawa.ac.jp

[2] Institute of Information Engineering, Automation and Mathematics, Faculty of Chemical and Food Technology, Slovak University of Technology in Bratislava, Bratislava, Slovakia
zuzana.ontkovicova@stuba.sk

[3] Department of Computing Science, Umeå University, Umeå, Sweden
vtorra@cs.umu.se

Abstract. The Radon-Nikodym derivative is a fundamental concept in probability theory, where it serves as the corresponding density function. Such a derivative is extensively used in applications, as it is the cornerstone of Hellinger distance, Kullback–Leibler divergence, and thus of entropy.

Replacing probabilities with fuzzy measures, where the additivity property is replaced by monotonicity, we aim to study derivatives with respect to the fuzzy measures in the context of the Sugeno integral, one of the most-common fuzzy integrals in practical applications. Specifically, the focus is on identifying the conditions for the existence of such derivatives and determining their form.

Two complementary approaches are used. The direct one allows the study of necessary and sufficient conditions for the existence of this type of derivative and provides particular examples illustrating its non-uniqueness. As an application, conditions for possibility measures are presented. The second - resulting measure approach - aims to find the form of the derivative by deriving the form of the resulting measure. The results are illustrated through a particular example, where the Sugeno derivative is explicitly computed.

Keywords: Measure derivatives · Sugeno integral · Fuzzy measures · Resulting measure approach

1 Introduction

The Radon-Nikodym derivative is a well known concept for probabilities (additive measures in general) considering Lebesgue integral. Assume two probabilities P_1 and P_2, where P_2 is absolutely continuous with respect to P_1 ($P_2 \ll P_1$). Then the (Lebesgue-)Radon-Nikodym derivative of P_2 with respect to P_1, commonly denoted as $\frac{dP_2}{dP_1}$, is the function that allows one to construct P_2 as the integral of the function with respect to P_1.

B. Vantaggi et al. (Eds.): IPMU 2026, CCIS 3019, pp. 31–42, 2026.
https://doi.org/10.1007/978-3-032-28994-0_3

The derivative plays a fundamental role, for example, in defining distances on probabilities. It serves as the basis for the f-divergence, which generalizes the Kullback–Leibler divergence, the Hellinger distance, the Rényi distance and the variation distance, among others.

The same type of derivative has also been considered when the measure is fuzzy. A few authors, [3] and [4] as the earliest ones, have studied Choquet-Radon-Nikodym (also Radon-Nikodym-like) derivatives for fuzzy measures considering the Choquet integral. The idea is basically the same. Given two fuzzy measures ν and μ, the Choquet-Radon-Nikodym derivative of ν with respect to μ is the function f that permits to construct ν as the Choquet integral of f with respect to μ. When ν and μ are probabilities, the Choquet-Radon-Nikodym derivative corresponds to the classical Radon-Nikodym derivative. The existence and calculation of the derivative remain difficult problems that continues to be studied by different authors, e.g., [5–7,9,11].

In this paper, we consider the same notion of derivatives for fuzzy measures, only with a different background, assuming integration with respect to the Sugeno integral. Introduced by Prof. Sugeno in his dissertation thesis [10], the Sugeno integral is one of the two most widely used integrals for fuzzy measures. Because of its high interpretability and close alignment with if-then rules, it is often used in fuzzy control systems, multi-criteria decision analysis, pattern recognition and AI and ML models. Unlike the Choquet integral with traditional arithmetic operations addition and multiplication, the Sugeno integral uses comparative operators minimum and maximum. It is therefore an appropriate integral for ordinal scales.

Here, we deal with the following problem. Given two fuzzy measures ν and μ, the Sugeno-Radon-Nikodym derivative of ν with respect to μ is the function f that allows one to construct ν as the Sugeno integral of f with respect to μ. In mathematical terms

$$\nu(A) = (S)\int_A f d\mu \qquad \Leftrightarrow \qquad f = \frac{d\nu}{d\mu}.$$

Our focus is on finding necessary and sufficient conditions for the existence of this derivative and ideally also investigating the form of the derivative itself.

The concept was briefly studied before. First proposed by Sugeno [10], followed up by Pucci and Candeloro [1], both provided only existence conditions, being too technical and complicated to verify.

The paper consists of five sections. Section 2 provides background theory concerning fuzzy measures and the Sugeno integral. The following two sections present main results on Sugeno-Radon-Nikodym derivatives, with direct approach for exploring existence conditions in Sect. 3, and resulting measure approach focused on finding the form of the derivatives in Sect. 4. Summarization and possible directions for future work are listed in Sect. 5.

2 Preliminaries

Let us consider the universal set $X := \{x_1, x_2. \cdots, x_n\}$ and review the definitions of fuzzy measure and the Sugeno integral as in [2,12,13].

Definition 1. *A set function $\mu : X \to R_0^+$ such that $\mu(\emptyset) = 0$ and is monotone with respect to the set inclusion (i.e., $\mu(A) \leq \mu(B)$ when $A \subset B$) is called a fuzzy measure (also non-additive measure, capacity or monotone game).*

It is often also considered that μ satisfies $\mu(X) = 1$. We do not require this condition here, although assume that $\mu(X) = a$ $(0 < a < \infty)$.

Definition 2. *A fuzzy measure μ on $(X, 2^X)$ is called a possibility measure, if $\mu(A \cup B) = \mu(A) \vee \mu(B)$ for all $A, B \in 2^X$, $\vee$ being the maximum on real line.*

Taking into account integration with respect to fuzzy measure, this paper focuses on the Sugeno integral.

Definition 3. *Let μ be a fuzzy measure and $f : X \to [0, \infty)$ a non-negative function. The Sugeno integral of the function f with respect to the fuzzy measure μ is defined by*

$$(S)\int f d\mu = \sup_{\alpha \geq 0} (\alpha \wedge \mu(\{x | f(x) \geq \alpha\})),$$

$\wedge$ being minimum on real line. Taking an arbitrary $A \subset X$, the Sugeno integral of the function f with respect to the fuzzy measure μ over the set A is defined by

$$(S)\int_A f d\mu = \sup_{\alpha \geq 0} (\alpha \wedge \mu(\{x | f(x) \geq \alpha\} \cap A)).$$

Since X is assumed finite in this paper, there exists a permutation σ on $\{1, 2, \ldots, n\}$ such that $f(x_{\sigma(1)}) \geq f(x_{\sigma(2)}) \geq \ldots f(x_{\sigma(n)})$ and the corresponding ordered set is given as $A_k := \{x_{\sigma(1)}, x_{\sigma(2)}, \ldots x_{\sigma(k)}\}$. Then the discrete Sugeno integral has the form

$$(S)\int f d\mu = \bigvee_{k=1}^{n} (f(x_{\sigma(k)}) \wedge \mu(A_k))$$

and for an arbitrary $A \subset X$

$$(S)\int_A f d\mu = \bigvee_{k=1}^{n} (f(x_{\sigma(k)}) \wedge \mu(A_k \cap A)).$$

3 The Direct Approach

In the following, let μ, ν be two fuzzy measures on $(X, 2^X)$ and assume a permutation σ on $\{1, 2, \ldots, n\}$ such that $\mu(\{x_{\sigma(1)}\}) \geq \mu(\{x_{\sigma(2)}\}) \geq \cdots \geq \mu(\{x_{\sigma(n)}\})$.

Suppose that there exists a derivative $f : X \to [0, \infty)$, that is,

$$\mu(A) = (S) \int_A f d\nu$$

for any $A \subset X$. Assuming singletons first, $\mu(\{x_i\}) = (S) \int_{\{x_i\}} f d\nu$ holds for each $i = 1, \ldots n$. Applying the definition of the discrete Sugeno integral,

$$\mu(\{x_i\}) = f(x_i) \wedge \nu(\{x_i\}).$$

Because of minimum, clearly $\mu(\{x_i\}) \leq \nu(\{x_i\})$, resulting in two options:
If $\mu(\{x_i\}) < \nu(\{x_i\})$, then $f(x_i) = \mu(\{x_i\})$.
If $\mu(\{x_i\}) = \nu(\{x_i\})$, then $f(x_i)$ can be any value greater or equal to $\mu(\{x_i\})$.
Therefore we have the next proposition.

Proposition 1. *Suppose there exists a derivative $f : X \to [0, \infty)$ such that,*

$$\mu(A) = (S) \int_A f d\nu$$

for all $A \subset X$. Then it holds $\mu(\{x_i\}) \leq \nu(\{x_i\})$ for all $i = 1, 2, \ldots n$.
Moreover, $f(x_i) = \begin{cases} \mu(\{x_i\}) & \text{if } \mu(\{x_i\}) < \nu(\{x_i\}) \\ (.) \geq \mu(\{x_i\}) & \text{if } \mu(\{x_i\}) = \nu(\{x_i\}). \end{cases}$

Notation $(.) \geq \mu(\{x_i\})$ means that the corresponding value of the derivative is guaranteed to be greater or equal to $\mu(\{x_i\})$. Whether it can be any such number, so the question of uniqueness, cannot be easily answered. The following example provides a clearer illustration of the problem.

Example 1. Let $X = \{x_1, x_2, x_3\}$ and the integration measure ν is given as

A	$\emptyset$	$\{x_1\}$	$\{x_2\}$	$\{x_3\}$	$\{x_1, x_2\}$	$\{x_2, x_3\}$	$\{x_1, x_3\}$	$\{x_1, x_2, x_3\}$
$\nu(A)$	0	0.01	0.2	0.03	0.4	0.2	0.05	0.6

First, knowing the derivative exists, we look at the problem from another perspective. Let us assume that we already have the derivative and want to find the resulting measure μ. Taking $f(x_1) = 0.3$, $f(x_2) = 0.1$ and $f(x_3) = 0.2$, μ values obtained after the Sugeno integration are

A	$\emptyset$	$\{x_1\}$	$\{x_2\}$	$\{x_3\}$	$\{x_1, x_2\}$	$\{x_2, x_3\}$	$\{x_1, x_3\}$	$\{x_1, x_2, x_3\}$
$\mu(A)$	0	0.01	0.1	0.03	0.1	0.1	0.05	0.1

where $\mu(X) = [f(x_1) \wedge \nu(\{x_1\})] \vee [f(x_3) \wedge \nu(\{x_1, x_3\})] \vee [f(x_2) \wedge \nu(\{X\})] = 0.1$ to illustrate the computation.
To check the derivative form from Proposition 1, we have

$$f(x_1) = \frac{d\mu(\{x_1\})}{d\nu(\{x_1\})} = 0.3 > \mu(\{x_1\}) \qquad \text{since}\, \mu(\{x_1\}) = \nu(\{x_1\})$$
$$f(x_2) = \frac{d\mu(\{x_2\})}{d\nu(\{x_2\})} = 0.1 = \mu(\{x_2\}) \qquad \text{since}\, \mu(\{x_2\}) < \nu(\{x_2\})$$
$$f(x_3) = \frac{d\mu(\{x_3\})}{d\nu(\{x_3\})} = 0.2 > \mu(\{x_3\}) \qquad \text{since}\, \mu(\{x_3\}) = \nu(\{x_3\}),$$

which aligns with the result.

The above problem of uniqueness arises when taking measure ν and different derivative g with $g(x_1) = 0.05$, $g(x_2) = 0.1$ and $g(x_3) = 0.3$. It is easy to see that the resulting measure μ is exactly the same as the one obtained for f. Thus, we have found two different functions which can be derivatives for the given μ and ν. Moreover, they are different not only in values, but also in their ordering. □

Remark 1. For the derivative values, we do not have one particular number, only half-open interval bounded from below. Because of this non-uniqueness and the issues associated with it, we choose the corresponding values as the lowest possible, so $f(x_i) = \mu(\{x_i\})$. However, it needs to be emphasized that it is only our choice and may be too restrictive in particular situations or applications.

Conversely, suppose that $\mu(\{x_i\}) \leq \nu(\{x_i\})$ for all i and set $f(x_i) = \mu(\{x_i\})$. From the construction, we have $\mu(\{x_i\}) = f(x_i) \wedge \nu(\{x_i\})$ and therefore for all i

$$\mu(\{x_i\}) = (S) \int_{\{x_i\}} f d\nu,$$

which leads to the following result.

Proposition 2. *Suppose that $\mu(\{x_i\}) \leq \nu(\{x_i\})$ for all $i = 1, \ldots, n$. Then there exists a function $f : X \to [0, \infty)$ such that*

$$\mu(A) = (S) \int_A f d\nu$$

for all $A \subset X$ where $|A| = 1$.[1]

Next, suppose that $\mu(\{x_i\}) \leq \nu(\{x_i\})$ for all i and $i < j$

$$\mu(\{x_{\sigma(i)}, x_{\sigma(j)}\}) = (S) \int_{\{x_{\sigma(i)}, x_{\sigma(j)}\}} f d\nu.$$

[1] The focus is only on singletons here, so nothing is said about μ values for non-singletons. As will be shown in the next section, this is a more complex problem in general, because the derivative does not exist for an arbitrary μ.

Then we have

$$\mu(\{x_{\sigma(i)}, x_{\sigma(j)}\}) = [f(x_{\sigma(i)}) \wedge \nu(\{x_{\sigma(i)}\}] \vee [f(x_{\sigma(j)} \wedge \nu(\{x_{\sigma(i)}, x_{\sigma(j)}\})].$$

Let us set again $f(x_i) = \mu(\{x_i\})$, so it holds $f(x_{\sigma(i)}) \geq f(x_{\sigma(j)})$ because of nonincreasing ordering by σ. Moreover, $f(x_{\sigma(i)}) \leq \nu(\{x_{\sigma(i)}\}) \leq \nu(\{x_{\sigma(i)}, x_{\sigma(j)}\})$ because of assumed relation between μ and ν and monotonicity of ν.

These inequalities result in

$$\begin{aligned}\mu(\{x_{\sigma(i)}, x_{\sigma(j)}\}) &= [\mu(\{x_{\sigma(i)}\}) \wedge \nu(\{x_{\sigma(i)}\}] \vee [\mu(\{x_{\sigma(j)}\}) \wedge \nu(\{x_{\sigma(i)}, x_{\sigma(j)}\})] \\ &= \mu(\{x_{\sigma(i)}\}) \vee \mu(\{x_{\sigma(j)}\}) \\ &= \mu(\{x_{\sigma(i)}\}).\end{aligned}$$

It is easy to see that, with the same logic as for two-element set, similar results can be shown with induction for a set with arbitrary finite number of elements, for any $\mu(\{x_{\sigma(i_1)}, x_{\sigma(i_2)}, \ldots, x_{\sigma(i_k)}\})$, where $1 \leq i_1 < i_2 < \cdots < i_k \leq n$. Also, the second line above suggests μ is a possibility measure, i.e., $\mu(\{x_{\sigma(i)}, x_{\sigma(j)}\}) = \mu(\{x_{\sigma(i)}\}) \vee \mu(\{x_{\sigma(j)}\})$. This fact is clear in all the induction steps.

Moreover, measure μ for $A = \{x_{\sigma(i_1)}, x_{\sigma(i_2)}, \ldots, x_{\sigma(i_k)}\}$ has the form

$$\mu(A) = \begin{cases} \mu(\{x_{i_1}\}) & \text{if } k = 1 \ (|A| = 1) \\ \mu(\{x_{\sigma(i_1)}\}) & \text{if } k \geq 2 \ (|A| \geq 2). \end{cases} \tag{1}$$

Clearly $\mu(\emptyset) = 0$ from the definition of fuzzy measure. Thus, the following proposition can be presented.

Proposition 3. *Suppose that there exists a derivative $f : X \to [0, \infty)$ that is*

$$\mu(A) = (S) \int_A f d\nu$$

for all $A \subset X$, $\mu(\{x_i\}) \leq \nu(\{x_i\})$ and $f(x_i) = \mu(\{x_i\})$ for all $i = 1, 2, \ldots n$. Then μ is a possibility measure with the form (1).

Example 2. Let $X := \{x_1, x_2, x_3\}$, and define fuzzy measures as

A	$\emptyset$	$\{x_1\}$	$\{x_2\}$	$\{x_3\}$	$\{x_1, x_2\}$	$\{x_2, x_3\}$	$\{x_1, x_3\}$	$\{x_1, x_2, x_3\}$
$\mu(A)$	0	0.8	0.5	0.2	-	-	-	-
$\nu(A)$	0	0.8	0.6	0.4	1.0	0.9	0.8	1.0

According to the derivation of Proposition 3, we only need values of measure μ on singletons to find the corresponding derivative. Thus, the derivative of μ with respect to ν for the Sugeno integral is given as $f(x_1) = \mu(\{x_1\}) = 0.8$, $f(x_2) = \mu(\{x_2\}) = 0.5$, and $f(x_3) = \mu(\{x_3\}) = 0.2$.

Now, by computing the remaining values of μ as the result after the corresponding Sugeno integration, we verify if it is a possibility measure as stated in Proposition 3. For example

$$\begin{aligned}\mu(\{x_2, x_3\}) = (S) \int_{\{x_2, x_3\}} f d\nu &= [f(x_2) \wedge \nu(\{x_2\})] \vee [f(x_3) \wedge \nu(\{x_2, x_3\})] \\ &= (0.5 \wedge 0.6) \vee (0.2 \wedge 0.9) = 0.5\end{aligned}$$

$$\mu(X) = (S)\int_X f d\nu = [f(x_1) \wedge \nu(\{x_1\})] \vee [f(x_2) \wedge \nu(\{x_1, x_2\})] \vee [f(x_3) \wedge \nu(X)]$$
$$= (0.8 \wedge 0.8) \vee (0.5 \wedge 1) \vee (0.2 \wedge 1) = 0.8$$

All the values for μ are listed below, from which it is clear that μ truly is a possibility measure.

A	$\emptyset$	$\{x_1\}$	$\{x_2\}$	$\{x_3\}$	$\{x_1, x_2\}$	$\{x_2, x_3\}$	$\{x_1, x_3\}$	$\{x_1, x_2, x_3\}$
$\mu(A)$	0	0.8	0.5	0.2	0.8	0.5	0.8	0.8

□

Conversely, let $A := \{x_{\sigma(i_1)}, x_{\sigma(i_2)}, \ldots, x_{\sigma(i_k)}\}$ $(1 \leq i_1 < i_2 < \cdots < i_k \leq n)$ be a subset of X and μ a possibility measure. We also assume that for all i $\mu(\{x_{\sigma(i)}\}) \leq \nu(\{x_{\sigma(i)}\})$.
Then define a function $f : X \to [0, \infty)$ by $f(x_i) = \mu(\{x_i\})$ for each i. From that, we obtain

$$(S)\int_A f d\nu = [f(x_{\sigma(i_1)}) \wedge \nu(\{x_{\sigma(i_1)}\}] \vee [f(x_{\sigma(i_2)}) \wedge \nu(\{x_{\sigma(i_1)}, x_{\sigma(i_2)}\}] \vee \ldots$$
$$\cdots \vee [f(x_{\sigma(i_k)}) \wedge \nu(A)].$$

Since $\nu(\{x_i\}) \leq \nu(\{x_i, x_j\}) \leq \cdots \leq \nu(A)$ from monotonicity of ν, and from comparison between μ, ν and f we have $f(x_i) \leq \nu(\{x_i\})$ for each i, it holds

$$(S)\int_A f d\nu = [f(x_{\sigma(i_1)}) \wedge \nu(\{x_{\sigma(i_1)}\})] \vee [f(x_{\sigma(i_2)}) \wedge \nu(\{x_{\sigma(i_2)}\})] \vee \ldots$$
$$\cdots \vee [f(x_{\sigma(i_k)}) \wedge \nu(\{x_{\sigma(i_k)}\})]$$
$$= f(x_{\sigma(i_1)}) \vee f(x_{\sigma(i_2)}) \vee \cdots \vee f(x_{\sigma(i_k)}).$$

Therefore
$$\mu(A) = (S)\int_A f d\nu = f(x_{\sigma(i_1)}) = \mu(\{x_{\sigma(i_1)}\}).$$

Since μ is a possibility measure, $\mu(A) = \mu(\{x_{\sigma(i_1)})\})$.

Proposition 4. *Suppose that μ is a possibility measure and $\mu(\{x_i\}) \leq \nu(\{x_i\})$ for all $i = 1, 2, \ldots n$. Then, assuming an arbitrary $A \subset X$, there exists a function (derivative) $f : X \to [0, \infty)$, that is*

$$\mu(A) = (S)\int_A f d\nu.$$

4 The Resulting Measure Approach

Previous section was concerned primarily with the existence of the Sugeno derivatives, while here we also want to examine their explicit form. There, we tried to directly make a conclusion for the derivative, assuming both measures are known. Now, let us look at the Sugeno integral from another perspective - by assuming the integration function f and measure ν and looking at the resulting measure μ. The approach is adopted from [8], where the authors deal with the same problem for the Choquet version of the derivatives.

Looking again at the definition of the discrete Sugeno integral and assuming $A = \{x_{\sigma(i_1)}, x_{\sigma(i_2)}, \dots, x_{\sigma(i_k)}\}$ with $1 \le i_1 < i_2 < \dots < i_k \le n$

$$\begin{aligned}\mu(A) &= (S)\int_A f d\nu \\ &= [f(x_{\sigma(i_1)}) \wedge \nu(\{x_{\sigma(i_1)}\})] \vee [f(x_{\sigma(i_2)}) \wedge \nu(\{x_{\sigma(i_1)}, x_{\sigma(i_2)}\})] \vee \dots \\ &\quad \dots \vee [f(x_{\sigma(i_k)}) \wedge \nu(\{x_{\sigma(i_1)}, x_{\sigma(i_2)}, \dots, x_{\sigma(i_k)}\})].\end{aligned}$$

It is clear that $\{f(x_{\sigma(i)})\}_{i=1}^n$ is non-increasing and $\{\nu(\{x_{\sigma(1)}, \dots, x_{\sigma(i)}\})\}_{i=1}^n$ is non-decreasing with respect to i. Dealing with minimum and maximum in the definition, three possible cases need to be considered:
If $f(x_i) \ge \nu(\{x_1, \dots, x_i\})$ for all i, then

$$\begin{aligned}\mu(A) &= \nu(\{x_{\sigma(i_1)}\}) \vee \nu(\{x_{\sigma(i_1)}, x_{\sigma(i_2)}\}) \vee \dots \vee \nu(\{x_{\sigma(i_1)}, x_{\sigma(i_2)}, \dots, x_{\sigma(i_k)}\}) \\ &= \nu(\{x_{\sigma(i_1)}, x_{\sigma(i_2)}, \dots, x_{\sigma(i_k)}\}) = \nu(A),\end{aligned}$$

resulting in measures μ and ν being identical. Thus function f can have any values if the initial condition is satisfied.
If $f(x_i) \le \nu(\{x_1, \dots, x_i\})$ for all i, then

$$\mu(A) = f(x_{\sigma(i_1)}) \vee f(x_{\sigma(i_2)}) \vee \dots \vee f(x_{\sigma(i_k)}) = f(x_{\sigma(i_1)}),$$

so resulting measure is a constant equal to the maximal value of f on A.
If there exists $\alpha \in \{2, \dots, n\}$ such that $f(x_{\sigma(i_j)}) \ge \nu(\{x_{\sigma(i_1)}, \dots, x_{\sigma(i_j)}\})$ for all $j < \alpha$ and $f(x_{\sigma(i_{j+1})}) < \nu(\{x_{\sigma(i_1)}, \dots, x_{\sigma(i_j)}, x_{\sigma(i_{j+1})}\})$ for all $j \ge \alpha$, then

$$\begin{aligned}\mu(A) &= \nu(\{x_{\sigma(i_1)}\}) \vee \dots \vee \nu(\{x_{\sigma(i_1)}, \dots, x_{\sigma(i_{\alpha-1}}\}) \vee f(x_{\sigma(i_\alpha)}) \vee \dots \vee f(x_{\sigma(i_k)}) \\ &= \nu(\{x_{\sigma(i_1)}, \dots, x_{\sigma(i_{\alpha-1})}\}) \vee f(x_{\sigma(i_\alpha)}).\end{aligned}$$

Introducing notation $B = \{x_{\sigma(i_1)}, \dots, x_{\sigma(i_j)}\}$, depending on the comparison between corresponding values of f and ν, μ in this case is either equal to $\nu(B)$ or the maximal value of f on $(A \setminus B)$.

From these cases, the result for the derivative can be directly deduced, as done in the following theorem. With this approach, answer for existence as well as form of the derivative can be provided.

Proposition 5. *Assume a permutation* $\sigma : \{1, 2, \dots, n\} \to \{1, 2, \dots, n\}$ *ordering values in a non-increasing way and two fuzzy measures* μ, ν *on a discrete set* $X = \{x_1, x_2, \dots, x_n\}$ *with an arbitrary* $A \subset X, A = \{x_{\sigma(i_1)}, x_{\sigma(i_2)}, \dots, x_{\sigma(i_k)}\}$, $1 \le i_1 < i_2 < \dots < i_k \le n$. *Then the corresponding Sugeno-Radon-Nikodym derivative* f *with* $\mu(A) = (S)\int_A f d\nu$ *exists if one of the following conditions is satisfied, with the corresponding form:*

I) $\mu \equiv \nu$; *then the derivative* f *has arbitrary values while condition* $f(x_{\sigma(i)}) \geq \nu(\{x_{\sigma(1)}, \ldots, x_{\sigma(i)}\})$ *holds for all* $i = 1, \ldots, n$.

II) $\mu(A) = \begin{cases} 0 & \text{if } A = \emptyset \\ c & \text{otherwise} \end{cases}$, $c \in \mathbb{R}^+$; *then* $f(x_{\sigma(1)}) = c$ *and other values of* f *are arbitrary, only satisfying* $f(x_{\sigma(i)}) \leq \nu(\{x_{\sigma(1)}, \ldots, x_{\sigma(i)}\})$ *for* $i > 1$.

III) $\exists \alpha \in \{2, \ldots, n\}$ $\mu(\{x_{\sigma(i_1)}, \ldots, x_{\sigma(i_j)}\}) = \begin{cases} \nu(\{x_{\sigma(i_1)}, \ldots, x_{\sigma(i_j)}\}) & \text{if } j < \alpha \\ c & \text{otherwise} \end{cases}$ *with* $c \in \mathbb{R}^+$ *not violating monotonicity of* μ; *then the derivative is given in the form*

$$f(x_{\sigma(i_j)}) = \begin{cases} (.) \geq \nu(\{x_{\sigma(i_1)}, \ldots, x_{\sigma(i_j)}\}) & \text{if } j < \alpha \\ c & \text{if } j = \alpha \\ \nu(\{x_{\sigma(1)}, \ldots, x_{\sigma(i_j)}\}) & \text{if } j > \alpha \end{cases}$$

where notation (.) *signifies a suitable value satisfying the given condition.*

Suitable value in the theorem above means exactly the same as in Proposition 1, since non-uniqueness is again included, as illustrated in Example 1.

Note that the form of ν is not particularly important in finding the derivative, the crucial aspect is the form of the measure μ. The proposition also suggests that if the form of μ is different from the three cases mentioned above, f as the derivative of μ with respect to any ν does not exist (cannot be determined).

Example 3. Let $X = \{x_1, x_2, x_3\}$ and we deal with three fuzzy measures ν, μ_1 and μ_2, which are given as

A	$\emptyset$	$\{x_1\}$	$\{x_2\}$	$\{x_3\}$	$\{x_1, x_2\}$	$\{x_2, x_3\}$	$\{x_1, x_3\}$	$\{x_1, x_2, x_3\}$
$\nu(A)$	0	0.1	0.2	0.3	0.7	0.5	0.4	0.9
$\mu_1(A)$	0	0.1	0.2	0.3	0.7	0.5	0.4	0.9
$\mu_2(A)$	0	0.6	0.6	0.6	0.6	0.6	0.6	0.6

First, let us find the derivative $f = \dfrac{d\nu}{d\mu_1}$.

Since $\nu \equiv \mu_1$, according to Theorem 5 I) it holds $f(x_{\sigma(1)}) \geq \nu(\{x_{\sigma(1)}\})$, $f(x_{\sigma(2)}) \geq \nu(\{x_{\sigma(1)}, x_{\sigma(2)}\})$, $f(x_{\sigma(3)}) \geq \nu(X)$, and from the ordering of derivative values $f(x_{\sigma(1)}) \geq f(x_{\sigma(2)}) \geq f(x_{\sigma(3)})$.

In particular, we take $f(x_2) \geq f(x_3) \geq f(x_1)$. Then, $f(x_2) \geq \nu(\{x_2\}) = 0.2$, $f(x_3) \geq \nu(\{x_2, x_3\}) = 0.4$, $f(x_1) \geq \nu(X) = 0.9$. Putting all the conditions together, clearly $f(x_2) \geq f(x_3) \geq f(x_1) \geq 0.9 = \nu(X)$.

In general, all the conditions can be replaced with just one, stating $f(x_{\sigma(i)}) \geq \nu(A)$ for all i.

Second, we find the derivative $g = \dfrac{d\nu}{d\mu_2}$.

Because μ_2 has constant values (except the empty set), using Theorem 5 II) we have $g(x_{\sigma(1)}) = \mu_2(\{x_{\sigma(1)}\})$, $g(x_{\sigma(2)}) \leq \nu(\{x_{\sigma(1)}, x_{\sigma(2)}\})$, $g(x_{\sigma(3)}) \leq \nu(X)$, and from the ordering of derivative values $g(x_{\sigma(1)}) \geq g(x_{\sigma(2)}) \geq g(x_{\sigma(3)})$.

Taking $g(x_1) \geq g(x_2) \geq g(x_3)$, $g(x_1) = \mu_2(\{x_1\}) = 0.6$, $g(x_2) \leq \nu(\{x_1, x_2\}) = 0.7$ and $g(x_3) \leq \nu(X) = 0.9$. Summarising all the conditions, $0.6 = g(x_1) \geq g(x_2) \geq g(x_3)$.
Taking $g(x_2) \geq g(x_3) \geq g(x_1)$, $g(x_2) = \mu_2(\{x_2\}) = 0.6$, $g(x_3) \leq \nu(\{x_2, x_3\}) = 0.4$ and $g(x_3) \leq \nu(X) = 0.9$. It results in one joint condition $0.6 = g(x_2) \geq \nu(\{x_2, x_3\}) = 0.4 \geq g(x_3) \geq g(x_1)$.
In general, provided conditions can be replaced by a new ones in the form $f(x_{\sigma(1)}) = \mu_2(\{x_{\sigma(1)}\})$ and $f(x_{\sigma(i)}) \leq [f(x_{\sigma(1)}) \wedge \nu(\{x_{\sigma(1)}, x_{\sigma(2)}\})]$ for all $i > 1$. □

Building on the observations and the simplified conditions from the example above, we now present the following theorem. It serves as a refined extension of Proposition 5, integrating all proposed relations into a more detailed and comprehensive form.

Theorem 1 (Modified Proposition 5). *Let $\sigma : \{1, 2, \ldots, n\} \to \{1, 2, \ldots, n\}$ be a permutation ordering values in a non-increasing way and μ, ν two fuzzy measures on a discrete set $X = \{x_1, x_2, \ldots, x_n\}$ with an arbitrary $A \subset X, A = \{x_{\sigma(i_1)}, x_{\sigma(i_2)}, \ldots, x_{\sigma(i_k)}\}$, $1 \leq i_1 < i_2 < \cdots < i_k \leq n$. Then the corresponding Sugeno-Radon-Nikodym derivative f with $\mu(A) = (S)\int_A f d\nu$ exists if one of the following conditions is satisfied, with the corresponding form:*

I) $\mu \equiv \nu$; then the derivative f has arbitrary values satisfying the condition $f(x_{\sigma(i)}) \geq \nu(A)$ for all $i = 1, \ldots, n$.

II) $\mu(A) = \begin{cases} 0 & \text{if } A = \emptyset \\ & \text{otherwise} \end{cases}, c \in \mathbb{R}^+$; then $f(x_{\sigma(1)}) = c$ and other values of f are arbitrary satisfying $f(x_{\sigma(i)}) \leq [f(x_{\sigma(1)}) \wedge \nu(A)]$ for all $i > 1$.

III) $\exists \alpha \in \{2, \ldots, n\}$ $\mu(\{x_{\sigma(i_1)}, \ldots, x_{\sigma(i_j)}\}) = \begin{cases} \nu(\{x_{\sigma(i_1)}, \ldots, x_{\sigma(i_j)}\}) & \text{if } j < \alpha \\ c & \text{otherwise} \end{cases}$, with $c \in \mathbb{R}^+$ not violating monotonicity of μ; then the derivative is given in the form

$$f(x_{\sigma(i_j)}) = \begin{cases} (.) \geq \nu(\{x_{\sigma(i_1)}, \ldots, x_{\sigma(i_j)}\}) & \text{if } j < \alpha \\ c & \text{if } j = \alpha \\ (.) \leq \nu(\{x_{\sigma(1)}, \ldots, x_{\sigma(i_j)}\}) & \text{if } j > \alpha \end{cases}$$

where notation (.) signifies a suitable value satisfying the given condition.

The following example illustrates the idea behind the third case in the theorem above. Moreover, it presents the most general case one can encounter when finding the derivative form. Without checking the conditions from Proposition 5, we try to obtain the same outcomes.

Example 4. Let $X = \{x_1, x_2, x_3\}$ and measures μ and ν are given as below.

A	$\emptyset$	$\{x_1\}$	$\{x_2\}$	$\{x_3\}$	$\{x_1, x_2\}$	$\{x_2, x_3\}$	$\{x_1, x_3\}$	$\{x_1, x_2, x_3\}$
$\mu(A)$	0	0.1	0.2	0.3	0.4	0.4	0.4	0.4
$\nu(A)$	0	0.1	0.2	0.3	0.5	0.6	0.7	0.8

First, $\mu \leq \nu$ from Proposition 1 holds, which is a necessary condition for existence of the derivative. Without loss of generality, let $f(x_1) \geq f(x_2) \geq f(x_3)$. Then

$$\begin{aligned}\mu(X) &= [f(x_1) \wedge \nu(\{x_1\})] \vee [f(x_2) \wedge \nu(\{x_1, x_2\})] \vee [f(x_3) \wedge \nu(X)] \\ &= [f(x_1) \wedge 0.1] \vee [f(x_2) \wedge 0.5] \vee [f(x_3) \wedge 0.8] = 0.4\end{aligned}$$

At a glance, no ν value is equal to the result, so at least one f value has to be. From that the maximal f value needs to be at least equal to 0.4, so $f(x_1) \geq 0.4$. Looking at the individual minimum comparisons, it is clear that the first one cannot give the resulting value. Therefore, the second highest f value should be at least 0.4, so $f(x_2) \geq 0.4$. Moreover, the second bracket also implies $f(x_2) < 0.5$ otherwise ν value is lower and $f(x_2) \leq 0.4$ for the final result to hold. By the same logic, third minimum comparison gives $f(x_3) < 0.8$ and $f(x_3) \leq 0.4$.

Thus, the joint condition is $f(x_1) \geq f(x_2) \geq 0.4 \geq f(x_2) \geq f(x_3)$, which can be modified to $f(x_1) \geq f(x_2) = 0.4 \geq f(x_3)$, fully corresponding to the conditions proposed in the Proposition 5. □

5 Conclusions

We have explored in this paper a novel insight into the concept of Radon-Nikodym derivatives, based on fuzzy measures and Sugeno integral, referred to as the Sugeno-Radon-Nikodym derivatives. The focus is on the existence conditions, with non-uniqueness illustrated in examples, and the corresponding form of the derivatives also being derived. Two complementary approaches were used, the direct one - knowing measures and finding the derivative, from which the existence conditions were derived, and the resulting measure approach - assuming the derivative and integration measure while deriving the resulting measure, which proved to be a more suitable perspective for obtaining the derivative form.

Exploring the topic of the Sugeno-Radon-Nikodym derivatives offers a wide range of possible directions for future research. Studying the derivatives for particular measures or gaining deeper insight into their non-uniqueness can be helpful in practical applications. From a theoretical standpoint, the problem of non-existence of the derivative when resulting measure μ is not in the form presented in theorems is particularly interesting.

Overall, while the concept shows considerable potential for significance in practical problems, a deeper and more systematic investigation is required - an effort that this paper aims to initiate.

Acknowledgements. This work was supported by the Wallenberg AI, Autonomous Systems and Software Program (WASP) funded by the Knut and Alice Wallenberg Foundation (prof. Torra), by JSPS KAKENHI Grant No. JP25K15266 from Japan Society for the Promotion of Science (Prof. Narukawa), and by VEGA 1/0318/25 grant provided by the Slovak Ministry of Education, Research, Development, and Youth (Dr. Ontkovičová).

References

1. Candeloro, D., Pucci, S.: Radon-Nikodym derivatives and conditioning in fuzzy measure theory. Stochastica **11**(2–3), 107–120 (1987)
2. Grabisch, M.: Set functions, games and capacities in decision making, vol. 46. Springer, Berlin (2016). https://doi.org/10.1007/978-3-319-30690-2
3. Graf, S.: A Radon-Nikodym theorem for capacities. Journal für die reine und angewandte Mathematik, 192-214 (1980). https://doi.org/10.1515/crll.1980.320.192
4. Huber, P.J., Strassen, V.: Minimax tests and the Neyman-Pearson lemma for capacities. The Annals of Statistics, 251–263 (1973)
5. Mesiar, R., Šipoš, J.: Radon-Nikodym-like theorem for fuzzy measures. J. Fuzzy Math. **1**, 873–878 (1993)
6. Narukawa, Y., Torra, V.: Derivative for discrete Choquet integrals. In: International Conference on Modeling Decisions for Artificial Intelligence, 138–147 (2019). https://doi.org/10.1007/978-3-030-26773-5_13
7. Ontkovičová, Z., and Kiseľák, J. (2022) A way to proper generalization of ϕ-divergence based on Choquet derivatives. Soft Comput. **26**(21), 11295–11314. https://doi.org/10.1007/s00500-022-07381-5
8. Ontkovičová, Z., and Torra, V. (2025). On measures resulting from the Choquet integration. In: Information Processing and Management of Uncertainty in Knowledge-Based Systems 2, 3-11. https://doi.org/10.1007/978-3-031-74000-8_1
9. Rébillé, R.: A Super Radon-Nikodym derivative for almost subadditive set functions. Int. J. Uncertainty, Fuzziness Knowl.-Based Syst. **21**(03), 347–365 (2013). https://doi.org/10.1142/S0218488513500189
10. Sugeno, M.: Theory of fuzzy integrals and its applications. Doctoral Thesis, Tokyo Institute of Technology (1974)
11. Sugeno, M.: A note on derivatives of functions with respect to fuzzy measures. Fuzzy Sets Syst. **222**, 1–17 (2013). https://doi.org/10.1016/j.fss.2012.11.003
12. Torra, V., Narukawa, Y., Sugeno, M. (eds.) Non-additive measures: theory and applications. Springer (2013)
13. Wang, Z., Klir, G.J.: Generalized measure theory (Vol. 25). Springer Science & Business Media (2010)

A New Construction Method for Uninorms on a Bounded Lattice Through Uninorms on Its Subintervals

Gül Deniz Çaylı(✉)

Department of Mathematics, Faculty of Science, Karadeniz Technical University, 61080 Trabzon, Turkey
guldeniz.cayli@ktu.edu.tr

Abstract. In this paper, we introduce two new methods for constructing uninorms on a bounded lattice L. These methods are based on the use of t-norms (or t-conorms) and uninorms defined on specific subsets of L. Unlike existing approaches that mainly rely on t-norms and t-conorms, our methods also use uninorms defined on subsets of L, which provide greater flexibility. We show that the proposed constructions extend several known methods in the literature and generate new classes of uninorms. Furthermore, several examples are given to illustrate the effectiveness and distinct features of the proposed methods.

Keywords: Bounded lattice · Neutral element · T-norm · T-conorm · Uninorm

1 Introduction

Uninorms, introduced by Yager and Rybalov [42], provide a natural generalization of t-norms and t-conorms by allowing the neutral element to take any value in the unit interval $[0,1]$. They reduce to t-norms and t-conorms when the neutral element is equal to 1 and 0, respectively, while proper uninorms correspond to the case where the neutral element lies in $]0,1[$. Owing to this flexibility, uninorms have attracted considerable attention in both theoretical investigations [15–17,20] and a wide range of applications, including fuzzy logic [31], fuzzy system modeling [43], decision-making [44], image processing [21], and neural networks [35].

While the theory of uninorms on the unit interval is well developed, their extension to bounded lattices introduces substantial structural complexity. Bounded lattices provide a richer and more general framework than the unit interval, but this generality makes the construction and analysis of aggregation operators considerably more challenging. In this context, Asmus et al. [1] proposed methods for constructing (a,b)-aggregation functions by utilizing t-norms, t-conorms, and uninorms defined on $[0,1]$, leading to applications such as max pooling in convolutional neural networks [26]. Karaçal and Mesiar [24] introduced the concept of uninorms on bounded lattices and showed that such operators can be generated using t-norms and t-conorms. Subsequently, Bodjanova and Kalina [7,8] developed two construction methods based on the simultaneous use of t-norms and t-conorms. Several further contributions have been

B. Vantaggi et al. (Eds.): IPMU 2026, CCIS 3019, pp. 43–58, 2026.
https://doi.org/10.1007/978-3-032-28994-0_4

made in this area. Çaylı [9] proposed methods for constructing uninorms that are neither conjunctive nor disjunctive. Dan et al. [13,14] examined structural properties of uninorms when either a t-norm or a t-conorm is given on a bounded lattice. In addition, Ç aylı [9,11] studied internal uninorms and introduced construction approaches based on both t-norms and t-conorms. The contribution of Xie and Li [40] identified the largest and smallest uninorms on bounded lattices. Moreover, Ouyang and Zhang [32] improved a construction method derived from closure and interior operators, encompassing special cases of approaches in [24]. Aşıcı and Mesiar [3,4] further contributed by proposing methods based on either a t-norm or a t-conorm. For additional developments on uninorms on bounded lattices, we refer to [22,25,29,30,33,34,37–39,46]. Despite these extensive studies, constructing uninorms on bounded lattices remains a challenging problem due to the structural complexity of these lattices. Most existing approaches are based on t-norms and t-conorms. More recently, Xiu and Zheng [41] introduced a method that constructs uninorms on a bounded lattice L by using uninorms defined on sublattices of L, providing a new perspective on the problem. However, a characterization of uninorms on bounded lattices is still not available. Motivated by these observations, this paper proposes a new approach for constructing uninorms on bounded lattices by utilizing uninorms defined on specific subsets of a bounded lattice L. This approach goes beyond traditional methods that rely solely on t-norms and t-conorms. In particular, we develop a construction based on a uninorm U' on $L\backslash I_a$, where I_a denotes the set of all elements incomparable with the fixed element $a \in L\backslash\{0,1\}$, together with a t-conorm (or, dually, a t-norm) on L. The proposed methods generate new classes of uninorms and extend several existing constructions in the literature.

A distinctive feature of our approach is that it allows greater structural flexibility. In particular, when the neutral element coincides with the indicated element a, the resulting uninorms significantly generalize previously known classes [3,4,11,24,41]. Furthermore, the proposed framework highlights essential differences from the method introduced in [41], especially in terms of how the operator behaves on specific subsets of L. More precisely, in the domains $[0,e]\times]a,1]$ and $(]e,a]\cup I_e^a)\times]a,1]\cup[a,1]^2$, the method in [41] yields the value y and $R(x\vee a,y)$, respectively, where R is a t-superconorm on $[a,1]^2$. In contrast, our approach uses the uninorm U' in these domains. Furthermore, on the domains $(I_a)^2$ and $I_e^a \times I_a$, our method produces the values $S(x,y)$ and y, respectively. The method in [41], however, relies on the t-superconorm R, whose values are always comparable with a, which restricts its flexibility. Both methods coincide on the remaining domains, especially when the elements of $]a,1[$ and I_a are incomparable. These differences highlight the broader structure of our construction and lead to new classes of uninorms on bounded lattices.

The remainder of the paper is organized as follows. Section 2 provides preliminary definitions and basic results on bounded lattices and uninorms on them. Section 3 presents two methods for constructing uninorms on a bounded lattice L using uninorms defined on certain subsets of L. These methods are based on either a t-conorm or a t-norm. They also allow the construction of new families of t-norms and t-conorms under certain conditions. Furthermore, we show that our methods are structurally different from the approaches in [3,4,11,24,40,41]. The final section concludes the paper and discusses possible directions for future research.

2 Preliminaries

In this section, we recall basic definitions and results related to bounded lattices and uninorms on them.

A lattice [6] is a nonempty set L equipped with an order relation $\leq$ such that any two elements $a,b \in L$ have a least upper bound (called the join or supremum), denoted by $a \vee b$, and a greatest lower bound (called the meet or infimum), denoted by $a \wedge b$.

For $a,b \in L$, we write $a < b$ if $a \leq b$ and $a \neq b$. If neither $a \leq b$ nor $b \leq a$, then a and b are said to be incomparable, denoted by $a \parallel b$. Otherwise, they are comparable. In this case, we use the notation $a \nparallel b$. We denote by I_a the set of all elements incomparable with a; that is, $I_a = \{x \in L : x \parallel a\}$. $I_{a,b}$ denotes the set of all elements incomparable with both a and b; that is, $I_{a,b} = \{x \in L : x \parallel a \text{ and } x \parallel b\}$. I_a^b denotes the set of all elements that are incomparable with a but comparable with b; that is, $I_a^b = \{x \in L : x \parallel a$ and $x \nparallel b\}$. For $a,b \in L$ with $a \leq b$, the subintervals $[a,b]$, $[a,b[$, $]a,b]$ and $]a,b[$ of L are defined in the usual way.

A lattice $(L,\leq)$ is called bounded if it has a bottom element 0 and a top element 1, that is, two elements $1,0 \in L$ exist such that $0 \leq x \leq 1$ for all $x \in L$. Throughout this paper, unless stated otherwise, we denote by L a bounded lattice with the bottom element 0 and the top element 1.

Definition 1 **([12,19,24]).** *A binary operation $U : L \times L \to L$ is called a uninorm if, for any $x,y,z \in L$, it satisfies:*

(i) $U(x,z) \leq U(y,z)$ for $x \leq y$ (increasingness);
(ii) $U(x,U(y,z)) = U(U(x,y),z)$ (associativity);
(iii) $U(x,y) = U(y,x)$ (commutativity);
(iv) there exists $e \in L$ such that $U(x,e) = x$ (neutral element).

A uninorm U on L is called idempotent if $U(x,x) = x$ for all $x \in L$. We denote by $\mathscr{U}_{id}$ the class of all idempotent uninorms U on L. It is called disjunctive (resp. conjunctive) if $U(0,1) = 1$ (resp. $U(0,1) = 0$). We denote by $\mathscr{U}_d$ (resp. $\mathscr{U}_c$) the class of all disjunctive (resp. conjunctive) uninorms U on L. A t-norm (resp. t-conorm) on L is a uninorm with the neutral element 1 (resp. 0) (refer to [2,18,27,28,36]).

Example 1. (i) The strongest t-norm on $[a,b]^2$ is $T_\wedge$, defined by $T_\wedge(x,y) = x \wedge y$ for all $x,y \in [a,b]$, while the weakest t-norm on $[a,b]^2$ is T_W, which takes the value $x \wedge y$ if $b \in \{x,y\}$ and a otherwise.
(ii) The weakest t-conorm on $[a,b]^2$ is $S_\vee$, defined by $S_\vee(x,y) = x \vee y$ for all $x,y \in [a,b]$, while the strongest t-conorm on $[a,b]^2$ is S_W, which takes the value $x \vee y$ if $a \in \{x,y\}$ and b otherwise.

Definition 2 **([23]).** *A binary operation R on L is called a t-superconorm (resp. t-subnorm) if it is increasing, associative, commutative, and satisfies $x \vee y \leq R(x,y)$ (resp. $R(x,y) \leq x \wedge y$) for all $x,y \in L$.*

Definition 3 **([45]).** *Let $e \in L \setminus \{0,1\}$. $\mathscr{U}_{\min}$ denotes the class of all uninorms U on L with the neutral element e such that $U(x,y) = y$ for all $(x,y) \in]e,1] \times L \setminus [e,1]$. Similarly, $\mathscr{U}_{\max}$ denotes the class of all uninorms U on L with the neutral element e such that $U(x,y) = y$ for all $(x,y) \in [0,e[\times L \setminus [0,e]$.*

3 Constructions of New Uninorms on Bounded Lattices

After the introduction of uninorms on the unit interval, their extension to bounded lattices has become an important research topic. Karaçal and Mesiar [24] introduced uninorms on bounded lattices and showed that they can be generated using t-norms and t-conorms. More recently, Xiu and Zheng [41] proposed a method based on uninorms defined on a subinterval of bounded lattices. However, a characterization of such uninorms is still not available.

In this section, we present two new methods for constructing uninorms on bounded lattices. These methods generalize several earlier approaches described in papers [3,4, 11,24,40] and provide new classes of uninorms. We also compare our methods with the one proposed in [41] and highlight the main differences. More specifically, we propose in Theorem 1 a method for constructing uninorms on a bounded lattice L that satisfies the following conditions:

$$x < y \text{ for all } x \in [0,e[\text{ and } y \in I_a, \tag{C1}$$

$$z < y \text{ for all } z \in I_e^a \text{ and } y \in I_a, \tag{C2}$$

$$t \| y \text{ for all } t \in]e,a[\cup]a,1[\text{ and } y \in I_a, \tag{C3}$$

for $a \in L \backslash \{0,1\}$ and $e \in]0,a[$. This way uses the existence of the uninorm U' on $L \backslash I_a$ with the neutral element e satisfying the following conditions:

$$U'(x,y) \in [0,e] \cup I_e^a \text{ iff } x,y \in [0,e] \cup I_e^a, \tag{C4}$$

$$U'(x,y) \neq e \text{ for all } x,y \in I_e^a. \tag{C5}$$

For clarity, we summarize the conditions together with their formal meanings and interpretations in Table 1. It is important to emphasize that $U'(x,1) = 1$ for all $x \in L \backslash I_a$ under condition (C4). It is apparent from [9] that $U'(0,1) \in \{0,1\} \cup I_e^a$. Then, by condition (C4), we observe that $U'(0,1) = 1$. So, the uninorm U' is disjunctive on $L \backslash I_a$. We infer from the increasingness of U' that $U'(x,1) = 1$ for all $x \in L \backslash I_a$.

Theorem 1. *Let $a \in L \backslash \{0,1\}$, $U' : (L \backslash I_a)^2 \to L \backslash I_a$ be a uninorm with the neutral element $e \in]0,a[$, and $S : L^2 \to L$ be a t-conorm. Suppose that the function $U_1 : L^2 \to L$ is given by the formula (1).*

$$U_1(x,y) = \begin{cases} U'(x,y) & if\ (x,y) \in (L \backslash I_a)^2, \\ y & if\ (x,y) \in ([0,e] \cup I_e^a) \times I_a, \\ x & if\ (x,y) \in I_a \times ([0,e] \cup I_e^a), \\ S(x,y) & if\ (x,y) \in I_a \times I_a, \\ 1 & otherwise. \end{cases} \tag{1}$$

Table 1. Conditions (C1)–(C5) with formal interpretation

Condition	Formal statement	Interpretation
(C1)	$x < y$ for all $x \in [0,e[$ and $y \in I_a$, i.e., $x \le y$ and $x \ne y$.	All elements below the neutral element e are strictly smaller than those incomparable with a, ensuring that the function formulated as (1) is increasing.
(C2)	$z < y$ for all $z \in I_e^a$ and $y \in I_a$, i.e., $z \le y$ and $z \ne y$.	All elements that are incomparable with e but comparable with a are strictly smaller than those incomparable with a, ensuring that the function formulated as (1) is increasing.
(C3)	$t \parallel y$ for all $t \in]e,a[\cup]a,1[$ and $y \in I_a$, i.e., neither $t \le y$ nor $y \le t$.	All elements in $]e,a[\cup]a,1[$ are incomparable with those incomparable with a, ensuring that the function formulated as (1) is increasing and associative.
(C4)	$U'(x,y) \in [0,e] \cup I_e^a$ iff $x,y \in [0,e] \cup I_e^a$.	The output of U' is restricted according to the regions of its inputs, ensuring that the function formulated as (1) is increasing and associative.
(C5)	$U'(x,y) \ne e$ for all $x,y \in I_e^a$.	The output of U' does not attain the neutral element e for inputs that are incomparable with e but comparable with a, ensuring that the function formulated as (1) is increasing.

(I) Let the conditions (C1)–(C5) be satisfied. In this case, U_1 is a uninorm on L with the neutral element e.
(II) Let $U' \in \mathscr{U}_{\mathrm{id}} \cup \mathscr{U}_{\max}$. If the conditions (C2)–(C5) are fulfilled, then U_1 is a uninorm on L with the neutral element e.
(III) Let $I_a \ne \emptyset$ and the conditions (C1)-(C3) be satisfied. U_1 is a uninorm on L with the neutral element e iff U' meets the conditions (C4) and (C5).
(IV) Let $U' \in \mathscr{U}_{\max}$ and the conditions (C1), (C3)-(C5) be satisfied. U_1 is a uninorm on L with the neutral element e iff the condition (C2) is fulfilled.
(V) Let U' have no 1-divisors and the conditions (C1), (C2), (C4), and (C5) be satisfied. U_1 is a uninorm on L with the neutral element e for all t-conorms S on L iff the condition (C3) is fulfilled.

Proof. (I) Let the conditions (C1)–(C5) be satisfied. We show that U_1 is a uninorm on L with the neutral element e. The commutativity of U_1 and the fact that e is its neutral element are obvious. It remains to verify the increasingness and associativity of U_1. On the domain $L \backslash I_a$, both properties follow directly from the corresponding properties of U'. It therefore suffices to consider in which at least one of arguments belongs to I_a.

Increasingness: Let $x,y,z \in L$ with $x \le y$. We show that $U_1(x,z) \le U_1(y,z)$. The inequality is clearly satisfied when the elements x and y belong to the same domain or when $1 \in \{x,y,z\}$. Hence, the proof is split into all possible remaining cases.

1. Let $z \in I_a$. We have $U_1(x,z) = U_1(y,z)$ for $(x,y) \in [0,e] \times I_e^a \cup]e,a[\times [a,1[$, while $U_1(x,z) = z \le S(y,z) = U_1(y,z)$ for $(x,y) \in ([0,e] \cup I_e^a) \times I_a$. Moreover, $U_1(x,z) = z \le 1 = U_1(y,z)$ for $(x,y) \in I_e^a \times [a,1[\cup [0,e] \times (]e,a[\cup [a,1[)$ .2. Let $(x,y) \in ([0,e] \cup I_e^a) \times I_a$. We have $U_1(x,z) = U'(x,z) \le y = U_1(y,z)$ for $z \in [0,e] \cup I_e^a$, while $U_1(x,z) = U'(x,z) \le 1 = U_1(y,z)$ for $z \in]e,a[\cup [a,1[$.3

Associativity: We demonstrate that $U_1(x, U_1(y,z)) = U_1(U_1(x,y), z)$ for all $x,y,z \in L$. The proof is split into all possible cases by considering the commutativity of U_1.

1. If $x,y \in [0,e] \cup I_e^a$ and $z \in I_a$, then $U_1(x,U_1(y,z)) = z = U_1(U_1(x,y),z)$.
2. If $x \in [0,e] \cup I_e^a$, $y,z \in I_a$, then $U_1(x,U_1(y,z)) = S(y,z) = U_1(U_1(x,y),z)$.
3. If $x,y,z \in I_a$, then $U_1(x,U_1(y,z)) = U_1(x,S(y,z)) = U_1(S(x,y),z) = U_1(U_1(x,y),z)$.
4. On all remaining regions, excluding the cases listed in (1)-(3) and their permutations arising from commutativity, we have $U_1(x,U_1(y,z)) = 1 = U_1(U_1(x,y),z)$.

(II) Assume that the conditions (C2)–(C5) are satisfied. If $U' \in \mathscr{U}_{id} \cup \mathscr{U}_{\max}$, then, even without the condition (C1), it can be verified that U_1 is a uninorm on L by arguments analogous to those used in (I).

(III) Assume that $I_a \neq \emptyset$ and that the conditions (C1)–(C3) hold. If the conditions (C4) and (C5) hold, it follows from (I) that U_1 is a uninorm on L. It remains to show that the conditions (C4) and (C5) are satisfied if U_1 is a uninorm on L. Let $z \in I_a$ be arbitrary.

Suppose that $x,y \in [0,e] \cup I_e^a$ and $U'(x,y) \notin [0,e] \cup I_e^a$. Then, we have $U_1(z,U_1(x,y)) = U_1(z,U'(x,y)) = 1$, while $U_1(U_1(z,x),y) = U_1(z,y) = z$. This discrepancy shows that associativity does not hold. Therefore, $U'(x,y) \in [0,e] \cup I_e^a$ for any $x,y \in [0,e] \cup I_e^a$.

Now suppose that $U'(x,y) \in [0,e] \cup I_e^a$ when at least one of x, y does not belong to this set. Let $x \notin [0,e] \cup I_e^a$ without loss of generality. Then, we have $U_1(z,U_1(x,y)) = U_1(z,U'(x,y)) = z$, whereas $U_1(U_1(z,x),y) = U_1(1,y) = U'(1,y) = 1$. Again, associativity fails. Hence, if $U'(x,y) \in [0,e] \cup I_e^a$, then both x and y must belong to this set. This proves that the condition (C4) is necessary.

Next suppose that there exists $p \in I_e^a$ such that $U'(p,p) = e$. Under the condition (C2), $p < z$ holds. By the increasingness of U_1, we have $e = U'(p,p) = U_1(p,p) \leq U_1(z,p) = z$. Thus $e \leq z$, and since $p < z$, we obtain $e \vee p \leq z$. Moreover, $e \vee p \in]e,a[$, which contradicts the condition (C3). Therefore, $U'(p,p) \neq e$ for any $p \in I_e^a$, which implies that the condition (C5) holds if U_1 is a uninorm on L.

(IV) Assume that $U' \in \mathscr{U}_{\max}$ and that the conditions (C1), (C3)-(C5) hold. If the condition (C2) is satisfied, then it follows from (I) that U_1 is a uninorm on L. It remains to verify that the condition (C2) holds if U_1 is a uninorm on L.

Let $k \in I_e^a$ and $l \in I_a$. By the increasingness of U_1, we observe $k = U'(0,k) = U_1(0,k) \leq U_1(l,k) = l$. Hence, $k < l$ for any $k \in I_e^a$ and $l \in I_a$, which establishes the condition (C2).

(V) Assume that U' has no 1-divisors and the conditions (C1), (C2), (C4), and (C5) hold. If the condition (C3) holds, it follows from (I) that U_1 is a uninorm on L for all t-conorms S on L. Conversely, assume that U_1 is a uninorm for all t-conorms S on L.

Suppose that there exist $k \in]a,1[$ and $l \in I_a$ such that $l < k$. By the increasingness of U_1, $1 = U_1(l,k) \leq U_1(k,k) = U'(k,k)$, which implies that $U'(k,k) = 1$. This conflicts the assumption that U' has no 1-divisors. Hence, $k \| l$ for any $k \in]a,1[$ and $l \in I_a$.

Now suppose that there exist $m \in]e,a[$ and $l \in I_a$ such that $m < l$. By the increasingness of U_1, we have $1 = U_1(m,l) \leq U_1(l,l) = S(l,l) = l$, for the t-conorm $S = S_\vee$ on L. This implies that $l = 1$, which is a contradiction with $l \in I_a$. Therefore, $m \| l$ for any $m \in]e,a[$ and $l \in I_a$, and the condition (C3) follows.

It is important to clarify the structural framework underlying the construction in Theorem 1. Although the requirement that the set of elements incomparable with a is nonempty appears explicitly only in (III), it plays a fundamental role throughout the construction. Both the definition of the function and the distinction between different regions of the lattice rely on the presence of such elements, which enables a decomposition of the lattice into comparable and incomparable parts. This structural feature ensures that the construction exhibits a richer and more comprehensive behavior.

Remark 1. We illustrate in Fig. 1 the structure of the uninorm U_1 on L in Theorem 1.

I_a	y	1	y	1	$S(x,y)$
$[a,1]$	$U'(x,y)$	$U'(x,y)$	$U'(x,y)$	$U'(x,y)$	1
I_e^a	$U'(x,y)$	$U'(x,y)$	$U'(x,y)$	$U'(x,y)$	x
$]e,a[$	$U'(x,y)$	$U'(x,y)$	$U'(x,y)$	$U'(x,y)$	1
$[0,e]$	$U'(x,y)$	$U'(x,y)$	$U'(x,y)$	$U'(x,y)$	x
	$[0,e]$	$]e,a[$	I_e^a	$[a,1]$	I_a

Fig. 1. Uninorm $U_1 : L^2 \to L$ in Theorem 1

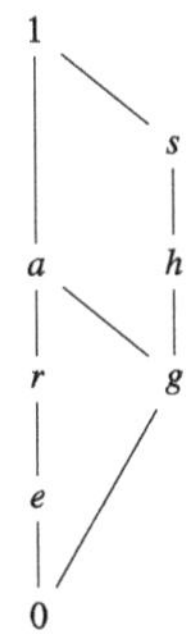

Fig. 2. Lattice L_1

The next example serves to deepen our understanding of uninorms in Theorem 1.

Example 2. Let L_1 be the bounded lattice characterized by the Hasse diagram in Fig. 2. In this situation, the method in Theorem 1 constructs the uninorm U_1 on L_1 with the neutral element e as shown in Table 2, provided that the t-conorm $S : L^2 \to L$ is determined by $S = S_\vee$. It is apparent from Table 2 that $U' = U_1|_{L_1 \setminus I_a}$ is a uninorm on $L_1 \setminus I_a$ that satisfies the conditions (C4) and (C5).

It is important to note that the condition (C1) in Theorem 1 cannot, in general, be omitted for U_1, defined by the formula (1), to be a uninorm on L. We illustrate this point by examining a bounded lattice that explicitly contradicts the condition (C1), thereby demonstrating that U_1 fails to qualify as a uninorm in this case.

Example 3. Let L_2 be the bounded lattice depicted by the Hasse diagram in Fig. 3. Since there exist elements $k \in [0,e[$ and $s \in I_a$ that are incomparable with each other, L_2 does not satisfy the condition (C1). Consider the uninorm U' defined on $L_2 \setminus I_a$ as given in Table 3. Constructing the operation U_1 on L_2 according to the method in Theorem 1, we observe that it is not increasing. Indeed, take elements $l, s \in L_2$ such that $l < s$. Then, by the definition of U_1, we have $U_1(l,l) = U'(l,l) = k$, while $U_1(s,l) = s$. Since $l < s$, the increasingness property requires that $U_1(l,l) \leq U_1(s,l)$, that is, $k \leq s$. However, from the structure of the lattice L_2, k and s are incomparable (i.e. neither $k \leq s$ nor $s \leq k$ holds). This contradicts the increasingness property. Hence, U_1 is not a uninorm on L_2.

For $e=0$ in Theorem 1, U' becomes a t-conorm S^* on $L\backslash I_a$, which induces the class of t-conorms on L given in Corollary 1.

Corollary 1. *Let $a\in L\backslash\{0,1\}$. Given the t-conorms $S:L^2\to L$ and $S^*:(L\backslash I_a)^2\to L\backslash I_a$, the function $U_{1,S^*}:L^2\to L$ defined by*

$$U_{1,S^*}(x,y)=\begin{cases} S^*(x,y) & if\ (x,y)\in(L\backslash I_a)^2,\\ y & if\ (x,y)\in\{0\}\times I_a,\\ x & if\ (x,y)\in I_a\times\{0\},\\ S(x,y) & if\ (x,y)\in I_a\times I_a,\\ 1 & otherwise,\end{cases}$$

is a t-conorm on L if $t\|k$ for all $t\in]0,a[\cup]a,1[$ and $k\in I_a$.

Choosing $a=e$ in Theorem 1 leads to a class of uninorms on L, as in Corollary 2, determined by a uninorm U' on $L\backslash I_e$ with neutral element e under the criteria below:

$$s\|m \text{ for all } m\in I_e \text{ and } s\in]e,1[, \qquad \text{(C1}')$$

$$x,y\in[0,e] \text{ if } U'(x,y)\in[0,e]. \qquad \text{(C2}')$$

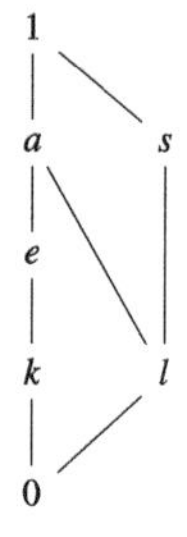

Fig. 3. Lattice L_2

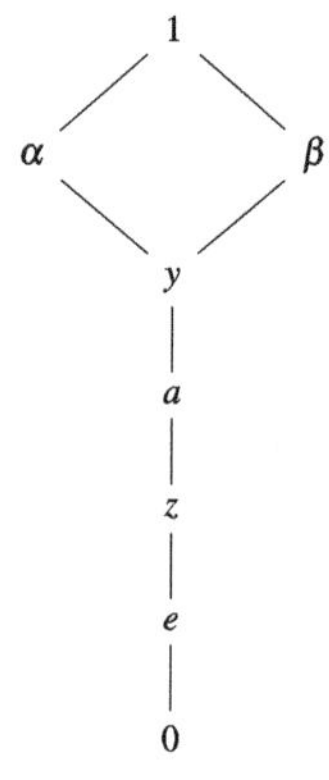

Fig. 4. Lattice L_3

Corollary 2. *Let $e\in L\backslash\{0,1\}$. Given the t-conorm $S:L^2\to L$ and the uninorm $U':(L\backslash I_e)^2\to L\backslash I_e$ with the neutral element e, the function $U_{1,U'}:L^2\to L$ is defined by*

$$U_{1,U'}(x,y)=\begin{cases} U'(x,y) & if\ (x,y)\in(L\backslash I_e)^2,\\ y & if\ (x,y)\in[0,e]\times I_e,\\ x & if\ (x,y)\in I_e\times[0,e],\\ S(x,y) & if\ (x,y)\in I_e\times I_e,\\ 1 & otherwise,\end{cases}$$

is a uninorm on L with the neutral element e if the conditions (C1′) and (C2′) hold.

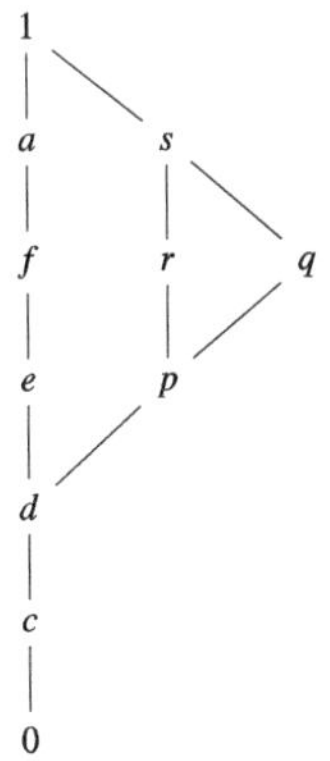

Fig. 5. Lattice L_4.

Table 2. Uninorm U_1 on L_1

U_1	0	e	g	r	a	h	s	1
0	0	0	g	r	a	h	s	1
e	0	e	g	r	a	h	s	1
g	g	g	g	a	a	h	s	1
r	r	r	a	r	a	1	1	1
a	a	a	a	a	a	1	1	1
h	h	h	h	1	1	h	s	1
s	s	s	s	1	1	s	s	1
1	1	1	1	1	1	1	1	1

Table 3. Uninorm U' on $L_2 \backslash I_a$

U'	0	k	e	l	a	1
0	0	0	0	0	a	1
k	0	0	0	0	a	1
e	0	0	e	l	a	1
l	0	0	l	k	a	1
a	a	a	a	a	1	1
1	1	1	1	1	1	1

Remark 2. We summarize the behavior of the construction given in Theorem 1 for special choices of the neutral element e.

If $e = 0$, then the uninorm U' defined on $L \backslash I_a$ reduces to a t-conorm on this domain. In particular, $U'(x,y) = 0$ holds iff $x = y = 0$. Consequently, the construction in Theorem 1 collapses to an operation whose neutral element coincides with the bottom element of the lattice. So, the resulting operator on L is a t-conorm. In this setting, it is sufficient that every element in $]0,a[\cup]a,1[$ is incomparable with each element incomparable with a.

If $e = a$, the construction in Theorem 1 takes a particularly structured form. In this case, the uninorm U' defined on $L \backslash I_e$ with the neutral element e behaves as a t-norm on $[0,e]^2$ and as a t-conorm on $[e,1]^2$. On the remaining regions, the operation is determined by the auxiliary components of the construction in Theorem 1. This decomposition reflects the classical structure of uninorms on L, and shows that the proposed method recovers several known constructions as special cases.

These observations show that the proposed method naturally extends classical constructions and unifies them within a single framework.

It is vital to underscore that the uninorms derived from the methodology in Theorem 1 encompass those developed in earlier foundational papers [3,4,11,24,40].

Table 4. Region-wise comparison between the proposed method and the method in [41]

Region of L^2	Method in [41]	Proposed method
$([0,e]\times]a,1[) \cup (]a,1[\times[0,e])$	$x \vee y$	$U'(x,y)$
$((]e,a[\cup I_e^a)\times]a,1[) \cup (]a,1[\times(]e,a[\cup I_e^a)) \cup [a,1[^2$	$R(x\vee a, y\vee a)$	$U'(x,y)$
$((]e,a[\cup[a,1[) \times I_a) \cup (I_a \times (]e,a[\cup[a,1[))$	$R(x\vee a, y\vee a)$	1
$I_e^a \times I_a$	$R(a, y\vee a)$	y
$I_a \times I_e^a$	$R(x\vee a, a)$	x
$(I_a)^2$	$R(x\vee a, y\vee a)$	$S(x,y)$
Other regions	Coincide	Coincide

Table 5. Region-wise comparison between the proposed method and the method in [41] under the condition (C3)

Region of L^2	Method in [41]	Proposed method
$R_1 = ([0,e]\times]a,1[) \cup (]a,1[\times[0,e])$	$x \vee y$	$U'(x,y)$
$R_2 = ((]e,a[\cup I_e^a)\times]a,1[) \cup (]a,1[\times(]e,a[\cup I_e^a))$	$R(x\vee a, y\vee a)$	$U'(x,y)$
$R_3 = I_e^a \times I_a$	1	y
$R_4 = I_a \times I_e^a$	1	x
$R_5 = [a,1[^2$	$R(x,y)$	$U'(x,y)$
$R_6 = (I_a)^2$	1	$S(x,y)$
Other regions	Coincide	Coincide

Remark 3. For the t-conorm $S : L^2 \to L$ and the uninorm $U' : (L\backslash I_e)^2 \to L\backslash I_e$, we consider the uninorm $U_1 : L^2 \to L$ identified by the formula (1) in Theorem 1, where $e = a$. If $T' = U' \mid_{[0,e]^2}$ is a t-norm on $[0,e]^2$ and $S' = U' \mid_{[e,1]^2}$ is a t-conorm on $[e,1]^2$, the following hold:

(i) Let U' be determined by $U'(x,y) = \begin{cases} T'(x,y) & if\ (x,y) \in [0,e]^2, \\ S'(x,y) & if\ (x,y) \in [e,1]^2, \\ x \vee y & otherwise. \end{cases}$ U_1 coincides with the uninorm constructed by the method in [11, Theorem 10] if $S = S_\vee$, while U_1 coincides with the uninorm using the method in [40, Theorem 3.1] if $S = S_W$.

(ii) Let U' be determined by $U'(x,y) = \begin{cases} T'(x,y) & if\ (x,y) \in [0,e]^2, \\ S_W(x,y) & if\ (x,y) \in [e,1]^2, \\ x \vee y & otherwise. \end{cases}$ U_1 coincides with the uninorm derived from the approach in [4, Theorem 6] if $S = S_\vee$, while U_1 coincides with the uninorm in [24, Theorem 1] if $S = S_W$.

(iii) Let U' be determined by $U'(x,y) = \begin{cases} T_\wedge(x,y) & if\ (x,y) \in [0,e]^2, \\ S'(x,y) & if\ (x,y) \in [e,1]^2, \\ x \vee y & otherwise. \end{cases}$ If $S = S_\vee$, then U_1 coincides with the uninorm based on the method in [3, Theorem 7].

Table 6. T-superconorm R on $[a,1]^2$

R	a	y	α	β	1
a	a	β	1	β	1
y	β	β	1	β	1
α	1	1	1	1	1
β	β	β	1	β	1
1	1	1	1	1	1

Table 7. Uninorm U' on L_3

U'	0	e	z	a	y	α	β	1
0	0	0	z	a	y	α	β	1
e	0	e	z	a	y	α	β	1
z	z	z	α	α	α	1	1	1
a	a	a	α	α	α	1	1	1
y	y	y	α	α	1	1	1	1
α	α	α	1	1	1	1	1	1
β	β	β	1	1	1	1	1	1
1	1	1	1	1	1	1	1	1

Table 8. Uninorm U_1 on L_4

U_1	0	c	d	e	f	a	p	q	r	s	1
0	0	0	0	0	f	a	p	q	r	s	1
c	0	0	0	c	f	a	p	q	r	s	1
d	0	0	d	d	f	a	p	q	r	s	1
e	0	c	d	e	f	a	p	q	r	s	1
f	f	f	f	f	f	a	1	1	1	1	1
a	a	a	a	a	a	a	1	1	1	1	1
p	p	p	p	p	1	1	p	q	s	s	1
q	q	q	q	q	1	1	q	q	s	s	1
r	r	r	r	r	1	1	s	s	1	1	1
s	s	s	s	s	1	1	s	s	1	1	1
1	1	1	1	1	1	1	1	1	1	1	1

Remark 4. To illustrate the difference between our method in Theorem 1 and the approach in [41], we present a comparison on the regions of L^2, summarized in Tables 4 and 5. Suppose that the restriction of the uninorm U', considered in Theorem 1, to the domain $[a,1]^2$ coincides with a t-superconorm R, which is identical to the one introduced in [41] and satisfies $R(a,a)=a$. Then, under the condition (C3), the uninorm U_1 defined in Theorem 1 is less than or equal to the uninorm U described in [41]. This comparison can be established by examining Table 5. More precisely:

(i) If $(x,y)\in R_1$, then $U_1(x,y)=U'(x,y)\le x\vee y=U(x,y)$.
(ii) If $(x,y)\in R_2$, then $U_1(x,y)=U'(x,y)\le U'(x\vee a,y\vee a)=R(x\vee a,y\vee a)=U(x,y)$.
(iii) If $(x,y)\in R_3$, then $U_1(x,y)=y\le 1=U(x,y)$.
(iv) If $(x,y)\in R_4$, then $U_1(x,y)=x\le 1=U(x,y)$.
(v) If $(x,y)\in R_6$, then $U_1(x,y)=S(x,y)\le 1=U(x,y)$.
(vi) On the remaining regions, two uninorms coincide.

Notice that if the restriction of the uninorm U' to $[a,1]^2$ is not identical to the t-superconorm R defined in the method in [41], then the uninorm U_1 in Theorem 1 is not necessarily comparable with the uninorm U in [41]. This situation can be illustrated by considering the lattice L_3 in Fig. 4.

In particular, assume that the t-superconorm R in [41] is given by Table 6, while the uninorm U' in Theorem 1 is defined by Table 7. Then, for $(z,y)\in R_2$, we obtain $U_1(z,y)=U'(z,y)=\alpha$, whereas $U(z,y)=R(z\vee a,y\vee a)=R(a,y)=\beta$. Since neither $\alpha\le\beta$ nor $\beta\le\alpha$ holds, it follows that U_1 and U are not comparable.

It is important to recognize that the uninorm derived from the method outlined in Theorem 1 does not need to coincide with the uninorms identified in the previous works [3,4,11,24,40,41]. This distinction is further clarified in the example provided below:

Example 4. Let L_4 be diagram in Fig. 5 and the uninorm $U' : (L\backslash I_a)^2 \to L\backslash I_a$ be defined by

$$U'(x,y) = \begin{cases} 0 & if\ (x,y) \in [0,d[^2 \cup [0,d[\times \{d\} \cup \{d\} \times [0,d[, \\ x\wedge y & if\ (x,y) \in \{d\}^2 \cup \{e\} \times [0,e] \cup [0,e] \times \{e\}, \\ x\vee y & otherwise. \end{cases}$$

By using the t-conorm $S : L^2 \to L$ specified by

$$S(x,y) = \begin{cases} y\vee q & if\ (x,y) \in]0,q] \times I_q, \\ x\vee q & if\ (x,y) \in I_q \times]0,q], \\ 1 & if\ (x,y) \in]q,1]^2 \cup]q,1] \times I_q \cup I_q \times]q,1] \cup I_q \times I_q, \\ x\vee y & otherwise, \end{cases}$$

we can describe the uninorm U_1 on L_4, as presented in Table 8, based on the procedure established in Theorem 1. In this case, the following outcomes emerge:

(i) The uninorm U on L_4 derived from [3, Theorem 7] satisfies that $U(d,c) = c$.
(ii) The uninorm U on L_4 derived from [4, Theorem 6] satisfies that $U(f,a) = 1$.
(iii) The uninorm U on L_4 derived from [11, Theorem 10] satisfies that $U(p,r) = r$.
(iv) The uninorms U on L_4 derived from [24, Theorem 1], [40, Theorem 3.1] and [41, Theorem 3.1] satisfies that $U(p,q) = 1$.
(v) The uninorm U_1 on L_4 established in Theorem 1 satisfies that $U_1(d,c) = 0$, $U_1(f,a) = a$, $U_1(p,r) = s$, and $U_1(p,q) = q$. This shows that U_1 is different from the uninorms produced by the methods discussed in the papers [3,4,11,24,40,41].

In the following, we consider the uninorm $U'' : (L\backslash I_b)^2 \to L\backslash I_b$ with the neutral element $e \in]b,1[$ and the t-norm $T : L^2 \to L$. Then, we propose a dual method for constructing uninorms on L under specific assumptions below:

$$y < x \text{ for all } x \in]e,1] \text{ and } y \in I_b, \tag{D1}$$

$$y < z \text{ for all } z \in I_e^b \text{ and } y \in I_b, \tag{D2}$$

$$t \| y \text{ for all } t \in]b,e[\cup]0,b[\text{ and } y \in I_b, \tag{D3}$$

$$U''(x,y) \in [e,1] \cup I_e^b \text{ iff } x,y \in [e,1] \cup I_e^b, \tag{D4}$$

$$U''(x,y) \neq e \text{ for all } x,y \in I_e^b. \tag{D5}$$

Theorem 2. *Let $b \in L\backslash\{0,1\}$, $U'' : (L\backslash I_b)^2 \to L\backslash I_b$ be a uninorm with the neutral element $e \in]b,1[$, and $T : L^2 \to L$ be a t-norm. Suppose that the function $U_2 : L^2 \to L$ is given by the formula (2).*

$$U_2(x,y) = \begin{cases} U''(x,y) & if\ (x,y) \in (L\backslash I_b)^2, \\ y & if\ (x,y) \in \left([e,1] \cup I_e^b\right) \times I_b, \\ x & if\ (x,y) \in I_b \times \left([e,1] \cup I_e^b\right), \\ T(x,y) & if\ (x,y) \in I_b \times I_b, \\ 0 & otherwise. \end{cases} \tag{2}$$

(I) Let the conditions (D1)-(D5) be satisfied. In this case, U_2 is a uninorm on L with the neutral element e.

(II) Let $U'' \in \mathscr{U}_{id} \cup \mathscr{U}_{\min}$. If the conditions (D2)-(D5) are fulfilled, then U_2 is a uninorm on L with the neutral element e.

(III) Let $I_b \neq \emptyset$ and the conditions (D1)-(D3) be satisfied. U_2 is a uninorm on L with the neutral element e iff U'' meets the conditions (D4) and (D5).

(IV) Let $U'' \in \mathscr{U}_{\min}$ and the conditions (D1), (D3)-(D5) be satisfied. U_2 is a uninorm on L with the neutral element e iff the condition (D2) is fulfilled.

(V) Let U'' have no 0-divisors and the conditions (D1), (D2), (D4), and (D5) be satisfied. U_2 is a uninorm on L with the neutral element e for all t-norms T on L iff the condition (D3) is fulfilled.

Setting $e = 1$ in Theorem 2, the uninorm U'' reduces to a t-norm T^* on $L \backslash I_b$, yielding a new structure of t-norms on L as described in Corollary 3.

Corollary 3. *Let $b \in L \backslash \{0,1\}$. Given the t-norms $T : L^2 \to L$ and $T^* : (L \backslash I_b)^2 \to L \backslash I_b$, the function $U_{2,T^*} : L^2 \to L$ defined by*

$$U_{2,T^*}(x,y) = \begin{cases} T^*(x,y) & if\ (x,y) \in (L \backslash I_b)^2, \\ y & if\ (x,y) \in \{1\} \times I_b, \\ x & if\ (x,y) \in I_b \times \{1\}, \\ T(x,y) & if\ (x,y) \in I_b \times I_b, \\ 0 & otherwise, \end{cases}$$

is a t-norm on L if $t \| k$ for all $t \in]0,a[\cup]a,1[$ and $k \in I_a$.

Setting $b = e$ in Theorem 2 yields a structure of uninorms on L, as in Corollary 4, based on a uninorm U'' on $L \backslash I_e$ with neutral element e satisfying the criteria below:

$$s \| m \text{ for all } m \in I_e \text{ and } s \in]0,e[, \tag{D1$'$}$$

$$x, y \in [e,1] \text{ if } U''(x,y) \in [e,1]. \tag{D2$'$}$$

Corollary 4. *Let $e \in L \backslash \{0,1\}$. Given the t-norm $T : L^2 \to L$ and the uninorm $U'' : (L \backslash I_e)^2 \to L \backslash I_e$ with the neutral element e, the function $U_{2,U''} : L^2 \to L$ is defined by*

$$U_{2,U^{\triangle}}(x,y) = \begin{cases} U''(x,y) & if\ (x,y) \in (L \backslash I_e)^2, \\ y & if\ (x,y) \in [e,1] \times I_e, \\ x & if\ (x,y) \in I_e \times [e,1], \\ T(x,y) & if\ (x,y) \in I_e \times I_e, \\ 0 & otherwise, \end{cases}$$

is a uninorm on L with the neutral element e if the conditions (D1$'$) and (D2$'$) hold.

4 Concluding Remarks

The extension of uninorms to a bounded lattice L has become an active research area following their development on the unit interval. While classical constructions mainly rely on t-norms and t-conorms, recent work by Xiu and Zheng [41] showed that uninorms can also be built from those defined on subintervals of L. Motivated by this, we proposed two new construction methods based on uninorms defined on specific subsets of L, incorporating t-norms and t-conorms to enhance flexibility. We further considered the neutral element as the top or bottom element of L, providing a clearer structural perspective on t-norms and t-conorms. Our approach generalizes several existing methods and offers a broader framework than approaches based only on t-norms and t-conorms. For future work, we plan to relax some of the conditions required for our constructions and to explore new structures for generating uninorms on bounded lattices.

Acknowledgements. The author would like to thank the editors and the reviewers for their valuable comments and suggestions, which have greatly contributed to improving the paper. This study was supported by Scientific and Technological Research Council of Turkey (TUBITAK) under the Grant Number 123F428. The authors thank to TUBITAK for their supports.

References

1. Asmus, T.C., Dimuro, G.P., Bedregal, B., Sanz, J.A., Fernandez, J., Martinez, I.R., Mesiar, R., Bustince, H.: A constuctive framework to define fusion functions with floating domains in arbitrary closed real intervals. Inf. Sci. **610**, 800–829 (2022)
2. Aşıcı, E., Mesiar, R.: New constructions of triangular norms and triangular conorms on an arbitrary bounded lattice. Int. J. Gen Syst **49**, 143–160 (2020)
3. Aşıcı, E., Mesiar, R.: On the construction of uninorms on bounded lattices. Fuzzy Sets Syst. **408**, 65–85 (2021)
4. Aşıcı, E., Mesiar, R.: On generating uninorms on some special classes of bounded lattices. Fuzzy Sets Syst. **439**, 102–125 (2022)
5. Benítez, J.M., Castro, J.L., Requena, I.: Are artificial neural networks black boxes? IEEE Trans. Neural Netw. **8**, 1156–1163 (1997)
6. Birkhoff, G.: Lattice Theory. American Mathematical Society Colloquium Publishers, Providence (1967)
7. Bodjanova, S., Kalina, M.: Uninorms on bounded lattices-recent development. In: Kacprzyk, J., et al. (eds.) IWIFSGN 2017, EUSFLAT 2017, AISC, vol. 641, pp. 224–234. Springer, Cham (2018)
8. Bodjanova, S., Kalina, M.: Uninorms on bounded lattices with given underlying operations. In: Halaš, R., et al. (eds.) AGOP 2019, AISC, vol. 981, pp. 183–194. Springer, Cham (2019)
9. Çaylı, G.D.: Uninorms that are neither conjunctive nor disjunctive on bounded lattices. In: Medina, J., Ojeda-Aciego, M., Verdegay, J.L., Pelta, D.A., Cabrera, I.P., Bouchon-Meunier, B., Yager, R.R. (eds.) IPMU 2018. CCIS, vol. 853, pp. 310–318. Springer, Cham (2018). https://doi.org/10.1007/978-3-319-91473-2_27
10. Çaylı, G.D.: On properties of internal uninorms on bounded lattices. In: Halaš, R., et al. (eds.) AGOP 2019, AISC, vol. 981, pp. 115–128. Springer, Cham (2019)
11. Çaylı, G.D.: Uninorms on bounded lattices with the underlying t-norms and t-conorms. Fuzzy Sets Syst. **395**, 107–129 (2020)

12. Çaylı, G.D.: Constructions of uninorms in bounded lattices leveraging uninorms in their sublattices. In: IEEE Int. Conf. Fuzzy Syst., pp. 1–6 (2025)
13. Dan, Y., Hu, B.Q.: A new structure for uninorms on bounded lattices. Fuzzy Sets Syst. **386**, 77–94 (2020)
14. Dan, Y., Hu, B.Q., Qiao, J.: New constructions of uninorms on bounded lattices. Int. J. Approx. Reason. **110**, 185–209 (2019)
15. De Baets, B.: Idempotent uninorms. Europ. J. Oper. Res. **118**, 631–642 (1999)
16. Drewniak, J., Drygaś, P.: On a class of uninorms. Int. J. Uncertain. Fuzziness Knowl. Based Syst. **10**, 5–10 (2002)
17. Drygaś, P.: On properties of uninorms with underlying t-norm and t-conorm given as ordinal sums. Fuzzy Sets Syst. **161**, 149–157 (2010)
18. Ertuğrul, Ü., Yeşilyurt, M.: Ordinal sums of triangular norms on bounded lattices. Inf. Sci. **517**, 198–216 (2020)
19. Ertuğrul, Ü., Yeşilyurt, M., Mesiar, R.: Element-based construction methods for uninorms on bounded lattices. Axioms **14**, 552 (2025)
20. Fodor, J., Yager, R.R., Rybalov, A.: Structure of uninorms. Int. J. Uncertain. Fuzziness Knowl. Based Syst. **5**, 411–427 (1997)
21. González-Hidalgo, M., Mir-Torres, A., Ruiz-Aguilera, D., Torrens, J.: Edge-images using a uninorm-based fuzzy mathematical morphology: opening and closing. In: Tavares, J., Jorge, N. (eds.) CMAS, vol. 13, pp. 137–157. Springer, Dordrecht (2009)
22. He, P., Wang, X.P.: Constructing uninorms on bounded lattices by using additive generators. Int. J. Approx. Reason. **136**, 1–13 (2021)
23. Ji, W.: Constructions of uninorms on bounded lattices by means of t-subnorms and t-subconorms. Fuzzy Sets Syst. **403**, 38–55 (2021)
24. Karaçal, F., Mesiar, R.: Uninorms on bounded lattices. Fuzzy Sets Syst. **261**, 33–43 (2015)
25. Karaçal, F., Ertuğrul, Ü., Mesiar, R.: Characterization of uninorms on bounded lattices. Fuzzy Sets Syst. **308**, 54–71 (2017)
26. Martinez, I.R., Asmus, T.C., Dimuro, G.P., Herrera, F., Takáč, Z., Bustince, H.: Generalizing max pooling via (a, b) -grouping functions for Convolutional Neural Networks. Inf. Fusion **99**, 101893 (2023)
27. Medina, J.: Characterizing when an ordinal sum of t-norms is a t-norm on bounded lattices. Fuzzy Sets Syst. **202**, 75–88 (2012)
28. Medina, J.: A characterization of ordinal sums being t-norms on bounded lattices by ordinal sums of drastic t-norms. In: IEEE World Congr. Comput. Intell. pp. 15–19 (2010)
29. Mesiarová-Zemánková, A., Mesiar, R., Su, Y., Wang, Z.: Idempotent uninorms on bounded lattices with at most a single point incomparable with the identity element: Part I. Int. J. Gen Syst **54**, 145–163 (2025)
30. Mesiarová-Zemánková, A., Mesiar, R., Su, Y., Wang, Z.: Idempotent uninorms on bounded lattices with at most a single point incomparable with the identity element: Part II. Int. J. Gen Syst **54**, 164–197 (2025)
31. Metcalfe, G., Montagna, F.: Substructural fuzzy logics. J. Symb. Log. **72**, 834–864 (2007)
32. Ouyang, Y., Zhang, H.P.: Constructing uninorms via closure operators on a bounded lattice. Fuzzy Sets Syst. **395**, 93–106 (2020)
33. Ouyang, Y., Zhang, H.P., Wang, Z., De Baets, B.: Idempotent uninorms on a complete chain. Fuzzy Sets Syst. **448**, 107–126 (2022)
34. Ouyang, Y., Zhang, H.P., Wang, Z., De Baets, B.: On the representation of internal uninorms on a bounded lattice. Fuzzy Sets Syst. **87**, 108994 (2024)
35. Pedrycz, W., Hirota, K.: Uninorm-based logic neurons as adaptive and inter-pretable processing constructs. Soft. Comput. **11**, 41–52 (2016)
36. Shi, J.Q., Zhao, B.: New constructions of t-norms and t-conorms on bounded lattices. Aequationes Math. **98**, 1527–1564 (2024)

37. Sun, X.R., Liu, H.W.: Further characterization of uninorms on bounded lattices. Fuzzy Sets Syst. **427**, 96–108 (2022)
38. Wen, H.,Wu, X., Çaylı, G. D.: Characterizing some of types of uninorms on bounded lattices. Int. J. Uncertain. Fuzziness Knowl. Based Syst. **31**, 533-549 (2023)
39. Wu, T.: New constructions of uni-nullnorms on certain classes of bounded lattices by closure (interior) operators. Kybernetika **60**, 624–651 (2024)
40. Xie, A., Li, S.: On constructing the largest and smallest uninorms on bounded lattices. Fuzzy Sets Syst. **386**, 95–104 (2020)
41. Xiu, Z., Zheng, X.: New construction methods of uninorms on bounded lattices via uninorms. Fuzzy Sets Syst. **465**, 108535 (2023)
42. Yager, R.R., Rybalov, A.: Uninorm aggregation operators. Fuzzy Sets Syst. **80**, 111–120 (1996)
43. Yager, R.R.: Uninorms in fuzzy systems modelling. Fuzzy Sets Syst. **122**, 167–175 (2001)
44. Yager, R.R.: Defending against strategic manipulation in uninorm-based multi-agent decision making. Fuzzy Sets Syst. **140**, 331–339 (2003)
45. Zhang, H.P., Wu, M., Wang, Z., Ouyang, Y., De Baets, B.: A characterization of the classes U_{min} and U_{max} of uninorms on a bounded lattice. Fuzzy Sets Syst. **423**, 107–121 (2021)
46. Zhao, B., Wu, T.: Some further results about uninorms on bounded lattices. Int. J. Approx. Reason. **130**, 22–49 (2021)

Fill-in Restrictions and Conditioning for Measure-Based Level-Set Functionals

Jana Borzová, Ondrej Hutník, and Miriam Kleinová(✉)

Institute of Mathematics, Faculty of Science, Pavol Jozef Šafárik University in Košice, Jesenná 5, 040 01 Košice, Slovakia
{jana.borzova,ondrej.hutnik,miriam.kleinova}@upjs.sk

Abstract. We study restriction procedures for aggregation functions that depend on a capacity and an $[0, 1]$-valued input only through the level sets of the input. This leads to measure-based level-set functionals determined by either the upper profile or the lower profile. We axiomatize restriction schemes by locality on a set and by exact localization of the relevant profile, obtaining canonical induced restrictions: fill-in-0 for upper-cut oriented functionals and fill-in-1 for lower-cut oriented ones. The framework clarifies the Gödel q-cointegral on $[0, 1]$ via its inf-crossing lower-cut representation and yields a matching operator-level restriction principle. We then compare fill-in restriction with capacity-side restriction: global agreement with conditioning is highly rigid in the upper-oriented case and impossible (for $n \geqslant 2$ under mild nondegeneracy) in the lower-oriented case. We also characterize when Bayes-type normalization reproduces the fill-in-0 upper profile.

Keywords: Measure-based level-set functionals · Upper and lower cuts · Capacity · Restriction schemes · Conditioning

1 Introduction

Restriction to a subset of coordinates $E \subseteq [n]$ is a basic operation in aggregation theory and in nonadditive integration: one may either modify the input vector $\mathbf{x}$ by suppressing information outside E, or modify the underlying capacity μ so that it reflects the fact that only E is relevant. While these two viewpoints coincide for classical additive measures in special situations, they typically diverge for nonadditive capacities and for nonlinear integrals. The aim of this paper is to provide a clean level-set based framework in which such restriction mechanisms can be compared and, in favorable cases, uniquely characterized.

Our starting point is the observation that many important functionals are determined by the level sets of the input. More precisely, for each $t \in [0, 1]$ they depend on $\mathbf{x}$ only through the upper cut $U_t(\mathbf{x}) = \{i : x_i \geqslant t\}$ or, dually, through the lower cut $L_t(\mathbf{x}) = \{i : x_i \leqslant t\}$, evaluated by a capacity μ or its dual μ^c. This leads to the notion of a *measure-based level-set functional*, specified by either the upper profile $P^{\uparrow}_{\mu,\mathbf{x}}$ or the lower profile $P^{\downarrow}_{\mu,\mathbf{x}}$. The class includes, in

B. Vantaggi et al. (Eds.): IPMU 2026, CCIS 3019, pp. 59–72, 2026.
https://doi.org/10.1007/978-3-032-28994-0_5

particular, the Sugeno integral and related semicopula-based universal integrals, as well as cointegral-type functionals such as the Gödel q-cointegral on $[0,1]$; on the other hand, it excludes operators that depend on the full pointwise structure of $\mathbf{x}$ rather than on its level sets. Thus, the framework isolates those functionals whose behavior is governed by the interaction between cuts and capacities.

This upper/lower dichotomy is not merely formal: it determines which data-side restriction is natural. To prevent coordinates outside E from distorting the cut structure that drives the operator, upper-cut oriented functionals are canonically localized by fill-in-0, whereas lower-cut oriented functionals are canonically localized by fill-in-1. We axiomatize this principle by requiring locality on E together with exact localization of the relevant profile, and show that within induced schemes these axioms uniquely select the corresponding fill-in restrictions.

The framework also accommodates operators that are not universal integrals. In particular, the Gödel q-cointegral on $[0,1]$ admits a robust inf-crossing representation in terms of the lower profile $P^{\downarrow}_{\mu,\mathbf{x}}$, which explains why fill-in-1 is the correct restriction mechanism. Moreover, its algebraic representation yields a complementary operator-level axiomatization of restriction, leading to the same canonical scheme and at the same time exposing the failure of naive masking.

Having identified the canonical data-side restrictions, we compare them with capacity-side restriction. Classical conditioning $\mu \mapsto \mu_E$ preserves the cut structure of $\mathbf{x}$ and only rescales the set function, whereas fill-in transforms alter the cuts themselves. We show that in the upper-oriented setting, global agreement between conditioning and fill-in-0 is extremely rigid and forces the capacity to be maximal, while in the lower-oriented setting, global agreement between conditioning and fill-in-1 is impossible for $n \geqslant 2$ under a mild nondegeneracy assumption. We also investigate Bayes-type normalization and characterize precisely when it reproduces the same upper-cut profile as fill-in-0.

Beyond their theoretical interest, these results are relevant for decision models based on fuzzy integrals and capacities, where restriction to a subset of criteria appears naturally in sensitivity analysis, preference elicitation, or scenario-based evaluation. Our results show that the appropriate notion of restriction is dictated by the cut structure underlying the model, and cannot in general be replaced by probabilistic conditioning.

2 Measure-Based Level-Set Functionals and Restrictions

Throughout this paper, we consider a fixed finite universe X, i.e., without loss of generality we may assume $X = [n] := \{1, 2, \ldots, n\}$. Let us denote by $\mathbf{M}^1_n$ the set of all capacities, (i.e., normalized grounded and monotone set functions) on 2^X and by $\mathbf{F}^1_n$ the set of all functions from X to $[0,1]$. For $\mathbf{x} \in \mathbf{F}^1_n$ and $t \in [0,1]$ define the upper and lower cuts

$$U_t(\mathbf{x}) := \{i \in [n] : x_i \geqslant t\}, \qquad L_t(\mathbf{x}) := \{i \in [n] : x_i \leqslant t\}.$$

For a set function μ on X with $\mu(X) = 1$ we use the dual $\mu^c(A) := 1 - \mu(X \setminus A)$.

Definition 1. For $n \in \mathbb{N}$ and $(\mathbf{x}, \mu) \in \mathbf{F}_n^1 \times \mathbf{M}_n^1$ define the profiles

$$P^{\uparrow}_{\mu,\mathbf{x}}(t) := \mu\big(U_t(\mathbf{x})\big), \quad t \in [0,1], \tag{1}$$
$$P^{\downarrow}_{\mu,\mathbf{x}}(t) := \mu^c\big(L_t(\mathbf{x})\big), \quad t \in [0,1]. \tag{2}$$

Easily, the profile $P^{\uparrow}_{\mu,\mathbf{x}}$ is a nonincreasing function, while $P^{\downarrow}_{\mu,\mathbf{x}}$ is nondecreasing. In what follows, put

$$\mathcal{D} := \bigcup_{n\in\mathbb{N}} (\mathbf{F}_n^1 \times \mathbf{M}_n^1).$$

Definition 2. A mapping $\mathcal{I}\colon \mathcal{D} \to [0,1]$ is called a *measure-based level-set functional* if one of the following holds:
(A) *Upper-cut oriented*: there exists a functional $\mathfrak{F}^{\uparrow}$ acting on functions $p\colon [0,1] \to [0,1]$ such that for every $n \in \mathbb{N}$ and every $(\mathbf{x}, \mu) \in \mathbf{F}_n^1 \times \mathbf{M}_n^1$,

$$\mathcal{I}(\mathbf{x}, \mu) = \mathfrak{F}^{\uparrow}\big(P^{\uparrow}_{\mu,\mathbf{x}}\big).$$

(B) *Lower-cut oriented*: there exists a functional $\mathfrak{F}^{\downarrow}$ acting on functions $q\colon [0,1] \to [0,1]$ such that for every $n \in \mathbb{N}$ and every $(\mathbf{x}, \mu) \in \mathbf{F}_n^1 \times \mathbf{M}_n^1$,

$$\mathcal{I}(\mathbf{x}, \mu) = \mathfrak{F}^{\downarrow}\big(P^{\downarrow}_{\mu,\mathbf{x}}\big).$$

In applications, one typically uses one of the following two profile functionals.
(i) Sup-type (upper cuts): for some $\Theta\colon [0,1]\times[0,1] \to [0,1]$ nondecreasing in the second argument,

$$\mathfrak{F}^{\uparrow}(P^{\uparrow}_{\mu,\mathbf{x}}(t)) = \bigvee_{t\in[0,1]} \Theta\big(t, P^{\uparrow}_{\mu,\mathbf{x}}(t)\big). \tag{3}$$

If Θ is a semicopula, the sup-type functional is the smallest semicopula-based universal integral, cf. [5]. Its special case, $\Theta(t,s) = t \wedge s$, is the famous Sugeno integral

$$\mathcal{I}(\mathbf{x}, \mu) = \bigvee_{t\in[0,1]} \big(t \wedge \mu(U_t(\mathbf{x}))\big) = \mathsf{Su}(\mathbf{x}, \mu).$$

(ii) Crossing-type (lower cuts): for some predicate $\Psi\colon [0,1] \times [0,1] \to \{0,1\}$ nondecreasing in the second argument,

$$\mathfrak{F}^{\downarrow}(P^{\downarrow}_{\mu,\mathbf{x}}(t)) = \inf\big\{t \in [0,1] : \Psi\big(t, P^{\downarrow}_{\mu,\mathbf{x}}(t)\big) = 1\big\}, \tag{4}$$

with the convention $\inf\emptyset := 1$. If $\Psi_{\mathsf{Gd}}(t,s) = \mathbf{1}(\{s > t\})$ where $\mathbf{1}(S)$ denotes the indicator function of a logical sentence S, then (4) yields

$$\mathcal{I}(\mathbf{x}, \mu) = \inf\big\{t \in [0,1] : \mu^c(L_t(\mathbf{x})) > t\big\} = \mathsf{Gd}(\mathbf{x}, \mu), \tag{5}$$

cf. [2], i.e. the (inf-)crossing representation of the Gödel q-cointegral with the Gödel fuzzy implication

$$x \to_{\mathsf{Gd}} y = \begin{cases} 1, & \text{if } x \leqslant y, \\ y, & \text{otherwise.} \end{cases}$$

We work on the numerical scale $[0,1]$, where the Gödel implication admits the standard form above and the corresponding cointegral is well defined via the lower-cut representation (5). Since this is the only fuzzy implication used throughout the paper, we omit the subscript Gd and simply write $\to$.

Here and throughout, the dimension n is implicit: whenever $\mathbf{x} \in \mathbf{F}_n^1$ and $\mu \in \mathbf{M}_n^1$, all sets E and all transformations are understood relative to the same ground set $[n]$. By $\mathbf{1}_E$ we denote the indicator function of a set $E \subseteq [n]$, that is, $\mathbf{1}_E(i) = 1$ if $i \in E$ and $\mathbf{1}_E(i) = 0$ otherwise. Specially, if $E = [n]$ the indicator function is denoted by $\mathbf{1}$ and corresponds to the unit vector on $[n]$. On the other hand, $\mathbf{0}$ denotes zero vector on $[n]$.

Definition 3. For $n \in \mathbb{N}$, $E \subseteq [n]$, and $\mathbf{x} \in \mathbf{F}_n^1$ define

$$R_E^0(\mathbf{x}) := \mathbf{x}\mathbf{1}_E + \mathbf{0} \cdot \mathbf{1}_{E^c}, \tag{6}$$

$$R_E^1(\mathbf{x}) := \mathbf{x}\mathbf{1}_E + \mathbf{1} \cdot \mathbf{1}_{E^c}. \tag{7}$$

Remark 1. The above restrictions are also important for general aggregation functions Agg, cf. [3]. If we consider the product aggregation function Prod, we have $\mathsf{Prod}(R_E^0(\mathbf{x})) \neq \mathsf{Prod}(R_E^1(\mathbf{x}))$. Analogously, $\mathsf{Min}(R_E^0(\mathbf{x})) \neq \mathsf{Min}(R_E^1(\mathbf{x}))$. Moreover, $\mathsf{Prod}(R_E^0(\mathbf{x})) = \mathsf{Min}(R_E^0(\mathbf{x})) = 0$ since both aggregation functions have 0 as annihilator. Moreover, the restricted aggregation function need not satisfy boundary condition, in general. For instance, $\mathsf{Agg}(R_E^0(\mathbf{1})) \neq 1$, cf. [4].

The following proposition makes the guiding principle explicit: upper-cut based operators are naturally localized by 0-filling outside E, while lower-cut based operators are localized by 1-filling outside E.

Proposition 1. *Fix $n \in \mathbb{N}$, $E \subseteq [n]$, and $\mathbf{x} \in \mathbf{F}_n^1$. Then*

(i) $U_t\big(R_E^0(\mathbf{x})\big) = E \cap U_t(\mathbf{x})$ *for all* $t \in (0,1]$ *and* $U_0\big(R_E^0(\mathbf{x})\big) = [n]$;
(ii) $L_t\big(R_E^1(\mathbf{x})\big) = E \cap L_t(\mathbf{x})$ *for all* $t \in [0,1)$ *and* $L_1\big(R_E^1(\mathbf{x})\big) = [n]$.

Proof. (i) If $i \in E^c$, then $(R_E^0(\mathbf{x}))_i = 0$, hence $i \notin U_t(\cdot)$ for all $t > 0$. If $i \in E$, then $(R_E^0(\mathbf{x}))_i = x_i$, so $i \in U_t(R_E^0(\mathbf{x}))$ iff $i \in U_t(\mathbf{x})$. For $t = 0$ it is immediate.

(ii) If $i \in E^c$, then $(R_E^1(\mathbf{x}))_i = 1$, hence $i \notin L_t(\cdot)$ for all $t < 1$. If $i \in E$, then $(R_E^1(\mathbf{x}))_i = x_i$, so $i \in L_t(R_E^1(\mathbf{x}))$ iff $i \in L_t(\mathbf{x})$. For $t = 1$ it is immediate. □

The restriction is designed so that coordinates outside E do not distort the cut structure that drives the given operator. Consequently, operators governed by upper cuts are naturally restricted by the "fill-in-0" transform (6), whereas operators governed by lower cuts require the "fill-in-1" transform (7). We now formalize this idea by axiomatizing restriction schemes directly in terms of level-set localization.

Definition 4. Let $\mathcal{I}\colon \mathcal{D} \to [0,1]$ be a measure-based level-set functional. A *restriction scheme* for $\mathcal{I}$ is a family $\mathcal{R} = (\mathcal{R}_E)_E$ with $\mathcal{R}_E\colon \mathcal{D} \to [0,1]$, where $\mathcal{R}_E(\mathbf{x},\mu)$ is defined whenever $\mathbf{x} \in \mathbf{F}_n^1$, $\mu \in \mathbf{M}_n^1$, and $E \subseteq [n]$. We say that $\mathcal{R}$ is *induced* if there exists a family of maps $\mathcal{X} = (\mathcal{X}_E)_E$ with $\mathcal{X}_E\colon \bigcup_{n\in\mathbb{N}} \mathbf{F}_n^1 \to \bigcup_{n\in\mathbb{N}} \mathbf{F}_n^1$, such that for every $\mathbf{x} \in \mathbf{F}_n^1$, $\mu \in \mathbf{M}_n^1$, and $E \subseteq [n]$,

$$\mathcal{R}_E(\mathbf{x},\mu) = \mathcal{I}\big(\mathcal{X}_E(\mathbf{x}),\mu\big). \tag{8}$$

We next introduce axioms capturing two principles: (i) the restriction should be local on E, and (ii) it should preserve the relevant cut structure of $\mathbf{x}$ within E. Since measure-based level-set functionals are determined by their level sets, this leads to two natural localization variants, depending on whether $\mathcal{I}$ is based on upper cuts $U_t(\mathbf{x})$ or lower cuts $L_t(\mathbf{x})$.

Definition 5. Let $\mathcal{I}$ be a measure-based level-set functional. A restriction scheme $\mathcal{R}$ for $\mathcal{I}$ is required to satisfy for each $n \in \mathbb{N}$ and each $E \subseteq [n]$:

(RS1) $\mathcal{R}_E(\mathbf{x}, \mu) = \mathcal{R}_E(\mathbf{y}, \mu)$ for all $\mu \in \mathbf{M}_n^1$ whenever $\mathbf{x}, \mathbf{y} \in \mathbf{F}_n^1$ satisfy $x_i = y_i$ for all $i \in E$.

(RS2) $\mathcal{R}_{[n]}(\mathbf{x}, \mu) = \mathcal{I}(\mathbf{x}, \mu)$ for all $(\mathbf{x}, \mu) \in \mathbf{F}_n^1 \times \mathbf{M}_n^1$.

(RS3$^\uparrow$) $\mathcal{R}$ is induced by $\mathcal{X}$ and for all $t \in (0, 1]$,

$$\mu\big(U_t(\mathcal{X}_E(\mathbf{x}))\big) = \mu(E \cap U_t(\mathbf{x}))\,. \tag{9}$$

(RS3$^\downarrow$) $\mathcal{R}$ is induced by $\mathcal{X}$ and for all $t \in [0, 1)$,

$$\mu^c\big(L_t(\mathcal{X}_E(\mathbf{x}))\big) = \mu^c(E \cap L_t(\mathbf{x}))\,. \tag{10}$$

Axioms (RS1)–(RS2) ensure that restriction is local to the subset E and that no information is lost when $E = [n]$. Axioms (RS3$^\uparrow$) and (RS3$^\downarrow$) encode the fundamental level-set principle: restriction should preserve the relevant cut structure of the input, so that coordinates outside E do not influence the evaluation of $\mathcal{I}$.

Proposition 2. *Let $\mathcal{I}$ be upper-cut oriented measure-based level-set functional. Set*

$$\mathcal{R}_E^\uparrow(\mathbf{x}, \mu) := \mathcal{I}\big(R_E^0(\mathbf{x}), \mu\big). \tag{11}$$

Then $\mathcal{R}^\uparrow$ is induced and satisfies (RS1), (RS2), *and* (RS3$^\uparrow$). *Moreover, if $\widetilde{\mathcal{R}}$ is any other induced scheme satisfying* (RS3$^\uparrow$), *then $\widetilde{\mathcal{R}} = \mathcal{R}^\uparrow$ pointwise.*

Proof. Fix $n \in \mathbb{N}$ and $E \subseteq [n]$. Then by Proposition 1(i), $U_t(R_E^0(\mathbf{x})) = E \cap U_t(\mathbf{x})$ for all $t \in (0, 1]$, hence

$$P^\uparrow_{\mu, R_E^0(\mathbf{x})}(t) = \mu\big(U_t(R_E^0(\mathbf{x}))\big) = \mu(E \cap U_t(\mathbf{x})).$$

This is exactly (9) for $\mathcal{X}_E = R_E^0$, so (RS3$^\uparrow$) holds. Locality (RS1) and (RS2) are immediate from the definition of R_E^0. For uniqueness among induced schemes, let $\widetilde{\mathcal{R}}_E(\mathbf{x}, \mu) = \mathcal{I}(\widetilde{\mathcal{X}}_E(\mathbf{x}), \mu)$ satisfy (RS3$^\uparrow$). Then (9) implies that $P^\uparrow_{\mu, \widetilde{\mathcal{X}}_E(\mathbf{x})}(t) = \mu(E \cap U_t(\mathbf{x})) = P^\uparrow_{\mu, R_E^0(\mathbf{x})}(t)$ for all t. Since $\mathcal{I}$ depends on $(\mathbf{x}, \mu)$ only through $P^\uparrow_{\mu, \mathbf{x}}$, we obtain

$$\widetilde{\mathcal{R}}_E(\mathbf{x}, \mu) = \mathcal{I}(\widetilde{\mathcal{X}}_E(\mathbf{x}), \mu) = \mathcal{I}(R_E^0(\mathbf{x}), \mu) = \mathcal{R}_E^\uparrow(\mathbf{x}, \mu),$$

which completes the proof. □

Example 1. The Sugeno integral Su is a $[0,1]$-valued discrete universal integral, and it is upper-cut oriented. Hence Proposition 2 yields the standard restriction

$$\mathcal{R}_E^{\uparrow}(\mathbf{x},\mu) = \mathsf{Su}(R_E^{\downarrow}(\mathbf{x}),\mu) = \mathsf{Su}(\mathbf{x}\mathbf{1}_E,\mu) = \bigvee_{t\in[0,1]} (t \wedge \mu(E \cap U_t(\mathbf{x}))).$$

Example 2. For the Gödel q-cointegral Gd on $[0,1]$, the appropriate level-set representation is the inf-crossing form (5). Thus the operator is naturally lower-cut oriented in the sense of Definition 2. Consequently, the fill-in-1 transform $\mathbf{x} \mapsto R_E^1(\mathbf{x})$ is the canonical induced restriction enforcing exact lower-cut localization (RS3$^{\downarrow}$).

The profile axioms (RS1), (RS2) and (RS3$^{\uparrow}$) explain why fill-in-1 restriction is the correct localization mechanism for Gd. At the same time, the Gödel q-cointegral also admits an equivalent algebraic representation

$$\mathsf{Gd}(\mathbf{x},\mu) = \bigwedge_{E\subseteq[n]} \Big(\mu^c(E) \to \mathsf{Max}_E(\mathbf{x})\Big),$$

cf. [2], which allows one to formulate restriction directly at the operator level. This yields an alternative axiomatization that does not mention profiles explicitly and nevertheless selects the same fill-in-1 restriction mechanism as above. Here $\mathsf{Max}_E(\mathbf{x}) := \max_{i\in E} x_i$.

Definition 6. A *Gödel domain restriction scheme* is a family $\mathcal{G} = (\mathcal{G}_E)_E$ with $\mathcal{G}_E : \mathcal{D} \to [0,1]$ being interpreted as the Gödel q-cointegral of $\mathbf{x} \in \mathbf{F}_n^1$ restricted to $E \subseteq [n]$. A Gödel restriction scheme $\mathcal{G} = (\mathcal{G}_E)_E$ is said to be *admissible* if for each $n \in \mathbb{N}$ and each $E \subseteq [n]$ it satisfies:

(GR1) $\mathcal{G}_E(\mathbf{x},\mu) = \mathcal{G}_E(\mathbf{y},\mu)$ for all $\mu \in \mathbf{M}_n^1$ whenever $\mathbf{x},\mathbf{y} \in \mathbf{F}_n^1$ satisfy $x_i = y_i$ for all $i \in E$.

(GR2) $\mathcal{G}_{[n]}(\mathbf{x},\mu) = \mathsf{Gd}(\mathbf{x},\mu)$ for all $(\mathbf{x},\mu) \in \mathbf{F}_n^1 \times \mathbf{M}_n^1$.

(GR3) For every $F \subseteq E$ and every $(\mathbf{x},\mu) \in \mathbf{F}_n^1 \times \mathbf{M}_n^1$,

$$\mathcal{G}_E(\mathbf{x},\mu) \leqslant \mu^c(F) \to \mathsf{Max}_F(\mathbf{x}). \tag{12}$$

(GR4) If $\mathcal{G}^*$ is any other family satisfying (GR1) and (GR3), then for all $E \subseteq [n]$ and all $(\mathbf{x},\mu)$,

$$\mathcal{G}_E^*(\mathbf{x},\mu) \leqslant \mathcal{G}_E(\mathbf{x},\mu). \tag{13}$$

Remark 2. Axioms (GR1)–(GR3) express that restricting to E should be local and should not violate any Gödel rule encoded by subsets $F \subseteq E$. There are many such schemes (e.g. the constant-zero scheme satisfies (GR1) and (GR3)). Axiom (GR4) is the selection principle: it picks the largest admissible restriction.

Theorem 1. *Let $\mathcal{G}$ be the admissible Gödel restriction scheme. Then for every $n \in \mathbb{N}$, $E \subseteq [n]$, $\mu \in \mathbf{M}_n^1$ and $\mathbf{x} \in \mathbf{F}_n^1$,*

$$\mathcal{G}_E(\mathbf{x},\mu) = \bigwedge_{F\subseteq E} \Big(\mu^c(F) \to \mathsf{Max}_F(\mathbf{x})\Big). \tag{14}$$

In particular, the restriction is unique: any two admissible Gödel schemes coincide.

Proof. Fix n, E, μ and $\mathbf{x}$. By (GR3), $\mathcal{G}_E(\mathbf{x}, \mu) \leqslant \mu^c(F) \to \mathsf{Max}_F(\mathbf{x})$ for every $F \subseteq E$. Taking the infimum over $F \subseteq E$ yields

$$\mathcal{G}_E(\mathbf{x}, \mu) \leqslant \mathcal{T}_E(\mathbf{x}, \mu) := \bigwedge_{F \subseteq E} \Big(\mu^c(F) \to \mathsf{Max}_F(\mathbf{x})\Big). \tag{15}$$

Then $\mathcal{T}_E$ satisfies (GR1) since $\mathsf{Max}_F(\mathbf{x})$ depends only on coordinates in $F \subseteq E$, and it satisfies (GR3) because it is an infimum of the right-hand sides in (12). Applying (GR4) with $\mathcal{G}_E^* := \mathcal{T}_E$ gives

$$\mathcal{T}_E(\mathbf{x}, \mu) \leqslant \mathcal{G}_E(\mathbf{x}, \mu). \tag{16}$$

Combining (15) and (16) yields (14). □

We now connect the canonical formula (14) with the fill-in-1 transform from Definition 3, showing that the operator-level axioms select exactly the restriction $\mathbf{x} \mapsto R_E^1(\mathbf{x})$.

Proposition 3. *For every $n \in \mathbb{N}$, $E \subseteq [n]$, $\mu \in \mathbf{M}_n^1$ and $\mathbf{x} \in \mathbf{F}_n^1$,*

$$\bigwedge_{F \subseteq E} \Big(\mu^c(F) \to \mathsf{Max}_F(\mathbf{x})\Big) = \mathsf{Gd}(R_E^1(\mathbf{x}), \mu). \tag{17}$$

Consequently, the unique admissible Gödel restriction scheme is given by

$$\mathcal{G}_E(\mathbf{x}, \mu) = \mathsf{Gd}(R_E^1(\mathbf{x}), \mu).$$

Proof. From the definition, we have

$$\mathsf{Gd}(R_E^1(\mathbf{x}), \mu) = \bigwedge_{F \subseteq [n]} \Big(\mu^c(F) \to \mathsf{Max}_F\big(R_E^1(\mathbf{x})\big)\Big).$$

If $F \cap E^c \neq \emptyset$, then $\mathsf{Max}_F(R_E^1(\mathbf{x})) = 1$, hence $\mu^c(F) \to 1 = 1$, and such sets do not affect the outer infimum. Therefore the infimum reduces to $F \subseteq E$, where $\mathsf{Max}_F(R_E^1(\mathbf{x})) = \mathsf{Max}_F(\mathbf{x})$. This yields (17). □

Finally, the commonly used masking restriction $\mathbf{x} \mapsto R_E^0(\mathbf{x})$ is not compatible with the maximality principle (GR4) except in degenerate cases, because it forces the complement E^c into every nontrivial lower cut and can collapse the cointegral.

Proposition 4. *Fix $n \geqslant 2$ and a nonempty $E \subsetneq [n]$, and put*

$$\mathcal{M}_E(\mathbf{x}, \mu) := \mathsf{Gd}(R_E^0(\mathbf{x}), \mu).$$

If there exists $i \in E^c$ such that $\mu([n] \setminus \{i\}) \neq 1$, then $\mathcal{M}_E(\mathbf{x}, \mu) = 0$ for every $\mathbf{x} \in \mathbf{F}_n^1$ with $x_i > 0$. In particular, $\mathcal{M}_E$ cannot coincide with the canonical restriction from Theorem 1.

Proof. Take $\mathbf{x}$ with $x_i > 0$ and consider $F = \{i\} \subseteq E^c$. Then $\mathsf{Max}_{\{i\}}(R_E^0(\mathbf{x})) = 0$ and $\mu^c(\{i\}) = 1 - \mu([n] \setminus \{i\}) > 0$. Hence $\mu^c(\{i\}) \to 0 = 0$, which implies $\mathcal{M}_E(\mathbf{x}, \mu) = 0$. On the other hand, the canonical value in (14) can be strictly positive for many inputs, so $\mathcal{M}_E$ cannot coincide with it. □

3 Restriction Schemes and Conditioning the Capacities

Since a measure-based level-set functional depends on $(\mathbf{x}, \mu)$ only through $P^{\uparrow}_{\mu,\mathbf{x}}$ (resp. $P^{\downarrow}_{\mu,\mathbf{x}}$), comparing different restriction procedures amounts to comparing the induced profiles. In particular, our conditioning arguments use simple test vectors such as $\mathbf{x} = \mathbf{1}_E$ or $\mathbf{x} = \mathbf{0}$, for which the resulting profiles are constant, i.e. consist of a single level, on the relevant range of cuts. To derive nontrivial structural information on μ from the equality of restricted values, we therefore impose a mild identifiability assumption requiring that the underlying profile functional distinguish such constant profiles.

Definition 7. Let $\mathfrak{F}$ be a profile functional acting on mappings $Q\colon [0,1] \to [0,1]$. We say that $\mathfrak{F}$ *separates constant profiles* if

$$\mathfrak{F}(Q_a) = \mathfrak{F}(Q_b) \implies a = b, \qquad a, b \in [0,1], \tag{18}$$

where $Q_a(t) \equiv a$ denotes the constant profile.

Example 3. The Sugeno-type profile functional $\mathfrak{F}^{\uparrow}(p) = \sup_{t\in[0,1]}(t \wedge p(t))$ satisfies $\mathfrak{F}^{\uparrow}(Q_a) = a$ for every constant profile Q_a. The same holds for the crossing-type functional $\mathfrak{F}^{\downarrow}(q) = \inf\{t \in [0,1] : q(t) > t\}$, for which $\mathfrak{F}^{\downarrow}(Q_a) = a$. Hence both separate constant profiles.

The separation property concerns only profiles that are constant on the relevant range of cuts, typically $(0,1]$ for upper cuts and $[0,1)$ for lower cuts. The values at the endpoints $t = 0$ or $t = 1$ play no role in the identifiability arguments used below and may be ignored without loss of generality.

3.1 Bayes Capacity Restriction vs. Fill-in Restrictions

Besides restricting the argument $\mathbf{x}$ by a fill-in transformation, one may restrict the underlying capacity itself. In analogy with classical probability, where conditioning on an event E corresponds to normalizing the measure on E, we consider the conditioned capacity

$$\mu_E(F) := \frac{\mu(F \cap E)}{\mu(E)}, \quad F \subseteq [n], \tag{19}$$

where $n \in \mathbb{N}$, $\mu \in \mathbf{M}^1_n$ and $E \subseteq [n]$ with $\mu(E) > 0$. This construction keeps the ambient space $[n]$ unchanged, but modifies the weight structure of sets so as to reflect the information that the relevant domain is E.

In the following, we compare this measure-based restriction $\mu \mapsto \mu_E$ with fill-in restrictions $\mathbf{x} \mapsto R^0_E(\mathbf{x})$ and $\mathbf{x} \mapsto R^1_E(\mathbf{x})$ at the level of measure-based level-set functionals.

Theorem 2. *Let $\mathcal{I}$ be an upper-cut oriented measure-based level-set functional whose profile functional $\mathfrak{F}^{\uparrow}$ separates constant profiles. Fix $n \in \mathbb{N}$. If for some capacity $\mu \in \mathbf{M}^1_n$ we have*

$$\mathcal{I}(R^0_E(\mathbf{x}), \mu) = \mathcal{I}(\mathbf{x}, \mu_E) \quad \textit{for all } \mathbf{x} \in \mathbf{F}^1_n \textit{ and all } E \subseteq [n] \textit{ with } \mu(E) > 0, \tag{20}$$

then $\mu = \mu^*$, *i.e.* $\mu(F) = 1$ *for every nonempty* $F \subseteq [n]$. *Conversely, if* $\mu = \mu^*$, *then* (20) *holds for every upper-cut oriented measure-based level-set functional* $\mathcal{I}$.

Proof. Fix $n \in \mathbb{N}$ and assume (20). For a nonempty $E \subseteq [n]$ take $\mathbf{x} = \mathbf{1}_E$. Then $R_E^0(\mathbf{1}_E) = \mathbf{1}_E$, hence

$$\mathcal{I}(\mathbf{1}_E, \mu) = \mathcal{I}(\mathbf{1}_E, \mu_E). \tag{21}$$

For every $t \in (0,1]$ we have $U_t(\mathbf{1}_E) = E$ and $U_0(\mathbf{1}_E) = [n]$. Therefore

$$P^{\uparrow}_{\mu,\mathbf{1}_E}(t) = \mu(E) \text{ and } P^{\uparrow}_{\mu_E,\mathbf{1}_E}(t) = \mu_E(E) = 1 \text{ for all } t \in (0,1].$$

By upper-cut orientation,

$$\mathcal{I}(\mathbf{1}_E, \mu) = \mathfrak{F}^{\uparrow}(P^{\uparrow}_{\mu,\mathbf{1}_E}) = \mathfrak{F}^{\uparrow}(Q_{\mu(E)}),$$
$$\mathcal{I}(\mathbf{1}_E, \mu_E) = \mathfrak{F}^{\uparrow}(P^{\uparrow}_{\mu_E,\mathbf{1}_E}) = \mathfrak{F}^{\uparrow}(Q_1).$$

Combining with (21) yields $\mathfrak{F}^{\uparrow}(Q_{\mu(E)}) = \mathfrak{F}^{\uparrow}(Q_1)$. By (18), this forces $\mu(E) = 1$. Since $E \neq \emptyset$ was arbitrary, we conclude $\mu(E) = 1$ for every nonempty $E \subseteq [n]$, i.e. $\mu = \mu^*$.

Conversely, assume $\mu = \mu^*$ and fix $E \subseteq [n]$ with $\mu(E) > 0$. For any $\mathbf{x} \in \mathbf{F}_n^1$ and any $t \in (0,1]$, Proposition 1(i) gives $U_t(R_E^0(\mathbf{x})) = E \cap U_t(\mathbf{x})$. Hence $\mu(U_t(R_E^0(\mathbf{x}))) = \mu(E \cap U_t(\mathbf{x}))$. On the other hand, $\mu(E) = 1$ and thus $\mu_E(F) = \mu(F \cap E)$ for all $F \subseteq [n]$, so in particular $\mu_E(U_t(\mathbf{x})) = \mu(E \cap U_t(\mathbf{x}))$. Therefore $P^{\uparrow}_{\mu,R_E^0(\mathbf{x})}(t) = P^{\uparrow}_{\mu_E,\mathbf{x}}(t)$ for all $t \in (0,1]$, and by upper-cut orientation of $\mathcal{I}$ we get $\mathcal{I}(R_E^0(\mathbf{x}), \mu) = \mathcal{I}(\mathbf{x}, \mu_E)$. □

Remark 3. The theorem shows that, within the class of upper-cut oriented measure-based level-set functionals, the compatibility between the fill-in-0 transform to the data vector $\mathbf{x}$ and conditioning the capacity μ on E is highly rigid. In fact, requiring (20) forces μ to coincide with the greatest capacity μ^*. Consequently, outside this degenerate case, restriction by masking the data and restriction by conditioning the capacity are genuinely distinct procedures and should not be expected to agree uniformly over all inputs.

In order to study the restriction $\mathbf{x} \mapsto R_E^1(\mathbf{x})$ and its relationship to conditioning $\mu \mapsto \mu_E$, we need to exclude trivial cases in which some coordinates carry zero weight under μ. Indeed, if $\mu(\{i\}) = 0$ for some i, then filling the i-th coordinate by 1 may have no effect on the conditioned capacity, which can obscure the comparison between the two restriction mechanisms. Therefore, we use capacities $\mu \in \mathbf{M}_n^1$ which are *strictly positive on singletons* meaning that

$$\mu(\{i\}) > 0 \quad \text{for every } i \in [n]. \tag{22}$$

Now the result follows.

Theorem 3. *Let $\mathcal{I}$ be a lower-cut oriented measure-based level-set functional whose profile functional $\mathfrak{F}^{\downarrow}$ separates constant profiles. Fix $n \in \mathbb{N}$ and take $\mu \in \mathbf{M}_n^1$ strictly positive on singletons. If*

$$\mathcal{I}(R_E^1(\mathbf{x}), \mu) = \mathcal{I}(\mathbf{x}, \mu_E) \text{ for all } \mathbf{x} \in \mathbf{F}_n^1 \text{ and all } E \subseteq [n] \text{ with } \mu(E) > 0, \quad (23)$$

then necessarily $n = 1$.

Proof. Assume, towards a contradiction, that $n \geqslant 2$ and (23). Fix $i \in [n]$ and put $E = \{i\}$; by (22) we have $\mu(E) > 0$, so μ_E is defined. Take $\mathbf{x} = \mathbf{0}$. Then $R_E^1(\mathbf{0}) = \mathbf{1}_{E^c}$. For every $t \in [0,1)$ we have $L_t(\mathbf{1}_{E^c}) = E$, hence $P^{\downarrow}_{\mu,\mathbf{1}_{E^c}}(t) = \mu^c(E)$ for all $t \in [0,1)$. Also, $L_t(\mathbf{0}) = [n]$ for every $t \in [0,1)$, hence $P^{\downarrow}_{\mu_E,\mathbf{0}}(t) = \mu_E^c([n]) = 1$ for all $t \in [0,1)$. By lower-cut orientation,

$$\mathcal{I}(\mathbf{1}_{E^c}, \mu) = \mathfrak{F}^{\downarrow}(Q_{\mu^c(E)}), \qquad \mathcal{I}(\mathbf{0}, \mu_E) = \mathfrak{F}^{\downarrow}(Q_1).$$

Using (23) with $\mathbf{x} = \mathbf{0}$ and $E = \{i\}$ yields $\mathfrak{F}^{\downarrow}(Q_{\mu^c(E)}) = \mathfrak{F}^{\downarrow}(Q_1)$. By the separation property (18), we must have $\mu^c(E) = 1$, i.e. $1 - \mu([n] \setminus E) = 1$ implies $\mu([n] \setminus E) = 0$. Since $n \geqslant 2$, the set $[n] \setminus E$ is nonempty, so it contains some $j \neq i$. By monotonicity, $0 < \mu(\{j\}) \leqslant \mu([n] \setminus E) = 0$, contradicting (22). Hence $n \geqslant 2$ is impossible.

Finally, for $n = 1$ the statement is consistent: the only nonempty subset is $E = [1]$, and then $R_E^1(\mathbf{x}) = \mathbf{x}$ and $\mu_E = \mu$, so (23) holds trivially. □

The obstruction is structural: fill-in-1 restriction removes E^c from all nontrivial lower cuts, while conditioning $\mu \mapsto \mu_E$ does not modify the cuts at all. For lower-cut oriented functionals, the cut structure is decisive, so these two mechanisms cannot agree globally. This explains why fill-in-1 is appropriate for cointegrals (such as the Gödel q-cointegral), yet it is fundamentally different from conditioning. Theorem 2 and Theorem 3 formalize this mismatch in the profile-based framework.

3.2 Bayes-Type Capacity Restriction vs. Fill-in Restrictions

Bayes-type normalization provides an alternative way to restrict a capacity to a subset E, see e.g. [1]. Fix $E \subseteq [n]$ and define the *Bayes-type restriction* of $\mu \in \mathbf{M}_n^1$ by

$$\mu^E(F) := \frac{\mu(F \cap E)}{\mu(F \cap E) + \mu^c(F^c \cap E)}, \quad F \subseteq [n], \quad (24)$$

whenever the denominator is nonzero.

The denominator in (24) is strictly positive whenever at least one of the terms $\mu(F \cap E)$ and $\mu^c(F^c \cap E)$ is positive. In particular, if $F \cap E = \emptyset$ and $\mu^c(E) > 0$, then $\mu^c(F^c \cap E) = \mu^c(E) > 0$, so (24) is well-defined and yields $\mu^E(F) = 0$. However, even under $\mu^c(E) > 0$ the denominator may vanish for some F (namely when $\mu(F \cap E) = 0$ and $\mu^c(F^c \cap E) = 0$ simultaneously). If $\mu^c(E) = 0$, then (24) is undefined at least for those F with $\mu(F \cap E) = 0$. In what follows, all statements are understood in the setting where (24) is well-defined for the sets under consideration (and one may adopt the convention $\mu^E(F) = 0$ when the numerator and denominator are both 0).

The next theorem describes when the Bayes-type restriction $\mu \mapsto \mu^E$ reproduces the same upper-cut profile as the fill-in-0 restriction $\mathbf{x} \mapsto R_E^0(\mathbf{x})$, and therefore yields the same value for any upper-cut oriented measure-based level-set functional.

Theorem 4. *Fix $n \in \mathbb{N}$, $E \subseteq [n]$, and $\mu \in \mathbf{M}_n^1$ such that $\mu^E \in \mathbf{M}_n^1$. Then the following assertions are equivalent:*

(i) *$\mathcal{I}(R_E^0(\mathbf{x}), \mu) = \mathcal{I}(\mathbf{x}, \mu^E)$ for every $\mathbf{x} \in \mathbf{F}_n^1$ and for every upper-cut oriented measure-based level-set functional $\mathcal{I}$;*
(ii) *$\mu^E(F) = \mu(F \cap E)$ for every $F \subseteq [n]$;*
(iii) *for every $F \subseteq [n]$ with $\mu(F \cap E) > 0$ we have*

$$\mu(F \cup E^c) = \mu(F \cap E). \tag{25}$$

Proof. (i)⇒(ii) Fix $F \subseteq [n]$ and put $\mathbf{x} = \mathbf{1}_F$. Then $R_E^0(\mathbf{x}) = \mathbf{1}_{F\cap E}$. Choose an upper-cut oriented functional $\mathcal{I}$ satisfying $\mathcal{I}(\mathbf{1}_A, \nu) = \nu(A)$ for all capacities ν and all $A \subseteq [n]$ (e.g. the Sugeno integral). Then

$$\begin{aligned} \mathcal{I}(R_E^0(\mathbf{x}), \mu) &= \mathcal{I}(\mathbf{1}_{F\cap E}, \mu) = \mu(F \cap E), \\ \mathcal{I}(\mathbf{x}, \mu^E) &= \mathcal{I}(\mathbf{1}_F, \mu^E) = \mu^E(F), \end{aligned}$$

and the assumed equality yields $\mu^E(F) = \mu(F \cap E)$.

(ii)⇒(iii) Fix $F \subseteq [n]$ with $\mu(F \cap E) > 0$. From (ii) and (24) we get

$$\mu(F \cap \ E) = \frac{\mu(F \cap E)}{\mu(F \cap E) + \mu^c(F^c \cap E)}.$$

Dividing by $\mu(F \cap E)$ yields $1 = \mu(F \cap E) + \mu^c(F^c \cap E)$. Since $\mu^c(F^c \cap E) = 1 - \mu([n] \setminus (F^c \cap E)) = 1 - \mu(F \cup E^c)$, we obtain $\mu(F \cup E^c) = \mu(F \cap E)$.

(iii)⇒(ii) Fix $F \subseteq [n]$. If $\mu(F \cap E) = 0$, then $\mu^E(F) = 0$ by (24), so $\mu^E(F) = \mu(F \cap E)$. If $\mu(F \cap E) > 0$, then by (iii) we have $\mu(F \cup E^c) = \mu(F \cap E)$ and therefore $\mu^c(F^c \cap E) = 1 - \mu(F \cup E^c) = 1 - \mu(F \cap E)$. Thus

$$\mu^E(F) = \frac{\mu(F \cap E)}{\mu(F \cap E) + 1 - \mu(F \cap E)} = \mu(F \cap E).$$

(ii)⇒(i) Fix $\mathbf{x} \in \mathbf{F}_n^1$ and $t \in (0, 1]$. By Proposition 1(i), $U_t(R_E^0(\mathbf{x})) = E \cap U_t(\mathbf{x})$, hence using (ii) we get

$$\mu\left(U_t(R_E^0(\mathbf{x}))\right) = \mu(E \cap U_t(\mathbf{x})) = \mu^E(U_t(\mathbf{x})).$$

Thus the upper profiles coincide: $P^{\uparrow}_{\mu, R_E^0(\mathbf{x})}(t) = P^{\uparrow}_{\mu^E, \mathbf{x}}(t)$ for all $t \in (0, 1]$. Since any upper-cut oriented $\mathcal{I}$ depends only on the upper profile, we obtain $\mathcal{I}(R_E^0(\mathbf{x}), \mu) = \mathcal{I}(\mathbf{x}, \mu^E)$. □

Remark 4. Condition (25) means that adding E^c to any set F does not increase its μ-value once F has positive μ-mass inside E. In this situation, the Bayes-type transform $\mu \mapsto \mu^E$ collapses to the simple setwise restriction $F \mapsto \mu(F \cap E)$, and therefore it matches fill-in-0 restriction for every upper-cut oriented measure-based level-set functional.

Example 4. Let $n = 2$, $E = \{1\}$ and define a capacity $\mu \in \mathbf{M}_2^1$ by

$$\mu(\emptyset) = 0, \quad \mu(\{1\}) = 0.4, \quad \mu(\{2\}) = 0.6, \quad \mu(\{1, 2\}) = 1.$$

Then $\mu^c(\{1\}) = 1 - \mu(\{2\}) = 0.4 > 0$ and μ^E is well-defined. We get $\mu^E(\{1\}) = 1$ while $\mu(\{1\} \cap E) = 0.4$, so (ii) fails. By Theorem 4, the identity $\mathcal{I}(R_E^0(\mathbf{x}), \mu) = \mathcal{I}(\mathbf{x}, \mu^E)$ cannot hold for all $\mathbf{x}$ and all upper-cut oriented measure-based level-set functionals $\mathcal{I}$. Indeed, choosing $\mathbf{x} = \mathbf{1}_{\{1\}}$ already yields different values for the standard Sugeno integral.

Remark 5. One may ask for a lower-cut analogue of Theorem 4, i.e. whether the Bayes-type restriction $\mu \mapsto \mu^E$ can reproduce the same *lower-cut profile* as the fill-in-1 restriction $\mathbf{x} \mapsto R_E^1(\mathbf{x})$. In general, such a compatibility cannot be expected except in degenerate situations. Indeed, for $\mathbf{x} = \mathbf{0}$ we have $R_E^1(\mathbf{0}) = \mathbf{1}_{E^c}$, and hence for every $t \in [0, 1)$, $L_t\big(R_E^1(\mathbf{0})\big) = E$, so that $P^{\downarrow}_{\mu,\, R_E^1(\mathbf{0})}(t) = \mu^c(E)$. On the other hand, $L_t(\mathbf{0}) = [n]$ for all $t \in [0, 1]$, hence $P^{\downarrow}_{\mu^E, \mathbf{0}}(t) = (\mu^E)^c([n]) = 1$. Therefore, for any lower-cut oriented measure-based level-set functional whose profile functional separates constant profiles, one obtains

$$\mathcal{I}(R_E^1(\mathbf{0}), \mu) \neq \mathcal{I}(\mathbf{0}, \mu^E)$$

whenever $\mu^c(E) \neq 1$. This shows that Bayes-type normalization is generally incompatible with the fill-in-1 restriction mechanism that is natural for lower-cut driven functionals.

3.3 Capacity Transformations Compatible with Fill-in Restrictions

The fill-in restrictions R_E^0 and R_E^1 are chosen so that, respectively, upper cuts or lower cuts outside E do not interfere with the level-set structure of the input. It is therefore natural to ask whether one can achieve the same localization effect by transforming the capacity μ instead of transforming $\mathbf{x}$.

For upper-cut oriented functionals the relevant profile is $P^{\uparrow}_{\mu,\mathbf{x}}(t) = \mu(U_t(\mathbf{x}))$. Since $U_t(R_E^0(\mathbf{x})) = E \cap U_t(\mathbf{x})$ for $t \in (0, 1]$, the restricted profile becomes $t \mapsto \mu(E \cap U_t(\mathbf{x}))$. Thus, the natural capacity-side counterpart of fill-in-0 is the setwise restriction $\widetilde{\mu}_E(F) := \mu(F \cap E)$.

For lower-cut oriented functionals, the relevant profile is $P^{\downarrow}_{\mu,\mathbf{x}}(t) = \mu^c(L_t(\mathbf{x}))$. Since $L_t(R_E^1(\mathbf{x})) = E \cap L_t(\mathbf{x})$ for $t \in [0, 1)$, the restricted profile becomes $t \mapsto \mu^c(E \cap L_t(\mathbf{x}))$. This suggests transforming the *dual* capacity, rather than μ itself.

Definition 8. Fix $n \in \mathbb{N}$, $\mu \in \mathbf{M}_n^1$, and $E \subseteq [n]$. Define the set function $\mu_{\langle E\rangle} : 2^{[n]} \to [0,1]$ by

$$\mu_{\langle E\rangle}(F) := \mu(F \cup E^c), \quad F \subseteq [n]. \tag{26}$$

Immediately, for every $F \subseteq [n]$, using complements, we have

$$\mu^c_{\langle E\rangle}(F) = 1 - \mu_{\langle E\rangle}(F^c) = 1 - \mu(F^c \cup E^c) = 1 - \mu\big((F \cap E)^c\big) = \mu^c(F \cap E).$$

The set function (26) need not be a capacity in general, since it may fail to be grounded. It is a capacity, for instance, if $\mu(E^c) = 0$, in which case $\mu_{\langle E\rangle}(\emptyset) = 0$. On the other hand, the following result shows that $\mu_{\langle E\rangle}$ is exactly the capacity transformation that reproduces, at the profile level, the lower-cut localization produced by fill-in-1.

Theorem 5. *Fix $n \in \mathbb{N}$, $E \subseteq [n]$, and $\mu \in \mathbf{M}_n^1$. Then the following assertions are equivalent:*

(i) $\mathcal{I}(R_E^1(\mathbf{x}), \mu) = \mathcal{I}(\mathbf{x}, \mu_{\langle E\rangle})$ *for every* $\mathbf{x} \in \mathbf{F}_n^1$ *and every lower-cut oriented measure-based level-set functional* $\mathcal{I}$*;*
(ii) $P^{\downarrow}_{\mu,\, R_E^1(\mathbf{x})}(t) = P^{\downarrow}_{\mu_{\langle E\rangle},\, \mathbf{x}}(t)$ *for every* $\mathbf{x} \in \mathbf{F}_n^1$ *and every* $t \in [0,1]$*;*
(iii) $\mu^c_{\langle E\rangle}(F) = \mu^c(F \cap E)$ *for every* $F \subseteq [n]$.

Proof. (iii)⇒(ii) Fix $\mathbf{x} \in \mathbf{F}_n^1$ and $t \in [0,1)$. By Proposition 1(ii), $L_t(R^{\uparrow}_{n,E}(\mathbf{x})) = E \cap L_t(\mathbf{x})$, hence

$$P^{\downarrow}_{\mu,\, R_E^1(\mathbf{x})}(t) = \mu^c(E \cap L_t(\mathbf{x})) = \mu^c_{\langle E\rangle}(L_t(\mathbf{x})) = P^{\downarrow}_{\mu_{\langle E\rangle},\, \mathbf{x}}(t),$$

where we used (iii). The case $t = 1$ is trivial since $L_1(\cdot) = [n]$.

(ii)⇒(i) Immediate, because any lower-cut oriented measure-based level-set functional $\mathcal{I}$ depends on $(\mathbf{x}, \mu)$ only through the profile $P^{\downarrow}_{\mu,\mathbf{x}}$.

(i)⇒(iii) Fix $F \subseteq [n]$ and take $\mathbf{x} = \mathbf{1}_{F^c}$. Then $L_t(\mathbf{x}) = F$ for every $t \in [0,1)$, hence

$$P^{\downarrow}_{\mu_{\langle E\rangle},\, \mathbf{x}}(t) = \mu^c_{\langle E\rangle}(F) \quad \text{and} \quad P^{\downarrow}_{\mu,\, R^{\uparrow}_{n,E}(\mathbf{x})}(t) = \mu^c(E \cap F), \quad t \in [0,1). \tag{27}$$

Choose a lower-cut oriented functional $\mathcal{I}$ whose profile functional separates constant profiles (e.g. a crossing-type template). Then (27) forces $\mu^c_{\langle E\rangle}(F) = \mu^c(E \cap F)$. □

Remark 6. The transformation $\mu \mapsto \mu_{\langle E\rangle}$ is not a normalization. Its role is purely profile-theoretic: it is the unique capacity-side modification that makes the lower-cut profile $t \mapsto \mu^c(E \cap L_t(\mathbf{x}))$ representable as $t \mapsto \mu^c(L_t(\mathbf{x}))$ for all $\mathbf{x}$.

Conclusions

We developed a profile-based approach to measure-based level-set functionals that isolates the role of upper and lower cuts in nonadditive integration. This perspective yields canonical restriction mechanisms: fill-in-0 for upper-cut oriented functionals and fill-in-1 for lower-cut oriented ones, each uniquely determined by level-set localization principles. Our results show that restriction by conditioning a capacity is, in general, incompatible with these canonical fill-in mechanisms, except in degenerate cases. Thus, masking the data and conditioning the measure represent fundamentally different operations. This structural mismatch clarifies why certain fuzzy integrals and cointegrals—particularly those used in decision making—require restriction at the data level rather than at the level of the capacity. These findings highlight that in fuzzy integration and decision theory, the appropriate notion of restriction is dictated by the underlying cut structure of the model, and not by probabilistic intuition alone.

Acknowledgement. This work was supported by the Slovak Research and Development Agency under contract No. APVV-21-0468. The third author's postdoctoral position is being carried out as part of the HRS4R Strategy at UPJŠ, see https://www.upjs.sk/en/hrs4r/.

References

1. Denneberg, D.: Conditioning (updating) non-additive measures. Annal. Operat. Res. **52**(1), 21–42 (1994). https://doi.org/10.1007/BF02032159
2. Dubois, D., Prade, H., Rico, A., Teheux, B.: Generalized qualitative Sugeno integrals. Inf. Sci. **415**, 429–445 (2017). https://doi.org/10.1016/j.ins.2017.05.037
3. M. Grabisch, J. Marichal, R. Mesiar, E. Pap: Aggregation Functions. Cambridge University Press, New York, 2009. https://doi.org/10.1017/CBO9781139644150
4. Kolesárová, A., Beganová, J., Stupňanová, A.: Aggregation-based extensions of fuzzy measures. Fuzzy Sets Syst. **194**, 1–14 (2012). https://doi.org/10.1016/j.fss.2011.11.003
5. Klement, E.P., Mesiar, R.: Discrete integrals and axiomatically defined functionals. Axioms **1**(1), 9–20 (2012). https://doi.org/10.3390/axioms1010009

More on the Inclusion–Exclusion Integral: Benchmark Interaction Operators and Equivalence Concepts

José Carlos R. Alcantud[1(✉)] and Aoi Honda[2]

[1] Unidad de Excelencia Gestión Económica para la Sostenibilidad GECOS and IME, University of Salamanca, 37007 Salamanca, Spain
jcr@usal.es

[2] Department of Mathematics, Faculty of Science, Kobe University, Kobe 657-8501, Japan
aoi@math.kobe-u.ac.jp
http://diarium.usal.es/jcr

Abstract. The inclusion-exclusion integral represents one of the numerous extensions of the Choquet integral introduced during the past decade. While other generalizations typically replace arithmetic operations within either the monotone measure-based or Möbius transform-based formulations of the discrete Choquet integral, the inclusion-exclusion integral incorporates a novel element (termed an interaction operator) into the computations. Just like the Möbius transform breaks down the monotone measure into interacting constituents, the interaction operator is responsible for decomposing the inputs, which are thereby distributed among negative and positive interactions too. In this work we revisit fundamental topics of the theory of inclusion-exclusion integrals, such as the properties of benchmark interaction operators, or the existence of unit elements. Then we carefully examine the case of two-component inputs. This case always produces non-negative inclusion–exclusion integrals. With general inputs, belief measures guarantee the production of non-negative inclusion–exclusion integrals, irrespectively of the interaction operator. We define two concepts of equivalence: one derived from the monotone measure, and the other based on the interaction operator. We give sufficient conditions for both properties. Finally, results from the founding literature are generalized. One conclusion is that the class of monotone measures defining inclusion–exclusion integrals that are independent of the interaction operator is characterized by additivity.

Keywords: Inclusion-exclusion integral · Interaction operator · Monotone measure · Aggregation

1 Introduction

Honda and Okazaki introduced the inclusion–exclusion integral (or IE integral) in both discrete and nondiscrete settings [13,14]. The aim was to generalize the

B. Vantaggi et al. (Eds.): IPMU 2026, CCIS 3019, pp. 73–86, 2026.
https://doi.org/10.1007/978-3-032-28994-0_6

Choquet integral with the help of interaction operators. This novel operator includes cases such as the product and the minimum (over the coordinates of the inputs), and is designed to distribute the inputs among negative and positive interacting constituents in the calculations. Fernández *et al.* [6] suggested that it should be possible to replace the product in these computations by suitable functions to further extend the scope of this approach. Boczek *et al.* [5] proved that their Choquet-Sugeno-like operator contains the IE integral as a particular case, and that conditional aggregation operators are more general than extended interaction operators.

A theoretical setback of IE integrals (and more general operators such as the Choquet-Sugeno-like operator in [5]) is that because they are so flexible, they in general fail to satisfy properties of the Choquet integral such as averageness, monotonicity, or idempotency. In connection with this issue, Honda and James [12] investigated the conditions for the IE integral to be an aggregation operator, and Honda and Alcantud [10] investigated monotonicity of the IE integral.

Lately, the Choquet integral has helped study intertemporal discounting [1,2], and IE integrals have found applications in classification and regression problems aligning with the interpretability of neural networks [7,11].

Here we address basic topics of the theory of IE integrals, including the definition and properties of benchmark interaction operators, and the existence of unit elements of the interaction operators. We perform an examination of the case of inputs with two components, and show that in this case all IE integrals are non-negative. We define two concepts of equivalence: one derived from the monotone measure, and the other based on the interaction operator. We give sufficient conditions for both properties. Finally, results from the founding literature are generalized. One conclusion is that the class of monotone measures defining inclusion–exclusion integrals that are independent of the interaction operator is characterized by additivity. We also observe that belief measures always produce non-negative inclusion–exclusion integrals, independently of the interaction operator chosen.

The remainder of this paper is organized as follows. We review the basic concepts of the theory in Sect. 2. Section 3 focuses on the case of two-component inputs. The main results are presented in Sect. 4. Finally, Sect. 5 provides the concluding remarks and outlines several avenues for future research.

2 A Critical Review of Concepts

In this section, we do two things. We fix the notation and recall the fundamental ingredients of the operator that we study in this paper. And we also add information on the theory underlying the inclusion–exclusion integral.

2.1 Basic Notation and Concepts

Henceforth, we work with $\Omega = \{1, 2, \ldots, n\}$, and $v : 2^{\Omega} \to [0, 1]$ will be a *monotone measure* on Ω. This means that v satisfies

$$v(\varnothing) = 0, \text{ and } A \subseteq B \subseteq \Omega \Rightarrow v(A) \leqslant v(B).$$

If in addition, v is normalized (i.e., $v(\Omega) = 1$), then we say that it is a fuzzy measure or a capacity on Ω.

The monotone measure v is *additive* when $v(A \cup B) = v(A) + v(B)$, for all disjoint $A, B \subseteq \Omega$.

As usual, m^v denotes the *Möbius transform* of v [4, Section 4.1]:

$$m^v(A) = \sum_{A \supseteq A'} (-1)^{|A \setminus A'|} v(A'), \text{ for each } A \subseteq \Omega.$$

We say that v is a *k-additive* monotone measure on Ω when $k < |A|$ implies $m^v(A) = 0$, and $m^v(A) \neq 0$ for some $A \subseteq \Omega$ with $|A| = k$ [8]. Additive monotone measures are characterized by 1-additivity [9, Theorem 2.33, Remark 2.51 (i)].

The (discrete) Choquet integral defined from v associates with each $\boldsymbol{f} = (f_1, \dots, f_n) \in [0, +\infty)^n$ the number

$$(C) \int \boldsymbol{f}\, dv = (f_{\rho(1)} - f_{\rho(2)}) v(\{\rho(1)\}) + (f_{\rho(2)} - f_{\rho(3)}) v(\{\rho(1), \rho(2)\}) + \dots +$$

$$(f_{\rho(n-1)} - f_{\rho(n)}) v(\{\rho(1), \dots, \rho(n-1)\}) + f_{\rho(n)} v(\Omega)$$

provided that $\rho : \Omega \longrightarrow \Omega$ is bijective and $f_{\rho(1)} \geqslant \dots \geqslant f_{\rho(n)}$ [4, Section 5.2]. We will need the following alternative expression that uses the Möbius transform of v [4, Section 5.2.1]: for each $\boldsymbol{f} = (f_1, \dots, f_n) \in [0, +\infty)^n$,

$$(C) \int \boldsymbol{f}\, dv = \sum_{B \subseteq \Omega} m^v(B) \cdot \min_{j \in B} f_j. \tag{1}$$

Henceforth, $K \in (0, +\infty)$ is fixed.

A mapping $\boldsymbol{f} : \Omega \longrightarrow [0, K]$ is interpreted as $\boldsymbol{f} \in [0, K]^n$. The identification uses $\boldsymbol{f} = (f_1, \dots, f_n) \in [0, K]^n$ with $f_i = \boldsymbol{f}(i)$ for all $i \in \Omega$.

The most characteristic feature of the inclusion–exclusion integral (or IE integral) is that it takes advantage of both monotone measures and the following type of functions defined in [13].

Definition 1. *An Ω-interaction operator on $[0, K]$ is a mapping $I(.|.) : [0, K]^n \times 2^\Omega \longrightarrow [0, K]$ with the next properties: when $\boldsymbol{f} \in [0, K]^n$,*

1. *$I(\boldsymbol{f}|\varnothing) = K$.*
2. *$I(\boldsymbol{f}|\{j\}) = f_j = \boldsymbol{f}(j)$, for each $j \in \{1, 2, \dots, n\}$.*
3. *$I(\boldsymbol{f}|A) \leqslant I(\boldsymbol{f}|B)$, for each $B \subseteq A \subseteq \Omega$.*

We drop the dependence on Ω and simply refer to interaction operators on $[0, K]$, when Ω is common knowledge.

The tuple $(\Omega, \mathcal{P}(\Omega), v, I, K)$ is called an *interactive monotone measure space* [13,14] when I is an Ω-interaction operator on $[0, K]$, $K \in (0, +\infty)$, and v is a monotone measure on Ω. Associated with it, the *inclusion–exclusion integral* is defined by the following equivalent formulas [13,14]: when $\boldsymbol{f} \in [0,K]^n$,

$$(I)\int \boldsymbol{f}\, dv = \sum_{A\subseteq\Omega}\left(\sum_{B\supseteq A}(-1)^{|B\setminus A|}I(\boldsymbol{f}\mid B)\right)v(A) = \sum_{A\subseteq\Omega} M^I(\boldsymbol{f}\mid A)\,v(A). \quad (2)$$

$$(I)\int \boldsymbol{f}\, dv = \sum_{A\subseteq\Omega} I(\boldsymbol{f}\mid A)\, m^v(A). \quad (3)$$

Note that in Eq. (2), we have implicitly defined M^I associated with I. An equivalent form for this functional declares that for all $A \subseteq \Omega$ and $\boldsymbol{f} \in [0,K]^n$:

$$M^I(\boldsymbol{f}\mid A) = \sum_{B\supseteq A}(-1)^{|B\setminus A|}I(\boldsymbol{f}\mid B) = \sum_{S\subseteq\Omega\setminus A}(-1)^S I(\boldsymbol{f}\mid A\cup S). \quad (4)$$

It is known that $f_i = \boldsymbol{f}(i) = \sum_{i\in A\subseteq\Omega} M^I(\boldsymbol{f}\mid A)$, for all $i \in \Omega$ and $\boldsymbol{f} \in [0,K]^n$ [13, Theorem 1].

We proceed to establish some fundamental examples and facts about interaction operators in the next section. Then Sect. 2.3 is concerned with the idea of interaction operators having a unit element. The interaction operator $I(.|.)$ is positive when $M^I(\mathbf{f}|A) \geqslant 0$ throughout.

2.2 Benchmark Interaction Operators

To give a systematic analysis of the notion in Definition 1, we proceed to propose benchmark interaction operators and to study their properties.

Firstly, note that we can identify both upper and lower bounds for the class of all Ω-interaction operators. The largest Ω-interaction operator on $[0,K]$ with $K \in (0,+\infty)$ is presented in the following example:

Example 1. [13] Fix $K \in (0,+\infty)$, then we define:

$$\text{for all } \boldsymbol{f} \in [0,K]^n \text{ and } A \subseteq \Omega,\ I_n^K(\boldsymbol{f}|A) = \begin{cases} K, & \text{when } A = \varnothing, \\ \min_{i\in A} f_i, & \text{otherwise.} \end{cases} \quad (5)$$

Clearly, this expression defines an Ω-interaction operator on $[0,K]$.

The axioms show that I_n^K is an upper bound for all Ω-interaction operators on $[0,K]$, i.e., if $I(.|.)$ is an Ω-interaction operator on $[0,K]$, then $I(\boldsymbol{f}|A) \leqslant I_n^K(\boldsymbol{f}|A)$ for all $\boldsymbol{f} \in [0,K]^n$ and $A \subseteq \Omega$. This justifies that hereafter I_n^K be called the *largest Ω-interaction operator* on $[0,K]$.

The Ω-interaction operator $I_n^K(.|.)$ belongs to the next structured family of interaction operators on $[0,K]$, which also contains the smallest Ω-interaction operator on $[0,K]$:

Example 2. Fix $k \in \Omega$ and $K \in (0, +\infty)$. We define the *k-min Ω-interaction operator* on $[0, K]$ such that for all $\boldsymbol{f} \in [0, K]^n$ and $A \subseteq \Omega$,

$$I_k^K(\boldsymbol{f}|A) = \begin{cases} K, \text{ when } A = \varnothing, \\ \min_{i \in A} f_i, \text{ when } 1 \leqslant |A| \leqslant k, \\ 0, \text{ otherwise.} \end{cases} \tag{6}$$

Observe that:

1. The case $k = n$ produces the largest Ω-interaction operator on $[0, K]$ described in Example 1. Hence the consistent notation I_n^K for the interaction operator defined in Example 1.
2. The case $k = 1$ obviously produces the *smallest Ω-interaction operator* on $[0, K]$, i.e., if $I(.|.)$ is an Ω-interaction operator on $[0, K]$, then $I(\boldsymbol{f}|A) \geqslant I_1^K(\boldsymbol{f}|A)$ for all $\boldsymbol{f} \in [0, K]^n$ and $A \subseteq \Omega$.

In addition, we note for further use that if $|A| \leqslant k < k'$, then $I_k^K(\boldsymbol{f}|A) = I_{k'}^K(\boldsymbol{f}|A) = \min_{i \in A} f_i$, for all $\boldsymbol{f} \in [0, K]^n$.

Example 3. Fix $K \in (0, +\infty)$. We let $m_{\boldsymbol{f}} = \min_{i \in \Omega} f_i$ for each $\boldsymbol{f} \in [0, K]^n$. Now we define the *min-interaction operator* on $[0, K]$ such that for all $\boldsymbol{f} \in [0, K]^n$ and $A \subseteq \Omega$,

$$I_m^K(\boldsymbol{f}|A) = \begin{cases} K, \text{ when } A = \varnothing, \\ f_i, \text{ when } A = \{i\}, \\ m_{\boldsymbol{f}}, \text{ otherwise.} \end{cases} \tag{7}$$

It is obvious that when $n = 2$, this construction produces the largest Ω-interaction operator on $[0, K]$ described in Example 1: $I_2^K(.|.) = I_m^K(.|.)$ if $n = 2$.

Under the inspiration of [13, Example 1], the next case is designed.

Example 4. Fix $K \leqslant 1$. We define the *product interaction operator* on $[0, K]$ by the expression: for all $\boldsymbol{f} \in [0, K]^n$ and $A \subseteq \Omega$,

$$I_\Pi^K(\boldsymbol{f}|A) = \begin{cases} K, \text{ when } A = \varnothing, \\ \prod_{i \in A} f_i, \text{ otherwise.} \end{cases} \tag{8}$$

Relatedly, the next variation of Example 4 is interesting:

Example 5. Fix $K \in (0, +\infty)$. The *normalized-product interaction operator* on $[0, K]$ is defined by the expression: for all $\boldsymbol{f} \in [0, K]^n$ and $A \subseteq \Omega$,

$$I_{\hat{\Pi}}^K(\boldsymbol{f}|A) = \begin{cases} K, \text{ when } A = \varnothing, \\ \frac{1}{K^{|A|-1}} \prod_{i \in A} f_i, \text{ otherwise.} \end{cases} \tag{9}$$

Note that:
a) Axiom 2 of an interaction operator (v., Definition 1) holds since $I_{\hat{\Pi}}^K(\boldsymbol{f}|\{i\}) = \frac{1}{K^0} f_i = f_i$.

b) Axiom 3 of an interaction operator (v., Definition 1) holds because $B \subseteq A$ implies $I_{\hat{\Pi}}^K(\boldsymbol{f}|A) = \frac{1}{K^{|A|-1}} \prod_{i \in A} f_i \leqslant \frac{1}{K^{|B|-1}} \prod_{i \in B} f_i = I_{\hat{\Pi}}^K(\boldsymbol{f}|B)$. Observe that this inequality boils down to $\prod_{i \in B \setminus A} \frac{f_i}{K} \leqslant 1$, which holds true.

In addition, $I_{\hat{\Pi}}^1(.|.) = I_{\Pi}^1(.|.)$.

2.3 The Existence of a Unit Element

In this section, we are concerned with a basic fact concerning unit elements. Following [13], we say that K is the *unit element* of the Ω-interaction operator $I(.|.)$ on $[0, K]$ if when $\boldsymbol{f} \in [0, K]^n$ is such that $f_i = K$ for some $i \in \Omega$, it must be the case that $I(\boldsymbol{f}|B) = I(\boldsymbol{f}|B \setminus \{i\})$ whenever $i \in B \subseteq \Omega$.

The following example proves that it is not true that K is the unit element of all interaction operators on $[0, K]$, even when $n = 2$. It clarifies which of the benchmark examples described in the previous section have a unit element.

Example 6. If we go through the examples in Sect. 2.2, then we observe the following facts:

1. K is the unit element of $I_n^K(.|.)$ defined in Example 1.
2. K is not the unit element of the k-min Ω-interaction operator $I_1^K(.|.)$ defined in Example 2 (i.e., $k = 1$) when $n = 2$. To see why, select $\boldsymbol{f} = (K, f_2)$ with $f_2 \neq 0$. Thus we assume $i = 1$ and $f_1 = K$. Fix $B = \Omega$, therefore $i \in B$. However, it is not true $I_1^K(\boldsymbol{f}|B) = I_1^K(\boldsymbol{f}|B \setminus \{i\})$ because $I_1^K(\boldsymbol{f}|B \setminus \{i\}) = I_1^K(\boldsymbol{f}|\{2\}) = f_2 \neq 0$ and $I_1^K(\boldsymbol{f}|B) = I_1^K(\boldsymbol{f}|\Omega) = 0$.
3. When $n = 2$, K is the unit element of the min-interaction operator $I_m^K(.|.)$ defined in Example 3.
   However, when $n > 2$ the opposite is true. To see why, consider the case $n = 3$, $\boldsymbol{f} = (\frac{K}{3}, \frac{K}{2}, K)$, $B = \{2, 3\}$ thus $i = 3$. Then $I_m^K(\boldsymbol{f}|B) = m_{\boldsymbol{f}} = \frac{K}{3} < \frac{K}{2} = f_2 = I(\boldsymbol{f}|B \setminus \{i\}) = I_m^K(\boldsymbol{f}|\{2\})$.
4. K is the unit element of the product and normalized-product interaction operators on $[0, K]$ defined in Examples 4 and 5, if and only if $K = 1$.

Characterization of the class of interaction operators that have a unit element is not yet available.

3 The Inclusion–Exclusion Integral: Analysis When $n = 2$

One crucial aspect of the research about inclusion–exclusion integrals is the form that they adopt when the interaction operators that underly them belong to certain benchmark classes. For illustration, we recall that the case of the largest interaction operator defined in Example 1 has been adequately studied in [13], and it is important because it produces an inclusion-exclusion integral that is a Choquet integral.

We now move on to explore the situation under other examples of interaction operators described in Sect. 2.2. Unless otherwise stated, in this section we assume $n = 2$ thus $\Omega = \{1,2\}$. This assumption enables us to represent the inclusion–exclusion integrals visually. Section 4 extends the inspection to the case of unrestricted values of n. These analyses may help to boost interest in interaction operators.

For simplicity, for each monotone measure v on $\Omega = \{1,2\}$ we denote $v_i = v(\{i\})$ $(i = 1,2)$ and $v_{12} = v(\Omega)$. Correspondingly, $m^v(\{i\}) = v_i$ $(i = 1,2)$ and $m^v(\Omega) = v_{12} - v_1 - v_2$.

Equation (3) is written as follows with the help of this auxiliary notation:

$$(I)\int \boldsymbol{f}\, dv = (f_1 - I(\boldsymbol{f}|\Omega)) \cdot v_1 + (f_2 - I(\boldsymbol{f}|\Omega)) \cdot v_2 + I(\boldsymbol{f}|\Omega) \cdot v_{12}. \tag{10}$$

The reason is that $(I)\int \boldsymbol{f}\, d\,\mathrm{v} = I(\boldsymbol{f}|\{1\}) \cdot v_1 + I(\boldsymbol{f}|\{2\}) \cdot v_2 + I(\boldsymbol{f}|\Omega) \cdot (v_{12} - v_1 - v_2)$. Using the axioms of an interaction operator, this expression becomes $(I)\int \boldsymbol{f}\, d\,\mathrm{v} = f_1 \cdot v_1 + f_2 \cdot v_2 + I(\boldsymbol{f}|\Omega) \cdot (v_{12} - v_1 - v_2)$.

3.1 Examples: Inclusion–Exclusion Integrals Defined from Particular Interaction Operators

We are ready to explore situations motivated by examples of interaction operators described and studied in Sect. 2.2, under the assumption $n = 2$.

Example 7. (Example 2 continued). Using Equation (10), when $n = 2$ one has

$$(I_1^K)\int \boldsymbol{f}\, dv = f_1 \cdot v_1 + f_2 \cdot v_2 + 0. \tag{11}$$

Therefore, when $n = 2$, the inclusion-exclusion integral defined from the 1-min interaction operator $I_1^K(.|.)$ is a weighted average mean with non-normalized weights (v_1, v_2). In particular, it is an additive Choquet integral.

Section 4.1 below studies this inclusion-exclusion integral when $n > 2$.

Example 8. (Example 3 continued). Using $I_2^K(.|.) = I_m^K(.|.)$ if $n = 2$, we conclude that for any monotone measure v, the inclusion-exclusion integral defined from the min-interaction operator I_m^K (which is now the largest interaction operator on $[0, K]$) and v is the Choquet integral defined from v.

Section 4.2 below computes the form of this IE integral when $n > 2$.

Despite these remarkable cases, the next negative example proves that not all inclusion-exclusion integrals are Choquet integrals when $n = 2$:

Example 9. (Example 4 continued). We revisit the product interaction operator $I_\Pi^K(.|.)$ on $[0, K]$ when $n = 2$. Now Equation (10) becomes

$$(I_\Pi^K)\int \boldsymbol{f} dv = f_1(1 - f_2)v_1 + f_2(1 - f_1)v_2 + f_1 f_2 v_{12}.$$

Fig. 1 represents the inclusion-exclusion integral in the case $K = 1$, with the fuzzy measure v such that $v(\{1\}) = 0.8$ and $v(\{2\}) = 0.9$.

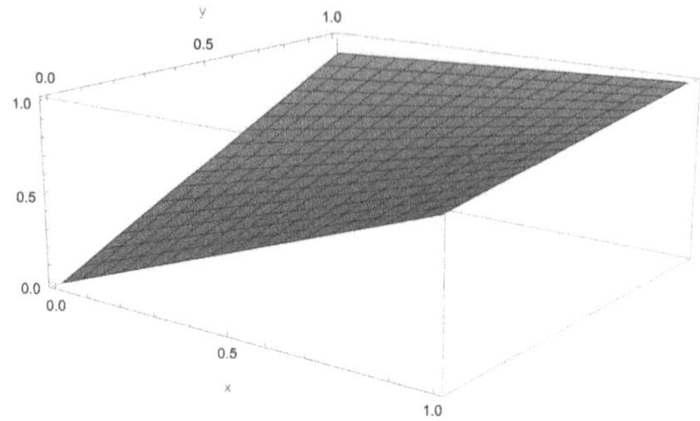

Fig. 1. An inclusion-exclusion integral that is not a Choquet integral when $n = 2$. We use $K = 1$ in Example 9.

Example 10. (Example 5 continued). We revisit the normalized-product interaction operator $I^K_{\hat{\Pi}}(.|.)$ on $[0, K]$ when $n = 2$. In this case, Equation (10) becomes

$$(I^K_{\hat{\Pi}}) \int \boldsymbol{f} dv = \frac{1}{K}\Big(f_1(K - f_2)v_1 + f_2(K - f_1)v_2 + f_1 f_2 v_{12}\Big).$$

3.2 A Result When $n = 2$

We know that positive interaction operators produce non-negative inclusion-exclusion integrals [13, Theorem 2 (a)]. The next particular case is interesting for intuition, as it shows how the process applies in a simple situation:

Proposition 1. *Fix $K \in (0, +\infty)$. When $n = 2$, all Ω-interaction operators on $[0, K]$ are positive. Therefore, all inclusion-exclusion integrals defined from an interactive monotone measure space $(\Omega = \{1, 2\}, \mathcal{P}(\Omega), v, I, K)$ are non-negative.*

Proof. Suppose $I(.|.)$ is an interaction operator on $[0, K]$. Fix $\boldsymbol{f} = (f_1, f_2) \in [0, K]^2$. For $i = 1, 2$, $M^I(\boldsymbol{f}|\{i\}) = f_i - I(\boldsymbol{f}|\Omega) \geqslant 0$, due to Axioms 2 and 3 in Definition 1, and $M^I(\boldsymbol{f}|\Omega) = I(\boldsymbol{f}|\Omega) \geqslant 0$. Therefore, $I(.|.)$ is positive.

The second claim follows from [13, Theorem 2 (a)].

We give valuable information about non-negative inclusion-exclusion integrals for unrestricted values of n in Sect. 4.5.

4 The Inclusion–Exclusion Integral: Analysis When n is Unrestricted

This section achieves various goals. Sections 4.1 and 4.2 add information to the computations performed in the previous section when the restriction on

n is removed. In this way, we give important insights regarding the inclusion–exclusion integral defined from benchmark interaction operators. Section 4.3 proposes two new concepts (I-equivalence of monotone measures, and v-equivalence of interaction operators) for which examples are given. Section 4.4 gives a converse to a theorem proven in [13]. With this result we prove that the monotone measures for which all inclusion–exclusion integrals coincide are exactly the additive measures. Finally, Sect. 4.5 identifies a class of monotone measures that always produces non-negative inclusion-exclusion integrals.

4.1 IE Integrals Defined from k-Min Interaction Operators

In continuation of Example 7, consider the case with arbitrary n. The 2-min interaction operator $I_2^K(.|.)$ coincides with the largest interaction operator on $[0, K]$ (Example 1). We mentioned that it produces inclusion–exclusion integrals that are Choquet integrals associated with the corresponding monotone measure.

In addition, note that we can draw consequences from the computation of the following evaluations by $M^{I_k^K}(.|.)$ for all $k \in \Omega$:

$$M^{I_k^K}(\boldsymbol{f}|A) = \begin{cases} 0, & \text{when } |A| > k, \\ I_k^K(\boldsymbol{f}|A), & \text{when } |A| = k. \end{cases} \tag{12}$$

These partial evaluations of the Möbius transform of I_k^K demonstrate that *the assignments of $v(A)$ for subsets A with more than k elements do not affect the value of the inclusion–exclusion integral* defined from the monotone measure v and I_k^K. Specifically, Eqs. (2) and (3) adopt the following simplified forms:

$$\begin{aligned} (I_k^K)\int \boldsymbol{f}\,dv &= \sum_{A\subseteq\Omega, |A|=k} I_k^K(\boldsymbol{f} \mid A)\, v(A) + \sum_{A\subseteq\Omega, |A|<k} M^{I_k^K}(\boldsymbol{f} \mid A)\, v(A) \\ &= \sum_{A\subseteq\Omega, |A|\leqslant k} I_k^K(\boldsymbol{f} \mid A)\, m^v(A), \text{ for all } \boldsymbol{f} \in [0, K]^n. \end{aligned} \tag{13}$$

4.2 IE Integrals Defined from the Min-Interaction Operator

In continuation of Example 8, in this section we calculate the inclusion–exclusion integral defined from a monotone measure v and the min-interaction operator I_m^K when $n > 2$. In this case, for all $\boldsymbol{f} \in [0, K]^n$,

$$(I_m^K)\int \boldsymbol{f}\,dv = \sum_{i\in\Omega} f_i\, v(\{i\}) + \sum_{A\subseteq\Omega, |A|>1} m_{\boldsymbol{f}} \cdot m^v(A). \tag{14}$$

This means that the inclusion-exclusion integral under inspection is a correction of a weighted average mean (determined by the values of v on singletons only). The correction adds a term that only depends on the minimum value attained by $\boldsymbol{f}$. Indeed, let $\boldsymbol{w} = (v(\{1\}), \dots, v(\{n\}))$ be a (non-normalized) vector of weights, and let $WAM_{\boldsymbol{w}}(\boldsymbol{f}) = \sum_{i\in\Omega} v(\{i\})f_i$ denote the weighted average mean defined from $\boldsymbol{w}$. Then, a basic property of the Möbius transform yields

$$(I_m^K)\int \boldsymbol{f}\, dv = WAM_{\boldsymbol{w}}(\boldsymbol{f}) + m_{\boldsymbol{f}} \cdot (v(\Omega) - \sum_{i\in\Omega} v(\{i\})). \tag{15}$$

In addition, we can argue that the inclusion-exclusion integral defined from the min-interaction operator behaves as an additive Choquet integral when $\sum_{i\in\Omega} v(\{i\}) \leqslant v(\Omega)$. The argument is as follows. With each $\boldsymbol{f} \in [0, K]^n$ we associate $\bar{\boldsymbol{f}} = (f_1, \ldots, f_n, m_{\boldsymbol{f}}) \in [0, K]^{n+1}$, and we define the additive monotone measure $\bar{v}$ on $\bar{\Omega} = \{1, 2, \ldots, n, n+1\}$ that satisfies $\bar{v}(\{i\}) = v(\{i\})$ when $i \in \Omega$, plus $\bar{v}(\{n+1\}) = v(\Omega) - \sum_{i\in\Omega} v(\{i\})$. Then we have shown that

$$(I_m^K)\int \boldsymbol{f}\, d\,\mathrm{v} = (C)\int \bar{\boldsymbol{f}}\, d\bar{v}.$$

Another feature that we disclose is the exact form of $M^{I_m^K}$: for all $\boldsymbol{f} \in [0, K]^n$ and $A \subseteq \Omega$, using the first formula defined by Equation (4), we claim

$$M^{I_m^K}(\boldsymbol{f}|A) = \begin{cases} m_{\boldsymbol{f}}, \text{ when } A = \Omega, \\ 0, \text{ when } A \subsetneq \Omega, |A| > 1, \text{ and} \\ f_i - m_{\boldsymbol{f}}, \text{ when } A = \{i\}. \end{cases} \tag{16}$$

To prove it, note first that when $|A| > 1$,

$$M^{I_m^K}(\boldsymbol{f}|A) = \Big(\sum_{B\supseteq A} (-1)^{|B\setminus A|}\Big) m_{\boldsymbol{f}} = \begin{cases} m_{\boldsymbol{f}}, \text{ when } A = \Omega, \\ 0, \text{ when } A \subsetneq \Omega, |A| > 1. \end{cases}$$

And when $A = \{i\}$,

$$M^{I_m^K}(\boldsymbol{f}|\{i\}) = I_m^K(\boldsymbol{f}|\{i\}) + \Big(\sum_{i\in B} (-1)^{|B\setminus A|}\Big) m_{\boldsymbol{f}} = f_i - m_{\boldsymbol{f}}.$$

Both computations use the following known combinatorial identity derived from the binomial theorem: for each non-empty set X with cardinality c,

$$\sum_{S\subseteq X} (-1)^{|S|} = \binom{c}{0} - \binom{c}{1} + \binom{c}{2} - \ldots + (-1)^c \binom{c}{c} = (1-1)^c = 0.$$

4.3 Equivalence in the Study of Inclusion–Exclusion Integrals

Properties that have been anticipated in the previous sections lead us to define two concepts with a common trait, namely, the production of equal inclusion–exclusion integrals when one of the defining factors (either the interaction operator or the monotone measure) is fixed. Consider the next two concepts:

Definition 2. *Let I be an Ω-interaction operator on $[0, K]$. The monotone measures v and v' on Ω are I-equivalent when $(I) \int \boldsymbol{f} dv = (I) \int \boldsymbol{f} dv'$, $\forall \boldsymbol{f} \in [0, K]^n$.*

Definition 3. *Let v be a monotone measure on Ω. The Ω-interaction operators I and I' on $[0, K]$ are v-equivalent when $(I) \int \boldsymbol{f} dv = (I') \int \boldsymbol{f} dv$, $\forall \boldsymbol{f} \in [0, K]^n$.*

For a fixed Ω-interaction operator I on $[0, K]$, I-equivalent monotone measures on Ω produce the same inclusion–exclusion integral when coupled with I. Thus when v and v' are I-equivalent, knowing $(I) \int \boldsymbol{f} dv$ suffices to know $(I) \int \boldsymbol{f} dv'$. And for a fixed monotone measure v on Ω, v-equivalent Ω-interaction operators produce the same inclusion–exclusion integral when coupled with v. Thus when we know that I and I' are v-equivalent, knowing $(I) \int \boldsymbol{f} dv$ suffices to know $(I') \int \boldsymbol{f} dv$. The next results identify cases with these properties.

First, we note that when v is additive, all interaction operators on $[0, K]$ are v-equivalent. This property is a corollary to the following result that we revisit in Sect. 4.4 below:

Theorem 1 (Honda and Okazaki [13], Theorem 4). *Let v be an additive monotone measure on Ω. Then for each interaction operator I on $[0, K]$, the inclusion-exclusion integral associated with $(\Omega, \mathcal{P}(\Omega), v, I, K)$ is the Choquet integral defined from v, i.e., $(I)\int \boldsymbol{f} dv = (C)\int \boldsymbol{f} dv$, for each $\boldsymbol{f} \in [0, K]^n$.*

Secondly, we obtain a representation of Choquet integrals defined from k-additive monotone measures by inclusion-exclusion integrals:

Proposition 2. *Let v be a k-additive monotone measure on Ω, with $k < n$. Then I_k^K, I_{k+1}^K, ..., I_n^K are v-equivalent interaction operators on $[0, K]$, and $(I_k^K)\int \boldsymbol{f} dv = \ldots = (I_n^K)\int \boldsymbol{f} dv = (C)\int \boldsymbol{f} dv$, for each $\boldsymbol{f} \in [0, K]^n$.*

Proof. The property follows from the fact that when $k < k' \leqslant n$, Eq. (13) states

$$(I_k^K) \int \boldsymbol{f} \, dv = \sum_{A \subseteq \Omega, |A| \leqslant k} I_k^K(\boldsymbol{f} \mid A) \, m^v(A) = \sum_{A \subseteq \Omega, |A| \leqslant k} I_{k'}^K(\boldsymbol{f} \mid A) \, m^v(A)$$

$$= (I_{k'}^K) \int \boldsymbol{f} \, dv.$$

The first equality holds by k-additivity of v, the second is a basic property (v. Example 2), and the last one holds by k-additivity of v. To conclude the proof, we recall the property that $(I_n^K)\int \boldsymbol{f} \, dv = (C)\int \boldsymbol{f} \, dv$ [13, Example 2].

Monotone measures on Ω are always n-additive. Consequently, the case $k = n$ of Proposition 2 produces a well-known representation of Choquet integrals:

Corollary 1 (Honda and Okazaki [13], Example 2). *Let v be a monotone measure on Ω. Then $(I_n^K)\int \boldsymbol{f} dv = (C)\int \boldsymbol{f} dv$, for each $\boldsymbol{f} \in [0, K]^n$.*

To conclude this section, our next result concerns the min-interaction operator on $[0, K]$. Its proof follows from inspection of Eq. (15):

Proposition 3. *Let v, v' be monotone measures on Ω that coincide on singletons. Then v and v' are I_m^K-equivalent.*

4.4 Characterization of Monotone Measures Producing IE Integrals Independent of the Interaction Operator

When v is an additive monotone measure on Ω, all Ω-interactive monotone measure spaces $(\Omega, \mathcal{P}(\Omega), v, I, K)$ produce the same inclusion–exclusion integral, which in fact coincides with the Choquet integral defined from v (v., Theorem 1). We proceed to prove that the converse holds true. Actually, we prove a stronger result, namely, that the converse implication holds as long as the largest and smallest interaction operators produce the same inclusion–exclusion integral:

Theorem 2. *Let v be a monotone measure on Ω such that for all $\boldsymbol{f} \in [0,K]^n$ $(I_1^K)\int \boldsymbol{f} dv = (I_n^K)\int \boldsymbol{f} dv$. Then v is additive.*

Proof. We prove 1-additivity of v (i.e., additivity). Suppose $|A| > 1$, $A \subseteq \Omega$. Then we use a recurrent argument to prove $m^v(A) = 0$. We take advantage of the equality $(C)\int \boldsymbol{f}\, dv = (I_n^K)\int \boldsymbol{f}\, dv$, for all $\boldsymbol{f} \in [0,K]^n$ (v., Sect. 4.3).

Suppose first $|A| = 2$, $A = \{i,j\}$. Define $\boldsymbol{f} \in [0,K]^n$ such that $f_i = f_j = K$, $f_k = 0$ otherwise. Then, we compute the value of its inclusion–exclusion integrals with respect to I_n^K and I_1^K:

$$(I_n^K)\int \boldsymbol{f}\, dv = (C)\int \boldsymbol{f}\, dv = f_i v(\{i\}) + f_j v(\{j\}) + \min\{f_i, f_j\} m^v(\{i,j\}) =$$

$$Kv(\{i\}) + Kv(\{j\}) + Km^v(\{i,j\}),$$

using Eq. (1). And $(I_1^K)\int \boldsymbol{f}\, dv = Kv(\{i\}) + Kv(\{j\})$, by Eq. (3) and (6). Because $(I_1^K)\int \boldsymbol{f}\, dv = (I_n^K)\int \boldsymbol{f}\, dv$ by assumption, we conclude $m^v(A) = 0$.

Suppose now that $m^v(A) = 0$ holds true for all $A \subseteq \Omega$ with $2 \leqslant |A| < k \leqslant n$. Let us show that if $|A| = k$, $A \subseteq \Omega$, then $m^v(A) = 0$.

Similarly to the first step, we resort to $\boldsymbol{f} \in [0,K]^n$ such that $f_i = K$ when $i \in A$, $f_i = 0$ otherwise. Using the induction hypothesis, Eq. (1) produces

$$(I_n^K)\int \boldsymbol{f}\, dv = (C)\int \boldsymbol{f}\, dv = K\sum_{i\in A} v(\{i\}) + Km^v(A).$$

And now $(I_1^K)\int \boldsymbol{f}\, dv = K\sum_{i\in A} v(\{i\})$, which yields $m^v(A) = 0$ by the assumption $(I_1^K)\int \boldsymbol{f}\, dv = (I_n^K)\int \boldsymbol{f}\, dv$. This ends our proof.

Coupling Theorems 1 and 2, we have a full characterization of monotone measures producing inclusion–exclusion integrals that do not depend on the interaction operator (v., Corollary 1 too):

Corollary 2. *Let v be a monotone measure on Ω. Then v is additive if and only if for each Ω-interaction operator I on $[0,K]$, it is the case that $(I)\int \boldsymbol{f} dv = (C)\int \boldsymbol{f} dv$ for each $\boldsymbol{f} \in [0,K]^n$.*

4.5 Monotone Measures Producing Non-negative IE Integrals

Section 3.2 used the fact that by Equation (3), the IE integral with respect to any interaction operator and fuzzy measure v on Ω that satisfies $m^v(B) \geqslant 0$ for all $B \subseteq \Omega$ is non-negative. The fuzzy measures with such property are exactly the belief measures [4, Section 2.9]. All supermodular fuzzy measures are belief measures [4, Section 10.3], and all additive fuzzy measures are supermodular [4, Section 2.7]. Therefore we conclude:

Proposition 4. *Fix $K \in (0, +\infty)$. All IE integrals defined from an interactive monotone measure space $(\Omega, \mathcal{P}(\Omega), v, I, K)$ where v is a belief measure are non-negative. In particular, this is true if v is either supermodular or additive.*

5 Conclusions and Future Research Perspectives

We have shown that some fundamental issues concerning the inclusion-exclusion integral deserve further attention. For example, we have given a counterexample proving that the problem of identifying interaction operators that possess a unit element is still open. We have proven that Ω-interaction operators produce non-negative inclusion-exclusion integrals when $\Omega = \{1, 2\}$. And that when Ω is bigger, belief measures produce non-negative inclusion-exclusion integrals with any chosen Ω-interaction operator. In addition, we have defined two concepts (I-equivalence of monotone measures and v-equivalence of interaction operators) that pose new problems for future investigation.

Several results proven in the founding articles have been generalized. Proposition 2 extends the types of interaction operators producing Choquet integrals in case of k-additivity of the monotone measure (see the discussion in Sect. 4.3). Theorem 2 proves that the sufficient condition identified in [13, Theorem 4] is also necessary, therefore the conclusion that the class of monotone measures producing inclusion–exclusion integrals independent of the interaction operator has been fully identified (and it is the class of additive monotone measures).

Other feasible avenues for future investigation include the use of IE integrals in data privacy. This topic is a natural continuation of existing studies for the Choquet integral [15] and its generalization by dissimilarities [3]. It is also reasonable to investigate the operators that stem from replacing the product in the computations of the IE integral –either Eq. (2) or Eq. (3)– by appropriate functions as done in [6] and other works.

Acknowledgments. Alcantud is grateful to the Department of Education of the Junta de Castilla y León and FEDER Funds (Reference: CLU-2025-2-03). Honda is supported by JSPS KAKENHI Grant-in-Aid for Scientific Research (C) (Grant N.: 24K06868).

Disclosure of Interests. The authors have no competing interests to declare that are relevant to the content of this article.

References

1. Alcantud, J.C.R.: The capacity compliance problem: refinements of time discounting to Choquet integrals with 2-additive fuzzy measures. Comput. Appl. Math. **44**, 424 (2025). https://doi.org/10.1007/s40314-025-03407-4
2. Alcantud, J.C.R.: A characterization of delay averse Choquet integrals for intertemporal analysis. Theor. Decis. **99**, 37–70 (2025). https://doi.org/10.1007/s11238-025-10047-x
3. Alcantud, J.C.R.: The differentially private d-Choquet integral: an extension of differentially private Choquet integrals. In: Torra, V. et al. (ed.) MDAI 2025. Lecture Notes in Artificial Intelligence 15957, Springer Nature, March 2025. https://doi.org/10.1007/978-3-032-00891-6_11
4. Beliakov, G., James, S., Wu, J.Z.: Choquet Capacities and Fuzzy Integrals. Theory and Applications of Computability. Springer (2026). https://doi.org/10.1007/978-3-031-97070-2
5. Boczek, M., Hutník, O., Kaluszka, M.: Choquet-Sugeno-like operator based on relation and conditional aggregation operators. Inf. Sci. **582**, 1–21 (2022). https://doi.org/10.1016/j.ins.2021.07.063
6. Fernandez, J., Bustince, H., Horanská, L., Mesiar, R., Stupňanová, A.: A generalization of the Choquet integral defined in terms of the Möbius transform. IEEE Trans. Fuzzy Syst. **28**(10), 2313–2319 (2020). https://doi.org/10.1109/TFUZZ.2019.2933803
7. Fukushima, Y., Fujimoto, K., James, S., Honda, A.: Inclusion–exclusion integral neural networks: a framework for explainable AI with non-additive measures. J. Adv. Comput. Intell. Intell. Inf. **29**(6), 1541–1551 (2025). https://doi.org/10.20965/jaciii.2025.p1541
8. Grabisch, M.: k-order additive discrete fuzzy measures and their representation. Fuzzy Sets Syst. **92**(2), 167–189 (1997). https://doi.org/10.1016/S0165-0114(97)00168-1
9. Grabisch, M.: Set functions, games and capacities in decision making, Theory and Decision Library C, vol. 46. Springer, Cham (2016). https://doi.org/10.1007/978-3-319-30690-2
10. Honda, A., Alcantud, J.C.R.: Revisiting monotonicity of the inclusion-exclusion integral: The case of the arithmetic-mean interaction operator. In: Vantaggi, B., et al. (eds.) IPMU 2026. Springer, CCIS series (2026)
11. Honda, A., Itabashi, M., James, S.: A neural network based on the inclusion-exclusion integral and its application to data analysis. Inf. Sci. **648**, 119549 (2023). https://doi.org/10.1016/j.ins.2023.119549
12. Honda, A., James, S.: Averaging aggregation functions based on inclusion-exclusion integrals. In: 17th World Congress of International Fuzzy Systems Association and 9th International Conference on Soft Computing and Intelligent Systems (IFSA-SCIS), pp. 1–6 (2017). https://doi.org/10.1109/IFSA-SCIS.2017.8023353
13. Honda, A., Okazaki, Y.: Theory of inclusion-exclusion integral. Inf. Sci. **376**, 136–147 (2017). https://doi.org/10.1016/j.ins.2016.09.063
14. Honda, A., Okazaki, Y.: Generalization of inclusion-exclusion integral for nondiscrete monotone measure space. Fuzzy Sets Syst. **355**, 42–58 (2019). https://doi.org/10.1016/j.fss.2018.06.005
15. Torra, V.: Differentially private Choquet integral: extending mean, median, and order statistics. Int. J. Inf. Secur. **24**, 68 (2025). https://doi.org/10.1007/s10207-025-00984-7

Revisiting Monotonicity of the Inclusion–Exclusion Integral: The Case of the Arithmetic–Mean Interaction Operator

Aoi Honda[1](✉) and José Carlos R. Alcantud[2]

[1] Department of Mathematics, Faculty of Science, Kobe University, Kobe 657-8501, Japan
aoi@math.kobe-u.ac.jp

[2] Unidad de Excelencia Gestión Económica para la Sostenibilidad GECOS and IME, Universidad de Salamanca, 37007 Salamanca, Spain
jcr@usal.es
http://diarium.usal.es/jcr

Abstract. The inclusion–exclusion (IE) integral is a flexible aggregation framework that extends classical nonlinear integrals by combining monotone measures with interaction operators. While monotonicity with respect to the input function is a fundamental requirement for aggregation models, a complete characterization of monotonicity for the IE integral is still lacking, and existing results rely on restrictive axioms imposed on the interaction operator. In order to analyze monotonicity in a precise manner, we consider interaction operators under mild assumptions, including non-negativity, and impose further structural conditions only when required. Within this framework, we systematically distinguish three types of monotonicity for the IE integral, namely monotonicity with respect to the input function, the underlying measure, and the interaction operator. We then revisit monotonicity of the IE integral by focusing on the interaction operator given by the arithmetic mean. Although this operator does not satisfy the classical sufficient conditions for monotonicity, we show that the corresponding IE integral nevertheless preserves input monotonicity, thereby demonstrating that these conditions are not necessary. We further prove that the arithmetic–mean IE integral unexpectedly admits an equivalent linear representation, whose coefficients coincide with the Shapley values of the underlying monotone measure. These results demonstrate that the known sufficient conditions for monotonicity of the IE integral are not necessary and can be substantially weakened, and they provide new insights into the structural origins of monotonicity in inclusion–exclusion based aggregation models.

Keywords: Inclusion–exclusion integral · Fuzzy measure · Monotonicity · Arithmetic–mean aggregation · Shapley value

B. Vantaggi et al. (Eds.): IPMU 2026, CCIS 3019, pp. 87–100, 2026.
https://doi.org/10.1007/978-3-032-28994-0_7

1 Introduction

Aggregation integrals with respect to non-additive measures play a central role in decision making, information fusion, and cooperative game theory [1,2,7,8,10]. Among them, the inclusion–exclusion (IE) integral provides a flexible framework that extends classical nonlinear integrals by allowing the use of general interaction operators in combination with monotone measures [9]. By replacing the minimum operator underlying the Choquet integral with a more general interaction operator, the IE integral is able to model complex interactions among criteria while retaining a closed-form representation based on inclusion–exclusion principles [3]. A fundamental requirement for aggregation models is monotonicity with respect to the input function: increasing the input values should not decrease the aggregated outcome. Although coordinatewise monotonicity is a standard requirement in aggregation theory, weaker monotonicity conditions have also been considered in information fusion, especially in the study of pre-aggregation functions and related Choquet-like operators. These frameworks relax full monotonicity while preserving meaningful order behavior in restricted directions; see, e.g., [5,6,11]. In the present paper, we focus on the classical notion of monotonicity. For the IE integral, monotonicity is still far from being fully understood. While the formal definition of the IE integral resembles that of classical nonlinear integrals with respect to a monotone measure, its monotonicity properties depend in a delicate way on both the underlying measure and the chosen interaction operator. Existing results therefore provide only partial answers.

The present study also admits a natural interpretation in cooperative game theory. Indeed, a fuzzy measure on Ω may be regarded as a transferable-utility game, where subsets of criteria are interpreted as coalitions. In the arithmetic–mean setting considered in this paper, the IE integral turns out to admit a linear representation whose coefficients coincide with the Shapley values of the underlying game. This provides a conceptual link between the monotonicity of the IE integral and the consistency of aggregation procedures based on game-theoretic importance indices.

In [10], monotonicity of the IE integral has mainly been established under restrictive assumptions on the interaction operator. In particular, sufficient conditions have been derived for commutative multi-ary interaction operators satisfying strong structural properties such as disjoint meet supermodularity and quasi-surjectivity. Under these assumptions, the IE integral is known to preserve input monotonicity. However, these conditions are difficult to verify in practice and exclude many natural interaction operators. Whether they are also necessary has remained an open question.

In order to analyze monotonicity in a precise and systematic manner, we adopt a relaxed axiomatic viewpoint. In particular, we do not impose classical axioms such as antitonicity with respect to set inclusion or disjoint meet supermodularity unless explicitly required. Rather than imposing standard axioms on interaction operators from the outset, we consider them in full generality and introduce several distinct notions of monotonicity for the IE integral. Specifically, we distinguish monotonicity with respect to the input function, the underlying measure, and the interaction operator itself. This separation allows us to clarify which aspects of monotonicity are preserved and which may fail, depending on the structural properties of the interaction operator.

Within this framework, we focus on the IE integral associated with the arithmetic–mean interaction operator. The arithmetic mean is one of the simplest and most widely used aggregation operators, making it a natural candidate for probing the necessity of existing monotonicity conditions. This operator does not satisfy the classical sufficient conditions for monotonicity and, in particular, fails to be antitone with respect to set inclusion. Somewhat surprisingly, we show that the corresponding IE integral preserves input monotonicity. Moreover, we prove that the arithmetic–mean IE integral admits an equivalent linear representation whose coefficients coincide with the Shapley values of the underlying monotone measure. This result provides a transparent interpretation of the aggregation process and establishes a direct link between the IE integral and cooperative game theory.

The contributions of this paper can be summarized as follows:

- we systematically distinguish three types of monotonicity for the IE integral and clarify their logical independence. These notions correspond respectively to variations in the input data, the weighting of coalitions, and the aggregation mechanism;
- we show that the arithmetic–mean IE integral is input monotone despite violating the classical sufficient conditions;
- we establish an equivalent linear representation of the arithmetic–mean IE integral based on the Shapley value.

These results demonstrate that the known sufficient conditions for monotonicity of the IE integral are not necessary and can be substantially weakened. The arithmetic–mean IE integral thus serves as a revealing test case for understanding the structural origins of monotonicity in inclusion–exclusion based aggregation models. Our analysis focuses primarily on input monotonicity, while the other types of monotonicity are discussed to clarify their independence and limitations.

2 Preliminaries

Throughout this paper, we consider a finite universe $\Omega = \{1, 2, \ldots, n\}$, and denote by $v : 2^{\Omega} \to [0, K]$ a monotone measure on Ω. That is,

$$v(\varnothing) = 0, \qquad A \subset B \subseteq \Omega \Rightarrow v(A) \leq v(B).$$

If, in addition, $v(\Omega) = 1$, then v is called a *fuzzy measure* or a *capacity* on Ω.

A mapping $\boldsymbol{f} : \Omega \to [0, K]$, with $K > 0$, can be naturally identified with a vector in $[0, K]^n$. More precisely, when $\Omega = \{1, \ldots, n\}$, we write

$$\boldsymbol{f} = (f_1, \ldots, f_n) \in [0, K]^n,$$

where $f_i = \boldsymbol{f}(i)$ for each $i \in \Omega$.

There is no loss of generality in assuming that the measure v is normalized so that $v(\Omega) = 1$, and that the input vector $\boldsymbol{f}$ is normalized so that $\boldsymbol{f} \in [0,1]^n$, since the general case $\boldsymbol{f} \in [0,K]^n$ can always be reduced to this setting by rescaling. Accordingly, throughout the paper we assume that both v and $\boldsymbol{f}$ are normalized.

Let $I : [0,1]^n \times 2^\Omega \to \mathbb{R}$ be an interaction operator. For each $\boldsymbol{f} \in [0,1]^n$ and each $A \subseteq \Omega$, the quantity $I(\boldsymbol{f} \mid A)$ denotes the interaction value associated with the subset A for the input vector $\boldsymbol{f}$. In general, $I(\boldsymbol{f} \mid A)$ may depend on the whole vector $\boldsymbol{f}$, and not only on the components indexed by A.

The IE integral associated with a fuzzy measure v on Ω and an interaction operator I is defined by

$$(I)\int \boldsymbol{f}\,dv = \sum_{A\subseteq\Omega}\left(\sum_{B\supseteq A}(-1)^{|B\setminus A|}\,I(\boldsymbol{f}\mid B)\right)v(A). \tag{1}$$

Introducing the Möbius transform of the set function $A \mapsto I(\boldsymbol{f} \mid A)$, defined for each $A \subseteq \Omega$ by

$$M^I(\boldsymbol{f}\mid A) = \sum_{B\supseteq A}(-1)^{|B\setminus A|}\,I(\boldsymbol{f}\mid B), \tag{2}$$

the IE integral can be equivalently written as

$$(I)\int \boldsymbol{f}\,dv = \sum_{A\subseteq\Omega} M^I(\boldsymbol{f}\mid A)\,v(A). \tag{3}$$

Equivalently, by means of the Möbius transform m_v of the fuzzy measure v, the IE integral admits the representation

$$(I)\int \boldsymbol{f}\,dv = \sum_{A\subseteq\Omega} I(\boldsymbol{f}\mid A)\,m_v(A), \tag{4}$$

where

$$m_v(A) = \sum_{B\subseteq A}(-1)^{|A\setminus B|}v(B), \qquad A \subseteq \Omega.$$

The transform $M^I(\boldsymbol{f} \mid A)$ in (2) can be viewed as the Möbius transform of the set function $A \mapsto I(\boldsymbol{f} \mid A)$ with respect to the reversed inclusion order $\supseteq$. In other words, it corresponds to a standard Möbius inversion on the Boolean lattice endowed with the reversed order.

When the interaction operator is chosen as

$$I(\boldsymbol{f}\mid A) = \min_{i\in A} f_i,$$

with the convention that $I(\boldsymbol{f} \mid \varnothing) = 1$, the corresponding IE integral coincides with the Choquet integral. In this case, the minimum operation plays the role of a conjunctive aggregation operator, which is well known to be compatible with fuzzy integration. In the initial definition of the IE integral, the interaction operator I is assumed to satisfy several conditions as follows [9,10]. For any $\boldsymbol{f}, \boldsymbol{g} \in [0,1]^n$, any $i \in \Omega$, and any subsets $A, B \subseteq \Omega$, the interaction operator I was requested to satisfy the following properties:

(I1) *Boundary condition (normalization at the empty set).*

$$I(\boldsymbol{f} \mid \varnothing) = 1.$$

(I2) *Singleton consistency (identity on singletons).*

$$I(\boldsymbol{f} \mid \{i\}) = f_i.$$

(I3) *Pointwise input monotonicity.* For every $A \subseteq \Omega$,

$$\boldsymbol{f} \leq \boldsymbol{g} \;\Rightarrow\; I(\boldsymbol{f} \mid A) \leq I(\boldsymbol{g} \mid A),$$

where $\boldsymbol{f} \leq \boldsymbol{g}$ means $f_i \leq g_i$ for all $i \in \Omega$ (i.e., $\boldsymbol{f}$ is less than or equal to $\boldsymbol{g}$ pointwise).

(I4) *Antitonicity with respect to set inclusion.*

$$A \subseteq B \;\Rightarrow\; I(\boldsymbol{f} \mid A) \geq I(\boldsymbol{f} \mid B).$$

In this paper, however, in order to investigate monotonicity properties of the IE integral in a precise and systematic manner, we do not impose these axioms as standing assumptions on the interaction operator. Throughout this work, the interaction operator I is not required to satisfy conditions (I1)–(I4), unless explicitly stated otherwise. Instead, the only general assumption we make is that

$$I(\boldsymbol{f} \mid A) \geq 0, \text{ for all } \boldsymbol{f} \in [0,1]^n \text{ and all } A \subseteq \Omega.$$

Accordingly, we consider interaction operators in full generality. In particular, we do not restrict I to be commutative or idempotent, nor do we assume any specific algebraic structure. While $I(\boldsymbol{f} \mid B)$ is often defined solely in terms of the components indexed by B, it may also depend explicitly on the remaining components of $\boldsymbol{f}$ indexed by $\Omega \backslash B$. This general viewpoint allows us to encompass a broad and flexible class of interaction operators and, consequently, a wide variety of IE integrals.

3 Monotonicity Properties of the IE Integral

Since the IE integral depends on several components, namely the input function, the underlying measure, and the interaction operator, different types of monotonicity naturally arise. In what follows, we distinguish three such types of monotonicity, which we refer to as input monotonicity (M1), measure monotonicity (M2), and operator monotonicity (M3).

(M1) *Monotonicity of the first kind (input monotonicity).* For a fixed interaction operator I and fuzzy measure v on Ω, when $\boldsymbol{f}, \boldsymbol{g} \in [0,1]^n$ and $\boldsymbol{f} \leq \boldsymbol{g}$, one has $(I)\int \boldsymbol{f}\, dv \leq (I)\int \boldsymbol{g}\, dv$.

(M2) *Monotonicity of the second kind (measure monotonicity).* For a fixed interaction operator I, when v, v' are fuzzy measures on Ω and $v \leq v'$, one has $(I)\int \boldsymbol{f}\, dv \leq (I)\int \boldsymbol{f}\, dv'$ for every $\boldsymbol{f} \in [0,1]^n$. In this case we refer to measure monotonicity.

(M3) *Monotonicity of the third kind (operator monotonicity).* For a fixed fuzzy measure v on Ω, when I, I' are interaction operators and $I \leq I'$, one has $(I)\int \boldsymbol{f}\, dv \leq (I')\int \boldsymbol{f}\, dv$ for every $\boldsymbol{f} \in [0,1]^n$. In this case we refer to operator monotonicity.

These three notions of monotonicity are logically independent. The examples provided in the following subsections demonstrate that satisfying one type of monotonicity does not imply the others, highlighting the necessity of distinguishing them explicitly.

In the remainder of this section, Sects. 3.1, 3.2 and 3.3 investigate the M1, M2 and M3, respectively.

3.1 Monotonicity of the IE Integral: Interpretation of the First Kind

This section is concerned with the first type of monotonicity, M1, namely input monotonicity.

The input monotonicity of the IE integral is still far from being fully understood. Although the definition of the IE integral bears a formal resemblance to that of classical nonlinear integrals with respect to a monotone measure, a complete characterization of its monotonicity properties has not yet been established. At present, only partial results are available.

In particular, a sufficient condition for the monotonicity of the IE integral has been obtained under the assumption that the interaction operator is a commutative multi-ary operator. This condition, stated precisely in [10, Propositions 4 and 13], shows that the IE integral is monotone whenever the underlying interaction operator satisfies the following two structural properties:

1. I is *disjoint meet supermodular of order* n, and
2. I is *quasi-surjective.*

We recall that an interaction operator I is said to be *disjoint meet supermodular of order* n if, for any integer $m < n$ and any $A \in 2^{\Omega}$ and any family of subsets $A_1, \ldots, A_m \in 2^{\Omega} \setminus \{A\}$ satisfying $A_i \cap A_j = A$ for all $i, j \in \{1, \ldots, m\}$, the following inequality holds:

$$I(\boldsymbol{f} \mid \mathrm{A}) \geq \sum_{\substack{B \subseteq \{1,\ldots,m\} \\ B \neq \varnothing}} (-1)^{|B|+1} I\left(\boldsymbol{f} \,\middle|\, \bigcup_{i \in B} A_i\right),$$

for all $\boldsymbol{f} \in [0,1]^n$. We note that, in the original definition, disjoint meet supermodularity is formulated for set functions. In the present setting, this notion is naturally extended to interaction operators by evaluating the defining inequality pointwise with respect to the input vector $\boldsymbol{f}$. Intuitively, this condition ensures that the multi-ary aggregation operator induced by the interaction operator I preserves a suitable form of higher-order monotonicity, which in turn guarantees that the inclusion–exclusion coefficients remain non-negative.

An interaction operator I is said to be *quasi-surjective* if, for any subset $A \subseteq \Omega$, any index $i \in A$, and any fixed vector $\boldsymbol{f}_{\hat{i}} \in [0,1]^{n-1}$, every value belonging to the range of the mapping

$$x \longmapsto I(f_1, \dots, f_{i-1}, x, f_{i+1}, \dots, f_n \mid A)$$

can be attained for some $x \in [0,1]$. That is, by varying the i-th component f_i while keeping all other components fixed, the interaction operator can generate any aggregation value that is admissible under the given configuration.

Under these assumptions, [10, Propositions 4 and 13] show that the IE integral satisfies fundamental properties such as non-negativity and input monotonicity. In particular, for any functions $\boldsymbol{f}, \boldsymbol{g} \in [0,1]^n$ satisfying $\boldsymbol{f} \leq \boldsymbol{g}$, one has

$$(I)\int \boldsymbol{f}\ \mathrm{dv} \leq (I)\int \boldsymbol{g}\, dv.$$

In [10], concrete examples are provided in terms of IE integrals constructed from interaction operators induced by suitable t-norms. More precisely, [10] identifies several t-norms that satisfy the above conditions, and shows that the interaction operators defined via these t-norms fulfill the required assumptions. In particular, this applies to the Dubois–Prade family of t-norms, which includes, as extremal cases, the minimum t-norm and the algebraic product t-norm. Thus, the examples covered in [10] include:

- the minimum t-norm, which yields the Choquet integral,
- the algebraic product t-norm, and
- the Dubois–Prade t-norms.

A complete characterization of monotonicity for more general interaction operators remains an open research problem. In this section, we investigate this issue in depth by focusing on the IE integral associated with the arithmetic–mean interaction operator. Although simple in structure, the arithmetic–mean IE integral turns out to be a particularly useful test case for exploring the monotonicity properties of the IE integral. Indeed, it provides valuable insight into the role played by the interaction operator and helps clarify which assumptions are essential for monotonicity and which can be relaxed.

Definition 1 (IE integral with arithmetic–mean interaction). *Let v be a fuzzy measure on Ω. The arithmetic–mean interaction operator I^{AM} is defined, for every $\boldsymbol{f} = (f_1, \dots, f_n) \in [0,1]^n$ and every nonempty subset $A \subseteq \Omega$, by*

$$I^{\mathrm{AM}}(\boldsymbol{f} \mid A) = \frac{1}{|A|} \sum_{i \in A} f_i.$$

The IE integral of $\boldsymbol{f} \in [0,1]^n$ with respect to v and I^{AM} and its representation are given by

$$(I^{\mathrm{AM}}) \int \boldsymbol{f}\, dv = \sum_{\substack{A \subseteq \Omega \\ A \neq \varnothing}} \left(\sum_{B \supseteq A} (-1)^{|B \setminus A|}\, I^{\mathrm{AM}}(\boldsymbol{f} \mid B) \right) v(A), \tag{5}$$

$$= \sum_{\substack{A \subseteq \Omega \\ A \neq \varnothing}} I^{\mathrm{AM}}(\boldsymbol{f} \mid A)\, m_v(A), \tag{6}$$

where m_v denotes the Möbius transform of the fuzzy measure v.

Proposition 1 (Input monotonicity of the IE integral with arithmetic–mean interaction). *Let v be a fuzzy measure on Ω, and let I^{AM} be the arithmetic–mean interaction operator. Then the IE integral with arithmetic–mean interaction is input monotone in the sense of* (M1). *That is, for any $\boldsymbol{f}, \boldsymbol{g} \in [0,1]^n$ satisfying $\boldsymbol{f} \leq \boldsymbol{g}$ componentwise, one has*

$$(I^{\mathrm{AM}}) \int \boldsymbol{f}\, dv \leq (I^{\mathrm{AM}}) \int \boldsymbol{g}\, dv.$$

For instance, when $\Omega = \{1,2\}$ and $v(\{1\}) = 0.3$, $v(\{2\}) = 0.5$, $v(\{1,2\}) = 1$, the arithmetic–mean IE integral reduces to

$$(I^{\mathrm{AM}}) \int \boldsymbol{f}\, dv = 0.3 f_1 + 0.5 f_2 + (1 - 0.3 - 0.5) \frac{f_1 + f_2}{2} = 0.4 f_1 + 0.6 f_2.$$

Hence, for $\boldsymbol{f} = (0.2, 0.4) \leq \boldsymbol{g} = (0.7, 0.4)$, one has

$$(I^{\mathrm{AM}}) \int \boldsymbol{f}\, dv = 0.32 < 0.52 = (I^{\mathrm{AM}}) \int \boldsymbol{g}\, dv,$$

which illustrates (M1) for the arithmetic–mean IE integral. However, this input monotonicity is not a consequence of the classical sufficient conditions, since the arithmetic–mean interaction operator fails to be disjoint meet supermodular. Indeed, the defining inequality of this property does not hold in general. For instance, consider the condition

$$f_1 \ \geq\ \frac{f_1 + f_2}{2} + \frac{f_1 + f_3}{2} - \frac{f_1 + f_2 + f_3}{3},$$

which is equivalent to

$$2 f_1 \ \geq\ f_2 + f_3.$$

Since this inequality is not satisfied for arbitrary choices of $(f_1, f_2, f_3) \in [0,1]^3$, the interaction operator I^{AM} is not disjoint meet supermodular.

Despite the failure of disjoint meet supermodularity, the IE integral associated with the arithmetic–mean interaction operator still satisfies input monotonicity. This is due to the remarkably simple structure of this integral, as shown in the following proposition.

Proposition 2. *For the IE integral associated with the arithmetic–mean interaction operator I^{AM} and a monotone measure v on Ω, there exists an equivalent linear representation. More precisely, the IE integral reduces to a (possibly non-normalized) weighted arithmetic mean of the inputs. In particular, there exists an additive measure μ on 2^{Ω} such that*

$$(I^{\mathrm{AM}}) \int \boldsymbol{f}\, dv = \sum_{i=1}^{n} \mu(\{i\})\, f_i, \tag{7}$$

for all $\boldsymbol{f} \in [0,1]^n$.

Proof. Substituting the definition of the arithmetic–mean interaction operator into the Möbius-transform representation of the IE integral yields

$$\begin{aligned}(I^{\mathrm{AM}}) \int \boldsymbol{f}\, dv &= \sum_{\substack{A\subseteq \Omega\\ A\neq\varnothing}} \left(\frac{1}{|A|}\sum_{i\in A} f_i\right) m_v(A) = \sum_{\substack{A\subseteq \Omega\\ A\neq\varnothing}} \sum_{i\in A} \frac{m_v(A)}{|A|}\, f_i \\ &= \sum_{i\in\Omega} f_i \sum_{\substack{A\subseteq \Omega\\ i\in A}} \frac{m_v(A)}{|A|}.\end{aligned}$$

Define, for each $i \in \Omega$,

$$\mu(\{i\}) := \sum_{\substack{A\subseteq \Omega\\ i\in A}} \frac{m_v(A)}{|A|}.$$

Then we obtain

$$(I^{\mathrm{AM}}) \int \boldsymbol{f}\, dv = \sum_{i\in\Omega} \mu(\{i\})\, f_i,$$

as claimed. Finally, extend μ to 2^{Ω} by additivity, i.e.,

$$\mu(S) := \sum_{i\in S} \mu(\{i\}), \qquad S \in 2^{\Omega},$$

so that μ is an additive measure on 2^{Ω}.

This linear representation suggests input monotonicity, once the coefficients are shown to be nonnegative.

We note that the additive measure μ introduced in the above proof is characterized by the Shapley value of the fuzzy measure v. Specifically, for each $i \in \Omega$, the coefficient $\mu(\{i\})$ is given by the i-th component of the Shapley value $\Phi(v) = (\phi_1(v), \ldots, \phi_n(v))$ of v, that is,

$$\begin{aligned}\mu(\{i\}) = \sum_{\substack{A\subseteq \Omega\\ i\in A}} \frac{m_v(A)}{|A|} \quad &= \sum_{A\subseteq \Omega\setminus\{i\}} \frac{|A|!\,(n-|A|-1)!}{n!}\big(v(A\cup\{i\}) - v(A)\big) \\ = \phi_i(v), \qquad &\text{taking advantage of [4, Eq. (3.11) and Def. 3.4].}\end{aligned}$$

By the definition of the arithmetic–mean interaction operator and the Möbius representation of the IE integral, the coefficient $\mu(\{i\})$ arising in the linear representation presented in Eq. (7) is given by exactly the same expression. Hence, the additive measure μ is fully determined by the Shapley value of v. It is well known that each coefficient $\mu(\{i\}) = \phi_i(v)$ is nonnegative by the monotonicity of v, and also that $\sum_{i\in\Omega} \mu(\{i\}) = \sum_{i\in\Omega} \phi_i(v) = v(\Omega)$ [4, Eq. (3.6)].

By exploiting the relationship described above between the arithmetic–mean IE integral and the Shapley value, one can recover the Shapley value of a fuzzy measure through the IE integral of indicator functions as follows:

Proposition 3. *Let v be a monotone measure on Ω, and let $\mathbf{1}_A$ denote the indicator function of a subset $A \subseteq \Omega$, that is,*

$$(\mathbf{1}_A)_i = \begin{cases} 1, & \text{if } i \in A, \\ 0, & \text{otherwise.} \end{cases}$$

Then the following equality holds:

$$(I^{\mathrm{AM}}) \int \mathbf{1}_A \; dv = \sum_{i\in A} \phi_i(v).$$

In particular, for each $i \in \Omega$, one has

$$(I^{\mathrm{AM}}) \int \mathbf{1}_{\{i\}} \; dv = \phi_i(v), \; (I^{\mathrm{AM}}) \int \mathbf{1}_{\Omega} \; dv = \mu(\Omega).$$

Remark 1. In the conditions of Proposition 2, the expression in Eq. (7) guarantees that the IE integral is additive too.

The arithmetic–mean interaction operator does not satisfy the monotonicity condition with respect to set inclusion required for the partition-based interpretation. Indeed, the ordering between $(f_1 + f_2)/2$ and $(f_1 + f_2 + f_3)/3$ depends on the value of f_3 and is therefore not fixed in general. The IE integral is commonly classified as a partition-type integral. This classification stems from the fact that the IE integral can be interpreted as a sum of volumes of partitioned hyperrectangles, whose edge lengths are given by $M^I(\boldsymbol{f} \mid A)$ and $v(A)$. In order for all such hyperrectangles to have nonnegative edge lengths, the above monotonicity condition on the interaction operator is at least necessary. When an interaction operator that does not satisfy this condition is used, as in the case of the arithmetic–mean interaction operator, negative contributions may appear. For instance, when $\Omega = \{1, 2\}$, the IE integral is decomposed into three terms, and one obtains

$$\begin{aligned} &(I^{\mathrm{AM}}) \int \boldsymbol{f} \, dv \\ &= \left(f_1 - \frac{f_1 + f_2}{2}\right) v(\{1\}) + \left(f_2 - \frac{f_1 + f_2}{2}\right) v(\{2\}) + \frac{f_1 + f_2}{2} v(\{1, 2\}). \end{aligned}$$

In this expression, at least one of the first two terms is necessarily negative, which illustrates the failure of the partition-based interpretation when the interaction operator does not satisfy the monotonicity condition with respect to set inclusion. Nevertheless, even in this case, the IE integral satisfies input monotonicity, as shown in Proposition 1.

3.2 Monotonicity of the IE Integral: Interpretation of the Second Kind

We now investigate IE integrals that satisfy monotonicity with respect to the underlying measure, that is, property (M2), for a fixed interaction operator I. In the case of Choquet integrals (i.e., when I is the minimum interaction operator), the measure monotonicity property is always satisfied. However, for general choices of the interaction operator I, this property is no longer guaranteed for the IE integral:

Example 1 (A counterexample to M2). Let $\Omega = \{1, 2\}$ and $K = 1$. Define an interaction operator I by

$$I(\boldsymbol{f} \mid \{1\}) = f_1, \qquad I(\boldsymbol{f} \mid \{2\}) = f_2, \qquad I(\boldsymbol{f} \mid \{1,2\}) = \min\{1, f_1 + f_2\}.$$

Now consider two monotone measures v, v' ($v \leq v'$) on 2^{Ω} defined by

$$v(\{1,2\}) = v'(\{2\}) = v'(\{1,2\}) = 1, \qquad v(\{1\}) = v(\{2\}) = v'(\{1\}) = 0.$$

Then for $\boldsymbol{f} = (1, 0.6)$, we have

$$(I)\int \boldsymbol{f}\, dv = 1 > (I)\int \boldsymbol{f}\, dv' = 0.6$$

despite the fact that v is monotonically dominated by v', i.e., $v \leq v'$.

Example 1 illustrates that measure monotonicity (M2) is far from automatic once one moves beyond the Choquet case, and that significantly restricts the class of admissible interaction operators. This naturally raises the question of identifying conditions under which M2 holds. At present, determining meaningful structural conditions on I that guarantee M2 remains an open problem.

3.3 Monotonicity of the IE Integral: Interpretation of the Third Kind

Finally, we turn to M3, which concerns monotonicity with respect to the interaction operator for a fixed fuzzy measure v on Ω. Throughout this subsection, we assume non-negativity of the interaction operator. As in the case of measure monotonicity (M2), we demonstrate that this property is not guaranteed in general.

Example 2 (A counterexample to M3). Let $\Omega = \{1, 2\}$ and $K = 1$. Consider the monotone measure v on 2^Ω defined by

$$v(\varnothing) = 0, \qquad v(\{1\}) = v(\{2\}) = 0.9, \qquad v(\{1, 2\}) = 1.$$

Then its Möbius transform m_v satisfies

$$m_v(\{1\}) = v(\{1\}) = 0.9, \qquad m_v(\{2\}) = v(\{2\}) = 0.9,$$
$$m_v(\{1, 2\}) = v(\{1, 2\}) - v(\{1\}) - v(\{2\}) = -0.8.$$

Define two interaction operators I and I', $I(\boldsymbol{f} \mid A) \leq I'(\boldsymbol{f} \mid A)$, by

$$I(\boldsymbol{f} \mid \{1\}) = I'(\boldsymbol{f} \mid \{1\}) = f_1 > 0, \qquad I(\boldsymbol{f} \mid \{2\}) = I'(\boldsymbol{f} \mid \{2\}) = f_2 > 0,$$

and

$$I(\boldsymbol{f} \mid \{1, 2\}) = 0, \qquad I'(\boldsymbol{f} \mid \{1, 2\}) = \min(f_1, f_2) > 0.$$

Using the Möbius representation of the IE integral, we obtain for $\boldsymbol{f} = (f_1, f_2)$

$$\begin{aligned}(I)\int \boldsymbol{f}\, dv &= f_1\, m_v(\{1\}) + f_2\, m_v(\{2\}) + I(\boldsymbol{f} \mid \{1, 2\})\, m_v(\{1, 2\}) \\ &= 0.9 f_1 + 0.9 f_2,\end{aligned}$$

whereas

$$(I')\int \boldsymbol{f}\, dv = 0.9 f_1 + 0.9 f_2 - 0.8 \min(f_1, f_2).$$

Hence,

$$(I)\int \boldsymbol{f}\, dv \;>\; (I')\int \boldsymbol{f}\, dv$$

despite the fact that I is monotonically extended to I', i.e., despite $I \leq I'$.

This naturally raises the question of which situations guarantee that M3 holds. A preliminary result about this problem follows.

A cursory inspection of Equation (4) shows that the IE integral is monotone with respect to the interaction operator for any fuzzy measure v on Ω whose Möbius transform satisfies $m_v(A) \geqslant 0$ for all $A \subset \Omega$, provided that the interaction operators under consideration take only non-negative values. This class of fuzzy measures is known to coincide with belief measures (also called totally monotonic, or k-monotonic for all $k > 1$) [4, Section 2.9], which contain all supermodular fuzzy measures [4, Section 10.3] and therefore all additive fuzzy measures [4, Section 2.7]. The next conclusion follows immediately:

Corollary 1. *Suppose that we restrict our attention to non-negative interaction operators. Then the IE integral is monotone with respect to any belief measure v on Ω. In particular, it is monotone with respect to the interaction operator for any supermodular, and hence any additive fuzzy measure v on Ω.*

Remark 2. When v is additive, Honda and Okazaki [9, Theorem 4] demonstrated that all interaction operators satisfying axioms (I1)-(I4) produce the Choquet integral defined by v. This result has been strengthened to a full characterization in [3, Theorem 2]. As a consequence, when v is additive and the interaction operator is restricted to satisfy axioms (I1)–(I4), the corresponding IE integral coincides with the Choquet integral and is therefore monotone with respect to variations of the interaction operator. This provides an alternative justification of operator monotonicity in the additive case, under the axiomatic framework considered in [9].

Remark 3. When v is a belief measure, [3, Section 4.5] explains that the IE integral is non-negative, for all non-negative interaction operators. The reason is that in Eq. (4), $I(\boldsymbol{f} \mid A) \geq 0$ and $m_v(A) \geq 0$ for all $A \subseteq \Omega$.

The question that naturally arises is: are belief measures the only fuzzy measures that make the IE integral monotonic in the sense of M3? We expect to come back to this problem in the future.

4 Conclusion

In this paper, we investigated monotonicity properties of the inclusion–exclusion (IE) integral from a structural point of view. By distinguishing three different notions of monotonicity, namely with respect to the input function, the underlying measure, and the interaction operator, we clarified several logical relationships among these properties.

Focusing on the IE integral associated with the arithmetic–mean interaction operator, we showed that input monotonicity may still hold even when classical sufficient conditions, such as disjoint meet supermodularity, are violated. Moreover, for the arithmetic–mean IE integral, we established an equivalent linear representation in terms of the Shapley value, providing a transparent interpretation of the underlying aggregation mechanism.

These results demonstrate that the known sufficient conditions for monotonicity of the IE integral, such as disjoint meet supermodularity, are not necessary and can be substantially weakened. While the present analysis provides new insights into input monotonicity through the arithmetic–mean IE integral, a complete characterization of monotonicity for more general interaction operators remains an open problem for future research. This includes input monotonicity, measure monotonicity and monotonicity with respect to the interaction operator. From a methodological perspective, this work also illustrates that relaxing the axiomatic requirements imposed on interaction operators can be a fruitful approach for identifying which structural properties are truly responsible for monotonicity.

Acknowledgments. This work was supported by JSPS KAKENHI Grant-in-Aid for Scientific Research (C) (Grant Number: 24K06868). Alcantud is grateful to the Department of Education of the Junta de Castilla y León and FEDER Funds (Reference: CLU-2025-2-03).

Disclosure of Interests. The authors have no competing interests to declare that are relevant to the content of this article.

References

1. Alcantud, J.C.R.: The capacity compliance problem: refinements of time discounting to Choquet integrals with 2-additive fuzzy measures. Comput. Appl. Math. **44**, 424 (2025). https://doi.org/10.1007/s40314-025-03407-4
2. Alcantud, J.C.R.: A characterization of delay averse Choquet integrals for intertemporal analysis. Theor. Decis. **99**, 37–70 (2025). https://doi.org/10.1007/s11238-025-10047-x
3. Alcantud, J.C.R., Honda, A.: More on the inclusion-exclusion integral: benchmark interaction operators and equivalence concepts. In: Vantaggi, B., et al. (eds.) IPMU 2026. CCIS, Springer, Cham (2026)
4. Beliakov, G., James, S., Wu, J.Z.: Choquet Capacities and Fuzzy Integrals. Theory and Applications of Computability. Springer, Cham (2026). https://doi.org/10.1007/978-3-031-97070-2
5. Bustince, H., et al.: Pre-aggregation functions: definition, properties and construction methods. In: 2016 IEEE International Conference on Fuzzy Systems (FUZZ-IEEE), pp. 294–300 (2016). https://doi.org/10.1109/FUZZ-IEEE.2016.7737700
6. Dimuro, G.P., et al.: The state-of-art of the generalizations of the Choquet integral: from aggregation and pre-aggregation to ordered directionally monotone functions. Inf. Fusion **57**, 27–43 (2020). https://doi.org/10.1016/j.inffus.2019.10.005
7. Fernandez, J., Bustince, H., Horanská, L., Mesiar, R., Stupňanová, A.: A generalization of the Choquet integral defined in terms of the Möbius transform. IEEE Trans. Fuzzy Syst. **28**(10), 2313–2319 (2020). https://doi.org/10.1109/TFUZZ.2019.2933803
8. Honda, A., James, S.: Averaging aggregation functions based on inclusion-exclusion integrals. In: 2017 Joint 17th World Congress of International Fuzzy Systems Association and 9th International Conference on Soft Computing and Intelligent Systems (IFSA-SCIS), pp. 1–6 (2017). https://doi.org/10.1109/IFSA-SCIS.2017.8023353
9. Honda, A., Okazaki, Y.: Theory of inclusion-exclusion integral. Inf. Sci. **376**, 136–147 (2017). https://doi.org/10.1016/j.ins.2016.09.063
10. Honda, A., Okazaki, Y.: Generalization of inclusion-exclusion integral for nondiscrete monotone measure space. Fuzzy Sets Syst. **355**, 42–58 (2019). https://doi.org/10.1016/j.fss.2018.06.005
11. Lucca, G., et al.: Preaggregation functions: construction and an application. IEEE Trans. Fuzzy Syst. **24**(2), 260–272 (2016). https://doi.org/10.1109/TFUZZ.2015.2453020

Using the Sugeno Integral with the Adaptive Power Measure in the Fuzzy Reasoning Method

Giancarlo Lucca[1(✉)], Graçaliz P. Dimuro[1], Tiago Asmus[3], Bruno Dalmazo[1], Abreu Quevedo[1], Rafael Berri[1], Renata Reiser[2], Adenauer Yamin[2], and Humberto Bustince[4]

[1] Centro de Ciências Computacionais (C3), Universidade Federal do Rio Grande, Rio Grande, Brazil
{giancarlo.lucca,gracalizdimuro,dalmazo,rafael.berri}@furg.br

[2] Centro de Desenvolvimento Tecnológico (CDTec), Universidade Federal de Pelotas, Pelotas, Brazil
{reiser,adenauer}@inf.ufpel.edu.br

[3] Instituto de Matemática, Estatística e Física (IMEF), Universidade Federal do Rio Grande, Rio Grande, Brazil
tiagoasmus@furg.br

[4] Departamento de Estadística, Informática y Matemáticas (DEIM), Universidad Pública de Navarra (UPNa), Pamplona, Spain
bustince@unavarra.es

Abstract. Fuzzy set theory provides effective mechanisms for managing uncertainty and imprecision in classification problems. In this context, the Sugeno Integral stands out as a relevant aggregation operator, particularly when combined with appropriate fuzzy measures. The primary objective of this work is to investigate the performance of the Sugeno Integral within the Fuzzy Reasoning Method (FRM) applied to Fuzzy Rule-Based Classification Systems (FRBCSs), with a specific focus on the application of an Adaptive Power Measure (APM). Unlike static approaches, the APM dynamically determines the measure's exponent utilizing heuristics such as the arithmetic mean, product, median, and geometric mean. To provide a comprehensive analysis, we benchmarked this adaptive approach against classical measures—including Cardinality, Dirac, Weighted Mean (Wmean), and Ordered Weighted Averaging (OWA)—using the FARC-HD fuzzy classifier across 33 datasets from the KEEL repository. The empirical results demonstrate that the Power Measure achieves the highest average accuracy among all tested measures. Moreover, the adaptive approach yields significant performance benefits in diverse scenarios. These findings corroborate the viability of employing adaptive measures within the fuzzy context and unveil new possibilities for developing more robust classifiers, capable of handling high data variability.

Keywords: Fuzzy Reasoning Method · Sugeno integral · Adaptive Fuzzy measures

B. Vantaggi et al. (Eds.): IPMU 2026, CCIS 3019, pp. 101–115, 2026.
https://doi.org/10.1007/978-3-032-28994-0_8

1 Introduction

Fuzzy set theory has established itself as a robust framework for modeling the uncertainty and imprecision inherent in various real-world problems [35,36]. Within this domain, fuzzy integrals [29] serve as a fundamental mechanism for information aggregation [5], particularly in scenarios where the additivity property of classical probability measures does not hold.

Among these operators, the Choquet Integral (CI) [6] is widely recognized. In a seminal application, Barrenechea et al. [4] proposed a Fuzzy Reasoning Method (FRM) utilizing the CI to aggregate class values within Fuzzy Rule-Based Classification Systems (FRBCSs) [14]. Furthermore, the authors introduced the Exponential Cardinality (or Power Measure - PM), a fuzzy measure [26] designed to adapt to different contexts.

This approach inspired a series of generalizations of the CI. Developments include C_T-integrals [18], which introduce the concept of pre-aggregation by replacing the conventional product with t-norms; CC-integrals [22], which employ copulas to generalize the expanded CI; and C_F-integrals [23], which utilize functions with left absorption to generate non-averaging behaviors. These concepts were further extended by C_{F1F2}-integrals [16] using pairs of functions, and subsequently by gC_{F1F2}-integrals [9], which incorporate ordered directional monotonicity. Regarding dissimilarity-based approaches, literature presents dC_F-integrals [33], combining Restricted Dissimilarity Functions (RDFs) with F-functions; dXC-integrals [30], operating on the basic expanded form; and dCC-integrals [20,28], which broaden functional relationships for diverse situations[1].

The Sugeno Integral (SI) [29] represents another significant operator in the fuzzy context. Empirical studies have demonstrated its efficiency in Brain-Computer Interfaces (BCI) [15], where it was benchmarked against the discrete Choquet Integral. The SI has also been applied to attention mechanisms in Transformer models [27] and generalized by Bardozo et al. [3]. Moreover, Wieczynski et al. [32] incorporated the SI into the FRM, utilizing the Power Measure.

Recent research has also explored adaptive fuzzy measures for specific problems. Such measures have been applied to edge detection [24,25] and combined with CI generalizations in FRBCS [21], yielding consistent results in both domains.

Based on these precedents, this work has two primary objectives:

(i) To apply the Sugeno Integral within the FRM using a diverse set of fuzzy measures—Cardinality, Dirac, Wmean, OWA, and PM—following the approach of [4] to broaden the application scope.
(ii) To implement the adaptive method with the Sugeno Integral and evaluate the classifier's performance.

[1] A review of theory and applications is presented in [8], while recent pre-aggregation applications are discussed in [17].

The remainder of this paper is organized as follows: Sect. 2 provides the theoretical concepts. Section 3 present the application of the approach in the FRM. Section 4 is the experimental framework. Section 5 is related with the obtained results and at the end the conclusions are made.

2 Theoretical Baseline

This section presents the fundamental concepts required to understand this work. To do so, consider $N = \{1, \ldots, n\}$ as the set of natural numbers up to n.

Definition 1 (Fuzzy Measure). *A fuzzy measure on N is a set function $\mathfrak{m} : 2^N \to [0,1]$ satisfying: (i) Boundary conditions: $\mathfrak{m}(\emptyset) = 0$ and $\mathfrak{m}(N) = 1$; and (ii) Monotonicity: For all $A, B \subseteq N$, if $A \subseteq B$ then $\mathfrak{m}(A) \leq \mathfrak{m}(B)$.*

The fuzzy measures utilized in this work are the same one presented in [4] which are defined as:

1. Cardinality or the uniform measure:
$$\mathfrak{m}(A) = \frac{|A|}{n}. \tag{1}$$
2. Dirac Measure: For a previously fixed $i \in N$,
$$\mathfrak{m}(A) = \begin{cases} 1 & \text{if } i \in A \\ 0 & \text{if } i \notin A. \end{cases} \tag{2}$$
3. Weighted Mean (Wmean): Consider an arbitrary weight vector $(w_1, \ldots, w_n) \in [0,1]^n$ such that $\sum_{i=1}^{n} w_i = 1$ and consider the fuzzy measure: $m(\{1\}) = w_1, \ldots, m(\{n\}) = w_n$. For $|A| > 1$, it is defined as:
$$\mathfrak{m}(A) = \sum_{i \in A} m(\{i\}). \tag{3}$$
4. Ordered Weighted Averaging (OWA): The values for the fuzzy measure are assigned as: $m(\{i\}) = w_j$, where i is the j-th largest component to be aggregated, i.e., considering an OWA operator. For $|A| > 1$, it is defined as:
$$\mathfrak{m}(A) = \sum_{i \in A} m(\{i\}). \tag{4}$$
5. Power Measure (PM):
$$\mathfrak{m}(A) = \left(\frac{|A|}{n}\right)^q, \text{ with } q > 0. \tag{5}$$

In this work, following the concept presented in [24,25], we utilize several alternatives for determining the q value (in addition to the adaptive approach proposed in [4]). Observe that this approach is used in the third step of the FRM to aggregate values per class, consequently the q value will not be zero under any circunstamce. In Table 1 details the employed heuristics:

Table 1. Approaches used for picking the parameter q in the PM.

Approach	ID	Definition
Maximum	MAX	$\max(x_1, x_2, \ldots, x_n)$
Minimum	MIN	$\min(x_1, x_2, \ldots, x_n)$
Product	PROD	$\prod_{i=1}^{n} x_i$
Arithmetic Mean	AM	$\frac{1}{n}\sum_{i=1}^{n} x_i$
Median	MED	$\begin{cases} x_{\left(\frac{n+1}{2}\right)}, & \text{if } n \text{ is odd,} \\ \frac{x_{\left(\frac{n}{2}\right)}+x_{\left(\frac{n}{2}+1\right)}}{2}, & \text{if } n \text{ is even.} \end{cases}$
Geometric Mean	GM	$\sqrt[n]{\prod_{i=1}^{n} x_i}$
Harmonic Mean	HM	$\frac{n}{\sum_{i=1}^{n}\frac{1}{x_i}}, x_i \neq 0$

Definition 2 (Discrete Sugeno Integral). *Let* $\mathfrak{m}$ *be a fuzzy measure and* $\boldsymbol{x} = (x_1, \ldots, x_n) \in [0,1]^n$ *be an input vector. The consider the discrete Sugeno integral with respect to* $\mathfrak{m}$ *is defined as:*

$$\mathfrak{S}_{\mathfrak{m}}(\boldsymbol{x}) = \bigvee_{i=1}^{n} \left[x_{(i)} \wedge \mathfrak{m}(A_{(i)})\right] \tag{6}$$

where $\vee$ *and* $\wedge$ *denote the maximum and minimum operators, respectively. Also,* $(\cdot)$ *is a permutation on* $\{1, \ldots, n\}$ *such that* $x_{(i-1)} \leq x_{(i)}$ *for all* $i = 1, \ldots, n$*, with* $x_{(0)} = 0$ *and* $A_{(i)} = \{(1), \ldots, (i)\}$.

Definition 3 (Discrete Choquet integral). *[6] Let* $\mathfrak{m}\colon 2^N \to [0,1]$ *be a fuzzy measure. The discrete Choquet Integral (CI) is the function* $\mathfrak{C}_{\mathfrak{m}}\colon [0,1]^n \to [0,1]$*, defined for all* $\mathbf{x} = (x_1, \ldots, x_n) \in [0,1]^n$*, by:*

$$\mathfrak{C}_{\mathfrak{m}}(\mathbf{x}) = \sum_{i=1}^{n} \left(x_{(i)} - x_{(i-1)}\right) \cdot \mathfrak{m}\left(A_{(i)}\right), \tag{7}$$

where $\left(x_{(1)}, \ldots, x_{(n)}\right)$ *is an increasing permutation on the input* $\mathbf{x}$*, that is,* $0 \leq x_{(1)} \leq \cdots \leq x_{(n)}$*, where* $x_{(0)} = 0$ *and* $A_{(i)} = \{(i), \ldots, (n)\}$ *is the subset of indices corresponding to the* $n - i + 1$ *largest components of* $\mathbf{x}$.

3 Application of the Discrete Sugeno Integral with the Adaptive PM in the Fuzzy Reasoning Method

Fuzzy Rule-Based Classification Systems (FRBCSs) [14] constitute an extension of traditional rule-based approaches by integrating fuzzy set theory into the rule antecedents. This integration not only enhances the interpretability of the model but also provides a framework for addressing the uncertainty and vagueness inherent in complex classification tasks.

The architecture of these systems relies on a Knowledge Base (KB), which is composed by a Rule Base (RB) and a Database (DB). The models analyzed in this work utilize fuzzy rules characterized by the following linguistic structure:

$$\text{Rule } R_j : \text{ If } x_{p1} \text{ is } A_{j1} \text{ and } \ldots \text{ and } x_{pn} \text{ is } A_{jn}, \text{ then Class is } C_j \text{ with } RW_j, \tag{8}$$

where R_j denotes the j-th rule, and A_{ji} represents the fuzzy sets modeled by triangular membership functions associated with the input variables. C_j indicates the predicted class label, and $RW_j \in [0, 1]$ represents the rule weight [13], which quantifies the certainty of the rule. In this study, the rule weight is computed using the Certainty Factor (CF) [7] method:

$$RW_j = CF_j = \frac{\sum_{\boldsymbol{x}_p \in \text{Class } C_j} \mu_{A_j}(\boldsymbol{x}_p)}{\sum_{p=1}^{N} \mu_{A_j}(\boldsymbol{x}_p)}, \tag{9}$$

where N corresponds to the total number of training patterns, and $\boldsymbol{x}_p = (x_{p1}, \ldots, x_{pm})$ denotes the p-th training example.

Once the fuzzy rules that constitutes the system have been generated from the training set, the Fuzzy Reasoning Method (FRM) is responsible for classifying new examples (test set). Let $\boldsymbol{x}_p = (x_{p1}, \ldots, x_{pn})$ be a new example to be classified, L the number of rules in the rule base, and M the number of classes. The inference process adopted in this study follows the method proposed in [4] for aggregating positive information. It is composed of four sequential steps:

1. **Matching Degree:** First, the compatibility between the example $\boldsymbol{x}_p$ and the antecedent of each fuzzy rule R_j is calculated. This is usually achieved by applying a t-norm T' (typically the product or minimum) to the membership degrees of the example in the corresponding fuzzy sets:

$$\mu_{A_j}(\boldsymbol{x}_p) = T'(\mu_{A_{j1}}(x_{p1}), \ldots, \mu_{A_{jn}}(x_{pn})), \quad j = 1, \ldots, L. \tag{10}$$

2. **Association Degree:** To incorporate the reliability of each rule into the reasoning process, the matching degree is weighted by the rule weight RW_j. This results in the association degree $b_j(\boldsymbol{x}_p)$ for the class predicted by rule R_j:

$$b_j(\boldsymbol{x}_p) = \mu_{A_j}(\boldsymbol{x}_p) \cdot RW_j. \tag{11}$$

   At this stage, we consider only positive information, meaning rules where $b_j(\boldsymbol{x}_p) > 0$.
3. **Classification Soundness Degree per Class:** The association degrees derived from rules predicting the same class C_k are aggregated to determine a single soundness degree S_k for that class. In this work, we propose the use of the discrete Sugeno Integral $\mathfrak{S}_\mathfrak{m}$ as the aggregation operator, combined with the adaptive fuzzy measures described in Sect. 2:

$$S_k = \mathfrak{S}_\mathfrak{m}\left(\{b_j(\boldsymbol{x}_p) \mid \text{Fired Rules } R_j \text{that predicts } C_k\}\right), \quad k = 1, \ldots, M. \tag{12}$$

   We highlight that in this step, for each class, the fired rules are used with the q exponent accordingly to the Table 1.

4. **Final Classification:** Finally, the system assigns the class with the highest classification soundness degree to the example $\boldsymbol{x}_p$:

$$\text{Class} = \arg \max_{k=1,\ldots,M} (S_k). \tag{13}$$

4 Experimental Framework

In this section, we describe the experimental framework adopted to validate the proposed method. To ensure a robust evaluation, we selected 33 datasets from the KEEL repository [2]. It is important to note that these datasets are identical to those used in previous studies on fuzzy measure generalizations, maintaining the same data partitions to ensure fair comparability (See for example [16,20,31,33].

For each dataset, we employed a 5-fold cross-validation approach [10]. We highlight that we use the split provided by KEEL. The performance of the fuzzy classifier—considering the varying heuristics for the adaptive parameter q—is measured by the mean accuracy rate across all folds. This metric was selected as these datasets are standard benchmarks in the KEEL repository.

It is available in Table 2 the list of selected datasets, detailing their reference number, identification acronym (ID), total number of examples (#Ex.), attributes (#Atts.), and classes (#Class). Following standard experimental protocols, six datasets—*Magic*, *Page-blocks*, *Penbased*, *Ring*, *Satimage*, and *Twonorm*—were stratified, and 10% of the examples were randomly sampled to reduce computational cost while preserving distribution. Furthermore, datasets containing missing values, such as *Wisconsin*, had incomplete instances removed to ensure analytical consistency.

Upon defining the datasets, we proceeded to the learning and classification stages. We adopted the Fuzzy Association Rule-based Classification model for High Dimensional problems (FARC-HD) [1] as the base classifier. All experiments were conducted using the model's standard parameter configuration[2].

Regarding the specific settings of FARC-HD, we utilized 5 linguistic labels per variable, with a minimum support of 0.05 and a minimum confidence of 0.8. The depth of the trees was limited to 3, and the parameter k was set to 2. For the evolutionary process, the population size was established at 50 individuals, with a maximum of 20,000 evaluations. The parameters alpha and bits per gene were set to 0.02 and 30, respectively. Finally, a fixed seed of 53743421 was used to ensure the reproducibility of the results. Finally, we highlight that the source code implementing the FARC-HD is open to the community at KEEL and different modified FRM can be found in https://github.com/Giancarlo-Lucca. The implementation related with this paper can be provided under request.

[2] The experiments were performed on a workstation equipped with an AMD Threadripper PRO 5955WX processor (16 cores, 32 threads, up to 4.5 GHz), 128 GB of DDR4-3200 ECC memory, a 1.96 TB SSD, and an NVIDIA RTX A4500 GPU with 20 GB of ECC GDDR6 memory.

Table 2. Properties of the datasets considered in this study

Id.	Dataset	#Samp.	#Feat.	#Class
App	Appendicitis	106	7	2
Bal	Balance	625	4	3
Ban	Banana	5300	2	2
Bnd	Bands	365	19	2
Bup	Bupa	345	6	2
Cle	Cleveland	297	13	5
Con	Contraceptive	1473	9	3
Eco	Ecoli	336	7	8
Gla	Glass	214	9	6
Hab	Haberman	306	3	2
Hay	Hayes-Roth	160	4	3
Ion	Ionosphere	351	33	2
Iri	Iris	150	4	3
Led	led7digit	500	7	10
Mag	Magic	1,902	10	2
New	Newthyroid	215	5	3
Pag	Pageblocks	5,472	10	5
Pen	Penbased	10,992	16	10
Pho	Phoneme	5,404	5	2
Pim	Pima	768	8	2
Rin	Ring	740	20	2
Sah	Saheart	462	9	2
Sat	Satimage	6,435	36	7
Seg	Segment	2,310	19	7
Shu	Shuttle	58,000	9	7
Son	Sonar	208	60	2
Spe	Spectfheart	267	44	2
Tit	Titanic	2,201	3	2
Two	Twonorm	740	20	2
Veh	Vehicle	846	18	4
Win	Wine	178	13	3
Wis	Wisconsin	683	11	2
Yea	Yeast	1,484	8	10

5 Experimental Results

The analysis of the experimental results is structured to provide a comprehensive validation of the proposed method. The analysis is organized into distinct phases to ensure a robust assessment: first, we evaluate the comparative performance (accuracy among the folds) of the discrete Sugeno Integral when combined with the different adaptive and classical fuzzy measures; second, we conduct a rigorous statistical assessment, comprising a group analysis to identify the most effective adaptive heuristic and a pairwise comparison to validate the superiority of the adaptive mechanism against the control variable; and finally, we benchmark the best-performing discrete Sugeno-based configuration against the classical discrete Choquet Integral.

5.1 Performance Analysis

This section presents and discusses the experimental outcomes. The accuracy rates obtained by the discrete Sugeno Integral using different fuzzy measures is shown in Table 3. The accuracy is obtained by computing the total of correct classified examples divided by the total of examples. In this table, the columns represent the evaluated measures. From column 1–5 we have classical fuzzy measures (observe that the WMEAN and OWA are aggregation operators) and from column 6–12 the measures related with our approach. Also, the rows correspond to the datasets.

To ease the comprehension of the results, the highest accuracy value for each dataset is highlighted in **bold**. The bottom rows present the average accuracy across all datasets and the number of datasets where each approach achieved the best performance (#Best).

Regarding the overall performance, the Power Measure (PM) achieved the highest mean accuracy (79.54%), followed closely by the PROD (79.43%) and MIN (79.28%) measures. Conversely, four other approaches yielded a general average of approximately 78%. It is worth noting that three of these lower-performing methods do not utilize the adaptive strategy, which underscores the benefits of the proposed approach.

Analyzing the performance per dataset, the PM achieved the best results in 7 distinct datasets. This is followed by the adaptive measures PROD, MEDIAN, and GM, with 5, 4, and 4 winning cases, respectively. The remaining fuzzy measures exhibited comparatively lower performance.

These findings align with the analysis proposed in [19], where the authors combined different discrete Choquet Integral generalizations with fuzzy measures. Consistent with the Choquet-based study, the PM demonstrated superiority, while measures exhibiting averaging characteristics yielded general results in the range of approximately 78–79%.

5.2 Statistical Analysis Among the Adaptive Approaches

In this section, we conduct a statistical analysis to determine the most suitable heuristic for the adaptive parameter q combining with the discrete Sugeno inte-

Table 3. Average accuracy obtained by the discrete Sugeno integral considering different fuzzy measures.

Dataset	CARD	DIRAC	WMEAN	OWA	PM	MAX	MIN	PROD	AM	MED	GM	HM
App	**86.80**	80.17	83.98	86.75	85.84	83.07	83.03	83.03	82.12	83.98	83.94	84.89
Bal	77.76	78.24	76.00	78.72	81.60	79.20	80.96	**82.40**	80.16	81.44	80.32	81.12
Ban	83.62	84.09	84.43	82.79	**85.26**	84.11	84.02	84.26	83.62	84.19	84.72	83.70
Ban	67.72	65.97	69.43	69.88	71.06	68.27	71.06	71.06	67.76	**71.89**	67.71	67.18
Bup	64.93	64.06	60.29	62.61	60.87	61.16	**65.22**	**65.22**	64.35	64.35	64.35	64.35
Cle	56.22	55.56	56.92	55.56	54.88	55.58	56.55	56.56	54.89	56.23	57.94	56.24
Con	51.05	50.24	51.93	51.93	52.61	52.07	51.59	50.78	51.32	52.89	**53.02**	52.00
Eco	77.70	77.70	78.58	77.10	77.09	75.61	77.99	**79.18**	77.10	77.70	78.27	77.11
Gla	65.90	64.98	63.58	65.44	**69.17**	64.02	65.90	66.37	64.49	64.02	64.97	64.51
Hab	**74.17**	71.23	72.21	71.23	74.17	70.89	70.58	71.56	69.92	71.23	71.89	72.22
Hay	79.49	78.69	80.26	79.54	**81.74**	81.00	78.72	79.46	78.72	79.49	78.72	78.72
Ion	88.61	88.61	88.60	87.48	88.89	87.76	88.90	88.61	89.20	88.61	**90.31**	89.18
Iri	92.00	93.33	92.67	93.33	92.67	92.67	93.33	93.33	**94.00**	**94.00**	93.33	93.33
Led	**68.80**	68.00	67.80	68.40	68.40	68.20	68.00	67.00	67.40	68.20	68.40	67.80
Mag	79.34	77.86	78.97	78.86	79.70	80.28	79.60	79.44	79.60	79.81	79.76	79.86
New	93.95	93.02	94.42	88.37	93.95	94.88	93.95	**95.81**	95.81	94.42	94.42	93.95
Pag	94.70	94.52	**94.70**	94.52	93.97	93.98	94.16	94.52	93.97	94.52	94.16	94.52
Pen	90.18	89.91	90.18	86.27	91.27	90.82	**91.82**	91.27	91.18	91.27	91.18	91.27
Pho	82.49	82.33	82.70	82.79	**82.94**	82.62	82.36	82.05	82.44	82.07	82.20	82.01
Pim	75.13	73.04	75.65	74.87	74.21	73.82	74.60	74.47	73.83	74.87	75.51	**76.17**
Rin	85.27	84.59	84.86	84.32	87.97	87.57	89.19	89.32	89.19	**89.59**	88.65	88.65
Sah	68.38	68.82	68.18	69.47	**70.78**	70.13	70.78	69.25	69.69	70.12	69.26	70.34
Sat	79.47	78.85	**80.72**	78.07	79.01	78.07	79.63	79.63	79.63	79.63	79.63	79.63
Seg	92.55	91.04	92.64	92.81	92.25	92.16	92.94	92.99	92.94	**93.29**	**93.29**	93.07
Shu	97.70	**98.57**	98.30	96.78	98.16	97.15	97.20	97.20	97.10	97.10	97.10	97.10
Son	78.87	76.48	73.10	77.42	76.95	79.33	79.80	**80.80**	78.82	73.62	77.91	79.83
Spe	76.74	77.88	73.40	78.64	**78.99**	75.25	75.29	75.29	75.29	75.29	75.29	75.29
Tit	78.87	**79.06**	78.87	78.87	78.87	78.87	78.87	78.87	78.87	78.87	78.87	78.87
Two	83.38	82.30	84.46	83.92	84.86	85.00	82.57	85.00	84.32	83.65	84.32	**85.54**
Veh	69.86	64.66	66.55	66.90	**69.86**	66.91	68.56	68.56	68.56	67.85	68.56	68.56
Win	92.70	96.06	94.95	93.76	93.83	94.37	96.05	95.49	95.49	95.49	**97.19**	94.37
Wis	96.05	95.90	95.46	95.61	95.90	95.61	**96.78**	96.34	95.32	95.46	95.90	96.34
Yea	57.14	57.21	57.48	**57.75**	57.01	56.27	56.20	56.20	56.20	56.20	56.20	56.20
Mean	79.02	78.27	78.55	78.51	**79.54**	78.69	79.28	79.43	78.89	79.13	79.31	79.21
#Best	3	2	2	1	7	1	3	5	1	4	4	2

gral. Initially, we apply the Aligned Friedman rank test [11] to detect statistical differences among the seven adaptive approaches, namely: MAX, MIN, PROD, AM, MED, GM, and HM.

We present in Fig. 1 a bar graph with the rankings obtained by each method. The algorithm with the lowest rank is identified as the control variable for the subsequent post-hoc analysis. In this case, the **PROD** approach achieved the best ranking, positioning itself as the representative of the adaptive measures. To verify whether the performance differences are significant, we employ Holm's post-hoc test [12]. The values of this test is available at the top of each bar. The Adjusted P-Values (APV) indicate that the control method significantly outperforms AM and MAX, rejecting the null hypothesis for these cases ($\alpha = 0.05$). However, for the remaining heuristics, the statistical differences are not significant, suggesting a similar behavior among the top-ranked adaptive versions.

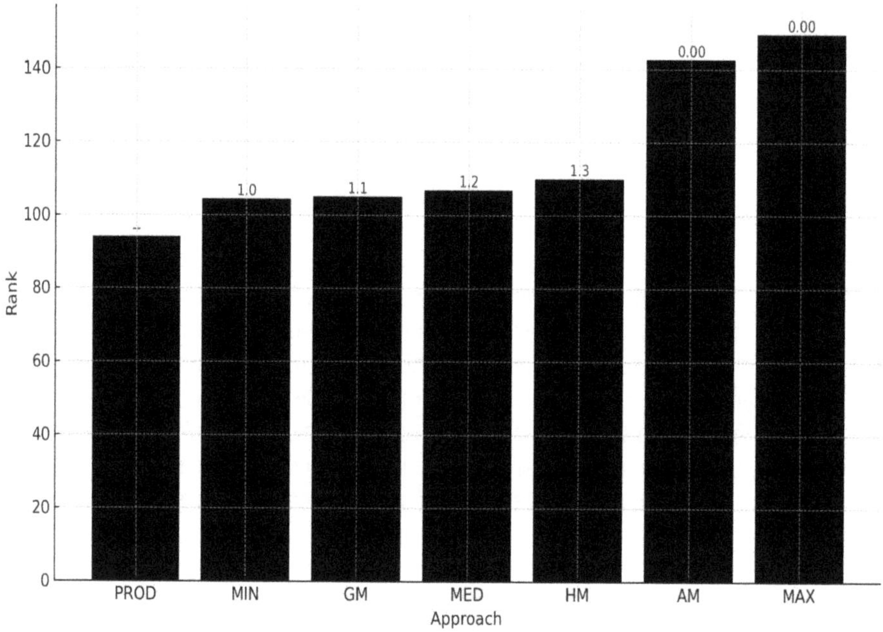

Fig. 1. Group comparison with Align Friedman Rank Test and Holm's post-hoc.

Considering that the adaptive measure based on PROD is considered as control variable. We have performed a pair-wise comparison against the PM. Precisely, the Wilcoxon signed rank test is considered [34].

By comparing the two approaches, we have that the Sum of positive ranks (related with the PM) is 832.5. On the other hand, the Sum of negative ranks (related with the PROD) is equal to 493.5. The obtained p-value is 0.11, indicating a similarity among the approaches.

Table 4. Performance comparison: discrete Sugeno Integral vs. discrete Choquet Integral (both using Adaptive PM_{PROD}).

Dataset	$\mathfrak{S}_{PM_{PROD}}$	$\mathfrak{C}_{PM_{PROD}}$
App	83.03	**83.98**
Bal	82.40	**84.64**
Ban	**84.26**	84.17
Bnd	**71.06**	69.98
Bup	**65.22**	63.19
Cle	**56.56**	**56.56**
Con	**50.78**	50.58
Eco	**79.18**	78.57
Gla	66.37	**67.79**
Hab	71.56	**72.21**
Hay	79.46	**80.23**
Ion	88.61	**90.32**
Iri	93.33	**94.00**
Led	67.00	**69.40**
Mag	79.44	**79.76**
New	**95.81**	94.42
Pag	94.52	**94.89**
Pen	**91.27**	91.00
Pho	82.05	**82.12**
Pim	74.47	**74.86**
Rin	89.32	**90.81**
Sah	69.25	**70.77**
Sat	**79.63**	79.00
Seg	**92.99**	92.86
Shu	**97.20**	96.60
Son	80.80	**81.31**
Spe	**75.29**	74.88
Tit	**78.87**	**78.87**
Two	85.00	**85.54**
Veh	68.56	**68.91**
Win	**95,49**	93.24
Wis	96.34	**96.78**
Yea	56.20	**57.61**
Mean	79.43	**79.69**
# Best	14	21

5.3 Comparing the Discrete Sugeno and the Discrete Choquet Integral with Adaptive Approach

Following the identification of the discrete Sugeno integral combined with the adaptive power measure ($\mathfrak{S}_{PM_{PROD}}$) as the best-performing approach within the proposed framework, this section provides a comparative analysis against the classical discrete Choquet integral ($\mathfrak{C}$).

It is worth noting that previous studies [21] have combined the discrete Choquet integral with adaptive measures, identifying the C_{F1F2}-integral as the optimal scenario. However, to ensure a fair comparison focused strictly on the aggregation operator (Sugeno vs. Choquet), we adopt the standard discrete Choquet integral combined with the same adaptive measure based on the Product heuristic ($\mathfrak{C}_{PM_{PROD}}$).

Table 4 details the accuracy obtained by both methods across the 33 datasets. The structure follows the previous analyses, with the best result for each dataset highlighted in **boldface**. In cases of a tie, both values are highlighted. The last rows present the average accuracy and the number of datasets where each method achieved the highest performance.

The discrete Sugeno integral achieved superior or equal performance in 14 datasets, while the discrete Choquet integral prevailed in 21 cases. Regarding the average accuracy, the Choquet integral presents a slight advantage (79.69%) compared to the discrete Sugeno integral (79.43%).

To determine whether this difference is statistically significant, we have applied once again the Wilcoxon Signed-Rank test (pairwise comparison). The obtained p-value was 0.10 with Sum of positive ranks equals to 776.5 and Sum of negative ranks with 448.5.

Considering a significance level of $\alpha = 0.05$, the test indicates that The statistical equivalence between the methods is a noteworthy finding. The discrete Sugeno integral, despite being a qualitative operator based on minimum and maximum operations (often considered less expressive than the sum-product based Choquet integral), proved to be a robust alternative when combined with the adaptive power measure. This suggests that for classification tasks with high uncertainty, the discrete Sugeno integral can offer comparable performance with potentially lower computational complexity.

6 Conclusion

In this paper, we have investigated the application of the discrete Sugeno Integral as an aggregation operator within the Fuzzy Reasoning Method (FRM) of Fuzzy Rule-Based Classification Systems (FRBCSs). Specifically, we focused on the integration of an Adaptive Power Measure (APM), where the measure's exponent q is dynamically determined for each instance using aggregation heuristics, aiming to enhance the classifier's adaptability without relying on static parameter tuning.

The comprehensive experimental study, conducted using the FARC-HD classifier across 33 datasets from the KEEL repository, allows us to draw three several conclusions regarding the performance and viability of the proposed approach.

First, regarding the efficacy of adaptive heuristics, the approach based on the Product (PROD) heuristic achieved the best average ranking among the seven adaptive strategies evaluated. The statistical analysis utilizing the Aligned Friedman and Holm's post-hoc tests confirmed its superiority over the Arithmetic Mean and Maximum heuristics, establishing it as the most robust representative of the adaptive approach in this context.

Secondly, the results demonstrate the competitiveness of the adaptive method against static measures. The pairwise comparison between the adaptive PROD approach and the static Power Measure revealed no statistically significant difference ($p = 0.11$). This is a highly relevant finding, as it indicates that the proposed adaptive mechanism can achieve performance levels equivalent to the best static measure without the need for the computational overhead associated with optimizing a fixed parameter, such as through genetic algorithms.

Finally, the benchmarking against the state-of-the-art Choquet Integral indicated no statistical difference ($p = 0.10$) between the two operators when both utilize the adaptive measure. This result highlights the robustness of the discrete Sugeno Integral. Despite being a qualitative operator relying solely on minimum and maximum operations, it proved to be a competitive alternative to the quantitative Choquet Integral. This suggests that the discrete Sugeno Integral is a viable choice for classification tasks, particularly in scenarios where lower computational complexity or qualitative modeling is prioritized.

Future work will focus on explore its application in Deep Learning architectures, specifically within the attention mechanisms of Transformer models. The combination of this approach with new discrete Sugeno based generalization is a possible path to follow.

Acknowledgments. This work was supported by the following Brazilian funding agencies: CAPES, FAPERGS (24/2551-0001396-2, 23/2551-0000773-8, 24/2551-0000723-7) and FAPERGS/CNPq (23/2551-0000126-8).

References

1. Alcala-Fdez, J., Alcala, R., Herrera, F.: A fuzzy association rule-based classification model for high-dimensional problems with genetic rule selection and lateral tuning. IEEE Trans. Fuzzy Syst. **19**(5), 857–872 (2011)
2. Alcalá-Fdez, J., et al.: Keel: a software tool to assess evolutionary algorithms for data mining problems. Soft. Comput. **13**(3), 307–318 (2009)
3. Bardozzo, F., et al.: Sugeno integral generalization applied to improve adaptive image binarization. Inf. Fusion **68**, 37–45 (2021). https://doi.org/10.1016/j.inffus.2020.10.020
4. Barrenechea, E., Bustince, H., Fernandez, J., Paternain, D., Sanz, J.A.: Using the Choquet integral in the fuzzy reasoning method of fuzzy rule-based classification systems. Axioms **2**(2), 208–223 (2013)

5. Beliakov, G., Pradera, A., Calvo, T.: Aggregation Functions: A Guide for Practitioners. Springer, Heidelberg (2007). https://doi.org/10.1007/978-3-540-73721-6
6. Choquet, G.: Theory of capacities. Annales de l'Institut Fourier **5**, 131–295 (1953–1954)
7. Cordón, O., del Jesus, M.J., Herrera, F.: A proposal on reasoning methods in fuzzy rule-based classification systems. Int. J. Approx. Reason. **20**(1), 21–45 (1999)
8. Dimuro, G.P., et al.: The state-of-art of the generalizations of the Choquet integral: From aggregation and pre-aggregation to ordered directionally monotone functions. Inf. Fusion **57**, 27–43 (2020). https://doi.org/10.1016/j.inffus.2019.10.005
9. Dimuro, G.P., et al.: Generalized cf1f2-integrals: From Choquet-like aggregation to ordered directionally monotone functions. Fuzzy Sets Syst. **378**, 44–67 (2020). https://doi.org/10.1016/j.fss.2019.01.009
10. Duda, R.O., Hart, P.E., Stork, D.G.: Pattern Classification, 2nd edn. Wiley-Interscience, New York (2000)
11. Hodges, J.L., Lehmann, E.L.: Ranks methods for combination of independent experiments in analysis of variance. Ann. Math. Stat. **33**, 482–497 (1962)
12. Holm, S.: A simple sequentially rejective multiple test procedure. Scand. J. Stat. **6**, 65–70 (1979)
13. Ishibuchi, H., Nakashima, T.: Effect of rule weights in fuzzy rule-based classification systems. IEEE Trans. Fuzzy Syst. **9**(4), 506–515 (2001)
14. Ishibuchi, H., Nakashima, T., Nii, M.: Classification and Modeling with Linguistic Information Granules, Advanced Approaches to Linguistic Data Mining. Advanced Information Processing, Springer, Heidelberg (2005). https://doi.org/10.1007/b138232
15. Ko, L., et al.: Multimodal fuzzy fusion for enhancing the motor-imagery-based brain computer interface. IEEE Comput. Intell. Mag. **14**(1), 96–106 (2019). https://doi.org/10.1109/MCI.2018.2881647
16. Lucca, G., Dimuro, G.P., Fernandez, J., Bustince, H., Bedregal, B., Sanz, J.A.: Improving the performance of fuzzy rule-based classification systems based on a nonaveraging generalization of CC-integrals named $C_{F_1F_2}$-integrals. IEEE Trans. Fuzzy Syst. **27**(1), 124–134 (2019). https://doi.org/10.1109/TFUZZ.2018.2871000
17. Lucca, G., Marco-Detchart, C., Dimuro, G., Rincon, J.A., Julian, V.: Recent applications of pre-aggregation functions. In: Quaresma, P., Camacho, D., Yin, H., Gonçalves, T., Julian, V., Tallón-Ballesteros, A.J. (eds.) IDEAL 2023. LNCS, vol. 14404, pp. 177–185. Springer, Cham (2023). https://doi.org/10.1007/978-3-031-48232-8_17
18. Lucca, G., et al.: Pre-aggregation functions: construction and an application. IEEE Trans. Fuzzy Syst. **24**(2), 260–272 (2016)
19. Lucca, G., Sanz, J.A., Dimuro, G.P., Borges, E.N., Santos, H., Bustince, H.: Analyzing the performance of different fuzzy measures with generalizations of the Choquet integral in classification problems. In: 2019 IEEE International Conference on Fuzzy Systems (FUZZ-IEEE), pp. 1–6 (2019). https://doi.org/10.1109/FUZZ-IEEE.2019.8858815
20. Lucca, G., et al.: dCC-integrals: a generalization of cc-integrals by restricted dissimilarity functions with applications on two different contexts. Appl. Soft Comput. **181**, 113517 (2025). https://doi.org/10.1016/j.asoc.2025.113517, https://www.sciencedirect.com/science/article/pii/S1568494625008282
21. Lucca, G., et al.: On the application of the adaptive power measure in a fuzzy rule-based classification system. In: 2025 IEEE International Conference on Fuzzy Systems (FUZZ), pp. 1–6 (2025). https://doi.org/10.1109/FUZZ62266.2025.11152038

22. Lucca, G., et al.: CC-integrals: Choquet-like copula-based aggregation functions and its application in fuzzy rule-based classification systems. Knowl.-Based Syst. **119**, 32–43 (2017)
23. Lucca, G., Sanz, J.A., Dimuro, G.P., Bedregal, B., Bustince, H., Mesiar, R.: CF-integrals: A new family of pre-aggregation functions with application to fuzzy rule-based classification systems. Inf. Sci. **435**, 94–110 (2018). https://doi.org/10.1016/j.ins.2017.12.029
24. Marco-Detchart, C., Lucca, G., Dimuro, G., Rincon, J.A., Julian, V.: Adaptative fuzzy measure for edge detection. In: Quaresma, P., Camacho, D., Yin, H., Gonçalves, T., Julian, V., Tallón-Ballesteros, A.J. (eds.) IDEAL 2023. LNCS, vol. 14404, pp. 497–505. Springer, Cham (2023). https://doi.org/10.1007/978-3-031-48232-8_45
25. Marco-Detchart, C., Lucca, G., Santos Silva, M.A., Rincon, J.A., Julian, V., Dimuro, G.: Sliding window based adaptative fuzzy measure for edge detection. Expert. Syst. **42**(2), e13730 (2025). https://doi.org/10.1111/exsy.13730
26. Murofushi, T., Sugeno, M., Machida, M.: Non-monotonic fuzzy measures and the Choquet integral. Fuzzy Sets Syst. **64**(1), 73–86 (1994)
27. Sartori, J., de Bem, R., Dimuro, G., Lucca, G.: The role of aggregation functions on transformers and vits self-attention for classification. In: 2023 36th SIBGRAPI Conference on Graphics, Patterns and Images (SIBGRAPI), pp. 97–102 (2023). https://doi.org/10.1109/SIBGRAPI59091.2023.10347163
28. Sartori, J., et al.: d-cc integrals: Generalizing cc-integrals by restricted dissimilarity functions with applications to fuzzy-rule based systems. In: Naldi, M.C., Bianchi, R.A.C. (eds.) BRACIS 2023. LNCS, vol. 14195, pp. 243–258. Springer, Cham (2023). https://doi.org/10.1007/978-3-031-45368-7_16
29. Sugeno, M.: Theory of Fuzzy Integrals and its Applications. Ph.D. thesis, Tokyo Institute of Technology, Tokyo (1974)
30. Wieczynski, J., et al.: d-XC integrals: on the generalization of the expanded form of the Choquet integral by restricted dissimilarity functions and their applications. IEEE Trans. Fuzzy Syst. **30**(12), 5376–5389 (2022). https://doi.org/10.1109/TFUZZ.2022.3176916
31. Wieczynski, J., et al.: Applying d-XChoquet integrals in classification problems. In: 2022 IEEE International Conference on Fuzzy Systems (FUZZ-IEEE), pp. 1–7 (2022). https://doi.org/10.1109/FUZZ-IEEE55066.2022.9882740
32. Wieczynski, J., et al.: Application of the sugeno integral in fuzzy rule-based classification. Appl. Soft Comput. **167**, 112265 (2024). https://doi.org/10.1016/j.asoc.2024.112265
33. Wieczynski, J., et al.: dc_F-integrals: Generalizing c_F-integrals by means of restricted dissimilarity functions. IEEE Trans. Fuzzy Syst. **31**(1), 160–173 (2023). https://doi.org/10.1109/TFUZZ.2022.3184054
34. Wilcoxon, F.: Individual comparisons by ranking methods. Biometrics **1**, 80–83 (1945)
35. Zadeh, L.A.: Fuzzy sets. Inf. Control **8**(3), 338–353 (1965)
36. Zadeh, L.A.: The concept of a linguistic variable and its application to approximate reasoning - I. Inf. Sci. **8**(3), 199–249 (1975)

Aggregation of Random Variables Under Weak Stochastic Orders

Juan Baz[1(✉)], Irene Díaz[2], and Susana Montes[3]

[1] Dipartimento di Scienze Matematiche, Politecnico di Torino, Torino, Italy
juan.bazgonzalez@polito.it
[2] Department of Computer Science, University of Oviedo, Gijón, Spain
sirene@uniovi.es
[3] Department of Statistics and I.O. and Didactic of Mathematics, University of Oviedo, Oviedo, Spain
montes@uniovi.es

Abstract. Aggregations of random variables map several random variables to a new random variable, satisfying monotonicity and boundary conditions with respect to a stochastic order. Typically, the usual stochastic order ($\leq_{st}$) is adopted, since it allows compositions of usual aggregation functions and random vectors to be aggregations of random variables. However, quite strong conditions are needed in order to have the usual stochastic order between two random vectors, reducing its applicability. In this paper, we replace the usual stochastic order by weaker orders, studying the usual aggregation functions that can still be used and properties concerning variability and positive-dependence bias.

Keywords: Aggregation · Stochastic Orders · Probability theory

1 Introduction

Many applications of aggregation functions include the fusion of observations of quantities measured over a population [10,18]. Following the usual statistical approach, it is reasonable to consider the inputs of the aggregation to be random variables. In this direction, the theory of aggregation of random variables has been developed in recent years [2–4,6].

In particular, an aggregation of random variables is a function that takes n random variables defined in the same probability space and taking values on a real interval I and returns another random variable also defined in such a probability space and taking values on I. In order to extend the monotonicity and the boundary conditions, stochastic orders are used to compare the location of the involved random variables and vectors. The choice of the stochastic order is

The authors are supported by the Ministry of Science and Innovation of Spain (PID2022-139886NB-I00) and the Asturian Agency for Science, Business Competitiveness and Innovation (SEK-25-GRU-GIC-24-018). I. Díaz and S. Montes are also supported by European Project UE23-AI4RA-101132914.

B. Vantaggi et al. (Eds.): IPMU 2026, CCIS 3019, pp. 116–130, 2026.
https://doi.org/10.1007/978-3-032-28994-0_9

crucial, since it determines what properties the aggregation of random variables satisfies or not. A preliminary study in [3] hints that the most natural choice is the usual stochastic order, since it works well with usual aggregation functions as a consequence of its preservation under increasing transformations. Actually, the usual stochastic order has been considered in almost any work of this type of functions [2,4], and is also behind the notion of monotonicity in some papers dealing with aggregation of probability distributions [9,21].

However, given a pair of random vectors, rather strong conditions are required to obtain the usual stochastic order between them. For instance, consider two random variables X and Y such that

$$Pr(X = 1) = 0.001, \quad Pr(X = -100) = 0.999, \quad Pr(Y = 0) = 1.$$

It is easy to check that $X \not\leq_{st} Y$, while it is intuitive that, in some sense, X takes smaller values than Y. Another interesting example is the case of Gaussian random variables, since they can only be compared if they have the same variance, regardless of the difference between the means [15].

In the multivariate case, the usual stochastic order is even stronger. Let $\boldsymbol{X}$ and $\boldsymbol{Y}$ be two random vectors of dimension n such that $X_i \leq_{st} Y_i$ for any $i \in \{1, \ldots, n\}$. In general, additional conditions such as having the same dependence structure [20] or a small overlapping between supports [16] are needed in order to have $\boldsymbol{X} \leq_{st} \boldsymbol{Y}$. These strong conditions means that relatively few pairs of random vectors are comparable, so the monotonicity cannot be applied frequently.

In this direction, this paper is devoted to study aggregations of random variables with respect to weaker stochastic orders. By doing that, we expand the set of pairs of random vectors that can be compared. This change is not free, there are aggregations of random variables with respect to the usual stochastic order that are no longer aggregations of random variables when we consider a weaker order. Moreover, some important properties can be lost when changing the stochastic order. On the other hand, there are some ways of combining random variables that do not satisfy the monotonicity with respect to the usual stochastic order but they do for weaker stochastic orders. We will consider the most common location stochastic orders that are implied by the usual stochastic order, taking [20] as the main reference in this regard. That is, in contrast to previous works, this paper provides a unified analysis of how weakening the stochastic order affects admissible aggregation mechanisms, explicitly identifying variability and dependence biases associated with each order, if any.

The rest of the paper is organized as follows. In Sect. 2, we introduce the basic notions on stochastic orders and aggregations of random variables. In Sects. 3, 4, 5 and 6 we study the aggregations of random variables with respect to, respectively, the increasing convex and concave orders, the order statistics order, the orthant orders and the Laplace transform order. The conclusions are discussed in Sect. 7.

2 Preliminaries

This section is devoted to introduce the main concepts needed for the development of the paper. A probability space (Ω, Σ, P) consists of a set Ω, a σ-algebra of subsets of Ω and a probability measure $P : \Sigma \longrightarrow [0, 1]$ [19]. A measurable function from a probability space to $\mathbb{R}^n$, considering the Borel σ-algebra on $\mathbb{R}^n$, is called a random vector [19]. In the following, we will consider all random vectors to be of dimension $n \in \mathbb{N}$. Given a random vector $\boldsymbol{X}$, their components, which are random variables, will be denoted as $X_1, \ldots, X_n$. A random variable that takes one value with probability one will be denoted just by that value. We recall that $E[\boldsymbol{X} \mid \boldsymbol{Y}]$ denotes the conditional expectation of $\boldsymbol{X}$ given $\boldsymbol{Y}$, which is also a random vector (see Chap. 8 in [13]). A random vector is said to be exchangeable if changing the order of its components keeps the distribution invariant [1]. In some results, we will consider the set of all permutations of $\{1, \ldots, n\}$, denoted as P. Given a random vector $\boldsymbol{X}$, let us consider a new random vector

$$\hat{\boldsymbol{X}} = \sum_{\pi \in P} Z_\pi \boldsymbol{X}_\pi, \tag{1}$$

where $(Z_\pi, \pi \in P)$ is a collection of Bernoulli random variables (i.e. they only take the values 0 or 1) such that $Pr(Z_\pi = 1) = \frac{1}{n!}$ and $Pr(\sum_{\pi \in P} Z_\pi = 1) = 1$. The interpretation of such a construction is simple, we choose with uniform probability and independently of $\boldsymbol{X}$ a permutation and we apply it to the indices of $\boldsymbol{X}$. The resulting random vector is, in fact, a uniform mixture (see [14]) of all possible permutations of $\boldsymbol{X}$. For more information in this regard, we refer the reader to [17]. In addition, we will denote as $(X_{(1)}, \ldots, X_{(n)})$ the order statistics of $\boldsymbol{X}$, i.e. the random vector consisting on the ordered values, from the smallest to the greatest, of $\boldsymbol{X}$.

2.1 Stochastic Orders

Stochastic orders are binary relations that compare random elements, mainly random vectors, in terms of location, variability or dependence. In this paper, we will focus mainly on location, for which the most known stochastic order is the usual stochastic order, defined as follows.

Definition 1. *[20] Let $\boldsymbol{X}$ and $\boldsymbol{Y}$ be two random vectors. If $E[\varphi(\boldsymbol{X})] \leq E[\varphi(\boldsymbol{Y})]$ for any measurable increasing function $\varphi : \mathbb{R}^n \longrightarrow \mathbb{R}$ such that $E[\varphi(\boldsymbol{X})]$ and $E[\varphi(\boldsymbol{Y})]$ exist, then $\boldsymbol{X}$ is said to be smaller than or equal to $\boldsymbol{Y}$ in the usual stochastic order and it is denoted as $\boldsymbol{X} \leq_{st} \boldsymbol{Y}$.*

A simple condition that implies the usual stochastic order is $Pr(\boldsymbol{X} \leq \boldsymbol{Y}) = 1$, denoted as $\boldsymbol{X} \leq_{a.s.} \boldsymbol{Y}$ [20]. If two random vectors satisfy $\boldsymbol{X} \leq_{st} \boldsymbol{Y}$ and $\boldsymbol{X} \geq_{st} \boldsymbol{Y}$, then they have the same distribution, i.e. they induce the same probability distribution on $\mathbb{R}^n$. This fact will be denoted by $\boldsymbol{X} =_{st} \boldsymbol{Y}$. The following result gives some preservation properties.

Proposition 1. *[20] Let $\boldsymbol{X}$, $\boldsymbol{Y}$, $\boldsymbol{X}'$ and $\boldsymbol{Y}'$ be random vectors such that $\boldsymbol{X} \leq_{st} \boldsymbol{Y}$ and $\boldsymbol{X}' \leq_{st} \boldsymbol{Y}'$. Then,*

(1) $g(\boldsymbol{X}) \leq_{st} g(\boldsymbol{Y})$ for any increasing measurable function $g : \mathbb{R}^n \to \mathbb{R}^m$,
(2) $(X_{(1)}, \ldots, X_{(n)}) \leq_{st} (Y_{(1)}, \ldots, Y_{(n)})$,
(3) $(X_{\pi(1)}, \ldots, X_{\pi(n)}) \leq_{st} (Y_{\pi(1)}, \ldots, Y_{\pi(n)})$ for any permutation π of $\{1, \ldots, n\}$,
(4) $Z\boldsymbol{X} + (1 - Z)\boldsymbol{X}' \leq_{st} Z\boldsymbol{Y} + (1 - Z)\boldsymbol{Y}'$ for any Bernoulli random variable Z that is independent of $\boldsymbol{X}$, $\boldsymbol{Y}$, $\boldsymbol{X}'$ and $\boldsymbol{Y}'$.

As a consequence of points (3) and (4), we have that $\boldsymbol{X} \leq_{st} \boldsymbol{Y}$ implies $\hat{\boldsymbol{X}} \leq_{st} \hat{\boldsymbol{Y}}$, with $\hat{\boldsymbol{X}}$ and $\hat{\boldsymbol{Y}}$ defined as Equation (1). A first technique that can be applied in order to construct weaker stochastic orders is to consider expectations of functions that are subsets of the set of increasing functions. This is the case of the increasing convex and increasing concave orders.

Definition 2. *[20] Let $\boldsymbol{X}$ and $\boldsymbol{Y}$ be two random vectors. If $E[\varphi(\boldsymbol{X})] \leq E[\varphi(\boldsymbol{Y})]$ for any measurable increasing convex (concave) function $\varphi : \mathbb{R}^n \to \mathbb{R}$ such that $E[\varphi(\boldsymbol{X})]$ and $E[\varphi(\boldsymbol{Y})]$ exist, then $\boldsymbol{X}$ is said to be smaller than or equal to $\boldsymbol{Y}$ in the increasing convex (concave) stochastic order and it is denoted as $\boldsymbol{X} \leq_{icx} (\leq_{icv})\boldsymbol{Y}$.*

Since any increasing convex or increasing concave function is increasing, it holds that $\boldsymbol{X} \leq_{st} \boldsymbol{Y} \Rightarrow \boldsymbol{X} \leq_{icx} (\leq_{icv})\boldsymbol{Y}$. Also notice that the function $f(x_1, \ldots, x_n) = x_i$ is increasing, convex and concave for any $i \in \{1, \ldots, n\}$, thus $\boldsymbol{X} \leq_{icx} (\leq_{icv})\boldsymbol{Y}$ implies $E[X_i] \leq E[Y_i]$ for any $i \in \{1, \ldots, n\}$. The following characterization will be useful later.

Theorem 1. *[20] Let $\boldsymbol{X}$ and $\boldsymbol{Y}$ be two random vectors. Then, $\boldsymbol{X} \leq_{icx} \boldsymbol{Y}$ if and only if there exists two random vectors $\hat{\boldsymbol{X}}$ and $\hat{\boldsymbol{Y}}$ defined in the same probability space such that $\hat{\boldsymbol{X}} =_{st} \boldsymbol{X}$, $\hat{\boldsymbol{Y}} =_{st} \boldsymbol{Y}$ and $E[\hat{\boldsymbol{Y}} \mid \hat{\boldsymbol{X}}] \geq \hat{\boldsymbol{X}}$.*

Another method for constructing orders that are weaker than the usual stochastic order is to loose the conditions in the multivariate case, while still having the usual stochastic order for random variables. A possibility is to consider probabilities over upper or lower rectangles, leading to the following orders.

Definition 3. *[20] Let $\boldsymbol{X}$ and $\boldsymbol{Y}$ be two random vectors. Then, if $Pr(\boldsymbol{X} \geq \boldsymbol{\lambda}) \leq Pr(\boldsymbol{X} \geq \boldsymbol{\lambda})$ ($Pr(\boldsymbol{X} \leq \boldsymbol{\lambda}) \geq Pr(\boldsymbol{X} \leq \boldsymbol{\lambda})$) for any $\boldsymbol{\lambda} \in \mathbb{R}^n$, it is said that $\boldsymbol{X}$ is smaller than $\boldsymbol{Y}$ in the upper (lower) orthant order and it is denoted as $\boldsymbol{X} \leq_{uo} (\leq_{lo})\boldsymbol{Y}$.*

These orders are related to the Positive Quadrant Dependence (PQD) order, defined as follows.

Definition 4. *[20] Let $\boldsymbol{X}$ and $\boldsymbol{Y}$ be two random vectors. Then, if $\boldsymbol{X} \leq_{uo} \boldsymbol{Y}$ and $\boldsymbol{X} \geq_{lo} \boldsymbol{Y}$, it is said that $\boldsymbol{X}$ is be smaller than $\boldsymbol{Y}$ in the Positive Quadrant Dependence order and it is denoted as $\boldsymbol{X} \leq_{PQD} \boldsymbol{Y}$.*

The PQD order is a positive dependence order, which means that, if $\boldsymbol{X} \leq_{PQD} \boldsymbol{Y}$, then the components of $\boldsymbol{Y}$ increase and decrease together more strongly than the components of $\boldsymbol{X}$. Moreover, $\boldsymbol{X} \leq_{PQD} \boldsymbol{Y}$ implies that $X_i =_{st} Y_i$ for any $i \in \{1, \ldots, n\}$, i.e. the components have the same distribution. Inspired by the scaled order statistics orders (see Sect. 6.G.2 in [20]), we introduce the following order.

Definition 5. *Let* $\boldsymbol{X}$ *and* $\boldsymbol{Y}$ *be two random vectors. Then, if* $(X_{(1)}, \ldots, X_{(n)}) \leq_{st} (Y_{(1)}, \ldots, Y_{(n)})$, *it is said that* $\boldsymbol{X}$ *is smaller than* $\boldsymbol{Y}$ *in the order statistics order and it is denoted as* $\boldsymbol{X} \leq_{ost} \boldsymbol{Y}$.

Notice that the inequality $\boldsymbol{X} \leq_{ost} \boldsymbol{Y}$ remains valid if we change the order of the components of $\boldsymbol{X}$ or $\boldsymbol{Y}$. Finally, we will also consider the Laplace transform order, which is only defined for positive random vectors.

Definition 6. *[20] Let* $\boldsymbol{X}$ *and* $\boldsymbol{Y}$ *be two positive random vectors. Then, if for any* $\boldsymbol{s} \in (\mathbb{R}^+)^n$,

$$E\left[e^{-\sum_{i=1}^n s_i X_i}\right] \geq E\left[e^{-\sum_{i=1}^n s_i X_i}\right],$$

$\boldsymbol{X}$ *is said to be smaller than or equal than* $\boldsymbol{Y}$ *in the Laplace transform order and it is denoted as* $\boldsymbol{X} \leq_{Lt} \boldsymbol{Y}$.

The implications between the introduced location stochastic orders are given in the next result, which is a compendium of results that can be found in [20] (in particular, see Theorem 7.A.12, Implication (6.G.9) and Theorem 7.D.3).

Theorem 2. *Let* $\boldsymbol{X}$ *and* $\boldsymbol{Y}$ *be two random vectors. Then,* $\boldsymbol{X} \leq_{st} \boldsymbol{Y}$ *implies* $\boldsymbol{X} \leq_{icx} \boldsymbol{Y}$, $\boldsymbol{X} \leq_{icv} \boldsymbol{Y}$, $\boldsymbol{X} \leq_{uo} \boldsymbol{Y}$, $\boldsymbol{X} \leq_{lo} \boldsymbol{Y}$ *and* $\boldsymbol{X} \leq_{Lt} \boldsymbol{Y}$. *Moreover, if* $\boldsymbol{X}$ *and* $\boldsymbol{Y}$ *are positive, then* $\boldsymbol{X} \leq_{Lt} \boldsymbol{Y}$ *is implied by* $\boldsymbol{X} \leq_{icv} \boldsymbol{Y}$ *and* $\boldsymbol{X} \leq_{lo} \boldsymbol{Y}$.

2.2 Aggregations of Random Variables

Aggregation functions take real values on a common, non-empty interval I and return another value in the same interval, satisfying monotonicity and some boundary conditions [8]. The concept of aggregation of random variables extends the notion of aggregation functions from real numbers to random variables, using stochastic orders for the monotonicity and the boundary conditions. Let us start introducing the set of random vectors we will work with. Considering a probability space (Ω, Σ, P) and a real non-empty interval I (bounded or not), we define the following set.

$$L_I^n(\Omega) = \{\boldsymbol{X} : \Omega \to I^n \mid \boldsymbol{X} \text{ is measurable}\}.$$

This set consists of the random vectors defined from the considered probability space to the Cartesian product of the interval I. If $n = 1$, $L_I^1(\Omega)$ will be denoted by $L_I(\Omega)$. In addition, (Ω) will be dropped, assuming that the probability space is rich enough (see [12]). Thus, we will denote them simply as L_I and L_I^n. A general definition of aggregation of random variables is the following one.

Definition 7. *[6] Let (Ω, Σ, P) be a probability space, $\leq_{so}$ a stochastic order and I a real non-empty interval. An aggregation function of random variables (with respect to $\leq_{so}$) is a function $A : L_I^n \to L_I$ which satisfies:*

- *For any $\boldsymbol{X}, \boldsymbol{Y} \in L_I^n$ such that $\boldsymbol{X} \leq_{so} \boldsymbol{Y}$, $A(\boldsymbol{X}) \leq_{so} A(\boldsymbol{Y})$.*
- *For any $X \in L_I$, there exist $\boldsymbol{X}_1, \boldsymbol{X}_2 \in L_I^n$ such that $A(\boldsymbol{X}_1) \leq_{so} X \leq_{so} A(\boldsymbol{X}_2)$.*

As already mentioned, the most common choice is the usual stochastic order $\leq_{st}$, while in this paper we will consider weaker orders. The following preliminary result states a link between aggregations of random variables with respect to different stochastic orders.

Lemma 1. *Let $A : L_I^n \to L_I$ be an aggregation of random variables with respect to $\leq_{so}$ and consider another stochastic order $\leq_{so'}$ such that $\boldsymbol{X} \leq_{so} \boldsymbol{Y} \Rightarrow \boldsymbol{X} \leq_{so'} \boldsymbol{Y}$ for any pair of random vectors $\boldsymbol{X}$ and $\boldsymbol{Y}$. The following statements are equivalent:*

- *A is an aggregation of random variables with respect to $\leq_{so'}$,*
- *For any $\boldsymbol{X}, \boldsymbol{Y} \in L_I^n$ such that $\boldsymbol{X} \leq_{so'} \boldsymbol{Y}$, $A(\boldsymbol{X}) \leq_{so'} A(\boldsymbol{X})$.*

Proof. By definition, if A is an aggregation of random variables with respect to $\leq_{so'}$, the other statement holds. For the other implication, we just need to check the boundary conditions. For any $X \in L_I$, since A is an aggregation of random variables with respect to $\leq_{so}$, there exists $\boldsymbol{X}_1, \boldsymbol{X}_2 \in L_I^n$ such that $A(\boldsymbol{X}_1) \leq_{so} X \leq_{so} A(\boldsymbol{X}_2)$, thus $A(\boldsymbol{X}_1) \leq_{so'} X \leq_{so'} A(\boldsymbol{X}_2)$ and the boundary conditions with respect to $\leq_{so'}$ also hold. □

If we consider $\leq_{so}$ to be the usual stochastic order, the result essentially says that for checking if an aggregation of random variables with respect to $\leq_{st}$ is also an aggregation of random variables with respect to a weaker order, it suffices to check the monotonicity. We have the following straightforward consequence.

Corollary 1. *Let $\leq_{so}$ and $\leq_{so'}$ be two stochastic orders such that for any pair of random vectors $\boldsymbol{X}$ and $\boldsymbol{Y}$, it holds $\boldsymbol{X} \leq_{so} \boldsymbol{Y} \Rightarrow \boldsymbol{X} \leq_{so'} \boldsymbol{Y}$ and for any pair of random variables X and Y it holds $X \leq_{so} Y \iff X \leq_{so'} Y$. Then, any aggregation of random variables with respect to $\leq_{so'}$ is an aggregation of random variables with respect to $\leq_{so}$.*

We end this section by remarking that the composition of measurable usual aggregation functions and random vectors is a particular case of aggregations of random variables with respect to the usual stochastic order.

Theorem 3. *[3] Let $\hat{A} : I^n \to I$ be a measurable aggregation function. Then, the function $A : L_I^n \to L_I$ defined as $A(\boldsymbol{X}) = \hat{A} \circ \boldsymbol{X}$ is an aggregation of random variables with respect to $\leq_{st}$.*

As we will see later, this result is no longer true if we replace $\leq_{st}$ by other stochastic orders.

3 Aggregation Under Increasing Convex and Concave Orders

Along this section, we will replace $\leq_{st}$ for $\leq_{icx}$ and $\leq_{icv}$ in Definition 7. Let us focus for the moment on the increasing convex order, since the study is similar in both cases. As a first consequence, Theorem 3 is no longer true, since the increasing convex order is not preserved when applying a general increasing function. However, when restricting our study to convex aggregation functions, we can obtain a similar result.

Proposition 2. *Let $\hat{A} : I^n \to I$ be a convex measurable aggregation function. Then, the function $A : L_I^n \to L_I$ defined as $A(\boldsymbol{X}) = \hat{A} \circ \boldsymbol{X}$ is an aggregation of random variables with respect to $\leq_{icx}$.*

Proof. The increasing convex order is preserved when applying increasing convex functions, see Theorem 7.A.5. (a) in [20], thus the monotonicity holds. Using Theorem 3, A is an aggregation of random variables with respect to $\leq_{st}$, thus applying Lemma 1 the result holds. □

The class of convex aggregation functions includes weighted means, Choquet integrals based on supermodular capacities [7] or the maximum, among others. On the other hand, there are aggregations of random variables with respect to $\leq_{icx}$ that are not aggregations of random variables with respect to $\leq_{st}$. We provide an example accordingly.

Example 1. Let the function $A : L^2_{[0,1]} \to L_{[0,1]}$ be defined as

$$A(X_1, X_2) = \begin{cases} 0 & \text{if } E[X_1] \in [0, 0.25), \\ 0.45 & \text{if } E[X_1] \in [0.25, 0.5), \\ U & \text{if } E[X_1] \in [0.5, 0.75), \\ 1 & \text{if } E[X_1] \in [0.75, 1], \end{cases}$$

where U is a uniform random variable over $[0,1]$. If V is a degenerate random variable, then it is clear that $E[U \mid V] = E[U]$, so using Theorem 1 we have $0 \leq_{icx} 0.45 \leq_{icx} U \leq_{icx} 1$. That is, $A(X_1, X_2)$ increases in the increasing convex order as a function of $E[X_1]$. Let $(X_1, X_2) \leq_{icx} (Y_1, Y_2)$. Then, $E[X_1] \leq E[Y_1]$, so $A(X_1, X_2) \leq_{icx} A(Y_1, Y_2)$, and we have the monotonicity with respect to $\leq_{icx}$. In addition, the boundary conditions are satisfied since $A(0,0) = 0$ and $A(1,1) = 1$.

However, it is easy to compute that $E[U^{\frac{1}{4}}] = 0.8$, while $E[0.45^{\frac{1}{4}}] = 0.45^{\frac{1}{4}} \approx 0.819$. Since $f(x) = x^{\frac{1}{4}}$ is increasing in $[0,1]$, we have that $0.45 \not\leq_{st} U$. In particular, $A(0.3, 0.5) \not\leq_{st} A(0.6, 0.5)$ while clearly $(0.3, 0.5) \leq_{st} (0.6, 0.5)$, so the monotonicity with respect to $\leq_{st}$ is not true.

Leaving aside this particular example, any aggregation of random variables with respect to the increasing convex order is increasing with respect the addition of an independent random vector with positive mean.

Proposition 3. *Let $A : L_I^n \to L_I$ be an aggregation of random variables with respect to $\leq_{icx}$. Then, for any random vectors $\boldsymbol{X}$ and $\boldsymbol{Z}$ such that $\boldsymbol{X}, \boldsymbol{X}+\boldsymbol{Z} \in L_I^n$, $\boldsymbol{X}$ and $\boldsymbol{Z}$ are independent and $E[\boldsymbol{Z}] \geq \boldsymbol{0}$, it holds that $A(\boldsymbol{X}) \leq_{icx} A(\boldsymbol{X}+\boldsymbol{Z})$.*

Proof. Notice that $E[\boldsymbol{X}+\boldsymbol{Z} \mid \boldsymbol{X}] = \boldsymbol{X} + E[\boldsymbol{Z}] \geq \boldsymbol{X}$, thus $\boldsymbol{X} \leq_{icx} \boldsymbol{X}+\boldsymbol{Z}$ by Theorem 1. The result holds by the monotonicity with respect to $\leq_{icx}$ of A. □

The case $E[\boldsymbol{Z}] = 0$ in the latter result is specially relevant, since it says that adding noise in the input makes the output to increase. Another result with a similar interpretation is the following one.

Proposition 4. *Let $A : L_I^n \to L_I$ be an aggregation of random variables with respect to $\leq_{icx}$. Then, for any $\epsilon \geq 0$ and any exchangeable random vector $\boldsymbol{X} \in L_I^n$, it holds*

$$A\left(\frac{1}{n}\sum_{i=1}^{n} X_i - \epsilon, \ldots, \frac{1}{n}\sum_{i=1}^{n} X_i - \epsilon\right) \leq_{icx} A(\boldsymbol{X}),$$

whenever $\sum_{i=1}^n w_i X_i - \epsilon \in L_I$.

Proof. Fix a $\boldsymbol{X} \in L_I^n$. Denote as P the set of all permutations of $\{1, \ldots, n\}$ and, for any $\pi \in P$, let $\boldsymbol{X}_\pi$ be the random vector $(X_{\pi(1)}, \ldots, X_{\pi(n)})$. Define the random vector $\hat{\boldsymbol{X}}$ as

$$\hat{\boldsymbol{X}} = \sum_{\pi \in P} Z_\pi \boldsymbol{X}_\pi,$$

where $(Z_\pi, \pi \in P)$ is a collection of Bernoulli random variables such that $Pr(Z_\pi = 1) = \frac{1}{n!}$ and $Pr(\sum_{\pi \in P} Z_\pi = 1) = 1$. Since $\boldsymbol{X}$ is exchangeable, $\hat{\boldsymbol{X}} =_{st} \boldsymbol{X}$. Moreover, suppose that $\boldsymbol{X} = \boldsymbol{\lambda}$. Then, consider $\mu = \frac{1}{n}\sum_{i=1}^n \lambda_i - \epsilon$ and compute the expected value of $\hat{\boldsymbol{X}}$ given $\boldsymbol{X} = \boldsymbol{\lambda}$.

$$\begin{aligned} E[\hat{\boldsymbol{X}} \mid \boldsymbol{X} = \boldsymbol{\lambda}] &= \frac{1}{n!}\sum_{\pi \in P} E[\boldsymbol{X}_\pi \mid \boldsymbol{X} = \boldsymbol{\lambda}] = \frac{1}{n}\sum_{i=1}^{n} E[X_i \mathbf{1} \mid \boldsymbol{X} = \lambda] = \\ &= \frac{1}{n}\sum_{i=1}^{n} \lambda_i \mathbf{1} \geq \frac{1}{n}\sum_{i=1}^{n} (\lambda_i - \epsilon)\mathbf{1} = \mu\mathbf{1}, \end{aligned}$$

where the second equality holds noticing that, among all permutations, the variable X_i is in the $k-th$ position exactly $(n-1)!$ times. Since the latter conditional expectation only depends on μ, we have

$$E\left[\hat{\boldsymbol{X}} \,\middle|\, \left(\frac{1}{n}\sum_{i=1}^{n} X_i - \epsilon, \ldots, \frac{1}{n}\sum_{i=1}^{n} X_i - \epsilon\right)\right] \geq \left(\frac{1}{n}\sum_{i=1}^{n} X_i - \epsilon, \ldots, \frac{1}{n}\sum_{i=1}^{n} X_i - \epsilon\right),$$

thus, using Theorem 1,

$$\left(\frac{1}{n}\sum_{i=1}^{n} X_i - \epsilon, \ldots, \frac{1}{n}\sum_{i=1}^{n} X_i - \epsilon\right) \leq_{icx} \boldsymbol{X}.$$

Finally, the result holds using the monotonicity with respect to $\leq_{icx}$ of A. □

If $\epsilon = 0$, this result says that replacing exchangeable inputs by their arithmetic mean makes the aggregation to take smaller values. The arithmetic mean has the property of reducing the variability of the inputs (see Theorem 3 in [5]), so this result confirms the interpretation of Proposition 3, more variability implies greater values. A consequence of the latter result is specially relevant.

Corollary 2. *Let $A : L_I^n \to L_I$ be an aggregation of random variables with respect to $\leq_{icx}$ such that for any random variables $X_1, \ldots, X_n$ such that $X_1 =_{a.s.} \cdots =_{a.s.} X_n$ it holds $A(X_1, \ldots, X_n) =_{a.s.} X_1$. Then,*

$$\frac{1}{n}\sum_{i=1} X_i \leq_{icx} A(\boldsymbol{X})$$

for any exchangeable vector $\boldsymbol{X} \in L_I^n$.

Proof. Notice that $\frac{1}{n}\sum_{i=1} X_i \in L_I$. Applying Proposition 4 for $\epsilon = 0$,

$$\frac{1}{n}\sum_{i=1} X_i =_{a.s.} A\left(\frac{1}{n}\sum_{i=1}^{n} X_i, \ldots, \frac{1}{n}\sum_{i=1}^{n} X_i\right) \leq_{icx} A\left(\boldsymbol{X}\right).$$

□

The property $X_1 =_{a.s.} \cdots =_{a.s.} X_n \Rightarrow A(X_1, \ldots, X_n) =_{a.s.} X_1$ is called almost surely idempotence, see [4] for more information in this regard. Let us end this section by writing the latter result in terms of the composition of usual aggregation functions (recall Theorem 3).

Corollary 3. *Let $\hat{A} : I^n \to I$ be a measurable, convex and idempotent aggregation function. Then, for any exchangeable random vector $\boldsymbol{X} \in L_I^n$, it holds that $\frac{1}{n}\sum_{i=1}^{n} X_i \leq_{icx} \hat{A} \circ \boldsymbol{X}$.*

That is, for exchangeable random vectors, the arithmetic mean is the smallest convex idempotent aggregation with respect to the increasing convex order. Analogous results can be derived for the increasing concave order using the same techniques. We provide them without proof. First, the compositions of concave aggregation functions with random vectors are aggregations of random variables with respect to $\leq_{icv}$.

Proposition 5. *Let $\hat{A} : I^n \to I$ be a concave measurable aggregation function. Then, the function $A : L_I^n \to L_I$ defined as $A(\boldsymbol{X}) = \hat{A} \circ \boldsymbol{X}$ is an aggregation of random variables with respect to $\leq_{icv}$.*

In addition, aggregations of random variables with respect to $\leq_{icv}$ have a negative bias with respect to dispersion.

Proposition 6. *Let $A : L_I^n \to L_I$ be an aggregation of random variables with respect to $\leq_{icv}$. Then, for any random vectors $\boldsymbol{X}$ and $\boldsymbol{Z}$ such that $\boldsymbol{X}, \boldsymbol{X} + \boldsymbol{Z} \in L_I^n$, $\boldsymbol{X}$ and $\boldsymbol{Z}$ are independent and $E[\boldsymbol{Z}] \geq \boldsymbol{0}$, it holds that $A(\boldsymbol{X}) \geq_{icv} A(\boldsymbol{X} - \boldsymbol{Z})$.*

Proposition 7. *Let $A : L_I^n \to L_I$ be an aggregation of random variables with respect to $\leq_{icv}$. Then, for any $\epsilon \geq 0$ and any exchangeable random vector $\boldsymbol{X} \in L_I^n$, it holds*

$$A\left(\frac{1}{n}\sum_{i=1}^{n} X_i + \epsilon, \ldots, \frac{1}{n}\sum_{i=1}^{n} X_i + \epsilon\right) \geq_{icv} A(\boldsymbol{X})$$

whenever $\sum_{i=1}^{n} w_i X_i + \epsilon \in L_I$.

Finally, the greatest almost surely idempotent aggregation of random variables with respect to the increasing concave stochastic order when working with exchangeable random vectors is the arithmetic mean.

Corollary 4. *Let $A : L_I^n \to L_I$ be an aggregation of random variables with respect to $\leq_{icx}$ such that for any random variables $X_1, \ldots, X_n$ such that $X_1 =_{a.s.} \cdots =_{a.s.} X_n$ it holds $A(X_1, \ldots, X_n) =_{a.s.} X_1$. Then,*

$$\frac{1}{n}\sum_{i=1} X_i \geq_{icv} A(\boldsymbol{X})$$

for any exchangeable vector $\boldsymbol{X} \in L_I^n$.

Corollary 5. *Let $\hat{A} : I^n \to I$ be a measurable, concave and idempotent aggregation function. Then, for any exchangeable random vector $\boldsymbol{X} \in L_I^n$, it holds $\frac{1}{n}\sum_{i=1}^{n} X_i \geq_{icv} \hat{A} \circ \boldsymbol{X}$.*

4 Aggregation Under the Order Statistics Order and Symmetry

Consider now the orders statistic order $\leq_{ost}$. As a consequence of Corollary 1, since $\leq_{st}$ and $\leq_{ost}$ are equivalent for random variables, we have that the set of aggregations of random variables with respect to $\leq_{ost}$ is a subset of aggregations of random variables with respect to $\leq_{st}$. Then, a natural question is to ask what are the properties that an aggregation of random variables with respect to $\leq_{st}$ should satisfy in order to be also an aggregation of random variables with respect to $\leq_{ost}$. We will start showing that, when working with exchangeable random vectors, we have a good behavior.

Lemma 2. *Let $A : L_I^n \to L_I$ be an aggregation of random variables with respect to $\leq_{st}$. Then, for any exchangeable random vectors $\boldsymbol{X}, \boldsymbol{Y} \in L_I^n$ such that $\boldsymbol{X} \leq_{ost} \boldsymbol{Y}$, it holds that $A(\boldsymbol{X}) \leq_{st} A(\boldsymbol{Y})$.*

Proof. Let P be the set of all permutations of $\{1, \ldots, n\}$. Denote as $\boldsymbol{O}^X$ and $\boldsymbol{O}^Y$ the order statistics of, respectively, $\boldsymbol{X}$ and $\boldsymbol{Y}$. Let $(Z_\pi, \pi \in P)$ be a collection of Bernoulli random variables such that $Pr(Z_\pi = 1) = \frac{1}{n!}$ for any $\pi \in P$ and $Pr(\sum_{\pi \in P} Z_\pi = 1) = 1$. Then, since $\boldsymbol{X}$ and $\boldsymbol{Y}$ are exchangeable,

$$\boldsymbol{X} =_{st} \sum_{\pi \in P} Z_\pi \cdot (O_{\pi(1)}^X, \ldots, O_{\pi(n)}^X), \quad \boldsymbol{Y} =_{st} \sum_{\pi \in P} Z_\pi \cdot (O_{\pi(1)}^Y, \ldots, O_{\pi(n)}^Y)$$

Then, if $\boldsymbol{X} \leq_{ost} \boldsymbol{Y}$, then $\boldsymbol{O}^X \leq_{st} \boldsymbol{O}^Y$ and $\boldsymbol{X} \leq_{st} \boldsymbol{Y}$ as a consequence of Proposition 1 (3) and (4). By the monotonicity of A with respect to the usual stochastic order, we obtain $A(\boldsymbol{X}) \leq_{st} A(\boldsymbol{Y})$. □

This result allows us to have the following characterization.

Proposition 8. *A function $A : L_I^n \to L_I$ is an aggregation of random variables with respect to $\leq_{ost}$ if and only if:*

(1) A is an aggregation of random variables with respect to $\leq_{st}$,
(2) For any $\boldsymbol{X}, \boldsymbol{Y} \in L_I^n$, $\boldsymbol{X} =_{ost} \boldsymbol{Y} \Rightarrow A(\boldsymbol{X}) =_{st} A(\boldsymbol{Y})$.

Proof. If A is an aggregation of random variables with respect to $\leq_{ost}$, (1) holds by Corollary 1 and (2) holds by the monotonicity, since $\boldsymbol{X} \leq_{ost} \boldsymbol{Y}$ and $\boldsymbol{X} \geq_{ost} \boldsymbol{Y}$ imply $A(\boldsymbol{X}) \leq_{st} A(\boldsymbol{Y})$ and $A(\boldsymbol{X}) \geq_{st} A(\boldsymbol{Y})$, so $A(\boldsymbol{X}) =_{st} A(\boldsymbol{Y})$.

For the other implication, let $(Z_\pi, \pi \in P)$ be a collection of Bernoulli random variables such that $Pr(Z_\pi = 1) = \frac{1}{n!}$ for any $\pi \in P$ and $Pr(\sum_{\pi \in P} Z_\pi = 1) = 1$. For any $\boldsymbol{X} \in L_I^n$, consider

$$\hat{\boldsymbol{X}} = \sum_{\pi \in P} Z_\pi \boldsymbol{X}$$

Since the values of $\hat{\boldsymbol{X}}$ are just a (random) reordering of the values of $\boldsymbol{X}$, the order statistics of $\boldsymbol{X}$ and $\hat{\boldsymbol{X}}$ coincide, so $\boldsymbol{X} =_{ost} \hat{\boldsymbol{X}}$. Then, by (2) we have that $A(\boldsymbol{X}) =_{st} A(\hat{\boldsymbol{X}})$. Moreover, $\hat{\boldsymbol{X}}$ is exchangeable. Then, it is possible to apply Lemma 2 to obtain that, for any $\boldsymbol{X}, \boldsymbol{Y} \in L_I^n$ such that $\boldsymbol{X} \leq_{ord} \boldsymbol{Y}$,

$$A(\boldsymbol{X}) =_{st} A(\hat{\boldsymbol{X}}) \leq_{st} A(\hat{\boldsymbol{Y}}) =_{st} A(\boldsymbol{Y}),$$

thus the monotonicity with respect to $\leq_{ord}$ holds. Then, the result holds using (1) and Lemma 1. □

As a consequence, we can prove the following composition theorem, that allows us to use, among others, OWA operators, the geometric mean and the harmonic mean [8] with $\leq_{ost}$.

Corollary 6. *Let A be a measurable symmetric aggregation function. Then, $A \circ \boldsymbol{X}$ is an aggregation of random variables with respect to $\leq_{ord}$.*

5 Aggregation Under Orthant Orders and Dependence

The orthant orders compare probabilities over upper and lower rectangles. Similarly as the order statistic order, any aggregation of random variables with respect to $\leq_{lo}$ or $\leq_{uo}$ is an aggregation of random variables with respect to $\leq_{st}$. Unfortunately, very few usual aggregation functions are suitable to be used when working with the orthant orders. For instance, the maximum and the minimum preserve, respectively, the lower and upper orthant orders (see Theorem 6.G.15. in [20]). For the product, which is an aggregation function only for some particular intervals, we only have that the expectations are ordered (see Theorem 6.G.1.

in [20]). Regarding the dependence of the inputs, these aggregations take greater or smaller values as the positive dependence increases. We recall that $\leq_{PQD}$ is a positive dependence order that implies both $\leq_{uo}$ and $\geq_{lo}$, see Definition 4, so the following results hold trivially.

Proposition 9. *Let $A : L_I^n \to L_I$ be an aggregation of random variables with respect to $\leq_{uo}$. Then, for any $\boldsymbol{X}, \boldsymbol{Y} \in L_I^n$ such that $\boldsymbol{X} \leq_{PQD} \boldsymbol{Y}$, $A(\boldsymbol{X}) \leq_{st} A(\boldsymbol{X})$.*

Proposition 10. *Let $A : L_I^n \to L_I$ be an aggregation of random variables with respect to $\leq_{lo}$. Then, for any $\boldsymbol{X}, \boldsymbol{Y} \in L_I^n$ such that $\boldsymbol{X} \leq_{PQD} \boldsymbol{Y}$, $A(\boldsymbol{X}) \geq_{st} A(\boldsymbol{X})$.*

That is, aggregations of random variables with respect to $\leq_{uo}$ increase if the positive dependence is stronger, while the behavior is the opposite one for $\leq_{lo}$.

6 Aggregation Under the Laplace Transform Order

The Laplace transform order is weaker than the increasing concave and lower orthant orders, but not equivalent to them in the univariate case. Since it is defined only for positive random vectors, during this section we will consider $I \subseteq \mathbb{R}^+$. Regarding usual aggregations, we known that the Laplace transform order is preserved under weighted means (see Theorem 7.D.5. in [20]). For the product, we also know that the expectations are ordered as a consequence of Theorem 7.D.6. in [20]. The following result states that this type of aggregations take greater values when the input random vector is replaced by the arithmetic mean of several independent random vectors with the same distribution.

Proposition 11. *Let $A : L_I^n \to L_I$ be an aggregation of random variables with respect to $\leq_{Lt}$ and let $\boldsymbol{X} \in L_I^n$. Consider $\boldsymbol{X}_1, \dots, \boldsymbol{X}_m$ to be independent random vectors such that $\boldsymbol{X}_k =_{st} \boldsymbol{X}$ for any $k \in \{1, \dots, m\}$. Then,*

$$A(\boldsymbol{X}) \leq_{Lt} A\left(\frac{1}{m}\sum_{k=1}^{m} \boldsymbol{X}_k\right).$$

Proof. Denote as X_{ki} the $i-th$ component of $\boldsymbol{X}_k$ and as X_i the $i-th$ component of X. For any $\boldsymbol{s} \in (\mathbb{R}^+)^n$, using independence,

$$E\left[e^{-\sum_{i=1}^{n} s_i \frac{1}{m}(\sum_{k=1}^{m} \boldsymbol{X}_{ki})}\right] = E\left[\prod_{k=1}^{m} e^{-\frac{1}{m}\sum_{i=1}^{n} s_i X_{ki}}\right] =$$

$$= \prod_{k=1}^{m} E\left[e^{-\frac{1}{m}\sum_{i=1}^{n} s_i X_{ki}}\right] = E\left[\sqrt[m]{e^{-\sum_{i=1}^{n} s_i X_i}}\right]^m$$

Since $f(x) = x^m$ is convex for positive values of x, by Jensen's inequality [11], we have that $E[X^m] \geq E[X]^m$ for any positive random variable, so we obtain

$$E\left[e^{-\sum_{i=1}^{n} s_i \frac{1}{m}(\sum_{k=1}^{m} \boldsymbol{X}_{ki})}\right] = E\left[\sqrt[m]{e^{-\sum_{i=1}^{n} s_i X_i}}\right]^m \leq E\left[e^{-\sum_{i=1}^{n} s_i X_i}\right],$$

thus $\boldsymbol{X} \leq_{Lt} \frac{1}{m}\sum_{k=1}^{m} \boldsymbol{X}_k$. The result holds by the monotonicity of A. □

Recall that the arithmetic mean reduces the variability [5], so we can interpret Proposition 11 as the aggregations increasing their value if the variability decrease. This aligns with the interpretation of the Laplace transform order as penalizing dispersion. It also coincides, since the increasing concave order implies the Laplace transform, with the intuition behind Propositions 6 and 7. These type of aggregations also have a direct relation with the PQD order, thus their output value increases if the positive dependence of the inputs is stronger.

Corollary 7. *Let* $A : L_I^n \to L_I$ *be an aggregation function with respect to* $\leq_{Lt}$*. Then, for any* $\boldsymbol{X}, \boldsymbol{Y} \in L_I^n$ *such that* $\boldsymbol{X} \leq_{PQD} \boldsymbol{Y}$*, it holds that* $A(\boldsymbol{X}) \geq_{Lt} A(\boldsymbol{Y})$*.*

Proof. The result holds since $\boldsymbol{X} \leq_{PQD} \boldsymbol{Y} \Rightarrow \boldsymbol{X} \geq_{lo} \boldsymbol{Y} \Rightarrow \boldsymbol{X} \geq_{Lt} \boldsymbol{Y}$, see Definition 4 and Theorem 2. □

7 Conclusion

In this paper, we have studied aggregations of random variables with respect to stochastic orders that are weaker than the usual stochastic order. For each case, we have focused on stating the usual aggregation functions that can be used when considering each of the orders, as well as the possible bias that the aggregations could have with respect to the variability and the dependence of the inputs. A summary of all cases can be found in Table 1. Note that no information about bias in such a figure represents that the behavior changes depending on the case, not the absence of bias. In general, changing the stochastic order makes the family of aggregations of random variables to be less rich than if one considers the usual stochastic order. Moreover, we lose the generalization of the classical theory of aggregation functions, not all of them are suitable to be used with stochastic orders different than the usual stochastic order, i.e. Theorem 3 does not hold. On the other hand, the capacity of compare more random vectors could be useful in cases in which the usual stochastic order is too restrictive.

Table 1. Different stochastic orders considered in the definition of aggregations of random variables, the usual aggregations that can be used in each case and their bias with respect to variability and positive dependence.

Stochastic order	Usual aggregations	Variability bias	Positive dependence bias
Usual stochastic order	Anyone		
Increasing convex order	Convex	Positive	
Increasing concave order	Concave	Negative	
Order statistics order	Symmetric		
Upper orthant order	Maximum		Negative
Lower orthant order	Minimum		Positive
Laplace transform order	Weighted means	Negative	Positive

Moreover, the increasing convex, increasing concave and the Laplace transform order allow new transformations of the inputs to be aggregations with respect to them. While the new aggregation mechanisms are limited, the analysis clarifies the structural constraints imposed by each order.

References

1. Aldous, D.J.: Exchangeability and related topics. In: Hennequin, P.L. (ed.) École d'Été de Probabilités de Saint-Flour XIII—1983. LNM, vol. 1117, pp. 1–198. Springer, Heidelberg (1985). https://doi.org/10.1007/BFb0099421
2. Baz, J., Beliakov, G., Díaz, I., Montes, S.: Taxonomy of aggregations of random variables. In: Lesot, M.J., et al. (eds.) IPMU 2024. LNNS, vol. 1175, pp. 158–170. Springer, Cham (2024). https://doi.org/10.1007/978-3-031-74000-8_14
3. Baz, J., Díaz, I., Montes, S.: The choice of an appropriate stochastic order to aggregate random variables. In: García-Escudero, L.A., et al. (eds.) SMPS 2022. AISC, vol. 1433, pp. 40–47. Springer, Cham (2022). https://doi.org/10.1007/978-3-031-15509-3_6
4. Baz, J., Díaz, I., Montes, S.: Idempotence and internality of aggregations of random variables. In: Baczyński, M., De Baets, B., Holčapek, M., Kreinovich, V., Medina, J. (eds.) EUSFLAT 2025. LNCS, vol. 15883, pp. 245–257. Springer, Cham (2025). https://doi.org/10.1007/978-3-031-97225-6_20
5. Baz, J., Pellerey, F., Díaz, I., Montes, S.: On the property of reduction of variability for mean functions. Comput. Appl. Math. **44**(6), 297 (2025)
6. Baz González, J., et al.: Aggregation of random structures. Ph.D. thesis, University of Oviedo (2025)
7. Beliakov, G., James, S., Wu, J.: Discrete Fuzzy Measures. Springer, Cham (2020). https://doi.org/10.1007/978-3-030-15305-2
8. Grabisch, M., Marichal, J.L., Mesiar, R., Pap, E.: Aggregation Functions, vol. 127. Cambridge University Press (2009)
9. Hora, S.C., Fransen, B.R., Hawkins, N., Susel, I.: Median aggregation of distribution functions. Decis. Anal. **10**(4), 279–291 (2013)
10. James, S.: An Introduction to Data Analysis Using Aggregation Functions in R. Springer, Cham (2016). https://doi.org/10.1007/978-3-319-46762-7
11. Jensen, J.L.W.V.: Sur les fonctions convexes et les inégalités entre les valeurs moyennes. Acta Math. **30**(1), 175–193 (1906)
12. Keisler, H.J., Sun, Y.: Why saturated probability spaces are necessary. Adv. Math. **221**(5), 1584–1607 (2009)
13. Klenke, A.: Probability Theory: A Comprehensive Course. Springer, Cham (2008). https://doi.org/10.1007/978-3-030-56402-5
14. McLachlan, G.J., Lee, S.X., Rathnayake, S.I.: Finite mixture models. Annu. Rev. Stat. Appl. **6**(1), 355–378 (2019)
15. Müller, A.: Stochastic ordering of multivariate normal distributions. Ann. Inst. Stat. Math. **53**(3), 567–575 (2001)
16. Müller, A., Scarsini, M.: Conditions for the multivariate stochastic order under dependence uncertainty. In: Ansari, J., et al. (eds.) SMPS 2024. AISC, vol. 1458, pp. 309–316. Springer, Cham (2024). https://doi.org/10.1007/978-3-031-65993-5_38
17. Navarro, J., Spizzichino, F.: On the relationships between copulas of order statistics and marginal distributions. Stat. Probab. Lett. **80**(5–6), 473–479 (2010)

18. Pollesch, N., Dale, V.H.: Applications of aggregation theory to sustainability assessment. Ecol. Econ. **114**, 117–127 (2015)
19. Rohatgi, V.K., Saleh, A.M.E.: An Introduction to Probability and Statistics. Wiley, Hoboken (2015)
20. Shaked, M., Shanthikumar, J.G.: Stochastic Orders. Springer, New York (2007). https://doi.org/10.1007/978-0-387-34675-5
21. Yager, R.R.: On the OWA aggregation with probabilistic inputs. Int. J. Uncertain. Fuzziness Knowl.-Based Syst. **23**(Suppl. 1), 143–162 (2015)

Supervised Learning the Joint Weighted Average – Unique Solutions and How to Find Them

Youssef Abdulghani[1(✉)], Christian Wagner[1], and Stephen B. Broomell[2]

[1] Lab for Uncertainty in Data and Decision Making (LUCID), School of Computer Science, University of Nottingham, Nottingham, UK
{youssef.abdulghani,christian.wagner}@nottingham.ac.uk

[2] GRID—Global Risk and Individual Decisions Laboratory, Purdue University, West Lafayette, IN 47907, USA
broomell@purdue.edu

Abstract. The recently introduced Joint Weighted Average (JWA) operator combines the Linear Weighted Average (LWA) and the non-linear Ordered Weighted Average (OWA), offering systematic and simultaneous consideration of both weighting strategies. The JWA therefore can represent complex aggregation behavior with interpretable ordered and linear weighting structures. Here, we investigate whether JWA weights can be uniquely learned from observed aggregates.

This is critical in applications from the physical sciences to the social sciences. For example, explaining how weighting of sensors interacts with weighting of the actual measurements, in a sensor fusion context, or explaining how humans make decisions in respect to both the information given and the information's origin.

The JWA's non-linear, interactive behavior makes it difficult to determine *a priori* the data requirements that guarantee weight uniqueness. In this paper, we articulate this challenge and discuss why it is difficult to find general conditions for uniqueness. We then show, through empirical analysis, that the main properties influencing uniqueness are connected to the permutations of evidence order found in training data. Specifically, we show that a unique solution will exist under the condition that several permutations are present in the training data. This paper thus sets out an initial exploration of the complex, yet exciting, behavior of the JWA and its weights, enhancing its interdisciplinary application for translating complex non-linear aggregation behavior into interpretable parameters.

Keywords: Aggregation Operators · Joint Weighted Average · Weight Identification · Behavioral Modeling · Explainable AI

1 Introduction

Information aggregation is the foundation of intelligent systems. In an uncertain world, sensors, experts, and experiences represent information sources to be fused

B. Vantaggi et al. (Eds.): IPMU 2026, CCIS 3019, pp. 131–144, 2026.
https://doi.org/10.1007/978-3-032-28994-0_10

into a single outcome to facilitate decision making [2,15]. In inter-disciplinary applications, aggregation is not only used for predictive performance but as a mechanism for modeling, describing, and understanding real-world behavior (e.g. human decision-making). In this scenario, the parameters of an appropriately parameterized aggregation operator can be exploited as meaningful behavioral descriptors of the original real-world process being modeled [3,12]. This interpretive role renders the *identifiability* of the operator essential; if the same observed behavior can be explained by multiple parameter sets, the semantics attached to the learned parameters can become more challenging to interpret.

Two distinct paradigms can be recognized in the aggregation literature according to *what* is being weighted. Source-centric operators, such as the Linear Weighted Average (LWA), attach weights to model the worth of specific sources, yielding a globally linear mapping from source-tied evidence to the output [3]. Evidence-centric operators, in contrast, attach weights dynamically to the evidence (modeling its worth), leveraging the numerical order of said evidence as the operational mechanism. The Ordered Weighted Averaging (OWA) operator introduced by Yager [17] is the canonical evidence-centric construction and has been widely studied and applied across decision making and fuzzy systems [7].

Motivated by the need to represent both source-worth and evidence-worth within a single semantically interpretable mechanism, the Joint Weighted Average (JWA) [3] operator was proposed as a simultaneous integration of LWA and OWA-style aggregation strategies. JWA jointly parametrizes the two notions: how much to weigh each source as well as how much to weigh each piece of evidence. This simultaneous integration is particularly compelling because it enables the modeling of complex behaviors that naturally combine these dual strategies, which cannot be captured equally by traditional combinations (more details in Sect. 2 and [3]) of LWA (purely source-tied, globally linear) or OWA (purely order-tied, source-agnostic) [3].

Unlike the OWA which incorporates ordering, JWA incorporates both ordering and interaction between source- and evidence-centric weighting. It thus exhibits non-linear properties. This raises a fundamental challenge for learning parameters from data: it is not evident *a priori* whether estimating the weights from observed training data will yield a unique set of identifiable weights.

In this work, we start addressing this issue by focusing on the following question: how can we find the dataset properties that afford the identification of a unique set of source-weights and order-weights for the JWA operator? As part of initial progress towards tackling this question, we adopt and discuss an empirically motivated approach. The paper's contributions are as follows.

- We characterize the JWA learning problem in terms of the possibility of identifying a unique solution for the underlying LWA/OWA weights and the associated challenges.
- We show that it *is possible* to identify JWA weights *uniquely*, subject to specific constraints on the diversity and scale of the training data.
- In respect to the data requirements, we show that the *order permutations* within any training data are key to the identifiability of the JWA weights.

The remainder of the paper is organized as follows. Section 2 reviews background on LWA, OWA, and JWA. Section 3 articulates the weight uniqueness problem and why it is a complex problem for the JWA. Section 4 details the empirical methodology we devised as a way to gain insight into this problem and presents illustrative results for the specific case involving aggregating three sources of information. Finally, Sect. 6 discusses implications, limitations, and future work.

2 Background

Let n be the number of information sources, the weight vector $\mathbf{w} = (\mathrm{w}_1, \ldots, \mathrm{w}_n)$ is the vector of convex source weights, where w_l corresponds to the weight of numbered source l. x_l is the evidence of the numbered source l. The linear weighted average (LWA) aggregation is then defined as the following linear combination: $\mathrm{LWA}(\mathbf{x}) = \sum_{l=1}^{n} \mathrm{w}_l \mathrm{x}_l$. Moreover, if there are k samples/data rows that need to be aggregated then the LWA aggregate can be calculated for each sample i by:

$$\mathrm{LWA}_i(\mathbf{x}) = \sum_{l=1}^{n} \mathrm{w}_l \mathrm{x}_{i,l}, \tag{1}$$

where $\mathrm{x}_{i,l}$ is the evidence value of source l in the i-th sample.

The Ordered Weighted Average (OWA) [17] requires ordering the evidence $\mathrm{x}_{i,l}$ to create $\mathbf{X}^{\pi}$ such that $\mathrm{x}^{\pi}_{i,1} > \ldots > \mathrm{x}^{\pi}_{i,n}$ for each row i. The OWA of the i-th sample can be expressed as:

$$\mathrm{OWA}_i(\mathbf{x}) = \sum_{l=1}^{n} \mathrm{v}_l \mathrm{x}^{\pi}_{i,l}. \tag{2}$$

where $\mathbf{v}$ is the vector of order weights, such that v_l is the weight of the l-th order position (i.e., associated with the value $\mathrm{x}^{\pi}_{i,l}$).

The value of combining the aforementioned LWA and OWA weighting has been recognized in earlier work [3,10,11,13,16]. Pioneering work by Torra introduced the weighted OWA (WOWA) operator [13] to unify LWA and OWA by incorporating both source weights and order weights within a single weighting structure. Subsequent research proposed different hybrid frameworks such as the Hybrid Weighted Average (HWA) [16], Ordered Weighted Average – Weighted Average (OWAWA) [11], and the Standard Deviation Weighted Average (SDOWA) [5]. Nevertheless, an important gap remained where none of these approaches consistently provided the desired/expected outcome *and* meaningful semantics in joint aggregation operations as articulated in [3].

By identifying this gap, the authors of [3] proposed the joint weighted average (JWA) operator, in which the source-weight vector and the position-weight vector are combined as

$$\mathbf{j}_i = \mathbf{w}_i^{\pi_i} \oplus \mathbf{v} = \left(\frac{w^{\pi_i}_{i,1} v_1}{\sum_{l=1}^{n} w^{\pi_i}_{i,l} v_l}, \ldots, \frac{w^{\pi_i}_{i,n} v_n}{\sum_{l=1}^{n} w^{\pi_i}_{i,l} v_l} \right). \tag{3}$$

Here, π_i denotes the permutation associated with sample i, that is, the ordering that sorts the evidence values into $\mathbf{x}_i^{\pi_i} = (x_{i,1}^{\pi_i}, \ldots, x_{i,n}^{\pi_i})$. The vector $\mathbf{w}_i^{\pi_i} = (w_{i,1}^{\pi_i}, \ldots, w_{i,n}^{\pi_i})$ is the corresponding permutation of the original source-weight vector $\mathbf{w}_i$, so that $w_{i,l}^{\pi_i}$ is the weight of the information source associated with the l-th ordered evidence value $x_{i,l}^{\pi_i}$. The vector $\mathbf{v} = (v_1, \ldots, v_n)$ contains the position weights. This combination method is known in compositional geometry[1] [1] as the perturbation operation ($\oplus$) [1]. Therefore, each sample i has its own permutation π_i, permuted source-weight vector $\mathbf{w}_i^{\pi_i}$, and joint weight vector $\mathbf{j}_i$. The JWA aggregate for sample i is then computed as

$$\text{JWA}_i(\mathbf{x}_i^{\pi_i}) = \sum_{l=1}^{n} j_{i,l}\, x_{i,l}^{\pi_i}. \tag{4}$$

As usual for aggregation operators, going beyond theoretical considerations of an operator to practical utility depends on the existence of suitably determined weights. The determination of the weight from examples, i.e. the supervised learning of weights, is one popular method of setting the operator weights [8,15]. For LWA and OWA, separately, weight learning can often be posed as constrained least squares with well-understood optimization behavior [15]. For combined aggregation operators, such as the WOWA operator, similar methods were proposed to learn weights from observed input/output pairs, e.g. [14]. While we can apply a similar least squares approach to the JWA aggregator, the interaction between the LWA and OWA weighting strategies complicates the question of weight uniqueness in the supervised learning regime of JWA.

3 Why Weight Uniqueness Is Difficult to Determine for JWA?

To understand the complexity of JWA weight uniqueness, we first consider the linear aggregation case. Assume an LWA operation performed with a ground-truth weight vector $\mathbf{w} = (\mathrm{w}_1, \ldots, \mathrm{w}_n)$. Equation (1) can be re-written as the following canonical linear algebra expression, where $\mathbf{X}$ is the evidence matrix and $\mathbf{y}$ is the output vector of LWA aggregation:

$$\mathbf{X}\mathbf{w} = \mathbf{y}. \tag{5}$$

Furthermore, assume there is no noise/uncertainties present–we adopt this assumption throughout this paper leaving more complex settings to future work. In this case, the uniqueness problem in supervised learning setting can be solved analytically using a fundamental result in linear algebra: a unique solution for the weights, given by $\mathbf{w} = \mathbf{X}^{-1}\mathbf{y}$, exists if and only if the matrix $\mathbf{X}$ is invertible. In other words, at least n independent samples (input/output pairs) are needed to uniquely solve this linear system of equations. However, the components of

[1] The study of vectors in a space where the components of any vector in that space have to sum to a certain constant, usually unity.

$\mathbf{w}$ are not all independent since we have the constraint that $\sum_{l=1}^{n} \mathrm{w}_l = 1$. This effectively relaxes the requirement of n independent examples to $n-1$ for the majority of learning cases.

Furthermore, consider that an OWA operation would only change this requirement slightly, since an OWA operation is linear with respect to $\mathbf{X}^{\pi}$ (the ordered evidence matrix). In particular, Eq. (2) can be re-written as

$$\mathbf{X}^{\pi}\mathbf{v} = \mathbf{y}, \tag{6}$$

with unique order weights $\mathbf{v}$ computed by $\mathbf{v} = (\mathbf{X}^{\pi})^{-1}\mathbf{y}$. The existence of a unique weight vector depends on the rank (linear independence) of the ordered matrix $\mathbf{X}^{\pi}$. Note that in general, the ordered evidence matrix might have different row rank than the evidence matrix. To illustrate this, consider the evidence matrix,

$$\mathbf{X} = \begin{bmatrix} 95 & 70 & 80 \\ 80 & 95 & 70 \end{bmatrix},$$

the row rank of this matrix is 2, because it is impossible to express any one of these rows as a linear combination of the other. If then the evidence matrix is ordered in descending order per row, then we obtain

$$\mathbf{X}^{\pi} = \begin{bmatrix} 95 & 80 & 70 \\ 95 & 80 & 70 \end{bmatrix},$$

since both rows are duplicates, the rank of the ordered matrix is 1, and the second row will not add to the constraints in the learning problem that enable obtaining a unique order weight vector $\mathbf{v}$.

In contrast to OWA and LWA, the JWA operation (Eq. (4)) cannot be reduced to a single *linear* system of unknown weights. The reason is that the effective weight applied to a given evidence is not fixed across samples. Instead, it depends on how that source's evidence is ordered within a given sample. Specifically, for each sample i, sorting the evidence vector $\mathbf{x}_i$ induces a permutation π_i and a corresponding permuted source-weight vector $\mathbf{w}_i^{\pi_i}$. The joint weights $\mathbf{j}_i$ are then obtained by combining $\mathbf{w}_i^{\pi_i}$ with the order-weight vector $\mathbf{v}$ and normalizing (see Eq. (3)). As a result, the weights are indexed by both the sample i and the ordered position l, rather than by a single index as in LWA or OWA.

It is still possible to express the JWA operation compactly, but doing so highlights why linear algebra intuition breaks down. Let $\mathbf{X}^{\pi} \in \mathbb{R}^{k\times n}$ be the row-wise ordered evidence matrix, and let $\mathbf{J} \in \mathbb{R}^{k\times n}$ be the matrix of weights whose i-th row is $\mathbf{j}_i$. With n sources, there are $n!$ possible orderings. Each ordering π_i defines a specific permuted weight vector $\mathbf{w}_i^{\pi_i}$, and a corresponding joint-weight vector (defined previously in Eq. (3)). The JWA outputs must satisfy,

$$\mathbf{y} = \mathrm{diag}(\mathbf{J}\mathbf{X}^{\pi}).$$

Each y_i is the dot product of row i of $\mathbf{J}$ with row i of $\mathbf{X}^{\pi}$.

If $\mathbf{J}$ were an arbitrary matrix, this system of equations would be massively under-determined: $\mathbf{y}$ provides k scalar constraints, while $\mathbf{J}$ has $k \times n$ free entries.

Fortunately, the JWA derivation of $\mathbf{J}$ is *not* entirely free: its rows are generated from two simplex-constrained vectors $(\mathbf{w}, \mathbf{v})$ and the observed permutations $\{\pi_i\}_{i=1}^{k}$. This makes the identification problem smaller in dimension, but still fundamentally *non-linear* because of the normalization in Eq. (3) and the permutation-dependent re-indexing of $\mathbf{w}$ across samples.

If we let all entries of $\mathbf{w}$ be distinct (as is done in our experiment in Sect. 5), then different evidence ordering permutations will lead to different ordered source-weights $\mathbf{w}_i^{\pi_i}$ with up to $n!$ unique joint weighting vectors $\mathbf{j}_i$. However, in practice, not all $n!$ orderings may be observed in a dataset, and even if they are observed, some can overlap when $\mathbf{w}$ has repeated components (so distinct permutations can generate the same $\mathbf{w}_i^{\pi_i}$ and thus the same $\mathbf{j}_i$). This directly ties identifiability to the diversity of permutations in the data: if the observed orderings are not rich or varied enough, multiple pairs $(\mathbf{w}, \mathbf{v})$ can yield identical input–output values.

Uncovering the conditions for uniqueness will therefore require a deeper understanding of the possible diversity of permutations that can manifest in training data. For intuition, consider an example with $n = 3$ sources and $k = 2$ samples. There are $n! = 3! = 6$ possible order permutations, and a training dataset can exhibit (possibly repeated) orderings, an example of such datasets are

$$C_a = \{(\mathrm{x}_1, \mathrm{x}_3, \mathrm{x}_2), (\mathrm{x}_2, \mathrm{x}_1, \mathrm{x}_3)\}, \quad C_b = \{(\mathrm{x}_2, \mathrm{x}_1, \mathrm{x}_3), (\mathrm{x}_2, \mathrm{x}_1, \mathrm{x}_3)\}$$

Here, a configuration C_m means the *multiset* of the k observed order permutations (i.e., which permutations appear, and with what multiplicities), while ignoring the order in which the samples are listed. Note that in this notation, having the evidence x_ℓ as the first element of the vector $(\ldots)$ means that source ℓ provided the evidence with the highest value and so on.

For a given number of sources n and samples k, the number of possible configurations is

$$\binom{n! + k - 1}{k}, \tag{7}$$

where $\binom{a}{b}$ (read 'a choose b') denotes the number of ways to select b items from a possibilities when the selection order does not matter; in our setting it counts multisets of size k drawn from the $n!$ possible order permutations with repetitions allowed. Note that Eq. (7) is the number of possible ways to form a joint order weight matrix $\mathbf{J}$ from specific LWA and OWA weight vectors. Although this number will grow quickly for large n and k, a detailed analysis for small n and k could pave the way to a general understanding of the conditions that lead to weight uniqueness. This is especially true if finding unique weight solutions is relatively efficient (with respect to usual metrics such as runtime/memory).

4 An Empirical Approach Towards Weight Uniqueness

Using simulation, we can construct all possible forms of $\mathbf{J}$ for a given $(\mathbf{w}, \mathbf{v})$ when n and k are small enough to remain tractable. This allows us to empirically test which order configurations yield unique LWA and OWA weights, and to examine the properties of configurations that do or do not lead to uniqueness. In this paper, we focus on the first task, identifying configurations that produce unique weights, and we leave a deeper analysis of why they do so for future work.

An overview of our devised method is that we first (i) generate a synthetic training data set. Then (ii) optimize the weights using an efficient supervised learning optimization algorithm. Finally, we (iii) probe the existence of more than one optimal pair of weight vectors ($\mathbf{w}$,$\mathbf{v}$) by leveraging multi-start optimization. In what follows, we describe each element in greater detail and then present the results of applying it to a subset of the general uniqueness question.

4.1 Synthetic Data Generation

The goal of data generation is to construct a dataset containing a prespecified number of samples, in which individual evidence values are random, but the overall outcomes are determined by a predefined set of LWA and OWA weights. The objective is then to recover these original weights from the simulated data and the JWA model.

We generate evidence matrices for n sources and k samples, while controlling the number of distinct order permutations per row. Specifically, we construct evidence matrices $\mathbf{X} \in \mathbb{Z}^{k\times n}$ such that, for each sample $i \in \{1,\ldots,k\}$, the relative order of the evidence values n between sources follows a prescribed permutation π_i of $(\mathrm{x}_l,\ldots,\mathbf{x}_u)$. In other words, we control for the number of samples that share the same ordering within the generated training data.

To construct all possible $\mathbf{J}$ for the given ($\mathbf{w}$,$\mathbf{v}$), the evidence values in $\mathbf{X}$ need to be assigned to sources according to the permutation π_i. More specifically, for each row i, we randomly draw n different evidence values from a bounded range. In general, evidence values can be any value in $\mathbb{R}$, but we bound them here since typical aggregation problems contain evidence values in a certain range. We then sort the evidence values in descending order to obtain $\mathbf{z}_i = (\mathrm{z}_{i,1},\ldots,\mathrm{z}_{i,n})$ with $\mathrm{z}_{i,1} > \cdots > \mathrm{z}_{i,n}$. We assign these ordered values to the n sources according to π_i. For example, if we randomly sampled $\mathbf{z}_2 = (97, 65, 8)$ and we had $\pi_2 = (\mathrm{x}_2, \mathrm{x}_1, \mathrm{x}_3)$, then $\mathbf{x}_2 = (65, 97, 8)$.

Note that in our experiments, we sample distinct values to avoid ties and ensure that each row induces a well-defined ordering. We avoid ties for simplicity and to focus on the core question of our current analysis. By choosing a set of $\{\pi_1,\ldots,\pi_k\}$, we can ensure we have datasets containing a small or large variety of order permutations, including multiple samples for the same ordering permutation or all-distinct orderings, which is central to probing uniqueness as discussed in Sect. 3.

Given the generated $\mathbf{X}$, the target outputs $\mathbf{y} \in \mathbb{R}^k$ are computed using fixed ground-truth weights $(\mathbf{w}, \mathbf{v})$ under the JWA model. Each row is ordered to form the overall ordered matrix $\mathbf{X}^{\pi}$, the corresponding permuted source-weight vector $\mathbf{w}^{\pi_i}$ is obtained, and the joint weights are computed through the perturbation operation, consistent with Eqs. (3)–(4). A diagram of the data generation procedure is shown in Fig. 1.

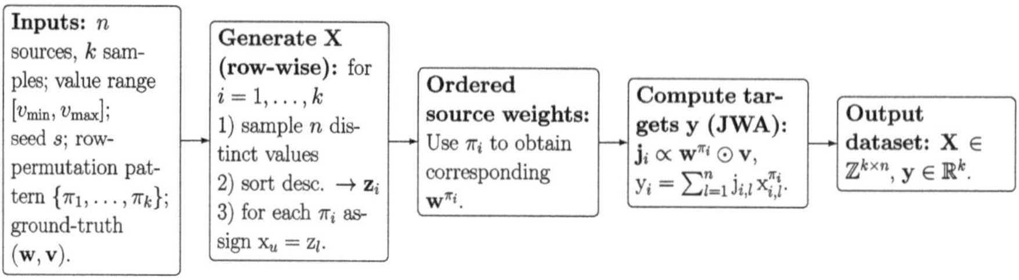

Fig. 1. A diagram of the synthetic data generation procedure.

4.2 Supervised Learning Optimization

Having described the training dataset generation process, in this section we formalize the supervised learning component of our analysis. Let n be the number of information sources, k the number of samples, $\mathbf{x}_i$ the input vector for the i-th sample, and y_i the ground truth value aggregated output of $\mathbf{x}_i$. Additionally, let $\hat{\mathbf{w}}$ and $\hat{\mathbf{v}}$ be candidate LWA and OWA weight vectors, respectively. Lastly, let $\hat{\mathrm{y}}_i$ be the output of a candidate JWA model with $\hat{\mathbf{w}}$ and $\hat{\mathbf{v}}$ applied to $\mathbf{x}_i$. From those definitions, the JWA weight learning problem can be formulated in a very general way as the following constrained optimization problem:

$$
\begin{aligned}
&\min_{\hat{\mathbf{w}}, \hat{\mathbf{v}}} \quad L(\hat{\mathrm{y}}_i, \mathrm{y}_i) \\
&\text{s.t.} \quad \sum_{l=1}^{n} \hat{\mathrm{w}}_l = 1, \quad \sum_{l=1}^{n} \hat{\mathrm{v}}_l = 1, \quad \hat{\mathrm{w}}_l \geq 0, \quad \hat{\mathrm{v}}_l \geq 0
\end{aligned}
\tag{8}
$$

where L is any loss function that measures the distance between the ground truth y_i and the estimated aggregate $\hat{\mathrm{y}}_i$. Efficiently solving this problem depends on the particular choice of L and the optimization technique but the overall procedure is well established.

In our experiments, we optimize Eq. (8) with mean squared error (MSE) loss and the limited memory Broyden–Fletcher–Goldfarb–Shanno (L-BFGS) algorithm. L-BFGS is a quasi-Newton method that incorporates curvature information by building an implicit approximation to the inverse Hessian from past gradient evaluations. In many smooth deterministic problems this can reduce the number of iterations compared to first-order methods such as gradient descent or Adam [9].

4.3 Multi-start Optimization and Solution Acceptance

For each synthetic dataset $(\mathbf{X}, \mathbf{y})$, our aim is to obtain reliable parameter estimates for weight vectors and to test whether the learning problem admits multiple distinct high-quality solutions (with respect to the LWA/OWA weights). Since gradient-based methods may converge to different optima depending on initialization, we perform N independent random restarts: in each trial we randomly initialize $(\hat{\mathbf{w}}, \hat{\mathbf{v}})$, run L-BFGS to minimize the training objective, and record the resulting candidate solution if it meets our success criteria. A solution is marked as successful if its final mean squared error (MSE) is below a small threshold ε. We choose ε to be stringent because the data are noise-free and the targets are produced by a JWA operator, consequently, an ideal fit should attain MSE ≈ 0.

Finally, by comparing the LWA and OWA weights estimates returned by successful restarts, we assess whether different initializations lead to *different* equally good solutions, rather than repeatedly converging to the same estimate of LWA and OWA weights.

Let $\mathcal{S}$ be the set of successful solutions returned by the N optimization restarts. To decide whether the dataset yields a unique identification, we calculate the standard deviation of each $(\hat{\mathbf{w}}, \hat{\mathbf{v}})$ in $\mathcal{S}$. In particular, for each weight component w_l and v_l, we look at how much that component varies across the accepted solutions by computing its standard deviation, and we take the largest standard deviation over all components and over both sets of weights. If this largest standard deviation is smaller than a chosen small tolerance σ, we decide that the solution is unique because all accepted runs are essentially converging to the same weight vector.

4.4 Testing the Empirical Approach: A Three-Source Experiment

We evaluate the proposed empirical approach for detecting uniqueness by applying it to a JWA weight-learning experiment with $n = 3$ information sources. For a given sample size k, the number of distinct ordering configurations is $\binom{3!+k-1}{k}$. Since $k = 1$ is trivially non-unique, we start at $k = 2$ and increase k incrementally. Because most configurations at $k + 1$ contain, as subsets, configurations already present at k, the additional benefit of increasing k diminishes beyond the smallest value at which some configurations yield uniquely identifiable LWA and OWA weights. Accordingly, we stop at the first such k. Table 1 lists the k values used in this experiment.

The following describes the exact experimental parameters. Evidence values are sampled as distinct integers from the range $[1, 100)$ (i.e., without replacement, thus avoiding ties), using 5 different random seeds $\{77, 57, 764, 89, 112\}$. Note that choosing certain seeds is done to ensure reproducibility.

Target values are computed from the generated $\mathbf{X}$ and the fixed ground-truth parameter vectors $\mathbf{w} = (0.6, 0.1, 0.3)$ and $\mathbf{v} = (0.45, 0.5, 0.05)$ using a python implementation of JWA based on *PyTorch*.

For each ordering configuration, we perform random restarts $N = 1000$ of the L-BFGS optimization algorithm as implemented in *PyTorch* `v2.8.0`. The L-BFGS parameters are set to default values with max iterations changed to 500 and line search changed to `strong_wolfe`. For numerical tolerances, we set $\varepsilon = 10^{-8}$ and $\sigma = 10^{-3}$. It should be noted that this experiment is designed to examine whether the proposed empirical approach can provide insight into the weight uniqueness problem, rather than to comprehensively cover all learning scenarios or mimic real-world data.

5 Empirical Results: Uniqueness in a Three-Source Scenario

Table 1. Empirical results summary for $n = 3$ across k with 5 different seeds (Sxxx). Total configuration counts are obtained from Eq. (7).

k	Total Configurations	Unique Weight Configurations				
		S77	S57	S764	S89	S112
2	21	0	0	0	0	0
3	56	0	0	0	0	0
4	126	44	50	46	44	43

A summary of results for the three-source setting ($n = 3$) are presented in Table 1. Across all five seeds, we observe no uniquely identifiable solutions for $k < 4$. In these datasets, multiple distinct pairs of LWA and OWA weights $(\hat{\mathbf{w}}, \hat{\mathbf{v}})$ consistently achieve a near-zero error (loss $L < 10^{-8}$) with standard deviations that are orders of magnitude greater than the threshold $\sigma = 10^{-3}$ (average maximum standard deviation $\overline{\sigma}_{\max} \approx 10^2\sigma$).

Figure 2 displays an example of non-unique LWA and OWA weight solution sets for $k = 3$. The three panels correspond to the three components of the OWA vector, with panel titles indicating the ground-truth values $\mathrm{v}_1 = 0.45$, $\mathrm{v}_2 = 0.5$, and $\mathrm{v}_3 = 0.05$. Additionally, in each panel, the horizontal black line marks the corresponding ground-truth v_l. Each accepted solution yields a pair $(\hat{\mathbf{w}}, \hat{\mathbf{v}})$. For a fixed panel l we plot $\hat{\mathrm{v}}_l$ (vertical axis) against each component $\hat{\mathrm{w}}_l$ (horizontal axis), using distinct markers for $l \in \{1, 2, 3\}$ (circles for $\hat{\mathrm{w}}_1$, squares for $\hat{\mathrm{w}}_2$, and triangles for $\hat{\mathrm{w}}_3$). Vertical reference lines indicate the ground-truth LWA weights $\mathrm{w}_1 = 0.6$, $\mathrm{w}_2 = 0.1$, and $\mathrm{w}_3 = 0.3$. The resulting scatter plot visualize how the accepted JWA solutions distribute in $(\hat{\mathbf{w}}, \hat{\mathbf{v}})$-space under stringent fit tolerance, supporting the empirical assessment of (non-)uniqueness via the dispersion criterion ($\sigma_{\max} < 10^{-3}$). It is evident from the figure that for the shown ordering configuration, multiple distinct solutions satisfy the acceptance threshold and have large standard deviations ($\sim 10^2\sigma$) across all weight components.

At sample size $k = 4$, uniqueness becomes possible, but only for a subset of the total 126 ordering configurations (see Table 1). Figure 3 shows an example from one of these unique solution sets. In contrast to Fig. 2, Fig. 3 shows the accepted runs collapsing to essentially single points in each panel. The points are tightly aligned with the ground-truth and exhibit far less dispersion (virtually zero, $\overline{\sigma}_{\max} < 10^{-3}$), consistent with a unique recovery of the ground-truth LWA and OWA weights $(\mathbf{w}, \mathbf{v})$ for that configuration.

Different seed values, which in turn yield different evidence values, appear to cause variation in the number of unique solutions identified by the standard deviation threshold. Across all seeds, there are 67 distinct configurations that

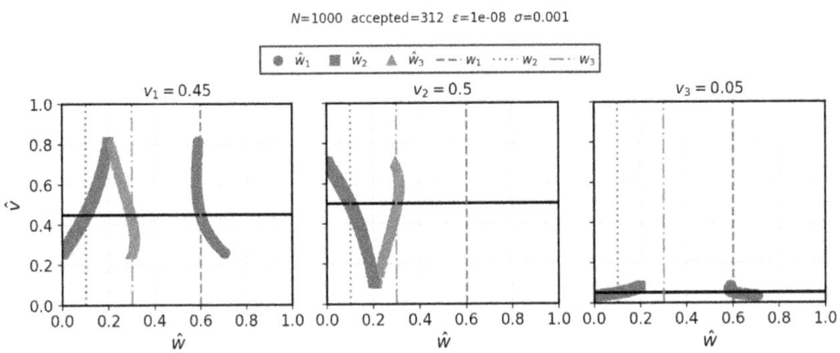

Fig. 2. Visualization of empirically-obtained optimal LWA and OWA weight sets in JWA aggregation. This is an example of a non-unique solution set ($n = 3$, $k = 3$, seed S89) with ordering configuration $\{(x_1, x_3, x_2), (x_2, x_3, x_1), (x_3, x_2, x_1)\}$.

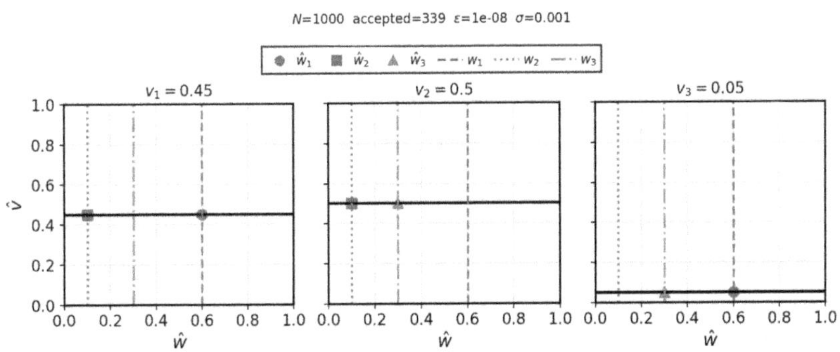

Fig. 3. Same as Fig. 2 but for an example unique solution set ($n = 3$, $k = 4$, seed S112) with ordering configuration $\{(x_1, x_2, x_3), (x_1, x_2, x_3)\ (x_2, x_3, x_1), (x_2, x_3, x_1)\}$.

produce a unique solution. Of these, 27 configurations consistently result in unique solutions for every seed (i.e., they are robust to changes in the evidence value). The mean pairwise Jaccard index (computed as the size of the intersection of unique-solution sets divided by the size of their union) is 0.65, suggesting a moderate degree of overlap in the configurations that lead to weight uniqueness between any two seeds.

6 Discussion and Conclusions

This paper addressed a prerequisite for using the Joint Weighted Average (JWA) as an interpretable aggregation model: whether supervised learning from input/output samples can recover a *unique* pair of weight vectors $(\mathbf{w}, \mathbf{v})$.

We present the JWA weight optimization task as a system of equations to reveal how its ordering-driven nonlinearity complicates an analytic expression of the conditions for unique solutions. We therefore introduced an empirical probe that generates controlled synthetic datasets, learns $(\hat{\mathbf{w}}, \hat{\mathbf{v}})$ via constrained optimization, and tests for non-uniqueness through multi-start learning and solution dispersion.

It is important to note that, although the empirical approach and the test experiment were sufficient to provide insight into the weight uniqueness problem, they also have several limitations.

For instance, the experiment use a fixed ground-truth parameterization. Different LWA and OWA weights (e.g., near-uniform weights, sparse/extreme weights, or boundary cases) could alter the prevalence of unique solutions and the geometry of the non-unique solution sets. We have shown the empirical results for the three-source scenario and small sample sizes. However, attempting to find general conditions for weight uniqueness will likely require conducting a similar analysis for multiple scenarios of n-sources with more values of k.

Moreover, uniqueness is assessed operationally through multi-start optimization in addition to acceptance/standard deviation thresholds (ε, σ). The characterization of LWA/OWA optimal weight sets, including the decision about whether a given set is unique, is sensitive to optimizer behavior, finite restart budgets, and numerical tolerances. Close-by optima may be considered unique or non-unique if their standard deviation falls slightly below or above the threshold, respectively. On the other hand, rare optima may be missed with finite restarts.

The results also suggest that the number of configurations that lead to weight uniqueness is dependent on the evidence values themselves. This variability was not expected, as a reasonable assumption is that evidence values should not play a strong role in determining whether a unique weight set is found or not. Our initial thoughts are that this might be partially explained by multiple numerical/precision artifacts of the empirical approach that are compounded together (see the limitations in the previous paragraph). Another possible explanation is that the affordability of unique solutions is in fact somewhat dependent on the numerical differences between the evidence value of each source and the aggregate value of the JWA. These two possible causes are not mutually exclusive. More detailed examination of the source of this variability will be carried out in future work.

It is important to emphasize that our empirical procedure, by definition, does not constitute a mathematical proof for conditions of uniqueness. An analytical characterization of when JWA weights are uniquely identifiable is challenging but not impossible. Pursuing such an analysis could yield a more robust and general understanding than empirical sweeps alone. One promising direction is to leverage tools from computational algebraic geometry. More specifically, after expressing the identification constraints as multivariate polynomial equations, one can analyze the solution set generated by reducing the equations to Gröbner basis utilizing the Bachberger algorithm [4,6].

Regardless of the limitations discussed, the empirical results presented in this paper provide the following clear insights:

1. Unique optimal LWA and OWA weights can be found in the JWA supervised learning setting.

2. There is a critical sample size that allows for uniqueness of the weights.
3. Some specific configurations of order permutations seem to produce unique weights, even when the evidence values are varied.

Notably, the final insight has implications in practical settings as it shifts attention from collecting more data to collecting or designing data that elicits sufficiently diverse orderings. This matters directly for the use-cases that motivated the development of JWA. If weights are to be interpreted as meaningful descriptors (e.g., source-worth and evidence-worth) for explanation or behavioral insight, then non-uniqueness complicates that interpretation, whereas suitably rich permutation structure enables a single, reproducible decomposition into the LWA and OWA weights $(\mathbf{w}, \mathbf{v})$.

Future work will focus on addressing some of the numerical artifacts/limitations in the current empirical approach to reach more robust findings. We plan to investigate why certain permutation configurations uniquely identify $(\mathbf{w}, \mathbf{v})$. Additionally, we hope to better understand why certain permutations might lead to uniqueness depending on the evidence. We aim to repeat this approach for other n scenarios/weight parameterizations and move from empirical observations to actionable conditions. Exploring the feasibility of translating both the explanations of why certain permutations induce uniqueness, and the results derived from other n-value settings into a general heuristic that predicts uniqueness based on the structure of the dataset, prior to any learning being performed.

Alongside this, we will explore relaxing idealized assumptions by incorporating noise and ties/near-ties, and by studying whether regularization or probabilistic learning can help with identification when uniqueness is weak or absent. Ultimately, such inquiries would support principled data collection and experimental design for JWA-based modeling, strengthening its use as both a flexible predictor and an explainable/behaviorally interpretable aggregation mechanism.

Acknowledgments. This study was funded by the joint *NSF* (SES-2343580) and *UKRI* (ES/Z000084/1) co-funded grant. We thank the anonymous reviewers for their suggested comments that improved some aspects of this article.

Disclosure of Interests. The authors have no competing interests to declare that are relevant to the content of this article.

References

1. Aitchison, J.: The statistical analysis of compositional data. J. Roy. Stat. Soc. Ser. B (Methodol.) **44**(2), 139–177 (1982). http://www.jstor.org/stable/2345821
2. Beliakov, G., Pradera, A., Calvo, T.: Aggregation Functions: A Guide for Practitioners, 1st edn. Springer, Cham (2008). https://doi.org/10.1007/978-3-540-73721-6
3. Broomell, S.B., Wagner, C.: The joint weighted average (JWA) operator. In: Ansari, J., et al. (eds.) SMPS 2024. AISC, vol. 1458, pp. 44–58. Springer, Cham (2024). https://doi.org/10.1007/978-3-031-65993-5_6

4. Buchberger, B.: A theoretical basis for the reduction of polynomials to canonical forms. SIGSAM Bull. **10**(3), 19–29 (1976). https://doi.org/10.1145/1088216.1088219
5. Cardin, M., Giove, S.: SDOWA: a new OWA operator for decision making. In: Esposito, A., Faundez-Zanuy, M., Morabito, F.C., Pasero, E. (eds.) Progresses in Artificial Intelligence and Neural Systems. SIST, vol. 184, pp. 305–315. Springer, Singapore (2021). https://doi.org/10.1007/978-981-15-5093-5_28
6. Cox, D.A., Little, J.B., O'Shea, D.: Ideals, Varieties, and Algorithms: An Introduction to Computational Algebraic Geometry and Commutative Algebra. Undergraduate Texts in Mathematics, 4th edn, corrected publication edn. Springer, Cham (2018). https://doi.org/10.1007/978-3-031-91841-4
7. Emrouznejad, A., Marra, M.: Ordered weighted averaging operators 1988–2014: a citation-based literature survey. Int. J. Intell. Syst. **29**(11), 994–1014 (2014). https://doi.org/10.1002/int.21673
8. Grabisch, M., Marichal, J.L., Mesiar, R., Pap, E.: Aggregation Functions. Encyclopedia of Mathematics and Its Applications. Cambridge University Press, Cambridge (2009)
9. Kingma, D.P., Ba, J.: Adam: a method for stochastic optimization. CoRR (2014)
10. Llamazares, B.: On generalizations of weighted means and OWA operators. In: Proceedings of the 7th Conference of the European Society for Fuzzy Logic and Technology (EUSFLAT-11), pp. 9–14. Atlantis Press (2011). https://doi.org/10.2991/eusflat.2011.114
11. Merigó, J.M., Gil-Lafuente, A.M., Martorell, O.: On the use of the uncertain induced OWA operator and the uncertain weighted average and its application in tourism management. In: 2009 Ninth International Conference on Intelligent Systems Design and Applications, pp. 856–861 (2009). https://doi.org/10.1109/ISDA.2009.239
12. Murray, B.J., et al.: Explainable AI for the Choquet integral. IEEE Trans. Emerg. Top. Comput. Intell. **5**(4), 520–529 (2021). https://doi.org/10.1109/TETCI.2020.3005682
13. Torra, V.: Weighted OWA operators for synthesis of information. In: Proceedings of IEEE 5th International Fuzzy Systems, vol. 2, pp. 966–971 (1996). https://doi.org/10.1109/FUZZY.1996.552309
14. Torra, V.: Learning weights for weighted OWA operators. In: 2000 26th Annual Conference of the IEEE Industrial Electronics Society. IECON 2000. 2000 IEEE International Conference on Industrial Electronics, Control and Instrumentation. 21st Century Technologies, vol. 4, pp. 2530–2535 (2000). https://doi.org/10.1109/IECON.2000.972396
15. Torra, V., Narukawa, Y.: Modeling Decisions: Information Fusion and Aggregation Operators (Cognitive Technologies). Springer, Heidelberg (2006). https://doi.org/10.1007/978-3-540-68791-7
16. Xu, Z.S., Da, Q.L.: An overview of operators for aggregating information. Int. J. Intell. Syst. **18**(9), 953–969 (2003). https://doi.org/10.1002/int.10127
17. Yager, R.: On ordered weighted averaging aggregation operators in multicriteria decisionmaking. IEEE Trans. Syst. Man Cybern. **18**(1), 183–190 (1988). https://doi.org/10.1109/21.87068

Imprecise Probabilities

A Polyhedral Approach to Learning Belief Functions from Imprecise Data

Václav Kratochvíl[1,2(✉)], Radim Jiroušek[1,2], and Milan Daniel[2,3]

[1] Faculty of Management, Prague University of Economics and Business, Jindrichuv Hradec, Czechia
radim@utia.cas.cz

[2] Institute of Information Theory and Automation, Czech Academy of Sciences, Prague, Czechia
velorex@utia.cas.cz

[3] Institute of Computer Science, Czech Academy of Sciences, Prague, Czechia
milan.daniel@cs.cas.cz

Abstract. We address the problem of learning belief functions from empirical data when observations may be imprecise. Our approach is based on the interpretation of belief functions as lower envelopes of sets of probability measures. Empirical data are first transformed into statistically justified lower bounds on event probabilities using confidence intervals. These bounds define a feasible polytope of belief functions compatible with the data. Since this polytope generally contains infinitely many belief functions, we propose to select representative solutions by optimizing linear criteria over the polytope.

Keywords: Belief function · Learning · Imprecise data · Jeffreys's confidence intervals · Convex polytopes · Linear programming

1 Introduction

Data-based belief function learning involves constructing a belief function that is consistent with empirical data. In this paper, we address situations in which some of the data may be uncertain, imprecise, or partially ambiguous. Unlike most probabilistic model learning approaches, ours naturally handles such data and utilizes all the information it contains.

This paper approaches the problem from a geometric perspective, representing belief functions as points in a multidimensional vector space. In this representation, all belief functions that are consistent with constraints derived from the data form a convex polytope.

In general, the information extracted from data does not directly define a belief function, but rather a set of admissible belief functions. Therefore, learning a belief function reduces to identifying the feasible polytope induced by these constraints and selecting a representative solution within it via an appropriate optimization criterion. The key feature of this approach is that the constraints

B. Vantaggi et al. (Eds.): IPMU 2026, CCIS 3019, pp. 147–160, 2026.
https://doi.org/10.1007/978-3-032-28994-0_11

derived from data and the considered selection criteria are all linear functions. This allows for efficient computation using linear programming solvers and provides a clear geometric interpretation of the solution space.

Statistical confidence intervals play a central role in deriving constraints from empirical data by providing interval estimates of event probabilities. In particular, Jeffreys confidence intervals (or other equally-tailed confidence intervals) provide the necessary information for constructing probability interval estimates. Combined with the accepted Fagin-Halpern semantics of the belief function, these intervals form the basis of the proposed process.

Only the lower bounds of the confidence intervals may be sufficient to define the required belief function. The reason for this will be clarified in Sect. 3.4, where the dual role of belief and plausibility is discussed.

The paper is organized as follows. Section 2 introduces the notation, and Sect. 3 presents the basic ideas of the proposed data-driven belief function learning approach. Section 4 describes the computational procedures based on polyhedral geometry. Section 5 reports results from computational experiments with artificially generated data, illustrating the three proposed optimality criteria and the efficiency of the computational procedures. The final section discusses open questions arising from this contribution.

2 Notation and Preliminaries

Let $\Omega = \{\omega_1, \dots, \omega_n\}$ be a finite frame of discernment. We denote by 2^Ω the power set of Ω.

Each *belief function* is uniquely determined by a *basic probability assignment*, which is a mapping

$$m : 2^\Omega \to [0, 1]$$

satisfying

$$m(\emptyset) = 0, \qquad \sum_{A \subseteq \Omega} m(A) = 1.$$

Subsets $A \subseteq \Omega$ such that $m(A) > 0$ are called *focal elements*. If all focal elements are singletons, the belief function (see below) will be referred to as a *Bayesian belief function*. Note that such a belief function coincides with a classical probability measure on Ω.

A basic probability assignment m and the corresponding *belief function* are linked by the following invertible transform:

$$bel_m(A) = \sum_{B \subseteq A} m(B), \qquad m(A) = \sum_{B \subseteq A} (-1)^{(|B|-|A|)} bel_m(B), \tag{1}$$

for all $A \subseteq \Omega$. The corresponding *plausibility function* $pl_m : 2^\Omega \to [0, 1]$ is given by

$$pl_m(A) = \sum_{B \cap A \neq \emptyset} m(B). \tag{2}$$

Belief and plausibility functions are related by the duality

$$pl_m(A) = 1 - bel_m(A^c), \tag{3}$$

where $A^c = \Omega \setminus A$ denotes the complement of A.

3 From Imprecise Data to Belief Functions

In this section, we describe the ideas behind the proposed process of data-based belief function learning. The process assumes the availability of empirical data, some of which may be noisy. More precisely: We assume that the data are produced by a random process that generates a series of outputs from a finite frame of discernment Ω. We assume that each trial produces exactly one element from the frame of discernment. However, due to limitations of the observation process, the outcome may not be identified uniquely. Instead, the observer reports a subset $B \subseteq \Omega$ such that $\omega \in B$, representing an imprecise observation of the true outcome. We call such a B a reported outcome. We assume that the reported set is the most specific one available from the observation, i.e., it contains exactly the information provided by that trial and no additional uncertainty/information is introduced.

The proposed belief function learning process is based on the Fagin–Halpern interpretation of belief functions [6]. According to this interpretation, belief and plausibility functions are viewed as the lower and upper envelopes of a family of probability measures, respectively. This interpretation suggests converting empirical data into inequalities that the probabilities of events must satisfy. Classical tools of mathematical statistics, namely confidence intervals, facilitate this transformation.

Thus, the proposed learning process is realized in two steps. First, information from data is condensed into a monotonic set function representing lower bounds on event probabilities. In the second step, this function serves as a basis for finding a resulting belief function that best fits these bounds.

In what follows, it is important to distinguish between the reported outcome and the actual outcome, which is always a single element $\omega \in \Omega$.

3.1 The Role of Confidence Intervals

To derive constraints on event probabilities, we consider, for each subset $A \subseteq \Omega$, an associated binary experiment indicating whether the true outcome ω belongs to respective A. (It is obvious that if $\omega \in A$ for k of total n realizations, then $\omega \in A^c$ for in $(n-k)$ realizations.) The probability that a single trial of the data-generating process produces an outcome satisfying $\omega \in A$ will be denoted by $p(A)$. Classical statistical methods provide point or interval estimates of this unknown parameter. For a given confidence level $1-\alpha$, a two-sided confidence interval $[a, b]$ for $p(A)$ provides lower and upper bounds such that, under repeated sampling, the interval contains the true value with probability $1-\alpha$.

Equivalently,

$$\Pr(a > p(A)) = \Pr(b < p(A)) = \frac{\alpha}{2},$$

where $\Pr(\cdot)$ refers to probability induced by the random sampling process, while $p(A)$ itself is a fixed (non-random) parameter.

Since we have accepted the generalized probability interpretation of belief functions, belief and plausibility functions can be viewed as the lower and upper envelopes of sets of probability measures. If we were to model only the aforementioned binary experiment, we could define

$$\text{bel}(A) = 1 - \text{pl}(A^c) = a, \quad \text{and} \quad \text{pl}(A) = 1 - \text{bel}(A^c) = b.$$

If $|\Omega| > 2$, we propose to apply the above binary construction separately to each pair $\{A, A^c\}$, $A \subseteq \Omega$. These interval estimates will serve as the basis for deriving constraints on belief functions in the subsequent sections.

Before explaining what to do with these confidence intervals, and how to use them to find a suitable belief function, let us illustrate the situation with a simple example.

3.2 Illustrative Example

Let $\Omega = \{\omega_1, \omega_2, \omega_3\}$ and consider a dataset of $n = 30$ independent trials. In each trial, exactly one element $\omega \in \Omega$ occurs, but the observation may be imprecise. Instead of the exact outcome, a subset $B \subseteq \Omega$ is reported, indicating that $\omega \in B$ and that no more specific information is available.

Let $o(A)$ denote the number of observations with reported outcome $A \subseteq \Omega$. The observations are summarized in Table 1. In 25 cases, the outcome was observed precisely. In 3 cases, it was only known that $\omega \in \{\omega_1, \omega_2\}$, i.e., $o(\{\omega_1, \omega_2\}) = 3$. In the remaining 2 cases, no information beyond $\omega \in \Omega$ was available, i.e., $o(\Omega) = 2$.

Table 1. Imprecise observations

Reported set A	$o(A)$
$\{\omega_1\}$	10
$\{\omega_2\}$	8
$\{\omega_3\}$	7
$\{\omega_1, \omega_2\}$	3
Ω	2

From Table 1, one can derive bounds on how many times each event $A \subseteq \Omega$ could have occurred. For example, the outcome ω_1 occurred at least 10 times (when observed precisely), but it could have occurred up to 15 times when ambiguous observations such as $\{\omega_1, \omega_2\}$ and Ω are taken into account. Similarly, ω_2 occurred at least 8 times and at most 13 times. More generally, for each subset $A \subseteq \Omega$, we can determine the minimal and maximal number of trials in which the true outcome belonged to A. These limits are listed in Table 2.

Table 2. Numbers of experiments producing element from $A \subseteq \Omega$

A	$k_{\min}(A)$	$k_{\max}(A)$
$\{\omega_1\}$	10	15
$\{\omega_2\}$	8	13
$\{\omega_3\}$	7	9
$\{\omega_1, \omega_2\}$	21	23
$\{\omega_1, \omega_3\}$	17	22
$\{\omega_2, \omega_3\}$	15	20
Ω	30	30

The minimal value $k_{\min}(A)$ counts observations that necessarily imply $\omega \in A$, while the maximal value $k_{\max}(A)$ includes all observations that are compatible with $\omega \in A$. More precisely,

$$k_{\min}(A) = \sum_{B \subseteq A} o(B) \qquad k_{\max}(A) = \sum_{B \cap A \neq \emptyset} o(B). \tag{4}$$

These quantities satisfy the complementarity relation

$$k_{\min}(A) = n - k_{\max}(A^c), \qquad \text{for all } A \subseteq \Omega. \tag{5}$$

Thus, $k_{\min}(A)$ and $k_{\max}(A)$ summarize the information provided by the data about how often the true outcome may have belonged to A.

For a fixed $A \subset \Omega$, Jeffreys's confidence interval [7] provides bounds on the probability $p(A)$ as a function of the number k of successes in n binomial trials. In the present setting, the exact value of k is unknown; we only know that

$$k \in [k_{\min}(A),\ k_{\max}(A)].$$

Since the bounds of Jeffreys's confidence interval[1] [2] are monotone in k (their values for selected k are listed in Table 3), the smallest admissible lower bound for $p(A)$ is obtained by evaluating the interval at $k_{\min}(A)$, while the largest admissible upper bound is obtained at $k_{\max}(A)$. These values are then used to construct the bounds on summarized in Table 4.

[1] The values of Jeffreys's confidence intervals are computed using the R function `qbeta`, which evaluates quantiles of the Beta distribution. In particular, the lower bound corresponds to the $\alpha/2$-quantile of the Beta distribution with parameters $(k{+}0.5,\ n{-}k+0.5)$, while the upper bound corresponds to the $(1-\alpha/2)$-quantile of the same distribution. In R, the lower bound is obtained as `qbeta(`$\alpha/2$`, `$k{+}0.5$`, `$n{-}k{+}0.5$`)`.

Table 3. Jeffreys confidence intervals for selected values of k in $n = 30$ binomial trials with $\alpha = 0.05$.

k	interval	k	interval	k	interval	k	interval
7	$\langle 0.111, 0.404 \rangle$	10	$\langle 0.186, 0.511 \rangle$	17	$\langle 0.390, 0.731 \rangle$	22	$\langle 0.559, 0.865 \rangle$
8	$\langle 0.135, 0.441 \rangle$	13	$\langle 0.269, 0.610 \rangle$	20	$\langle 0.489, 0.814 \rangle$	23	$\langle 0.596, 0.889 \rangle$
9	$\langle 0.160, 0.477 \rangle$	15	$\langle 0.328, 0.672 \rangle$	21	$\langle 0.523, 0.840 \rangle$	30	$\langle 0.920, 1.000 \rangle$

Table 4. Jeffreys's bounds for $p(A)$ computed from $k_{\min}(A)$ and $k_{\max}(A)$ ($\alpha = 0.05$).

A	$k_{\min}(A)$	$k_{\max}(A)$	$p(A)$ (Jeffreys')	
			lower bound	upper bound
$\{\omega_1\}$	10	15	0.186	0.672
$\{\omega_2\}$	8	13	0.135	0.610
$\{\omega_3\}$	7	9	0.111	0.477
$\{\omega_1, \omega_2\}$	21	23	0.523	0.889
$\{\omega_1, \omega_3\}$	17	22	0.390	0.865
$\{\omega_2, \omega_3\}$	15	20	0.328	0.814
Ω	30	30	0.920	1.000

3.3 Lower Bounds on Belief Functions

According to the Fagin–Halpern interpretation [6], a belief function bel_m can be viewed as the lower envelope of a family of probability measures compatible with the available evidence. This interpretation allows us to accept the probabilistic bounds derived in the previous section as constraints on belief functions. Thus, for each $A \subseteq \Omega$, we define a function $g(A)$ as the lower bound of Jeffreys's confidence interval evaluated at $k_{\min}(A)$. It provides a statistically justified lower bound on the probability $p(A)$, and therefore also for the sought-after belief function

$$\mathrm{bel}_m(A) \geq g(A).$$

The function g therefore provides a lower bound that any admissible belief function must satisfy. However, the function g usually does not satisfy the definition of a belief function and therefore cannot be used directly as a solution.

In the example above, the values of $g(A)$ correspond to the lower bounds reported in Table 4. Since any belief function satisfies $\mathrm{bel}(\Omega) = 1$, we set $g(\Omega) = 1$ without loss of generality.

3.4 Upper Bounds on Plausibility Functions

Analogously to the lower bound $k_{\min}(A)$, the data also induce an upper bound $k_{\max}(A)$ on the number of trials in which the true outcome could have belonged to A. Note that the definition of k_{max} (Eq. 4) closely corresponds to the definition of the plausibility function (see Eq. (2)), as both quantify the maximal support that can be assigned to the set A.

The plausibility function represents the upper envelope of the set of compatible probability measures. Therefore, it provides an upper bound on the probability $p(A)$ of the event A.

When equal-tailed confidence intervals are used, such as Jeffreys's intervals, an analogous dual relation holds for the corresponding probabilistic bounds. If $g(A)$ denotes the lower bound of the confidence interval for $p(A)$, then the corresponding upper bound can be expressed as $1 - g(A^c)$. It must satisfy

$$\mathrm{pl}_m(A) \leq 1 - g(A^c).$$

Using the well-known duality between belief and plausibility (see Eq. (3)), this inequality is equivalent to

$$\mathrm{bel}_m(A^c) \geq g(A^c),$$

which coincides with the previously derived constraint $\mathrm{bel}_m(A) \geq g(A)$. Therefore, the lower bounds $g(A)$ fully capture the information extracted from the data, and no additional constraints arise from the upper bounds.

4 Geometrical Approach to Belief Function Learning

In this section, data-based belief function learning is formulated as a geometric problem in the space of basic probability assignments. The key idea is to represent all belief functions consistent with a given set of constraints as a convex polytope and to interpret the final step of learning as the selection of a representative point from this polytope.

4.1 Polyhedral Representation

Our goal is to characterize the set of belief functions that satisfy the bounds induced by the data. Since both belief and plausibility functions are linear mappings of basic probability assignments, it is convenient to express all constraints directly in terms of the basic probability assignment m.

In particular, lower bounds on belief functions of the form $bel_m(A) \geq g(A)$ can be rewritten using Eq. (1) as linear inequalities

$$\sum_{B \subseteq A} m(B) \geq g(A). \tag{6}$$

As discussed above, upper bounds on plausibility do not provide any additional information. Therefore, the function g fully captures the information extracted from the data and represents the only set of constraints used in the second step of learning the belief function.

To exploit this structure, each assignment is represented by a vector

$$m = \big(m(A)\big)_{A \subseteq \Omega}.$$

This vector can be viewed as a point in the Euclidean space[2] $\mathbb{R}^{2^{|\Omega|}-1}$, where each coordinate corresponds to a non-empty subset $A \subseteq \Omega$.

The set of all basic probability assignments forms a polytope

$$\mathcal{M} = \left\{ m \in \mathbb{R}^{2^{|\Omega|}-1} \;\middle|\; m(A) \geq 0 \text{ for all } A \subseteq \Omega, \sum_{A \subseteq \Omega} m(A) = 1 \right\}.$$

In this geometric setting, finding a belief function bel_m such that $bel_m \geq g$ is equivalent to finding a point $m \in \mathcal{M}$ satisfying the linear constraints (6). This leads to the polytope

$$\mathcal{M}_g = \left\{ m \in \mathcal{M} \;\middle|\; \sum_{B \subseteq A} m(B) \geq g(A) \;\; \text{for all } A \subseteq \Omega \right\},$$

which we call the *feasible polytope.* It represents the set of all belief functions consistent with the imposed bounds.

Such a description of a convex set as the intersection of finitely many linear half-spaces is called its *H-representation.* For a general background on polyhedral representations and their properties, see, e.g., [11]. This formulation naturally enables the use of linear programming methods.

Example 1. Consider the imprecise observations summarized in Table 1 on the frame $\Omega = \{\omega_1, \omega_2, \omega_3\}$, with a total number of observations $n = 30$. For these values, Jeffreys confidence intervals for the binomial parameter $p(A)$ are computed with significance level $\alpha = 0.05$. The resulting bounds are reported in Table 4. In the construction of the feasible polytope, the lower endpoint of each interval (the fourth column of Table 4) is taken as the lower bound $g(A)$ (recall that we set $g(\Omega) = 1$).

The feasible polytope $\mathcal{M}_g$ is then defined as the set of all basic probability assignments m satisfying the standard belief-function constraints (i.e., non-negativity and normalization constraints) together with the dominance constraints (thus lower-bound constraints) $bel_m(A) \geq g(A)$ for all $A \subseteq \Omega$. For the present example, these conditions translate into the explicit system of linear constraints. The full system is given here explicitly for clarity.

Non-negativity constraints: $m(\{\omega_1\}) \geq 0$, $m(\{\omega_2\}) \geq 0$, $m(\{\omega_3\}) \geq 0$, $m(\{\omega_1, \omega_2\}) \geq 0$, $m(\{\omega_1, \omega_3\}) \geq 0$, $m(\{\omega_2, \omega_3\}) \geq 0$, $m(\{\omega_1, \omega_2, \omega_3\}) \geq 0$.

Normalization constraint: $m(\{\omega_1\}) + m(\{\omega_2\}) + m(\{\omega_3\}) + m(\{\omega_1, \omega_2\}) + m(\{\omega_1, \omega_3\}) + m(\{\omega_2, \omega_3\}) + m(\{\omega_1, \omega_2, \omega_3\}) = 1$.

[2] The empty set is excluded since $m(\emptyset) = 0$.

Lower-bound constraints: $m(\{\omega_1\}) \geq 0.186$, $m(\{\omega_2\}) \geq 0.135, m(\{\omega_3\}) \geq 0.111$, $m(\{\omega_1\}) + m(\{\omega_2\}) + m(\{\omega_1, \omega_2\}) \geq 0.523$,
$m(\{\omega_1\}) + m(\{\omega_3\}) + m(\{\omega_1, \omega_3\}) \geq 0.390$,
$m(\{\omega_2\}) + m(\{\omega_3\}) + m(\{\omega_2, \omega_3\}) \geq 0.328$.

4.2 Optimization

In the present setting, the polytope $\mathcal{M}_g$ is non-empty by construction, as the lower bounds g are derived from empirical data in a way that guarantees the existence of at least one compatible basic probability assignment. In particular, one may always construct a Bayesian belief function corresponding to a distribution induced by empirical frequencies. Hence, whenever the feasible polytope $\mathcal{M}_g$ is defined in the described manner from data, it is always non-empty.

In general, the feasible polytope $\mathcal{M}_g$ contains an infinite number of belief functions. To obtain a single representative, an additional selection criterion is required. When using a linear criterion function, the search for the best representation of the data using belief functions is naturally formulated as a linear optimization problem over the polytope $\mathcal{M}_g$. Such optimization problems over convex polytopes are well understood, and it is well known that linear objective functions attain their optima on faces of the feasible polytope [1].

Therefore, in this paper, we restrict to criteria that can be expressed as linear functions of the basic probability assignments:

$$\sum_{A \subseteq \Omega} w_A \, m(A), \tag{7}$$

where the coefficients w_A encode a specific preference over focal sets. This restriction allows the use of efficient linear programming solvers.

Different choices of the weight vector $(w_A)_{A \subseteq \Omega}$ correspond to different selection principles. In particular, we consider three linear criteria, denoted throughout the paper as L1, HD, and CW.

L1 Criterion. The L1 criterion corresponds to selecting a belief function that is as close as possible to the given lower bound g in terms of the L_1 distance, i.e., $\sum_{A \subseteq \Omega} |bel(A) - g(A)|$. As shown in [3], this is equivalent to *minimizing* the objective function (7) with weights $w_A = 2^{|\Omega|-|A|}$, i.e.,

$$\sum_{A \subseteq \Omega} 2^{|\Omega|-|A|} \, m(A).$$

HD (Entropy-Based) Criterion. To favor belief functions representing higher uncertainty, we consider the HD criterion, defined as the *maximization* of the Dubois–Prade measure of information [5],

$$\sum_{A \subseteq \Omega} \log_2 |A| \, m(A).$$

This criterion promotes mass allocation on larger subsets and yields more imprecise admissible dominating belief functions. In this case, the weights are given by $w_A = \log_2 |A|$.

Entropy-based measures for belief functions have been extensively studied, and their interpretation in terms of informativeness and imprecision has been critically discussed in the literature (e.g., [8]).

CW (Cardinality-Weighted) Criterion. The CW criterion is defined by weights $w_A = 1/|A|$ for $A \neq \emptyset$, i.e.,

$$\sum_{A \subseteq \Omega} \frac{1}{|A|} m(A).$$

In this case, the objective is *minimized.* This choice assigns larger weights to smaller subsets, which encourages solutions that place more mass on larger, more general focal sets. Similarly to the L1 and HD criterion, this leads to solutions that assign more mass to larger focal elements, thereby promoting belief functions with higher ignorance.

Although the three criteria differ in how they treat smaller sets, they lead to the same results in the following example with $|\Omega| = 3$. This is because in this trivial example, the respective function g is a belief function. As will be shown later such a situation is extremely rare when the cardinality of Ω grows.

Example 2. Table 5 illustrates the solutions of the linear optimization problems over the feasible polytope $\mathcal{M}_g$ constructed from the data from Example 1. All three considered criteria L1, HD, and CW, yield the same result in this case. Recall that o denotes the reported outcomes (taken from Table 1) and g the corresponding lower bound. The remaining columns in Table 5 present the corresponding belief functions and basic probability assignments corresponding to the optimal solutions of all three linear optimization problems.

Table 5. Optimal solutions for data taken from Table 1. All three criteria yield identical solutions.

A	o	g	bel_{L1}	m_{L1}	bel_{HD}	m_{HD}	bel_{CW}	m_{CW}
$\{\omega_1\}$	10	0.1860	0.1860	0.1860	0.1860	0.1860	0.1860	0.1860
$\{\omega_2\}$	8	0.1349	0.1349	0.1349	0.1349	0.1349	0.1349	0.1349
$\{\omega_3\}$	7	0.1109	0.1109	0.1109	0.1109	0.1109	0.1109	0.1109
$\{\omega_1, \omega_2\}$	3	0.5235	0.5235	0.2025	0.5235	0.2025	0.5235	0.2025
$\{\omega_1, \omega_3\}$	–	0.3901	0.3901	0.0932	0.3901	0.0932	0.3901	0.0932
$\{\omega_2, \omega_3\}$	–	0.3280	0.3280	0.0822	0.3280	0.0822	0.3280	0.0822
Ω	2	1	1	0.1903	1	0.1903	1	0.1903
L1 (minimum)				**2.6734**		2.6734		2.6734
HD (maximum)				0.6795		**0.6795**		0.6795
CW (minimum)				0.6842		0.6842		**0.6842**

5 Results from Experiments

In this section, we report on empirical experiments conducted to study how the proposed learning procedure behaves for increasing cardinalities of the frame of discernment. In particular, we examine whether different linear selection criteria lead to identical or distinct optimal belief functions, and how this behavior depends on the size of Ω.

We start with the case $\Omega = \{\omega_1, \omega_2, \omega_3, \omega_4\}$. The data used in this example are reported in the second column of Table 6, and the corresponding lower bound function g obtained from Jeffreysn's confidence intervals is reported in the third column.

The feasible polytope $\mathcal{M}_g$ was constructed (note that it has 11 451 vertices, illustrating its combinatorial complexity), and all three linear criteria introduced in the previous section were used to select representative belief functions. For each criterion, the resulting optimal basic probability assignment m is reported in Table 6.

Table 6. Optimal solutions for an example with $|\Omega| = 4$.

A	o	g	bel_{L1}	m_{L1}	bel_{HD}	m_{HD}	bel_{CW}	m_{CW}
$\{\omega_1\}$	16	0.1425	0.1526	0.1526	0.1526	0.1526	0.1425	0.1425
$\{\omega_2\}$	20	0.1901	0.1901	0.1901	0.2009	0.2009	0.1901	0.1901
$\{\omega_3\}$	8	0.0555	0.0640	0.0640	0.0640	0.0640	0.0555	0.0555
$\{\omega_4\}$	1	0.0015	0.0015	0.0015	0.0015	0.0015	0.0015	0.0015
$\{\omega_1, \omega_2\}$	–	0.3986	0.3986	0.0559	0.3986	0.0451	0.3986	0.0660
$\{\omega_1, \omega_3\}$	–	0.2398	0.2398	0.0232	0.2398	0.0232	0.2398	0.0418
$\{\omega_1, \omega_4\}$	–	0.1542	0.1542	0	0.1542	0	0.1542	0.0102
$\{\omega_2, \omega_3\}$	–	0.2912	0.2912	0.0370	0.2912	0.0262	0.2912	0.0455
$\{\omega_2, \omega_4\}$	–	0.2024	0.2024	0.0107	0.2025	0	0.2024	0.0107
$\{\omega_3, \omega_4\}$	–	0.0656	0.0656	0	0.0656	0	0.0656	0.0085
$\{\omega_1, \omega_2, \omega_3\}$	–	0.5120	0.5228	0	0.5120	0	0.5415	0
$\{\omega_1, \omega_2, \omega_4\}$	9	0.5414	0.5414	0.1305	0.5414	0.1412	0.5414	0.1204
$\{\omega_1, \omega_3, \omega_4\}$	–	0.2525	0.2525	0.0111	0.2525	0.0111	0.2600	0
$\{\omega_2, \omega_3, \omega_4\}$	16	0.5267	0.5267	0.2232	0.5267	0.2339	0.5267	0.2148
Ω	–	1	1	0.1000	1	0.1001	1	0.0925
L1 (minimum)				**4.6033**		4.6034		4.6108
HD (maximum)				0.9052		**0.9070**		0.8989
CW (minimum)				0.6183		0.6201		**0.6158**

All three linear criteria considered in this study tend to select solutions with more mass assigned to larger focal elements.[3] At the same time, the lower bound g imposes mandatory constraints on all subsets, in particular on singletons, which must receive at least the belief mass prescribed by g. As Table 6 shows, these lower bounds are often attained.

Although the three criteria share this general structural preference, they differ in how the remaining degrees of freedom within the feasible polytope are resolved. In particular, the CW criterion places relatively stronger emphasis on smaller focal sets than the HD criterion, and therefore tends to select solutions with relatively more mass on intermediate-size focal elements and less mass on the largest sets than the HD solution, as illustrated in Table 6.

We also conducted a series of numerical experiments to assess how often the three criteria (L1, HD, and CW) yield a triple of different optimal belief functions. In particular, we distinguish between cases where we received different belief functions with the same values of a given criterion and cases where we received different belief functions with different values of a given criterion. In more detail, although different criteria may select different optimal basic probability assignments, these assignments can attain the same value when evaluated using one of the objective functions. In such cases, the corresponding solutions lie on the same optimal face of the feasible polytope associated with that criterion. (The last three rows of Table 6 and Table 5 report the values of the respective objective functions for the obtained solutions.) We refer to the latter cases, where the optimal values differ, as *genuinely different* outcomes.

For the ternary frame $|\Omega| = 3$, the resulting lower-bound function g was always a belief function, and all three criteria therefore recovered the same solution.

For the quaternary case $|\Omega| = 4$, genuinely different optimal solutions were observed only very rarely. Specifically, among 5,000 randomly generated datasets constructed from both precise and ambiguous observations, such cases occurred only three times. The example discussed above is one of them.

The situation changes markedly for higher-dimensional frames. Starting from $|\Omega| = 5$, the proportion of such cases increases rapidly. Approximately 50% of randomly generated datasets in the five-element space led to genuinely different optimal solutions. This proportion increases to around 90% for $|\Omega| = 6$ and to approximately 99% for $|\Omega| = 7$. These frequencies should be interpreted as empirical observations obtained under the specific data-generation mechanism and selection criteria used in our experiments, and do not constitute a general theoretical claim.

Overall, these results indicate that as the dimension of the frame increases, the feasible polytope $\mathcal{M}_g$ becomes richer in structure. As a consequence, different

[3] This preference reflects a conservative modeling principle: larger focal sets encode imprecision inherent in the data, whereas concentrating mass on smaller sets would introduce unwarranted specificity (comming from the applied optimizing criteria) not justified by the observations.

linear objective functions are more likely to attain different optima, leading to genuinely distinct optimal belief functions.

These results confirm that the choice of selection criterion becomes increasingly important as the size of the frame grows.

6 Conclusions and Open Problems

The present paper should be understood primarily as a methodological and conceptual contribution: its aim is to formulate the polyhedral learning framework and to identify the main open questions that arise from it. In this paper, we proposed a polyhedral approach to learning belief functions from data based on lower bounds derived from confidence intervals. The method provides a natural link between statistical estimation and the theory of belief functions, and allows the set of admissible belief functions to be represented as a convex polytope.

From a computational perspective, the proposed procedure is very efficient for problems with small frame sizes. In particular, for frames up to $|\Omega| \approx 10$, all steps of the method can be performed very quickly in practice.

Nevertheless, for larger frames, the method can still be applied in a structured way by decomposing the problem into smaller subsets of variables. This naturally leads to structured models, such as belief networks [10] or compositional models [9]. Preliminary experiments in this direction, including polyhedral approximations of belief functions applied to real cybersecurity data [4], indicate that this approach is promising for practical applications.

The experimental results show that the choice of the selection criterion becomes increasingly important as the size of the frame grows. Thus, the problem of a proper criterion selection goes hand in hand with problems arising from the space complexity of belief functions.

Several open problems remain for future research. On the statistical side, the impact of the choice of confidence intervals (e.g., Jeffreys, Wilson, or Clopper–Pearson) on the resulting belief functions and the geometry of the feasible polytope deserves further investigation. In addition, when confidence intervals are applied simultaneously to a large number of subsets, it may be necessary to consider relaxed or approximate formulations that allow controlled violations of some constraints.

Another important direction concerns the selection criteria used in the optimization step. Although the L1, HD, and CW criteria share similar qualitative properties, their behavior differs in higher-dimensional settings, and it is not yet clear which criterion is most appropriate for a given application. This suggests studying broader families of criteria, as well as possible combinations of existing ones, in order to better capture different modeling preferences.

Finally, an important open problem is how to ensure consistency when combining locally constructed belief functions into larger models. Addressing this issue is essential for extending the proposed approach to high-dimensional applications.

Acknowledgements. This research was partially supported by the research programme of the Strategy AV21 AI: Artificial Intelligence for Science and Society.

References

1. Boyd, S., Vandenberghe, L.: Convex Optimization. Cambridge University Press, Cambridge (2004)
2. Crawley, M.J.: The R Book. Wiley, New York (2012)
3. Daniel, M., Jiroušek, R., Kratochvíl, V.: From confidence bounds to belief functions. Kybernetika (2025, submitted)
4. Daniel, M., Jiroušek, R., Kratochvíl, V.: How Sir Harold Jeffreys would create a belief function based on data. In: Proceedings of the 13th Workshop on Uncertainty Processing (WUPES'25), pp. 92–103 (2025)
5. Dubois, D., Prade, H.: Properties of measures of information in evidence and possibility theories. Fuzzy Sets Syst. **24**(2), 161–182 (1987)
6. Halpern, J.Y., Fagin, R.: Two views of belief: belief as generalized probability and belief as evidence. Artif. Intell. **54**(3), 275–317 (1992)
7. Jeffreys, H.: An invariant form for the prior probability in estimation problems. Proc. Roy. Soc. Lond. Ser. A. Math. Phys. Sci. **186**(1007), 453–461 (1946)
8. Jiroušek, R., Kratochvíl, V.: About twenty-five naughty entropies in belief function theory: do they measure informativeness? Int. J. Approx. Reason. 109454 (2025)
9. Jiroušek, R., Shenoy, P.P.: Compositional models in valuation-based systems. Int. J. Approx. Reason. **55**(1), 277–293 (2014)
10. Shenoy, P.P., Shafer, G.: Propagating belief functions with local computations. IEEE Expert **1**(3), 43–52 (1986)
11. Ziegler, G.M.: Lectures on Polytopes, vol. 152. Springer, Cham (2012). https://doi.org/10.1007/978-1-4613-8431-1

Weighted Total Variation Distances for Contextual Robustification

David Nieto-Barba[1(✉)], Sébastien Destercke[2], and Enrique Miranda[1]

[1] University of Oviedo, Department of Statistics and O.R., Asturies, Spain
{nietodavid,mirandaenrique}@uniovi.es

[2] University of Technology of Compiègne, Heudiasyc, UMR CNRS 7253, Hauts-de-France, France
sebastien.destercke@cnrs.fr

Abstract. This work investigates the robustification of probability measures, on finite-dimensional possibility spaces, through the family of Weighted Total Variation distances. This collection is indexed by a set of vectors of weights, each of which grades the willingness to change the probability initially assigned to each singleton, and embraces the Total Variation distance when the weights are uniform. Thus, these distances allow to create a neighbourhood around a probability measure taking into account the importance of singletons due to application-specific needs. After motivating the interpretation and potential applications of a robustifying procedure with such characteristics, we demonstrate explicit formulae for the extreme points of the neighbourhood models and the coherent lower previsions that characterise them. Finally, we show that these neighbourhood models are 2-monotone, essentially, if and only if the weights are uniform, and provide insights into future research directions.

Keywords: Robustification · Contextual distortion · Total Variation distance · Neighbourhood models · Credal sets · Lower previsions

1 Introduction

The vast majority of phenomena involving human decision-making are inherently subject to uncertainty, and experimental data and prior information are classically used to estimate precise probabilities accounting for the uncertainty in the experimental outcomes. However, to avoid misleading consequences of an erroneous elicitation/estimation process, decision-makers may want to consider a set of plausible probability measures that are "close" to the initially estimated model, thereby allowing them to make more robust decisions [7].

This notion of closedness may be captured through neighbourhood models [11,12], by means of a suitable distorting function quantifying the dissimilarity between probability measures. An example of such distorting function is the Total Variation distance [12]. While under this distance the difference on each

B. Vantaggi et al. (Eds.): IPMU 2026, CCIS 3019, pp. 161–175, 2026.
https://doi.org/10.1007/978-3-032-28994-0_12

singleton is equally pondered, the main goal of this paper is to illustrate the usefulness of modifying this ponderation, and to characterise the induced neighbourhoods through the lens of imprecise probability theory. Such modifications give rise to weighted versions [5, App.D] of the Total Variation distance, which enable the expression of varying degrees of relevance or reliability for the estimated probability on each singleton. In this way, it may be chosen beforehand how cautious one may want to be about the initial probability assigned to each singleton, permitting thus a contextual distortion in the spirit of [4,9,14].

This paper is structured as follows. In Sect. 2 we summarise the theoretical aspects that are used throughout the paper, while Sect. 3 synthesises our contributions in different subsections ranging from the motivation, formalisation and basic properties of Weighted Total Variation distances, to the analysis and characterisation of their extreme points and associated coherent lower previsions. We finally give some concluding remarks and establish future research lines in Sect. 4.

2 Preliminaries

Let $\mathcal{X} = \{x_1, \dots, x_n\}$ be a finite *possibility space* with cardinality $|\mathcal{X}| = n$. We denote by $\mathbb{P}(\mathcal{X})$ the set of probability measures on $\mathcal{X}$, which we shall identify with the standard $(n-1)$-simplex of the Euclidean space $\mathbb{R}^n$; hence, the former inherits the convexity and norm (and thus the topological) structures. We define $\mathbb{P}^*(\mathcal{X})$ as the set of probability measures satisfying $P(A) > 0$ for each non-empty *event* $A \subseteq \mathcal{X}$, and use $A \subset \mathcal{X}$ to refer to proper events.

Any closed and convex set $\mathcal{M} \subseteq \mathbb{P}(\mathcal{X})$ shall be called *credal set.* We use $\text{ext}(\mathcal{M})$ to denote the set of extreme points of $\mathcal{M}$, i.e. the set of probabilities in $\mathcal{M}$ that cannot be written as a non-trivial convex combination of two different elements in $\mathcal{M}$.

2.1 Coherent Lower Previsions and Probabilities

Let $\mathcal{L}(\mathcal{X})$ denote the set of real-valued functionals on $\mathcal{X}$, also known as *gambles.* A *lower prevision on* $\mathcal{L}(\mathcal{X})$ [1,16,17] is a functional $\underline{P} : \mathcal{L}(\mathcal{X}) \to \mathbb{R}$. Its associated credal set $\mathcal{M}(\underline{P})$ is formed by its dominating probability measures:

$$\mathcal{M}(\underline{P}) := \big\{P \in \mathbb{P}(\mathcal{X}) \mid P(f) \geq \underline{P}(f) \quad \forall f \in \mathcal{L}(\mathcal{X})\big\}, \tag{1}$$

where $P(f)$ stands for the expectation operator of the probability P on f.

Coherent lower previsions [10,17] may be defined as lower previsions $\underline{P}$ satisfying $\mathcal{M}(\underline{P}) \neq \emptyset$ and $\underline{P}(f) = \min\big\{P(f) \mid P \in \mathcal{M}(\underline{P})\big\}$ for all $f \in \mathcal{L}(\mathcal{X})$, and are in a one-to-one correspondence with non-empty credal sets. While such a $\underline{P}$ determines a non-empty credal set through Eq. (1), any non-empty credal set $\mathcal{M}$ univocally determines a lower prevision $\underline{P}$ satisfying $\mathcal{M}(\underline{P}) = \mathcal{M}$, by taking its *lower envelope on gambles*, i.e. $\underline{P}(f) := \min\big\{P(f) \mid P \in \mathcal{M}\big\}$ for each $f \in \mathcal{L}(\mathcal{X})$. The conjugate *upper* prevision on $\mathcal{L}(\mathcal{X})$ of a coherent $\underline{P}$, denoted by $\overline{P}$, is defined as $\overline{P}(f) := \max\big\{P(f) \mid P \in \mathcal{M}(\underline{P})\big\}$ for every $f \in \mathcal{L}(\mathcal{X})$.

A lower prevision $\underline{P}$ is called *2-monotone* [3] when it satisfies:

$$\underline{P}(f_1 \vee f_2) + \underline{P}(f_1 \wedge f_2) \geq \underline{P}(f_1) + \underline{P}(f_2) \quad \forall f_1, f_2 \in \mathcal{L}(\mathcal{X}),$$

where $\wedge, \vee$ refer to the pointwise minimum and maximum of gambles. 2-monotone lower previsions are in particular coherent whenever the normalisation conditions $\underline{P}(I_\emptyset) = 0$ and $\underline{P}(I_\mathcal{X}) = 1$ are satisfied.

Coherent lower probabilities are coherent lower previsions restricted to the set of indicator functions of events, $\{I_A \mid A \subseteq \mathcal{X}\} \subseteq \mathcal{L}(\mathcal{X})$. For each event $A \subseteq \mathcal{X}$, we use $\underline{P}(A)$ to denote $\underline{P}(I_A)$. By restricting the previous definitions to the indicator functions of events, we may analogously define the associated credal set, conjugate upper probabilities, coherence and 2-monotonicity for lower probabilities, and lower envelopes on events of non-empty credal sets.

Remarkably, while different coherent lower previsions may determine the same coherent lower probability through their restriction to events, it occurs that 2-monotone lower previsions are in a one-to-one correspondence with 2-monotone lower probabilities. In particular, the restriction to events of a 2-monotone lower prevision is a 2-monotone lower probability and has the same associated credal set.

2.2 Neighbourhood Models and the Total Variation Distance

Given $P_0 \in \mathbb{P}(\mathcal{X})$, a *distorting function* $d : \mathbb{P}(\mathcal{X}) \times \mathbb{P}(\mathcal{X}) \to [0, +\infty)$ and a *distortion parameter* $\delta \geq 0$, the *neighbourhood of* P_0 *through* d *with parameter* δ is defined as:

$$B_d^\delta(P_0) := \{P \in \mathbb{P}(\mathcal{X}) \mid d(P, P_0) \leq \delta\}. \tag{2}$$

A possible choice of a distorting function is a distance. We recall that a distance $d : \mathbb{P}(\mathcal{X}) \times \mathbb{P}(\mathcal{X}) \to [0, +\infty)$ satisfies the following properties:

(ia) $d(Q, P) = 0$ for certain $P, Q \in \mathbb{P}(\mathcal{X})$ implies that $P = Q$;
(ib) $d(P, P) = 0$ for each $P \in \mathbb{P}(\mathcal{X})$;
(ii) (Symmetry) If $P, Q \in \mathbb{P}(\mathcal{X})$, then $d(Q, P) = d(P, Q)$;
(iii) (Triangle inequality) For every $P, Q, R \in \mathbb{P}(\mathcal{X})$, it holds $d(Q, P) \leq d(Q, R) + d(R, P)$.

In particular, we may use as distorting function the *Total Variation distance* (henceforth abbreviated by TV-distance), which is given by:

$$d_{\mathrm{TV}}(P, P_0) := \max_{A \subseteq \mathcal{X}} |P(A) - P_0(A)| = \frac{1}{2} \sum_{x \in \mathcal{X}} |P(\{x\}) - P_0(\{x\})|, \tag{3}$$

where the last equality was proved in [8, Prop.4.2].

The TV-distance is continuous and convex (hence quasi-convex) with respect to its first argument. Consequently, the neighbourhood model it determines by Eq. (2) is a credal set [11, Prop.3.4].

Moreover, the lower envelope on events of $B_{d_{\mathrm{TV}}}^\delta(P_0)$, denoted by $\underline{P}_{\mathrm{TV}}$, is a 2-monotone lower probability [12, Prop.2.4], and as a consequence it holds that

$\mathcal{M}(\underline{P}_{\mathrm{TV}}) = B^{\delta}_{d_{\mathrm{TV}}}(P_0)$ [12, Thm.2.2]. This lower probability is known as the *Total Variation Model* [6, Sec.3] (TV-Model, for short) and is given by:

$$\underline{P}_{\mathrm{TV}}(A) := \max\left\{P_0(A) - \delta, 0\right\} \quad \forall A \subset \mathcal{X}, \quad \text{and} \quad \underline{P}_{\mathrm{TV}}(\mathcal{X}) := 1.$$

It is of particular interest for this work that, whenever $P_0 \in \mathbb{P}^*(\mathcal{X})$ and $\delta < \min_{x\in\mathcal{X}} P_0(\{x\})$ hold (conditions that guarantee $B^{\delta}_{d_{\mathrm{TV}}}(P_0) \subseteq \mathbb{P}^*(\mathcal{X})$), then $B^{\delta}_{d_{\mathrm{TV}}}(P_0)$ has exactly $n(n-1)$ extreme points [12, Prop.2.5], a computationally interesting property. In addition, under these assumptions, the lower envelope on gambles of this neighbourhood is given by [13,15]:

$$\underline{P}_{\mathrm{TV}}(f) := P_0(f) - \delta(\max f - \min f) \quad \forall f \in \mathcal{L}(\mathcal{X}). \tag{4}$$

3 Distorting Through Weighted Total Variation Distances

In this section, we first motivate the modifications of the TV-distance under which non-uniform weights may be considered for robustifying probability measures in preferential directions, and exemplify their use in a practical context. Our analysis begins with the formalisation and analysis of some of their basic properties, some of which allow us to construct neighbourhood models around probability measures. Then, we find closed expressions for the extreme points of these neighbourhoods and for the coherent lower previsions and probabilities associated with the corresponding neighbourhood models, proving also that when $n \geq 3$ the model is 2-monotone only for uniform weights.

There are many contexts in which we may aim for a non-uniform distortion of a precise model:

- P_0 may represent a distribution of resources, and we may want to allow for transfers of resources that depend on the initial wealth.
- If P_0 is in the interior of the simplex, we may want the neighbourhood to stay in the interior so as to avoid zero lower probabilities, and this would require a smaller distortion in the directions that are closer to the boundary.
- P_0 may represent normalised utilities in a multicriteria decision making problem, and we may use weights to highlight the importance of each of the criteria.

Another context of interest is illustrated in the following example.

3.1 Illustrative Example

A council of experts that prescribed a probability measure P_0 for the modelling of certain phenomenon may want to be cautious about the inferences and decision-making built upon that model, as these may be misleading due to mistakes of different nature in the elicitation process. To this aim, they may want to add imprecision by considering a neighbourhood around the initial model P_0, by means of Eq. (2) for a suitable distorting function, so that any probability in this set is considered plausible.

If the experts are equally unsure (or want to be equally cautious) about the value of P_0 on each singleton, a possibility is to use the TV-distance given by Eq. (3), since in this distance the differences between $P_0(\{x\})$ and $P(\{x\})$ for each $P \in \mathbb{P}(\mathcal{X})$ are equally weighted for any $x \in \mathcal{X}$. However, they may also want to change the weights so that the importance of the difference in one singleton increases or decreases with respect to the others. Our next example illustrates such a situation.

Example 1. Imagine that the governing authority in charge of the emergency services of a certain region want to be prepared in order to intervene in a situation of heavy rain, which may devastate several towns within this region. Being prepared for such an intervention in extreme situations requires the advance mobilisation of resources, accompanied by the corresponding economic cost, hence a balance should be found between excessive anticipation and passivity, given that the latter may lead to the loss of lives.

For simplicity, assume that climate experts prescribed, on the basis of the historical weather information and available methodologies of inference, the uniform probability on a three element possibility space $\mathcal{X} = \{x_1, x_2, x_3\}$, where $x_1 =$ "Dry", $x_2 =$ "Light rain" and $x_3 =$ "Heavy rain", i.e., $P_0 = (1/3, 1/3, 1/3)$.

Modifying Eq. (3), let us define $d(P, P_0)$, for each $P \in \mathbb{P}(\mathcal{X})$ and $\alpha_3 \geq 0$, as:

$$\frac{1}{2}\big|P(\{x_1\}) - P_0(\{x_1\})\big| + \frac{1}{2}\big|P(\{x_2\}) - P_0(\{x_2\})\big| + \alpha_3\big|P(\{x_3\}) - P_0(\{x_3\})\big|.$$

We remark that the just introduced parameter α_3 graduates in d the significance of the difference that P and P_0 assign to $\{x_3\}$, recovering for $\alpha_3 = 1/2$ the TV-distance. Figure 1 graphically represents in the simplex the neighbourhood $B_d^{\delta}(P_0)$ of radius $\delta = 3/20$ through Eq. (2), for different values of α_3.

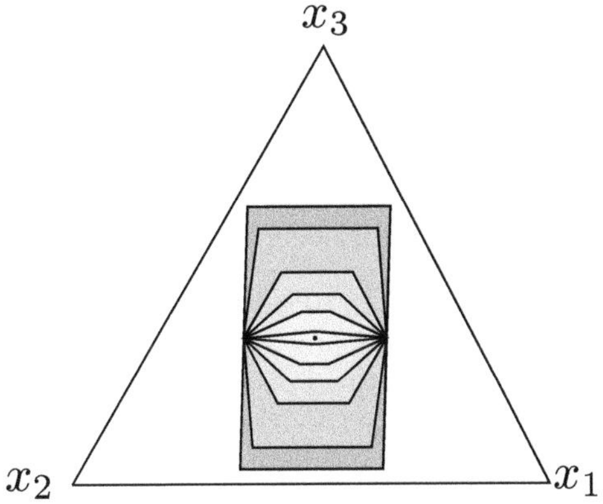

Fig. 1. Neighbourhoods with radius $\delta = 3/20$ for $\alpha_3 \in \{0, 0.1, 0.5, 1, 2, 10\}$ in Barycentric coordinates for Example 1.

Table 1. Lower and upper envelopes on singletons of the neighbourhoods in Example 1.

α	$\underline{P}(\{x_1\})$	$\overline{P}(\{x_1\})$	$\underline{P}(\{x_2\})$	$\overline{P}(\{x_2\})$	$\underline{P}(\{x_3\})$	$\overline{P}(\{x_3\})$
0	$0.0\widehat{3}$	$0.6\widehat{3}$	$0.0\widehat{3}$	$0.6\widehat{3}$	$0.0\widehat{3}$	$0.6\widehat{3}$
0.1	$0.08\widehat{3}$	$0.58\widehat{3}$	$0.08\widehat{3}$	$0.58\widehat{3}$	$0.08\widehat{3}$	$0.58\widehat{3}$
0.5	$0.18\widehat{3}$	$0.48\widehat{3}$	$0.18\widehat{3}$	$0.48\widehat{3}$	$0.18\widehat{3}$	$0.48\widehat{3}$
1	$0.18\widehat{3}$	$0.48\widehat{3}$	$0.18\widehat{3}$	$0.48\widehat{3}$	$0.2\widehat{3}$	$0.48\widehat{3}$
2	$0.18\widehat{3}$	$0.48\widehat{3}$	$0.18\widehat{3}$	$0.48\widehat{3}$	$0.27\widehat{3}$	$0.39\widehat{3}$
10	$0.18\widehat{3}$	$0.48\widehat{3}$	$0.18\widehat{3}$	$0.48\widehat{3}$	0.319..	0.347..

From Table 1 and Fig. 1 we observe that, as α_3 increases with respect to the value $\alpha_3 = 1/2$ (which gives the TV-distance), the neighbourhoods become narrower. Remarkably, this is done without altering the lowest and highest possible probability values on the singletons $\{x_1\}$ and $\{x_2\}$ of the TV-model, while the probability values possibly assigned to $\{x_3\}$ among the probabilities in the neighbourhood become more similar to $P_0(\{x_3\})$. On the other side, as α_3 decreases, the allowed disparity between $P(\{x_3\})$ and $P_0(\{x_3\})$, where $P \in B_d^\delta(P_0)$, is augmented. In contradistinction to the previous case, this forces the width of feasible values of $P(\{x_1\})$ and $P(\{x_2\})$ to be increased as well. We can however see that the resulting probability set is larger in the direction of $P(\{x_3\})$. ♦

3.2 Formalisation and Basic Properties

Given $\alpha := (\alpha_1, \dots, \alpha_n) \in \mathbb{R}^n$, we use the notation $\alpha \succeq 0$ (resp. $\alpha \succ 0$) to mean that $\alpha_i \geq 0$ (resp. $\alpha_i > 0$) for each $i \in \{1, \dots, n\}$.

Definition 1. *Let $\alpha := (\alpha_1, \dots, \alpha_n) \in \mathbb{R}^n$ be such that $\alpha \succeq 0$. We define $d_{\text{TV}}^\alpha : \mathbb{P}(\mathcal{X}) \times \mathbb{P}(\mathcal{X}) \to [0, +\infty)$ as:*

$$d_{\text{TV}}^\alpha(P, P_0) := \sum_{i=1}^n \alpha_i |P(\{x_i\}) - P_0(\{x_i\})| \quad \forall P, P_0 \in \mathbb{P}(\mathcal{X}),$$

*and call it the α-*Weighted Total Variation *(α-WTV, for short).*

The above definition gives the TV-distance for $\alpha = (1/2, \dots, 1/2)$ (i.e. $d_{\text{TV}}^\alpha = d_{\text{TV}}$ for this choice of α). In addition, any other vector of uniform weights gives a scalar transformation of the TV-distance. We also observe that the normalisation requirement $\sum_{i=1}^n \alpha_i = n/2$ (satisfied by the TV-distance) may be imposed in order to compare the neighbourhood models.

We stress that when a weight α_i is null for certain $i \in \{1, \dots, n\}$, then the value assigned by the α-WTV does not depend on the probabilities on the singleton $\{x_i\}$. Our first result determines the continuity, convexity and distance-like properties, and proves that if more than one weight is null, then d_{TV}^α is not a distance.

Proposition 1. *Let α and d_{TV}^{α} be as in Definition 1. Then, for any $P_0 \in \mathbb{P}(\mathcal{X})$, $d_{\mathrm{TV}}^{\alpha}(\cdot, P_0)$ is continuous and convex. Moreover, d_{TV}^{α} satisfies the distance properties (ib), (ii) and (iii), and it is a distance if and only if at most one of the weights in α is null.*

Proof (Sketch). Continuity and convexity and properties (ib), (ii), (iii) are easily shown to be satisfied for any $\alpha \succeq 0$. On the other hand, (ia) is clearly satisfied when $\alpha \succ 0$, whereas if there exists a unique $k^* \in \{1, \dots, n\}$ for which $\alpha_{k^*} = 0$, then $d_{\mathrm{TV}}^{\alpha}(P, P_0) = 0$ implies $P(\{x\}) = P_0(\{x\})$ for each $x \neq x_{k^*}$, so $P_0 = P$ holds.

Conversely, if there exist $k^*, j \in \{1, \dots, n\}$, with $k^* \neq j$ and $\alpha_{k^*} = \alpha_j = 0$, consider P_0 given by $P_0(\{x\}) = 1/n$ for all $x \in \mathcal{X}$, let $\beta \neq 1/2$ and $P_\beta \in \mathbb{P}(\mathcal{X})$ given by $P_\beta(\{x_{k^*}\}) = \frac{2\beta}{n}$, $P_\beta(\{x_j\}) = \frac{2(1-\beta)}{n}$ and $P_\beta(\{x\}) = P_0(\{x\})$, if $x \neq x_{k^*}, x_j$. Then, $d_{\mathrm{TV}}^{\alpha}(P_\beta, P_0) = 0$, but $P_\beta \neq P_0$. □

The convexity and continuity properties guarantee, together with (ib), that the neighbourhood model that d_{TV}^{α} determines through Eq. (2) is in correspondence with a coherent lower prevision. However, if more than one weight is null, then the neighbourhood $B_{d_{TV}^{\alpha}}^{\delta}(P_0)$ thus produced is never contained in $\mathbb{P}^*(\mathcal{X})$, not even when $P_0 \in \mathbb{P}^*(\mathcal{X})$ and $\delta = 0$. This undesirable behaviour, which is related to (ia) not being satisfied, leads us to discard this situation in the forthcoming subsections.

We also observe that, since $\mathbb{P}(\mathcal{X})$ is a polytope, the maximum value of the α-WTVs over all choices of P once P_0 has been fixed must be achieved (from the continuity and convexity properties and the compactness of the simplex) at some of its extreme points, $\mathrm{ext}(\mathbb{P}(\mathcal{X})) = \{P^{\{x_i\}} := I_{\{x_i\}} \mid i \in \{1, \dots, n\}\}$. Thus, from:

$$d_{\mathrm{TV}}^{\alpha}(P^{\{x_i\}}, P_0) = \alpha_i(1 - P_0(\{x_i\})) + \sum_{j|j\neq i} \alpha_j P_0(\{x_j\}) = \sum_{j|j\neq i} (\alpha_i + \alpha_j) P_0(\{x_j\}),$$

$\mathrm{ext}(\mathbb{P}(\mathcal{X}) \times \mathbb{P}(\mathcal{X})) = \mathrm{ext}(\mathbb{P}(\mathcal{X})) \times \mathrm{ext}(\mathbb{P}(\mathcal{X}))$ and $d_{\mathrm{TV}}^{\alpha}(P^{\{x_i\}}, P^{\{x_j\}}) = \alpha_i + \alpha_j$ for each $i, j \in \{1, \dots, n\}$ with $i \neq j$, we get the following result.

Proposition 2. *Let α and d_{TV}^{α} be as in Definition 1. Given $P_0 \in \mathbb{P}(\mathcal{X})$, there exists $i^* \in \{1, \dots, n\}$ for which*

$$\max_{P \in \mathbb{P}(\mathcal{X})} d_{\mathrm{TV}}^{\alpha}(P, P_0) = \sum_{j|j\neq i^*} (\alpha_{i^*} + \alpha_j) P_0(\{x_j\})$$

holds. Moreover,

$$\max_{P, P_0 \in \mathbb{P}(\mathcal{X})} d_{\mathrm{TV}}^{\alpha}(P, P_0) = \max_{i,j|i\neq j} \{\alpha_i + \alpha_j\}, \quad \text{hence} \quad R(d_{\mathrm{TV}}^{\alpha}) = \left[0, \max_{i,j|i\neq j} \{\alpha_i + \alpha_j\}\right],$$

where $R(d_{\mathrm{TV}}^{\alpha})$ denotes the range of d_{TV}^{α}.

3.3 Characterisation of Extreme Points and Lower Envelopes

We obtain now the extreme points of the neighbourhood model determined by the α-WTV-distances when this neighbourhood is included in $\mathbb{P}^*(\mathcal{X})$. In particular, we prove that the complexity of these neighbourhood models is the same as the TV-Model when all the weights are strictly positive, while it is smaller when only one weight is null.

Proposition 3. *Let α and d_{TV}^{α} be as in Definition 1. Given $P_0 \in \mathbb{P}^*(\mathcal{X})$ and $\delta > 0$, we distinguish two cases:*

Case 1. *If $\alpha \succ 0$ and*

$$\delta < \min\left\{(\alpha_i + \alpha_j)P_0(\{x_j\}) \mid i, j \in \{1, \dots, n\},\ i \neq j\right\} =: \overline{\delta}, \tag{5}$$

then:

$$ext\big(B^{\delta}_{d_{\mathrm{TV}}^{\alpha}}(P_0)\big) = \{P_{ij} \mid i, j \in \{1, \dots, n\},\ i \neq j\},$$

where, for each $i, j \in \{1, \dots, n\}$ with $i \neq j$:

$$P_{ij}(\{x\}) := \begin{cases} P_0(\{x\}) + (\alpha_i + \alpha_j)^{-1}\delta, & \text{if } x = x_i; \\ P_0(\{x\}) - (\alpha_i + \alpha_j)^{-1}\delta, & \text{if } x = x_j; \\ P_0(\{x\}), & \text{if } x \neq x_i, x_j. \end{cases} \tag{6}$$

As a consequence, $B^{\delta}_{d_{\mathrm{TV}}^{\alpha}}(P_0)$ has exactly $n(n-1)$ extreme points.

Case 2. *If $\alpha \succeq 0$, there exists a unique $k^* \in \{1, \dots, n\}$ for which $\alpha_{k^*} = 0$ and*

$$\delta < \min\Big\{ \min\left\{\alpha_i P_0(\{x_{k^*}\}) \mid i \in \{1, \dots, n\} \setminus \{k^*\}\right\}, \\ \min\left\{\alpha_j P_0(\{x_j\}) \mid j \in \{1, \dots, n\} \setminus \{k^*\}\right\}\Big\} =: \overline{\delta}, \tag{7}$$

then:

$$ext\big(B^{\delta}_{d_{\mathrm{TV}}^{\alpha}}(P_0)\big) = \{P_{k^*j} \mid j \in \{1, \dots, n\} \setminus \{k^*\}\} \cup \{P_{ik^*} \mid i \in \{1, \dots, n\} \setminus \{k^*\}\},$$

where P_{k^*j} and P_{ik^*} are given by Eq. (6). Therefore, $B^{\delta}_{d_{\mathrm{TV}}^{\alpha}}(P_0)$ has exactly $2(n-1)$ extreme points.

Proof (Sketch). Let us prove case 1 in first place. Indeed, for each $i, j \in \{1, \dots, n\}$ with $i \neq j$ it holds $P_{ij} \in \mathbb{P}(\mathcal{X})$, using the assumption $\delta < P_0(\{x_j\})(\alpha_i + \alpha_j)$, and moreover $d_{\mathrm{TV}}^{\alpha}(P_{ij}, P_0) = \delta$. In addition, $P_{ij} \in \mathrm{ext}\big(B^{\delta}_{d_{\mathrm{TV}}^{\alpha}}(P_0)\big)$: if this were not the case, there would exist $\beta \in (0,1)$ and $Q_1, Q_2 \in B^{\delta}_{d_{\mathrm{TV}}^{\alpha}}(P_0)$ such that $P_{ij} = \beta Q_1 + (1-\beta)Q_2$. It can be shown that this would imply:

$$\alpha_i(Q_l(\{x_i\}) - P_0(\{x_i\})) + \alpha_j(P_0(\{x_j\}) - Q_l(\{x_j\})) = d_{\mathrm{TV}}^{\alpha}(Q_l, P_0) = \delta,$$

for each $l \in \{1, 2\}$. As a consequence it holds:

(a) $Q_1(\{x\}) = Q_2(\{x\}) = P_0(\{x\}) = P_{ij}(\{x\})$ for each $x \in \mathcal{X} \setminus \{x_i, x_j\}$;
(b) $Q_1(\{x_i\}), Q_2(\{x_i\}) \geq P_0(\{x_i\})$ and $Q_1(\{x_j\}), Q_2(\{x_j\}) \leq P_0(\{x_j\})$;
(c) $\alpha_i\big[(Q_1(\{x_i\}) - P_0(\{x_i\})) - (Q_2(\{x_i\}) - P_0(\{x_i\}))\big]$
$= \alpha_j\big[(Q_1(\{x_j\}) - P_0(\{x_j\})) - (Q_2(\{x_j\}) - P_0(\{x_j\}))\big]$.

On the one side, (a) implies $Q_l(\{x_i\}) - P_0(\{x_i\}) = P_0(\{x_j\}) - Q_l(\{x_j\})$ for each $l \in \{1,2\}$, whence we obtain, together with (b):

$$K_l := Q_l(\{x_i\}) - P_0(\{x_i\}) = P_0(\{x_j\}) - Q_l(\{x_j\}) \geq 0 \quad \forall l \in \{1,2\}.$$

Thus, (c) boils down to $\alpha_i(K_1 - K_2) = -\alpha_j(K_1 - K_2)$, which implies, from the hypothesis $\alpha_i \neq 0 \neq \alpha_j$, that $K_1 = K_2$, hence $Q_1 = Q_2 = \beta Q_1 + (1-\beta)Q_2 = P_{ij}$. We conclude that $\{P_{ij} \mid i,j \in \{1,\ldots,n\},\ i \neq j\} \subseteq \operatorname{ext}\big(B^{\delta}_{d^{\alpha}_{\mathrm{TV}}}(P_0)\big)$.

On the other side, let $Q^* \in \operatorname{ext}\big(B^{\delta}_{d^{\alpha}_{\mathrm{TV}}}(P_0)\big)$, $\mathcal{X}_1 := \{x \in \mathcal{X} \mid Q^*(\{x\}) > P_0(\{x\})\}$, which is non-empty since $Q^* \neq P_0$, and define:

$$\mathbb{B} := \{Q \in \mathbb{P}(\mathcal{X}) \mid Q(\{x\}) \geq P_0(\{x\}) \text{ if } x \in \mathcal{X}_1, Q(\{x\}) \leq P_0(\{x\}) \text{ if } x \notin \mathcal{X}_1\},$$

which is non-empty as well from $Q^* \in \mathbb{B}$. In fact, $Q^* \in \operatorname{ext}\big(B^{\delta}_{d^{\alpha}_{\mathrm{TV}}}(P_0) \cap \mathbb{B}\big)$. Note that the probabilities Q in $B^{\delta}_{d^{\alpha}_{\mathrm{TV}}}(P_0) \cap \mathbb{B}$ are characterised by:

(C1) $0 \leq Q(\{x\}) \leq 1$ for each $x \in \mathcal{X}$;
(C2) $d^{\alpha}_{\mathrm{TV}}(Q, P_0) \leq \delta$;
(C3) $Q(\{x\}) \geq P_0(\{x\})$ for each $x \in \mathcal{X}_1$;
(C4) $Q(\{x\}) \leq P_0(\{x\})$ for each $x \notin \mathcal{X}_1$.

Since $Q^* \in \operatorname{ext}\big(B^{\delta}_{d^{\alpha}_{\mathrm{TV}}}(P_0) \cap \mathbb{B}\big)$, it must saturate $n-1$ linearly independent restrictions [2, Sec.2.2] among (C1)–(C4). We note that, by the assumptions on δ and P_0, none of the inequalities in (C1) is saturated, whereas (C2) must be saturated so, from (C3) and (C4), Q^* must be equal to P_0 in $n-2$ singletons; i.e., $|\mathcal{X}_1| = 1 = |\mathcal{X}_2|$, where: $\mathcal{X}_2 := \{x \in \mathcal{X} \mid Q^*(\{x\}) < P_0(\{x\})\}$.

Letting $x_{i^*} \in \mathcal{X}_1, x_{j^*} \in \mathcal{X}_2$ be the only elements in $\mathcal{X}_1, \mathcal{X}_2$, it must then hold $Q^* = P_{i^*j^*}$. Indeed, letting $K := Q^*(\{x_{i^*}\}) - P_0(\{x_{i^*}\}) = P_0(\{x_{j^*}\}) - Q^*(\{x_{j^*}\}) > 0$, it holds $\delta = d^{\alpha}_{\mathrm{TV}}(Q^*, P_0) = (\alpha_{i^*} + \alpha_{j^*})K$, thus $K = (\alpha_{i^*} + \alpha_{j^*})^{-1}\delta$, $Q^* = P_{i^*j^*}$ and case 1 is proved. Case 2 is proved in a similar way. □

Our next result shows that the restrictions over δ in the previous proposition characterise the radius for which the neighbourhoods are contained in $\mathbb{P}^*(\mathcal{X})$.

Proposition 4. *Let α and d^{α}_{TV} be as in Definition 1. Given $P_0 \in \mathbb{P}^*(\mathcal{X})$ and $\delta > 0$, let $\overline{\delta}$ be given by Eq.* (5) *or Eq.* (7)*, depending on the considered subcase for α as in Proposition 3. Then, $B^{\delta}_{d^{\alpha}_{\mathrm{TV}}}(P_0) \subseteq \mathbb{P}^*(\mathcal{X})$ if and only if $\delta < \overline{\delta}$.*

Proof (Sketch). From previous proposition, $\delta < \overline{\delta}$ entails $\operatorname{ext}\big(B^{\delta}_{d^{\alpha}_{\mathrm{TV}}}(P_0)\big) \subseteq \mathbb{P}^*(\mathcal{X})$, hence $B^{\delta}_{d^{\alpha}_{\mathrm{TV}}}(P_0) \subseteq \mathbb{P}^*(\mathcal{X})$ as well, both in case 1 and 2.

Conversely, in case 1, assume that $\delta \geq \overline{\delta}$ holds, where $\overline{\delta} = P_0(\{x_{j^*}\})(\alpha_{i^*} + \alpha_{j^*})$ for certain $i^*, j^* \in \{1, \ldots, n\}$ with $i^* \neq j^*$. The probability given by

$$Q(\{x\}) = \begin{cases} P_0(\{x\}), & \text{if } x \neq x_{i^*}, x_{j^*}; \\ 0, & \text{if } x = x_{j^*}; \\ P_0(\{x\}) + P_0(\{x_{j^*}\}), & \text{if } x = x_{i^*}, \end{cases}$$

satisfies $d^{\alpha}_{\mathrm{TV}}(Q, P_0) = (\alpha_{i^*} + \alpha_{j^*})P_0(\{x_{j^*}\}) = \overline{\delta} \leq \delta$, so $Q \in B^{\delta}_{d^{\alpha}_{\mathrm{TV}}}(P_0) \setminus \mathbb{P}^*(\mathcal{X})$.

Regarding case 2, if $\delta \geq \overline{\delta}$ holds and there exists $i^* \neq k^*$ such that $\overline{\delta} = \alpha_{i^*} P_0(\{x_{k^*}\})$, then the probability Q given by:

$$Q(\{x\}) = \begin{cases} P_0(\{x\}), & \text{if } x \neq x_{i^*}, x_{k^*}; \\ 0, & \text{if } x = x_{k^*}; \\ P_0(\{x\}) + P_0(\{x_{k^*}\}), & \text{if } x = x_{i^*}. \end{cases}$$

satisfies $d^{\alpha}_{\mathrm{TV}}(Q, P_0) = \alpha_{i^*} P_0(\{x_{k^*}\}) = \overline{\delta} \leq \delta$, thus $Q \in B^{\delta}_{d^{\alpha}_{\mathrm{TV}}}(P_0) \setminus \mathbb{P}^*(\mathcal{X})$. If, on the other hand, there exists $i^* \neq k^*$ such that $\overline{\delta} = \alpha_{i^*} P_0(\{x_{i^*}\})$ it suffices to define a probability Q as before, but assigning null probability to $\{x_{i^*}\}$ and adding this probability to $\{x_{k^*}\}$, to get the same conclusion. □

The explicit expressions for the extreme points obtained in Proposition 3 allow us to determine the lower envelopes on gambles of the neighbourhoods.

Proposition 5. *Let α and d^{α}_{TV} be as in Definition 1. Given $P_0 \in \mathbb{P}^*(\mathcal{X})$, let $0 < \delta < \overline{\delta}$, where $\overline{\delta}$ is given by Eq.* (5) *or Eq.* (7)*, depending on the considered subcase for α as in Proposition 3. Moreover, let $\underline{P}^{\alpha}_{\mathrm{TV}}$ the lower envelope on gambles of $B^{\delta}_{d^{\alpha}_{\mathrm{TV}}}(P_0)$. Then, for the case 1 it holds:*

$$\underline{P}^{\alpha}_{\mathrm{TV}}(f) = P_0(f) - \delta \max_{i \neq j} \left\{ |f(x_i) - f(x_j)|(\alpha_i + \alpha_j)^{-1} \right\} \quad \forall f \in \mathcal{L}(\mathcal{X}), \tag{8}$$

whereas in the case 2 we get:

$$\underline{P}^{\alpha}_{\mathrm{TV}}(f) = P_0(f) - \delta \max_{i \neq k^*} \left\{ |f(x_i) - f(x_{k^*})|\alpha_i^{-1} \right\} \quad \forall f \in \mathcal{L}(\mathcal{X}). \tag{9}$$

Proof. The lower envelope on a gamble is achieved on the extreme points. Hence, for case 1, Proposition 3 yields:

$$\begin{aligned} \underline{P}^{\alpha}_{\mathrm{TV}}(f) &= \min_{i \neq j} P_{ij}(f) = P_0(f) + \delta \min_{i \neq j} \left\{ (f(x_i) - f(x_j))(\alpha_i + \alpha_j)^{-1} \right\} \\ &= P_0(f) - \delta \max_{i \neq j} \left\{ |f(x_i) - f(x_j)|(\alpha_i + \alpha_j)^{-1} \right\}. \end{aligned}$$

Analogously, in case 2 we obtain:

$$\begin{aligned} \underline{P}^{\alpha}_{\mathrm{TV}}(f) &= \min \left\{ \min_{j \neq k^*} \{P_{k^*j}(f)\}, \min_{i \neq k^*} \{P_{ik^*}(f)\} \right\} \\ &= P_0(f) + \delta \min \left\{ \min_{j \neq k^*} \{(f(x_{k^*}) - f(x_j))\alpha_j^{-1}\}, \min_{i \neq k^*} \{(f(x_i) - f(x_{k^*}))\alpha_i^{-1}\} \right\} \\ &= P_0(f) - \delta \max_{i \neq k^*} \left\{ |f(x_i) - f(x_{k^*})|\alpha_i^{-1} \right\}, \end{aligned}$$

as claimed. □

We observe that in the case $\alpha = (1/2, \dots, 1/2)$, from Eq. (8) we get:

$$\underline{P}^{\alpha}_{\mathrm{TV}}(f) = P_0(f) - \delta \max_{i \neq j}\{f(x_i) - f(x_j)\} = P_0(f) - \delta(\max f - \min f) \quad \forall f \in \mathcal{L}(\mathcal{X}),$$

which, as it should be, is consistent with Eq. (4). This proposition also permits us to characterise the lower envelope on events of the neighbourhoods by evaluating Eqs. (8),(9) on indicator functions of events.

Corollary 1. *Let α and d^{α}_{TV} be as in Definition 1. Given $P_0 \in \mathbb{P}^*(\mathcal{X})$, let $0 < \delta < \overline{\delta}$, where $\overline{\delta}$ is given by Eq. (5) or Eq. (7), depending on the considered subcase for α as in Proposition 3. Moreover, let $\underline{P}^{\alpha}_{\mathrm{TV}}$ the lower envelope on events of $B^{\delta}_{d^{\alpha}_{\mathrm{TV}}}(P_0)$. Then:*

$$\underline{P}^{\alpha}_{\mathrm{TV}}(A) = P_0(A) - \delta\left(\min_{i|x_i \notin A} \alpha_i + \min_{j|x_j \in A} \alpha_j\right)^{-1} \quad \forall A \neq \emptyset, \mathcal{X}. \tag{10}$$

Proof (Sketch). For case 1, we let $f = I_A$ for $A \neq \emptyset, \mathcal{X}$, so Eq. (8) yields:

$$\begin{aligned} \underline{P}^{\alpha}_{\mathrm{TV}}(A) &= \underline{P}^{\alpha}_{\mathrm{TV}}(f) = P_0(f) - \delta \max_{i \neq j}\left\{|f(x_i) - f(x_j)|(\alpha_i + \alpha_j)^{-1}\right\} \\ &= P_0(f) - \delta \max_{\substack{i,j|x_i \notin A,\\ x_j \in A}}\left\{(\alpha_i + \alpha_j)^{-1}\right\} = P_0(A) - \delta\left(\min_{i|x_i \notin A} \alpha_i + \min_{j|x_j \in A} \alpha_j\right)^{-1}. \end{aligned}$$

On the other side, for case 2, given an event $A \neq \emptyset, \mathcal{X}$, from Eq. (9) it suffices to compute $\max_{i \neq k^*}\left\{|I_A(x_i) - I_A(x_{k^*})|\alpha_i^{-1}\right\}$. If $x_{k^*} \in A$, then this quantity equals:

$$\max_{i \neq k^*}\left\{\left(I_A(x_{k^*}) - I_A(x_i)\right)\alpha_i^{-1}\right\} = \max_{i|x_i \notin A}\left\{\alpha_i^{-1}\right\} = \left(\min_{i|x_i \notin A} \alpha_i\right)^{-1}.$$

Finally, $x_{k^*} \notin A$ yields the same result, replacing the index with $\{i \mid x_i \in A\}$ in the last expressions. We thus deduce that Eq. (10) holds as well, since $\alpha_{k^*} = 0$. □

Putting together the characterisation of the lower envelope on gambles and on events, we prove next that the associated credal sets do not coincide unless the weights are uniform or $n = 2$. Thus, the lower prevision (which characterises the neighbourhood) is 2-monotone only in these particular scenarios.

Proposition 6. *In the conditions and notation of the Corollary 1, it holds:*

$$B^{\delta}_{d^{\alpha}_{\mathrm{TV}}}(P_0) = \mathcal{M}(\underline{P}^{\alpha}_{\mathrm{TV}}) \Leftrightarrow \left[n = 2 \text{ or } \alpha_1 = \cdots = \alpha_n > 0\right]. \tag{11}$$

Consequently, $\underline{P}^{\alpha}_{\mathrm{TV}}$ is 2-monotone if and only if the previous condition holds.

Proof (Sketch). For $n = 2$, any coherent model is 2-monotone; while if all the weights coincide, we already know that the equality holds, since the neighbourhood is described by a TV-Model, modifying the radius when the constant is different from 1/2, so 2-monotonicity holds as well and the equality is satisfied.

Conversely, assume that $n > 2$ and there exist $i^*, j^* \in \{1, \ldots, n\}$ with $i^* \neq j^*$ and $\max_i \alpha_i = \alpha_{i^*} > \alpha_{j^*} = \min_j \alpha_j$, and let us prove that the equality does not hold. While $B^{\delta}_{d^{\alpha}_{\mathrm{TV}}}(P_0) \subseteq \mathcal{M}(\underline{P}^{\alpha}_{\mathrm{TV}})$ is satisfied in general, we aim to prove that there exists $P \in \mathcal{M}(\underline{P}^{\alpha}_{\mathrm{TV}}) \setminus B^{\delta}_{d^{\alpha}_{\mathrm{TV}}}(P_0)$.

For case 1, we distinguish two subcases. First, assume there exists $k^* \neq i^*, j^*$ such that $\alpha_{k^*} < \alpha_{i^*}$ and define the probability P determined by:

$$P(\{x\}) = \begin{cases} P_0(\{x\}), & \text{if } x \neq x_{i^*}, x_{j^*}, x_{k^*}; \\ P_0(\{x\}) - \delta(\alpha_{k^*} + \alpha_{j^*})^{-1}, & \text{if } x = x_{j^*}; \\ P_0(\{x\}) + \delta(\alpha_{i^*} + \alpha_{j^*})^{-1}, & \text{if } x = x_{i^*}; \\ P_0(\{x\}) + \delta(\alpha_{k^*} + \alpha_{j^*})^{-1} - \delta(\alpha_{i^*} + \alpha_{j^*})^{-1}, & \text{if } x = x_{k^*}. \end{cases}$$

Indeed, from the definition of i^*, j^*, k^*, it can be proven $P \in \mathcal{M}(\underline{P}^{\alpha}_{\mathrm{TV}})$, since $P(A) \geq \underline{P}^{\alpha}_{\mathrm{TV}}(A)$ is satisfied for each $A \subseteq \mathcal{X}$. However, $P \notin B^{\delta}_{d^{\alpha}_{\mathrm{TV}}}(P_0)$, since:

$$d^{\alpha}_{\mathrm{TV}}(P, P_0) > \alpha_{i^*}\delta(\alpha_{i^*} + \alpha_{j^*})^{-1} + \alpha_{j^*}\delta(\alpha_{k^*} + \alpha_{j^*})^{-1} > \delta$$

follows from $\alpha_{k^*} < \alpha_{i^*}$. Assume now that for each $k \neq i^*, j^*$ the equalities $\alpha_k = \alpha_{i^*} = \max_i \alpha_i$ hold. Letting k^* be any of these index k, we define

$$P(\{x\}) = \begin{cases} P_0(\{x\}), & \text{if } x \neq x_{i^*}, x_{j^*}, x_{k^*}; \\ P_0(\{x\}) + \delta(\alpha_{i^*} + \alpha_{k^*})^{-1} - \delta(\alpha_{i^*} + \alpha_{j^*})^{-1}, & \text{if } x = x_{j^*}; \\ P_0(\{x\}) + \delta(\alpha_{i^*} + \alpha_{j^*})^{-1}, & \text{if } x = x_{i^*}; \\ P_0(\{x\}) - \delta(\alpha_{i^*} + \alpha_{k^*})^{-1}, & \text{if } x = x_{k^*}. \end{cases}$$

As in the previous subcase, it can be prove $P \in \mathcal{M}(\underline{P}^{\alpha}_{\mathrm{TV}})$, while $P \notin B^{\delta}_{d^{\alpha}_{\mathrm{TV}}}(P_0)$ follows from $\alpha_{j^*} \leq \alpha_{k^*}$, which yields:

$$d^{\alpha}_{\mathrm{TV}}(P, P_0) = \delta\left(1 + \frac{\alpha_{k^*} - \alpha_{j^*}}{\alpha_{i^*} + \alpha_{k^*}}\right) > \delta.$$

We now prove that, in case 2, the aforementioned equality neither holds. For this, let $i^*, j^*, k^* \in \{1, \ldots, n\}$, where k^* is the unique weight for which $\alpha_{k^*} = 0$ and $i^* \neq j^* \neq k^*$. Define $P \in \mathbb{P}(\mathcal{X})$ as:

$$P(\{x\}) = \begin{cases} P_0(\{x\}), & \text{if } x \neq x_{i^*}, x_{j^*}, x_{k^*}; \\ P_0(\{x\}) - \delta\alpha_{i^*}^{-1}, & \text{if } x = x_{i^*}; \\ P_0(\{x\}) + \delta\alpha_{j^*}^{-1}, & \text{if } x = x_{j^*}; \\ P_0(\{x\}) - \delta\alpha_{j^*}^{-1} + \delta\alpha_{i^*}^{-1}, & \text{if } x = x_{k^*}, \end{cases}$$

which is such that $P \in \mathcal{M}(\underline{P}^{\alpha}_{\mathrm{TV}})$. However, $\alpha_{k^*} = 0$ yields $d^{\alpha}_{\mathrm{TV}}(P, P_0) = 2\delta$, hence $P \notin B^{\delta}_{d_{\mathrm{TV}}}(P_0)$.

It remains to prove the converse implication of the 2-monotonicity assertion. Since this property implies the equality in Eq. (11), a necessary condition for this equality to take place is that the weights are constant or $n = 2$, which concludes the proof. $\square$

Our next example illustrates the results obtained in this subsection.

Example 2. In the context and notation of Example 1, fixing $\alpha_3 = 1$, Fig. 2 represents $B^{\delta}_{d_{\mathrm{TV}}}(P_0)$ (Proposition 3) and its restriction to events $\mathcal{M}(\underline{P}^{\alpha}_{\mathrm{TV}})$ (Cor. 1). It holds $B^{\delta}_{d^{\alpha}_{\mathrm{TV}}}(P_0) \subsetneq \mathcal{M}(\underline{P}^{\alpha}_{\mathrm{TV}})$, which is the most usual situation (Proposition 6).

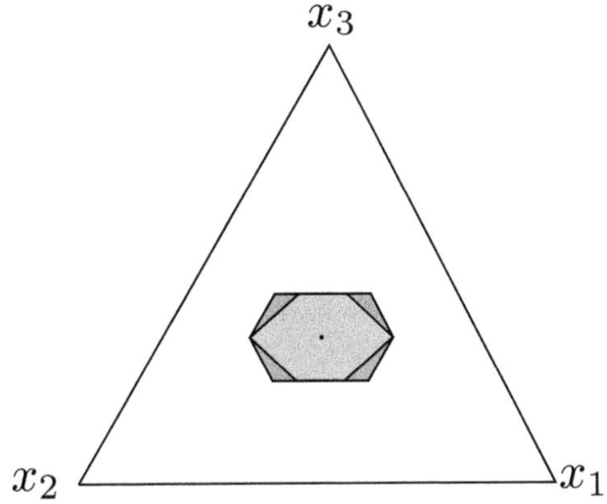

Fig. 2. Representation of $B^{\delta}_{d_{\mathrm{TV}}}(P_0)$ (lighter grey) and the credal set of its restriction to events, $\mathcal{M}(\underline{P}^{\alpha}_{\mathrm{TV}})$ (darker grey), in Barycentric coordinates for Example 2.

4 Conclusions and Future Lines

In this paper we have motivated and exemplified the use of WTV-distances for the contextual distortion or robustification of probability measures through the neighbourhood models that they determine. First, we proved the convexity, continuity, distance-like properties and the range of these weighted versions of the TV-distance, which in fact fail to be a distance whenever more than one weight is null.

Moreover, we characterised the radius for which the neighbourhoods of these distances are composed of strictly positive probability measures, provided that the initial probability also is. Under this assumption, we found closed expressions for their extreme points and the coherent lower prevision that characterise each of them. In combination to being nice mathematical characterisations, these provide efficient computational tools to reason with the proposed model. In doing so, we also found that the neighbourhoods of WTV-distances preserve the complexity of the TV-distance for strictly positive weights, while the number of extreme points is reduced when only one weight is null. This allowed us to compute in a exact manner the restriction to events and to prove that 2-monotonicity holds only when the weights are uniform or $n = 2$, thus the neighbourhoods rarely can be reduced to their lower envelope on events.

Our work opens a number of future research lines: continuing the analysis of the properties of these models, such as their invariance under conditioning; generalising the distances by considering weights that depend on the initial probability itself or extending them to the comparison of already imprecise models, following the work in [15]. We may also study their use in the aggregation of sources of information or opinion, probabilistic values in game theory, risk measures, optimal allocation of resources or multi-criteria decision-making.

Acknowledgments. We acknowledge the support by project PID2022-140585NB-I00 funded by MICIU/AEI/10.13039/501100011033 and "FEDER/UE", as well as funding from the UTC foundation for innovation given to the SAFE AI Chair. David Nieto-Barba is also funded by the Severo Ochoa predoctoral program by the Principality of Asturias NAC-AT-PUB-ASV-2025 BP24-18. We would also like to thank Ignacio Montes for his helpful comments.

Disclosure of Interests. The authors have no competing interests to declare that are relevant to the content of this article.

References

1. Augustin, T., Coolen, F., de Cooman, G., Troffaes, M. (eds.): Introduction to Imprecise Probabilities. Wiley Series in Probability and Statistics. Wiley, New York (2014)
2. Bertsimas, D., Tsitsiklis, J.: Introduction to Linear Optimization. Athena Scientific (1997)
3. de Cooman, G., Troffaes, M., Miranda, E.: n-Monotone lower previsions. J. Intell. Fuzzy Syst. **16**, 253–263 (2005)
4. Destercke, S.: A new contextual discounting rule for lower probabilities. In: Hüllermeier, E., Kruse, R., Hoffmann, F. (eds.) Proceedings of IPMU'10, Part II, pp. 198–207 (2010)
5. Douc, R., Moulines, E., Priouret, P., Soulier, P.: Markov Chains. Springer Series in Operations Research and Financial Engineering. Springer, Cham (2018). https://doi.org/10.1007/978-3-319-97704-1
6. Herron, T., Seidenfeld, T., Wasserman, L.: Divisive conditioning: further results on dilation. Philos. Sci. **64**, 411–444 (1997)
7. Huber, P.J.: Robust Statistics. Wiley, New York (1981)
8. Levin, D.A., Peres, Y., Wilmer, E.L.: Markov Chains and Mixing Times. American Mathematical Society (2009)
9. Mercier, D., Quost, B., Denoeux, T.: Refined modeling of sensor reliability in the belief function framework using contextual discounting. Inf. Fusion **9**, 246–258 (2008)
10. Miranda, E.: A survey of the theory of coherent lower previsions. Int. J. Approx. Reason. **48**(2), 628–658 (2008)
11. Montes, I., Miranda, E., Destercke, S.: Unifying neighbourhood and distortion models: Part I - new results on old models. Int. J. Gen Syst **49**(6), 602–635 (2020)
12. Montes, I., Miranda, E., Destercke, S.: Unifying neighbourhood and distortion models: Part II - new models and synthesis. Int. J. Gen Syst **49**(6), 636–674 (2020)

13. Moral, S.: Discounting imprecise probabilities. In: Gil, E., Gil, E., Gil, J., Gil, M.Á. (eds.) The Mathematics of the Uncertain. SSDC, vol. 142, pp. 685–697. Springer, Cham (2018). https://doi.org/10.1007/978-3-319-73848-2_63
14. Moral, S., del Sagrado, J.: Aggregation of imprecise probabilities. In: Bouchon-Meunier, B. (ed.) Aggregation and Fusion of Imperfect Information. Studies in Fuzziness and Soft Computing, vol. 12, pp. 162–188. Springer, Cham (1998). https://doi.org/10.1007/978-3-7908-1889-5_10
15. Nieto-Barba, D., Montes, I., Miranda, E.: The imprecise total variation model and its connections with game theory. Fuzzy Sets Syst. **517**, 109448 (2025)
16. Troffaes, M., de Cooman, G.: Lower Previsions. Wiley Series in Probability and Statistics. Wiley, New York (2014)
17. Walley, P.: Statistical Reasoning with Imprecise Probabilities. Chapman and Hall, London (1991)

Propagation of Interval Belief Structures and Imprecise Copulas for Neural Network Verification

Francesc Pifarre-Esquerda(✉), Eric Goubault(✉), and Sylvie Putot(✉)

LIX, CNRS, École polytechnique, Institut Polytechnique de Paris, Palaiseau, France
{francesc.pifarre-esquerda,goubault,putot}@lix.polytechnique.fr

Abstract. Quantitative verification of neural networks requires reasoning about probabilities under substantial uncertainty in both input distributions and their dependence structure. In realistic settings, this information is often only partially specified, and assuming precise probabilistic models can lead to unreliable results.

We propose a sound framework for quantitative verification under imprecise probabilistic information, combining interval belief structures to represent marginal uncertainty with imprecise copulas to model uncertain dependence. We develop a propagation method for imprecisely coupled interval belief structures through feed-forward neural networks. Using mixed imprecise copula volumes, we derive sound push-forward constructions through affine transformations and activation functions. The resulting output can provide guaranteed lower and upper bounds on probabilistic safety properties, valid for all probability models compatible with the specified imprecise inputs.

Keywords: Imprecise probability · Neural networks · Interval belief structures · Imprecise copulas · Verification

1 Introduction

Neural networks (NNs) are increasingly deployed in safety-critical and high-risk domains, making the verification of their behaviour a central concern. Over the past years, significant progress has been made in the qualitative verification of NNs, where one seeks to determine whether a given safety specification is satisfied or violated for all admissible inputs. Sound and scalable techniques based on abstract interpretation have been developed [12,19,22].

By contrast, quantitative or probabilistic verification of neural networks taking probabilistic elements of the inputs into account remains comparatively underdeveloped. A central challenge in these quantitative approaches to neural network analysis is to represent both marginal uncertainty of each input feature and uncertainty about the dependence structure between features while still enabling sound forward propagation through affine layers and non-linear activations. However, in realistic applications, input uncertainty is rarely known

B. Vantaggi et al. (Eds.): IPMU 2026, CCIS 3019, pp. 176–189, 2026.
https://doi.org/10.1007/978-3-032-28994-0_13

precisely as marginal distributions may be only partially specified, and assumptions about dependence can be heuristic or unjustified. Collapsing epistemic uncertainty into a single precise probabilistic model can lead to a false sense of confidence [1,6] and remains a key obstacle to deploying trustworthy and interpretable NN models [20].

This challenge is particularly relevant for probabilistic verification of NNs, where the objective is to bound the probability that a safety property holds under uncertain inputs. Existing approaches often rely on sampling-based methods [2,17,25], and therefore cannot provide guaranteed bounds. Recent guaranteed methods include probability stars [21], branch-and-bound algorithms [4], and Dempster-Shafer structures [8].

Imprecise probability theory provides a principled mathematical framework to address these issues by explicitly representing both aleatoric uncertainty (intrinsic randomness) and epistemic uncertainty (lack of knowledge). Rather than committing to a single probability distribution, uncertainty is modelled by credal sets consistent with available information. This approach has proved valuable in a variety of fields, including engineering analysis [3] or dynamical systems [9].

The central contribution of this work is the application of imprecise probability tools to the verification of NNs. We develop a sound propagation method for marginal interval belief structures joined by an imprecise copula through feed-forward neural networks. The propagation relies on imprecise copula volumes evaluated on conservative/optimistic quantile rectangles, yielding computable lower and upper bounds on the probability mass assigned to each input cell. We then derive push-forward constructions through affine transformations and activation functions to obtain both output marginal IBSs and an output imprecise copula that captures both the specified dependencies between inputs and dependencies induced by the network itself. This enables sound evaluation of probabilistic safety properties at the network output.

2 Imprecise Model: Marginal Interval Belief Structures and Imprecise Copulas

2.1 Interval Belief Structures

We use as basic imprecise probability structure the probability box [7], usually referred to as p-box in short. P-boxes represent the credal sets (sets of probability distributions) that lie between a pair of bounding or envelope CDFs. The probability distributions within the credal set capture the aleatoric element of uncertainty while the set itself represents the lack of full epistemic knowledge.

Performing operations on p-boxes can be done through convolutions [26], but analytical solutions to these are not generally available. To facilitate operations on p-boxes, Interval Dempster-Shafer structures (DSIs) are commonly used [7, 27]. DSIs offer discrete outer approximations of p-boxes and provide a way to perform sound approximations of arithmetic operations on them. They have also been applied to NN contexts in [8].

Interval Belief Structures (IBSs) further generalize these classical interval Dempster-Shafer structures by allowing the basic probability masses attached to focal sets to be imprecise and given in terms of intervals. They were introduced simultaneously as generalization of DSIs in [27] and focusing on their induced belief functions in [5]. IBSs have previously been successfully applied both to general evidential reasoning [24] and to domain specific tasks such as diabetes diagnostics [18]. In our propagation through neural networks, IBSs will be used as the basic unit of computation for marginal distributions.

Definition 1 (Interval belief structure). *Let $\mathcal{F} = \{F_1, \ldots, F_N\}$ be a family of non-empty subsets of $\mathcal{X}$, referred to as focal sets. An interval belief structure on $\mathcal{X}$ is specified by a collection of intervals*

$$I = \{\langle F_i,\, [\underline{m}_i, \overline{m}_i]\rangle \mid i = 1, \ldots, N\},$$

with $0 \leq \underline{m}_i \leq \overline{m}_i \leq 1$ for all i, together with the requirement that there exists at least one basic probability assignment m such that

$$m(F_i) \in [\underline{m}_i, \overline{m}_i], \quad i = 1, \ldots, N, \qquad \sum_{i=1}^{N} m(F_i) = 1,$$

which means that the IBS is not empty.

The set of all probability assignments compatible with the IBS I is the credal set of beliefs

$$\mathcal{M}(I) = \big\{m \mid m(F_i) \in [\underline{m}_i, \overline{m}_i],\ \sum_{i=1}^{N} m(F_i) = 1\big\}.$$

For an IBS to be well-defined, it needs to be non-empty in the credal set sense, meaning that its bounds must allow for at least one valid distribution. This non-emptiness property can be characterized as follows:

Proposition 1 (Non-emptiness of IBS). *A necessary and sufficient condition for the existence of at least one compatible m (non-emptiness of $\mathcal{M}(I)$) is $\sum_{i=1}^{N} \underline{m}_i \leq 1 \leq \sum_{i=1}^{N} \overline{m}_i$ as given in Proposition 1 of [5].*

Moreover, the idea of the normalization of IBS is also relevant. This relates to the tightness of the mass bounds with respect to their associated credal set. If an IBS is normalized, the mass bounds can be realized by a particular mass assignment or DSI within the credal set. We will aim to work with normalized IBSs for increased tightness and well-defined quantile grids in relevant calculations.

Definition 2 (Normalized interval belief structure). *Consider an interval belief structure $I = \{\langle F_i,\, [\underline{m}_i, \overline{m}_i]\rangle \mid i = 1, \ldots, N\}$ with $0 \leq \underline{m}_i \leq \overline{m}_i \leq 1$ for all i, and assume it is non-empty so that $\mathcal{M}(I) \neq \emptyset$.*

We say that I is a normalized interval belief structure (in the sense of Wang and Elhag [18, 23]) if:

$$\sum_{j=1}^{N} \overline{m}_j - (\overline{m}_i - \underline{m}_i) \geq 1 \quad \text{and} \quad \sum_{j=1}^{N} \underline{m}_j + (\overline{m}_i - \underline{m}_i) \leq 1, \qquad \forall i \in \{1, \dots, n\}.$$

Equivalently, for every i the whole interval $[\underline{m}_i, \overline{m}_i]$ consists of admissible values $m(F_i)$ for some $m \in \mathcal{M}(I)$. In this sense normalized interval belief structures form a tight representation of their associated credal set. This condition is also equivalent to: $\underline{m}_i = \inf_{m \in \mathcal{M}(I)} m(F_i)$ and $\overline{m}_i = \sup_{m \in \mathcal{M}(I)} m(F_i)$.

Proposition 2 (IBS normalization). *Let $I = \{\langle F_i, [\underline{m}_i, \overline{m}_i] \rangle \mid i = 1, \dots, N\}$ be an IBS. It can be normalized by retaking the mass bounds at each focal element i such that the bounds are given by:*

$$\max \left[\underline{m}_i, \ 1 - \sum_{j \neq i} \overline{m}_j \right] \ \leq \ m(F_i) \ \leq \ \min \left[\overline{m}_i, \ 1 - \sum_{j \neq i} \underline{m}_j \right], \qquad i = 1, \dots, N.$$

This construction has been adapted from Sect. 4 of [23].

In the semantics of probability distributions, IBSs induce belief functions on their elements. We restrict ourselves here to the unidimensional case where $\mathcal{X} = \mathbb{R}$ and all focal sets F_i are intervals. IBSs represent univariate distributions and their associated uncertainty. IBSs become DSIs in the "degenerate" or limit case where the upper and lower mass bounds coincide.

A p-box can be recovered from an IBS by taking the broadest envelopes possible. By doing so, a lot of extra information contained by the IBS on the internal structure of the resulting p-box credal set is lost, but the p-box credal set is an outer approximation of the original IBS.

Definition 3 (IBS belief, plausibility, and induced p-box). *Let I be an IBS with credal set $\mathcal{M}(I)$. For any $m \in \mathcal{M}(I)$ and $A \subseteq X$, we define $Bel_m(A) = \sum_{F_i \subseteq A} m(F_i)$, $Pl_m(A) = \sum_{F_i \cap A \neq \emptyset} m(F_i)$ which induce bounds:*

$$\underline{Bel}(A) = \inf_{m \in \mathcal{M}(I)} Bel_m(A), \quad \overline{Pl}(A) = \sup_{m \in \mathcal{M}(I)} Pl_m(A).$$

These define the IBS's CDF envelopes:

$$\underline{F}(x) := \underline{Bel}((-\infty, x]), \qquad \overline{F}(x) := \overline{Pl}((-\infty, x]).$$

It holds that $\underline{F} \leq \overline{F}$, both are non-decreasing, and $[\underline{F}, \overline{F}]$ is a p-box representing all distributions compatible with I.

To relate IBSs to copulas, we will use the quantile levels. These lie in the CDF codomain as the accumulated probability in each focal element. For IBSs, these quantile levels are imprecise and given only within intervals.

Proposition 3 (Quantile levels for IBS). *Let I be a normalized IBS. We define its quantile levels as given by its lower belief and upper plausibility:*

$$\underline{\alpha}_i = \max\left\{\sum_{k=1}^{i} \underline{m}_k \,,\, 1 - \sum_{k=i+1}^{N} \overline{m}_k\right\} \qquad \overline{\alpha}_i = \min\left\{\sum_{k=1}^{i} \overline{m}_k \,,\, 1 - \sum_{k=i+1}^{N} \underline{m}_k\right\}.$$

We use the boundary conventions $\underline{\alpha}_0 = \overline{\alpha}_0 = 0$ and $\underline{\alpha}_N = \overline{\alpha}_N = 1$.

Since the upper and lower masses need not add to 1, the second argument on the min/max assigns the minimum mass to the first i elements, unless the maximum/minimum mass of the remaining elements is not enough/too much to reach 1 for the last quantile level. This construction follows Definition 3 of [23].

We refer to the interval quantile bounds $[\underline{\alpha}_i, \overline{\alpha}_i]$ jointly as α_i. For quantile levels and IBSs indices to be well-defined we require a total order between the focal elements. By convention when working with p-boxes, we will take the lexicographical order on the pair given by the focal interval bounds [7].

2.2 Imprecise Copulas

The same arguments that justify the employment of imprecise probability structures to model marginal distributions can also be raised for imprecise dependence structures. Copulas allow to separate the information in the joint dependence of random variables and their marginal distribution through Sklar's seminal theorem [13]. Imprecise copulas allow us to do the same while accounting for uncertainty in their dependence.

The main result justifying our decision to employ IBS marginals joined by an imprecise copula, which we will refer to jointly as (imprecisely) coupled IBSs, is the extension of Sklar's theorem to the imprecise domain. Coherent imprecise copulas allow to relate imprecise marginals to imprecise multivariate distributions with results following from Sklar's seminal theorem for "precise" copulas [11,15,16]. In what follows, when we speak of coupled IBSs we mean a multivariate distribution such that each marginal basic probability assignment lies in the IBSs marginal credal sets and the dependence is described by some unknown copula C lying between the quasi-copula envelopes $\underline{Q} \leq C \leq \overline{Q}$.

This section introduces necessary structures and results to justify this modelling decision, and lays down the groundwork to later define the propagation of coupled IBSs through a NN. The basic building blocks of imprecise copulas are not properly copulas, but a relaxed version of them called quasi-copulas.

Definition 4 (Quasi-copulas). *For any point $(u_1, \ldots, u_{j-1}, u_{j+1}, \ldots, u_n) \in \mathbb{I}^{n-1}$ and any $t \in \mathbb{I}$ (respectively $\overline{\mathbb{I}}$). A n-dimensional quasi-copula Q is a function $Q : \mathbb{I}^n \to \mathbb{I}$ that satisfies the following conditions:*

(i) For every $j = 1, \ldots, n$ we have $Q(1, \ldots, 1, u_j, 1, \ldots, 1) = u_j$.
(ii) Q is increasing in each of its variables, i.e., for every $j = 1, \ldots, n$ and for every point $(u_1, \ldots, u_n) \in \mathbb{I}^n$ the value $Q(\mathbf{u})$ is non-decreasing as any u_j increases with the rest remaining fixed.

(iii) Q *is Lipschitz, i.e., if* $\mathbf{u}, \mathbf{v} \in \mathbb{I}^n$*, then* $|Q(\mathbf{v}) - Q(\mathbf{u})| \leq \sum_{j=1}^{n} |v_j - u_j|$.
(iv) for every $j = 1, \ldots, n$ *and for every point* $(u_1, \ldots, u_{j-1}, u_{j+1}, \ldots, u_n) \in \mathbb{I}^{n-1}$ *we have* $Q(u_1, \ldots, u_{j-1}, 0, u_{j+1}, \ldots, u_n) = 0$.

Quasi-copulas give the envelopes of the credal set which defines an imprecise copula. To have an imprecise copula, however, care is needed to ensure that they are well-defined. This refers to issues of non-emptiness and coherence, which remained open for some time after the original introduction of imprecise copulas in [11]. In essence, the original characterization of imprecise copulas given in [11] was shown to be flawed in that it allowed for imprecise copulas which had no copula within (counterexample given in [14]). Therefore we follow the tighter characterization of a well-defined imprecise copula of [14] and its generalization by the same authors to higher-dimensional cases in [16].

Definition 5 (Avoiding sure loss or non-emptiness). *We consider a pair of quasi-copulas* $(\underline{Q}, \overline{Q})$ *to avoid sure loss (or to be non-empty in the credal set sense) if there exists a proper copula* C *with* $\underline{Q} \leq C \leq \overline{Q}$.

Definition 6 (Coherent imprecise copulas). *We will call a pair* $[\underline{Q}, \overline{Q}]$ *of* n*-variate quasi-copulas a coherent imprecise copula if they are non-empty (avoid sure loss) and:* $\underline{Q} = \inf\{C \mid \underline{Q} \leq C \leq \overline{Q}\}$*, and* $\overline{Q} = \sup\{C \mid \underline{Q} \leq C \leq \overline{Q}\}$.

The infimum and supremum are taken pointwise with respect to the product order. This definition follows the characterization of multivariate imprecise copulas introduced after Th. 16 of [16]. We will call the quasi-copulas the bounds or envelopes of the imprecise copula.

We point out the similarity of the notion of a coherent imprecise copula to the normalization of an IBS: both require the envelopes describing the credal sets (either masses on IBS or quasi-copulas in the imprecise copula) to be tight. The volumes of imprecise copula, which will be used for propagation, generalize the precise copula volumes which are the measure induced by copulas on rectangles. For an imprecise copula, we can derive two dual induced volumes:

Definition 7 (Mixed imprecise copula volume). *Let* $[\underline{Q}, \overline{Q}]$ *be an imprecise copula and let*

$$P = [\underline{p}_1, \overline{p}_1] \times \cdots \times [\underline{p}_n, \overline{p}_n] \subseteq [0,1]^n$$

be a rectangle. We will refer to as the lower and upper mixed imprecise volumes of P*, denoted* $\underline{V}_{[\underline{Q},\overline{Q}]}(P)$ *and* $\overline{V}_{[\underline{Q},\overline{Q}]}(P)$ *as:*

$$\underline{V}_{[\underline{Q},\overline{Q}]}(P) = \sum_{\substack{\mathbf{p} \in \mathrm{vertices}(P) \\ \mathrm{sign}(\mathbf{p}) > 0}} \mathrm{sign}(\mathbf{p})\, \underline{Q}(\mathbf{p}) + \sum_{\substack{\mathbf{p} \in \mathrm{vertices}(P) \\ \mathrm{sign}(\mathbf{p}) < 0}} \mathrm{sign}(\mathbf{p})\, \overline{Q}(\mathbf{p})$$

$$\overline{V}_{[\underline{Q},\overline{Q}]}(P) = \sum_{\substack{\mathbf{p} \in \mathrm{vertices}(P) \\ \mathrm{sign}(\mathbf{p}) > 0}} \mathrm{sign}(\mathbf{p})\, \overline{Q}(\mathbf{p}) + \sum_{\substack{\mathbf{p} \in \mathrm{vertices}(P) \\ \mathrm{sign}(\mathbf{p}) < 0}} \mathrm{sign}(\mathbf{p})\, \underline{Q}(\mathbf{p})$$

where the sum is over all vertices $\mathbf{p} = (p_1, \dots, p_n)$ *with* $p_i \in \{\underline{p}_i, \overline{p}_i\}$, *and*

$$\text{sign}(\mathbf{p}) = \begin{cases} +1, & \textit{if}\, \mathbf{p} \textit{ has an even number of lower bounds } \underline{p}_i, \\ -1, & \textit{if}\, \mathbf{p} \textit{ has an odd number of lower bounds } \underline{p}_i. \end{cases}$$

These mixed volumes are based on the L operator of [14], which corresponds to our $\overline{V}_{[\underline{Q},\overline{Q}]}$, and $\underline{V}_{[\underline{Q},\overline{Q}]}$ is constructed as its dual counterpart. As $\underline{Q} = \overline{Q} = C$, we have a precise copula (if the more restrictive copula axioms are satisfied for C). Then $\underline{V}_{[\underline{Q},\overline{Q}]}(P) = \overline{V}_{[\underline{Q},\overline{Q}]}(P) = V_C(P)$ gives the standard copula volume. For quasi-copula bounds, $\underline{V}_{[\underline{Q},\overline{Q}]}(P)$ may be negative as quasi-copulas need not be n-increasing. Also note that while the usual copula volume is a measure and additive with respect to disjoint unions of rectangles, the mixed imprecise copula volumes are not. Neither of the mixed volumes is a proper measure and $\overline{V}_{[\underline{Q},\overline{Q}]}$ is only super-additive while $\underline{V}_{[\underline{Q},\overline{Q}]}$ is sub-additive.

Mixed volumes will be key in our arithmetic to propagate coupled IBSs, but are also useful in the characterizations of the non-emptiness, and therefore the coherence, of an imprecise copula, by Theorem 1.

Proposition 4 (Mixed volumes order). *Let* $[\underline{Q}, \overline{Q}]$ *be an imprecise copula and* $C \in [\underline{Q}, \overline{Q}]$. *For any rectangle* R: $\underline{V}_{[\underline{Q},\overline{Q}]}(R) \leq V_C(R) \leq \overline{V}_{[\underline{Q},\overline{Q}]}(R)$.

Theorem 1 (Characterization of non-emptiness). *Let* $\underline{Q} \leq \overline{Q}$ *be (discrete) quasi-copulas defined on* $D \subseteq \mathbb{I}^n$. *Then, there exists a copula* C *defined on* D *with* $\underline{Q} \leq C \leq \overline{Q}$ *if and only if* $\overline{V}_{[\underline{Q},\overline{Q}]} \geq 0$ *for all* $R \in \mathcal{R}_D$ *(set of all finite disjoint unions of rectangles with vertices on* D*). This result corresponds to Theorem 15 of [16] adapted to our notation.*

3 Propagation Through Neural Networks

In this section, we propagate IBSs and imprecise copulas through feed-forward neural networks in such a way that they over-approximate the distributions of the random variables in each layer. Two operations are composed to define an arbitrary feed-forward neural network: affine steps and activation functions.

Definition 8 (Feed-forward Neural Network). *We consider an* $L-$*layer fully-connected feed-forward neural network, for* $L \in \mathbb{N}$ *and* $h_0, \dots, h_L \in \mathbb{N}$ *the layer widths, specified by* $\{(W^k, b^k, \sigma^k)\}_{k=0}^{L-1}$, *where for each layer* $k = 0, \dots, L-1$, $W^k \in \mathbb{R}^{h_{k+1} \times h_k}$, *and* $\sigma^k : \mathbb{R}^{h_{k+1}} \to \mathbb{R}^{h_{k+1}}$ *is an activation map applied coordinate-wise:* $\sigma^k(s) = (\sigma_1^k(s_1), \dots, \sigma_{h_{k+1}}^k(s_{h_{k+1}}))$ *for* $s \in \mathbb{R}^{h_{k+1}}$.

Given an input $x = x^0 \in \mathbb{R}^{h_0}$, *the network output* $f_\theta(x) \in \mathbb{R}^{h_L}$ *is defined recursively as:* $s^{k+1} = W^k x^k + b^k$, $x^{k+1} = \sigma^k(s^{k+1})$, *for* $k = 0, \dots, L-1$, *and* $f_\theta(x) := x^L$. *We denote the corresponding random vectors in the propagation as:* $\mathbf{X}^0 := \mathbf{X}$, $\mathbf{S}^{k+1} := W^k \mathbf{X}^k + b^k$, $\mathbf{X}^{k+1} := \sigma^k(\mathbf{S}^{k+1})$.

First, we will define how to soundly apply the operation, affine or activation, on our marginal distributions represented by the IBSs. Secondly, we develop push-forward constructions to propagate the imprecise copulas through the same operations. We refer to this propagation method as a push-forward as the constructions propagate the quasi-copula envelopes through their induced volume on select rectangles defined on the IBS's quantile levels.

3.1 Affine Step

Let $(X_i)_{i=1}^n$ be represented by normalized IBSs $I_{X_i} = \{\mathbf{x}^i_{j_i}, \mathbf{m}^i_{j_i}\}$, where j_i will be used as a running index iterating over the focal elements of the different marginals X_i. Also let $(X_i)_{i=1}^n$ be coupled by the multivariate imprecise copula with envelopes $[\underline{Q}, \overline{Q}]$ and with associated quantile levels $[\underline{\alpha}^i_{j_i}, \overline{\alpha}^i_{j_i}]$. We define two possible rectangles upon which we will calculate the mixed copula volume: a lower and upper one:

$$\underline{R}_{j_1,\ldots,j_n} = {}^{\;n}_{i=2}[\overline{\alpha}^i_{j_i-1}, \underline{\alpha}^i_{j_i}] \quad \text{and} \quad \overline{R}_{j_1,\ldots,j_n} = {}^{\;n}_{i=2}[\underline{\alpha}^i_{j_i-1}, \overline{\alpha}^i_{j_i}]$$

Note that $\underline{R}j_1, \ldots, j_n$ uses the highest possible previous quantile $(\overline{\alpha}^i_{j_i-1})$ and the lowest possible current quantile $(\underline{\alpha}^i_{j_i})$, creating the smallest possible quantile rectangle (empty if $\overline{\alpha}^i_{j_i-1} > \underline{\alpha}^i_{j_i}$) that could represent this focal element's probability mass in the copula space. This ensures we never overestimate the lower bound. Analogously, $\overline{R}_{j_1,\ldots,j_n}$ uses the lowest possible previous quantile $(\underline{\alpha}^i_{j_i-1})$ and the highest possible current quantile $(\overline{\alpha}^i_{j_i})$ to get the largest possible quantile rectangle so that we never underestimate the upper bound.

Proposition 5 (Addition of imprecisely coupled IBSs). *Let* $Z = \sum_{i=1}^n X_i$. *Then* $I_Z = \{\langle \mathbf{z}_{j_1,\ldots,j_n}, \mathbf{r}_{j_1,\ldots,j_n}\rangle\}$ *such that for all* $j_i = 1, \ldots, N_i$ *for* $i = 1, \ldots, n$ *we have*

$$\mathbf{z}_{j_1,\ldots,j_n} = \mathbf{x}^1_{j_1} + \cdots + \mathbf{x}^n_{j_n} \quad \textit{and} \quad \mathbf{r}_{j_1,\ldots,j_n} = \left[\underline{V}_{[\underline{Q},\overline{Q}]}(\underline{R}_{j_1,\ldots,j_n}), \overline{V}_{[\underline{Q},\overline{Q}]}(\overline{R}_{j_1,\ldots,j_n})\right].$$

For the focal elements, we use traditional interval arithmetic. For the upper bound, if the imprecise copula is coherent (or only non-empty), the upper mixed volume is guaranteed to be non-negative (Th. 1). We also note that the number of focal elements explodes after the affine transformation, with a new element for each input-cell combination $(j_1, \ldots, j_n)$.

This IBS sum construction gives an outer approximation of the operation on its credal set. This quality holds as for $\underline{R}_{j_1,\ldots,j_n} \subset R \subset \overline{R}_{j_1,\ldots,j_n}$ a rectangle and $C \in [\underline{Q}, \overline{Q}]$ a copula we have the inequalities $V_C(R) \leq V_C(\overline{R}) \leq \overline{V}_{[\underline{Q},\overline{Q}]}(\overline{R})$.

Note that, however, the resulting IBSs may not be tight, as the proposed affine propagation does not preserve normalization. For further propagation, since we will need quantile levels which are only well-defined for normalized IBSs (Prop. 3) the IBS is normalized by applying Proposition 2.

We also need to propagate the imprecise copula through the affine operation to obtain the dependence between the new variables created by the affine layer. Let $\mathbf{S} = (S_1, \ldots, S_m)$ be the output variables defined by the linear sums $S_k = \sum_{i \in I_k} a_i X_i$ with a_i scalars. The input space is discretized by the focal elements of $\mathbf{X}$. For every multi-index $\mathbf{J} = (j_1, \ldots, j_n)$, we determine the mass interval $[\underline{m}_{\mathbf{J}}, \overline{m}_{\mathbf{J}}]$ associated with the input cell $R_{\mathbf{J}}$. The focal elements and their mass bounds are computed using the mixed volumes of the input imprecise copula on the conservative and optimistic quantile rectangles $\underline{R}_{\mathbf{J}}, \overline{R}_{\mathbf{J}}$ as given in Prop. 5.

Let I_{S_k} be the resulting marginal IBS for each sum variable S_k, consisting of focal intervals $\{\mathbf{s}_\ell^k\}$ obtained by applying Proposition 5 and normalized by Prop. 2, and their associated quantile levels given by $\left\{\{\gamma_{j_k}^k\}_{j_k=1}^{N_k}\right\}_{k=1}^{m}$. There exists a deterministic index mapping $\mathbf{L}^{\mathrm{aff}}(\mathbf{J}) = (L_1^{\mathrm{aff}}(\mathbf{J}), \ldots, L_m^{\mathrm{aff}}(\mathbf{J}))$ defined by the affine transformation such that the image of any input rectangle under T is strictly contained within a specific output cell by tracking which focal elements of the original IBSs are added to form a new focal element on the output IBSs.

The $\mathbf{L}^{\mathrm{aff}}$ memory map is defined such that the indices of the focal elements of the variable resulting from the affine transform $I_Z = \{\langle \mathbf{z}_k, \mathbf{r}_k \rangle\}$ are in correspondence with the indices of the intervals of the input X_i that yielded each focal element by interval arithmetic. I.e., if interval $\mathbf{z}_k$ was obtained by the interval sum of $\mathbf{x}_{j_1}^1 + \cdots + \mathbf{x}_{j_n}^n$ then $\mathbf{L}^{\mathrm{aff}}(j_1, \ldots, j_n) = k$. This alignment ensures that probability mass assigned to an input multi-index $\mathbf{J}$ can be pushed-forward to the output index $\mathbf{L}^{\mathrm{aff}}(\mathbf{J})$.

Proposition 6 (Push-forward of an imprecise multivariate copula through IBS addition). *Let $u^* = (\gamma_{\ell_1}^1, \ldots, \gamma_{\ell_m}^m)$ be a target grid point on the output discrete quasi-copula domain and define the index set*

$$\mathcal{I}(u^*) := \left\{ \mathbf{J} \;\middle|\; L_k^{\mathit{aff}}(\mathbf{J}) \leq \ell_k \textit{ for all } k = 1, \ldots, m \right\}.$$

The value of the output imprecise copula at u^* is obtained by:

$$\underline{Q}_{\mathbf{S}}(u^*) = \max\left(\sum_{\mathbf{J} \in \mathcal{I}(u^*)} \underline{m}_{\mathbf{J}},\quad 1 - \sum_{\mathbf{J} \notin \mathcal{I}(u^*)} \overline{m}_{\mathbf{J}} \right),$$

$$\overline{Q}_{\mathbf{S}}(u^*) = \min\left(\sum_{\mathbf{J} \in \mathcal{I}(u^*)} \overline{m}_{\mathbf{J}},\quad 1 - \sum_{\mathbf{J} \notin \mathcal{I}(u^*)} \underline{m}_{\mathbf{J}} \right).$$

These are discrete quasi-copulas defining a coherent discrete imprecise copula.

Remark 1. The propagation is exact at the grid nodes of the focal intervals because they align perfectly with the output focal elements via the affine map. This method implicitly constructs a stepwise constant function. The discrete quasi-copula envelopes could be extended to full quasi-copulas via patchwork methods [10]. While the constructed imprecise copula is coherent in the discrete sense, the coherence of an extension on the continuous sense would need to be considered.

3.2 Activation Functions

We distinguish two cases of activation functions: first univariate, monotone, injective activations, such as sigmoids, hyperbolic tangent, leaky ReLU. Secondly, we consider the particular case of ReLU, still monotone but not injective. IBS propagation is the same in both cases:

Proposition 7 (Monotone activation of an IBS). *Let X be a variable represented by a normalized IBS $I_X = \{\langle \mathbf{x}_j, [\underline{m}_j, \overline{m}_j] \rangle \mid j = 1, \ldots, N\}$, where the focal sets $\mathbf{x}_j = [\underline{x}_j, \overline{x}_j] \subset \mathbb{R}$ are intervals ordered in increasing order.*

Let $\sigma : \mathbb{R} \to \mathbb{R}$ be a monotone (non-decreasing) measurable function and define $Z = \sigma(X)$. For each focal element $\mathbf{x}_j$, define its image $\mathbf{z}_j := \sigma(\mathbf{x}_j) := [\sigma(\underline{x}_j), \sigma(\overline{x}_j)]$ and construct the IBS $I_Z := \{\langle \mathbf{z}_j, [\underline{m}_j, \overline{m}_j] \rangle : j = 1, \ldots, N\}$ which is a sound outer approximation of the credal set under the activation.

The lack of injectivity in ReLU is a source of difficulties. The first one relates to the appearance of a mass atom in the quasi-copula envelopes below which they become ill-defined. The second relates to the identification of where this mass atom appears. In our imprecise setting, this identification is not possible, so we develop a sound way to approximate it.

Let $\mathbf{X} = (X_1, \ldots, X_n)$ be variables described by normalized IBS I_{X_i} and dependent according to a coherent imprecise copula $[\underline{Q}_{\mathbf{X}}, \overline{Q}_{\mathbf{X}}]$. Let I_{Z_i} be the ReLUed IBSs of I_{X_i} obtained by applying Proposition 7 with $Z_i = \mathrm{ReLU}(X_i)$.

For each i, let $\underline{w}_i = \underline{\mathrm{Bel}}_{X_i}((-\infty, 0])$ and $\overline{w}_i = \overline{\mathrm{Pl}}_{X_i}((-\infty, 0])$ denote the lower and upper probability bounds of the event $\{X_i < 0\}$ induced by the IBS I_{X_k} (conservatively taken on the broadest p-box sense given by Prop. 3). These bounds satisfy $0 \le \underline{w}_i \le \overline{w}_i \le 1$ and represent the minimal and maximal probability mass that will collapse to the atom $\{0\}$ after ReLU.

We then split the copula domain $[0,1]^n$ into two regions: $U^+ = \Big\{\mathbf{u} = (u_1, \ldots, u_n) \in [0,1]^n \mid u_i > \overline{w}_i \Big\}$ and $U^- = [0,1]^n \setminus U^+$. For every $\mathbf{u} \in U^-$, the ReLU transform may collapse a non-trivial probability mass to $\{0\}$ on at least one coordinate k, creating additional uncertainty about the joint allocation of that mass.

To restrict all future evaluations to the well-defined domain beyond the degenerate mass atoms, we selectively merge focal elements of the marginal IBSs which collapse to 0 after the ReLU. This choice ensures that all quasi-copula envelope evaluations only take place in its well-defined domain, therefore implicitly becoming quasi-sub-copulas on the quantile domain above the degenerate probability atom. This approach to handling dependencies after ReLU comes at the cost of a conservative outer-approximation.

Proposition 8 (ReLU-aware merger of IBS focal elements). *Let X be a real-valued random variable represented by a normalized interval belief structure $I_X = \{\langle \mathbf{x}_j, [\underline{m}_j, \overline{m}_j] \rangle \mid j = 1, \ldots, N\}$. Let $\sigma = \mathrm{ReLU}$ and define $Z = \sigma(X) = \max(0, X)$. We define*

$$j_0 := \max\{j \in \{0, \ldots, N\} \mid \underline{x_j} \le 0\},$$

with the convention $j_0 = 0$ *if* $\underline{x_1} > 0$.

We construct the merged focal intervals $\mathbf{z}_1 := [0, \max_{1\leq j\leq j_0} \max(0, \overline{x}_j)]$. *For* $\ell = 2, \ldots, N - j_0 + 1$, *we then have:*

$$\mathbf{z}_\ell := [\underline{x}_{j_0+\ell-1}, \overline{x}_{j_0+\ell-1}].$$

Therefore the strictly positive focal intervals are left unchanged under ReLU. The resulting merged IBS is then given by $I_Z^{\mathrm{m}} := \{\langle \mathbf{z}_\ell, [\underline{n}_\ell, \overline{n}_\ell]\rangle \mid \ell = 1, \ldots, N - j_0 + 1\}$, *with mass bounds*

$$\underline{n}_1 := Bel_X((-\infty, 0]), \qquad \overline{n}_1 := Pl_X((-\infty, 0]),$$

and for $\ell \geq 2$,

$$\underline{n}_\ell := \underline{m}_{j_0+\ell-1}, \qquad \overline{n}_\ell := \overline{m}_{j_0+\ell-1}.$$

In the merged IBS, z_1 *is the unique focal element of* I_Z^{m} *containing* 0, *and it aggregates all mass that may be mapped to* 0 *by ReLU (i.e., originating from values* ≤ 0 *before activation). Moreover,* I_Z^{m} *is a sound outer approximation of applying ReLU to the credal set defined by the original IBS.*

After merging, all quantile grid points satisfy $u_i \geq \overline{w}_i$ or $u_i = 0$ for the edges, where the quasi-copulas are 0 by definition. Therefore once the merger has taken place, the imprecise copula can be evaluated and propagated through the activation function. In the case of injective activations, no merger is required.

Let $\sigma_i : \mathbb{R} \to \mathbb{R}$ be measurable activation functions and define $Z_i = \sigma_i(X_i)$, $Z = (Z_1, \ldots, Z_n)$. For each marginal i, construct an output IBS I_{Z_i} by applying Prop. 7 and the ReLU-aware merger if the activation in question is ReLU (Prop. 8). Let $\left\{\{\gamma^i_{j_i}\}_{j_i=1}^{M_i}\right\}_{i=1}^{n}$ be the resulting quantile grid for Z_i. There exists a memory index map $\mathbf{L}^{\mathrm{act}} : \prod_i\{1, \ldots, N_i\} \to \prod_i\{1, \ldots, M_i\}$, constructed analogously to $\mathbf{L}^{\mathrm{aff}}$, such that each $R_\mathbf{J}$ maps into a unique output cell.

Proposition 9 (Push-forward of an imprecise copula through an activation). *For any point in the output quantile grid* $u^* = (\gamma^1_{\ell_1}, \ldots, \gamma^n_{\ell_n})$ *define*

$$\mathcal{I}(u^*) := \left\{\mathbf{J} \;\middle|\; L_i^{act}(\mathbf{J}) \leq \ell_i \text{ for all } i = 1, \ldots, n\right\}.$$

We define the push-forward copula envelopes

$$\underline{Q}_Z(u^*) := \max\left\{\sum_{\mathbf{J}\in\mathcal{I}(u^*)} \underline{m}_\mathbf{J},\ 1 - \sum_{\mathbf{J}\notin\mathcal{I}(u^*)} \overline{m}_\mathbf{J}\right\},$$

$$\overline{Q}_Z(u^*) := \min\left\{\sum_{\mathbf{J}\in\mathcal{I}(u^*)} \overline{m}_\mathbf{J},\ 1 - \sum_{\mathbf{J}\notin\mathcal{I}(u^*)} \underline{m}_\mathbf{J}\right\}.$$

Then $[\underline{Q}_Z, \overline{Q}_Z]$ *defines a coherent discrete imprecise copula for* Z *on the output quantile grid.*

Algorithm 1. Coupled IBS propagation through a neural network

Input: Input p-boxes $\{[\underline{F}_i, \overline{F}_i]\}_{i=1}^{h_0}$; grids $\{\alpha_j^{i,0}\}_{j=0}^{N_{i,0}}$; input imprecise copula $C^0 = [\underline{Q}_{\mathbf{X}^0}, \overline{Q}_{\mathbf{X}^0}]$; network $\{(W^k, b^k, \sigma^k)\}_{k=0}^{L-1}$.
Ensure: $\{d_{X_r^L}^L\}_{r=1}^{h_L}$ and imprecise copula $[\underline{Q}_L, \overline{Q}_L]$ on $\mathcal{U}^L = \prod_{r=1}^{h_L}\{\alpha_j^{r,L}\}$.
Init: $(d_{X_i^0}^0, \{\alpha_j^{i,0}\}) \leftarrow$ PBoxToIBS$([\underline{F}_i, \overline{F}_i], \{\alpha_j^{i,0}\})$ for $i = 1, \dots, h_0$; $C^0(\mathbf{u}) \leftarrow C_{\mathbf{X}^0}(\mathbf{u})$ for all $\mathbf{u} \in \mathcal{U}^0$.
for $k = 0$ to $L-1$ **do**
  Affine: $S^{k+1} = W^k X^k + b^k$
  $(\{d_{S_r^{k+1}}^{k+1}\}, \{\gamma^{r,k+1}\}, L^{k,\text{aff}}) \leftarrow$ AffineStep$(\{d_{X_i^k}^k\}, \{\alpha^{i,k}\}, C^k, W^k, b^k)$ ▷ Prop. 5
  $C^{k+1,\text{aff}} \leftarrow$ PushFwdCopula$(C^k, \{\alpha^{i,k}\}, \{\gamma^{r,k+1}\}, L^{k,\text{aff}})$ ▷ Prop. 6
  Activation: $X^{k+1} = \sigma^k(S^{k+1})$
  $(\{d_{X_r^{k+1}}^{k+1}\}) \leftarrow$ ActIBS$(\{d_{S_r^{k+1}}^{k+1}\}, \sigma^k)$ ▷ Prop. 7
  $(\{d_{X_r^{k+1}}^{k+1}\}, \{\alpha^{r,k+1}\}, L^{k,\text{act}}) \leftarrow$ Merge$(\{d_{X_r^{k+1}}^{k+1}\}, \sigma^k)$ ▷ Prop. 8
  $C^{k+1} \leftarrow$ PushFwdCopula$(C^{k+1,\text{aff}}, \{\gamma^{r,k+1}\}, \{\alpha^{r,k+1}\}, L^{k,\text{act}})$ ▷ Prop. 9
end for
return $(\{d_{X_r^L}^L\}_{r=1}^{h_L}, C^L)$

3.3 Full Propagation Algorithm

We can now compose the affine and activation operations on coupled IBSs to propagate them through a full feed-forward neural network, in Algorithm 1.

The algorithm has exponential complexity first with respect to the amount of neurons per layer which leads to an exponential explosion of the copula quantile grid domain; and with respect to the number of focal elements in the IBS marginals, which also grow exponentially after each affine step.

3.4 Quantitative Verification

The propagation of coupled IBSs through a neural network provides the reachable states with sound probabilistic information and a rich description of the domain of the outputs of the neural networks and their dependencies.

The resulting structure allows us, in particular, to verify probabilistic properties. Given a linear safety property $Hy \leq w$ on the network output vector y we can compute sound bounds for the probability of the property being satisfied. Practically, an extra affine step on the coupled IBS is used to evaluate $z = Hy - w$. The probability bounds of the linear property of interest are then given by the belief and plausibility (Prop. 3) of the z IBS evaluated at 0. The copula volumes also allow us to verify a conjunction of linear properties.

4 Conclusions

We have developed a pipeline to propagate imprecisely coupled interval belief structures through affine transforms and activation layers. While these operations may be of interest in other fields, we use them for neural networks reachability analysis, obtaining imprecise descriptions of the network's outputs and their dependence, with application to quantitative verification.

Future work includes a computational implementation in order to evaluate this methodology on well-established benchmarks for probabilistic verification. This may require developing more careful heuristic merger strategies through the propagation to keep computation tractable. Difficulties may also arise in modelling features and copulas in a fully imprecise manner. Finally, the probabilistic information obtained after the propagation is much more detailed than needed for the verification of linear safety properties. This paves the way for further interpretability applications on the imprecise multivariate distributions obtained such as robustness certification or sensitivity analysis.

Acknowledgment. This work was partially supported by the SAIF project, funded by the "France 2030" government investment plan managed by the French National Research Agency, under the reference ANR-23-PEIA-0006.

Disclosure of Interests. The authors have no competing interests.

References

1. Balch, M.S., Martin, R., Ferson, S.: Satellite conjunction analysis and the false confidence theorem. In: Proceedings of the Royal Society A: Mathematical, Physical and Engineering Sciences **475**(2227), 20180565 (2019)
2. Baluta, T., Chua, Z.L., Meel, K.S., Saxena, P.: Scalable quantitative verification for deep neural networks. In: 2021 IEEE/ACM 43rd International Conference on Software Engineering (ICSE), Madrid, ES, pp. 312–323. IEEE (2021)
3. Beer, M., Ferson, S., Kreinovich, V.: Imprecise probabilities in engineering analyses. Mech. Syst. Signal Process. **37**(1–2), 4–29 (2013)
4. Boetius, D., Leue, S., Sutter, T.: Solving probabilistic verification problems of neural networks using branch and bound (2024)
5. Denœux, T.: Reasoning with imprecise belief structures. Int. J. Approximate Reasoning **20**(1), 79–111 (1999)
6. Ferson, S., Ginzburg, L., Akçakaya, R.: Whereof one cannot speak: when input distributions are unknown. Risk Anal. (1996)
7. Ferson, S., Kreinovich, V., Ginzburg, L.R., Myers, D.S.: Constructing probability boxes and dempster-shafer structures, Sandia National Laboratories, Albuquerque, New Mexico. SAND2002-4015 Technical Report (2003)
8. Goubault, E., Putot, S.: A zonotopic dempster-shafer approach to the quantitative verification of neural networks. In: Platzer, A., Rozier, K.Y., Pradella, M., Rossi, M. (eds.) FM 2024. LNCS, vol. 14933, pp. 324–342. Springer, Cham (2025). https://doi.org/10.1007/978-3-031-71162-6_17
9. Gray, A., Forets, M., Schilling, C., Ferson, S., Benet, L.: Verified propagation of imprecise probabilities in non-linear ODEs. Int. J. Approximate Reasoning **164**, 109044 (2024)
10. Kokol Bukovšek, D., Košir, T., Mojškerc, B., Omladič, M.: Extending multivariate sub-quasi-copulas. J. Math. Anal. Appl. **540**(1), 128582 (2024)

11. Montes, I., Miranda, E., Pelessoni, R., Vicig, P.: Sklar's theorem in an imprecise setting. Fuzzy Sets Syst. **278**, 48–66 (2015)
12. Müller, M.N., Makarchuk, G., Singh, G., Püschel, M., Vechev, M.: Prima: general and precise neural network certification via scalable convex hull approximations. Proc. ACM Program. Lang 6(POPL) (2022)
13. Nelsen, R.B.: An Introduction to Copulas, 2. ed. Springer Series in Statistics, Springer, New York (2006). corr. 2. pr. softcover version of original hardcover edition 2006 edn. (2010)
14. Omladič, M., Stopar, N.: Final solution to the problem of relating a true copula to an imprecise copula. Fuzzy Sets Syst. **393**, 96–112 (2020)
15. Omladič, M., Stopar, N.: A full scale Sklar's theorem in the imprecise setting. Fuzzy Sets Syst. **393**, 113–125 (2020)
16. Omladič, M., Stopar, N.: Multivariate imprecise Sklar type theorems. Fuzzy Sets Syst. **428**, 80–101 (2022)
17. Pautov, M., Tursynbek, N., Munkhoeva, M., Muravev, N., Petiushko, A., Oseledets, I.: CC-CERT: a probabilistic approach to certify general robustness of neural networks. In: Proceedings of the AAAI Conference on Artificial Intelligence **36**(7), 7975–7983 (2022)
18. Sevastianov, P., Dymova, L., Bartosiewicz, P.: A framework for rule-base evidential reasoning in the interval setting applied to diagnosing type 2 diabetes. Expert Syst. Appl. **39**(4), 4190–4200 (2012)
19. Singh, G., Gehr, T., Püschel, M., Vechev, M.: An abstract domain for certifying neural networks. Proceedings of the ACM on Programming Languages **3**(POPL), 1–30 (2019)
20. Singh, G., Laurel, J., Misailovic, S., Banerjee, D., Singh, A., Xu, C., Ugare, S., Zhang, H., et al.: Safety and trust in artificial intelligence with abstract interpretation. Foundations and Trends® in Programming Languages **8**(3-4), 250–408 (2025)
21. Tran, H.D., Choi, S., Okamoto, H., Hoxha, B., Fainekos, G., Prokhorov, D.: Quantitative Verification for Neural Networks using ProbStars. In: Proceedings of the 26th ACM International Conference on Hybrid Systems: Computation and Control, pp. 1–12. ACM, San Antonio TX USA (2023)
22. Tran, H.D., et al.: Star-based reachability analysis of deep neural networks. In: Formal Methods The Next 30 Years: Third World Congress, FM 2019, Porto, Portugal, October 711, 2019, Proceedings. p. 670686. Springer, Heidelberg (2019)
23. Wang, Y., Yang, J., Xu, D., Chin, K.: On the combination and normalization of interval-valued belief structures. Inf. Sci. **177**(5), 1230–1247 (2007)
24. Wang, Y.M., Yang, J.B., Xu, D.L., Chin, K.S.: The evidential reasoning approach for multiple attribute decision analysis using interval belief degrees. Eur. J. Oper. Res. **175**(1), 35–66 (2006)
25. Weng, T.W., Chen, P.Y., Nguyen, L.M., Squillante, M.S., Oseledets, I., Daniel, L.: PROVEN: certifying robustness of neural networks with a probabilistic approach (2018)
26. Williamson, R.C., Downs, T.: Probabilistic arithmetic. I. Numerical methods for calculating convolutions and dependency bounds. Int. J. Approximate Reasoning **4**(2), 89–158 (1990)
27. Yager, R.R.: Dempster-Shafer belief structures with interval valued focal weights. Int. J. Intell. Syst. **16**(4), 497–512 (2001)

An Order-Theoretic Study of the Credal Sets Generated by Comparative Probabilities

Darío Tagarro(✉), Enrique Miranda(✉), and Raúl Pérez-Fernández(✉)

Department of Statistics and Operations Research and Mathematics Didactics, University of Oviedo, Oviedo, Spain
{tagarrodario,mirandaenrique,perezfernandez}@uniovi.es

Abstract. We study the complexity of the credal set determined by a comparative probability order on the singletons of a finite possibility space. We show that the bound established by Miranda and Destercke in [15] can be reduced under some conditions on the associated graph, and give sufficient conditions for this new bound to be attained. We focus in particular on the case where the order relation associated with the comparative probability is either bounded above or below, and discuss specific cases of these in detail. In addition we investigate the properties of the lower probability determined by a comparative probability ordering.

Keywords: Comparative probabilities · partial orders · credal sets · belief functions · 2-monotonicity

1 Introduction

In situations of ambiguous, contradictory or imprecise information, probability measures have been deemed inadequate as a model of uncertainty with sufficient guarantees. This has motivated the rise of a number of alternative approaches, that are usually encompassed under the term *imprecise probabilities* [2]. These include in particular coherent lower previsions [17], Choquet capacities [4], belief functions [16] and possibility measures [5]. Among the many models that are covered under the imprecise probability umbrella, there are a few of them that are interesting due to the simplicity in their elicitation. This is the case of probability intervals [3], that only require the specification of the lower and upper probabilities on the singletons, p-boxes [7], where lower and upper bounds of the distribution function are established, or the model under study in this paper, comparative probabilities.

Comparative probabilities spring from the specification of a partial probability ordering among the events, so that $A \succeq B$ is interpreted as the assessment "the probability of A is at least as large as the probability of B". They were first considered by Bruno de Finetti in [9] and subsequently analysed by Koopman

B. Vantaggi et al. (Eds.): IPMU 2026, CCIS 3019, pp. 190–203, 2026.
https://doi.org/10.1007/978-3-032-28994-0_14

[13], Fine [8] and Fishburn [10], among others. Due to their formulation in terms of partial orders, the analysis of comparative probability models may also be of interest in other contexts. To see an example, we may for instance consider a problem of resource distribution where a number of constraints are placed on the final allocation; the set of compatible ones, once some normalization conditions are put in place, is equivalent to the set of probability measures compatible with some comparability ordering. Similarly, we may also connect comparative probabilities with solutions of coalitional games under partial information [12] or with imprecise compositional data [1].

In this paper, we follow up some recent work [6,15] and analyse the complexity that entails working with comparative probabilities. More specifically, a comparative probability relation determines a convex set of compatible probability measures. In order to work with this set, it is useful to determine the number and form of its extreme points, since they allow to obtain the associated lower and upper probabilities and expectations, as well as the updated models. The study of extreme points may also be useful in the numerical handling of partial preferences, commonly encountered in multi-criteria decision making [14] or in preference learning [11]. The maximum number of extreme points was shown in [15] to be comparable to the one determined by a possibility measure if the comparisons are established only on the singletons, while in [6] it was shown to increase significantly in the general case where they are made on events.

While these results are undoubtedly of interest, a number of questions remain: for instance, is the maximal number of extreme points attained frequently or can the bound be reduced in the majority of cases? How does the complexity of the set of compatible probability measures change when we remove some of the comparative relations? Which are the properties of the lower and upper probabilities associated with the order? These are some of the issues that we shall tackle in this work. We shall focus on the case where the comparative ordering is established on the singletons, and improve on a number of results established in [15].

The paper is organized as follows: in Sect. 2, we shall recall a number of preliminary notions that are necessary to follow the rest of the paper. In Sect. 3, we shall determine the maximum number of extreme points in the case of relations that are bounded either above or below. Our results shall be used in Sect. 4 to investigate the properties of the associated lower and upper probabilities, showing that they correspond to belief functions under some conditions. Finally, we shall conclude with some additional discussion in Sect. 5. Due to the space limitations, proofs have been omitted.

2 Preliminaries

Consider a finite possibility space $\mathscr{X} = \{x_1, \ldots, x_n\}$, and let $\mathbb{P}_{\mathscr{X}}$ denote the set of probability measures on $\mathscr{X}$. Our focus in this paper is on sets of elementary comparative assessments over $\mathscr{X}$, that is, comparative judgments of the form "the probability of x_i is at least that of x_j". These elementary comparative assessments can be expressed in terms of a binary relation, and denoted as $x_i \succsim x_j$;

equivalently, we can represent them via the set $\mathscr{L} \subseteq \{1, \dots, n\} \times \{1, \dots, n\}$ defined as $(i, j) \in \mathscr{L}$ if $x_i \succsim x_j$.

The set of those probability measures compatible with our comparative judgments is denoted by $\mathscr{P}(\mathscr{L})$:

$$\mathscr{P}(\mathscr{L}) = \{P \in \mathbb{P}_{\mathscr{X}} : P(\{x_i\}) \geq P(\{x_j\}),\ \forall (i, j) \in \mathscr{L}\}. \tag{1}$$

Note that $\mathscr{P}(\mathscr{L})$ is always non-empty since it includes the uniform probability distribution on $\mathscr{X}$. It is moreover closed and convex, so it is a *credal set.*

The *transitive and reflexive closure* of a relation modeled by $\mathscr{L}$ will be denoted by $\mathscr{C}(\mathscr{L})$ and we shall denote $x_i \succeq x_j$ if $(i, j) \in \mathscr{C}(\mathscr{L})$. We shall assume throughout that $\mathscr{L}$ is the covering relation of $\mathscr{C}(\mathscr{L})$, i.e., that it has no redundancies under transitivity. As pointed out in [15], it is equivalent to work with the credal set associated with a relation and with its transitive and reflexive closure, so they will be used indistinctly in this paper.

Lower Probability of the Credal Set. The credal set $\mathscr{P}(\mathscr{L})$ determines a *coherent lower probability* $\underline{P}$ by taking lower envelopes on events [17]: $\underline{P}(A) = \min\{P(A) : P \in \mathscr{P}(\mathscr{L})\}, \forall A \subseteq \mathscr{X}$. This lower probability can be equivalently represented by means of its *Möbius inverse* $m_{\underline{P}} : 2^{\mathscr{X}} \mapsto \mathbb{R}$, given by $m_{\underline{P}}(A) = \sum_{C \subseteq A} (-1)^{|A \setminus C|} \underline{P}(C)$ for all $A \subseteq \mathscr{X}$; it holds that $\underline{P}(A) = \sum_{C \subseteq A} m_{\underline{P}}(C)$ for every $A \subseteq \mathscr{X}$.

As particular cases of coherent lower probabilities, we have 2-monotone capacities or belief functions. A lower probability $\underline{P}$ is *2-monotone* when $\underline{P}(A \cup B) + \underline{P}(A \cap B) \geq \underline{P}(A) + \underline{P}(B)$ for all $A, B \subseteq \mathscr{X}$, and it is a *belief function* [16] when its Möbius inverse $m_{\underline{P}}$ is non-negative. Any belief function is 2-monotone.

Since $\mathscr{P}(\mathscr{L})$ is closed and convex, it is uniquely determined by its extreme points, which are those $P \in \mathscr{P}(\mathscr{L})$ that cannot be expressed as $P = \alpha P_1 + (1 - \alpha) P_2$ for some $P_1 \neq P_2 \in \mathscr{P}(\mathscr{L})$ and some $\alpha \in (0, 1)$. If we denote by $\operatorname{Ext}(\mathscr{P}(\mathscr{L}))$ the set of extreme points of $\mathscr{P}(\mathscr{L})$, it holds that [17, Thm. 3.6.2]

$$\underline{P}(A) = \min\{P(A) : P \in \operatorname{Ext}(\mathscr{P}(\mathscr{L}))\}. \tag{2}$$

Graphical Representation. Miranda and Destercke used in [15] a graphical approach to characterize the extreme points of the credal set generated by a set of comparative probabilities. They represented judgments through a (directed) graph $\mathscr{G} = (\mathscr{X}, \mathscr{L})$, where the elements of the possibility space $\mathscr{X}$ are the nodes of the graph, and a directed edge is drawn between x_i and x_j when $(i, j) \in \mathscr{L}$.

A relation whose associated graph is acyclic will be called an *acyclic* relation, and a relation whose associated graph is weakly connected will be called a *connected* relation. According to [15, Props. 2–3], in the study of the set of extreme points of $\mathscr{P}(\mathscr{L})$ we can focus without loss of generality to acyclic and connected relations. For this reason, in what follows we shall assume our relation to be acyclic and connected unless explicitly stated otherwise.

In order to characterize the set of extreme points of the credal set associated with a relation $\mathcal{L}$, it will play a key role the set of ancestors generated by a given set $B \subseteq \mathcal{X}$, defined as $\langle B \rangle_{\mathcal{L}} := \{x_i \in \mathcal{X} : \exists x_j \in B \text{ such that } x_i \succeq x_j\}$. This concept leads to the definition of the family of sets *closed by ancestors* of a relation $\mathcal{L}$:

$$\mathcal{H}_{\mathcal{L}} := \{\langle B \rangle_{\mathcal{L}} : B \subseteq \mathcal{X}\}.$$

When there is no ambiguity regarding the relation $\mathcal{L}$ under study, $\langle B \rangle_{\mathcal{L}}$ and $\mathcal{H}_{\mathcal{L}}$ will be simply denoted by $\langle B \rangle$ and $\mathcal{H}$ for simplicity.

In this paper, we shall pay special attention to two types of relations. An order relation is said to be *bounded-above* if there exists $x_1 \in \mathcal{X}$ such that $x_1 \succeq x_i$ for all $x_i \in \mathcal{X}$, that is, x_1 is the unique maximal element of $\mathcal{L}$ and $\langle\{x_1\}\rangle = \{x_1\}$. Analogously, a relation is said to be *bounded-below* if there exists $x_n \in \mathcal{X}$ such that $x_i \succeq x_n$ for all $x_i \in \mathcal{X}$, that is, if x_n is the unique minimal element of $\mathcal{L}$ and $\langle\{x_n\}\rangle = \mathcal{X}$. A relation is said to be *bounded* if it is both bounded below and bounded above. In these cases, x_1 and x_n shall usually denote the unique maximal and minimal elements of the relation, respectively.

A particular type of bounded-above relations are out-arborescences. Recall that an *out-arborescence* is a connected acyclic graph in which every element has indegree 1 except one element called *root* that has indegree 0. A relation whose associated graph is an out-arborescence will also be called an out-arborescence. One instance of out-arborescence is given by modal relations: we shall say that $\mathcal{L}$ is a *modal relation* if there exists $x_1 \in \mathcal{X}$ such that $\mathcal{L} = \{(1, i) : i \neq 1\}$.

Similarly, an *in-arborescence* is a particular type of bounded-below relation that is a connected acyclic graph in which every element has outdegree 1 except one element called *root* that has outdegree 0. A relation whose associated graph is an in-arborescence will also be called an in-arborescence. One instance of in-arborescence are antimodal relations: we say that $\mathcal{L}$ is an *antimodal relation* if there exists $x_n \in \mathcal{X}$ such that $\mathcal{L} = \{(i, n) : i \neq n\}$.

There are two operations that we shall make on a relation in this paper. On the one hand, we shall at times remove an element x_k from $\mathcal{X}$; the resulting relation on the set $\mathcal{X} \setminus \{x_k\}$ shall be denoted $\mathcal{L}_{x_k} := \{(i, j) \in \mathcal{C}(\mathcal{L}) : i, j \neq k\}$.

Secondly, we shall sometimes consider the *transpose* of a relation $\mathcal{L}$ that is the relation given by $\mathcal{L}^T = \{(i, j) : (j, i) \in \mathcal{L}\}$. The associated graph is obtained by reversing the arcs. Note that the transpose of a bounded-below relation is a bounded-above relation and vice versa; the transpose of an in-arborescence is an out-arborescence and vice versa; and also the transpose of a modal relation is an antimodal relation and vice versa.

Computation of the Extreme Points. Miranda and Destercke proved in [15] the following result relating the extreme points of the credal set $\mathcal{P}(\mathcal{L})$ and $\mathcal{H}$.

Theorem 1. *[15, Thm. 1] Let $\mathcal{L}$ be an acyclic relation, and let $\mathcal{P}(\mathcal{L})$ be the credal set it induces by Eq.* (1)*. For any $B \subseteq \mathcal{X}$, let P_B denote the uniform probability measure on the set B. Then $Ext(\mathcal{P}(\mathcal{L}))$ is given by*

$$\{P_B : B \in \mathcal{H}, \nexists B_1, B_2 \in \mathcal{H} \text{ such that } B_1 \cup B_2 = B \text{ and } B_1 \cap B_2 = \emptyset\}.$$

Given this correspondence, we shall identify throughout an extreme point with its support, so we will indistinctly refer to $\mathrm{Ext}(\mathscr{P}(\mathscr{L}))$ as the subsets of $\mathscr{X}$ for which the associated uniform probability is an extreme point of $\mathscr{P}(\mathscr{L})$.

The above connection between $\mathrm{Ext}(\mathscr{P}(\mathscr{L}))$ and $\mathscr{H}$ leads us to analyse in more detail this family. In this respect, we observe that, for any $B \subseteq \mathscr{X}$, if there exist $x_i, x_j \in B$ such that $x_i \succeq x_j$, it follows that $\langle B\rangle = \langle B \setminus \{x_i\}\rangle$; thus, two different sets can generate the same ancestors, and this happens when there are comparable elements in the generating set. For this reason, in order to determine the set $\mathscr{H}$ it suffices to compute the sets of ancestors generated by elements that are pairwise incomparable with respect to $\succeq$. A set of pairwise incomparable elements is called an *antichain*, and the set of antichains of a relation $\mathscr{L}$ is denoted by $\mathscr{A}(\mathscr{L})$, so it follows that $\mathscr{H} = \{\langle A\rangle : A \in \mathscr{A}(\mathscr{L})\}$. Since every singleton is an antichain the set $\mathscr{A}(\mathscr{L})$ can never be empty.

On the other hand, since the extreme points will be generated by those elements of $\mathscr{H}$ that cannot be decomposed as a disjoint union of two other sets, we should find which antichains will generate indecomposable sets. An antichain A will be said to be *connected* if the restriction of $\mathscr{L}$ to $\langle A\rangle$ is connected, meaning that there do not exist $A_1, A_2 \in \mathscr{A}(\mathscr{X})$ such that $\langle A\rangle = \langle A_1\rangle \cup \langle A_2\rangle$ and $\langle A_1\rangle \cap \langle A_2\rangle = \emptyset$. According to that, the extreme points will be those generated by connected antichains, so $\mathrm{Ext}(\mathscr{P}(\mathscr{L})) = \{\langle A\rangle : A \in \mathscr{A}(\mathscr{L}) \text{ connected}\}$.

3 Analysis of the Number of Extreme Points

In this section, we shall bound the number of extreme points of the credal set associated with elementary comparative assessments in terms of the structure of the order relation. We begin our analysis with the case in which the relation is bounded above, next we study the case in which the relation is bounded below, and we conclude with the case in which the relation is bounded.

3.1 Bounded-Above Relations

Since in this paper we are dealing with finite possibility spaces and the relation $\mathscr{L}$ is assumed to be acyclic, there will always be elements x_i that are maximal, in the sense that there is no other x_j with $x_j \succeq x_i$. What is particular about bounded-above relations is that for them there is only one such maximal element. From the point of view of partial probability orderings, they correspond to a scenario where we specify an element whose probability cannot be smaller than any other. On the other hand, if we regard $\mathscr{L}$ as constraints on a resource allocation problem, being bounded above means that there is one individual that is bound to receive the maximum portion of the resources in the group, whichever is the final distribution to be decided.

A key feature of bounded-above relations is that they are the only ones for which all the antichains are connected; as a consequence, for them the sets $\mathrm{Ext}(\mathscr{P}(\mathscr{L}))$ and $\mathscr{H}$ coincide.

Lemma 1. *$Ext(\mathscr{P}(\mathscr{L})) = \mathscr{H}$ if and only if $\mathscr{L}$ is bounded above.*

In [15, Thm. 4], it was established that the maximum number of extreme points of $\text{Ext}(\mathscr{P}(\mathscr{L}))$ is $2^{|\mathscr{X}|-1}$ and that this bound is tight, being attained for instance in the case where the relation is modal. In what follows, we shall establish that the modal case is actually the *only* scenario with such a large number of extreme points, and that for the other cases a significantly smaller bound can be established. Specifically, our main result in this section shall be the following.

Theorem 2. *The number of extreme points of* $\mathscr{P}(\mathscr{L})$ *of a bounded-above relation* $\mathscr{L}$ *is* $2^{|\mathscr{X}|-1}$ *if and only if the relation is modal. If the relation* $\mathscr{L}$ *is non modal, the maximum number of extreme points of* $\mathscr{P}(\mathscr{L})$ *is* $3 \cdot 2^{|\mathscr{X}|-3}$.

It is immediate that when $|\mathscr{X}| < 3$ every bounded relation is modal. When $|\mathscr{X}| = 3$, there is only one non-modal bounded-above relation, given by $\mathscr{L} = \{(1,2),(2,3)\}$. In that case, it follows from Theorem 1 that the extreme points of $\mathscr{P}(\mathscr{L})$ are determined by $\{x_1\}$, $\{x_1, x_2\}$ and $\{x_1, x_2, x_3\}$. As a consequence, when $|\mathscr{X}| = 3$, the maximum number of extreme points of $\mathscr{P}(\mathscr{L})$ is $3 = 3 \cdot 2^0 = 3 \cdot 2^{|\mathscr{X}|-3}$.

The proof of Theorem 2 is made applying induction on the cardinality of $\mathscr{X}$. For this, we remove in the induction step an element x_i from $\mathscr{X}$ for which we prove that $\mathscr{L}_{x_i}$, restriction of the relation $\mathscr{L}$ to $\mathscr{X} \setminus \{x_i\}$, is still non modal and bounded above, and relate the extreme points of $\mathscr{L}$ with those of $\mathscr{L}_{x_i}$.

Let us show that the bound on the number of extreme points in the non modal case is tight.

Example 1. Let $\mathscr{X} = \{x_1, \ldots, x_n\}$ and consider the relation given by $\mathscr{L} = \{(2,n)\} \cup \{(1,i) : i \in \{2, \ldots, n-1\}\}$, which is clearly non modal and bounded above, and its associated graph (Fig. 1).

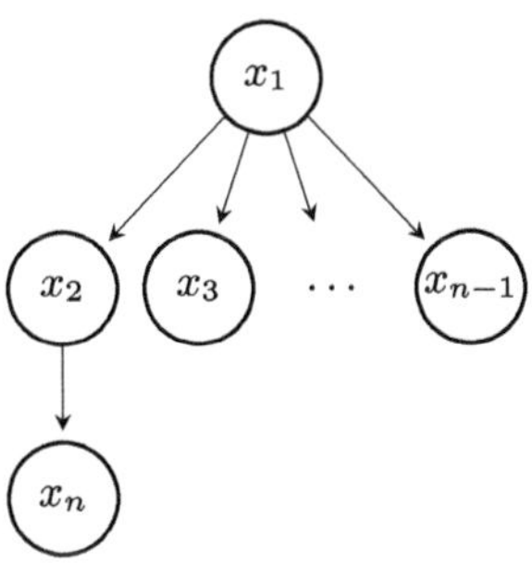

Fig. 1. Graph associated with $\mathscr{L}$ in Example 1.

Applying Theorem 1, the extreme points of the credal set associated with this relation are those uniform probabilities whose support is the union of one set of $\{\{x_1\}, \{x_1, x_2\}, \{x_1, x_2, x_n\}\}$ with any subset of $\{x_3, \ldots x_{n-1}\}$. That is, we may identify $\text{Ext}(\mathscr{L}) = \{\{x_1\}, \{x_1, x_2\}, \{x_1, x_2, x_n\}\} \times 2^{\{x_3,\ldots x_{n-1}\}}$, and therefore $|\text{Ext}(\mathscr{L})| = |\{\{x_1\}, \{x_1, x_2\}, \{x_1, x_2, x_n\}\}| \cdot |2^{\{x_3,\ldots x_{n-1}\}}| = 3 \cdot 2^{n-3}$. ♦

Our proof of Theorem 2 hinges on the successive elimination of minimal elements of the graph associated with the comparative probability relation. Next we analyse the effect of removing the maximal element.

Proposition 1. *Let $\mathscr{L}$ be a bounded-above relation with maximal element x_1, and let $\{\mathscr{X}_i\}_{i=1}^m$ be the connected components of $\mathscr{L}_{x_1}$. Denote by $\mathscr{L}_i$ the restriction of $\mathscr{L}$ to $\mathscr{X}_i$. Then the following mapping f*

$$f : \mathscr{H}_{\mathscr{L}} \to \times_{i=1}^m (\mathscr{H}_{\mathscr{L}i} \cup \{\emptyset\})$$
$$B \mapsto \times_{i=1}^m (B \cap \mathscr{X}_i),$$

is a bijection. As a consequence, $|\mathscr{H}_{\mathscr{L}}| = \prod_{i=1}^m (|\mathscr{H}_{\mathscr{L}i}| + 1)$.

This result shows us how, for bounded-above relations with maximal element $\{x_1\}$, the set $\mathscr{H}_{\mathscr{L}}$ can be expressed in terms of the sets $\mathscr{H}_{\mathscr{L}i}$ associated with the connected components of $\mathscr{X} \setminus \{x_1\}$. According to Lemma 1, each $\mathscr{H}_{\mathscr{L}i}$ determines the extreme points of $\mathrm{Ext}(\mathscr{P}(\mathscr{L}_{\mathscr{L}i}))$ when $\mathscr{L}_i$ is bounded above, and in that case we may express the extreme points of the original relation in terms of the extreme points of its restriction to these connected components. Interestingly, there is one special type of relations in which every connected subset is bounded above: out-arborescences.

Indeed, if $\mathscr{L}$ is an out-arborescence, it will clearly have one maximal element: its root, and thus it will be bounded above. Moreover, every connected subgraph of an out-arborescence is still an out-arborescence. Taking this into account, we deduce that, on this particular type of bounded-above relations, $\mathrm{Ext}(\mathscr{P}(\mathscr{L}_i)) = \mathscr{H}_{\mathscr{L}_i}$ for every connected component. Proposition 1 leads then immediately to the following result.

Theorem 3. *Let $\mathscr{L}$ be an out-arborescence with root x_1, and let $\{\mathscr{X}_i\}_{i=1}^m$ be the connected components of $\mathscr{L}_{x_1}$. Denote by $\mathscr{L}_i$ the restriction of $\mathscr{L}$ to $\mathscr{X}_i$. Then the following mapping*

$$f : Ext(\mathscr{P}(\mathscr{L})) \to \times_{i=1}^m (Ext(\mathscr{P}(\mathscr{L}_i)) \cup \{\emptyset\})$$
$$B \mapsto \times_{i=1}^m (B \cap \mathscr{X}_i),$$

is a bijection, and as a consequence $|Ext(\mathscr{P}(\mathscr{L}))| = \prod_{i=1}^m (|Ext(\mathscr{P}(\mathscr{L}_i))| + 1)$.

Applying Theorem 3 recursively gives a procedure to determine the extreme points of the credal set in the case of out-arborescences: we first eliminate its root and determine the connected components of the resulting relation, and relate the extreme points of the initial relation with those of the connected components. Since every connected component is again an out-arborescence with a smaller cardinality, we can iterate this method until we get to singletons or to a structure with already known number of extreme points, such as chains or modal relations.

It also follows from Theorem 3 that we can determine the number of extreme points by multiplying the number of extreme points of the restrictions of the relation to the connected components adding one. As we shall show next, the maximum number of extreme points in the global relation will be obtained when we have as many connected components as possible, even if these are of a very small cardinality.

Lemma 2. *Let $\mathscr{L}$ be an out-arborescence over $\mathscr{X}$ with root x_1, and let $\{\mathscr{X}_i\}_{i=1}^m$ be the connected components of $\mathscr{L}_{x_1}$. If there exists some $\mathscr{X}_j$ that is not a singleton, then for any minimal element $x_k \in \mathscr{X}_j$ the relation $\tilde{\mathscr{L}}$ given by $\tilde{\mathscr{L}} = \{(i,j) : (i,j) \in \mathscr{L}, j \neq k\} \cup \{(1,k)\}$ is an out-arborescence and $|Ext(\mathscr{P}(\mathscr{L}))| \leq |Ext(\mathscr{P}(\tilde{\mathscr{L}}))|$.*

If we apply this result recursively until every connected component is a singleton we will obtain a modal relation, and the number of extreme points will be $2^{|\mathscr{X}|-1}$, as it was previously stated. Indeed, this is the maximum number of extreme points not only for out-arborescences but also for general relations. If instead we want the out-arborescence to be non-modal, then its maximum number of extreme points will be obtained when we can apply the result recursively until every connected component is a singleton except one; we obtain then the relation described in Example 1, with $3 \cdot 2^{|\mathscr{X}|-3}$ different extreme points, as it was also previously stated in the case of non modal bounded-above relations.

The fact that the bounds on the maximum number of extreme points in modal and non modal out-arborescences coincide with the ones given for modal and non modal bounded-above relations is no coincidence: it is because any bounded-above relation can be embedded into an out-arborescence, and this allows to establish a relationship between their associated credal sets and as a consequence between the extreme points.

Proposition 2. *For any bounded above $\mathscr{L}$ there exists an out-arborescence $\tilde{\mathscr{L}}$ that satisfies $\tilde{\mathscr{L}} \subseteq \mathscr{L}$. Moreover, it holds that $Ext(\mathscr{P}(\mathscr{L})) \subseteq Ext(\mathscr{P}(\tilde{\mathscr{L}}))$, and consequently $|Ext(\mathscr{P}(\mathscr{L}))| \leq |Ext(\mathscr{P}(\tilde{\mathscr{L}}))|$.*

3.2 Bounded-Below Relations

We shift our attention now to bounded-below relations, i.e., those for which there exists a unique minimal element. They correspond to the symmetric scenario with respect to the bounded-above ones: here, we specify an element whose probability cannot be greater than any other. From the perspective of a resource allocation problem within a group, it means that there is an individual that is always bound to receive the minimum in the group.

Since the transpose of a bounded-below relation is a bounded-above relation, we shall try to use the results established in Sect. 3.1 for bounded-above relations to bound the number of extreme points. In this respect, our next result shows that there exists a connection between the sets $\mathscr{H}$ determined by a relation and its transpose:

Lemma 3. *Consider a relation $\mathscr{L}$ and its transpose $\mathscr{L}^T$. A set $\emptyset \neq B \neq \mathcal{X}$ belongs to $\mathscr{H}_{\mathscr{L}}$ if and only if its complement $\mathscr{X} \setminus B$ belongs to $\mathscr{H}_{\mathscr{L}^T}$. Consequently, $|\mathscr{H}_{\mathscr{L}}| = |\mathscr{H}_{\mathscr{L}^T}|$.*

Taking this result into account together with Lemma 1, we deduce that $\text{Ext}(\mathscr{P}(\mathscr{L}^T)) = \mathscr{H}_{\mathscr{L}^T}$. Since moreover $\text{Ext}(\mathscr{P}(\mathscr{L})) \subseteq \mathscr{H}_{\mathscr{L}}$, it follows that

$$|\text{Ext}(\mathscr{P}(\mathscr{L}))| \leq |\mathscr{H}_{\mathscr{L}}| = |\mathscr{H}_{\mathscr{L}^T}| = |\text{Ext}(\mathscr{P}(\mathscr{L}^T))|.$$

Note that if the bounded-below relation $\mathscr{L}$ is not bounded-above we shall have $\text{Ext}(\mathscr{P}(\mathscr{L})) \subsetneq \mathscr{H}_{\mathscr{L}}$, and then $|\text{Ext}(\mathscr{P}(\mathscr{L}))| < |\text{Ext}(\mathscr{P}(\mathscr{L}^T))|$. In other words, if we want to have the same number of extreme points in a bounded-below relation as on its transpose, the relation has to be bounded.

The comments above and Theorem 2 allow us to deduce the following:

Corollary 1. *Let $\mathscr{L}$ be a non antimodal bounded-below relation. Then the number of extreme points of $\mathscr{P}(\mathscr{L})$ is at most $3 \cdot 2^{|\mathscr{X}|-3}$.*

However, and in contradistinction with the results established in Sect. 3.1, this bound is not tight. To see this, note that tightness would require the transpose $\mathscr{L}^T$ of $\mathscr{L}$ to be akin to the one in Example 1; however, in that case the relation $\mathscr{L}$ obtained would not be bounded above, meaning that $|\text{Ext}(\mathscr{P}(\mathscr{L}))| < |\text{Ext}(\mathscr{P}(\mathscr{L}^T))| = 3 \cdot 2^{|\mathscr{X}|-3}$.

In order to establish a tight bound on the number of extreme points for bounded-below relations, we need to analyse what happens to them when their unique minimal element x_n is removed.

Lemma 4. *Let $\mathscr{L}$ be a bounded-below relation with minimal element x_n. Then $Ext(\mathscr{P}(\mathscr{L})) = Ext(\mathscr{P}(\mathscr{L}_{x_n})) \cup \{\mathscr{X}\}$, whence $|Ext(\mathscr{P}(\mathscr{L}))| = |Ext(\mathscr{P}(\mathscr{L}_{x_n}))| + 1$. Moreover, if $\{\mathscr{X}_i\}_{i=1}^m$ are the connected components of $\mathscr{L}_{x_n}$, then $Ext(\mathscr{P}(\mathscr{L})) = \cup_{i=1}^m Ext(\mathscr{P}(\mathscr{L}_i)) \cup \{\mathscr{X}\}$, whence $|Ext(\mathscr{P}(\mathscr{L}))| = \sum_{i=1}^m |Ext(\mathscr{P}(\mathscr{L}_i))| + 1$.*

This allows us to deduce the following:

Corollary 2. *The number of extreme points of $\mathscr{P}(\mathscr{L})$ for a non antimodal bounded-below relation $\mathscr{L}$ is at most $2^{|\mathscr{X}|-2} + 1$.*

The bound on the number of extreme points of a non antimodal bounded-below relation is reached no matter the cardinality of the set over which it is established the relation, as can be seen in the next example.

Example 2. Let $\mathscr{X} = \{x_1, \ldots, x_n\}$ and consider the relation given by $\mathscr{L} = \{(1, i) : i \in \{2, \ldots, n-1\}\} \cup \{(i, n) : i \in \{2, \ldots, n-1\}\}$, which is clearly non antimodal and bounded-below, and its associated graph (Fig. 2).

Since the resulting relation $\mathscr{L}_{x_n}$ is a modal relation over a set with cardinality $n-1$, it follows from [15, Thm. 4] that it will have $2^{(n-1)-1} = 2^{n-2}$ extreme points. If we now apply Lemma 4, we deduce that $|\text{Ext}(\mathscr{P}(\mathscr{L}))| = |\text{Ext}(\mathscr{P}(\mathscr{L}_{x_n}))| + 1 = 2^{n-2} + 1 = 2^{|\mathscr{X}|-2} + 1$, reaching the bound given by Corollary 2. ♦

Lemma 4 also shows us how, for bounded-below relations with minimal element $\{x_n\}$, the set of extreme points $\text{Ext}(\mathscr{P}(\mathscr{L}))$ can be expressed in terms of the sets $\text{Ext}(\mathscr{P}(\mathscr{L}_i))$ associated with the connected components of $\mathscr{X} \setminus \{x_n\}$,

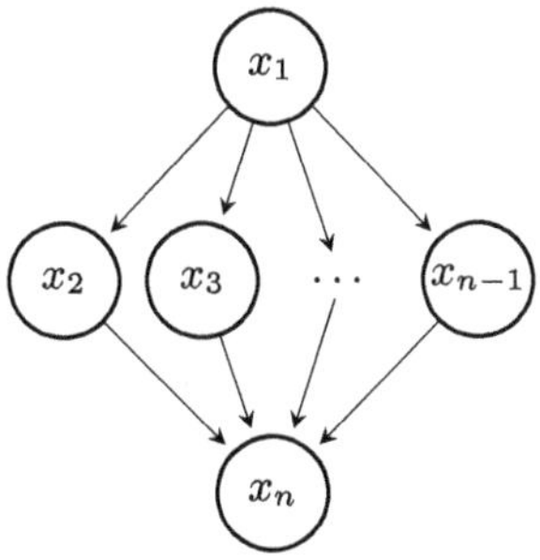

Fig. 2. Graph associated with $\mathscr{L}$ in Example 2.

similarly to what we did for bounded-above relations in Theorem 2. However, there are two notorious differences between these two cases. Firstly, in the case of bounded-below relations we can directly relate the sets of extreme points of the original relation with those of the connected components, whereas for bounded-above relations we can only relate the sets $\mathscr{H}_{\mathscr{L}}$. Secondly, in the case of bounded-below relations, the relation between the sets is given by a union, whereas in the case of bounded-above relations the relation is given by the Cartesian product. This results in a very different structure of the set of extreme points and therefore in a different cardinality.

Analogously to the case of bounded-above relations, our aim is to apply the result recursively, and for this we need every connected component to be also a bounded-below relation. It comes as no surprise that there is one special type of relations where this happens: those whose associated graph is an in-arborescence. Similarly to what happened in the case of out-arborescences, if $\mathscr{L}$ is an in-arborescence, it will clearly have one minimal element: its root, and thus it will be bounded below. Moreover, it also holds that every connected subgraph of an in-arborescence is still an in-arborescence. Applying then Lemma 4 recursively in this case for in-arborescences, we obtain the explicit structure of the set of extreme points:

Theorem 4. *The extreme points of $\mathscr{P}(\mathscr{L})$ for an in-arborescence $\mathscr{L}$ are those generated by singletons of $\mathscr{X}$, and $|Ext(\mathscr{P}(\mathscr{L}))| = |\mathscr{X}|$.*

3.3 Bounded Relations

As announced, the previous results on the number of extreme points of bounded-below relations will now be used to determine the maximum number of extreme points for bounded relations. For this, we shall remove the unique minimal element of the bounded relation, resulting on a bounded-above relation, and apply the results established for that case.

Corollary 3. *Consider a bounded relation $\mathscr{L}$ with minimal element x_n.*

(a) If $\mathscr{L}_{x_n}$ is modal, the number of extreme points of $\mathscr{P}(\mathscr{L})$ is $2^{|\mathscr{X}|-2}+1$.

(b) If $\mathscr{L}_{x_n}$ is not modal, the number of extreme points of $\mathscr{P}(\mathscr{L})$ is at most $3 \cdot 2^{|\mathscr{X}|-4} + 1$.

To see that the bounds on the number of extreme points established in Corollary 3 are reached, note that the case in which the resulting relation $\mathscr{L}_{x_n}$ is modal has been already studied in Example 2, as a specific case of a bounded-below relation. The case in which the resulting relation is non modal is analysed in our next example.

Example 3. Consider the relation $\mathscr{L} = \{(2, n-1)\} \cup \{(1, i) : i \in \{2, \dots, n-2\}\}$ over the set $\mathscr{X} = \{x_1, \dots, x_{n-1}\}$. Reasoning as in Example 1, we deduce that $|\text{Ext}(\mathscr{P}(\mathscr{L}))| = 3 \cdot 2^{(n-1)-3}$.

If we now add to $\mathscr{X}$ a new element x_n and consider the relation $\tilde{\mathscr{L}} = \mathscr{L} \cup \{(i, n) : i \in \{3, \dots, n-1\}\}$, we obtain that the new relation $\tilde{\mathscr{L}}$ is bounded, with maximal element x_1 and minimal element x_n. Applying Lemma 4, it follows that $|\text{Ext}(\mathscr{P}(\tilde{\mathscr{L}}))| = |\text{Ext}(\mathscr{P}(\mathscr{L}))| + 1 = 3 \cdot 2^{n-4} + 1 = 3 \cdot 2^{|\mathscr{X}|-4} + 1$. ♦

4 Properties of the Associated Lower Probability

The results on the structure and number of extreme points of $\mathscr{P}(\mathscr{L})$ allow us to determine more efficiently the coherent lower probability induced by some comparative assessments $\mathscr{L}$ by means of Eq. (2). In this section, we shall give in some cases the expression of $\underline{P}$ and study if in some cases it is a 2-monotone capacity or a belief function.

We should give a word of caution here, though: the lower probability $\underline{P}$ does not keep all the information about $\mathscr{L}$, in the sense that the credal set $\mathscr{M}(\underline{P}) := \{P \in \mathbb{P}_{\mathscr{X}} : P(A) \geq \underline{P}(A)\ \forall A \subseteq \mathscr{X}\}$ shall in general be a strict superset of $\mathscr{P}(\mathscr{L})$. This means that the use of $\underline{P}$ will be in general an *outer approximation* of the available information, and that, in order to properly summarize $\mathscr{P}(\mathscr{L})$, we should use the richer language of coherent lower *previsions* [17]. It was in this framework where it was established in [15, Thm. 7] that the lower prevision determined by $\mathscr{P}(\mathscr{L})$ does not satisfy 2-monotonicity for $|\mathscr{X}| \geq 3$ except in the trivial cases where $\mathscr{P}(\mathscr{L})$ is equal to either $\mathbb{P}_{\mathscr{X}}$ or to $P_{\mathscr{X}}$, the uniform probability measure on $\mathscr{X}$.

Nevertheless, it may still be that the coherent lower probability $\underline{P}$ complies with 2 or n-monotonicity; some results in this direction were established in [15, Sect. 4.3], showing that it is a belief function when $|\mathscr{X}| = 3$ but not necessarily 2-monotone for larger cardinalities. This is the problem we shall investigate in this section.

4.1 2-Monotonicity

As shown in [15, Ex. 6] the lower probability $\underline{P}$ determined by $\mathscr{L}$ by means of Eq. (2) need not be 2-monotone. Our next result shows that this is not an accidental finding: there is a quite large family of relations for which 2-monotonicity is violated.

Proposition 3. *Consider a relation* $\mathscr{L}$ *over* $\mathscr{X} = \{x_1, \dots, x_n\}$*, such that there exist* $x_i, x_{i-1}, x_{i-2} \in \mathscr{X}$ *that verify* $\{x_{i-2}\} \subsetneq \langle x_{i-2}\rangle, \langle x_{i-1}\rangle = \langle x_{i-2}\rangle \cup \{x_{i-1}\}$ *and* $\langle x_i\rangle = \langle x_{i-2}\rangle \cup \{x_{i-1}, x_i\}$*. Then the lower probability determined by Eq.* (2) *is not 2-monotone.*

Although the conditions imposed on the relation in the last result may seem rather restrictive, they are in fact quite general. It is only required that there exists at least a chain of length three x_i, x_{i-1}, x_{i-2}, with x_{i-2} having at least one ancestor different from itself, and with x_i, and x_{i-1} having no more ancestors than the ones on the chain and those of x_{i-2}. This situation is illustrated in Fig. 3.

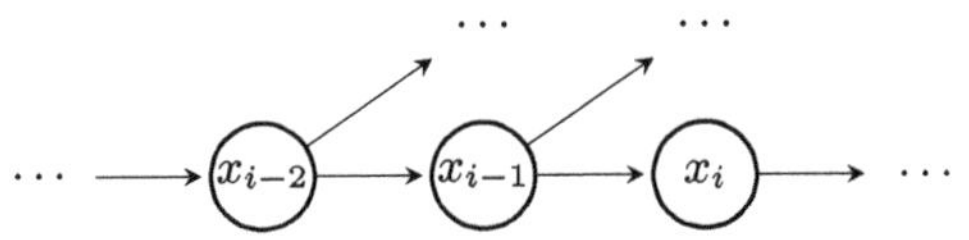

Fig. 3. Graph associated with the conditions required in Proposition 3.

4.2 Belief Functions

Although it has previously been shown that a large number of comparative probability orderings are not 2-monotone, there are two special types of order relations for which their associated lower probability is not only 2-monotone but also a belief function: modal and antimodal comparative probability orderings. These correspond to the case where we only have one element that is deemed to have more (resp., less) probability than the rest, while the others are incomparable to each other, and constitute therefore the minimal bounded-above and bounded-below relations. If we regard the problem from a perspective of resource allocation, this would mean that we explicit one individual that cannot receive less (resp., more) than any other in the distribution.

Theorem 5. *Let* $\mathscr{L}$ *be a comparative probability ordering on* $\mathscr{X}$ *and let* $\underline{P}$ *be the lower probability it induces by means of Eq.* (2)*.*

1. *If* $\mathscr{L}$ *is modal with maximal element* x_1*, then* $\underline{P}$ *is given by*

$$\underline{P}(A) = \begin{cases} 0, & \text{if } x_1 \notin A \\ \dfrac{1}{n - |B|}, & \text{if } A = B \mathbin{\dot\cup} \{x_1\}. \end{cases}$$

2. *If* $\mathscr{L}$ *is antimodal with minimal element* x_n*, then* $\underline{P}$ *is given by*

$$\underline{P}(A) = \begin{cases} 0, & \text{if } \exists x_i \in \mathscr{X} \setminus A \quad x_i \neq x_n \\ \dfrac{n-1}{n}, & \text{if } A = \{x_1, \dots, x_{n-1}\} \\ 1, & \text{if } A = \mathscr{X}. \end{cases}$$

In both cases, $\underline{P}$ is a belief function.

In fact, the lower probability induced by an antimodal ordering is not only a belief function: it is a minitive measure, because its focal elements are nested.

5 Conclusions

Elementary comparative probability orderings were studied by means of a graphical approach in [15], where the explicit structure of the extreme points of the associated credal set, its maximum cardinality and the properties of its associated lower probability were established. In this paper, we have focused on the particular case of comparative probability orderings that are induced by bounded-above and bounded-below relations. We have shown that, in spite of the apparent symmetry between these two cases, the behavior of the set of extreme points enormously differs in them. By suppressing the minimal and maximal elements of these relations and studying the resulting structure we have established tighter bounds of the maximum number of the extreme points of the credal set, and in the case of in- and out-arborescences we have also given the precise structure of the set of extreme points and a procedure of computation.

An intriguing case of relations are the modal and the antimodal, for which we have shown that their associated lower probabilities are belief functions. However, as previously pointed out in [15], belief functions and 2-monotone capacities are not expressive enough models when it comes to comparative assessments, in that they do not allow to determine the associated lower and upper previsions. We have found a large family of comparative probability orderings that do not even satisfy 2-monotonicity, which includes most bounded-below and bounded-above relations, but not all of them. Nevertheless, an exhaustive characterization of which relations induce a 2-monotone lower probability has yet to be established.

Another interesting open problem would be to explore the connection between a comparative probability ordering and its transpose. In this respect, it has been shown that the maximum number of extreme points is reached in modal relations while in their transposes, antimodal relations, the minimum is reached. This suggests a connection between the extreme points of the credal set induced by a relation and the ones induced by its transpose that would be worth examining.

It should be relatively straightforward to generalise some of our results to the case where the graph associated with the order relation is of a hierarchical type, in the sense that we can establish a partition of the nodes that are at the same hierarchical level and make a correspondence with a graph over these sets. This could be of interest for instance in a resource allocation problem where different levels are determined on the individuals and an assessment is of the type "every individual from group i should receive at least as much as any individual from group j".

And finally, it would also be interesting to investigate the problems tackled in this paper in more general scenarios, such as comparative orderings on events, infinite possibility spaces or graded versions of the ratios between the probabilities of the elements. In all of these problems, we expect the theory of coherent sets of desirable gambles [17] to be of assistance. While we expect the complexity of these matters to be significantly higher than the one we have considered in this paper, their investigation should help to complete the picture on the usefulness of comparative probability orderings as an uncertainty model.

Acknowledgments. This work has been supported by grant PID2022-140585NB-I00 funded by MICIU/AEI/10.13039/501100011033 and "FEDER/UE".

Disclosure of Interests. The authors have no competing interests to declare that are relevant to the content of this article.

References

1. Aitchison, J.: The statistical analysis of compositional data. J. Royal Stat. Soc. Ser. B (Methodol.) **44**(2), 139–177 (1982)
2. Augustin, T., Coolen, F., de Cooman, G., Troffaes, M. (eds.): Introduction to Imprecise Probabilities. Wiley Ser. Prob. Stat. Wiley (2014)
3. de Campos, L., Huete, J., Moral, S.: Probability intervals: a tool for uncertain reasoning. Internat. J. Uncertain. Fuzziness Knowl.-Based Syst. **2**, 167–196 (1994)
4. Choquet, G.: Theory of capacities. Annales de l'Institut Fourier **5**, 131–295 (1953–1954)
5. Dubois, D., Prade, H.: Possibility Theory. Plenum Press, New York (1988)
6. Erreygers, A., Miranda, E.: A graphical study of comparative probabilities. J. Math. Psychol. **104**, 102582 (2021)
7. Ferson, S., Kreinovich, V., Ginzburg, L., Myers, D.S., Sentz, K.: Constructing probability boxes and Dempster-Shafer structures. Tech. Rep. SAND2002–4015, Sandia National Laboratories (2003)
8. Fine, T.: An argument for comparative probability. In: Butts, R., Hintikka, J. (eds.) Basic Problems in Methodology and Linguistics, pp. 105–119. Reidel (1979)
9. de Finetti, B.: Sul significato soggettivo della probabilità. Fundam. Math. **17**, 298–329 (1931)
10. Fishburn, P.: The axioms of subjective probability. Stat. Sci. **1**, 335–345 (1986)
11. Fürnkranz, J., Hüllermeier, E.: Preference Learning. Springer (2010)
12. Grabisch, M.: Set functions, games and capacities in decision making. Springer (2016)
13. Koopman, B.: The axioms and algebra of intuitive probability. Ann. Math. **41**, 269–292 (1940)
14. Labreuche, C.: On the Robustness for the Choquet Integral. In: Hüllermeier, E., Kruse, R., Hoffmann, F. (eds.) IPMU 2010. LNCS (LNAI), vol. 6178, pp. 484–493. Springer, Heidelberg (2010). https://doi.org/10.1007/978-3-642-14049-5_50
15. Miranda, E., Destercke, S.: Extreme points of the credal sets generated by comparative probabilities. J. Math. Psychol. **64**(65), 44–57 (2015)
16. Shafer, G.: A Mathematical Theory of Evidence. Princeton University Press, New Jersey (1976)
17. Walley, P.: Statistical Reasoning with Imprecise Probabilities. Chapman and Hall, London (1991)

On the Commutativity of Aggregation and Natural Extension for Lower Probabilities

Ignacio Montes(✉) and Enrique Miranda

Department of Statistics and O.R. and D.M., University of Oviedo, C/Leopoldo Calvo Sotelo 18, 33007 Oviedo, Spain
{imontes,mirandaenrique}@uniovi.es

Abstract. Starting from a finite number of lower probabilities, we study the problem of their aggregation into a global coherent lower prevision on gambles. We follow two approaches: on the one hand, we may first apply the natural extension to each lower probability, obtaining a lower prevision, and then combine these using an aggregation rule; or we may first apply an aggregation rule to the lower probabilities and then take the natural extension of the output. In this paper, we analyse whether the resulting models coincide. In addition, we study if any of the two approaches preserves the property of k-monotonicity.

Keywords: Lower probability · Coherent lower prevision · k-monotonicity · Natural extension · Aggregation rules

1 Introduction

In a decision making problem under uncertainty, experts commonly provide their model about the uncertainty separately, and these are then aggregated into a global model. Although in most situations experts employ probability measures, some recent works such as [7] suggest the use of more flexible models such as lower probabilities [2] (also known as capacities, or as non-additive or fuzzy measures), belief functions [12], necessity and possibility measures [16], or even more advanced tools from imprecise probability theory [15].

Among the many interesting models within imprecise probability theory, two of them offer a good balance between generality and practicality: credal sets [8] and (coherent) lower previsions [15]. Credal sets are closed and convex sets of probability measures, while (coherent) lower previsions provide lower bounds on the expectation operator associated with an unknown or only partially known probability measure. These two models are mathematically equivalent, in the sense that they constitute different representations of the same probabilistic information, and lower probabilities can be seen as particular cases of (coherent) lower previsions in which bounds are specified only on indicators of events.

When the information provided by experts is expressed in terms of a lower prevision, a natural problem is how to aggregate these into a global model, and

B. Vantaggi et al. (Eds.): IPMU 2026, CCIS 3019, pp. 204–218, 2026.
https://doi.org/10.1007/978-3-032-28994-0_15

for this purpose a number of aggregation rules have been proposed in the literature. Among the most popular are conjunction, disjunction, and convex mixture. Firstly, the conjunction rule [5,14] defines the aggregated credal set as the intersection of the given credal sets, meaning that it contains only the probability measures that are deemed valid by all the experts. Secondly, the disjunction rule [5,14], also called convex pooling in [13], defines the aggregated credal set as the convex hull of the union of the credal sets, meaning that it contains the probability measures that are valid for at least one expert. Thirdly, the convex mixture rule [5,14], also called linear opinion pooling in [13], combines the coherent lower previsions through a convex combination. We refer to [14] for a detailed account of the problem of belief aggregation, to our recent contribution [10] for an in-depth analysis of these and other aggregation rules, and to [1,6,11] for further related work on the aggregation of imprecise probability models.

When experts use instead lower probabilities to model uncertainty, it is possible to extend them to a lower prevision, thereby obtaining lower bounds not only on the values of a probability measure but also on its associated expectation operator. This can be achieved through a procedure called natural extension [15]. However, this raises the question of whether we should first aggregate the models into a global lower probability and then compute its natural extension, or instead extend them first to a lower prevision and then apply the aggregation rule on these extensions. In other words, do the aggregation and the natural extension commute? This is the first problem we shall investigate in this paper for the conjunction, disjunction and convex mixture rules.

A subsequent problem is to analyse whether the two approaches (aggregate first and then take the natural extension or apply natural extension and then aggregate) preserve the properties of the lower probabilities, in the sense that if the initial models are k-monotone (or in particular belief functions) the resulting lower prevision is also k-monotone. This would be an extension of the analysis we carried out in [9].

The rest of the paper is organised as follows. In Sect. 2 we explain the basic notions regarding lower previsions and probabilities, paying special attention to the procedure of natural extension. In Sect. 3 we introduce the three main aggregation rules considered in this paper and the problem to be studied. Later, we devote Sects. 4–6 to investigate the commutativity between the aggregation and natural extension for the conjunction, disjunction and convex mixture rules, studying as well if they preserve k-monotonicity. In Sect. 7 we further complete the work by considering other aggregation rules and analysing the preservation of a stronger property than k-monotonicity: minitivity. The paper concludes in Sect. 8 with some additional discussion.

2 Lower Probabilities and Previsions

2.1 Lower Previsions

Let $\mathcal{X}$ be a (not necessarily finite) possibility space, and denote by $\mathcal{L}(\mathcal{X})$ the set of real-valued random variables $f : \mathcal{X} \to \mathbb{R}$, usually called *gambles*. We denote by $\mathbb{P}(\mathcal{X})$ the set of finitely additive probability measures on $\mathcal{P}(\mathcal{X})$.

Given $\mathcal{K} \subseteq \mathcal{L}(\mathcal{X})$, a lower prevision is a function $\underline{P} : \mathcal{K} \to \mathbb{R}$ assigning a real value to each gamble in $\mathcal{K}$. It determines an *upper prevision* $\overline{P} : \mathcal{K}^c \to \mathbb{R}$ by the conjugacy relation $\overline{P}(f) = -\underline{P}(-f)$, where $f \in \mathcal{K}^c = \{f \in \mathcal{L}(\mathcal{X}) \mid -f \in \mathcal{K}\}$. Any lower prevision determines a (possibly empty) *credal set* $\mathcal{M}(\underline{P}) = \{P \in \mathbb{P}(\mathcal{X}) \mid E_P(f) \geq \underline{P}(f)\ \forall f \in \mathcal{K}\}$, where E_P denotes the expectation operator with respect to the probability measure P.

The lower prevision *avoids sure loss* (ASL, for short) when $\mathcal{M}(\underline{P}) \neq \emptyset$ and it is called *coherent* when $\underline{P}(f) = \min\{E_P(f) \mid P \in \mathcal{M}(\underline{P})\}$ for any $f \in \mathcal{K}$. We shall denote by $\underline{\mathbb{P}}(\mathcal{X})$ the family of lower previsions, and by $\underline{\mathbb{P}}'(\mathcal{X})$ the subfamily of coherent lower previsions.

A coherent lower prevision $\underline{P}$ defined on a domain $\mathcal{K} \subseteq \mathcal{L}(\mathcal{X})$ can be extended to a greater domain $\mathcal{K}' \supseteq \mathcal{K}$ using the *natural extension*, given by $\underline{E}_{\underline{P}}(f) = \min\{E_P(f) \mid P \in \mathcal{M}(\underline{P})\}$ for any $f \in \mathcal{K}'$. In particular, any coherent lower prevision $\underline{P}$ defined on $\mathcal{K}$ can be extended to $\mathcal{L}(\mathcal{X})$. Moreover, the natural extension can also be applied to a lower prevision $\underline{P}$ avoiding sure loss; in that case, it gives rise to the smallest coherent lower prevision dominating $\underline{P}$.

A coherent lower prevision $\underline{P}$ defined on $\mathcal{L}(\mathcal{X})$ is *k-monotone*, for some $k \geq 2$, when for any $p \in \{1, \ldots, k\}$ and any $f_1, \ldots, f_p \in \mathcal{L}(\mathcal{X})$ it holds that $\underline{P}\left(\bigvee_{i=1}^p f_i\right) \geq \sum_{\emptyset \neq I \subseteq \{1,\ldots,p\}} (-1)^{|I|+1} \underline{P}\left(\bigwedge_{i \in I} f_i\right)$, where $\wedge$ and $\vee$ refer to the pointwise minimum and maximum, respectively. One instance of 2-monotone lower previsions are the *vacuous* ones on some $C \subseteq \mathcal{X}$, given by $\underline{P}_C(f) = \inf_{x \in C} f(x)$. Their credal set is given by $\mathcal{M}(\underline{P}_C) = \{P \in \mathbb{P}(\mathcal{X}) \mid P(C) = 1\}$.

2.2 Lower Probabilities

A lower probability is a function $\mu : \mathcal{P}(\mathcal{X}) \to [0, 1]$ that is normalised ($\mu(\emptyset) = 0$ and $\mu(\mathcal{X}) = 1$) and monotone increasing ($\mu(A) \leq \mu(B)$ if $A \subseteq B$). It can be seen as a lower prevision $\underline{P}$ defined on $\mathcal{K} = \{I_A \mid A \subseteq \mathcal{X}\}$ by $\underline{P}(I_A) := \mu(A)$ for any $A \subseteq \mathcal{X}$. Thus, we say that μ is *coherent* when $\mu(A) = \min\{P(A) \mid P \in \mathcal{M}(\mu)\}$ for all $A \subseteq \mathcal{X}$, where $\mathcal{M}(\mu) = \{P \in \mathbb{P}(\mathcal{X}) \mid P(A) \geq \mu(A)\ \forall A \subseteq \mathcal{X}\}$. Moreover, any coherent lower prevision $\underline{P}$ defined on $\mathcal{L}(\mathcal{X})$ determines a coherent lower probability by $\mu(A) = \underline{P}(I_A)$ for any $A \subseteq \mathcal{X}$. However, two different coherent lower previsions may determine the same coherent lower probability. The smallest coherent extension to $\mathcal{L}(\mathcal{X})$ of a coherent lower probability is the natural extension, that gives rise to the coherent lower prevision $\underline{E}_\mu(f) = \min\{E_P(f) \mid P \in \mathcal{M}(\mu)\}$ for all $f \in \mathcal{L}(\mathcal{X})$ and satisfies $\mathcal{M}(\mu) = \mathcal{M}(\underline{E}_\mu)$.

A coherent lower probability μ is k-monotone for $k \geq 2$ when for any $1 \leq p \leq k$ and any $A_1, \ldots, A_k \subseteq \mathcal{X}$, $\mu\left(\bigcup_{i=1}^p A_i\right) \geq \sum_{\emptyset \neq I \subseteq \{1,\ldots,p\}} (-1)^{|I|+1} \mu\left(\bigcap_{i \in I} A_i\right)$. A lower probability that is k-monotone for any $k \in \mathbb{N}$ is usually called *belief function*. When $\mathcal{X}$ is finite, belief functions μ can be equivalently represented via the *Möbius inverse*, given by $m(A) = \sum_{B \subseteq A} (-1)^{|A \setminus B|} \mu(B)$ for all $A \subseteq \mathcal{X}$. Given m, the initial μ can be recovered by $\mu(A) = \sum_{B \subseteq A} m(B)$ for all $A \subseteq \mathcal{X}$. While the alternative representation using the Möbius inverse holds for any lower probability, m is non-negative on all events if and only if μ is a belief function.

The restriction of a k-monotone lower prevision $\underline{P}$ to (indicator of) events is a k-monotone lower probability, but more importantly, given a k-monotone lower probability μ, it has a unique k-monotone extension to $\mathcal{L}(\mathcal{X})$, which is the natural extension $\underline{E}_{\mu}$, and it also coincides with the Choquet integral [2] with respect to μ. Thus, under k-monotonicity, the information provided by the restriction of the lower prevision to events determines all its values.

One example of a completely monotone lower prevision is the vacuous lower prevision $\underline{P}_C$ on an event $C \subseteq \mathcal{X}$. Its restriction to events is the belief function μ_C given by $\mu_C(A) = 1$ if $C \subseteq A$ and $\mu_C(A) = 0$ otherwise, and when $\mathcal{X}$ is finite its Möbius inverse satisfies $m(C) = 1$ and $m(A) = 0$ for any $A \neq C$.

3 Aggregation Rules

Definition 1 ([10]). *An* aggregation rule *for coherent lower previsions is a function* $\mathcal{A}_n : \left(\underline{\mathbb{P}}(\mathcal{X})\right)^n \to \underline{\mathbb{P}}(\mathcal{X})$.

The subscript n in $\mathcal{A}_n$ indicates the number of coherent lower previsions to be aggregated, and it will be omitted whenever no confusion can occur.

3.1 Aggregation Rules Under Study

In this paper we consider three of the most popular aggregation rules [5,14]: the conjunction, disjunction and convex mixture.

Conjunction rule ($\mathcal{A}_C$): It gives $\mathcal{A}_C(\underline{P}_1, \ldots, \underline{P}_n)(f) = \underline{E}_{\max\{\underline{P}_1,\ldots,\underline{P}_n\}}(f)$ for any gamble $f \in \mathcal{L}(\mathcal{X})$, and it takes a finite value if $\max\{\underline{P}_1, \ldots, \underline{P}_n\}$ ASL and the value $+\infty$ otherwise. This means that the conjunction rule gives rise to a coherent lower prevision if, and only if, $\max\{\underline{P}_1, \ldots, \underline{P}_n\}$ ASL or, equivalently, when $\mathcal{M}(\underline{P}_1) \cap \ldots \cap \mathcal{M}(\underline{P}_n) \neq \emptyset$. It also follows that $\mathcal{M}\big(\mathcal{A}_C(\underline{P}_1, \ldots, \underline{P}_n)\big) = \mathcal{M}(\underline{P}_1) \cap \ldots \cap \mathcal{M}(\underline{P}_n)$.

Disjunction rule ($\mathcal{A}_D$): It produces the coherent lower prevision given by $\mathcal{A}_D(\underline{P}_1, \ldots, \underline{P}_n)(f) = \min\{\underline{P}_1(f), \ldots, \underline{P}_n(f)\}$ for any $f \in \mathcal{L}(\mathcal{X})$. Its credal set is $\mathcal{M}\big(\mathcal{A}_D(\underline{P}_1, \ldots, \underline{P}_n)\big) = \mathcal{CH}\big(\mathcal{M}(\underline{P}_1) \cup \ldots \cup \mathcal{M}(\underline{P}_n)\big)$, where $\mathcal{CH}$ denotes the convex hull.

Convex mixture ($\mathcal{A}_M$): Given $\alpha_1, \ldots, \alpha_n \in [0,1]$ satisfying $\alpha_1 + \ldots + \alpha_n = 1$, the convex mixture rule they determine is given by $\mathcal{A}_M(\underline{P}_1, \ldots, \underline{P}_n)(f) = \sum_{i=1}^n \alpha_i \underline{P}_i(f)$ for any $f \in \mathcal{L}(\mathcal{X})$. Its credal set is given by:

$$\begin{aligned}\mathcal{M}\big(\mathcal{A}_M(\underline{P}_1, \ldots, \underline{P}_n)\big) &= \alpha_1 \mathcal{M}(\underline{P}_1) \oplus \ldots \oplus \alpha_n \mathcal{M}(\underline{P}_n) \\ &= \{\alpha_1 P_1 + \ldots \alpha_n P_n \mid P_1 \in \mathcal{M}(\underline{P}_1), \ldots, P_n \in \mathcal{M}(\underline{P}_n)\},\end{aligned}$$

where $\oplus$ denotes the Minkowski sum.

These rules satisfy the inequalities

$$\mathcal{A}_D(\underline{P}_1, \ldots, \underline{P}_n) \leq \mathcal{A}_M(\underline{P}_1, \ldots, \underline{P}_n) \leq \mathcal{A}_C(\underline{P}_1, \ldots, \underline{P}_n)$$

for any coherent lower previsions $\underline{P}_1, \ldots, \underline{P}_n$, regardless of the weights considered in the convex mixture rule. For a thorough study of these and other aggregation rules, we refer to [10].

3.2 Aggregation Rules Applied to Lower Probabilities

The aggregation rules presented in the previous subsection can be applied to lower probabilities $\mu_1, \ldots, \mu_n$ by restricting the definition to indicators of events. This produces $\mathcal{A}_C(\mu_1, \ldots, \mu_n)(A) = \underline{E}_{\max\{\mu_1,\ldots,\mu_n\}}(A)$, $\mathcal{A}_D(\mu_1, \ldots, \mu_n)(A) = \min\{\mu_1(A), \ldots, \mu_n(A)\}$ and $\mathcal{A}_M(\mu_1, \ldots, \mu_n)(A) = \sum_{i=1}^{n} \alpha_i \mu_i(A)$ for any $A \subseteq \mathcal{X}$.

In our recent contribution [9] we investigated the problem of the closedness of the aggregation rules applied to lower probabilities, in the sense that if all the lower probabilities belong to a given subfamily of coherent lower probabilities (2- or k-monotone, belief functions, minitive measures) the aggregated model also belongs to the same subfamily. In particular, we showed that (i) $\mathcal{A}_C$ does not preserve k-monotonicity in general, although it preserves 2-monotonicity in the particular case of $n = 2$ and $\mathcal{M}(\mu_1) \cup \mathcal{M}(\mu_2)$ convex; (ii) $\mathcal{A}_D$ does not preserve k-monotonicity in general; and (iii) k-monotonicity is instead preserved by $\mathcal{A}_M$.

3.3 Statement of the Problem

In this study, we investigate whether the aggregation of coherent lower probabilities $\mu_1, \ldots, \mu_n$ commutes with the procedure of the natural extension. Formally, in order to obtain an aggregated model evaluated on $\mathcal{L}(\mathcal{X})$, we have two avenues:

First approach: We apply the natural extension to the lower probabilities, obtaining $\underline{E}_{\mu_1}, \ldots, \underline{E}_{\mu_n}$, and then we aggregate them by means of an aggregation rule $\mathcal{A}$: $\mathcal{A}(\underline{E}_{\mu_1}, \ldots, \underline{E}_{\mu_n})$.

Second approach: We aggregate the lower probabilities by means of a rule $\mathcal{A}$ (on events), giving rise to $\mathcal{A}(\mu_1, \ldots, \mu_n)$, and later we compute the natural extension to $\mathcal{L}(\mathcal{X})$: $\underline{E}_{\mathcal{A}(\mu_1,\ldots,\mu_n)}$.

The question now is: do both approaches give rise to the same model? In other words, do $\mathcal{A}(\underline{E}_{\mu_1}, \ldots, \underline{E}_{\mu_n})$ and $\underline{E}_{\mathcal{A}(\mu_1,\ldots,\mu_n)}$ coincide? This problem is graphically summarised in Fig. 1. A second question of interest is whether these two approaches preserve k-monotonicity. Formally, if $\mu_1, \ldots, \mu_n$ are k-monotone, are $\mathcal{A}(\underline{E}_{\mu_1}, \ldots, \underline{E}_{\mu_n})$ and/or $\underline{E}_{\mathcal{A}(\mu_1,\ldots,\mu_n)}$ k-monotone (on gambles) as well? This would intuitively be the case, given that 2-monotone lower probabilities have a unique extension to a 2-monotone lower prevision (its Choquet integral), but we should also take into account the implications of the aggregation rule.

Next, we investigate these problems for the three aggregation rules introduced in Sect. 3.1.

4 The Conjunction Rule

We start our analysis considering the conjunction rule. Our first result shows that the two approaches described in the previous section coincide.

Theorem 1. *Given coherent lower probabilities* $\mu_1, \ldots, \mu_n$, $\mathcal{M}(\underline{E}_{\mathcal{A}_C(\mu_1,\ldots,\mu_n)}) = \mathcal{M}(\mathcal{A}_C(\underline{E}_{\mu_1}, \ldots, \underline{E}_{\mu_n}))$. *Equivalently,* $\underline{E}_{\mathcal{A}_C(\mu_1,\ldots,\mu_n)} = \mathcal{A}_C(\underline{E}_{\mu_1}, \ldots, \underline{E}_{\mu_n})$.

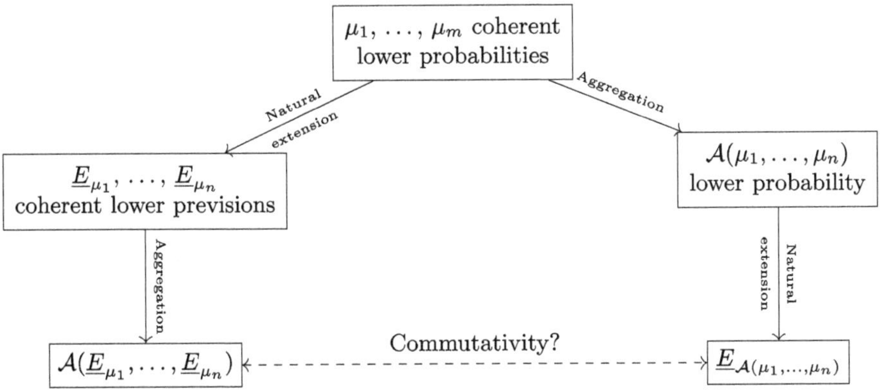

Fig. 1. Graphical representation of the problem.

Proof. Let us prove the equality of the credal sets. For this aim, note that $\mathcal{M}(\underline{E}_{\mathcal{A}_C(\mu_1,\ldots,\mu_n)}) = \mathcal{M}(\mathcal{A}_C(\mu_1, \ldots, \mu_n))$ because $\underline{E}_{\mathcal{A}_C(\mu_1,\ldots,\mu_n)}$ is the natural extension of $\mathcal{A}_C(\mu_1, \ldots, \mu_n)$. Also, $\mathcal{M}(\mu_1) \cap \ldots \cap \mathcal{M}(\mu_n) = \mathcal{M}(\underline{E}_{\mu_1}) \cap \ldots \cap \mathcal{M}(\underline{E}_{\mu_n}) = \mathcal{M}(\mathcal{A}_C(\underline{E}_{\mu_1}, \ldots, \underline{E}_{\mu_n}))$, considering the definition of the conjunction and using again that $\underline{E}_{\mu_i}$ is the natural extension of μ_i. Therefore,

$$\begin{aligned} P \in \mathcal{M}(\underline{E}_{\mathcal{A}_C(\mu_1,\ldots,\mu_n)}) &\Leftrightarrow P \in \mathcal{M}(\mathcal{A}_C(\mu_1, \ldots, \mu_n)) \Leftrightarrow P \geq \mathcal{A}_C(\mu_1, \ldots, \mu_n) \\ &\Leftrightarrow P \geq \max\{\mu_1, \ldots, \mu_n\} \Leftrightarrow P \geq \mu_i \ \ \forall i \Leftrightarrow P \in \mathcal{M}(\mu_i) \ \ \forall i \\ &\Leftrightarrow P \in \mathcal{M}(\mu_1) \cap \ldots \cap \mathcal{M}(\mu_n) = \mathcal{M}(\mathcal{A}_C(\underline{E}_{\mu_1}, \ldots, \underline{E}_{\mu_n})). \end{aligned}$$

To see the equality between $\underline{E}_{\mathcal{A}_C(\mu_1,\ldots,\mu_n)}$ and $\mathcal{A}_C(\underline{E}_{\mu_1}, \ldots, \underline{E}_{\mu_n})$ observe on one side that if the credal sets are non-empty, their lower envelopes $\underline{E}_{\mathcal{A}_C(\mu_1,\ldots,\mu_n)}$ and $\mathcal{A}_C(\underline{E}_{\mu_1}, \ldots, \underline{E}_{\mu_n})$ coincide; and if the credal sets are empty, this means that $\mathcal{M}(\mu_1) \cap \ldots \cap \mathcal{M}(\mu_n) = \mathcal{M}(\underline{E}_{\mu_1}) \cap \ldots \cap \mathcal{M}(\underline{E}_{\mu_n}) = \emptyset$, so $\mathcal{A}_C(\underline{E}_{\mu_1}, \ldots, \underline{E}_{\mu_n}) = +\infty$. Also, $\mathcal{M}(\underline{E}_{\mathcal{A}_C(\mu_1,\ldots,\mu_n)}) = \emptyset$ means that $\mathcal{A}_C(\mu_1, \ldots, \mu_n)$ does not avoid sure loss, and thus $\underline{E}_{\mathcal{A}_C(\mu_1,\ldots,\mu_n)} = +\infty$. □

Despite this positive property, as shown in [9, Ex.1, Ex.6], the conjunction rule may not preserve the property of 2-monotonicity. Nevertheless, our next result provides a sufficient condition for this preservation.

Theorem 2. *Let μ_1 and μ_2 be 2-monotone lower probabilities. If $\mathcal{M}(\mu_1) \cup \mathcal{M}(\mu_2)$ is convex, then $\mathcal{A}_C(\underline{E}_{\mu_1}, \underline{E}_{\mu_2})(f) = \max\{\underline{E}_{\mu_1}(f), \underline{E}_{\mu_2}(f)\}$ for any $f \in \mathcal{L}(\mathcal{X})$ and $\mathcal{A}_C(\underline{E}_{\mu_1}, \underline{E}_{\mu_2})$ is a 2-monotone lower prevision.*

Proof. From [4, Thm. 9], $\underline{E}_{\mu_1}$ and $\underline{E}_{\mu_2}$ are 2-monotone lower previsions. Noting that two gambles $f, g \in \mathcal{L}(\mathcal{X})$ are comonotone if $f(x) < f(y)$ implies $g(x) \leq g(y)$, by [4, Thm. 15] it follows that $\underline{E}_{\mu_i}(f+g) = \underline{E}_{\mu_i}(f) + \underline{E}_{\mu_i}(g)$ for any comonotone $f, g \in \mathcal{L}(\mathcal{X})$ and $i \in \{1, 2\}$, that is, $\underline{E}_{\mu_1}$ and $\underline{E}_{\mu_2}$ are comonotone additive.

Consider two comonotone gambles $f, g \in \mathcal{L}(\mathcal{X})$. From the coherence of $\underline{E}_{\mu_1}$ and $\underline{E}_{\mu_2}$ there exists $P_1 \in \mathcal{M}(\underline{E}_{\mu_1}) = \mathcal{M}(\mu_1)$ such that

$$E_{P_1}(f+g) = \underline{E}_{\mu_1}(f+g) \leq \max\{\underline{E}_{\mu_1}(f+g), \underline{E}_{\mu_2}(f+g)\} \leq \mathcal{A}_C(\underline{E}_{\mu_1}, \underline{E}_{\mu_2})(f+g),$$

where the second inequality follows because $\mathcal{A}_C(\underline{E}_{\mu_1}, \underline{E}_{\mu_2})$ is by definition the natural extension of $\max\{\underline{E}_{\mu_1}(f+g), \underline{E}_{\mu_2}(f+g)\}$; similarly, there exists $P_2 \in \mathcal{M}(\underline{E}_{\mu_2}) = \mathcal{M}(\mu_2)$ such that

$$E_{P_2}(f+g) = \underline{E}_{\mu_2}(f+g) \leq \max\{\underline{E}_{\mu_1}(f+g), \underline{E}_{\mu_2}(f+g)\} \leq \mathcal{A}_C(\underline{E}_{\mu_1}, \underline{E}_{\mu_2})(f+g).$$

Since $\mathcal{M}(\mu_1) \cup \mathcal{M}(\mu_2)$ is convex, it follows from [17, Thm. 6] that there is some $\alpha \in [0,1]$ such that $P^\alpha = \alpha P_1 + (1-\alpha) P_2$ belongs to $\mathcal{M}(\mu_1) \cap \mathcal{M}(\mu_2) = \mathcal{M}(\mathcal{A}_C(\underline{E}_{\mu_1}, \underline{E}_{\mu_2}))$, and therefore P^α dominates $\mathcal{A}_C$. Since moreover

$$E_{P^\alpha}(f+g) \leq \max\{\underline{E}_{P_1}(f+g), \underline{E}_{P_2}(f+g)\} \leq \mathcal{A}_C(\underline{E}_{\mu_1}, \underline{E}_{\mu_2})(f+g),$$

we deduce that

$$\mathcal{A}_C(\underline{E}_{\mu_1}, \underline{E}_{\mu_2})(f+g) = E_{P^\alpha}(f+g) = \max\{\underline{E}_{\mu_1}(f+g), \underline{E}_{\mu_2}(f+g)\}.$$

Using that the zero gamble is comonotone with any other gamble f, we conclude that $\mathcal{A}_C(\underline{E}_{\mu_1}, \underline{E}_{\mu_2})(f) = \max\{\underline{E}_{\mu_1}(f), \underline{E}_{\mu_2}(f)\}$ for any $f \in \mathcal{L}(\mathcal{X})$.

Assume w.l.o.g. that $\mathcal{A}_C(\underline{E}_{\mu_1}, \underline{E}_{\mu_2})(f+g) = \underline{E}_{\mu_1}(f+g)$. Then we obtain

$$\begin{aligned}\mathcal{A}_C(\underline{E}_{\mu_1}, \underline{E}_{\mu_2})(f+g) &= \underline{E}_{\mu_1}(f+g) = \underline{E}_{\mu_1}(f) + \underline{E}_{\mu_1}(g)\\ &\leq \mathcal{A}_C(\underline{E}_{\mu_1}, \underline{E}_{\mu_2})(f) + \mathcal{A}_C(\underline{E}_{\mu_1}, \underline{E}_{\mu_2})(g),\end{aligned}$$

and since $\mathcal{A}_C(\underline{E}_{\mu_1}, \underline{E}_{\mu_2})$ is super-additive,

$$\mathcal{A}_C(\underline{E}_{\mu_1}, \underline{E}_{\mu_2})(f+g) = \mathcal{A}_C(\underline{E}_{\mu_1}, \underline{E}_{\mu_2})(f) + \mathcal{A}_C(\underline{E}_{\mu_1}, \underline{E}_{\mu_2})(g).$$

Therefore, $\mathcal{A}_C(\underline{E}_{\mu_1}, \underline{E}_{\mu_2})$ is comonotone additive and by [4, Thm. 9] it is 2-monotone. □

Note that Theorem 2 cannot be extended to the aggregation of more than two lower probabilities. For example, if μ_1 and μ_2 are 2-monotone lower probabilities such that $\mathcal{A}_C(\mu_1, \mu_2)$ is not 2-monotone and let μ_3 be the vacuous lower probability on $\mathcal{X}$, it holds that $\mathcal{M}(\mu_1) \cup \mathcal{M}(\mu_2) \cup \mathcal{M}(\mu_3) = \mathcal{M}(\mu_3) = \mathbb{P}(\mathcal{X})$, which is convex, but $\mathcal{A}_C(\mu_1, \mu_2, \mu_3) = \mathcal{A}_C(\mu_1, \mu_2)$ is not 2-monotone. On the other hand, Theorem 2 assures the preservation of 2-monotonicity, similar hypotheses do not ensure the preservation of k-monotonicity for $k \geq 3$, as we show in [9, Ex. 6].

5 The Disjunction Rule

We next turn our attention on the disjunction rule. Our first result shows a relation between the two approaches described in Sect. 3.3.

Theorem 3. *Let $\mu_1, \ldots, \mu_n$ be coherent lower probabilities. Then, it holds that $\mathcal{M}(\mathcal{A}_D(\underline{E}_{\mu_1}, \ldots, \underline{E}_{\mu_n})) \subseteq \mathcal{M}(\underline{E}_{\mathcal{A}_D(\mu_1,\ldots,\mu_n)})$. Equivalently $\mathcal{A}_D(\underline{E}_{\mu_1}, \ldots, \underline{E}_{\mu_n}) \geq \underline{E}_{\mathcal{A}_D(\mu_1,\ldots,\mu_n)}$.*

Proof. Let us see the inclusion between the credal sets. For this aim, note that:

$$\begin{aligned}
&\mathcal{M}(\mathcal{A}_D(\underline{E}_{\mu_1}, \ldots, \underline{E}_{\mu_n})) \\
&\qquad = \{P \in \mathbb{P}(\mathcal{X}) \mid E_P(f) \geq \mathcal{A}_D(\underline{E}_{\mu_1}, \ldots, \underline{E}_{\mu_n})(f) \quad \forall f \in \mathcal{L}(\mathcal{X})\} \\
&\qquad = \{P \in \mathbb{P}(\mathcal{X}) \mid E_P(f) \geq \min\{\underline{E}_{\mu_1}(f), \ldots, \underline{E}_{\mu_n}(f)\} \quad \forall f \in \mathcal{L}(\mathcal{X})\}. \\
&\mathcal{M}(\underline{E}_{\mathcal{A}_D(\mu_1,\ldots,\mu_n)}) = \mathcal{M}(\mathcal{A}_D(\mu_1, \ldots, \mu_n)) \\
&\qquad = \{P \in \mathbb{P}(\mathcal{X}) \mid P(A) \geq \min\{\mu_1(A), \ldots, \mu_n(A)\} \quad \forall A \subseteq \mathcal{X}\}.
\end{aligned}$$

The inclusion is then trivial, once we note that any probability measure P satisfying $E_P(f) \geq \min\{\underline{E}_{\mu_1}(f), \ldots, \underline{E}_{\mu_n}(f)\}$ for any $f \in \mathcal{L}(\mathcal{X})$, in particular satisfies $P(A) \geq \min\{\mu_1(A), \ldots, \mu_n(A)\}$ for any $A \subseteq \mathcal{X}$, simply by taking $f = I_A$. □

In the following example we show that the converse inclusion does not always hold and that $\mathcal{A}_D(\mu_1, \ldots, \mu_n)$ may not preserve k-monotonicity.

Example 1. Consider a three-element space $\mathcal{X}$, and the probability measures $P_1 = (1/3, 1/3, 1/3)$ and $P_2 = (1/2, 1/4, 1/4)$, which are in particular k-monotone for any $k \geq 2$ (i.e., belief functions). The values of P_1 and P_2 and the disjunction rule $\mathcal{A}_D(P_1, P_2)$ on events are:

A	$\{x_1\}$	$\{x_2\}$	$\{x_3\}$	$\{x_1,x_2\}$	$\{x_1,x_3\}$	$\{x_2,x_3\}$	$\mathcal{X}$
$P_1(A)$	$1/3$	$1/3$	$1/3$	$2/3$	$2/3$	$2/3$	1
$P_2(A)$	$1/2$	$1/4$	$1/4$	$3/4$	$3/4$	$1/2$	1
$\mathcal{A}_D(P_1,P_2)(A)$	$1/3$	$1/4$	$1/4$	$2/3$	$2/3$	$1/2$	1
$m_D(A)$	$1/3$	$1/4$	$1/4$	$1/12$	$1/12$	0	0

The previous table also shows the Möbius inverse of $\mathcal{A}_D(P_1, P_2)$, which is non-negative, meaning that $\mathcal{A}_D(P_1, P_2)$ is a belief function, and hence a k-monotone lower probability for any $k \geq 2$, and that its natural extension $\underline{E}_{\mathcal{A}_D(P_1,P_2)}$ is a k-monotone lower prevision.

Consider also the gambles f and g reported in the table below, where $f \wedge g$, $f \vee g$ and their evaluation on $\mathcal{A}_D(\underline{E}_{P_1}, \underline{E}_{P_2})$ are also shown:

	x_1	x_2	x_3	P_1	P_2	$\mathcal{A}_D(\underline{E}_{P_1}, \underline{E}_{P_2})$
f	0	4	-2	$2/3$	$1/2$	$1/2$
g	-2	-3	4	$-1/3$	$-3/4$	$-3/4$
$f \wedge g$	-2	-3	-2	$-7/3$	$-9/4$	$-7/3$
$f \vee g$	0	4	4	$8/3$	2	2

Note that $\mathcal{A}_D(\underline{E}_{P_1}, \underline{E}_{P_2})(h) = \min\{\underline{E}_{P_1}(h), \underline{E}_{P_2}(h)\} = \min\{E_{P_1}(h), E_{P_2}(h)\}$ for any gamble $h \in \mathcal{L}(\mathcal{X})$. Considering the gamble f, we get

$$\begin{aligned}
\underline{E}_{\mathcal{A}_D(P_1,P_2)}(f) &= \min\{E_P(f) \mid P \in \text{ext}(\mathcal{M}(\underline{E}_{\mathcal{A}_D(P_1,P_2)}))\} \\
&= \min\{E_P(f) \mid P \in \text{ext}(\mathcal{M}(\mathcal{A}_D(P_1, P_2)))\},
\end{aligned}$$

implying that $\underline{E}_{\mathcal{A}_D(P_1,P_2)}(f) = 1/3 < \mathcal{A}_D(\underline{E}_{\mu_1}, \underline{E}_{\mu_2})(f)$, so the inequality in Theorem 3 may be strict. Moreover, $\mathcal{A}_D(\underline{E}_{P_1}, \underline{E}_{P_2})(f \wedge g) + \mathcal{A}_D(\underline{E}_{P_1}, \underline{E}_{P_2})(f \vee g) = -1/3$ and $-\mathcal{A}_D(\underline{E}_{P_1}, \underline{E}_{P_2})(f) - \mathcal{A}_D(\underline{E}_{P_1}, \underline{E}_{P_2})(g) = -1/4$, meaning that $\mathcal{A}_D(\underline{E}_{P_1}, \underline{E}_{P_2})$ is not even 2-monotone. ♦

6 The Convex Mixture Rule

For the convex mixture rule it is not difficult to establish the following.

Theorem 4. *Given coherent lower probabilities $\mu_1, \ldots, \mu_n$, $\mathcal{M}(\underline{E}_{\mathcal{A}_M(\mu_1,\ldots,\mu_n)}) \supseteq \mathcal{M}(\mathcal{A}_M(\underline{E}_{\mu_1}, \ldots, \underline{E}_{\mu_n}))$. Equivalently, $\underline{E}_{\mathcal{A}_M(\mu_1,\ldots,\mu_n)} \leq \mathcal{A}_M(\underline{E}_{\mu_1}, \ldots, \underline{E}_{\mu_n})$.*

Proof. Since $\underline{E}_{\mathcal{A}_M(\mu_1,\ldots,\mu_n)}$ is the natural extension of $\mathcal{A}_M(\mu_1, \ldots, \mu_n)$, $P \in \mathcal{M}(\underline{E}_{\mathcal{A}_M(\mu_1,\ldots,\mu_n)}) = \mathcal{M}(\mathcal{A}_M(\mu_1, \ldots, \mu_n)) \Leftrightarrow P(A) \geq \sum_{i=1}^n \alpha_i \mu_i(A)\ \forall A \subseteq \mathcal{X}$ and $P \in \mathcal{M}(\mathcal{A}_M(\underline{E}_{\mu_1}, \ldots, \underline{E}_{\mu_n})) \Leftrightarrow E_P(f) \geq \sum_{i=1}^n \alpha_i \underline{E}_{\mu_i}(f) \quad \forall f \in \mathcal{L}(\mathcal{X})$.

We deduce that $\mathcal{M}(\underline{E}_{\mathcal{A}_M(\mu_1,\ldots,\mu_n)}) \supseteq \mathcal{M}(\mathcal{A}_M(\underline{E}_{\mu_1}, \ldots, \underline{E}_{\mu_n}))$, since if P satisfies $E_P(f) \geq \sum_{i=1}^n \alpha_i \underline{E}_{\mu_i}(f)$ for any gamble $f \in \mathcal{L}(\mathcal{X})$, in particular taking $f = I_A$ for some event $A \subseteq \mathcal{X}$ we reach $P(A) \geq \sum_{i=1}^n \alpha_i \mu_i(A)$. □

As the next example shows, the dominance may be strict, meaning that both approaches do not coincide in general.

Example 2. Let $\mathcal{X} = \{x_1, x_2, x_3, x_4\}$ and let μ_1, μ_2 and $\mathcal{A}_M(\mu_1, \mu_2) = 0.5\mu_1 + 0.5\mu_2$ be given by:

A	$\mu_1(A)$	$\mu_2(A)$	$\mathcal{A}_M(\mu_1, \mu_2)(A)$
$\{x_1\}$	0.25	0	0.125
$\{x_2\}$	0.25	0	0.125
$\{x_3\}$	0	0	0
$\{x_4\}$	0	0	0
$\{x_1, x_2\}$	0.5	0	0.25
$\{x_1, x_3\}$	0.5	0	0.25
$\{x_1, x_4\}$	0.5	0	0.25
$\{x_2, x_3\}$	0.5	0	0.25
$\{x_2, x_4\}$	0.5	0	0.25
$\{x_3, x_4\}$	0	0	0
$\{x_1, x_2, x_3\}$	0.75	0.25	0.5
$\{x_1, x_2, x_4\}$	0.75	0.25	0.5
$\{x_1, x_3, x_4\}$	0.5	0.25	0.375
$\{x_2, x_3, x_4\}$	0.5	0.25	0.375
$\mathcal{X}$	1	1	1

It can be checked that both μ_2 and $\mathcal{A}_M(\mu_1, \mu_2)$ are belief functions, and as a consequence also 2-monotone, while μ_1 is coherent, being the lower envelope of the probability mass functions $(0.25, 0.25, 0.25, 0.25)$ and $(0.5, 0.5, 0, 0)$, but not 2-monotone. If we now consider the gamble f given by $f(x_1) = 1, f(x_2) = 3, f(x_3) = 2$ and $f(x_4) = 2$, it follows that $\underline{E}_{\mu_1}(f) = 2$ and $\underline{E}_{\mu_2}(f) = \frac{5}{4}$, whence $\mathcal{A}_M(\underline{E}_{\mu_1}, \underline{E}_{\mu_2})(f) = 13/8$, while $\underline{E}_{\mathcal{A}_M(\mu_1,\mu_2)}(f) = 1.5$. As a consequence, the procedures of convex mixture and natural extension do not commute. ♦

In spite of this negative result, our next result shows not only that both approaches preserve k-monotonicity, but also that when the lower probabilities are k-monotone for some $k \geq 2$, they coincide. This is a consequence of the linearity of the Choquet integral and its connection with the natural extension in the case of k-monotone lower probabilities.

Theorem 5. *Given k-monotone lower probabilities $\mu_1, \ldots, \mu_n$, $\underline{E}_{\mathcal{A}_M(\mu_1,\ldots,\mu_n)} = \mathcal{A}_M(\underline{E}_{\mu_1}, \ldots, \underline{E}_{\mu_n})$ and they are k-monotone lower previsions.*

Proof. It is an immediate consequence of the definition that a convex mixture of k-monotone lower previsions (resp., lower probabilities) is again k-monotone. Also, the natural extension $\underline{E}_{\mathcal{A}_M(\mu_1,\ldots,\mu_n)}$ of a k-monotone lower probability is a k-monotone lower prevision.

Finally, to see that $\mathcal{A}_M(\underline{E}_{\mu_1}, \ldots, \underline{E}_{\mu_n})$ and $\underline{E}_{\mathcal{A}_M(\mu_1,\ldots,\mu_n)}$ coincide, simply note that for any event $A \subseteq \mathcal{X}$, $\underline{E}_{\mathcal{A}_M(\mu_1,\ldots,\mu_n)}(A) = \mathcal{A}_M(\mu_1, \ldots, \mu_n)(A) = \sum_{i=1}^n \alpha_i \mu_i(A)$ and $\mathcal{A}_M(\underline{E}_{\mu_1}, \ldots, \underline{E}_{\mu_n}) = \sum_{i=1}^n \alpha_i \underline{E}_{\mu_i}(A) = \sum_{i=1}^n \alpha_i \mu_i(A)$. Since their restriction to events coincide, and they are k-monotone, their extension to gambles coincide as well. □

7 Further Comments

7.1 Other Aggregation Rules for Lower Previsions

So far, we have investigated the conjunction, disjunction, and convex mixture rules. However, other rules have also been proposed in the literature for aggregating coherent lower previsions. In the following, we summarise some of them:

Pareto rule ($\mathcal{A}_P$): It is defined as [14]

$$\mathcal{A}_P(\underline{P}_1, \ldots, \underline{P}_n)(f) = \min\left\{ \max_{i=1,\ldots,n} \underline{P}_i(f), \min_{i=1,\ldots,n} \overline{P}_i(f) \right\} \quad \forall f \in \mathcal{L}(\mathcal{X}).$$

Conjunction-Disjunction (CD) rule ($\mathcal{A}_{CD}$): It is defined as [6]

$$\mathcal{A}_{CD}(\underline{P}_1, \ldots, \underline{P}_n) = \begin{cases} \mathcal{A}_C(\underline{P}_1, \ldots, \underline{P}_n), & \text{if } \max\{\underline{P}_1, \ldots, \underline{P}_n\} \text{ ASL.} \\ \mathcal{A}_D(\underline{P}_1, \ldots, \underline{P}_n), & \text{otherwise.} \end{cases}$$

Maximal consistent subsets (MCS) rule ($\mathcal{A}_{MCS}$): A set $I \subseteq \{1, \ldots, n\}$ is a maximal consistent subset if $\cap_{i \in I} \mathcal{M}(\underline{P}_i) \neq \emptyset$ and it is maximal with this property with respect to the order determined on $\{1, \ldots, n\}$ by set inclusion. If $I_1, \ldots, I_k$ are the maximal consistent subsets, the maximal consistent subsets rule considers the lower prevision determined by the credal set [14]:

$$\mathcal{M}(\mathcal{A}_{MCS}(\underline{P}_1, \ldots, \underline{P}_n)) = \mathcal{CH}\left(\bigcup_{j=1}^{k} \bigcap_{i \in I_j} \mathcal{M}(\underline{P}_i)\right).$$

The Pareto rule is justified from a behavioral point of view in [14], while the CD and MCS rules are modifications of the conjunction rule for cases in which it leads to a non-coherent aggregated model. Specifically, $\mathcal{A}_{CD}$ applies $\mathcal{A}_C$ whenever it results in a coherent model (i.e., when $\max\{\underline{P}_1, \ldots, \underline{P}_n\}$ ASL, or equivalently, when $\mathcal{M}(\underline{P}_1) \cap \ldots \cap \mathcal{M}(\underline{P}_n) \neq \emptyset$), and applies $\mathcal{A}_D$ otherwise. In contrast, $\mathcal{A}_{MCS}$ identifies the maximal consistent sets, applies $\mathcal{A}_C$ to them, and subsequently applies $\mathcal{A}_D$ to those sets. These three rules were extensively investigated in our recent contribution [10].

These three rules are undoubtedly interesting, but we have not focused on them in this paper for the following reasons:

- The Pareto rule may give rise to a non-coherent lower prevision. Indeed, when $\max\{\underline{P}_1, \ldots, \underline{P}_n\}$ ASL (a condition that guarantees the coherence of $\mathcal{A}_C$), then $\mathcal{A}_P(\underline{P}_1, \ldots, \underline{P}_n) = \max\{\underline{P}_1, \ldots, \underline{P}_n\}$ (see [10, Prop.7(i)]), meaning that $\mathcal{A}_C$ is the natural extension of $\mathcal{A}_P$ (which in this case ASL but may not be coherent). Moreover, when $\max\{\underline{P}_1, \ldots, \underline{P}_n\}$ is coherent, then $\mathcal{A}_P$ and $\mathcal{A}_C$ coincide and both are coherent lower prevision. Otherwise, if $\max\{\underline{P}_1, \ldots, \underline{P}_n\}$ is not coherent, neither the commutativity between aggregation and the natural extension nor the preservation of k-monotonicity for $\mathcal{A}_P$ can be guaranteed. These observations lead us to conclude that the behaviour of $\mathcal{A}_P$ in the setting of this paper is worse than that of $\mathcal{A}_C$.
- When all the lower probabilities are compatible, in the sense that $\mathcal{M}(\mu_1) \cap \ldots \cap \mathcal{M}(\mu_n) \neq \emptyset$, $\mathcal{A}_{CD}$ coincides with $\mathcal{A}_C$. Hence, in this case Theorems 1 and 2 hold under the same hypotheses for $\mathcal{A}_C$. Otherwise, $\mathcal{A}_{CD}$ coincides with $\mathcal{A}_D$, which implies from Theorem 3 that $\mathcal{A}_{CD}(\underline{E}_{\mu_1}, \ldots, \underline{E}_{\mu_n}) \geq \underline{E}_{\mathcal{A}_{CD}(\mu_1, \ldots, \mu_n)}$, but equality cannot be guaranteed even under 2-monotonicity, and k-monotonicity is not preserved (see Example 1).
- Finally, when all the lower probabilities are compatible, $\mathcal{A}_{MCS}$ coincides with $\mathcal{A}_C$ (as well as with $\mathcal{A}_{CD}$), meaning that Theorems 1 and 2 also apply to this rule. Otherwise, $\mathcal{A}_{MCS}$ applies first the conjunction to the maximal consistent subsets and then the disjunction. Since $\mathcal{A}_D$ only satisfies a dominance relation between the two approaches, and it does not preserve k-monotonicity, $\mathcal{A}_{MCS}$ inherits the same (negative) traits as $\mathcal{A}_C$ and $\mathcal{A}_D$.

7.2 Preservation of Minitivity

So far, we have investigated the preservation of k-monotonicity, but we may take a look to a more restrictive condition: minitivity. Consider throughout this subsection a finite possibility space $\mathcal{X}$. A lower probability μ is called *minitive* if it satisfies $\mu(A \cap B) = \min\{\mu(A), \mu(B)\}$ for any $A, B \subseteq \mathcal{X}$; minitive measures are particular cases of belief functions. The situation is more restrictive if we consider minitivity for lower previsions. Following [3], a coherent lower prevision $\underline{P}$ is minitive preserving when its conjugate upper prevision $\overline{P}$, defined as $\overline{P}(f) = -\underline{P}(-f)$ for any $f \in \mathcal{L}(\mathcal{X})$, is *supremum preserving*, that is when $\overline{P}(f) = \sup_{x\in\mathcal{X}} f(x)\overline{P}(\{x\})$ for any $f \in \mathcal{L}(\mathcal{X})$. It follows from the results in [3, Sect. 8] that the natural extension $\underline{E}_\mu$ of a minitive measure μ from events to gambles is minimum-preserving if and only if μ is $0-1$-valued in addition to being minitive, meaning that μ is vacuous in some event C. Since this is a very restrictive situation, we can easily obtain the following result.

Proposition 1. *Let $\mathcal{X}$ be a finite possibility space and let $\mu_1, \ldots, \mu_n$ be vacuous models on $C_1, \ldots, C_n$, respectively. Then $\underline{E}_{\mathcal{A}_C(\mu_1,\ldots,\mu_n)}$ and $\mathcal{A}_C(\underline{E}_{\mu_1}, \ldots, \underline{E}_{\mu_n})$ are coherent if and only if $C_1 \cap \ldots \cap C_n \neq \emptyset$. In such case, $\mathcal{A}_C(\mu_1, \ldots, \mu_2)$ is the vacuous model on $C_1 \cap \ldots \cap C_n$.*

Proof. It suffices to consider that $\mathcal{M}(\underline{E}_{\mathcal{A}_C(\mu_1,\ldots,\mu_n)}) = \mathcal{M}(\mathcal{A}_C(\mu_1, \ldots, \mu_n)) = \mathcal{M}(\mu_1) \cap \ldots \cap \mathcal{M}(\mu_n) = \{P \in \mathbb{P}(\mathcal{X}) \mid P(C_1 \cap \ldots \cap C_n) = 1\}$, which is empty if and only if $C_1 \cap \cdots \cap C_n \neq \emptyset$. In that case, we deduce from Theorem 1 that $\underline{E}_{\mathcal{A}_C(\mu_1,\ldots,\mu_n)} = \mathcal{A}_C(\underline{E}_{\mu_1}, \ldots, \underline{E}_{\mu_n})$. □

Concerning the disjunction, we obtain the following result; a related result was established in [9, Prop. 22].

Proposition 2. *Let $\mathcal{X}$ be a finite possibility space and let $\mu_1, \ldots, \mu_n$ be vacuous models on $C_1, \ldots, C_n$, respectively. Then $\mathcal{A}_D(\mu_1, \ldots, \mu_n)$ is a vacuous model on $C_1 \cup \ldots \cup C_n$, $\underline{E}_{\mathcal{A}_D(\mu_1,\ldots,\mu_n)} = \mathcal{A}_D(\underline{E}_{\mu_1}, \ldots, \underline{E}_{\mu_n})$ and $\underline{E}_{\mathcal{A}_D(\mu_1,\ldots,\mu_n)}$ preserves minitivity.*

Proof. First of all, for any $A \subseteq \mathcal{X}$ it holds that:

$$\mathcal{A}_D(\mu_1, \ldots, \mu_n) = \min\{\mu_1(A), \ldots, \mu_n(A)\} = \begin{cases} 1, & \text{if } A \supseteq C_1, \ldots, A \supseteq C_n. \\ 0, & \text{otherwise.} \end{cases}$$

Hence, $\mathcal{A}_D(\mu_1, \ldots, \mu_n)$ is the vacuous model on $C_1 \cup \ldots \cup C_n$ and its credal set is given by $\mathcal{M}(\mathcal{A}_D(\mu_1, \ldots, \mu_n)) = \{P \in \mathbb{P}(\mathcal{X}) \mid P(C_1 \cup \ldots \cup C_n) = 1\}$. Secondly,

$$\begin{aligned} \mathcal{M}(\mathcal{A}_D(\underline{E}_{\mu_1}, \ldots, \underline{E}_{\mu_n})) &= \mathcal{CH}(\mathcal{M}(\underline{E}_{\mu_1}) \cup \ldots \cup \mathcal{M}(\underline{E}_{\mu_n})) \\ &= \mathcal{CH}(\mathcal{M}(\mu_1) \cup \ldots \cup \mathcal{M}(\mu_n)) = \mathcal{CH}\Big(\{P \in \mathbb{P}(\mathcal{X}) \mid \max_{i=1,\ldots,n} P(C_i) = 1\}\Big) \\ &\subseteq \{P \in \mathbb{P}(\mathcal{X}) \mid P(C_1 \cup \ldots \cup C_n) = 1\}. \end{aligned}$$

The other inclusion also holds: take P such that $P(C_1 \cup \ldots \cup C_n) = 1$, and define $\alpha_1 = P(C_1)$ and $\alpha_i = P(C_i \setminus (C_1 \cup \ldots \cup C_{i-1}))$ for any $i = 1, \ldots, n$. Also, take $P_1 \in \mathcal{M}(\mu_1)$ such that $P(C_1) = 1$, and for any $i \in \{2, \ldots, n\}$ such that $\alpha_i > 0$, take $P_i \in \mathcal{M}(\mu_i)$ such that $P(C_i \setminus (C_1 \cup \ldots \cup C_{i-1})) = 1$. Then, $P = \alpha_1 P_1 + \sum_{i>1|\alpha_i>0} \alpha_i P_i$. Thus, both approaches coincide and preserve minitivity. □

Finally, contrary to the conjunction and disjunction rules, the convex mixture rule does not preserve minitivity. To see it, note that

$$\begin{aligned}\mathcal{M}(\mathcal{A}_M(\underline{E}_{\mu_1}, \ldots, \underline{E}_{\mu_n})) &= \{\alpha_1 P_1 + \ldots + \alpha_n P_n \mid P_i \in \mathcal{M}(\mu_i) \ \forall i = 1, \ldots, n\} \\ &= \{P \in \mathbb{P}(\mathcal{X}) \mid P(C_1) \geq \alpha_1, \ldots, P(C_n) \geq \alpha_n\},\end{aligned}$$

but this means that the obtained model is not $0-1$ valued. See also [9, Sect. 8.3] for additional comments in this direction.

8 Conclusions

This paper investigates the commutativity between the aggregation of coherent lower probabilities and the natural extension to gambles. The first approach computes the natural extensions ($\underline{E}_{\mu_1}$, $\ldots$, $\underline{E}_{\mu_n}$) and later aggregates them ($\mathcal{A}(\underline{E}_{\mu_1}, \ldots, \underline{E}_{\mu_n})$), while the second approach consists in aggregating the lower probabilities ($\mathcal{A}(\mu_1, \ldots, \mu_n)$) and later applies natural extension ($\underline{E}_{\mathcal{A}(\mu_1, \ldots, \mu_n)}$).

After analysing this problem for $\mathcal{A}_C$, $\mathcal{A}_D$ and $\mathcal{A}_M$, we conclude that the only rule for which the aggregation and the natural extension commute is the conjunction (Theorem 1), while for the disjunction and the convex mixtures only a dominance relation between them holds (Theorems 3 and 4). However, when the initial models are k-monotone in addition to coherent, commutativity also holds for the convex mixture rule (Theorem 5). When the two approaches do not coincide, the choice between them could be based on which is the base representation we favour: if we consider the associated credal sets, there is no harm in computing first the natural extension to a lower prevision and then to aggregate this; while if the focus is on the lower probabilities, we should go for the less informative model, that results from first applying aggregation and then natural extension.

With respect to the preservation of k-monotonicity, we have shown that the conjunction rule only preserves 2-monotonicity for two models and with an additional restriction (Theorem 2), while the convex mixture rule preserves k-monotonicity for any $k \in \mathbb{N}$ (Theorem 5). In contradistinction, the disjunction rule does not preserve k-monotonicity regardless of the chosen approach.

Table 1. A summary of the results.

Rule	Commutativity?	2-monotone preservation?	k -monotone preservation?
$\mathcal{A}_C$	$\mathcal{A}_C(\underline{E}_{\mu_1},\ldots,\underline{E}_{\mu_n}) = \underline{E}_{\mathcal{A}_C(\mu_1,\ldots,\mu_n)}$	Yes *(if $n=2$ and $\mathcal{M}(\mu_1)\cup\mathcal{M}(\mu_2)$ is convex)*	No
$\mathcal{A}_D$	$\mathcal{A}_D(\underline{E}_{\mu_1},\ldots,\underline{E}_{\mu_n}) \geq \underline{E}_{\mathcal{A}_D(\mu_1,\ldots,\mu_n)}$	No	No
$\mathcal{A}_M$	$\mathcal{A}_M(\underline{E}_{\mu_1},\ldots,\underline{E}_{\mu_n}) \geq \underline{E}_{\mathcal{A}_M(\mu_1,\ldots,\mu_n)}$	Yes *(and both approaches coincide)*	Yes *(and both approaches coincide)*

A summary of the results can be seen in Table 1
While the conjunction rule is the unique rule for which both approaches always coincide, we should remark that it may give rise to a non-coherent model when the initial lower probabilities are conflicting, while the disjunction and convex mixture rules does not suffer from this issue. We may then consider alternative aggregation rules to the conjunction in situations of conflict, similarly to the ideas mentioned in this paper for the CD or MCS rules.

From the research presented in this paper, several open questions arise. On the one hand, we may look at the problem for some particular cases of coherent lower probabilities, such as belief functions; in this respect, there are several aggregation rules tailor made for belief functions whose extension to lower previsions should be explored. And on the other hand, we may approach the problem from a more general perspective: instead of focusing on whether a specific rule satisfies commutativity, we may investigate which axiomatic properties should be imposed on an aggregation rule in order to ensure commutativity, or at least a dominance relation between the two approaches.

Acknowledgments. This contribution is part of grant PID2022-140585NB-I00 funded by MICIU/AEI/10.13039/501100011033 and "FEDER/UE". We would also like to thank the reviewers for their helpful comments.

References

1. Bradley, S.: Aggregating belief models. In: Proceedings of the Eleventh International Symposium on Imprecise Probabilities: Theories and Applications, vol. 103, pp. 38–48. PMLR (2019)
2. Choquet, G.: Theory of capacities. Annales de l'Institut Fourier **5**, 131–295 (1953–1954)
3. de Cooman, G., Aeyels, D.: Supremum preserving upper probabilities. Inf. Sci. **118**, 173–212 (1999). https://doi.org/10.1016/S0020-0255(99)00007-9
4. de Cooman, G., Troffaes, M.C.M., Miranda, E.: n-Monotone exact functionals. J. Math. Anal. Appl. **347**, 143–156 (2008). https://doi.org/10.1016/j.jmaa.2008.05.071
5. Destercke, S., Dubois, D., Chojnacki, E.: Possibilistic information fusion using maximal coherent subsets. IEEE Trans. Fuzzy Syst. **17**(1), 79–92 (2009). https://doi.org/10.1109/TFUZZ.2008.2005731

6. Dubois, D., Liu, W., Ma, J., Prade, H.: The basic principles of uncertain information fusion. an organised review of merging rules in different representation frameworks. Inf. Fusion **32**, 12–39 (2016). https://doi.org/10.1016/j.inffus.2016.02.006
7. Keith, A., Ahner, D.: A survey of decision making and optimization under uncertainty. Ann. Oper. Res. **300**, 319–353 (2021). https://doi.org/10.1007/s10479-019-03431-8
8. Levi, I.: The Enterprise of Knowledge. MIT Press, Cambridge (1980)
9. Miranda, E., Montes, I.: On the closedness of imprecise probability models under aggregation. Submitted (2025)
10. Miranda, E., Salamanca, J., Montes, I.: A comparative analysis of aggregation rules for coherent lower previsions. Int. J. Approximate Reasoning **185**, 109474 (2025). https://doi.org/10.1016/j.ijar.2025.109474
11. Moral, S., del Sagrado, J.: Aggregation of imprecise probabilities. In: Bouchon-Meunier, B. (eds.) Aggregation and Fusion of Imperfect Information, pp. 162–188. Springer, Heidelberg (1998). https://doi.org/10.1007/978-3-7908-1889-5_10
12. Shafer, G.: A Mathematical Theory of Evidence. Princeton University Press, New Jersey (1976)
13. Stewart, R., Quintana, I.: Probabilistic opinion pooling with imprecise probabilities. J. Philos. Logic **47**(1), 17–45 (2018). https://doi.org/10.1007/s10992-016-9415-9
14. Walley, P.: The elicitation and aggregation of beliefs. Stat. Res. Report (1982)
15. Walley, P.: Statistical Reasoning with Imprecise Probabilities. Chapman and Hall, London (1991)
16. Zadeh, L.A.: Fuzzy sets as a basis for a theory of possibility. Fuzzy Sets Syst. **1**, 3–28 (1978). https://doi.org/10.1016/S0165-0114(99)80004-9
17. Zaffalon, M., Miranda, E.: Probability and time. Artif. Intell. **198**, 1–51 (2013). https://doi.org/10.1016/j.artint.2013.02.005

Decision Making with Generalised Distortion Models

Nicolás Carrizosa(✉), Ignacio Montes, and Enrique Miranda

Department of Statistics and O.R. and D.M., University of Oviedo, C/Leopoldo Calvo Sotelo 18, 33007 Oviedo, Spain
{carrizosanicolas,imontes,mirandaenrique}@uniovi.es

Abstract. We introduce linear variational models, which include as particular cases some of the most prominent distortion models in the literature, and investigate their interest in a decision making problem under uncertainty and imprecision. We compare five optimality criteria: Γ-maximin, Γ-maximax, E-admissibility, maximality and interval dominance, and provide an expression of the optimal alternatives when the credal set modelling the uncertainty is determined by a linear variational model. In addition, we measure the extent of the distortion that should be put in place for an alternative to be optimal.

Keywords: Coherent lower previsions · Expected utility · Distortion models · Sensitivity analysis

1 Introduction

In a problem of decision making under uncertainty, it is customary to model this uncertainty by means of a probability measure. When we know the utility of the consequences of each alternative, it has been proven [1,24] that we should choose those alternatives that maximise the expected utility.

There are however situations where this paradigm is not applicable because the available information does not allow us to uniquely determine the probability measure or the utility function involved in the problem, and in those cases a number of alternatives have been proposed [8,20,28]. In this paper, we focus on the case where our imprecise knowledge of the probability measure only permits us to consider a closed and convex set of probability measures, or credal set [12]. This links our problem with that of decision making with imprecise probabilities [27], which is the term used to encompass those mathematical models that serve as an alternative to probability theory in contexts of ambiguous, imprecise or contradictory information.

There are several mathematical models that are covered under the imprecise probabilities umbrella, such as belief functions [25] or possibility measures [7]. In this paper, we shall focus on *distortion models* [6,18,19], that arise as neighbourhoods determined by a probability measure P_0 and a distorting factor δ

B. Vantaggi et al. (Eds.): IPMU 2026, CCIS 3019, pp. 219–232, 2026.
https://doi.org/10.1007/978-3-032-28994-0_16

via a suitable distorting function. They have the advantage of combining mathematical simplicity, ease of interpretation as well as interesting mathematical properties.

In this work, we take advantage of the similarities between some of them to define a new family of distortion models that includes a number of cases of interest as particular instances. We shall call them *linear variational models*, and, as we shall see, their generality will allow us on the one hand to have more flexibility in the definition of the distortion and on the other in allowing for a unified analysis of the decision problem that can later be particularised.

In this respect, when our uncertainty about the states of nature is modelled using a set of probability measures, expected utility can be generalised in a number of different ways, as summarised in [26]. It is then of interest to look for simpler expressions of the optimality criteria that render their use in applications more direct. This is the problem we shall investigate in this paper. We shall on the one hand provide formulae for the optimal alternatives according to each criterion when imprecision is modelled by a linear variational model, and on the other hand perform a sensitivity analysis that determines the extent of the distortion that should be applied in order for an alternative to become optimal.

The paper is organised as follows: in Sect. 2, we recall some basic notions from imprecise probabilities and introduce the linear variational models; in Sect. 3, we compare the optimality criteria in [26] that extend expected utility to the imprecise case and provide a simpler expression in the case of linear variational models; then in Sect. 4 we investigate if it is possible to characterise the optimality of an alternative in terms of the distorting factor that enlarges our model; and finally, in Sect. 5 we give some additional comments and remarks. Due to space limitations, proofs have been omitted.

2 Preliminaries

Let us recall some concepts from imprecise probability (IP) models that shall be used in this paper; we refer to [2,14,27] for a more detailed account.

2.1 Lower Probabilities and Lower Previsions

Let Ω be a finite possibility space of cardinality n. We shall denote by $\mathbb{P}(\Omega)$ the set of probability measures defined on the power set $\mathcal{P}(\Omega)$, and by $\mathbb{P}^*(\Omega)$ the set of probabilities which are strictly positive in the singletons. A closed and convex $\mathcal{M} \subseteq \mathbb{P}(\Omega)$ is called a *credal set*.

A *lower probability* on Ω is a function $\underline{P} : \mathcal{P}(\Omega) \to [0,1]$ satisfying monotonicity (if $A \subseteq B$, then $\underline{P}(A) \leq \underline{P}(B)$) and normalisation ($\underline{P}(\emptyset) = 0$ and $\overline{P}(\Omega) = 1$). Any lower probability determines a conjugate *upper probability* by $\overline{P}(A) = 1 - \underline{P}(A^c)$ for any $A \subseteq \Omega$. The lower probability also determines a credal set formed by the probability measures that dominate it:

$$\mathcal{M}(\underline{P}) = \{P \in \mathbb{P}(\Omega) \mid \underline{P}(A) \leq P(A)\ \forall A \subseteq \Omega\}.$$

A lower probability $\underline{P}$ is said to *avoid sure loss* if there exists at least one probability measure compatible with $\underline{P}$, that is, when $\mathcal{M}(\underline{P}) \neq \emptyset$. Also, $\underline{P}$ is *coherent* when, in addition to avoiding sure loss, it satisfies $\underline{P}(A) = \min\{P(A) \mid P \in \mathcal{M}(\underline{P})\}$ for any $A \subseteq \Omega$.

A more general model than lower probabilities are lower previsions, which are defined on *gambles*, i.e. real-valued functions $f : \Omega \to \mathbb{R}$. If we denote by $\mathcal{L}(\Omega)$ the set of all gambles on Ω, a lower prevision is a function $\underline{P} : \mathcal{L}(\Omega) \to \mathbb{R}$ assigning a real value to each gamble. Its conjugate upper prevision $\overline{P}$ is given by $\overline{P}(f) = -\underline{P}(-f)$ for any $f \in \mathcal{L}(\Omega)$. In a similar manner, a lower prevision determines a credal set by:

$$\mathcal{M}(\underline{P}) = \{P \in \mathbb{P}(\Omega) \mid \underline{P}(f) \leq P(f)\ \forall f \in \mathcal{L}(\Omega)\},$$

where we also use P to denote the expectation operator associated with P. The properties of avoiding sure loss and coherence are defined in an analogous manner to lower probabilities: $\underline{P}$ avoids sure loss when $\mathcal{M}(\underline{P}) \neq \emptyset$ and it is coherent when $\underline{P}(f) = \min\{P(f) \mid P \in \mathcal{M}(\underline{P})\}$ for any gamble $f \in \mathcal{L}(\Omega)$.

A coherent lower prevision $\underline{P}$ determines a coherent lower probability $\underline{Q}$ by $\underline{Q}(A) = \underline{P}(I_A)$ for any $A \subseteq \Omega$. While different coherent lower previsions may induce the same coherent lower probability, it is possible to make a one-to-one correspondence under the additional condition of *2-monotonicity*. A coherent lower prevision is 2-monotone if

$$\underline{P}(f \vee g) + \underline{P}(f \wedge g) \geq \underline{P}(f) + \underline{P}(g) \quad \forall f, g \in \mathcal{L}(\Omega),$$

while a coherent lower probability $\underline{Q}$ is 2-monotone if

$$\underline{Q}(A \cup B) + \underline{Q}(A \cap B) \geq \underline{Q}(A) + \underline{Q}(B) \quad \forall A, B \subseteq \Omega.$$

It holds that if $\underline{Q}$ is a 2-monotone lower probability, it has a unique 2-monotone lower prevision $\underline{P}$ that extends it, which can be computed by applying the Choquet integral [4] with respect to $\underline{Q}$.

2.2 Distortion Models

A particularly interesting and interpretable family of IP models are *distortion models*. Let us introduce them following the paradigm from [18,19].

Definition 1. *Let $P_0 \in \mathbb{P}(\Omega)$, $d : \mathbb{P}(\Omega) \times \mathbb{P}(\Omega) \to \mathbb{R}$ a distortion function and $\delta \geq 0$ a distortion factor. The* distortion model *associated with P_0, d and δ is given by the following set of probability measures:*

$$B_d^{\delta}(P_0) = \{P \in \mathbb{P}(\Omega) \mid d(P, P_0) \leq \delta\}. \tag{1}$$

When the distorting function d satisfies the following properties:

1. $d(P, P) = 0$ for any $P \in \mathbb{P}(\Omega)$,
2. d is continuous in the first argument,

3. d is quasiconvex, meaning that for any $\lambda \in [0,1], P, P', P_0 \in \mathbb{P}(\Omega)$ it holds that $d(\lambda P + (1-\lambda)P', P_0) \leq \max\{d(P, P_0), d(P', P_0)\}$,

it follows that $B_d^\delta(P_0)$ is closed, convex and non-empty [18, Prop. 3.1]. It determines a coherent lower prevision $\underline{P}_d$ by:

$$\underline{P}_d(f) = \min\left\{P(f) \mid P \in B_d^\delta(P_0)\right\} = \min\{P(f) \mid d(P, P_0) \leq \delta\} \quad \forall f \in \mathcal{L}(\Omega).$$

Next, we recall three particular instances of distortion models: the linear vacuous, pari-mutuel and total variation models.

Linear Vacuous Models. *Linear vacuous models* [27], also known as ε-contamination models [11], have their origin in robust statistics and constitute a prominent example of distortion models.

Definition 2. *Given $\delta \in [0,1]$ and $P_0 \in \mathbb{P}(\Omega)$, the associated linear vacuous (LV, in short) model is given by the lower probability:*

$$\underline{P}_{LV}(A) := \begin{cases} (1-\delta)\, P_0(A), & \text{if } A \subset \Omega, \\ 1, & \text{if } A = \Omega. \end{cases}$$

The interpretation of this model is that we have a proportion δ of contaminated/unreliable data that stems from an arbitrary and unknown probability $P \in \mathbb{P}(\Omega)$, while the remaining $1-\delta$ is modelled by the distribution P_0. The associated credal set can be expressed as:

$$\mathcal{M}(\underline{P}_{LV}) = \{(1-\delta)P_0 + \delta P \mid P \in \mathbb{P}(\Omega)\}.$$

The lower probability $\underline{P}_{LV}$ is 2-monotone[1] in addition to being coherent. Thus, it has a unique 2-monotone extension to gambles, which is the lower prevision given by [27]:

$$\underline{P}_{LV}(f) = (1-\delta)\, P_0(f) + \delta \min f, \quad \overline{P}_{LV}(f) = (1-\delta)\, P_0(f) + \delta \max f$$

for any gamble $f \in \mathcal{L}(\Omega)$. Moreover, when $P_0 \in \mathbb{P}^*(\Omega)$, $\mathcal{M}(\underline{P}_{LV}) \subseteq \mathbb{P}^*(\Omega)$ if and only if $\delta \in [0,1)$.

LV models can be seen as an instance of distortion models because $\mathcal{M}(\underline{P}_{LV})$ can be expressed as in Eq. (1) using as distortion function d_{LV} [18,21] given by

$$d_{LV}(P, P_0) = \max_{A \mid P_0(A)>0} \tfrac{P_0(A)-P(A)}{P_0(A)}.$$

Pari Mutuel Models. The second model analysed in this contribution is the *Pari-mutuel*, which has its origin in betting schemes from horse racetracks. It was formally defined in [27] and studied in detail in [17,18,22].

[1] In fact, it is also a belief function; see e.g. [18, Sect. 5.1].

Definition 3. *Given $\delta \in [0,\infty)$ and $P_0 \in \mathbb{P}(\Omega)$, the associated Pari-mutuel (PM, in short) model is given by the lower probability:*

$$\underline{P}_{PM}(A) := \max\{(1+\delta)\,P_0(A) - \delta, 0\} \quad \forall A \subseteq \Omega. \tag{2}$$

When $P_0 \in \mathbb{P}^*(\Omega)$ and δ satisfies

$$\delta < \min_{\omega\in\Omega} \tfrac{P_0(\{\omega\})}{1-P_0(\{\omega\})}, \tag{3}$$

the maximum in Eq. (2) can be omitted for any non-empty event, and $\mathcal{M}(\underline{P}_{PM}) \subseteq \mathbb{P}^*(\Omega)$.

The lower probability $\underline{P}_{PM}$ in Eq. (2) is 2-monotone, hence it has a unique 2-monotone extension to gambles. Its expression was given in [27], but a more handy, yet less general expression was given in [21] when $P_0 \in \mathbb{P}^*(\Omega)$ and δ satisfies the condition in Eq. (3):

$$\underline{P}_{PM}(f) = (1+\delta)\,P_0(f) - \delta\,\max f, \quad \overline{P}_{PM}(f) = (1+\delta)\,P_0(f) - \delta\,\min f.$$

When $P_0 \in \mathbb{P}^*(\Omega)$, PM models can be seen as distortion models in the sense that $\mathcal{M}(\underline{P}_{PM})$ can be expressed as in Eq. (1) with distortion function d_{PM} [18] given by

$$d_{PM}(P, P_0) = \max_{A\subset\Omega} \tfrac{P_0(A)-P(A)}{1-P_0(A)}.$$

Total Variation Models. The *total variation model* corresponds to the distortion model determined by the total variation distance [13] d_{TV} given by

$$d_{TV}(P, P_0) = \max_{A\subset\Omega} \left|P(A) - P_0(A)\right|, \quad \forall P, P_0 \in \mathbb{P}(\Omega),$$

which can be interpreted as the maximal absolute difference between probability measures P and P_0 across the events.

Definition 4. *Given $P_0 \in \mathbb{P}(\Omega)$ and $\delta \in [0,1]$, the total variation (TV, in short) model associated with P_0 and δ is given by the lower probability,*

$$\underline{P}_{TV}(A) = \begin{cases} \max\{P_0(A) - \delta, 0\}, & \text{if } A \subset \Omega. \\ 1, & \text{if } A = \Omega. \end{cases} \tag{4}$$

The TV model was first proposed in [10], and it was later thoroughly studied in [19]. When $P_0 \in \mathbb{P}^*(\Omega)$ and the distorting factor δ satisfies

$$\delta < \min_{\omega\in\Omega} P_0(\{\omega\}), \tag{5}$$

then it holds that $\mathcal{M}(\underline{P}_{TV}) \subseteq \mathbb{P}^*(\Omega)$ and the expression in Eq. (4) simplifies to $\underline{P}_{TV}(A) = P_0(A) - \delta$ for $A \neq \emptyset, \Omega$, $\underline{P}_{TV}(\emptyset) = 0$ and $\underline{P}_{TV}(\Omega) = 1$.

Again, the lower probability $\underline{P}_{TV}$ in Eq. (4) is 2-monotone, meaning that it has a unique 2-monotone extension to gambles. When $P_0 \in \mathbb{P}^*(\Omega)$ and δ satisfies the condition in Eq. (5), it was shown in [21] that:

$$\underline{P}_{TV}(f) = P_0(f) - \delta(\sup f - \inf f), \quad \overline{P}_{TV}(f) = P_0(f) + \delta(\sup f - \inf f).$$

Remark 1. Given a fixed P_0 and δ, the TV model associated with such parameters is more imprecise than both LV and PM, since

$$\underline{P}_{TV}(f) \leq \min\{\underline{P}_{LV}(f), \underline{P}_{PM}(f)\} \quad \forall f \in \mathcal{L}(\Omega),$$

which in terms of credal sets means that $\mathcal{M}(\underline{P}_{TV}) \supseteq \mathcal{M}(\underline{P}_{LV})$ and $\mathcal{M}(\underline{P}_{TV}) \supseteq \mathcal{M}(\underline{P}_{PM})$. In particular this implies that whenever $P_0 \in \mathbb{P}^*(\Omega)$ and δ satisfies the condition in Eq. (5), the three credal sets are included in $\mathbb{P}^*(\Omega)$. Also, the LV and PM models are incomparable, as shown in [19, Prop. 5.1]. ♦

2.3 Linear Variational Models

If we consider $P_0 \in \mathbb{P}^*(\Omega)$ and δ satisfying the restriction in Eq. (5), the lower and upper previsions for the LV, PM and TV models bear a noticeable similarity. Indeed, for any $f \in \mathcal{L}(\Omega)$, it holds that:

$$\begin{aligned}
\underline{P}_{LV}(f) &= P_0(f) - \delta\,(P_0(f) - \min f)\,, & \overline{P}_{LV}(f) &= P_0(f) + \delta\,(\max f - P_0(f))\,,\\
\underline{P}_{PM}(f) &= P_0(f) - \delta\,(\max f - P_0(f))\,, & \overline{P}_{PM}(f) &= P_0(f) + \delta\,(P_0(f) - \min f)\,,\\
\underline{P}_{TV}(f) &= P_0(f) - \delta\,(\max f - \min f)\,, & \overline{P}_{TV}(f) &= P_0(f) + \delta\,(\max f - \min f)\,.
\end{aligned}$$

All of them can be expressed as the expectation of the gamble f for P_0 plus a δ-scaled increment/decrement that somewhat reflects the variability of f.

This motivates the introduction of the following family of models, that we shall call *linear variational models.* Note that in the following definition, we do not require δ to satisfy Eq. (5); instead, we replace it with condition 2.

Definition 5. *Consider* $P_0 \in \mathbb{P}^*(\Omega)$, $\delta \geq 0$ *and an operator* $\underline{\Delta} : \mathcal{L}(\Omega) \to [0, +\infty)$ *satisfying*

1. $\underline{\Delta} f = 0 \Leftrightarrow f$ *is a constant gamble.*
2. $\delta \underline{\Delta} f \leq P_0(f) - \min f$ *for any* $f \in \mathcal{L}(\Omega)$. (6)
3. $\underline{\Delta}(\alpha f) = \alpha\,\underline{\Delta} f$ *for any* $\alpha \geq 0$.
4. $\underline{\Delta}(f + g) \leq \underline{\Delta} f + \underline{\Delta} g$ *for any* $f, g \in \mathcal{L}(\Omega)$.

The conjugate lower and upper previsions given by:

$$\underline{P}_{\underline{\Delta}}(f) = P_0(f) - \delta\,\underline{\Delta} f, \qquad \overline{P}_{\underline{\Delta}}(f) = P_0(f) + \delta\,\overline{\Delta} f, \tag{7}$$

where $\overline{\Delta} f = \underline{\Delta}(-f)$, *determine an IP model called* linear variational *(LVar, in short) model induced by* $(P_0, \underline{\Delta}, \delta)$.

The first condition in Definition 5 guarantees that $\underline{P}_{\underline{\Delta}}(f) = P_0(f)$ for any constant gamble and the second establishes an upper bound on δ for which the model is properly defined. Thus, the LVar coincides with the initial model P_0 on gambles without variability. Moreover, LVar models can be shown to be coherent.

Proposition 1. *Under the conditions of Definition 5, the lower prevision* $\underline{P}_{\underline{\Delta}}$ *in Eq. (7) is coherent and satisfies* $P_0 \in \mathcal{M}(\underline{P}_{\underline{\Delta}})$.

It is worth mentioning that the LV, PM and TV models are indeed particular cases of LVar models. Their associated operators are given by

$$\underline{\Delta}_{LV} f = P_0(f) - \min f, \qquad \overline{\Delta}_{LV} f = \max f - P_0(f). \tag{8}$$

$$\underline{\Delta}_{PM} f = \max f - P_0(f), \qquad \overline{\Delta}_{PM} f = P_0(f) - \min f. \tag{9}$$

$$\underline{\Delta}_{TV} f = \max f - \min f = \overline{\Delta}_{TV} f. \tag{10}$$

If we compare the operators $\underline{\Delta}_{LV}$ and $\underline{\Delta}_{PM}$ in Eq. (8) and (9), we observe a certain duality between both models. On the other hand, it holds that:

$$\underline{\Delta}_{TV} f = \underline{\Delta}_{LV} f + \underline{\Delta}_{PM} f \geq \max\left\{\underline{\Delta}_{LV} f, \underline{\Delta}_{PM} f\right\} \quad \forall f \in \mathcal{L}(\Omega),$$

whence $\underline{P}_{TV} \leq \min\left\{\underline{P}_{LV}, \underline{P}_{PM}\right\}$, reflecting the behaviour discussed in Remark 1.

Our last result in this section shows for which values of δ these models satisfy condition 2 in Definition 5.

Proposition 2. *Consider the operators* $\underline{\Delta}_{LV}$, $\underline{\Delta}_{PM}$ *and* $\underline{\Delta}_{TV}$ *defined in Eqs.* (8)–(10), *respectively.*

(i) $\underline{\Delta}_{LV}$ *satisfies properties 1–4 in Definition 5* $\Leftrightarrow \delta \in [0,1]$.
(ii) $\underline{\Delta}_{PM}$ *satisfies properties 1–4 in Definition 5* $\Leftrightarrow \delta \leq \min_{\omega\in\Omega} \frac{P_0(\{\omega\})}{1-P_0(\{\omega\})}$.
(iii) $\underline{\Delta}_{TV}$ *satisfies properties 1–4 in Definition 5* $\Leftrightarrow \delta \leq \min_{\omega\in\Omega} P_0(\{\omega\})$.

3 Decision Making with LVar Models

Consider a decision making problem where a choice must be made between a finite set D of alternatives. We shall associate with each $d \in D$ a gamble $J_d : \Omega \to \mathbb{R}$ representing its utility, so that $J_d(\omega)$ represents the value obtained if d is chosen and $\omega \in \Omega$ is the state of nature that is observed.

We shall assume that no two gambles $J_d, J_{d'}$ are equal for $d \neq d' \in D$, in addition to *act-state independence* [26], meaning that the outcome ω is independent of the decision d that is chosen. In order to choose an element of D, we can first of all discard those alternatives that are dominated by another one, leaving us with the so-called *feasible* or *Pareto-optimal alternatives*[2]:

$$\text{opt}_{\geq}(D) = \{d \in D \mid \forall e \in D, J_e \ngtr J_d\}.$$

In [26, Appendix A2], it was proven that $\text{opt}_{\geq}(D) \neq \emptyset$ if $\{J_d \mid d \in D\}$ is non-empty and weakly compact as a subset of $\mathcal{L}(\Omega)$; this is in particular the case when both D and Ω are finite, as we shall assume in this paper.

While $\text{opt}_{\geq}(D)$ may be regarded as a set of optimal alternatives if we have no additional information about Ω, when we know the probability distribution

[2] In what follows, $J_e \geq J_d$ denotes $J_e(\omega) \geq J_d(\omega)$ for any $\omega \in \Omega$, $J_e \ngeq J_d$ denotes that there exists $\omega \in \Omega$ such that $J_e(\omega) < J_d(\omega)$, and $J_e > J_d$ means that $J_e \geq J_d$ and $J_e \neq J_d$.

$P \in \mathbb{P}(\Omega)$ of the states of nature in Ω it is arguable that we should consider only those that maximise the *expected utility* [24]:

$$\mathrm{opt}_P(D) = \{d \in \mathrm{opt}_{\geq}(D) \mid P(J_d) \geq P(J_e)\ \forall e \in \mathrm{opt}_{\geq}(D)\}. \tag{11}$$

It holds that $\mathrm{opt}_P(D) \neq \emptyset$ if $\mathrm{opt}_{\geq}(D) \neq \emptyset$. In what follows, for the sake of simplicity we shall denote $\mathrm{opt}_P(D)$ and $\mathrm{opt}_{\geq}(D)$ as opt_P and $\mathrm{opt}_{\geq}$ respectively, whenever no confusion is possible.

Nevertheless, in the uncertainty modelling about Ω there are intermediate scenarios between the total absence of information and the precise case; as argued in [26], in such cases it may be more adequate to consider imprecise probability models, and this requires us to generalise the expected utility criterion.

3.1 Optimality Criteria

Assume thus that our beliefs about Ω are modelled by a coherent lower prevision $\underline{P}$ on $\mathcal{L}(\Omega)$ with conjugate upper prevision $\overline{P}$. In this scenario, the expected utility criterion can be extended in different manners, as summarised in [26].

Γ-maximin. The first criterion we consider is Γ-maximin, in which the expectation operator in Eq. (11) is replaced by the lower prevision. This gives rise to the following set of optimal alternatives [9]:

$$\mathrm{opt}_{\underline{P}}(D) = \{d \in \mathrm{opt}_{\geq} \mid \underline{P}(J_d) \geq \underline{P}(J_e)\ \forall e \in \mathrm{opt}_{\geq}\}.$$

This criterion accounts for maximising the utility in the worst-case scenario.

Γ-maximax. Similarly, we may also replace the expectation operator in Eq. (11) by the upper prevision [9]:

$$\mathrm{opt}_{\overline{P}}(D) = \{d \in \mathrm{opt}_{\geq} \mid \overline{P}(J_d) \geq \overline{P}(J_e)\ \forall e \in \mathrm{opt}_{\geq}\}.$$

This criterion accounts for maximising the utility in the best-case scenario.

Maximality. Under this criterion, an alternative is deemed optimal when exchanging it for any other alternative is not a desirable gamble in the sense of Walley [27]. This leads to the following set of optimal alternatives:

$$\mathrm{opt}_{\geq_{\underline{P}}}(D) = \{d \in \mathrm{opt}_{\geq} \mid \underline{P}(J_e - J_d) \leq 0\ \forall e \in \mathrm{opt}_{\geq}\}.$$

Interval Dominance. This criterion compares the intervals determined by the lower and upper previsions for each gamble, discarding an alternative when its interval is dominated by another one [30]:

$$\mathrm{opt}_{\sqsupseteq_{\underline{P}}}(D) = \{d \in \mathrm{opt}_{\geq} \mid \overline{P}(J_d) \geq \underline{P}(J_e)\ \forall e \in \mathrm{opt}_{\geq}\}.$$

E-Admissibility. An alternative is optimal according to E-admissibility if there exists a precise probability measure compatible with our beliefs for which it maximises the expected utility. In other words, if there exists $P \in \mathcal{M}(\underline{P})$ such that $P(J_d)$ is maximal among $\{P(J_e)\}_{e \in \text{opt}_{\geq}}$:

$$\text{opt}_{\mathcal{M}(\underline{P})}(D) = \{d \in \text{opt}_{\geq} \mid \exists P \in \mathcal{M}(\underline{P}),\, d \in \text{opt}_P\}.$$

We shall denote the sets of optimal alternatives under these criteria using $\text{opt}_{\cdot}$ rather than $\text{opt}_{\cdot}(D)$ when no confusion is possible. All five criteria reduce to maximising the expected utility when $\underline{P}$ is precise (i.e., when $\underline{P} = \overline{P}$). In the imprecise case, though, some of them are stricter than others, in the sense that they render a smaller number of optimal alternatives. We shall say that criterion opt_1 is *stricter* than opt_2 if $\text{opt}_1 \subseteq \text{opt}_2$. The relationships among the presented criteria (see [26]) are graphically shown in Fig. 1.

$$\begin{array}{ccccccc} \text{opt}_{\overline{P}} & \subseteq & \text{opt}_{\mathcal{M}(\underline{P})} & \subseteq & \text{opt}_{\geq_{\underline{P}}} & \subseteq & \text{opt}_{\sqsupset_{\underline{P}}} \\ & & & & \cup\!\mid & & \\ & & & & \text{opt}_{\underline{P}} & & \end{array}$$

Fig. 1. Relationships between optimality criteria.

We see that the Γ-maximin and Γ-maximax criteria are the strictest ones while interval dominance is the most lenient. Some of these criteria also show a monotone behaviour as imprecision increases, as proven in [15, Props.17-19].

Proposition 3. *Let $\underline{P}$ and $\underline{Q}$ be two coherent lower previsions such that $\underline{P} \leq \underline{Q}$. Then $\text{opt}_{\mathcal{M}(\underline{Q})} \subseteq \text{opt}_{\mathcal{M}(\underline{P})}$, $\text{opt}_{\geq_{\underline{Q}}} \subseteq \text{opt}_{\geq_{\underline{P}}}$ and $\text{opt}_{\sqsupset_{\underline{Q}}} \subseteq \text{opt}_{\sqsupset_{\underline{P}}}$.*

E-admissibility differs from the other criteria in that it is not directly defined via the lower/upper previsions. It is nonetheless possible to give an alternative formulation using the notion of randomised alternatives:

Definition 6. *Given a set D of alternatives, a* randomised alternative $\lambda \equiv (\lambda_e)_{e \in D}$, *where $\lambda_e \geq 0$ for any $e \in D$ and $\sum_{e \in D} \lambda_e = 1$, corresponds to a gamble J_λ defined as the convex combination $J_\lambda := \sum_{e \in D} \lambda_e J_e$.*

Let us denote by $G(D)$ the set of randomised alternatives:

$$G(D) := \left\{ \lambda \equiv (\lambda_e)_{e \in D} \;\middle|\; \lambda_e \geq 0,\, \sum_{e \in D} \lambda_e = 1 \right\}.$$

The elements of $G(D)$ can be understood as the alternatives arising from randomly selecting an alternative $e \in D$ with probability λ_e.

E-admissibility can be characterised in terms of the lower prevision by taking into account the set of randomised alternatives; see [26, Sec. 4] for an earlier proof of the necessity part.

Proposition 4. *Given $\underline{P}$ a coherent lower prevision and $d \in opt_{\geq}$, it holds that:*

$$d \in opt_{\mathcal{M}(\underline{P})}(D) \iff \underline{P}(J_\lambda - J_d) \leq 0 \quad \forall \lambda \in G(opt_{\geq}). \tag{12}$$

The above characterisation of E-admissibility resembles that of maximality, but considering instead the randomised decisions in the right-hand side of Eq. (12). It is related to the results in [26,27] stating that, under convexity of D, E-admissibility and maximality coincide. Instead, Proposition 4 establishes a connection between E-admissibility and maximality for randomised alternatives for general, non necessarily convex, sets of alternatives D.

3.2 Optimality Rules for LVar Models

Next, we consider that uncertainty is modelled by a LVar model. In that case, we obtain alternative expressions for the five optimality criteria enumerated in the previous subsection.

Proposition 5. *Consider $P_0 \in \mathbb{P}^*(\Omega)$, $\delta \geq 0$ and an operator $\underline{\Delta}$, and let $\underline{P}_{\Delta}$ be the LVar model determined by Eq. (7). Then the optimality criteria can be expressed as follows:*

(i) $d \in opt_{\underline{P}_{\Delta}} \Leftrightarrow P_0(J_d) \geq \max_{e \in opt_{\geq}} \{P_0(J_e) - \delta\,(\underline{\Delta} J_e - \underline{\Delta} J_d)\}$.
(ii) $d \in opt_{\overline{P}_{\Delta}} \Leftrightarrow P_0(J_d) \geq \max_{e \in opt_{\geq}} \{P_0(J_e) - \delta\,(\overline{\Delta} J_d - \overline{\Delta} J_e)\}$.
(iii) $d \in opt_{\mathcal{M}(\underline{P}_{\Delta})} \Leftrightarrow P_0(J_d) \geq \max_{\lambda \in G(opt_{\geq})} \{P_0(J_\lambda) - \delta\,\underline{\Delta}(J_\lambda - J_d)\}$.
(iv) $d \in opt_{\geq_{\underline{P}_{\Delta}}} \Leftrightarrow P_0(J_d) \geq \max_{e \in opt_{\geq}} \{P_0(J_e) - \delta\,\underline{\Delta}(J_e - J_d)\}$.
(v) $d \in opt_{\sqsupseteq_{\underline{P}_{\Delta}}} \Leftrightarrow P_0(J_d) \geq \max_{e \in opt_{\geq}} \{P_0(J_e) - \delta\,(\underline{\Delta} J_e + \overline{\Delta} J_d)\}$.

On the other hand, since the LV, PM and TV models can be seen as particular cases of LVar models, it is possible to reformulate for them the expressions in Proposition 5. Our next result does this for the LV model:

Corollary 1. *Given $P_0 \in \mathbb{P}^*(\Omega)$ and $\delta \in [0, 1)$, it holds that:*

(i) $d \in opt_{\underline{P}_{LV}} \Leftrightarrow P_0(J_d) \geq \max_{e \in opt_{\geq}} \left\{P_0(J_e) - \frac{\delta}{1-\delta}\,(\min J_d - \min J_e)\right\}$.
(ii) $d \in opt_{\overline{P}_{LV}} \Leftrightarrow P_0(J_d) \geq \max_{e \in opt_{\geq}} \left\{P_0(J_e) - \frac{\delta}{1-\delta}\,(\max J_e - \max J_d)\right\}$.
(iii) $d \in opt_{\mathcal{M}(\underline{P}_{LV})} \Leftrightarrow P_0(J_d) \geq \max_{\lambda \in G(opt_{\geq})} \left\{P_0(J_\lambda) - \frac{\delta}{1-\delta} \max(J_d - J_\lambda)\right\}$.
(iv) $d \in opt_{\geq_{\underline{P}_{LV}}} \Leftrightarrow P_0(J_d) \geq \max_{e \in opt_{\geq}} \left\{P_0(J_e) - \frac{\delta}{1-\delta} \max(J_d - J_e)\right\}$.
(v) $d \in opt_{\sqsupseteq_{\underline{P}_{LV}}} \Leftrightarrow P_0(J_d) \geq \max_{e \in opt_{\geq}} \left\{P_0(J_e) - \frac{\delta}{1-\delta}\,(\max J_d - \min J_e)\right\}$.

Using the values of $\underline{\Delta}$ and $\overline{\Delta}$ in Eqs. (9) and (10), similar expressions for the optimality criteria can be given for the PM and TV models.

4 Optimal Alternatives in Terms of the Parameter δ

So far, our results assume that the parameter δ is fixed. In this section, we consider instead $P_0 \in \mathbb{P}^*(\Omega)$, an operator $\underline{\Delta}$ and the δ-dependent coherent lower and upper previsions $\underline{P}_{\underline{\Delta}}$ and $\overline{P}_{\underline{\Delta}}$ in Eq. (7), and study when a given alternative d is optimal for each criterion in terms of δ.

Note that $\underline{P}_{\underline{\Delta}}$ is defined in terms of $(P_0, \delta, \underline{\Delta})$, and Condition 2 in Definition 5 already imposes an upper bound on δ. In what follows, we derive additional bounds on δ for an alternative to be optimal, which may conflict with the one given by Eq. (6). In such cases, the alternative would never be optimal for any LVar model defined by those P_0 and $\underline{\Delta}$.

4.1 Γ-Maximin

We begin our study with the Γ-maximin criterion. In the following result, we give conditions on d under which the alternative is not optimal for any $\delta > 0$ as well as a characterisation of the distortion parameters δ rendering d optimal when those conditions are not satisfied.

Proposition 6. *Let $\underline{P}_{\underline{\Delta}}$ be the LVar model determined by $(P_0, \delta, \underline{\Delta})$ by means of Definition 5, and let $d \in opt_{\geq}$. Then,*

(i) If there exists $e \in opt_{\geq}$ such that $P_0(J_d) \leq P_0(J_e)$ and $\underline{\Delta} J_d \geq \underline{\Delta} J_e$, with at least one inequality being strict, then $d \notin opt_{\underline{P}_{\underline{\Delta}}}$ for any $\delta > 0$.

(ii) If there is no such $e \in opt_{\geq}$, then $d \in opt_{\underline{P}_{\underline{\Delta}}}$ if and only if

$$\max_{e \in D^{d-}_{\underline{P}_{\underline{\Delta}}}} \left\{ \frac{P_0(J_e) - P_0(J_d)}{\underline{\Delta} J_e - \underline{\Delta} J_d} \right\} \leq \delta \leq \min_{e \in D^{d+}_{\underline{P}_{\underline{\Delta}}}} \left\{ \frac{P_0(J_e) - P_0(J_d)}{\underline{\Delta} J_e - \underline{\Delta} J_d} \right\}, \tag{13}$$

where

$$D^{d-}_{\underline{P}_{\underline{\Delta}}} = \left\{ e \in opt_{\geq} \mid \underline{\Delta} J_d < \underline{\Delta} J_e \right\}, \quad D^{d+}_{\underline{P}_{\underline{\Delta}}} = \left\{ e \in opt_{\geq} \mid \underline{\Delta} J_d > \underline{\Delta} J_e \right\}$$

and the bounds on Eq. (13) are rendered trivial when $D^{d-}_{\underline{P}_{\underline{\Delta}}} = \emptyset$ and $D^{d+}_{\underline{P}_{\underline{\Delta}}} = \emptyset$, respectively.

4.2 Γ-Maximax

Since Γ-maximin maximises the upper prevision instead of the lower prevision, a result akin to Proposition 6 can be obtained involving $\overline{\Delta}$ instead of $\underline{\Delta}$.

Proposition 7. *Let $\underline{P}_{\underline{\Delta}}$ be the LVar model determined by $(P_0, \delta, \underline{\Delta})$ by means of Definition 5, and let $d \in opt_{\geq}$. Then,*

(i) If there exists $e \in opt_{\geq}$ such that $P_0(J_d) \leq P_0(J_e)$ and $\overline{\Delta} J_d \leq \overline{\Delta} J_e$, with at least one inequality being strict, then $d \notin opt_{\overline{P}_{\underline{\Delta}}}$ for any $\delta > 0$.

(ii) If there is no such $e \in opt_{\geq}$*, then* $d \in opt_{\overline{P}_{\Delta}}$ *if and only if*

$$\max_{e \in D^{d-}_{\overline{P}_{\Delta}}} \left\{ \frac{P_0(J_e) - P_0(J_d)}{\overline{\Delta} J_d - \overline{\Delta} J_e} \right\} \leq \delta \leq \inf_{e \in D^{d+}_{\overline{P}_{\Delta}}} \left\{ \frac{P_0(J_e) - P_0(J_d)}{\overline{\Delta} J_d - \overline{\Delta} J_e} \right\}, \tag{14}$$

where

$$D^{d-}_{\overline{P}_{\Delta}} = \{ e \in opt_{\geq} \mid \overline{\Delta} J_d > \overline{\Delta} J_e \}, \quad D^{d+}_{\overline{P}_{\Delta}} = \{ e \in opt_{\geq} \mid \overline{\Delta} J_d < \overline{\Delta} J_e \}$$

and the bounds on Eq. (14) *are rendered trivial when* $D^{d-}_{\overline{P}_{\Delta}} = \emptyset$ *and* $D^{d+}_{\overline{P}_{\Delta}} = \emptyset$*, respectively.*

4.3 E-Admissibility

Regarding E-admissibility, it is a consequence of Proposition 4 that an alternative $d \in \text{opt}_{\geq}$ will not be optimal when it is not feasible in the enlarged set of randomised alternatives. This leads to the following result.

Proposition 8. *Let* $\underline{P}_{\Delta}$ *be the LVar model determined by* $(P_0, \delta, \underline{\Delta})$ *by means of Definition 5, and let* $d \in opt_{\geq}$*. Then,*

(i) If $\exists \lambda \in G(opt_{\geq})$ *such that* $J_\lambda > J_d$*, then* $d \notin opt_{\mathcal{M}(\underline{P}_{\Delta})}$ *for any* $\delta \geq 0$*.*
(ii) If there is no such J_λ*, then* $d \in opt_{\mathcal{M}(\underline{P}_{\Delta})}$ *if and only if*

$$\delta \geq \max_{\lambda \in G(opt_{\geq}) \mid J_\lambda \neq J_d} \left\{ \frac{P_0(J_\lambda) - P_0(J_d)}{\underline{\Delta}(J_\lambda - J_d)} \right\}.$$

4.4 Maximality

Considering the similarity between the conditions for E-admissibility and Maximality highlighted in Proposition 4, it comes as no surprise that the results associated with maximality will resemble those in Proposition 8.

Proposition 9. *Let* $\underline{P}_{\Delta}$ *be the LVar model determined by* $(P_0, \delta, \underline{\Delta})$ *by means of Definition 5, and let* $d \in opt_{\geq}$*. Then,* $d \in opt_{\geq_{\underline{P}_{\Delta}}}$ *if and only if*

$$\delta \geq \max_{e \in opt_{\geq} \mid J_e \neq J_d} \left\{ \frac{P_0(J_e) - P_0(J_d)}{\underline{\Delta}(J_e - J_d)} \right\}.$$

4.5 Interval Dominance

Finally, optimality in terms of interval dominance requires the comparison of the upper prevision of J_d with the lower prevision of J_e. This means that for a sufficiently large distortion parameter, an alternative d will always be optimal.

Proposition 10. *Let* $\underline{P}_{\Delta}$ *be the LVar model determined by* $(P_0, \delta, \underline{\Delta})$ *by means of Definition 5, and let* $d \in opt_{\geq}$*. Then,* $d \in opt_{\sqsupseteq_{\underline{P}_{\Delta}}}$ *if and only if*

$$\delta \geq \max_{e \in opt_{\geq}} \left\{ \frac{P_0(J_e) - P_0(J_d)}{\underline{\Delta} J_e + \overline{\Delta} J_d} \right\}.$$

5 Conclusions

By observing that the lower previsions associated with distortion models are usually defined by means of a suitable function that depends on the variability of the gamble, in this paper we have introduced linear variational models as a unified paradigm that encompasses as particular cases some of the most popular distortion models in the literature. We have characterised their coherence in terms of the distorting function $\underline{\Delta}$ that determines them, and applied these models in a decision making problem under uncertainty and imprecision.

We have shown that the optimal alternatives can be determined by pairwise comparing their expected utility with respect to the original probability measure and their respective distortions via the functional $\underline{\Delta}$, and made a sensitivity analysis that determines for which distorting factors δ an alternative is optimal for each criterion. This allows in a number of cases to establish certain "break-down points" where the set of optimal alternatives progressively enlarges, which should be of interest when using these models in practice.

One important underlying assumption in this paper is that, by considering coherent lower previsions, the utility function of the problem is assumed to be measured in a linear scale; it would be of interest to tackle this problem in more general contexts, such as the extension carried out in [16], which could be of interest given the useful properties of sets of desirable gambles in this context [28,29]. In addition, the properties of the linear variational models should be investigated more broadly, as well as their connection with other general families of distortion models, such as vertical barrier models [5]. Finally, we may also investigate the use of distortion models in connection with other alternatives to expected utility in situations of ambiguity, such as [3,23].

Acknowledgments. This work is part of grant PID2022-140585NB-I00, funded by MICIU/AEI/10.13039/501100011033 and "FEDER/UE". Nicolás Carrizosa acknowledges the financial support by the FPU grant FPU24/03037 from the Ministry of Science, Innovation and Universities of Spain. We also acknowledge the comments and suggestions of the anonymous reviewers.

References

1. Anscombe, F.J., Aumann, R.J.: A definition of subjective probability. Ann. Math. Stat. **34**, 199–2005 (1963)
2. Augustin, T., Coolen, F., de Cooman, G., Troffaes, M. (eds.): Introduction to Imprecise Probabilities. Wiley Series in Probability and Statistics, Wiley (2014)
3. Bell, D.: Regret in decision making under uncertainty. Oper. Res. **30**(5), 961–981 (1982)
4. Choquet, G.: Theory of capacities. Annales de l'Institut Fourier **5**, 131–295 (1953–1954)
5. Corsato, C., Pelessoni, R., Vicig, P.: Nearly-Linear uncertainty measures. Int. J. Approximate Reasoning **114**, 1–28 (2019)

6. Destercke, S., Montes, I., Miranda, E.: Processing distortion models: a comparative study. Int. J. Approximate Reasoning **145**, 91–120 (2022)
7. Dubois, D., Prade, H.: Possibility Theory. Plenum Press, New York (1988)
8. Galaabaatar, T., Karni, E.: Subjective expected utility with incomplete preferences. Econometrica **81**(1), 255–284 (2013)
9. Gilboa, I., Schmeidler, D.: Maxmin expected utility with a non-unique prior. J. Math. Econ. **18**, 141–153 (1989)
10. Herron, T., Seidenfeld, T., Wasserman, L.: Divisive conditioning: further results on dilation. Philos. Sci. **64**, 411–444 (1997)
11. Huber, P.J.: Robust Statistics. Wiley, New York (1981)
12. Levi, I.: The Enterprise of Knowledge. MIT Press, Cambridge (1980)
13. Levin, D.A., Peres, Y., Wilmer, E.L.: Markov Chains and Mixing Times. American Mathematical Society (2009)
14. Miranda, E.: A survey of the theory of coherent lower previsions. Int. J. Approximate Reasoning **48**(2), 628–658 (2008)
15. Miranda, E., Montes, I., Presa, A.: Inner approximations of coherent lower probabilities and their application to decision making problems. Ann. Oper. Res. **355**, 2777–2815 (2025)
16. Miranda, E., Zaffalon, M.: Nonlinear desirability theory. Int. J. Approximate Reasoning **154**, 176–199 (2023)
17. Montes, I., Miranda, E., Destercke, S.: Pari-mutuel probabilities as an uncertainty model. Inf. Sci. **481**, 550–573 (2019)
18. Montes, I., Miranda, E., Destercke, S.: Unifying neighbourhood and distortion models: Part I- New results on old models. Int. J. Gen. Syst. **49**(6), 602–635 (2020)
19. Montes, I., Miranda, E., Destercke, S.: Unifying neighbourhood and distortion models: Part II- New models and synthesis. Int. J. Gen. Syst. **49**(6), 636–674 (2020)
20. Nau, R.: The shape of incomplete preferences. Ann. Stat. **34**(5), 2430–2448 (2006)
21. Nieto-Barba, D., Montes, I., Miranda, E.: The imprecise Vertical Barrier models for distorting lower probabilities (2026). submitted for publication
22. Pelessoni, R., Vicig, P., Zaffalon, M.: Inference and risk measurement with the pari-mutuel model. Int. J. Approximate Reasoning **51**, 1145–1158 (2010)
23. Quiggin, J.: Generalized expected utility theory. The rank-dependent model. Kluwer Academic (1993)
24. Savage, L.J.: The Foundations of Statistics. Dover, New York (1972). second revised edition, first published 1954
25. Shafer, G.: A Mathematical Theory of Evidence. Princeton University Press, New Jersey (1976)
26. Troffaes, M.C.M.: Decision making under uncertainty using imprecise probabilities. Int. J. Approximate Reasoning **45**(1), 17–29 (2007)
27. Walley, P.: Statistical Reasoning with Imprecise Probabilities. Chapman and Hall, London (1991)
28. Zaffalon, M., Miranda, E.: Axiomatising incomplete preferences through sets of desirable gambles. J. Artif. Intell. Res. **60**, 1057–1126 (2017)
29. Zaffalon, M., Miranda, E.: Desirability foundations of robust rational decision making. Synthese **198**(Suppl. 27), 6529–6570 (2021)
30. Zaffalon, M., Wesnes, K., Petrini, O.: Reliable diagnoses of dementia by the naive credal classifier inferred from incomplete cognitive data. Artif. Intell. Med. **29**, 61–79 (2003)

A Preliminary Study of Notions of Independence for Choice Functions

Justyna Dąbrowska(✉), Banda Norimarna, and Arthur Van Camp(✉)

Eindhoven University of Technology, Den Dolech 2, 5612AZ Eindhoven, The Netherlands

a.van.camp@tue.nl

Abstract. We study independence concepts for imprecise-probabilistic choice functions. Leveraging the idea that a choice function is represented by a collection of coherent sets of desirable gambles, we introduce representational independence as the requirement of having an independent representation. We derive the representational product, which is the smallest coherent choice function that marginalises to given choice functions and satisfies representational independence. By applying similar proof techniques, we also obtain the independent product for the existing S-independence. We compare these products, together with the existing epistemic product, and derive some of their properties. Finally, we discuss open questions concerning the independence notions.

Keywords: Independence · Sets of desirable gamble sets · Choice functions · Natural extension

1 Introduction

If an agent's joint beliefs about two uncertain variables (X, Y) are described by a probability mass function (pmf) p on their joint finite possibility space,[1] then X and Y are (stochastically) independent if conditioning p on any value of one variable does not change the agent's beliefs about the other. Given marginal mass functions p_X and p_Y, the (unique) independent joint distribution with these marginals is their product $p_X p_Y$. This construction is a form of *independent natural extension*, which we study here in an imprecise-probabilistic setting.

In this paper we investigate independence for choice functions, one of the most expressive belief models in the imprecise-probabilistic framework. Their added flexibility allows expressing alternative notions of independence, such as requiring independence in every element of a representation, or judging it unreasonable to use observations of X to make decisions about Y. We introduce two new notions of independence and relate them to two existing ones.

The paper is organised as follows. In Sect. 2, we introduce the relevant results about choice functions, or their equivalent model of sets of desirable gamble

[1] For convenience, we assume all probabilities are positive.

B. Vantaggi et al. (Eds.): IPMU 2026, CCIS 3019, pp. 233–247, 2026.
https://doi.org/10.1007/978-3-032-28994-0_17

sets. Section 3 contains the main results: after reviewing marginalisation and conditioning, we introduce the independence notions. Section 4 concludes with a brief discussion and directions for future research. In order to adhere to the page limit, we have omitted the proofs.

2 Choice Functions

Consider an uncertain variable X taking values in a possibility space $\mathcal{X}$, which we assume to be *finite* throughout this paper. A gamble f is a real-valued function on $\mathcal{X}$ that maps each possibility x in $\mathcal{X}$ to a reward $f(x)$, expressed in unites of a predetermined utility scale. If the agent accepts a gamble f, she accepts to receive the – possibly negative – reward $f(x)$ if the possibility x is realised.

Because X is an *uncertain* variable, a gamble f on $\mathcal{X}$ involves risk so it is a risky transaction. An agent's preferences between gambles therefore reveal her beliefs about X. A *choice function* C is a function that describes the agent's preference between gambles in a very general way, without assuming that they are determined by a binary preference order [7,12]. In this paper, we study choice functions as a belief model, but for mathematical convenience, we shall focus on the equivalent model of *sets of desirable gamble sets* [4,5].

To introduce choice functions, we first need to introduce some relevant notation. We denote all gambles on $\mathcal{X}$ as $\mathcal{L}(\mathcal{X})$ – or simply $\mathcal{L}$ when it is clear from the context what the domain is. The set of all gambles $\mathcal{L}(\mathcal{X})$ is an $|\mathcal{X}|$-dimensional linear space under the pointwise addition and scalar multiplication of gambles. For two gambles f and g, we use $f \leq g$ to denote $f(x) \leq g(x)$ for all x in $\mathcal{X}$, and we use $f < g$ for '$f \leq g$ and $f(x) < g(x)$ for some x in $\mathcal{X}$'. A constant gamble is a gamble that returns the same value α everywhere, and we identify such gamble with a real number α. We collect the gambles that result in a partial gain in the *set of positive gambles* $\mathcal{L}_{>0}(\mathcal{X}) := \{f \in \mathcal{L}(\mathcal{X}) : f > 0\}$, and the gambles that cannot make you win utility in the *set of non-positive gambles* $\mathcal{L}_{\leq 0}(\mathcal{X}) := \{f \in \mathcal{L}(\mathcal{X}) : f \leq 0\}$ – or simply $\mathcal{L}_{>0}$ and $\mathcal{L}_{\leq 0}$ respectively, when the domain is clear from the context

Choice functions take a *finite* set of gambles, called *gamble set*, as an argument. We denote the set of all gamble sets on $\mathcal{X}$ as $\mathcal{Q}(\mathcal{X}) := \{F \subseteq \mathcal{L}(\mathcal{X}) : |F| \in \mathbb{N}\}$, or simply $\mathcal{Q}$. A choice function C on $\mathcal{X}$ is a function $\mathcal{Q}(\mathcal{X}) \to \mathcal{Q}(\mathcal{X})$ such that a set of admissible gambles $C(F)$ is a subset of F for every F in $\mathcal{Q}(\mathcal{X})$. The corresponding set of rejected gambles $R(F) := F \setminus C(F)$ is an equivalent representation of this assessment.

Imprecise-probabilistic choice functions have first been introduced by Seidenfeld et al. [7,12], where they have provided an axiomatisation for coherent choice between *horse lotteries* rather than gambles. Since then, Refs. [4,5,13,14,17,20], among others, have proposed an axiomatisation based on it, but specified to gambles. Due to page limitations, we will not give an overview of the rationality axioms for choice functions here, but rather introduce them directly in Sect. 2.1 in their equivalent and more convenient form – sets of desirable gamble sets – established in Refs. [4,5]. We stress that the rationality axioms allow for a gamble f to be admissible from both $\{f, g\}$ and $\{f, h\}$, while being inadmissible from $\{f, g, h\}$, which proves that choice functions can express more than pairwise preferences.

2.1 Sets of Desirable Gamble Sets

In this section, we discuss relevant results about coherent sets of desirable gamble sets, which were introduced in Refs. [4,5] as an equivalent representation of coherent choice functions. Given the equivalence, everything we establish for sets of desirable gamble sets, will immediately hold for choice functions too, *mutatis mutandis.*

Definition 1 (Sets of desirable gamble sets). *A set of desirable gamble sets K on $\mathcal{X}$ is a subset of $\mathcal{Q}(\mathcal{X})$.*

The idea is that a set of desirable gamble sets K contains all the gamble sets F that have at least one gamble that the agent prefers to the constant gamble 0, called the *status quo*. Such a gamble set F is then called a *desirable gamble set.*

Given a rejection function R, if $0 \in R(\{0\} \cup F)$ then we interpret this as meaning that the agent finds at least one gamble f in F desirable, or in other words, prefers f to 0, and thus F should be a desirable gamble set. Then $K := \{F \in \mathcal{Q} : 0 \in R(\{0\} \cup F)\}$ is the set of desirable gamble sets corresponding to R. Conversely, given a set of desirable gamble sets K, the corresponding rejection function R is given by $R(F) := \{f \in F : F - \{f\} \in K\}$, where $F - \{f\} := \{g - f : g \in F\}$ for every F in $\mathcal{Q}$. Under conditions implied by coherence, both operations commute; see Ref. [4].

Definition 2 (Coherent sets of desirable gamble sets [4, Definition 4]). *A set of desirable gamble sets $K \subseteq \mathcal{Q}$ is called* coherent *if:*

K_0. *$\emptyset \notin K$;*
K_1. *$F \in K \Rightarrow F \setminus \{0\} \in K$;*
K_2. *$\{f\} \in K$ for all f in $\mathcal{L}_{>0}$;*
K_3. *if $F, G \in K$ and $(\lambda^{f,g}, \mu^{f,g}) > 0$ for every pair (f, g) in $F \times G$, then $\{\lambda^{f,g} f + \mu^{f,g} g : f \in F, g \in G\} \in K$;*[2]
K_4. *if $F \in K$ and $F \subseteq G$, then $G \in K$.*

We collect all the coherent sets of desirable gamble sets in the collection $\overline{\mathcal{K}}(\mathcal{X})$, or simply $\overline{\mathcal{K}}$ when the possibility space is clear from the context.

We refer to Refs. [4,5] for a justification of the coherence axioms.

A set of desirable gamble sets K_1 is called *at least as informative as* a set of desirable gamble sets K_2 when $K_2 \subseteq K_1$, simply because an agent with K_1 finds more gamble sets desirable than an agent with K_2. The resulting partially ordered set $(\overline{\mathcal{K}}, \subseteq)$ is a complete meet-semilattice [4, Theorem 8]. This guarantees

[2] We use $(\lambda^{f,g}, \mu^{f,g}) > 0$ to mean '$\lambda^{f,g} \geq 0$ and $\mu^{f,g} \geq 0$ but not $\lambda^{f,g} = \mu^{f,g} = 0$.'

that if a partially specified set of desirable gamble sets $\mathcal{A} \subseteq \mathcal{Q}$ has a coherent superset, in which case $\mathcal{A}$ is called *consistent*, then it has a unique smallest (or least informative) coherent superset $\mathrm{cl}_{\overline{\mathcal{K}}}(\mathcal{A}) := \bigcap\{K \in \overline{\mathcal{K}} : \mathcal{A} \subseteq K\}$, called the *natural extension* of $\mathcal{A}$ [4, Theorem 9].

The natural extension $\mathrm{cl}_{\overline{\mathcal{K}}}(\mathcal{A})$ of a consistent assessment $\mathcal{A}$ obtains a closed-form expression; however, we focus on its more convenient formulation in terms of *representations*, which we discuss in Sects. 2.2 and 2.3.

2.2 Sets of Desirable Gambles

Given a coherent rejection function R, the gambles in $D_R := \{f \in \mathcal{L} : 0 \in R(\{0, f\})\}$ are preferred in a *pairwise preference* to 0. Similarly, for a coherent set of desirable gamble sets K, the set $D_K := \{f \in \mathcal{L} : \{f\} \in K\}$ consists of the gambles that are preferred to 0. If R and K contain the same information, the sets D_R and D_K coincide. We therefore call D_K the *binary part* of K.

The set D_K is more commonly known as a *set of desirable gambles*: it contains the gambles that the agent prefers to 0. Sets of desirable gambles were introduced by Seidenfeld et al. [10], and have been further developed by a range of authors, for instance in Refs. [2,3,9,19,21,22].

Definition 3 (Sets of desirable gambles). *A set of desirable gambles D on $\mathcal{X}$ is a subset of $\mathcal{L}(\mathcal{X})$.*

The idea is that the set of desirable gambles D contains all the gambles f that are preferred to 0. Sets of desirable gambles have the following rationality axioms.

Definition 4 (Coherent sets of desirable gambles). *A set of desirable gambles $D \subseteq \mathcal{L}$ is called* coherent *if:*

D$_1$. *$0 \notin D$;*
D$_2$. *$\mathcal{L}_{>0} \subseteq D$;*
D$_3$. *if $f, g \in D$ and $(\lambda, \mu) > 0$, then $\lambda f + \mu g \in D$.*

We collect all the coherent sets of desirable gambles in $\overline{\mathbf{D}}(\mathcal{X}) \subseteq \mathscr{P}(\mathcal{L}(\mathcal{X}))$,[3] or simply $\overline{\mathbf{D}}$ when the possibility space is clear from the context.

Coherent sets of desirable gambles are convex cones – sets $A \subseteq \mathcal{L}$ for which $\mathrm{posi}(A) := \{\sum_{k=1}^{n} \lambda_k f_k : n \in \mathbb{N}, \lambda_k \in \mathbb{R}_{>0}, f_k \in A\} \subseteq A$ – that do not contain 0 but contain all the positive gambles. Given a pmf p, we let $D_p := \{f \in \mathcal{L} : E_p(f) > 0 \text{ or } f > 0\}$ be the corresponding set of desirable gambles, which collects all the gambles whose p-expectation E_p is positive, and the set $\mathcal{L}_{>0}$. It is a matter of straightforward verification that D_p is a coherent set of desirable gambles. If $p(x) > 0$ for all x in $\mathcal{X}$ then D_p is an open half space.

[3] In this paper, we denote the power set of a given set A by $\mathscr{P}(A)$, and the set of all non-empty subsets of A by $\mathscr{P}^{+}(A) = \mathscr{P}(A) \setminus \{\emptyset\}$.

A set of desirable gambles D_1 is called *at least as informative as* a set of desirable gambles D_2 when $D_2 \subseteq D_1$. The resulting partially ordered set $(\overline{\mathcal{D}}, \subseteq)$ is also a complete meet-semilattice, and if a partially specified set of desirable gambles $A \subseteq \mathcal{L}$ has a coherent superset, in which case A is called *consistent*, then it has a unique smallest (or least informative) coherent superset $\mathrm{cl}_{\overline{\mathcal{D}}}(A) := \bigcap\{D \in \overline{\mathcal{D}} : A \subseteq D\}$, called the *natural extension* of A. The natural extension for sets of desirable gambles has a convenient closed-form expression.

Theorem 1. **([19, Theorem 1]).** *Consider any assessment $A \subseteq \mathcal{L}$. Then A is consistent iff $0 \notin \mathrm{posi}(\mathcal{L}_{>0} \cup A)$. If this is the case, then $\mathrm{cl}_{\overline{\mathcal{D}}}(A) = \mathrm{posi}(\mathcal{L}_{>0} \cup A)$.*

Maximal Sets of Desirable Gambles. The maximal elements of the partially ordered set $(\overline{\mathcal{D}}(\mathcal{X}), \subseteq)$ are called *maximal sets of desirable gambles*. We collect them in the set $\mathcal{M}(\mathcal{X})$, or simply $\mathcal{M}$ when the possibility space is clear from the context.

Maximal sets of desirable gambles have an easy characterisation: a coherent set of desirable gambles D is maximal if and only if $f \in D$ or $-f \in D$ for all gambles $f \neq 0$ [19, Proposition 2]. This implies [3, Lemma 17] that every element of $\mathcal{M}(\mathcal{X})$ is a superset of D_p, where p is a pmf. As such, elements M of $\mathcal{M}(\mathcal{X})$ can be seen as more informative than probabilities: if a non-zero gamble f's expectation $E_p(f)$ is zero, then M still contains either f or $-f$.

For any set of gambles $A \subseteq \mathcal{L}$, denote the set of its dominating maximal sets of desirable gambles by $m(A) := \{M \in \mathcal{M} : A \subseteq M\}$. Given a coherent set of desirable gambles D, the set $m(D)$ can be viewed as a representation of D.

Theorem 2. **([19, Corollary 4]).** *A set of desirable gambles A is consistent iff $m(A) \neq \emptyset$. Moreover, its natural extension can be obtained by $\mathrm{cl}_{\overline{\mathcal{D}}}(A) = \bigcap m(A)$.*

In particular, Theorem 2 implies that any coherent set of desirable gambles D can be represented by the maximal sets of desirable gambles above it.

2.3 Representation

Given a coherent set of desirable gambles D, there may be multiple coherent sets of desirable gamble sets K such that $D_K = D$, but the smallest – or least informative – of them is $K_D := \{F \in \mathcal{Q} : F \cap D \neq \emptyset\}$ [15, Proposition 5]. Because K_D is completely determined by D, and hence by *binary comparisons*, we call any coherent K_D a *binary* set of desirable gamble sets. Binary sets of desirable gambles are useful because they allow for a representation of any coherent set of desirable gamble sets.

Theorem 3. **([5, Theorem 9]).** *For any sets of desirable gamble sets K, the following two expressions are equivalent:*

(i) K is coherent;
(ii) there is a non-empty set $\mathcal{D} \subseteq \overline{\mathcal{D}}$ of coherent sets of desirable gambles such that $K = \bigcap\{K_D : D \in \mathcal{D}\}$. If this is the case, then K is said to be represented *by $\mathcal{D}$, and $\mathcal{D}$ is a* representation *of K.*

Moreover, K's (unique) largest representing set is $\mathcal{D}_K := \{D \in \overline{\mathbf{D}} : K \subseteq K_D\}$.

Ref. [20, Equation (24)] guarantees that Theorem 3 implies the following convenient expression for the natural extension.

Theorem 4. *An assessment* $\mathcal{A} \subseteq \mathcal{Q}$ *is consistent iff* $\mathcal{D}_{\mathcal{A}} \neq \emptyset$. *Moreover, if this is the case, then* $\mathrm{cl}_{\overline{\mathbf{K}}}(\mathcal{A}) = \bigcap\{K_D : D \in \mathcal{D}_{\mathcal{A}}\}$.

3 Three Concepts of Independence

In this section, we compare three notions of independence for sets of desirable gamble sets: epistemic independence, representational independence and S-independence. Each of them captures a different intuitive concept of independence. The most widely used one, epistemic independence, has been introduced in Ref. [21, Sections 9.1 and 9.2] for lower previsions and further developed for sets of desirable gambles in Ref [18] and sets of desirable gamble sets in Ref. [14]. S-independence has been introduced in Ref. [12] and studied in more detail for choice functions in Ref. [6]. We introduce a new notion in this context – which we call representational independence – based on epistemic and strong products for sets of desirable gambles; see Ref. [18].

To prioritise conceptual clarity and minimise technicalities, we have decided to focus on independence between two uncertain variables X and Y, with finite possibility spaces $\mathcal{X}$ and $\mathcal{Y}$, respectively.

3.1 Marginalisation and Conditioning

In this section, we discuss sets of desirable gamble sets that represent beliefs about X and Y *jointly*, necessary to our discussion of independence next. The discussion and results in Sect. 2 above hold for the possibility space $\mathcal{X}\times\mathcal{Y}$ without restriction.

For any gamble f in the $|\mathcal{X}||\mathcal{Y}|$-dimensional linear space $\mathcal{L}(\mathcal{X} \times \mathcal{Y})$ and any $x \in \mathcal{X}$, the partial map $f(x, \cdot)$ is a gamble on $\mathcal{Y}$; and similarly, for any $y \in \mathcal{Y}$, the partial map $f(\cdot, y)$ is a gamble on $\mathcal{X}$. In this section, the roles of X and Y are symmetric; to avoid repetition we decide to focus on one of them, but *swapping* X *for* Y would yield analogous statements or results. It will be convenient to relate a gamble f on $\mathcal{X}$ to a gamble on $\mathcal{X} \times \mathcal{Y}$.

Definition 5. (Cylindrical extension). *Given any gamble* f *on* $\mathcal{X}$, *we let its* cylindrical extension f^Y *to* $\mathcal{X} \times \mathcal{Y}$ *be defined by* $f^Y(x, y) := f(x)$ *for all* x *in* $\mathcal{X}$ *and* y *in* $\mathcal{Y}$. *Similarly, given any set of gambles* $F \subseteq \mathcal{L}(\mathcal{X})$, *we let its* cylindrical extension $F^Y \subseteq \mathcal{L}(\mathcal{X} \times \mathcal{Y})$ *be defined as* $F^Y := \{f^Y : f \in F\}$.

Formally, f is a gamble on $\mathcal{X}$, while f^Y is a gamble on $\mathcal{X} \times \mathcal{Y}$, but since it is constant on $\mathcal{Y}$, its behavioural content is contained in $\mathcal{X}$ – just like for f. We will therefore, from now on, *make no notational distinction between a gamble and its cylindrical extension.* This notational trick allows us to regard f as an element of $\mathcal{L}(\mathcal{X} \times \mathcal{Y})$, and $\mathcal{L}(\mathcal{X})$ as a subset of $\mathcal{L}(\mathcal{X} \times \mathcal{Y})$ – even though their dimensions might differ – and similarly for $\mathcal{Q}(\mathcal{X}) \subseteq \mathcal{Q}(\mathcal{X} \times \mathcal{Y})$.

Marginalisation. Suppose that we have a coherent belief model D or K about (X, Y) jointly and we are interested in marginalising to X, or extracting the information about X solely. For a set of desirable gambles D, we collect the gambles that belong to D but only depend on $\mathcal{X}$ in its X-marginal $\operatorname{marg}_X D$.

Definition 6. ([15]). *For any set of desirable gambles $D \subseteq \mathcal{L}(\mathcal{X} \times \mathcal{Y})$, its X-marginal $\operatorname{marg}_X D \subseteq \mathcal{L}(\mathcal{X})$ is defined as $\operatorname{marg}_X D := D \cap \mathcal{L}(\mathcal{X})$.*

Similarly, for a set of desirable gamble sets K, we collect the gamble sets that belong to K, but only depend on $\mathcal{X}$, in its X-marginal $\operatorname{Marg}_X K$.

Definition 7. ([15]). *For any set of desirable gamble sets $K \subseteq \mathcal{Q}(\mathcal{X} - \times \mathcal{Y})$, its X-marginal $\operatorname{Marg}_X K \subseteq \mathcal{Q}(\mathcal{X})$ is defined as $\operatorname{Marg}_X K := K \cap \mathcal{Q}(\mathcal{X})$.*

Definition 7 generalises Definition 6, in the sense that for all K' in $\overline{\mathcal{K}}$ and D' in $\overline{\mathcal{D}}$, we have [15, Proposition 10] $\operatorname{Marg}_X K_{D'} = K_{\operatorname{marg}_X D'}$ and $\operatorname{marg}_X D_{K'} = D_{\operatorname{Marg}_X K'}$. Marginalisation preserves the order for both sets of desirable gambles and set of desirable gamble sets: if $D_1 \subseteq D_2$, then $\operatorname{marg}_X D_1 \subseteq \operatorname{marg}_X D_2$ and if $K_1 \subseteq K_2$, then $\operatorname{Marg}_X K_1 \subseteq \operatorname{Marg}_X K_2$. Likewise, marginalisation preserves coherence: if a set of desirable gambles D is coherent, then so is $\operatorname{marg}_X D$; and if a set of desirable gamble sets K is coherent, then so is $\operatorname{Marg}_X K$. Moreover, using the lifted version $\operatorname{marg}_X \mathcal{D} := \{\operatorname{marg}_X D : D \in \mathcal{D}\}$, if a coherent set of desirable gamble sets K is represented by $\mathcal{D}$, then $\operatorname{Marg}_X K$ is represented by $\operatorname{marg}_X \mathcal{D}$; see Ref. [14, Proposition 8].

Conditioning. Assume that we have a model D or K representing the agent's beliefs about (X, Y) jointly. Suppose we receive new information that X takes values in some event $E \in \mathscr{P}^+(\mathcal{X})$. We aim to update our model to reflect this information, which is to *condition* on the event E.

Calling off a gamble f on $E \times \mathcal{Y}$ with respect to E yields the gamble $\mathbb{I}_E f \in \mathcal{L}(\mathcal{X} \times \mathcal{Y})$ defined, for all $(x, y) \in \mathcal{X} \times \mathcal{Y}$ by

$$\mathbb{I}_E f(x,y) := \begin{cases} f(x,y), & \text{if } x \in E; \\ 0, & \text{otherwise.} \end{cases}$$

This is a *called-off* version of f: the risky transaction occurs only if E happens; if not, the gamble gets called off. In turn, calling off the gamble set F on the event E yields $\mathbb{I}_E F = \{\mathbb{I}_E f : f \in F\}$.

Conditioning D on E yields the conditional set of desirable gambles $D\rfloor E := \{f \in \mathcal{L}(E \times \mathcal{Y}) : \mathbb{I}_E f \in D\}$ and if D is coherent, then so is $D\rfloor E$. We refer to [21, Appendix F] and [19, Section 3.2] for more information.

Similarly, conditioning K on E yields the conditional set of desirable gamble sets $K\rfloor E := \{F \in \mathcal{Q}(E \times \mathcal{Y}) : \mathbb{I}_E F \in K\}$ and if K is coherent, then so is $K\rfloor E$. Moreover, if $\mathcal{D}$ is some representation of K, then $K\rfloor E$ is represented by $\mathcal{D}\rfloor E = \{D\rfloor E : D \in \mathcal{D}\}$ [14, Proposition 7].

3.2 Independence Concepts

In this section we provide an overview of three concepts of independence. In order to streamline the discussion, let K denote a coherent set of desirable gamble sets on the joint (finite) possibility space $\mathcal{X} \times \mathcal{Y}$.

Epistemic Independence. The idea of epistemic irrelevance from X to Y is:

> Learning that a non-empty event $E_X \subseteq \mathcal{X}$ obtains does not affect the beliefs about Y.

The set K is said in Ref. [14, Section 6] to satisfy *epistemic irrelevance from X to Y* when conditioning on any non-empty event $E_X \subseteq \mathcal{X}$ leaves the marginal beliefs about Y unchanged. Formally, for all E_X in $\mathscr{P}^+(\mathcal{X})$, $\mathrm{Marg}_Y\ (K\rfloor E_X) = \mathrm{Marg}_Y\ K$. Epistemic irrelevance is asymmetric, and to obtain its symmetric counterpart – called *epistemic independence* – one must require it in both directions. For K, this requirement is

$$\mathrm{Marg}_Y\ (K\rfloor E_X) = \mathrm{Marg}_Y\ K \text{ and } \mathrm{Marg}_X\ (K\rfloor E_Y) = \mathrm{Marg}_X\ K \tag{1}$$

for all E_X in $\mathscr{P}^+(\mathcal{X})$ and E_Y in $\mathscr{P}^+(\mathcal{Y})$. If Equation (1) holds for all such events, we say that K satisfies *epistemic independence.*

A K on $\mathcal{X} \times \mathcal{Y}$ is called an *epistemic product* of coherent K_X on $\mathcal{X}$ and K_Y on $\mathcal{Y}$ if it satisfies epistemic independence and has K_X and K_Y as its marginals. It is established in Ref. [14, Theorem 15] that the smallest epistemic product of K_X and K_Y exists, and we denote it by $K_1 \otimes K_2$.

The requirement of epistemic irrelevance can also be applied on sets of desirable gambles. A coherent set of desirable gambles D on $\mathcal{X} \times \mathcal{Y}$ is said in Ref. [18] to satisfy *epistemic irrelevance from X to Y* if $\mathrm{marg}_Y\ (D\rfloor E_X) = \mathrm{marg}_Y\ D$ for all E_X in $\mathscr{P}^+(\mathcal{X})$. This notion is again asymmetric, and to obtain a symmetric counterpart – called *epistemic independence* – one must require it in both directions. Similarly as for sets of desirable gamble sets, given two coherent sets of desirable gambles D_X on $\mathcal{X}$ and D_Y on $\mathcal{Y}$, a set D on $\mathcal{X} \times \mathcal{Y}$ is called an *epistemic product* of D_X and D_Y if it satisfies epistemic independence and has D_X and D_Y as its marginals. It is established in Ref. [18, Theorem 19] that the smallest epistemic product of D_X and D_Y exists, and we denote it by $D_X \otimes D_Y$.

Fortunately, for pmfs, the epistemic product for sets of desirable gambles coincides with the standard independence definition, in the following sense.

Proposition 1. *Consider a pmf p on $\mathcal{X}$ and a pmf q on $\mathcal{Y}$ such that $p(x) > 0$ for all x in $\mathcal{X}$ and $q(y) > 0$ for all y in $\mathcal{X}$. Then $D_{pq} = D_p \otimes D_q$.*

Representational Independence. Consider a *committee of experts* in which each member expresses their beliefs by a coherent set of desirable gambles D. The collective information of the committee is captured by its collection $\mathcal{D}$ of the individual Ds, which, by Theorem 3, represents a coherent set of desirable gamble sets K. The independence requirement for K we introduce here, which we call *representational independence*, is that the each member of the committee must agree about the independence:

There is an *independent representation*, that is, a representation whose every member satisfies epistemic independence.

Definition 8 (Representational independence). *A coherent set of desirable gamble sets K on $\mathcal{X} \times \mathcal{Y}$ satisfies* representational independence *if it has a representation $\mathcal{D}$ such that every D in $\mathcal{D}$ satisfies epistemic independence.*

Recall from Theorem 3 that a coherent K may obtain multiple representations. Representational independence is the requirement that *at least one such representation* is independent.

Given two coherent sets of desirable gamble sets K_X on $\mathcal{X}$ and K_Y on $\mathcal{Y}$, we call K on $\mathcal{X} \times \mathcal{Y}$ a *representational product* of K_X and K_Y if it satisfies representational independence and has K_X and K_Y as its marginals. We establish that the smallest representational product of K_X and K_Y – which we call the *representationally independent natural extension of K_X and K_Y* – exists and has a convenient representation in terms of the epistemically independent natural extension of the elements in the representations of K_X and K_Y.

Theorem 5. *Consider any coherent marginal sets of desirable gamble sets $K_X \in \overline{\mathcal{K}}(\mathcal{X})$ and $K_Y \in \overline{\mathcal{K}}(\mathcal{Y})$. Then the representationally independent natural extension of K_X and K_Y exists and is given by*

$$K_X \boxdot K_Y := \bigcap\nolimits_{D_X \in \mathcal{D}_{K_X}, D_Y \in \mathcal{D}_{K_Y}} K_{D_X \otimes D_Y}, \tag{2}$$

which has $\{D_X \otimes D_Y : D_X \in \mathcal{D}_{K_X}, D_Y \in \mathcal{D}_{K_Y}\}$ as an independent representation.

In Definition 8 we have used epistemic independence for sets of desirable gambles. Another popular type of independence for sets of desirable gambles is *strong independence*. Given coherent sets of desirable gambles D_X on $\mathcal{X}$ and D_Y on $\mathcal{Y}$, their strong product is defined as $D_X \boxtimes D_Y := \bigcap\{M_X \otimes M_Y : M_X \in m(D_X), M_Y \in m(D_Y)\}$. Similarly to the representationally independent product, the strong product is an intersection of epistemic products of the members of representations $m(D_X)$ and $m(D_Y)$ of D_X and D_Y, respectively. In the context of coherent sets of desirable gambles, [18, Proposition 27] establishes that $D_X \boxtimes D_Y$ is indeed an epistemic product of D_X and D_Y, but not necessarily the smallest one [18, Appendix A.3].

This tells us that there is a choice to be made in Eq. (2) about the type of product of the D_X and D_Y. In our Definition 8 of representational independence, we have chosen to require *epistemic* independence, but the results in Ref. [18] allows us to use a *strong* product instead. We thus obtain a different independence notion, which we call *strong representational independence.*

Definition 9 (Strong representational independence). *A coherent set of desirable gamble sets K on $\mathcal{X} \times \mathcal{Y}$ satisfies* strong representational independence *if it has a representation $\mathcal{D}$ such that every D in $\mathcal{D}$ is a strong product.*

Since every strong product is an epistemic product, if K satisfies strong representational independence, then it also satisfies representational independence. Similar to what we have done above, we call K on $\mathcal{X}\times\mathcal{Y}$ a *strong representational product* of the two coherent sets of desirable gamble sets K_X on $\mathcal{X}$ and K_Y on $\mathcal{Y}$, if it satisfies strong representational independence and has K_X and K_Y as its marginals. Here too, it turns out that the smallest strong representational product of K_X and K_Y – which we call the *strong representationally independent natural extension of* K_X *and* K_Y – exists and has a convenient representation in terms of strong products of elements in the representations of K_X and K_Y.

Theorem 6. *Consider any coherent marginal sets of desirable gamble sets* $K_X \in \overline{\mathcal{K}}(\mathcal{X})$ *and* $K_Y \in \overline{\mathcal{K}}(\mathcal{Y})$*. Then the strong representationally independent natural extension of* K_X *and* K_Y *exists and is given by*

$$K_X \boxdot K_Y \coloneqq \bigcap\nolimits_{K_X \in \mathcal{D}_{K_X}, K_Y \in \mathcal{D}_{K_Y}} K_{D_X \boxtimes D_Y},$$

which has $\{D_X \boxtimes D_Y : D_X \in \mathcal{D}_{K_X}, D_Y \in \mathcal{D}_{K_Y}\}$ *as an independent representation.*

Interestingly, epistemic independence is a weaker requirement than strong representational independence.

Proposition 2. *Consider any* $K \in \overline{\mathcal{K}}(\mathcal{X} \times \mathcal{Y})$*. If* K *satisfies (strong) representational independence, then* K *satisfies epistemic independence.*

As a consequence, the strong representational product of two coherent sets of desirable gamble sets K_X and K_Y is an epistemic product of K_X and K_Y, but it is not necessarily the smallest one.

Corollary 1. *Consider any* $K_X \in \overline{\mathcal{K}}(\mathcal{X})$ *and* $K_Y \in \overline{\mathcal{K}}(\mathcal{Y})$*. Then* $K_X \otimes K_Y \subseteq K_X \circledcirc K_Y \subseteq K_X \boxdot K_Y$.

S-Independence. The idea of *S-irrelevance* of X to Y is [6, Section 4.1]:

> It is unreasonable to *spend resources* in order to use the observed value of X to choose between gambles that only depend on Y.

When X is S-irrelevant to Y and Y is S-irrelevant to X, the two uncertain variables are called *S-independent.*

Observing the value of X is modelled by selecting a partition $\mathcal{P}$ of the possibility space $\mathcal{X}$ and determining which event $E \in \mathcal{P}$ occurs, so that $X \in E$. For each event E in the partition, the agent chooses the gamble f_E on $\mathcal{Y}$. The action of observing X and then selecting a gamble on Y in this manner corresponds to the composite gamble $\sum_{E\in\mathcal{P}} \mathbb{I}_E(X) f_E(Y)$.

If X is S-irrelevant to Y, the requirement is that the agent choosing between the gambles on Y should reject the option to pay any real $\epsilon > 0$ for the composite gamble: from the gamble set $\{f_E : E \in \mathcal{P}\} \cup \{\sum_{G\in\mathcal{P}} \mathbb{I}_G f_G - \epsilon\}$, the agent should reject the latter gamble. Translated to sets of desirable gamble sets, this requirement becomes as follows [6, Definition 9].

Definition 10 (S-independence). *A coherent set of desirable gamble sets* K *on* $\mathcal{X} \times \mathcal{Y}$ *satisfies* S-irrelevance from X to Y *if* $\{\sum_{G \in \mathcal{P} \setminus \{E\}} \mathbb{I}_G[f_E - f_G] + \epsilon : E \in \mathcal{P}\} \in K$*, for all partitions* $\mathcal{P}$ *of* $\mathcal{X}$*, all* $f_E \in \mathcal{L}(\mathcal{Y})$ *and all* $\epsilon > 0$*.* K *satisfies* S-independent *if it satisfies S-irrelevance both from* X *to* Y *and from* Y *to* X*.*

Using representations of K, we can simplify the requirement in Definition 10, which will be useful later on this paper, thereby generalising [6, Proposition 12].

Proposition 3. *Consider any coherent set of desirable gamble sets* K *on* $\mathcal{X} \times \mathcal{Y}$*, and any representation* $\mathcal{D}$ *of* K*. Then* K *satisfies S-irrelevance from* X *to* Y *iff for all* D *in* $\mathcal{D}$*, the binary* K_D *satisfies S-irrelevance from* X *to* Y*.*

The theory of S-independence was significantly developed in Ref. [6]. To fully appreciate and build upon this work, we must introduce two additional axioms for sets of desirable gamble sets, the first being *mixingness.* A coherent set of desirable gamble sets K satisfies mixingness if

K_5. If $G \in K$ and $F \subseteq G \subseteq \mathrm{posi}F$, then also $F \in K$.

The effect of adding this axiom, is that any mixing set of desirable gamble sets K has a representation $\mathcal{D}$ – see Theorem 3 – that consists of *mixing sets of desirable gambles*, which are coherent sets of desirable gambles D for which the complement is also a convex cone: $\mathrm{posi}(D^c) = D^c$.[4] All maximal sets of desirable gambles, as well as all D_p for pmfs p such that $p(x) > 0$ for every x in $\mathcal{X}$, are mixing.

The second additional axiom is *Archimedeanity*, for which we refer to Ref. [17] for a detailed description. What matters for our analysis is that, once this requirement is imposed on K, it can be represented by $\mathcal{D}$ containing only sets of desirable gambles of the form $D_{\underline{P}} := \{f \in \mathcal{L} : \underline{P}(f) > 0\}$, where $\underline{P}$ is a coherent lower prevision. A coherent lower prevision is a lower expectation functional that satisfies certain rationality axioms; we refer to [8,21] for more information about lower previsions. This means that we can represent an Archimedean set of desirable gamble sets K by a set $\underline{\mathcal{P}}$ of coherent lower previsions, and its largest representation in terms of lower previsions is $\underline{\mathcal{P}}_K := \{\underline{P} \text{ coherent lower prevision} : K \subseteq K_{D_{\underline{P}}}\}$; see Ref. [17] for more details.

A *linear prevision*, or (precise) expectation operator, is a lower prevision that corresponds to a precise probability. Imposing both Archimedeanity and mixingness on K has the effect that the set $\underline{\mathcal{P}}_K$ consists of linear previsions only; see [6, Theorem 2]. Together with a technical condition called *credible indeterminacy,*[5] the following surprising result is established in Ref [6].

---

[4] Such sets of desirable gambles have also been called *lexicographic* in Refs. [1,16].

[5] For convenience, we use a stronger version of credible indeterminacy than in Ref. [6], but we give it the same name. This guarantees that under our more restrictive requirements, the results in Ref. [6] remain valid. We call a set of desirable gamble sets K_X on $\mathcal{X}$ *credibly indeterminate* if for every outcome x in $\mathcal{X}$ there is a real $\epsilon > 0$ such that $\{\mathbb{I}_{\{x\}} - \epsilon\} \in K$.

Theorem 7 (**[6, Theorem 10]**). *Consider any Archimedean set of desirable gamble sets K on $\mathcal{X} \times \mathcal{Y}$ whose X- and Y-marginals are credibly indeterminate. If K satisfies S-independence, then every $\underline{P}$ in $\underline{\mathcal{P}}_K$ is a linear prevision that moreover satisfies independence.*

Theorem 7 and Proposition 1 imply that Archimedean and credibly indeterminate sets of desirable gamble sets that satisfy S-independence, also satisfy representational independence. We call K on $\mathcal{X} \times \mathcal{Y}$ an *S-independent product* of two coherent sets of desirable gamble sets K_X on $\mathcal{X}$ and K_Y on $\mathcal{Y}$ if it is Archimedean, satisfies S-independence and has K_X and K_Y as its marginals. It turns out that this independence concept, too, has a smallest S-independent product of K_X and K_Y, at least when K_X and K_Y are mixing, Archimedean and credibly indeterminate, which we call the *S-independent natural extension.*

Theorem 8. *Consider Archimedean, mixing and credibly indeterminate sets of desirable gamble sets $K_X \in \overline{\mathcal{K}}(\mathcal{X})$ and $K_Y \in \overline{\mathcal{K}}(\mathcal{Y})$. Then the S-independent natural extension of K_X and K_Y exists and is given by*

$$K_X \circledast K_Y := \bigcap\nolimits_{P_X \in \underline{\mathcal{P}}_{K_X}, P_Y \in \underline{\mathcal{P}}_{K_Y}} K_{D_{P_X P_Y}},$$

which has $\{D_{P_X P_Y} : P_X \in \underline{\mathcal{P}}_{K_X}, P_Y \in \underline{\mathcal{P}}_{K_Y}\}$ as an (independent) representation.

It turns out that the new notion of representational independence is expressive enough to connect K to S-independence without the need to impose Archimedeanity, as is required in Theorem 7.

Proposition 4. *Given any mixing set of desirable gamble sets K on $\mathcal{X} \times \mathcal{Y}$, if K satisfies (strong) representational independence, then K satisfies S-independence.*

Together with Theorem 7 and Proposition 1, Proposition 4 implies that for Archimedean, mixing and credibly inderterminate sets of desirable gamble sets S-independence and representational independence are equivalent.

4 Discussion

We introduced a new notion of independence for sets of desirable gamble sets – representational independence – together with its variant, strong representational independence. For these notions, as well as for the existing S-independence, we established independent natural extensions of marginal sets of desirable gamble sets, and compared them with the epistemically independent natural extension.

We verify that epistemic independence, representational independence, and S-independence all coincide with the standard notion of independence for probability measures, in the following sense. Let p and q be pmfs on $\mathcal{X}$ and $\mathcal{Y}$, respectively, such that $p(x) > 0$ and $q(y) > 0$ for all $x \in \mathcal{X}$ and $y \in \mathcal{Y}$, and define $K_p := K_{D_p}$, and analogously for q and pq. Then the results in this paper guarantee that

$$K_p \otimes K_q = K_p \boxcircle K_q = K_p \circledast K_q = K_{pq}.$$

Indeed, Proposition 1 yields $K_p \otimes K_q = K_{pq}$. Since K_p is Archimedean, mixing, and credibly indeterminate with singleton representation $\underline{\mathcal{P}}_{K_p} = \{E_p\}$ (and similarly for q and pq), Theorem 8 implies $K_p \circledast K_q = K_{pq}$. As the S-independent product is a representational product, it is a superset of the smallest such product $K_p \boxcircle K_q$. Together with Proposition 2, this gives $K_{pq} = K_p \otimes K_q \subseteq K_p \boxcircle K_q \subseteq K_p \circledast K_q = K_{pq}$, and hence all three products coincide in this case.

Several directions for further research remain open. We have shown that strong representational independence for mixing sets of desirable gamble sets implies S-independence, but it is still an open question whether this result can be strengthened to an equivalence, and under which conditions this would be possible. Additionally, the relation with mixingness opens up more questions, such as whether there are products – other than the S-independent product – that preserve mixingness without imposing Archimedeanity. We also wonder to which extent the Archimedeanity condition is necessary in Ref. [6], and whether there are ways to obtain a closed-form expression for the S-independent product without relying on Archimedeanity.

One of the motivations for this work is to obtain a suitable notion of independence for use in Bayesian networks with sets of desirable gambles as local models. For this purpose, the associated independent product should ideally be associative. Whether any of the proposed products satisfies associativity is still unknown, which is why we introduced all notions for two uncertain variables only. Furthermore, for iterative applications of independent products, we must either find a canonical representation of the product, or allow for the representations of the marginals to be arbitrary, neither of which is currently established for any of the products.

Acknowledgments. The authors thank Enrique Miranda for stimulating discussions on independence notions for desirability and lower previsions, and three anonymous reviewers for their insightful and detailed comments, which greatly improved this paper.

Disclosure of Interests. The authors have no competing interests to declare that are relevant to the content of this article.

References

1. Benavoli, A., Facchini, A., Zaffalon, M., Vicente-Pérez, J.: A polarity theory for sets of desirable gambles. In: Antonucci, A., Corani, G., Couso, I., Destercke, S. (eds.) Proceedings of the Tenth International Symposium on Imprecise Probability: Theories and Applications. Proceedings of Machine Learning Research, vol. 62, pp. 37–48. PMLR (2017)
2. Casanova, A.: Rationality and desirability – a foundational study. Ph.D. thesis, Università della Svizzera Italiana (2023)

3. Couso, I., Moral, S.: Sets of desirable gambles: conditioning, representation, and precise probabilities. Int. J. Approximate Reason. **52**(7), 1034–1055 (2011). https://doi.org/10.1016/j.ijar.2011.04.004
4. De Bock, J., De Cooman, G.: A desirability-based axiomatisation for coherent choice functions. In: Uncertainty Modelling in Data Science (Proceedings of SMPS 2018), pp. 46–53 (2018). https://doi.org/10.1007/978-3-319-97547-4_7
5. De Bock, J., De Cooman, G.: Interpreting, axiomatising and representing coherent choice functions in terms of desirability. Proc. Mach. Learn. Res. **103**, 125–134 (2019), ISIPTA 2019 — Proceedings of the Eleventh International Symposium on Imprecise Probability: Theories and Applications
6. De Bock, J., De Cooman, G.: On a notion of independence proposed by Teddy Seidenfeld. In: Augustin, T., Cozman, F.G., Wheeler, G. (eds.) Reflections on the Foundations of Probability and Statistics: Essays in Honor of Teddy Seidenfeld, pp. 243–284. Springer, Cham (2023). https://doi.org/10.1007/978-3-031-15436-2_11
7. Kadane, J.B., Schervish, M.J., Seidenfeld, T.: A Rubinesque theory of decision. In: DasGupta, A. (ed.) A Festschrift for Herman Rubin, Institute of Mathematical Statistics Lecture Notes – Monograph Series, vol. 45, pp. 45–55 (2004). https://doi.org/10.1214/lnms/1196285378
8. Miranda, E.: A survey of the theory of coherent lower previsions. Int. J. Approximate Reason. **48**(2), 628–658 (2008). https://doi.org/10.1016/j.ijar.2007.12.001
9. Quaeghebeur, E.: Introduction to imprecise probabilities. chap. Desirability. John Wiley & Sons (2014). https://doi.org/10.1002/9781118763117.ch1
10. Seidenfeld, T., Schervish, M.J., Kadane, J.B.: Decisions without ordering. In: Sieg, W. (ed.) Acting and reflecting: The Interdisciplinary Turn in Philosophy, Synthese Library, vol. 211, pp. 143–170. Kluwer, Dordrecht (1990). https://doi.org/10.1007/978-94-009-2476-5_11, reprinted in [11], pp. 40–68
11. Seidenfeld, T., Schervish, M.J., Kadane, J.B.: Rethinking the Foundations of Statistics. Cambridge University Press, Cambridge (1999). https://doi.org/10.1017/CBO9781139173230.001
12. Seidenfeld, T., Schervish, M.J., Kadane, J.B.: Coherent choice functions under uncertainty. Synthese **172**(1), 157–176 (2010). https://doi.org/10.1007/s11229-009-9470-7
13. Van Camp, A.: Choice functions as a tool to model uncertainty. Ph.D. thesis, Universiteit Gent (2018). https://hdl.handle.net/1854/LU-8546928
14. Van Camp, A., Blackwell, K., Konek, J.: Independent natural extension for choice functions. Int. J. Approximate Reasoning **152**, 390–413 (2023). https://doi.org/10.1016/j.ijar.2022.11.003
15. Van Camp, A., Miranda, E.: Modelling epistemic irrelevance with choice functions. Int. J. Approximate Reasoning **125**, 49–72 (2020). https://doi.org/10.1016/j.ijar.2020.06.010
16. Van Camp, A., De Cooman, G., Miranda, E.: Lexicographic choice functions. Int. J. Approximate Reasoning **92**, 97–119 (2018). https://doi.org/10.1016/j.ijar.2017.10.011
17. De Cooman, G.: Coherent and Archimedean choice in general Banach spaces. Int. J. Approximate Reasoning **140**, 255–281 (2022). https://doi.org/10.1016/j.ijar.2021.09.005
18. De Cooman, G., Miranda, E.: Irrelevant and independent natural extension for sets of desirable gambles. J. Artif. Intell. Res. **45**, 601–640 (2012). https://doi.org/10.1613/jair.3770

19. De Cooman, G., Quaeghebeur, E.: Exchangeability and sets of desirable gambles. International J. Approximate Reasoning **53**(3), 363–395 (2012). https://doi.org/10.1016/j.ijar.2010.12.002, special issue in honour of Henry E. Kyburg, Jr.
20. De Cooman, G., Van Camp, A., De Bock, J.: The logic behind desirable sets of things, and its filter representation. Int. J. Approximate Reasoning **172**, 109241 (2024). https://doi.org/10.1016/j.ijar.2024.109241
21. Walley, P.: Statistical Reasoning with Imprecise Probabilities. Chapman and Hall, London (1991)
22. Walley, P.: Towards a unified theory of imprecise probability. Int. J. Approximate Reasoning **24**, 125–148 (2000). https://doi.org/10.1016/S0888-613X(00)00031-1

Allowing for Imprecision in the Game-Theoretic Characterisation of the Poisson Process

Alexander Erreygers(✉)

Foundations Lab for imprecise probabilities, Ghent University, Ghent, Belgium
alexander.erreygers@ugent.be

Abstract. In their 1993 paper 'Forecasting point and continuous processes: Prequential analysis' in *Test*, Vovk put forward a game-theoretic definition of the Poisson process. A key assumption therein is that the rate of the Poisson process is known or specified exactly. In contrast, I replace this assumption with the less stringent—and arguably more realistic—one that the available information about the process takes the form of bounds on the rate rather than a single, exact value. The resulting process has properties similar to the standard, 'precise' Poisson process, albeit with an imprecise flavour to them, thus justifying the moniker 'imprecise Poisson process'.

Keywords: Counting process · Capital process · Bid–ask spread

1 Introduction

More than twenty years ago, Vovk [14] put forward a 'prequential' definition of the Poisson and Wiener processes,[1] with an (upper) expectation operator that is derived from the capital in a gambling game. Nowadays, this approach towards modelling uncertainty is known as the *game-theoretic* one, as laid out and popularised by Shafer & Vovk in their seminal monographs [11,12]. Discrete-time processes have been studied extensively in this game-theoretic framework, often allowing for imprecision in the local uncertainty models. Continuous-time processes have also received quite some attention in this framework; in contrast to discrete-time processes, I'm not aware of work in the setting of continuous time that allows for imprecision. This is why in this contribution, I set out to allow for imprecision, or a bid–ask spread, in Vovk's [14] game-theoretic definition of the Poisson process.

I lay down the foundation for doing so in Sect. 2, in the form of basic notation and terminology regarding (counting) paths, variables and processes. Section 3

[1] More generally, he considers the reduction of continuous martingales to these processes through a change of time.

B. Vantaggi et al. (Eds.): IPMU 2026, CCIS 3019, pp. 248–262, 2026.
https://doi.org/10.1007/978-3-032-28994-0_18

introduces, in a relatively general manner, the basics of Shafer & Vovk's game-theoretic foundations for modelling uncertainty regarding a continuous-time process. Next, I specialise this to the imprecise Poisson process in Sect. 4, and investigate the properties of the resulting conditional upper expectation operator in Sect. 5. Section 6 concludes this contribution.

In order to comply with the page limit, I state most results without proof; the sole exceptions are Propositions 5 and 7 and Theorem 2. Unless mentioned otherwise, the omitted proofs are modifications of the proofs of related results in [14]; the interested reader can find these proofs in the extended version of this contribution available on arXiv: 2604.00598.

2 Counting Paths, Variables and Processes

The set-up for this contribution is essentially standard, and follows Vovk's [14] rather closely; for the reader's sake, I feel it's nonetheless necessary to take some care in introducing it clearly. Let Ω be the set of all *counting paths*: those paths $\omega\colon \mathbb{R}_{\geq 0} \to \mathbb{Z}_{\geq 0}$ that start in 0, are increasing with *unit* jumps and right-continuous; these paths also have limits from the left, whence they form a subset of the well-known càdlàg paths [5, Ch. 3, § 5].

An *extended real partial variable* is a map from a subset of Ω to the set $\overline{\mathbb{R}}$ of extended real numbers.[2] We drop the adjective 'partial' if the domain is Ω and/or the adjective 'extended' if the codomain is $\mathbb{R}$. So $\overline{\mathbb{V}} := \overline{\mathbb{R}}^{\Omega}$ is the set of extended real variables, and for any time point $t \in \mathbb{R}_{\geq 0}$, the corresponding *coordinate variable*

$$N_t\colon \Omega \to \mathbb{Z}_{\geq 0}\colon \omega \mapsto \omega(t)$$

is a real variable; with $g\colon \mathbb{Z}_{\geq 0} \to \mathbb{R}$ and $t \in \mathbb{R}_{\geq 0}$, the composition

$$g(N_t) := g \circ N_t\colon \Omega \to \mathbb{R}\colon \omega \mapsto g(\omega(t))$$

is a real variable that is bounded if and only if g is bounded. Indicator variables are also bounded real variables: for any *event* $A \subseteq \Omega$, its corresponding *indicator* $\mathbb{I}_A$ is the $\{0,1\}$-valued variable that is 1 on A and 0 elsewhere.

An essential class of extended real variables are the *stopping times*: this class $\mathfrak{T}$ consists of the positive extended real variables τ—that is, maps from Ω to $\overline{\mathbb{R}}_{\geq 0}$—such that for all $\omega_1, \omega_2 \in \Omega$, if $\omega_1|_{[0,\tau(\omega_1)]\cap\mathbb{R}_{\geq 0}} = \omega_2|_{[0,\tau(\omega_1)]\cap\mathbb{R}_{\geq 0}}$ then $\tau(\omega_1) = \tau(\omega_2)$. Note that the constant real variable $t\colon \omega \mapsto t$ is a stopping time, and that for all stopping times $\tau_1, \tau_2 \in \mathfrak{T}$, their pointwise minimum $\tau_1 \wedge \tau_2$ and maximum $\tau_1 \vee \tau_2$ are also stopping times. For any stopping time $\tau \in \mathfrak{T}$ and path ω, we let $\mathcal{I}_\tau(\omega)$ be the set of counting paths that agree with ω on $[0, \tau(\omega)] \cap \mathbb{R}_{\geq 0}$:

$$\mathcal{I}_\tau(\omega) := \{\varpi \in \Omega\colon \varpi|_{[0,\tau(\omega)]\cap\mathbb{R}_{\geq 0}} = \omega|_{[0,\tau(\omega)]\cap\mathbb{R}_{\geq 0}}\}.$$

---

[2] I adhere to the same extension of addition and multiplication from $\mathbb{R}$ to $\overline{\mathbb{R}}$ as Shafer & Vovk [12, p. 420], so in particular $+\infty - \infty = +\infty$.

An extended real partial variable f is *τ-measurable* if for all $\omega_1, \omega_2 \in \operatorname{dom} f$,

$$\omega_1|_{[0,\tau(\omega_1)]\cap\mathbb{R}_{\geq 0}} = \omega_2|_{[0,\tau(\omega_1)]\cap\mathbb{R}_{\geq 0}} \implies f(\omega_1) = f(\omega_2);$$

differently put, f is constant on $\mathcal{I}_\tau(\omega)$ for all $\omega \in \operatorname{dom} f$. Although a stopping time τ can take the value $+\infty$, we are typically interested in the set of paths for which it is finite/real; we denote this set by $\{\tau < +\infty\} := \{\omega \in \Omega \colon \tau(\omega) < +\infty\}$. For example, for any stopping time τ, we denote the set of extended real partial variables whose domain includes $\{\tau < +\infty\}$ by $\overline{\mathbb{V}}_\tau$, and for any $\omega \in \{\tau < +\infty\}$, we shorten $\omega(\tau(\omega))$ to $\omega(\tau)$.

Finally, a *process* is a family of real variables $\mathcal{S}_\bullet = (\mathcal{S}_t)_{t\in\mathbb{R}_{\geq 0}}$ such that $\mathcal{S}_t$ is t-measurable for all $t \in \mathbb{R}_{\geq 0}$. Such a process $\mathcal{S}_\bullet$ is *bounded below* if

$$\inf \mathcal{S}_\bullet := \inf\{\mathcal{S}_t(\omega) \colon t \in \mathbb{R}_{\geq 0}, \omega \in \Omega\} > -\infty.$$

The canonical example of a process that is bounded below is the *coordinate process* $N_\bullet$. For any process $\mathcal{S}_\bullet$ and stopping time τ, we'll often consider the 'stopped process' $\mathcal{S}_\tau \colon \{\tau < +\infty\} \to \mathbb{R} \colon \omega \mapsto \mathcal{S}_{\tau(\omega)}(\omega(\tau))$ and the extended real variable

$$\liminf \mathcal{S}_\bullet \colon \Omega \to \overline{\mathbb{R}} \colon \omega \mapsto \liminf_{t\to+\infty} \mathcal{S}_t(\omega);$$

note that if $\mathcal{S}_\bullet$ is bounded below, then so is $\liminf \mathcal{S}_\bullet$.

3 Game-Theoretic Upper Expectations

In this contribution, we'll use Shafer & Vovk's game-theoretic approach to model the uncertain (future) evolution of the coordinate process $N_\bullet$. A lot can be said about their powerful game-theoretic framework, but we'll stick to what is necessary for the remainder of this contribution; we refer the interested reader to their monographs [11,12] and references therein for more background. In the setting of continuous time, Shafer & Vovk consider a game between two players, called *trader* and *market*: first trader announces their strategy to trade in a number of securities, then market determines the price path of the securities. As in discrete time, one can also imagine a third player, called *forecaster*: they choose the securities that are available to trader. In the context of this contribution, the securities are derived from the coordinate process $N_\bullet$ and market chooses one realisation ω from Ω.

Trader's strategy has to obey some restrictions for this game to make sense. For example, it makes sense to assume that at time $t \in \mathbb{R}_{\geq 0}$, they are uncertain about the future prices of the securities, or differently put, only have exact information about the prices of the securities in the past. We'll get back to these restrictions in Sect. 4 further on. For now, we'll assume that each allowed trading strategy gives rise to a process $\mathcal{K}_\bullet$, which we'll call trader's *capital process* under this strategy; recall from Sect. 2 that for $\mathcal{K}_\bullet$ to be a process, it must be that $\mathcal{K}_t$ is t-measurable for all $t \in \mathbb{R}_{\geq 0}$, meaning that it's completely defined by the value of the paths on $[0, t]$—or, in other words, doesn't depend on the future values of the prices of the securities.

The set $\mathfrak{K}$ collects the capital processes corresponding to all allowed trading strategies. Then the conditional upper expectation $\overline{\mathrm{E}}_{\mathfrak{K}}[\bullet|\tau] : \overline{\mathbb{V}}_\tau \times \{\tau < +\infty\} \to \overline{\mathbb{R}}$ is defined for all $f \in \overline{\mathbb{V}}_\tau$ and $\omega \in \{\tau < +\infty\}$ by

$$\overline{\mathrm{E}}_{\mathfrak{K}}[f|\tau](\omega) := \inf\{\mathcal{K}_\tau(\omega) : \mathcal{K}_\bullet \in \mathfrak{K}, \inf \mathcal{K}_\bullet > -\infty, \liminf \mathcal{K}_\bullet \geq_{\mathcal{I}_\tau(\omega)} f\},$$

where here and in the remainder, we write '$\liminf \mathcal{K}_\bullet \geq_{\mathcal{I}_\tau(\omega)} f$' as a shorthand for '$\liminf \mathcal{K}_\bullet(\varpi) \geq f(\varpi)$ for all $\varpi \in \mathcal{I}_\tau(\omega)$'. This conditional expectation $\overline{\mathrm{E}}_{\mathfrak{K}}[f|\tau](\omega)$ is the infimum capital trader needs at time $\tau(\omega)$ to ('in the long run') superhedge f in 'all possible futures' $\mathcal{I}_\tau(\omega)$ using an allowed trading strategy for which the losses are bounded below a priori. Differently put, if trader has capital $c > \overline{\mathrm{E}}_{\mathfrak{K}}[f|\tau](\omega)$ at $\tau(\omega)$ (and knowing the partial counting path $\omega|_{[0,\tau(\omega)]}$), they can trade according to an allowed trading strategy such that they'll have $f(\varpi)$ in the long run, whatever the actual realisation $\varpi \in \mathcal{I}_\tau(\omega)$ turns out to be. Consequently, we can interpret $\overline{\mathrm{E}}_{\mathfrak{K}}[f|\tau](\omega)$ as trader's infimum selling price for the uncertain pay-off f, given the information they have at time $\tau(\omega)$. Since $\omega(0) = 0$ for all $\omega \in \Omega$, $\mathcal{K}_0$ is constant on Ω, and the same is true for $\overline{\mathrm{E}}_{\mathfrak{K}}[f|0]$, which for this reason we'll shorten to $\overline{\mathrm{E}}_{\mathfrak{K}}[f]$ from now on; this can be interpreted as the infimum initial capital trader needs at time 0 to superhedge f 'in the long run', or alternatively, their infimum selling price for the uncertain pay-off f.

For every stopping time $\tau \in \mathfrak{T}$ and extended variable $f \in \overline{\mathbb{V}}_\tau$, our definition ensures that the extended real partial variable $\omega \mapsto \overline{\mathrm{E}}_{\mathfrak{K}}[f|\tau](\omega)$ is constant on $\mathcal{I}_\tau(\omega)$, and therefore τ-measurable. Furthermore, for every extended variable $f \in \overline{\mathbb{V}}$ and path $\omega \in \Omega$, the function $t \mapsto \overline{\mathrm{E}}_{\mathfrak{K}}[f|t](\omega)$ is increasing because the map $t \mapsto \mathcal{I}_t(\omega)$ is decreasing.

Our calling $\overline{\mathrm{E}}_{\mathfrak{K}}[\bullet|\bullet]$ a (conditional) upper expectation—after [17]—is justified under some mild assumptions on $\mathfrak{K}$.

Proposition 1. *Suppose $\mathfrak{K}$ contains all constant processes and is a cone—that is, closed under pointwise addition and multiplication with positive scalars. Then for all $\tau \in \mathfrak{T}$, $f, g \in \overline{\mathbb{V}}_\tau$ and $\mu \in \mathbb{R}$,*

E1. $\overline{\mathrm{E}}_{\mathfrak{K}}[f|\tau] \leq \sup f$;
E2. $\overline{\mathrm{E}}_{\mathfrak{K}}[f + g|\tau] \leq \overline{\mathrm{E}}_{\mathfrak{K}}[f|\tau] + \overline{\mathrm{E}}_{\mathfrak{K}}[g|\tau]$;
E3. $\overline{\mathrm{E}}_{\mathfrak{K}}[\mu f|\tau] = \mu \overline{\mathrm{E}}_{\mathfrak{K}}[f|\tau]$ *whenever* $\mu > 0$;
E4. $\overline{\mathrm{E}}_{\mathfrak{K}}[f|\tau] \leq \overline{\mathrm{E}}_{\mathfrak{K}}[g|\tau]$ *whenever* $f \leq g$;
E5. $\overline{\mathrm{E}}_{\mathfrak{K}}[f + \mu|\tau] = \overline{\mathrm{E}}_{\mathfrak{K}}[f|\tau] + \mu$.

Following Vovk [14, p. 196], we call the set $\mathfrak{K}$ of allowed capital processes *coherent* if

$$\inf\{\liminf \mathcal{K}_\bullet(\varpi) : \varpi \in \mathcal{I}_t(\omega)\} \leq \mathcal{K}_t(\omega) \quad \text{for all } \mathcal{K}_\bullet \in \mathfrak{K}, t \in \mathbb{R}_{\geq 0}, \omega \in \Omega; \quad (1)$$

in other words, this coherence condition ensures that no trading strategy can result in a guaranteed profit for trader. That we demand coherence should come to no surprise to the reader who is familiar with coherent (conditional) upper expectations a la de Finetti [6], Williams [17] and/or Walley [15]—see also [13].

As is customary in that setting, we define the conditional lower expectation through conjugacy:

$$\underline{\mathrm{E}}_{\mathfrak{K}}[f|\tau](\omega) := -\overline{\mathrm{E}}_{\mathfrak{K}}[-f|\tau](\omega) \quad \text{for all } \tau \in \mathfrak{T}, f \in \overline{\mathbb{V}}_{\tau}, \omega \in \{\tau < +\infty\};$$

the value $\underline{\mathrm{E}}_{\mathfrak{K}}[f|\tau](\omega)$ can be thought of as trader's supremum buying price for f given the information they have at $\tau(\omega)$. If $\mathfrak{K}$ is coherent, trader's buying price is never higher than their selling price.

Proposition 2. *If $\mathfrak{K}$ satisfies the conditions in Proposition 1 and is coherent, then for all $\tau \in \mathfrak{T}$, $f \in \overline{\mathbb{V}}_{\tau}$ and $\omega \in \{\tau < +\infty\}$,*

E6. $\inf f|_{\mathcal{I}_{\tau}(\omega)} \leq \overline{\mathrm{E}}_{\mathfrak{K}}[f|\tau](\omega) \leq \sup f|_{\mathcal{I}_{\tau}(\omega)}$;
E7. $\underline{\mathrm{E}}_{\mathfrak{K}}[f|\tau](\omega) \leq \overline{\mathrm{E}}_{\mathfrak{K}}[f|\tau](\omega)$.

4 Betting Strategies and Capital Processes for the Poisson Process

As announced in the Introduction, this contribution aims to extend Vovk's [14] game-theoretic description of the Poisson process to allow for imprecision. Their game-theoretic characterisation draws inspiration from Watanabe's martingale characterisation of the Poisson process [16, Theorem 2.3 and following Remark]: the coordinate process $N_{\bullet}$ is a Poisson process with rate $\lambda \in \mathbb{R}_{\geq 0}$ if and only if the compensated process $(N_t - \lambda t)_{t \in \mathbb{R}_{\geq 0}}$ is a martingale—that is, if conditional on the information up to the current time point $s \in \mathbb{R}_{\geq 0}$, for every future time point $t \in]s, +\infty[$ the expectation of $N_t - \lambda t$ is $N_s - \lambda s$, or differently put, the expectation of the increment $N_t - N_s$ is $\lambda(t-s)$. Vovk's allowed trading strategies are exactly those that involve this compensated increment.

If forecaster puts forth some *rate* $\lambda \in \mathbb{R}_{\geq 0}$, trader is allowed to bet on a series of compensated increments of the form $N_{\tau_{k+1}} - N_{\tau_k} - \lambda(\tau_{k+1} - \tau_k)$, for stopping times $\tau_k \leq \tau_{k+1}$. More formally, a *two-sided elementary trading strategy* G is an increasing sequence of stopping times $\tau_1 \leq \tau_2 \leq \cdots \leq \tau_n \leq \tau_{n+1}$ and a sequence $h_1, \dots, h_n$ of variables such that for all $k \in \{1, \dots, n\}$, the *stake* h_k is a (possibly partial) bounded real variable with $\operatorname{dom} h_k \supseteq \{\tau_k < +\infty\}$ that is τ_k-measurable. We interpret such an elementary trading strategy G as follows: at time τ_k, trader puts stake h_k on the increment $N_{\tau_{k+1}} - N_{\tau_k} - \lambda(\tau_{k+1} - \tau_k)$—or more accurately, they 'pay' $h_k(\omega)(\omega(\tau_k) - \lambda\tau_k(\omega))$ to receive $h_k(\omega)(\omega(\tau_{k+1}) - \lambda\tau_{k+1}(\omega))$ at time τ_{k+1} of their choice. Consequently, if trader starts with initial capital $c \in \mathbb{R}$ and follows the two-sided elementary trading strategy G, their capital at time $t \in \mathbb{R}_{\geq 0}$ is the real variable

$$\mathcal{K}_t^{G,c} := c + \sum_{k=1}^{n} h_k \cdot \big(N_{\tau_{k+1} \wedge t} - N_{\tau_k \wedge t} - \lambda(\tau_{k+1} \wedge t - \tau_k \wedge t)\big), \tag{2}$$

where $\cdot$ indicates pointwise multiplication of two real variables and where we ignore the zero terms in the sum that arise when $\tau_k(\omega) \wedge t = \tau_{k+1}(\omega) \wedge t$. Our assumptions on the stopping times τ_k and stakes h_k ensure that $(\mathcal{K}_t^{G,c})_{t\in\mathbb{R}_{\geq 0}}$ is a real process, which we call a *two-sided elementary capital process*. We collect these capital processes in the set $\mathfrak{K}_\lambda$, and denote the corresponding conditional upper and lower expectation by $\overline{\mathrm{E}}_\lambda[\bullet|\bullet]$ and $\underline{\mathrm{E}}_{[\lambda}[\bullet|\bullet]$, respectively. It's easy to see that $\mathfrak{K}_\lambda$ includes the constant processes and is closed under scalar multiplication, but it takes a bit more work to verify that $\mathfrak{K}_\lambda$ is coherent and closed under pointwise addition; we don't prove this here separately, since it's a special case of Proposition 3 further on.

In the two-sided betting strategies, trader bets on the increment $N_{\tau_{k+1}} - N_{\tau_k}$ being 'large'—greater than $\lambda(\tau_{k+1} - \tau_k)$—when $h_k \geq 0$, and on $N_{\tau_{k+1}} - N_{\tau_k}$ being 'small'—smaller than $\lambda(\tau_{k+1} - \tau_k)$—when $h_k \leq 0$. In the one-sided betting strategies that we're going introduce next, there's a spread between the prices for these two bets. This time around, forecaster puts forth *rate bounds* $\underline{\lambda}, \overline{\lambda} \in \mathbb{R}_{\geq 0}$ such that $\underline{\lambda} \leq \overline{\lambda}$, and trader can take a *positive* stake on a series of bets $N_{\tau_{k+1}} - N_{\tau_k} - \overline{\lambda}(\tau_{k+1} - \tau_k)$ and $\underline{\lambda}(\tau_{k+1} - \tau_k) - (N_{\tau_{k+1}} - N_{\tau_k})$. More formally, a *one-sided elementary trading strategy* G is an increasing sequence of stopping times $\tau_1 \leq \tau_2 \leq \cdots \leq \tau_n \leq \tau_{n+1}$ and a sequence $\overline{h}_1, \underline{h}_1, \dots, \overline{h}_n, \underline{h}_n$ of variables such that for all $k \in \{1, \dots, n\}$, the *stakes* $\overline{h}_k$ and $\underline{h}_k$ are τ_k-measurable (possibly partial) bounded *positive* real variables whose domain includes $\{\tau_k < +\infty\}$. If trader starts with initial capital $c \in \mathbb{R}$ and follows the one-sided elementary trading strategy G, their corresponding capital at time $t \in \mathbb{R}_{\geq 0}$ is the real variable

$$\mathcal{K}_t^{G,c} := c + \sum_{k=1}^{n} \overline{h}_k \cdot \big(N_{\tau_{k+1}\wedge t} - N_{\tau_k \wedge t} - \overline{\lambda}(\tau_{k+1} \wedge t - \tau_k \wedge t)\big) \\ + \underline{h}_k \cdot \big(\underline{\lambda}(\tau_{k+1} \wedge t - \tau_k \wedge t) - N_{\tau_{k+1}\wedge t} + N_{\tau_k \wedge t}\big). \quad (3)$$

Our assumptions on the stopping times τ_k and stakes $\overline{h}_k$ and $\underline{h}_k$ ensure that $(\mathcal{K}_t^{G,c})_{t\in\mathbb{R}_{\geq 0}}$ is a real process, which we call a *one-sided elementary capital process*. We collect these capital processes in the set $\mathfrak{K}_{[\underline{\lambda},\overline{\lambda}]}$, and denote the corresponding conditional upper and lower expectations by $\overline{\mathrm{E}}_{[\underline{\lambda},\overline{\lambda}]}[\bullet|\bullet]$ and $\underline{\mathrm{E}}_{[\underline{\lambda},\overline{\lambda}]}[\bullet|\bullet]$, respectively.

For every capital process $\mathcal{K}_\bullet^{G,c} \in \mathfrak{K}_{[\underline{\lambda},\overline{\lambda}]}$, index $k \in \{1, \dots, n\}$, counting path $\omega \in \Omega$ and time points $t, r \in [\tau_k(\omega), \tau_{k+1}(\omega)] \cap \mathbb{R}_{\geq 0}$ such that $t \leq r$, it follows from Eq. (3) that, with $\underline{\overline{h}}_k := \overline{h}_k - \underline{h}_k$,

$$\mathcal{K}_r^{G,c}(\omega) - \mathcal{K}_t^{G,c}(\omega) = \underline{\overline{h}}_k(\omega)\big(\omega(r) - \omega(t) - \underline{\lambda}(r - t)\big) - \overline{h}_k(\omega)(\overline{\lambda} - \underline{\lambda})(r - t). \quad (4)$$

This equality makes it obvious that for all $\lambda \in \mathbb{R}_{\geq 0}$, the set $\mathfrak{K}_{\{\lambda\}}$ of one-sided elementary capital processes for $[\lambda, \lambda] = \{\lambda\}$ is equal to the set $\mathfrak{K}_\lambda$ of two-sided elementary capital processes for λ.

Recall from Sect. 3 that it's crucial that the set of capital processes $\mathfrak{K}_{[\underline{\lambda},\overline{\lambda}]}$ satisfies the conditions in Proposition 2.

Proposition 3. *For all $\underline{\lambda}, \overline{\lambda} \in \mathbb{R}_{\geq 0}$ with $\underline{\lambda} \leq \overline{\lambda}$, the set $\mathfrak{K}_{[\underline{\lambda},\overline{\lambda}]}$ of one-sided elementary capital processes includes the constants, is a cone and is coherent.*

5 Properties of the Conditional Upper Expectation for the Poisson Process

In the remainder of this contribution, I list some properties of the conditional upper expectation operator $\overline{\mathrm{E}}_{[\underline{\lambda},\overline{\lambda}]}[\bullet|\bullet]$ which I hope should convince the reader of the sensibility of the game-theoretic characterisation of the imprecise Poisson process.

5.1 Properties Related to the Rate Bounds

The first property looks at nested rate bounds: the conditional upper expectation for $[\underline{\lambda}_{\mathrm{i}},\overline{\lambda}_{\mathrm{i}}]$ is dominated by the one for $[\underline{\lambda}_{\mathrm{o}},\overline{\lambda}_{\mathrm{o}}]$ whenever $[\underline{\lambda}_{\mathrm{i}},\overline{\lambda}_{\mathrm{i}}] \subseteq [\underline{\lambda}_{\mathrm{o}},\overline{\lambda}_{\mathrm{o}}]$.

Proposition 4. *For all* $\underline{\lambda}_{\mathrm{o}},\underline{\lambda}_{\mathrm{i}},\overline{\lambda}_{\mathrm{i}},\overline{\lambda}_{\mathrm{o}} \in \mathbb{R}_{\geq 0}$ *with* $\underline{\lambda}_{\mathrm{o}} \leq \underline{\lambda}_{\mathrm{i}} \leq \overline{\lambda}_{\mathrm{i}} \leq \overline{\lambda}_{\mathrm{o}}$,

$$\overline{\mathrm{E}}_{[\underline{\lambda}_{\mathrm{i}},\overline{\lambda}_{\mathrm{i}}]}[f|\tau] \leq \overline{\mathrm{E}}_{[\underline{\lambda}_{\mathrm{o}},\overline{\lambda}_{\mathrm{o}}]}[f|\tau] \quad \textit{for all } \tau \in \mathfrak{T}, f \in \overline{\mathbb{V}}_{\tau}.$$

The second property involves the interpretation of the rate bounds $\overline{\lambda}$ and $\underline{\lambda}$ as proportionality constants for forecaster's selling and buying prices. Since, as explained in Sect. 3, $\overline{\mathrm{E}}_{[\underline{\lambda},\overline{\lambda}]}[N_\tau - N_\sigma|\sigma](\omega)$ can be interpreted as trader's infimum selling price for the uncertain increment $N_\tau - N_\sigma$ given the information they have at time $\sigma(\omega)$, one would expect that like forecaster's price, this is proportional to $\overline{\lambda}$; the next result confirms that this is indeed the case, at least when these stopping times are *constant.*

Proposition 5. *For any two time points* $s,t \in \mathbb{R}_{\geq 0}$ *such that* $s \leq t$,

$$\overline{\mathrm{E}}_{[\underline{\lambda},\overline{\lambda}]}[N_t - N_s|s] = \overline{\lambda}(t-s) \quad \textit{and} \quad \underline{\mathrm{E}}_{[\underline{\lambda},\overline{\lambda}]}[N_t - N_s|s] = \underline{\lambda}(t-s).$$

Proof. We prove first that

$$\overline{\mathrm{E}}_{[\underline{\lambda},\overline{\lambda}]}[N_t - N_s|s] \leq \overline{\lambda}(t-s) \quad \text{and} \quad \overline{\mathrm{E}}_{[\underline{\lambda},\overline{\lambda}]}[-(N_t - N_s)|s] \leq -\underline{\lambda}(t-s). \tag{5}$$

Fix any $m \in \mathbb{N}$, let $c_m := \overline{\lambda}(t-s)/m$ and observe that for the trading strategy G_m with stopping times $\tau_1 := s$ and $\tau_2 := t$ and stakes $\overline{h}_1 := 1/m$ and $\underline{h}_1 := 0$,

$$\mathcal{K}_r^{G_m,c_m} = \begin{cases} \frac{1}{m}\overline{\lambda}(t-s) & \text{if } r \leq s \\ \frac{1}{m}\left(\overline{\lambda}(t-r) + N_r - N_s\right) & \text{if } s < r < t \\ \frac{1}{m}(N_t - N_s) & \text{if } r \geq t \end{cases} \quad \text{for all } r \in \mathbb{R}_{\geq 0}.$$

Since $\mathcal{K}_\bullet^{G_m,c_m}$ is non-negative and superhedges $(N_t - N_s)/m$, we've shown that

$$\overline{\mathrm{E}}_{[\underline{\lambda},\overline{\lambda}]}[(N_t - N_s)/m|s] \leq \frac{1}{m}\overline{\lambda}(t-s).$$

Setting $m = 1$ gives the first inequality in (5).

Proving the second inequality is a bit more involved. Let $c := -\underline{\lambda}(t-s)$. For all $m \in \mathbb{N}$, consider the trading strategy G'_m with $\tau_1^m = s$, $\overline{h}_1^m := 0$, $\underline{h}_1^m := 1$ and

$$\tau_2^m : \Omega \to \overline{\mathbb{R}}_{\geq 0} : \omega \mapsto \inf\{r \in [s, +\infty[: \omega(r) \geq \omega(s) + m\} \cup \{t\}.$$

Then for all $\omega \in \Omega$ and $r \in \mathbb{R}_{\geq 0}$,

$$\mathcal{K}_r^{G'_m, c}(\omega) = \begin{cases} -\underline{\lambda}(t-s) & \text{if } r \leq s \\ -\underline{\lambda}(t-r) - \big(\omega(r) - \omega(s)\big) & \text{if } s < r < \tau_2^m(\omega) \\ -\big(\omega(t) - \omega(s)\big) & \text{if } r \geq \tau_2^m(\omega) = t \\ -\underline{\lambda}(t - \tau_2^m(\omega)) - m & \text{if } r \geq \tau_2^m(\omega) < t. \end{cases}$$

This equality tells us that $\mathcal{K}_\bullet^{G'_m, c}$ is bounded below and superhedges $-(N_t - N_s)$ on $\{\omega \in \Omega : \omega(t) < \omega(s) + m\}$. Since $\mathcal{K}_\bullet^{G_m, c_m}$ is bounded below and superhedges $(N_t - N_s)/m$, it follows that $\mathcal{K}_\bullet^{G'_m, c} + \underline{\lambda}(t-s)\mathcal{K}_\bullet^{G_m, c_m}$ is bounded below and superhedges $-(N_t - N_s)$. Consequently,

$$\overline{\mathrm{E}}_{[\underline{\lambda}, \overline{\lambda}]}[-(N_t - N_s)|s] \leq \mathcal{K}_s^{G'_m, c} + \underline{\lambda}(t-s)\mathcal{K}_s^{G_m, c_m} = -\underline{\lambda}(t-s) + \frac{1}{m}\underline{\lambda}\overline{\lambda}(t-s)^2.$$

Since this inequality holds for arbitrary $m \in \mathbb{N}$, it implies the second inequality in (5).

If $\underline{\lambda} = \lambda = \overline{\lambda}$, we infer from the two inequalities in (5) that

$$\lambda(t-s) \leq \underline{\mathrm{E}}_\lambda[N_t - N_s|s] \leq \overline{\mathrm{E}}_\lambda[N_t - N_s|s] \leq \lambda(t-s).$$

If $\underline{\lambda} < \overline{\lambda}$, the equality follows from (5) and the equality above for $\lambda = \overline{\lambda}$ and $\lambda = \underline{\lambda}$ due to Proposition 4 [with $\underline{\lambda}_{\mathrm{i}} = \lambda = \overline{\lambda}_{\mathrm{i}}$, $\underline{\lambda}_{\mathrm{o}} = \underline{\lambda}$ and $\overline{\lambda}_{\mathrm{o}} = \overline{\lambda}$]. □

The next property we turn to is the alternative characterisation of the rate parameter λ of the 'classical' Poisson process as the inverse of the expected time until the next increment. The time until the next increment after the stopping time $\tau \in \mathfrak{T}$ is the partial variable

$$\rho_\tau : \{\tau < +\infty\} \to \overline{\mathbb{R}}_{\geq 0} : \omega \mapsto \inf\{r \in]\tau(\omega), +\infty[: \omega(r) > \omega(\tau)\};$$

note that we can extend the domain of ρ_τ to Ω by setting it equal to $+\infty$ on $\{\tau < +\infty\}^c$, which makes this variable a stopping time. It's fairly easy to verify that the upper and lower expectation of $\rho_\tau - \tau$ conditional on τ are the inverse of the forecaster's rate bounds.

Proposition 6. *For every stopping time $\tau \in \mathfrak{T}$,*

$$\overline{\mathrm{E}}_{[\underline{\lambda}, \overline{\lambda}]}[\rho_\tau - \tau|\tau] = \frac{1}{\underline{\lambda}} \quad \text{and} \quad \underline{\mathrm{E}}_{[\underline{\lambda}, \overline{\lambda}]}[\rho_\tau - \tau|\tau] = \frac{1}{\overline{\lambda}},$$

where here we follow the convention $1/0 = +\infty$.

The proof is similar to but a bit more involved as the one for Proposition 5, and therefore omitted.

5.2 The Strong Markov Property

The next property of the 'classical' Poisson process on the list is that it satisfies the (strong) Markov property. We'll actually show a stronger 'memorylessness'-like result first: that the conditional upper expectation $\overline{\mathrm{E}}_{[\underline{\lambda},\overline{\lambda}]}[\bullet|\tau]$ can be 'shifted' from the stopping time τ to 0—intuitively, this is a straightforward consequence of the fact that trading strategies can be 'shifted'. In the formal statement of this result, we need to stitch together two counting paths; following [10], we stitch together paths $\omega, \varpi \in \Omega$ at the stopping time $\tau \in \mathfrak{T}$ as follows:

$$\omega \oplus_\tau \varpi : \mathbb{R}_{\geq 0} \to \mathbb{Z}_{\geq 0} : t \mapsto \begin{cases} \omega(t) & \text{if } t < \tau(\omega), \\ \omega(\tau(\omega)) + \varpi(t - \tau(\omega)) & \text{if } t \geq \tau(\omega); \end{cases}$$

the reader will have no trouble verifying that $\omega \oplus_\tau \varpi$ is indeed a counting path. Similarly, for any time point $s \in \mathbb{R}_{\geq 0}$ and counting path $\omega \in \Omega$, we'll need to look at the derived counting path

$$\omega_{[s,+\infty[} : \mathbb{R}_{\geq 0} \to \mathbb{Z}_{\geq 0} : t \mapsto \omega(t+s) - \omega(s)$$

which looks only at the increments of ω starting from s.

Proposition 7. *For all $\tau \in \mathfrak{T}$, $f \in \overline{\mathbb{V}}_\tau$ and $\omega \in \{\tau < +\infty\}$,*

$$\overline{\mathrm{E}}_{[\underline{\lambda},\overline{\lambda}]}[f|\tau](\omega) = \overline{\mathrm{E}}_{[\underline{\lambda},\overline{\lambda}]}[f(\omega \oplus_\tau \bullet)] \quad \textit{where } f(\omega \oplus_\tau \bullet) : \Omega \to \overline{\mathbb{R}} : \varpi \mapsto f(\omega \oplus_\tau \varpi).$$

Proof. We'll verify the equality in the statement by proving that the left-hand side of the equality is lower than or equal to the right-hand side and vice versa.

First, we show that the left-hand side of the equality is lower than or equal to the right-hand side. Consider any bounded below capital process $\mathcal{K}_\bullet^{G,c} \in \mathfrak{K}_{[\underline{\lambda},\overline{\lambda}]}$ that superhedges $f(\omega \oplus \bullet)$. Let us enumerate the stopping times and stakes of G as $\tau_1, \ldots, \tau_{n+1}$ and $\overline{h}_1, \ldots, \underline{h}_{n+1}$, respectively. Consider the trading strategy G' with stopping times $\tau'_1, \ldots, \tau'_{n+1}$ defined for all $k \in \{1, \ldots, n+1\}$ as

$$\tau'_k : \Omega \to \overline{\mathbb{R}}_{\geq 0} : \varpi \mapsto \begin{cases} \tau(\omega) + \tau_k(\varpi_{[\tau(\omega),+\infty[}) & \text{if } \varpi \in \mathcal{I}_\tau(\omega) \\ +\infty & \text{if } \varpi \notin \mathcal{I}_\tau(\omega) \end{cases}$$

and, for all $k \in \{1, \ldots, n\}$, stakes defined on $\mathcal{I}_\tau(\omega)$ by

$$\overline{h}'_k(\varpi) := \overline{h}_k(\varpi_{[\tau(\omega),+\infty[}) \quad \text{and} \quad \underline{h}'_k(\varpi) := \underline{h}_k(\varpi_{[\tau(\omega),+\infty[}) \quad \text{for all } \varpi \in \mathcal{I}_\tau(\omega).$$

Our construction ensures that $\mathcal{K}_\bullet^{G',c} \in \mathfrak{K}_{[\underline{\lambda},\overline{\lambda}]}$ is bounded below with $\mathcal{K}_\tau^{G',c}(\omega) = c$ and

$$\mathcal{K}_r^{G',c}(\varpi) = \mathcal{K}_{r-\tau(\omega)}^{G,c}(\varpi_{[\tau(\omega),+\infty[}) \quad \text{for all } \varpi \in \mathcal{I}_\tau(\omega), r \in [\tau(\omega), +\infty[.$$

For all $\varpi \in \mathcal{I}_\tau(\omega)$, we infer from all this that

$$\liminf \mathcal{K}_\bullet^{G',c}(\varpi) = \liminf \mathcal{K}_\bullet^{G,c}(\varpi_{[\tau(\omega),+\infty[}) \geq f(\omega \oplus_\tau \varpi_{[\tau(\omega),+\infty[}) = f(\varpi),$$

where for the last equality we used that $\varpi = \omega \oplus_\tau \varpi_{[\tau(\omega),+\infty[}$. So for any bounded below capital process $\mathcal{K}_\bullet^{G,c} \in \mathfrak{K}_{[\underline{\lambda},\overline{\lambda}]}$ that superhedges $f(\omega \oplus_\tau \bullet)$, there is some bounded below capital process $\mathcal{K}_\bullet^{G',c} \in \mathfrak{K}_{[\underline{\lambda},\overline{\lambda}]}$ with $\mathcal{K}_\tau^{G'c}(\omega) = c$ that superhedges f on $\mathcal{I}_\tau(\omega)$. From this, we infer that indeed

$$\overline{\mathrm{E}}_{[\underline{\lambda},\overline{\lambda}]}[f|\tau](\omega) \leq \overline{\mathrm{E}}_{[\underline{\lambda},\overline{\lambda}]}[f(\omega \oplus_\tau \bullet)].$$

The proof of the reverse inequality is similar and therefore omitted. □

The Markov property—see, for example, [5, Ch. 4, Eq. (1.2)]—follows almost immediately from this memoryless character of the conditional upper expectation: for all time points $t \in \mathbb{R}_{\geq 0}$ and time periods $\Delta \in \mathbb{R}_{\geq 0}$,

$$\overline{\mathrm{E}}_{[\underline{\lambda},\overline{\lambda}]}[g(N_{t+\Delta})|t](\omega) = \overline{\mathrm{E}}_{[\underline{\lambda},\overline{\lambda}]}[g(\omega(t) + N_\Delta)] \quad \text{for all } g \in \overline{\mathbb{R}}^{\mathbb{Z}_{\geq 0}}, \omega \in \Omega;$$

so does the strong Markov property [5, Ch. 4, Eq. (1.17)]: for all stopping times $\tau \in \mathfrak{T}$ and time periods $\Delta \in \mathbb{R}_{\geq 0}$,

$$\overline{\mathrm{E}}_{[\underline{\lambda},\overline{\lambda}]}[g(N_{t+\Delta})|\tau](\omega) == \overline{\mathrm{E}}_{[\underline{\lambda},\overline{\lambda}]}[g(\omega(\tau) + N_\Delta)] \quad \text{for all } g \in \overline{\mathbb{R}}^{\mathbb{Z}_{\geq 0}}, \omega \in \{\tau < +\infty\}.$$

5.3 The Law of Iterated Upper Expectations

Next up is the crucial *law of iterated (upper) expectations*, also known as the tower property. For the sake of simplicity, we'll only establish a version of this law for constant stopping times and bounded and so-called finitary variables: those that depend only on the value of the counting path at finitely many time points. Obviously, a variable $f \in \overline{\mathbb{V}}$ is bounded and finitary if and only if $f = g(N_{t_1}, \ldots, N_{t_k})$ for some $k \in \mathbb{N}$, $t_1 \leq \cdots \leq t_k \in \mathbb{R}_{\geq 0}$ and some $g \in \mathbb{G}_k$, where here and in the remainder we let $\mathbb{G}_k$ be the set of bounded real functions on $(\mathbb{Z}_{\geq 0})^k$—for $k = 1$, we'll simply write $\mathbb{G}$.

Theorem 1. *For all natural numbers $k \in \mathbb{N}$, time points $t_1, \ldots, t_{k+1} \in \mathbb{R}_{\geq 0}$ such that $t_1 < t_2 < \cdots < t_{k+1}$ and gambles $g \in \mathbb{G}_{k+1}$,*

$$\overline{\mathrm{E}}_{[\underline{\lambda},\overline{\lambda}]}[g(N_{t_1}, \ldots, N_{t_{k+1}})|t_1] = \overline{\mathrm{E}}_{[\underline{\lambda},\overline{\lambda}]}\left[\overline{\mathrm{E}}_{[\underline{\lambda},\overline{\lambda}]}[g(N_{t_1}, \ldots, N_{t_{k+1}})|t_k]\Big| t_1\right].$$

My proof is inspired by Shafer & Vovk's [11, Proposition 8.7] proof for a similar result in discrete time, but adds a move to ensure the 'cut' is finite. In order to abide the page limit, I've had to make the tough decision of omitting this proof.

One can turn the law of iterated upper expectations in Theorem 1 into a (theoretical) recursive computational scheme to compute $\overline{\mathrm{E}}_{[\underline{\lambda},\overline{\lambda}]}[g(N_{t_1}, \ldots, N_{t_k})|t_1]$, at least once one realises that due to Proposition 7, the variable

$$\varpi \mapsto \overline{\mathrm{E}}_{[\underline{\lambda},\overline{\lambda}]}[g(N_{t_1}, \ldots, N_{t_{k+1}}|t_k](\varpi)$$

in the conditional upper expectation on the right-hand side of the equality in Theorem 1 is only functionally dependent on the values ϖ takes in $t_1, \ldots, t_k$ rather than on the values it takes on the entire interval $[0, t_k]$—so only on a countable set rather than an uncountable one.

Corollary 1. *For all natural numbers $k \in \mathbb{N}$, time points $t_1, \dots, t_{k+1} \in \mathbb{R}_{\geq 0}$ such that $t_1 < \cdots < t_{k+1}$, bounded functions $g \in \mathbb{G}_{k+1}$ and paths $\omega \in \Omega$, and with $\Delta := t_{k+1} - t_k$,*

$$\overline{\mathrm{E}}_{[\underline{\lambda},\overline{\lambda}]}[g(N_{t_1}, \dots, N_{t_{k+1}})|t_k](\omega) = \overline{\mathrm{E}}_{[\underline{\lambda},\overline{\lambda}]}[g(\omega(t_1), \dots, \omega(t_k), \omega(t_k) + N_\Delta)].$$

5.4 Connection to the Sublinear Poisson Semigroup

Corollary 1 tells us that it's important to be able to compute conditional upper expectations of the form $\overline{\mathrm{E}}_{[\underline{\lambda},\overline{\lambda}]}[g(N_t)|s]$ for bounded functions $g \in \mathbb{G}$ and time points $s, t \in \mathbb{R}_{\geq 0}$ such that $s < t$. For the classical Poisson process with rate λ, and for Vovk's measure-theoretic Poisson process [14, Theorem 5], these conditional expectations are related to the Poisson distribution $\psi_{\lambda(t-s)}$ with parameter $\lambda(t-s)$:

$$\overline{\mathrm{E}}_\lambda[g(N_t)|s](\omega) = \underline{\mathrm{E}}_\lambda[g(N_t)|s](\omega) = \sum_{z \in \mathbb{Z}_{\geq 0}} g(\omega(s) + z)\psi_{\lambda(t-s)}(z).$$

To generalise this property to our imprecise setting, it will be elucidative to express the right-hand side of this equality using the so-called *Poisson semigroup* $(\mathrm{S}_\Delta)_{\Delta \in \mathbb{R}_{\geq 0}}$ for $\Delta = t - s$:

$$\overline{\mathrm{E}}_\lambda[g(N_t)|s](\omega) = \underline{\mathrm{E}}_\lambda[g(N_t)|s](\omega) = [\mathrm{S}_{(t-s)}g](\omega(s)).$$

This family $\mathrm{S}_\bullet$ of linear operators—linear maps from $\mathbb{G}$ to $\mathbb{G}$—is generated by the Poisson generator $\mathrm{G}\colon \mathbb{G} \to \mathbb{G}$, which maps any $g \in \mathbb{G}$ to

$$\mathrm{G}g\colon \mathbb{Z}_{\geq 0} \to \mathbb{R}\colon n \mapsto \lambda(g(n+1) - g(n)),$$

as follows:

$$\mathrm{S}_\Delta = e^{\Delta \mathrm{G}} = \lim_{k \to +\infty} \left(\mathrm{I} + \frac{\Delta}{k}\mathrm{G}\right)^k \quad \text{for all } \Delta \in \mathbb{R}_{\geq 0}. \tag{6}$$

Crucially, a similar result holds for the imprecise game-theoretic Poisson process, at least if we replace the Poisson semigroup $\mathrm{S}_\bullet$ by the sublinear Poisson semigroup $\overline{\mathrm{S}}_\bullet$. As explained in [3], this family of sublinear operators is generated by the sublinear Poisson generator $\overline{\mathrm{G}}\colon \mathbb{G} \to \mathbb{G}$, which maps any $g \in \mathbb{G}$ to

$$\overline{\mathrm{G}}g\colon \mathbb{Z}_{\geq 0} \to \mathbb{R}\colon n \mapsto \max\{\lambda\big(g(n+1) - g(n)\big)\colon \lambda \in \{\underline{\lambda}, \overline{\lambda}\}\},$$

through the operator exponential:

$$\overline{\mathrm{S}}_\Delta := e^{\Delta \overline{\mathrm{G}}} = \lim_{k \to +\infty} \left(\mathrm{I} + \frac{\Delta}{k}\overline{\mathrm{G}}\right)^k \quad \text{for all } \Delta \in \mathbb{R}_{\geq 0}. \tag{7}$$

Theorem 2. *For all time points $s, t \in \mathbb{R}_{\geq 0}$ such that $s \leq t$ and $g \in \mathbb{G}$,*

$$\overline{\mathrm{E}}_{[\underline{\lambda},\overline{\lambda}]}[g(N_t)|s] = [\overline{\mathrm{S}}_{t-s}g](N_s).$$

As an intermediary step towards proving this result, we establish the following 'generalisation'[3] of Vovk's [14] Theorem 5; the proof is a rather straightforward modification of the original one, essentially replacing the 'Bernouilli approximation' of Eq. (6) with that of Eq. (7) and replacing the derived two-sided trading strategy with the natural one-sided counterpart.

Proposition 8. *For all $s, t \in \mathbb{R}_{\geq 0}$ such that $s \leq t$ and $g \in \mathbb{G}$,*

$$\overline{\mathrm{E}}_{[\underline{\lambda},\overline{\lambda}]}[g(N_t)|s] \leq (\overline{\mathrm{S}}_{t-s}g)(N_s).$$

Proving Theorem 2 is now a matter of combining Proposition 8 with a couple of other previously obtained results.

Proof of Theorem 2. Recall from Proposition 7 that

$$\overline{\mathrm{E}}_{[\underline{\lambda},\overline{\lambda}]}[g(N_t)|s](\omega) = \overline{\mathrm{E}}_{[\underline{\lambda},\overline{\lambda}]}[g(\omega(s) + N_{t-s})] \quad \text{for all } \omega \in \Omega.$$

Consequently, it suffices to show that

$$\overline{\mathrm{E}}[g(z + N_\Delta)] = [\overline{\mathrm{S}}_\Delta g](z) \quad \text{for all } g \in \mathbb{G}, z \in \mathbb{Z}_{\geq 0}, \Delta \in \mathbb{R}_{\geq 0}.$$

So for all $\Delta \in \mathbb{R}_{\geq 0}$, let $\overline{\mathrm{T}}_\Delta \colon \mathbb{G} \to \mathbb{G}$ map $g \in \mathbb{G}$ to

$$\overline{\mathrm{T}}_\Delta g \colon \mathbb{Z}_{\geq 0} \to \mathbb{R} \colon z \mapsto \overline{\mathrm{E}}[g(z + N_\Delta)].$$

It follows immediately from the properties of the upper expectation that $\overline{\mathrm{T}}_\Delta$ is a sublinear transition operator, from Proposition 8 and [4, Lemma 53] that $\overline{\mathrm{T}}_\Delta$ is dominated by $\overline{\mathrm{S}}_\Delta$, and from 2 that $\overline{\mathrm{T}}_0 = \mathrm{I}$.

Furthermore, we can use the law of iterated upper expectations [Theorem 1] to show that $\overline{\mathrm{T}}_\bullet$ is a semigroup. To this end, fix some $\Delta_1, \Delta_2 \in \mathbb{R}_{>0}$, $g \in \mathbb{G}$ and $z \in \mathbb{Z}_{\geq 0}$, and observe that

$$[\overline{\mathrm{T}}_{\Delta_1+\Delta_2}g](z) = \overline{\mathrm{E}}_{[\underline{\lambda},\overline{\lambda}]}[g(z + N_{\Delta_1+\Delta_2})] = \overline{\mathrm{E}}_{[\underline{\lambda},\overline{\lambda}]}[\overline{\mathrm{E}}_{[\underline{\lambda},\overline{\lambda}]}[g(z + N_{\Delta_1+\Delta_2})|\Delta_1]].$$

Now for all $\omega \in \Omega$, it follows from Proposition 7 that

$$\overline{\mathrm{E}}_{[\underline{\lambda},\overline{\lambda}]}[g(z + N_{\Delta_1+\Delta_2})|\Delta_1](\omega) = \overline{\mathrm{E}}_{[\underline{\lambda},\overline{\lambda}]}[g(z + \omega(\Delta_1) + N_{\Delta_2})] = [\overline{\mathrm{T}}_{\Delta_2}g](z+\omega(\Delta_1)).$$

Substituting into the preceding equality, we find that

$$[\overline{\mathrm{T}}_{\Delta_1+\Delta_2}g](z) = \overline{\mathrm{E}}\big[[\overline{\mathrm{T}}_{\Delta_2}g](z + N_{\Delta_1})\big] = [\overline{\mathrm{T}}_{\Delta_1}\overline{\mathrm{T}}_{\Delta_2}g](z),$$

as required.

[3] We only generalise their result in the particular case $A_t = \lambda t$.

For any $\lambda \in [\underline{\lambda}, \overline{\lambda}]$ and $\Delta \in \mathbb{R}_{\geq 0}$, let $\mathrm{T}^{\lambda}_{\Delta}$ map $g \in \mathbb{G}$ to

$$\mathrm{T}^{\lambda}_{\Delta} g \colon \mathbb{Z}_{\geq 0} \to \mathbb{R} \colon z \mapsto \overline{\mathrm{E}}_{\lambda}[g(z + N_{\Delta})].$$

Now from Proposition 8, it follows that for all $\Delta \in \mathbb{R}_{\geq 0}$ and $g \in \mathbb{G}$,

$$\mathrm{T}^{\lambda}_{\Delta} g \leq \mathrm{S}^{\lambda}_{\Delta} g \quad \text{and} \quad -\mathrm{T}^{\lambda}_{\Delta}(-g) \geq -\mathrm{S}^{\lambda}_{\Delta}(-g) = \mathrm{S}^{\lambda}_{\Delta} g,$$

where $\mathrm{S}^{\lambda}_{\bullet}$ is the Poisson semigroup with rate λ. Consequently, $\mathrm{T}^{\lambda}_{\Delta} = \mathrm{S}^{\lambda}_{\Delta}$ for all $\Delta \in \mathbb{R}_{\geq 0}$ and $\lambda \in [\underline{\lambda}, \overline{\lambda}]$. From this, Propositions 4 and 8, it follows that

$$\mathrm{S}^{\lambda}_{\Delta} g = \mathrm{T}^{\lambda}_{\Delta} g \leq \overline{\mathrm{T}}_{\Delta} g \leq \overline{\mathrm{S}}_{\Delta} g \quad \text{for all } \lambda \in [\underline{\lambda}, \overline{\lambda}], \Delta \in \mathbb{R}_{\geq 0}, g \in \mathbb{G}.$$

Since $\overline{\mathrm{S}}_{\bullet}$ is equal to Nendel's [9] so called *Nisio semigroup* induced by the family $\{\mathrm{S}^{\lambda}_{\bullet} \colon \lambda \in [\underline{\lambda}, \overline{\lambda}]\}$ [3, Proposition 5.2], and this Nisio semigroup is the point-wise smallest semigroup that dominates the family $\{\mathrm{S}^{\lambda}_{\bullet} \colon \lambda \in [\underline{\lambda}, \overline{\lambda}]\}$ [9, Remark 5.3], it follows from these inequalities that $\overline{\mathrm{T}}_{\Delta} = \overline{\mathrm{S}}_{\Delta}$ for all $\Delta \in \mathbb{R}_{\geq 0}$, which concludes our proof. □

6 Conclusion

I am by no means the first to construct an 'imprecise' Poisson process. To the best of my knowledge, Hu and Peng [7, Section 6] were the first to construct a sublinear expectation for $\mathbb{R}^d$-valued Lévy processes, through the viscosity solution to an integro-partial differential equation characterised by a set of Lévy triples; see their Example 43 for the special case of the Poisson process. This inspired Neufeld and Nutz [10] to construct an upper expectation for $\mathbb{R}^d$-valued Lévy processes through the upper envelope of the expectations with respect to the set of probability measures whose 'differential characteristics' take values in the set of triplets; their Example 2.6 treats the Poisson process as a special case.

Unaware of this work, and inspired by work on imprecise finite-state Markov processes [8], Jasper De Bock and I [4] constructed a sublinear expectation for the Poisson process as the upper envelope of the expectations with respect to the set of 'compatible' counting processes—a much less technical condition than the one in [10]. Inspired by [1], I then took an arguably more fruitful approach to the problem in [2, Section 6], constructing a sublinear expectation directly from the sublinear Poisson semigroup.

These earlier approaches have in common with the approach in the present contribution that the upper expectation of $g(N_t)$ can be retrieved as the (viscosity) solution to what is essentially the same differential equation; compare the differential equations in [7, Eq. (9)] and [10, Eq. (2.5)] to the one in [3, Proposition 3.6]. Except for [2], these earlier approaches suffer from the same limitation: they only (practically) determine the upper expectation of finitary variables.

Under the game-theoretic approach, the upper expectation of such (bounded) finitary variables can be determined by means of Theorems 1 and 2 and Corollary 2. However, in Proposition 6 I've also explicitly determined the upper and lower expectation of a non-finitary variable—the time $\rho_\tau - \tau$ until the next increment. Another benefit of the game-theoretic approach over the other approaches is that it involves fewer technicalities—there's no need for measurability, for example, and conditional expectations are defined uniquely and naturally.

Whether the (conditional) upper expectation of other non-finitary variables can also be determined easily is one of the many possible lines of follow-up research I envision. A related future research topic is the continuity of the game-theoretic upper expectation with respect to point-wise convergence of variables. More generally, one could see this work as a first step in the study of imprecise renewal processes, or even imprecise countable-state Markov processes, in the game-theoretic framework.

Acknowledgments. My work on this contribution was funded by Ghent University's Special Research Fund. I'd like to express my gratitude to the three anonymous reviewers; their constructive comments have significantly improved this contribution. I dedicate this contribution to Milena and Dolores, in part for their putting up with my mental and/or physical absence during the preparation of this contribution, but mostly for their love.

Disclosure of Interests. Nothing to disclose.

References

1. Denk, R., Kupper, M., Nendel, M.: Kolmogorov-type and general extension results for nonlinear expectations. Banach J. Math. Anal. **12**(3), 515–540 (2018). https://doi.org/10.1215/17358787-2017-0024
2. Erreygers, A.: Convex expectations for countable-state uncertain processes with càdlàg sample paths. Int. J. Approx. Reason. **175**, 109308 (2024). https://doi.org/10.1016/j.ijar.2024.109308
3. Erreygers, A.: Uniformly continuous semigroups of sublinear transition operators. Electron. J. Differ. Equ. **2025**(122) (2025). https://doi.org/10.58997/ejde.2025.122
4. Erreygers, A., De Bock, J.: First steps towards an imprecise Poisson process. In: Proceedings of the Eleventh International Symposium on Imprecise Probabilities: Theories and Applications. Proceedings of Machine Learning Research, vol. 103. PMLR (2019). https://doi.org/10.48550/arXiv.1905.05734
5. Ethier, S.N., Kurtz, T.G.: Markov Processes: Characterization and Convergence. Wiley (1986). https://doi.org/10.1002/9780470316658
6. de Finetti, B.: Theory of Probability: A Critical Introductory Treatment. Wiley (2017). https://doi.org/10.1002/9781119286387
7. Hu, M., Peng, S.: G-Lévy processes under sublinear expectations. Probab. Uncertain. Quant. Risk **6**(1), 1–22 (2021). https://doi.org/10.3934/puqr.2021001
8. Krak, T., De Bock, J., Siebes, A.: Imprecise continuous-time Markov chains. Int. J. Approx. Reason. **88**, 452–528 (2017). https://doi.org/10.1016/j.ijar.2017.06.012
9. Nendel, M.: On nonlinear expectations and Markov chains under model uncertainty. Int. J. Approx. Reason. **130**, 226–245 (2021). https://doi.org/10.1016/j.ijar.2020.12.013
10. Neufeld, A., Nutz, M.: Nonlinear Lévy processes and their characteristics. Trans. Am. Math. Soc. **369**(1), 69–95 (2017). https://doi.org/10.1090/tran/6656

11. Shafer, G., Vovk, V.: Probability and Finance: It's Only a Game! Wiley Series in Probability and Statistics. Wiley (2001). https://doi.org/10.1002/0471249696
12. Shafer, G., Vovk, V.: Game-Theoretic Foundations for Probability and Finance. Wiley Series in Probability and Statistics. Wiley (2019). https://doi.org/10.1002/9781118548035
13. Troffaes, M.C.M., De Cooman, G.: Lower Previsions. Wiley (2014). https://doi.org/10.1002/9781118762622
14. Vovk, V.G.: Forecasting point and continuous processes: prequential analysis. TEST **2**, 189–217 (1993). https://doi.org/10.1007/bf02562675
15. Walley, P.: Statistical Reasoning with Imprecise Probabilities. Chapman and Hall (1991)
16. Watanabe, S.: On discontinuous additive functionals and Lévy measures of a Markov process. Jpn. J. Math. Trans. Abstracts **34**, 53–70 (1964). https://doi.org/10.4099/jjm1924.34.0_53
17. Williams, P.M.: Notes on conditional previsions. Technical report, School of Mathematical and Physical Sciences, University of Sussex (1975). Reprinted as [18]
18. Williams, P.M.: Notes on conditional previsions. Int. J. Approx. Reason. **44**(3), 366–383 (2007). https://doi.org/10.1016/j.ijar.2006.07.019

Minimum Expected Utility and Non-maximal Credal Sets in the Uncertain Evidence Framework for Belief Functions

Pierre Pomeret-Coquot(✉)

IRIT, Université de Toulouse, CNRS, Toulouse INP, UTC, IUT Rodez, Toulouse, France
pierre.pomeret@irit.fr

Abstract. Decision making in the multi-prior model often relies on the minimum expected utility criterion. When dealing with non-maximal credal sets, the classical Choquet integral cannot be used, as it may lead to reversed preferences. In this paper, we propose an accurate definition and an efficient algorithm for this criterion within the *Uncertain Evidence Framework* for belief functions, which involves non-maximal credal sets bounded by belief and plausibility functions.

Keywords: Multi-prior model · Minimum Expected Utility · Non-Maximal Credal Sets · Belief Functions · Uncertain Evidence

1 Introduction

Decision-making under uncertainty is a fundamental challenge in artificial intelligence, economics and operations research. The multi-prior model, which considers sets of possible probability distributions (credal sets), provides a flexible framework for representing imprecise knowledge. However, traditional approaches typically assume maximal credal sets, significantly limiting their expressiveness (as in imprecise probabilities [26], probability intervals [5], belief functions [6,22], etc.).

In this paper, we focus on the Uncertain Evidence framework for belief functions that we developed in [18]. This framework allows the representation of non-maximal credal sets through evidence functions, which provide an accurate representation of uncertainty when evidence reliability is questionable – whether due to modeling choices or Bayesian updating. However, the minimum expected utility (minEU) criterion, which is well-justified both empirically and axiomatically, cannot be computed accurately using the Choquet integral when credal sets are not maximal. We demonstrate that it can lead to reversed preferences.

Our main contributions are twofold: we provide a constructive mathematical characterization of minEU for non-maximal credal sets in the Uncertain Evidence framework and we develop an efficient algorithm for computing minEU with complexity linear in the size of the evidence function.

B. Vantaggi et al. (Eds.): IPMU 2026, CCIS 3019, pp. 263–276, 2026.
https://doi.org/10.1007/978-3-032-28994-0_19

The paper is organized as follows: Sect. 2 presents the necessary background on belief functions and the Uncertain Evidence framework. Section 3.1 characterizes minEU. Section 3.2 develops our computational algorithm and analyzes the algorithm's complexity. Finally, Sect. 4 concludes with potential extensions.

2 Background Definitions

Belief Function Theory [6,22] allows representing explicitly imprecise knowledge. We focus here on its imprecise probability interpretation, where uncertainty arises from two sources: the inherent variability of the situation (described probabilistically) and our ignorance about it (considered through multiple possible probability distributions).

Let Ω be a finite set of n possible "states of the world." A probability distribution expresses precise knowledge about the "chances" of all $\omega \in \Omega$.

Definition 1 (Probability Distribution). *A function $p : \Omega \to [0,1]$ is a probability distribution if and only if $\sum_{\omega \in \Omega} p(\omega) = 1$.*

We denote by $\mathrm{Pr}_p : 2^\Omega \to [0,1]$ the probability measure defined by p, where $\mathrm{Pr}_p(A) = \sum_{\omega \in A} p(\omega)$ for all $A \subseteq \Omega$. Let $\mathrm{Prob}(\Omega)$ be the set of all probability distributions on Ω.

When p is not known precisely, knowledge can be expressed as the set of the possible distributions $\mathcal{F} \subseteq \mathrm{Prob}(\Omega)$, called the credal set [11,16]. The extreme probabilities in this set are referred to as lower and upper probabilities.

Definition 2 (Lower and Upper Probability). *Let $\mathcal{F} \subseteq \mathrm{Prob}(\Omega)$ be a credal set. Its lower and upper probabilities are $\mathrm{P}^-_\mathcal{F} : 2^\Omega \to [0,1]$ and $\mathrm{P}^+_\mathcal{F} : 2^\Omega \to [0,1]$ such that $\mathrm{P}^-_\mathcal{F}(A) = \inf_{p \in \mathcal{F}} \mathrm{Pr}_p(A)$ and $\mathrm{P}^+_\mathcal{F}(A) = \sup_{p \in \mathcal{F}} \mathrm{Pr}_p(A)$, $\forall A \subseteq \Omega$.*

Lower and upper probabilities generally do not fully characterize a credal set (as illustrated in Examples 1 and 2). Many authors therefore restrict their study to *maximal* credal sets only (also called "convex", though not in the usual set-theoretic sense) for they are in one-to-one correspondence with lower and upper probabilities.

Definition 3 (Maximal Credal Set). *A credal set $\mathcal{F} \subseteq \mathrm{Prob}(\Omega)$ is maximal if and only if $\mathcal{F} = \{p \in \mathrm{Prob}(\Omega),\ \ \forall A, \mathrm{P}^-_\mathcal{F}(A) \leq \mathrm{Pr}_p(A) \leq \mathrm{P}^+_\mathcal{F}(A)\}$.*

Belief Function Theory can be interpreted in terms of credal sets. We first recall the basics of the classical framework, which relies on three set functions: the mass function m, the belief function P^-_m and the plausibility function P^+_m. These functions represent different views of the same knowledge, related by:

$$\mathrm{P}^-_m(A) = \sum_{B \subseteq A} m(B) \quad \text{and} \quad \mathrm{P}^+_m(A) = \sum_{B \cap A \neq \emptyset} m(B).$$

These functions are well defined if and only if $m(\emptyset) = 0$, $\sum_{B \subseteq \Omega} m(B) = 1$ and $\forall B, m(B) \geq 0$.

A mass function, interpreted as a random set, encodes a partially known probability distribution: each $m(\{\omega\})$ represents the amount of probability allocated with certainty to ω, while for $|B| \geq 2$, $m(B)$ represents the amount of probability that cannot be precisely allocated among the states $\omega \in B$ (see [4] for more intuition). Formally, an allocation $(\gamma_B)_{B \subseteq \Omega}$ is compatible with m if for each $B \subseteq \Omega$, $\gamma_B : B \to [0,1]$ satisfies $\sum_{\omega \in B} \gamma_B(\omega) = m(B)$. This leads to the distribution $p^\gamma(\omega) = \sum_B \gamma_B(\omega)$. The credal set associated with m is $\mathcal{F}_m = \{p^\gamma : \omega \mapsto \sum_B \gamma_B(\omega),\ \ \forall B, \sum_{\omega \in B} \gamma_B(\omega) = m(B)\}$. The credal set $\mathcal{F}_m$ is always maximal, with lower and upper probabilities given by P^-_m and P^+_m respectively. Note that there exist maximal credal sets whose lower probabilities are not belief functions (in this case, $\exists B, m(B) < 0$): Belief Function Theory is a sub-theory of imprecise probabilities.

Example 1 (Modeling with Mass Functions). Consider an urn U_1 containing exactly 100 balls: 25 red balls, 25 black balls, 25 balls that are red or white, and 25 balls that are black or white. We model this situation with $\Omega = \{r, b, w\}$ and $m_1(\{r\}) = m_1(\{b\}) = m_1(\{r,w\}) = m_1(\{b,w\}) = 0.25$. This leads to the belief and plausibility functions listed in Table 1. The credal set $\mathcal{F}_1 = \{(0.25 + x_r, 0.25 + y_b, x_w + y_b),\ x_r + x_w = y_r + y_w = 0.25\}$ is maximal (Fig. 1).

Table 1. The mass function m_1 and the corresponding belief and plausibility functions.

A	$\emptyset$	$\{r\}$	$\{b\}$	$\{w\}$	$\{r,b\}$	$\{r,w\}$	$\{b,w\}$	$\{r,b,w\}$
$m_1(A)$		0.25	0.25			0.25	0.25	
$\mathrm{P}^-_1(A)$	0	0.25	0.25	0	0.5	0.5	0.5	1
$\mathrm{P}^+_1(A)$	0	0.5	0.5	0.5	1	0.75	0.75	1

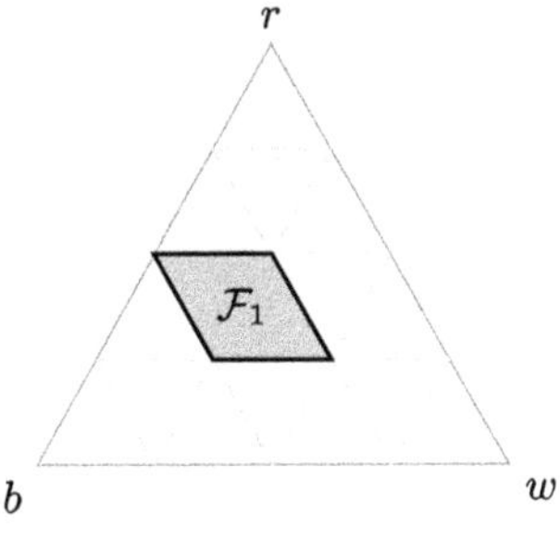

Fig. 1. The credal set $\mathcal{F}_1$ in the simplex. (The simplex represents all possible distributions $(p_r, p_b, p_w) \in \mathrm{Prob}(\{r,b,w\})$ as barycenters of its vertices.)

In [18], we proposed an alternative framework for Belief Function Theory based on *evidence functions*, which map subsets of Ω to $\mathbb{R}_+$-valued intervals rather than to probability values. These intervals represent commensurable quantities (i.e., values with the same unit, such as numbers of colored balls), indicating the ignorance we have about some pieces of evidence.

Let $\mathbb{I}(\mathbb{R}_+)$ denote the set of closed intervals in $\mathbb{R}_+$ (where for any $[x, y] \in \mathbb{I}(\mathbb{R}_+), 0 \leq x \leq y$).

Definition 4 (Evidence Function). *A function* $\mathrm{M} : 2^\Omega \to \mathbb{I}(\mathbb{R}_+)$ *is an evidence function if and only if* $\mathrm{M}(\emptyset) = [0, 0]$.

For an evidence function M, we define M^- and M^+ as the functions yielding the lower and upper bounds of M respectively, such that for any $B \subseteq \Omega$, $\mathrm{M}(B) = [\mathrm{M}^-(B), \mathrm{M}^+(B)]$. Each B with $\mathrm{M}(B) \neq [0, 0]$ is called a focal element, indicating that the amount x of evidence stating B is such that $\mathrm{M}^-(B) \leq x \leq \mathrm{M}^+(B)$. We denote by $\mathcal{S}(\mathrm{M}) = \{B, \mathrm{M}(B) \neq [0, 0]\}$ the set of all focal elements. To avoid divisions by zero, we assume there exists at least one B with $\mathrm{M}^-(B) > 0$.

From an evidence function M, we can derive the minimum and maximum quantities for any event $A \subseteq \Omega$:

$$\mathrm{Q}^-_\mathrm{M}(A) = \sum_{B \subseteq A} \mathrm{M}^-(B) \quad \text{and} \quad \mathrm{Q}^+_\mathrm{M}(A) = \sum_{B \cap A \neq \emptyset} \mathrm{M}^+(B).$$

The minimum and maximum proportions are then:

$$\mathrm{P}^-_\mathrm{M}(A) = \frac{\mathrm{Q}^-_\mathrm{M}(A)}{\mathrm{Q}^-_\mathrm{M}(A) + \mathrm{Q}^+_\mathrm{M}(A^c)} \quad \text{and} \quad \mathrm{P}^+_\mathrm{M}(A) = \frac{\mathrm{Q}^+_\mathrm{M}(A)}{\mathrm{Q}^+_\mathrm{M}(A) + \mathrm{Q}^-_\mathrm{M}(A^c)}.$$

For any evidence function M, P^-_M and P^+_M are dual belief and plausibility functions [18, Theorem 3]. Evidence functions thus provide an alternative framework for Belief Function Theory. Certain evidence functions (where $\mathrm{M}^- = \mathrm{M}^+$) are equivalent to non-normalized mass functions, with the same expressiveness. In contrast, uncertain evidence functions (where $\mathrm{M}^- \neq \mathrm{M}^+$) convey information that cannot be expressed using mass functions, even though their lower and upper proportions are proper belief and plausibility functions (as in Example 2). The Uncertain Evidence framework is therefore more expressive than the classical framework, as made explicit by its interpretation in terms of credal sets.

As with mass functions, evidence functions can be interpreted as random sets expressing unknown quantities: each $\mathrm{M}(B)$ denotes a quantity $x \in \mathrm{M}(B)$ that cannot be precisely allocated to the states $\omega \in B$.

Definition 5 (Compatible Allocation). *Let* M *be an evidence function. A compatible allocation is a family of functions* $(\gamma_B)_{B \subseteq \Omega}$ *such that for each* $B \subseteq \Omega$, $\gamma_B : \Omega \to \mathbb{R}_+$ *satisfies the predicate* compatible(M, γ_B) *defined by:*

$$\text{compatible}(\mathrm{M}, \gamma_B) = \left(\sum\nolimits_{\omega \in B} \gamma_B(\omega) \in \mathrm{M}(B)\right) \ \wedge \ \left(\forall \omega \notin B, \gamma_B(\omega) = 0\right).$$

Each compatible allocation $(\gamma_B)_{B \subseteq \Omega}$ defines a compatible *configuration.*

Definition 6 (Configuration). *Let* $(\gamma_B)_{B \subseteq \Omega}$ *be an allocation. The configuration* $q^\gamma : \Omega \to \mathbb{R}_+$ *that it defines is such that* $\forall \omega \in \Omega,\ q^\gamma(\omega) = \sum_{B \subseteq \Omega} \gamma_B(\omega)$.

A configuration represents a "quantity distribution", and its normalization $p^\gamma : \omega \mapsto q^\gamma(\omega) / \sum_{\omega' \in \Omega} q^\gamma(\omega')$ is a proper probability distribution. The credal set of an evidence function is the set of normalized compatible configurations.

Definition 7 (Credal Set of an Evidence Function). *Let* M *be an evidence function. Its credal set is:*

$$\mathcal{F}_{\mathrm{M}} = \left\{ p^\gamma : \omega \mapsto \frac{\sum_{B \subseteq \Omega} \gamma_B(\omega)}{\sum_{B \subseteq \Omega} \sum_{\omega' \in B} \gamma_B(\omega')},\quad \forall B \subseteq \Omega, \text{compatible}(\mathrm{M}, \gamma_B) \right\}.$$

The lower and upper probabilities of such credal sets correspond to the minimum and maximum proportions: $\mathrm{P}^-_{\mathrm{M}}(A) = \inf_{p \in \mathcal{F}_{\mathrm{M}}} \mathrm{Pr}_p(A)$ and $\mathrm{P}^+_{\mathrm{M}}(A) = \sup_{p \in \mathcal{F}_{\mathrm{M}}} \mathrm{Pr}_p(A)$, $\forall A \subseteq \Omega$. However, these credal sets are generally not maximal when the evidence is uncertain ($\mathrm{M}^- \neq \mathrm{M}^+$), as shown in Example 2.

Example 2 (Modeling with Evidence Functions). Consider an urn U_2 containing between 50 and 100 balls: 25 red balls, 25 black balls, and 0 to 50 white balls. We model it using $\Omega = \{r, b, w\}$ and $\mathrm{M}_2(\{r\}) = \mathrm{M}_2(\{b\}) = [25, 25]$ and $\mathrm{M}_2(\{w\}) = [0, 50]$. This leads to the quantities and proportions listed in Table 2. Note that we recover the same proportions as in Example 1 ($\mathrm{P}^-_2 = \mathrm{P}^-_1$ and $\mathrm{P}^+_2 = \mathrm{P}^+_1$). However, the credal set $\mathcal{F}_2 = \left\{ \left(\frac{25}{50+x}, \frac{25}{50+x}, \frac{x}{50+x} \right),\ 0 \leq x \leq 50 \right\}$ clearly differ from $\mathcal{F}_1$. It is not maximal, e.g., $p = (0.3, 0.5, 0.2) \in \mathcal{F}_1$ but $p \notin \mathcal{F}_2$ (Fig. 2).

Table 2. Minimum and maximum quantities and proportions derived from M_2.

A	$\emptyset$	$\{r\}$	$\{b\}$	$\{w\}$	$\{r,b\}$	$\{r,w\}$	$\{b,w\}$	$\{r,b,w\}$
$\mathrm{M}_2(A)$		$[25,25]$	$[25,25]$	$[0,50]$				
$\mathrm{Q}^-_2(A)$	0	25	25	0	50	25	25	50
$\mathrm{Q}^+_2(A)$	0	25	25	50	50	75	75	100
$\mathrm{P}^-_2(A)$	0	0.25	0.25	0	0.5	0.5	0.5	1
$\mathrm{P}^+_2(A)$	0	0.5	0.5	0.5	1	0.75	0.75	1

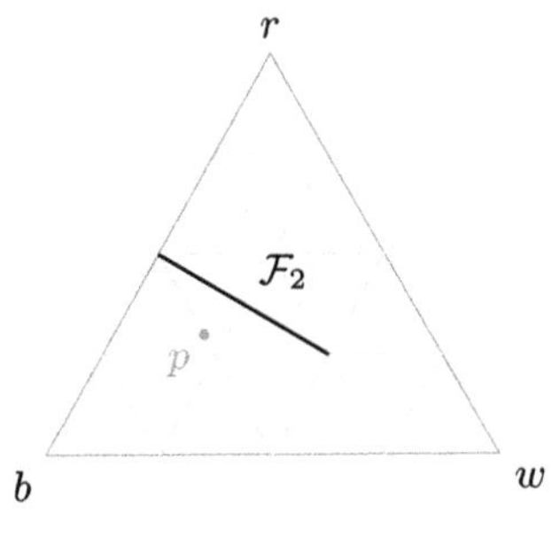

Fig. 2. The non-maximal credal set $\mathcal{F}_2$ of M_2 and $p = (0.3, 0.5, 0.2) \notin \mathcal{F}_2$.

The Uncertain Evidence framework is very expressive, as it allows distinguishing between pieces of knowledge that share the same lower and upper probabilities (when expressible in the belief function theory) by accurately delimiting non-maximal credal sets. Such knowledge may arise directly from modeling (when the reliability of the evidence is uncertain, hence the name of the framework), or in dynamic contexts, where the Bayesian update of prior maximal credal sets typically results in posterior credal sets that are not maximal (see [18, Section 6] for further details).

3 Minimum Expected Utility

Expectation is a fundamental tool in Probability Theory. In particular, the expectation of a utility function has been widely used to model decision-making from the 18th century to the present day [1,17,20].

We consider Savage's framework [20], where decision-making amounts to evaluating *acts* (and typically selecting the "best" one). An act is a function $a : \Omega \to \mathbb{X}$ that maps states to consequences. Intuitively, $a(\omega)$ is the consequence of choosing act a when the actual state of the world is ω. The evaluation of consequences is given by a quantitative utility function $u : \mathbb{X} \to \mathbb{R}$. Many authors have concluded (for various reasons) that the overall evaluation of an act is related to the expectation of its utility given a (potentially subjective) probability distribution [17,20]. Formally, $a \succeq b \iff \mathrm{EU}_{p,u}(a) \geq \mathrm{EU}_{p,u}(b)$.

Definition 8 (Expected Utility). *Let $p : \Omega \to [0,1]$ be a probability distribution, $u : \mathbb{X} \to \mathbb{R}$ a utility function and $a : \Omega \to \mathbb{X}$ an act. The expected utility of a is $\mathrm{EU}_{p,u}(a) = \sum_{\omega\in\Omega} p(\omega) \times u(a(\omega))$.*

In the case of ignorance, multiple probability distributions are possible, leading to multiple expected utility values for a given act. Considering the minimum expected utility (minEU) is strongly justified, as it captures observed decision-makers preferences (see, e.g., Ellsberg's experiment [10]) and is supported by axiomatic arguments [2,7,21] (see, e.g., [9, Chapter 10] for further information).

Definition 9 (Minimum Expected Utility). *Let $\mathcal{F}$ be a credal set, $u : \mathbb{X} \to \mathbb{R}$ an utility function and $a : \Omega \to \mathbb{X}$ an act. Its minimum expected utility is:*

$$\mathrm{minEU}_{\mathcal{F},u}(a) = \inf_{p\in\mathcal{F}} \mathrm{EU}_{p,u}(a).$$

When knowledge is described by a maximal credal set, the minEU value of an act equals its Choquet integral [3] (also called "Choquet utility" or CEU) [12,13,21]. For a credal set derived from a mass function m, we have [6,23]: $\mathrm{minEU}_{\mathcal{F}_m,u}(a) = \mathrm{CEU}_{m,u}(a) = \sum_{B\subseteq\Omega} m(B) \times \min_{\omega\in B} u(a(\omega))$.

By analyzing this formula carefully, we see that the minEU value is obtained by considering the expected utility of the "worst case" allocations $(\gamma_B)_B$ compatible with m: these allocations map each mass $m(B)$ to the "worst case" $\omega \in B$, whose utility is therefore $\min_{\omega\in B} u(a(\omega))$. By applying this approach to all focal elements, we obtain the given formula.

The CEU value is only suitable for maximal credal sets. For non-maximal credal sets, the CEU value does not equal the minEU value. Moreover, it cannot be considered an approximation, as comparing CEU values may lead to reversed preferences (see Example 3).

Example 3 (Reversed Preferences). Consider the credal set $\mathcal{F}_2$ from Example 2 and the two acts a and a' defined by:

$$u(a(r)) = 0 \qquad u(a(b)) = 5 \qquad u(a(w)) = 2$$
$$u(a'(r)) = 0 \qquad u(a'(b)) = 8 \qquad u(a'(w)) = 0$$

The CEU value is easily computed using m_1 (recall that $\mathrm{P}_1^- = \mathrm{P}_2^-$ and $\mathrm{P}_1^+ = \mathrm{P}_2^+$), yielding $\mathrm{CEU}_{m_1,u}(a) = 1.75 < \mathrm{CEU}_{m_1,u}(a') = 2$. However, mathematical analysis of $\mathcal{F}_2$ reveals that $\mathrm{minEU}_{\mathcal{F}_2,u}(a) = 2.25 > \mathrm{minEU}_{\mathcal{F}_2,u}(a') = 2$, leading to the conclusion that $a \succ a'$.

Note that two other decision-making criteria are closely related to minEU and fall within the scope of this paper: the maximum expected utility $\mathrm{maxEU}_{\mathcal{F},u}(a) = -\mathrm{minEU}_{\mathcal{F},-u}(a)$, and the Hurwicz-like trade-off $H^{\alpha}_{\mathcal{F},u}(a) = \alpha\,\mathrm{minEU}_{\mathcal{F},u}(a) + (1-\alpha)\,\mathrm{maxEU}_{\mathcal{F},u}(a)$ [14,25]. Conversely, Jaffray's [15] and pignistic criteria [24] are not included, as they involve notions that we do not consider here (e.g., density of credal sets; see [18, Section 5.1]) and require a more in-depth study. A comprehensive review of decision-making criteria can be found in [8].

3.1 Minimum Expected Utility and Uncertain Evidence

As shown in Example 3, the CEU formula is not suitable for the Uncertain Evidence framework. For this entire subsection, let $\mathrm{M} : 2^{\Omega} \to \mathbb{I}(\mathbb{R}_+)$ be an evidence function, $a : \Omega \to \mathbb{X}$ an act, and $u : \mathbb{X} \to \mathbb{R}$ a utility function. We seek a constructive definition of:

$$\mathrm{minEU}_{\mathcal{F}_{\mathrm{M}},u}(a) = \inf_{p \in \mathcal{F}_{\mathrm{M}}} \mathrm{EU}_{p,u}(a).$$

To compute $\mathrm{minEU}_{\mathcal{F}_{\mathrm{M}},u}(a)$, we can identify a "worst-case" probability distribution compatible with M and compute the expected utility with respect to this distribution. Note that there may be multiple "worst-case" distributions (if $\exists \omega \neq \omega'$ such that $u(a(\omega)) = u(a(\omega'))$). For simplicity, we rank the states according to $u \circ a$ and denote them $\omega_1, \ldots, \omega_n$ such that $i < j \implies u(a(\omega_i)) \leq u(a(\omega_j))$. Ties are broken arbitrarily to establish a total order.

We define any $\omega_i \in B$ such that $u(a(\omega_i)) = \min_{\omega \in B} u(a(\omega))$ as *B*-minimal, and denote by $\omega^B = \min_{i,\omega_i \in B} \omega_i$ the *B*-minimal state with the lowest index.

An allocation γ and its corresponding configuration q^{γ} and distribution p^{γ} are called minimal if $\mathrm{EU}_{p^{\gamma},u}(a) = \mathrm{minEU}_{\mathcal{F}_{\mathrm{M}},u}(a)$.

In the following, we will construct a minimal compatible configuration, enabling a direct computation of the minEU value. To achieve this, we will prove several lemmas that eventually reduce the set of candidate configurations to $n+1$ configurations, one of which is minimal. First, note that:

Lemma 1. *Let* $(\gamma_B)_B$ *be an allocation.*

$$\mathrm{EU}_{p^\gamma,u}(a) = \frac{1}{K^\gamma} \sum_{(\omega_i,B)\in\Omega\times 2^\Omega} \gamma_B(\omega_i) \times u(a(\omega_i)),$$

where $K^\gamma = \sum_{\omega_i,B} \gamma_B(\omega_i)$ *is the positive normalization factor of* p^γ*.*

Proof. This follows directly from Definitions 5 and 6. □

For all B, compatible allocations allocate a quantity $x \in \mathrm{M}(B)$ among one or several $\omega \in B$. A minimal allocation must allocate $x \in \mathrm{M}(B)$ only to B-minimal states. In particular, one such allocation allocates it to ω^B.

Lemma 2. *There exists a minimal compatible allocation* $(\gamma_B)_B$ *such that, for all* $B \subseteq \Omega$*:*

$$\gamma_B(\omega^B) \in \mathrm{M}(B) \quad \text{and} \quad \gamma_B(\omega_i) = 0 \text{ otherwise.}$$

Proof. Suppose there exists A, $\omega_i \in A$ with $\omega_i \neq \omega^A$, and a minimal compatible allocation $(\gamma_B)_B$ such that $\gamma_A(\omega_i) > 0$. Define $(\mu_B)_B$ by $\mu_A(\omega_i) = 0$, $\mu_A(\omega^A) = \gamma_A(\omega^A) + \gamma_A(\omega_i)$ and $\mu_B(\omega_j) = \gamma_B(\omega_j)$ otherwise. Since $(\gamma_B)_B$ is compatible with M, so is $(\mu_B)_B$. From Lemma 1, it holds that $K^\gamma = K^\mu > 0$ and:

$$\begin{aligned}
&K^\gamma \left(\mathrm{EU}_{p^\gamma,u}(a) - \mathrm{EU}_{p^\mu,u}(a)\right) \\
&= \left(\gamma_A(\omega_i) - \mu_A(\omega_i)\right) \times u(a(\omega_i)) + \left(\gamma_A(\omega^A) - \mu_A(\omega^A)\right) \times u(a(\omega^A)) \\
&= \gamma_A(\omega_i) \times \left(u(a(\omega_i)) - u(a(\omega^A))\right).
\end{aligned}$$

If $u(a(\omega_i)) = u(a(\omega^A))$, then $\mathrm{EU}_{p^\gamma,u}(a) = \mathrm{EU}_{p^\mu,u}(a)$, making μ also minimal. Otherwise, $u(a(\omega_i)) > u(a(\omega^A))$ implies $\mathrm{EU}_{p^\gamma,u}(a) > \mathrm{EU}_{p^\mu,u}(a)$, contradicting the minimality of $(\gamma_B)_B$. □

Equivalently, Lemma 2 can be expressed in terms of a configuration. Since a quantity $x \in \mathrm{M}(B)$ is allocated to ω^B for all B, each ω_i receives an amount equal to the sum of allocated quantities for all B such that $\omega_i = \omega^B$ is the state in B with the lowest index. We first define these minimal and maximal quantities.

Definition 10 (Minimal and maximal allocated quantities). *For all* $\omega_i \in \Omega$*, the minimal and maximal quantities allocated to* ω_i *are, respectively:*

$$\lambda_i^- = \sum_{B,\omega_i=\omega^B} \mathrm{M}^-(B) \quad \text{and} \quad \lambda_i^+ = \sum_{B,\omega_i=\omega^B} \mathrm{M}^+(B).$$

Lemma 2 can then be restated in terms of a configuration:

Corollary 1. *There exists a minimal compatible configuration* q^γ *such that, for all* $\omega_i \in \Omega$*:*

$$q^\gamma(\omega_i) \in [\lambda_i^-, \lambda_i^+].$$

Proof. This follows by rewriting Definitions 6 and 10 in Lemma 2. □

In the following, we will compare the expected utilities of configurations that differ in only one value. We factorize the proofs with the following lemma:

Lemma 3. *Let ω_i, q^γ and q^μ such that $q^\gamma(\omega_i) < q^\mu(\omega_i)$ and $q^\gamma(\omega_j) = q^\mu(\omega_j)$ otherwise. Then:*

$$\begin{aligned} u(a(\omega_i)) < \mathrm{EU}_{p^\gamma,u}(a) &\iff \mathrm{EU}_{p^\gamma,u}(a) > \mathrm{EU}_{p^\mu,u}(a)\\ u(a(\omega_i)) = \mathrm{EU}_{p^\gamma,u}(a) &\iff \mathrm{EU}_{p^\gamma,u}(a) = \mathrm{EU}_{p^\mu,u}(a)\\ u(a(\omega_i)) > \mathrm{EU}_{p^\gamma,u}(a) &\iff \mathrm{EU}_{p^\gamma,u}(a) < \mathrm{EU}_{p^\mu,u}(a) \end{aligned}$$

Proof. First, recall that $\forall x, y, z$ and t such that $z > 0$ and $t > 0$, it holds that $\frac{x+y}{z+t} < \frac{y}{t} \iff \frac{x}{z} < \frac{y}{t}$ and similarly for $>$ and for $=$.

According to Lemma 1, we can rewrite $\mathrm{EU}_{p^\gamma,u}(a) = \frac{x^\gamma}{K^\gamma}$ and $\mathrm{EU}_{p^\mu,u}(a) = \frac{x^\mu}{K^\mu}$, where $x^\mu = x^\gamma + \delta_i \times u(a(\omega_i))$ and $K^\mu = K^\gamma + \delta_i$ with $\delta_i = q^\mu(\omega_i) - q^\gamma(\omega_i) > 0$. Thus: $\mathrm{EU}_{p^\mu,u}(a) = \frac{x^\gamma + \delta_i \times u(a(\omega_i))}{K^\gamma + \delta_i}$.

The result follows by comparing this with $\mathrm{EU}_{p^\gamma,u}(a) = \frac{x^\gamma}{K^\gamma}$. □

Corollary 1 ensures that the minimal configuration q^γ we seek satisfies $q^\gamma(\omega_i) \in [\lambda_i^-, \lambda_i^+]$, for all $\omega_i \in \Omega$. However, we need not consider the entire interval; we can restrict our attention to the bounds λ_i^- and λ_i^+ only.

Lemma 4. *There exists a minimal compatible configuration q^γ such that, for all $\omega_i \in \Omega$,*

$$q^\gamma(\omega_i) \in \{\lambda_i^-, \lambda_i^+\}.$$

Proof. Let q^γ be a minimal compatible configuration satisfying Corollary 1's requirement and suppose ω_i such that $\lambda_i^- < q(\omega_i) < \lambda_i^+$.

- If $u(a(\omega_i)) < \mathrm{EU}_{p^\gamma,u}(a)$, let q^μ be such that $q^\mu(\omega_i) = \lambda_i^+$ and $q^\mu(\omega_j) = q^\gamma(\omega_j)$ otherwise. By Lemma 3, $\mathrm{EU}_{p^\gamma,u}(a) > \mathrm{EU}_{p^\mu,u}(a)$, a contradiction.
- If $u(a(\omega_i)) > \mathrm{EU}_{p^\gamma,u}(a)$, let q^μ be such that $q^\mu(\omega_i) = \lambda_i^-$ and $q^\mu(\omega_j) = q^\gamma(\omega_j)$ otherwise. By Lemma 3, $\mathrm{EU}_{p^\gamma,u}(a) > \mathrm{EU}_{p^\mu,u}(a)$, a contradiction.
- If $u(a(\omega_i)) = \mathrm{EU}_{p^\gamma,u}(a)$, let q^μ be such that $q^\mu(\omega_i) = \lambda_i^+$ and $q^\mu(\omega_j) = q^\gamma(\omega_j)$ otherwise. By Lemma 3, $\mathrm{EU}_{p^\gamma,u}(a) = \mathrm{EU}_{p^\mu,u}(a)$, q^μ is minimal. □

Lemma 4 reduces the set of candidate minimal configurations to 2^n configurations (the 2^n ways to select either λ_i^- or λ_i^+ for all $\omega_i \in \Omega$).

We now show that there is a threshold x such that any minimal configuration q^γ satisfies $q^\gamma(\omega_i) = \lambda_i^+$ if $u(a(\omega_i)) < x$ and $q^\gamma(\omega_i) = \lambda_i^-$ if $u(a(\omega_i)) > x$ (if $u(a(\omega_i)) = x$, any $q^\gamma(\omega_i) \in [\lambda_i^-, \lambda_i^+]$ is valid, and we arbitrary choose $q^\gamma(\omega_i) = \lambda_i^-$. This reduces the set of candidate minimal configurations to only $n+1$ configurations. More precisely, we show that this threshold is $x = \mathrm{minEU}_{\mathcal{F}_\mathrm{M},u}(a)$.

Lemma 5. *The following compatible configuration q^γ is minimal:*

$$q^\gamma(\omega_i) = \begin{cases} \lambda_i^+ & \text{if } u(a(\omega_i)) \leq \mathrm{minEU}_{\mathcal{F}_\mathrm{M},u}(a) \\ \lambda_i^- & \text{otherwise.} \end{cases}$$

Proof. Let q^γ be a minimal configuration such that $q^\gamma(\omega) \in \{\lambda_i^-, \lambda_i^+\}$ (which exists by Lemma 4). By definition, $\text{minEU}_{\mathcal{F}_\text{M},u}(a) = \text{EU}_{p^\gamma,u}(a)$.

- Suppose there exists ω_i such that $q^\gamma(\omega_i) = \lambda_i^-$ and $u(a(\omega_i)) < \text{EU}_{p^\gamma,u}(a)$. Let q^μ be such that $q^\mu(\omega_i) = \lambda_i^+$ and $q^\mu(\omega_j) = q^\gamma(\omega_j)$ otherwise. By Lemma 3, $\text{EU}_{p^\mu,u}(a) < \text{EU}_{p^\gamma,u}(a)$, a contradiction.
- Symmetrically, suppose ω_i such that $q^\gamma(\omega_i) = \lambda_i^+$ and $u(a(\omega_i)) > \text{EU}_{p^\gamma,u}(a)$. Let q^μ be such that $q^\mu(\omega_i) = \lambda_i^-$ and $q^\mu(\omega_j) = q^\gamma(\omega_j)$ otherwise. By Lemma 3, $\text{EU}_{p^\mu,u}(a) < \text{EU}_{p^\gamma,u}(a)$, a contradiction.
- Finally, suppose there exists an ω_i such that $q^\gamma(\omega_i) \neq \lambda_i^-$ and $u(a(\omega_i)) = \text{EU}_{p^\gamma,u}(a)$. Let q^μ be such that $q^\mu(\omega_i) = \lambda_i^-$ and $q^\mu(\omega_j) = q^\gamma(\omega_j)$ otherwise. By Lemma 3, $\text{EU}_{p^\mu,u}(a) = \text{EU}_{p^\gamma,u}(a)$, so $(\mu_B)_B$ is also minimal. □

For $0 \leq i \leq n$, let $q^{(i)}$ be the configuration such that:

$$q^{(i)}(\omega_j) = \begin{cases} \lambda_{\omega_j}^+ & \text{if } j \leq i \\ \lambda_{\omega_j}^- & \text{otherwise.} \end{cases}$$

Let $p^{(i)}$ be its normalized distribution. One of $n+1$ configurations $q^{(0)}, \ldots, q^{(n)}$ satisfies Lemma 5's requirements and is therefore minimal.

Theorem 1 (Minimum Expected Utility). *Let* $\text{M} : 2^\Omega \to \mathbb{I}(\mathbb{R}_+)$ *be an evidence function,* $u : \mathbb{X} \to \mathbb{R}$ *a utility function and* $a : \Omega \to \mathbb{X}$ *an act. The minimum expected utility of* a *is:*

$$\text{minEU}_{\mathcal{F}_\text{M},u}(a) = \min_{i=0\ldots n} \text{EU}_{p^{(i)},u}(a) = \min_{i=0\ldots n} \frac{1}{K^{(i)}} \sum_{\omega \in \Omega} q^{(i)}(\omega) \times u(a(\omega))$$

where $K^{(i)} = \sum_{\omega\in\Omega} q^{(i)}(\omega)$ *is the normalization factor of* $p^{(i)}$*.*

Proof. This follows from Lemma 5 by considering the $n+1$ configurations. □

3.2 An Efficient Algorithm to Compute MinEU

In the previous section, we demonstrated that there exists a rank $i^* \in \{0, \ldots, n\}$ such that $q^{(i^*)}$ is a minimal configuration, i.e., $\text{minEU}_{\mathcal{F}_\text{M},u}(a) = \text{EU}_{p^{(i^*)},u}(a)$.

A naive algorithm to compute $\text{minEU}_{\mathcal{F}_\text{M},u}(a)$ follows from Theorem 1: constructing the $n+1$ configurations and comparing their expected utility. However, this approach is inefficient. Let us observe that:

$$\text{EU}_{p^{(i+1)},u}(a) = \frac{x^{(i)} + (\lambda_i^+ - \lambda_i^-) \times u(a(\omega_{i+1}))}{K^{(i)} + \lambda_i^+ - \lambda_i^-}$$

can be efficiently computed from $\text{EU}_{p^{(i)},u}(a) = \frac{x^{(i)}}{K^{(i)}}$. We can therefore first compute $\text{EU}_{p^{(0)},u}(a)$ and then iteratively compute up to $\text{EU}_{p^{(n)},u}(a)$.

Moreover, we only need to iterate until reaching the rank i^* where we have $\text{minEU}_{\mathcal{F}_\text{M},u}(a) = \text{EU}_{p^{(i^*)},u}(a)$. This rank is easily identified since the function $f := i \mapsto \text{EU}_{p^{(i)},u}(a)$ is decreasing for $i \leq i^*$ and increasing for $i \geq i^*$.

Lemma 6. *Let $f : \{0, \dots, n\} \to \mathbb{R} := i \mapsto \mathrm{EU}_{p^{(i)},u}(a)$. There exists i^* such that f is decreasing on $\{0, \dots, i^*\}$ and f is increasing on $\{i^*, \dots, n\}$.*

Proof. From Lemma 5, we know that i^* satisfies $f(i^*) = \mathrm{minEU}_{\mathcal{F}_{\mathrm{M}},u}(a)$. From Lemma 3, we have for all i that $f(i+1) \geq f(i) \iff u(a(\omega_{i+1})) \geq f(i)$.

- For all i, define the predicate $P(i) = u(a(\omega_{i+1})) \geq f(i)$. Since $P(i)$ is equivalent to $f(i+1) \geq f(i)$, it follows from Lemma 5 that $P(i^*)$ holds. Now, suppose $i \geq i^*$ such that $P(i)$.
  From Lemma 1, we can write $f(i) = x^{(i)}/K^{(i)}$. Let $\delta = \lambda^+_{i+1} - \lambda^-_{i+1}$. From $P(i)$, we have $\frac{x^{(i)}}{K^{(i)}} \leq u(a(\omega_{i+1})) = \frac{\delta \cdot u(a(\omega_{i+1}))}{\delta}$, which implies:
  $$\frac{x^{(i)} + \delta \cdot u(a(\omega_{i+1}))}{K^{(i)} + \delta} \leq \frac{\delta \cdot u(a(\omega_{i+1}))}{\delta},$$
  i.e., $f(i+1) \leq u(a(\omega_{i+1}))$. Since $u(a(\omega_{i+1})) \leq u(a(\omega_{i+2}))$, $P(i+1)$ holds. By induction, $P(i)$ holds for all $i \geq i^*$ and f is increasing on $\{i^*, \dots, n\}$.
- Now, define the predicate $Q(i) = u(a(\omega_{i-1})) \geq f(i)$, which is equivalent to $f(i-1) \geq f(i)$. Similarly, $Q(i^*)$ holds and $Q(i)$ implies $Q(i-1)$ when $i \leq i^*$. By induction $Q(i)$ holds for all $i \leq i^*$ and f is decreasing on $\{0, \dots, i^*\}$. □

The inflection point i^* of f is its global minimum, and by definition $f(i^*) = \mathrm{minEU}_{\mathcal{F}_{\mathrm{M}},u}(a)$. We can therefore find i^* and $f(i^*)$ by computing values $f(0)$, $f(1)$, etc. until f stops decreasing, leading to Algorithm 1. Note that more sophisticated search methods like dichotomy will not improve the algorithm's efficiency since $f(i+1)$ can be computed from $f(i)$ in constant time $\mathcal{O}(1)$. The most computationally intensive part of the algorithm is its initialization.

Algorithm 1. Compute $\mathrm{minEU}_{\mathcal{F}_{\mathrm{M}},u}(a)$

```
Sort Ω such that
    i < j ⟹ u(a(ω_i)) ≤ u(a(ω_j))
for 1 ≤ i ≤ n do
    λ_i^- ← 0
    λ_i^+ ← 0
end for
for B ∈ S(M) do
    i ← argmin_{ω_i ∈ B} u(a(ω))
    λ_i^- ← λ_i^- + M^-(B)
    λ_i^+ ← λ_i^+ + M^+(B)
end for
y ← 0
z ← 0
for 1 ≤ i ≤ n do
    y ← y + λ_i^- × u(a(ω_i))
    z ← z + λ_i^-
end for
f^(0) ← y/z
for 1 ≤ i ≤ n do
    y ← y + (λ_i^+ − λ_i^-) × u(a(ω_i))
    z ← z + λ_i^+ − λ_i^-
    f^(i) ← y/z
    if f^(i) > f^(i−1) then
        return f^(i−1)
    end if
end for
return f^(n)
```

Theorem 2 (Correctness). *Algorithm 1 returns* $\text{minEU}_{\mathcal{F}_{\text{M}},u}(a)$.

Proof. The initialization of Algorithm 1's (first column) computes the λ_i^- and λ_i^+ values according to Definition 10. In the second column, the first "for" loop initializes y and z such that $f^{(0)} = y/z = \text{EU}_{p^{(0)},u}(a)$. In the second "for" loop, at each step i, $f^{(i)} = \text{EU}_{p^{(i)},u}(a)$ is computed by increasing both the numerator y and the denominator z according to Lemma 1. The algorithm returns $f^{(i-1)}$ when the sequence $(f^{(i)})_{0\leq i\leq n}$ starts increasing, i.e., when the global minimum $i^* = i-1$ is reached, hence $f^{(i-1)} = \text{minEU}_{\mathcal{F}_{\text{M}},u}(a)$ (Lemma 6). □

We now analyze the complexity of Algorithm 1, showing that it is linear in the size of the evidence function: $\mathcal{O}(\text{Size}(\text{M})) = \mathcal{O}(sn)$, where $s = |\mathcal{S}(\text{M})|$ is the number of focal elements and $n = |\Omega|$ is the number of states. This complexity is comparable to computing a Choquet integral on a mass function, making it equally tractable (tractability depends on the number s of focal elements, which might be $2^n - 1$ in general, but is usually bound to be polynomial in n). We assume realistically that $s \gg \log n$ and that all set operations are $\mathcal{O}(n)$.

Theorem 3 (Complexity). *Let* M *be an evidence function on a set of* n *states with* s *focal elements. Algorithm 1 requires* $\mathcal{O}(sn)$ *time and* $\mathcal{O}(n)$ *space.*

Proof.
- Time complexity: Initialization (first column) involves sorting the n states in $\mathcal{O}(n \log n)$ and computing the λ_ω^- and λ_ω^+ in a loop over s elements, each step requiring a set operation, resulting in $\mathcal{O}(sn)$. The second column's first loop iterates over n elements, each step being $\mathcal{O}(1)$, hence $\mathcal{O}(n)$. Its second loop also iterates over at most n elements, each step being $\mathcal{O}(1)$, hence $\mathcal{O}(n)$. Assuming $s \gg \log n$, we have $\mathcal{O}(n \log n + sn + n + n) = \mathcal{O}(sn)$.
- Space complexity: The algorithm requires storing the $2n$ values λ_i^- and λ_i^+, the two values y and z and at most $n+1$ values $v^{(i)}$ (naively). The space complexity is therefore $\mathcal{O}(2n + 2 + n + 1) = \mathcal{O}(n)$. □

The main cost is the initialization loop, which runs in $\mathcal{O}(sn)$. This is comparable to the computation of a Choquet integral for a mass function. Note that this loop can easily be parallelized by distributing the set of focal elements $\mathcal{S}(\text{M})$ across several cores, computing local sums, and then aggregating the results.

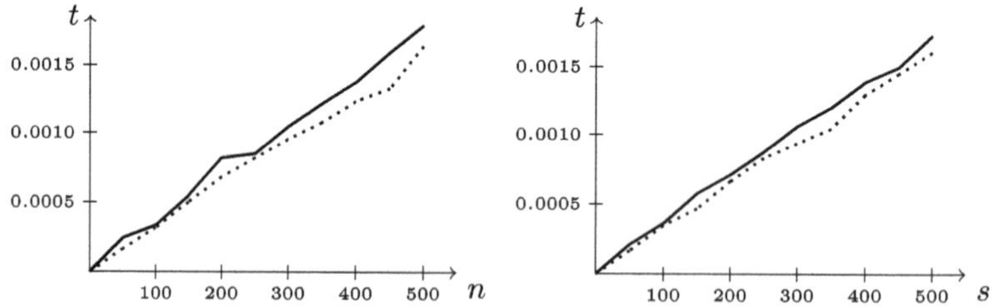

Fig. 3. Average execution time t (in seconds) of Algorithm 1 on evidence functions (bold line) and of Choquet integral on mass functions (dotted line) for various values of $n = |\Omega|$ (left, using $s = 100$) and of $s = |\mathcal{S}(m)| = |\mathcal{S}(\text{M})|$ (right, using $n = 100$).

Finally, we implemented Algorithm 1 and compared its execution time with that of the Choquet integral on random data [19]. This confirms the complexity analysis and shows that both algorithms are equally efficient (Fig. 3).

4 Conclusion

In this paper, we demonstrate the necessity of an exact computation of the Minimal Expected Utility for non-maximal credal sets, as the Choquet integral may lead to reversed preferences. We propose a constructive definition and a tractable algorithm for this computation when the credal set derives from an evidence function, with complexity linear in the size of the evidence function. This enables the development of a decision theory based on the Uncertain Evidence framework for Belief Function Theory. Our work opens several important research directions.

First, the impact on the axiomatic arguments supporting the use of the Choquet Integral (particularly the co-monotonicity axiom) needs to be studied. Since accurate minEU may lead to opposite preferences, it violates this axiom. We must determine whether this violation is reasonable and whether there exists a proper formulation suitable for both certain and uncertain evidence.

Then, empirical justifications for accurate minEU should be explored. Do decision-makers actually exhibit preferences captured by this criterion in case of uncertain evidence? Are real-world data computed efficiently? Experimental validation is clearly needed.

Last, we focused here on pessimistic decision making in the Uncertain Evidence Framework for belief functions. On the one hand, the extension of other decision criteria to non-maximal credal sets should be explored. On the other hand, belief functions cannot express the full generality of imprecise probabilities, and this larger scope should also be investigated.

We believe these open questions are of paramount importance. Non-maximal credal sets are essential for modeling and updating knowledge expressed in imprecise probability theory and its sub-theories, but cannot be approximated by maximal sets in a decision-making context. They therefore require more in-depth study.

References

1. Charreton, R.: Esquisse d'une théorie nouvelle de mesure du sort – Traduction of Bernoulli, D.: Specimen Theoriae Novae de Mensura Sortis (1738). Cahiers du séminaire d'histoire des mathématiques **6**, 61–77 (1985)
2. Chateauneuf, A., Cohen, M., Kast, R.: A review of some results related to comonotonicity. Cahiers Eco & Maths **97**(32) (1997)
3. Choquet, G.: Theory of capacities. In: Annales de l'institut Fourier. vol. 5, pp. 131–295 (1954). https://doi.org/10.5802/aif.53
4. Cuzzolin, F.: The Geometry of Uncertainty: The Geometry of Imprecise Probabilities. Springer (2020). https://doi.org/10.1007/978-3-030-63153-6

5. De Campos, L.M., Huete, J.F., Moral, S.: Probability intervals: a tool for uncertain reasoning. Int. J. Uncertain. Fuzziness Knowl.-Based Syst. **2**(02), 167–196 (1994). https://doi.org/10.1142/S0218488594000146
6. Dempster, A.P.: Upper and lower probabilities induced by a multivalued mapping. Ann. Math. Stat. **38**(2), 325–339 (1967). https://doi.org/10.1214/aoms/1177698950
7. Denneberg, D.: Non-Additive Measure and Integral. Theory and Decision Library B. Springer (1994). https://doi.org/10.1007/978-94-017-2434-0
8. Denœux, T.: Decision-making with belief functions: a review. Int. J. Approximate Reasoning **109**, 87–110 (2019). https://doi.org/10.1016/j.ijar.2019.03.009
9. Dubois, D., Prade, H., Pirlot, M., Bouyssou, D.: Decision Making Process: Concepts and Methods. Wiley (2013). https://doi.org/10.1002/9780470611876
10. Ellsberg, D.: Risk, ambiguity, and the Savage axioms. Q. J. Econ. 643–669 (1961). https://doi.org/10.2307/1884324
11. Fine, T.L.: Lower probability models for uncertainty and nondeterministic processes. J. Stat. Planning and inference **20**(3), 389–411 (1988). https://doi.org/10.1016/0378-3758(88)90099-7
12. Gilboa, I., Schmeidler, D.: Maxmin expected utility with non-unique prior. J. Math. Econ. **18**(2), 141–153 (1989). https://doi.org/10.1016/0304-4068(89)90018-9
13. Gilboa, I., Schmeidler, D.: Additive representations of non-additive measures and the choquet integral. Ann. Oper. Res. **52**(1), 43–65 (1994). https://doi.org/10.1007/BF02032160
14. Hurwicz, L.: Optimality criteria for decision making under ignorance. Tech. rep., Cowles Commission discussion paper, statistics (1951). https://doi.org/10.1017/CBO9780511752940.015
15. Jaffray, J.Y.: Linear utility theory for belief functions. Oper. Res. Lett. **8**(2), 107–112 (1989). https://doi.org/10.1016/0167-6377(89)90010-2
16. Levi, I.: The Enterprise of Knowledge: An Essay on Knowledge, Credal Probability, and Chance. MIT Press (1980). https://doi.org/10.1086/289214
17. Morgenstern, O., Von Neumann, J.: Theory of Games and Economic Behavior. Princeton University Press (1944). https://doi.org/10.1515/9781400829460
18. Pomeret-Coquot, P.: Modeling and updating uncertain evidence within belief function theory. Int. J. Approximate Reasoning **182**, 109428 (2025). https://doi.org/10.1016/j.ijar.2025.109428
19. Pomeret-Coquot, P.: Jupyter notebook for the experiment. GitHub repository (2026). https://github.com/pPomCo/minEU. Accessed 01 Apr 2026
20. Savage, L.J.: The Foundations of Statistics. Wiley (1954). https://doi.org/10.1002/nav.3800010316
21. Schmeidler, D.: Integral representation without additivity. Proc. Am. Math. Soc. **97**(2), 255–261 (1986). https://doi.org/10.2307/2046508
22. Shafer, G.: A Mathematical Theory of Evidence. Princeton University Press (1976). https://doi.org/10.2307/j.ctv10vm1qb
23. Shafer, G.: Constructive probability. Synthese **48**(1), 1–60 (1981). https://doi.org/10.1007/BF01064627
24. Smets, P., Kennes, R.: The transferable belief model. Artif. Intell. **66**(2), 191–234 (1994). https://doi.org/10.1016/0004-3702(94)90026-4
25. Strat, T.M.: Decision analysis using belief functions. Int. J. Approximate Reasoning **4**(5–6), 391–417 (1990). https://doi.org/10.1016/0888-613X(90)90014-S
26. Walley, P.: Statistical Reasoning with Imprecise Probabilities. Chapman & Hall (1991)

Knowledge Representation and Modelling

Implicative Fuzzy Rules Systems in Water Quality Evaluation and Reasoning

Mārtiņš Zemlītis(✉) and Olga Grigorenko

University of Latvia, Riga, LV 1004, Latvia
martins.zemlitis@lu.lv, olga.grigorenko@lu.lv

Abstract. This study presents a framework for river water quality assessment using implicative fuzzy rule-based systems, designed to support decision-making under uncertainty. Building on the existing Latvian One-out–all-out approach, which evaluates water quality in a non-compensatory manner, our method models expert judgments of chemical indicators, such as dissolved oxygen, nitrogen, phosphorus, ammonium, and biochemical oxygen demand, using fuzzy sets. The proposed system preserves information near decision boundaries, addresses the subjectivity inherent in qualitative assessments, and ensures monotonicity, so that improvements in water quality indicators are reflected in higher evaluations. Results demonstrate the construction of fuzzy rules and the generation of outputs for payoff functions, enabling the estimation of costs associated with degraded water quality. This work lays the foundation for future evaluation of the Value of Information in water quality systems, providing a pathway toward more informed environmental management decisions.

Keywords: Implicative fuzzy rules systems · Water quality analysis systems · Payoff function

1 Introduction

This study proposes a modeling framework for river water quality assessment aimed at supporting subsequent decision-making processes. It addresses situations in which decisions are based on qualitative judgments provided by domain experts, who interpret quantitative measurements of water constituents, such as dissolved oxygen (O_2), total nitrogen (N), total phosphorus (P), ammonium (NH_4^+), and biochemical oxygen demand over five days (BSP_5), rather than relying on statistical analyses. To manage the uncertainty inherent in this type of information, an implicative fuzzy rule–based system is used, enabling the model to be constructed directly from qualitative expert assessments.

We use tables containing information on chemical measurements for rivers in Latvia, together with expert assessments that evaluate each parameter over the specified value ranges. For each interval, experts classify the water quality as very good, good, medium, bad, or very bad, which can alternatively be interpreted as very clean, clean, medium, dirty, or very dirty.

B. Vantaggi et al. (Eds.): IPMU 2026, CCIS 3019, pp. 279–290, 2026.
https://doi.org/10.1007/978-3-032-28994-0_20

The quality of water in a fixed river is deduced using rules in the form:

$$\text{AND} \begin{cases} \textbf{IF } P \text{ is Low and } N \text{ is Low and ... } \textbf{THEN } Y \text{ is Clean} \\ \textbf{IF } P \text{ is Low and } N \text{ is Medium and ... } \textbf{THEN } Y \text{ is Medium} \\ \ldots \\ \textbf{IF } P \text{ is High and } N \text{ is High and ... } \textbf{THEN } Y \text{ is Dirty} \end{cases} \tag{1}$$

The system is constructed in accordance with the One-out–all-out principle, as stipulated in the current Latvian regulations. Under this principle, the overall evaluation is non-compensatory: poor performance in any single criterion cannot be offset by better performance in others. Consequently, the final output corresponds to the worst individual evaluation.

While the current approach in Latvia is performed by evaluating crisp values, our aim is to develop an approach, that is similar to one described in [3], but with fuzzy sets. The crisp classification methods are inherently limited in their ability to handle the subjectivity and inherent vagueness in environmental measurements, leading to abrupt class changes and a loss of information when values fall near decision boundaries. Our interests in fuzzification of water quality evaluation stems from our current work, that deals with development of an alternative of Value of Information (VoI) [4], that uses fuzzy sets, instead of probability theory. Thus our overarching objective is to evaluate the Value of Information (VoI) for water quality assessment systems. In the context of river water quality, the VoI problem consists in quantifying the benefit of acquiring additional or more precise measurements of water quality indicators in order to reduce uncertainty, for example such as the One-out–all-out classification, and thereby improve environmental management decisions. In this paper, we focus on preliminary work toward the evaluation of the Value of Information in water quality assessment systems. Specifically, we develop and implement fuzzy rule-based systems and generate output values for payoff functions, which are subsequently used to evaluate costs associated with degraded or unclean water quality.

In VoI, one of our tasks is to define the payoff function, with respect to which the value is evaluated. This motives to develop the fuzzy approach, because, when performing actions with fuzzy values, we can retain all the information and only compress it (deffuzify it) when required, thus having the final evaluation based on all the possible information. The objective of this paper is to detail the methodology for constructing a fuzzy rule base, that is based on the principles of the crisp Latvian method, and to demonstrate how this system performs.

Looking back at the example rule base (1), such system can be expressed as aggregation of rules in form:

$$\textbf{IF } X \text{ is } A_i \textbf{ THEN } Y \text{ is } B_i \tag{2}$$

for $i \in 1, \ldots, n$, where n is the total number of rules. Let us denote the fuzzy sets of input domain as $\mathcal{F}(U)$. In our work, the set U contains all the relevant measurements of water for evaluating water quality and the set $\mathcal{F}(U)$ contains the fuzzy sets over this domain. Similarly, we define the fuzzy sets for output domain $\mathcal{F}(V)$. The fuzzy rule (2) can be modeled as a fuzzy relation $R_i \in \mathcal{F}(U \times V)$.

One of the approaches to model these fuzzy relations is the *Mamdani–Assilian* approach [5], that models R_i as conjunction using some T-norm: $R_i(x, y) = A_i(x) * B_i(y)$ and aggregates them, by taking maximum, thus:

$$\check{R}(x, y) = \bigvee_{i=1}^{n} A_i(x) * B_i(y). \tag{3}$$

In this work we do not investigate this approach due to lack of results, that would make it mathematically appealing.

Another widely used approach, which is particularly appealing due to its desirable theoretical properties, is the implicative model [6]. Instead of employing a T-norm for conjunction, this approach is based on implication, such that

$$R_i(x, y) = A_i(x) \to B_i(y),$$

and the individual relations are aggregated by taking the minimum:

$$\hat{R}(x, y) = \bigwedge_{i=1}^{n} A_i(x) \to B_i(y). \tag{4}$$

In this work, we are using the implicative approach to model the water quality. One of the key desirable properties of the implicative approach is monotonicity, which guarantees that for any two vectors of water quality indicators, if one vector dominates the other in terms of improved chemical conditions, then the resulting water quality evaluation is not worse.

The remainder of the paper is structured as follows. In the next section, we present the necessary mathematical background on implicative fuzzy rule-based systems and discuss their main properties. Section 3 describes the water quality evaluation framework, while Sect. 4 outlines the current implementation. In Sect. 5, we demonstrate the construction of the payoff function. Finally, conclusions are drawn in Sect. 6.

2 Preliminaries

For this work, we fix some residuated lattice $\mathcal{L} = \langle [0, 1], \wedge, \vee, *, \to, 0, 1 \rangle$, where $*$ is a left-continuous t-norm and its residual implication $\to$, which is defined as: $a \to b = sup\{x \in [0, 1] : a * x \leq b\}$. While the results stated further allow for an arbitrary t-norm, for our work we fix the t-norm as the Łukasiewicz t-norm.

Definition 1. *The Core and Support of a fuzzy set $A \in \mathcal{F}(U)$ are defined as:*
$Core(A) = \{x \ ; \ A(x) = 1\}$,
$Supp(A) = \{x \ ; \ A(x) > 0\}$.

Definition 2. *[1] A subset $\mathcal{C}$ of $F(U)$ is called a fuzzy covering of U if*

$$\bigcup_{A \in \mathcal{C}} Supp(A) = U.$$

Definition 3. *[1] Let $\mathcal{C} = \{A_1, \ldots, A_K\}$ be a linearly ordered set of normal convex fuzzy sets such that $\text{Core}(A_k) = [a_k^L, a_k^R]$. If $\mathcal{C}$ is a fuzzy covering of U, then it is called*

1. *a **strong** (or 1-strong) fuzzy covering of U if for any $k = 1, \ldots, K-1$ it holds that*
$$A_k(x) + A_{k+1}(x) \geq 1 \tag{5}$$
for any $x \in [a_k^R, a_{k+1}^L]$;
2. *a p-**strong** fuzzy covering of U, with $p \in \mathbb{N}, p \geq 2$, if it is $(p-1)$-strong and if for any $k = 1, \ldots, K-p$ it holds that*
$$A_k(x) + A_{k+p}(x) \geq 1 \tag{6}$$
for any $x \in [a_k^R, a_{k+p}^L]$.

Definition 4. 1. *The function $FoM(A) = \inf Core(A)$ is called the **first of maxima defuzzification function.***
2. *The function $LoM(A) = \sup Core(A)$ is called the **last of maxima defuzzification function.***
3. *The function $MoM(A) = \frac{FoM(A)+LoM(A)}{2}$ is called the **mean of maxima defuzzification function.***

We consider a fuzzy rule base with m input variables and a single output variable, i.e. a fuzzy rule base consisting of rules of the type:

$$\textbf{IF } X_1 \text{ is } A_{i_1}^1 \textbf{ AND} \ldots \textbf{AND} X_m \text{ is } A_{i_m}^m, \textbf{THEN } Y \text{ is } B_{\varphi(i_1,\ldots,i_m)} \tag{7}$$

where $i_s \in \{1, \ldots, n_s\}$ for $s = 1, \ldots, m$, and $\varphi(i_1, \ldots, i_m) \in \{1, \ldots, r\}$. Each input variable X_s, $s = 1, \ldots, m$, $U = U_1 \times U_2 \times \ldots \times U_m$ takes values in a universe U_s, while the output variable Y takes values in a universe V.

Definition 5. *[1] Let $C \in \mathcal{F}(U)$, then the fuzzy sets $C^{\uparrow}, C^{\downarrow} \in \mathcal{F}(U)$ are defined by*

- $C^{\uparrow}(x) = \sup\{C(t) \mid t \in U \textit{ and } t \leq x\}$
- $C^{\downarrow}(x) = \sup\{C(t) \mid t \in U \textit{ and } t \geq x\}$

In the image 1 the examples of both $At - Most$ and $At - Least$ are shown.

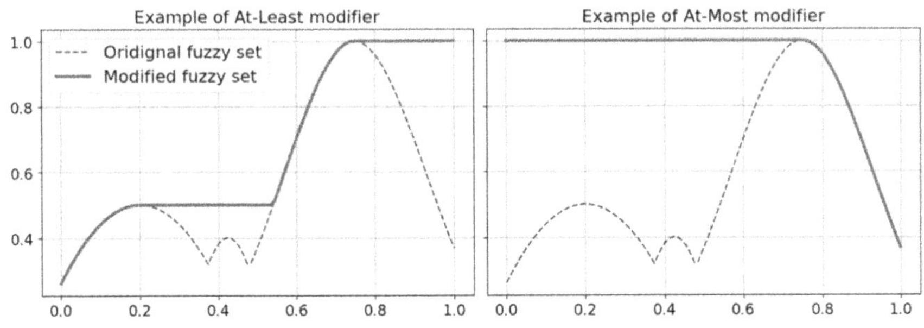

Fig. 1. Examples of $At - Least$ and $At - Most$ modifiers

Definition 6. *[1] Consider fuzzy rule base (7). The corresponding "**at least**" (**ATL** for short) fuzzy rule base consists of the following fuzzy rules:*

$$\textbf{\textit{IF}}\ X_1\ \textbf{\textit{is}}\ (A^1_{i_1})^{\uparrow}\ \textbf{\textit{AND}}\ \ldots\ \textbf{\textit{AND}}\ X_m\ \textbf{\textit{is}}\ (A^m_{i_m})^{\uparrow},\ \textbf{\textit{THEN}}\ Y\ \textbf{\textit{is}}\ B^{\uparrow}_{\varphi(i_1,\ldots,i_m)}.$$

These rules can be modeled by the fuzzy relation $R^{\uparrow}_{(i_1,\ldots,i_m)} \in \mathcal{F}(U \times V)$ given by

$$R^{\uparrow}_{(i_1,\ldots,i_m)}(x_1,\ldots,x_m,y) = \left((A^1_{i_1})^{\uparrow}(x_1) \wedge \cdots \wedge (A^m_{i_m})^{\uparrow}(x_m)\right) \rightarrow B^{\uparrow}_{\varphi(i_1,\ldots,i_m)}(y).$$

The ATL fuzzy rule base is then modelled by the fuzzy relation $R^{\uparrow} \in \mathcal{F}(U \times V)$ given by

$$R^{\uparrow}(x_1,\ldots,x_m,y) = \bigwedge_{i_1=1}^{n_1} \cdots \bigwedge_{i_m=1}^{n_m} R^{\uparrow}_{(i_1,\ldots,i_m)}(x_1,\ldots,x_m,y).$$

The definition for rule base for "at most" (**ATM** for short) and fuzzy relation $R^{\uparrow} \in \mathcal{F}(U \times V)$ is defined similarly.

Definition 7. *[1] Consider fuzzy rule base (12). The corresponding "**at least-at most**" (**ATLM** for short) fuzzy rule base consists of the 2n rules given by (13) and (14) and is modelled by the fuzzy relation $R^{\uparrow} \in \mathcal{F}(U \times V)$ given by*

$$R^{\updownarrow}(x_1,\ldots,x_m,y) = R^{\downarrow}(x_1,\ldots,x_m,y) \wedge R^{\uparrow}(x_1,\ldots,x_m,y). \tag{8}$$

In this work, each membership function corresponds to quality measure, for example, **Good** or **Bad**. in other words, they form a linear order and thus we can speak of monotone and smooth rule bases. If $A_{i_1} \preceq A_{i_2}$ correspond this linear order, then for a monotone rule base, we expect for inequality to hold for output $B_{\varphi(i_1)} \preceq B_{\varphi(i_2)}$. For a smooth rule base, we expect for $\varphi(i_1 + 1) = \varphi(i_1) + p$, where $p = \{0, 1\}$. In other words, looking at better quality membership function at input should translate to looking at not worse quality ones at output. The definitions for a smooth and monotone rule bases used in this work can be found at [1].

Definition 8. *[1] An implicative model R of fuzzy rule base is called* **coherent** *if for any $(x_1, \ldots, x_m) \in U_1 \times \cdots \times U_m$ there exists $y \in V$ such that $R(x_1, \ldots, x_m, y) = 1$.*

Theorem 1. *[1] Consider fuzzy rule base (7). The fuzzy relations $R^{\uparrow}$ and $R^{\downarrow}$ are coherent. Moreover, the resulting functions $\mathrm{FoM}(R^{\uparrow}(x_1, \ldots, x_m, \cdot))$ and $\mathrm{LoM}(R^{\downarrow}(x_1, \ldots, x_m, \cdot))$ are monotone.*

Corollary 1. *[1] Consider a fuzzy rule base (7) such that $R^{\updownarrow}$ is coherent. The resulting function $\mathrm{MoM}(R^{\uparrow}(x_1, \ldots, x_m, \cdot))$ is monotone.*

The previous results are valid for a single rule (7), if we modify it by both ATM and ATL modifiers. But if we consider such rules getting aggregated, we might lose the Coherence.

Theorem 2. *[1] The fuzzy relation $R^{\updownarrow} \in \mathcal{F}(U_1 \times \cdots \times U_m \times V)$ is coherent for any smooth monotone fuzzy rule base (7 and the corresponding* ATLM *fuzzy rule base if and only if the consequent fuzzy sets form an m-strong fuzzy covering of V.*

Theorem 3. *[2] Suppose that, for all $i \in \{1, \ldots, n_j\}$ and $j \in \{1, \ldots, m\}$ (and $k \in \{1, \ldots, k\}$), the antecedent fuzzy sets $A_i^j \in \mathcal{F}(U)$ are continuous and the consequent fuzzy sets $B_k \in \mathcal{F}(V)$ are continuous, normal, and strictly convex. Further assume that R is coherent. Then the functions $FoM(R)$ and $Lom(R^{\updownarrow})$ (and consequently $MoM(R)$ too) are continuous if, for all indexes, at least one of the following properties holds:*

1. $\overline{\mathrm{Supp}(A_i^j)} = U_j$,
2. $\overline{\mathrm{Supp}(B_k)} = V$,

Because of the Ruspini's condition, we cannot have the first condition, but because for the consequent membership functions, it is not required, that they form a Ruspini's condition, it is quite simple to have $\overline{\mathrm{Supp}(B_k)} = V$, by taking B_k as the Gaussian membership function. But because of the Theorem (2), we are required to make some changes to these Gaussian membership function, so that they form a m-strong covering.

3 Water Quality Evaluation

As mentioned in the introduction, the current evaluation of water quality is performed using crisp values. In this work, we only consider such measurements as: $O_2, N_{total}, P_{total}, NH_4^+, BSP_5$, and evaluation of smaller rivers. The evaluation follows the *One out - all out* principle. In other words, the final evaluation is equal to the worst individual evaluation, that is, in Eq. (7), the mapping φ is chosen to be **max**. In the Table 1 it is shown, how the evaluation is done for each measurement. Based on the measured value, in which interval it falls in, the respective quality is assigned.

Table 1. The quality intervals of each measurement.

Meas.	VG	G	M	B	VB
O_2	>8	6,0 – 8,0	4,0 – 6,0	2,0 – 4,0	<2
BSP_5	<2,0	2,0 – 2,5	2,5 – 3,0	3,0 – 3,5	>3,5
$N/NH_4{}^+$	0,09	0,09 – 0,12	0,12 – 0,15	0,15 – 0,18	>0,18
N_{total}	<1,5	1,5 – 2,0	2,0 – 2,5	2,5 – 3,0	>3,0
P_{total}	<0,04	0,04 – 0,065	0,065 – 0,090	0,090 – 0,115	>0,115

Table 2. Example of evaluation on sample *G*327.

Station name	O_2	BSP_5	$N/NH_4{}^+$	N_{total}	P_{total}	Final quality
Gosupe, grīva	7,95	1,89	0,143	2,7	0,074	**Bad** (4)

If we look at example (2), the final evaluation is **Bad**, because the measurement for the Nitrogen falls in the interval with evaluation **Bad**.

One can see the issue from this one example, if we care about the evaluation of water quality in order to determine the possible cost of cleaning this water body, the current approach will give a very pessimistic result. That is, if we consider example of all measurements being **Very Bad** and a water body with only one being **Very Bad** and other being **Very Good**, they both will be evaluated as having the same quality, while it would make sense to assume, that cleaning one type of pollution is cheaper, to clean all of them.

4 Current Implementation

In order to construct the fuzzy rule system, we first must define the membership functions for the input and output values.

4.1 Membership Functions for Input

We construct the membership functions for input values based on the intervals given by the current quality evaluation. We define the membership function (triangle function) such that their Core is the middle of respective interval. For example, looking at the Table (1), for membership function corresponding to quality **Medium**, the core is 2.25. To have Ruspini's partition, the triangle is defined as $(1.75, 2.25, 2.75)$. For the membership function for both end values, that have only lower and upper bounds for the intervals. We assume, that the membership functions are distributed uniformly and, for example, in (Table 1), for **Very Bad**, we assume, that the interval is $(1.25, 1.5)$. We note that, for the end values we have one sided triangles and for very extreme values, that might fall outside our assumed intervals, we simply project them back.

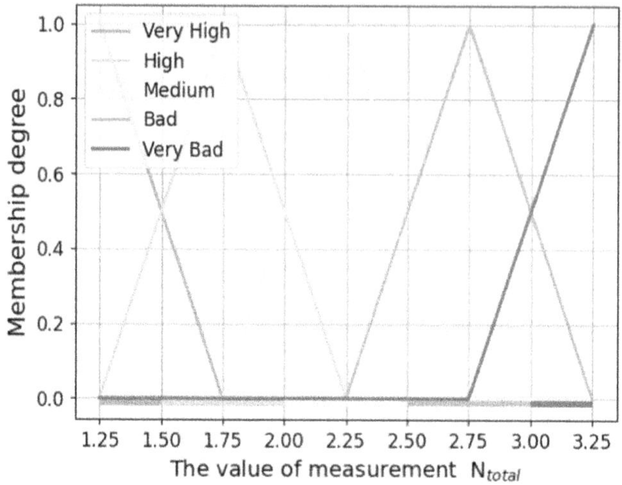

Fig. 2. The membership function for N_{total}

For example, if a Nitrogen values would fall below 1.25 (outside the defined interval seen in 2), we simply project it back to the 1.25.[1]

4.2 Membership Functions for Output

When it comes to choosing the type of membership functions for the output, these functions have to satisfy more criteria. They have to both perform an m-strong covering and their support has to be equal to the whole output domain. For these reasons, we chose to use the Gaussian membership functions visualized in Fig. 3.

4.3 Resulting Water Quality Evaluation

When applying the described system to the date in Table 2, the output is seen in the Fig. 4. We can see, that the Mean of Maxima defuziffication falls inside the **Bad** quality evaluation, but it is not too far off from being in **Medium** quality.

5 From Water Quality to Payoff

One of the motivations for construction of this system was to acquire a water quality in order to evaluate a payoff function. For now, we consider a simple function that depends on whether or not we decide to clean the water body and the water quality itself. Because once we introduce fuzzy evaluation of water

[1] The code for making all the calculations and plots in this work can be found at https://github.com/maartinjshz/Fuzzy-Rule-Base.

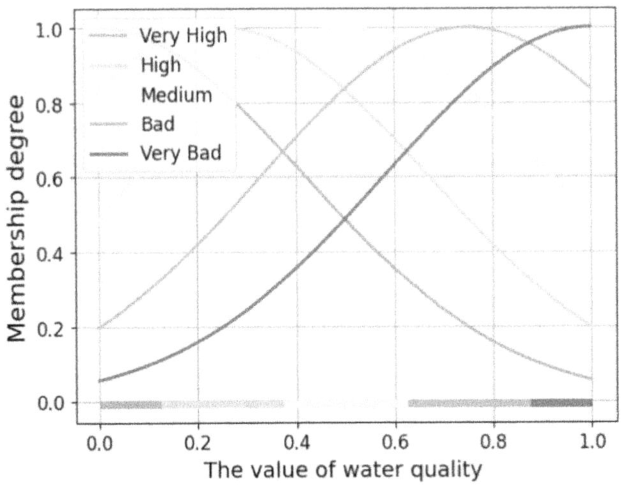

Fig. 3. The membership functions for output

quality, we cannot tell, if the water is good or bad, so we cannot define the payoff function the same way as in the crisp setting [7].

$$v(\mu, u) = \begin{cases} N \cdot (1-\mu), & \text{if } u = 0 \text{ (no action is taken)} \\ N - \mu \cdot c, & \text{if } u = 1 \text{ (action to clean water is taken)} \end{cases} \tag{9}$$

where N and c are some fuzzy numbers and μ is the water quality. This function evaluates the payoff based on water quality and if the decision to clean the water is made ($u = 1$) or not ($u = 0$). When calculating the function value using the number in Fig. 4, we get numbers seen in the Fig. 5. For the final evaluation, we want to choose the one, that gives the most payoff. Because we have a discrete function, we propose to simply compare the defuziffied values of the fuzzy numbers, to choose the biggest one. In this example, the numbers N, c were chosen as triangle numbers, where $N = (80, 100, 120)$ and $c = (30, 45, 60)$. Here, the N is the payoff that we would get, if the water was clean and c is the cost for cleaning the water.

Another experiment we ran was to see, how changing the numbers N, c would affect the final payoff. We fixed the center for both triangles to be $N_{min} = 100$ and $c_{mid} = 45$ and changed the size of the support for both numbers. The results can be seen in the Fig. 6. On the Y-axis, the values should be interpreted as - $(c_{mid} - c_i, c_{min}, c_{mid} + c_i)$ and similarly for X-axis. We can see that on top left corner, the values changes, because $N - \mu c$ is bigger, than $N\mu$, while on right side, the $N\mu$ gets bigger and thus the values does not depend on c anymore. Here, we defuzzified the values using the Center of Gravity defuzification, simply because using Mean of Maxima gives the same output no matter what the support of the numbers is, the MoM stays the same. We did run numerical tests for monotonicity of CoG and they did not fail.

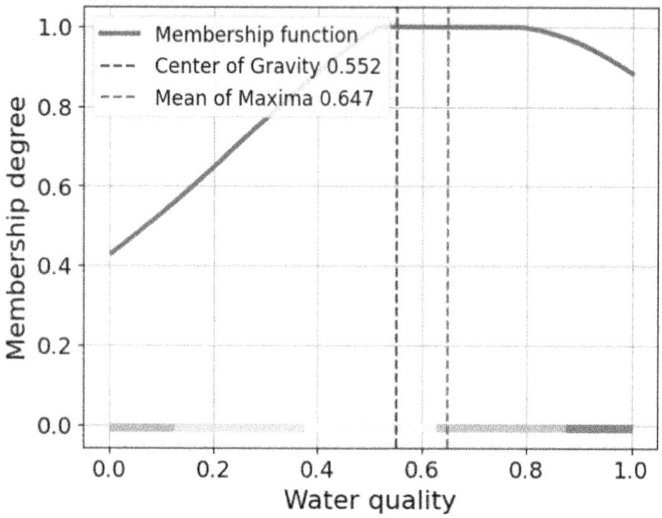

Fig. 4. The waterquality of Gosupe

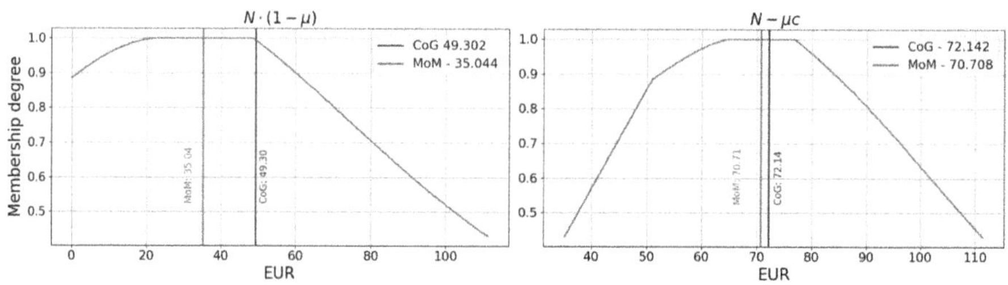

Fig. 5. The payoff values of Gosupe example

6 Conclusions

In this work, we showed how to perform fuzzy water quality evaluation, that mimics the crisp case, using the methodology used for rivers in Latvia. To achieve this, we constructed fuzzy rule system, that uses implicative rules with modifiers, in order to have monotonicity. We used gaussian membership functions for modeling the consequent, because that makes the system continuous. And for the system to be coherent, we want these consequent gaussian functions to perform a p-strong covering. We also showed, that if we have less consequent membership functions, than input dimensions, the theorem still holds.

While the monotonicity of MoM defuzzification is ensured, this method of defuzzification is not satisfactory, because when calculating the payoff values with water quality evaluation, the final result does not change on the number as a whole, but only based on its Core. This was shown in Fig. 6, where MoM

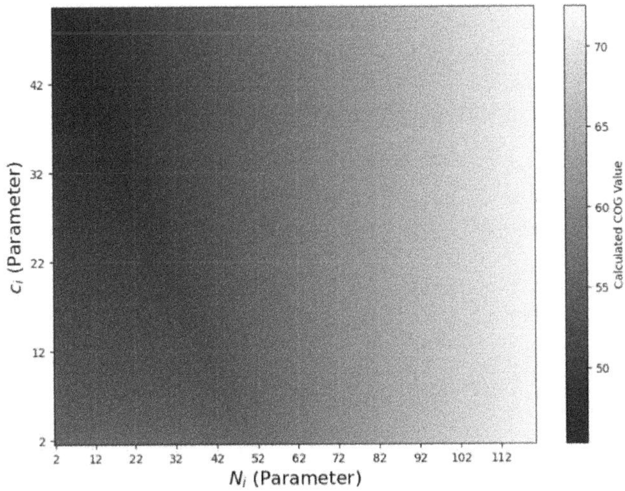

Fig. 6. The evaluation of payoff for different cost values

would just make the same values not matter how big or small was the support of the numbers.

One of the issues not discussed previously is that in some cases, this system gives unsatisfactory results. For example, if we were to consider a case, where one water body has all measurements **Very Bad**, while another has all **Very Good** besides one, that is **Very Bad**, this system would evaluate both of these the same. Which, if we consider the costs of cleaning these water bodies, it would make more sense, that having just one parameter as **Very Bad** will cost less, than cleaning all of them. And it can be seen in data, that a lot of rivers have **Very Bad** evaluation of Nitrogen levels, while other parameters are good.

Acknowledgments. This research is funded by the Latvian Council of Science, project "A fuzzy logic-based approach to the value of information estimation in optimal control problems under uncertainty with applications to ecological management", Project No. lzp-2024/1-0188.

References

1. Štěpnička, M., De Baets, B.: Implication-based models of monotone fuzzy rule bases. Fuzzy Sets Syst. **232**, 134–155 (2013). https://doi.org/10.1016/j.fss.2013.01.011
2. Štěpnička, M., Bodenhofer, U., Daňková, M., Novák, V.: Continuity issues of the implicational interpretation of fuzzy rules. Fuzzy Sets Syst. **161**(14), 1959–1972 (2010). https://doi.org/10.1016/j.fss.2009.12.008
3. Vides, L.: ģeoloģijas un meteoroloģijas centrs: Pārskats par virszemes un pazemes ūdeņu stāvokli 2023. gadā (2024). https://videscentrs.lvgmc.lv/lapas/udens-kvalitate. Accessed 3 Feb 2026

4. Howard, R.A.: Information value theory. IEEE Trans. Syst. Sci. Cybern. **2**(1), 22–26 (1966). https://doi.org/10.1109/TSSC.1966.300074
5. Mamdani, E.H., Assilian, S.: An experiment in linguistic synthesis with a fuzzy logic controller. Int. J. Man-Mach. Stud. **7**(1), 1–13 (1975). https://doi.org/10.1016/S0020-7373(75)80002-2
6. Bodenhofer, U., Dankova, M., Stepnicka, M., Novak, V.: A plea for the usefulness of the deductive interpretation of fuzzy rules in engineering applications. In: 2007 IEEE International Fuzzy Systems Conference, pp. 1–6 (2007). https://doi.org/10.1109/FUZZY.2007.4295600
7. Luhede, A., Yaqine, H., Bahmanbijari, R., Römer, M., Upmann, T.: The value of information in water quality monitoring and management. Ecol. Econ. **219**, 108128 (2024). https://doi.org/10.1016/j.ecolecon.2024.108128

Bipolar Max-Product Equations with Ceiling Negation

David Lobo(✉) and Pablo López-Molina

Department of Mathematics, University of Cádiz, Cádiz, Spain
{david.lobo,pablo.lopezmolina}@uca.es

Abstract. This work introduces the notion of ceiling negation, a modification of a negation operator which coincides with the original negation above a certain threshold, and takes the maximum value 1 below that threshold. Bipolar max-product equations with ceiling negations will be studied afterwards, with a particular focus on their solvability and the existence and determination of maximal and minimal solutions.

Keywords: bipolar equations · max-product composition · ceiling negation · involutive negation

1 Introduction

A fuzzy relation equation (FRE) models the composition of two fuzzy relations, one of which is unknown, leading to a third fuzzy relation. The problem consists of determining the unknown fuzzy relation, which is usually solved according to the properties of the underlying partially ordered set and the composition operator. The theory of FRE emerged in 1976 under the assumption of fuzzy relations in the unit interval and a max-min composition operator [21]. After this seminal work, the topic focused on the resolution of FRE in general frameworks, such as FRE defined in lattices with different families of composition operators [2, 9,11,20], in parallel with applying FRE in a broad variety of fields [1,3,8,13,18, 19].

In 2013, involved in the context of an optimization problem, bipolar fuzzy relation equations (BFRE) were introduced as a generalization of FRE [14]. In the theory of BFRE, usually referred to as bipolar equations, the unknown fuzzy relation appears together with its negation, so that the properties of the negation operator directly affect to the resolution of the problem. The work developed in [14] considers bipolar equations defined with max-min composition and the standard negation, which is the most common involutive negation in the literature. Similarly to the non-bipolar case, many studies have addressed the solvability of bipolar equations defined with different operators, like the max-product composition [4,5,17], although most of them maintain the hypothesis of involutivity in the negation operator [16,22–24].

The fact that bipolar equations are usually defined with involutive negations significantly reduces their generality, and therefore the scope of applications. This

B. Vantaggi et al. (Eds.): IPMU 2026, CCIS 3019, pp. 291–302, 2026.
https://doi.org/10.1007/978-3-032-28994-0_21

motivates the research carried out in this paper, which handles the resolution of bipolar equations defined with max-product composition and ceiling negations, a new uniparametric family of non-involutive negations. These negations are introduced here as a modification of an involutive negation such that it takes the value 1 on elements below a preset threshold, while above this threshold it coincides with the underlying involutive negation. The resolution study includes a characterization of the solvability of bipolar equations with ceiling negations and a characterization of the greatest, least, maximal and minimal solutions.

2 Motivation

In this section, we recall the notion of bipolar equation and present the motivation of this work. In the first place, we recall the notions of residuated pair and negation operator.

Definition 1. *[15] Given two mappings* $*, \leftarrow : [0,1] \times [0,1] \to [0,1]$*, we say that* $\leftarrow$ *is the residuated implication of* $*$ *and* $(*, \leftarrow)$ *is a residuated pair if, for any* $x, y, z \in [0,1]$*, the adjoint property is satisfied, that is:*

$$y \leq z \leftarrow x \quad \textit{if and only if} \quad x * y \leq z$$

Example 1. The product residuated pair $(*, \leftarrow_P)$ is formed by the following operators:

$$x * y = x \cdot y \qquad \textit{(product operator)}$$

$$z \leftarrow_P x = \begin{cases} 1 & \text{if } x \leq z \\ \dfrac{z}{x} & \text{otherwise} \end{cases} \qquad \textit{(residuated implication of } *\textit{)}$$

Definition 2. *Let* $\neg \colon [0,1] \to [0,1]$ *be a mapping. We say that* $\neg$ *is a negation operator if it is order-reversing and* $\neg(0) = 1$*,* $\neg(1) = 0$*. Moreover,* $\neg$ *is an involutive negation if* $\neg \circ \neg(x) = x$*, for all* $x \in [0,1]$*.*

In the absence of any ambiguity, we will consider $\neg x$ instead of $\neg(x)$.

Example 2. The mappings $\neg_S, \neg_Y, \neg_P \colon [0,1] \to [0,1]$, given as follows, are negation operators:

$$\neg_S x = 1 - x \qquad \textit{(Standard negation)}$$

$$\neg_Y x = \sqrt{1 - x^2} \qquad \textit{(Yager negation)}$$

$$\neg_P x = \begin{cases} 1 \text{ if } x = 0 \\ 0 \text{ if } x > 0 \end{cases} \qquad \textit{(Product negation)}$$

The following definition presents the notion of bipolar equation.

Definition 3. *Let $(*, \leftarrow)$ be a residuated pair and $\neg$ a negation operator. A bipolar equation is an expression of the form:*

$$\bigvee_{j=1}^{m} (a_j^+ * x_j) \vee (a_j^- * \neg x_j) = b \tag{1}$$

where $x_1, \ldots, x_m$ are unknown variables and $a_j^+, a_j^-, b \in [0,1]$, $j \in \{1, \ldots, m\}$.

The underlying idea of a bipolar equation is that both the presence, that is high values, and the absence, that is low values, of the unknown variables have an influence on the right-hand side of the equation. In other words, for each variable x, both expressions $a^+ * x$ (presence of relation) and $a^- * \neg x$ (absence of relation) are being taken into account to determine the independent term b.

In the vast majority of studies on bipolar equations carried out in the literature, an involutive negation is considered. This prevents the equation from modelling some situations like the toy example presented below.

Suppose that we want to model the instability level of a patient undergoing treatment against an illness, where the following statements must be taken into account:

i) An excessively high concentration of medication has some secondary effects, progressively increasing the patient's instability.
ii) In general, the instability of the patient decreases proportionally with respect to the treatment concentration.
iii) There exists a minimum treatment concentration under which the treatment has no positive effect on the patient. In this case, the disease will continue, increasing the patient's instability to its maximum value.

Let $x \in [0,1]$ represent the concentration of medication the patient is receiving. According to statement i), we can model the instability of the patient due to secondary effects as $a^+ * x$, where a^+ symbolizes how an excess of medication progressively affects the patient's instability.

Now, if $a^- \in [0,1]$ is the maximum possible instability, which is obtained when the patient receives no treatment, we can model the instability related to statement ii) employing a negation operator $\neg$ as $a^- * \neg x$. As a result, taking into account both statements i) and ii), the patient's instability can be represented as $(a^+ * x) \vee (a^- * \neg x)$.

Finally, if $\alpha \in [0,1]$ is the minimum treatment concentration, any concentration value $x < \alpha$ should lead to the maximum patient's instability a^-, similarly to the case $x = 0$. As a consequence, if we want the expression $(a^+ * x) \vee (a^- * \neg x)$ to properly model the three statements i), ii) and iii), $\neg x$ should be 1 for any element $x \in [0, \alpha[$. This requires the use of a non-injective negation, and therefore a non-involutive negation.

As a first approach to the investigation of bipolar equations with non-involutive negations, we introduce below the concept of ceiling negation, a uniparametric family of non-involutive negations which coincide with an involutive negation except for values under a certain threshold, in which case they take the value 1.

More precisely, given a threshold $\alpha \in [0,1]$ and a negation operator $\neg$, the image of any element $x \in [0,1]$ with $x < \alpha$ by the α-ceiling negation of $\neg$ is 1, while the image of any element $x \in [0,1]$ with $x \geq \alpha$ coincides with $\neg x$.

Definition 4. *Let $\neg$ be an involutive negation and $\alpha \in [0,1]$. The α-ceiling negation of $\neg$ is the mapping $\neg^\alpha \colon [0,1] \to [0,1]$ given as:*

$$\neg^\alpha x = \begin{cases} 1 & \text{if } x < \alpha \\ \neg x & \text{if } x \geq \alpha \end{cases}$$

The following result states that the α-ceiling negation of an involutive negation is, indeed, a negation operator.

Proposition 1. *Let $\neg$ be an involutive negation and $\alpha \in [0,1]$, then the α-ceiling negation of $\neg$ is a negation operator.*

3 Solving Bipolar Max-Product Equations with a Ceiling Negation

In what follows, we will focus on studying the solvability of a bipolar max-product equation defined with a ceiling negation, that is an expression of the form:

$$\bigvee_{j=1}^{m} (a_j^+ * x_j) \vee (a_j^- * \neg^\alpha x_j) = b \tag{2}$$

where $\neg^\alpha$ is the α-ceiling negation of an involutive negation $\neg$ and $*$ is the usual product operator. From here on, the residuated implication of $*$ will be denoted as $\leftarrow$.

The results presented in this section are founded upon the resolution strategy presented in [6,7], which is applicable to bipolar equations defined with an involutive negation and a residuated pair under certain requirements. Following such approach, in order to characterize the solvability of (2), the following two tuples are defined:

$$g^+ = (b \leftarrow a_1^+, \ldots, b \leftarrow a_m^+)$$

$$\neg g^- = (\neg(b \leftarrow a_1^-), \ldots, \neg(b \leftarrow a_m^-))$$

One of the main results of [7] proves that a bipolar equation with involutive negation is solvable if and only if g^+ is a solution or $\neg g^-$ is a solution. Nevertheless, this characterization is not valid for bipolar equations with non-involutive negations. In particular, it does not hold for bipolar equations with ceiling negations. The following example illustrates that, indeed, it is not possible to characterize the solvability of Eq. (2) exclusively in terms of the tuples g^+ and $\neg g^-$.

Example 3. Consider the 2/3-ceiling negation of the standard negation (Example 2), which is defined as follows:

$$\neg^{2/3} x = \begin{cases} 1 & \text{if } x < \frac{2}{3} \\ \neg_S x & \text{if } x \geq \frac{2}{3} \end{cases}$$

Let the following bipolar max-product equation defined with the 2/3-ceiling negation of the standard negation:

$$(0.2 * x_1) \vee (0.8 * \neg^{2/3} x_1) \vee (0.1 * x_2) \vee (0.4 * \neg^{2/3} x_2) = 0.4 \qquad (3)$$

The corresponding tuples g^+ and $\neg_S g^-$ are given by:

$$\begin{aligned} g^+ &= (0.4 \leftarrow 0.2, 0.4 \leftarrow 0.1) \\ &= (1, 1) \\ \neg_S g^- &= (\neg_S(0.4 \leftarrow 0.8), \neg_S(0.4 \leftarrow 0.4)) \\ &= (\neg_S 0.5, \neg_S 1) \\ &= (0.5, 0) \end{aligned}$$

A simple evaluation reveals that none of the tuples g^+ or $\neg_S g^-$ is a solution of Eq. 3:

$$(0.2 * 1) \vee (0.8 * \neg^{2/3} 1) \vee (0.1 * 1) \vee (0.4 * \neg^{2/3} 1) = 0.2 \vee 0 \vee 0.1 \vee 0 = 0.2$$

$$(0.2 * 0.5) \vee (0.8 * \neg^{2/3} 0.5) \vee (0.1 * 0) \vee (0.4 * \neg^{2/3} 0) = 0.1 \vee 0.8 \vee 0 \vee 0.4 = 0.8$$

Nevertheless, one can easily verify that Eq. 3 is solvable. For instance, the tuple $(g_1^+, \neg g_2^-) = (1, 0)$ is a solution of Eq. 3:

$$(0.2 * 1) \vee (0.8 * \neg^{2/3} 1) \vee (0.1 * 0) \vee (0.4 * \neg^{2/3} 0) = 0.2 \vee 0 \vee 0 \vee 0.4 = 0.4$$

Therefore, the characterization presented in [7] for the solvability of bipolar equations with involutive negations is not fulfilled for bipolar equations with ceiling negations.

□

As illustrated in Example 3, it is not possible to characterize the solvability of bipolar equations with the product operator and a ceiling negation in terms of tuples g^+ and $\neg g^-$, in contrast to the situation for bipolar equations endowed with an involutive negation [7]. This is a crucial difference between the two studies, which also serves to illustrate the usefulness of the involutive property.

Paying attention to the counterexample presented in Example 3, the solution $(g_1^+, \neg g_2^-)$ shown thereupon is actually a combination of the tuples g^+ and

$\neg g^-$. This fact motivates the next theorem, which characterizes the solvability of bipolar equations with the product operator and a ceiling negation in terms of certain combinations of the tuples g^+ and $\neg g^-$.

Theorem 1. *Equation* (2) *is solvable if and only if either g^+ is a solution or there is $k \in \{1,\dots,m\}$ such that $b \leq a_k^-$ and $(g_1^+,\dots,g_{k-1}^+,\neg g_k^-,g_{k+1}^+,\dots,g_m^+)$ is a solution.*

Theorem 1 simplifies the process of determining whether a bipolar equation with product operator and a ceiling negation is solvable as a direct evaluation of, at most, $m+1$ tuples. It is important to note that, despite the fact that Theorem 1 provides a characterization of solvability in terms of the tuples g^+ and g^- , the number of evaluations has increased considerably with respect to the case of bipolar equations with involutive negations, where only the evaluation of two tuples is required [7]. Below, an alternative characterization to Theorem 1 will be presented, where the solvability of a bipolar equation with ceiling negation is characterized in terms of the evaluation of just two tuples.

As shown in [10–12], a (non-bipolar) fuzzy equation defined with a residuated composition is solvable if and only if its corresponding tuple g^+ is a solution. Therefore, it seems natural that if the solvability of (2) can be characterized in terms of the evaluation of two tuples, then g^+ must be one of them. The idea now comes from defining a mapping ϕ so that the characterization is established exclusively in terms of the tuples g^+ and $\phi(g^-)$. Clearly, according to Example 3, the mapping ϕ cannot coincide with the underlying involutive negation $\neg$. Indeed, a feasible mapping ϕ consists of modifying the involutive negation $\neg$ in a similar manner to a ceiling negation. Formally, we define the mapping $\overset{\alpha}{\neg}\colon [0,1] \to [0,1]$ as follows:

$$\overset{\alpha}{\neg} x = \begin{cases} \neg x & \text{if } x \leq \neg\alpha \text{ or } x = 1 \\ 1 & \text{otherwise} \end{cases}$$

As shown below, the solvability of Eq. (2) can be characterized in terms of the following tuples:

$$g^+ = (b \leftarrow a_1^+, \dots, b \leftarrow a_m^+)$$

$$\overset{\alpha}{\neg} g^- = (\overset{\alpha}{\neg}(b \leftarrow a_1^-), \dots, \overset{\alpha}{\neg}(b \leftarrow a_m^-))$$

Theorem 2. *Equation* (2) *is solvable if and only if either g^+ is a solution or $\overset{\alpha}{\neg} g^-$ is a solution.*

As intended, Theorem 2 enables to reduce the problem of determining the solvability of a bipolar max-product equation with ceiling negation to a straightforward evaluation of exclusively two tuples g^+ and $\overset{\alpha}{\neg} g^-$.

Note that, in comparison with Theorem 1, Theorem 2 simplifies the process of checking whether a bipolar max-product equation with a ceiling negation is solvable or not. In fact, the following algorithm provides a recipe for studying the solvability of a bipolar equation of the form (2) according to Theorem 2:

Algorithm 1: Resolution method for bipolar max-product equations defined with ceiling negations

---

Input: Bipolar max-product equation with ceiling negation
Output: **True** if the bipolar equation is solvable, **False** otherwise

Compute the tuple g^+;
Evaluate the tuple g^+ ;
if *g^+ is a solution* **then**
    return True;
else
    Compute the tuple $\overset{\alpha}{\neg} g^-$;
    Evaluate the tuple $\overset{\alpha}{\neg} g^-$;
    if *$\overset{\alpha}{\neg} g^-$ is a solution* **then**
        return True;
    else
        return False;
    end
end

As aforementioned, Theorem 2 states that checking the solvability of a bipolar max-product equation defined with a ceiling negation can be reduced to evaluating two predefined tuples, which means that the number of operations required to determine whether a bipolar equation is solvable or not, is very low or negligible. In particular, Algorithm 1 runs in $O(m)$ time where m denotes the number of unknown variables.

The following example illustrates the usefulness of Theorems 1 and 2.

Example 4. Consider the 1/2-ceiling negation of the Yager negation (Example 2) given as:

$$\overset{1/2}{\neg} x = \begin{cases} 1 & \text{if } x < 1/2 \\ \sqrt{1-x^2} & \text{if } x \geq 1/2 \end{cases}$$

In this example, we will discuss the solvability of the following bipolar max-product equation with 1/2-ceiling negation:

$$(0.2 * x_1) \vee (0.8 * \overset{1/2}{\neg} x_1) \vee (0.5 * x_2) \vee (0.4 * \overset{1/2}{\neg} x_2) = 0.75 \tag{4}$$

In this example, we will study the solvability of Eq. (4) by applying both Theorems 1 and 2. In this case, both theorems lead to the evaluation of two tuples.

On the one hand, basing on Theorem 1, we can determine the solvability of Eq. (4) is solvable by checking the tuples g^+ and $(\neg_Y g_1^-, g_2^+)$, which are respectively given by:

$$g^+ = (0.75 \leftarrow 0.2, 0.75 \leftarrow 0.5) = (1, 1)$$

$$\neg_Y g^- = (\neg_Y(0.75 \leftarrow 0.8), \neg_Y(0.75 \leftarrow 0.4)) = (\neg_Y 0.9375, \neg_Y 1) = (\neg_Y 0.9375, 0)$$

Making the corresponding computation, we obtain that none of the previous tuples are solutions of (4):

$$(0.2 * 1) \vee (0.8 * \neg^{1/2} 1) \vee (0.5 * 1) \vee (0.4 * \neg^{1/2} 1) = 0.2 \vee 0 \vee 0.5 \vee 0 = 0.5$$

$$(0.2 * \neg_Y g_1^-) \vee (0.8 * \neg^{1/2} \neg_Y g_1^-) \vee (0.5 * 1) \vee (0.4 * \neg^{1/2} 1) = 0.07 \vee 0.8 \vee 0.5 \vee 0 = 0.8$$

Therefore, applying Theorem 1, we conclude that (3) is not solvable.

On the other hand, applying Theorem 2, we could also check the solvability of Eq. (4) by evaluating the tuples g^+ and $\overset{1/2}{\neg} g^-$, which is defined as follows:

$$\overset{1/2}{\neg} g^- = (\overset{1/2}{\neg}(0.75 \leftarrow 0.8), \overset{1/2}{\neg}(0.75 \leftarrow 0.4)) = (\neg_Y 0.9375, 0)$$

As already shown, g^+ is not a solution of (4), so it remains to check the case of the tuple $\overset{1/2}{\neg} g^-$:

$$(0.2 * \neg_Y 0.9375) \vee (0.8 * \neg^\alpha \neg_Y 0.9375) \vee (0.5 * 0) \vee (0.4 * \neg^\alpha 0) = 0.07 \vee 0.8 \vee 0 \vee 0.4 = 0.8$$

Again, applying Theorem 2, we conclude that (4) has no solutions.

□

4 Maximal and Minimal Solutions

This section is devoted to studying the boundary elements of the solution set of a bipolar max-product equation with ceiling negation. In particular, we will focus on characterizing the existence of the greatest, maximal, least and minimal solutions of (2), besides determining their form.

The following result characterizes the existence of the greatest solution and the existence of maximal solutions of (2). As it can be seen, there is a strong connection between the characterization of the solvability presented in Theorem 1 and the existence of a greatest or maximal solutions.

Theorem 3. *If Eq. (2) is solvable, then the following statements hold:*

- *If g^+ is a solution, then it is the greatest.*
- *If g^+ is not a solution, then the set of maximal solutions is given as follows:*

$$\mathcal{M} = \{(g_1^+, \dots, g_{k-1}^+, \neg g_k^-, g_{k+1}^+, \dots, g_m^+) \in [0,1]^m \mid \alpha \leq \neg g_k^-\}$$

Notice that, Theorem 3 implies that the existence of maximal solutions of a solvable bipolar equation with ceiling negation is not guaranteed, in general. Indeed, the set $\mathcal{M}$ defined in Theorem 3 could be empty. This is another major difference with respect to the study of bipolar equations with involutive negations, since in that case there always exist maximal solutions [7].

The following result establishes sufficient and necessary conditions for the existence of the least solution and minimal solutions of a bipolar max-product equation with ceiling negation.

Theorem 4. *If Eq.* (2) *is solvable, then the following statements hold:*

- *It the tuple* $(x_1^\alpha, \ldots, x_m^\alpha)$ *given as:*

$$x_j^\alpha = \begin{cases} \neg g_j^- & \text{if } \neg g_j^- \notin]0, \alpha[\\ \alpha & \text{if } \neg g_j^- \in]0, \alpha[\end{cases}$$

is a solution of (2)*, then it is the least solution.*

- *On the contrary, the non-empty set of minimal solutions is given as:*

$$\mathcal{M} = \{(x_1^\alpha, \ldots, x_{k-1}^\alpha, g_k^+, x_{k+1}^\alpha, \ldots, x_m^\alpha) \mid a_k^+ \geq b\}$$

where x_j^α *is defined for each* $j \in \{1, \ldots, m\}$ *as:*

$$x_j^\alpha = \begin{cases} \neg g_j^- & \text{if } \neg g_j^- \notin]0, \alpha[\\ \alpha & \text{if } \neg g_j^- \in]0, \alpha[\end{cases}$$

As a consequence of Theorem 4, we conclude that if $\neg g^-$ is a solution of (2), then it is the least solution, which reminds to the case of bipolar equations with involutive negations [7].

Corollary 1. *If* $\neg g^-$ *is a solution of Eq.* (2)*, then it is the least solution.*

Additionally, Theorem 4 guarantees the existence of minimal solutions for a solvable bipolar max-product equation with ceiling negation, as it happens in the case of bipolar equations with an involutive negation [7].

The following example illustrates the process of determining the maximal and minimal solutions of a solvable bipolar max-product equation with a ceiling negation.

Example 5. Consider the operators and the bipolar equation given in Example 3. In particular, we will study the extremal solutions of the following bipolar equation:

$$(0.2 * x_1) \vee (0.8 * \neg^{2/3} x_1) \vee (0.1 * x_2) \vee (0.4 * \neg^{2/3} x_2) = 0.4 \tag{5}$$

Note that, in Example 3, it has already been shown that Eq. (5) is solvable by considering a specific solution. However, this analysis can be carried out directly as a consequence of Theorems 1 and 2, as shown below.

We firstly compute the tuples g^+ and $\neg_S g^-$ like in Example 3:

$$\begin{aligned} g^+ &= (0.4 \leftarrow 0.2, 0.4 \leftarrow 0.1) \\ &= (1, 1) \end{aligned}$$

$$\begin{aligned} \neg_S g^- &= (\neg_S(0.4 \leftarrow 0.8), \neg_S(0.4 \leftarrow 0.4)) \\ &= (\neg_S 0.5, \neg_S 1) \\ &= (0.5, 0) \end{aligned}$$

As we proved in Example 3, none of the tuples g^+ or $\neg_S g^-$ is a solution of Eq. (5). Therefore, according to Theorem 1, we proceed to evaluate the tuples $(g_1^+, \neg_S g_2^-)$ and $(\neg_S g_1^-, g_2^+)$:

$$(0.2 * 1) \vee (0.8 * \neg^{2/3} 1) \vee (0.1 * 0) \vee (0.4 * \neg^{2/3} 0) = 0.2 \vee 0 \vee 0 \vee 0.4 = 0.4$$

$$(0.2 * 0.5) \vee (0.8 * \neg^{2/3} 0.5) \vee (0.1 * 1) \vee (0.4 * \neg^{2/3} 1) = 0.1 \vee 0.8 \vee 0.1 \vee 0 = 0.8$$

Since the tuple $(g_1^+, \neg_S g_2^-) = (1, 0)$ is a solution of Eq. (5), it is solvable.

Now, we intend to determine the extremal solutions of Eq. (5). Since g^+ is not a solution, according to Theorem 3, the set of maximal solutions is given as follows:

$$\mathcal{M} = \{(g_1^+, \dots, g_{k-1}^+, \neg g_k^-, g_{k+1}^+, \dots, g_m^+) \in [0,1]^m \mid \alpha \leq \neg g_k^-\}$$

Notice that, $\alpha = \frac{2}{3} > \neg_S g_j^-$ for $j = 1, 2$. Therefore, we conclude that the set M is empty, consequently, there are no maximal solutions.

On the other hand, we compute the tuple $(x_1^\alpha, x_2^\alpha) = (\frac{2}{3}, 0)$ defined in Theorem 4, and we evaluate such tuple in Eq. (5):

$$(0.2 * \frac{2}{3}) \vee (0.8 * \neg^{2/3} \frac{2}{3}) \vee (0.1 * 0) \vee (0.4 * \neg^{2/3} 0) = \frac{2}{15} \vee \frac{8}{3} \vee 0 \vee 0.4 = 0.4$$

Since the tuple $(x_1^\alpha, x_2^\alpha) = (\frac{2}{3}, 0)$ is a solution of Eq. (5), applying Theorem 4, we conclude that $(\frac{2}{3}, 0)$ is the least solution of Eq. (5).

5 Conclusions and Future Work

The objective of this study is to undertake an initial investigation into the solvability of bipolar equations defined with non-involutive negations. To this aim, ceiling negations have been defined as a non-involutive modified version of involutive negations. The resolution approach focuses on characterizing the solvability and the existence of the greatest, least, maximal and minimal solutions of bipolar max-product equations with ceiling negations. This represents an advance in the study of non-involutive negations and establishes an intermediate step between the study of involutive negations and non-involutive negations.

In the future, we will analyse the resolution of systems of bipolar max-product equations with ceiling negations, and the resolution of bipolar equations defined with a ceiling negation and an arbitrary residuated pair.

Acknowledgments. Partially supported by the project PID2022-137620NB-I00 funded by MICIU/AEI/10.13039/501100011033 and FEDER, UE, by the grant TED2021-129748B-I00 funded by MCIN/AEI/10.13039/501100011033 and European Union Next GenerationEU/PRTR and project FEDER-UCA-2024-A2-04 funded by Programa Operativo FEDER Andalucía 2021–2027 and by Consejería de Universidad, Investigación e Innovación, Junta de Andalucía.

Disclosure of Interests. The authors declare that they have no known competing financial interest or personal relationships that could have appeared to influence the work reported in this paper.

References

1. Alcalde, C., Burusco, A., Díaz-Moreno, J.C., Medina, J.: Fuzzy concept lattices and fuzzy relation equations in the retrieval processing of images and signals. Int. J. Uncertainty, Fuzziness Knowl.-Based Syst. **25**(Supplement-1), 99–120 (2017). https://doi.org/10.1142/s0218488517400050
2. Bělohlávek, R.: Fuzzy Relational Systems: Foundations and Principles. Kluwer Academic Publishers, New York (2002)
3. Cornejo, M.E., Díaz-Moreno, J.C., Medina, J.: Multi-adjoint relation equations: a decision support system for fuzzy logic. Int. J. Intell. Syst. **32**(8), 778–800 (2017). https://doi.org/10.1002/int.21889
4. Cornejo, M.E., Lobo, D., Medina, J.: Bipolar fuzzy relation equations systems based on the product t-norm. Math. Methods Appl. Sci. **42**(17), 5779–5793 (2019). https://doi.org/10.1002/mma.5646
5. Cornejo, M.E., Lobo, D., Medina, J.: On the solvability of bipolar max-product fuzzy relation equations with the standard negation. Fuzzy Sets Syst. **410**, 1–18 (2021). https://doi.org/10.1016/j.fss.2020.02.010
6. Cornejo, M.E., Lobo, D., Medina, J.: Bipolar multi-adjoint relation equations with join-irreducible right-hand side. Comput. Appl. Math. **45**, 307 (2026). https://doi.org/10.1007/s40314-026-03669-6
7. Cornejo, M.E., Lobo, D., Medina, J., De Baets, B.: Bipolar equations on complete distributive symmetric residuated lattices: the case of a join-irreducible right-hand side. Fuzzy Sets Syst. **442**, 92–108 (2022). https://doi.org/10.1016/j.fss.2022.02.003
8. Cornejo, M.E., Lobo, D., Medina, J.: Optimization of partially monotonic functions subject to bipolar fuzzy relation equations. Inf. Sci. **648**, 119497 (2023). https://doi.org/10.1016/j.ins.2023.119497
9. De Baets, B.: Analytical solution methods for fuzzy relational equations. In: Dubois, D., Prade, H. (eds.) Fundamentals of Fuzzy Sets, vol. 7, pp. 291–340. Springer US, Boston, MA (2000). https://doi.org/10.1007/978-1-4615-4429-6_7
10. De Baets, B., Kerre, E.E.: A primer on solving fuzzy relational equations on the unit interval. Internat. J. Uncertain. Fuzziness Knowl.-Based Syst. **02**(02), 205–225 (1994). https://doi.org/10.1142/s021848859400016x
11. Di Nola, A., Sanchez, E., Pedrycz, W., Sessa, S.: Fuzzy Relation Equations and Their Applications to Knowledge Engineering. Kluwer Academic Publishers, Norwell, MA, USA (1989)
12. Díaz, J.C., Medina, J.: Multi-adjoint relation equations: definition, properties and solutions using concept lattices. Inf. Sci. **253**, 100–109 (2013). https://doi.org/10.1016/j.ins.2013.07.024
13. Feng, J.e., Lv, H., Cheng, D.: Multiple fuzzy relation and its application to coupled fuzzy control. Asian J. Control **15**(5), 1313–1324 (2013). https://doi.org/10.1002/asjc.656
14. Freson, S., De Baets, B., De Meyer, H.: Linear optimization with bipolar max–min constraints. Inf. Sci. **234**, 3–15 (2013). https://doi.org/10.1016/j.ins.2011.06.009
15. Hájek, P.: Metamathematics of fuzzy logic. Trends in Logic, Kluwer Academic Publishers (1998)
16. Li, P., Jin, Q.: On the resolution of bipolar max-min equations. Kybernetika **52**(4), 514–530 (2016). https://doi.org/10.14736/kyb-2016-4-0514
17. Liu, C.C., Lur, Y.Y., Wu, Y.K.: Some results of bipolar max-product fuzzy relational equations. In: Proceedings of the International Multi-Conference of Engineers and Computer Scientists, vol. 2 (2017)

18. Lobo, D., Cornejo, M.E., Medina, J.: Abductive reasoning in normal residuated logic programming via bipolar max-product fuzzy relation equations. In: 2019 Conference of the International Fuzzy Systems Association and the European Society for Fuzzy Logic and Technology (EUSFLAT 2019). Atlantis Studies in Uncertainty Modelling, vol. 1, pp. 588–594. Atlantis Press (2019). https://doi.org/10.2991/eusflat-19.2019.81
19. Lobo, D., Medina, J., Merkl, T.C., Pichler, R.: Minimal solutions of fuzzy relation equations via maximal independent elements. Inf. Sci. **690**, 121558 (2025). https://doi.org/10.1016/j.ins.2024.121558
20. Peeva, K., Kyosev, Y.: Fuzzy Relational Calculus: Theory. World Scientific Publishing Company, Applications and Software (2004)
21. Sanchez, E.: Resolution of composite fuzzy relation equations. Inf. Control **30**(1), 38–48 (1976). https://doi.org/10.1016/S0019-9958(76)90446-0
22. Tiwari, V.L., Thapar, A.: Covering problem for solutions of max-archimedean bipolar fuzzy relation equations. Internat. J. Uncertain. Fuzziness Knowl.-Based Syst. **28**(04), 613–634 (2020). https://doi.org/10.1142/s0218488520500269
23. Yang, X.P.: Resolution of bipolar fuzzy relation equations with max-łukasiewicz composition. Fuzzy Sets Syst. **397**, 41–60 (2020). https://doi.org/10.1016/j.fss.2019.08.005
24. Zhou, J., Yu, Y., Liu, Y., Zhang, Y.: Solving nonlinear optimization problems with bipolar fuzzy relational equation constraints. J. Inequalities Appl. **2016**, 126 (2016). https://doi.org/10.1186/s13660-016-1056-6

Empirical Likelihood Stacking for Remaining Useful Life Estimation

Jonas Karlsson[1(✉)], Alexander Karlsson[1], Sunith Bandaru[2], and Ebru Turanoglu Bekar[3]

[1] School of Informatics, University of Skövde, Skovde, Sweden
{jonas.karlsson,alexander.karlsson}@his.se
[2] School of Engineering Science, Skövde University, Skovde, Sweden
sunith.bandaru@his.se
[3] Department of Industrial and Materials Science, Chalmers University of Technology, Gothenburg, Sweden
ebrut@chalmers.se

Abstract. Predictive maintenance (PdM) plays an important role in the transition toward Industry 4.0, offering the potential to increase operational efficiency and reduce unexpected downtime. A central application of PdM involves the estimation of a system component's remaining useful life (RUL) to enable informed maintenance decisions. Deep learning (DL) models have demonstrated strong performance in RUL prediction tasks. However, these models often lack the capability to reliably quantify predictive uncertainty, which is essential for risk-aware decision-making in industrial applications. Bayesian approximation models, like Stochastic Weight Averaging Bayesian and Variational Inference, can yield a distribution of predictions while avoiding the prohibitively costly process of true Bayesian inference. This distribution can be used to reason about the uncertainty of the model, but often shows the model being overconfident. We propose empirical likelihood stacking, a method for improving uncertainty quantification for DL models. By applying stacking and deep ensembles to estimate the RUL of turbofan engines, we show the trade-offs between these two methods when applied to DL models. We find that the stacked model has a better calibrated uncertainty at a small cost to point prediction accuracy, when compared to the ensemble.

Keywords: Artificial Intelligence · Stacking · Deep Learning · Uncertainty · Remaining Useful Life

1 Introduction

Predictive Maintenance (PdM) has been identified as a key aspect of *Industry 4.0* [27]. Due to the increasing availability of sensors and real-time monitoring, the health of a machine can be tracked over time, and components can be changed before a breakdown occurs. These large datasets allow for the application of data-driven methods, such as Deep Learning (DL) models, which have been applied

B. Vantaggi et al. (Eds.): IPMU 2026, CCIS 3019, pp. 303–317, 2026.
https://doi.org/10.1007/978-3-032-28994-0_22

to maintenance prognostics with great effect [21]. A popular method of estimating when a machine (or a component within a machine) will suffer a fault is by predicting its remaining useful life (RUL) [22]. The RUL value describes how long the component in question will operate until it requires repair or replacement. Thus, accurately predicting a machine's RUL and performing preventive maintenance before a fault occurs can prevent critical stops in production.

It is expected to have some deviation between the true RUL value and that predicted by the model. This means that the RUL prediction carries some inherent uncertainty. Quantifying this uncertainty is essential when making a decision based on the prediction of a PdM system [4]. For example, a maintenance engineer might want to take extra precautions when dealing with a high uncertainty prediction for a critical component. In this way, the reliability of a RUL prediction is affected by the quality of its associated uncertainty. This motivates the use of predictions that are represented by a distribution of RUL estimates, rather than a point RUL estimate. By providing these probabilistic RUL prognostics, we can increase the reliability of the PdM system.

Although Deep Neural Networks (DNNs) have exhibited great promise in predicting RUL, they are commonly deterministic, meaning they provide a single output per prediction. Probabilistic DL models, often utilizing Bayesian methods, represent the parameters (weights and biases) of a Neural Network (NN) as random variables. This results in probabilistic DL models that yield a distribution of RUL values per prediction. This predictive distribution can then be used to represent the uncertainty associated with the prediction. Variational Inference (VI) [3] approximates Bayesian inference and is a popular method used within probabilistic DL. Using VI with NNs, the weights and biases of the neural network are represented as probability distributions. Similarly, Stochastic Weight Averaging Gaussian (SWAG) [15] is a baseline probabilistic model for obtaining probabilistic output from a NN. The predictive distribution of a VI or SWAG model provides better uncertainty estimation than a single RUL value. This is due to the models consisting of multiple sets of NN parameters, where each unique set of parameters values yield a different prediction. However, we can improve the prediction further by using multiple models, gathered over separate training runs. This process of aggregating many trained DL models is known as *deep ensembles* [9]. Although using multiple models can improve the total predictive output, there is still a potential gain to be had by adding some logic to the ensembling process. Stacking [26] does this by weighing the output of each model before including it in the final prediction. Since stacking involves additional computations when compared to regular ensembling, we would expect the added complexity to contribute to better performance of the final aggregated model.

In this paper, we propose *empirical likelihood stacking*; a pragmatic stacking approach for probabilistic DL. To obtain the weights of the stacked distribution, our proposal is to use the fitness of each model sample on the validation dataset. To show its effect in practice, an empirical comparison between ensembling and stacking approaches on SWAG and VI was conducted on a well known RUL prognostic dataset. Although the experiment focuses on measuring uncertainty quantification, we also include point prediction accuracy in our result.

2 Related Work

Various Machine Learning (ML) methods have been applied to the area of RUL prognostics before the current focus on DNNs. Khan and Yairi outline [11] some of these methods in their review. Previous methods include autoencoders, k-means clustering, decision trees and random forests. They also bring up NN architectures, such as the Convolutional Neural Network (CNN) and the Long Short-Term Memory (LSTM). We direct interested readers to that article for additional preliminaries of the application area.

In the article by Staber and Da Viega [23], quality of the uncertainty estimation among multiple Bayesian NNs are evaluated. They find that, among the methods tested, deep ensembles (of single NN parameters) are able to strike a balance between predictive accuracy and prediction coverage. SWAG, on the other hand, was shown to have excellent performance on prediction accuracy, while underestimating the uncertainty of its predictions. Our paper extends this work, by exploring the gains of ensembling models containing multiple sets of network parameters, like SWAG models.

Mitici et al. [16] implemented Monte Carlo Dropout (MC Dropout) with a CNN to achieve uncertainty estimation for RUL predictions on the Commercial Modular Aero-Propulsion System Simulation (C-MAPSS) dataset. They found that MC Dropout performed well with regard to uncertainty calibration as the α-Coverage was close to ideal for all subsets of the data. Xiang et al. [25] also used MC Dropout for estimating the (epistemic) uncertainty of a gated transformer NN on the same prognostic dataset. Their results included the Prediction Interval Coverage Probability (PICP), and Prediction Interval Normalized Averaged Width (PINAW) metrics. Similarly, Nguyen et al. [17] used the PICP and ormalized Mean Prediction Interval Width (NMPIW) when evaluating their proposed lognorm-LSTM model. In their paper, they explored *system RUL* by using the validation set for quantifying the system level prognostic uncertainty. Neither work [17,25] make explicit arguments regarding the uncertainty calibration of the models. In fact, complementary analysis regarding uncertainty calibration seems uncommon in many works using the PICP and NMPIW metrics.

Stacking methods have previously been applied on RUL prognostics. Han et al. [8] implemented a multi-objective evolutionary algorithm to optimize both the accuracy and diversity of the RUL prediction on a bearings dataset. The selected models were stacked to create the final RUL (point) prediction. However, the article does not deal with the uncertainty estimation of the proposed stacking method. In fact, uncertainty estimation is a topic that has recently been identified as in need of further research within predictive health management [24].

This paper aims to bridge the research gap between stacking and uncertainty estimation in the context of RUL prognostics, as well as providing a large surface area for comparison by utilizing multiple metrics for evaluating uncertainty estimation.

3 Preliminaries

3.1 Probabilistic Deep Learning

Hamiltonian Monte Carlo (HMC) [1] is a well known probabilistic method which has previously been applied for RUL prognostics [2]. In the context of DL, HMC is a method for obtaining samples from the probability distribution of the NN weights given the training data, called the posterior distribution. Asymptotically, this sampling gives a complete description of fitness of the model for all NN weights. However, the process of sampling network weights with HMC is difficult to tune, and costly in computing resources and time. Thus, HMC is not suitable for practical applications [10]. Instead of exploring the posterior distribution, VI [3] instead uses a surrogate distribution. This (simpler) distribution is then made as close to the true posterior as possible by minimizing the KullbackLeibler (KL) divergence between the two. Since calculating the true posterior is intractable, this in turn means that the KL divergence cannot be computed. Instead the Evidence Lower Bound (ELBO) is introduced to be equal to the KL divergence, plus some unknown constant. The VI surrogate can then be made similar to the true posterior (up to some unknown constant) by optimizing the ELBO.

SWAG has been proposed by Maddox et al. [15] as a method to approximate full Bayesian inference, making it an alternative probabilistic approach to HMC. This method saves samples of model weights during standard optimization (usually at the end of an epoch). These samples are viewed as being drawn from a Gaussian distribution which is fitted over the model weights. The distribution then acts as the posterior distribution after training has been completed. At inference time, network weights can be drawn from this distribution to sample as many models as necessary. Although calculating the SWAG takes some additional compute time, this method can be used to cheaply enable uncertainty representation in DNNs.

Deep ensembling techniques [9] aggregates the outputs of multiple DNNs in order to increase prediction accuracy and generalizability of the total system [6]. DNNs may end up in different optima based on their randomized initial parameters. This can highlight disagreements between the models, which will be lead to a broader predictive distribution. Bayesian stacking [26], on the other hand, has been proposed as a method of creating posterior distributions from non-mixing HMC chains. This can be seen as an alternative to naive ensembling of NNs. Instead of weighing the contributions to the aggregate prediction uniformly, the proposed stacking method assigns weights to each model depending on some criteria. Applied to HMC chains, this form of stacking can aggregate parallel inferences in order to cover as many posterior modes as possible. By constructing weights for each contributing distribution, stacking can reduce the influence from models that fit poorly to the data.

3.2 Metrics

Point estimation metrics are usually based on the mean value $\bar{y}$ of the predictive set $\hat{y}$. For a dataset with n number of data points, where the prediction set consists of m number of predictions we have $\hat{y}_{i,j}$, $i \in \{1, 2, ..., n\}$, $j \in \{1, 2, ..., m_i\}$. The mean prediction per data instance can then be described as:

$$\bar{y}_i = \frac{1}{m_i} \sum_{j=1}^{m_i} \hat{y}_{i,j} \tag{1}$$

Root Mean Squared Error (RMSE) measures the squared deviations between the mean value of the predictive distribtution $\bar{y}_i$ and the target value y_i. By taking the square root over the sum of all squared deviations, the RMSE emphasizes outliers, more so than the Mean Absolute Error (MAE), but produces a result on the same scale. The PICP metric [12] captures the frequency with which the target value is covered by the prediction interval. Ideally, the true target value should be covered by the prediction interval in relation to the width of the interval. The 95% prediction interval is commonly used [17,25]. As such, that PICP interval will also be used in this paper. However, model that naively yields a very wide prediction interval will also achieve a high PICP. The NMPIW metric [12], complements the PICP by measuring the (normalized) width of the prediction interval. As the metric only measures the width of the predictive distribution, a model can reduce the distribution to a single point prediction in order to obtain a perfect score, regardless of the accuracy of the model. Therefore, in this paper the PICP and NMPIW will be viewed jointly. Together they describe both the coverage of the model's prediction interval, and the width of the distribution.

Continuous Ranked Probability Score. Continuous Ranked Probability Score (CRPS) [7] measures how centered a distribution is around a target value, while also taking into account the distribution's width. This metric can serve as a probabilistic generalization of the MAE, as for a point prediction it becomes equivalent to the MAE. We define $F_{\hat{y}_i}(x)$ as the empirical cumulative distribution function (CDF) of the predictive distribution for data sample i.

$$\begin{aligned} CRPS &= \frac{1}{n} \sum_{i=1}^{n} CRPS_i \\ CRPS_i &= \int_{-\infty}^{\infty} (F_{\hat{y}_i}(x) - \mathbb{1}\{y_i \leq x\})^2 dx \\ \mathbb{1}\{y_i \leq x\} &= \begin{cases} 1, & y_i \leq x \\ 0, & \text{otherwise} \end{cases} \end{aligned} \tag{2}$$

Weighted CRPS. In real-world settings, overestimating the RUL (a late prediction) usually leads to more severe consequences [14]. To address this, Ingeborg and Mitici [18] propose the Weighted Continuous Ranked Probability Score

(CRPS^{W}), which modifies the CRPS to further penalize predictions that fall after the target RUL. The CRPS^{W} is defined as:

$$\begin{aligned} CRPS^W &= \frac{1}{n}\sum_{i=1}^{n} CRPS_i^W \\ CRPS_i^W &= (2-\beta)\int_{-\infty}^{y_i} (F_{\hat{y}_i}(x) - \mathbb{1}\{y_i \le x\})^2 dx \\ &\quad + \beta \int_{y_i}^{\infty} (F_{\hat{y}_i}(x) - \mathbb{1}\{y_i \le x\})^2 dx \\ &= (2-\beta)\int_{-\infty}^{y_i} (F_{\hat{y}_i}(x))^2 dx + \beta \int_{y_i}^{\infty} (F_{\hat{y}_i}(x) - 1)^2 dx \end{aligned} \tag{3}$$

with $0 \le \beta \le 2$ being a user-specified parameter that controls the weighing of early versus late predictions. Ingeborg and Mitici [18] utilize a β value of 1.5 on the same dataset as used in this paper to give greater weight to late predictions, thus we use the same β value in our experiments.

α-Coverage and Ranked Probability α-Coverage [18] is introduced as a complement to the accuracy and sharpness measurement of the CRPS. This metric constructs a credible interval around the median predicted value with a width α. For example, when ordering the predictions $\hat{y}_i$, the span $[\hat{y}_i^{0.30}, \hat{y}_i^{0.70}]$ represents all predictions between the 30th and the 70th percentiles. The α-Coverage for a dataset with n data points can then be defined as:

$$\alpha\text{-Coverage} = \frac{1}{n}\sum_{i=1}^{n} \mathcal{I}(\alpha)_i$$

$$\mathcal{I}(\alpha)_i = \begin{cases} 1, & y_i \in [\hat{y}_i^{\,0.5-0.5\alpha}, \hat{y}_i^{\,0.5+0.5\alpha}] \\ 0, & \text{otherwise} \end{cases}$$

Reliability Score (RS) [18] is a calibration curve for regression (as opposed to classification) tasks. It is obtained by measuring the α-Coverage for different values of α. If the target value falls inside the predicted interval significantly more or less than α percent of the time, then the model's uncertainty estimates are not well-calibrated. The RS metric can be visualized in a diagram by plotting the measured α-Coverage for varying values of α.

4 Empirical Likelihood Stacking

In this section we describe the proposed methodology of the empirical likelihood stacking procedure for creating a meta-model from trained NNs. Our contribution is based on previous work done by Yao et al. [26], and we direct interested readers to that paper for further reading.

The stacking model is constructed by obtaining a model-wise weight $\mathbf{w} = (w_1, w_2, ..., w_K)$ where K is the number of models at our disposal. In this paper, we propose using the validation data as a simple and computationally cheap way for calculating the weights $\mathbf{w}$. The rationale for basing the stacking weights on the validation dataset is that the validation set is a common target for regularization techniques, such as early stopping, and is often included in modern DL experiments by default. It is therefore straightforward for practitioners to implement this extra step of weight optimization. In light of these aspects, we propose basing the weights on the models' empirical performance on the validation set. Thus, to compute the weights of the k-th model we first calculate the predictive density p with a kernel density estimation (KDE)[1] using a (normalized) gaussian kernel $\mathbf{K}$:

$$p_k(y_i, (\hat{y}_{i,j})_{j=1}^{m}) = \sum_{j=1}^{m} \mathbf{K}(y_i - \hat{y}_{i,j}; h)$$

where $\hat{y}_i$ are the prediction samples, and y_i is the target RUL for datapoint $i \in \{1, 2, ..., n_v\}$ in a validation dataset of size n_v. The result of the KDE is highly dependent on the the kernel width h, as a misspecified value of h can lead to either an under- or over-smoothed estimation. During initial experimentation, it was observed that the predictions from both SWAG and VI were approximately normal in shape. Because of this, Scott's rule [20] should perform well, and was used to set the width parameter h. Then, as proposed by Yao et al. [26], we solve

$$\mathbf{w}^*_{1,...,K} = \arg \max_{\mathbf{w} \in \mathbb{S}(K)} \sum_{i=1}^{n_v} \log \sum_{k=1}^{K} w_k p_k(y_i, (\hat{y}_{i,j})_{j=1}^{m_k}) + \log(p_{\text{prior}}(\mathbf{w})),$$

where m_k is the number of parameter samples from k-th model, and $\mathbb{S}(K)$ is the space of a $(K-1)$-dimensional simplex

$$\mathbb{S}(K) = \{\mathbf{w} : 0 \leq w_k \leq 1, \forall\, k\, ; \sum_{k=1}^{K} w_k = 1\}$$

$p_{\text{prior}}(\mathbf{w})$ is a Dirichlet prior, tuned by a scaling parameter λ that forces convexity of the optimization of $\mathbf{w}$ for all $\lambda > 1$. The Dirichlet prior and λ term is further described in the original work [26]. For this paper, the proposed rule of thumb of $\lambda = 1.001$ was used. To optimize the weights $\mathbf{w}$, the same method[2] and parameters are used as by Yao et al. [26]. Lastly, we perform importance resampling by selecting parameter draws from each model proportional to its weight. This allows us to calculate the Monte Carlo estimate as described in [26]: For the K model functions f parameterized by θ as

$$\mathbb{E}(f(\theta)|\mathbf{w}) \approx \sum_{k=1}^{K} w_k \sum_{m=1}^{m_k} \frac{f(\theta_{km})}{m_k}$$

where m_k is the number of NN parameter samples for the k-th model.

[1] https://scikit-learn.org/stable/modules/density.html#kernel-density.

[2] https://github.com/yao-yl/Multimodal-stacking-code.

5 Experiments

This section contains details about the setup of the experiment. First we describe the dataset and the data-processing steps taken in Sect. 5.1. In Sect. 5.2 we briefly outline the NN architecture used in this paper.

5.1 Description of the Dataset

The proposed method was applied to a well known turbofan degradation dataset consisting of measurements from simulated engines. The data was generated by the tool C-MAPSS [19], developed by NASA. The dataset contains four subsets: FD001, FD002, FD003, and FD004. These subsets are of varying complexity with one or more fault- and operating conditions. For each subset, the data samples are divided into predefined training and test sets. The data processing followed the same process as outlined by Costa and Sánchez [5]. The training data was split into 80-20% training and validation sets. All data is scaled with a standard scaler with respect to operating condition. The data are likely to contain some noise, which may cause problems for the DL models. Therefore, the sensor data are also passed through an exponential weighted smoothing process [5]. Of the total 21 sensors, 7 show constant measurement over time for subsets FD001 and FD003. During data preparation, these sensors were discarded for these two subsets, leaving a total of 14 sensor values for subsets FD001 and FD003, and 21 sensors for FD002 and FD004. When a machine operates without signs of degradation, it is reasonable to assume that the sensor values will be nearly constant until the engine starts degrading. This assumption is supported by looking at the sensor data. The data seem to be constant (with some measurement noise) until a point, after which they increasingly deviate until a fault occurs. Therefore, previous work [2,5] on the turbofan data apply a piece-wise linear function on the RUL. This bounds the maximum RUL for all training and validation data to 125. Another common processing step introduced in [14] was to apply a sliding window over the time axis of the data. This transforms the time series into an image-like two dimensional object, which fits a CNN well. This also allows the NN to view the immediate history of a component, which can assist in detecting ongoing trends. Similar to related work [2,18], the window sizes were chosen as 30, 20, 30, and 15 for subsets FD001, FD002, FD003, and FD004, respectively.

5.2 Model Architecture

A CNN architecture is proposed, inspired by previous work [14,18]. The model consists of 5 convolutional layers, followed by a dense (fully connected layer). The convolutional layers has a one dimensional kernel and a tanh activation function. The first four convolutional layers has a kernel size of 10 (along the time axis), while the fifth layer has a size of 3. For regularization, dropout layers were applied after convoluational layers 2, 3, and 4 during training. Each dropout layer has a probability of 0.5 for dropping any given neuron in the previous layer, which is the same probability as used in [18]. The dense layer has 420 neurons and a Leaky

ReLU activation function. The SWAG CNN is trained with the Adam optimizer [13] for 250 epochs, and with a constant learning rate of 0.005. The learning rate was kept constant to increase the diversity of the parameter samples. The weights of the NN is initialized with the default PyTorch initialization scheme for SWAG, and set to normal distributions with a prior scale of 0.1 for VI. Finally, the last 30% of the epochs are saved and added to the SWAG weights. The VI model is similarly trained with the Adam optimizer for 250 epochs, with a decaying learning rate from 0.01 to 0.001. Fifty SWAG and VI NNs were trained on each turbofan data subset. The relative high number of models were chosen to ensure statistical validity of the result. Prior to the experiments, the hyper-parameters for each model were fine tuned by manual search, in the cases where they were not already explored by previous work. For both methods, the *single* NN with the highest likelihood on the validation data was chosen as a point of comparison against the stacking and ensembling methods. The deep ensemble was constructed by uniformly aggregating the predictions from all 50 networks. The stacking was conducted on the 50 networks as detailed in Sect. 4.

6 Results and Discussion

The PICP and NMPIW offer complementary descriptions of the predictive distributions. As seen in Table 1, the NMPIW follow a clear pattern where the single model has the smallest distribution width, followed by stacking and finally the ensemble. This holds true for all subsets of the data. For the PICP, the metric tends to favor the stacking model over the ensemble, with the single model clearly performing the worst. Figure 1 shows the NMPIW and PICP metrics for the three variants of the SWAG and VI models on each subset of the data. Although not always best in either metric, the stacking model manages to often come closest to the combined optimal point (this is most clear for subset FD002 in Fig. 3). As is shown in Table 2, there is clear evidence that both empirical likelihood stacking and ensembling provides better uncertainty estimation than a

Table 1. PICP and NMPIW of the three models, per subset. For PICP higher is better, for NMPIW lower is better.

Subset	Metric	SWAG			VI		
		Single	Stacking	Ensemble	Single	Stacking	Ensemble
FD001	PICP ↑	0.43	0.71	0.79	0.43	0.68	0.64
	NMPIW ↓	0.16	0.38	0.50	0.30	0.45	0.64
FD002	PICP ↑	0.37	0.57	0.50	0.46	0.52	0.51
	NMPIW ↓	0.14	0.26	0.49	0.31	0.36	0.56
FD003	PICP ↑	0.42	0.61	0.61	0.49	0.62	0.61
	NMPIW ↓	0.14	0.28	0.36	0.38	0.55	0.70
FD004	PICP ↑	0.34	0.47	0.45	0.35	0.47	0.45
	NMPIW ↓	0.18	0.28	0.38	0.32	0.51	0.67

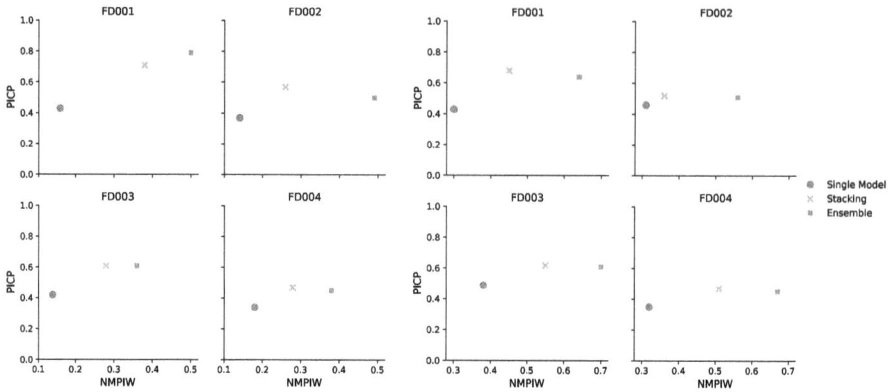

Fig. 1. PICP and NMPIW scores for SWAG (left) and VI (right). Each plot shows the result for one data subset, with the three model configurations (Single, Stacked, and Ensemble). Top left corner corresponds to perfect PICP and NMPIW scores.

single DNN. For the PICP, a wider prediction interval will have an increased RUL coverage, and thus a higher score. Therefore, it is expected that the ensemble model, which uses all predictions, achieves the highest PICP score. However, this is not always the case as the stacking model often performs as well, if not better, than the ensemble model in this regard. The NMPIW penalizes the width of the prediction interval, heavily favoring the single model. An interesting observation is that the stacking model often achieves a similar PICP as the ensemble, but with a lower NMPIW score. This indicates that the prediction intervals of the stacking model is of higher quality than either the single model, or the ensemble.

For RMSE and CRPS, the ensemble consistently outperforms the other models in the SWAG case. However, for VI the situation is the opposite, with the stacking model often performing best with respect to CRPS and CRPS^{W}. Since the mean prediction is used to calculate the RMSE, having more predictions available seems to allow the ensemble to achieve a better RMSE than both the stacking and single model variants in most cases. The CRPS measures the closeness of all predictions to the target RUL value. Similarly, the findings indicate a clear trend in which a larger number of predictions result in better CRPS performance. In terms of RS, the stacking model achieves the best score, closely followed by the ensemble. This can be seen in Fig. 2, where the stacking model falls closer to the ideal line for the majority of different credible interval widths. This shows that the additional effort of stacking and ensembling trained models yields better-calibrated uncertainty. Notably, the stacking model slightly outperforms the ensemble here, which indicates that the act of weighing the models further improves the uncertainty calibration. As stated in the introduction, DNNs are known for underestimating their uncertainty. Although stacking and ensembling improves the uncertainty calibration Fig. 2 shows that these models still underestimate their predictive uncertainty.

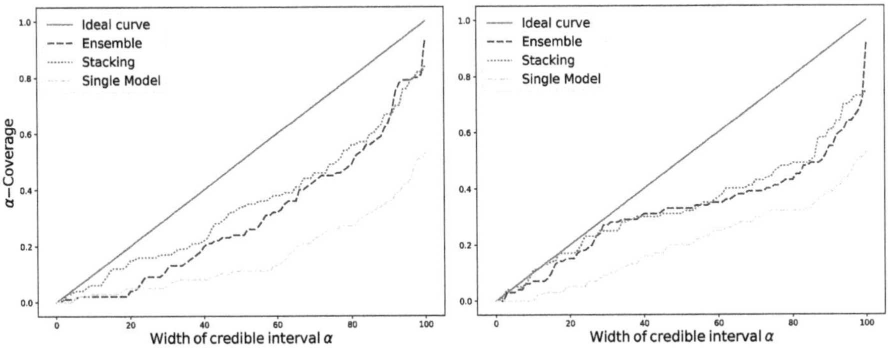

Fig. 2. Reliability diagram for SWAG (left) and VI (right), of the three models for the FD001 dataset. Lines falling below the ideal curve indicate models which are underestimating their predictive uncertainty.

Table 2. RMSE, CRPS, $CRPS^W$, and RS of the single best, stacked, and ensemble models for SWAG and VI per data subset. Top performing model for SWAG and VI (separately) highlighted in bold. Total number of times each model achieved the top performance is summarized at the bottom.

Subset	Metric	SWAG			VI		
		Single	Stacking	Ensemble	Single	Stacking	Ensemble
FD001	RMSE ↓	14.65	14.08	**13.96**	25.68	**24.22**	24.38
	CRPS ↓	9.94	9.04	**8.53**	17.39	**14.43**	15.26
	$CRPS^W$ ↓	10.79	**8.91**	9.44	17.40	**15.14**	16.31
	RS ↓	0.34	**0.17**	0.21	0.30	**0.16**	0.18
FD002	RMSE ↓	26.73	27.01	**26.69**	**31.44**	31.59	31.68
	CRPS ↓	16.98	15.87	**15.79**	21.38	20.30	**20.27**
	$CRPS^W$ ↓	16.98	11.75	**11.69**	21.38	**17.65**	17.71
	RS ↓	0.35	**0.27**	0.29	0.30	0.28	**0.27**
FD003	RMSE ↓	15.18	15.60	**15.03**	28.52	28.09	**28.04**
	CRPS ↓	9.76	9.31	**9.04**	18.96	**17.51**	17.85
	$CRPS^W$ ↓	9.76	**9.32**	9.37	22.31	**20.15**	21.33
	RS ↓	0.34	**0.20**	0.21	0.27	0.23	**0.21**
FD004	RMSE ↓	**28.64**	29.27	29.44	35.55	35.45	**35.34**
	CRPS ↓	19.55	**19.20**	19.26	25.3	**22.53**	23.99
	$CRPS^W$ ↓	15.31	**14.38**	14.47	24.81	**19.98**	22.37
	RS ↓	0.34	**0.29**	0.30	0.34	**0.28**	0.30
# of top performing		1	**8**	7	1	**10**	5

As shown in Table 2 for SWAG, the ensemble generally achieves a lower (better) CRPS score, while for VI, stacking has lowers scores in both CRPS and CRPS^{W}. For both SWAG and VI, stacking outperforms in terms of RS in the majority of cases.

Overall, there is a clear advantage of using stacking or ensembling for SWAG and VI models in all compared metrics. Judging from the combined PICP and NMPIW scores, the stacking model consistently dominates the ensemble in the trade-off for both SWAG and VI. This notion is also supported by the RS metric, where stacking often beats the ensemble.

7 Summary and Conclusions

In this paper, we propose empirical likelihood stacking, inspired by Yao et al. [26], we propose to use the validation dataset together with KDE, instead of the cross-validated training set for calculating the stacking weights. We have evaluated and compared the proposed stacking method with ensembling for DNN models trained with SWAG and VI. The models were implemented and trained on the well known C-MAPSS dataset for simulated turbofan engines. While both deep ensemble and stacking improves most aspects of the prediction when compared to the single best model, we find that stacking improved the quality of the prediction intervals of both the VI and SWAG models when compared with the ensemble. Results also showed that stacking improved the uncertainty calibration of SWAG in comparison to the deep ensemble, leading to a general reduction in over-confidence. This can be highly important for maintenance decision making, as well calibrated uncertainty is a requirement for informed decision-making in scenarios with high risk. In addition, in the case of VI, stacking outperformed the ensemble in most metrics. The predictions of the stacking model also tended to underestimate the RUL more often than the ensemble, which may be desirable in a real-world scenario where missed maintenance is more costly than early maintenance. Regardless of using stacking or ensembling, an argument can be made regarding the additional computational cost of training multiple models. However, this process is highly parallelizable as the training of the individual models can be done in complete separation. Once the models have been trained, the computational cost of calculating the stacking weights is negligible.

Questions arise about why stacking tends to outperform the ensemble to a higher degree when applied to VI, compared to SWAG. One reason for this discrepancy might be the initialization of the model weights and biases. For SWAG, these parameters are likely less diverse than the parameters sampled from the distributions used for VI. As shown by Yao et al. [26] stacking performs better on over-dispersed Markov Chain Monte Carlo (MCMC) chains. This might be a key reason for limited improvements in various metrics when comparing stacking with ensembling for the SWAG models. As the initialization of the weights follow the same distribution for all models, it might be that the final models are too similar to fully utilize the benefits of stacking. Hence, potential future work is to increase the diversity among the trained models and identifying the factors that can improve the quality of stacking weights. Second, this paper used the validation set as the basis for the stacking weights. This was done due to the ubiquitous nature of the validation dataset, as it is commonly used in the DL context for regularization methods. Pareto smoothed importance sampling (PSIS) is used to estimate the leave-one-out (LOO) cross-validation in [26] for calculating the stacking weights. Finding the differences in empirical performance between stacking weights based on estimated LOO cross-validation versus the validation set would provide an interesting point of comparison for future work. Finally, the regularization term λ should be fine-tuned and the effect on the stacking weights evaluated.

Acknowledgments. The authors would like to thank the Advanced and Innovative Digitalization Program funded by VINNOVA for their funding of the research projects TPdM-Trustworthy Predictive Maintenance (Grant No. 2022-01710) and AIMOps-Advanced AI Architectures for Integrated and Enhanced Manufacturing Operations (Grant No. 2025-01110), within which this study has been conducted.

References

1. Andrieu, C., De Freitas, N., Doucet, A., Jordan, M.I.: An introduction to MCMC for machine learning. Mach. Learn. **50**, 5–43 (2003)
2. Benker, M., Furtner, L., Semm, T., Zaeh, M.F.: Utilizing uncertainty information in remaining useful life estimation via Bayesian neural networks and Hamiltonian Monte Carlo. J. Manuf. Syst. **61**, 799–807 (2021)
3. Blei, D.M., Kucukelbir, A., McAuliffe, J.D.: Variational inference: a review for statisticians. J. Am. Stat. Assoc. **112**(518), 859–877 (2017)
4. Chen, C., Shi, J., Lu, N., Zhu, Z.H., Jiang, B.: Data-driven predictive maintenance strategy considering the uncertainty in remaining useful life prediction. Neurocomputing **494**, 79–88 (2022)
5. Costa, N., Sánchez, L.: Variational encoding approach for interpretable assessment of remaining useful life estimation. Reliab. Eng. Syst. Saf. **222**, 108353 (2022)
6. Ganaie, M.A., Hu, M., Malik, A.K., Tanveer, M., Suganthan, P.N.: Ensemble deep learning: a review. Eng. Appl. Artif. Intell. **115**, 105151 (2022)
7. Gneiting, T., Raftery, A.E.: Strictly proper scoring rules, prediction, and estimation. J. Am. Stat. Assoc. **102**(477), 359–378 (2007)
8. Han, T., Pang, J., Tan, A.C.: Remaining useful life prediction of bearing based on stacked autoencoder and recurrent neural network. J. Manuf. Syst. **61**, 576–591 (2021)
9. Hansen, L.K., Salamon, P.: Neural network ensembles. IEEE Trans. Pattern Anal. Mach. Intell. **12**(10), 993–1001 (1990)
10. Izmailov, P., Vikram, S., Hoffman, M.D., Wilson, A.G.G.: What are Bayesian neural network posteriors really like? In: International Conference on Machine Learning, pp. 4629–4640. PMLR (2021)
11. Khan, S., Yairi, T.: A review on the application of deep learning in system health management. Mech. Syst. Signal Process. **107**, 241–265 (2018)
12. Khosravi, A., Nahavandi, S., Creighton, D., Atiya, A.F.: Lower upper bound estimation method for construction of neural network-based prediction intervals. IEEE Trans. Neural Netw. **22**(3), 337–346 (2010)

13. Kingma, D.P., Ba, J.: Adam: a method for stochastic optimization (2017). https://arxiv.org/abs/1412.6980
14. Li, X., Ding, Q., Sun, J.Q.: Remaining useful life estimation in prognostics using deep convolution neural networks. Reliab. Engi. Syst. Safe. **172**, 1–11 (2018)
15. Maddox, W.J., Izmailov, P., Garipov, T., Vetrov, D.P., Wilson, A.G.: A simple baseline for Bayesian uncertainty in deep learning. In: Advances in Neural Information Processing Systems, vol. 32 (2019)
16. Mitici, M., de Pater, I., Barros, A., Zeng, Z.: Dynamic predictive maintenance for multiple components using data-driven probabilistic RUL prognostics: The case of turbofan engines. Reliab. Eng. Syst. Saf. **234**, 109199 (2023)
17. Nguyen, K.T., Medjaher, K., Gogu, C.: Probabilistic deep learning methodology for uncertainty quantification of remaining useful lifetime of multi-component systems. Reliab. Engi. Syst. Saf. **222**, 108383 (2022)
18. de Pater, I., Mitici, M.: Novel metrics to evaluate probabilistic remaining useful life prognostics with applications to turbofan engines. In: PHM Society European Conference, vol. 7, pp. 96–109 (2022)
19. Saxena, A., Goebel, K., Simon, D., Eklund, N.: Damage propagation modeling for aircraft engine run-to-failure simulation. In: 2008 International Conference on Prognostics and Health Management, pp. 1–9. IEEE (2008)
20. Scott, D.W.: On optimal and data-based histograms. Biometrika **66**(3), 605–610 (1979)
21. Serradilla, O., Zugasti, E., Rodriguez, J., Zurutuza, U.: Deep learning models for predictive maintenance: a survey, comparison, challenges and prospects. Appl. Intell. **52**(10), 10934–10964 (2022)
22. Si, X.S., Wang, W., Hu, C.H., Zhou, D.H.: Remaining useful life estimation-a review on the statistical data driven approaches. Eur. J. Oper. Res. **213**(1), 1–14 (2011)
23. Staber, B., Da Veiga, S.: Benchmarking Bayesian neural networks and evaluation metrics for regression tasks. arXiv preprint arXiv:2206.06779 (2022)
24. Thelen, A., Huan, X., Paulson, N., Onori, S., Hu, Z., Hu, C.: Probabilistic machine learning for battery health diagnostics and prognostics—review and perspectives. NPJ Mater. Sustain. **2**(1), 14 (2024)
25. Xiang, F., Zhang, Y., Zhang, S., Wang, Z., Qiu, L., Choi, J.H.: Bayesian gated-transformer model for risk-aware prediction of aero-engine remaining useful life. Expert Syst. Appl. **238**, 121859 (2024)
26. Yao, Y., Vehtari, A., Gelman, A.: Stacking for non-mixing Bayesian computations: the curse and blessing of multimodal posteriors. J. Mach. Learn. Res. **23**(79), 1–45 (2022)
27. Zonta, T., Da Costa, C.A., da Rosa Righi, R., de Lima, M.J., Da Trindade, E.S., Li, G.P.: Predictive maintenance in the industry 4.0: a systematic literature review. Comput. Ind. Eng. **150**, 106889 (2020)

Tucker Unimodal Decomposition of Probability Distributions

Jiří Vomlel[1,2](✉)

[1] Institute of Information Theory and Automation, Czech Academy of Sciences, Prague, Czechia
[2] Institute for Research and Applications of Fuzzy Modeling, University of Ostrava, Ostrava, Czechia
vomlel@utia.cas.cz

Abstract. The research reported in this paper is motivated by the application of probabilistic graphical models in the social sciences. In this field, models are often learned from data collected in survey questionnaires. A Likert scale is typically used to collect respondents' opinions. For instance, in the seven point Likert scale, the possible responses are (1) strongly disagree, (2) disagree, (3) somewhat disagree, (4) neutral, (5) somewhat agree, (6) agree, and (7) strongly agree. Naturally, the dividing lines between these categories are vague, so it is reasonable to interpret them using fuzzy numbers instead of integers. This approach yields a new representation of the probability distributions learned from the collected data. The original state space of each measured variable is transformed into a new, typically reduced, state space. A function describes the correspondence to the original state space. For this function to have a natural interpretation, it must be unimodal, meaning it either increases to a peak and then decreases or decreases to a trough and then increases. Since each probability distribution can be viewed as a tensor, the problem of finding a new, compact representation can be formalized as a unimodal Tucker decomposition. We find these decompositions by combining the alternating least squares algorithm with projections of the columns of the factor matrices onto unimodal vectors. We tested the algorithm's performance using data from the Dividing Lines in Czech Society survey.

Keywords: Probability · Tucker tensor decomposition · Likert scale · Fuzzy sets · Fuzzy transform

1 Introduction

Our work reported in this paper is motivated by the application of probabilistic models in the social sciences, where surveys and questionnaires are commonly used to collect respondents' opinions via a Likert scale. Likert scales consist of several states, which are usually represented by a set of consecutive integers. A seven-point Likert scale, for example, has the following states: (1) strongly

B. Vantaggi et al. (Eds.): IPMU 2026, CCIS 3019, pp. 318–331, 2026.
https://doi.org/10.1007/978-3-032-28994-0_23

disagree, (2) disagree, (3) somewhat disagree, (4) neutral, (5) somewhat agree, (6) agree, and (7) strongly agree.

Typically, several modeling options are available. For analyzing individual item responses, *ordinal regression models* are the gold standard, as they respect the ordered nature of Likert scales [1,7]. For identifying latent dimensions across diverse political, social, and personal items, *Item Response Theory models* (such as the Graded Response Model) or *factor analysis for ordinal data* can be used to reveal underlying constructs [9,14].

We take a conceptually different approach. We believe that the dividing lines between the states of a Likert scale are vague, so it seems natural to interpret them using fuzzy sets. This idea is not entirely new, since Gil and González-Rodríguez [6] have already suggested identifying each Likert response category with a fuzzy set. Each response in a survey or questionnaire can be viewed as a fuzzy observation of a hidden continuous variable. In [8] we proposed to approximate probability distributions using the F-transform [10,11]. In this paper, we extend the approach presented in [8] to multidimensional probability distributions. We consider discrete multidimensional probability distributions P defined on the grid

$$\mathbb{X} = \mathbb{X}_1 \times \cdots \times \mathbb{X}_d = \{1, \ldots, N_1\} \times \cdots \times \{1, \ldots, N_d\} \enspace ,$$

where each set $\{1, \ldots, N_i\}, i = 1, \ldots, d$ is a numerical representation of the Likert scale used for the corresponding variable. Each multidimensional probability distribution can be represented as a d-dimensional tensor $\mathcal{P} \in \mathbb{R}^{\mathbb{X}_1 \times \cdots \times \mathbb{X}_d}$. For simplicity, we will assume that $N_1 = \ldots = N_d = N$, though this is not necessary.

A fuzzy set is a pair (U, A) where U is a set (often required to be non-empty) and A is a mapping from the universe U to $[0, 1]$, referred to as the membership function. The fuzzy set is often identified by its membership function. In this paper, the universe U will be an interval of real numbers $[1, N]$. An observation $X = k$ of a random variable X, where k is a value from the Likert scale $\{1, \ldots, N\}$, will be interpreted as a fuzzy set $A_k : [1, N] \to [0, 1]$.

A family of fuzzy sets $\{A_k,\ k = 1, \ldots, n\}$, $n \in \mathbb{N}$, all defined on a common universe U, is called a fuzzy partition[1]. Two conditions on the A_k are frequently imposed in the literature: *normality*, $\max_{x \in U} A_k(x) = 1$ for each k, and the *Ruspini condition* [13], $\sum_{k=1}^{n} A_k(x) = 1$ for all $x \in U$. This paper imposes only normality. The reason is substantive rather than technical: in Likert-scale survey data, certain response categories (e.g., endpoints or the middle value) are used far more frequently than others, and requiring the Ruspini condition would force the partition to distort this empirical structure.

Each fuzzy partition can be represented using a matrix $\boldsymbol{A}$ as

$$a_{ki} = A_k(x_i), i = 1, \ldots, N,\ k = 1, \ldots, n \tag{1}$$

$$\mathbf{A} = \left(a_{ki}\right)_{k=1,i=1}^{n,N} \tag{2}$$

[1] We use small n to indicate that $n \leq N$.

where each row k corresponds to the values of a membership function A_k evaluated at $x = (x_1, \ldots, x_N)$. Its row-normalized version[2] will be denoted as:

$$\tilde{\mathbf{A}} = \left(\tilde{a}_{ki}\right)_{k=1,i=1}^{n,N} \tag{3}$$

Using this notation, the definition of the F-transform [10,11] becomes a matrix product formula. Its generalization to multidimensional probability distributions is then defined as follows.

Definition 1. *The F-transform of the probability distribution P represented as a tensor $\mathcal{P}$ is*

$$\mathcal{G} = \mathcal{P} \times_1 \tilde{\mathbf{A}}^{(1)} \times_2 \tilde{\mathbf{A}}^{(2)} \cdots \times_d \tilde{\mathbf{A}}^{(d)} \ , \tag{4}$$

where, for dimension $k = 1, \ldots, d$, the symbol $\times_k$ denotes the mode-k tensor-matrix product,

$$\mathbf{A}^{(k)} = \left(a_{ij}\right)_{i=1,j=1}^{n_k,N_k} \tag{5}$$

is the k-th fuzzy partition matrix, and $\tilde{\mathbf{A}}^{(k)}$ is the row-normalized matrix $\mathbf{A}^{(k)}$.

Following [10,11] the inverse F-transform can be defined for multidimensional functions as follows.

Definition 2. *The inverse F-transform is*

$$\hat{\mathcal{P}} = \mathcal{G} \times_1 (\hat{\mathbf{A}}^{(1)})^T \times_2 (\hat{\mathbf{A}}^{(2)})^T \cdots \times_d (\hat{\mathbf{A}}^{(d)})^T \ , \tag{6}$$

where $\hat{\mathbf{A}}^{(k)}$ are column-normalized matrices $\mathbf{A}^{(k)}$ for $k = 1, \ldots, d$.

The key observation is that the inverse F-transform can be viewed as a constrained low-rank approximation; more precisely, it is the *Tucker decomposition.* This means that we need to work with prescribed fuzzy partitions; instead, we can use algorithms for Tucker decomposition not only to find the tensor $\mathcal{G}$, called the core, but also the matrices $\boldsymbol{A}$. However, to achieve desirable interpretation properties, we require the rows of matrices $\hat{\mathbf{A}}^{(k)}$ to represent unimodal functions. On the other hand, to avoid complex computations, we do not require the matrices to be column normalized; instead, we normalize the factor matrices and the resulting tensor.

In this paper, we will proceed as follows: In Sect. 2 we describe Alternating Optimization for Unimodal Tucker Decomposition. This algorithm exploits the Unimodal Projection Algorithm presented in Sect. 3. The factor normalization is described in Sect. 4. We conclude the paper by performing experimental comparisons on real data from a large survey in Sect. 5 and summarizing the results in Sect. 6.

[2] Row-normalization is performed by dividing each row by its sum; column-normalization is performed likewise.

2 Tucker Decomposition with Unimodal Constraints

Figure 1 shows an example of a rank-2, one-dimensional ($d = 1$) unimodal Tucker decomposition of a vector of length $N_1 = 7$. The core G is the vector $(0.0935, 0.1422)$, and the two columns of the factor matrix (left) are both unimodal. The right-hand plot shows the original vector (blue curve with small circles) together with its rank-2 Tucker approximation (red curve with small triangles),which is already relatively good at such a low rank.

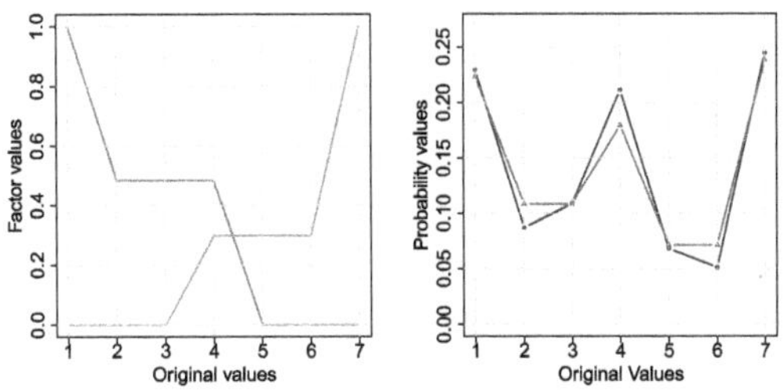

Fig. 1. One-dimensional unimodal Tucker decomposition

Given a d-way tensor $\mathcal{X} \in \mathbb{R}^{N_1 \times N_2 \times \cdots \times N_d}$ and target ranks $n_1, n_2, \ldots, n_d$, we seek a Tucker decomposition [15]:

$$\mathcal{X} \approx \mathcal{G} \times_1 \boldsymbol{U}_1 \times_2 \boldsymbol{U}_2 \times_3 \cdots \times_d \boldsymbol{U}_d$$

where $\mathcal{G} \in \mathbb{R}^{N_1 \times N_2 \times \cdots \times N_d}$ is the core tensor and $\boldsymbol{U}_k \in \mathbb{R}^{n_k \times N_k}$ are factor matrices[3], subject to the constraint that each column of each $\boldsymbol{U}_k$ is *unimodal*. The optimization problem is:

$$\min_{\mathcal{G}, \{\boldsymbol{U}_k\}_{k=1}^d} \quad \|\mathcal{X} - \mathcal{G} \times_1 \boldsymbol{U}_1 \times_2 \boldsymbol{U}_2 \cdots \times_d \boldsymbol{U}_d\|_F^2$$
$$\text{subject to} \quad \text{each column of } \boldsymbol{U}_k \text{ is unimodal}, \quad k = 1, \ldots, d$$

A vector $\boldsymbol{u} \in \mathbb{R}^n$ is *unimodal* if it satisfies one of two forms:

1. *Maximum-type* (∩-shape): There exists an index $p \in \{1, \ldots, n\}$ such that:

$$u_1 \leq u_2 \leq \cdots \leq u_p \geq u_{p+1} \geq \cdots \geq u_n \tag{7}$$

2. *Minimum-type* (∪-shape): There exists an index $t \in \{1, \ldots, n\}$ such that:

$$u_1 \geq u_2 \geq \cdots \geq u_t \leq u_{t+1} \leq \cdots \leq u_n \tag{8}$$

---

[3] Since the presentation of the algorithms is independent of the intended interpretation provided in the previous section, we use $\boldsymbol{U}_k, k = 1, \ldots, d$ to denote factor matrices. They can be interpreted as the matrices of the inverse F-transform as defined in Definition 2. Similar arguments apply for the tensor $\mathcal{X}$.

We additionally require $u_i \geq 0$ for all i (non-negativity) for maximum-type unimodality and $u_i \leq 0$ for all i (non-positivity) for minimum-type unimodality. This requirement is motivated by the application domain considered in this paper. Under the above requirements, the columns of factor matrices can have the desired interpretation since they can be easily transformed into unimodal maximum-type functions taking values from the interval $[0, 1]$; see Sect. 4.

2.1 ALS with Unimodal Constraints

We extend the standard Tucker decomposition [15] commonly computed via Higher-Order Orthogonal Iteration (HOOI) [5] with unimodal constraints on factor matrices. The initialization uses Higher-Order SVD (HOSVD) [4]. The unimodality constraint was studied by Bro and Sidiropoulos [2], and we build on their algorithm. We employ a block coordinate descent strategy with projection-based constraint enforcement, combining efficient precomputed Gram matrices with the unimodality projection algorithm.

Algorithm 1. HOSVD Initialization with Unimodal Constraints

for $k = 1, \ldots, d$ **do**
  Unfold $\mathcal{X}$ along mode k: $\boldsymbol{X}_{(k)} \in \mathbb{R}^{N_k \times \prod_{j \neq k} N_j}$
  Compute truncated SVD: $\boldsymbol{X}_{(k)} \approx \boldsymbol{U}_k \boldsymbol{\Sigma}_k \boldsymbol{V}_k^\top$.
  Keep n_k left singular vectors $\boldsymbol{u}_{k,j}$, $j = 1, \ldots, n_k$ from $\boldsymbol{U}_k$.
  for $j = 1, \ldots, n_k$ **do**
    $\boldsymbol{u}_{k,j}^{(0)} = \Pi_{\mathcal{U}}(\boldsymbol{u}_{k,j})$ ▷ Project each vector to the unimodal constraint set
  end for
end for
Return: $\{\mathbf{U}_k^{(0)}\}_{k=1}^d$.

The algorithm is initialized using the Higher-Order Singular Value Decomposition (HOSVD) as specified in Algorithm 1. After initialization of the factor matrices $\{\boldsymbol{U}_k^{(0)}\}_{k=1}^d$, the initial core tensor is computed exactly via the pseudoinverse of each factor matrix individually, $\mathcal{G}^{(0)} = \mathcal{X} \times_1 (\boldsymbol{U}_1^{(0)})^\dagger \times_2 \cdots \times_d (\boldsymbol{U}_d^{(0)})^\dagger$, where $\boldsymbol{U}_k^\dagger = (\boldsymbol{U}_k^\top \boldsymbol{U}_k)^{-1} \boldsymbol{U}_k^\top$. The main loop of the ALS algorithm is presented as Algorithm 2. The symbol $\Pi_{\mathcal{U}}(\cdot)$ denotes the unimodality projection operator described in Sect. 3. Diverse criteria can be used to check for convergence, e.g., the factor change, objective change, stagnation check, and limit cycle criterion. In our experiments reported in Sect. 5, we used a combination of all these.

The key features of the algorithm are: (1) *HOSVD Initialization*, which provides a good starting point near the global optimum, based on the best rank-n_k approximation of each mode, (2) *Exact Core Recovery*, which computes the core tensor as the exact optimum for the current factor matrices via per-mode pseudoinverses rather than the full Kronecker product. This avoids the ill-conditioning that arises at high ranks, since the conditioning of $\boldsymbol{U}_k^\top \boldsymbol{U}_k \in$

$\mathbb{R}^{n_k \times n_k}$ depends only on the individual factor matrix rather than the full Kronecker structure, and (3) *Unconstrained Least Squares with Unimodal Projection*, which computes the unconstrained optimum $\bar{\boldsymbol{U}}_k = \boldsymbol{X}_{(k)} \boldsymbol{V}^\top (\boldsymbol{V}\boldsymbol{V}^\top)^{-1}$ and projects each column onto the unimodal constraint via $\Pi_{\mathcal{U}}(\cdot)$. This solve is well-conditioned because $\boldsymbol{V}\boldsymbol{V}^\top \in \mathbb{R}^{n_k \times n_k}$ is a small matrix whose conditioning depends only on the current core and factor matrices, not on the full Kronecker product. A proposed update is accepted if it reduces the objective and rejected otherwise.

Algorithm 2. Alternating Optimization for Unimodal Tucker Decomposition

Initialize $\{\mathbf{U}_k^{(0)}\}_{k=1}^d$ using HOSVD with Unimodal Constraints (Algorithm 1)
Compute initial core via pseudoinverses:
  $\mathcal{G}^{(0)} = \mathcal{X} \times_1 (\boldsymbol{U}_1^{(0)})^\dagger \times_2 (\boldsymbol{U}_2^{(0)})^\dagger \times_3 \cdots \times_d (\boldsymbol{U}_d^{(0)})^\dagger$
  where $\boldsymbol{U}_k^\dagger = (\boldsymbol{U}_k^\top \boldsymbol{U}_k)^{-1} \boldsymbol{U}_k^\top$ is the pseudoinverse of $\boldsymbol{U}_k$
Compute initial objective: $E^{(0)} = \left\| \mathcal{X} - \mathcal{G}^{(0)} \times_1 \boldsymbol{U}_1^{(0)} \times_2 \cdots \times_d \boldsymbol{U}_d^{(0)} \right\|_F$
for $t = 1, 2, \ldots, T_{\max}$ **do**
  $E_{\text{start}} \leftarrow E^{(t-1)}$
  for $k = 1, \ldots, d$ **do** ▷ Update Each Factor Matrix
    Unfold $\mathcal{X}$ and $\mathcal{G}^{(t-1)}$ along mode k:
      $\boldsymbol{X}_{(k)} \in \mathbb{R}^{N_k \times \prod_{j \neq k} N_j}, \quad \boldsymbol{G}_{(k)} \in \mathbb{R}^{n_k \times \prod_{j \neq k} n_j}$
    Compute Kronecker product of factor matrices from other modes:
      $\boldsymbol{Z} = \boldsymbol{U}_d^{(t-1)} \otimes \cdots \otimes \boldsymbol{U}_{k+1}^{(t-1)} \otimes \boldsymbol{U}_{k-1}^{(t-1)} \otimes \cdots \otimes \boldsymbol{U}_1^{(t-1)}$
    $\boldsymbol{V} = \boldsymbol{G}_{(k)} \boldsymbol{Z}^\top \in \mathbb{R}^{n_k \times \prod_{j \neq k} N_j}$ ▷ Compute auxiliary matrix
    $\bar{U}_k = \boldsymbol{X}_{(k)} \boldsymbol{V}^\top (\boldsymbol{V}\boldsymbol{V}^\top)^{-1} \in \mathbb{R}^{N_k \times n_k}$ ▷ Solve unconstrained least squares
    for $j = 1, \ldots, n_k$ **do** ▷ Project Each Column to Unimodal Constraint
      $\boldsymbol{u}_{k,j}^* = \Pi_{\mathcal{U}}(\bar{\boldsymbol{u}}_{k,j})$
    end for
    $\boldsymbol{U}_k^* \leftarrow [\boldsymbol{u}_{k,1}^*, \ldots, \boldsymbol{u}_{k,n_k}^*]$
    ▷ Compute candidate core exactly via pseudoinverses
    $\mathcal{G}^* = \mathcal{X} \times_1 (\boldsymbol{U}_1^{(t)})^\dagger \times_2 \cdots \times_k (\boldsymbol{U}_k^*)^\dagger \times_{k+1} \cdots \times_d (\boldsymbol{U}_d^{(t-1)})^\dagger$
    ▷ Compute candidate objective
    $E^* = \left\| \mathcal{X} - \mathcal{G}^* \times_1 \boldsymbol{U}_1^{(t)} \times_2 \cdots \times_k \boldsymbol{U}_k^* \times_{k+1} \cdots \times_d \boldsymbol{U}_d^{(t-1)} \right\|_F$
    if $E^* \leq E^{(t-1)}$ **then** ▷ Accept Update Only If Error Does Not Increase
      $\boldsymbol{U}_k^{(t)} \leftarrow \boldsymbol{U}_k^*, \quad \mathcal{G}^{(t-1)} \leftarrow \mathcal{G}^*, \quad E^{(t-1)} \leftarrow E^*$
    else
      $\boldsymbol{U}_k^{(t)} \leftarrow \boldsymbol{U}_k^{(t-1)}$ ▷ Reject Update Entirely
    end if
  end for
  $E^{(t)} \leftarrow E^{(t-1)}$ ▷ Final Error After All Mode Updates
  $\delta^{(t)} = \dfrac{|E^{(t)} - E_{\text{start}}|}{E_{\text{start}}}$ ▷ Relative change in objective
  if CHECKCONVERGENCE(t, $\delta^{(t)}$, $\{E^{(i)}\}_{i=1}^t$) **then STOP**
  end if
end for

Lemma 1. *The computational complexity of one iteration of the ALS algorithm with the unimodal constraints is:*

$$O\left(d \cdot \prod_{k=1}^{d} N_k + \sum_{k=1}^{d}\left(n_k^2 \prod_{j\neq k} N_j + n_k N_k^2\right)\right) .$$

Proof. In one iteration, these computations are performed:

- *Unfolding:* $O\left(d \cdot \prod_{k=1}^{d} N_k\right)$
- *Kronecker products:* $O\left(\sum_{k=1}^{d} \prod_{j\neq k} N_j \cdot \prod_{j\neq k} n_j\right)$
- *Matrix multiplications:* $O\left(\sum_{k=1}^{d} N_k n_k \prod_{j\neq k} N_j\right)$
- *Full mode least squares:* $O\left(\sum_{k=1}^{d}\left(n_k^2 \prod_{j\neq k} N_j + n_k^3\right)\right)$
- *Unimodality projections:* $O\left(\sum_{k=1}^{d} n_k N_k^2\right)$
- *Core updates via pseudoinverses:* Computing each $\boldsymbol{U}_k^{\dagger} = (\boldsymbol{U}_k^{\top}\boldsymbol{U}_k)^{-1}\boldsymbol{U}_k^{\top}$ costs $O(N_k n_k^2 + n_k^3)$ per mode, giving $O\left(\sum_{k=1}^{d}(N_k n_k^2 + n_k^3)\right)$ in total. Since $N_k \geq n_k$, this is dominated by the matrix multiplication term $N_k n_k \prod_{j\neq k} N_j$. The subsequent tensor contraction costs $O\left(d \cdot \prod_{k=1}^{d} N_k\right)$.
- *Error evaluations:* $O\left(d \cdot \prod_{k=1}^{d} N_k\right)$

This gives the total per iteration:
$O\left(d \cdot \prod_{k=1}^{d} N_k + \sum_{k=1}^{d}\left(n_k^2 \prod_{j\neq k} N_j + n_k N_k^2\right)\right)$.

3 Unimodal Projection Algorithm

The key component of our proposal is the unimodal projection. We will use the following lemma published in [2].

Lemma 2. *The unimodal least squares problem*

$$\boldsymbol{x}^{\star} = \arg\min_{\boldsymbol{x}} \|\boldsymbol{Y} - \boldsymbol{x}\boldsymbol{b}^T\|_F^2 \quad \textit{subject to } \boldsymbol{x} \textit{ being unimodal}$$

is equivalent to solving

$$\begin{aligned}
\boldsymbol{b}^{\star} &= \arg\min_{\boldsymbol{b}} \|\boldsymbol{\beta} - \boldsymbol{b}\|_2^2 \quad \textit{subject to } \boldsymbol{b} \textit{ being unimodal, where} \\
\boldsymbol{\beta} &= \arg\min_{\boldsymbol{x}} \|\boldsymbol{Y} - \boldsymbol{x}\boldsymbol{b}^T\|_F^2 \ .
\end{aligned}$$

This lemma implies that to solve the unimodal least squares problem, we can first solve the unconstrained least squares problem and then find the unimodal solution by minimizing the Euclidean distance from the unconstrained solution.

The projection operator $\Pi : \mathbb{R}^n \to \mathbb{R}^n$ finds the closest unimodal vector to the input:

$$\Pi(\boldsymbol{v}) = \arg\min_{\boldsymbol{u}} \|\boldsymbol{v} - \boldsymbol{u}\|_2^2 \quad \text{subject to } \boldsymbol{u} \text{ is unimodal.}$$

Following [2], the unimodal regression problem is *not* equivalent to simply solving two independent monotone regression subproblems for the segments before and after the peak (or trough). The key insight is that the peak/trough value must be handled consistently to ensure that the resulting vector is truly unimodal. For a *maximum-type* unimodal vector with a peak at position p, the left segment $\boldsymbol{u}_{1:p}$ must be non-decreasing, and the right segment $\boldsymbol{u}_{p:n}$ must be non-increasing, with $\boldsymbol{u}_p$ being the maximum value that satisfies both monotonicity constraints. For a *minimum-type* unimodal vector with a trough at position t, the left segment $\boldsymbol{u}_{1:t}$ must be non-increasing, and the right segment $\boldsymbol{u}_{t:n}$ must be non-decreasing, with $\boldsymbol{u}_t$ being the minimum value that satisfies both monotonicity constraints.

Algorithm 3. Project to Unimodal

Input: vector $\boldsymbol{v} \in \mathbb{R}^n$, sign $s \in \{+, -\}$
Initialize: $\boldsymbol{u}^* \leftarrow \boldsymbol{0}$, $e^* \leftarrow \|\boldsymbol{v}\|^2$
for $p = 1$ to n **do**
  Construct candidate unimodal vector $\boldsymbol{u}^{(p)}$ with peak at position p:
  if $s = +$ **then**

$$u_i^{(p)} = \begin{cases} \text{Isotonic}_{\uparrow}(\boldsymbol{v}_{1:p-1})_i & \text{if } i < p \\ \max(v_p, 0) & \text{if } i = p \\ \text{Isotonic}_{\downarrow}(\boldsymbol{v}_{p+1:n})_{i-p} & \text{if } i > p \end{cases}$$

    where $u_i^{(p)} \geq 0$ (projection onto non-negative cone)
  else

$$u_i^{(p)} = \begin{cases} \text{Isotonic}_{\downarrow}(\boldsymbol{v}_{1:p-1})_i & \text{if } i < p \\ \min(v_p, 0) & \text{if } i = p \\ \text{Isotonic}_{\uparrow}(\boldsymbol{v}_{p+1:n})_{i-p} & \text{if } i > p \end{cases}$$

    where $u_i^{(p)} \leq 0$ (projection onto non-positive cone)
  end if
  if ($s = +$ and $u_p^{(p)} \geq u_i^{(p)}\ \forall i$) or ($s = -$ and $u_p^{(p)} \leq u_i^{(p)}\ \forall i$) **then**
    Compute error: $e^{(p)} = \|\boldsymbol{v} - \boldsymbol{u}^{(p)}\|^2$
    if $e^{(p)} < e^*$ **then**
      $\boldsymbol{u}^* \leftarrow \boldsymbol{u}^{(p)}$
      $e^* \leftarrow e^{(p)}$
    end if
  end if
end for
Return: $\boldsymbol{u}^*$

In Algorithm 3 we present an efficient implementation based on Bro's *ulsr* (Unimodal Least Squares Regression) algorithm [2] that exploits the structure of the problem to avoid unnecessary recomputations: The unimodality constraint is enforced via projection onto the set of unimodal vectors. We define two constraint sets:

$$\mathcal{U}^+ = \{\boldsymbol{u} \in \mathbb{R}^n : u_1 \leq \cdots \leq u_p \geq u_{p+1} \geq \cdots \geq u_n,\ u_i \geq 0,\ p \in \{1, \ldots, n\}\}$$
$$\mathcal{U}^- = \{\boldsymbol{u} \in \mathbb{R}^n : u_1 \geq \cdots \geq u_p \leq u_{p+1} \leq \cdots \leq u_n,\ u_i \leq 0,\ p \in \{1, \ldots, n\}\}$$

where $\mathcal{U}^+$ contains non-negative unimodal vectors and $\mathcal{U}^-$ contains non-positive unimodal vectors. Given a vector $\boldsymbol{v} \in \mathbb{R}^n$ and a sign $s \in \{+, -\}$, the projection $\Pi_{\mathcal{U}^s}(\boldsymbol{v})$ is computed as described in Algorithm 3, where $\text{Isotonic}_\uparrow(\boldsymbol{x})$ and $\text{Isotonic}_\downarrow(\boldsymbol{x})$ denote isotonic regression for monotone increasing and decreasing sequences, respectively, as suggested by Robertson et al. [12].

The final projection chooses the better from the non-negative and non-positive unimodal projections:

$$\Pi_{\mathcal{U}}(\boldsymbol{v}) = \arg \min_{\boldsymbol{u} \in \{\Pi_{\mathcal{U}^+}(\boldsymbol{v}), \Pi_{\mathcal{U}^-}(\boldsymbol{v})\}} \|\boldsymbol{v} - \boldsymbol{u}\|^2$$

This approach allows the algorithm to handle both positive-peaked and negative-peaked unimodal shapes, selecting the one with minimal projection error.

4 Factor Normalization

After convergence, factor matrices are normalized so that each column attains a peak value of 1; see Algorithm 4. This step improves interpretability while preserving the tensor reconstruction exactly. The normalization transfers the scaling from the factors to the core tensor $\tilde{\mathcal{G}}$, making factor matrices directly comparable across modes.

Lemma 3. *The normalization satisfies reconstruction preservation:*

$$\mathcal{G} \times_1 \mathbf{U}_1 \times_2 \cdots \times_d \mathbf{U}_d = \tilde{\mathcal{G}} \times_1 \tilde{\mathbf{U}}_1 \times_2 \cdots \times_d \tilde{\mathbf{U}}_d \ .$$

Each normalized column satisfies:

$$\|\tilde{\mathbf{u}}_{k,j}\|_\infty = \max_i |\tilde{u}_{k,j,i}| \quad = \quad 1 \ .$$

Proof. The first statement of this lemma follows directly from the comparison of the two expressions for the decomposition with the original and the normalized tensor. They differ only in the scaling factors $\sigma_j, j = 1, \ldots, n_k, k = 1, \ldots, d$ that cancel in the normalized decomposition. The second statement is a direct consequence of the algebraic operations performed in steps 6–19 of Algorithm 4.

The normalization is particularly useful for visualizing, comparing, and interpreting unimodal factors, as all their columns are scaled so that their peak values equal 1 while maintaining their shape characteristics.

Algorithm 4. Normalize Factor Matrices

Input: Factor matrices $\{\mathbf{U}_k\}_{k=1}^d$, core tensor $\mathcal{G}$, ranks $\{n_k\}_{k=1}^d$
Output: Normalized factors $\{\tilde{\mathbf{U}}_k\}_{k=1}^d$, adjusted core $\tilde{\mathcal{G}}$
Initialize: $\tilde{\mathcal{G}} \leftarrow \mathcal{G}$
for $k = 1$ to d **do**
  for $j = 1$ to n_k **do**
    Compute extremal values of column j:
      $m_j^{\min} = \min_i (U_k)_{i,j}$
      $m_j^{\max} = \max_i (U_k)_{i,j}$
    Determine dominant extremum and its sign:
      $\ell^* = \arg\max_{\ell \in \{\min,\max\}} |m_j^\ell|$
      $\sigma_j = \text{sign}(m_j^{\ell^*})$
      $c_j = |m_j^{\ell^*}|$
    Compute scaling factor:
    if $c_j = 0$ **then**
      $s_j \leftarrow 0$
    else
      $s_j \leftarrow \sigma_j / c_j$
    end if
    Normalize column: $\tilde{\mathbf{u}}_{k,j} \leftarrow s_j \cdot \mathbf{u}_{k,j}$
  end for
  Construct diagonal scaling matrix:
    $\mathbf{S}_k = \text{diag}(\sigma_1 c_1, \sigma_2 c_2, \ldots, \sigma_{n_k} c_{n_k}) \in \mathbb{R}^{n_k \times n_k}$
  Adjust core tensor: $\tilde{\mathcal{G}} \leftarrow \tilde{\mathcal{G}} \times_k \mathbf{S}_k$
end for
Return: $\{\tilde{\mathbf{U}}_k\}_{k=1}^d$, $\tilde{\mathcal{G}}$

5 Experimental Comparisons

We perform an experiment using data from a survey conducted by the STEM Institute for Empirical Research [3] in 2022. A total of 1,661 Czech citizens over the age of 18 were surveyed. Respondents provided their opinions on 30 key topics of public life and 14 assessments of their own life situations, as well as their demographic data. The data from this study provided the analytical basis for the publication [3] and served to demonstrate the enhancement through the incorporation of MLR and OLR models as CPTs within the framework of BN structural learning [16]. We used this data and computed 20 probability distributions of dimension $d = 2, 3, 4, 5$ consisting of correlated variables according to [16]. In the experiments, we used equal ranks $n_i = n$ for all $i = 1, \ldots, d$, taking values $n = 2, \ldots, 7$. The approximation of the original tensor is computed as:

$$\hat{\mathcal{X}} = \tilde{\mathcal{G}} \times_1 \tilde{\mathbf{U}}_1 \times_2 \cdots \times_d \tilde{\mathbf{U}}_d \ .$$

To ensure that the approximation is a probability distribution, we divide each tensor value by the total sum of all tensor values. To measure the error, we use the Frobenius norm of the difference between the original and reconstructed tensors. The Frobenius norm is the square root of the sum of the absolute squares of tensor elements. The relative reconstruction error is:

$$\epsilon_{\mathrm{rel}} = \frac{\|\mathcal{X} - \hat{\mathcal{X}}\|_F}{\|\mathcal{X}\|_F}$$

Figure 2 compares the relative error of three selected probability distributions with $d = 3, 4, 5$ as a function of the selected rank n. The comparison is made for (1) the general Tucker decomposition and (2) the proposed unimodal Tucker decomposition implemented using an ALS algorithm.

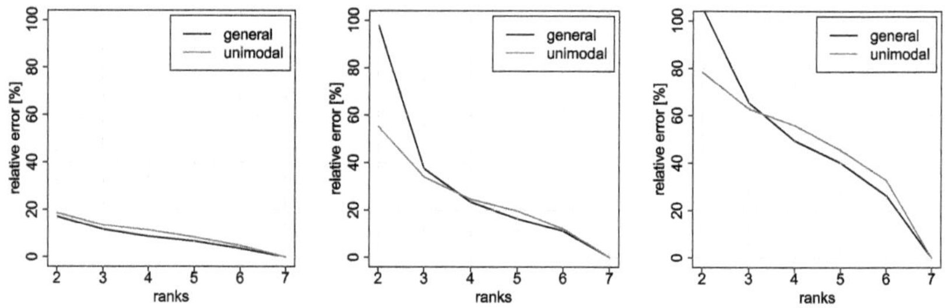

Fig. 2. The relative errors of the general algorithm and the unimodal ALS for different ranks and three different probability tables with $d = 3, 4, 5$, respectively.

In Fig. 3, we present the mean relative error as a function of ranks. The error decreases with higher ranks, and there are no significant differences between the unimodal and general Tucker decompositions, both having zero error at the maximal rank of 7. Rank 3 approximations seem to be a good compromise between complexity and the quality of approximations. The unimodality requirement looks natural for the tested probability distributions and does not restrict the approximation quality.

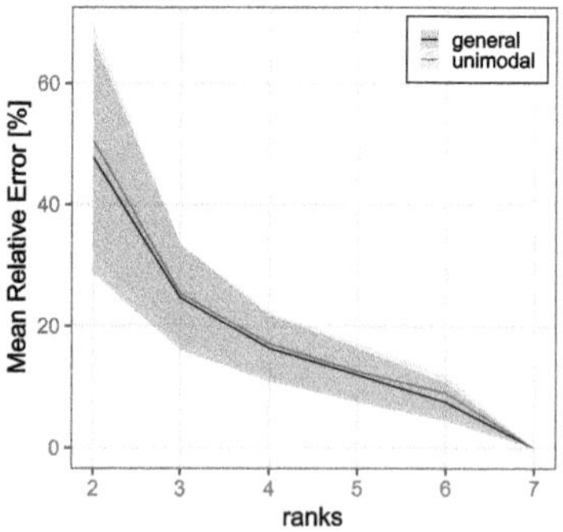

Fig. 3. The mean relative error ϵ_{rel} with respect to the ranks n.

We examine the probability distribution[4] $P(D_{11}, A_{15}, A_{18}, A_{19})$, representative of $d = 4$ in Fig. 2. Figure 4 shows the normalized membership functions of the unimodal rank-3 solution, which naturally correspond to three survey opinion types: *disagree, neutral, agree.* The reconstructed 1D marginals (Fig. 5) preserve the general trends of the originals. Mosaic plots of the original and reconstructed tensors of $P(D_{11}, A_{15}, A_{18}, A_{19})$ for ranks $(3, 3, 3, 3)$ are compared in Fig. 6, where rectangle sizes are proportional to probabilities and colors encode the last tensor dimension. The main patterns are reproduced despite some visible differences. Notably, the original tensor requires $7^4 = 2401$ parameters, while the reconstruction needs only $4 \cdot 3 \cdot 7 + 3^4 = 165$.

The experiments were implemented in R; the code is publicly available on GitHub and archived at Zenodo [17].

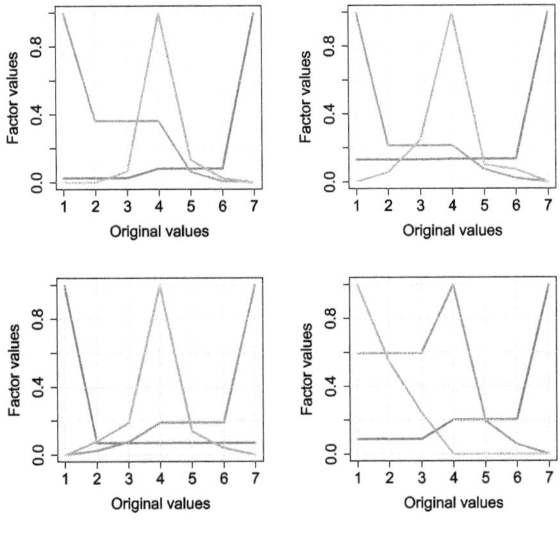

Fig. 4. The normalized unimodal membership functions.

[4] For variable descriptions, see [3, 16].

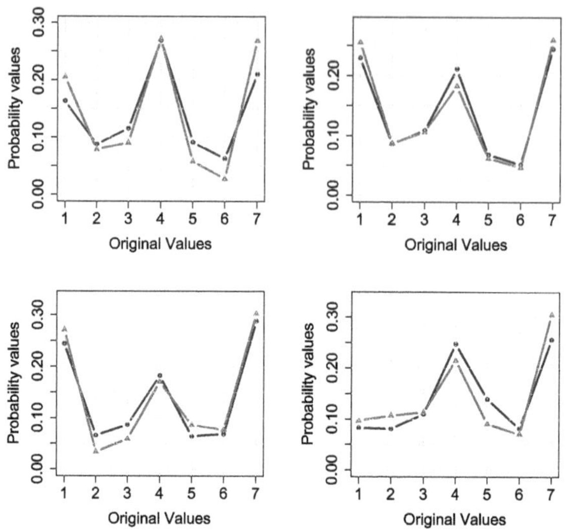

Fig. 5. Original (blue with dots) and reconstructed (red with triangles) marginals. (Color figure online)

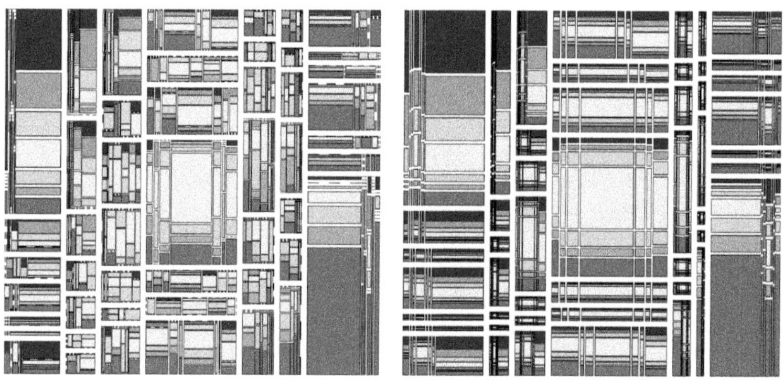

Fig. 6. The original (left) and the reconstructed (right) tensors.

6 Conclusions

We propose a computational method based on Unimodal Tucker Decomposition for representing multidimensional probability distributions. The approach offers two key benefits: (1) improved interpretability of the observed variables' states via Fuzzy Partitions, which naturally capture the fuzzy nature of these variables, and (2) a significantly more compact representation, with strong potential to reduce the computational complexity of probabilistic inference in the learned models.

Acknowledgments. Developed within the project of the University of Ostrava:

Social Dimension of New Technologies in the Energy Sector in the Ostrava Metropolitan Area (reg. number CZ.02.01.01/00/23_021/000859) with financial support from the European Union through the Jan Amos Komenský Operational Program.

Disclosure of Interests. The author has no competing interests to declare that are relevant to the content of this article.

References

1. Agresti, A.: Analysis of Ordinal Categorical Data, 2nd edn. Wiley, Hoboken, NJ (2010)
2. Bro, R., Sidiropoulos, N.: Least squares algorithms under unimodality and non-negativity constraints. J. Chemom. **12**(4), 223–247 (1998)
3. Buchtík, M.: Různá vyprávění o jedné společnosti. Friedrich-Ebert-Stiftung and Masarykova demokratická akademie Praha (2023)
4. De Lathauwer, L., De Moor, B., Vandewalle, J.: A multilinear singular value decomposition. SIAM J. Matrix Anal. Appl. **21**(4), 1253–1278 (2000)
5. De Lathauwer, L., De Moor, B., Vandewalle, J.: On the best rank-1 and rank-$(R_1, R_2, \ldots, R_N)$ approximation of higher-order tensors. SIAM J. Matrix Anal. Appl. **21**(4), 1324–1342 (2000)
6. Gil, M.A., González-Rodríguez, G.: Fuzzy vs. likert scale in statistics. In: Trillas, E., Bonissone, P.P., Magdalena, L., Kacprzyk, J. (eds.) Combining Experimentation and Theory: A Hommage to Abe Mamdani, pp. 407–420. Springer Berlin Heidelberg (2012). https://doi.org/10.1007/978-3-642-24666-1_27
7. McCullagh, P.: Regression models for ordinal data. J. Roy. Stat. Soc.: Ser. B (Methodol.) **42**(2), 109–127 (1980)
8. Mrógala, J., Perfilieva, I., Vomlel, J.: Fuzzy Bayesian networks with Likert scales. In: Proceedings of the 13th Workshop on Uncertainty Processing (WUPES'25), Třešť, Czech Republic. pp. 164–165. MatfyzPres (2025)
9. Muthén, B.: A general structural equation model with dichotomous, ordered categorical, and continuous latent variable indicators. Psychometrika **49**(1), 115–132 (1984). https://doi.org/10.1007/BF02294210
10. Perfilieva, I.: Fuzzy transforms: theory and applications. Fuzzy Sets Syst. **157**, 993–1023 (2006). https://doi.org/10.1016/j.fss.2005.11.012
11. Perfilieva, I., Novák, V., Dvořák, A.: Fuzzy transform in the analysis of data. Int. J. Approximate Reasoning **48** (2008). https://doi.org/10.1016/j.ijar.2007.06.003
12. Robertson, T., Wright, F., Dykstra, R.L.: Order restricted statistical inference. John Wiley & Sons (1988)
13. Ruspini, E.H.: A new approach to clustering. Inf. Control **15**, 22–32 (1969)
14. Samejima, F.: Estimation of latent ability using a response pattern of graded scores. Psychometrika Monograph Suppl. **34**(4, Pt. 2) (1969)
15. Tucker, L.R.: Some mathematical notes on three-mode factor analysis. Psychometrika **31**(3), 279–311 (1966)
16. Vomlel, J.: Enhancing Bayesian networks through logistic regression: a case study of Czech society divisions. Kybernetika (2026). Accepted for publication
17. Vomlel, J.: Unimodal Tucker decomposition (2026). https://doi.org/10.5281/zenodo.19431213

Discounting Operators in Belief Functions Theory: Taxonomies and Operational Analysis

Mustapha Reda Senouci[1](✉), Faouzi Sebbak[1], and Latifa Oukhellou[2]

[1] Computer Science Department, Ecole Militaire Polytechnique, Algiers, Algeria
mrsenouci@gmail.com

[2] Grettia Laboratory, Gustave Eiffel University, Champs-sur-Marne, France

Abstract. Belief Functions Theory (BFT) supports rich uncertainty modeling and information fusion, but its effectiveness hinges on the management of unreliable or conflicting evidence. Discounting operators address this issue by adjusting source contributions according to their reliability. However, the field still lacks a structured and up-to-date survey that clearly distinguishes existing operators and provides guidance on their selection. This paper fills that gap through two complementary taxonomies: a multidimensional characterization of operator behavior and a classification based on the information used to derive discount rates. We review representative operators, analyze their mathematical structure and practical requirements, and compare their qualitative behavior across key operational dimensions. The survey provides clear guidance for selecting and deploying discounting operators in systems that must handle unreliable evidence under diverse constraints.

Keywords: Belief Functions Theory · Dempster-Shafer Theory · Discounting Operators · Evidence Reliability · Uncertainty Management

1 Introduction

Belief Functions Theory (BFT), also known as Dempster–Shafer theory, provides a formal framework for representing and combining uncertain information [33,34]. Its ability to model epistemic uncertainty and aggregate heterogeneous evidence underpins applications in sensor fusion [30], decision support [17], communication networks [29,31], and intelligent transportation systems [32]. In practice, however, the quality of fusion depends critically on the reliability of the sources involved. When sources differ in credibility or produce conflicting reports, direct combination may yield distorted or misleading results [28].

Discounting operators address this issue by adjusting mass functions according to estimated source reliability. Over the years, many variants have been proposed, ranging from classical formulations [33] to adaptive [15], contextual [22],

B. Vantaggi et al. (Eds.): IPMU 2026, CCIS 3019, pp. 332–347, 2026.
https://doi.org/10.1007/978-3-032-28994-0_24

and data-driven approaches [6]. These contributions are scattered across the literature, and existing reviews either address discounting only tangentially [1,17,31] or focus on specific application domains [28]. As a result, a consolidated view of available operators, their underlying assumptions, and their trade-offs remains lacking.

This paper presents the first dedicated survey of discounting operators in BFT. Our contributions are threefold: (i) a primary taxonomy based on the type of information used to compute discount rates (external meta-knowledge, conflict or distance measures, intrinsic uncertainty indicators, or empirical performance data), complemented by a secondary perspective addressing temporal adaptation, granularity, and processing structure; (ii) a structured review of representative operators and their mathematical properties; and (iii) practical guidance and open problems that emerge from this synthesis.

The remainder of the paper is organized as follows. Section 2 summarizes the fundamentals of BFT and the standard discounting mechanism. Section 3 introduces the proposed taxonomies and surveys major operators. Section 4 analyzes their properties. Finally, Sect. 5 concludes with perspectives for future work.

2 Background on Belief Functions and Discounting

This section summarizes the essentials of BFT and the classical discounting mechanism.

2.1 Foundations of Belief Functions Theory

The core concept in BFT is the *basic belief assignment* (BBA), denoted by $m : 2^{\Theta} \rightarrow [0,1]$, where Θ represents the frame of discernment, defined as a finite set of mutually exclusive and exhaustive hypotheses. A BBA satisfies

$$\sum_{A \subseteq \Theta} m(A) = 1, \qquad m(\emptyset) = 0, \tag{1}$$

where $m(A)$ represents the belief committed exactly to $A \subseteq \Theta$ [33]. From m, the *belief* and *plausibility* functions are derived as:

$$Bel(A) = \sum_{\emptyset \neq B \subseteq A} m(B), \quad Pl(A) = \sum_{\substack{B \subseteq \Theta \\ B \cap A \neq \emptyset}} m(B) = 1 - Bel(\overline{A}),$$

where $Bel(A)$ measures the total belief committed to A, while $Pl(A)$ quantifies how much support does not contradict A [34].

When multiple sources provide evidence, BFT offers fusion rules to combine their BBAs [28]. The most widely used is *Dempster's rule*:

$$m_{1 \cap 2}(A) = \frac{1}{1-K} \sum_{\substack{B, C \subseteq \Theta \\ B \cap C = A}} m_1(B)\, m_2(C), \qquad A \neq \emptyset, \tag{2}$$

where

$$K = \sum_{\substack{B,C \subseteq \Theta \\ B \cap C = \emptyset}} m_1(B)\, m_2(C) \quad (3)$$

is the global conflict [2]. This rule assumes reliable sources, an assumption that rarely holds in practice.

Alternative rules are often employed when reliability is uncertain or when conflict is high [28]. The *disjunctive rule* combines m_1 and m_2 as:

$$m_{1\cup 2}(A) = \sum_{\substack{B,C \subseteq \Theta \\ B \cup C = A}} m_1(B)\, m_2(C). \quad (4)$$

Decision-making commonly uses Bel, Pl, or the *pignistic probability* ($BetP$) from the transferable belief model [34]:

$$BetP(\theta) = \sum_{\substack{A \subseteq \Theta \\ \theta \in A}} \frac{m(A)}{|A|}, \qquad \theta \in \Theta. \quad (5)$$

2.2 Motivation for Discounting Operators

Real-world sources often differ in reliability, and failing to account for this variability may amplify conflict or distort combined beliefs [28,33]. Discounting incorporates a reliability estimate $\alpha \in [0, 1]$, where $\alpha = 0$ denotes full reliability and $\alpha = 1$ complete unreliability.

Shafer's classical operator [33] produces a discounted BBA m^α as follows:

$$\begin{aligned} m^\alpha(A) &= (1-\alpha)\, m(A), \qquad A \subset \Theta,\, A \neq \emptyset, \\ m^\alpha(\Theta) &= \alpha + (1-\alpha)\, m(\Theta). \end{aligned} \quad (6)$$

This reallocation of mass toward Θ captures the uncertainty induced by partial trust in the source [8]. Discounting is therefore a fundamental step in fusion pipelines: it embeds source reliability into the BBA, improves robustness against unreliable or malicious sources, and supports adaptive or context-dependent reliability modeling. The next section introduces two complementary taxonomies of discounting operators and reviews their properties.

3 Discounting Operators: Taxonomies and Survey

Discounting can be characterized along several independent dimensions that capture how discount rates are defined and applied. Figure 1 presents a multidimensional taxonomy that classifies operators along four principal axes, enabling a more nuanced understanding of their properties and applicability.

The *information source* dimension specifies what determines the discount factor. The *temporal* dimension indicates whether discounting parameters are

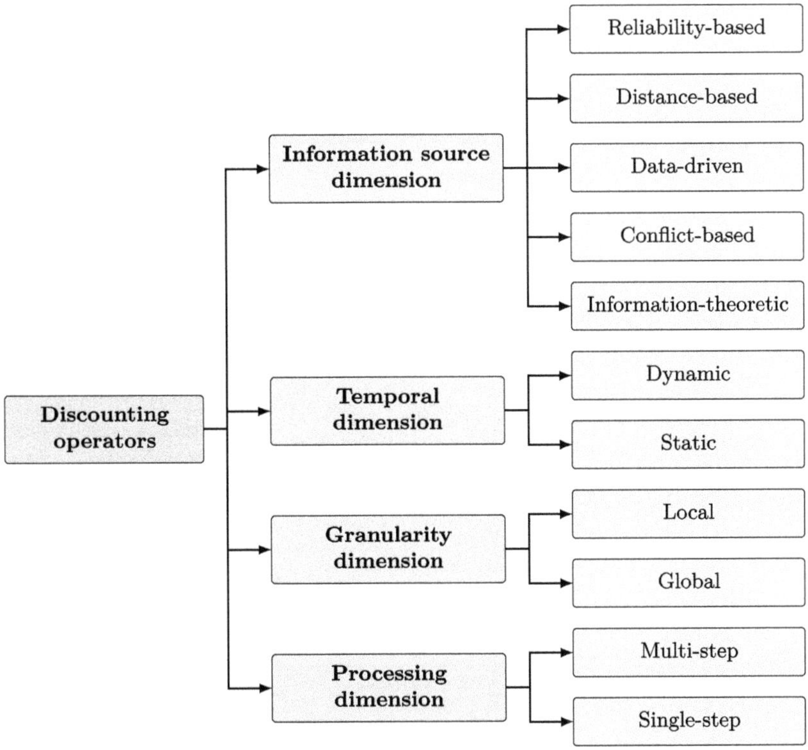

Fig. 1. Multidimensional taxonomy of discounting operators in BFT.

fixed or adapt over time. The *granularity* dimension describes whether a single factor is applied globally or varies across propositions. The *processing* dimension distinguishes between direct one-step computations and multi-stage procedures.

Discounting operators differ fundamentally in the type of information they use to determine the discount rate. Figure 2 provides an orthogonal classification into four mutually exclusive categories. *Source reliability*-based operators rely on external meta-knowledge such as sensor specifications, expert assessments, or contextual cues. *Conflict- and distance-based* operators compute discount rates from the interaction between BBAs, typically using conflict, divergence, or distance measures. *Information-theoretic* operators derive rates from intrinsic uncertainty indicators of one or more BBAs, such as entropy or non-specificity. *Data-driven* operators adjust discounting based on external performance signals, including ground truth or validation statistics.

Although the taxonomy presented in Fig. 2 is exhaustive, space constraints limit the discussion to representative operators. Accordingly, the information-source axis serves as the primary guide for this survey, while the remaining dimensions are discussed only when they provide additional insight.

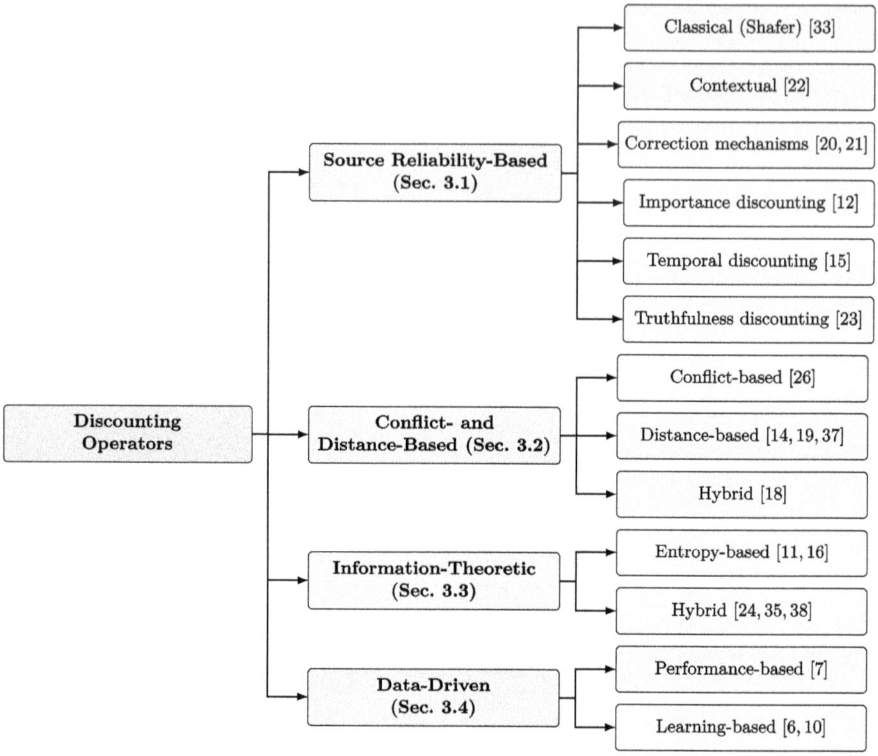

Fig. 2. Taxonomy of discounting operators in BFT.

3.1 Source Reliability-Based Operators

Source reliability-based operators constitute the classical foundation for handling imperfect information sources. Their objective is straightforward: weaken a source's BBA according to its assessed credibility, based on meta-knowledge about the origin, quality, or acquisition conditions of the evidence. The classical discounting operation (Sect. 2.2) applies a single factor α to all focal elements and transfers the discounted mass to Θ.

Contextual discounting [22] generalizes this by allowing reliability to vary across *contexts*, typically defined by a partition of the frame. Let $\Omega = \{\theta_1, \ldots, \theta_L\}$ be a partition of the frame Θ, where each block θ_ℓ corresponds to a specific context with reliability β_ℓ and unreliability $\alpha_\ell = 1 - \beta_\ell$. Given a BBA m, contextual discounting builds a corrected BBA by combining m with a context-induced BBA m^Ω through the disjunctive rule:

$$m^{\alpha}_{\Omega} = m \cup m^{\Omega}. \tag{7}$$

The BBA m^Ω is defined as the disjunctive combination of L elementary BBAs $m_1, \ldots, m_L$, one per context: $m^\Omega = m_1 \cup m_2 \cup \ldots \cup m_L$, where each m_ℓ,

$\ell \in \{1, \ldots, L\}$, is defined as

$$m_\ell(A) = \begin{cases} 1 - \alpha_\ell & \text{if } A = \emptyset, \\ \alpha_\ell & \text{if } A = \theta_\ell, \\ 0 & \text{otherwise.} \end{cases} \tag{8}$$

Several extensions refine this mechanism. Some operators [12,20,21] redirect discounted mass to specific subsets rather than to Θ only, enabling more fine-grained reliability modeling. Others decompose reliability into multiple dimensions, such as separating *relevance* from *truthfulness* [23], or introduce temporal dynamics that decrease credibility as information becomes outdated [15].

3.2 Conflict and Distance-Based Operators

Conflict- and distance-based operators derive discounting factors from inter-source disagreement. High conflict or large epistemic distances induce stronger discounting, reflecting the intuition that mutually inconsistent evidence should be down-weighted [19,26].

Conflict-Based Operators. A representative approach is Schubert's sequential incremental discounting [26]. It discounts each belief function in proportion to its *degree of falsity*, defined as the reduction in conflict when that belief function e_q is removed from the ensemble χ. Let $c^{(d,0)}$ be the unnormalized conflict (mass on $\emptyset$) after combining the currently discounted BBAs at iteration d, and $c^{(d,q)}$ the conflict when e_q is excluded. The degree of falsity is $m_{\Delta\chi}(e_q \notin \chi) = \frac{c^{(d,0)} - c^{(d,q)}}{1 - c^{(d,q)}}$. The credibility of e_q follows as $\alpha_q^{(d)} = 1 - m_{\Delta\chi}(e_q \notin \chi) = \frac{1 - c^{(d,0)}}{1 - c^{(d,q)}}$. Schubert applies updates incrementally using a gain $\varepsilon \in (0,1]$: $\alpha_\varepsilon^{(d,q)} = 1 - \varepsilon \cdot \frac{c^{(d,0)} - c^{(d,q)}}{1 - c^{(d,q)}}$.

The discounted BBA at the next iteration is

$$m_q^{(d+1)}(A) = \begin{cases} \alpha_\varepsilon^{(d,q)}\, m_q^{(d)}(A), & A \subset \Omega,\ A \neq \Omega, \\ \alpha_\varepsilon^{(d,q)}\, m_q^{(d)}(\Omega) + (1 - \alpha_\varepsilon^{(d,q)}), & A = \Omega. \end{cases}$$

At each iteration, all BBAs are updated using the current conflict values and then recombined via Dempster's rule. The process terminates when the total conflict $c^{(d,0)}$ falls below a predefined threshold $k \in (0, 1)$.

Distance-Based Operators. Classical conflict measures, such as $k = m(\emptyset)$ (Eq. 3), conflates genuine disagreement with auto-conflict due to non-idempotent combination rules. Distance-based operators sidestep this issue by quantifying disagreement geometrically. They rely on measures like the Jousselme distance [13], which derives discount rates from how far a source's BBA lies from a reference (e.g., a prototype or the aggregated belief state). This approach anchors discounting directly in the geometric structure of belief functions.

This geometric perspective is exemplified by operators such as [14,19,37], which estimate source reliability directly from observed inter-source disagreement. A representative example is the method proposed by Martin et al. [19]. Their procedure first quantifies pairwise dissimilarity by means of the Jousselme distance between belief functions: $d_J(m_1, m_2) = \sqrt{\frac{1}{2}(m_1 - m_2)^\top \mathbf{D}(m_1 - m_2)}$, where $\mathbf{D}$ is the standard $2^{|\Theta|} \times 2^{|\Theta|}$ similarity matrix,

$$\mathbf{D}_{A,B} = \begin{cases} 1, & A = B = \emptyset, \\ \dfrac{|A \cap B|}{|A \cup B|}, & A, B \subseteq \Theta,\ A \cup B \neq \emptyset, \\ 0, & \text{otherwise.} \end{cases}$$

Given M sources $m_1, \ldots, m_M$, the conflict of source i w.r.t. the ensemble is the mean distance to all other sources: $\mathrm{Conf}(i, E) = \frac{1}{M-1} \sum_{\substack{j=1 \\ j \neq i}}^{M} d_J(m_i, m_j)$.

Reliability is then obtained through a nonlinear mapping,

$$\alpha_i = \left(1 - \mathrm{Conf}(i, E)^{\lambda}\right)^{1/\lambda}, \quad \lambda > 0,$$

typically with $\lambda \in \{1.5, 2\}$. Higher disagreement drives α_i downward.

These operators rely either on conflict measures or on geometric distances. Hybrid schemes also exist; for example, Liu et al. [18] combine both types of indicators to derive discounting factors.

3.3 Information-Theoretic Operators

Information-theoretic operators derive discount rates from measures of a source's internal uncertainty (e.g., entropy, non-specificity, or mass variance) rather than from external assessments of reliability. Sources exhibiting higher entropy or imprecision provide less informative evidence and are therefore discounted more aggressively. The discount factor is thus directly tied to the informational value of each BBA.

Huynh [11] defines an entropy-based discount rate $\delta(m_i)$ by applying Shannon entropy to the pignistic distribution BetP_{m_i}. The ambiguity of m_i is $H(m_i) = -\sum_{\theta \in \Theta} \mathrm{BetP}_{m_i}(\theta) \log_2(\mathrm{BetP}_{m_i}(\theta))$, with range $[0, \log_2(|\Theta|)]$. The normalized entropy, $\delta(m_i) = \frac{H(m_i)}{\log_2(|\Theta|)}$, yields a discount rate that increases with the source's internal uncertainty.

Another widely used measure is the *Deng entropy* [3], defined as

$$E_d(m) = - \sum_{A \subseteq \Theta,\, m(A) > 0} m(A) \log_2 \left(\frac{m(A)}{2^{|A|} - 1} \right), \tag{9}$$

which reduces to Shannon entropy when all focal elements are singletons. Larger values of $E_d(m)$ indicate higher uncertainty and typically lead to stronger discounting in fusion and conflict-mitigation frameworks [16,38].

Another established measure is the *generalized Hartley-like non-specificity* introduced by Dubois and Prade [5]: $NS(m) = \sum_{A \subseteq \Theta, m(A)>0} m(A) \log_2 |A|$, which captures imprecision independently of conflict. Larger focal sets, weighted by their masses, increase $NS(m)$. Although variants have been proposed to address known limitations [36], $NS(m)$ remains the standard reference.

In practice, non-specificity is frequently combined with other indicators to derive adaptive discounting rates [35]. Other approaches follow the same direction by integrating criteria from different categories; for instance, [24,38] jointly employ information-theoretic and conflict-based indicators.

3.4 Data-Driven Operators

Data-driven approaches estimate dynamic discount factors using empirical validation data or learning-based techniques. Performance-based methods exploit historical performance metrics, such as confusion matrices or classification accuracies, to quantify sensor reliability. For example, Elouedi et al. [7] derive discounting rates directly from a classifier's confusion matrix, which captures a classifier's past performance on objects where the truth is known. Their framework combines classical discounting using a global reliability rate (Tf), defined as the overall classification accuracy, with contextual discounting using local rates ($Tf[\omega_\ell]$ or $Tfd[\omega_\ell]$) that depend on the true class ω_ℓ.

Learning-based approaches instead optimize discounting parameters by training on labeled datasets. This line traces back to Denoeux's evidential k-nearest-neighbour classifiers [4], which estimate per-class source reliability from distances; subsequent work frames discount-factor estimation as a formal optimization problem. These methods minimize the distance between belief outputs after discounting and ground-truth labels. In [6], this distance is defined as the sum of Euclidean distances between the pignistic probabilities (BetP) derived from the discounted sensor evidence (${}^{\alpha}m$) and the indicator vector ($\delta_{A,i}$) of the true class label, making unreliability directly measurable as a deviation from correctness.

More recent work, such as [10], embeds discounting within deep learning architectures. The model learns class-specific reliability coefficients β_{tk} for each modality t conditioned on the true class θ_k, using contextual discounting. Training is performed end-to-end with a two-term loss: one term penalizes modality-level prediction errors, and the other penalizes errors after evidence fusion. The result is a data-driven, class-aware reliability model learned jointly with the task.

3.5 Multi-criteria Operators

Multi-criteria approaches argue that no single indicator can capture the full spectrum of source imperfections. Instead of relying on one factor (conflict, distance, entropy, or performance), they aggregate multiple heterogeneous criteria to estimate a more faithful reliability score. These methods do not constitute a new family; they simply combine evidence drawn from the four categories discussed earlier. The final discount rate comes from an MCDM/MCDA aggregation step that fuses several reliability indicators into a single score.

A representative example is [9], which applies the PROMETHEE II method to merge six criteria capturing both expert imperfection and inter-source conflict. Building on this work, the authors in [25] extend the framework by incorporating eight additional dissimilarity measures, yielding a total of fourteen metrics that jointly characterize internal and external conflict. The underlying rationale is straightforward: discounting based on richer and complementary criteria yields a more stable and discriminative estimation of source reliability than any single-criterion approach.

4 Operational Analysis and Selection Guidelines

This section analyzes the operational behavior of discounting rules, including their requirements and differences, through a multidimensional characterization, a comparative illustration, and a qualitative comparison.

4.1 Multidimensional Characterization

Table 1 maps representative operators across the four dimensions of our taxonomy to support systematic selection.

This characterization highlights clear structural and semantic differences that govern applicability. Classical and contextual discounting rely on fixed, reliability-based factors with static timing and single-step processing. More recent methods increase modeling fidelity by introducing temporal dynamics (e.g., falsity-based discounting, IDRC), allowing discount rates to evolve during fusion. The granularity dimension separates operators that apply a global factor, redirecting discounted mass solely to Θ, from those that use local, hypothesis- or context-specific factors, as in contextual discounting. The most significant shift along the information-source dimension is the emergence of multi-criteria methods, which aggregate heterogeneous indicators from distance-based, conflict-based, and information-theoretic approaches into multi-step reliability estimation, rather than relying on a single cue.

Overall, the multidimensional view clarifies trade-offs among flexibility and tractability, expert-supplied meta-knowledge and data-driven adaptation, and semantic simplicity and expressive power, helping practitioners align operator choice with application constraints and epistemic assumptions.

4.2 Comparative Illustration

We compare five schemes, classical [33], contextual [22], entropy-based [11], distance-based [19], and falsity-based [26], using a standard aerial-target example [15]. The primary sensor provides $m_1(\{a\}) = 0.5$, $m_1(\{r\}) = 0.5$, with a, h, r denoting airplane, helicopter, and rocket. Meta-knowledge indicates the sensor is over-reliable when the true target belongs to $\{h, r\}$, motivating contextual or adaptive discounting.

Table 1. Multidimensional characterization of representative discounting operators.

Discounting Operator	Information Source	Temporal Dimension	Granularity Dimension	Processing Dimension
Classical discounting [33]	Reliability-based	Static	Global	Single-step
Contextual discounting [22]	Reliability-based	Static	Local	Single-step
Importance discounting [12]	Reliability-based	Static	Global	Multi-step
Temporal discounting [15]	Reliability-based	Dynamic	Local	Single-step
Correction mechanisms [20,21]	Reliability-based	Static	Local	Single-step
Truthfulness discounting [23]	Reliability-based	Static	Local	Single-step
Falsity-based discounting [26]	Conflict-based	Dynamic	Local	Multi-step
IDRC [14]	Distance-based	Dynamic	Global	Multi-step
Disagreement-based discounting [37]	Distance-based	Dynamic	Global	Multi-step
DismP-based discounting [18]	Distance-based + Conflict-based	Static	Global	Multi-step
Distance-based discounting [19]	Distance-based	Static	Global	Multi-step
Entropy-based discounting [11]	Information-theoretic	Dynamic	Global	Single-step
Negation discounting [16]	Information-theoretic	Static	Global	Multi-step
Weighted discounting [38]	Distance-based + Information-theoretic	Static	Global	Multi-step
Generic discounting [24]	Distance-based + Information-theoretic	Static	Global	Multi-step
Non-specificity discounting [35]	Distance-based + Information-theoretic	Static	Global	Multi-step
Assessment-based discounting [6]	Data-driven (Learning-based)	Static	Global	Multi-step
Confusion matrix discounting [7]	Data-driven (Performance-based)	Static	Local	Multi-step
Deep evidential discounting [10]	Data-driven (Learning-based)	Static	Local	Multi-step
Sequential discounting [25]	Multi-criteria	Dynamic	Global	Multi-step
Multi-criteria discounting [9]	Multi-criteria	Static	Global	Multi-step

Classical, contextual, and entropy-based rules operate directly on m_1. Distance- and conflict-based methods require multiple sources; therefore, we introduce a slightly perturbed BBA: $m_2(\{a\}) = 0.45$, $m_2(\{r\}) = 0.45$, $m_2(\{a, r\}) = 0.10$.

Table 2 summarizes the discounted BBAs and reveals distinct behaviors across discounting paradigms. Classical discounting applies a uniform correction, which unnecessarily penalizes even the reliable $\{a\}$ belief. In contrast, contextual discounting, using the partition $\Omega = \{\{a\}, \{h, r\}\}$, exhibits its characteristic behavior: it eliminates belief in $\{r\}$ and creates belief in the composite $\{a, r\}$ through disjunctive correction. This reflects its semantic assumption that unreliability applies conditionally on the true state. Entropy-based discounting imposes a strong global reduction. This results from the pignistic transformation of m_1 having entropy $H = 1.0$; given a frame size of $|\Theta| = 3$ and a maximum entropy of $\log_2 3 \approx 1.585$, the resulting discount rate is $\delta = H/\log_2 3 \approx 0.6309$. Distance-based discounting applies only a minimal correction due to the high similarity between m_1 and m_2. Finally, the conflict-based method applies no discounting, as the initial conflict remains below the decision threshold of 0.5, reflecting its design goal of intervening only when fusion failure is imminent.

Table 2. Effect of discounting rules on m_1 under context $\{h, r\}$ with reliability 0.6.

Operator	$m(\{a\})$	$m(\{r\})$	$m(\{a,r\})$	$m(\Omega)$
Original m_1	0.5000	0.5000	0.0000	0.0000
Classical discounting [33]	0.3000	0.3000	0.0000	0.4000
Contextual discounting [22]	0.3000	0.0000	0.3000	0.4000
Entropy-based discounting [11]	0.1845	0.1845	0.0000	0.6309
Distance-based discounting [19]	0.4994	0.4994	0.0000	0.0013
Falsity-based discounting [26]	0.5000	0.5000	0.0000	0.0000

Figure 3 illustrates the mass redistribution. Only the contextual operator assigns mass to $\{a, r\}$, a direct consequence of its disjunctive mechanism (Eq. 7–8). All other operators redirect discounted mass exclusively to Θ, preserving the original focal structure. This example underscores a key point: discounting is not merely a preprocessing step; it encodes assumptions about evidence quality that directly shape fusion outcomes. Selecting an appropriate discounting rule is, therefore, a critical modeling decision in belief-functions-based systems.

4.3 Qualitative Comparison

Table 3 provides a qualitative assessment of representative operators across key practical dimensions, including their operational requirements, complexity, and strategies for redistributing discounted mass.

The following discussion covers the failure modes and limitations of each category; source reliability-based operators [12,15,20–23,33] rely on external

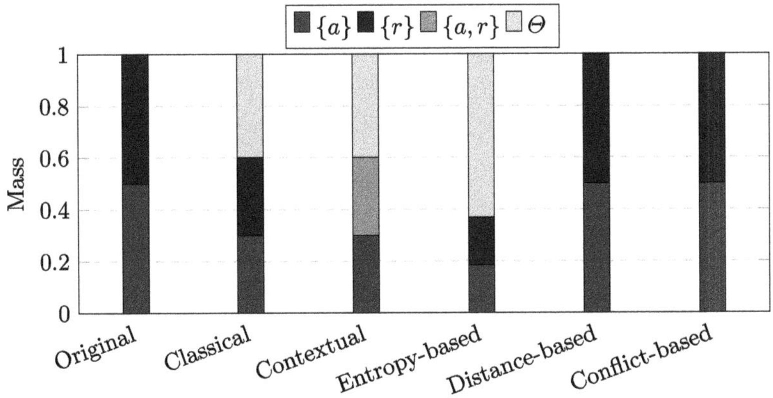

Fig. 3. Mass redistribution across focal elements under five discounting operators.

meta-knowledge, allowing single-source operation with low computational cost. However, their effectiveness depends on accurate *a priori* reliability estimates, which may be unavailable or degrade over time. Conflict- and distance-based methods [9,14,16,18,19,25,26,37] eliminate this requirement by deriving discount factors from inter-source disagreement, yielding self-calibrating behavior at the expense of higher complexity and the need for simultaneous multi-BBA availability. Information-theoretic operators [11,35,38] use intrinsic uncertainty measures to compute discount rates without meta-knowledge or extensive multi-source comparisons; however, internal uncertainty may not tightly correlate with true source reliability in all contexts. Data-driven approaches [6,7,10,24] anchor discounting in empirical performance using ground truth, optimizing parameters through error minimization, but their effectiveness depends on dataset representativeness and the availability of sufficient labeled data.

A central structural distinction concerns how discounted mass is redistributed. Operators transferring all discounted mass to Θ [6,7,9,11,14,19,23–26,33] follow the classical paradigm of expressing unreliability as total ignorance, offering semantic clarity but potentially losing finer-grained distinctions. Operators that redistribute mass to specific subsets [10,12,15,20–22,35,38] capture proposition-dependent uncertainty more precisely but require richer parameterization and risk mischaracterizing focal-specific reliability.

Finally, many advanced methods face scalability constraints. Optimization steps in [6,24], iterative post-weight combination in [35,38], and complex internal–external metric computation in [9,16,25] hinder real-time deployment. Only a small subset [11,23,33] remains suitable for real-time use due to their low computational overhead, highlighting the persistent tension between expressive reliability modeling and feasibility in latency-constrained applications.

Table 3. Operational characterization of representative discounting operators.

Discounting operator	Meta-knowledge required?	Multiple BBAs required?	Training data required?	Suitable for real-time use?	Transfers discounted mass to Θ?
Classical discounting [33]	✓	✗	✗	✓	✓
Contextual discounting [22]	✓	✗	✗	✗	✗
Importance discounting [12]	✓	✗	✗	✗	✗
Temporal discounting [15]	✓	✗	✗	✗	✗
Correction mechanisms [20,21]	✓	✗	✗	✗	✗
Truthfulness discounting [23]	✓	✗	✗	✓	✓
Falsity-based discounting [26]	✗	✓	✗	✗	✓
IDRC [14]	✗	✓	✗	✗	✓
Disagreement-based discounting [37]	✗	✓	✗	✗	✓
DismP-based discounting [18]	✗	✓	✗	✗	✓
Distance-based discounting [19]	✗	✓	✗	✗	✓
Entropy-based discounting [11]	✗	✗	✗	✓	✓
Negation discounting [16]	✗	✓	✗	✗	✓
Weighted discounting [38]	✗	✓	✗	✗	✗
Generic discounting [24]	✗	✓	✓	✗	✓
Non-specificity discounting [35]	✗	✓	✗	✗	✗
Assessment-based discounting [6]	✗	✗	✓	✗	✓
Confusion matrix discounting [7]	✗	✗	✓	✗	✓
Deep evidential discounting [10]	✗	✓	✓	✗	✗
Sequential discounting [25]	✗	✓	✗	✗	✓
Multi-criteria discounting [9]	✗	✓	✗	✗	✓

5 Conclusion

This paper introduced two complementary taxonomies for discounting operators in belief functions theory and used them to clarify operator behavior and guide informed selection in multi-source fusion. The analysis shows that operator effectiveness is inherently context-dependent, shaped by conflict structure, availability of meta-knowledge, computational constraints, and the temporal stability of the environment.

Several challenges remain. First, the lack of a shared reference implementation for discounting operators hampers reproducibility and slows cumulative progress; our earlier EDST framework [27] offers a concrete baseline that can be extended to cover a broader range of operators and to support large-scale empirical benchmarks. Second, composite strategies are still underexplored, including sequential schemes (e.g., global discounting followed by focal-specific refinement) and adaptive mechanisms that switch operators based on runtime indicators, such as increasing conflict. Third, many advanced operators, particularly data-driven and multi-criteria approaches, suffer from limited interpretability, which restricts their adoption in safety-critical and regulated applications. Fourth, formal cross-category relationships and stability or robustness bounds for each operator family remain uncharacterized. Finally, the interaction between discounting operators and non-Dempster combination rules remains poorly understood, with little systematic guidance on compatible or antagonistic pairings.

References

1. Belmessous, K., Sebbak, F., Mataoui, M., Senouci, M.R., Cherifi, W.: Dempster-shafer theory in recommender systems: a survey. Internat. J. Uncertain. Fuzziness Knowl. Based Syst. **32**(05), 747–780 (2024)
2. Dempster, A.P.: Upper and lower probabilities induced by a multivalued mapping. Ann. Math. Stat. **38**(2), 325–339 (1967)
3. Deng, Y.: Deng entropy. Chaos, Solitons Fractals **91**, 549–553 (2016)
4. Denoeux, T.: A k-nearest neighbor classification rule based on dempster-shafer theory. IEEE Trans. Syst. Man Cybern. **25**(5), 804–813 (1995)
5. Dubois, D., Prade, H.: A note on measures of specificity for fuzzy sets. Int. J. Gen Syst **10**(4), 279–283 (1985)
6. Elouedi, Z., Mellouli, K., Smets, P.: Assessing sensor reliability for multisensor data fusion within the transferable belief model. IEEE Trans. Syst. Man Cybern. **34**(1), 782–787 (2004)
7. Elouedi, Z., Lefevre, E., Mercier, D.: Discountings of a belief function using a confusion matrix. In: 22nd IEEE International Conference on Tools with Artificial Intelligence, vol. 1, pp. 287–294 (2010)
8. Elouedi, Z., Mellouli, K., Smets, P.: The evaluation of sensors' reliability and their tuning for multisensor data fusion within the transferable belief model. In: European Conference on Symbolic and Quantitative Approaches with Uncertainty, pp. 350–361. Springer, Berlin, Heidelberg (2001)
9. Frikha, A.: On the use of a multi-criteria approach for reliability estimation in belief function theory. Inf. Fusion **18**, 20–32 (2014)
10. Huang, L., Ruan, S., Decazes, P., Denœux, T.: Deep evidential fusion with uncertainty quantification and reliability learning for multimodal medical image segmentation. Inf. Fusion **113**, 102648 (2025)
11. Huynh, V.N.: Application of dempster-shafer theory to ensemble classification and user preferences. In: 6th School on Belief Functions and Their Applications. Japan Advanced Institute of Science and Technology, Ishikawa, Japan (2023), lecture presented 27–31 Oct 2023

12. Jiao, L., Pan, Q., Liang, Y., Feng, X., Yang, F.: Combining sources of evidence with reliability and importance for decision making. CEJOR **24**(1), 87–106 (2013)
13. Jousselme, A.L., Grenier, D.: Éloi Bossé: a new distance between two bodies of evidence. Inf. Fusion **2**(2), 91–101 (2001)
14. Klein, J., Colot, O.: Automatic discounting rate computation using a dissent criterion. In: Workshop on the Theory of Belief Functions, pp. 1–6. Brest, France (2010)
15. Kurdej, M., Cherfaoui, V.: Conservative, proportional and optimistic contextual discounting in the belief functions theory. In: Proceedings of the 16th International Conference on Information Fusion, pp. 2012–2018 (2013)
16. Li, S., Xiao, F., Abawajy, J.H.: Conflict management of evidence theory based on belief entropy and negation. IEEE Access **8**, 37766–37774 (2020)
17. Li, T., Sun, J., Fei, L.: Dempster-shafer theory in emergency management: a review. Nat. Hazards **121**(6), 6413–6440 (2025)
18. Liu, Z., Dezert, J., Pan, Q., Mercier, G.: Combination of sources of evidence with different discounting factors based on a new dissimilarity measure. Decis. Support Syst. **52**(1), 133–141 (2011)
19. Martin, A., Jousselme, A.L., Osswald, C.: Conflict measure for the discounting operation on belief functions. In: 2008 11th International Conference on Information Fusion, pp. 1–8 (2008)
20. Mercier, D., Denoeux, T., Masson, M.H.: General correction mechanisms for weakening or reinforcing belief functions. In: 9th International Conference on Information Fusion, pp. 1–7 (2006)
21. Mercier, D., Éric Lefèvre, Delmotte, F.: Belief functions contextual discounting and canonical decompositions. Int. J. Approx. Reason. **53**(2), 146–158 (2012). theory of Belief Functions (BELIEF 2010)
22. Mercier, D., Quost, B., Denœux, T.: Contextual discounting of belief functions. In: Godo, L. (ed.) Symbolic and Quantitative Approaches to Reasoning with Uncertainty, pp. 552–562. Springer, Berlin Heidelberg, Berlin, Heidelberg (2005)
23. Pichon, F., Dubois, D., Denœux, T.: Relevance and truthfulness in information correction and fusion. Int. J. Approx. Reason. **53**(2), 159–175 (2012)
24. Samet, A., Lefèvre, E., Hammami, I., Ben Yahia, S.: Reliability estimation measure: generic discounting approach. Int. J. Pattern Recognit Artif Intell. **29**(07), 1559011 (2015)
25. Sarabi-Jamab, A., Araabi, B.N.: How to decide when the sources of evidence are unreliable: a multi-criteria discounting approach in the dempster-shafer theory. Inf. Sci. **448–449**, 233–248 (2018)
26. Schubert, J.: Conflict management in dempster–shafer theory using the degree of falsity. Int. J. Approx. Reason **52**(3), 449–460 (2011). dependence Issues in Knowledge-Based Systems
27. Sebbak, F., Senouci, M.R.: Optimizing cardinality-aware combination rules in belief functions theory: an enhanced framework. In: 2024 27th International Conference on Information Fusion (FUSION), pp. 1–8. IEEE (2024)
28. Sebbak, F., Senouci, M.R., Benhammadi, F., Mataoui, M., Cherifi, W.: Towards cardinality-aware evidential combination rules in dempster-shafer theory (2024). KI - Künstliche Intelligenz
29. Senouci, M.A., Senouci, M.R., Hoceini, S., Mellouk, A.: An evidential approach for network interface selection in heterogeneous wireless networks. In: 2016 IEEE Global Communications Conference (GLOBECOM), pp. 1–7 (2016)
30. Senouci, M.R., Mellouk, A., Oukhellou, L., Aissani, A.: An evidence-based sensor coverage model. IEEE Commun. Lett. **16**(9), 1462–1465 (2012)

31. Senouci, M.R., Mellouk, A., Senouci, M.A., Oukhellou, L.: Belief functions in telecommunications and network technologies: an overview. Ann. Telecommun. - annales des télécommunications **69**(3–4), 135–145 (2014)
32. Senouci, M.R., Sebbak, F., Chibani, N.: Reliability-aware belief functions combination in intelligent transportation systems. In: 2025 7th International Conference on Pattern Analysis and Intelligent Systems (PAIS), pp. 1–6 (2025)
33. Shafer, G.: A Mathematical Theory of Evidence. Princeton University Press (1976)
34. Smets, P., Kennes, R.: The transferable belief model. Artif. Intell. **66**(2), 191–234 (1994)
35. Song, Y., Wang, X., Wu, W., Quan, W., Huang, W.: Evidence combination based on credibility and non-specificity. Pattern Anal. Appl. **21**(1), 167–180 (2016)
36. Yang, Y., Han, D., Dezert, J.: A new non-specificity measure in evidence theory based on belief intervals. Chin. J. Aeronaut. **29**(3), 704–713 (2016)
37. Yang, Y., Han, D., Han, C.: Discounted combination of unreliable evidence using degree of disagreement. Int. J. Approx. Reason. **54**(8), 1197–1216 (2013)
38. Yuan, K., Xiao, F., Fei, L., Kang, B., Deng, Y.: Conflict management based on belief function entropy in sensor fusion. Springerplus **5**(1), 1–12 (2016). https://doi.org/10.1186/s40064-016-2205-6

Efficient Exact Decombination for Belief Functions Theory: A Commonality-Based Framework for Dynamic Reasoning

Faouzi Sebbak(✉) and Mustapha Reda Senouci

Computer Science Department, Ecole Militaire Polytechnique, Algiers, Algeria
faouzi.sebbak@gmail.com

Abstract. Belief Functions Theory (BFT) enables robust reasoning under uncertainty through the combination of evidence. In dynamic environments, previously fused evidence must be retracted when sources become unreliable, a process called *decombination.* Despite its theoretical importance, decombination remains computationally prohibitive for real-time applications. This paper presents a scalable and high-performance, exact decombination framework, introducing two computational strategies: a linear-system formulation with focal-element reduction, and a commonality-based method using Möbius transforms and element-wise ratios. The framework supports conjunctive, normalized, and cardinality-aware rules. Extensive experiments demonstrate that the commonality-ratio method achieves near-constant runtime for frames with up to $|\Theta| = 10$ elements ($\approx$2 ms) and sub-second performance for $|\Theta| = 21$, outperforming linear-system approaches by orders of magnitude. This establishes commonality-based decombination as a reference method for dynamic BFT reasoning. The complete implementation is publicly available, enabling practical belief revision in information fusion systems.

Keywords: Belief Functions Theory · Dempster–Shafer Theory · Decombination · Evidence Retraction · EDST Framework · Dynamic Reasoning · Uncertainty Management

1 Introduction

Belief Functions Theory (BFT), also known as Dempster–Shafer theory [2,11], has established itself as a principled framework for combining uncertain, imprecise, and conflicting information from multiple sources. By assigning belief masses to subsets of a finite frame of discernment Θ, BFT captures epistemic uncertainty beyond classical probability, enabling robust fusion in applications ranging from sensor networks [9,16] and machine learning [4] to autonomous systems [10] and recommender systems [1].

Reasoning under uncertainty in information fusion systems requires both evidence aggregation and evidence retraction. While evidence combination through Dempster's rule [11] and its variants is well understood, real-world fusion systems

B. Vantaggi et al. (Eds.): IPMU 2026, CCIS 3019, pp. 348–362, 2026.
https://doi.org/10.1007/978-3-032-28994-0_25

face a critical challenge: previously aggregated evidence may become obsolete or unreliable. Sensor failures, outdated measurements, adversarial inputs, and evolving contexts necessitate the removal of specific evidence contributions from accumulated beliefs, a process termed *decombination* or *belief retraction* [6,12]. Unlike monotonic combination, decombination is an inverse operation: given a combined mass $m = m_1 \oplus m_2$, recover the residual belief $m_1 = m \ominus m_2$ after removing source m_2.

Despite its fundamental importance for non-monotonic reasoning and temporal fusion, decombination has received limited attention compared to combination operators. While previous works [6,12] establish the theoretical basis for decombination, they lack the high-performance implementations required for large frames and advanced combination rules. The exponential growth of the power set 2^{Θ} renders naive enumeration intractable as the frame size increases, creating a computational bottleneck for dynamic BFT applications.

The Enhanced Dempster–Shafer Toolbox (EDST) [7] addresses scalability for evidence combination through bit-encoded power-set representations, vectorized focal operations, and optimized Möbius transforms. It supports classical rules (conjunctive, Dempster) as well as advanced operators such as PCR6 variants [13] and cardinality-aware rules (ZCR, JCR) [8,15]. However, EDST and more generally existing BFT toolkits lack efficient and exact decombination operators that scale to practical frame sizes, which makes dynamic belief revision infeasible in systems where evidence must be added and removed over time. To address this limitation, this paper extends EDST with a comprehensive, scalable decombination framework and makes the following contributions:

(i) Computational unification: A unified computational framework that bridges existing theoretical foundations of decombination with a scalable implementation supporting conjunctive, normalized, and cardinality-aware rules.
(ii) Dual computational strategies: (a) A linear-system formulation with focal-element reduction, and (b) a commonality-based method exploiting Möbius transforms and element-wise division for near-optimal complexity.
(iii) Scalability analysis: Extensive experiments showing that the commonality-ratio method achieves constant-time performance for moderate frames ($|\Theta| \leq 10$) and sub-second execution for $|\Theta| = 21$, establishing it as the reference exact decombination method.
(iv) Open-source integration: Full implementation within EDST[1], providing the BFT community with production-ready tools for dynamic reasoning.

The remainder of the paper is organized as follows. Section 2 reviews BFT fundamentals, combination rules, and existing decombination approaches. Section 3 presents the proposed framework with detailed algorithmic descriptions. Section 4 provides computational validation and scalability analysis. Section 5 concludes with impact assessment and future directions.

[1] https://github.com/LeSinus/EDST2.

2 Background and Related Work

This section recalls core BFT notions, summarizes combination rules, and reviews decombination approaches.

2.1 Fundamentals of Belief Function Theory

BFT [11] generalizes probability by assigning masses to subsets of a finite frame of discernment $\Theta = \{\theta_1, \ldots, \theta_n\}$. A mass function is defined as

$$m : 2^\Theta \to [0, 1], \qquad \sum_{A \subseteq \Theta} m(A) = 1, \tag{1}$$

with focal elements A such that $m(A) > 0$. From m, several equivalent representations are derived:

$$Bel(A) = \sum_{B \subseteq A} m(B), \qquad Pl(A) = \sum_{B \cap A \neq \emptyset} m(B), \qquad q(A) = \sum_{B \supseteq A} m(B).$$

Bel and *Pl* measure committed and possible support, respectively. The commonality function q, the Möbius transform of m, is central to efficient combination and decombination.

2.2 Combination of Evidence

For mass functions m_1, m_2 on 2^Θ, the main operators are:

Conjunctive Rule.

$$m_\cap(A) = \sum_{B \cap C = A} m_1(B) m_2(C), \tag{2}$$

with $m_\cap(\emptyset)$ denoting conflict.

Dempster's Normalized Rule.

$$m_\oplus(A) = \frac{1}{1-K} \sum_{B \cap C = A} m_1(B) m_2(C), \qquad K = \sum_{B \cap C = \emptyset} m_1(B) m_2(C). \tag{3}$$

Disjunctive Rule.

$$m_\cup(A) = \sum_{B \cup C = A} m_1(B) m_2(C). \tag{4}$$

Extensions address conflict, reliability, and specificity, including PCR rules [13], cautious fusion [3], and cardinality-aware rules [8]. Zhang's rule [15] introduced intersection-based weighting:

$$m^D_{1,\ldots,s}(H) = \frac{1}{K^D} \sum_{\substack{H_1,\ldots,H_s \\ H_1 \cap \cdots \cap H_s = H}} D(H_1, \ldots, H_s) \prod_i m_i(H_i), \tag{5}$$

with

$$D^Z = \frac{|H_1 \cap \cdots \cap H_s|}{|H_1| \cdots |H_s|}, \qquad D^J = \frac{|H_1 \cap \cdots \cap H_s|}{|H_1 \cup \cdots \cup H_s|}.$$

Such rules improve specificity control but increase computational cost over 2^Θ, motivating optimized toolkits such as EDST [7].

2.3 Decombination Operator

The decombination operator [6,12] aims to reverse evidence aggregation.

Definition 1 (Decombination problem). *Given mass functions m and m_2 on 2^Θ, find m_1 such that: $m = m_1 \oplus m_2 \iff m_1 = m \ominus m_2$.*

Decombination enables belief revision but is computationally challenging due to the combinatorial structure of the power set.

Commonality-Domain Formulation. For conjunctive and normalized rules, the commonality function $q_m(A) = \sum_{A \subseteq B} m(B)$ yields the multiplicative relation

$$q_m(A) = q_{m_1}(A)\, q_{m_2}(A), \qquad q_{m_1}(A) = \frac{q_m(A)}{q_{m_2}(A)}. \tag{6}$$

The mass function m_1 is recovered via the inverse Möbius transform:

$$m_1(A) = \sum_{A \subseteq B} (-1)^{|B-A|} \frac{q_m(B)}{q_{m_2}(B)}. \tag{7}$$

This exact method requires the enumeration of all supersets of A, yielding exponential complexity.

Linear-System Formulation. Alternatively, decombination can be formulated as a linear system over focal masses [6]. For the conjunctive rule,

$$m(A) = \sum_{B \cap C = A} m_1(B)\, m_2(C),$$

each focal element $A \subseteq \Theta$ yields one linear equation in the unknowns $\{m_1(B)\}_{B \subseteq \Theta}$, with coefficients determined by m_2. While mathematically elegant, this approach constructs a system of size $\mathcal{O}(2^{2|\Theta|})$ in the worst case, limiting scalability.

Existing decombination methods [6,12] provide essential theoretical foundations but remain primarily conceptual. They lack optimized toolkit support, exclude cardinality-aware rules, and make limited use of vectorized transform-domain representations. These gaps motivate the unified, scalable framework integrated into EDST and presented in the following section.

3 Proposed Decombination Framework

This section introduces the EDST-based decombination framework.

3.1 Framework Overview and Design Principles

EDST [7] is a modular MATLAB framework for efficient belief functions computation, extending earlier toolkits [5] via a layered architecture separating powerset encoding, computational primitives, fusion operators, and decision modules.

Mass functions are represented as fixed-length vectors indexed over 2^Θ using a canonical ordering enabling direct addressing and efficient manipulation of focal elements. For $\Theta = \{\theta_1, \theta_2, \theta_3\}$,

$$2^\Theta = [\emptyset, \{\theta_1\}, \{\theta_2\}, \{\theta_1, \theta_2\}, \{\theta_3\}, \{\theta_1, \theta_3\}, \{\theta_2, \theta_3\}, \{\theta_1, \theta_2, \theta_3\}].$$

This representation supports vectorized cardinality, set operations, conflict computation, and focal-element reduction via sparse matrices, enabling efficient implementation of both classical and advanced fusion rules, including PCR6 variants [13], CBF [14], ZCR, and JCR [15].

Dynamic reasoning requires inverse operations for evidence removal. This decombination process [6,12] is essential for belief revision and non-monotonic inference. We extend EDST with a decombination module providing:

- a unified interface for fusion and defusion,
- two strategies: commonality-based ratios and linear-system inversion,
- compatibility with cardinality-aware rules.

EDST uses bit-encoded subsets, enabling constant-time set operations via bitwise arithmetic, where each subset is encoded as an n-bit integer, which accelerates focal-set manipulation.

Throughout this work, we assume that the mass to be decombined is non-dogmatic.

Non-dogmatic Regularization. To ensure invertibility, EDST applies

$$m'(\Theta) = m(\Theta) + \varepsilon, \qquad m'(A) = (1 - \varepsilon)m(A),$$

with $\varepsilon \in [10^{-6}, 10^{-3}]$, equivalent to discounting with reliability factor $\alpha = 1 - \varepsilon$. This purely computational step guarantees stable decombination when $m(\Theta) = 0$. EDST automatically checks the condition $m(\Theta) > 0$ and applies an infinitesimal discounting step when necessary, ensuring that all decombination operations are well posed.

3.2 Building the Linear System

Given $m = m_1 \oplus m_2$, decombination recovers $m_1 = m \ominus m_2$. For the unnormalized conjunctive rule,

$$m(A) = \sum_{B \cap C = A} m_1(B)m_2(C),$$

each focal element A yields one equation, and an additional normalization constraint ensures uniqueness.

For $\Theta = \{a, b, c\}$ with focal sets $\{a\}, \{b\}, \{a, b\}$,

$$\begin{bmatrix} m_2(\{a\}) + m_2(\{a,b\}) & 0 & m_2(\{a\}) \\ 0 & m_2(\{b\}) + m_2(\{a,b\}) & m_2(\{b\}) \\ 0 & 0 & m_2(\{a,b\}) \\ 1 & 1 & 1 \end{bmatrix} \begin{bmatrix} m_1(\{a\}) \\ m_1(\{b\}) \\ m_1(\{a,b\}) \end{bmatrix} = \begin{bmatrix} m(\{a\}) \\ m(\{b\}) \\ m(\{a,b\}) \\ 1 \end{bmatrix}$$

The matrix is triangular up to normalization, allowing a polynomial-time solution. In general,

$$m(A_k) = \sum_{\substack{B \cap C = A_k \\ B \in \mathcal{F}_{m_2}, C \in \mathcal{F}_m}} m_2(B) m_1(C), \tag{8}$$

with $\mathcal{F}_{m_2}$ and $\mathcal{F}_m$ denote the focal sets of m_2 and m, respectively, together with the constraint $\sum_A m_1(A) = 1$.

3.3 Algorithmic Implementation: Commonality-Based Solution

The commonality domain provides a direct route to decombination, as Eq. (6) reduces the operation to pointwise division. Once q_{m_1} is obtained, the mass function is recovered via the inverse Möbius transform in Eq. (7).

Algorithm 1 implements this approach in two stages. First, the mass functions m and m_2 are mapped to their commonality representations using the routine `mtoq`, which runs in $\mathcal{O}(n2^n)$ time, where $n = |\Theta|$. Second, depending on the selected strategy, the algorithm either applies the ratio to all subsets followed by inversion through `qtom`, also in $\mathcal{O}(n2^n)$ time, or injects the ratio directly into the Möbius inversion, evaluating only over supersets.

Under the bit-encoded power-set representation, all set-theoretic operations (intersection, difference, and subset testing) are executed in constant time via bitwise arithmetic. For normalized decombination, the resulting mass is renormalized after inversion. Overall, the commonality-based procedure has time complexity $\mathcal{O}(n2^n)$ and space complexity $\mathcal{O}(2^n)$, independently of the number of focal elements.

In the sparse variant (Strategy 2), the inner summation is restricted to subsets B such that $q_m(B) > 0$, yielding a complexity of $\mathcal{O}(n2^n\ell)$, where $\ell = |\mathcal{F}(m)|$. While still exponential in the worst case, this variant is significantly more efficient when the combined mass has a compact focal support.

3.4 Algorithmic Implementation: Linear-System Solution

For a binary frame $\Theta = \{\theta_1, \theta_2\}$, recovering m_1 from (m, m_2) such that $m = m_1 \oplus m_2$ reduces to solving a linear system $\mathbf{Ax} = \mathbf{b}$ with

$$\mathbf{x} = \left[m_1(\{\theta_1\})\ m_1(\{\theta_2\})\ m_1(\{\theta_1, \theta_2\})\right]^\top, \qquad \mathbf{b} = m.$$

Algorithm 1: Commonality-Based Decombination

Input : m (combined mass), m_2 (mass to forget)
type: unnormalized (0) or normalized (1) decombination
strategy: ratio (1) or explicit inversion (2)
Output: Recovered mass m_1

Step 1: Convert mass functions to commonality functions
$q_m \leftarrow \text{mtoq}(m), \quad q_{m_2} \leftarrow \text{mtoq}(m_2)$
Extract focal elements $\mathcal{F}_{q_m}$

Step 2: Compute q_{m_1} according to chosen strategy
if *strategy* $= 1$ **then**
  `// Strategy 1: Direct ratio + transform`
  foreach $A_i \in \mathcal{F}_{q_m}$ **do**
    $q_{m_1}(A_i) \leftarrow q_m(A_i)/q_{m_2}(A_i)$
  end
  $m_1 \leftarrow \text{qtom}(q_{m_1})$
end
if *strategy* $= 2$ **then**
  `// Strategy 2: Ratio integrated into Möbius inversion`
  foreach *each subset* A_i **do**
    $S \leftarrow 0$
    foreach $B_j \in \mathcal{F}_m$ **do**
      if $A_i \cap B_j = A_i$ **then**
        $k \leftarrow |B_j \setminus A_i|$
        $S \leftarrow S + (-1)^k \cdot q_m(B_j)/q_{m_2}(B_j)$
      end
    end
    $m_1(A_i) \leftarrow S$
  end
end

Step 3: Normalize if required
if *type* $= 1$ **then**
  $K \leftarrow \sum_{A_i} m_1(A_i)$
  $m_1 \leftarrow m_1/K$
end

return m_1

The conjunctive rule induces the nearly triangular coefficient matrix

$$\mathbf{A} = \begin{bmatrix} m_2(\{\theta_1\}) + m_2(\{\theta_1, \theta_2\}) & 0 & m_2(\{\theta_1\}) \\ 0 & m_2(\{\theta_2\}) + m_2(\{\theta_1, \theta_2\}) & m_2(\{\theta_2\}) \\ 0 & 0 & m_2(\{\theta_1, \theta_2\}) \end{bmatrix},$$

whose sparsity follows from the intersection structure of focal elements. This property extends to arbitrary frames and is exploited in Algorithm 2.

Algorithm 2: Linear-System Decombination

Input : m (combined mass), m_2 (mass to forget)
type: unnormalized (0), normalized (1), cardinality-aware (2)
Output: Recovered mass m_1.

Step 1: Extract focal elements $\mathcal{F}_m$ and $\mathcal{F}_{m_2}$
Step 2: Build the coefficient matrix A:
foreach $B_i \in \mathcal{F}_{m_2}$ **do**
    foreach $C_j \in \mathcal{F}_m$ **do**
        if $B_i \cap C_j \in \mathcal{F}_m$ **then**
            $A[i,j] \leftarrow A[i,j] + m_2(B_i)$
            if *type* $= 2$ **then**
                $A[i,j] \leftarrow A[i,j] \cdot \text{distance}(B_i, C_j)$
            end
        end
    end
end
Step 3: Solve the linear system
if *type* $= 0$ **then**
    $b \leftarrow m$
    Solve $Ax = b$
    $m_1(C_j) \leftarrow x_j$
end
if *type* $= 1$ *or* 2 **then**
    Introduce normalization variable x_K
    Construct normalization row
        $A_{\text{full}}(1,:) \leftarrow \sum_r A_{\text{full}}(r,:)$
    Restrict to active focal elements
        $A_{\text{reduced}} \leftarrow A_{\text{full}}$, $b_{\text{reduced}} \leftarrow b$
    Prepare reduced linear system $\mathbf{A}_{\text{reduced}}\mathbf{x} = 0$
        $A_{\text{reduced}} \leftarrow -A_{\text{reduced}}$
        $A_{\text{reduced}}(:,1) \leftarrow b_{\text{reduced}}$ **(insert RHS into first column)**
        $A_{\text{reduced}}(1,1) \leftarrow 1$ **(enforce normalization for** x_K**)**
    Solve reduced system with: $\mathbf{x} = (x_K, m_1(C_1), \ldots, m_1(C_k))^\top$
    Extract recovered masses: $m_1(C_j) \leftarrow x_j$ for $j = 2, \ldots, k$
end
return m_1

Coefficient Matrix Construction. For each $A \in \mathcal{F}_m$, all pairs $(C, B) \in \mathcal{F}_m \times \mathcal{F}_{m_2}$ such that $C \cap B = A$ are enumerated. In the worst case, this yields complexity $\mathcal{O}(\ell\ell_2)$, where $\ell_2 = |\mathcal{F}(m_2)|$. For cardinality-aware rules (JCR or ZCR), each valid pair requires additional cardinality computation, introducing a factor $\mathcal{O}(n)$. Although EDST restricts variables to $\mathcal{F}_m$, the explicit allocation of the coefficient matrix induces a dominant time and space cost of $\mathcal{O}(2^{2n})$ in the worst case.

Solving the Linear System. After removing redundant equations and enforcing normalization when required, the system involves ℓ unknowns (or $\ell+1$ for normalized and cardinality-aware rules). Solving the resulting triangular or constrained system incurs time complexity $\mathcal{O}(\ell^3)$, with memory requirements proportional to the number of nonzero coefficients. The overall complexity is $\mathcal{O}(2^{2n} + \ell^3)$.

Proposition 1 (Focal-element reduction). *Let m_1 and m_2 be mass functions on Θ, and let $m = m_1 \oplus m_2$ be their unnormalized conjunctive combination. If m_2 is non-dogmatic ($m_2(\Theta) > 0$), then an unknown $m_1(C)$ is required in the linear system only if $C \in \mathcal{F}(m)$.*

Proof. Since $m_2(\Theta) > 0$, every focal element $C \in \mathcal{F}(m_1)$ appears in m through $C \cap \Theta = C$, implying $\mathcal{F}(m_1) \subseteq \mathcal{F}(m)$. Hence, only focal elements of m are required when assembling Eq. (8), eliminating the need to enumerate 2^Θ.

Normalized Conjunctive and Cardinality-Aware Rules. For Dempster's normalized rule, a scalar consensus factor is introduced, and the resulting homogeneous system is solved together with the normalization constraint. Cardinality-aware rules (JCR and ZCR) follow the same procedure, with the sole modification occurring during coefficient construction, where Jaccard or Zhang distances weight each valid focal intersection. All subsequent steps remain unchanged.

Example: Reduction of the Linear System. Consider mass functions

$$m_1(\{a\}) = 0.4, \quad m_1(\{b,c\}) = 0.6, \qquad m_2(\{a\}) = 0.3, \quad m_2(\{a,b,c\}) = 0.7.$$

After restricting the system to the active focal elements of m (i.e., those with nonzero mass), the reduced system becomes

$$\mathbf{A} = \begin{bmatrix} m_2(\{a\}) + m_2(\{a,b,c\})\; 0\,0\,0\,0 & 0 & 0 \\ 0 & 0\,0\,0\,0\; m_2(\{a,b,c\}) & 0 \end{bmatrix} = \begin{bmatrix} 1\,0\,0\,0\,0 & 0 & 0 \\ 0\,0\,0\,0\,0 & 0.7 & 0 \end{bmatrix}$$

Only the focal elements $\{a\}$ and $\{b,c\}$ (the ones present in m) are kept, which preserves sparsity and substantially decreases the system size.

A normalization constraint enforcing $\sum_{A \in \mathcal{F}_m} m_1(A) = 1$ is added to the system. The constraint is restricted to active focal elements in $\mathcal{F}_m$ (e.g. $\{a\}$ and $\{b,c\}$), preserving sparsity, and is integrated by augmenting the reduced matrix with the corresponding normalization row.

For the normalized Dempster's rule, the scalar x_C representing the consensus factor is introduced to the linear system :

$$m(A)\, x_C = \sum_{B \cap C = A} m_2(B)\, m_1(C), \qquad A \subseteq \Theta.$$

For the example above, the system becomes

$$\begin{aligned} x_C - [m_2(\{a\}) + m_2(\{a,b,c\})]\, m_1(\{a\}) - m_2(\{a,b,c\})\, m_1(\{b,c\}) &= 0, \\ x_C\, m(\{a\}) - [m_2(\{a\}) + m_2(\{a,b,c\})]\, m_1(\{a\}) &= 0, \\ x_C\, m(\{b\}) - m_2(\{a,b,c\})\, m_1(\{b,c\}) &= 0. \end{aligned}$$

The corresponding matrix is

$$\mathbf{A} = \begin{bmatrix} 1 & -m_2(\{a\}) - m_2(\{a,b,c\}) & 0 & 0 & 0 & 0 & -m_2(\{a,b,c\}) & 0 \\ m(\{a\}) & -m_2(\{a\}) - m_2(\{a,b,c\}) & 0 & 0 & 0 & 0 & 0 & 0 \\ m(\{b\}) & 0 & 0 & 0 & 0 & 0 & -m_2(\{a,b,c\}) & 0 \end{bmatrix}$$

and the unknown vector is

$$\mathbf{x} = \left[x_C,\ m_1(\{a\}),\ m_1(\{b\}),\ m_1(\{a,b\}),\ m_1(\{c\}),\ m_1(\{a,c\}),\ m_1(\{b,c\}),\ m_1(\{a,b,c\})\right]^\top$$

The final estimate of m_1 is obtained by solving $\mathbf{Ax} = 0$ together with the normalization constraint.

4 Results and Discussion

This section reports a comparative evaluation of commonality-based and linear-system decombination strategies, focusing on runtime and scalability.

4.1 Experimental Protocol and Evaluation Criteria

Experiments were conducted in MATLAB R2015a using EDST extended with the proposed decombination operators (Sect. 3). Computations ran on an Intel i9 workstation (2.2 GHz, 32 GB RAM). Each configuration was evaluated over 500 Monte–Carlo trials, and reported runtimes are empirical means.

Three exact decombination strategies were compared: (i) commonality–ratio decombination (CR, Strategy 1), (ii) commonality-based decombination with explicit Möbius inversion (Strategy 2), and (iii) linear-system decombination. Each strategy was tested under unnormalized conjunctive, normalized (Dempster), and cardinality-aware (JCR/ZCR) rules. All mass functions contained six randomly selected focal elements in order to simulate the typical sparse belief functions encountered in practice, and the removed source m_2 satisfied $m_2(\Theta) > 0$, ensuring invertibility. While this setting enables controlled and reproducible comparisons, denser focal structures may lead to increased computational complexity and are left for future investigation.

All methods achieved reconstruction errors $\|m_1 - \widehat{m}_1\|_2 \approx 10^{-12}$, confirming exactness. Runtime is therefore the sole evaluation criterion.

4.2 Comparative Runtime Behavior

Table 1 and Fig. 1 report execution times for $2 \leq |\Theta| \leq 10$, revealing clear differences between strategies. The commonality–ratio method exhibits nearly constant runtime across frame sizes for both unnormalized and normalized rules. This behavior follows directly from its implementation as pointwise division in the commonality domain combined with Fast Möbius Transforms. Execution times remain close to 2 ms even at $|\Theta| = 10$, with negligible impact from normalization.

Table 1. Execution times (s) for decombination.

$\|\Theta\|$	Unnormalized			Normalized			Cardinality-Aware	
	Ratio	Exhaustive	Linear	Ratio	Exhaustive	Linear	Linear (JCR)	Linear (ZCR)
2	0.0015	0.0030	0.0032	0.0020	0.0046	0.0050	0.0052	0.0053
3	0.0014	0.0046	0.0081	0.0017	0.0075	0.0175	0.0122	0.0121
4	0.0018	0.0119	0.0128	0.0013	0.0065	0.0102	0.0188	0.0203
5	0.0014	0.0167	0.0189	0.0011	0.0133	0.0161	0.0292	0.0311
6	0.0012	0.0307	0.0249	0.0013	0.0444	0.0457	0.0426	0.0425
7	0.0013	0.0712	0.0331	0.0014	0.0675	0.0352	0.0590	0.0544
8	0.0015	0.1831	0.0501	0.0015	0.1941	0.0511	0.0735	0.0672
9	0.0017	0.4726	0.0577	0.0017	0.5341	0.0610	0.0816	0.0824
10	0.0020	1.3768	0.0787	0.0020	1.3739	0.0791	0.1033	0.1049

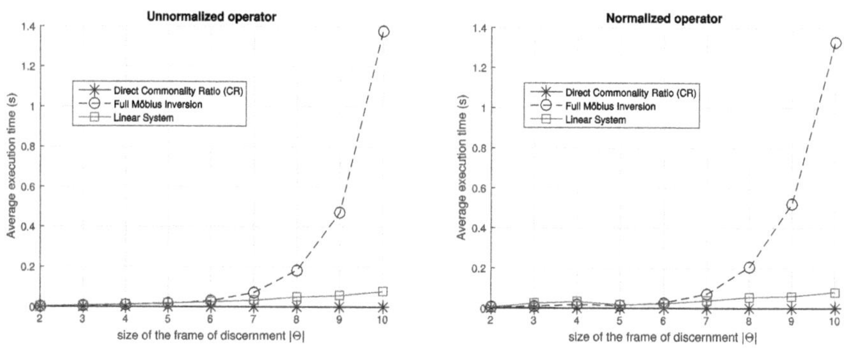

Fig. 1. Mean execution time (500 trials) of decombination methods.

These experiments directly address the feasibility of *real-time belief revision* in operational fusion systems. For context, sensor fusion in autonomous vehicles operates at 10–100 Hz, requiring evidence updates every 10–100 ms. Similarly, intrusion detection systems must respond to evolving threat assessments within milliseconds. The 2 ms runtime achieved by CR decombination at $|\Theta| = 10$ comfortably satisfies these latency requirements, enabling continuous belief revision in safety-critical applications.

In contrast, the exhaustive commonality-based inversion (Strategy 2) shows rapid growth with $|\Theta|$. Runtimes increase from a few milliseconds at $|\Theta| = 2$ to over one second at $|\Theta| = 10$, reflecting the exponential complexity of explicit inversion despite EDST optimizations.

The linear-system approach performs reasonably for small frames but scales poorly as $|\Theta|$ increases. Even with focal-element reduction (Proposition 1), the cost of solving a linear system of size $\ell = |\mathcal{F}(m)|$ dominates, leading to approximately cubic growth and limited practicality beyond $|\Theta| \geq 7$.

The near-constant runtime of the commonality-ratio method across frame sizes reflects the theoretical $\mathcal{O}(n2^n)$ complexity of fast Möbius transforms, which grows slowly compared to the $\mathcal{O}(2^{2n})$ matrix allocation in the linear-system approach. For $|\Theta| = 10$ (1024 subsets), the CR method requires only $\approx$10,000 operations, whereas the linear system potentially allocates a 1024×1024 matrix (>1M entries) even with focal-element reduction. This fundamental asymmetry explains the observed performance gap.

Figure 1 and Table 1 further show that normalization imposes negligible overhead on all decombination methods, as it merely rescales the result vector in the commonality domain or introduces a single column for the consensus variable in the linear-system formulation.

Cardinality-aware decombination (JCR and ZCR) relies on the linear-system formulation and therefore incurs additional computational cost. As reported in Table 1, JCR and ZCR runtimes consistently exceed those of normalized CR decombination, yet remain below 0.11 s up to $|\Theta| = 10$ under the considered sparse-focal configuration. These results quantitatively illustrate the trade-off between expressive fusion rules incorporating cardinality information and increased computational burden.

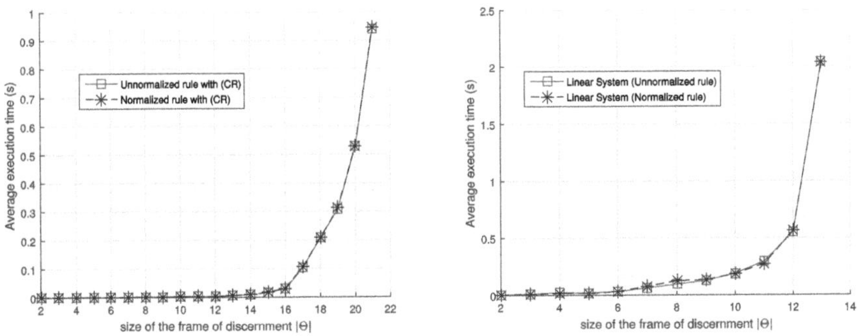

Fig. 2. Mean execution time (500 trials) of CR and linear systems decombination for unnormalized and normalized rules.

4.3 Scalability to Large Frames

The scalability of the commonality–ratio and linear-system methods was further evaluated for larger frames. Table 2 and Fig. 2 show results for $2 \leq |\Theta| \leq 21$.

These results represent a significant advance for practical BFT systems. Prior work has emphasized the prohibitive computational cost of exact decombination as the frame size increases, effectively restricting its applicability in real-time settings [6]. The proposed commonality–ratio method markedly extends this practical frontier, enabling exact decombination on much larger frames, including cases with $|\Theta| = 21$ (over two million subsets), processed in under one second.

Table 2. Execution times (s) for large $|\Theta|$.

$\|\Theta\|$	Commonality–ratio		Linear system	
	conjunctive	normalized	conjunctive	normalized
2	0.0013	0.0012	0.0048	0.0050
4	0.0014	0.0013	0.0232	0.0167
6	0.0012	0.0012	0.0327	0.0316
8	0.0026	0.0024	0.0950	0.1258
10	0.0032	0.0030	0.1893	0.1852
11	0.0039	0.0038	0.2924	0.2738
12	0.0037	0.0038	0.5537	0.5647
13	0.0064	0.0071	2.0440	2.0345
14	0.0097	0.0106	-	-
15	0.0165	0.0176	-	-
16	0.0302	0.0319	-	-
18	0.2071	0.2086	-	-
20	0.5288	0.5294	-	-
21	0.9413	0.9451	-	-

By contrast, the linear-system method rapidly becomes impractical as the frame size grows, due to the cubic cost of solving the associated matrix system; it exhibits a sharp increase in runtime, exceeding one second for a frame size of $|\Theta| = 13$, after which experiments were halted. In our tests, this approach results in runtimes exceeding 2 s, which is roughly three orders of magnitude slower than commonality–ratio decombination (about 0.006 s).

Overall, these results confirm that commonality–ratio decombination offers the best compromise between exactness, robustness, and scalability. Linear-system approaches remain suitable for specialized settings, such as cardinality-aware fusion, but are restricted to small frames or offline use.

Practical Implications. The commonality-ratio method establishes a new standard for dynamic BFT reasoning. Systems requiring belief revision at 1–10 Hz can now operate with frames up to $|\Theta| \approx 15$, sufficient for many real-world applications including multi-class recognition (∼10 classes), sensor fusion in autonomous systems (∼5–10 hypotheses), and medical diagnosis (∼10–15 diseases). For offline analysis or batch processing, $|\Theta| = 21$ becomes tractable, enabling retrospective belief auditing and forensic analysis of fusion decisions.

5 Conclusion

This paper introduced a scalable and high-performance, exact decombination framework for BFT, integrated into the Enhanced Dempster–Shafer Toolbox

(EDST). By exploiting commonality-domain representations and optimized Möbius transforms, the proposed framework overcomes the computational barrier that has historically limited decombination to theoretical studies and small-scale demonstrations.

Among the investigated methods, the commonality–ratio decombination (CR) approach consistently delivers superior performance across conjunctive, normalized, and cardinality-aware rules. For frames up to $|\Theta| = 10$, CR decombination achieves near-constant runtime (≈2 ms), satisfying latency requirements for real-time fusion systems operating at 10–100 Hz. Scalability extends to $|\Theta| = 21$ with sub-second execution, establishing a new state-of-the-art for exact inverse operations in BFT. The linear-system formulation, while less efficient, provides essential support for cardinality-aware rules that cannot be expressed in the commonality domain. Its focal-element reduction strategy (Proposition 1) enables practical decombination for specialized applications where expressive fusion justifies the computational cost.

By bridging theoretical developments and practical deployment, the enhanced EDST framework is made available to the community to support further research and applications. Future work will explore specialized optimizations for structured belief functions. In particular, investigating decombination for k-additive belief functions, p-boxes, and quasi-Bayesian models may enable more efficient algorithms by exploiting sparsity and underlying lattice structures inherent to these representations.

References

1. Belmessous, K., Sebbak, F., Mataoui, M., Senouci, M.R., Cherifi, W.: Dempster-Shafer theory in recommender systems: a survey. Internat. J. Uncertain. Fuzziness Knowl.-Based Syst. **32**(05), 747–780 (2024)
2. Dempster, A.P.: Upper and lower probabilities generated by a random closed interval. Ann. Math. Stat. 957–966 (1968)
3. Denoeux, T.: Conjunctive and disjunctive combination of belief functions induced by nondistinct bodies of evidence. Artif. Intell. **172**(2), 234–264 (2008)
4. Denœux, T.: Logistic regression, neural networks and Dempster-Shafer theory: a new perspective. Knowl.-Based Syst. **176**, 54–67 (2019)
5. Martin, A.: Implementing general belief function framework with a practical codification for low complexity. In: Advances and Applications of DSmT for Information Fusion, pp. 217–273. American Research Press Rehoboth (2009)
6. Pinto Prieto, D., Haan, R.D., Destercke, S.: How to efficiently decombine belief functions? In: International Conference on Information Processing and Management of Uncertainty in Knowledge-Based Systems, pp. 91–102. Springer (2024)
7. Sebbak, F., Senouci, M.R.: Optimizing cardinality-aware combination rules in belief functions theory: an enhanced framework. In: 2024 27th International Conference on Information Fusion (FUSION), pp. 1–8 (2024)
8. Sebbak, F., Senouci, M.R., Benhammadi, F., Mataoui, M., Cherifi, W.: Towards cardinality-aware evidential combination rules in Dempster-Shafer theory. KI-Künstliche Intelligenz **39**(04), 273–288 (2025)

9. Senouci, M.R., Mellouk, A., Senouci, M.A., Oukhellou, L.: Belief functions in telecommunications and network technologies: an overview. Ann. Telecommun.-annales des télécommunications **69**(3), 135–145 (2014)
10. Senouci, M.R., Sebbak, F., Chibani, N.: Reliability-aware belief functions combination in intelligent transportation systems. In: 2025 7th International Conference on Pattern Analysis and Intelligent Systems (PAIS), pp. 1–6 (2025)
11. Shafer, G.: A Mathematical Theory of Evidence, vol. 42. Princeton University Press (1976)
12. Shenoy, P.P.: Conditional independence in valuation-based systems. Int. J. Approximate Reasoning **10**(3), 203–234 (1994)
13. Smarandache, F., Dezert, J.: Modified PCR rules of combination with degrees of intersections. In: 2015 18th International Conference on Information Fusion (Fusion), pp. 2100–2107. IEEE (2015)
14. Tang, Y., Zhang, X., Zhou, Y., Huang, Y., Zhou, D.: A new correlation belief function in Dempster-Shafer evidence theory and its application in classification. Sci. Rep. **13**(1) (2023)
15. Zhang, L.: Representation, independence, and combination of evidence in the Dempster-Shafer theory. In: Advances in the Dempster-Shafer Theory of Evidence, pp. 51–69. Wiley (1994)
16. Zhang, P., et al.: Information fusion and feature selection for multi-source data utilizing Dempster-Shafer evidence theory and k-nearest neighbors. Inf. Sci. 122408 (2025)

A Possibilistic Calculus of Guarantees

Ismaïl Baaj[1(✉)] and Henri Prade[2]

[1] Lemma, Paris II Panthéon-Assas University, Paris, France
ismail.baaj@assas-universite.fr
[2] IRIT - Toulouse University, 31062 Toulouse Cedex 9, France
henri.prade@irit.fr

Abstract. In possibility theory, four set functions can be defined from a possibility distribution. While the use of possibility and necessity measures in knowledge representation and reasoning has been widely studied, the guaranteed possibility function and its dual have received little attention. This article is devoted to the study of the latter. In particular, it shows how the calculation of guaranteed possibility and its dual, which has an inductive flavor, differs from the treatment of possibility and necessity measures, although it is parallel to it in a certain sense. A new max-min matrix calculation based on conditional guaranteed possibility is presented, which allows us to develop a propagation mechanism similar to that used with layered neural networks.

Keywords: possibility theory · knowledge representation · duality

1 Introduction

Possibility theory is a particularly interesting setting since it is midway between logic and probability theory [23]. Its qualitative version [18] leads to the emergence of a neuro-symbolic approach that combines a low-level perception task performed by a neural network with a high-level reasoning task performed by a possibilistic rule-based system [2]. In other words, the framework of possibility theory makes it an interesting candidate for interfacing "System 1"-like tasks (rapid classification abilities) and "System 2"-like tasks (deliberative and logical inference) in the sense of Kahneman [28]. The max and min operations, on which possibility theory is based, seem physiologically more plausible than sum and product operations.

Most of the applications of possibility theory to the handling of reasoning tasks are based on the use of possibility and necessity measures associated to a possibility distribution; see [13] for a survey. However, possibility theory benefits from the existence of two other set functions: the guaranteed possibility and its dual. Like their counterparts in the evidence theory (the commonality [32] and its dual), these two possibilistic set functions have hardly been taken into consideration. We can only mention their use in the representation of some types of preference [5], in the modeling of positive desires [11], and in reasoning with both generic knowledge and examples [33].

The purpose of this paper is to propose *a systematic investigation of the calculus underlying guaranteed possibility and its dual.* Although it parallels in some

B. Vantaggi et al. (Eds.): IPMU 2026, CCIS 3019, pp. 363–377, 2026.
https://doi.org/10.1007/978-3-032-28994-0_26

sense the calculus based on possibility and necessity measures, it deviates significantly from it, since the guaranteed possibility is a decreasing set function and often behaves as a necessity.

The paper is organized as follows. Section 2 first recalls the four possibilistic set functions, highlighting their respective meanings and how they can be used to provide upper and lower approximations of a possibility distribution. Then the conditioning of guaranteed possibility is discussed in detail, and we finally recall how a pair consisting of a guaranteed possibility and a standard possibility can be interpreted as bracketing a likelihood function. Section 3 is dedicated to the propagation of uncertainty using guaranteed possibility, first in logical terms, and then in terms of a matrix calculus using conditional guaranteed possibility. In both sections, the behavior of guaranteed possibility functions and their duals is compared and contrasted with that of possibility and necessity measures. A concluding discussion suggests how these findings can be used in practice and proposes avenues for future research.

2 Background on Possibility Theory

The basic building block of possibility theory is the notion of a possibility distribution, which is a mapping π from a set of interpretations $\mathcal{I}$ (e.g., the set of interpretations induced by a propositional language, or the set of values of a variable of interest) to a linearly ordered bounded scale $\mathcal{S}$ (e.g., a finite scale, or the interval $[0,1]$, or a subset thereof). π is essentially a way of encoding a total preorder. If $\omega \in \mathcal{I}$, the possibility level $\pi(\omega) \in \mathcal{S}$ is understood as a level of plausibility of ω (when modeling knowledge), or a level of acceptability of ω (when modeling preferences). The greatest lower (resp. least upper) bound of $\mathcal{S}$ is denoted by 0 (resp. 1). In the setting of possibility theory, the available information is supposed to be represented by a possibility distribution.

2.1 Possibilistic Set Functions

Let p be a proposition, $[p] \subseteq \mathcal{I}$ its set of models, $\mathcal{I}$ being the set of interpretations. Four set functions can be associated with a possibility distribution $\pi : \mathcal{I} \to \mathcal{S}$ [18], where $\mathcal{S}$ is a linearly ordered scale; $\mathcal{S}$ may be finite ($1 - (\cdot)$ is then an order-reversing map), or taken as the real interval $[0,1]$. These four set functions are:

- the (weak) possibility measure $\Pi([p]) = \sup_{\omega \in [p]} \pi(\omega)$;
- the (strong) necessity measure $N([p]) = 1 - \Pi(\neg p) = \inf_{\omega \notin [p]} 1 - \pi(\omega)$;
- the (strong) possibility measure $\Delta([p]) = \inf_{\omega \in [p]} \pi(\omega)$;
- the (weak) necessity measure $\nabla([p]) = 1 - \Delta(\neg p) = \sup_{\omega \notin [p]} 1 - \pi(\omega)$.

By convention, $\Pi(\emptyset) = 0$ and $\Delta(\emptyset) = 1$, and thus $N(\mathcal{I}) = 1$ and $\nabla(\mathcal{I}) = 0$. By upper normalization of π, i.e., $\exists \omega \in \mathcal{I}, \pi(\omega) = 1$, we ensure $\Pi(\mathcal{I}) = 1$ and thus $N(\emptyset) = 0$. By lower normalization of π, i.e., $\exists \omega \in \mathcal{I}, \pi(\omega) = 0$, we ensure $\Delta(\mathcal{I}) = 0$ and thus $\nabla(\emptyset) = 1$.

$\Pi([p])$ estimates the consistency of p with the information represented by π on the basis of the existence of at least a model of p with a high level of plausibility/acceptability. The upper normalization that ensures $\Pi(\mathcal{I}) = 1$ means the π and the set of interpretations are fully consistent: at least one interpretation reaches the maximum level of plausibility/acceptability. Equivalently $N(\emptyset) = 0$ ensures that the contradiction (which has an empty set of models) has no certainty/priority at all. More generally, the duality $N([p]) = 1 - \Pi([\neg p])$ states that p is all the more certain/prioritized as $\neg p$ is not plausible/acceptable.

The strong possibility, or guaranteed possibility $\Delta([p])$ estimates to what extent *all* the models of p have a high level of possibility. The lower normalization stating the existence of an interpretation with a zero possibility ensures that $\Delta(\mathcal{I}) = 0$ means that the guaranteed possibility of the whole set of interpretations is minimal. The duality relation $\nabla([p]) = 1 - \Delta([\neg p])$ states that as soon as a model of $\neg p$ has a zero possibility, $\nabla([p]) = 1$, which means there is at least one argument in favor of the certainty/acceptabiliy of p (the complete certainty/acceptability requires that all the models of $\neg p$ have a zero possibility and is measured by N).

In the following, in place of $\Pi([p]), N([p]), \Delta([p]), \nabla([p])$, we shall write $\Pi(p)$, $N(p), \Delta(p), \nabla(p)$ for simplicity. We shall use the notations $\bot$ and $\top$ for the contradiction and the tautology, which are such that $[\bot] = \emptyset$ and $[\top] = \mathcal{I}$ respectively.

It can be easily checked that these set functions have the following properties:

$$\Pi(p \vee q) = \max(\Pi(p), \Pi(q)), \quad N(p \wedge q) = \min(N(p), N(q)), \tag{1}$$

$$\Delta(p \vee q) = \min(\Delta(p), \Delta(q)), \quad \nabla(p \wedge q) = \max(\nabla(p), \nabla(q)). \tag{2}$$

In (1), $\Pi(p \vee q)$ expresses that the consistency of $p \vee q$ with the information requires the consistency of p or the consistency of q, while $N(p \wedge q)$ expresses that the certainty of $p \wedge q$ is all the greater as both the certainty of p and the certainty of q are higher. In (2), $\Delta(p \vee q)$ expresses that the guaranteed possibility of $p \vee q$ requires both the guaranteed possibility of p and the guaranteed possibility of q, while the meaning of $\nabla(p)$ being less easy to grasp, the intuition conveyed by $\nabla(p \wedge q)$ is harder to lay bare. Let us say that if something contributes to the weak necessity of p or of q, it also contributes to the weak necessity of $p \wedge q$. Letting $q = \neg p$ in (1) yields

$$\max(\Pi(p), \Pi(\neg p)) = 1 \quad \text{and} \quad \min(N(p), N(\neg p)) = 0 \tag{3}$$

as a result of the upper normalization. This makes clear that at least one of p and $\neg p$ should be fully possible, while p and $\neg p$ cannot be simutaneously somewhat certain at the risk of inconsistency. Due to (2), the lower normalization enforces

$$\min(\Delta(p), \Delta(\neg p)) = 0 \quad \text{and} \quad \max(\nabla(p), \nabla(\neg p)) = 1. \tag{4}$$

The first equality says that p and $\neg p$ cannot be simultaneously guaranteed; the second states that there is at least one argument in favor of p or of $\neg p$. Here, the available information is represented by a possibility distribution π. What can be said on a proposition p of interest is qualitatively summarized by the 4 estimates $\Pi(p), \Delta(p), N(p), \nabla(p)$ which reflect the maximum and the minimum of π over $[p]$ and over $[\neg p]$.
When the upper and the lower normalizations hold, we have the following inequality:

$$\max(N(p), \Delta(p)) \leq \min(\Pi(p), \nabla(p)) \quad \text{for all } p \neq \bot, p \neq \top. \tag{5}$$

When $p = \bot$, we have $N(p) = \Pi(p) = 0$ and $\Delta(p) = \nabla(p) = 1$, but $\Delta(\bot) = 1 > \Pi(\bot) = 0$. When $p = \top$, we have $N(p) = \Pi(p) = 1$ and $\Delta(p) = \nabla(p) = 0$, but $N(\top) = 1 > \nabla(\top) = 0$. Each member of the inequality (5) combines two functions of different nature: an increasing one with a decreasing one. This inequality shows the parallel importance of the independent set functions N and Δ when they have high values. Indeed $N(p) = 1$ means that *all* the counter-models of p are fully impossible, while $\Delta(p) = 1$ means that *all* the models of p are fully possible. When $N(p) = 1$, $\forall \omega \vDash \neg p, \pi(\omega) = 0$; if $p \vDash q$ then $[\neg q] \subseteq [\neg p]$ and thus $\forall \omega \vDash \neg q, \pi(\omega) = 0$, which means $N(q) = 1$; this is the basis of the semantic deduction of q from p. Besides, when $\Delta(p) = 1$, $\forall \omega \vDash p, \pi(\omega) = 1$; if $q \vDash p$ then $[q] \subseteq [p]$ and thus $\forall \omega \vDash q, \pi(\omega) = 1$, which means $\Delta(q) = 1$; it looks a bit like induction: something more specific is inferred from knowledge about a less specific proposition.[1]

The mutual behavior of the N-Π and of the Δ-∇ possibilistic set functions can be better understood by means of two squares of opposition. In these squares, the thick black line means mutual exclusion, dotted diagonals express contradiction, arrows picture implications, and double lines relate statements, at least one of which is true. The square of Fig. 1 appears as a graded version (through the threshold $\alpha > 0$) of the traditional square of modalities. Note that since $N(p) = 1 - \Pi(\neg p)$, the negation of $N(p) \geq \alpha \Leftrightarrow \Pi(\neg p) \leq 1 - \alpha$ is indeed $\Pi(\neg p) > 1 - \alpha$. Moreover $N(p) \geq \alpha$ entails $\Pi(p) > 1 - \alpha$ for any $\alpha > 0$, since, by (3), $N(p) > 0$ entails $N(\neg p) = 0 \Leftrightarrow \Pi(p) = 1$. This contrasts with the square of Fig. 2, which is unusual, although it mirrors the one of Fig. 1. Note that $\Delta(p) \geq \gamma \Leftrightarrow \nabla(\neg p) \leq 1 - \gamma$ since $\nabla(p) = 1 - \Delta(\neg p)$. The larger γ, the higher the possibility of all the models of p, this can be understood as offering guarantees for p. See [24] for a detailed study of the structures of opposition induced by the four set functions N, Π, Δ, ∇.

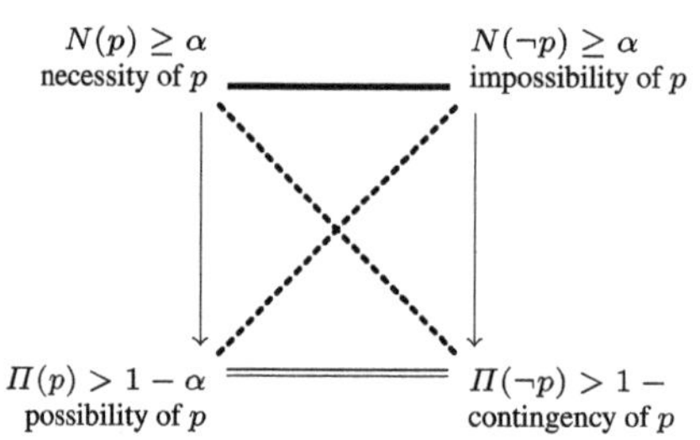

Fig. 1. The N-Π square of opposition ($p \neq \bot, p \neq \top$)

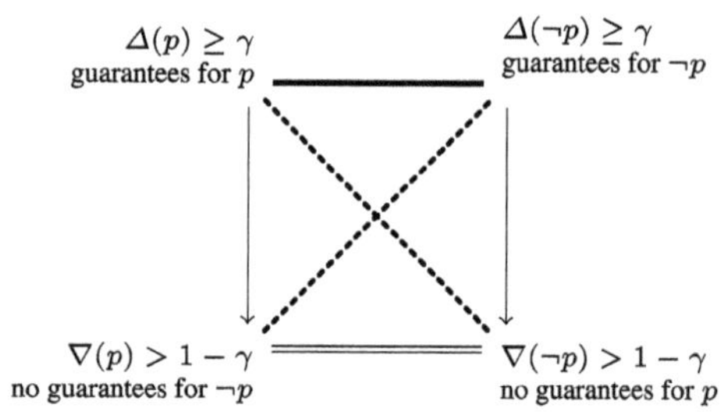

Fig. 2. The Δ-∇ square of opposition ($p \neq \bot$, $p \neq \top$)

2.2 Upper and Lower Approximations of a Possibility Distribution

A possibility distribution π compatible with the constraint $N(p) \geq \alpha$ must be such that

$$\forall \omega \in \mathcal{I}, \pi(\omega) \leq \max([p](\omega), 1 - \alpha) \tag{6}$$

[1] This also recalls the following plausible inference model: if $q \vDash p$ and p is true then q becomes more plausible; see vol. 2 of [30].

where $[p]$ is the characteristic function of the set of models of p, namely $[p](\omega) = 1$ if $\omega \models p$ and $[p](\omega) = 0$ otherwise. The inequality (6) is a direct consequence of the fact that $N(p) \geq \alpha$ is equivalent to $\Pi(\neg p) \leq 1 - \alpha$; $\pi^*(\omega) = \max([p](\omega), 1 - \alpha)$ is the greatest possibility distribution obeying (6).
Let $K = \{N(p_i) \geq \alpha_i, i = 1, ..., m\}$ be a set of such constraints. Then K induces a family of possibility distributions whose greatest element is [9]:

$$\pi^*_K(\omega) = \min_{i=1}^{m} \max([p_i](\omega), 1 - \alpha_i) \tag{7}$$

A constraint $\Delta(p) \geq \gamma$ corresponds to a family of possibility distributions δ such that

$$\forall \omega \in \mathcal{I}, \delta(\omega) \geq \min([p](\omega), \gamma) \tag{8}$$

In other words, $\Delta(p) \geq \gamma$ means that every model ω such that $\omega \models p$ is such that $\delta(\omega) \geq \gamma$, i.e., all models of p are guaranteed to be possible to at least level γ.

Then a set of constraints $P = \{\Delta(p_j) \geq \gamma_j | j = 1, \ldots, k\}$ corresponds to a family of possibility distributions whose greatest lower bound is [4]:

$$\delta_{*P}(\omega) = \max_{j=1}^{k} \min([p_j](\omega), \gamma_j) \tag{9}$$

obtained by cumulating the guaranteed possibilities.
Thus, a possibility distribution can be approximated from above by means of necessity-based constraints, see (7), and from below by means of guaranteed possibility-based constraints, see (9). The distribution δ_{*P} based on Δ correspond to the idea of focusing only on what has been actually observed, while π^*_K based on N correspond to what cannot be definitively rejected given what it is hold as certain to some extent.

2.3 Conditioning

The conditioning $\Pi(q \mid p)$ of q by p, in possibility theory, obeys the identity [18]

$$\Pi(p \wedge q) = \Pi(q \mid p) \star \Pi(p) \tag{10}$$

where $\star$ is min or the product, depending on whether we choose to be within a qualitative or a quantitative framework. Here we stick to a qualitative setting. For $\star = \min$, the greatest, least restrictive solution of the above equation is

$$\Pi(q \mid p) = \begin{cases} \Pi(p \wedge q) & \text{if } \Pi(p \wedge q) < \Pi(p) \\ 1 & \text{otherwise} \end{cases}. \tag{11}$$

We have the following:

Property 1. *$\Pi(q \mid p) = 1$ or $\Pi(p \mid q) = 1$ if and only if $\Pi(p \wedge q) = \min(\Pi(p), \Pi(q))$.*

Proof. Note that $\Pi(q \mid p) < 1$ if $\Pi(p) > \Pi(p \wedge q)$. If $\Pi(q \mid p) = 1$ then $\Pi(p) = \Pi(p \wedge q) \leq \Pi(q)$ (by monotony of Π). If $\Pi(p \mid q) = 1$ then $\Pi(q) = \Pi(p \wedge q) \leq \Pi(p)$. Hence $\Pi(p \wedge q) = \min(\Pi(p), \Pi(q))$. Conversely, assume $\Pi(p) \leq \Pi(q)$, then $\Pi(p \wedge q) = \Pi(p)$ and $\Pi(q \mid p) = 1$. □

When p and q are such that $\Pi(p \wedge q) = \min(\Pi(p), \Pi(q))$, they are said to be *unrelated* [29]. Conditional necessity is defined by duality: $N(q|p) = 1 - \Pi(\neg q|p)$.

Conditioning can be also defined for guaranteed possibility measures [4]. See also [11]. As for the inference, it works in a reversed way with respect to (10). Namely, conditioning obeys the following equation: $\Delta(p \wedge q) = \max(\Delta(q \mid p), \Delta(p))$. It means that $p \wedge q$ is guaranteed possible either because p is so or because, in the context p, q is guaranteed possible. Since $\Delta(p) = \min(\Delta(p \wedge q), \Delta(p \wedge \neg q))$, the smallest, most restrictive solution of the above equation (since Δ plays the role of a lower bound) is

$$\Delta(q \mid p) = \begin{cases} \Delta(p \wedge q) & \text{if } \Delta(p) < \Delta(p \wedge q) \\ 0 & \text{if } \Delta(p) = \Delta(p \wedge q) \leq \Delta(p \wedge \neg q). \end{cases} \tag{12}$$

Note the unusual behavior of this conditioning: $\Delta(q \mid p) = 0$ as soon as $\Delta(p) = \Delta(p \wedge q)$; thus we have $\Delta(p \mid p) = 0$, which may look strange. But having p true is not the same as guaranteeing that *all* the models of p are feasible. We have the following:

Property 2. $\Delta(q \mid p) = 0$ *or* $\Delta(p \mid q) = 0$ *if and only if* $\Delta(p \wedge q) = \max(\Delta(p), \Delta(q))$.

Proof. Observe that $\Delta(q \mid p) > 0$ if $\Delta(p) < \Delta(p \wedge q)$. $\Delta(q \mid p) = 0$ if and only if $\Delta(p) = \Delta(p \wedge q)$. Moreover $\Delta(p \wedge q) \geq \Delta(q)$ since Δ is decreasing. □

When p and q are such that $\Delta(p \wedge q) = \max(\Delta(p), \Delta(q))$, they are said to be Δ-*unrelated*. As shown by Property 2, p and q are Δ-unrelated as soon as the possibility of having q true when p is true, or the possibility of having p true when q is true is not guaranteed at all. Note also that $\Delta(p \mid q) = 0$ does not entail $\Delta(\neg p \mid q) = 0$. $\Delta(p \mid q) = 0 = \Delta(\neg p \mid q)$ holds only if $\Delta(p \wedge q) = \Delta(p \wedge \neg q)$ (two quantities that are also equal to $\Delta(p)$ in this case).

With respect to the values of $\Delta(q \mid p)$ and $\Delta(p \mid q)$, the following four situations can be encountered (and only these four):

$$\begin{cases} \Delta(q \mid p) = \Delta(p \mid q) > 0 \ \ if \ \ \Delta(p \wedge q) > \max(\Delta(p), \Delta(q)) \\ \Delta(q \mid p) > 0, \Delta(p \mid q) = 0 \ \ if \ \ \Delta(p \wedge q) = \Delta(q) > \Delta(p) \\ \Delta(q \mid p) = 0, \Delta(p \mid q) > 0 \ \ if \ \ \Delta(p \wedge q) = \Delta(p) > \Delta(q) \\ \Delta(q \mid p) = \Delta(p \mid q) = 0 \ \ if \ \ \Delta(p \wedge q) = \Delta(p) = \Delta(q) \end{cases} . \tag{13}$$

This shows that $\Delta(q \mid p)$ and $\Delta(p \mid q)$ are not always equal and may be different.

Forms of independence in the setting of possibility theory in terms of weak possibility and strong necessity is discussed in [7] where situations such as $N(q \mid p) = N(q) > 0$ or $N(q \mid p) = N(q) = 0$ are considered). Without developing here a similar axiomatic study for strong possibility, let us note that it follows from (12) and (13) that

- $\Delta(q \mid p) = \Delta(q) > 0$ if $\Delta(p \wedge q) = \Delta(q)$, and then we have $\Delta(p \mid q) = 0$ and $\Delta(p \wedge q) = \max(\Delta(p), \Delta(q))$.
- $\Delta(q \mid p) = \Delta(q) = 0$. Then $\Delta(p) = \Delta(p \wedge q) \geq \Delta(q) = 0$. Again $\Delta(p \wedge q) = \max(\Delta(p), \Delta(q))$.

Moreover, thanks to Property 2, $\Delta(p \wedge q) = \max(\Delta(p), \Delta(q))$ entails $\Delta(q \mid p) = 0$ or $\Delta(p \mid q) = 0$, which means that $\Delta(q \mid p) = \Delta(q) > 0$, or $\Delta(p \mid q) = \Delta(p) > 0$, or $\Delta(q \mid p) = \Delta(p \mid q) = 0$, with $\Delta(p) = \Delta(q)$ (but not necessarily equal to 0). Thus $\Delta(q \mid p) = \Delta(q) > 0$ is a *stronger form of independence* than the Δ-unrelatedness. Lastly, note that $\Delta(p \wedge p') = \Delta(p)$ if $\Delta(p' \mid p) = 0$ or $\Delta(p \mid p') = 0$ and $\Delta(p) \geq \Delta(p')$, since then $\Delta(p \wedge p') = \max(\Delta(p), \Delta(p'))$. This means that the guarantee attached to a proposition p is not affected by the presence of a Δ-unrelated feature p'.

2.4 Possibility and Likelihood

One of the proposed understandings of a numerical possibility distribution [20] is in terms of likelihood function in non-Bayesian statistics [6]. A likelihood function $\lambda(\theta) = P(d|\theta)$, viewed as a representation of uncertainty about θ, where $P(\cdot|\theta)$ is a statistical model with parameter θ, and d is an observed dataset. Likelihood functions are defined up to a multiplicative constant. They behave like relative possibility distributions.

Moreover it holds that $P(d|A) \leq \max_{\theta \in A} P(d|\theta)$ when a priori probability on θ is unknown and A is a disjunction of hypotheses [12]: thus denoting by Λ the extension of the likelihood function to subsets of hypotheses $A \subseteq \Theta$, we have $\Lambda(A) \leq \max_{\theta \in A} \lambda(\theta)$ where $\Lambda(\{\theta\}) = \lambda(\theta)$. Besides, Λ should be monotonic, i.e., $A \subseteq B$ implies $\Lambda(A) \leq \Lambda(B)$. So we have $\Lambda(A) \geq \max_{\theta \in A} \lambda(\theta)$. If we want to keep the same scale as probability functions, it leads to $\Lambda(A) = \max_{\theta \in A} \lambda(\theta)$ with $\lambda(\theta) = \frac{P(d|\theta)}{\max_{\theta \in \Theta} P(d|\theta)}$, assuming $\Lambda(\Theta) = 1$ [20]. Thus Λ behaves as a possibility measure [12].

Noticing that $P(d|A) \geq \min_{\theta \in A} P(d|\theta)$, one may similarly build a guaranteed possibility function $\Delta(A) = \min_{\theta \in A} \lambda(\theta)$ associated with the likelihood function λ. Thus, "the pair $(\Delta(A), \Pi(A))$ is interpreted as the minimum and the maximum of the probabilities to get the observation d given that we are in A, over a convex set of probabilities. This clearly estimates the plausibility to be in A when d is observed from an abductive reasoning point of view, that is, when the aim is to find a set of hypotheses explaining the current observations" [12]. Hence, one can report the bracketing $[\Delta(A), \Pi(A)]$, which allows us to distinguish between "A contains at least one good explanation" (large $\Pi(A)$) and "all explanations in A remain good enough" (large $\Delta(A)$).

3 A Calculus of Guarantees Using Decreasing Possibilistic Set Functions

In this section, we study the possibilistic inference in terms of the Δ function, first in logical form, and then, in terms of conditional functions, making a parallel in both cases with inference based on Π/N measures.

3.1 A Reversed Logic for Guarantees

Formulas in basic possibilistic logic [9] are pairs of the form (p, α) where p is a propositional logic formula and α is an element of a linearly ordered scale. The formula

(p, α) is semantically understood as the constraint $N(p) \geq \alpha$ where N is a necessity measure and α is a certainty (or priority) level associated with p. The basic possibilistic logic [9,13,19,21] relies on the following weighted resolution rule for the propositional case:

$$N(p \vee r) \geq \alpha, N(\neg p \vee q) \geq \beta \vDash N(q \vee r) \geq \min(\alpha, \beta). \tag{14}$$

This clearly extends the cut rule in propositional logic retrieved when $\alpha = \beta = 1$. The deductive inference rule (14) can be equivalently rewritten in terms of possibility:

$$\Pi(\neg p \wedge \neg r) \leq 1-\alpha, \Pi(p \wedge \neg q) \leq 1-\beta \vDash \Pi(\neg q \wedge \neg r) \leq \max(1-\alpha, 1-\beta). \tag{15}$$

If we consider the particular case of the *modus ponens*, i.e., if $r = \bot$, we get

$$\Pi(\neg p) \leq 1-\alpha, \Pi(p \wedge \neg q) \leq 1-\beta \vDash \Pi(\neg q) \leq \max(1-\alpha, 1-\beta)$$

which reads the higher α and β, the more impossible $\neg p$ and the more impossible the exceptions of the implication $p \rightarrow q$, then the more impossible $\neg q$. Interestingly, this can be put in matrix form ($\Box_{\max}^{\min}$ (resp. $\Box_{\min}^{\max}$) is the min-max (resp. max-min) matrix product)[2]:

$$\begin{bmatrix} \Pi(q) \\ \Pi(\neg q) \end{bmatrix} \leq \begin{bmatrix} \Pi(\neg p \wedge q) & \Pi(p \wedge q) \\ \Pi(\neg p \wedge \neg q) & \Pi(p \wedge \neg q) \end{bmatrix} \Box_{\max}^{\min} \begin{bmatrix} \Pi(p) \\ \Pi(\neg p) \end{bmatrix}. \tag{16}$$

Moreover there exists a deductive inference rule [15] that mixes lower bounds of necessity and possibility measures:

$$N(p \vee q) \geq \gamma, \Pi(\neg p \vee r) \geq \delta \vDash \Pi(q \vee r) \geq \delta \text{ if } \gamma > 1-\delta. \tag{17}$$

This is a weighted version of a deductive inference rule that holds in modal logics [25]. All these infererence patterns have a clear deductive flavor.

We are now in position to present the inference patterns with weights in terms of Δ and ∇. Although the patterns governing Δ and ∇ mirror inference patterns (14), (15) and (17), they have a completely different meaning, as we are going to see. As a summary, one can say that with N, we propagate degrees of certainty (or priority) deductively. In contrast, with Δ, we propagate degrees of guaranteed possibility (for sets of models that are feasible/observed at least at some level), which gives the calculation an essentially inductive flavor. This is what we detail now.

As already said, a constraint of the form $\Delta(p) \geq \gamma$ means that *any* model of p is possible for sure to an extent at least equal to γ. This may be understood as saying that all the models of p have been observed (or reported). This offers a form of guarantee about p. The following pattern of inference [8,16]

$$\Delta(p \wedge q) \geq \gamma, \Delta(\neg p \wedge r) \geq \delta \vDash \Delta(q \wedge r) \geq \min(\gamma, \delta) \tag{18}$$

agrees with this semantics in terms of observations and guarantees. For instance if we consider the special case $q = \top$, it writes $\Delta(p) \geq \gamma, \Delta(\neg p \wedge r) \geq \delta \vDash \Delta(r) \geq$

[2] This is the dual counterpart of $\begin{bmatrix} N(q) \\ N(\neg q) \end{bmatrix} \geq \begin{bmatrix} N(\neg p \vee q) & N(p \vee q) \\ N(\neg p \vee \neg q) & N(p \vee \neg q) \end{bmatrix} \Box_{\min}^{\max} \begin{bmatrix} N(p) \\ N(\neg p) \end{bmatrix}$ [22].

$\min(\gamma, \delta)$, and indeed if all models of p have guarantees because observed, this applies in particular to the models of $p \wedge r$, and since the models of $\neg p \wedge r$ have guarantees, all the models of r have guarantees. A matrix form exists which is the counterpart of (16):

$$\begin{bmatrix} \Delta(q) \\ \Delta(\neg q) \end{bmatrix} \geq \begin{bmatrix} \Delta(\neg p \wedge q) & \Delta(p \wedge q) \\ \Delta(\neg p \wedge \neg q) & \Delta(p \wedge \neg q) \end{bmatrix} \Box_{\min}^{\max} \begin{bmatrix} \Delta(p) \\ \Delta(\neg p) \end{bmatrix} \tag{19}$$

The pattern of inference (18) is equivalent to

$$\nabla(\neg p \vee \neg q) \leq 1 - \gamma, \nabla(p \vee \neg r) \leq 1 - \delta \vDash \nabla(\neg q \vee \neg r) \leq \max(1 - \gamma, 1 - \delta) \tag{20}$$

Letting $\neg q = s$ and taking $r = \top$, we obtain as a special case: $\nabla(\neg p \vee s) \leq 1 - \gamma, \nabla(p) \leq 1 - \delta \vDash \nabla(s) \leq \max(1 - \gamma, 1 - \delta)$. We recognize an instance of the *modus ponens* weighted in terms of upper bounds of the weak necessity ∇. This can be rewritten as: $1 - \nabla(\neg p \vee s) \geq \gamma, 1 - \nabla(p) \geq \delta \vDash 1 - \nabla(s) \geq \min(\gamma, \delta)$.

If we assume that γ and δ have high values, this means that the upper bounds of the weak necessity ∇ are close to 0 for the different propositions under consideration. Due to the inequalities (5), this also means that the corresponding certainties and guaranteed possibilities are close to 0. Thus, viewed as a pattern of logical deduction, the pattern of inference (18) offers no certainty, no guarantee. As we shall see, this is rather an inductive pattern. Besides, the following inference rule [10] mirrors (17):

$$\Delta(p \wedge q) \geq \gamma, \nabla(\neg p \wedge r) \geq \delta \vDash \nabla(q \wedge r) \geq \delta \text{ if } \gamma > 1 - \delta \tag{21}$$

Following the square of Fig. 2, it expresses, when $r = \top$, that if $p \wedge q$ has guarantees high enough and if p has no guarantee, then $\neg q$ has no guarantee. Indeed if the models of $p \wedge q$ have been observed, and if not all models of p have been observed, it means that not all models of $p \wedge \neg q$, and consequently not all models of $\neg q$ have been observed.

3.2 A Matrix Calculation of Guarantees

The oriented nature of if-then rules is better captured in terms of conditioning. A matrix calculus using conditional possibility was proposed in [26]; see also [14,31]. Noticing

$$\Pi(q) = \max(\Pi(p \wedge q), \Pi(\neg p \wedge q)) = \max(\min(\Pi(q|p), \Pi(p)), \min(\Pi(q|\neg p), \Pi(\neg p)))$$

the propagation of uncertainty takes the form of a max-min matrix product noted $\Box_{\min}^{\max}$:

$$\begin{bmatrix} \Pi(q) \\ \Pi(\neg q) \end{bmatrix} = \begin{bmatrix} \Pi(q|p) & \Pi(q|\neg p) \\ \Pi(\neg q|p) & \Pi(\neg q|\neg p) \end{bmatrix} \Box_{\min}^{\max} \begin{bmatrix} \Pi(p) \\ \Pi(\neg p) \end{bmatrix} \tag{22}$$

This max-min matrix product equation holds with equality, in contrast with (16). Due to constraints (3), each column of the conditional matrix must be normalized, i.e., $\max(\Pi(q \mid p), \Pi(\neg q \mid p)) = 1$ and $\max(\Pi(q \mid \neg p), \Pi(\neg q \mid \neg p)) = 1$, so each column has at least one entry equal to 1.

The general form of the conditional matrix is $\begin{bmatrix} 1 & s \\ r & 1 \end{bmatrix}$ thus representing the rule "if p then q" with certainty $1 - r$ together with the rule "if $\neg p$ then $\neg q$" with certainty

$1 - s$. $\begin{bmatrix} 1 & 1 \\ r & 1 \end{bmatrix}$ encodes only the first rule with complete ignorance about the second rule.

Matrices such that $\begin{bmatrix} 1 & 1 \\ r & s \end{bmatrix}$ (resp. $\begin{bmatrix} r & s \\ 1 & 1 \end{bmatrix}$) are not considered since they express that q (resp. $\neg q$) holds unconditionally (with certainty $\max(1-r, 1-s)$) The $\Box^{\max}_{\min}$ product preserves the normalisation condition $\max(\Pi(p), \Pi(\neg p)) = 1$.
Following a construction made in [27] (see also [22]), we move to a min-max matrix for handling rules in parallel. See [2,3] for the complete theory. In what follows, the min-max matrix calculus for parallel rules is recalled using a new presentation.

Matrix Calculation for Π Functions. Let us focus on matrices of the form $\begin{bmatrix} 1 & s \\ r & 1 \end{bmatrix}$, then the matrix product $\Box^{\max}_{\min}$ in Eq. (22) can be simplified if we take into account the normalization condition on the input vector, i.e., $\max(\Pi(p), \Pi(\neg p)) = 1$. Indeed, let $\begin{bmatrix} \Pi(p) \\ \Pi(\neg p) \end{bmatrix} = \begin{bmatrix} \lambda \\ \rho \end{bmatrix}$, then $\begin{bmatrix} \Pi(q) \\ \Pi(\neg q) \end{bmatrix} = \begin{bmatrix} 1 & s \\ r & 1 \end{bmatrix} \Box^{\max}_{\min} \begin{bmatrix} \lambda \\ \rho \end{bmatrix} = \max(\begin{bmatrix} s \\ r \end{bmatrix}, \begin{bmatrix} \lambda \\ \rho \end{bmatrix}) = \begin{bmatrix} \max(s, \lambda) \\ \max(r, \rho) \end{bmatrix}$ as soon as $\max(\lambda, \rho) = 1$, as it can be easily checked.

Let us consider two rules "if p_1 then q_1" and "if p_2 then q_2" in parallel respectively represented by the matrices $\begin{bmatrix} 1 & s_1 \\ r_1 & 1 \end{bmatrix}$ and $\begin{bmatrix} 1 & s_2 \\ r_2 & 1 \end{bmatrix}$, with respective inputs $\begin{bmatrix} \lambda_1 \\ \rho_1 \end{bmatrix}$ and $\begin{bmatrix} \lambda_2 \\ \rho_2 \end{bmatrix}$.

Then the combination of the two results $\Pi(q)$ and $\Pi(q')$ is performed by a min combination, i.e., $\Pi(q \wedge q') = \min(\Pi(q), \Pi(q'))$, assuming unrelatedness[3], i.e.,

$$\begin{bmatrix} \Pi(q_1 \wedge q_2) \\ \Pi(q_1 \wedge \neg q_2) \\ \Pi(\neg q_1 \wedge q_2) \\ \Pi(\neg q_1 \wedge \neg q_2) \end{bmatrix} = \begin{bmatrix} \min(\Pi(q_1), \Pi(q_2)) \\ \min(\Pi(q_1), \Pi(\neg q_2)) \\ \min(\Pi(\neg q_1), \Pi(q_2)) \\ \min(\Pi(\neg q_1), \Pi(\neg q_2)) \end{bmatrix} \tag{23}$$

Combining (22) and (23) leads to a $\Box^{\min}_{\max}$ matrix product, indeed we get

$$\begin{bmatrix} \Pi(q_1 \wedge q_2) \\ \Pi(q_1 \wedge \neg q_2) \\ \Pi(\neg q_1 \wedge q_2) \\ \Pi(\neg q_1 \wedge \neg q_2) \end{bmatrix} = \begin{bmatrix} \min(\max(s_1, \lambda_1), \max(s_2, \lambda_2)) \\ \min(\max(s_1, \lambda_1), \max(r_2, \rho_2)) \\ \min(\max(r_1, \rho_1), \max(s_2, \lambda_2)) \\ \min(\max(r_1, \rho_1), \max(r_2, \rho_2)) \end{bmatrix} = \begin{bmatrix} s_1 & 1 & s_2 & 1 \\ s_1 & 1 & 1 & r_2 \\ 1 & r_1 & s_2 & 1 \\ 1 & r_1 & 1 & r_2 \end{bmatrix} \Box^{\min}_{\max} \begin{bmatrix} \lambda_1 \\ \rho_1 \\ \lambda_2 \\ \rho_2 \end{bmatrix} \tag{24}$$

What is obtained is a possibility distribution, since $q_1 \wedge q_2$, $q_1 \wedge \neg q_2$, $\neg q_1 \wedge q_2$, $\neg q_1 \wedge \neg q_2$ are mutually exclusive and form a partition of the set of interpretations induced by q_1 and q_2. In case, some of the above conjunctions are equal to $\bot$, the partition reduces to the non contradictory conjunctions. The obtained distribution is normalized in the usual possibilistic sense, i.e., at least one of the values in the vector $\begin{bmatrix} \Pi(q_1 \wedge q_2) \\ \Pi(q_1 \wedge \neg q_2) \\ \Pi(\neg q_1 \wedge q_2) \\ \Pi(\neg q_1 \wedge \neg q_2) \end{bmatrix}$ is equal to 1 as soon as $\max(\lambda_1, \rho_1) = 1$ and $\max(\lambda_2, \rho_2) = 1$.

If one considers the particular case $p_1 = p_2 = p$ and $q_1 = q_2 = q$ (and thus $\lambda_1 = \lambda_2, \rho_1 = \rho_2, s_1 = s_2, r_1 = r_2$), one obtains, getting rid of the second and third

[3] In any case, we are computing upper bounds, since we have $\Pi(q \wedge q') \leq \min(\Pi(q), \Pi(q'))$.

lines of the matrices that correspond to contradictions $\neg q \wedge q \equiv \bot$:

$$\begin{bmatrix} \Pi(q) \\ \Pi(\neg q) \end{bmatrix} = \begin{bmatrix} \max(s,\lambda) \\ \max(r,\rho) \end{bmatrix} = \begin{bmatrix} s & 1 \\ 1 & r \end{bmatrix} \Box^{\min}_{\max} \begin{bmatrix} \lambda \\ \rho \end{bmatrix} \tag{25}$$

We now follow a similar path using conditioned Δ set functions. But before, we present the treatment of rules in parallel in the setting of the guaranteed possibility measures. This shows how one can move from a logical-like knowledge representation to a functional view where uncertainty propagation reduces to a matrix calculus.

A Matrix Calculation for $\boldsymbol{\Delta}$ Functions. First observe that $\Delta(q) = \Delta((\neg p \wedge q) \vee (p \wedge q)) = \min(\Delta(\neg p \wedge q), \Delta(p \wedge q)) = \min(\max(\Delta(q|p), \Delta(p)), \max(\Delta(q|\neg p), \Delta(\neg p)))$. This leads to the min-max matrix product $\Box^{\min}_{\max}$ equality, in contrast with (19):

$$\begin{bmatrix} \Delta(q) \\ \Delta(\neg q) \end{bmatrix} = \begin{bmatrix} \Delta(q|p) & \Delta(q|\neg p) \\ \Delta(\neg q|p) & \Delta(\neg q|\neg p) \end{bmatrix} \Box^{\min}_{\max} \begin{bmatrix} \Delta(p) \\ \Delta(\neg p) \end{bmatrix}. \tag{26}$$

Due to the constraint (4), each column of the conditional matrix must be normalized from below, that is, $\min(\Delta(q \mid p), \Delta(\neg q \mid p)) = 0$ and $\min(\Delta(q \mid \neg p), \Delta(\neg q \mid \neg p)) = 0$, so each column has at least one entry equal to 0. The general form of the conditional matrix is $\begin{bmatrix} t & 0 \\ 0 & u \end{bmatrix}$ thus representing the rules if p then q with guaranteed possibility t, together with the rule if $\neg p$ then $\neg q$ with guaranteed possibility u.

As already seen in the general case in Subsect. 2.2, while Π provides upper approximations of possibility distributions, Δ gives lower approximations. This is again the case for the conditioned set functions. Indeed here $\begin{bmatrix} t & 0 \\ 0 & u \end{bmatrix}$ is always smaller than $\begin{bmatrix} 1 & s \\ r & 1 \end{bmatrix}$, which provides a bracketing of a conditional possibility distribution. This kind of bracketing has been already encountered in the representation of fuzzy rules [17].

If we focus on matrices of the form $\begin{bmatrix} t & 0 \\ 0 & u \end{bmatrix}$, then the matrix product $\Box^{\min}_{\max}$ in equation (26) can be simplified if we take into account the normalization condition on the input vector, i.e., $\min(\Delta(p), \Delta(\neg p)) = 0$. Indeed, let $\begin{bmatrix} \Delta(p) \\ \Delta(\neg p) \end{bmatrix} = \begin{bmatrix} \delta \\ \epsilon \end{bmatrix}$, then $\begin{bmatrix} \Delta(q) \\ \Delta(\neg q) \end{bmatrix} = \begin{bmatrix} t & 0 \\ 0 & u \end{bmatrix} \Box^{\min}_{\max} \begin{bmatrix} \delta \\ \epsilon \end{bmatrix} = \min(\begin{bmatrix} t \\ u \end{bmatrix}, \begin{bmatrix} \epsilon \\ \delta \end{bmatrix}) = \begin{bmatrix} \min(t,\epsilon) \\ \min(u,\delta) \end{bmatrix}$ as soon as $\min(\delta, \epsilon) = 0$, as it can easily checked.

Let us consider two rules "if p_1 then q_1" and "if p_2 then q_2" in parallel respectively represented by the matrices $\begin{bmatrix} t_1 & 0 \\ 0 & u_1 \end{bmatrix}$ and $\begin{bmatrix} t_2 & 0 \\ 0 & u_2 \end{bmatrix}$, with respective inputs $\begin{bmatrix} \delta_1 \\ \epsilon_1 \end{bmatrix}$ and $\begin{bmatrix} \delta_2 \\ \epsilon_2 \end{bmatrix}$.

Then the combination of the two results $\Delta(q)$ and $\Delta(q')$ is performed by a max combination, i.e., $\Delta(q \wedge q') = \max(\Delta(q), \Delta(q'))$, assuming Δ-unrelatedness[4], i.e.,

$$\begin{bmatrix} \Delta(q_1 \wedge q_2) \\ \Delta(q_1 \wedge \neg q_2) \\ \Delta(\neg q_1 \wedge q_2) \\ \Delta(\neg q_1 \wedge \neg q_2) \end{bmatrix} = \begin{bmatrix} \max(\Delta(q_1), \Delta(q_2)) \\ \max(\Delta(q_1), \Delta(\neg q_2)) \\ \max(\Delta(\neg q_1), \Delta(q_2)) \\ \max(\Delta(\neg q_1), \Delta(\neg q_2)) \end{bmatrix} \tag{27}$$

[4] In any case, we are computing lower bounds, since we always have $\Delta(q \wedge q') \geq \max(\Delta(q), \Delta(q'))$. Thus it is a cautious evaluation.

It leads to a min-max matrix product $\Box_{\min}^{\max}$, indeed we get

$$\begin{bmatrix} \Delta(q_1 \wedge q_2) \\ \Delta(q_1 \wedge \neg q_2) \\ \Delta(\neg q_1 \wedge q_2) \\ \Delta(\neg q_1 \wedge \neg q_2) \end{bmatrix} = \begin{bmatrix} \max(\min(t_1, \epsilon_1), \min(t_2, \epsilon_2)) \\ \max(\min(t_1, \epsilon_1), \min(u_2, \delta_2)) \\ \max(\min(u_1, \delta_1), \min(t_2, \epsilon_2)) \\ \max(\min(u_1, \delta_1), \min(u_2, \delta_2)) \end{bmatrix} = \begin{bmatrix} 0 & t_1 & 0 & t_2 \\ 0 & t_1 & u_2 & 0 \\ u_1 & 0 & 0 & t_2 \\ u_1 & 0 & u_2 & 0 \end{bmatrix} \Box_{\min}^{\max} \begin{bmatrix} \delta_1 \\ \epsilon_1 \\ \delta_2 \\ \epsilon_2 \end{bmatrix} \tag{28}$$

What is obtained is possibility distribution of guarantees, since $q_1 \wedge q_2$, $q_1 \wedge \neg q_2$, $\neg q_1 \wedge q_2$, $\neg q_1 \wedge \neg q_2$ are mutually exclusive and form a partition of the set of interpretations induced by q_1 and q_2. In case, some of the above conjunctions are equal to $\perp$, the partition reduces to the non contradictory conjunctions. The obtained distribution is normalized in the sense of guaranteed possibility, i.e., at least one of the values in the vector $\begin{bmatrix} \Delta(q_1 \wedge q_2) \\ \Delta(q_1 \wedge \neg q_2) \\ \Delta(\neg q_1 \wedge q_2) \\ \Delta(\neg q_1 \wedge \neg q_2) \end{bmatrix}$ is equal to 0 as soon as $\min(\delta_1, \epsilon_1) = 0$ and $\min(\delta_2, \epsilon_2) = 0$.

This is for two rules, and this can be generalized to n rules, which is done now.

Let $H = \{1, 2, \ldots, n\}$ be the index set of the propositions $q_1, q_2, \ldots, q_n$. Let 2^H denote the power set of H. For each subset $S \subseteq H$, we associate the conjunction $\phi_S := \left(\bigwedge_{i \in S} q_i\right) \wedge \left(\bigwedge_{i \in H \setminus S} \neg q_i\right)$. In general, some ϕ_S may be inconsistent (i.e., $\phi_S \equiv \perp$) due to logical dependencies between the q_i's. We therefore restrict the construction to the feasible index family

$$\mathcal{F} := \{ S \subseteq H \mid \phi_S \not\equiv \perp \} \qquad \text{(equivalently: } \phi_S \text{ is satisfiable).}$$

We introduce the mapping τ which, given a subset $S \subseteq H$, constructs a row matrix of size $(1, 2n)$ by block concatenation:

$$\tau(S) := \begin{bmatrix} L_1 \ L_2 \cdots L_n \end{bmatrix}, \qquad L_i = \begin{cases} \begin{bmatrix} 0 & t_i \end{bmatrix} & \text{if } i \in S, \\ \begin{bmatrix} u_i & 0 \end{bmatrix} & \text{if } i \notin S. \end{cases}$$

We equip 2^H with the lexicographic order $<$. Let $S_1, S_2 \subseteq H$, $S_1 \neq S_2$, and define:

$$\text{for } k = 1, 2, \quad \xi_k(i) := \begin{cases} 1 & \text{if } i \in S_k, \\ 0 & \text{if } i \notin S_k. \end{cases}$$

Let $j := \min\{ i \in H \mid \xi_1(i) \neq \xi_2(i) \}$., then $S_1 < S_2 \Longleftrightarrow \xi_1(j) < \xi_2(j)$.
We use the restriction of $<$ to $\mathcal{F}$ and enumerate the feasible subsets as $\mathcal{F} = \{S_1, S_2, \ldots, S_m\}$ with $S_1 < S_2 < \cdots < S_m$, where $m := |\mathcal{F}|$.
For each $k = 1, \ldots, m$, write $\phi_k := \phi_{S_k}$. We build a column vector $O \in [0, 1]^{m \times 1}$, a

matrix $M \in [0,1]^{m\times 2n}$ and a column vector $I \in [0,1]^{2n\times 1}$ by

$$O := \begin{bmatrix} \Delta(\phi_1) \\ \Delta(\phi_2) \\ \vdots \\ \Delta(\phi_m) \end{bmatrix}, \qquad M := \begin{bmatrix} \tau(S_1) \\ \tau(S_2) \\ \vdots \\ \tau(S_m) \end{bmatrix}, \qquad I := \begin{bmatrix} \delta_1 \\ \epsilon_1 \\ \delta_2 \\ \epsilon_2 \\ \vdots \\ \delta_n \\ \epsilon_n \end{bmatrix}.$$

Finally, the max–min system is $O = M \,\Box^{\max}_{\min}\, I$. For each $k \in \{1,\ldots,m\}$, letting the k-th row of M be $\tau(S_k) = [m_{k1},\ldots,m_{k,2n}]$, the max-min composition gives

$$O_k \;=\; \big(\tau(S_k)\big)\,\Box^{\max}_{\min}\, \mathrm{I} \;=\; \max_{j=1}^{2n}\, \min\!\big(m_{kj},\, I_j\big).$$

Using the block structure of $\tau(S_k)$, this simplifies to $O_k \;=\; \max_{i\in H}\, \min\!\big(\alpha_{k,i},\, \beta_{k,i}\big)$, where $\alpha_{k,i} := \begin{cases} t_i & \text{if } \xi_k(i) = 1, \\ u_i & \text{if } \xi_k(i) = 0 \end{cases}$ and $\beta_{k,i} := \begin{cases} \epsilon_i & \text{if } \xi_k(i) = 1, \\ \delta_i & \text{if } \xi_k(i) = 0. \end{cases}$

This matrix calculus is also relevant for machine learning applications. In the Π-based setting, rule parameters can be learned from training samples by solving, for each sample, a system of min-max equations: the right-hand side vector encodes a targeted output possibility distribution, the matrix is constructed from the premise degrees induced by the sample, and the unknowns are the rule parameters s_i, r_i [1]. The same construction can be applied here: using Δ-based propagation, one can build a max-min system from data to learn the rule parameters t_i and u_i. Hence, learning procedures based on (Δ, ∇) can be developed in direct analogy with existing schemes based on (Π, N), and can support applications such as neuro-symbolic ones [2].

4 Conclusion

This paper highlights the interest of having two complementary reasoning modes in possibility theory. Alongside the usual use of (Π, N), we have focused on the pair (Δ, ∇) and the corresponding tools: the meaning of guarantees captured by Δ, its conditioning rule, and its use for uncertainty propagation, both in logical form and in a matrix form based on conditional values.

This makes it possible to compare, on the same problem, what follows from Π-based propagation and what follows from Δ-based propagation. The former relies on the existence of at least one sufficiently plausible model, while the latter relies on the minimum possibility level shared by all models of a statement. This difference is also reflected by the propagation schemes for Π and for Δ, with different normalization constraints on conditional matrices.

Overall, the paper highlights a dual reading: the available information yields two complementary assessments of a logical proposition, via (Π, N) and via (Δ, ∇), while, under the likelihood reading, the bracketing $[\Delta(A), \Pi(A)]$ offers a similar assessment for a set of hypotheses A given the observation. As a perspective, this highlights the need to understand the complementary information provided by Π-propagation and that provided by Δ-propagation using their respective matrix calculus, in terms of likelihood.

Disclosure of Interests. The authors have no competing interests to declare that are relevant to the content of this article.

References

1. Baaj, I.: Learning rule parameters of possibilistic rule-based system. In: 2022 IEEE International Conference on Fuzzy Systems (FUZZ-IEEE), pp. 1–8. IEEE (2022)
2. Baaj, I., Marquis, P.: Π-nesy: a possibilistic neuro-symbolic approach. CoRR, abs/2504.07055 (2025)
3. Baaj, I., Poli, J.-P., Ouerdane, W., Maudet, N.: Min-max inference for possibilistic rule-based system. In: FUZZ-IEEE, pp. 1–6. IEEE (2021)
4. Benferhat, S., Dubois, D., Kaci, S., Prade, H.: Bipolar possibilistic representations. In: Darwiche, A., Friedman, N. (eds.) UAI 2002, Proceedings of 18th Conference in Uncertainty in Artificial Intelligence, Univ. of Alberta, Edmonton, August 1–4, pp. 45–52. Morgan Kaufmann (2002)
5. Benferhat, S., Dubois, D., Prade, H.: Towards a possibilistic logic handling of preferences. Appl. Intell. **14**(3), 303–317 (2001)
6. Coletti, G., Petturiti, D., Vantaggi, B.: Fuzzy memberships as likelihood functions in a possibilistic framework. Int. J. Approximate Reasoning **88**, 547–566 (2017)
7. Dubois, D., Fariñas del Cerro, L., Herzig, A., Prade, H.: A roadmap of qualitative independence. In: Dubois, D., Prade, H., Klement, E.P. (eds.) Fuzzy Sets, Logics and Reasoning about Knowledge, pp. 325–350. Kluwer Academic Publishers (1999)
8. Dubois, D., Hájek, P., Prade, H.: Knowledge-driven versus data-driven logics. J. Log. Lang. Inf. **9**(1), 65–89 (2000)
9. Dubois, D., Lang, J., Prade, H.: Possibilistic logic. In: Gabbay, D.M., Hogger, C.J., Robinson, J.A., Nute, D. (eds.) Handbook of Logic in Artificial Intelligence and Logic Programming, vol. 3, pp. 439–513. Oxford University Press (1994)
10. Dubois, D., Lorini, E., Prade, H.: Bipolar possibility theory as a basis for a logic of desires and beliefs. In: Liu, W., Subrahmanian, V.S., Wijsen, J. (eds.) SUM 2013. LNCS (LNAI), vol. 8078, pp. 204–218. Springer, Heidelberg (2013). https://doi.org/10.1007/978-3-642-40381-1_16
11. Dubois, D., Lorini, E., Prade, H.: The strength of desires: a logical approach. Minds Mach. **27**(1), 199–231 (2017)
12. Dubois, D., Moral, S., Prade, H.: A semantics for possibility theory based on likelihoods. J. Math. Anal. Appl. **205**, 359–380 (1997)
13. Dubois, D., Prade, H.: 40 years of research in possibilistic logic - a survey. In: Proceedings of 34th International Joint Conference on Artificial Intelligence (IJCAI 2025), Montreal, August 16-22, pp. 10427–10435 (2025)
14. Dubois, D., Prade, H.: Possibilistic inference under matrix form. In: Negoita, C., Prade, H. (eds.) Fuzzy Logic in Knowledge Engineering, pp. 112–126. Verlag TÜV Rheinland (1986)
15. Dubois, D., Prade, H.: Resolution principles in possibilistic logic. Int. J. Approximate Reasoning **4**, 1–21 (1990)

16. Dubois, D., Prade, H.: Possibility theory as a basis for preference propagation in automated reasoning. In: Proceedings of 1st IEEE International Conference on Fuzzy Systems (FUZZ-IEEE'92), San Diego, Ca., March 8–12, pp. 821–832 (1992)
17. Dubois, D., Prade, H.: Basic issues on fuzzy rules and their application to fuzzy control. In: Driankov, D., Eklund, P.W., Ralescu, A.L. (eds.) IJCAI 1991. LNCS, vol. 833, pp. 1–14. Springer, Heidelberg (1994). https://doi.org/10.1007/3-540-58279-7_14
18. Dubois, D., Prade, H.: Possibility theory: qualitative and quantitative aspects. In: Quantified Representation of Uncertainty and Imprecision, Handbook of Defeasible Reasoning and Uncertainty Management Systems, vol. 1, pp. 169–226. Kluwer (1998)
19. Dubois, D., Prade, H.: Possibilistic logic - an overview. In: Siekmann, J.H. (ed.) Computational Logic, Handbook of the History of Logic, vol. 9, pp. 283–342. Elsevier (2014)
20. Dubois, D., Prade, H.: Practical methods for constructing possibility distributions. Int. J. Intell. Syst. **31**(3), 215–239 (2016)
21. Dubois, D., Prade, H.: Possibilistic logic: from certainty-qualified statements to two-tiered logics – a prospective survey. In: Calimeri, F., Leone, N., Manna, M. (eds.) JELIA 2019. LNCS (LNAI), vol. 11468, pp. 3–20. Springer, Cham (2019). https://doi.org/10.1007/978-3-030-19570-0_1
22. Dubois, D., Prade, H.: From possibilistic rule-based systems to machine learning - a discussion paper. In: Davis, J., Tabia, K. (eds.) SUM 2020. LNCS (LNAI), vol. 12322, pp. 35–51. Springer, Cham (2020). https://doi.org/10.1007/978-3-030-58449-8_3
23. Dubois, D., Prade, H.: Reasoning and learning in the setting of possibility theory - overview and perspectives. Int. J. Approx. Reason. **171**, 109028 (2024)
24. Dubois, D., Prade, H.: Structures of opposition in possibility theory-based logic and related logics. In: Proceedings of IEEE International Conference on Fuzzy Systems (FUZZ 2025), Reims, July 6–10, pp. 1–6 (2025)
25. Fariñas del Cerro, L., Penttonen, M.: A note of the complexity of the satisfiability of modal horn clauses. J. Log. Program. **4**(1), 1–10 (1987)
26. Farreny, H., Prade, H.: A possibility theory-based approach to default and inexact reasoning. Commun. Cogn. **17**(4), 85–99 (1984)
27. Farreny, H., Prade, H.: Positive and negative explanations of uncertain reasoning in the framework of possibility theory. In: Proceedings of 5th Conference on Uncertainty in Artificial Intelligence (UAI 1989), Windsor, ON, August 18–20, pp. 95–101 (1989)
28. Kahneman, D.: Thinking, Fast and Slow. Macmillan (2011)
29. Nahmias, S.: Fuzzy variables. Fuzzy Sets Syst. **1**, 97–110 (1978)
30. Polya, G.: Mathematics and Plausible Reasoning-Vol.1: Induction and analogy in Mathematics, Vol. 2: Patterns of Plausible Inference, 2nd edn. Princeton University Press (1968, 1954)
31. Prade, H.: A simple inference technique for dealing with uncertain facts in terms of possibility. Kybernetes **15**(1), 19–24 (1986). Errata, Vol.15, p.214
32. Shafer, G.: A Mathematical Theory of Evidence. Princeton University Press (1976)
33. Ughetto, L., Dubois, D., Prade, H.: Implicative and conjunctive fuzzy rules - a tool for reasoning from knowledge and examples. In: Proceedings of 16th National Conference on Artificial Intelligence (AAAI), July 18–22 Orlando, pp. 214–219 (1999)

Extended Predecessor Decoding for Coherent MAP Inference in Non-linear Bayesian Models

Branislav Rudić[1(✉)], Veronika Putz[1], Markus Pichler-Scheder[1], and Dmitry Efrosinin[2]

[1] Linz Center of Mechatronics GmbH, Altenberger Str. 69, 4040 Linz, Austria
{branislav.rudic,veronika.putz,markus.pichler-scheder}@lcm.at

[2] Institute of Stochastics, Johannes Kepler University, Altenberger Str. 69, 4040 Linz, Austria
dmitry.efrosinin@jku.at

Abstract. Recursive Bayesian inference in state observation models is commonly addressed through marginal inference techniques such as prediction, filtering, and smoothing. While these methods provide distributions over individual states, marginal Maximum A Posteriori (MAP) estimates obtained independently at each time step may become temporally inconsistent in the presence of multimodal posteriors, particularly in non-linear and non-Gaussian Bayesian models. Predecessor decoding is a MAP-based inference method that recursively infers the most probable predecessor state conditioned on a given successor state and past observations, thereby enabling coherent MAP inference in the sense of temporally consistent successive state estimates. So far, this approach has primarily been studied under linear Gaussian assumptions. In this paper, predecessor decoding is extended to non-linear state observation models by employing local linearization techniques analogous to those used in extended Kalman filtering and smoothing. This results in an approximate yet fully recursive decoding scheme for non-linear Bayesian models with Gaussian noise. Furthermore, the approach is discussed for models with multimodal uncertainties represented by Gaussian mixture models, where predecessor decoding preserves temporal coherence of MAP estimates across time and avoids inconsistencies inherent to marginal MAP inference. The presented results contribute to Bayesian information processing by clarifying the role of decoding-based inference for decision-making under uncertainty.

Keywords: MAP Inference · Predecessor Decoding · Temporal Coherence · State Observation Models · Non-linear Bayesian Models · Gaussian Mixtures Models

1 Introduction

State observation models constitute a central class of probabilistic models for describing dynamic systems with latent states that evolve over time and are indirectly observed through noisy measurements. Such models are widely used across signal processing, navigation, control, telecommunications, finance, physics, and related fields [10,20]. Inference in state observation models aims at extracting information about the hidden

B. Vantaggi et al. (Eds.): IPMU 2026, CCIS 3019, pp. 378–391, 2026.
https://doi.org/10.1007/978-3-032-28994-0_27

state trajectory from a sequence of observations under uncertainty, typically by exploiting the conditional independence structure induced by the Markov property.

Classical Bayesian inference tasks in state observation models include prediction, filtering, and smoothing, all of which focus on estimating posterior distributions of marginal state variables conditioned on past, present, or future observations [7,10,20]. In many applications, however, the marginal distributions themselves are not the final objective. Instead, one often seeks a sequence of representative state estimates that can be used for interpretation, decision-making, or as input to downstream processing.

A common approach to obtain point estimates from posterior distributions is Maximum A Posteriori (MAP) inference, where state estimates are obtained by maximizing the corresponding marginal posterior distributions. While marginal MAP estimates are straightforward to compute once the marginals are available, they suffer from a fundamental limitation: successive marginal MAP estimates are obtained independently at each time step and may therefore be temporally inconsistent. In non-linear, non-Gaussian, and in particular multimodal settings, this may result in state sequences that combine incompatible modes of the posterior distribution across time, potentially leading to implausible trajectories [15,17]. In particular, sequences obtained by concatenating marginal MAP estimates may even be invalid if they violate the transition model, for example by containing state teleportations or transitions with zero probability. Such incoherent trajectories may be perceived as implausible and can even lead to incorrect conclusions and flawed decision-making in practical applications.

Temporal consistency can, in principle, be enforced by computing the joint MAP state sequence, i.e., by maximizing the joint posterior distribution over all states given the observations. For discrete-state models, this problem is efficiently solved by the Viterbi algorithm [25]. In linear Gaussian models, marginal inference and joint MAP inference coincide, as the posterior distribution is unimodal and Gaussian, and the marginal means equal the joint MAP assignment [11,14]. Beyond these special cases, however, computing the joint MAP sequence becomes intractable. For general nonlinear continuous-state models, particularly mixture-based ones acting as universal approximators, no analytical recursive solutions are available, and particle-based methods often suffer from high computational cost and the curse of dimensionality [8].

To address this gap, a novel MAP inference paradigm, referred to as predecessor decoding, has been introduced in recent work [15,19]. Instead of maximizing marginal posteriors independently or attempting to solve the full joint MAP problem, predecessor decoding recursively infers MAP predecessors. Each state estimate is obtained as the most probable predecessor of a given successor state conditioned on past observations. By construction, this recursive procedure enforces temporal coherence of successive estimates, while retaining a computational complexity comparable to marginal inference.

The advantages of predecessor decoding become particularly apparent in models with multimodal posterior distributions, such as Gaussian mixture models. In such settings, marginal MAP inference is especially prone to producing incoherent state sequences by switching between incompatible modes across time. It has been shown that predecessor decoding yields valid and coherent trajectories in Gaussian mixture models, preserving consistency with the underlying transition structure even in the presence of strong multimodal ambiguities [15]. More generally, predecessor decoding has been analyzed as a recursive Bayesian decoding framework applicable to a wide range of state observation models [17].

While predecessor decoding is defined abstractly for general state observation models, practical realizations depend on the ability to evaluate or approximate the required conditional distributions. Existing closed-form formulations have primarily focused on linear Gaussian and linear Gaussian mixture models. However, many real-world systems exhibit non-linear dynamics or observation models, where linear assumptions are insufficient. This situation closely mirrors the development of classical marginal inference methods, where linear Gaussian models led to the Stratonovich-Kalman-Bucy filter [11,12,24] and the Rauch-Tung-Striebel smoother [14], which were later extended to non-linear models using local linearization techniques [9,21,22]. The abstract relationships between recursive filtering, recursive smoothing and predecessor decoding have been recently clarified in [16,17,19].

In this paper, we extend predecessor decoding to non-linear Bayesian state observation models by employing local linearization techniques analogous to those used in extended filtering and smoothing. The resulting formulation yields an approximate yet fully recursive decoding scheme that preserves temporal coherence of MAP estimates in non-linear settings. The proposed extension broadens the applicability of predecessor decoding to a wider class of models and contributes to the understanding of coherent MAP inference for decision-making under uncertainty.

2 Inference in Non-linear Models

For state observation models, the joint distribution factorizes into

$$p(\boldsymbol{x}_{0:T}, \boldsymbol{o}_{1:T}) = p(\boldsymbol{x}_0) \prod_{t=1}^{T} p(\boldsymbol{x}_t \mid \boldsymbol{x}_{t-1})\, p(\boldsymbol{o}_t \mid \boldsymbol{x}_t), \tag{1}$$

where $p(\boldsymbol{x}_0)$ is the initial state, $p(\boldsymbol{x}_t \mid \boldsymbol{x}_{t-1})$ is the Markovian state transition model, and $p(\boldsymbol{o}_t \mid \boldsymbol{x}_t)$ is the state observation model. In this section, we assume that the initial distribution is Gaussian, and that both the transition and observation models are non-linear Gaussians. Under these assumptions, two analogous approaches have emerged, one stemming from probability theory, and the other from system theory, to formulate the factors of such a continuous-state Hidden Gauss-Markov Model [1,2]:

probabilistic representation		*state-space representation*	
$p(\boldsymbol{x}_0) = \mathcal{N}_{\boldsymbol{x}_0}(\vec{\boldsymbol{\mu}}_0, \vec{\boldsymbol{\Sigma}}_0)$	$\equiv$	$\boldsymbol{x}_0 = \vec{\boldsymbol{\mu}}_0 + \boldsymbol{u}_0, \quad \boldsymbol{u}_0 \sim \mathcal{N}(\boldsymbol{0}, \vec{\boldsymbol{\Sigma}}_0)$	(2)
$p(\boldsymbol{x}_t \mid \boldsymbol{x}_{t-1}) = \mathcal{N}_{\boldsymbol{x}_t}(\boldsymbol{f}_t(\boldsymbol{x}_{t-1}), \boldsymbol{Q}_t)$	$\equiv$	$\boldsymbol{x}_t = \boldsymbol{f}_t(\boldsymbol{x}_{t-1}) + \boldsymbol{v}_t, \; \boldsymbol{v}_t \sim \mathcal{N}(\boldsymbol{0}, \boldsymbol{Q}_t)$	(3)
$p(\boldsymbol{o}_t \mid \boldsymbol{x}_t) = \mathcal{N}_{\boldsymbol{o}_t}(\boldsymbol{h}_t(\boldsymbol{x}_t), \boldsymbol{R}_t)$	$\equiv$	$\boldsymbol{o}_t = \boldsymbol{h}_t(\boldsymbol{x}_t) + \boldsymbol{w}_t, \; \boldsymbol{w}_t \sim \mathcal{N}(\boldsymbol{0}, \boldsymbol{R}_t)$	(4)

Parameters are grouped per time frame in the tuple

$$\lambda_t = \langle \boldsymbol{f}_t, \boldsymbol{Q}_t, \boldsymbol{h}_t, \boldsymbol{R}_t \rangle, \tag{5}$$

for all $t \geq 1$, where $\boldsymbol{f}_t$ is the non-linear transition function, $\boldsymbol{Q}_t$ is the process noise covariance matrix, $\boldsymbol{h}_t$ is the non-linear observation function and $\boldsymbol{R}_t$ is the observation noise covariance matrix. Specification (5) underscores the use of model-based parametrization as opposed to data-driven approaches. In this work, we define these factors using a small number of distribution parameters to ensure the efficient execution of inference tasks.

To distinguish between inference contexts without introducing additional indices, overset notation is employed. In particular, $\overset{\mapsto}{\boldsymbol{v}}$, $\vec{\boldsymbol{v}}$, $\overleftrightarrow{\boldsymbol{v}}$, $\widehat{\boldsymbol{v}}$, and $\overset{\hookrightarrow}{\boldsymbol{v}}$ indicate predicting, filtering, smoothing, sequence-decoding, and predecessor-decoding contexts of a variable $\boldsymbol{v}$, respectively. This notation is consistently applied in present and prior works [15–19] to emphasize the inference setting while keeping expressions compact.

2.1 Marginal Inference

This section provides a brief summary of how marginal inference can be achieved in non-linear models by linearization. In recursive filtering, the distribution $p(\boldsymbol{x}_{t-1} \mid \boldsymbol{o}_{1:t-1})$ is first propagated through the transition function $\boldsymbol{f}_t$, yielding the prior $p(\boldsymbol{x}_t \mid \boldsymbol{o}_{1:t-1})$. The prior is then updated using the observation function $\boldsymbol{h}_t$ to obtain the filtered distribution $p(\boldsymbol{x}_t \mid \boldsymbol{o}_{1:t})$. For differentiable transition and observation functions $\boldsymbol{f}_t$ and $\boldsymbol{h}_t$, local Taylor linearization can applied in both prediction and update, leading to Gaussian marginal approximations:

$$\begin{aligned} \boldsymbol{f}_t(\boldsymbol{x}_{t-1}) &\approx \boldsymbol{f}_t(\vec{\boldsymbol{\mu}}_{t-1}) + \boldsymbol{F}_t(\boldsymbol{x}_{t-1} - \vec{\boldsymbol{\mu}}_{t-1}) \\ &= \boldsymbol{F}_t\, \boldsymbol{x}_{t-1} + \underbrace{(\boldsymbol{f}_t(\vec{\boldsymbol{\mu}}_{t-1}) - \boldsymbol{F}_t\, \vec{\boldsymbol{\mu}}_{t-1})}_{=:\boldsymbol{a}_t}, \end{aligned} \tag{6}$$

$$\begin{aligned} \boldsymbol{h}_t(\boldsymbol{x}_t) &\approx \boldsymbol{h}_t(\overset{\mapsto}{\boldsymbol{\mu}}_t) + \boldsymbol{H}_t\,(\boldsymbol{x}_t - \overset{\mapsto}{\boldsymbol{\mu}}_t) \\ &= \boldsymbol{H}_t\, \boldsymbol{x}_t + \underbrace{(\boldsymbol{h}_t(\overset{\mapsto}{\boldsymbol{\mu}}_t) - \boldsymbol{H}_t\, \overset{\mapsto}{\boldsymbol{\mu}}_t)}_{=:\boldsymbol{b}_t}, \end{aligned} \tag{7}$$

with Jacobian matrices

$$\boldsymbol{F}_t = \left.\frac{\partial \boldsymbol{f}_t(\boldsymbol{x})}{\partial \boldsymbol{x}}\right|_{\boldsymbol{x}=\vec{\boldsymbol{\mu}}_{t-1}}, \quad \boldsymbol{H}_t = \left.\frac{\partial \boldsymbol{h}_t(\boldsymbol{x})}{\partial \boldsymbol{x}}\right|_{\boldsymbol{x}=\overset{\mapsto}{\boldsymbol{\mu}}_t}.$$

Substituting (6) into (3), and (7) into (4) at each time step yields linear Gaussian approximations for transition and observation models

$$p(\boldsymbol{x}_t \mid \boldsymbol{x}_{t-1}) \approx \mathcal{N}_{\boldsymbol{x}_t}(\boldsymbol{F}_t \boldsymbol{x}_{t-1} + \boldsymbol{a}_t, \boldsymbol{Q}_t), \tag{8}$$

$$p(\boldsymbol{o}_t \mid \boldsymbol{x}_t) \approx \mathcal{N}_{\boldsymbol{o}_t}(\boldsymbol{H}_t \boldsymbol{x}_t + \boldsymbol{b}_t, \boldsymbol{R}_t). \tag{9}$$

Standard inference techniques can be applied to linearized model (3), (8), (9) to infer marginal distributions

$$p(\boldsymbol{x}_t \mid \boldsymbol{o}_{1:t-1}) \approx \mathcal{N}_{\boldsymbol{x}_t}(\overset{\mapsto}{\boldsymbol{\mu}}_t, \overset{\mapsto}{\boldsymbol{\Sigma}}_t), \tag{10}$$

$$p(\boldsymbol{x}_t \mid \boldsymbol{o}_{1:t}\quad) \approx \mathcal{N}_{\boldsymbol{x}_t}(\vec{\boldsymbol{\mu}}_t, \overrightarrow{\boldsymbol{\Sigma}}_t), \tag{11}$$

$$p(\boldsymbol{x}_t \mid \boldsymbol{o}_{1:T}\quad) \approx \mathcal{N}_{\boldsymbol{x}_t}(\overleftrightarrow{\boldsymbol{\mu}}_t, \overleftrightarrow{\boldsymbol{\Sigma}}_t). \tag{12}$$

The extended or rather linearized approaches for (one-step) predicting (10), filtering (11) and smoothing (12) in non-linear Gaussian models are summarized in Table 1, and can be found for instance in [7,20].

2.2 MAP Inference

While Sect. 2.1 focuses on estimating marginal state distributions under non-linear model assumptions (3)–(4), this section addresses the estimation of single best state estimates. In the Bayesian framework, this task is referred to as decoding or maximum a posteriori (MAP) inference.

Posterior Decoding, also known as marginal MAP, is obtained by maximizing the filtered or smoothed marginals,

$$\vec{\boldsymbol{x}}_t := \arg\max_{\boldsymbol{x}_t} p(\boldsymbol{x}_t \,|\, \boldsymbol{o}_{1:t}) \qquad \forall t, \tag{13}$$

$$\overset{\leftrightarrows}{\boldsymbol{x}}_t := \arg\max_{\boldsymbol{x}_t} p(\boldsymbol{x}_t \,|\, \boldsymbol{o}_{1:T}) \qquad \forall t. \tag{14}$$

For general models, the resulting sequences $\vec{\boldsymbol{x}}_{0:T}$ and $\overset{\leftrightarrows}{\boldsymbol{x}}_{0:T}$ may become implausible, as the temporal coherence inherent in successive marginal distributions does not generally extend to their modes. In (11) and (12) the marginals in (13) and (14) are approximated by Gaussian distributions, hence $\vec{\boldsymbol{x}}_t \approx \vec{\boldsymbol{\mu}}_t$ and $\overset{\leftrightarrows}{\boldsymbol{x}}_t \approx \overset{\leftrightarrows}{\boldsymbol{\mu}}_t$.

Sequence Decoding, or joint MAP, refers to maximizing the joint posterior,

$$\widehat{\boldsymbol{x}}_{0:T} := \arg\max_{\boldsymbol{x}_{0:T}} p(\boldsymbol{x}_{0:T} \,|\, \boldsymbol{o}_{1:T}). \tag{15}$$

While sequence decoding yields coherent trajectories, direct computation of (15) is infeasible for general models. When all factors in (1) are approximated by Gaussians, cf. (3), (8), and (9), their product remains Gaussian with joint mean $\overset{\leftrightarrows}{\boldsymbol{\mu}}_{0:t}$, thus $\widehat{\boldsymbol{x}}_{0:t} \approx \overset{\leftrightarrows}{\boldsymbol{\mu}}_{0:t}$. In more general models, e.g., where the factors in (1) are Gaussian mixtures, solving (15) becomes intractable. Particle-based methods are commonly employed for this task, e.g. [8], but are known to suffer from the curse of dimensionality [6]. This difficulty motivates decoding strategies that retain coherence while remaining tractable.

Predecessor Decoding, illustrated in Fig. 1, has recently been studied for linear state observation models in [15–17,19]. It is based on recursively computing

$$\overset{\curvearrowright}{\boldsymbol{x}}_t := \arg\max_{\boldsymbol{x}_t} p(\boldsymbol{x}_t \,|\, \overset{\curvearrowright}{\boldsymbol{x}}_{t+1}, \boldsymbol{o}_{1:t}) \quad \text{for} \quad t = T-1 \rightarrow 0. \tag{16}$$

By iterating the recursion (16), a temporally coherent state sequence $\overset{\curvearrowright}{\boldsymbol{x}}_{0:T}$ is obtained, where the terminal state $\overset{\curvearrowright}{\boldsymbol{x}}_T$ may be initialized freely. For linear Gaussian mixture models, it has been shown in [15,17] that predecessor decoding can be implemented efficiently and yields improved estimation performance compared to posterior decoding, both at the state level and in terms of overall trajectory accuracy.

In the following, predecessor decoding is extended from linear [17] to non-linear Gaussian models by applying the local linearization techniques described in Sect. 2.1. As stated in Theorem 1, the resulting predecessor recursion can be expressed entirely in terms of the prediction and filtering quantities summarized in Table 1.

Table 1. Local Gaussian approximations for predicting, filtering and smoothing in non-linear Gaussian models

	EXTENDED SMOOTHING		
	EXTENDED FILTERING		CORRECTION
	EXTENDED PREDICTION	UPDATE	
marginal	$p(\boldsymbol{x}_t \mid \boldsymbol{o}_{1:t-1})$	$p(\boldsymbol{x}_t \mid \boldsymbol{o}_{1:t})$	$p(\boldsymbol{x}_t \mid \boldsymbol{o}_{1:T})$
recursion	$\int p(\boldsymbol{x}_t \mid \boldsymbol{x}_{t-1})\, p(\boldsymbol{x}_{t-1} \mid \boldsymbol{o}_{1:t-1})\, \mathrm{d}\boldsymbol{x}_{t-1}$	$\frac{p(\boldsymbol{o}_t \mid \boldsymbol{x}_t)\, p(\boldsymbol{x}_t \mid \boldsymbol{o}_{1:t-1})}{p(\boldsymbol{o}_t \mid \boldsymbol{o}_{1:t-1})}$	$p(\boldsymbol{x}_t \mid \boldsymbol{o}_{1:t}) \int \frac{p(\boldsymbol{x}_{t+1} \mid \boldsymbol{x}_t)}{p(\boldsymbol{x}_{t+1} \mid \boldsymbol{o}_{1:t})}\, p(\boldsymbol{x}_{t+1} \mid \boldsymbol{o}_{1:T})\, \mathrm{d}\boldsymbol{x}_{t+1}$
graph	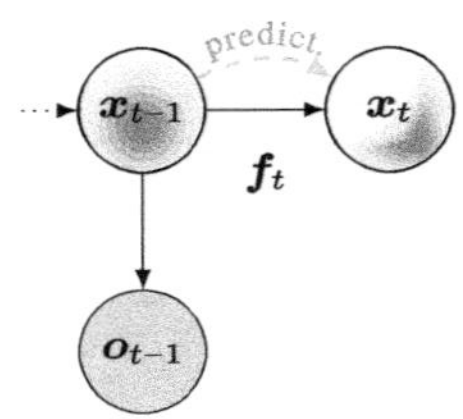	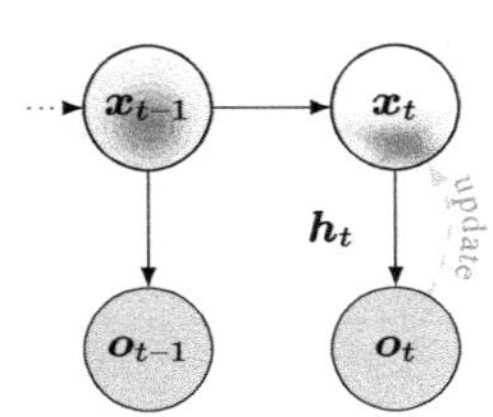	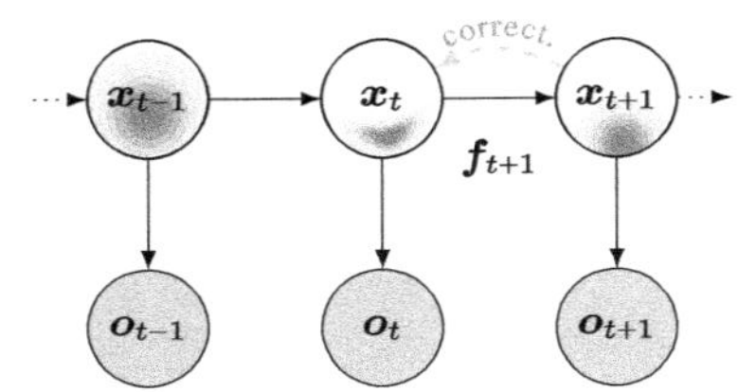
non-linearity	$\boldsymbol{f}_t(\boldsymbol{x}_{t-1})$	$\boldsymbol{h}_t(\boldsymbol{x}_t)$	$\boldsymbol{f}_{t+1}(\boldsymbol{x}_t)$
linearization	$\boldsymbol{f}_t(\vec{\boldsymbol{\mu}}_{t-1}) + \boldsymbol{F}_t(\boldsymbol{x}_{t-1} - \vec{\boldsymbol{\mu}}_{t-1})$	$\boldsymbol{h}_t(\vec{\boldsymbol{\mu}}_t) + \boldsymbol{H}_t\,(\boldsymbol{x}_t - \vec{\boldsymbol{\mu}}_t)$	$\boldsymbol{f}_{t+1}(\vec{\boldsymbol{\mu}}_t) + \boldsymbol{F}_{t+1}(\boldsymbol{x}_t - \vec{\boldsymbol{\mu}}_t)$
Jacobian	$\boldsymbol{F}_t = \left.\frac{\partial \boldsymbol{f}_t(\boldsymbol{x})}{\partial \boldsymbol{x}}\right\|_{\boldsymbol{x}=\vec{\boldsymbol{\mu}}_{t-1}}$	$\boldsymbol{H}_t = \left.\frac{\partial \boldsymbol{h}_t(\boldsymbol{x})}{\partial \boldsymbol{x}}\right\|_{\boldsymbol{x}=\vec{\boldsymbol{\mu}}_t}$	$\boldsymbol{F}_{t+1} = \left.\frac{\partial \boldsymbol{f}_{t+1}(\boldsymbol{x})}{\partial \boldsymbol{x}}\right\|_{\boldsymbol{x}=\vec{\boldsymbol{\mu}}_t}$
mean	$\vec{\boldsymbol{\mu}}_t = \boldsymbol{f}_t(\vec{\boldsymbol{\mu}}_{t-1})$	$\vec{\boldsymbol{\mu}}_t = \vec{\boldsymbol{\mu}}_t + \boldsymbol{K}_t(\boldsymbol{o}_t - \boldsymbol{h}_t(\vec{\boldsymbol{\mu}}_t))$	$\overleftrightarrow{\boldsymbol{\mu}}_t = \vec{\boldsymbol{\mu}}_t + \boldsymbol{G}_t(\overleftrightarrow{\boldsymbol{\mu}}_{t+1} - \vec{\boldsymbol{\mu}}_{t+1})$
covariance	$\vec{\boldsymbol{\Sigma}}_t = \boldsymbol{F}_t\, \vec{\boldsymbol{\Sigma}}_{t-1}\, \boldsymbol{F}_t^{\top} + \boldsymbol{Q}_t$	$\vec{\boldsymbol{\Sigma}}_t = \vec{\boldsymbol{\Sigma}}_t - \boldsymbol{K}_t\, \boldsymbol{H}_t\, \vec{\boldsymbol{\Sigma}}_t$	$\overleftrightarrow{\boldsymbol{\Sigma}}_t = \vec{\boldsymbol{\Sigma}}_t + \boldsymbol{G}_t(\overleftrightarrow{\boldsymbol{\Sigma}}_{t+1} - \vec{\boldsymbol{\Sigma}}_{t+1})\boldsymbol{G}_t^{\top}$
gains		$\boldsymbol{K}_t = \vec{\boldsymbol{\Sigma}}_t\, \boldsymbol{H}_t^{\top}(\boldsymbol{H}_t\, \vec{\boldsymbol{\Sigma}}_t\, \boldsymbol{H}_t^{\top} + \boldsymbol{R}_t)^{-1}$	$\boldsymbol{G}_t = \vec{\boldsymbol{\Sigma}}_t\, \boldsymbol{F}_{t+1}^{\top}\, \vec{\boldsymbol{\Sigma}}_{t+1}^{-1}$

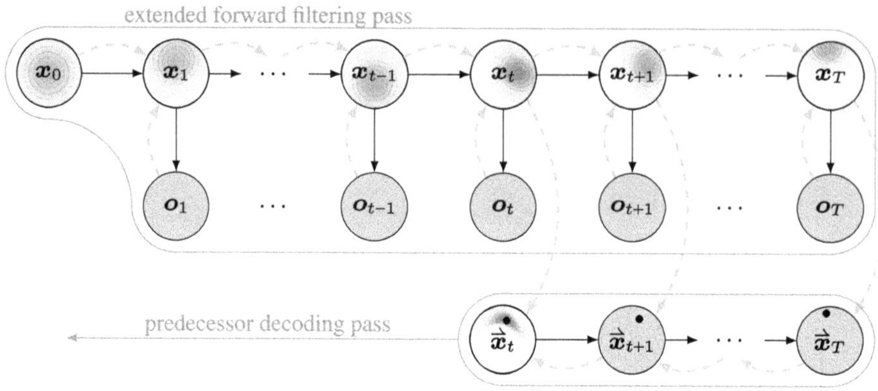

Fig. 1. Graphical interpretation of coherent MAP inference in a forward-filtering/predecessor-decoding scheme. Prediction and update are performed in a forward pass using Gaussian approximations, while predecessor decoding proceeds backward and gives rise to non-Gaussian distributions, motivating the linearization approach developed in this paper.

Theorem 1. *Consider the non-linear state observation model* (3)–(4) *with linear approximations* (6)–(9)*. The MAP predecessor $\vec{\bar{x}}_t$ for any given $\vec{\bar{x}}_{t+1}$, is approximately*

$$\vec{\bar{x}}_t \approx \vec{\mu}_t + \vec{\Sigma}_t \, F_{t+1}^\top \, \overleftrightarrow{\Sigma}_{t+1}^{-1} (\vec{\bar{x}}_{t+1} - \overleftrightarrow{\mu}_{t+1}), \tag{17}$$

where $\vec{\mu}_t$, $\vec{\Sigma}_t$ and $\overleftrightarrow{\mu}_{t+1}$, $\overleftrightarrow{\Sigma}_{t+1}$ denote the filtered and predicted means and covariance matrices, respectively, and with Jacobian matrix $F_{t+1} = \left.\frac{\partial f_{t+1}(x)}{\partial x}\right|_{x=\vec{\mu}_t}$.

Proof. From Definition (16) we have $\vec{\bar{x}}_t := \arg\max_{x_t} p(x_t \mid o_{1:t}, \vec{\bar{x}}_{t+1})$. This is equivalent to $\vec{\bar{x}}_t = \arg\max_{x_t} p(x_t, \vec{\bar{x}}_{t+1} \mid o_{1:t})$, since $p(\vec{\bar{x}}_{t+1} \mid o_{1:t})$ does not depend on x_t. The joint density factorizes as

$$p(x_t, \vec{\bar{x}}_{t+1} \mid o_{1:t}) = p(x_t \mid o_{1:t})\, p(\vec{\bar{x}}_{t+1} \mid x_t, o_{1:t}) = p(x_t \mid o_{1:t})\, p(\vec{\bar{x}}_{t+1} \mid x_t)$$

where the last equality follows from the Markov property of the model. Using the Gaussian approximation $p(x_t \mid o_{1:t}) \approx \mathcal{N}_{x_t}(\vec{\mu}_t, \vec{\Sigma}_t)$ and the linearized transition model $p(x_{t+1} \mid x_t) \approx \mathcal{N}_{x_{t+1}}(F_{t+1}\, x_t + a_{t+1}, Q_{t+1})$, we obtain

$$p(x_t, \vec{\bar{x}}_{t+1} \mid o_{1:t}) \approx \mathcal{N}_{x_t}(\vec{\mu}_t, \vec{\Sigma}_t)\, \mathcal{N}_{\vec{\bar{x}}_{t+1}}(F_{t+1}\, x_t + a_{t+1}, Q_{t+1}). \tag{18}$$

Both factors are Gaussian functions of x_t. Applying the Affine Gaussian Refactorization Lemma (AGRL, Lemma 2 in Appendix), their product can be written as

$$\mathcal{N}_{x_t}(\vec{\mu}_t, \vec{\Sigma}_t)\, \mathcal{N}_{\vec{\bar{x}}_{t+1}}(F_{t+1}\, x_t + a_{t+1}, Q_{t+1}) = \mathcal{N}_{x_t}(\xi, \Gamma)\, \mathcal{N}_{\vec{\bar{x}}_{t+1}}(\zeta, \Phi) \propto \mathcal{N}_{x_t}(\xi, \Gamma),$$

with

$$\begin{aligned}
\boldsymbol{\zeta} &= \boldsymbol{F}_{t+1}\,\vec{\boldsymbol{\mu}}_t + \boldsymbol{a}_{t+1} = \boldsymbol{F}_{t+1}\,\vec{\boldsymbol{\mu}}_t + (\boldsymbol{f}_{t+1}(\vec{\boldsymbol{\mu}}_t) - \boldsymbol{F}_{t+1}\,\vec{\boldsymbol{\mu}}_t) = \boldsymbol{f}_{t+1}(\vec{\boldsymbol{\mu}}_t),\\
\boldsymbol{\Phi} &= \boldsymbol{F}_{t+1}\,\vec{\boldsymbol{\Sigma}}_t\,\boldsymbol{F}_{t+1}^{\top} + \boldsymbol{Q}_{t+1},\\
\boldsymbol{\xi} &= \vec{\boldsymbol{\mu}}_t + \boldsymbol{G}\,(\overleftrightarrow{\boldsymbol{x}}_{t+1} - (\boldsymbol{F}_{t+1}\,\vec{\boldsymbol{\mu}}_t + \boldsymbol{a}_{t+1})) = \vec{\boldsymbol{\mu}}_t + \boldsymbol{G}\,(\overleftrightarrow{\boldsymbol{x}}_{t+1} - \boldsymbol{f}_{t+1}(\vec{\boldsymbol{\mu}}_t)),\\
\boldsymbol{\Gamma} &= \vec{\boldsymbol{\Sigma}}_t - \boldsymbol{G}\,\boldsymbol{F}_{t+1}\,\vec{\boldsymbol{\Sigma}}_t,
\end{aligned}$$

and $\boldsymbol{G} = \vec{\boldsymbol{\Sigma}}_t\,\boldsymbol{F}_{t+1}^{\top}\,\overleftarrow{\boldsymbol{\Sigma}}_{t+1}^{-1}$. As the mode of a Gaussian equals its mean, applying arg max to (18) yields $\overleftrightarrow{\boldsymbol{x}}_t \approx \boldsymbol{\xi}$. Noting that $\boldsymbol{f}_{t+1}(\vec{\boldsymbol{\mu}}_t) = \overleftarrow{\boldsymbol{\mu}}_{t+1}$ under the extended prediction step (Table 1), this yields (17). □

Based on Theorem 1, Algorithm 1 summarizes an extended predecessor decoding scheme for non-linear state observation models. The algorithm has complexity $\mathcal{O}(T\,D^3)$ and consists of a forward pass implementing an Extended Kalman Filter ($\mathcal{O}(D^3)$) to compute predicted and filtered marginals, followed by a backward pass that recursively decodes coherent predecessors of a terminal state $\overleftrightarrow{\boldsymbol{x}}_T$, which can be chosen freely. If no initialization is specified, the decoder proceeds with the filtered mean,

$$\overleftrightarrow{\boldsymbol{x}}_T = \underset{\boldsymbol{x}_T}{\arg\max}\, p(\boldsymbol{x}_T|\boldsymbol{o}_{1:T}) \approx \underset{\boldsymbol{x}_T}{\arg\max}\, \mathcal{N}_{\boldsymbol{x}_T}(\vec{\boldsymbol{\mu}}_T, \vec{\boldsymbol{\Sigma}}_T) = \vec{\boldsymbol{\mu}}_T,$$

which is justified since mode and mean coincide for Gaussian distributions. More generally, the initialization may be chosen arbitrarily to reflect application-specific constraints or prior information (points of interest).

In addition to the decoded trajectory, Algorithm 1 also returns the filtered marginal of the last state, thereby providing both a real-time state estimate and a temporally coherent retrospective trajectory. In practical applications, the backward predecessor recursion need not be carried out to the initial time, instead, it may be truncated after a finite number of steps to obtain locally coherent trajectory segments. In the following, this framework is extended to Gaussian mixture models, where multimodality necessitates additional mode-finding and mixture-reduction steps.

3 Inference in Non-linear Mixture Models

In this section, we consider state observation models in which the factors in (1) are convex mixtures of non-linear Gaussian distributions,

$$p(\boldsymbol{x}_0) = \sum\nolimits_{k=1}^{\vec{N}_0} \vec{\omega}_0^k\,\mathcal{N}_{\boldsymbol{x}_0}(\vec{\boldsymbol{\mu}}_0^k, \vec{\boldsymbol{\Sigma}}_0^k), \tag{19}$$

$$p(\boldsymbol{x}_t\,|\,\boldsymbol{x}_{t-1}) = \sum\nolimits_{i=1}^{N_t^{\mathrm{x}}} \alpha_t^i\,p^i(\boldsymbol{x}_t\,|\,\boldsymbol{x}_{t-1}), \tag{20}$$

$$p(\boldsymbol{o}_t\,|\,\boldsymbol{x}_t) = \sum\nolimits_{j=1}^{N_t^{\mathrm{o}}} \beta_t^j\,p^j(\boldsymbol{o}_t\,|\,\boldsymbol{x}_t), \tag{21}$$

where each mixture component in (20) and (21) is a non-linear Gaussian. Each component is linearized locally around corresponding means $\vec{\boldsymbol{\mu}}_{t-1}^k$ and $\overleftarrow{\boldsymbol{\mu}}_t^{\ell}$, yielding Gaussian approximations of the form

$$p^i(\boldsymbol{x}_t \mid \boldsymbol{x}_{t-1}) = \mathcal{N}_{\boldsymbol{x}_t}(\boldsymbol{f}_t^i(\boldsymbol{x}_{t-1}), \boldsymbol{Q}_t^i) \\ \approx \mathcal{N}_{\boldsymbol{x}_t}(\boldsymbol{F}_t^{i,k}\, \boldsymbol{x}_{t-1} + \boldsymbol{a}_t^{i,k}, \boldsymbol{Q}_t^i), \tag{22}$$

$$p^j(\boldsymbol{o}_t \mid \boldsymbol{x}_t) = \mathcal{N}_{\boldsymbol{o}_t}(\boldsymbol{h}_t^j(\boldsymbol{x}_t), \boldsymbol{R}_t^j) \\ \approx \mathcal{N}_{\boldsymbol{o}_t}(\boldsymbol{H}_t^{j,\ell}\, \boldsymbol{x}_t + \boldsymbol{b}_t^{j,\ell}, \boldsymbol{R}_t^j), \tag{23}$$

with

$$\boldsymbol{F}_t^{i,k} = \left.\frac{\partial \boldsymbol{f}_t^i(\boldsymbol{x})}{\partial \boldsymbol{x}}\right|_{\boldsymbol{x}=\vec{\boldsymbol{\mu}}_{t-1}^k}, \boldsymbol{a}_t^{i,k} = \boldsymbol{f}_t^i(\vec{\boldsymbol{\mu}}_{t-1}^k) - \boldsymbol{F}_t^{i,k}\, \vec{\boldsymbol{\mu}}_{t-1}^k, \tag{24}$$

$$\boldsymbol{H}_t^{j,\ell} = \left.\frac{\partial \boldsymbol{h}_t^j(\boldsymbol{x})}{\partial \boldsymbol{x}}\right|_{\boldsymbol{x}=\overleftarrow{\boldsymbol{\mu}}_t^\ell}, \quad \boldsymbol{b}_t^{j,\ell} = \boldsymbol{h}_t^j(\overleftarrow{\boldsymbol{\mu}}_t^\ell) - \boldsymbol{H}_t^{j,\ell}\, \overleftarrow{\boldsymbol{\mu}}_t^\ell. \tag{25}$$

Algorithm 1 extended filtering and predecessor decoder for non-linear models

function ExtDecoder($\vec{\boldsymbol{\mu}}_{0:t-1}, \vec{\boldsymbol{\Sigma}}_{0:t-1}, \boldsymbol{o}_t[, \overleftrightarrow{\boldsymbol{x}}_t]; \lambda_{1:t}$)
  $\boldsymbol{f}_t, \boldsymbol{Q}_t, \boldsymbol{h}_t, \boldsymbol{R}_t \leftarrow \lambda_t$
  ▷ linearized prediction
  $\boldsymbol{F}_t \leftarrow \left.\frac{\partial \boldsymbol{f}_t(\boldsymbol{x})}{\partial \boldsymbol{x}}\right|_{\boldsymbol{x}=\vec{\boldsymbol{\mu}}_{t-1}}$
  $\overleftarrow{\boldsymbol{\mu}}_t \leftarrow \boldsymbol{f}_t(\vec{\boldsymbol{\mu}}_{t-1})$
  $\overleftarrow{\boldsymbol{\Sigma}}_t \leftarrow \boldsymbol{Q}_{t-1} + \boldsymbol{F}_t\, \vec{\boldsymbol{\Sigma}}_{t-1}\, \boldsymbol{F}_{t-1}^\top$
  ▷ linearized update
  $\boldsymbol{H}_t \leftarrow \left.\frac{\partial \boldsymbol{h}_t(\boldsymbol{x})}{\partial \boldsymbol{x}}\right|_{\boldsymbol{x}=\overleftarrow{\boldsymbol{\mu}}_t}$
  $\boldsymbol{K}_t \leftarrow \overleftarrow{\boldsymbol{\Sigma}}_t\, \boldsymbol{H}_t^\top\, (\boldsymbol{H}_t\, \overleftarrow{\boldsymbol{\Sigma}}_t\, \boldsymbol{H}_t^\top + \boldsymbol{R}_t)^{-1}$
  $\vec{\boldsymbol{\mu}}_t \leftarrow \overleftarrow{\boldsymbol{\mu}}_t + \boldsymbol{K}_t\, (\boldsymbol{o}_t - \boldsymbol{h}_t(\overleftarrow{\boldsymbol{\mu}}_t))$
  $\vec{\boldsymbol{\Sigma}}_t \leftarrow \overleftarrow{\boldsymbol{\Sigma}}_t - \boldsymbol{K}_t\, \boldsymbol{H}_t\, \overleftarrow{\boldsymbol{\Sigma}}_t$
  ▷ linearized predecessor decoding
  if no $\overleftrightarrow{\boldsymbol{x}}_t$ **then**
    $\overleftrightarrow{\boldsymbol{x}}_t \leftarrow \vec{\boldsymbol{\mu}}_t$
  end if
  for $s = t-1$ **to** 0 **do**
    $\boldsymbol{f}_{s+1}, \boldsymbol{Q}_{s+1} \leftarrow \lambda_{s+1}$
    $\boldsymbol{F}_{s+1} \leftarrow \left.\frac{\partial \boldsymbol{f}_{s+1}(\boldsymbol{x})}{\partial \boldsymbol{x}}\right|_{\boldsymbol{x}=\vec{\boldsymbol{\mu}}_s}$
    $\boldsymbol{G}_s \leftarrow \vec{\boldsymbol{\Sigma}}_s\, \boldsymbol{F}_{s+1}^\top\, (\boldsymbol{F}_{s+1}\, \vec{\boldsymbol{\Sigma}}_s\, \boldsymbol{F}_{s+1}^\top + \boldsymbol{Q}_{s+1})^{-1}$
    $\overleftrightarrow{\boldsymbol{x}}_s \leftarrow \vec{\boldsymbol{\mu}}_s + \boldsymbol{G}_s\, \left(\overleftrightarrow{\boldsymbol{x}}_{s+1} - \boldsymbol{f}_{s+1}(\vec{\boldsymbol{\mu}}_s)\right)$
  end for
  return $\vec{\boldsymbol{\mu}}_t, \vec{\boldsymbol{\Sigma}}_t, \overleftrightarrow{\boldsymbol{x}}_{0:t}$
end function

$$
\begin{aligned}
p(\boldsymbol{x}_t \,|\, \boldsymbol{o}_{1:t-1}) &\approx \sum\nolimits_{\ell=1}^{\overset{\mapsto}{N}_t} \overset{\mapsto}{\omega}_t^{\ell}\, \mathcal{N}_{\boldsymbol{x}_t}(\overset{\mapsto}{\boldsymbol{\mu}}_t^{\ell}, \overset{\mapsto}{\boldsymbol{\Sigma}}_t^{\ell}), && (26)\\
p(\boldsymbol{x}_t \,|\, \boldsymbol{o}_{1:t} \quad) &\approx \sum\nolimits_{k=1}^{\overrightarrow{N}_t} \overrightarrow{\omega}_t^{k}\, \mathcal{N}_{\boldsymbol{x}_t}(\overrightarrow{\boldsymbol{\mu}}_t^{k}, \overrightarrow{\boldsymbol{\Sigma}}_t^{k}), && (27)\\
p(\boldsymbol{x}_t \,|\, \boldsymbol{o}_{1:T} \quad) &\approx \sum\nolimits_{\iota=1}^{\overleftrightarrow{N}_t} \overleftrightarrow{\omega}_t^{\iota}\, \mathcal{N}_{\boldsymbol{x}_t}(\overleftrightarrow{\boldsymbol{\mu}}_t^{\iota}, \overleftrightarrow{\boldsymbol{\Sigma}}_t^{\iota}). && (28)
\end{aligned}
$$

The resulting marginals of the linearized model take the form of Gaussian mixtures, providing approximations to the corresponding marginals of the non-linear model, Recursive inference in Gaussian mixture models has been pioneered in [3,23]. Recursive formulations for the mixture parameters of (26) and (27) can be found in [15,26]. The prediction formulas for mean and covariance matrix are explicitly provided within Theorem 2. The recursive solution to the smoothing problem (28) in mixture models is elusive as discussed in [16,18].

In the following, these mixture-based marginal approximations (26) and (27) are used for extending predecessor decoding to non-linear Gaussian mixture models.

Theorem 2. *Consider the non-linear mixture model* (19)–(21) *with linear approximations* (22)–(25). *The MAP predecessor* $\overset{\rightharpoondown}{\boldsymbol{x}}_t$, *of given* $\overset{\rightharpoondown}{\boldsymbol{x}}_{t+1}$ *can be approximated by solving*

$$
\overset{\rightharpoondown}{\boldsymbol{x}}_t \approx \arg\max_{\boldsymbol{x}_t} \sum\nolimits_{i=1}^{N_{t+1}^{\mathrm{x}}} \sum\nolimits_{k=1}^{\overrightarrow{N}_t} \overset{\rightharpoondown}{\omega}_t^{i,k}\, \mathcal{N}_{\boldsymbol{x}_t}(\overset{\rightharpoondown}{\boldsymbol{\mu}}_t^{i,k}, \overset{\rightharpoondown}{\boldsymbol{\Sigma}}_t^{i,k}), \tag{29}
$$

with

$$
\begin{aligned}
\overset{\rightharpoondown}{\omega}_t^{i,k} &= \overrightarrow{\omega}_t^{k}\, \alpha_{t+1}^{i}\, \mathcal{N}_{\overset{\rightharpoondown}{\boldsymbol{x}}_{t+1}}(\overset{\mapsto}{\boldsymbol{\mu}}_{t+1}^{i,k}, \overset{\mapsto}{\boldsymbol{\Sigma}}_{t+1}^{i,k}), && (30)\\
\overset{\rightharpoondown}{\boldsymbol{\mu}}_t^{i,k} &= \overrightarrow{\boldsymbol{\mu}}_t^{k} + \boldsymbol{G}^{i,k}(\overset{\rightharpoondown}{\boldsymbol{x}}_{t+1} - \overset{\mapsto}{\boldsymbol{\mu}}_{t+1}^{i,k}), && (31)\\
\overset{\rightharpoondown}{\boldsymbol{\Sigma}}_t^{i,k} &= \overrightarrow{\boldsymbol{\Sigma}}_t^{k} - \boldsymbol{G}^{i,k}\, \boldsymbol{F}_{t+1}^{i,k}\, \overrightarrow{\boldsymbol{\Sigma}}_t^{k}, && (32)
\end{aligned}
$$

where

$$
\begin{aligned}
\boldsymbol{G}^{i,k} &= \overrightarrow{\boldsymbol{\Sigma}}_t^{k}\, (\boldsymbol{F}_{t+1}^{i,k})^{\top}\, (\overset{\mapsto}{\boldsymbol{\Sigma}}_{t+1}^{i,k})^{-1},\\
\overset{\mapsto}{\boldsymbol{\mu}}_{t+1}^{i,k} &= \boldsymbol{F}_{t+1}^{i,k}\, \overrightarrow{\boldsymbol{\mu}}_t^{k} + \boldsymbol{a}_{t+1}^{i,k},\\
\overset{\mapsto}{\boldsymbol{\Sigma}}_{t+1}^{i,k} &= \boldsymbol{F}_{t+1}^{i,k}\, \overrightarrow{\boldsymbol{\Sigma}}_t^{k}\, (\boldsymbol{F}_{t+1}^{i,k})^{\top} + \boldsymbol{Q}_{t+1}^{i}.
\end{aligned}
$$

Proof. By definition, $\overset{\rightharpoondown}{\boldsymbol{x}}_t$ maximizes $p(\boldsymbol{x}_t \,|\, \overset{\rightharpoondown}{\boldsymbol{x}}_{t+1}, \boldsymbol{o}_{1:t}) \propto p(\boldsymbol{x}_t, \overset{\rightharpoondown}{\boldsymbol{x}}_{t+1} \,|\, \boldsymbol{o}_{1:t})$. Applying Bayes' theorem and the Markov property, we obtain

$$
p(\boldsymbol{x}_t, \overset{\rightharpoondown}{\boldsymbol{x}}_{t+1} \,|\, \boldsymbol{o}_{1:t}) = p(\overset{\rightharpoondown}{\boldsymbol{x}}_{t+1} \,|\, \boldsymbol{x}_t)\, p(\boldsymbol{x}_t \,|\, \boldsymbol{o}_{1:t}). \tag{33}
$$

For the right side in (33) we have Gaussian mixture approximations (20)+(22) and (27).

$$p(\vec{\boldsymbol{x}}_{t+1} \mid \boldsymbol{x}_t)\, p(\boldsymbol{x}_t \mid \boldsymbol{o}_{1:t}) \tag{34}$$

$$\approx \sum_{i=1}^{N_{t+1}^{\mathrm{x}}} \alpha_{t+1}^i\, \mathcal{N}_{\vec{\boldsymbol{x}}_{t+1}}(\boldsymbol{F}_{t+1}^{i,k}\, \boldsymbol{x}_t + \boldsymbol{a}_{t+1}^{i,k}, \boldsymbol{Q}_{t+1}^i) \sum_{k=1}^{\vec{N}_t} \vec{\omega}_t^k\, \mathcal{N}_{\boldsymbol{x}_t}(\vec{\boldsymbol{\mu}}_t^k, \vec{\boldsymbol{\Sigma}}_t^k) \tag{35}$$

$$= \sum_i \sum_k \alpha_{t+1}^i\, \vec{\omega}_t^k\, \mathcal{N}_{\vec{\boldsymbol{x}}_{t+1}}(\boldsymbol{F}_{t+1}^{i,k}\, \boldsymbol{x}_t + \boldsymbol{a}_{t+1}^{i,k}, \boldsymbol{Q}_{t+1}^i)\, \mathcal{N}_{\boldsymbol{x}_t}(\vec{\boldsymbol{\mu}}_t^k, \vec{\boldsymbol{\Sigma}}_t^k) \tag{36}$$

$$= \sum_i \sum_k \gamma^{i,k}\, \mathcal{N}_{\boldsymbol{x}_t}(\boldsymbol{\xi}^{i,k}, \boldsymbol{\Gamma}^{i,k}), \tag{37}$$

where in (37) the AGRL (Appendix, Lemma 2) was applied component-wise, yielding

$$\begin{aligned}
\gamma^{i,k} &= \alpha_{t+1}^i\, \vec{\omega}_t^k\, \mathcal{N}_{\vec{\boldsymbol{x}}_{t+1}}(\boldsymbol{\zeta}^{i,k}, \boldsymbol{\Phi}^{i,k}),\\
\boldsymbol{\xi}^{i,k} &= \vec{\boldsymbol{\mu}}_t^k + \boldsymbol{G}^{i,k}(\vec{\boldsymbol{x}}_{t+1} - \boldsymbol{\zeta}^{i,k}),\\
\boldsymbol{\Gamma}^{i,k} &= \vec{\boldsymbol{\Sigma}}_t^k - \boldsymbol{G}^{i,k}\, \boldsymbol{F}_{t+1}^{i,k}\, \vec{\boldsymbol{\Sigma}}_t^k,
\end{aligned}$$

with

$$\begin{aligned}
\boldsymbol{\zeta}^{i,k} &= \boldsymbol{F}_{t+1}^{i,k}\, \vec{\boldsymbol{\mu}}_t^k + \boldsymbol{a}_{t+1}^{i,k},\\
\boldsymbol{\Phi}^{i,k} &= \boldsymbol{F}_{t+1}^{i,k}\, \vec{\boldsymbol{\Sigma}}_t^k\, (\boldsymbol{F}_{t+1}^{i,k})^\top + \boldsymbol{Q}_{t+1}^i,\\
\boldsymbol{G}^{i,k} &= \vec{\boldsymbol{\Sigma}}_t^k\, (\boldsymbol{F}_{t+1}^{i,k})^\top\, (\boldsymbol{\Phi}^{i,k})^{-1}.
\end{aligned}$$

As $\vec{\boldsymbol{x}}_t$ maximizes (34), the MAP predecessor is approximated by maximizing the Gaussian mixture in (37), yielding the stated result. □

In contrast to the unimodal case, multimodal posteriors do not have a mode-mean equivalence, and the arg max operator therefore does not vanish from the predecessor recursion. Consequently, practical realization requires methods for mode-finding in approximated Gaussian mixtures [4,13]. Moreover, a tractable inference algorithm must incorporate mixture reduction techniques to control the growth of mixture components, for example as described in [5,26]. The efficient combination of linearization, mode-finding, and mixture reduction constitutes an algorithmic extension that lies beyond the scope of this paper and is addressed in ongoing and future work.

4 Conclusion

In this paper, we addressed the problem of coherent Maximum A Posteriori (MAP) inference in state observation models, with particular emphasis on the limitations of marginal MAP estimation in non-linear and multimodal settings. While marginal inference methods yield coherent posterior distributions, independently maximizing these marginals can result in temporally inconsistent or even invalid state trajectories, which may negatively affect interpretation and decision-making.

Predecessor decoding offers an alternative MAP inference paradigm that enforces temporal coherence by recursively inferring conditional MAP predecessors. Building on this principle, we extended predecessor decoding to non-linear Bayesian state observation models using local linearization techniques analogous to those employed in extended filtering and smoothing. The resulting formulation leads to an approximate yet fully recursive decoding scheme that preserves temporal coherence of successive MAP estimates beyond linear model assumptions.

This extension broadens the applicability of predecessor decoding to a wider class of models relevant for practical inference under uncertainty. Moreover, it clarifies the role of decoding-based MAP inference as a complementary alternative to marginal inference in scenarios where coherent state estimates are essential for reliable reasoning and decision-making. Future work may investigate alternative approximation strategies, such as unscented transformations, data-driven observation models or other higher-order moment-matching methods, as well as efficient combinations with mode-finding and mixture-reduction techniques within the presented framework.

Acknowledgments. This work has been supported by the COMET-K2 Center of the Linz Center of Mechatronics (LCM) funded by the Austrian federal government and the federal state of Upper Austria.

Disclosure of Interests. Branislav Rudić, Veronika Putz and Markus Pichler-Scheder are employed by the Linz Center of Mechatronics GmbH. The remaining authors have no competing interests to declare that are relevant to the content of this article.

Appendix

The proofs make use of a Gaussian product identity provided in Lemma 2, which is an affine variant of the Gaussian Refactorization Lemma (GRL) from [1], which is recalled in Lemma 1 for completeness. Both lemmas are Gaussian instances of Bayes' theorem $p(\boldsymbol{x})\, p(\boldsymbol{y} \mid \boldsymbol{x}) = p(\boldsymbol{x} \mid \boldsymbol{y})\, p(\boldsymbol{y})$.

Lemma 1. (GRL, [1], [2]**).**

$$\mathcal{N}_x(\boldsymbol{\mu}, \boldsymbol{\Sigma})\, \mathcal{N}_y(\boldsymbol{F}\, \boldsymbol{x}, \boldsymbol{Q}) = \mathcal{N}_x(\boldsymbol{\xi}, \boldsymbol{\Gamma})\, \mathcal{N}_y(\boldsymbol{\zeta}, \boldsymbol{\Phi})$$

where

$$\begin{aligned} \boldsymbol{\zeta} &= \boldsymbol{F}\, \boldsymbol{\mu}, \\ \boldsymbol{\Phi} &= \boldsymbol{F}\, \boldsymbol{\Sigma}\, \boldsymbol{F}^\top + \boldsymbol{Q}, \\ \boldsymbol{\xi} &= \boldsymbol{\mu} + \boldsymbol{G}\, (\boldsymbol{y} - \boldsymbol{F}\, \boldsymbol{\mu}), \\ \boldsymbol{\Gamma} &= \boldsymbol{\Sigma} - \boldsymbol{G}\, \boldsymbol{F}\, \boldsymbol{\Sigma}, \end{aligned}$$

and $\boldsymbol{G} = \boldsymbol{\Sigma}\, \boldsymbol{F}^\top\, \boldsymbol{\Phi}^{-1}$.

Proof. See Appendix A of [1].

Lemma 2 **(AGRL).**

$$\mathcal{N}_x(\boldsymbol{\mu}, \boldsymbol{\Sigma})\, \mathcal{N}_y(\boldsymbol{F}\,\boldsymbol{x} + \boldsymbol{d}, \boldsymbol{Q}) = \mathcal{N}_x(\boldsymbol{\xi}, \boldsymbol{\Gamma})\, \mathcal{N}_y(\boldsymbol{\zeta}, \boldsymbol{\Phi})$$

where

$$\begin{aligned}
\boldsymbol{\zeta} &= \boldsymbol{F}\,\boldsymbol{\mu} + \boldsymbol{d}, \\
\boldsymbol{\Phi} &= \boldsymbol{F}\,\boldsymbol{\Sigma}\,\boldsymbol{F}^\top + \boldsymbol{Q}, \\
\boldsymbol{\xi} &= \boldsymbol{\mu} + \boldsymbol{G}\,\big(\boldsymbol{y} - (\boldsymbol{F}\,\boldsymbol{\mu} + \boldsymbol{d})\,\big), \\
\boldsymbol{\Gamma} &= \boldsymbol{\Sigma} - \boldsymbol{G}\,\boldsymbol{F}\,\boldsymbol{\Sigma},
\end{aligned}$$

and $\boldsymbol{G} = \boldsymbol{\Sigma}\,\boldsymbol{F}^\top\,\boldsymbol{\Phi}^{-1}$.

Proof. The statement follows immediately after applying the GRL to the transformed Gaussian in (38) of

$$\begin{aligned}
\mathcal{N}_x(\boldsymbol{\mu}, \boldsymbol{\Sigma})\, \mathcal{N}_y(\boldsymbol{F}\,\boldsymbol{x} + \boldsymbol{d}, \boldsymbol{Q}) & \\
&= \mathcal{N}_x(\boldsymbol{\mu}, \boldsymbol{\Sigma})\, \mathcal{N}_{y-d}(\boldsymbol{F}\,\boldsymbol{x}, \boldsymbol{Q}) \\
&= \mathcal{N}_x(\boldsymbol{\xi}, \boldsymbol{\Gamma})\, \mathcal{N}_{y-d}(\boldsymbol{F}\,\boldsymbol{\mu}, \boldsymbol{\Phi}) \qquad (38) \\
&= \mathcal{N}_x(\boldsymbol{\xi}, \boldsymbol{\Gamma})\, \mathcal{N}_y(\boldsymbol{F}\,\boldsymbol{\mu} + \boldsymbol{d}, \boldsymbol{\Phi}) \\
&= \mathcal{N}_x(\boldsymbol{\xi}, \boldsymbol{\Gamma})\, \mathcal{N}_y(\boldsymbol{\zeta}, \boldsymbol{\Phi}).
\end{aligned}$$

pagination □

References

1. Ainsleigh, P.L.: Theory of continuous-state hidden Markov models and hidden Gauss-Markov models. Tech. Rep. 11274, Naval Undersea Warfare Cent., Newport, RI, US (2001)
2. Ainsleigh, P.L., Kehtarnavaz, N., Streit, R.L.: Hidden Gauss-Markov models for signal classification. IEEE Trans. Signal Process. **50**(6), 1355–1367 (2002). https://doi.org/10.1109/TSP.2002.1003060
3. Alspach, D.L., Sorenson, H.W.: Nonlinear Bayesian estimation using Gaussian sum approximations. IEEE Trans. Autom. Control **17**(4), 439–448 (1972). https://doi.org/10.1109/TAC.1972.1100034
4. Carreira-Perpiñán, M.Á.: Mode-finding for mixtures of Gaussian distributions. IEEE Trans. Pattern Anal. Mach. Intell. **22**(11), 1318–1323 (2000). https://doi.org/10.1109/34.888716
5. Crouse, D.F., Willett, P., Pattipati, K., Svensson, L.: A look at Gaussian mixture reduction algorithms. In: Proceedings of the 14th International Conference on Information Fusion, pp. 531–538 (2011)
6. Daum, F.E., Huang, J.: Curse of dimensionality and particle filters. In: Proceedings of the IEEE Aerospace Conference (Cat. No.03TH8652), vol. 4, pp. 1979–1993 (2003). https://doi.org/10.1109/AERO.2003.1235126
7. Einicke, G.A.: Smoothing, Filtering and Prediction: Estimating the Past, Present and Future (2nd edn.), Prime Publishing, Northbrook, IL, US (2019)
8. Godsill, S., Doucet, A., West, M.: Maximum a posteriori sequence estimation using Monte Carlo particle filters. Ann. Inst. Stat. Math. **53**, 82–96 (2001). https://doi.org/10.1023/A:1017968404964

9. Jazwinski, A.H.: Stochastic Processes and Filtering Theory. No. 64 in Mathematics in Science and Engineering, Academic Press, New York, NY, US (1970)
10. Koller, D., Friedman, N.: Probabilistic graphical models: principles and techniques. MIT Press, Adaptive Computation and Machine Learning (2009)
11. Kálmán, R.E.: A new approach to linear filtering and prediction problems. J. Basic Eng. **82**, 35–45 (1960). https://doi.org/10.1115/1.3662552
12. Kálmán, R.E., Bucy, R.S.: New results in linear filtering and prediction theory. J. Basic Eng. **83**(1), 95–108 (1961). https://doi.org/10.1115/1.3658902
13. Pulkkinen, S., Mäkelä, M.M., Karmitsa, N.: A continuation approach to mode-finding of multivariate Gaussian mixtures and kernel density estimates. J. Global Optim. **56**(2), 459–487 (2013). https://doi.org/10.1007/s10898-011-9833-8
14. Rauch, H.E., Tung, F., Striebel, C.T.: Maximum likelihood estimates of linear dynamic systems. AIAA J. **3**(8), 1445–1450 (1965). https://doi.org/10.2514/3.3166
15. Rudić, B., Pichler-Scheder, M., Efrosinin, D.: Valid decoding in Gaussian mixture models. In: Proceedings of the 2024 IEEE 3rd Conference on Information Technology and Data Science (CITDS), pp. 175–180 (2024). https://doi.org/10.1109/CITDS62610.2024.10791365
16. Rudić, B.: Recursive Bayesian Inference in Dynamic Models: Advances and Applications. Ph.D. thesis, Johannes Kepler University Linz, Austria (2025). https://resolver.obvsg.at/urn:nbn:at:at-ubl:1-94646
17. Rudić, B., Pichler-Scheder, M., Efrosinin, D.: Recursive Bayesian decoding in state observation models: theory and application in quantum-based inference. Mathematics **13**(12) (2025). https://doi.org/10.3390/math13122012
18. Rudić, B., Sturm, V., Efrosinin, D.: On the analytic solution to recursive smoothing in mixture models. In: Proceedings of the 2024 58th Asilomar Conference on Signals, Systems, and Computers, pp. 1301–1305 (2024). https://doi.org/10.1109/IEEECONF60004.2024.10942739
19. Rudić, B., Sturm, V., Efrosinin, D.: On recursive marginal and MAP inference in state observation models. In: Dudin, A., Nazarov, A., Moiseev, A. (eds.) Information Technologies and Mathematical Modelling. Queueing Theory and Related Fields, pp. 85–97. Springe Nature Switzerland, Cham (2025). https://doi.org/10.1007/978-3-031-88307-1_7
20. Särkkä, S., Svensson, L.: Bayesian Filtering and Smoothing. Institute of Mathematical Statistics Textbooks, Cambridge University Press, Cambridge, UK, 2 edn. (2023). https://doi.org/10.1017/9781108917407
21. Särkkä, S., Svensson, L.: Bayesian Filtering and Smoothing, chap. Extended Rauch-Tung-Striebel Smoothing, pp. 267–277. Institute of Mathematical Statistics Textbooks, Cambridge University Press, 2 edn. (2023). https://doi.org/10.1017/9781108917407.014
22. Smith, G.L., Schmidt, S.F., McGee, L.A.: Application of statistical filter theory to the optimal estimation of position and velocity on board a circumlunar vehicle. NASA technical report, National Aeronautics and Space Administration, Washington, DC, US (1962)
23. Sorenson, H.W., Alspach, D.L.: Recursive Bayesian estimation using Gaussian sums. Automatica **7**(4), 465–479 (1971). https://doi.org/10.1016/0005-1098(71)90097-5
24. Stratonovich, R.L.: Conditional Markov processes. Theory Probab. Appl. **5**(2), 156–178 (1960). https://doi.org/10.1137/1105015
25. Viterbi, A.J.: Error bounds for convolutional codes and an asymptotically optimum decoding algorithm. IEEE Trans. Inf. Theory **13**(2), 260–269 (1967). https://doi.org/10.1109/TIT.1967.1054010
26. Wills, A.G., Hendriks, J., Renton, C., Ninness, B.: A numerically robust Bayesian filtering algorithm for Gaussian mixture models. IFAC-PapersOnLine **56**(1), 67–72 (2023). https://doi.org/10.1016/j.ifacol.2023.02.012, 12th IFAC Symposium on Nonlinear Control Systems NOLCOS 2022

A Mixed Integer Programming Approach to Solve Probabilistic Argumentation Tasks

Marco Baioletti, Andrea Capotorti, and Francesco Santini(✉)

Dipartimento di Matematica e Informatica, Università degli Studi di Perugia, Perugia, Italy
{marco.baioletti,andrea.capotorti,francesco.santini}@unipg.it

Abstract. This paper uses *Mixed Integer Programming* (*MIP*) to solve key computational tasks in *Probabilistic Abstract Argumentation*. In this framework, degrees of belief are assigned to arguments, enabling quantitative reasoning under uncertainty. From an epistemic perspective, probabilities represent an agent's beliefs about the acceptability of arguments and must satisfy rationality postulates. We encode four tasks as MIP problems with polynomial space complexity, namely, *checking* compatibility, *extending* partial assessments, *computing* probability intervals, and *correcting* incoherent assignments. Using sparsity results from probabilistic satisfiability, we derive compact encodings. Experiments on 2160 instances with up to 100 arguments demonstrate good scalability: most instances are solved in a reasonable time; extension tasks are harder but still show near-linear growth in computation time.

Keywords: Probabilistic Argumentation · Mixed Integer Programming · Coherence · Epistemic Uncertainty

1 Introduction

Abstract Argumentation [12] provides a formal model for reasoning with conflicting information, where arguments are atomic entities connected by an attack relation, abstracting away from domain-specific details. The central problem is determining which arguments can be reasonably accepted, rejected, or left undecided in the presence of conflicts. Argumentation semantics provide formal criteria for evaluating the status of an argument using labeling-based approaches [4,8], in which each argument is labeled as accepted, rejected, or undecided.

In realistic scenarios, an argumentation involves quantitative uncertainty about the reliability of arguments, the existence of attacks, and agents' degrees of belief. *Probabilistic Abstract Argumentation* [18,19] uses probability values to evaluate argument acceptability, extending classical qualitative methods to handle uncertain evidence, incomplete structures, and subjective beliefs [6,22].

B. Vantaggi et al. (Eds.): IPMU 2026, CCIS 3019, pp. 392–405, 2026.
https://doi.org/10.1007/978-3-032-28994-0_28

Applications include decision support, legal reasoning, dialog systems, and explainable AI.

This paper adopts the *epistemic approach*, where probabilities encode the degrees of belief of an agent in arguments, subject to some rationality postulates, such as *coherence* (*COH*), *rationality* (*RAT*), *semi-foundedness* (*SFOU*), and *semi-optimism* (*SOPT*) [18,19]. These postulates extend classical semantics to a quantitative setting. COH requires that a strong belief in an attacker lowers the belief in the attacked argument. RAT requires that if an argument is believed (probability > 0.5), then none of its targets is also believed. SFOU requires that unattacked arguments have a probability of at least 0.5. SOPT requires that an argument's belief be at least one minus the total belief in its attackers, under certain conditions.

Starting from partial probability assignments (that is, beliefs assigned to some arguments), we address four computational tasks: (i) *checking* whether the assignment is compatible with given postulates; (ii) *extending* the assessment to unassigned arguments; (iii) *computing* probability intervals for arguments; and (iv) *correcting* incoherent assignments at minimal distance.

We propose a *Mixed Integer Programming* (*MIP*) encoding that solves these tasks in polynomial space by exploiting the sparsity of probabilistic satisfiability: if a solution with k probability assessments exists, then one with at most $k+1$ nonzero probabilities exists. This supports efficient handling of medium- to large-scale frameworks. We implemented our approach in CPLEX and evaluated it on 2,160 balanced instances with 20–100 arguments, across different postulates (COH, RAT, SFOU, SOPT) and tasks. Although extension tasks are systematically harder, most instances are solved quickly with near-linear scaling. This advances the goal of making probabilistic epistemic Argumentation computationally practical and scalable, though some key reasoning tasks remain challenging because they can still be exponentially large, despite the graded beliefs ensured by the epistemic approach under rationality postulates.

The paper is organized as follows: Sect. 2 reviews Abstract Argumentation, probabilistic extensions, and rationality postulates. Section 3 presents the MIP encoding for all tasks. Section 4 reports experimental results, and Sect. 5 concludes with future directions.

2 Abstract Argumentation and Probabilistic Extensions

In the following sections, we present the basics of Abstract Argumentation and labeling semantics (Sect. 2.1) and Probabilistic Argumentation (Sect. 2.2).

2.1 Abstract Argumentation and Semantics

An *Abstract Argumentation Framework* AF is a directed graph $AF = \langle \mathcal{A}, \rightarrow \rangle$, where $\mathcal{A} = \{a_1, \ldots, a_n\}$ is a finite set of arguments, and $\rightarrow \subseteq \mathcal{A} \times \mathcal{A}$ is the attack relation [12]. For an argument $a \in \mathcal{A}$, we denote by $a^- = \{b \in \mathcal{A} \mid b \rightarrow a\}$ the set of its attackers. Argument evaluation is expressed by assigning a status to each argument. We first introduce *labeling-based* semantics [8]: in Caminada's labeling semantics, a label is *legal* if it is justified by the attack structure of the AF, meaning an assigned status is structurally warranted rather than arbitrary:[1]

Definition 1 (Labeling Semantics [8]). *Let* $AF = \langle \mathcal{A}, \rightarrow \rangle$ *be an AF. A labeling is a total function* $L : \mathcal{A} \rightarrow \{\text{in}, \text{out}, \text{undec}\}$. *For* $a \in \mathcal{A}$, *we can label it as follows:*

i. a *is legally* in *iff* $\forall b \in a^-,\ L(b) = \text{out}$;
ii. a *is legally* out *iff* $\exists b \in a^-$ *such that* $L(b) = \text{in}$;
iii. a *is* undec *iff it is not labeled* in *and not labeled* out, *that is iff* $\nexists b \in a^-$ *such that* $L(b) = \text{in}$ *and* $\exists c \in a^-$ *such that* $L(c) = \text{undec}$.

A labeling L *is:*

- admissible *(*adm*) iff every* in*-labeled argument is legally* in *and every* out*-labeled argument is legally* out*;*
- complete *(*com*) iff for all* $a \in \mathcal{A}$, $L(a) = \text{in} \iff a$ *is legally* in *and* $L(a) = \text{out} \iff a$ *is legally* out*;*
- preferred *(*prf*) iff* L *is a complete labeling whose set* $\mathsf{in}(L)$ *is maximal w.r.t. set inclusion;*
- stable *(*stb*) iff* L *is a complete labeling without undecided arguments: hence,* $\text{undec}(L) = \emptyset$*;*
- grounded *(*grd*) iff* L *is the unique complete labeling whose set* $\mathsf{in}(L)$ *is minimal w.r.t. set inclusion.*

An alternative way to evaluate arguments is through *extension-based* semantics, introduced by Dung in [12], before labeling semantics. Instead of assigning each argument a status (*in*, *out*, *undec*), extension-based semantics identify sets of jointly acceptable arguments, called *extensions*. Two fundamental properties that all the classical semantics in [12] satisfy are *conflict-freeness* and *defense*:

Definition 2 (Conflict-free extension and defense [12]). *A set of arguments* $A \in \sigma(AF) \subseteq 2^{\mathcal{A}}$ *is* conflict-free *w.r.t. an AF iff there are no arguments* $a, b \in A$ *such that* $b \rightarrow a$. *An argument* $a \in \mathcal{A}$ *is* defended by A *iff for every* $b \in \mathcal{A}$ *such that* $b \rightarrow a$, *there exists* $c \in A$ *such that* $c \rightarrow b$.

A semantics associates with each AF a collection of subsets of arguments satisfying collective acceptability conditions:

Definition 3 (Extension-based Semantics [12]). *Given* $AF = \langle \mathcal{A}, \rightarrow \rangle$, *an* extension-based semantics $\sigma \in \{com, prf, stb, grd\}$ *[12] associates with* AF *a set* $\sigma(AF) \subseteq 2^{\mathcal{A}}$ *whose elements are called* extensions, *representing sets of jointly acceptable arguments. Extension-based semantics can be related to labeling-based semantics in Definition 2.1 by considering labelings* L *such that, for each extension* $E \in \sigma(AF)$, $E = \{a \in \mathcal{A} \mid L(a) = \text{in}\}$.

[1] Note that label *undec* represents the absence of such justification, and this is why the notion of "legal" is not used for it.

For example, if we select $\sigma = \text{com}$, $E \in \text{com}(AF)$ iff *i)* E is conflict-free, *ii)* all arguments $a \in E$ are defended by E, and *iii)* for every argument $a \in \mathcal{A}$, if a is defended by E, then $a \in E$. If $E \in \text{com}(AF)$, then if $a \in E$ we have $L(a) = \text{in}$.

Given the framework F in Fig. 1, for example, we have $com(F) = \{\{a_6\}, \{a_1, a_3, a_6\}, \{a_2, a_4, a_6\}\}$, $prf(F) = \{\{a_1, a_3, a_6\}, \{a_2, a_4, a_6\}\}$, and $grd(F) = \{\{a_6\}\}$.

A key difference between extension-based and labeling-based semantics is that the latter provide a finer-grained representation by explicitly assigning the label *undec* to arguments, thereby capturing unresolved conflicts or insufficient defense that extension-based semantics represent only implicitly.

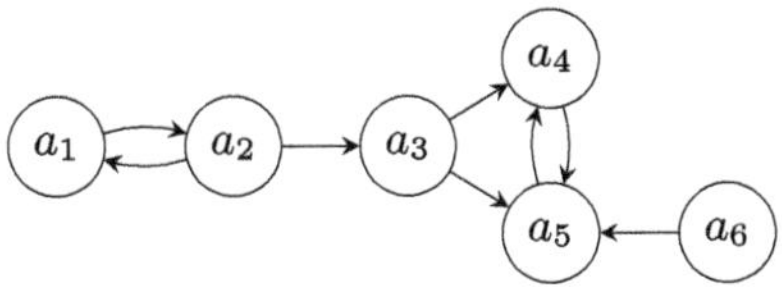

Fig. 1: An Abstract Argumentation Framework.

Table 1: A (total) probability assignment for the AF in Fig. 1.

	a_1	a_2	a_3	a_4	a_5	a_6
P_1	0.2	0.7	0.6	0.3	0.6	1
P_2	0.7	0.3	0.5	0.5	0.2	0.4
P_3	0.7	0.3	0.7	0.3	0	1
P_4	0.7	0.8	0.9	0.8	0.7	1
P_5	0.5	0.5	0.5	0.5	0.5	0.5

2.2 Probabilistic Argumentation

Probabilistic Abstract Argumentation is based on (discrete or "mass") probability distributions $P : 2^{\mathcal{A}} \to [0,1]$, with $\sum_{E \subseteq \mathcal{A}} P(E) = 1$, where $P(E)$ denotes the degree of belief in the acceptability of the extension $E \subseteq \mathcal{A}$. Note that in [19,23], the different name of "probability function" is used, but the name we adopt here is more in line with the usual one adopted in the probabilistic literature. Hence, there is a biunivocal correspondence between extensions and elementary events (atoms) through the following equivalence:

$$E \equiv \left(\bigwedge_{a_i \in E} a_i \right) \wedge \left(\bigwedge_{a_j \notin E} \neg a_j \right), \tag{1}$$

where $\wedge$ and $\neg$ denote logical conjunction and negation, respectively. Probability values derive from a probability distribution by additivity:

$$P(H) = \sum_{E \subseteq H} P(E) \text{ for any } H \in 2^{2^{\mathcal{A}}}. \tag{2}$$

As described in [23], we focus on extensions $E \subseteq \mathcal{A}$ (defined in Definition 3), which are the outcomes of inference in Argumentation; given a probability distribution, the probability value of a single argument

$$P(a) = \sum_{E \subseteq a} P(E) \tag{3}$$

for any $a \in \mathcal{A}$, represents the total belief. We adopt the usual small abuse of notation by using the same letter P to denote a probability distribution and the probability values it induces by additivity (2 or 3) in the presence (i.e., acceptance) of the specific argument a in the final output of the argumentation analysis. As described in [19], it is possible to associate a labeling with a probability distribution:

Definition 4 (Epistemic labeling [17]). *Let* $AF = \langle \mathcal{A}, \rightarrow \rangle$ *be an* AF *and* $P : 2^{\mathcal{A}} \rightarrow [0, 1]$ *a probability distribution on* AF*. An* epistemic labeling *is defined as* $L_P : \mathcal{A} \rightarrow \{\text{in}, \text{out}, \text{undec}\}$ *defined as* $L_P(a) = \text{in}$ *iff* $P(a) > 0.5$, $L_P(a) = \text{out}$ *iff* $P(a) < 0.5$, $L_P(a) = \text{undec}$ *iff* $P(a) = 0.5$.

Through the subjective approach to probability [13], the probabilistic perspective can be inverted: probabilities can be assigned directly to (some) arguments, as in the example in Table 1, e.g., through audience interviews [19].

Definition 5 (Partial probability assignment). *Let* $AF = \langle \mathcal{A}, \rightarrow \rangle$*, a* partial probability assignment *is a function* $P : A \rightarrow [0, 1]$*, where* $A \subseteq \mathcal{A}$*. For each* $a \in \mathcal{A}$*, the value* $P(a)$ *represents the degree of belief in the acceptability of argument* a*, while no probability value is specified for arguments in* $\mathcal{A} \setminus A$*.*

In the literature, coherence for partial probability assignments, understood as compatibility with a probability distribution, admits several equivalent definitions from semantic, syntactic, or operational perspectives (see, e.g., [9,10,13,20]). Any such formulation can be easily translated into the others (see, in particular, the characterization results in [9,10]). For our proposal, it is more convenient to adopt the operational point of view used in [3], which enables us to directly address the problem of coherence using mathematical programming tools. Operationally, the values $P(a)$, with $a \in A$, of a partial probability assignment, together with any structural zeros for impossible configurations, define the constraints that any probability distribution $P' : 2^{\mathcal{A}} \rightarrow [0, 1]$ compatible with P must satisfy (see, e.g., [1]). If at least one such probability distribution exists, the assignment is called "de Finetti coherent" (*dF-coherent*)[2], as shown in Definition 6.

Definition 6 (dF-coherence [10,13]). *A partial probability assignment* $P : A \rightarrow [0, 1]$*, with* $A \subseteq \mathcal{A}$*, is* dF-coherent *iff there exists at least a probability distribution* $P' : 2^{\mathcal{A}} \rightarrow [0, 1]$ *compatible with* P*, i.e.* $P'(a) = P(a)$*, for all* $a \in A$ *(in [18] notation, such* P' *is named a* P-compliant*).*

If the arguments in the domain A are logically independent (i.e., no structural zeros arise from incompatibility conditions), then any partial probability assignment $P : A \rightarrow [0, 1]$ is dF-coherent (see [13], vol. 1, p. 109 of the English translation, or [10], p. 32).

[2] We use the notation "dF-coherent" to distinguish this property of a partial assignment from the following coherence property "COH" of a probability distribution P w.r.t. AF.

If A contains an incompatible configuration (like those used among attacks in an AF to ensure conflict-free extensions (Definition 2), the dF-coherence of a partial probability assignment P must be verified via a suitable linear program with linear constraints. Any additional reasonable constraint on a P-compliant probability model P' can be incorporated into the initial probability assignment P to assess the probabilistic compatibility. A key consequence of dF-coherence is that any partial assignment P yields interval-coherent probabilities for every combination of arguments, and thus also for any single argument $a' \in \mathcal{A} \setminus A$:

Theorem 1 (Foundamental theorem of probabilties [13,20]). *If P is a dF-coherent assignment on $A \subseteq \mathcal{A}$, then for any element $H \in 2^{2^{\mathcal{A}}}$, and hence in particular for any single argument $H \equiv a' \in \mathcal{A} \setminus A$, there is a closed interval of coherent values $[\underline{P}(a'), \overline{P}(a')]$, i.e. the partial assignment $extP : A \cup \{a'\} \to [0,1]$ with $extP(a) = P(a)$ for all $a \in A$ and $extP(a') \in [\underline{P}(a'), \overline{P}(a')]$ is dF-coherent.*

In the operational approach to coherence, such intervals $[\underline{P}(a'), \overline{P}(a')]$ are obtained through linear programming optimization algorithms.

In this paper, we adopt the *epistemic* approach [19,23], where the structure of AF is fixed, and probabilities represent an agent's degree of belief in the acceptability of individual arguments: uncertainty concerns belief rather than structure. In contrast, the *constellation* approach [18,21] assigns probabilities to alternative graphs or subgraphs, modeling uncertainty about which arguments or attacks are present.

The following *rationality postulates* are conditions on probability distributions that ensure degrees of belief respect the attack relation. They extend classical semantic principles in Argumentation (e.g., conflict-freeness and defense) from a qualitative to a quantitative setting, constraining how belief in one argument should affect belief in its attackers or targets; they are *standard* postulates [19]:

COH P is *coherent* w.r.t. AF if for every $a, b \in \mathcal{A}$, whenever $a \to b$ then $P(a) \leq 1 - P(b)$.
SFOU P is *semi-founded* w.r.t. AF if $P(a) \geq 0.5$ for every $a \in \mathcal{A}$ with $a^- = \emptyset$.
FOU P is *founded* w.r.t. AF if $P(a) = 1$ for every $a \in \mathcal{A}$ with $a^- = \emptyset$.
SOPT P is *semi-optimistic* w.r.t. AF if $P(a) \geq 1 - \sum_{b \in a^-} P(b)$ for every $a \in \mathcal{A}$ with $a^- = \emptyset$.
OPT P is *optimistic* w.r.t. AF if $P(a) \geq 1 - \sum_{b \in a^-} P(b)$ for every $a \in \mathcal{A}$.
JUS P is *justifiable* w.r.t. AF if P is coherent and optimistic.
TER P is *ternary* w.r.t. AF if $P(a) \in \{0, 0.5, 1\}$ for every $a \in \mathcal{A}$.

The literature also considers *non-standard* postulates [19], which typically encode specific or highly constrained probability assignments, often in boundary or degenerate regions of the probability space $[0,1]^{\mathcal{A}}$.[3] Such conditions may determine belief values independently of the attack structure or constrain probability forms; therefore, they are used primarily for technical, comparative, or modeling purposes rather than as criteria for rational belief:

[3] A region of $[0,1]^{\mathcal{A}}$ is degenerate if it has strictly lower dimension than the ambient space.

RAT P is *rational* w.r.t. AF if, for every $a, b \in \mathcal{A}$ such that $a \to b$, $P(a) > 0.5$ implies $P(b) \leq 0.5$.
NEU P is *neutral* w.r.t. AF if $P(a) = 0.5$ for every $A \in \mathcal{A}$.
INV P is *involutary* w.r.t. AF if for every $a, b \in \mathcal{A}$ such that $a \to b$, then $P(a) = 1 - P(b)$.
MAX P is *maximal* w.r.t. AF if $P(a) = 1$ for every $a \in \mathcal{A}$.
MIN P is *minimal* w.r.t. AF if $P(a) = 0$ for every $a \in \mathcal{A}$.

The complete set $\mathcal{P}(\mathcal{A})$ of probability distributions is usually restricted to $\mathcal{P}_T(\mathcal{A})$, the distributions that satisfy a subset T of the above postulates (standard or non-standard), excluding those involving boundary or degenerate regions of $[0,1]^{\mathcal{A}}$. In what follows, we consider only $\mathcal{P}_T(\mathcal{A})$ with $T \subseteq \{COH, RAT, SFOU, SOPT\}$.

From a partial probability assessment $P : A \to [0,1]$, with $A \subseteq \mathcal{A}$, different computational tasks are possible. In fact, as also outlined in [19], we can perform the following tasks

check task: check if P is compatible with some subset T of postulates, i.e., to find if there exists a probability distribution $P' \in \mathcal{P}_T(\mathcal{A})$ extending P (i.e., P' is a P-compliant probability model) and respecting the postulates in T;
extension task: whenever P is compatible with some subset T of postulates, complete the assessment with some probability value on $\mathcal{A} \setminus A$ continuing to respect the postulates in T;
interval task: whenever P is compatible with some subset T of the postulates, for any $b \in \mathcal{A} \setminus A$ compute the interval of the legitimate values $[\underline{P}(b), \overline{P}(b)]$, continuing to respect the postulates in T;
correction task: whenever P is not compatible with some subset T of postulates, find another partial assessment that respects the postulates in T and is at some minimal distance from P.

Note that the correction task has been investigated for Probabilistic Argumentation in [19], under the name "Distance-Based Consolidation", while in the probabilistic coherence setting it was studied in [1,2].

All of these tasks can be formulated as optimization problems. For *check*, *extension*, and *interval* tasks, the optimization problems are fully linear. For the *correction* task, the constraints are linear, but the objective function depends on the chosen distance (see [19] for details).

In this paper, to benefit from the mixed integer programming implementation described in the next section, we use the *Manhattan distance*, also known as d_1:

$$d_1(P, P') = \sum_{a \in \mathcal{A}} |P(a) - P'(a)| \quad \text{with } P, P' \in \mathcal{P}(\mathcal{A}) \tag{4}$$

$$d_1(P, \mathcal{P}_T(\mathcal{A})) = \min_{P' \in \mathcal{P}_T(\mathcal{A})} d_1(P, P') \quad \text{with } P \in \mathcal{P}(\mathcal{A}). \tag{5}$$

Note that this distance, although not strictly convex and thus inducing a set of corrections that may not be connected, convex, or closed, still allows us to define an inconsistency index with the usual properties of consistency, monotonicity, separability, and super-additivity (see [19] for details). However, as mentioned, we chose d_1 because the corresponding correction problem is fully linear, with all associated implementation and efficiency benefits.

3 MIP Encoding

In this section, we describe how we encoded the tasks in Sect. 2.2.[4] These tasks could require an exponential number of variables, since the number of atoms is $2^{|\mathcal{A}|}$. Consequently, any "brute force" approach that explicitly considers all the $2^{|\mathcal{A}|}$ atoms can handle only tasks of limited size.

This problem is well known in the probabilistic community about satisfiability problems PSAT,[5] (see, e.g., [14]), and different specific algorithms have been proposed to simplify the computations (among the many, see, e.g., [3,15]). More recently, in [1,2] we proposed, inspired by the seminal paper [11], an efficient approach to solve any probabilistic satisfiability problem (as in the tasks of the previous section) via mixed-integer programming (MIP). This method is based on the following property:

Proposition 1 (Sparsity of PSAT solutions [14]). *If a satisfying probability distribution (on atoms) for an instance of PSAT with k probability assessments exists, then there exists one with at most $k + 1$ non-zero probabilities, and with entries rationals with total precision $O(k^2)$.*[6]

This result enables the search for a sparse solution with at most $k+1$ atoms and, through specific mixed-integer linear constraints, yields the probabilities of these atoms as part of the solution.

Consequently, tasks *check*, *extension*, *interval*, and *correction* can be solved by casting them as mixed integer programming problems and then using a fast MIP solver. Actually, in this approach, the *check* task is more or less equivalent to the *extension* task, since, checking the existence of a P-compliant P' that satisfies the postulates in T, a probability distribution P' must be found, and by the additivity property (2) the values $P'(a')$ can be computed for any $a' \in \mathcal{A} \setminus A$.

The structure of the MIP encoding is basically the same for all three tasks. In what follows, for any partial probability assessment $P : A \to [0, 1]$, we assume without loss of generality $\mathcal{A} = \{a_1, \ldots, a_n\}$ with $n = |\mathcal{A}|$ and $A = \{a_1, \ldots, a_k\}$ ($k = |A|$). Any atom E_j, or equivalently any extension intended as in (1), will have a vectorial representation with n binary elements: 0 if $a_i \notin E_j$, 1 if $a_i \in E_j$.

[4] A Python encoding of this project can be found at https://github.com/francesco-santini/MIP_probabilisticAF.

[5] The PSAT problem aims to check whether a given probability assignment on a finite set of disjunctive clauses is compatible with a probability distribution on the set of all logical assignments.

[6] The total precision of a rational vector is the total number of bits needed to encode all its entries, i.e., the sum of the bit-lengths of the numerators and denominators of its rational components, ensuring the solution admits a polynomial-size encoding.

In most cases, three sets of variables are used. The first set is composed of $n(k+1)$ binary variables a_{ij}, for each $i = 1, \ldots, n$ and $j = 1, \ldots, k+1$. The variable a_{ij} represents the logical value of the argument a_i in the vectorial representation of the atom E_j.

The second set is composed of $k+1$ real variables q_j, for $j = 1, \ldots, k+1$. The generic variable q_j contains the probability of the atom E_j.

The third set is composed of $n(k+1)$ real variables b_{ij}, for each $i = 1, \ldots, n$ and $j = 1, \ldots, k+1$. The generic variable b_{ij} allows us to express the products $a_{ij} \cdot q_j$ through linear constraints

$$0 \leq b_{ij} \leq a_{ij} \quad , \quad a_{ij} - 1 + q_j \leq b_{ij} \leq q_j \tag{6}$$

for $i = 1, \ldots, n$ and $j = 1, \ldots, k+1$.

In fact, if $a_{ij} = 0$, then $b_{ij} = 0$ also holds, and consequently $b_{ij} = 0 = a_{ij} \cdot q_j$. On the other hand, if $a_{ij} = 1$, then $a_{ij} - 1 + q_j \leq b_{ij} \leq q_j$ reduces to $q_j \leq b_{ij} \leq q_j$, and hence $b_{ij} = q_j = a_{ij} \cdot q_j$.

The constraints imposed by the probability assessments are as follows.

$$\sum_{j=1}^{k+1} b_{ij} = P(a_i), \quad i = 1, \ldots, k \tag{7}$$

with the addition of the normalization constraint

$$\sum_{j=1}^{k+1} q_j = 1. \tag{8}$$

The constraints for the different postulates are of direct translation, through the substitution of $P(a_i)$ with the expressions $\sum_{j=1}^{k+1} b_{ij}$. For example, the postulate COH induces constraints

$$\sum_{j=1}^{k+1} b_{rj} \leq 1 - \sum_{j=1}^{k+1} b_{sj} \text{ for each } (a_r \to a_s) \in AF. \tag{9}$$

The *extension* task can use any fictitious objective function, e.g.

$$\sum_{j=1}^{k+1} q_j \tag{10}$$

since the goal is to find any feasible solution.

For the *correction* task, two additional sets of real variables $\{r_i\}$ and $\{s_i\}$, for $i = 1, \ldots, k$, are used to express the constraint (11) that replaces (7)

$$\sum_{j=1}^{k+1} b_{ij} = P(a_i) + r_i - s_i, \quad i = 1, \ldots, k. \tag{11}$$

The objective function is

$$\sum_{a_i \in A} r_i + s_i. \tag{12}$$

For the *interval* task, the variables and constraints are the same as those for the *extension* task, while the objective function is the following:

$$\sum_{j=1}^{k+1} b_{lj}. \tag{13}$$

The objective function is the same for both optimization problems: one for the minimization sub-task and the other for the maximization sub-task.

The solutions of all these MIP problems contain both the explicit expression of at most $k+1$ atoms E_j, through the values a_{ij}, $i = 1, \ldots, n$, and their probability values, through the values q_j. With this probability function, any probability of interest can be obtained by additivity through the b_{ij}'s.

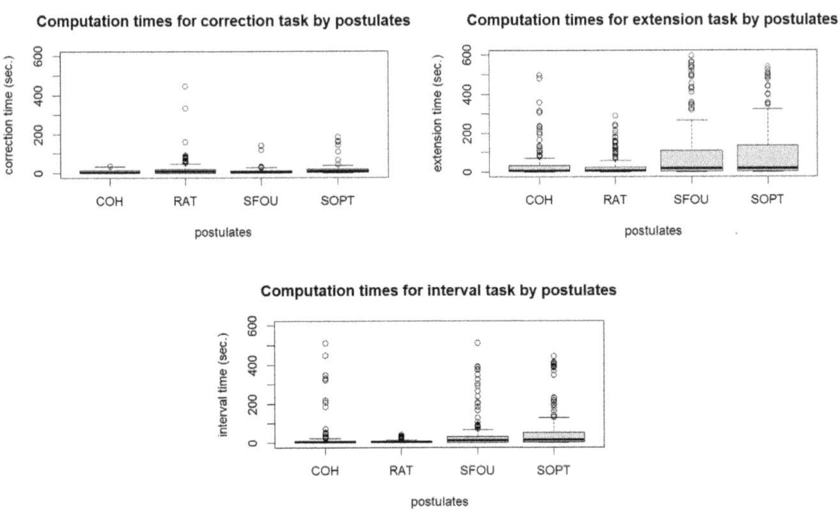

Fig. 2: Boxplots of computation times by postulates for *correction* (top-left), *extension* (top-right), *interval* (bottom).

4 Experiments

As already mentioned in the previous section, the advantage of implementing in MIP problems is that we can handle Probabilistic Argumentation tasks with polynomial space complexity. Although such tasks remain NP-hard or worse (for a detailed complexity study, see [19]), the MIP implementation solves most instances in a reasonable time, including those of medium to large size.

To demonstrate this benefit, we generated 2160 instances of Probabilistic Argumentation, perfectly balanced across the number of arguments, the set of postulates, and the task type. In particular, the AFs have been generated with the Erdős–Rényi method, with a number n of arguments varying from 20 to 100 by 10, the number of attacks is always the 10% of the maximum number (i.e., $0.1n(n-1)$) chosen randomly, the number of probability assignments is always $k = n/2$, with the k arguments chosen randomly in $\mathcal{A}$ and the k probability values chosen randomly in the interval $[0.1, 0.9]$.

Thus, we had 20 Probabilistic Argumentation instances for each combination of the number of variables n, the postulate $t \in \{COH, RAT, SFOU, SOPT\}$[7], and the task among the three types: *check*/*extension*, *correction*, *interval*. We focus on $COH, RAT, SFOU, SOPT$ because the other postulates require extremal probability values.

The Computations used the CPLEX (v13) optimization package through a Python MIP interface, with a time limit of 600 seconds (10 minutes). For the *interval* task, which involves two optimization steps, the reported computation time is the average of the two, and thus its value is comparable to the times of the other two tasks. Among the 2160 instances, the procedure did not obtain an optimal solution before time-out in only 60 instances. We ignore such instances in the following considerations.

As shown in Fig. 3 (top-left), *correction* and *interval* tasks have similar computational times, while *extension* tasks are more demanding. Still, most instances are solved in a reasonable time: for *correction* tasks, the interquartile range is $[0.62, 15.47]$. for *interval* tasks $[1.00, 36.51]$; for *extension* tasks $[1.10, 71.55]$. Comparing the postulates, we observe similar solving times (see Fig. 3 (top-right)), with SFOU and SOPT marginally harder but usually solved in a reasonable time: interquartile ranges $[0.46, 14.40]$ for COH, $[0.62, 14.86]$ for RAT, $[0.87, 25.72]$ for SFOU, and $[1.14, 42.31]$ for SOPT.

Among the correction tasks, all four postulates show similar times, while inside the *extension* tasks, SFOU and SOPT instances result in harder problems than COH and RAT ones, and inside the *interval* tasks, there is a linear increase in times (see Fig. 2 (bottom)).

But what is more relevant to highlight is that, at least for frameworks with up to 100 arguments, as we can appreciate from Fig. 3 (bottom), the computational times do not explode as the number of arguments increases (and consequently, the number of attacks and of arguments with assigned probabilities increases). Note that, even if solver competitions in Abstract Argumentation (e.g., [7]) adopt benchmarks with AF instances with up to thousands of arguments, empirical argument maps derived from real debates (e.g., *DebateGraph*[8] or the examples in [16]) typically count tens of arguments.

In fact, even though among the worst cases (outliers) we can observe an exponential growth (R^2 of 0.75 for the logarithmic scale transformation of times),

[7] In this first experimentation, we limit ourselves to considering one single postulate at a time, and in the future, we will also experiment with subsets T of them.

[8] DebateGraph: https://debategraph.org/.

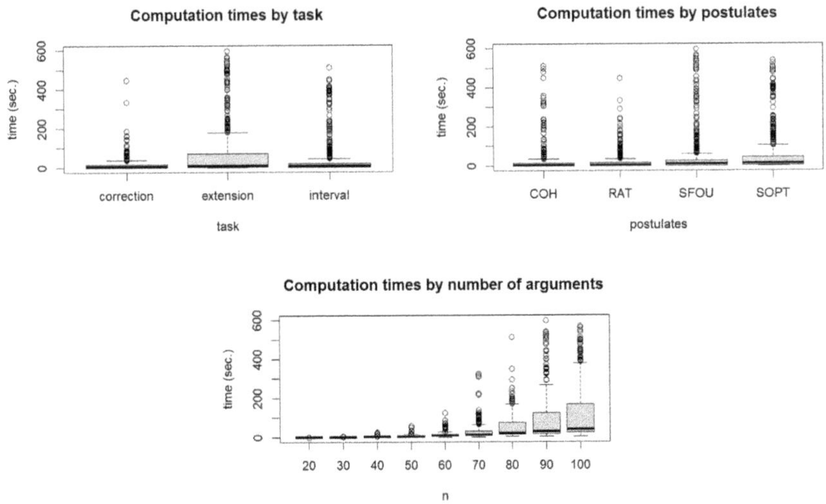

Fig. 3: Boxplots of computation times divided by task type (top-left), by postulates (top-right), and by the number of arguments n (bottom).

for the most common instances, the increase of times is linear (R^2 of 0.82 for ordinary least squares regression among the means, of 0.87 among the medians, of 0.79 among the third quartiles). These initial results are promising for applying our method to large-scale Probabilistic AFs.

5 Conclusions and Future Work

In this paper, we show that Mixed-Integer Programming provides a unified and scalable framework for solving key computational tasks in epistemic Probabilistic Argumentation. Using sparsity results from probabilistic satisfiability, we derived compact encodings with polynomial space complexity, enabling practical handling of AFs with up to 100 arguments. The experimental results confirm that, although the underlying problems remain computationally hard, the proposed MIP approach scales well in typical cases and keeps computational time under control even as the AF size increases.

From a theoretical perspective, this work strengthens the connection between Probabilistic Argumentation and Mathematical Programming, showing that epistemic rationality postulates can be translated into linear constraints in a principled and modular way. From a practical perspective, it demonstrates that Probabilistic Argumentation is not merely a theoretical extension of Abstract Argumentation, but a computationally viable tool for reasoning under uncertainty.

Several directions for future work remain open. First, a deeper analysis of why extension tasks are systematically harder than correction and interval tasks could lead to refined encodings or symmetry-breaking techniques that further improve performance. Second, while we adopted the Manhattan distance for computational reasons, alternative distance measures could be explored to better capture semantic proximity between belief states. Third, an important challenge is to approximate or incorporate maximum-entropy principles within a linear MIP framework, without resorting to nonlinear optimization while preserving desirable informational properties.

Moreover, future research should investigate combinations of multiple postulates simultaneously, as well as additional rationality principles such as the *rp-justifiability* proposed in [5]. Finally, extending the present approach to dynamic settings, where beliefs are updated iteratively, or to the constellation approach [18,21] to Probabilistic Argumentation would further bridge the gap between theoretical models and real-world decision-support systems.

Acknowledgements. Andrea Capotorti is a member of the "INdAM Research group GNAMPA". Francesco Santini is a member of the "INdAM Research group GNCS" and "Consorzio CINI". This work has been partially supported by the University of Perugia - "Fondo Ricerca di Ateneo (2022)" – Project RATIONALISTS.

References

1. Baioletti, M., Capotorti, A.: A further step for efficient corrections of inconsistent probabilistic data sets. Int. J. Approximate Reasoning **161**, 108942 (2023)
2. Baioletti, M., Capotorti, A.: A l1 based probabilistic merging algorithm and its application to statistical matching. Appl. Intell. **49**(1), 112–124 (2019)
3. Baioletti, M., Capotorti, A., Tulipani, S., Vantaggi, B.: Elimination of boolean variables for probabilistic coherence. Soft. Comput. **4**, 81–88 (2000)
4. Baroni, P., Caminada, M., Giacomin, M.: An introduction to argumentation semantics. Knowl. Eng. Rev. **26**(4), 365–410 (2011)
5. Baroni, P., Giacomin, M., Vicig, P.: On rationality conditions for epistemic probabilities in abstract argumentation. In: Proceedings of the 5th International Conference on Computational Models of Argument (COMMA 2014), vol. 266, pp. 121–132. IOS Press (2014)
6. Bistarelli, S., David, V., Monnin, P., Santini, F., Taticchi, C.: Fast computing of dung semantics in acyclic probabilistic argumentation frameworks. In: Thirty-Ninth AAAI Conference on Artificial Intelligence, AAAI 2025, pp. 14798–14805. AAAI Press (2025)
7. Bistarelli, S., et al.: The third and fourth international competitions on computational models of argumentation: design, results and analysis. Argument Comput. **16**(2), 236–299 (2025)
8. Caminada, M.: On the issue of reinstatement in argumentation. In: Fisher, M., van der Hoek, W., Konev, B., Lisitsa, A. (eds.) JELIA 2006. LNCS (LNAI), vol. 4160, pp. 111–123. Springer, Heidelberg (2006). https://doi.org/10.1007/11853886_11
9. Coletti, G.: Coherent numerical and ordinal probabilistic assessments. IEEE Trans. Syst. Man Cybern. **24**(12), 1747–1754 (1994)
10. Coletti, G., Scozzafava, R.: Probabilistic Logic in a Coherent Setting, vol. 15. Springer, Dordrecht (2002)
11. Cozman, F.G., Fargoni di Ianni, L.: Probabilistic satisfiability and coherence checking through integer programming. Int. J. Approx. Reasoning **58**(C), 57–70 (2015)

12. Dung, P.M.: On the acceptability of arguments and its fundamental role in nonmonotonic reasoning, logic programming and n-person games. Artif. Intell. **77**(2), 321–358 (1995)
13. de Finetti, B.: Teoria della probabilita. Nuova biblioteca scientifica Einaudi, Einaudi (1970). https://books.google.it/books?id=8OlAQwAACAAJ
14. Georgakopoulos, G., Kavvadias, D., Papadimitriou, C.H.: Probabilistic satisfiability. J. Complex. **4**(1), 1–11 (1988)
15. Hansen, P., Jaumard, B.: Algorithms for the maximum satisfiability problem. Computing **44**(4), 279–303 (1990). https://link.springer.com/article/10.1007/BF02241270
16. Harrell, M.: Representing the structure of a debate. Argumentation **36**(4), 595–610 (2022)
17. Hunter, A.: A probabilistic approach to modelling uncertain logical arguments. Int. J. Approximate Reasoning **54**(1), 47–81 (2013)
18. Hunter, A., Polberg, S., Potyka, N., Rienstra, T., Thimm, M.: Probabilistic argumentation: a survey. In: Gabbay, D., Giacomin, M., Simari, G.R., Thimm, M. (eds.) Handbook of Formal Argumentation (Volume 2), vol. 2, chap. 7. College Publications (2021)
19. Hunter, A., Thimm, M.: Probabilistic reasoning with abstract argumentation frameworks. J. Artif. Intell. Res. **59**, 565–611 (2017)
20. Lad, F.: Operational subjective statistical methods : a mathematical, philosophical, and historical introduction. Wiley Series in Probability and Statistics. Applied Probability and Statistics. Wiley, New York (1996)
21. Li, H., Oren, N., Norman, T.J.: Probabilistic argumentation frameworks. In: Modgil, S., Oren, N., Toni, F. (eds.) TAFA 2011. LNCS (LNAI), vol. 7132, pp. 1–16. Springer, Heidelberg (2012). https://doi.org/10.1007/978-3-642-29184-5_1
22. Santini, F., Jøsang, A., Pini, M.S.: Are my arguments trustworthy? Abstract argumentation with subjective logic. In: 21st International Conference on Information Fusion, FUSION, pp. 1982–1989. IEEE (2018)
23. Thimm, M., Baroni, P., Giacomin, M., Vicig, P.: Probabilities on extensions in abstract argumentation. In: Proceedings of the 2017 International Workshop on Theory and Applications of Formal Argument (TAFA 2017) (2017)

Statistical Inference and Data Analysis

Susceptibility of Skin Lesion CNN Classifiers to Increasing Gaussian Noise

Giuliana Ramella[1](✉) and Luca Serino[2]

[1] C.N.R., National Research Council, Institute for the Applications of Calculus Mauro Picone, Naples, Italy
giuliana.ramella@cnr.it

[2] C.N.R., National Research Council, Institute for High Performance Computing and Networking, Naples, Italy
luca.serino@cnr.it

Abstract. Noise is a realistic source of corruption in dermoscopic imaging, stemming from sensor limitations, low-light acquisition, and uncontrolled capture conditions. This study examines how this type of degradation alters the behavior of CNN-based skin lesion classifiers by systematically perturbing a balanced ISIC 2018 subset with increasing noise intensities. Four representative CNN architectures are compared under a unified training protocol, and their performance is analyzed across evaluation setups that separate matched and mismatched noise conditions between training and inference. Beyond standard Accuracy, we report Precision, F1 score, and Matthews Correlation Coefficient to capture changes in both overall and class-sensitive reliability. The analysis shows that the main performance loss occurs when models are tested at noise levels higher than those encountered during training, whereas degradation is less disruptive when the noise distribution is consistent across both phases. These results underscore the importance of explicitly accounting for noise variability when deploying a skin lesion classifier in real-world clinical settings.

Keywords: Convolutional Neural Network · Skin lesion classification · Gaussian Noise degradation

1 Introduction

In clinical practice, skin lesion assessment aims to reach the most accurate classification possible, since diagnostic errors can lead to delayed treatment or unnecessary procedures [4,8]. As clinicians—and AI decision-support tools—derive crucial information from what is visible in the image, the quality of the dermoscopic image plays a central role [5,16]. When images are degraded (e.g., blur, poor focus, uneven lighting, noise, shadows, or compression artifacts), diagnostically relevant details may be obscured or distorted, which can significantly bias interpretation and increase the risk of misclassification as well as to propagate

B. Vantaggi et al. (Eds.): IPMU 2026, CCIS 3019, pp. 409–422, 2026.
https://doi.org/10.1007/978-3-032-28994-0_29

errors to earlier stages of the pipeline, including lesion segmentation [14,15] and color quantization [3].

Noise is one of the most harmful forms of image degradation because it disrupts fine textural details and adds artificial pixel-level fluctuations, obscuring clinically relevant structures. It often arises during image acquisition, especially when images are captured with heterogeneous, non-standardized devices (e.g., smartphones or low-cost dermatoscopes) or when imaging practices are suboptimal. Its effects can be further intensified by underexposure, downstream post-processing, compression processing, and in-camera pipelines (e.g., sharpening/denoising) that may introduce or amplify grain-like patterns.

In this study, we quantify the effect of image noise on skin lesion classification across four representative CNN families commonly used in skin cancer detection [13]: DenseNet [11,19], InceptionNet [2,18], MobileNet [1,10], and VGGNet [7, 17].

To mitigate potential confounding due to class imbalance [9,16], we adopt an experimental setup aligned with [16]. Specifically, we adopt the same baseline Computational Models (CMs) pretrained on a balanced subset (BDS) of the ISIC 2018 benchmark [6]. Starting from this reference configuration, we generate a collection of noise-corrupted datasets by injecting controlled perturbations into the BDS images at progressively higher intensities. We then benchmark the CMs on these noisy variants to quantify how performance degrades as noise increases and to characterize robustness trends across architectures. The resulting analysis clarifies each model's vulnerability to noisy acquisitions, anticipates potential failure modes in clinical deployments with heterogeneous acquisition conditions, and provides actionable evidence to develop strategies that improve resilience to noise-induced artifacts.

In summary, we propose a systematic, quantitative framework to investigate how image noise and, more importantly, train–test mismatches in noise conditions affect CNN-based skin lesion classifiers. Our broader objective is to study the role of image quality in this domain across its various facets, a topic that has been seldom examined through rigorous quantitative analyses in prior work.

2 The Gaussian Noise Image Datasets

The considered starting balanced dataset, BDS [16], contains 3,000 dermoscopic images, equally distributed across three diagnostic categories: Melanoma (MEL), Melanocytic Nevi (NV), and Benign Keratosis Lesions (BKL), with 1,000 samples per class. Following the standard 70–20–10 protocol, the dataset is divided into 2,100 images for training, 600 for validation, and 300 for testing. The first two subsets are used during model development (hereafter collectively referred to as the training set), whereas the test subset is reserved exclusively for the final evaluation of classification performance.

These datasets constitute the starting point of our investigation and define the baseline noise level V_0, which we refer to as "noise-free" for convenience, despite the possible presence of mild acquisition noise in the original images. To investigate the impact of noise [12], we have created corrupted counterparts of each BDS subset by adding zero-mean Gaussian noise to every image. Specifically, we have generated five degraded datasets with progressively increasing perturbation strengths, denoted $V_1, \ldots, V_5$. For readability, we do not explicitly specify whether a given subset corresponds to training, validation, or testing, since this is clear from the context.

Rather than spacing the perturbation levels uniformly in variance, we used approximately equal increments in the noise standard deviation (σ), since σ directly controls the typical perturbation amplitude in the image domain. Specifically, we fixed the minimum and maximum noise variances to 0.01 and 0.20, corresponding to $\sigma_{\min} = \sqrt{0.01} = 0.10$ and $\sigma_{\max} = \sqrt{0.20} \approx 0.447$, and we selected five σ values evenly spaced between these endpoints according to:

$$\begin{aligned} V_i &= \sigma_i^2, \\ \sigma_i &= \sigma_{\min} + \frac{i-1}{4}\left(\sigma_{\max} - \sigma_{\min}\right), \qquad i = 1, \ldots, 5. \end{aligned} \tag{1}$$

This yielded the following noise variances $V_1, \ldots, V_5$:

$$(V_1, \ldots, V_5) = (0.010,\ 0.035,\ 0.075,\ 0.130,\ 0.200). \tag{2}$$

The maximum variance has been set to $V_5 = 0.200$ because higher values lead to excessive image degradation, making lesion borders and internal structures largely indistinguishable. This choice is consistent with our aim of investigating susceptibility under strong yet still interpretable corruptions, rather than under extreme perturbations of limited practical relevance. This decision is further supported by the experimental results (see Sect. 4), which show that performance in the mismatched settings already collapses at the highest considered noise levels. Consequently, extending the analysis beyond V_5 would likely provide only marginal additional insight. Moreover, spacing the intermediate noise levels uniformly by standard deviation yields more evenly spaced corruption severities in terms of perturbation magnitude. This avoids over-representing low-noise conditions that can arise when spacing uniformly by variance, resulting in a more interpretable Accuracy-versus-noise robustness profile for classification.

The degraded image datasets have been generated using the imnoise MATLAB function (Gaussian option), with the noise mean fixed at 0 and the variance levels $V_1, \ldots, V_5$. We note that fixing the noise mean to zero ensures that corruption severity is controlled solely by the variance, while avoiding a systematic shift in average image intensity (i.e., global brightness bias), so that performance differences across noise levels reflect increased noise magnitude rather than an intensity offset.

Figure 1 provides a qualitative illustration of the noise corruption process: starting from the clean image (V_0), zero-mean Gaussian noise is added with increasing strength to obtain progressively more challenging variants ($V_1, \ldots, V_5$), which gradually hide lesion boundaries and fine structural details.

3 Implementation Details and Training

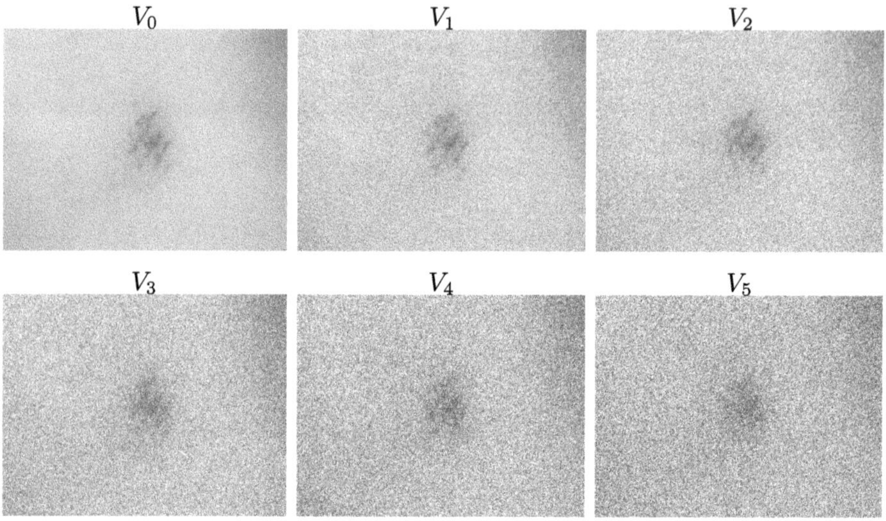

Fig. 1. Illustrative example of the noise corruption process: the same dermoscopic image at the baseline condition V_0 and after adding progressively stronger zero-mean Gaussian noise (V_1-V_5).

All RGB images have been resized to 224×224 to ensure a uniform input size across the considered CMs and to enable a fair architectural comparison under a common input resolution. They have then been fed into the networks using the corresponding model-specific routine to preserve the preprocessing pipeline associated with each CM. We note that resizing may interact with the added noise, as resampling can affect both fine dermoscopic details and the spatial distribution of the injected perturbations. Therefore, the reported robustness trends should also be interpreted in light of the adopted resizing procedure.

Training data have been augmented with random rotations (25°), horizontal shifts (0.1), vertical shifts (0.1), zoom (0.15), and horizontal flips, while validation images have been preprocessed only. Each CM was initialized with ImageNet weights and then fine-tuned end-to-end to better align the pretrained backbones with the skin-lesion classification domain. To this end, we appended a lightweight classification head consisting of Global Average Pooling (GAP), Batch Normalization (BN), a 256-unit fully connected layer with ReLU activation, Dropout (0.4), and a final Softmax layer. Models were trained with Adamax ($\text{lr} = 10^{-4}$), categorical cross-entropy, a batch size of 16, and Accuracy as the primary metric, for up to 100 epochs, with early stopping on validation loss (patience = 12, restoring the best weights) and best-model checkpointing. The same training pipeline was applied to each degraded dataset to assess robustness across increasing levels of corruption.

Implementations have been run in Keras/TensorFlow on a workstation (Intel Xeon Gold 6134, 128 GB RAM, NVIDIA Quadro 6000 24 GB VRAM).

4 Quantitative Performance Analysis Under Increasing Noise

To make the role of image quality explicit, we report results in terms of train–test image-quality alignment, as model performance is strongly influenced by the quality gap between the data used for learning and that used for classification. To this end, we adopt a pair notation $(\cdot,\cdot)$, where the first element denotes the training dataset and the second the test dataset. This notation is used throughout the paper to clearly identify the dataset version involved in each stage and to avoid considering training and testing conditions in isolation. Explicitly accounting for this distinction is essential for assessing robustness and generalization under controlled degradations, and for providing a more nuanced view of performance trends across different image qualities.

Accordingly, we consider the (BDS, BDS) combination at the baseline noise level V_0, which can be regarded as an "ideal" scenario where the training and test datasets are drawn from the same distribution and share the same image quality and acquisition conditions, since no additional degradation is introduced. Then we consider the following combinations at the increasing noise levels $V_1,\ldots,V_5$:

1. (BDS, BDS_n)
2. (BDS_n, BDS)
3. (BDS_n, BDS_n)

Tables 1, 2, 3 and 4 summarize the outcomes obtained for the dataset pairings introduced above. For each setting, we report the mean (%) and standard deviation of Accuracy (A), Precision (P), F1-score ($F1$), and Matthews Correlation Coefficient (MCC) computed over 10 independent runs, while progressively varying the noise intensity starting at level V_0 and moving through the five levels $V_1,\ldots,V_5$ using different random seeds. For each run, all CMs were initialized using the same seed to ensure paired comparisons.

From the experimental results reported in Table 1 for the (BDS, BDS) combination at level V_0, all CMs achieve high and stable performance. In terms of Accuracy, VGG16 attains the highest mean value (78.17%), closely followed by DenseNet121 (77.90%), while InceptionV3 is the lowest (75.67%). A consistent trend is observed for $F1$ and MCC: VGG16 yields the best $F1$ (78.17%) and the highest MCC (67.49%), with DenseNet121 being very close (MCC = 67.25%). Conversely, DenseNet121 achieves the highest P (79.07%), suggesting slightly more reliable positive predictions. The relatively small standard deviations across the 10 runs, roughly (1–3)% for $A/F1$ and (1.7–3.3)% for MCC, indicate good reproducibility, with VGG16 and DenseNet121 emerging as the most consistent models under this baseline condition.

The experimental results for the remaining dataset pairings under progressively increasing noise levels are as follows.

Table 1. Mean percentage (%) and standard deviation of *A*, *P*, *F1*, *MCC* over 10 runs, with training and test performed on the original BDS dataset.

(BDS, BDS)				
	$A\uparrow$	$P\uparrow$	$F1\uparrow$	$MCC\uparrow$
V_0				
DenseNet121	77.90 ± 2.13	**79.07 ± 2.01**	78.03 ± 2.13	67.25 ± 3.10
InceptionV3	75.67 ± 1.13	75.91 ± 1.21	75.67 ± 1.18	63.59 ± 1.69
MobileNet	75.93 ± 1.88	76.42 ± 2.06	75.91 ± 1.85	64.11 ± 2.91
VGG16	**78.17 ± 2.21**	78.74 ± 2.07	**78.17 ± 2.17**	**67.49 ± 3.29**

1. (BDS, BDS_n) (cfr. Table 2)
   In the (BDS, BDS_n) combination, CMs are trained on clean images (BDS) but tested on noisy versions (BDS_n) with increasing noise level. Performance declines steadily as noise intensifies. As expected, performance drops markedly as the perturbation level increases from V_1 to V_5 across all metrics. The degradation is already substantial at V_1, e.g., A in the (43–58)% range, and becomes severe from V_2 onward, where A falls to roughly (37–40)% and *MCC* to about (10–15)%. For stronger noise levels (V_3–V_5), A converges near chance-level behaviour - around (32–36)% - while *MCC* approaches zero and even becomes negative for VGG16 at V_5 (-1.17%), suggesting performance no better (or worse) under extreme corruption. Across architectures, DenseNet121 tends to be the most resilient in terms of A and maintains comparatively higher *MCC* at most noise levels (e.g., *MCC* is 39.32 at V_1 and 12.97 at V_2). However, P values are less informative here: they fluctuate widely (often with very large standard deviations, especially from V_2 onward), reflecting unstable decision thresholds when the models' outputs collapse under heavy noise. The increasing standard deviations—particularly for P, *F1*, and *MCC*—further highlight that robustness degrades not only in mean performance but also in consistency across runs as the test data become more corrupted.
2. (BDS_n, BDS) (cfr. Table 3)
   The (BDS_n, BDS) combination tests the presence of a strong degradation during the training. From Table 3, performance deteriorates as the noise level during training increases from V_1 to V_5, confirming that strong corruption of the training images hampers the ability to learn features that transfer to clean inputs. Already at V_1, A ranges from 46.63% (MobileNet) to 58.60% (DenseNet121), with *MCC* between 28.07% and 39.64%. From V_2 onward, all models approach a low-performance regime: A falls to roughly (38–41)% and *MCC* to about (10–18)%, suggesting that training on moderately corrupted data yields representations that generalize poorly to clean images. Under heavier training noise (V_3–V_5), A remains close to chance-level behaviour (about (33–37)%), while *MCC* stays near zero and exhibits large variability, highlighting unstable learning and strong sensitivity to the particular train-

Table 2. Mean percentage and standard deviation of *A*, *P*, *F1*, *MCC* over 10 runs for the (BDS, BDS_n) combination.

(BDS, BDS_n)				
	$A\uparrow$	$P\uparrow$	$F1\uparrow$	$MCC\uparrow$
V_1				
DenseNet121	**57.50 ± 3.26**	63.36 ± 3.91	**54.65 ± 3.78**	**39.32 ± 4.27**
InceptionV3	54.67 ± 4.22	63.47 ± 4.17	50.93 ± 5.24	35.69 ± 5.58
MobileNet	43.50 ± 7.89	**64.75 ± 2.02**	34.24 ± 10.68	22.31 ± 10.34
VGG16	50.77 ± 9.71	64.50 ± 5.15	45.25 ± 13.33	31.90 ± 12.77
V_2				
DenseNet121	38.97 ± 6.09	48.63 ± 18.17	28.05 ± 8.68	**12.97 ± 8.67**
InceptionV3	**39.57 ± 5.32**	**50.54** ± 17.92	**30.90 ± 6.89**	12.26 ± 9.40
MobileNet	37.34 ± 3.76	46.13 ± 19.61	25.79 ± 7.08	9.76 ± 5.58
VGG16	39.00 ± 5.59	**59.55 ± 13.07**	27.24 ± 8.40	14.58 ± 8.35
V_3				
DenseNet121	34.97 ± 4.16	33.30 ± 15.86	21.34 ± 6.76	4.46 ± 7.14
InceptionV3	35.47 ± 3.46	31.95 ± 12.99	**25.48 ± 5.04**	4.71 ± 6.45
MobileNet	34.83 ± 1.91	33.34 ± 17.82	22.02 ± 5.21	3.93 ± 4.03
VGG16	**35.77 ± 4.95**	**48.06 ± 17.65**	23.48 ± 6.54	**7.02 ± 9.69**
V_4				
DenseNet121	**34.16 ± 4.20**	18.74 ± 16.70	19.36 ± 6.34	1.11 ± 7.55
InceptionV3	33.47 ± 1.11	19.78 ± 5.95	**21.71 ± 4.51**	0.14 ± 3.51
MobileNet	33.97 ± 1.26	26.52 ± 14.71	20.74 ± 4.72	**1.77 ± 2.87**
VGG16	32.30 ± 5.57	**30.80 ± 19.24**	19.99 ± 3.75	0.49 ± 12.21
V_5				
DenseNet121	**35.16 ± 4.07**	17.56 ± 10.13	20.45 ± 6.93	**3.41 ± 7.56**
InceptionV3	33.37 ± 1.28	21.03 ± 10.33	**20.95 ± 4.20**	0.77 ± 3.17
MobileNet	33.40 ± 0.64	22.22 ± 14.41	19.74 ± 3.76	0.57 ± 3.20
VGG16	32.00 ± 5.68	**22.93 ± 16.69**	19.21 ± 4.76	-1.17 ± 13.14

ing run. Comparing architectures, no single CM dominates at all levels, but DenseNet121 tends to achieve the best performance at mild noise (V_1) and remains competitive across the table. MobileNet occasionally yields higher *F1* (e.g., V_5), yet its lower Accuracy at mild noise suggests a less reliable overall behaviour. The increasing standard deviations—especially for *P*, *F1*, and *MCC*—indicate that training on highly noisy data not only reduces mean performance but also makes results less reproducible across runs.

3. (BDS_n, BDS_n) (cfr. Table 4)
The (BDS_n, BDS_n) combination tests whether models can adapt when both training and testing share the same noise level. From Table 4, compared with

Table 3. Mean percentage and standard deviation of *A*, *P*, *F1*, *MCC* over 10 runs for the (BDS_n, BDS) combination.

(BDS_n, BDS)				
	$A\uparrow$	$P\uparrow$	$F1\uparrow$	$MCC\uparrow$
V_1				
DenseNet121	**58.60 ± 3.75**	59.98 ± 5.29	**56.40 ± 4.26**	**39.64 ± 5.88**
InceptionV3	52.40 ± 5.61	58.71 ± 4.83	48.81 ± 6.27	33.21 ± 7.33
MobileNet	46.63 ± 4.65	**63.99 ± 3.75**	40.28 ± 7.07	28.07 ± 5.56
VGG16	50.97 ± 11.28	61.72 ± 9.95	45.18 ± 16.17	32.24 ± 14.22
V_2				
DenseNet121	38.43 ± 4.79	53.34 ± 15.42	28.38 ± 5.74	12.69 ± 7.32
InceptionV3	38.20 ± 3.72	48.65 ± 14.95	28.47 ± 5.07	10.14 ± 6.71
MobileNet	**41.27 ± 4.69**	52.31 ± 8.21	**33.83 ± 9.36**	16.30 ± 5.62
VGG16	40.50 ± 7.33	**61.03 ± 10.86**	29.79 ± 10.53	**17.70 ± 11.05**
V_3				
DenseNet121	35.80 ± 4.04	34.39 ± 11.33	21.95 ± 4.58	5.76 ± 8.24
InceptionV3	35.67 ± 4.15	42.61 ± 16.82	25.97 ± 5.12	7.06 ± 9.02
MobileNet	**37.37 ± 4.34**	**44.22 ± 11.23**	**27.42 ± 8.58**	**9.11 ± 7.33**
VGG16	34.80 ± 1.68	42.94 ± 19.78	19.79 ± 3.37	7.30 ± 5.82
V_4				
DenseNet121	35.87 ± 5.37	26.18 ± 11.38	21.33 ± 5.22	5.73 ± 8.73
InceptionV3	34.73 ± 4.50	32.24 ± 14.96	22.30 ± 4.24	4.27 ± 8.54
MobileNet	**36.57 ± 2.61**	**40.51 ± 9.89**	**26.29 ± 6.94**	**8.37 ± 4.25**
VGG16	34.76 ± 5.78	32.60 ± 16.52	22.36 ± 7.90	4.11 ± 11.90
V_5				
DenseNet121	33.80 ± 4.23	24.73 ± 15.16	20.15 ± 4.79	2.39 ± 7.18
InceptionV3	33.40 ± 3.06	17.80 ± 9.40	19.64 ± 2.94	0.04 ± 7.13
MobileNet	33.73 ± 3.49	33.19 ± 6.43	**26.80 ± 4.29**	1.55 ± 7.65
VGG16	**36.60 ± 6.65**	**35.68 ± 19.78**	24.65 ± 9.57	**5.82 ± 13.87**

the cross-condition scenarios, performance is generally higher and more stable because the train–test distributions are matched: the CMs are trained and tested under the same noise settings. At mild noise (V_1), all CMs achieve strong results, with accuracies around 69–73% and MCCs around 55–60%. InceptionV3 shows the best overall performance, reaching A = 73.40%, *F1* = 73.35%, and MCC = 60.24%. At moderate noise (V_2), all CMs exhibit a clear performance drop. However, InceptionV3 remains the most robust, with A = 71.67% and MCC = 57.93%, whereas MobileNet degrades more sharply, down to A = 5 6.37% and MCC = 36.96%. Interestingly, performance partially recovers at V_3 for several CMs. For instance, DenseNet121 and VGG16 achieve accuracy values of about 68%, suggesting that this noise level may act as a form of regularization when both the training and test data are similarly corrupted. Beyond this point, heavier perturbations (V_4–V_5) again reduce all metrics. The decline is most pronounced for MobileNet, which drops to $A = 51.87\%$ and $MCC = 29.72\%$ at V_5. Across runs, standard deviations tend to increase at higher noise levels—especially for MobileNet and VGG16—indicating reduced training stability under severe corruption. Overall, these results highlight the importance of distribution matching: when the noise characteristics are consistent across training and testing, models perform considerably better than when noise is present in only one of the two datasets.

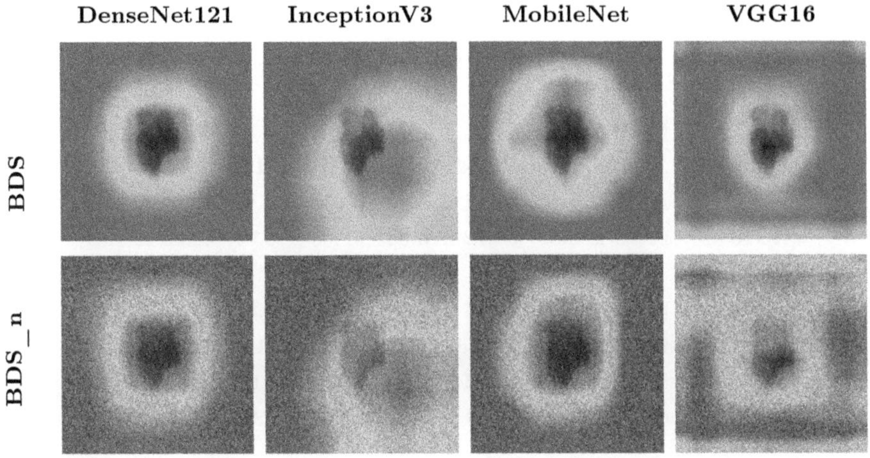

Fig. 2. Grad-CAM maps for all CMs on an example image under noise conditions. The maps highlight the regions that most strongly drive each model's prediction.

For each CM, Grad-CAM maps have been generated for all test images to examine the spatial patterns that guide the models' decisions. Figure 2 shows a representative example from the full collection of visualizations, highlighting how each CM allocates attention to lesion-relevant areas in both correctly and incorrectly classified samples, even under noisy conditions. The resulting attention maps indicate which image regions most strongly drive the model's predictions, revealing that CMs typically concentrate on clinically meaningful lesion structures and preserve coherent localization patterns despite noise.

Table 4. Mean percentage and standard deviation of A, P, $F1$, MCC over 10 runs for the (BDS_n, BDS_n) combination.

(BDS_n, BDS_n)				
	$A\uparrow$	$P\uparrow$	$F1\uparrow$	$MCC\uparrow$
V_1				
DenseNet121	71.73 ± 2.70	72.20 ± 2.54	71.76 ± 2.59	57.77 ± 4.06
InceptionV3	**73.40 ± 2.11**	73.63 ± 2.07	**73.35 ± 2.14**	**60.24 ± 3.11**
MobileNet	69.73 ± 4.22	70.39 ± 3.35	69.18 ± 4.99	55.17 ± 5.68
VGG16	71.83 ± 1.71	**73.64 ± 2.05**	71.85 ± 1.72	58.37 ± 2.55
V_2				
DenseNet121	67.60 ± 3.40	67.95 ± 3.41	67.44 ± 3.54	51.65 ± 5.02
InceptionV3	**71.67 ± 1.80**	**72.84 ± 2.04**	**71.73 ± 1.73**	**57.93 ± 2.79**
MobileNet	56.37 ± 6.13	60.44 ± 4.63	53.40 ± 7.84	36.96 ± 8.49
VGG16	68.10 ± 4.32	69.12 ± 3.63	67.63 ± 5.01	52.83 ± 5.81
V_3				
DenseNet121	68.63 ± 2.35	69.04 ± 2.19	68.37 ± 2.55	53.31 ± 3.33
InceptionV3	**69.07 ± 1.47**	**70.23 ± 1.28**	**68.95 ± 1.47**	**54.13 ± 2.08**
MobileNet	55.30 ± 4.22	59.83 ± 2.84	52.72 ± 6.01	36.10 ± 5.11
VGG16	68.00 ± 2.89	69.81 ± 2.71	67.93 ± 3.02	52.73 ± 4.10
V_4				
DenseNet121	64.90 ± 4.29	65.65 ± 4.11	64.40 ± 4.90	47.93 ± 6.02
InceptionV3	**68.60 ± 1.41**	**70.14 ± 1.29**	**68.59 ± 1.42**	**53.49 ± 2.02**
MobileNet	60.23 ± 7.63	61.73 ± 6.57	59.16 ± 8.51	41.49 ± 10.88
VGG16	62.77 ± 7.05	68.73 ± 3.19	61.11 ± 9.55	46.50 ± 8.90
V_5				
DenseNet121	**65.67 ± 1.78**	66.30 ± 2.08	**65.35 ± 2.02**	**48.95 ± 2.63**
InceptionV3	65.20 ± 3.11	**66.74 ± 3.76**	64.68 ± 3.04	48.67 ± 4.92
MobileNet	51.87 ± 4.27	54.51 ± 4.95	49.30 ± 6.00	29.72 ± 5.72
VGG16	62.60 ± 7.60	64.82 ± 10.65	60.47 ± 11.13	47.94 ± 6.64

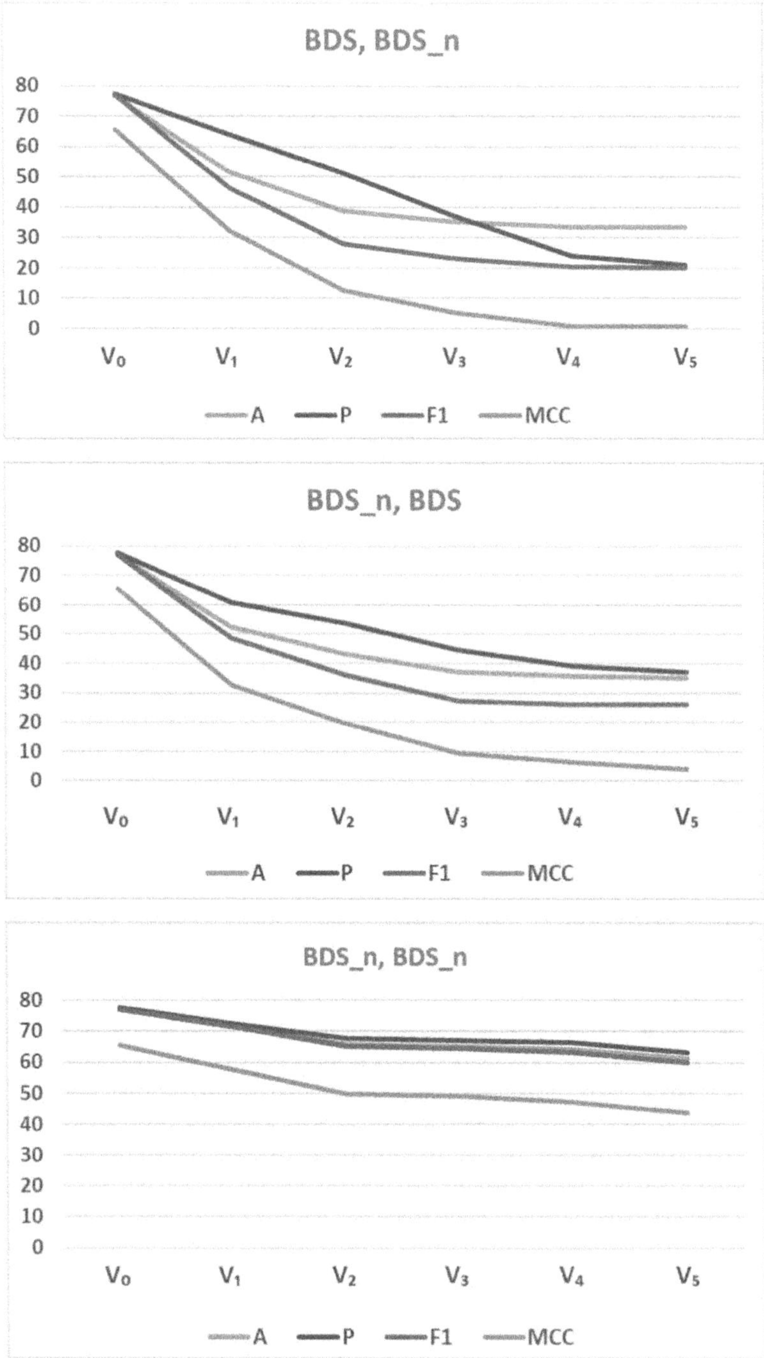

Fig. 3. Trend curve of noise effect with: (a) training on BDS and test on BDS_n, (b) training on BDS_n and test on BDS, and (c) training and test on degraded datasets BDS_n.

Figure 3 provides a compact visualization of the metrics for each train–test combination. The trend curves highlight the effect of increasing Gaussian noise across the experimental combinations. When training and testing conditions are mismatched—i.e., in (BDS, BDS_n) or (BDS_n, BDS)—performance drops sharply as the noise level increases from V_1 to V_5. In the (BDS, BDS_n) combination, all metrics deteriorate rapidly: *A* and *F1* fall from the baseline (V_0) to low values already at V_1, and *MCC* collapses toward zero at strong noise levels (V_4–V_5), indicating little to no agreement with the reference annotations. A similar decline is observed in (BDS_n, BDS), confirming that learning on heavily corrupted inputs does not transfer well to clean images, and that noise-induced domain shift is highly detrimental. In contrast, the matched setting (BDS_n, BDS_n) exhibits a markedly more stable behaviour. Although a moderate decrease is visible as noise increases, the models retain substantially higher *A*/*F1* and, crucially, consistently positive, comparatively high *MCC* values across all levels. This indicates that when the noise characteristics of the training and test data are aligned, networks can learn noise-adapted representations and maintain robust decision boundaries even under severe perturbations. Overall, these results suggest that training–test condition misalignment is more detrimental than degradation alone.

Beyond the global trends, architectural differences also emerge. Under mismatched conditions, lightweight architectures tend to degrade more abruptly, whereas deeper models exhibit greater resilience to mild-to-moderate noise. Conversely, in the matched (BDS_n, BDS_n) regime, all architectures exhibit lower performance fluctuations, suggesting more reliable learning despite corruption.

From a practical standpoint, these results underscore the importance of accounting for noise at training time to reduce domain shift and improve robustness in real-world skin lesion classification settings.

5 Conclusion

This study investigates the susceptibility of CNN-based skin lesion classifiers to additive Gaussian noise. Experiments across four representative architectures show that the extent of performance degradation is largely determined by the alignment between training and testing conditions.

In the mismatched settings -either training on clean data and testing on noisy images or training on noisy data and testing on clean images - all metrics deteriorate rapidly as noise increases. In particular, robustness collapses at moderate-to-high corruption levels, with *MCC* approaching zero (and occasionally becoming very small), suggesting that each CM becomes nearly unreliable when training and test conditions are misaligned.

By contrast, when noise is consistently present in both training and testing, the models exhibit substantially more stable behaviour, retaining comparatively high *A*/*F1* and consistently positive *MCC* values even at higher degradation levels. These results confirm that distribution mismatch is more detrimental than the noise itself and that CNNs can adapt effectively when trained on representative corruptions.

Overall, the findings emphasize the need to explicitly account for variations in image quality in skin lesion classification pipelines. From a practical perspective, the results suggest the following guidelines for designing more robust classifiers: (1) characterize as realistically as possible the image-quality conditions expected at deployment time; (2) reduce train-test mismatch by incorporating representative corruptions during training; (3) evaluate models under both matched and mismatched corruption settings rather than only on clean test images; and (4) prefer architectures and training strategies that preserve stable MCC and F1 values under progressive degradation. Accordingly, noise-aware training, realistic augmentation, acquisition standardization, domain adaptation, and possibly preprocessing or ensemble strategies appear as promising directions for improving robustness in real clinical scenarios.

Taken together, these guidelines and design principles provide a practical basis for developing more reliable skin lesion classifiers and highlight the need for further research on robustness-oriented training and evaluation protocols.

Acknowledgements. The research has been partially supported by the Gruppo Nazionale per il Calcolo Scientifico, Istituto Nazionale di Alta Matematica (GNCS INdAM).

Disclosure of Interests. The authors have no competing interests to declare that are relevant to the content of this article.

References

1. Babatunde, A.N., Balogun, B.F., Babatunde, A.J., Isiaka, S.O., Awotunde, J.B., Adeniyi, A.E.: Improving skin lesion classification using k-means, transfer learning and mobilenet architecture. Network Modeling Analysis in Health Informatics and Bioinformatics **14**, 70 (2025). https://doi.org/10.1007/s13721-025-00569-3
2. Bijoy, M.H.I., Rahman, M.M., Sattar, A., Haque, A., Arefin, M.S., K, D.P., Shimamura, T.: Skinincept: an ensemble transfer learning-based approach for multiclass skin disease classification using inceptionv3 and inceptionresnetv2. Discover Appl. Sci. **7**, 433 (2025). https://doi.org/10.1007/s42452-025-06596-z
3. Bruni, V., Ramella, G., Vitulano, D.: Automatic perceptual color quantization of dermoscopic images. In: VISAPP 2015 - 10th International Conference on Computer Vision Theory and Applications; VISIGRAPP, Proceedings, vol. 1, p. 323–330 (2015). https://doi.org/10.5220/0005304903230330
4. Chaki, J., Ucar, A.: Current Applications of Deep Learning in Cancer Diagnostics. CRC Press, Boca Raton, FL (2023). https://doi.org/10.1201/9781003277002
5. Chow, L.S., Paramesran, R.: Review of medical image quality assessment. Biomed. Signal Process. Control **27**, 145–154 (2016). https://doi.org/10.1016/j.bspc.2016.02.006
6. Codella, N., et al.: Skin lesion analysis toward melanoma detection 2018: a challenge hosted by the international skin imaging collaboration (ISIC). ArXiv (2018). https://arxiv.org/abs/1902.03368
7. Faghihi, A., Fathollahi, M., Rajabi, R.: Diagnosis of skin cancer using vgg16 and vgg19 based transfer learning models. Multimedia Tools Appl. **83**, 57495–57510 (2024). https://doi.org/10.1007/s11042-023-17735-2

8. Hasan, M.K., Ahamad, M.A., Yap, C.H., Yang, G.: A survey, review, and future trends of skin lesion segmentation and classification. Comput. Biol. Med. **155**, 106624 (2023). https://doi.org/10.1016/j.compbiomed.2023.106624
9. Hoang, V.D., Vo, X.T., Jo, K.H.: Categorical weighting domination for imbalanced classification with skin cancer in intelligent healthcare systems. IEEE Access **11**, 105170–105181 (2023). https://doi.org/10.1109/ACCESS.2023.3319087
10. Howard, A.G., et al.: Mobilenets: efficient convolutional neural networks for mobile vision applications. arXiv: abs/1704.04861 (2017). https://api.semanticscholar.org/CorpusID:12670695
11. Huang, G., Liu, Z., Van Der Maaten, L., Weinberger, K.: Densely connected convolutional networks. In: 2017 IEEE Conference on Computer Vision and Pattern Recognition (CVPR), pp. 2261–2269 (2017). https://doi.org/10.1109/CVPR.2017.243
12. Kamal, M., Al-Atabany, W.: Mpdenoisenet: Resource-efficient deep learning approach for image denoising. Neural Process. Lett. **58**, 7 (2026). https://doi.org/10.1007/s11063-025-11803-4, article number 7
13. Larasati, S.S.A., Rahmaniati, A.F., Ms, F.I.S., Utomo, Y.C., Ariadi, F., Utaminingrum, F.: Advancement in deep learning for skin detection: a comprehensive review. Biomed. Signal Process. Control **112**, 108738 (2026). https://doi.org/10.1016/j.bspc.2025.108738
14. Ramella, G.: Automatic skin lesion segmentation based on saliency and color. In: Proceedings of the 15th International Joint Conference on Computer Vision, Imaging and Computer Graphics Theory and Applications (VISIGRAPP 2020) - Volume 4: VISAPP, pp. 452–459. INSTICC, SciTePress (2020). https://doi.org/10.5220/0009144904520459
15. Ramella, G., Sanniti di Baja, G.: Image segmentation based on representative colors detection and region merging. In: Carrasco-Ochoa, J.A., Martínez-Trinidad, J.F., Rodríguez, J.S., di Baja, G.S. (eds.) MCPR 2013. LNCS, vol. 7914, pp. 175–184. Springer, Heidelberg (2013). https://doi.org/10.1007/978-3-642-38989-4_18
16. Ramella, G., Serino, L.: Cnn issues in skin lesion classification: data distribution and quantity. IEEE Access **13**, 58848–58862 (2025). https://doi.org/10.1109/ACCESS.2025.3556479
17. Simonyan, K., Zisserman, A.: Very deep convolutional networks for large-scale image recognition. CoRR abs/1409.1556 (2014)
18. Szegedy, C., Vanhoucke, V., Ioffe, S., Shlens, J., Wojna, Z.: Rethinking the inception architecture for computer vision. In: 2016 IEEE Conference on Computer Vision and Pattern Recognition (CVPR), pp. 2818–2826 (2016). https://doi.org/10.1109/CVPR.2016.308
19. Zhang, K., Guo, Y., Wang, X., Yuan, J., Ding, Q.: Multiple feature reweight densenet for image classification. IEEE Access **7**, 9872–9880 (2019). https://doi.org/10.1109/ACCESS.2018.2890127

A Machine Learning Pipeline for Freight Transport Pricing

Alessandro Bottino[1,2], Salvatore Cuomo[1], and Vincenzo Vocca[1(✉)]

[1] Università degli Studi di Napoli Federico II, Napoli, Italy
vincenzo.vocca@unina.it

[2] Istituto per la Protezione Sostenibile delle Piante, Consiglio Nazionale delle Ricerche (CNR), Portici, NA, Italy

Abstract. Freight pricing in brokerage platforms is a challenging regression problem characterised by high heterogeneity across shipment types, temporal non-stationarity of costs, and sparse multi-quotation structures. We present an end-to-end machine learning pipeline that addresses these challenges through four methodological contributions: (i) a domain-driven price actualisation formula that decomposes inflation into fuel and macroeconomic components; (ii) a similarity-based matching algorithm that groups single-quotation orders with comparable shipments, enriching the effective training signal; (iii) a stratified modelling strategy that trains separate Random Forest regressors for three structurally distinct shipment categories—Full Truck Load, Less-than-Truck Load, and Groupage; and (iv) a Gaussian Mixture Model-based confidence estimator that quantifies prediction reliability. Evaluated on a real-world dataset of approximately 58,000 historical quotations spanning nine years, our system achieves a Mean Absolute Percentage Error of 3.23% for full loads, 5.60% for partial loads, and 10.76% for groupage shipments on a held-out temporal test set, representing a 57–68% relative improvement over the incumbent rule-based pricing engine.

Keywords: freight pricing · random forest regression · feature engineering · similarity matching · confidence estimation · transportation logistics

1 Introduction

The freight transport industry constitutes a fundamental pillar of global supply chains, with road freight accounting for over 75% of inland goods transport in the European Union [8]. Within this market, *brokerage platforms* act as intermediaries between shippers and carriers, collecting transport requests and soliciting competitive quotations. A critical challenge for such platforms is accurate price estimation: underestimates lead to unprofitable contracts, while overestimates risk losing shippers to competitors.

Traditional pricing engines are rule-based systems that query historical transactions within tolerance windows and return weighted averages of normalised

B. Vantaggi et al. (Eds.): IPMU 2026, CCIS 3019, pp. 423–438, 2026.
https://doi.org/10.1007/978-3-032-28994-0_30

costs. These systems suffer from structural limitations: (i) they cannot capture non-linear feature interactions; (ii) they degrade when queries fall outside well-populated regions; and (iii) they provide no prediction uncertainty measure.

We propose a complete machine learning pipeline addressing these limitations through four methodological components:

C1 Price actualisation. A decomposition formula adjusting historical prices for fuel and macroeconomic inflation (Sect. 4).
C2 Similarity matching. An algorithm grouping single-quotation orders with comparable shipments, enriching the training signal (Sect. 5).
C3 Stratified modelling. Independent Random Forest regressors for FTL, LTL, and Groupage categories, respecting distinct pricing dynamics (Sect. 6).
C4 Confidence estimation. A GMM-calibrated score providing per-prediction reliability (Sect. 6).

Evaluated on ~58,000 quotations over nine years with a temporal train-test split, the system achieves MAPE of 3.23%, 5.60%, and 10.76% for the three categories, representing 57–68% improvement over the rule-based engine.

The paper is organised as follows. Section 2 surveys related work. Section 3 formalises the problem. Sections 4–6 describe the pipeline. Section 7 presents experimental results, and Sect. 8 concludes.

2 Related Work

Freight Rate Prediction
Early approaches to freight cost estimation relied on hedonic pricing models [3], decomposing price as a linear function of shipment attributes. More recently, Lindsey et al. [11] demonstrated that gradient boosted trees outperform linear benchmarks for truckload pricing when interaction effects are significant, while Wang et al. [18] applied deep learning to maritime spot-rate forecasting.

Random Forests in Regression
Random forests [4] remain among the most effective ensemble methods for tabular regression, combining robustness to overfitting with native mixed-type feature handling. Their theoretical consistency under mild regularity conditions has been established, and they have been successfully applied to travel time prediction and demand forecasting in the transportation domain.

Outlier Detection and Data Cleaning
The IQR method [15] provides a robust, non-parametric outlier criterion. Its stratified variant—computing thresholds within homogeneous subgroups—is advocated when distributions vary across categories [5,9].

Similarity Matching
Enriching sparse labels through similarity-based grouping connects to the broader literature on semi-supervised learning [6]. In logistics, lane-based clustering pools shipments along similar corridors for stable rate estimates [14].

Confidence Estimation
For ensemble methods, tree-prediction dispersion provides a natural epistemic uncertainty measure [17]. Gaussian Mixture Models [2] offer flexible target-distribution modelling for confidence calibration.

Price Index Adjustment
Temporal price adjustment is standard in procurement analytics. In the transport sector, composite indices blending fuel costs with sectoral deflators are widely adopted [10]. Our actualisation formula draws on this tradition, combining weekly fuel prices with quarterly B2B transport service indices.

Our work differs from the above in its *integrated* treatment: from raw quotations through price actualisation, similarity-based label enrichment, stratified modelling, and calibrated confidence estimation—a combination that, to our knowledge, has not been previously addressed.

3 Problem Formulation

We frame freight pricing as a supervised regression problem over a historical dataset of carrier quotations. The three shipment categories—FTL, LTL, and GRP—exhibit fundamentally different pricing structures, motivating a stratified treatment with one model per category.

3.1 Mathematical Framework

Let $\mathcal{D} = \{(\mathbf{x}_i, y_i)\}_{i=1}^{N}$ denote a dataset of N transport quotations, where $\mathbf{x}_i \in \mathcal{X} \subseteq \mathbb{R}^d$ is the feature vector and $y_i \in \mathbb{R}_{>0}$ the associated price. Each quotation belongs to an *order* $o_i \in \mathbb{N}$; multiple quotations may share the same order id, reflecting competing carrier bids. The feature space $\mathcal{X}$ comprises continuous attributes (route distance, cargo weight, computed cargo space, latitudinal displacement, truck occupancy fraction), categorical attributes (shipment category, transport type, equipment configuration, island/international flags, pallet class), and temporal attributes (order month, fuel price, macroeconomic coefficient).

The goal is to learn $f : \mathcal{X} \rightarrow \mathbb{R}_{>0}$ minimising:

$$\min_{f \in \mathcal{F}} \mathbb{E}_{(\mathbf{x},y)\sim P} \left[\ell(y, f(\mathbf{x}))\right]. \tag{1}$$

We adopt the Mean Absolute Error (MAE) as training criterion and the Mean Absolute Percentage Error (MAPE) as evaluation metric:

$$\text{MAPE} = \frac{100}{n} \sum_{i=1}^{n} \frac{|y_i - \hat{y}_i|}{|y_i| + \varepsilon}. \tag{2}$$

The per-category decomposition yields three independent sub-problems:

$$f_c : \mathcal{X}_c \rightarrow \mathbb{R}_{>0}, \qquad c \in \{\text{FTL}, \text{LTL}, \text{GRP}\}. \tag{3}$$

3.2 Temporal Evaluation Protocol

Prices evolve over time due to fuel fluctuations, regulatory changes, and market dynamics. A random train-test split would introduce look-ahead bias. We therefore adopt a **temporal split**: given a cutoff time t^*,

$$\mathcal{D}_{\text{train}} = \{(\mathbf{x}_i, y_i) : t_i \leq t^*\}, \tag{4}$$

$$\mathcal{D}_{\text{test}} = \{(\mathbf{x}_i, y_i) : t_i > t^*\}, \tag{5}$$

ensuring that evaluation faithfully simulates the deployment scenario.

4 Data Preprocessing and Feature Engineering

The raw dataset comprises $N = 58{,}294$ quotation records spanning approximately nine years of platform operations (2016–2025), with over 25 raw fields per record. Preprocessing addresses three challenges: data quality, temporal non-stationarity of prices, and feature representation. After cleaning and filtering, the dataset is reduced to approximately 35,000 records; the full pipeline yields $\sim$39,000 training records following similarity matching (Sect. 5).

4.1 Price Actualisation

A central challenge is the *temporal non-stationarity* of transport costs: a quotation of EUR 500 in 2017 corresponds to a different economic reality than the same amount in 2024. Training on raw prices would bias the model, as older records appear systematically cheaper.

Definition 1 (Actualised price). *Given a quotation with price y^{raw} at time t, fuel price p_t^{fuel}, and macroeconomic coefficient γ_t, the actualised price is:*

$$y^{\text{act}} = y^{\text{raw}} \cdot \left(\alpha \cdot \frac{p_{\text{now}}^{\text{fuel}}}{p_t^{\text{fuel}}} + \beta \cdot \frac{\gamma_t}{\gamma_{\text{now}}} \right), \tag{6}$$

where $\alpha, \beta > 0$ with $\alpha + \beta = 1$ are mixing weights.

The formula decomposes temporal adjustment into two channels:

- **Fuel component** ($\alpha = 0.3$): the ratio $p_{\text{now}}^{\text{fuel}}/p_t^{\text{fuel}}$ captures direct fuel cost impact, sourced from the Italian Ministry of Environment weekly diesel price data.
- **Macroeconomic component** ($\beta = 0.7$): the ratio $\gamma_t/\gamma_{\text{now}}$ accounts for labour, insurance, depreciation, and regulatory costs, derived from the quarterly ISTAT B2B transport price index [10] (ATECO 494, base year 2021).

The weights reflect the empirical share of fuel in total operating expenses ($\approx$25–35%), consistent with ECMT estimates [7].

Proposition 1 (Consistency). *If $p_t^{\text{fuel}} = p_{\text{now}}^{\text{fuel}}$ and $\gamma_t = \gamma_{\text{now}}$ for all t, then $y^{\text{act}} = y^{\text{raw}}$.*

Proof. Immediate from (6) with $\alpha + \beta = 1$.

4.2 Data Preparation and Feature Engineering

Data Cleaning. Columns with systematic missingness are imputed from alternative fields where available. Records missing critical columns (distance, weight, coordinates, category) are dropped. Domain constraints eliminate data entry errors: $|\lambda|, |\varphi| \leq 100$; $w \geq 20$ kg; $d \geq 20$ km; $y \in [20, 7000]$ EUR; order date $\geq$ January 2016.

Computed Features. The computed cargo space is defined as:

$$s = \max\left(\frac{w}{\kappa}, A\right), \quad \kappa = \begin{cases} 0.0919 & \text{Italy–Italy,} \\ 0.0735 & \text{EU cross-border,} \end{cases} \tag{7}$$

where A is the declared cargo area and κ derives from the ratio of payload capacity to standard semi-trailer area (1360 × 240 cm), accounting for Italian (30,000 kg) vs. European (24,000 kg) weight limits. Truck occupancy is $\rho = s/S_{\max}$ with $S_{\max} = 340{,}000\ \text{cm}^2$. The directional feature $\delta^{\text{lat}} = \varphi_{\text{dest}} - \varphi_{\text{orig}}$ captures North–South route directionality, which influences pricing due to asymmetric demand [13]. For Groupage, a pallet class $\pi \in \{1, \ldots, 8\}$ is assigned via a joint height–weight scheme. Equipment type is reduced to its dominant category and one-hot encoded; transport type is multi-label binarised into 28 indicator variables.

Outlier Removal. A two-stage strategy is applied after actualisation but before matching. *Stage 1* applies domain filters on normalised cost metrics (cost per km, per kg, and normalised cost index $c_{\text{norm}} = 10^5 \cdot y^{\text{act}}/(d \cdot s)$) with category-specific bounds. *Stage 2* applies a stratified IQR criterion: within each category, for each metric v:

$$Q_{50} - k \cdot \text{IQR}_{50,85} \leq v \leq Q_{85} + k \cdot \text{IQR}_{50,85}, \tag{8}$$

with $k = 1.0$. The asymmetric quantiles (Q_{50}–Q_{85}) reflect right-skewed cost distributions.

5 Similarity Matching and Label Enrichment

Approximately 72% of orders in the dataset are associated with a single quotation, providing a weak training signal. Orders with multiple quotations allow robust "market price" estimation via the median bid. We address this sparsity through a three-phase similarity matching algorithm that groups structurally similar orders, enriching the effective training signal. After matching, ∼16,750 of 19,250 singletons are successfully matched, yielding a final training set of ∼39,000 records.

5.1 Matching Algorithm

Matching Rule.

Definition 2. (Matching rule). *A matching rule* $\mathcal{R} = (\mathcal{E}, \mathcal{T})$ *consists of exact-match keys* $\mathcal{E} = \{e_1, \ldots, e_p\}$ *(categorical features that must coincide) and tolerance-based features* $\mathcal{T} = \{(v_j, \tau_j, \sigma_j)\}_{j=1}^{q}$ *(numerical features with tolerance* $\tau_j > 0$ *and type* $\sigma_j \in \{abs, rel\}$*).*

In our implementation:

$$\mathcal{E} = \{\texttt{tipo\_pallet},\ \texttt{tipo\_carico},\ \texttt{is\_isola},\ \texttt{estero}\}, \tag{9}$$

$$\mathcal{T} = \{(\rho, 0.05, \text{abs}),\ (\tau_{\text{tass}}, 0.05, \text{abs}),\ (d, 0.10, \text{rel}),\ (\delta^{\text{lat}}, 0.30, \text{rel})\}. \tag{10}$$

The tolerance semantics for a pair (i, j):

$$\text{match}(v_i, v_j) = \begin{cases} |v_i - v_j| \le \tau & \text{if } \sigma = \text{abs}, \\ |v_i - v_j| \le \tau \cdot |v_i| & \text{if } \sigma = \text{rel}. \end{cases} \tag{11}$$

Three-Phase Procedure. Phase 1 (Partition): Orders are split into base orders $\mathcal{B} = \{o : n_q(o) \ge 2\}$ and singletons $\mathcal{S} = \{o : n_q(o) = 1\}$. A representative feature vector is computed for each (medians for numerics, first valid value for categoricals). *Phase 2 (Best-match assignment):* For each singleton s and each base group sharing the same exact keys, a normalised score is computed:

$$\text{score}(s, b) = \sum_{j=1}^{q} \frac{|v_j^{(s)} - v_j^{(b)}|}{\tau_j(s)}. \tag{12}$$

The singleton is assigned to the base with minimum score, provided all tolerances are satisfied:

$$b^*(s) = \arg\min_{b \in \mathcal{B}_{\mathcal{E}(s)}} \text{score}(s, b) \quad \text{s.t.} \quad \forall j : \text{match}(v_j^{(s)}, v_j^{(b)}). \tag{13}$$

Phase 3 (Singleton clustering): Unmatched singletons are clustered via bucketing: each tolerance-feature vector is discretised into a hash key,

$$h(v_j) = \begin{cases} \lfloor v_j / \tau_j \rfloor & \text{if } \sigma_j = \text{abs}, \\ (\text{sgn}(v_j),\ \lfloor \ln|v_j| / \ln(1 + \tau_j) \rfloor) & \text{if } \sigma_j = \text{rel}, \end{cases} \tag{14}$$

and singletons sharing a bucket are grouped, achieving $O(|\mathcal{S}|)$ complexity per group.

Target Calibration.

Definition 3 (Calibrated target). *For group* g *with quotations* $\{(y_i^{\text{act}}, d_i, s_i)\}_{i \in g}$*, the normalised cost median is* $\tilde{c}_g = \text{median}_{i \in g}\{10^5 \cdot y_i^{\text{act}} / (d_i \cdot s_i)\}$*, and the calibrated target is:*

$$\tilde{y}_i = \frac{\tilde{c}_g \cdot d_i \cdot s_i}{10^5}. \tag{15}$$

This normalisation ensures that medians across structurally similar orders are meaningful regardless of shipment size, effectively denoising labels while preserving feature diversity.

5.2 Complexity and Effect on Label Quality

The algorithm is designed to scale to the dataset size. Phase 1 requires a single $O(N)$ pass; Phase 2 operates within exact-key groups, with worst-case $O(|\mathcal{S}|\cdot|\mathcal{B}|)$ per group but typically much less due to partitioning; Phase 3 bucketing runs in $O(|\mathcal{S}|)$ by construction. A pre-grouping step indexes base orders by their exact-key tuple, restricting Phase 2 comparisons to candidates sharing all categorical features.

Matching has two complementary effects on training data quality. First, it increases the *effective sample size*: orders that would have contributed a single noisy quotation instead contribute a group-level median that captures market consensus. Second, it reduces *label variance* within similar shipments: the normalised-cost calibration (Definition 3) ensures that $\tilde{y}_i$ varies smoothly with shipment geometry. The matched singletons account for ~43% of the final training set; removing them increases FTL MAPE by +2.64 percentage points (Sect. 7), confirming that this label enrichment is a substantial contributor to overall accuracy.

6 Modelling

Three independent Random Forest regressors are trained, one per category $c \in \{\text{FTL}, \text{LTL}, \text{GRP}\}$. Each is embedded in a scikit-learn pipeline comprising a column transformer (median imputation for numerics, mode imputation + one-hot encoding for categoricals) followed by a `RandomForestRegressor`. This stratified design respects the fundamentally different pricing structures of each category, as confirmed by the feature importance analysis of Sect. 7.

6.1 Random Forest Regressors

Feature Sets. All models share a common feature base (distance, weight, occupancy, directional displacement, island/international flags, equipment indicators, month). Groupage retains cargo height and maximum vehicle length, critical for pallet-level pricing; FTL/LTL exclude these, as the occupancy fraction ρ suffices. All models exclude target-derived columns, administrative identifiers, and raw coordinates.

Model. A Random Forest [4] constructs B regression trees $\{T_b\}_{b=1}^{B}$, each on a bootstrap sample with random feature subsampling. The prediction is:

$$\hat{y}(\mathbf{x}) = \frac{1}{B}\sum_{b=1}^{B} T_b(\mathbf{x}). \tag{16}$$

The MAE splitting criterion is preferred over MSE for two reasons: (i) the price distribution is right-skewed, with large orders that MSE would disproportionately weight; and (ii) MAE-trained leaves approximate conditional medians, aligning the training objective with the normalised-cost calibration.

Hyperparameters. The number of trees $B = 750$ was selected via grid search over $\{200, 500, 750, 1000\}$ on a held-out validation fold; performance stabilises beyond $B = 500$. The 750-tree setting keeps inference latency under 50 ms per request via the REST API. The maximum feature fraction per split follows the scikit-learn default of $d/3$ for regressors, providing good bias-variance trade-off for this tabular dimensionality.

Training and Inference Pipeline. At training time, for each category c: (i) apply the column transformer; (ii) fit RF_c on $\mathcal{D}_{\mathrm{train},c}$ with calibrated targets $\tilde{y}$; (iii) fit a GMM on $\{\tilde{y}_i\}_{i\in\mathcal{D}_{\mathrm{train},c}}$. At inference time, given a new request $\mathbf{x}$: (i) apply the column transformer (fitted on training data only); (ii) obtain B tree predictions and compute $\hat{y}(\mathbf{x})$, $\hat{\sigma}_{\mathrm{pred}}(\mathbf{x})$, and $\mathrm{PI}_{50}(\mathbf{x})$; (iii) compute $\mathrm{conf}(\mathbf{x})$ and return $(\hat{y}, \mathrm{conf}, \mathrm{PI}_{50})$ to the caller. This design ensures that the inference path is stateless and thread-safe, enabling horizontal scaling.

6.2 Uncertainty Estimation

Tree-Level Variance. The dispersion of individual tree predictions estimates epistemic uncertainty [17]:

$$\hat{\sigma}_{\mathrm{pred}}(\mathbf{x}) = \left[\frac{1}{B-1}\sum_{b=1}^{B}\left(T_b(\mathbf{x}) - \hat{y}(\mathbf{x})\right)^2\right]^{1/2}. \tag{17}$$

GMM-Based Target Scale. The training-set target distribution is modelled as a Gaussian Mixture [2]:

$$p(y) = \sum_{k=1}^{K} \pi_k \mathcal{N}(y \mid \mu_k, \sigma_k^2), \tag{18}$$

with $K \in \{1, \ldots, 4\}$ selected by BIC. The global mixture standard deviation provides the reference scale:

$$\sigma_{\mathrm{target}} = \sqrt{\sum_{k=1}^{K} \pi_k \left(\sigma_k^2 + (\mu_k - \bar{\mu})^2\right)}. \tag{19}$$

Confidence Score.

$$\mathrm{conf}(\mathbf{x}) = 1 - \frac{\hat{\sigma}_{\mathrm{pred}}(\mathbf{x})}{\hat{\sigma}_{\mathrm{pred}}(\mathbf{x}) + \sigma_{\mathrm{target}} + \varepsilon}, \tag{20}$$

where $\varepsilon > 0$ is a stabilisation constant. This score lies in $[0, 1]$: values near 1 indicate high tree agreement relative to target variability.

Proposition 2 (Monotonicity). *For fixed* σ_{target}*,* $\text{conf}(\mathbf{x})$ *is strictly decreasing in* $\hat{\sigma}_{\text{pred}}(\mathbf{x})$.

Proof. Let $g(\sigma) = 1 - \sigma/(\sigma + c)$ with $c = \sigma_{\text{target}} + \varepsilon > 0$. Then $g'(\sigma) = -c/(\sigma + c)^2 < 0$.

Additionally, per-prediction intervals are obtained from tree quantiles:

$$\text{PI}_\alpha(\mathbf{x}) = \left[Q_{\frac{100-\alpha}{2}}(\{T_b(\mathbf{x})\}),\ Q_{\frac{100+\alpha}{2}}(\{T_b(\mathbf{x})\}) \right], \tag{21}$$

with coverage $\alpha = 50\%$ in our experiments.

7 Experimental Results

The effective training dataset after preprocessing and matching comprises ~39,000 records: FTL (13,880), LTL (11,785), GRP (13,404). A temporal 90/10 split is adopted, with the test set consisting of the most recent orders. We compare against two baselines: (1) the **rule-based engine (RBE)**, the incumbent SQL system computing $\hat{y} = \bar{c}_{\text{km}} \cdot s \cdot d/1000$ over tolerance-matched historical records; and (2) a **preliminary ML (PML)** iteration using absolute tolerances, simple median targets, and no temporal split.

7.1 Performance Evaluation

Table 1. Test-set performance comparison (MAPE %/MAE in EUR).

	FTL		LTL		GRP	
System	MAPE	MAE	MAPE	MAE	MAPE	MAE
RBE	10.23	—	13.50	—	17.00	—
PML	7.56	—	11.91	—	14.81	—
Proposed	**3.23**	43.11	**5.60**	50.98	**10.76**	31.84

The proposed system achieves relative MAPE reductions of 68.4% (FTL), 58.5% (LTL), and 36.7% (GRP) over the rule-based engine, and 57.3%, 53.0%, 27.3% over the preliminary ML baseline. Training-set MAPE values of 1.26% (FTL), 2.32% (LTL), and 3.81% (GRP) indicate good generalisation without severe overfitting (Table 1).

Figure 1 displays the top-10 features by Gini importance. The differential importance profiles justify the stratified modelling approach: FTL is distance-dominated, while GRP pricing depends more evenly on multiple factors.

Figure 2 shows predicted vs. actual prices on the test set. Figure 3 validates the confidence estimator by partitioning test predictions into confidence bins: higher confidence consistently corresponds to lower APE, confirming Proposition 2. Predictions with conf > 0.7 exhibit median APE below 3% (FTL) and 8% (GRP), while low-confidence predictions should be flagged for human review.

7.2 Ablation Study and Discussion

Table 2 reports the impact of key components on FTL test-set MAPE. Each component contributes meaningfully: stratification yields the largest gain (+4.73 pp without it), followed by matching (+2.64 pp) and actualisation (+2.18 pp). The random-split result (2.81%) is optimistically biased, underscoring the necessity of temporal evaluation.

Table 2. Ablation study on FTL test-set MAPE (%).

Configuration	MAPE (%)
Full pipeline (proposed)	3.23
– Price actualisation	5.41
– Similarity matching	5.87
– Normalised-cost calibration	4.10
– Category stratification (single model)	7.96
– Temporal split (random split)	2.81

*Optimistically biased due to look-ahead leakage.

Category-Level Performance Gap. The GRP segment exhibits substantially higher error (10.76% MAPE) compared to FTL (3.23%) and LTL (5.60%). This is consistent with the more distributed feature importance profile seen in Fig. 1: Groupage pricing is governed by a richer set of interacting factors—pallet class, height, vehicle type, island surcharges, and destination—making the regression surface more complex. Furthermore, the Groupage market tends to pool shipments from multiple clients on a single truck, introducing additional pricing variability that is not fully captured by the available features.

Generalisation and Overfitting. The gap between training-set MAPE (1.26%, 2.32%, 3.81%) and test-set MAPE across all three categories remains bounded and proportionate, suggesting that the Random Forest is not severely overfitting despite the relatively small dataset size (13–14k records per category). This can be attributed to: (i) the bootstrapping and feature subsampling inherent to Random Forests; (ii) the normalised-cost calibration, which reduces label noise; and (iii) the temporal split, which prevents the model from memorising recent price patterns.

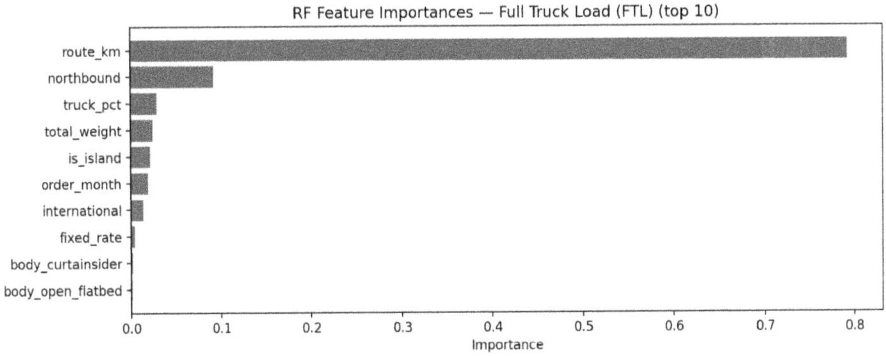

(a) FTL

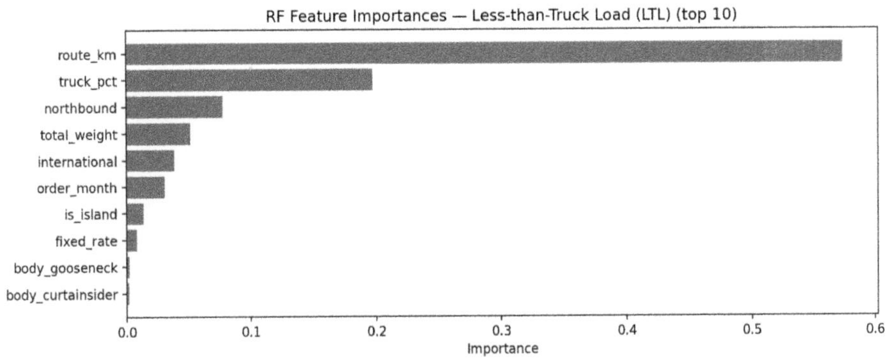

(b) LTL

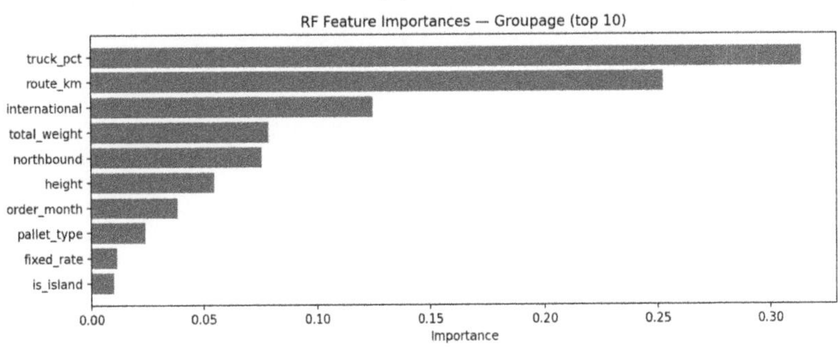

(c) GRP

Fig. 1. Feature importances (top 10). Route distance dominates FTL (> 60%), while GRP exhibits a more distributed importance profile across distance, space, weight, and direction.

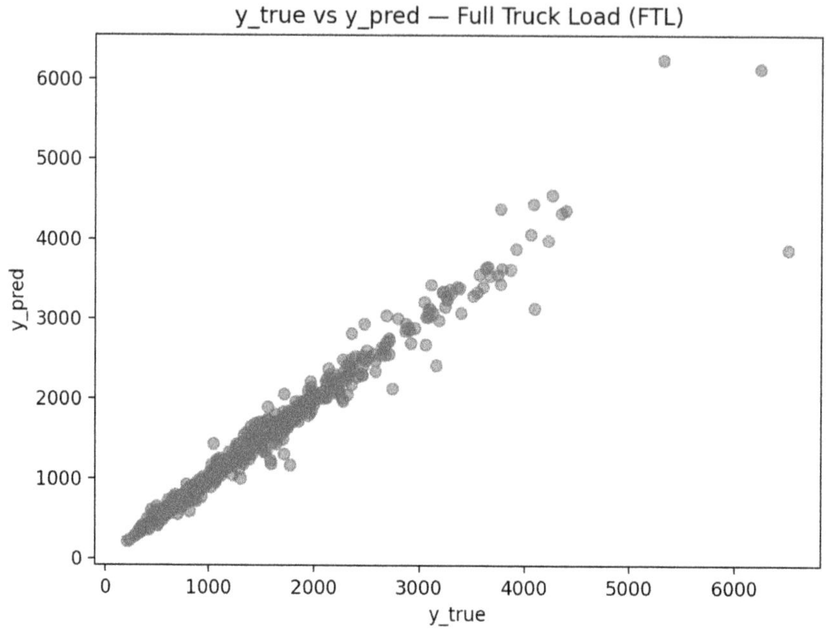

(a) FTL: $R^2 \approx 0.98$

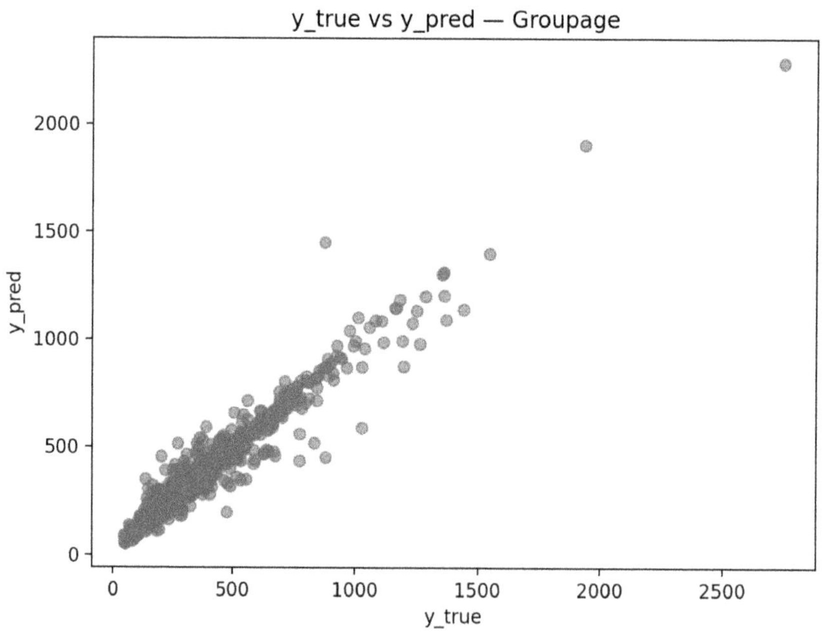

(b) GRP: $R^2 \approx 0.91$

Fig. 2. Predicted vs. actual prices. Strong diagonal alignment confirms accuracy; GRP shows slightly more dispersion.

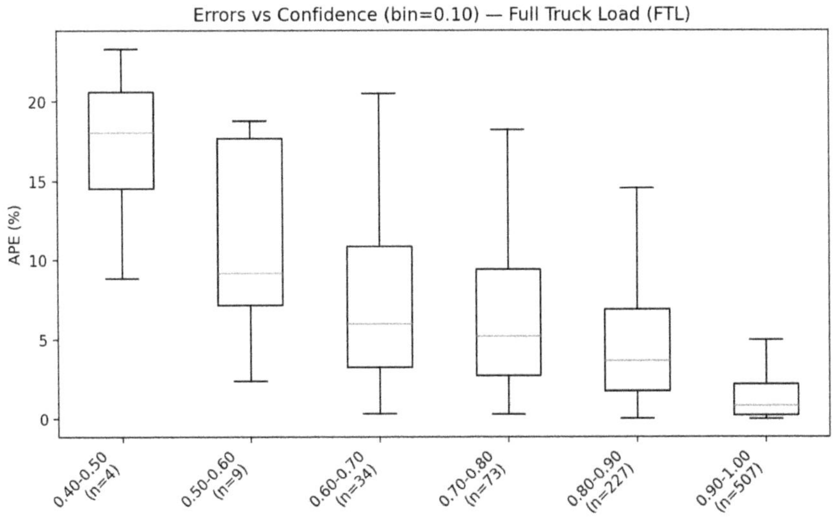

(a) FTL

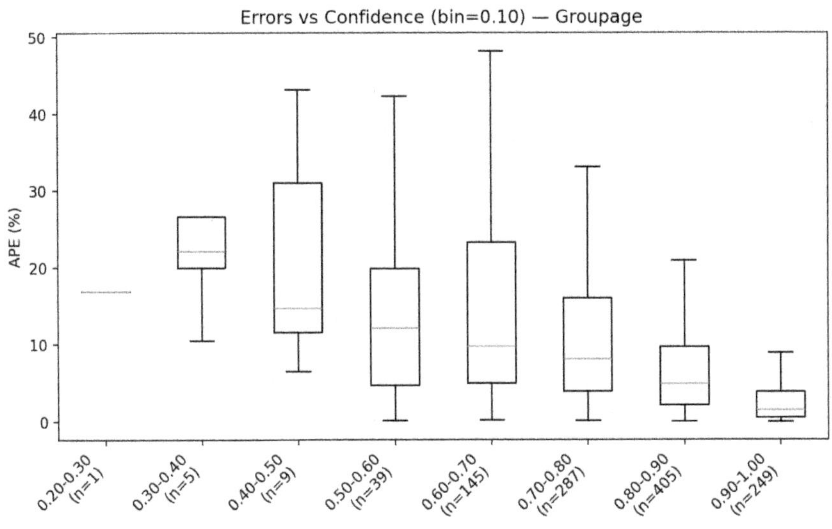

(b) GRP

Fig. 3. APE distribution by confidence bin. Higher confidence yields lower and tighter errors.

Operational Interpretation. From a business perspective, the achieved MAPE translates to concrete monetary savings. For a typical FTL shipment of EUR 1,000, a 3.23% error corresponds to a margin of approximately EUR 32, well within acceptable procurement tolerance. For GRP, the median price is lower ($\sim$ EUR 300 per shipment based on the MAE of EUR 31.84), so the absolute error is smaller even though the percentage error is larger. Low-confidence predictions (conf < 0.5) are flagged in the platform UI for manual review, allowing operators to intervene on structurally novel requests where the model is likely to be less reliable.

8 Conclusion

We have presented an end-to-end machine learning pipeline for freight transport pricing that integrates composite price actualisation, similarity-based matching, stratified Random Forest modelling, and GMM-calibrated confidence estimation. On a real-world dataset of $\sim$58,000 quotations, the system reduces MAPE from 10.23% to 3.23% (FTL), 13.50% to 5.60% (LTL), and 17.00% to 10.76% (GRP), representing 37–68% relative improvements over the rule-based engine.

These results are particularly significant in light of the intrinsic nature of the available labels. The dataset does not contain ground-truth prices in any strict economic sense: each quotation reflects a carrier's bid under a specific market context, influenced by fleet availability, route backhaul demand, seasonal pressure, and individual carrier strategy. As such, the target variable y is not a deterministic function of the shipment features, but rather a noisy market signal shaped by dynamics that are only partially observable. Achieving a test-set MAPE of 3.23% on FTL under these conditions is, in our assessment, a strong result—one that compares favourably with regression benchmarks on tabular datasets where clean ground-truth labels are available.

Iterative Development and Domain Validation. The pipeline reached its final form through a structured sequence of development and validation cycles conducted in close collaboration with the domain-expert team at the operating brokerage company. Each methodological component—price actualisation, similarity matching, stratified modelling, and confidence estimation—was introduced incrementally, with intermediate results reviewed against the company's operational experience and cross-checked against known pricing patterns. This iterative process was essential: domain feedback guided the choice of actualisation weights, the definition of matching tolerances, and the pallet classification scheme. The ablation results of Sect. 7.5 directly reflect this progression, quantifying the marginal contribution of each component as it was validated and integrated into the pipeline.

Limitations. The three category models are fully independent, potentially missing cross-category information. The actualisation weights ($\alpha = 0.3$, $\beta = 0.7$) are fixed and could be refined via cross-validation. The confidence estimator, while empirically validated, lacks formal coverage guarantees.

Future Directions. Promising extensions include: (i) benchmarking gradient boosted trees and tabular deep learning (TabNet [1]), particularly for the heterogeneous GRP segment; (ii) conformal prediction [16] for distribution-free prediction intervals; and (iii) SHAP-based explanations [12] to increase transparency for platform operators.

The pipeline is deployed in production, serving real-time pricing requests via a REST API, and constitutes a concrete demonstration that principled machine learning methodology, when developed in partnership with domain experts, can substantially outperform incumbent rule-based systems even in settings where label quality is inherently constrained by market noise.

References

1. Arik, S.Ö., Pfister, T.: TabNet: attentive interpretable tabular learning. In: Proceedings of the AAAI Conference on Artificial Intelligence, vol. 35, pp. 6679–6687 (2021)
2. Bishop, C.M.: Pattern Recognition and Machine Learning. Springer, New York (2006)
3. Bolis, S., Maggi, R.: Logistics strategy and transport service choices: an adaptive stated preference experiment. Growth Chang. **34**(4), 490–504 (2003)
4. Breiman, L.: Random forests. Mach. Learn. **45**(1), 5–32 (2001)
5. Chandola, V., Banerjee, A., Kumar, V.: Anomaly detection: a survey. ACM Comput. Surv. **41**(3), 1–58 (2009)
6. Chapelle, O., Schölkopf, B., Zien, A.: Semi-Supervised Learning. MIT Press (2006)
7. European Conference of Ministers of Transport. Bentien, et al. cost structures of road freight transport. OECD/ITF Transport Research Centre. Round Table 127 (2006)
8. Eurostat. Freight transport statistics – modal split (2023). https://ec.europa.eu/eurostat/statistics-explained/index.php?title=Freight_transport_statistics_-_modal_split. Accessed 15 Jan 2025
9. Hodge, V.J., Austin, J.: A survey of outlier detection methodologies. Artif. Intell. Rev. **22**(2), 85–126 (2004)
10. ISTAT. Indice dei prezzi alla produzione dei servizi di trasporto – business-to-business (2024). https://esploradati.istat.it/databrowser/. Serie trimestrale, base 2021=100, ATECO 494
11. Lindsey, C., Mahmassani, H.S., Mullarkey, M., Nash, T., Rothberg, S.: Regional freight demand forecasting using machine learning methods. Transp. Res. Rec. **2379**(1), 90–98 (2013)
12. Lundberg, S.M., Lee, S.-I.: A unified approach to interpreting model predictions. In: Advances in Neural Information Processing Systems, vol. 30 (2017)
13. McKinsey & Company. Route to the Future: The Outlook for European Road Freight. McKinsey Center for Future Mobility (2018)
14. Özbayrak, M., Akgün, M., Türkcan, A.: Activity-based cost estimation in a push/pull advanced manufacturing system. Int. J. Prod. Econ. **87**(1), 49–65 (2004)
15. John, W.: Exploratory Data Analysis. Addison-Wesley, Tukey (1977)
16. Vovk, V., Gammerman, A., Shafer, G.: Algorithmic Learning in a Random World. Springer, Heidelberg (2005)

17. Wager, S., Hastie, T., Efron, B.: Confidence intervals for random forests: the jackknife and the infinitesimal jackknife. J. Mach. Learn. Res. **15**(1), 1625–1651 (2014)
18. Wang, X., Meng, Q.: Deep learning approaches for freight rate forecasting in maritime shipping. In: Proceedings of the Transportation Research Board Annual Meeting (2020)

A Fuzzy Approach for Catastrophic Data Enhanced with Resampling and GAN Algorithms

Maciej Romaniuk[1,2(✉)] and Weronika Kamińska[3]

[1] Systems Research Institute PAS, Newelska 6, 01-447 Warszawa, Poland
mroman@ibspan.waw.pl

[2] Warsaw School of Information Technology, Newelska 6, 01-447 Warszawa, Poland

[3] Faculty of Mathematics and Information Science, Warsaw University of Technology, Koszykowa 75, 00-662 Warsaw, Poland

Abstract. To calculate the ruin probability, insurers need samples of sufficient quality and quantity that include data on claims. One remedy is to apply resampling algorithms to "multiply" such samples. This paper proposes a construction procedure that yields an LR fuzzy number describing the insurer's ruin probabilities. This fuzzy assessment is based on statistical properties of the resampled datasets. We apply the proposed approach to compare the results of three resampling algorithms (smoothed bootstrap, smoothed bootstrap based on the kernel density estimator, and GAN) and also the "classical" real-valued estimator of the ruin probability. The numerical analysis of simulations based on real-life catastrophic data provides some helpful insights into the quality of these resampling methods.

Keywords: Risk process · Smoothed bootstrap · GAN method · Expert opinion · Monte Carlo simulations

1 Introduction

As in other real-life problems, the quality and quantity of datasets are also vital for the insurers. Usually samples consisting of values and moments of claims for various kinds of events (like natural catastrophes, car crashes, etc.) are gathered by the insurers to propose new models, analyze them, calculate the probability of ruin, issue polices, reinsurance contracts or even new kinds of financial-insurance instruments (like catastrophe bonds) [8,17,20], etc. However, in the case of catastrophic events, these samples may not be of sufficient quality due to the rarity of such extreme claims and problems with their modeling.

One possible remedy to "get more data" is to "multiply" samples using a resampling method. Some of these algorithms are known for many years (like the classical Efron's bootstrap [7]), others, based on machine learning (ML), are pretty new and can be considered as state-of-the-art for developing generative models, like Generative Adversarial Network (GAN) [14,25]. It is tempting

B. Vantaggi et al. (Eds.): IPMU 2026, CCIS 3019, pp. 439–450, 2026.
https://doi.org/10.1007/978-3-032-28994-0_31

to compare the obtained resampled datasets in some way, e.g., to check the differences between the estimated probabilities of the insurer's ruin (i.e., the probability that the insurer's reserves given as a difference between the rates paid by the insureds and their claims are negative for some time horizon [1,20]).

In this paper, we propose a method to construct a fuzzy description of the insurer's ruin probability based on the statistical characteristics of resampled datasets. We significantly enhance our previous approach presented in [6]. In some way, the resulting fuzzy number (FN for short) [2] related to the simulated objective values can replace the expert's subjective opinion or at least can help in forming it. Instead of a simpler triangular FN, as in [6], more quantiles are used to get the more complex and detailed form of the membership function for the considered fuzzy description. Hence, an LR-fuzzy number [18] (LRFN for short), a kind of FNs widely considered in the literature, is obtained in this way. Then, we apply the introduced fuzzy assessment of the ruin probability to compare the outputs from three resampling methods (smoothed bootstrap, smoothed bootstrap based on the kernel density estimator, and GAN). In [6], the simpler methods, like the classical bootstrap and bootknife, were used. The real-life dataset concerning worldwide mass disasters [4] is used as our initial sample during this analysis. We focus on the distances calculated with the help of the metric proposed by Bertoluzza et al. [3,23] between the LRFNs obtained with the above-mentioned resampling methods. We also consider the similar distances between our fuzzy descriptions and the "classical" real-valued estimators of the ruin probability. This analysis provides an additional tool for verifying the quality of datasets generated by the applied resampling methods. On the contrary, the obtained fuzzy- and crisp-valued results were not compared in [6].

Hence, we enrich the approach presented in [6] by using a more general class of FNs, applying new, more complex resampling methods, and comparing the resulting crisp- and fuzzy-valued estimators of the ruin probabilities with the respective measures. These new ideas allow us to analyze better the usefulness of resampling methods for "getting more catastrophic data".

This paper is organized as follows. In Sect. 2, the preliminaries concerning the ruin probability, applied resampling algorithms, and FNs are recalled. The numerical experiments concerning the real-valued estimators of the ruin probability and introduction of the assessment of its fuzzy counterpart are described in Sect. 3. These two approaches (i.e., the "crisp" and fuzzy) are also compared. Some final remarks and possible future research are summarized in Sect. 4.

2 Preliminaries

This section presents some preliminaries concerning notation and algorithms considered in the following.

2.1 Risk Process and Claims

The **classical risk reserve process** R_t [1,20] is a function of time t describing the financial reserves of an insurer

$$R_t = u + pt - S_t \tag{1}$$

where u is an initial reserve of the insurer, p is a rate of premiums paid by the insureds per unit of time, and S_t is a claim process given by

$$S_t = \sum_{i=1}^{N_t} C_i \tag{2}$$

where $C_1, C_2, \ldots$ are *iid* random values of the claims, and N_t is a random number of these claims till time t. Usually, the values of the claims are described by some probability distribution, e.g., the exponential one [5,20], and N_t is given by the homogeneous (HPP for short) or the nonhomogeneous Poisson process (NHPP) [5,8,20].

For the insurer, calculation of **probability of an ultimate ruin** (i.e., a ruin with an infinite time horizon)

$$\psi(u) = \Pr\left(\inf_{t \geq 0} R_t < 0\right) \tag{3}$$

and **probability of a ruin** before the time T (i.e., a ruin with a finite time horizon)

$$\psi(u, T) = \Pr\left(\inf_{t \in [0,T]} R_t < 0\right) \tag{4}$$

are the points of interest [1]. In many situations, there are no analytical formulas to calculate these values, and numerical approximations or simulations are then necessary.

2.2 Bootstrap and Other Resampling Methods

The **Generative Adversarial Network** (GAN, [9]) consists of two neural networks, known as a generator and discriminator. They compete with each other in a zero-sum game. The GAN aims to generate samples with statistical properties similar to those of the initial set [25] after training on it. This non-parametric approach is considered state-of-the-art for developing generative models. To overcome existing problems (e.g., related to the incorporation of the experts' knowledge), various generalizations of the GAN (like the **DATGAN** method [14]) were also proposed.

The **bootstrap** method (or Efron's bootstrap) [7] is a classical resampling method. It generates B secondary (bootstrap) samples $\mathbb{X}^{*j} = (X_1^{*j}, \ldots, X_n^{*j})$, where $j = 1, \ldots, B$, consisting of values randomly drawn from the initial sample $\mathbb{X} = (X_1, \ldots, X_n)$ with repetitions. The bootstrap algorithm is widely used, e.g., in estimation problems, to approximate the p-value of a statistical test (also for fuzzy numbers [10,11,22]), etc. Because of known problems, many extensions of the classical approach have been proposed. For example, in the **smoothed bootstrap**, special noise is added to the bootstrapped samples to overcome repeating the same values as in Efron's bootstrap [12,13]. These "altered" samples can be drawn from a density estimate, e.g., using the kernel density estimation (KDE) with the Gaussian kernel, instead of directly drawing them from the initial dataset.

2.3 Fuzzy Numbers

For a more detailed introduction concerning fuzzy numbers, see, e.g., [2].

A **fuzzy number** (abbreviated further as FN) is an imprecise value characterized by a mapping $\tilde{A} : \mathbb{R} \to [0,1]$ (a **membership function**), such that its α-cut is defined by

$$\tilde{A}_\alpha = \begin{cases} \{x \in \mathbb{R} : \tilde{A}(x) \geqslant \alpha\} & \text{if} \quad \alpha \in (0,1], \\ cl\{x \in \mathbb{R} : \tilde{A}(x) > 0\} & \text{if} \quad \alpha = 0, \end{cases} \tag{5}$$

is a nonempty compact interval for each $\alpha \in [0,1]$. Operator cl in (5) denotes the closure. Conventionally, every FN is characterized by its membership function $\tilde{A}(x)$ or a family of α-cuts $\{\tilde{A}_\alpha\}_{\alpha \in [0,1]} = \left[a_\alpha^L, a_\alpha^R\right]_{\alpha \in [0,1]}$. There are two special α-cuts: the **core** $\tilde{A}_1 = \text{core}(\tilde{A})$, and the **support** $\tilde{A}_0 = \text{supp}(\tilde{A})$. The core contains all values fully compatible with the concept modeled by $\tilde{A}$, while the support – their counterparts compatible to some extent with $\tilde{A}$. A family of all FNs will be denoted by $\mathbb{F}(\mathbb{R})$ further on.

There exist many kinds of membership functions, like the **LR-fuzzy numbers** [18] (LRFNs for short) that are described by

$$\tilde{A}(x) = \begin{cases} 0 & \text{if} \quad x < a_1, \\ L\left(\frac{x-a_1}{a_2-a_1}\right) & \text{if} \quad a_1 \leqslant x < a_2, \\ 1 & \text{if} \quad a_2 \leqslant x < a_3, \\ R\left(\frac{a_4-x}{a_4-a_3}\right) & \text{if} \quad a_3 \leqslant x < a_4, \\ 0 & \text{if} \quad x \geq a_4, \end{cases} \tag{6}$$

where $L, R : [0,1] \to [0,1]$ are continuous and strictly increasing functions such that $L(0) = R(0) = 0$, $L(1) = R(1) = 1$, and $a_1, a_2, a_3, a_4 \in \mathbb{R}$, where $a_1 \leqslant a_2 \leqslant a_3 \leqslant a_4$. When $L(x)$ and $R(x)$ are linear functions, then we get a trapezoidal fuzzy number (**TPFN** for short). If additionally $a_2 = a_3$, we say about a triangular fuzzy number (**TRFN**).

Many measures can be used to calculate the distance (hence, the similarity) between two FNs [2]. In the following, we apply the so-called Bertoluzza metric [3,23], given by

$$D(\tilde{A}, \tilde{B}) = \left(\int_0^1 D_f^2\left(\tilde{A}_\alpha, \tilde{B}_\alpha\right) d\phi(\alpha)\right)^{1/2}, \tag{7}$$

where

$$D_f^2([a,b],[c,d]) = \int_0^1 (t|a-c| + (1-t)|b-d|)^2 df(t), \tag{8}$$

and f is normalized weighting measure on $[0,1]$, function $\phi(\alpha)$ satisfies the conditions $\phi(\alpha) \geq 0$, while $\alpha_1 \leq \alpha_2$ implies $\phi(\alpha_1) \leq \phi(\alpha_2)$, and $\int_0^1 \phi(\alpha)d\alpha = 1$.

3 Numerical Simulations

In our experiments, we used the dataset from the EM-DAT website [4], which contains data on worldwide mass disasters. We focused only on values of the claims in \$1000 adjusted to the inflation rate and times of their occurrences, i.e., the pairs $(\mathbb{C}, \mathbf{t}) = \{(C_i, t_i)_{i=1}\}$. Moreover, only material claims (i.e., the claims with values greater than zero) without 5% of the highest values from the years 1990–2023 for the USA were considered in the following. From this dataset, we extracted 281 cases related to 1990–2011.

We start by fitting both models: the HPP N_t (hence, its intensity λ) and the distribution of claim values C_i to the original data from the initial set. In the first case, we use the intervals between consecutive events (described by the exponential distribution $\text{Exp}(\lambda)$ for the HPP) to estimate the parameter λ using the moments method. For the significance level $\alpha = 0.01$, both the Kolmogorov-Smirnov (KS for short) and Cramer-von Mises (CvM) goodness-of-fit tests did not reject the null hypothesis for the estimated value $\hat{\lambda} = 12.8424$.

To find the best probability distribution function (pdf) for modeling C_i, we applied various distributions: $\text{Exp}(\lambda)$, the lognormal distribution with the logarithm of location μ and logarithm of scale σ parameters (abbreviated further by $\text{LN}(\mu,\sigma)$), gamma distribution with the shape α and scale β parameters (i.e., $\Gamma(\alpha,\beta)$), and Weibull distribution with the shape λ and scale k parameters ($W(\lambda,k)$). The procedures from the R package *EnvStats* [15] were used to calculate the maximum likelihood estimators of their parameters. The obtained values for the original training dataset are shown in Table 1. Only for $\text{LN}(\mu,\sigma)$, the KS and CvM tests did not reject the null hypothesis. However, to compare the overall results, all these distributions were considered in our further analysis. We focused on the above-mentioned "classical" pdfs (rather than the heavy-tailed ones also used for modeling catastrophic data) to improve the numerical performance of the presented method. Additionally, as mentioned, we deleted 5% of the highest values from the dataset, removing possible outliers in this way.

Table 1. The estimated parameters of the pdfs describing C_i for the original dataset.

Distribution	$\text{Exp}(\lambda)$	$\text{LN}(\mu,\sigma)$	$\Gamma(\alpha,\beta)$	$W(\lambda,k)$
Parameters	0.000001458	12.7167, 1.2135	0.8197, 83675.25	0.8139, 54269.99

The premiums paid by the insureds were modeled [21] as a function of time t with

$$p(t) = (1 + \theta)\, \mathbb{E}N_t\, \mathbb{E}C_i, \tag{9}$$

where θ is a safety loading (security loading).

Based on (1) and the previously estimated values of the parameters of the models for the original dataset, the Monte Carlo (MC) simulations were conducted to approximate the probability of the ruin $\hat{\psi}(u, T)$ for different ends of periods $T = \{10, 20, 50, 100\}$. Each experiment was repeated 10000 times to limit the influence of randomness with the following parameters: $u = 10^6, \theta = 0.05$. The obtained real-valued estimates of $\hat{\psi}(u, T)$ based on the MC means can be found in Table 2. As expected, these probabilities increase with the bigger values of the time T.

Table 2. The estimated (crisp) ruin probabilities $\hat{\psi}(u, T)$ for the original data.

Distribution	$T = 10$	$T = 20$	$T = 50$	$T = 100$
LN(μ, σ)	0.9007	0.9161	0.9395	0.9435
Exp(λ)	0.9213	0.9363	0.9479	0.9518
$\Gamma(\alpha, \beta)$	0.9124	0.9263	0.9377	0.943
W(k, λ)	0.9059	0.9251	0.9358	0.9393

3.1 Obtaining the Fuzzy-Valued Results

Then, 500 datasets of the same size as the original sample were generated using three resampling methods: the smoothed bootstrap based on the noise from the normal distribution (abbreviated as "Smoothed" further on), smoothed bootstrap with the Gaussian kernel for KDE ("KDE" for short) using the Python library *scikit-learn* [19], and DATGAN algorithm ("GAN") with the help of the Python library DATGAN [14].

Because of the resampling, we got many bootstrapped samples, which could be used to re-evaluate all the model parameters (including the intensity parameter for N_t and the parameters for the pdfs modeling the claims). Hence, we estimated the new set of these parameters for each bootstrapped sample. They can be used directly to obtain MC estimators of the ruin probabilities in the same manner as for the original data, as previously described. It will be helpful for the user if these values are aggregated in some way. Apart from the straightforward answer (i.e., calculating their overall mean), they can be treated as imprecise inputs. Hence, they can be transformed into fuzzy values, such as experts' opinions.

In [6], the simple solution to obtain such an FN was proposed. The three quantiles (minimum, median, and maximum) calculated for the set of obtained estimators were transformed into a TRFN. The support of the obtained TRFN was equal to the range defined by values from the minimum to the maximum, and the core was set to the median. An earlier, simpler approach in this manner may be found in [16]. This idea can be easily generalized to more complex types of fuzzy numbers, such as LRFNs.

Let us suppose that $q(r)$ is the quantile of the rank r for the considered sample. Then, we get a LRFN $\tilde{A}$ described by the α-cuts of the form

$$\left[a_{\alpha}^{L}, a_{\alpha}^{R}\right] = \left[q\left(\frac{\alpha}{2}\right), 1 - q\left(\frac{\alpha}{2}\right)\right]. \tag{10}$$

Hence, the support of such an LRFN is given by the interval $[q(0), q(1)]$ (i.e., the range from the minimum to maximum), and its core by $[q(0.5), q(0.5)]$ (the median), as in [6]. However, because more quantiles are used than previously, a fuzzy number's shape is more complex and detailed than in the simpler case given by a TRFN.

We applied this approach to calculate LRFNs for all the considered pdfs modeling the claims and values of the time T that are the same as in Table 2. The calculation of the MC estimators for each bootstrapped sample was repeated 1000 times to reduce the effect of randomness. Examples of the obtained LRFNs for $T = 10$ can be found in Fig. 1, where the outputs for the different resampling methods are compared with the real-valued estimators of the ruin probability for the initial sample (presented in Table 2). The respective results are marked with the following colors: KDE – red, Smoothed – green, GAN – blue, the crisp estimator of the ruin probability – black line. Other outputs and graphs are available upon reasonable request.

The obtained FNs can not be described as "triangular ones", their shapes are too complex for such a simplification. Therefore, if we are interested in a more detailed "expert's opinion", our results give us more information than simple TRFNs. The same applies to other possible approaches, like the classical "crisp" or interval-valued estimators. For example, interval-valued assessments of the ruin probability give us some insight into the estimator's error (e.g., its standard deviation), but without deeper knowledge of the behavior of this error. On the contrary, the introduced approach is completely non-parametric and provides us with more precise knowledge of the estimated value; e.g., we can directly check whether the obtained LRFN is a symmetrical FN or assess the influence of α on the width of the α-cuts.

3.2 Comparison of the Fuzzy and Crisp Outputs

As shown in Fig. 1, the LRFNs describing fuzzy assessments of ruin probabilities differ significantly across resampling methods. They have (generally) similar shapes, but are shifted relative to each other. Therefore, we focus on the distances among them in the following, instead of their other possible characteristics.

Hence, we calculated the values of the Bertoluzza metric (7) between all of these LRFNs with the help of the R package *SAFD* [24]. Examples of the results are given in Table 3. They are pretty varied depending on the pdf used

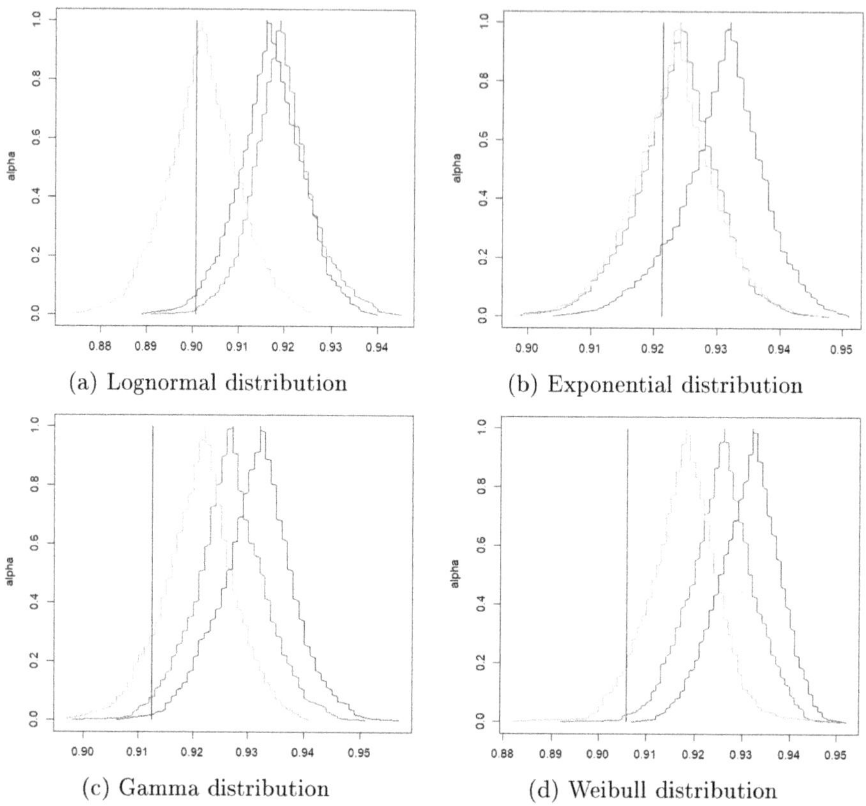

(a) Lognormal distribution

(b) Exponential distribution

(c) Gamma distribution

(d) Weibull distribution

Fig. 1. Comparisons of the fuzzy- (KDE – red line, Smoothed – green line, GAN – blue line) and real-valued (black line) estimators for the ruin probabilities for $T = 10$. (Color figure online)

for modeling C_i. Usually, the distances between LRFNs based on the KDE and GAN are the smallest (these values are emboldened in Table 3), while those for Smoothed and GAN are the largest (and emphasized in the respective table).

We can also be interested in analyzing differences between the crisp and fuzzy assessments of the ruin probabilities. The respective crisp estimators are also shown in Fig. 1 with black lines. Because the Bertoluzza metric can also be used to measure the distance between an FN and a crisp value, we apply it to conduct the analysis described above. Examples of the results can be found in Table 4. As previously mentioned, the lowest values are emboldened, while their biggest counterparts are emphasized there. As shown in Fig. 1, LRFNs for Smoothed are usually closest to the crisp estimators, while those for GAN are furthest. Interestingly, KDE and GAN lead to higher assessments of ruin probabilities than their crisp counterparts. Similar outputs were obtained for other values of T.

Table 3. The Bertoluzza distances between the fuzzy estimators of the ruin probabilities for $T = 10, 20, 50, 100$.

	KDE	Smoothed	GAN	KDE	Smoothed	GAN
$LN(\mu, \sigma)$		$T = 10$			$T = 20$	
KDE	0	*0.0171*	**0.0025**	0	*0.0115*	**0.0013**
Smoothed	*0.0171*	0	0.0148	*0.0115*	0	0.0104
GAN	**0.0025**	0.0148	0	**0.0013**	0.0104	0
Exp(λ)		$T = 10$			$T = 20$	
KDE	0	**0.0008**	0.0075	0	**0.0007**	0.0048
Smoothed	**0.0008**	0	*0.0081*	**0.0007**	0	*0.0053*
GAN	0.0075	*0.0081*	0	0.0048	*0.0053*	0
$\Gamma(\alpha, \beta)$		$T = 10$			$T = 20$	
KDE	0	0.0054	**0.0051**	0	0.0033	**0.0031**
Smoothed	0.0054	0	*0.0105*	0.0033	0	*0.0064*
GAN	**0.0051**	*0.0105*	0	**0.0031**	*0.0064*	0
W(k, λ)		$T = 10$			$T = 20$	
KDE	0	0.0078	**0.006**	0	0.0053	**0.0037**
Smoothed	0.0078	0	*0.0137*	0.0053	0	*0.0089*
GAN	**0.006**	*0.0137*	0	**0.0037**	*0.0089*	0
	KDE	Smoothed	GAN	KDE	Smoothed	GAN
$LN(\mu, \sigma)$		$T = 50$			$T = 100$	
KDE	0	*0.0067*	**0.0007**	0	*0.0043*	**0.0005**
Smoothed	*0.0067*	0	0.0064	*0.0043*	0	0.0041
GAN	**0.0007**	0.0064	0	**0.0005**	0.0041	0
Exp(λ)		$T = 50$			$T = 100$	
KDE	0	**0.0007**	0.0026	0	**0.0008**	0.0009
Smoothed	**0.0007**	0	*0.0030*	**0.0008**	0	*0.0014*
GAN	0.0026	*0.0030*	0	0.0009	*0.0014*	0
$\Gamma(\alpha, \beta)$		$T = 50$			$T = 100$	
KDE	0	0.0019	**0.0009**	0	*0.0013*	**0.0007**
Smoothed	0.0019	0	*0.0026*	*0.0013*	0	0.0012
GAN	**0.0009**	*0.0026*	0	**0.0007**	0.0012	0
W(k, λ)		$T = 50$			$T = 100$	
KDE	0	0.0027	**0.0013**	0	0.0014	**0.0007**
Smoothed	0.0027	0	*0.0039*	0.0014	0	*0.0019*
GAN	**0.0013**	*0.0039*	0	**0.0007**	*0.0019*	0

Table 4. The Bertoluzza distances between the fuzzy and crisp estimators of the ruin probabilities for $T = 10, 20, 50, 100$.

Distribution	KDE	Smoothed	GAN	KDE	Smoothed	GAN
		$T = 10$			$T = 20$	
LN(μ, σ)	*0.0191*	**0.0059**	0.017	*0.0174*	**0.0075**	0.0164
Exp (λ)	0.0053	**0.0051**	*0.0111*	**0.0045**	0.0046	*0.0069*
$\Gamma(\alpha, \beta)$	0.015	**0.01**	*0.0199*	0.0129	**0.0099**	*0.0157*
W(k, λ)	0.0205	**0.0132**	*0.0262*	0.0138	**0.0091**	*0.0172*
Distribution	KDE	Smoothed	GAN	KDE	Smoothed	GAN
		$T = 50$			$T = 100$	
LN(μ, σ)	*0.0062*	**0.0048**	0.0059	*0.0067*	**0.0044**	*0.0067*
Exp (λ)	**0.0042**	**0.0042**	*0.0044*	0.0043	*0.0045*	**0.0041**
$\Gamma(\alpha, \beta)$	0.0106	**0.0091**	*0.0113*	0.0085	**0.0077**	*0.0086*
W(k, λ)	0.0120	**0.0095**	*0.0132*	0.0117	**0.0104**	*0.0122*

Based on these results, we can say that Smoothed seems to be the best resampling method from the practical point of view. It leads to fuzzy assessments of the ruin probabilities that are close to the crisp estimators, while preserving the overall shape of the membership function, similar to other LRFNs obtained. Moreover, the fuzzy assessments of various resampling methods can vary significantly in their closeness.

4 Conclusions

In this paper, we proposed a construction procedure for the LR fuzzy number to describe the insurer's imprecise assessment of the ruin probability. Three different resampling methods (smoothed bootstrap, smoothed bootstrap based on the kernel density estimator, and GAN) were used to increase the size of the applied real-life catastrophic data. Then, based on the statistical properties of the resampled datasets, the respective LRFNs were constructed. Together with their real-valued counterparts for the initial sample, they were compared with the help of the Bertoluzza metric. In the considered case, the smoothed bootstrap led to the best overall results. Moreover, we showed that the obtained LRFNs provide additional knowledge (compared with simpler approaches such as "crisp" or interval-valued estimators, or those based only on TRFNs) about the estimated ruin probability. Then, these LRFNs can be treated as an expert's opinion (or at least one's first evaluation) about the considered parameter.

Further experiments and new ideas concerning this subject will be valuable. They can be concerned with other resampling methods and new ways to compare the obtained LRFNs, including their other fuzzy characteristics, such as the shapes of their membership functions.

References

1. Asmussen, S., Albrecher, H.: Ruin Probabilities. World Scientific, 2nd edn. (2010). https://doi.org/10.1142/7431
2. Ban, A., Coroianu, L., Grzegorzewski, P.: Fuzzy Numbers: Approximations, Ranking and Applications. Polish Academy of Sciences, Warsaw (2015)
3. Bertoluzza, C., Corral, N., Salas, A.: On a new class of distances between fuzzy numbers. Mathware Soft Comput. **2**(2), 71–84 (1995). https://eudml.org/doc/39054
4. Centre for Research on the Epidemiology of Disasters: The international disaster database (2024). https://www.emdat.be/, Accessed 10 Jan 2024
5. Chernobai, A., Burnecki, K., Rachev, S., Trück, S., Weron, R.: Modelling catastrophe claims with left-truncated severity distributions. Comput. Stat. 537–555 (2006). https://doi.org/10.1007/s00180-006-0011-2
6. Dzadz, N., Romaniuk, M.: Improving insurance catastrophic data with resampling and GAN methods. In: Atanassov, K.T., et al. (eds.) Uncertainty and Imprecision in Decision Making and Decision Support - New Advances, Challenges, and Perspectives, pp. 213–222. Springer, Cham (2026). https://doi.org/10.1007/978-3-031-99178-3_20
7. Efron, B.: Bootstrap methods: another look at the jackknife. Ann. Stat. **7**, 1–26 (1979). https://doi.org/10.1214/aos/1176344552
8. Giuricich, M.N., Burnecki, K.: Modelling of left-truncated heavy-tailed data with application to catastrophe bond pricing. XXPhys. A **525**, 498–513 (2019). https://doi.org/10.1016/j.physa.2019.03.073
9. Goodfellow, I., et al.: Generative adversarial nets. In: Ghahramani, Z., Welling, M., Cortes, C., Lawrence, N., Weinberger, K. (eds.) Advances in Neural Information Processing Systems, vol. 27, pp. 2672–2680. Curran Associates, Inc. (2014). https://doi.org/10.48550/arXiv.1406.2661
10. Grzegorzewski, P., Hryniewicz, O., Romaniuk, M.: Flexible bootstrap for fuzzy data based on the canonical representation. Int. J. Comput. Intell. Syst. **13**(1), 1650–1662 (2020). https://doi.org/10.2991/ijcis.d.201012.003
11. Grzegorzewski, P., Romaniuk, M.: Bootstrap methods for epistemic fuzzy data. Int. J. Appl. Math. Comput. Sci. **32**(2), 285 297 (2022). https://doi.org/10.34768/amcs-2022-0021
12. Hesterberg, T.: Unbiasing the bootstrap- bootknife sampling vs. smoothing. In: Proceedings of the Section on Statistics and the Environment, pp. 2924–2930 (2004)
13. Hesterberg, T.: Bootstrap. WIREs Comput. Stat. **3**(6), 497–526 (2011). https://doi.org/10.1002/wics.182
14. Lederrey, G., Hillel, T., Bierlaire, M.: DATGAN: integrating expert knowledge into deep learning for synthetic tabular data (2022). https://doi.org/10.48550/arXiv.2203.03489
15. Millard, S.P.: EnvStats: An R Package for Environmental Statistics. Springer, New York (2013). https://www.springer.com
16. Nowak, P., Romaniuk, M.: A fuzzy approach to option pricing in a Levy process setting. Int. J. Appl. Math. Comput. Sci. **23**(3), 613–622 (2013). https://doi.org/10.2478/amcs-2013-0046
17. Nowak, P., Romaniuk, M.: Valuing catastrophe bonds involving correlation and CIR interest rate model. Comput. Appl. Math. **37**(1), 365–394 (2018). https://doi.org/10.1007/s40314-016-0348-2

18. Parchami, A., Grzegorzewski, P., Romaniuk, M.: Statistical simulations with LR random fuzzy numbers. Stat. Pap. **65**(6), 3583–3600 (2024). https://doi.org/10.1007/s00362-024-01533-5
19. Pedregosa, F.: Scikit-learn: machine learning in Python. J. Mach. Learn. Res. **12**, 2825–2830 (2011)
20. Romaniuk, M.: Analysis of the insurance portfolio with an embedded catastrophe bond in a case of uncertain parameter of the insurer's share. In: Wilimowska, Z., Borzemski, L., Grzech, A., Świątek, J. (eds.) Information Systems Architecture and Technology: Proceedings of 37th International Conference on Information Systems Architecture and Technology – ISAT 2016 – Part IV. AISC, vol. 524, pp. 33–43. Springer, Cham (2017). https://doi.org/10.1007/978-3-319-46592-0_3
21. Romaniuk, M.: Imprecise approaches to analysis of insurance portfolio with catastrophe bond. In: Lesot, M.-J., et al. (eds.) IPMU 2020. CCIS, vol. 1239, pp. 3–16. Springer, Cham (2020). https://doi.org/10.1007/978-3-030-50153-2_1
22. Romaniuk, M., Grzegorzewski, P.: Resampling fuzzy numbers with statistical applications: FuzzyResampling package. The R J. **15**, 271–283 (2023). https://doi.org/10.32614/RJ-2023-036
23. Trutschnig, W., González-Rodríguez, G., Colubi, A., Ángeles Gil, M.: A new family of metrics for compact, convex (fuzzy) sets based on a generalized concept of mid and spread. Inf. Sci. **179**(23), 3964–3972 (2009). https://doi.org/10.1016/j.ins.2009.06.023
24. Trutschnig, W., Lubiano, M.A., Lastra, J.: SAFD — an R package for statistical analysis of fuzzy data. In: Borgelt, C., Gil, M.Á., Sousa, J.M., Verleysen, M. (eds.) Towards Advanced Data Analysis by Combining Soft Computing and Statistics, pp. 107–118. Springer, Heidelberg (2013). doi: https://doi.org/10.1007/978-3-642-30278-7_10
25. Wang, Z., She, Q., Ward, T.E.: Generative adversarial networks in computer vision: a survey and taxonomy. ACM Comput. Surv. **54**(2) (2021). https://doi.org/10.1145/3439723, article 37

A Bayesian Framework for Ranking Healthcare Facilities Under Uncertainty

Matteo Castano, Davide Cazzorla(✉), and Corrado Mencar

Università degli Studi di Bari Aldo Moro, Bari, Italy
m.castano@alumni.uniba.it, d.cazzorla@phd.uniba.it,
corrado.mencar@uniba.it

Abstract. Medicare's VBP Program has fundamentally reshaped hospital reimbursement by linking payments to multidimensional quality metrics. However, several empirical studies highlight its inability to consistently incentivize improvement and identify substantial limitations in its performance evaluation framework, most notably the neglect of statistical uncertainty in composite scores used for hospital ranking. This paper proposes a Bayesian methodology that models hospital performance measures—specifically, the PaCE score derived from the HCAHPS survey—as probabilistic quantities with credible intervals rather than fixed values. Using publicly available CMS data from the 2023 performance period, we apply Beta-binomial modeling and Monte Carlo approximation to characterize posterior distributions of relevant quality indicators. Hospitals are ranked according to the lower bound of the 90% central credible interval, emphasizing the most conservative plausible performance and directly penalizing facilities with higher uncertainty due to limited survey data. Experimental results demonstrate that nearly half of the top 50 hospitals undergo a change of at least five positions when uncertainty is taken into account, suggesting tangible real-world consequences for resource allocation and reputation. In addition to producing fairer and more informative rankings, the proposed approach generates natural incentives for hospitals to improve data quality and survey participation, and is generalizable to other domains within pay-for-performance schemes.

Keywords: Bayesian uncertainty quantification · healthcare facility ranking · credible intervals · performance assessment · value-based purchasing

1 Introduction

The Hospital Value-Based Purchasing (VBP) Program[1] represents a transformative initiative implemented by the Centers for Medicare and Medicaid Services

[1] https://www.cms.gov/medicare/quality/initiatives/hospital-quality-initiative/hospital-value-based-purchasing.

B. Vantaggi et al. (Eds.): IPMU 2026, CCIS 3019, pp. 451–462, 2026.
https://doi.org/10.1007/978-3-032-28994-0_32

(CMS) under the Patient Protection and Affordable Care Act of 2010. Operationalized in 2013, the VBP Program adjusts Medicare payments to hospitals participating in the Inpatient Prospective Payment System (IPPS) based on their performance across multiple quality dimensions, thereby creating financial incentives for providers to prioritize patient outcomes and care efficiency rather than service volume [1,10].

The program withholds a percentage of each participating hospital's Diagnosis-Related Group (DRG) payments, which is subsequently redistributed through a budget-neutral mechanism based on hospital performance measured by a Total Performance Score (TPS). This composite metric aggregates performance across four weighted domains: Clinical Outcomes (encompassing mortality and complication rates for specific conditions), Safety (measuring healthcare-associated infections and adverse events), Efficiency and Cost Reduction (assessed through Medicare Spending per Beneficiary), and Person and Community Engagement (derived from the Hospital Consumer Assessment of Healthcare Providers and Systems survey).

The Person and Community Engagement (PaCE) domain score constitutes a critical component of the VBP Program's TPS, derived exclusively from the Hospital Consumer Assessment of Healthcare Providers and Systems (HCAHPS) Survey—a standardized, nationally implemented instrument designed to capture patients' perspectives of their inpatient hospital experience [6]. The HCAHPS Survey comprises 29 questions administered to a random sample of adult inpatients between 48 h and six weeks post-discharge. From this survey instrument, eight distinct measures are extracted and utilized in the VBP evaluation framework: six composite measures (Communication with Nurses, Communication with Doctors, Responsiveness of Hospital Staff, Communication about Medicines, Care Transition, and Discharge Information), two individual measures (Cleanliness and Quietness of the Hospital Environment, which are subsequently combined into a single metric), and one global measure (Overall Hospital Rating).

The PaCE score calculation methodology involves multiple sequential steps:[2] first, computing the top-box raw score for each measure—defined as the unrounded percentage of patients selecting the most positive response category; second, applying patient-mix adjustments to account for demographic characteristics such as age and education level that may influence survey responses independent of hospital performance; third, applying survey mode adjustments to correct for systematic differences in response patterns across data collection modalities.

Following these adjustments, dimension scores are aggregated across four quarters of the performance period (weighted by the number of eligible discharges), and Achievement Points and Improvement Points are calculated for each dimension by comparing hospital performance against national benchmarks and baseline performance, respectively. The final PaCE score, ranging from 0 to

[2] https://www.hcahpsonline.org/globalassets/hcahps/vbp/hospital-vbp-domain-score-calculation-step-by-step-guide-february-2018.pdf.

100 points, represents the sum of the Base Score (derived from the maximum of Achievement or Improvement Points across all eight dimensions) and the Consistency Points (which incentivizes uniformly high performance across all dimensions by penalizing hospitals with any dimension falling below the achievement threshold) [3]. Hospitals must accumulate at least 100 completed surveys during the performance period to receive a PaCE score, ensuring sufficient statistical reliability in the patient experience assessment.

The current VBP Program exhibits several critical limitations that may compromise the fairness and validity of hospital performance evaluations. Several empirical investigations have documented that the VBP Program may not effectively incentivize quality improvement across participating institutions; specifically, Ryan *et al.* analyzed the initial implementation period and found no evidence of greater improvements in participating hospitals compared to non-participating facilities [9], while Figueroa *et al.* demonstrated that three years after program inception, no causal relationship could be established between VBP participation and improved patient outcomes [4].

Norton *et al.* identified fundamental structural flaws in the incentive mechanism, revealing substantial heterogeneity in marginal financial incentives [8]. Most critically, Friedson *et al.* exposed the program's systematic disregard for statistical uncertainty inherent in performance estimates, identifying three principal sources of estimation difficulty: the high variance in metrics caused by insufficient sample sizes (producing large standard errors that emphasize uncertainty), the large number of evaluated hospitals (making it statistically challenging to establish confidently correct rankings), and the bunched distribution characteristics of VBP metrics (creating arbitrary assignment zones containing substantial proportions of hospitals where point assignment depends not solely on true quality but also on statistical noise) [5].

This methodological deficiency is particularly problematic because the VBP Program treats hospital quality measures as known with certainty, computing the TPS as the arithmetic mean of domain scores while entirely ignoring the uncertainty associated with these estimates—thereby collapsing information from multiple patients into single metrics that fail to account for estimation reliability. Consequently, hospitals with small sample sizes may receive artificially inflated or deflated scores due to random variation rather than true performance differences, fundamentally undermining the program's objective of equitable resource allocation and potentially resulting in higher-quality hospitals receiving lower rewards than inferior-performing institutions.

The principal objective of this study is to propose an alternative hospital ranking methodology that explicitly incorporates statistical uncertainty into the evaluation process of the Medicare VBP Program. Specifically, the study aims to address the critical limitation of the current VBP approach by employing a Bayesian framework to quantify uncertainty in each hospital's TPS. The guiding principle of this methodological intervention is to handle performance information with appropriate skepticism, endorsing estimates only when supported by sufficient statistical evidence.

The proposed approach quantifies the uncertainty of each hospital's TPS through the 90% central credible interval of its posterior distribution, subsequently ranking hospitals according to the lower bound of these intervals (the 95% least plausible value). This conservative ranking strategy has a twofold objective:

1. Given two hospitals with the same score, the one with more data (i.e., with a more certain score) is favored;
2. Given two hospitals with the same amount of data (i.e., the same certainty), the one with the higher score is favored.

The methodology has been specifically applied to the Person and Community Engagement (PaCE) domain score, derived from the HCAHPS Survey, intending to demonstrate how accounting for uncertainty can significantly alter evaluation outcomes and create natural incentives for hospitals to improve data quality and survey participation.

The next section describes the datasets and the method adopted by CMS to calculate PaCE. In the successive Sect. 3, the proposed Bayesian methodology is reported by highlighting the assumed data-generating process, the Bayesian model, and the final ranking. Experimental results are collected and commented in Sect. 4, while some final notes, including the limitations of the study, are reported in Sect. 5.

2 Problem Statement

2.1 Datasets

The dataset employed in this study consists of publicly available data from CMS through the Provider Data Catalog[3] (PDC), specifically focused on the Hospital VBP Program for Fiscal Year 2025. The analysis utilizes three primary datasets that collectively provide information on facility performance metrics.

HCAHPS Survey Dataset. This dataset constitutes the largest component, comprising 442,215 rows representing individual outcomes for each HCAHPS question across all participating hospitals. The dataset contains 22 columns organized into several categories:

- **Hospital metadata:** Eight columns including Facility ID, Facility Name, Address, City/Town, State, ZIP Code, County/Parish, and Telephone Number
- **Survey measures:** Three columns identifying specific outcomes (HCAHPS Measure ID, HCAHPS Question, HCAHPS Answer Description)
- **Performance values:** Five columns containing outcome values and associated footnotes, including Patient Survey Star Rating and HCAHPS Answer Percent

[3] https://data.cms.gov/provider-data/about.

- **Survey participation metrics:** Four columns documenting Number of Completed Surveys, Survey Response Rate Percent, and related footnotes
- **Temporal information:** Two columns representing the observation timeframe (Start Date, End Date)

The HCAHPS Survey measures patient experiences across nine dimensions: six composite measures (Communication with Nurses, Communication with Doctors, Responsiveness of Hospital Staff, Communication about Medicines, Care Transition, Discharge Information), two individual measures (Cleanliness and Quietness of Hospital Environment), and one global measure (Hospital Rating).

PaCE Score Dataset. This dataset contains 2,489 rows, with one observation per hospital, and includes 74 columns:

- One column for Fiscal Year identification
- Seven columns containing hospital metadata
- For each of the eight HCAHPS measures, eight columns representing: Floor, Achievement Threshold, Benchmark, Baseline Rate, Performance Rate, Achievement Points, Improvement Points, and Dimension Score (totaling 64 columns)
- Two columns containing final aggregated scores: HCAHPS Base Score and HCAHPS Consistency Points

TPS Dataset. This dataset comprises 2,489 rows (one per hospital) with 17 columns:

- One column for Fiscal Year
- Seven columns of hospital metadata
- Eight columns containing domain scores (both unweighted and weighted versions) for: Clinical Outcomes, Person and Community Engagement, Safety, and Efficiency and Cost Reduction
- One column for the Total Performance Score

Data Collection. The HCAHPS Survey data were collected during the Performance Period, defined as the calendar year from January 1, 2023, to December 31, 2023, which serves as the basis for FY 2025 payment adjustments. The survey is administered to a random sample of adult patients between 48 h and six weeks after discharge, using various modalities including mail, telephone, mail with telephone follow-up, or active interactive voice recognition.

After preprocessing, which included removing hospitals with incomplete data or too few surveys, the final analytical sample retained hospitals with sufficient data quality for Bayesian inference. The number of completed surveys per hospital varied substantially, ranging from institutions with minimal survey responses to those with several hundred completed questionnaires, creating heterogeneity in measurement precision across facilities.

The dataset incorporates patient-mix adjustments to account for patient characteristics such as age and education that may influence survey responses but are unrelated to hospital performance. Additionally, survey mode adjustments correct for systematic differences in response patterns across different data collection methods, based on a randomized Mode Experiment involving 27,229 discharges from 45 hospitals.

2.2 PaCE Calculation

The PaCE score in the Medicare VBP Program is calculated using the HCAHPS Survey, based on several steps. For each dimension, CMS calculates two scores:

- **Achievement Points** (AP) compare a hospital's performance to all hospitals nationally, using thresholds (Floor, Achievement Threshold, Benchmark) derived from the baseline period. The points range from 0 to 10, with higher scores for better performance relative to the benchmark.
- **Improvement Points** (IP) compare a hospital's performance to its baseline period. Points range from 0 to 9, with higher scores for greater improvement.

The **Base Score** is the sum, over all eight dimensions, of the maximum between Achievement Points and Improvement Points for each dimension. (The maximum possible Base Score is therefore 80.) The **Consistency Points** (CP) rewards hospitals that perform well across all dimensions. It is calculated as follows:

1. If all dimension scores are above the Achievement Threshold, the hospital earns 20 CP.
2. If any dimension score is below the Floor, the hospital earns 0 CP.
3. Otherwise, the hospital earns between 0 and 19 points, calculated using a formula that considers the distance from the Floor and Achievement Threshold for each dimension.

The final **PaCE Score** is the sum of the Base Score and the Consistency Points, ranging from 0 to 100. Formally, let h be a hospital and M be the set of eight HCAHPS measures. The PaCE Score is calculated as:

$$\text{PaCE}_h = \sum_{m \in M} \max\{\text{AP}_{h,m}, \text{IP}_{h,m}\} + \text{CP}_h$$

3 Methodology

The adopted methodology models the PaCE score for each hospital using a Bayesian framework. The PaCE Score is derived from the HCAHPS Survey across eight dimensions, where each dimension score is treated as an estimate of the true underlying performance, and the uncertainty in these estimates is explicitly modeled.

3.1 Data-Generating Process

The model assumes that for each hospital h and each HCAHPS question q, the observed dimension score $s_{h,q}$ is an estimate of the true dimension score $\theta_{h,q}$. The true score is modeled as a probability parameter, and the observed data are assumed to follow a binomial distribution:

$$y_{h,q} \sim \text{Binomial}(N_h, \theta_{h,q})$$

where $y_{h,q}$ is the number of patients who selected the top-box response for question q at hospital h, and N_h is the total number of completed surveys for hospital h.

3.2 Bayesian Model

A non-informative prior is chosen to avoid biasing the results towards hospitals with historically high performance. Specifically, a uniform (i.e., Beta$(1,1)$) distribution is used as the prior for each $\theta_{h,q}$. This choice ensures that the prior does not favor any particular hospital and allows the data to dominate the posterior inference.

Given the Binomial likelihood and the Beta prior, the posterior distribution for $\theta_{h,q}$ is also a Beta distribution:

$$\theta_{h,q}|y_{h,q}, N_h \sim \text{Beta}(1 + y_{h,q}, 1 + N_h - y_{h,q})$$

This posterior distribution quantifies the uncertainty in the estimate of $\theta_{h,q}$ for each hospital and question (Fig. 1).

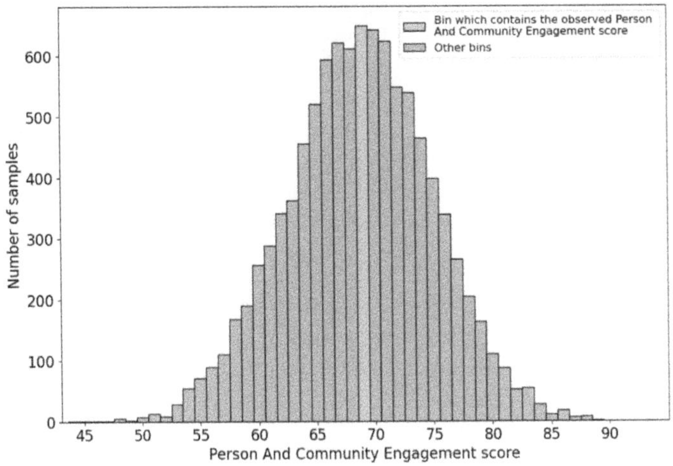

Fig. 1. Granular representation of PaCE vs. original numerical estimate.

To obtain the posterior distribution of the PaCE Score, which is a non-trivial function of the eight dimension scores, a Monte Carlo approximation is used. For each hospital, 10,000 samples are drawn from the posterior distribution of each dimension score, and these samples are aggregated to approximate the posterior distribution of the PaCE Score.

3.3 Ranking

The posterior distribution of the PaCE Score is summarized using the 5th percentile (determined by the lower bound of the 90% central credible interval), which represents a conservative estimate of the hospital's performance. Hospitals are then ranked based on this value, which penalizes institutions with greater uncertainty (often due to small sample sizes) when scores are equal (Fig. 2).

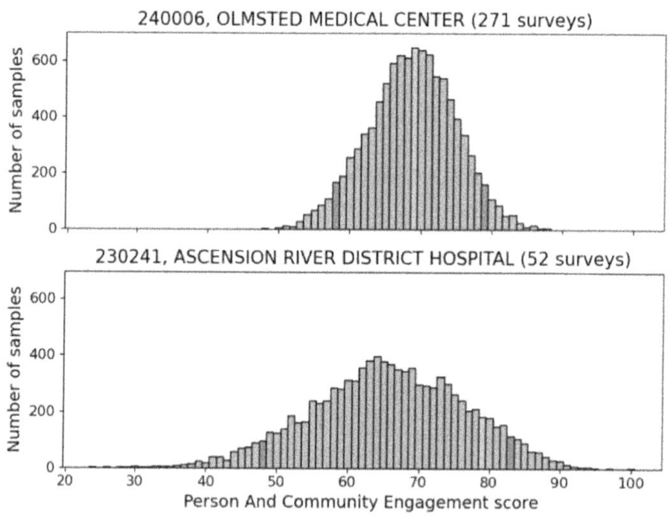

Fig. 2. Approximate posterior distribution of PaCE score for facilities "230241, Ascension River District Hospital" and "240006, Olmsted Medical Center". The orange bar contains the observed PaCE score, while the red bars delimit the 90% central credible interval (the lower bound corresponds to the 95% least plausible value).

The same Bayesian approach is applied to the TPS. The posterior distribution of the TPS is obtained by aggregating the posterior distributions of the domain scores, and hospitals are ranked based on the 5th percentile of the TPS posterior distribution.

4 Results

Thanks to Bayesian modeling, the original ranking based on observed TPS can now be interpreted with an additional layer of information: it becomes possible to assess how confident we are when evaluating a hospital. For some hospitals, the credible intervals are relatively narrow, which suggests high confidence in the corresponding original estimate, i.e., the hospital's reported TPS. For others, the intervals are much wider, reflecting a greater degree of uncertainty about the hospital's true score.

For example, we can consider Ascension River District Hospital (ARDH), which occupies the 3rd position, and Mayo Clinic Health System - Albert Lea and Austin (MCHS-ALA), in 6th position. Figure 3 shows that ARDH has a higher TPS but a wider credible interval than MCHS-ALA, for which we are highly confident of the estimate. For this reason, we cannot be sure that the ARDH truly deserves a higher position: its strong result could simply be the outcome of high statistical variance caused by the small number of surveys collected.

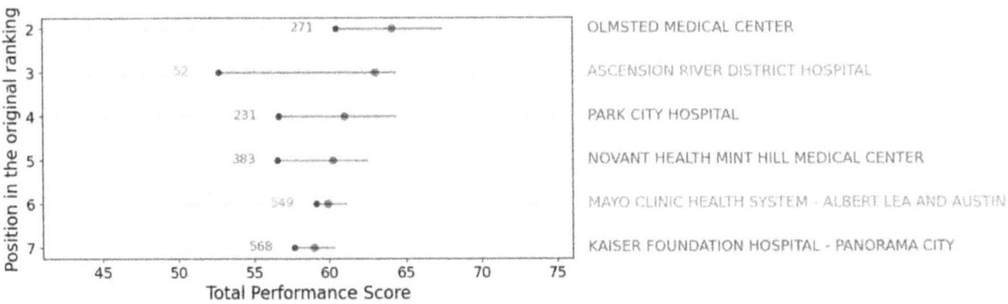

Fig. 3. The posterior distributions of the TPS for the top 7 hospitals. Blue points indicate the 95% least plausible value, red points the observed TPS values, and blue lines the 90% central credible intervals. The number of completed surveys for each hospital is displayed to the left of each interval. The hospitals highlighted are discussed in the text. (Color figure online)

The proposed new ranking is based on the 95% least plausible value of each posterior distribution, as shown in Fig. 4. The first aspect to highlight is the difference in the underlying *rationale* between the proposed ranking and the original one. While the original approach relies on point estimates derived from the data without accounting for uncertainty, the proposed methodology ranks hospitals according to the lower bound of the 90% central credible interval.

This adjustment favors hospitals with a larger amount of data and penalizes those with higher levels of uncertainty. Consequently, hospitals characterized by wider credible intervals tend to occupy lower positions in the new ranking. In this new ranking, ARDH now occupies the 21st position, whereas it held the 3rd highest value in the original TPS ranking. The penalization of this hospital is due to the small number of surveys it has—just 52 completed surveys—which significantly increases the uncertainty of its estimate.

For comparison, the hospital in the 20th position of the proposed ranking, SSM Health St. Clare Hospital—Baraboo (SCH-B), had a much lower original TPS but less uncertainty in its estimate due to a larger number of surveys (306).

As a result, SCH-B reaches a higher position than ARDH, regardless of the lower original TPS.

On the other hand, MCHS-ALA, is advantaged by the proposed ranking. In fact, its 95% least plausible value does not differ substantially from the original TPS; therefore, it is not penalized and attains the 3rd position in the proposed ranking. For comparison, the hospital in 6th position, Park City Hospital, had a slightly higher original TPS, but its smaller number of surveys prevented it from maintaining a higher placement.

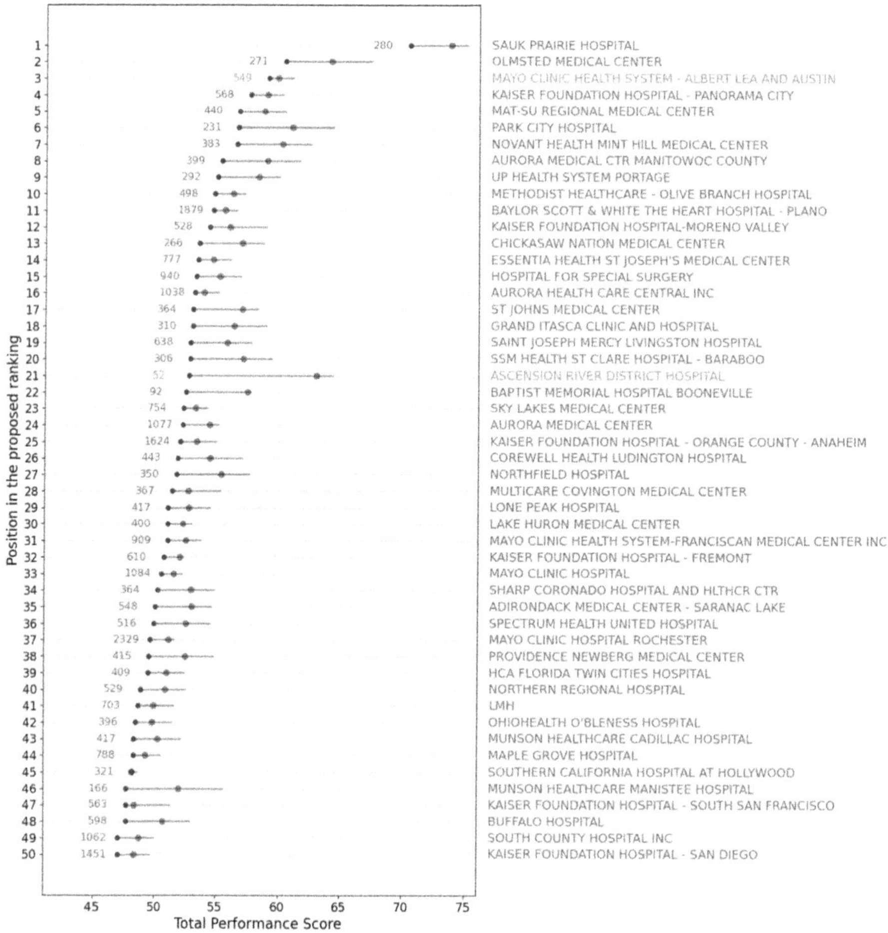

Fig. 4. Facility ranking with the proposed method. The posterior distributions of the TPS for the top 50 hospitals are shown with 90% central credible intervals (blue lines). Blue points indicate the new TPS estimates, red points the observed TPS values. The number of completed surveys for each hospital is displayed to the left of each interval. (Color figure online)

An important consideration is that the number of surveys influences the width of the credible interval, but it is not the only determining factor. For instance, we observe that HCA Florida Twin Cities Hospital, with 409 completed surveys, exhibits a narrower interval than Northern Regional Hospital, which has 529 surveys. This counterintuitive observation is a direct consequence of the skewness of the posterior Beta distributions in the Beta-Binomial model.

Actually, the posterior distribution of the PaCE score is more complex, as it results from aggregating the Beta posterior distributions of multiple HCAHPS dimension scores. This aggregation produces skewed distributions, meaning that the width of the resulting credible interval depends not only on the total number of surveys but also on the relative performance of each dimension.

In summary, by re-ranking the facilities according to the proposed methodology, almost half (23 out of 50) facilities undergo a change of at least 5 positions. This highlights that incorporating uncertainty in hospital evaluations can significantly alter the ranking outcomes.

5 Conclusion

This study has proposed and examined a Bayesian methodology for the ranking of healthcare facilities, specifically within the framework of the VBP Program. Uncertainty has been explicitly quantified using the 90% central credible interval of each hospital's TPS; thus, the approach yields a more robust and informative interpretation of hospital performance compared to traditional point-estimate-based rankings. Ranking hospitals according to the lower bound of these intervals penalizes institutions with greater statistical uncertainty—often due to small sample sizes—and rewards those supported by more substantial evidence.

Experimental results illustrate that incorporating uncertainty can substantially affect hospital ranking outcomes, as nearly half of the top 50 hospitals experience a change of at least five positions under the proposed method. This adjustment directly impacts hospital reputation and funding, resulting in a practical consequence of modeling uncertainty. Further, the methodology creates natural incentives for hospitals to improve data quality and survey participation, aligning with the objectives of the CMS to reward reliable measures of performance.

Despite limitations resulting from the unavailability of complete raw survey data and simplifying modeling assumptions, the proposed Bayesian approach proves to be a meaningful improvement. It offers fairer allocation of incentives, increases the credibility of the VBP Program, and provides a generalizable framework suitable for extension to other performance domains and pay-for-performance programs. Future research can explore the integration of uncertainty modeling into additional TPS domains—such as Clinical Outcomes, Safety, and Efficiency and Cost Reduction—and develop models that account for dependencies among domain scores or intelligently incorporate informative prior distributions guided by historical data.

Finally, in this work, we employed Bayesian modeling to estimate the uncertainty derived from ignorance of the true scores of hospitals. However, there is also uncertainty derived from the imprecision of questionnaire responses, which could be addressed using fuzzy set techniques. A possible future direction is to integrate these techniques into the methodology. Some approaches that could be considered include [2,7].

Acknowledgements. The research of Davide Cazzorla is funded by a Ph.D. fellowship within the framework of the project of the University of Bari Aldo Moro "Patti territoriali dell'alta formazione per le imprese" Ph.D. Project "Predictive AI in Value Based Procurement (VBP)", co-supported by InnovaPuglia S.p.A. D.C. and C.M. are INdAM members - GNCS. Generative AI has been used as writing support.

Disclosure of Interests. The authors have no competing interests to declare that are relevant to the content of this article.

References

1. Blumenthal, D., Jena, A.B.: Hospital value-based purchasing. J. Hosp. Med. **8**(5), 271–277 (2013)
2. Calcagnì, A., Grzegorzewski, P., Romaniuk, M.: Bayesianize fuzziness in the statistical analysis of fuzzy data. Int. J. Approximate Reasoning **186**, 109495 (2025)
3. Carter, J.C., Silverman, F.N.: Using HCAHPS data to improve hospital care quality. TQM J. **28**(6), 974–990 (2016)
4. Figueroa, J.F., Tsugawa, Y., Zheng, J., Orav, E.J., Jha, A.K.: Association between the value-based purchasing pay for performance program and patient mortality in US hospitals: observational study. BMJ i2214 (2016). https://doi.org/10.1136/bmj.i2214, https://www.bmj.com/lookup/doi/10.1136/bmj.i2214
5. Friedson, A.I., Horrace, W.C., Marier, A.F.: So many hospitals, so little information: how hospital value-based purchasing is a game of chance. South. Econ. J. **86**(2), 773–799 (2019)
6. Giordano, L.A., Elliott, M.N., Goldstein, E., Lehrman, W.G., Spencer, P.A.: Development, implementation, and public reporting of the HCAHPS survey. Med. Care Res. Rev. **67**(1), 27–37 (2010)
7. Marhamati, N., Buxton, E.K., Rahimi, S.: Integration of Z-numbers and Bayesian decision theory: a hybrid approach to decision making under uncertainty and imprecision. Appl. Soft Comput. **72**, 273–290 (2018)
8. Norton, E.C., Li, J., Das, A., Chen, L.M.: Moneyball in medicare. J. Health Econ. **61**, 259–273 (2018)
9. Ryan, A.M., Burgess, J.F., Pesko, M.F., Borden, W.B., Dimick, J.B.: The early effects of Medicare's mandatory hospital pay-for-performance program. Health Serv. Res. **50**(1), 81–97 (2015)
10. Yu, Z.A., Gorgone, M.B.: Pay-for-performance and value-based care. In: StatPearls. StatPearls Publishing, Treasure Island (FL) (2025). http://www.ncbi.nlm.nih.gov/books/NBK607995/

Bootstrap Methods for Interval-Valued Time Series

Maciej Romaniuk[1,2](✉) and Przemysław Grzegorzewski[1,2]

[1] Systems Research Institute PAS, Newelska 6, 01-447 Warszawa, Poland
mroman@ibspan.waw.pl

[2] Faculty of Mathematics and Information Science, Warsaw University of Technology, Koszykowa 75, 00-662 Warsaw, Poland
przemyslaw.grzegorzewski@pw.edu.pl

Abstract. Time series play a key role in research on phenomena and processes that change over time. Time series analysis is fundamental to the study of dynamic phenomena in many scientific fields. Classical stochastic models are often inadequate for modern data due to increasing complexity and the presence of imprecise, rather than purely random, observations. Such data are naturally represented by interval-valued or fuzzy time series and require new inferential tools. The bootstrap has proven to be a powerful and versatile method for complex data. However, bootstrap procedures for time series with imprecise values have not yet been systematically studied. In this paper, we address this gap by proposing bootstrap approaches for interval-valued time series that combine established resampling techniques for real-valued time series with bootstrap methods for fuzzy data within an epistemic framework. As our numerical analysis suggests, the stationary bootstrap should be preferred for bootstrapping the interval-valued time series.

Keywords: Block bootstrap · Interval-valued data · Random intervals · Time series · Autocorrelation function · Long-run variance · Correlogram

1 Introduction

Time series play a crucial role in contemporary research on phenomena and processes that evolve over time, particularly in economics and finance, natural and environmental sciences, astronomy and geophysics, medicine, epidemiology, public health and life sciences, engineering and manufacturing, transportation, social sciences, etc. Some time ago, researchers and practitioners were quite satisfied with various types of stochastic time series models, such as those described in the famous monograph by Box and Jenkins [4]. However, the rapid progress in almost all areas of life that we have been experiencing in recent years means that these classical methods are not always sufficient. This is due to the ever-increasing complexity of data problems, including their dimensionality, complexity, and temporal interdependence. We are also encountering new types of data that are

B. Vantaggi et al. (Eds.): IPMU 2026, CCIS 3019, pp. 463–476, 2026.
https://doi.org/10.1007/978-3-032-28994-0_33

no longer realizations of real-valued stochastic processes, as in classical time series analysis, but also observations whose uncertainty is not caused by randomness but rather by a lack of precision. Interval or fuzzy data are suitable for modeling this type of data. In turn, the analysis of complex time series requires new analytical tools and computational techniques that enable understanding of the phenomena under study and their effective forecasting, classification, and so on.

One such universal statistical tool that has made a stunning career in recent years, proving extremely useful and efficient for drawing conclusions from complex and unusual data, was the bootstrap, proposed by Efron [10]. Since this foundational monograph, many modifications and improvements have been made to the original concept of the bootstrap method. In particular, to deal with time series, it was necessary to develop a bootstrap approach taking into account the temporal relationships between observations, including the block bootstrap [7,17,24], sieve bootstrap [5], stationary bootstrap [24], and so on. Several methods have also been proposed for imprecise data analysis, like [11–13,26]. However, there appear to be no proposals for bootstrapping methods for time series with imprecise values. In this contribution, we try to at least partially fill this gap by considering time series with interval-valued data. In our study, we decided to creatively combine three commonly used bootstrap methods for real-valued time series with bootstrap approaches aimed for fuzzy numbers [12,19,26] viewed from the epistemic perspective [8].

The paper is organized as follows. We begin by reviewing the basic concepts of random intervals and establishing the notation (Sect. 2). Next, we discuss bootstrap methods used for real-valued time series (Sect. 3). In Sect. 4, we explain the algorithm for simulating interval-valued time series. Section 5, the most important part of the contribution, begins by outlining methods for generating bootstrap time series with interval-valued data. Then, we move on to methods for assessing the quality of the resulting bootstrap series and describe a comparative study of three methods for generating bootstrap series and the results obtained. Section 6 describes a case study in which we analyze bootstrap series obtained from daily USD/EUR currency exchange rates. Some concluding remarks and ideas concerning possible future scientific research can be found in Sect. 7.

2 Random Intervals

Let $\mathcal{K}_c(\mathbb{R})$ be the family of all non-empty bounded and closed intervals in the real line $\mathbb{R}$ endowed with a semi-linear structure induced by the Minkowski addition, and scalar product. Moreover, let $(\Omega, \mathcal{A}, P)$ be a probability space.

Definition 1. *A mapping $\boldsymbol{X} : \Omega \to \mathcal{K}_c(\mathbb{R})$ is said to be a* ***random interval*** *(interval-valued random set) associated with $(\Omega, \mathcal{A}, P)$ if and only if $\boldsymbol{X}$ is a measurable function with respect to the Borel σ-field generated by the topology induced by the Hausdorff metric d_H on $\mathcal{K}_c(\mathbb{R})$.*

The concept of the random interval is not new in statistics, as, e.g., a confidence interval by Neyman [23] is a particular random interval. However, systematic development of the probability-based theory for random sets began after the publication of Matheron's seminal book [20] (see also [21]).

If $\boldsymbol{X}$ is a random interval, then the expected value of $\boldsymbol{X}$ in Aumann's sense [1] is defined (if it exists) by the following set

$$\mathrm{E}(\boldsymbol{X}|P) = \left\{\mathrm{E}(f|P) : \ f\colon \Omega \to \mathbb{R}, f \in L^1(\Omega, \mathcal{A}, P), f \in \boldsymbol{X}\, a.s.[P]\right\}. \qquad (1)$$

It is worth noting that if $\boldsymbol{X}$ is a random interval, then $X^l := \inf \boldsymbol{X}$ and $X^r := \sup \boldsymbol{X}$ are real-valued random variables and vice versa. Hence, for any two random variables X^l and X^r in $\mathbb{R}$ such that $X^l \leqslant X^r$, we obtain a random interval $\boldsymbol{X} = \left[X^l, X^r\right]$. Consequently, the Aumann expectation of $\boldsymbol{X}$ is given by

$$\mathrm{E}(\boldsymbol{X}) = \left[\mathrm{E}\, X^l, \mathrm{E}\, X^r\right]. \qquad (2)$$

Sometimes, instead of the endpoints, it is more convenient to represent a random interval by its center and spread (radius), i.e.

$$\boldsymbol{X} = \left[\mathrm{mid}(\boldsymbol{X}) - \mathrm{spr}(\boldsymbol{X}), \mathrm{mid}(\boldsymbol{X}) + \mathrm{spr}(\boldsymbol{X})\right], \qquad (3)$$

where $\mathrm{mid}(\boldsymbol{X}) = \frac{1}{2}\left(X^l + X^r\right)$ and $\mathrm{spr}(\boldsymbol{X}) = \frac{1}{2}\left(X^r - X^l\right)$.

Although the Hausdorff metric is useful in formalizing the measurability of random sets, d_H is not the most convenient metric in $\mathcal{K}_c(\mathbb{R})$, especially for statistical applications. For this purpose Bertoluzza et al. [2] proposed the L^2-type distance defined for any $\boldsymbol{x}, \boldsymbol{y} \in \mathcal{K}_c(\mathbb{R})$ as follows

$$D_\theta(\boldsymbol{x}, \boldsymbol{y}) = \sqrt{\left(\mathrm{mid}(\boldsymbol{x}) - \mathrm{mid}(\boldsymbol{y})\right) + \theta\left(\mathrm{spr}(\boldsymbol{x}) - \mathrm{spr}(\boldsymbol{y})\right)}, \qquad (4)$$

where $\theta > 0$ is a relative weight for the difference between centers and spreads. Distance (4) is useful in defining the Fréchet variance [3] of a random interval

$$\mathrm{Var}(\boldsymbol{X}) = \mathrm{E}\left[D_\theta^2(\boldsymbol{X}, \mathrm{E}(\boldsymbol{X}))\right] = \mathrm{Var}\left(\mathrm{mid}(\boldsymbol{X})\right) + \theta\, \mathrm{Var}\left(\mathrm{spr}(\boldsymbol{X})\right). \qquad (5)$$

We used this kind of variance rather than alternatives (e.g., Kruse variance) to directly compare the respective real-valued outputs (rather than intervals) during our analysis.

Because of the semilinearity of $\mathcal{K}_c(\mathbb{R})$, a direct generalization of the classical covariance concept is not straightforward. For this reason, the covariance of random intervals is commonly defined as the covariance between elements in a Hilbert space (see [15]). Specifically, the covariance between two random intervals $\boldsymbol{X}$ and $\boldsymbol{Y}$ is defined by

$$\begin{aligned}\mathrm{Cov}(\boldsymbol{X}, \boldsymbol{Y}) &= \mathrm{E}\left[\left(\mathrm{mid}(\boldsymbol{X}) - \mathrm{E}(\mathrm{mid}(\boldsymbol{X}))\right)\left(\mathrm{mid}(\boldsymbol{Y}) - \mathrm{E}(\mathrm{mid}(\boldsymbol{Y}))\right)\right] \\ &\quad + \theta\, \mathrm{E}\left[\left(\mathrm{spr}(\boldsymbol{X}) - \mathrm{E}(\mathrm{spr}(\boldsymbol{X}))\right)\left(\mathrm{spr}(\boldsymbol{Y}) - \mathrm{E}(\mathrm{spr}(\boldsymbol{Y}))\right)\right] \qquad (6) \\ &= \mathrm{Cov}\left(\mathrm{mid}(\boldsymbol{X}), \mathrm{mid}(\boldsymbol{Y})\right) + \theta\, \mathrm{Cov}\left(\mathrm{spr}(\boldsymbol{X}), \mathrm{spr}(\boldsymbol{Y})\right).\end{aligned}$$

Based on the last two equations, we obtain the correlation coefficient for two random intervals defined in the usual manner as

$$\mathrm{corr}(\boldsymbol{X}, \boldsymbol{Y}) = \frac{\mathrm{Cov}(\boldsymbol{X}, \boldsymbol{Y})}{\sqrt{\mathrm{Var}(\boldsymbol{X})\, \mathrm{Var}(\boldsymbol{Y})}}. \qquad (7)$$

3 Bootstrap Methods for Time Series

The bootstrap, introduced by Efron [10], has proven to be an extremely effective method for estimating the sampling distribution of a statistic $T_n = T_n(X_1, \ldots, n)$ for independent and identically distributed (i.i.d.) observations from the unknown distribution F. This goal was achieved by resampling with replacement from the empirical distribution $\widehat{F}_n$. However, as Singh [27] showed, the classical i.i.d. bootstrap fails in the time-series setting $\{X_t\}_{t\in\mathbb{Z}}$ because resampling individual observations destroys temporal dependence, leading to inconsistent variance estimation and unreliable inference. Therefore, various approaches have been developed to extend the bootstrap for time series, like the block bootstrap [7,17,24], sieve bootstrap [5], stationary bootstrap [24], and so on (for the review of the methods we refer the reader to [6,14,16,18]).

Below, we briefly recall some of the bootstrap methods applied to usual real-valued time series. Let us consider a finite time series $\mathbb{X} = (X_t)_{t=1}^n$. Following one of the oldest bootstrap approach dedicated to time series, called the **nonoverlaping bootstrap** (NBB) [7], we divide our series into blocks $Y_1, \ldots, Y_b$, such that $Y_i = \big(X_{(i-1)l+1}, \ldots, X_{il}\big)$, where l is the length of the block specified by the user, and $b = n/l$ (we assume for simplicity that n is divisible by l). Then, we draw b blocks $Y_1^*, \ldots, Y_b^*$ with replacements from $Y_1, \ldots, Y_b$, and concatenate them to form the bootstrapped series $\mathbb{X}^* = (Y_1^*, \ldots, Y_b^*)$ while its realization is denoted by $\mathbb{x}^*$. The whole procedure can be repeated B times, so we obtain the entire set of the realized B bootstrapped series $\mathbb{x}_1^*, \ldots, \mathbb{x}_B^*$.

The key idea of the **moving block bootstrap** (MBB) [17] is quite similar. We partition the data into $N = n-l+1$ overlapping blocks $Y_i = (X_i, \ldots, X_{i+l-1})$ for $i = 1, \ldots, N$. Next, we draw b blocks $Y_1^*, \ldots, Y_b^*$ with replacement from $Y_1, \ldots, Y_N$, and concatenate to form the bootstrapped series $\mathbb{X}^* = (Y_1^*, \ldots, Y_b^*)$.

In both methods, the length of each block l is fixed. As noted in [18], the optimal value of l should be proportional to $n^{-\frac{1}{3}}$. Whereas in the **stationary bootstrap** (SB) [24] the block lengths l_i are selected randomly – usually from the geometric distribution, i.e. $l_i \sim \mathrm{Geom}(p)$. Moreover, each block $Y_i = (X_i, \ldots, X_{i+l_i-1})$ has randomly chosen starting point from $\{1, \ldots, n\}$. Finally, data are wrapped circularly to maintain stationarity. If the total length of all selected blocks exceeds n, then the redundant elements at the end of the last block are removed.

It is worth noting that the MBB preserves short-range dependence within blocks while treating blocks as approximately independent. Under mixing conditions and appropriate choice of block length, the MBB yields consistent estimators. The SB produces stationary resampled series and has been shown to possess desirable asymptotic properties, including consistency for the mean and smooth functions of the mean.

4 Interval-Valued Time Series Generation

Before we move on to the main challenge of this contribution, let us recall some notation related to well-known types of time series. We devote a few words to methods for generating time series with interval-valued observations, and then consider bootstrap methods for such time series.

Suppose that $(\varepsilon_t)_{t\in\mathbb{N}_+}$ is a purely random process, i.e., a sequence of i.i.d. random variables (so called **innovations**) drawn from the density distribution f_ϵ with the zero mean and standard deviation σ_ε. Then, a process $(X_t)_{t\in\mathbb{N}_+}$ defined by

$$X_t = \beta_0\varepsilon_t + \beta_1\varepsilon_{t-1} + \ldots + \beta_q\varepsilon_{t-q}, \tag{8}$$

where $\beta_0, \ldots, \beta_q \in \mathbb{R}$ are constants, is the so-called **moving average process** of order q, denoted usually as MA(q). After the respective scaling, we obtain $\beta_0 = 1$. On the other hand, a process $(X_t)_{t\in\mathbb{N}_+}$ described by

$$X_t = \alpha_1 X_{t-1} + \alpha_2 X_{t-2} + \ldots + \alpha_p X_{t-p} + \varepsilon_t, \tag{9}$$

where $\alpha_1, \ldots, \alpha_p \in \mathbb{R}$ are constants, is an **autoregressive process** of order p, denoted as AR(p).

Our method for generating interval-valued time series is a modification of the idea presented in [19], which leverages some results from our earlier results on bootstrapping for fuzzy data [12,26]. It essentially comes down to the following three steps described below (and synthetically shown as Algorithm 1):

1. Let $\mathbb{X}^O = \left(X_t^O\right)_{t=1}^n$ denote a finite real-valued time series with a known structure, e.g., AR(1) process. It can be interpreted from the epistemic perspective [8] as a series of consecutive **originals**, i.e., the true but not observed values of the interval-valued time series.
2. To obtain random intervals, we must determine the lower and upper bounds of the interval observation at each time point, ensuring that the former is no greater than the latter. This goal is easier to achieve by generating two non-negative random variables, which we will then subtract and add, respectively, from the previously generated original (see Step 1). Thus we simulate two independent samples $\mathbb{X}^L = \left(X_1^L, \ldots X_n^L\right)$ and $\mathbb{X}^R = \left(X_1^R, \ldots X_n^R\right)$ of i.i.d. random variables from the distributions with densities f_L, f_R, respectively. For example, we can set $X_t^L \sim U[0,1]$ and $X_t^R \sim U[0,1]$ for $t = 1, \ldots, n$, where $U[a,b]$ stands for the uniform distribution on $[a,b]$.
3. Finally, all subsequent elements of the desired interval-valued time series $(\boldsymbol{X}_t)_{t=1}^n$ are obtained from the following formula

$$\boldsymbol{X}_t = \left[X_t^O - X_t^L, X_t^O + X_t^R\right], \quad t = 1, \ldots, n. \tag{10}$$

It is worth noting that, following (10), the original of the observation in each time point does not necessarily coincide with the middle of the interval, as results from the method proposed in [19]. Both spreads for each $\boldsymbol{X}_t$ were given by the same random value (i.e., $X_t^L = X_t^R$) there, so X_t^O was always equal to the midpoint. We believe that the approach proposed in this paper is more accurate. Indeed, when looking at interval data from an epistemic perspective, we assume that each interval observation contains an unobserved actual value. However, we still have no idea in which part of the interval it lies (cf. [8]).

Algorithm 1. Interval-valued time series simulation

Require: Density distribution f_ε for generating innovations and two nonegative densities f_L, f_R for generating interval's endpoints.

Ensure: Interval-valued time series $(\boldsymbol{X}_t)_{t=1}^n$

1: Generate time series originals $\mathbb{X}^O = \left(X_1^O, \ldots X_n^O\right)$ following the selected real-valued time series model and innovations drawn from f_ε.

2: **for** $t = 1, \ldots, n$ **do**

3: Generate independently random variables $X_t^L \sim f_L$ and $X_t^R \sim f_R$.

4: Calculate $\boldsymbol{X}_t$ using (10).

5: **return** $(\boldsymbol{X}_t)_{t=1}^n = (\boldsymbol{X}_1, \ldots, \boldsymbol{X}_n)$.

5 Interval-Valued Time Series and the Bootstrap

In this section, we will demonstrate how to bootstrap interval-valued time series and describe a numerical experiment evaluating the considered methods.

5.1 Method

Before we proceed to bootstrap, we need to generate an interval-valued time series $(\boldsymbol{X}_t)_{t=1}^n$. It would be done using the method proposed in Sect. 4 (see Algorithm 1). We will refer to the time series realization generated in this way as the **primary** time series and denote it by $\mathbb{x} = (\boldsymbol{x}_t)_{t=1}^n$.

Next, we will create B bootstrap series $\mathbb{x}_1^*, \ldots, \mathbb{x}_B^*$ based on the primary time series, applying the three bootstrap methods described in Sect. 3 typically used for ordinary time series, i.e., NBB – nonoverlapping, MBB – moving block, and SB – stationary bootstrap. In fact, the algorithm for generating bootstrap samples from a series with interval-valued observations for each of these methods does not differ from the approach for an ordinary real-valued time series, because bootstrapping concerns whole objects within each block, regardless of their mathematical form.

At this point, one might ask about the novelty of this contribution, i.e., what fundamentally distinguishes bootstrap for interval-valued time series from the known algorithms for their real-valued counterparts. This novelty essentially concerns the method of evaluating such a bootstrap. Firstly, we need methods for generating time series, and secondly, methods for assessing the quality of the generated bootstrap series. The first of these issues was discussed in Sect. 3. Let us now turn to methods for assessing the quality of the generated bootstrap series. This raises the fundamental question of what constitutes such a quality. In the classical bootstrap, it is assumed that such a determinant is the ability of the bootstrap series to reproduce the distribution of its primary counterpart. In practice, this is primarily assessed by estimating typical statistical characteristics, such as the mean, variance, and correlation, the latter of which helps detect autocorrelation and plot correlograms (cf. [9]). Among more sophisticated tools, let us mention the Long-Run Variance, i.e., a special variability characteristic used for time series, and some measure of the series' location, such as the time series coverage.

Let us recall that the **Long-Run Variance** (LRV) of a real-valued time series $(X_t)_{t=1}^{\infty}$ with finite autocovariances is defined by

$$\mathrm{LRV} = \phi_X(0) + 2\sum_{k=1}^{\infty} \phi_X(k), \tag{11}$$

where $\phi_X(0)$ is the variance and $\phi_X(k) = \mathrm{Cov}(X_t, X_{t-k})$ is the covariance at lag k. Given the time series realization $(x_t)_{t=1}^{n}$ we may estimate LRV with, e.g., the Newey-West estimator $\widehat{\mathrm{LRV}} = \widehat{\phi}_x(0) + 2\sum_{k=1}^{L} w_k \widehat{\phi}_x(k)$, where $\widehat{\phi}_x(k)$ denote empirical covariances, w_k are some weights and L is the number of lags.

Let us now consider a realization of the primary interval-valued time series $\mathbb{x} = (\boldsymbol{x}_t)_{t=1}^{n}$. Keeping in mind equations from Sect. 2 we obtain the desired estimator, i.e. its sample mean $\overline{\boldsymbol{x}} = \left[\frac{1}{n}\sum_{t=1}^{n} \boldsymbol{x}_t^l, \frac{1}{n}\sum_{t=1}^{n} \boldsymbol{x}_t^r\right]$ and the sample real-valued covariance at lag k

$$\begin{aligned}\widehat{\phi}_{\mathbb{x}}(k) = \frac{1}{n} &\sum_{t=k+1}^{n-k} \big(\mathrm{mid}(\boldsymbol{x}_t) - \mathrm{mid}(\overline{\boldsymbol{x}})\big)\big(\mathrm{mid}(\boldsymbol{x}_{t-k}) - \mathrm{mid}(\overline{\boldsymbol{x}})\big) \\ &+ \theta\,\frac{1}{n} \sum_{t=k+1}^{n-k} \big(\mathrm{spr}(\boldsymbol{x}_t) - \mathrm{spr}(\overline{\boldsymbol{x}})\big)\big(\mathrm{spr}(\boldsymbol{x}_{t-k}) - \mathrm{spr}(\overline{\boldsymbol{x}})\big),\end{aligned} \tag{12}$$

where $\mathrm{mid}(\boldsymbol{x}_t) = \frac{1}{2}(\boldsymbol{x}_t^i + \boldsymbol{x}_t^r)$ and $\mathrm{spr}(\boldsymbol{x}_t) = \frac{1}{2}(\boldsymbol{x}_t^r - \boldsymbol{x}_t^i)$. Now we can determine the empirical LRV for the interval-valued time series $\mathbb{x} = (\boldsymbol{x}_t)_{t=1}^{n}$

Definition 2. *Let* $\mathbb{x} = (\boldsymbol{x}_t)_{t=1}^{n}$ *be a realization of the interval-valued time series* $(\boldsymbol{X}_t)_{t=1}^{n}$ *with finite autocovariances* $\phi_{\boldsymbol{X}}(k) = \mathrm{Cov}(\boldsymbol{X}_t, \boldsymbol{X}_{t-k})$*. Then the* ***empirical long-run variance*** *is defined by*

$$\widehat{\mathrm{LRV}}(\mathbb{x}) = \widehat{\phi}_{\mathbb{x}}(0) + 2\sum_{k=1}^{L} w_k \widehat{\phi}_{\mathbb{x}}(k), \tag{13}$$

where w_k *denote weights and* L *is the number of lags.*

Please note that the estimator (13) is given by a real value (i.e., "crisp"), similarly to its covariance components (12). Although the user can choose the number of lags and the weights, L should be set to the time series length, while the weights should depend on both k and L. Usually, we use the so-called Bartlett weight, i.e. $w_k = 1 - \frac{k}{L+1}$ and $L \sim n^{1/4}$.

After creating B bootstrap series $\mathbb{x}_1^*, \ldots, \mathbb{x}_B^*$ based on the primary series, we can use the notion of the empirical LRV to evaluate the quality of the bootstrap method. Firstly, we have to determine $\widehat{\mathrm{LRV}}(\mathbb{x}_i^*)$ for each bootstrap replication $i = 1, \ldots, B$. Then we compute the average empirical LRV, further called the **bootstrap LRV**, defined as $\widehat{\mathrm{LRV}}(\mathbb{x}^*) = \frac{1}{B}\sum_{i=1}^{B} \widehat{\mathrm{LRV}}(\mathbb{x}_i^*)$. Assuming that

$\widehat{\mathrm{LRV}}(\mathbb{x})$ denotes the LRV obtained for the primary time series, the **relative bias** of a given bootstrap method is given by

$$\mathrm{RBias}_{\mathrm{LRV}} = \frac{\widehat{\mathrm{LRV}}(\mathbb{x}^*) - \widehat{\mathrm{LRV}}(\mathbb{x})}{\widehat{\mathrm{LRV}}(\mathbb{x})}. \tag{14}$$

It can be seen that (14) quantifies the relative systematic error of the given bootstrap method, i.e., whether LRV typically overestimates or underestimates. One can also be interested in the **relative mean squared error** of the bootstrap LRV, defined as

$$\mathrm{RMSE}_{\mathrm{LRV}} = \sqrt{\frac{1}{B}\sum_{i=1}^{B}\left(\frac{\widehat{\mathrm{LRV}}(\mathbb{x}_i^*) - \widehat{\mathrm{LRV}}(\mathbb{x})}{\widehat{\mathrm{LRV}}(\mathbb{x})}\right)^2}. \tag{15}$$

Looking back on (12) one can clearly notice that $\widehat{\phi}_{\boldsymbol{x}}(0) = s^2(\boldsymbol{x})$ is the sample variance and the ratio $\widehat{\rho}(k) = \frac{\widehat{\phi}_{\boldsymbol{x}}(k)}{\widehat{\phi}_{\boldsymbol{x}}(0)}$ stands for the **autocorrelation** at lag k, while a function ACF which attributes $\widehat{\rho}(k)$ to each $k \in \{0, 1, \ldots, n\}$ is called the sample **autocorrelation function**. Having B bootstrap replications, we can determine all desired sample characteristics, like $\overline{\boldsymbol{x}}_i^*$, $s^2(\boldsymbol{x}_i^*)$, and $\mathrm{ACF}(\boldsymbol{x}_i^*)$, for $i = 1, \ldots, B$. Then, according to the bootstrap paradigm, we may calculate the overall estimators $\overline{\boldsymbol{x}}^*$, $s^2(\boldsymbol{x}^*)$, and $\widehat{\mathrm{ACF}}(\boldsymbol{x}^*)$ based on the respective averages for the whole bootstrapped set $\mathbb{x}^*$, e.g., $\overline{\boldsymbol{x}}^* = \frac{1}{B}\sum_{i=1}^{B}\overline{\boldsymbol{x}}_i^*$.

5.2 Numerical Experiments and Their Results

To evaluate and compare the quality of the considered bootstrap methods, we generated finite-length interval-valued time series. In particular, we considered several time series models specified in Table 1, both of relatively small and large length (i.e., with $n = 100$ and $n = 1000$ elements, respectively).

Table 1. Time series model specifications.

Type	Model of the time series original	f_ε	f_L, f_R
AR(1)	$X_t = 0.8X_{t-1} + \varepsilon_t$	$N(0, 2)$	$U[0, 1]$
AR(2)	$X_t = X_{t-1} - 0.25X_{t-2} + \varepsilon_t$		
MA(1)	$X_t = \varepsilon_t + 0.7\varepsilon_{t-1} + 0.5\varepsilon_{t-2} + 0.2\varepsilon_{t-3}$		

Then using three bootstrap methods described in Sect. 3 (NBB, MBB, and SB) to interval-valued time series, we created $B = 500$ bootstrap replications $\mathbb{x}_1^*, \ldots, \mathbb{x}_{500}^*$ based on each of the primary series. In our simulations, we considered three block lengths for the bootstrap procedures: $l = 5, 10$, and 20. Notably, two of these choices are close to the theoretically optimal block length [18] associated with a time series of length n, namely $n^{1/3}$. For the values of n considered here, this yields $10^{1/3} \approx 4.642$ and $1000^{1/3} = 10$.

Next, we determined various statistical characteristics described in Sect. 5.1 and plot the correlograms (cf. [9]) that might help to evaluate the quality of the considered bootstrap methods. We now briefly summarize the main results of our numerical analysis. Below we provided only some figures (Fig. 1 and 2) and numerical outcomes (Table 2). More detailed results can be found in the special supplementary file [25] and are available upon request.

Table 2. Comparisons of the bootstrap methods for the interval-valued time series ($B = 500$, $n = 100$ and $l = 10$)

	Measure	Primary	NBB	MBB	SB
AR(1)	$\overline{x}$	$[-0.501, 0.472]$	$[-0.564, 0.410]$	$[-0.845, 0.149]$	$[\mathbf{-0.557}, \mathbf{0.416}]$
	$\widehat{\mathrm{LRV}}$	57.360	**44.945**	43.750	44.685
	$\mathrm{RBias}_{\mathrm{LRV}}$	–	**−0.216**	−0.237	−0.221
	$\mathrm{RMSE}_{\mathrm{LRV}}$	–	**0.087**	0.109	0.101
AR(2)	$\overline{x}$	$[-0.429, 0.545]$	$[-0.496, 0.479]$	$[-0.792, 0.202]$	$[\mathbf{-0.481}, \mathbf{0.492}]$
	$\widehat{\mathrm{LRV}}$	53.059	**43.092**	40.986	43.030
	$\mathrm{RBias}_{\mathrm{LRV}}$	–	**−0.189**	−0.228	−0.189
	$\mathrm{RMSE}_{\mathrm{LRV}}$	–	0.098	0.111	**0.090**
MA(1)	$\overline{x}$	$[-0.465, 0.521]$	$[\mathbf{-0.497}, \mathbf{0.490}]$	$[-0.734, 0.257]$	$[-0.503, 0.483]$
	$\widehat{\mathrm{LRV}}$	24.496	**22.252**	18.199	20.534
	$\mathrm{RBias}_{\mathrm{LRV}}$	–	**−0.092**	−0.257	−0.162
	$\mathrm{RMSE}_{\mathrm{LRV}}$	–	0.080	0.108	**0.074**

Let us now briefly summarize the results from the numerical studies (the best results in Table 2 are emboldened). Taking the mean value into account, NBB and SB yielded results that are usually close to the sample statistics $\bar{x}$. The differences between NBB and SB seem to be negligible. On the contrary, MBB led to significantly bigger errors for the means of any considered models. For longer primary time series (i.e., when n was increased to 1000), errors for all bootstrap methods decreased significantly, while the influence of the block length l was not completely clear.

The LRV analysis confirmed that for the NBB and SB methods, we obtained results closer to the primary time series, with NBB noticeably dominating over SB. As before, better statistical properties were obtained for longer time series.

Some interesting conclusions were obtained from the ACF and correlogram analyses (see Fig. 1 and the left panel of Fig. 2). The rectangles in the figures denote bootstrap estimators for each of the considered methods, where the red color indicates NBB, green – MBB, and blue – SB, respectively. Additionally,

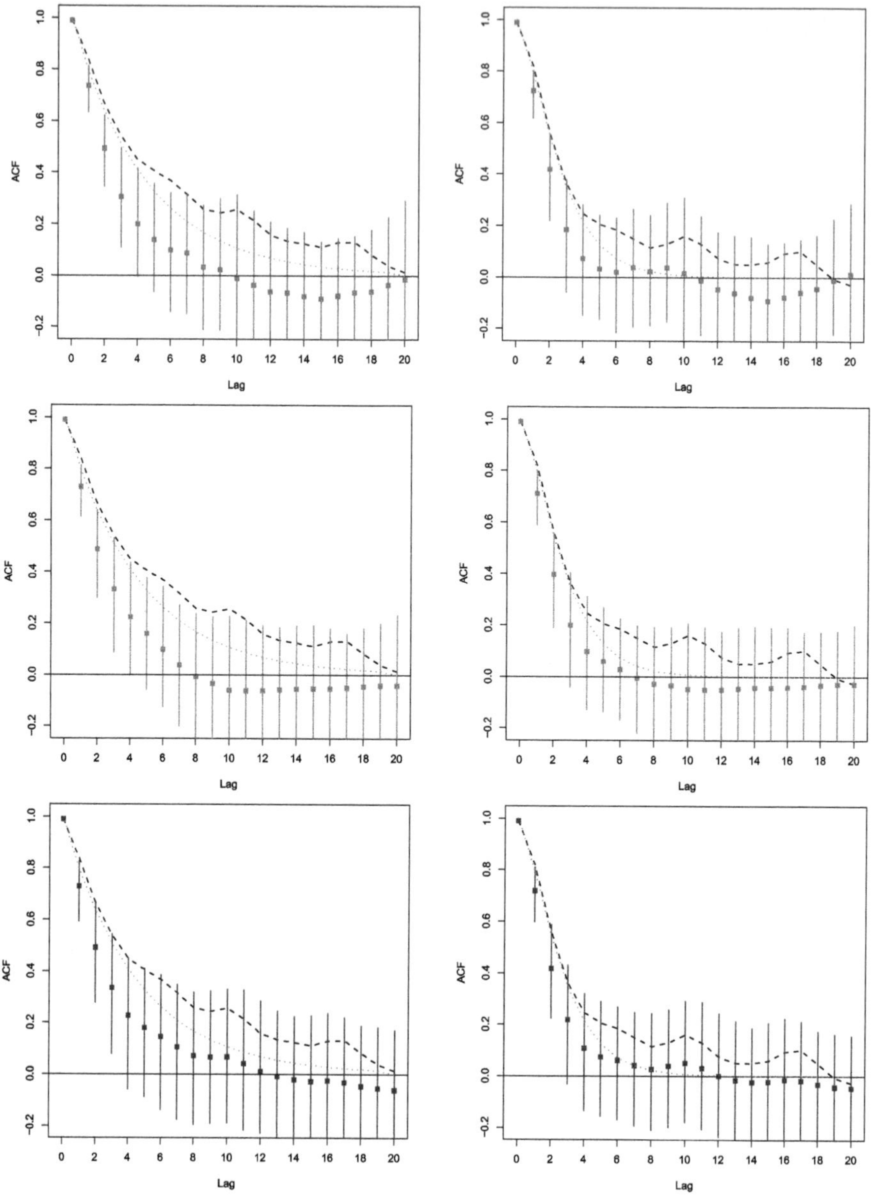

Fig. 1. Correlograms of three bootstrap methods: NBB (red), MBB (green), and SB (blue) for two models of the interval-valued time series: AR(1) - left column, and AR(2) - right column; $n = 100$ and $l = 10$. (Color figure online)

to better illustrate the uncertainty, the vertical lines passing through the boxes correspond to the 90% percentile confidence intervals.

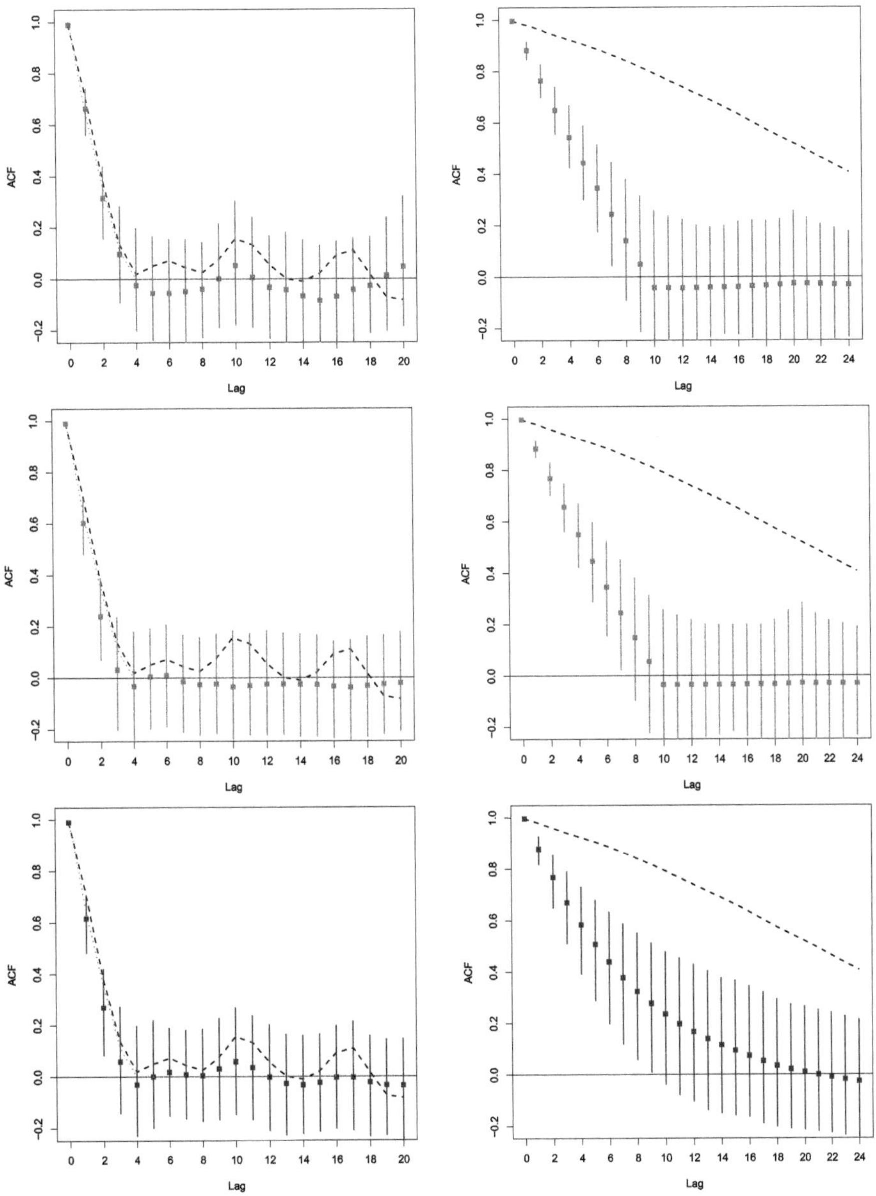

Fig. 2. Correlograms of three bootstrap methods: NBB (red), MBB (green), and SB (blue) for two the interval-valued time series: MA(1), $n = 100$ and $l = 10$ - left column, and USD/EUR (case study), $l = 10$ - right column. (Color figure online)

In general, the autocorrelation estimators decreased more slowly for SB as the lag increased. They were closer to both the respective sample statistics (black dashed line) and their true theoretical values (brown dotted line). Moreover, the correlogram for SB could even mimic the overall shape of $\widehat{\mathrm{ACF}}(\mathbb{x})$ with its unexpected changes in slope. On the contrary, the correlograms for NBB and MBB decreased rapidly with respect to the primary time series and true values, indicating overall larger errors. Some strange "artifacts" (i.e., unexpected "hills" or "valleys") appeared for NBB, but were not present in the respective sample statistics of the primary series. It is worth noting that larger values of the l parameter led to better-fitting correlograms based on bootstrap resampling.

To sum up, taking all benchmarks into account, SB and NBB provided the best overall results (with a slight preference for SB). We can also compare bootstrap methods on the basis of some theoretical characteristics of the originals with their subsequent transformation into the interval time series (via Algorithm 1), e.g., the respective expected values. Some results of this kind can be found in the supplementary file [25]. Here, due to a lack of space, we limit ourselves to the analysis of the realization of the primary series (i.e., "without knowing" its inner generation mechanism).

6 Case Study: USD/EUR Exchange Rates

We further conducted a numerical comparison of the bootstrap methods for interval-valued time series using a real-world dataset of daily USD/EUR currency exchange rates for 2010, available in [22]. For each trading day, the corresponding interval was constructed using the lowest and highest observed exchange rates. The resulting interval-valued time series consists of $n = 261$ observations. Accordingly, we applied block lengths $l = 6, 10$, and 12, with the smallest value being close to the theoretically optimal block length for the given sample size. Numerical outcomes of the respective statistical characteristics are given in Table 3.

The results for the correlograms were also similar to the ones for the synthetic samples (see, e.g., Fig. 2). Both NBB and MBB showed decreasing ACF values very rapidly as a function of lag. Then, their errors were larger than for SB. The slope of this function for SB was smaller and therefore closer to $\widehat{\mathrm{ACF}}(\mathbb{x})$. As previously mentioned, the longer block length improved the results. To sum up, it seems that SB should be preferred as the bootstrap method for ITS.

Table 3. Comparisons of the bootstrap methods for the interval-valued time series of daily USD/EUR exchange rates, $l = 10$

Measure	Primary	NBB	MBB	SB
$\overline{x}$	[0.751,0.759]	[0.752,0.760]	[0.752,0.760]	**[0.752, 0.760]**
$\widehat{\mathrm{LRV}}$	0.007	0.005	0.005	**0.005**
$\mathrm{RBias}_{\mathrm{LRV}}$	–	**−0.234**	**−0.235**	**−0.226**
$\mathrm{RMSE}_{\mathrm{LRV}}$	–	**0.087**	0.090	0.100

7 Conclusions

Interval-valued data are commonly used to represent imprecision, yet the literature lacks bootstrap methods designed explicitly for interval-valued time series. To address this gap, we numerically compared the nonoverlapping block (NBB), moving block (MBB), and stationary (SB) bootstraps using both synthetic and real datasets, and proposed a dedicated simulation algorithm for generating synthetic interval-valued time series. The evaluation relied on standard statistical measures adapted to the interval-valued setting. Our results suggest that SB (and NBB to some extent) yields the lowest errors and is therefore the most promising approach for interval-valued time series.

These findings are preliminary, as no bootstrap methods have yet been developed explicitly for interval-valued time series. Further research may consider alternative error measures and data-generation schemes, as well as extensions to fuzzy-valued time series, which generalize interval-valued data and are widely used in practice. Non-stationary time series may also be analyzed using specifically tailored bootstrap methods.

Acknowledgments. This work acknowledges the support from the project "ExplainMe: Explainable Artificial Intelligence for Monitoring Acoustic Features extracted from Speech" (FENG.02.02-IP.05-0302/23) carried out within the First Team programme of the Foundation for Polish Science, co-financed by the European Union under the European Funds for Smart Economy 2021–2027 (FENG).

References

1. Aumann, R.: Integrals of set-valued function. J. Math. Anal. Appl. **12**, 1–12 (1965)
2. Bertoluzza, C., Corral, N., Salas, A.: On a new class of distances between fuzzy numbers. Mathware Soft Comput. **2**(2), 71–84 (1995)
3. Blanco-Fernández, A., Corral, N., González-Rodríguez, G.: Estimation of a flexible simple linear model for interval data based on set arithmetic. Comput. Stat. Data Anal. **55**, 2568–2578 (2011). https://doi.org/10.1016/j.csda.2011.03.005
4. Box, G., Jenkins, G.: Time Series Analysis: Forecasting and Control. Holden-Day, Oakland (1976)
5. Buhlmann, P.: Sieve bootstrap for time series. Bernoulli **3**(2), 123–148 (1997). https://doi.org/10.2307/3318584
6. Bühlmann, P.: Bootstraps for time series. Stat. Sci. **17**(1), 52–72 (2002). https://doi.org/10.1214/ss/1023798998
7. Carlstein, E.: The use of subseries values for estimating the variance of a general statistic from a stationary sequence. Ann. Stat. **14**(3), 1171–1179 (1986). https://doi.org/10.1214/aos/1176350057
8. Couso, I., Dubois, D.: Statistical reasoning with set-valued information: ontic vs. epistemic views. Int. J. Approximate Reason. **55**(7), 1502–1518 (2014). https://doi.org/10.1016/j.ijar.2013.07.002
9. Cowpertwait, P.S., Metcalfe, A.V.: Introductory Time Series with R. Springer, New York (2009)

10. Efron, B.: Bootstrap methods: another look at the jackknife. Ann. Stat. **7**, 1–26 (1979)
11. Gil, M., Montenegro, M., González-Rodríguez, G., Colubi, A., Casals, M.: Bootstrap approach to the multi-sample test of means with imprecise data. Comput. Stat. Data Anal. **51**, 148–162 (2006). https://doi.org/10.1016/j.csda.2006.04.018
12. Grzegorzewski, P., Romaniuk, M.: Bootstrap methods for epistemic fuzzy data. Int. J. Appl. Math. Comput. Sci. **32**(2), 285–297 (2022). https://doi.org/10.34768/amcs-2022-0021
13. Grzegorzewski, P., Romaniuk, M.: Bootstrap methods for epistemic fuzzy data. Int. J. Appl. Math. Comput. Sci. **34**(2), 277–289 (2022). https://doi.org/10.61822/amcs-2024-0020
14. Härdle, W., Horowitz, J., Kreiss, J.P.: Bootstrap methods for time series. Int. Stat. Rev. **71**(2), 453–459 (2003)
15. Korner, R.: On the variance of fuzzy random variables. Fuzzy Sets Systems **92**, 83–93 (1997). https://doi.org/10.1016/S0165-0114(96)00169-8
16. Kreiss, J.P., Lahiri, S.N.: Bootstrap methods for time series. In: Subba Rao, T., Subba Rao, S., Rao, C. (eds.) Time Series Analysis: Methods and Applications, Handbook of Statistics, vol. 30, pp. 3–26. Elsevier (2012). https://doi.org/10.1016/B978-0-444-53858-1.00001-6
17. Künsch, H.R.: The jackknife and the bootstrap for general stationary observations. Ann. Stat. **17**(3), 1217–1241 (1989). https://doi.org/10.1214/aos/1176347265
18. Lahiri, S.: Theoretical comparisons of block bootstrap methods. Ann. Stat. **27**(1), 386–404 (1999). https://doi.org/10.1214/aos/1018031117
19. Maia, A.L.S., de A.T. de Carvalho, F., Ludermir, T.B.: Forecasting models for interval-valued time series. Neurocomputing **71**(16), 3344–3352 (2008). https://doi.org/10.1016/j.neucom.2008.02.022
20. Matheron, G.: Random Sets and Integral Geometry. Wiley, New York (1975)
21. Molchanov, I.: Theory of Random Sets. Springer, London (2005)
22. Narne, P.: https://www.kaggle.com/datasets/pavankrishnanarne/daily-currency-exchange-rates-2008-present/data
23. Neyman, J.: On the two different aspects of the representative method: the method of stratified sampling and the method of purposive selection. J. Roy. Stat. Soc. **97**, 558–625 (1934)
24. Politis, D.N., Romano, J.P.: The stationary bootstrap. J. Am. Stat. Assoc. **89**(428), 1303–1313 (1994). https://doi.org/10.2307/2290993
25. Romaniuk, M., Grzegorzewski, P.: Bootstrap methods for interval-valued time series (supplementary material). https://doi.org/10.13140/RG.2.2.20196.85122, https://www.researchgate.net/publication/399823687_Bootstrap_Methods_for_interval-Valued_Time_Series_supplementary_material
26. Romaniuk, M., Grzegorzewski, P., Parchami, A.: FuzzySimRes: epistemic bootstrap – an efficient tool for statistical inference based on imprecise data. R J. **16**(2), 175–190 (2024). https://doi.org/10.32614/RJ-2024-016
27. Singh, K.: On the asymptotic accuracy of Efron's bootstrap. Ann. Stat. **9**, 1187–1195 (1981). https://doi.org/10.1214/aos/1176345636

Uncertainty-Aware Repeated-Measures ANOVA for Interval-Valued Data with an Application to Longitudinal CT Tumor Imaging

Przemysław Grzegorzewski[1,2], Maha Moussa[3], Yan Sun[3](✉), and Said Elshafae[4]

[1] Faculty of Mathematics and Information Science, Warsaw University of Technology, Warsaw, Poland
[2] Systems Research Institute, Polish Academy of Sciences, Warsaw, Poland
[3] Department of Mathematics and Statistics, Utah State University, Logan, UT, USA
yan.sun@usu.edu
[4] School of Medicine and Huntsman Cancer Institute, University of Utah, Salt Lake City, UT, USA

Abstract. Repeated-measures ANOVA is widely used in clinical and longitudinal studies as an extension of the classical analysis of variance to test differences in means between related groups. The standard method assumes real-valued responses. However, in many applications, outcomes are naturally reported as intervals in the presence of various uncertainty factors, such as measurement imprecision, aggregation, rounding, and privacy preservation. To fill this gap, we propose an uncertainty-aware RM-ANOVA test that accounts for inherent uncertainty in interval-valued data. Using a distance-based approach for the center–radius representation, we construct interval-valued variance decomposition and a test statistic, analogous to their real-valued counterparts. For inference, we use a within-subject permutation test that is finite-sample exact under the repeated-measures null hypothesis and avoids the normality assumption, which is unrealistic for interval-valued responses. Simulation studies under various correlated longitudinal designs demonstrate satisfactory Type I error control and strong power gains when different uncertainty structures are present. Finally, we apply the proposed test to a publicly available longitudinal CT tumor imaging dataset with manual segmentations (Longitudinal-CT), where the interval-valued analysis yields stronger evidence of a time effect than corresponding center-only repeated-measures analyses, highlighting the value of explicitly accounting for segmentation-induced measurement uncertainty.

Keywords: interval-valued data · repeated measures · longitudinal data · random intervals · ANOVA · permutation test

B. Vantaggi et al. (Eds.): IPMU 2026, CCIS 3019, pp. 477–491, 2026.
https://doi.org/10.1007/978-3-032-28994-0_34

1 Introduction

Repeated-measures analysis of variance (RM-ANOVA) is a classical tool for assessing whether mean responses change across multiple levels or experimental conditions when the same units are observed repeatedly. Standard RM-ANOVA and related mixed-effects models are formulated for scalar outcomes, and rely on normality assumptions that may be unfeasible in reality [4,10]. In many modern applications, however, responses are more naturally represented as *intervals* rather than point values. Examples include imaging-derived tumor measurements subject to segmentation variability, repeated assessments summarized over time windows, and uncertainty-aware reporting that explicitly records imprecision. Interval-valued data provide a more realistic representation of epistemic uncertainty and partial observability, and have been studied extensively under the frameworks of symbolic and set-valued data analysis, primarily for cross-sectional settings [2,5,7]. Collapsing such data to single points necessarily discards uncertainty information that may be scientifically meaningful.

This paper develops an uncertainty-aware repeated-measures ANOVA test for interval-valued responses. To our knowledge, this is the first RM-ANOVA model that provides both an explicit variance decomposition and an ANOVA test for interval-valued longitudinal data. Based on an L_2 metric on the space of intervals, we construct an interval-valued RM-ANOVA variance decomposition and an F-type statistic with an interpretable weight controlling sensitivity to uncertainty dynamics. For inference, we employ a randomization procedure that generates the sampling distribution of F by randomly permuting group labels within each subject; under the repeated-measures null hypothesis of no treatment effect, this strategy provides an exact ANOVA test while preserving between-group dependences. We carry out systematic simulation studies under correlated longitudinal designs and distribution settings, and the results show that our test achieves stable Type I error control and competitive power across a range of uncertainty regimes. To demonstrate applicability, we apply the proposed test to a publicly available longitudinal CT tumor imaging dataset with manual segmentations, where interval-valued tumor volumes are derived from repeated masks across baseline and follow-up visits.

2 Classical RM-ANOVA

Suppose n subjects are measured under multiple (say, k) time points or various conditions. Let Y_{it} denote the response from subject i at time t, for $i = 1, \dots, n$ and $t = 1, \dots, k$. The so-called **repeated-measures ANOVA** (RM-ANOVA) model is usually formulated as

$$Y_{it} = \mu + \tau_t + s_i + \varepsilon_{it}, \tag{1}$$

where μ stands for the grand mean, τ_t denotes the t-th time effect, s_i is a random effect of subject i, and ε_{it} is a residual error. Our main goal is to test whether the mean response differs across time while accounting for within-subject dependence. For this purpose, we verify the null hypothesis

$$H_0 : \tau_1 = \tau_2 = \ldots = \tau_k, \tag{2}$$

of no time effect, against the alternative $H_1 : \exists\, t \neq t'$ such that $\tau_t \neq \tau_{t'}$. Assuming μ_t is the expected value of the outcome when the experiment is in time t, i.e. $\mu_t = \mu + \tau_t$, we can express the null hypothesis in the following equivalent form: $H_0 : \mu_1 = \ldots = \mu_k$.

To solve the problem we decompose the total variability SS_{total} into three components: SS_{time}, SS_{subj}, and SS_{error}, responsible for the time effects, variability between subjects and unexplained residuals, respectively, i.e. we have

$$SS_{total} = SS_{time} + SS_{subj} + SS_{error}, \tag{3}$$

where $SS_{total} = \sum_{i=1}^{n}\sum_{t=1}^{k}(Y_{it} - \bar{Y}_{..})^2$, $SS_{\text{time}} = n\sum_{t=1}^{k}(\bar{Y}_{.t} - \bar{Y}_{..})^2$, $SS_{\text{subj}} = k\sum_{i=1}^{n}(\bar{Y}_{i.} - \bar{Y}_{..})^2$ and where $\bar{Y}_{..} = \frac{1}{nk}\sum_{i=1}^{n}\sum_{t=1}^{k} Y_{it}$, $\bar{Y}_{i.} = \frac{1}{k}\sum_{t=1}^{k} Y_{it}$ and $\bar{Y}_{.t} = \frac{1}{n}\sum_{i=1}^{n} Y_{it}$ denote various kinds of sample means.

Classical RM-ANOVA requires a number of assumptions to be met, such as: normality: $\varepsilon_{it} \sim \mathcal{N}(0, \sigma^2)$; independence of observations across subjects and fixed correlation of observations within each subject and *sphericity*, i.e. $\text{Var}(Y_{.t} - Y_{.t'}) =$ constant for any t, t'. Under these assumptions we obtain a quite simple decision criterion, i.e. we reject H_0 if $(n-1)SS_{time}/SS_{error} > F_{1-\alpha}^{k-1,\,(n-1)(k-1)}$, where $F_{1-\alpha}^{k-1,\,(n-1)(k-1)}$ is the $(1-\alpha)100\%$ quantile of the F-Snedecor distribution with $k-1$, $(n-1)(k-1)$ degrees of freedom.

Unfortunately, generalizing RM-ANOVA to the case of imprecise data turns out to be far from trivial. This is due to the structure of interval-valued data, which creates various arithmetic and probabilistic obstacles that we will discuss in the next section.

3 Interval-Valued Data

Let $\mathcal{K}_c(\mathbb{R})$ denote the family of all non-empty bounded and closed intervals in the real line $\mathbb{R}$. Each interval $A \in \mathcal{K}_c(\mathbb{R})$ can be expressed by its endpoints L_A, U_A. Alternatively, we may consider the notation based on its center and radius denoted by C_A and R_A, respectively, where $C_A = \frac{1}{2}(L_A + U_A)$ and $R_A = \frac{1}{2}(U_A - L_A)$. Hence, for any $A \in \mathcal{K}_c(\mathbb{R})$ we have

$$A = [L_A, U_A] = [C_A - R_A, C_A + R_A],$$

where $L_A, U_A \in \mathbb{R}$, $L_A \leqslant U_A$ and $C_A \in \mathbb{R}$, $R_A \geqslant 0$. The Minkowski addition and scalar multiplication is defined in $\mathcal{K}_c(\mathbb{R})$, i.e. $\forall A, B \in \mathcal{K}_c(\mathbb{R})$ and $\forall \lambda \in \mathbb{R}$

$$A + B = \{a + b : a \in A, b \in B\}, \qquad \lambda \cdot A = \{\lambda a : a \in A\}.$$

However, $(\mathcal{K}_c(\mathbb{R}), +, \cdot)$ is not a linear space due to the lack of the opposite element with respect to the Minkowski addition: in general, $A + (-1)\cdot A \neq \{0\}$, unless $A = \{a\}$ is a singleton.

Definition 1. *Let $(\Omega, \mathcal{A}, P)$ be a probability space. A* ***random interval*** *(interval-valued random set) is a mapping $X : \Omega \to \mathcal{K}_c(\mathbb{R})$, which is a measurable function with respect to the Borel σ-field induced by the Hausdorff metric.*

Equivalently, a mapping $X : \Omega \to \mathcal{K}_c(\mathbb{R})$ is a random interval if $C_X : \Omega \to \mathbb{R}$ and $R_X : \Omega \to \mathbb{R}_+ \cup \{0\}$ are (real-valued) random variables defined as the center and radius of $X(\omega)$, respectively, $\forall \omega \in \Omega$. The *Aumann expectation* of X is given by the interval

$$\mathcal{E}(X) = \big[\mathbb{E}(L_X), \mathbb{E}(U_X)\big] = \big[\mathbb{E}(C_X) - \mathbb{E}(R_X), \mathbb{E}(C_X) + \mathbb{E}(R_X)\big]. \tag{4}$$

It is worth noting that, unlike the statistical analysis of numerical data, the reasoning with interval-valued data faces several inherent difficulties. These include complications with subtraction, which often necessitate avoiding this operation altogether; the absence of realistic and widely accepted probabilistic models for random intervals, leading to the exclusion of parametric approaches; and the lack of a universally accepted total ordering of intervals, which precludes the use of rank-based nonparametric methods.

4 RM-ANOVA for Interval-Valued Data

4.1 Model and Hypotheses

We consider a balanced repeated-measures design in which related samples are observed on n experimental subjects across k time points (or conditions). Let

$$X_{it} = [L_{it}, U_{it}] = [C_{it} - R_{it}, C_{it} + R_{it}], \qquad i = 1, \ldots, n, \quad t = 1, \ldots, k,$$

denote the bounded interval-valued response for subject i in time point t. Assume that, within each time point t, the interval observations are i.i.d. across units and share a common center–radius covariance structure. Equivalently, for each $t = 1, \ldots, k$, i.e.

$$\begin{bmatrix} C_{it} \\ R_{it} \end{bmatrix} \overset{i.i.d.}{\sim} F\left(\begin{bmatrix} \mu_t^C \\ \mu_t^R \end{bmatrix}, \begin{bmatrix} \sigma_C^2 & \sigma_{CR} \\ \sigma_{CR} & \sigma_R^2 \end{bmatrix} \right), \qquad i = 1, \ldots, n, \tag{5}$$

where $\mu_t^C, \sigma_{CR} \in \mathbb{R}$ and $\mu_t^R, \sigma_C^2, \sigma_R^2 > 0$.

Following (4), let $\boldsymbol{\mu}_t = \big[\mu_t^C - \mu_t^R, \mu_t^C + \mu_t^R\big]$ denote the expected value of the explained random variable X in time t. Then the repeated-measures null hypothesis of no time effect is that the k interval-valued means are equal

$$H_0 : \boldsymbol{\mu}_1 = \boldsymbol{\mu}_2 = \ldots, \boldsymbol{\mu}_k, \tag{6}$$

against the alternative $H_1 : \boldsymbol{\mu}_t \neq \boldsymbol{\mu}_{t'}$ for at least one pair $t \neq t'$.

4.2 RM-ANOVA Variance Decomposition

For the repeated-measures data, the grand mean $\bar{X}_{..}$ is defined by the following center and radius components

$$\bar{C}_{..} = \frac{1}{nk}\sum_{i=1}^{n}\sum_{t=1}^{k} C_{it}, \qquad \bar{R}_{..} = \frac{1}{nk}\sum_{i=1}^{n}\sum_{t=1}^{k} R_{it}. \tag{7}$$

The time-specific and subject-specific means $\bar{X}_{.t}$ and $\bar{X}_{.i}$ are given by

$$\bar{C}_{.t} = \frac{1}{n}\sum_{i=1}^{n} C_{it}, \qquad \bar{R}_{.t} = \frac{1}{n}\sum_{i=1}^{n} R_{it}, \qquad t = 1, \ldots, k, \tag{8}$$

and

$$\bar{C}_{i.} = \frac{1}{k}\sum_{t=1}^{k} C_{it}, \qquad \bar{R}_{i.} = \frac{1}{k}\sum_{t=1}^{k} R_{it}, \qquad i = 1, \ldots, n, \tag{9}$$

respectively. Keeping in mind the problem with subtraction in $\mathcal{K}_c(\mathbb{R})$, mentioned in Sect. 3, the total sum of squares is defined using the square of the L^2-type metric on $\mathcal{K}_c(\mathbb{R})$ as follows

$$SS_{\text{total}} = \sum_{i=1}^{n}\sum_{t=1}^{k} d_w^2\left(X_{it}, \bar{X}_{..}\right) = \sum_{i=1}^{n}\sum_{t=1}^{k}\left[\left(C_{it} - \bar{C}_{..}\right)^2 + w\left(R_{it} - \bar{R}_{..}\right)^2\right], \tag{10}$$

where $w > 0$ can be interpreted as a relative weight for the difference between radii and the difference between spreads (see [1,3]). Similarly, the time and subject sums of squares based on the weighted squared distance d_w are defined as

$$SS_{\text{time}} = n\sum_{t=1}^{k} d_w^2\left(X_{.t}, \bar{X}_{..}\right) = n\sum_{t=1}^{k}\left[\left(\bar{C}_{.t} - \bar{C}_{..}\right)^2 + w\left(\bar{R}_{.t} - \bar{R}_{..}\right)^2\right], \tag{11}$$

$$SS_{\text{subj}} = k\sum_{i=1}^{n} d_w^2\left(X_{i.}, \bar{X}_{..}\right) = k\sum_{i=1}^{n}\left[\left(\bar{C}_{i.} - \bar{C}_{..}\right)^2 + w\left(\bar{R}_{i.} - \bar{R}_{..}\right)^2\right]. \tag{12}$$

The residual sum of squares is obtained by

$$SS_{\text{error}} = SS_{\text{total}} - SS_{\text{time}} - SS_{\text{subj}}. \tag{13}$$

Analogous to classical repeated-measures ANOVA, we define the interval-valued test statistic

$$F_w = \frac{SS_{\text{time}}/(k-1)}{SS_{\text{error}}/((k-1)(n-1))}. \tag{14}$$

Here it should be noticed that although F_w resembles a conventional F statistic, its sampling distribution depends on the joint behavior of the center and radius components and may deviate substantially from F distribution, especially for small samples and non-Gaussian center and radius components. This is the reason why a nonparametric resampling procedure will be further used.

4.3 Random Permutation Test

Permutation inference is adopted, instead of the more time-consuming bootstrap resampling, to compute the p-value. Under the repeated-measures null hypothesis of no time effect, group labels are exchangeable within each subject. Thus, by randomizing group labels within each subject, the permutation test constructs the reference distribution in a completely nonparametric manner, yielding the finite-sample exact inference without any distributional assumptions [4, 10]. More precisely, the permutation p-value is computed as follows:

1. Compute the observed statistic F_w^{obs}.
2. For $b = 1, \ldots, B$, randomly permute the k group labels for each subject and recompute the statistic $F_w^{(b)}$.
3. Compute the p-value as

$$p_{\text{perm}} = \frac{1 + \sum_{b=1}^{B} \mathbb{1}\{F_w^{(b)} \geq F_w^{\text{obs}}\}}{B+1}. \tag{15}$$

In the above formula, the $+1$ correction in the numerator and denominator treats the observed statistic as one of the $B+1$ exchangeable realizations under the null hypothesis, preventing zero p-values and ensuring finite-sample exact inference [4]. It is easily seen that the total number of permutation samples $B = (k!)^n$ for computing the exact p-value. In practice, if this number is too large, one can choose a sufficiently large B to approximate the p-value. In our simulation study, we approximate the permutation p-value using $B = 1000$ within-subject permutations to balance accuracy and computation time. For the real-data application with $k = 2$, the within-subject permutation reduces to label swaps; we use $B = 5{,}000$ random swaps to obtain a stable Monte Carlo approximation.

5 Simulation Study

5.1 Data-Generating Mechanism

We consider balanced repeated-measures designs with $n \in \{5, 10, 15, 20\}$ subjects observed at $k = 3$ time points. For subject $i = 1, \ldots, n$ and occasion $t = 1, \ldots, k$, the interval-valued response $X_{it} = [L_{it}, U_{it}]$ is represented in center–radius form

$$X_{it} = [L_{it}, U_{it}] \quad \longleftrightarrow \quad (C_{it}, R_{it}), \qquad C_{it} = \frac{L_{it} + U_{it}}{2}, \quad R_{it} = \frac{U_{it} - L_{it}}{2}.$$

The center and radius components are generated by the additive model

$$\begin{bmatrix} C_{it} \\ R_{it} \end{bmatrix} = \begin{bmatrix} \mu_t^C \\ \mu_t^R \end{bmatrix} + \begin{bmatrix} b_i^C \\ b_i^R \end{bmatrix} + \begin{bmatrix} \varepsilon_{it}^C \\ \varepsilon_{it}^R \end{bmatrix}, \qquad i = 1, \ldots, n, \quad t = 1, \ldots, k, \tag{16}$$

where (μ_t^C, μ_t^R) are time points mean functions, (b_i^C, b_i^R) are subject-specific random effects, and $(\varepsilon_{it}^C, \varepsilon_{it}^R)$ are random errors.

Subject-Specific Random Intercepts. Between-subject heterogeneity is modeled by a bivariate Gaussian random intercept

$$\mathbf{b}_i = \begin{bmatrix} b_i^C \\ b_i^R \end{bmatrix} \sim \mathcal{N}\left(\begin{bmatrix} 0 \\ 0 \end{bmatrix}, \begin{bmatrix} \sigma_{bC}^2 & \rho\,\sigma_{bC}\sigma_{bR} \\ \rho\,\sigma_{bC}\sigma_{bR} & \sigma_{bR}^2 \end{bmatrix} \right).$$

Here $(\sigma_{bC}, \sigma_{bR})$ correspond to the component-wise standard deviations supplied via `sd_subject` in the simulator, and $\rho \in (-1, 1)$ controls the correlation between center and radius random intercepts.

Within-Subject Errors Via a Gaussian-Copula Dependence Model. For each subject i, we generate a latent Gaussian vector

$$\mathbf{Z}_i = \left[Z_{i1}^C, \ldots, Z_{ik}^C,\, Z_{i1}^R, \ldots, Z_{ik}^R \right]^T \sim \mathcal{N}(0, \mathrm{Corr}_e),$$

where the $2k \times 2k$ correlation matrix has the block form

$$\mathrm{Corr}_e = \begin{bmatrix} R_\phi & \rho\,R_\phi \\ \rho\,R_\phi & R_\phi \end{bmatrix}, \qquad (R_\phi)_{tt'} = \phi^{|t-t'|},$$

with $\phi \in (-1, 1)$ controlling AR(1) dependence across occasions within each component (as implemented in the code, the same ρ also controls the cross-component correlation in the within-subject errors).

To obtain potentially non-Gaussian margins while preserving Corr_e, we apply a Gaussian-copula transform: set $U = \Phi(\mathbf{Z}_i)$ elementwise and map U to the desired marginal family using its quantile function. The resulting errors are standardized to mean 0 and variance 1 within each component, then scaled by component-wise noise standard deviations

$$\varepsilon_{it}^C = \sigma_e^C\, \varepsilon_{it,C}^{\mathrm{std}}, \qquad \varepsilon_{it}^R = \sigma_e^R\, \varepsilon_{it,R}^{\mathrm{std}},$$

where (σ_e^C, σ_e^R) correspond to `sd_noise` in the simulator.

Finally, to ensure valid intervals, radii are truncated below at a nonnegative floor

$$R_{it} \leftarrow \max(R_{it}, r_0),$$

where r_0 corresponds to `radius_floor` (set to 0 in our experiments).

5.2 Time Effects and Alternatives

Under the repeated-measures null hypothesis, the mean functions are constant across time-points, i.e.

$$\mu_t^C \equiv 0, \qquad \mu_t^R \equiv \mu_R > 0, \qquad t = 1, \ldots, k.$$

We set μ_R to a moderate positive baseline to reflect non-degenerate measurement uncertainty; specifically, μ_R is chosen as a fixed fraction (one-half in our main experiments) of the marginal standard deviation of the center component.

To assess power, we introduce monotone trend alternatives through a heterogeneity factor $\eta \geq 1$ by allowing both the center and radius mean functions to vary across time-points

$$\mu_t^C = \frac{t-1}{k-1}\kappa_C\,(\eta - 1), \qquad \mu_t^R = \mu_R + \frac{t-1}{k-1}\kappa_R\,(\eta - 1), \tag{17}$$

where κ_C and κ_R control signal strength for center and radius trends, respectively. In all experiments, we set $\kappa_C = 2.0$ and $\kappa_R = 1.5$. Different signal strengths are used for the center and radius components to reflect the empirically smaller variability of radius measurements relative to centers in imaging-derived interval data. We consider $\eta \in \{1, 1.2, 1.4, 1.6, 1.8, 2.0\}$, with $\eta = 1$ corresponding to the null hypothesis.

5.3 Distributional Models

We examine three distributional designs, referred to as Models I–III. In all cases, dependence across time and between the center and radius components is introduced through a Gaussian-copula construction. Specifically, latent Gaussian variables are mapped to $U = \Phi(Z)$ and then transformed to the target marginal family via the corresponding quantile function. For non-Gaussian families, the resulting draws are standardized to have mean 0 and variance 1 before being scaled by component-specific noise standard deviations.

Model I (Normal Center, Uniform Radius). For Model I, we explicitly enforce normal center noise and uniform radius noise via separate marginal specifications in the simulator. The random errors satisfy

$$\varepsilon_{it}^C \sim \mathcal{N}(0,1), \qquad \varepsilon_{it}^R \sim \mathrm{Unif}(-\sqrt{3}, \sqrt{3}), \tag{18}$$

so that both error components have mean 0 and variance 1 prior to scaling. Note that the standardization to mean 0 and variance 1 applies to the error components ε_{it}^C and ε_{it}^R; the radius response R_{it} has a positive baseline mean $\mu_R > 0$ through the population-level mean function in (16)–(17).

Model II (Standardized Gamma Family). Let G_{it}^C, G_{it}^R denote random variables from the Gamma distribution with shape parameter 2 and rate 2. We define standardized errors by

$$\varepsilon_{it}^C = \frac{G_{it}^C - \mathbb{E}(G_{it}^C)}{\sqrt{\mathrm{Var}(G_{it}^C)}}, \qquad \varepsilon_{it}^R = \frac{G_{it}^R - \mathbb{E}(G_{it}^R)}{\sqrt{\mathrm{Var}(G_{it}^R)}}, \tag{19}$$

yielding mean 0 and variance 1 while retaining right-skewness.

Model III (Standardized Poisson Family). Let K_{it}^C, K_{it}^R denote random variables from the Poisson distribution with parameter $\lambda = 6$ and define

$$\varepsilon_{it}^C = \frac{K_{it}^C - \lambda}{\sqrt{\lambda}}, \qquad \varepsilon_{it}^R = \frac{K_{it}^R - \lambda}{\sqrt{\lambda}}, \tag{20}$$

so that both components have mean 0 and variance 1 prior to scaling.

In all models, standardized errors are scaled by component-specific within-subject standard deviations (implemented in the simulator via `sd_noise`), and radii are constrained to be nonnegative through $R_{it} \leftarrow \max(R_{it}, 0)$, ensuring valid interval-valued observations. Standardization ensures that differences across distributional models reflect distributional shape rather than scale, enabling a fair assessment of robustness and power.

5.4 Weighting Schemes and Inference

The proposed repeated-measures test is evaluated under weighting choices $w \in \{0.3, 0.6, 1, w^*\}$, where $w^* = \hat{\sigma}_C/\hat{\sigma}_R$ denotes a data-driven scaling weight and is the natural choice in many scenarios of interval-valued data analysis [8].

For each configuration, 1000 Monte Carlo replicates are generated, and permutation p-values are computed using 1000 within-subject permutations at significance level $\alpha = 0.05$. Performance is summarized by the false rejection rate at $\eta = 1$ and the correct rejection rate for $\eta > 1$.

6 Results and Discussion

Table 1 summarizes calibration performance across sample sizes, weighting choices, and radius-noise distributions, while Fig. 1 illustrates power performance for the representative Model I setting. Across all designs, the false rejection rate at $\eta = 1$ is close to the significance level, indicating stable finite-sample calibration even under non-Gaussian interval components. The correct rejection rate for $\eta > 1$ increases monotonically with both the effect magnitude η and the sample size n, as expected for a consistent repeated-measures test. These findings empirically confirm the finite-sample validity of the proposed permutation procedure.

Across simulation settings, power curves differ systematically across weighting choices. These differences are most pronounced when temporal changes occur primarily in the radius component, where larger values of w yield higher sensitivity. When the dominant signal is in the center, smaller values of w are often preferable.

From an interpretive perspective, the weighting parameter w provides a transparent mechanism for controlling sensitivity to uncertainty dynamics. By tuning w, practitioners can emphasize either location-driven or uncertainty-driven temporal effects, aligning inference with specific scientific goals. When prior knowledge about the dominant source of temporal variation is limited, a simple data-driven scaling choice offers a robust default across designs.

Finally, the within-subject permutation strategy plays a central role in ensuring valid inference. By relying on exchangeability of time labels within each subject under the repeated-measures null, the procedure avoids fragile parametric assumptions and yields stable finite-sample calibration even for small samples and non-Gaussian interval components.

7 Real Data Illustration: Interval-Valued Tumor Volumes

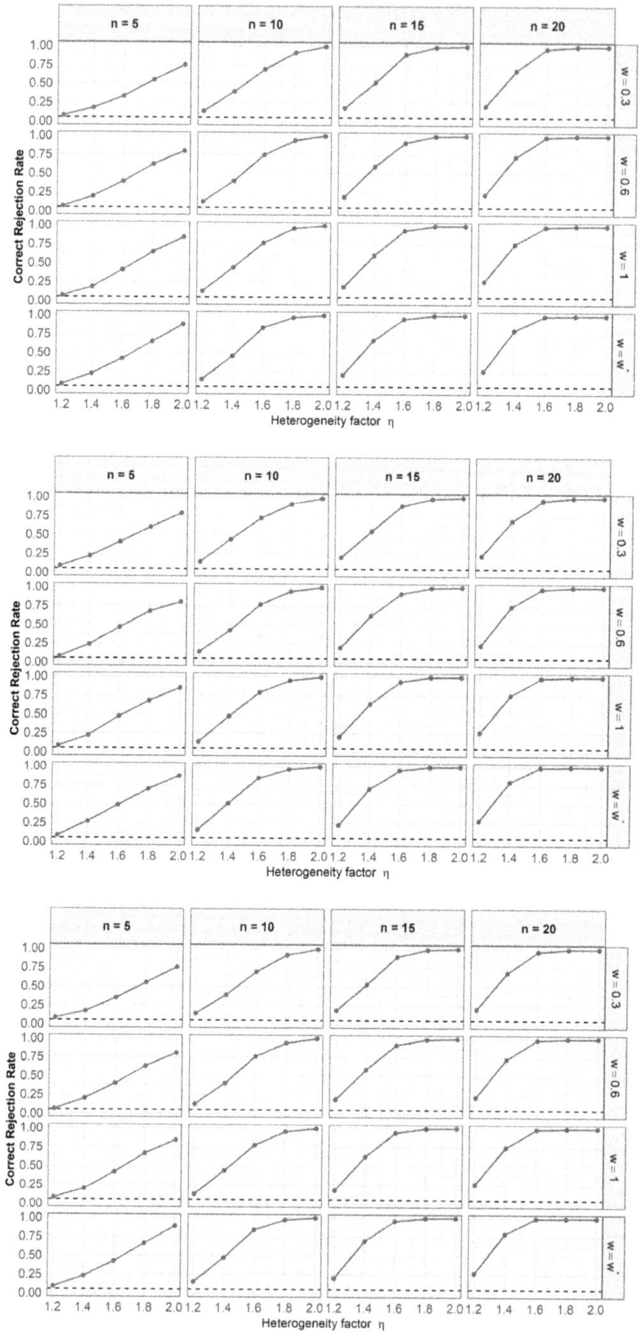

Fig. 1. Correct rejection rate versus η ($\eta > 1$), faceted by w (rows) and sample size n (columns) for Models I–III (Sect. 5.1). Curves are Monte Carlo estimates using within-subject permutation p-values.

Table 1. False rejection rates at $\eta = 1$ across sample sizes n and weights w under the three simulation models. Results are based on within-subject permutation p-values with significance level $\alpha = 0.05$.

Model	Weight w	$n = 5$	$n = 10$	$n = 15$	$n = 20$
Model I	0.3	0.044	0.038	0.047	0.043
Model I	0.6	0.045	0.052	0.050	0.050
Model I	1	0.058	0.047	0.059	0.052
Model I	w^*	0.048	0.051	0.048	0.059
Model II	0.3	0.050	0.039	0.044	0.043
Model II	0.6	0.052	0.052	0.053	0.052
Model II	1	0.064	0.049	0.061	0.050
Model II	w^*	0.046	0.046	0.042	0.049
Model III	0.3	0.042	0.042	0.047	0.048
Model III	0.6	0.046	0.056	0.053	0.055
Model III	1	0.056	0.057	0.061	0.049
Model III	w^*	0.051	0.048	0.039	0.058

We illustrate the proposed uncertainty-aware repeated-measures ANOVA using a publicly available longitudinal tumor imaging dataset from the *Longitudinal-CT* collection hosted by the FDAT research data repository at the University of Tübingen [9]. The dataset was released to support the study of therapy response and measurement variability in longitudinal computed tomography (CT) imaging and includes paired baseline and follow-up scans with associated manual tumor segmentations.

The dataset consists of contrast-enhanced thoracic CT images acquired at two time points corresponding to baseline (BL) and follow-up (FU). In addition to the raw CT images, the dataset provides multiple manually annotated tumor segmentation masks for a subset of subjects, enabling direct assessment of segmentation-induced measurement uncertainty. Figure 2 shows a representative axial CT slice at follow-up for one subject, with the corresponding tumor segmentation overlaid, illustrating the image-level data from which interval-valued tumor measurements are derived.

The full dataset contains $n = 191$ subjects, each observed at both BL and FU. For each subject i and time-point t, tumor volume was computed directly from the available segmentation masks. Specifically, the number of voxels labeled as tumor was multiplied by the physical voxel volume obtained from the corresponding DICOM image spacing metadata, yielding tumor volume measurements in mm^3. When multiple segmentation masks were available for the same subject–timepoint pair, these repeated measurements reflect segmentation-induced variability.

Following the interval representation introduced in Sect. 4, tumor volume at each (i, t) was summarized as an interval $X_{it} = [L_{it}, U_{it}]$, where L_{it} and U_{it}

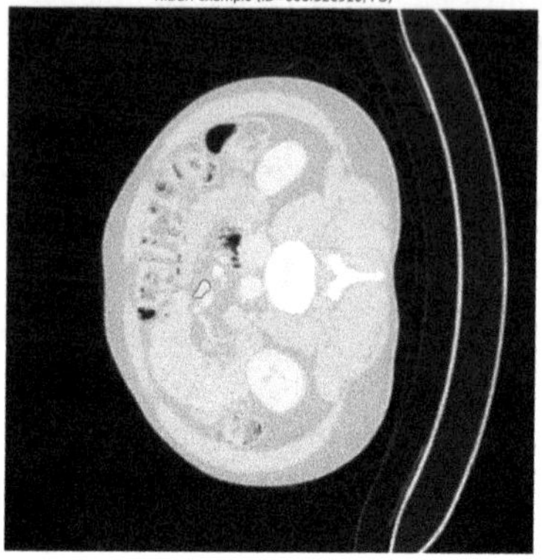

Fig. 2. Representative axial CT slice from the Longitudinal-CT dataset at follow-up (FU) for one subject. The manually annotated tumor segmentation mask is overlaid in red, illustrating how tumor volume measurements are derived from image-based segmentations. (Color figure online)

denote the minimum and maximum tumor volumes observed across all available segmentations at that visit. When only a single segmentation was available, the resulting interval was degenerate with $L_{it} = U_{it}$. Each interval was equivalently represented in center–radius form (C_{it}, R_{it}).

Most subjects had only a single segmentation per timepoint, yielding degenerate intervals with radius $R_{it} = 0$. Because the proposed method is designed to capture temporal changes in measurement uncertainty, our primary analysis focused on subjects exhibiting interval-valued information. Specifically, we retained subjects who were observed at both time points and had $R_{it} > 0$ at least one of the two visits. This filtering resulted in a final analysis cohort of $n = 24$ subjects, each contributing paired baseline and follow-up interval-valued measurements. Figure 3 displays boxplots of the tumor volume centers at baseline and follow-up for this subset. The figure illustrates both between-subject variability and an overall shift in tumor volume distributions across time, providing an intuitive visualization of the paired longitudinal structure underlying the formal inference.

The proposed interval-valued repeated-measures ANOVA was then applied to this filtered dataset using the center–radius representation and within-subject permutation inference described in Sect. 4. With $k = 2$ time points, the permutation procedure corresponds to random swapping of within-subject time labels and yields finite-sample exact inference under the repeated-measures null hypothesis. Using 5,000 within-subject permutations, the interval-valued test produced observed statistics and permutation p-values of $(F_w, p) = (2.200, 0.033)$ for $w = 1$, $(2.142, 0.037)$ for $w = 3$, $(2.062, 0.044)$ for $w = 6$, and $(1.969, 0.051)$ for the data-driven choice $w^* = 9.775$. These results suggest somewhat stronger evidence when moderate emphasis is placed on the radius component and illustrate how the proposed framework enables valid longitudinal inference while

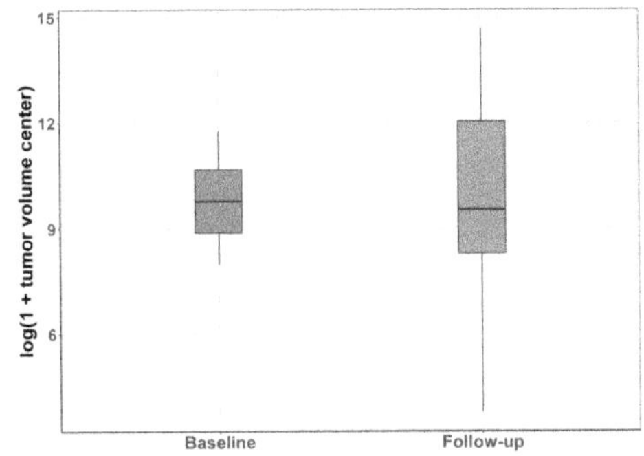

Fig. 3. Boxplot of tumor volume centers at baseline and follow-up for the subset of subjects with observable segmentation uncertainty.

explicitly accounting for measurement uncertainty encoded in interval-valued tumor volumes. To assess whether reducing interval-valued data to point-valued summaries leads to different inferential conclusions, we compared the proposed interval-valued analysis with standard center-only repeated-measures methods. For the same analysis cohort ($n = 24$), we reduced each interval-valued tumor measurement to its center and applied standard repeated-measures analyses to the resulting point-valued data. The corresponding center-only analyses were not statistically significant (paired t-test: $p = 0.149$; classical repeated-measures ANOVA on centers: $p = 0.149$; Wilcoxon signed-rank test: $p = 0.157$). In contrast, the interval-valued analysis yielded substantially stronger evidence of a time effect, suggesting that explicitly accounting for interval uncertainty can improve sensitivity relative to approaches based solely on tumor-volume centers (Table 2).

Table 2. Comparison of interval-valued and center-only repeated-measures analyses for the longitudinal CT tumor imaging example ($n = 24$). The cohort includes subjects observed at both time points with nonzero radius at least one visit.

Method	Statistic	p-value
Interval RM-ANOVA ($w = 1$)	2.200	0.033
Interval RM-ANOVA ($w = 3$)	2.142	0.037
Interval RM-ANOVA ($w = 6$)	2.062	0.044
Interval RM-ANOVA ($w = w^*$)	1.969	0.051
Paired t-test on centers	−1.493	0.149
Wilcoxon signed-rank on centers	100	0.157
RM-ANOVA on centers	2.229	0.149

8 Reproducibility and Code Availability

An open-source implementation of the proposed interval-valued RM-ANOVA with within-subject permutation inference, along with the simulation pipeline used to generate the results and figures in this paper, is available at https://github.com/Mahamoussa321/Interval-RM-ANOVA [6].

9 Conclusion

We propose an uncertainty-aware repeated-measures ANOVA framework for interval-valued outcomes that combines a weighted distance-based test statistic with a within-subject permutation procedure that is finite-sample exact under the repeated-measures null hypothesis. Simulation studies under correlated designs and non-Gaussian interval components demonstrate reliable control of Type I error and competitive power across a broad range of uncertainty regimes. Practically, the proposed method facilitates longitudinal inference that explicitly captures both location and uncertainty dynamics. Smaller weighting values prioritize center-driven effects, whereas larger values enhance sensitivity to temporal changes driven by uncertainty. In the absence of strong prior guidance, a simple data-driven scaling strategy provides a robust default choice. In the longitudinal CT tumor imaging application, the interval-valued analysis yielded stronger evidence of a time effect than corresponding center-only repeated-measures analyses. This empirical comparison highlights that explicitly incorporating segmentation-induced uncertainty can improve sensitivity relative to approaches that rely only on tumor-volume centers.

The framework currently assumes balanced repeated-measures designs and exchangeability of time labels under the null hypothesis. Extensions to unbalanced designs, missing data, and more complex dependence structures represent natural avenues for future research. Moreover, while this work focuses on permutation-based inference, integration with mixed-effects models or hierarchical representations of uncertainty may further improve interpretability and scalability in large longitudinal studies.

References

1. Bertoluzza, C., Corral Blanco, N., Salas, A.: On a new class of distances between fuzzy numbers. Mathware Soft Comput. **2**, 71–84 (1995)
2. Billard, L., Diday, E.: Symbolic Data Analysis: Conceptual Statistics and Data Mining. Wiley (2006). https://doi.org/10.1002/9780470090183
3. Gil, M., Lubiano, M., Montenegro, M., Lopez, M.: Least squares fitting of an affine function and strength of association for interval-valued data. Metrika **56**, 97–111 (2002). https://doi.org/10.1007/s001840100160
4. Good, P.I.: Permutation, Parametric and Bootstrap Tests of Hypotheses. Springer (2005). https://doi.org/10.1007/b138696

5. Lima Neto, E.A., de Carvalho, F.A.T.: Constrained linear regression models for symbolic interval-valued variables. Comput. Stat. Data Anal. **54**(2), 333–347 (2010). https://doi.org/10.1016/j.csda.2009.08.010
6. Moussa, M., Sun, Y., Grzegorzewski, P.: Interval-valued repeated-measures anova with permutation inference (2026). https://github.com/Mahamoussa321/Interval-RM-ANOVA, gitHub repository
7. Noirhomme-Fraiture, M., Brito, P.: Far beyond the classical data models: symbolic data analysis. Stat. Anal. Data Min. ASA Data Sci. J. (2011). https://doi.org/10.1002/sam.10112
8. Sinova, B., Cobubi, A., Gil, M., González-Rodríguez, G.: Interval arithmetic-based simple linear regression between interval data: Discussion and sensitivity analysis on the choice of the metric. Inf. Sci. **199**, 109–124 (2012). https://doi.org/10.1016/j.ins.2012.02.040
9. Longitudinal-CT: Annotated Longitudinal CT Scans for Therapy Response Assessment, University of Tübingen (2024)
10. Winkler, A.M., Ridgway, G.R., Webster, M.A., Smith, S.M., Nichols, T.E.: Permutation inference for the general linear model. NeuroImage **92**, 381–397 (2014). https://doi.org/10.1016/j.neuroimage.2014.01.060

Classification-Aligned Quality Criteria for Fuzzy Linguistic Summaries

Ansh Jay Kapadia, Katarzyna Kaczmarek-Majer(✉), and Olgierd Hryniewicz

Systems Research Institute Polish Academy of Sciences, Newelska 6, 01-147 Warsaw, Poland
{k.kaczmarek,olgierd.hryniewicz}@ibspan.waw.pl

Abstract. Fuzzy linguistic summaries provide compact, human-readable descriptions of complex data. In explainable artificial intelligence (XAI), they have been used to transform numerical model explanations into natural-language statements. Traditional quality criteria, such as the degree of truth and the degree of support, are exclusively data-driven and do not necessarily capture domain knowledge. In clinical settings, experts often reason contrastively and relative to baseline expectations: a pattern is informative if it differentially characterizes one diagnostic state versus others and if it increases the concentration of that state under the observed pattern. In this paper, we introduce two new quality criteria, contrast and surprise, for assessing fuzzy linguistic summaries in the classification contexts. In the current formulation, the proposed criteria are defined for the qualifier-summarizer pattern and do not directly depend on the quantifier, so they are intended to complement, rather than replace, summary-level criteria such as the degree of truth and degree of support. We provide illustrative experiments on real-life data to show their complementarity with the truth value and support.

Keywords: Fuzzy Linguistic Summaries · Contrastive Explanations · Bayesian Surprise · Explainable AI · Clinical Decision Support

1 Introduction

Fuzzy linguistic summarization translates complex large datasets into human-consistent statements by defining protoforms, i.e., fuzzy qualifiers linking data attributes to summarizer outputs. A key challenge is selecting a small subset of candidate summaries that is both faithful to the data and useful to domain experts.

Protoform selection is often driven by *sigma*-count criteria such as Degree of Truth (DoT) and Degree of Support (DoS) [16], which quantify semantic validity and coverage. However, high values of these criteria do not necessarily imply practical usefulness in clinical decision support. Clinicians often rate highly valid, high-coverage summaries as non-discriminative, while valuing lower-coverage patterns that capture diagnostically relevant structure. We address this

B. Vantaggi et al. (Eds.): IPMU 2026, CCIS 3019, pp. 492–505, 2026.
https://doi.org/10.1007/978-3-032-28994-0_35

gap proposing to complement data-centric quality measures by criteria aligned with clinical reasoning, in which useful patterns (i) distinguish a target diagnosis from alternative diagnoses, analogous to odds ratios [3,17], and (ii) shift belief from prior to posterior similar to the concept of Bayesian surprise [4,12]. Consistent with findings in XAI that users prefer contrastive explanations [1,10], we introduce the **contrast** criterion to capture differential occurrence of a pattern across classes, and the **surprise** criterion to capture the increase in the target-class rate relative to its base rate.

The remainder of this paper is organized as follows. Section 2 introduces fuzzy linguistic summaries and the classical quality criteria. Section 3 then presents the proposed class-dependent criteria, contrast and surprise, and discusses how they complement DoT and DoS for selecting clinically useful summaries. Section 4 reports experiments, including the classification models (MLP and XGBoost) applied for a particular applied scenario of bipolar-disorder speech monitoring, SHAP-based feature selection, protoform selection under different metrics, and evaluation via positive control, negative control, and bootstrap rank-stability analyses. Finally, Sect. 5 concludes the paper and outlines directions for future work.

2 Fuzzy Linguistic Summaries

2.1 Preliminaries

In this work, we rely on fuzzy linguistic summaries (FLS) formulated using extended protoforms [16]. These summaries provide interpretable descriptions in natural-language of structured numerical data.

Let $Y = \{y_1, \ldots, y_n\}$ denote a finite set of objects described by numerical attributes. Linguistic expressions (e.g., *low*, *high*) are modeled as fuzzy sets with membership functions $\mu : X \to [0,1]$. Linguistic quantifiers (e.g., *few*, *most*) are defined on $[0,1]$. We recall the general form of fuzzy linguistic summaries [11]:

$$S : Q\ R_1 \star \ldots \star R_k\ x \text{ are } P_1 \diamond \ldots \diamond P_l, \tag{1}$$

where $\star, \diamond \in \{\text{AND, OR}\}$, Q is a linguistic quantifier, $R_1, \ldots, R_k$ are qualifiers, and $P_1, \ldots, P_l$ are summarizers.

Although richer protoforms with multiple qualifiers/summarizers have been studied, see e.g., [11], this work focuses on the quintuple case with a single qualifier ($k = 1$) and a single summarizer ($l = 1$) to isolate the effect of the proposed usefulness criteria. Hence, we define a linguistic summary as

$$S = (Y, A, P, R, Q),$$

where Y is the set of objects, A the set of attributes, P the summarizer (fuzzy predicate), R the qualifier (possibly empty), and Q the linguistic quantifier. In this work, we adopt the evaluation framework and criteria proposed in [11], which serve as the basis for further extensions introduced in the following sections.

2.2 Quality Criteria

The Degree of Truth (DoT) measures the semantic validity of a linguistic summary under fuzzy logic [14,15]. It is defined as

$$\mathrm{DoT}(Q,R,P)=\mu_Q\left(\frac{\sum_{i=1}^{n}T(\mu_R(y_i),\mu_P(y_i))}{\sum_{i=1}^{n}\mu_R(y_i)}\right),$$

provided that $\sum_{i=1}^{n}\mu_R(y_i)>0$, and $\mathrm{DoT}=0$ otherwise.

The DoT quantifies the degree to which the proportion of objects satisfying both the qualifier and the summarizer matches the meaning of the linguistic quantifier. Higher values indicate stronger semantic agreement between the data and the linguistic statement.

The Degree of Support (DoS) measures the extent to which a linguistic summary covers the dataset [5]. It is defined as

$$\mathrm{DoS}(R,P)=\frac{1}{n}\sum_{i=1}^{n}\mathbf{1}(\mu_R(y_i)>0\wedge\mu_P(y_i)>0)\,,$$

where $\mathbf{1}(\cdot)$ denotes the indicator function.

The DoS reflects the proportion of objects for which the summary is applicable, independently of the linguistic quantifier. While a high DoS indicates broad coverage, it does not necessarily imply that the summary is informative or discriminative with respect to specific target classes.

3 The Proposed Criteria for Class-Dependent Linguistic Summaries

We consider a setting where each object $y_i\in Y$ is associated with a class label $c_i\in\mathcal{C}$, where $\mathcal{C}$ is a finite set of diagnostic states (e.g., $\{0,1,2\}$). For a fixed target class $c\in\mathcal{C}$, we define:

$$C=\{i\mid c_i=c\},\qquad \neg C=\{i\mid c_i\neq c\},$$

and $|C|,|\neg C|$ denote their cardinalities.

Given a fuzzy linguistic summary $S=(Y,A,P,R,Q)$, we interpret the conjunction of summarizer and qualifier as a fuzzy pattern. Note that this definition is class-independent (it does not depend on C), and class information is only used later when counting occurrences within and outside the target class. In our experiments, we use the Gödel t-norm, denoted by $\wedge$. Other t-norms can be investigated in future research, but are not considered in this work.

At an intuitive level, the *contrast* criterion answers the question: *How much more typical is this pattern for class c compared to the rest?* The *surprise* criterion answers: *How much does the presence of this pattern increase our belief that an object belongs to class c?* Hence, by definition, they are correlated but provide different interpretations of summary quality.

These criteria are designed to complement $DoT(S)$ and $DoS(S)$ by adding class-dependent information, without altering the underlying fuzzy-number representation of linguistic terms and quantifiers.

Let $\mu_{P \wedge R}(y_i)$ denote the fuzzy membership degree of object y_i to the combined protoform (P, R). We define a crisp activation of the pattern via a threshold Tr as

$$\mathbf{1}_{P \wedge R}(y_i) = \mathbf{1}(\mu_{P \wedge R}(y_i) > Tr), \tag{2}$$

where $Tr \geq 0$ is a fixed activation threshold. In this work, we focus on preliminary introduction of these criteria, hence for simplicity we assume crisp value, however we aim to extend the framework for fuzzy values in future work. In the implementation, $Tr = 0$ is used. We refer to objects with $\mathbf{1}_{P \wedge R}(y_i) = 1$ as *pattern-active.*

We now discuss the quantification of occurrences inside and outside the target class.

Let C denote the set of indices belonging to the target class c, and $\neg C$ its complement. Using the crisp activations, we define the empirical occurrence counts of the pattern within and outside the target class as

$$p_c = \sum_{i \in C} \mathbf{1}_{P \wedge R}(y_i), \qquad p_{\neg c} = \sum_{i \in \neg C} \mathbf{1}_{P \wedge R}(y_i). \tag{3}$$

The total number of pattern-active objects is $p_c + p_{\neg c}$.

In diagnostic medicine, the *odds ratio* expresses how much more likely a positive test result is in subjects with the condition than in those without it [17]. Large values indicate strong discriminative evidence.

A direct odds-ratio–style contrast would be given by

$$\mathrm{LR}(P, R; c) = \frac{p_c}{p_{\neg c}},$$

which is unbounded and numerically unstable when $p_{\neg c}$ is small. To obtain a bounded and robust alternative, we define the scaled contrast criterion as

$$\mathrm{Contr}_{\mathrm{scaled}}(P, R; c) = \frac{|p_c - p_{\neg c}|}{p_c + p_{\neg c} + \varepsilon}, \qquad \varepsilon > 0. \tag{4}$$

Here, ε is a small constant added for numerical stability (we use $\varepsilon = 10^{-12}$ in all experiments). The contrast takes values in $[0, 1]$. Values close to zero indicate that the pattern occurs with similar frequency inside and outside the target class, whereas values close to one indicate strong discriminative behavior, with the pattern being characteristic of either the target class or its complement.

Next, let $n = |Y|$ denote the number of objects. Then,

$$\mathrm{base}_c = \frac{|C|}{n} \tag{5}$$

denotes the base frequency of class c in the population. We estimate the conditional probability of class c given pattern activation as

$$p(c \mid P \wedge R) = \frac{p_c}{p_c + p_{\neg c}}, \tag{6}$$

with the convention that $p(c \mid P \wedge R) = 0$ if no object activates the pattern, that is, if $p_c = p_{\neg c} = 0$.

The difference between the conditional probability under the pattern and the class base frequency indicates how strongly the pattern is associated with class c. Inspired by Bayesian surprise and risk amplification notions [4,12], we quantify this effect by defining the scaled surprise criterion as

$$\mathrm{Surp}_{\mathrm{scaled}}(P, R; c) = \left[\frac{p(c \mid P \wedge R) - \mathrm{base}_c}{\mathrm{base}_c + \varepsilon} \right]_0^1, \qquad \varepsilon > 0, \tag{7}$$

where $[\cdot]_0^1$ denotes clipping to $[0, 1]$. This measure captures the relative increase in the conditional probability of class c under the pattern compared with its base frequency, with saturation at 1 for very large increases. High values of $\mathrm{Surp}_{\mathrm{scaled}}$ indicate that the pattern is associated with a substantial increase in the likelihood of class c, consistent with the idea that clinically interesting patterns are those that strongly update prior beliefs about diagnoses.

The new contrast and surprise criteria are designed to complement the traditional DoT and DoS criteria, which provide data-based global information about the validity and coverage of the protoform. The $\mathrm{Contr}_{\mathrm{scaled}}(P, R; c)$ and $\mathrm{Surp}_{\mathrm{scaled}}(P, R; c)$ aim to provide class-dependent information about differential behavior and belief update. Together, they lift fuzzy linguistic summaries from purely descriptive statements to class-aware explanatory tools, aligning the evaluation of summaries with clinical reasoning and contrastive explanation principles.

4 Experiments

4.1 About Classification Models

To evaluate the proposed criteria across different model families, we employed two widely used classifiers: a multilayer perceptron (MLP) and a gradient-boosted decision tree model based on XGBoost.

The MLP is a fully connected feedforward neural network designed to capture nonlinear relationships between input features and class labels. The architecture consists of two hidden layers with 64 and 16 neurons respectively, both using ReLU activations. A dropout layer with rate 0.1 is applied after the first hidden layer to mitigate overfitting. The output layer uses a softmax activation to produce class probabilities for the multi-class setting. The model is trained using standard backpropagation with categorical cross-entropy loss.

As a tree-based baseline, we use an XGBoost classifier configured for multi-class classification. The model employs 1000 boosting rounds with a learning rate of 0.1 and a maximum tree depth of 10, allowing it to capture complex feature interactions. The objective function is set to produce probabilistic outputs over the three target classes.

Together, these models enable a more comprehensive evaluation of the proposed explanatory criteria.

4.2 Mental Health Survey Dataset

The dataset used for evaluating the proposed criteria is derived from a longitudinal mental health survey involving individuals diagnosed with Bipolar Disorder. All data were collected with informed consent, and the study protocol adhered to applicable ethical and data protection guidelines [7]. The dataset comprises eleven speech-derived acoustic and behavioral features capturing voice perturbation, prosody, energy, temporal structure, and sleep-related activity.

Each row in the dataset corresponds to a single recording session for a given participant on a specific date. Recordings are annotated with a discrete clinical state label, denoted by the `state` variable, which represents the mental health condition assessed at the time of recording. The longitudinal nature of the resulting dataset and clinically grounded annotations make it suitable for evaluating feature-level criteria under real-world conditions.

The three clinical classes considered in this study are *depression*, *euthymia*, and *weak depression*. In the subsequent sections, these are encoded as follows: class 0 corresponds to depression, class 1 to euthymia, and class 2 to weak depression.

4.3 Feature Selection Prior to Linguistic Summarization

Given the use of a deliberately simple baseline classifier, we first performed feature selection to reduce dimensionality and improve the reliability of downstream explanation and summarization. The MLP model was first trained using all eleven features. SHAP values were then computed for a subset of the training samples, and feature importance was quantified as the mean absolute SHAP value aggregated across samples and output classes [9]. This explanation-first workflow aligns with prior approaches that combine neural networks and fuzzy linguistic summaries to explain acoustic markers of mental state [6].

The top five features with the highest mean absolute SHAP values were selected. The model was subsequently retrained using only this reduced feature set, and all final SHAP values used for fuzzy linguistic summarization were computed from this retrained model. Importantly, feature selection was performed exclusively on the training data to avoid information leakage into the test set.

This two-stage procedure ensures that the selected features are both informative for the predictive model and stable with respect to the explanation method, while maintaining compatibility with the subsequent fuzzy linguistic summary construction and evaluation.

As seen in Table 1 SHAP-based feature selection leads to a consistent improvement in accuracy and macro-averaged F1 score, suggesting that the selected features retain most of the discriminative information while yielding a lower-dimensional representation. This supports the use of explanation-driven feature selection as a reliable preprocessing step prior to fuzzy linguistic summarization.

To provide qualitative context for the classification and summarization task, we additionally visualize class-conditional kernel density estimates for the

Table 1. MLP and XGBoost performance before and after feature selection

Feature set	MLP		XGBoost	
	Accuracy	Macro F1	Accuracy	Macro F1
All features (11)	0.59	0.54	0.43	0.38
Selected features (5)	0.63	0.57	0.53	0.53

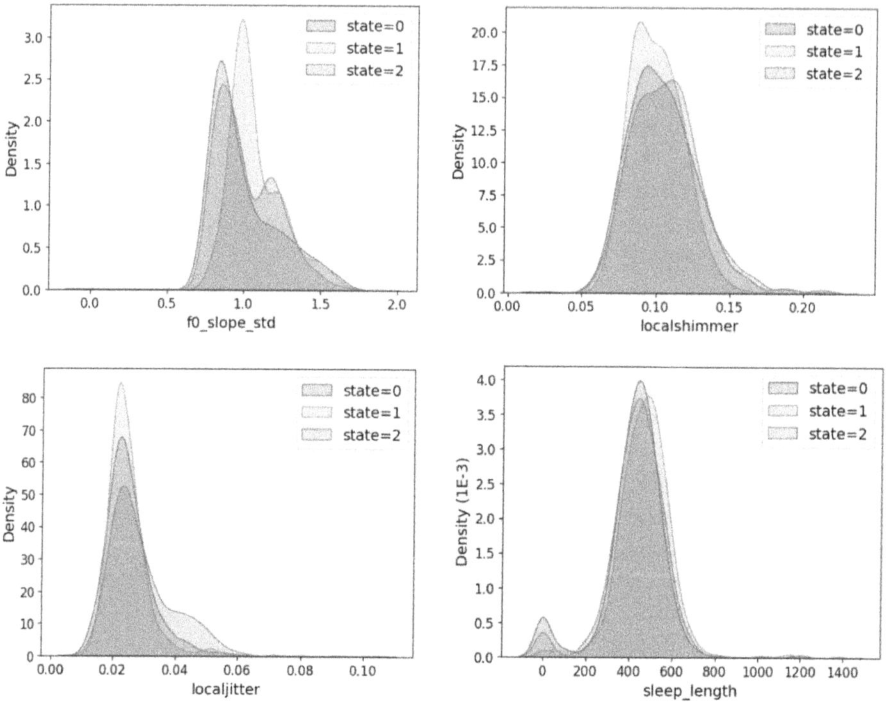

Fig. 1. Class-conditional kernel density estimates for the four acoustic features.

selected features (Fig. 1). These plots reveal weak separability between classes at the univariate level. This highlights the intrinsic difficulty of the problem and motivates the need for explanation-aware criteria and fuzzy linguistic summarization.

4.4 Fuzzy Linguistic Summaries Selected Based on Various Criteria

Both models were trained using the SHAP-selected feature subset and evaluated on the held-out test set. For each numerical feature, fuzzy memberships were constructed using quartile-based fuzzification over the empirical range of the data. Specifically, the linguistic terms low and high were modeled by trapezoidal membership functions, and medium by a triangular membership function, with breakpoints determined by the minimum, first quartile, median, third quartile, and maximum of the feature values. Using the resulting predictions and SHAP explanations, fuzzy linguistic protoforms were generated for all admissible feature–linguistic term combinations. For each protoform, DoT, DoS, Contrast, and Surprise criteria were computed.

To identify the most informative linguistic summaries, protoforms were filtered using thresholding criteria on the proposed criteria, discarding low-support and low-specificity candidates. From the remaining set, the top three protoforms were selected based on metric values.

Table 2. Top 3 protoforms for different models and thresholding

MLP-selected protoform using DoT and DoS	DoT	DoS	Contr	Surp
Among records that contribute against predicting depression, most of them have sleep length-related features at high level.	0.57	0.27	0.20	0.80
Among records that contribute against predicting weak depression, most of them have sleep length-related features at high level.	0.57	0.27	0.20	0.20
Among records that contribute positively to predicting depression, most of them have sleep length-related features at high level.	0.44	0.23	0.98	0.97
MLP-selected protoform using Contr and Surp	**DoT**	**DoS**	**Contr**	**Surp**
Among records that contribute positively to predicting depression, most of them have sleep length-related features at high level.	0.44	0.23	0.98	0.97
Among records that contribute against predicting depression, most of them have localshimmer-related features at high level.	0.30	0.27	0.83	0.74
Among records that contribute positively to predicting weak depression, most of them have localshimmer-related features at high level.	0.29	0.23	0.78	0.66
XGBoost-selected protoform using DoT and DoS	**DoT**	**DoS**	**Contr**	**Surp**
Among records that contribute positively to predicting euthymia, most of them have localshimmer-related features at high level.	0.39	0.28	0.13	0.30
Among records that contribute positively to predicting depression, most of them have localshimmer-related features at high level.	0.38	0.24	0.24	0.14
Among records that contribute against predicting depression, most of them have f0 slope std-related features at low level.	0.23	0.27	0.11	0.34
XGBoost-selected protoform using Contr and Surp	**DoT**	**DoS**	**Contr**	**Surp**
Among records that contribute positively to predicting weak depression, most of them have localshimmer-related features at high level.	0.39	0.28	0.63	0.44
Among records that contribute positively to predicting depression, most of them have localjitter-related features at high level.	0.38	0.24	0.54	0.31
Among records that contribute against predicting weak depression, most of them have f0 slope std-related features at low level.	0.23	0.27	0.52	0.28

Table 2 highlights the limitations of selecting protoforms using only DoT and DoS. These criteria reward statistical support and internal consistency, but they do not account for discriminative relevance. As a result, several top-ranked protoforms are redundant or even contradictory. For example, in the MLP model, sleep length–related features at a high level appear both for "contribute positively to predicting depression" and "contribute against predicting depression."

A similar pattern is visible in XGBoost, where the same acoustic feature (e.g., local shimmer at high level) appears across different classes, limiting interpretability.

When Contrast and Surprise are included, the selected protoforms become more class-specific and less redundant. Consequently, the chosen protoforms are not only data-supported but also more discriminative and clinically meaningful.

4.5 Evaluation

The proposed quality criteria, *Contrast* (Contr) and *Surprise* (Surp), are designed to quantify the perceived usefulness of fuzzy linguistic summaries in a class-dependent manner. Since explicit expert-provided usefulness scores are unavailable, we evaluate these criteria using three complementary strategies: a positive control experiment, a negative control experiment, and a bootstrap-based rank stability analysis. Together, these evaluations assess discriminative validity, resistance to spurious explanations, and robustness under data perturbation.

4.6 Positive Control Evaluation

We performed a sensitivity analysis using a positive control in which a synthetic feature was injected with class-dependent structure.
For a given target class c, feature values were generated as:

$$X \sim \begin{cases} \mathcal{N}(\delta, 1), & \text{if state} = c, \\ \mathcal{N}(0, 1), & \text{if state} \neq c, \end{cases}$$

introducing a controlled class-conditional shift while preserving overlap between classes. By varying δ, we explicitly controlled the degree of class separation induced by the injected feature. In this experiment, two of the original features were substituted with such class-informative positive control features. This setup allowed us to assess robustness under partial feature replacement. The ability of the proposed criteria to discriminate the injected feature from non-informative features was quantified using the AUROC.

Figure 2 shows the resulting AUROC as a function of δ for both Contrast and Surprise, across all target classes.

Surprise exhibits a more consistent and monotonic increase in AUROC with δ across classes, reaching near-perfect discrimination at moderate values of δ. This behavior indicates that Surprise is particularly sensitive to distributional deviations that emerge only when the injected feature becomes informative.

Contrast shows greater variability across classes and values of δ, with occasional non-monotonic behavior. This may be influenced by sampling variability or partial alignment between the injected and baseline distributions.

4.7 Negative Control Evaluation

To assess whether the proposed criteria spuriously attribute usefulness to irrelevant features, we conducted a negative control evaluation. A synthetic feature was introduced into the dataset, generated as independent Gaussian noise and designed to have no class-conditional structure or correlation with the target labels. SHAP values were recomputed on the modified dataset and the resulting metric values for the irrelevant feature were then compared against those

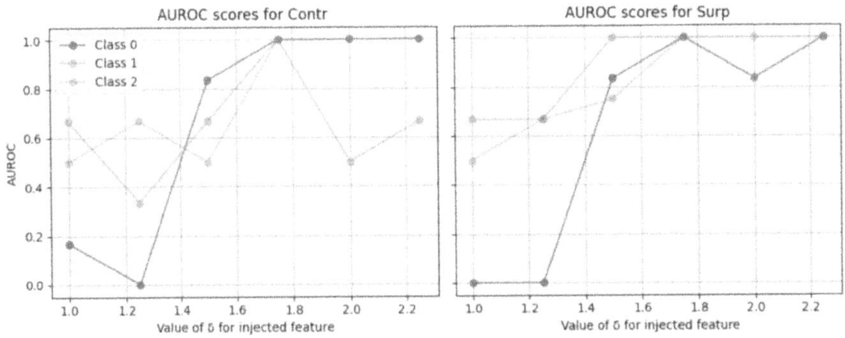

(a) MLP

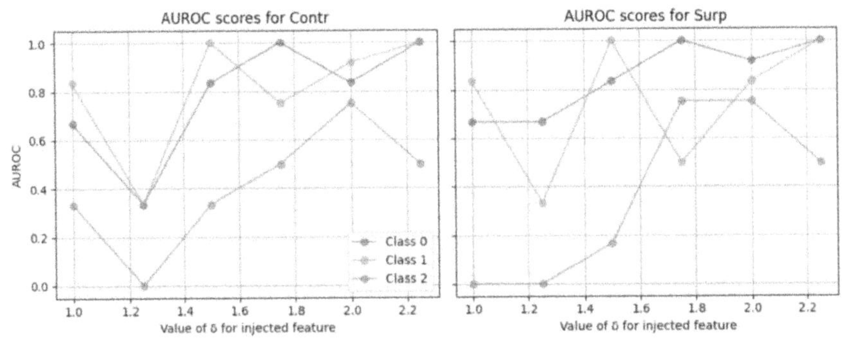

(b) XGBoost

Fig. 2. AUROC of Contrast (left) and Surprise (right) as a function of the mean shift δ used to generate a class-dependent injected feature.

obtained for real features across all target classes. As we can see in Fig. 3, the irrelevant feature shows SHAP values tightly concentrated around zero across all classes, while the real feature exhibits clear class-dependent shifts. This confirms that the injected synthetic feature behaves as intended.

Upon examining the behaviour of the proposed criteria (Table 3 and Fig. 4) we see a clear separation between irrelevant and real features for the surprise metric. Contrast exhibits greater sensitivity to relative deviations and may occasionally assign comparable values to irrelevant features at isolated protoforms, but these effects are neither dominant nor structured.

4.8 Bootstrap Rank Stability Evaluation

To assess the robustness of feature rankings induced by the proposed Contrast and Surprise criteria, we performed a bootstrap rank stability evaluation using a stratified resampling procedure. For each target class, 100 bootstrap samples were generated by resampling with replacement within each class. Protoform

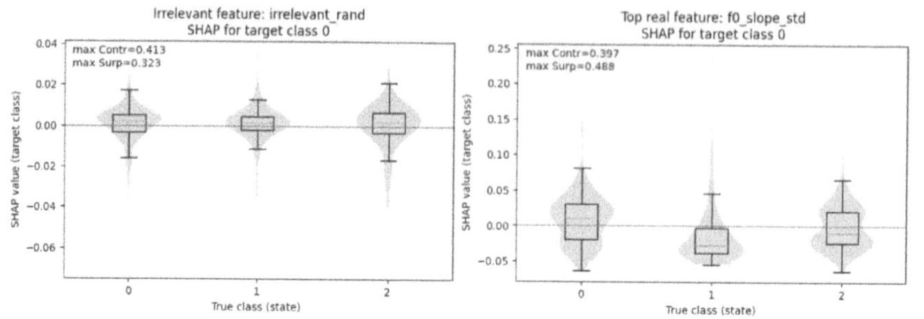

Fig. 3. Class-conditional SHAP value distributions for an irrelevant feature (left) and a real feature (right) for the target class.

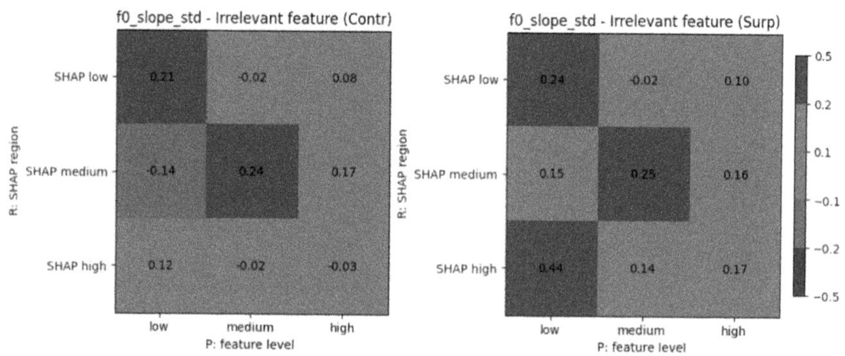

Fig. 4. Protoform-level heatmaps showing the difference between metric values computed for the real feature and the irrelevant feature. Values close to zero indicate comparable informativeness, positive values favor the real feature, and negative values indicate undesirable dominance of the irrelevant feature.

rankings derived from each bootstrap sample were then compared against the ranking obtained from the full dataset. The analysis focused on the top-k ranked protoforms ($k = 10$).

Ranking stability was quantified using Kendall's τ rank correlation coefficient, a non-parametric measure of agreement between two rankings. Given two rankings of the same n features, Kendall's τ is defined as

$$\tau = \frac{n_c - n_d}{\frac{1}{2}n(n-1)},$$

where n_c denotes the number of concordant protoform pairs and n_d denotes the number of discordant protoform pairs. Kendall's τ takes values in the range $[-1, 1]$, with larger values indicating stronger agreement [8].

The results in Table 4 indicate that both Contrast and Surprise yield highly stable feature rankings across all target classes, with consistently high Kendall's τ values within the top-10 protoforms indicating robustness to sampling perturbations.

Table 3. Negative control evaluation: irrelevant versus real features

Target class	Feature type	MLP				XGBoost			
		Contrast		Surprise		Contrast		Surprise	
		Mean	Std.	Mean	Std.	Mean	Std.	Mean	Std.
0	Irrelevant	0.34	0.10	0.13	0.09	0.33	0.07	0.09	0.07
	Real	0.36	0.27	0.34	0.32	0.36	0.26	0.35	0.36
1	Irrelevant	0.17	0.20	0.19	0.21	0.15	0.22	0.19	0.21
	Real	0.31	0.22	0.37	0.21	0.32	0.24	0.36	0.25
2	Irrelevant	0.60	0.25	0.25	0.16	0.68	0.15	0.36	0.27
	Real	0.67	0.26	0.64	0.56	0.67	0.28	0.67	0.51

Table 4. Rank stability (Kendall's τ) for top-10 protoforms

Target class	Metric	MLP		XGBoost	
		Mean τ	Std.	Mean τ	Std.
0	Contrast	0.86	0.08	0.61	0.15
	Surprise	0.74	0.13	0.59	0.13
1	Contrast	0.82	0.09	0.69	0.13
	Surprise	0.74	0.12	0.58	0.14
2	Contrast	0.85	0.08	0.58	0.17
	Surprise	0.74	0.15	0.60	0.15

5 Conclusions and Future Work

The overall evaluation supports the complementary use of these quality criteria, with Surprise providing robustness against noise-driven artifacts and Contrast contributing sensitivity to class-specific effects when such a structure is present. The positive control experiment shows that both Contrast and Surprise reliably recover known, class-dependent explanatory structure when it is explicitly injected into the data, while the negative control confirms that the quality criteria remain resistant to spurious or non-informative explanations. The bootstrap analysis further establishes the robustness and reproducibility of the resulting feature rankings under resampling variability.

Several directions can be explored to further strengthen and generalize the proposed quality criteria. The current formulation relies on a hard threshold Tr to determine pattern activation, resulting in a binary indicator. A natural extension is to replace this with the corresponding fuzzy membership value of the pattern, which may provide a more informative and robust characterization of explanatory structure, especially in borderline cases [13].

Second, a broader empirical evaluation is necessary across diverse domains to assess the generality of the criteria. Although the general formulation is not inherently limited to numerical variables, the present implementation assumes quantitative inputs when constructing fuzzy memberships. Extending the methodology to support appropriate membership constructions for categorical variables would broaden the practical applicability of the approach. In addition, a theoretical analysis of the proposed criteria, focusing on their mathematical properties and enhancements to other evaluation frameworks for fuzzy quantification [2], would further strengthen the framework.

Acknowledgement. The project "ExplainMe: Explainable Artificial Intelligence for Monitoring Acoustic Features extracted from Speech" (FENG.02.02-IP.05-0302/23) is carried out within the First Team programme of the Foundation for Polish Science co-financed by the European Union under the European Funds for Smart Economy 2021–2027 (FENG).

References

1. Buçinca, Z., Swaroop, S., Paluch, A.E., Doshi-Velez, F., Gajos, K.Z.: Contrastive explanations that anticipate human misconceptions can improve human decision-making skills. CHI 2025, ACM (2025). https://doi.org/10.1145/3706598.3713229
2. Delgado, M., Ruiz, M., Sánchez, D., Vila, M.A.: Fuzzy quantification: a state of the art. Fuzzy Sets Syst. **242**, 1–30 (2014)
3. Hayden, S.R., Brown, M.D.: Likelihood ratio: a powerful tool for incorporating the results of a diagnostic test into clinical decisionmaking. Ann. Emerg. Med. **33**(5), 575–580 (1999). https://doi.org/10.1016/S0196-0644(99)70346-X
4. Itti, L., Baldi, P.: Bayesian surprise attracts human attention **49**(10), 1295–1306 (2009). https://doi.org/10.1016/j.visres.2008.09.007
5. Kacprzyk, J., Wilbik, A., Zadrożny, S.: Linguistic summarization of time series using a fuzzy quantifier driven aggregation. Fuzzy Sets Syst. **159**(12), 1485–1499 (2008). https://doi.org/10.1016/j.fss.2008.01.025
6. Kaczmarek-Majer, K.: Explaining neural networks in natural language. In: Watson, P., Farahani, H., Bezdan, T. (eds.) Introduction to Intricate Artificial Psychology with Python (2026). https://doi.org/10.1016/B978-0-443-30248-0.00009-7
7. Kaczmarek-Majer, K., et al.: Święcicki,: acoustic features from speech as markers of depressive and manic symptoms in bipolar disorder: a prospective study. Acta Psychiatr. Scand. **151**(3), 358–374 (2025). https://doi.org/10.1111/acps.13735
8. Kendall, M.G.: A new measure of rank correlation. Biometrika **30**(1–2), 81–93 (1938). https://doi.org/10.1093/biomet/30.1-2.81
9. Lundberg, S., Lee, S.I.: A unified approach to interpreting model predictions (2017). https://arxiv.org/abs/1705.07874
10. Miller, T.: Contrastive explanation: a structural-model approach **36**, e14 (2021). https://doi.org/10.1017/S0269888921000102
11. Miś, K., Kaczmarek-Majer, K., Baczyński, M.: Fuzzy linguistic summaries and the double negation property. TechRxiv (2025). https://doi.org/10.36227/techrxiv.173747538.86263707/v2
12. Modirshanechi, A., Brea, J., Gerstner, W.: A taxonomy of surprise definitions **107**, 102712 (2022). https://doi.org/10.1016/j.jmp.2022.102712
13. Niewiadomski, A.: A type-2 fuzzy approach to linguistic summarization of data. IEEE Trans. Fuzzy Syst. **16**(1), 198–212 (2008). https://doi.org/10.1109/TFUZZ.2007.902025

14. Yager, R.R.: A new approach to the summarization of data **28**(1), 69–86 (1982). https://doi.org/10.1016/0020-0255(82)90036-1
15. Zadeh, L.: A computational approach to fuzzy quantifiers in natural languages. Comput. Linguist. 149–184 (1983)
16. Zadeh, L.A.: A computational approach to fuzzy quantifiers in natural languages **9**(1), 149–184 (1983). https://doi.org/10.1016/0898-1221(83)90013-5
17. Zhou, X.H., Obuchowski, N.A., McClish, D.K.: Statistical Methods in Diagnostic Medicine. Wiley Series in Probability and Statistics, Wiley, 2 edn. (2011). https://doi.org/10.1002/9780470906514

Consistency of Explanations in Evolving Supervised Learning Contexts

Marcin Ostrowski[1(✉)], Katarzyna Kaczmarek-Majer[1,2], and Jose M. Alonso-Moral[3]

[1] Systems Research Institute Polish Academy of Sciences, Newelska 6, 01-147 Warsaw, Poland
{Marcin.Ostrowski,k.kaczmarek}@ibspan.waw.pl
[2] Institute for Research and Applications of Fuzzy Modeling, University of Ostrava, Ostrava, Czech Republic
[3] Centro Singular de Investigación en Tecnoloxías Intelixentes (CiTIUS), Universidade de Santiago de Compostela, 15782 Santiago de Compostela, Spain
josemaria.alonso.moral@usc.es

Abstract. In many real-world scenarios, explanations are not perceived as isolated entities, but rather as streams accompanying models that operate over extended periods of time. In such contexts, users are exposed not to a single explanation, but to a sequence of explanations whose evolution may influence trust, understanding, and decision-making. In this work, we aim to capture the evolution of explanations that exhibit sudden changes, contradict prior explanations, or demonstrate erratic fluctuations, as these may compromise their practical utility, even when maintaining a high level of predictive performance. We propose a framework aimed at supporting the assessment of the consistency of explanations for evolving supervised learning contexts, taking into account the variability of the input datasets, and the uncertainty of the model. We introduce a model-agnostic and explanation-agnostic index for quantifying the temporal consistency of automated explanations. We empirically demonstrate that the proposed index facilitates the quantification and localization of temporal instability in explanation streams. Experimental results for simulated multivariate time series underscores the ability of the proposed index to capture instantaneous changes and their relative impact in relation to historical patterns.

Keywords: Explainable Artificial Intelligence · Online Learning · Stability · Classification · Fuzzy Linguistic Summarization

1 Introduction

Explanations are the foundation of trustworthy Artificial Intelligence (AI) systems, playing a central role in improving transparency and user confidence across various decision-support systems [1,6,8,10,18]. The Rashomon effect was first

B. Vantaggi et al. (Eds.): IPMU 2026, CCIS 3019, pp. 506–519, 2026.
https://doi.org/10.1007/978-3-032-28994-0_36

introduced by Breiman [3] and then made popular in the context of Explainable AI (XAI) by Rudin [20]. This effect justifies why sometimes different models explain the data-generating process equally well, but they may contradict each other because their predictions are built in a different way, i.e., following a different rational (e.g., relying on different features). Accordingly, in case that multiple, equally good models exist, their interpretations should be carefully compared before drawing any conclusion. If this is the case, selecting one specific model for a particular task should depend on multiple factors (e.g., performance, interpretability, explainability, fairness, sparsity, stability or consistency).

In this work, we focus on real-world scenarios, when observations are accumulated over time, often in batches, reflecting the evolution of the environment and the transformation of data-generating processes [7,22]. We observe that despite the growing body of research on XAI, most existing approaches implicitly assume static tabular data or static data distributions. The field of temporal scenarios has traditionally focused on generating explanations within designated sliding or expanding time windows [19]. This process commonly involves applying smoothing or aggregation techniques to static explanation methods in the temporal domain [11,21]. While these approaches facilitate temporal attribution analysis, they offer limited insight into the consistency of explanations themselves. Research areas that are closely related, such as statistical process control and data distribution drift detection, study temporal changes in data or model outputs [2,7]. However, these areas are not designed to assess explanations as structured, semantic objects. Another direction of research explores explainable online classification approaches, e.g., using prototypes [4]. In this research, we further extend previous work by proposing a pipeline for monitoring the consistency of explanations in evolving supervised learning contexts.

In this study, we posit that the temporal consistency of explanations constitutes a complementary dimension for model evaluation alongside predictive performance. Our research question focuses on developing and validating a convenient measure to capture how explanations change over time, accounting for their history and the various assumptions underlying both predictive modeling and the procedure used to derive explanations. The analysis of this question facilitates comparisons not only between explanations within a single model, but also between different models that may demonstrate similar performance, yet yield explanations of differing temporal reliability. To summarize, the main contribution of this work is the introduction of a novel index for measuring the temporal consistency of automated explanations as the quantification of the deviations from the expected temporal behavior of explanation signals. The proposed index is model-agnostic and explanation-agnostic, relying solely on the temporal progression of explanatory quantities. We demonstrate through a series of illustrative experiments that temporal consistency can reveal significant information about explanation reliability. In particular, it is demonstrated that models with comparable accuracy may exhibit substantial discrepancies in the temporal stability of their explanations. This underscores the significance of explanation consistency as a criterion for model selection and implementation in evolving environments.

The rest of the manuscript is organized as follows. Section 2 introduces the new index. Section 3 describes the experimental settings. Section 4 presents the main reported results. Section 5 provides readers with concluding remarks and outlines future work.

2 Temporal Consistency Assessment of Explanations

Figure 1 provides a schematic overview of the proposed temporal consistency assessment pipeline adapted to a showcase example. The aim of this pipeline is to provide a quantitative measure of explanation consistency based on the input data. The design is intended to be both model- and explanation-agnostic. The proposed approach consists of three main sequential steps: (i) predictive modeling; (ii) explanation generation; and (iii) consistency monitoring.

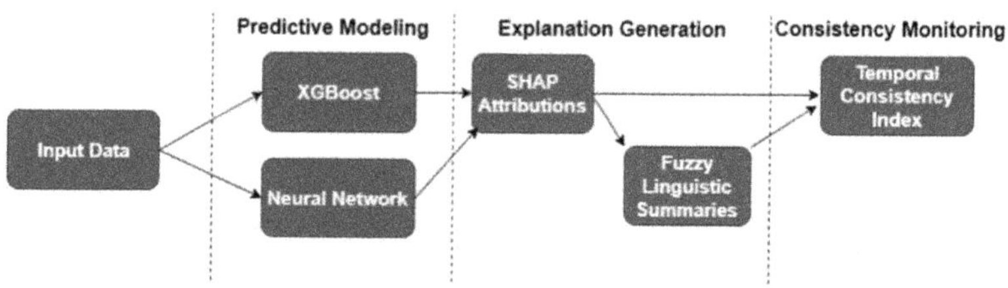

Fig. 1. Overview of the temporal consistency assessment pipeline adapted to an example. Explanatory signals generated by a predictive model over successive time windows are treated as temporal processes and evaluated using the proposed index, yielding a quantitative measure of explanation consistency.

2.1 Predictive Modeling

The field of predictive modeling in evolving environments has seen significant attention in the context of concept drift and online learning. The overarching aim is to preserve the efficacy of predictive models in environments where data distributions are constantly fluctuating [7,22]. In the domain of XAI, predictive models are commonly regarded as fixed structures, with explanations automatically generated after the learning process and examined independently from the underlying learning mechanics [8,11]. However, comparatively little attention has been paid to how the selection and development of the predictive model itself influences the temporal behavior of explanations.

In this study, predictive models are utilized as sources of explanatory signals, rather than as subjects of optimization. As a result, the focus is intentionally limited to well-established supervised learning models. Specifically, we consider gradient-boosted decision trees implemented via XGBoost [5] and a simple neural network represented by a multilayer perceptron classifier from the scikit-learn [17]. The present work does not seek to provide a comprehensive comparison of predictive models. Instead, it focuses on assessing explanation consistency under representative modeling choices.

2.2 Automated Explanation Generation

Contemporary explanation techniques, encompassing feature attribution and rule-based methodologies, are predominantly designed to provide local explanations for individual predictions or global explanations for static models [14,18]. In the context of temporal data analysis, explanations are typically generated independently at each temporal interval and subsequently integrated or smoothed for visualization [11].

In this work, the features' attributions derived from SHAP framework [11] are regarded as time-indexed explanatory signals. For a given feature j, Shapley values are computed for individual observations at a specific time step. In addition to numerical attribution streams, we construct fuzzy linguistic summaries (FLS) [9] that encapsulate global, human-interpretable statements regarding the behavior of explanations. These summaries are formulated using extended protoforms [13,23], where the relation between SHAP-derived quantities and feature values serves as the underlying numerical evidence. In case of having big datasets with many attributes, the so-called SHAP length metric can be used to select the most informative attributes for the desired degree of explanation completeness [12]. The proposed framework is explanation-agnostic and operates on arbitrary scalar explanatory streams. The present work focuses on SHAP-based attributions and fuzzy linguistic summaries.

2.3 Temporal Consistency Monitoring

Let $F = \{F_t\}_{t=1}^{T}, T > 1$, denote a real-valued temporal process describing the evolution of an explanatory quantity over discrete time steps, where $F_t \in \mathbb{R}$ summarizes the explanatory information available at time t, for example via aggregation over a batch of observations. Our objective is to quantify the temporal consistency of the process F, understood as the extent to which its evolution can be regarded as stable and predictable over time, as opposed to exhibiting abrupt or erratic deviations.

To assess deviations from expected temporal behavior, we construct a one-step predictor $\hat{F}_t$ of F_t based on past values. In this work, we employ a modified exponentially weighted moving average (EWMA) with a drift correction term, allowing the predictor to adapt to smooth trends while remaining sensitive to gradual changes in the underlying process

$$\hat{F}_t = (1-\lambda)\hat{F}_{t-1} + \lambda F_{t-1} + \beta d_{t-1}, \qquad d_t = (1-\mu)d_{t-1} + \mu(F_t - F_{t-1}),$$

with initialization $\hat{F}_1 = F_1$ and $d_1 = 0$.

The parameter $\lambda \in [0, 1]$ governs the degree to which the one-step predictor $\hat{F}_t$ adapts to the most recent observed value $\hat{F}_{t-1}$. Setting λ to a higher value, results in the predictor reacting in a stronger way to recent changes in the observed explanatory signal. This can be interpreted as the predictor becoming more responsive to short-term fluctuations. Conversely, setting λ to a smaller value, yields a smoother and more inertial baseline due to the predictor relying more heavily on its previous estimate $\hat{F}_{t-1}$.

The parameter $\beta \in [0, 1]$ determines the influence of the estimated drift term d_{t-1} on the predictor $\hat{F}_t$. With larger values of β, the predictor incorporates more information about the recent trend of the process. This improves the ability of the predictor to follow gradual systematic changes. When the parameter β is smaller, the predictor behaves more like a standard exponentially weighted moving average without explicit trend adjustment.

The parameter $\mu \in [0, 1]$ controls the update rate of the drift term d_t. This term summarizes the recent tendency of the signal to increase or decrease. Larger values of μ assign greater importance to the most recent difference $F_t - F_{t-1}$, making the drift estimate more sensitive to newly emerging trends. Smaller values of μ produce a more stable and slowly varying drift estimate, reflecting longer-term directional behavior rather than short-lived changes.

Deviations from expected behavior are quantified using normalized residuals. Let

$$s = \mathrm{MAD}\big(\{F_t\}_{t=1}^{T}\big)\,,$$

denote a robust scale estimator of the process based on the median absolute deviation (MAD). The normalized residuals are defined as

$$r_t = \frac{F_t - \hat{F}_t}{s}, \qquad t = 2, \ldots, T.$$

If $s = 0$, indicating a constant process, we define the temporal consistency as equal to its maximum value.

The Temporal Consistency Index (TCI) of the process F is defined as

$$\mathrm{TCI}(F) = 1 - \sum_{t=2}^{T} \omega_t\, \ell(r_t)\,, \quad \ell(r) = \frac{r^2}{\tau^2 + r^2}, \tau > 0.$$

where $\omega_t \geq 0$, $\sum_{t=2}^{T} \omega_t = 1$, and the parameter τ controls the sensitivity of the loss function to normalized residual magnitude. When τ is set to a smaller value, even moderate changes produce relatively large loss values, making the TCI more sensitive to deviations from predicted behavior. Conversely, applying large values of τ results in the loss growing more slowly, leading to only substantial deviations reducing the overall consistency.

In this work, a bounded quadratic-type loss is used to smoothly interpolate between quadratic penalization for small deviations and saturation for large deviations. By default, uniform weights $\omega_t = \frac{1}{T-1}$ are used, ensuring that all time points contribute equally to the consistency assessment. In addition to the overall index, the above formulation inherently incorporates a per-step inconsistency contribution. For each time step $t = 2, \dots, T$ we define

$$a_t := \omega_t \, \ell(r_t)$$

which quantifies the contribution of time step t to the overall inconsistency of the explanatory signal. By construction, $a_t \geq 0$. The quantities a_t thus facilitate the identification of time points at which the explanation stream exhibits the most significant deviation from its anticipated temporal behavior.

TCI ranges from 0 to 1, with higher values denoting greater stability and predictability in temporal behavior. Conversely, lower values indicate increased variability or abrupt changes over time. It is imperative to note that the index is model-agnostic and explanation-agnostic, contingent solely on the temporal progression of the explanatory signal. In scenarios where multiple explanatory signals are available, the index is computed independently for each signal. This results in a set of consistency scores that can be analyzed collectively.

3 Experimental Settings

3.1 About Data and Evaluation Protocol

We illustrate our framework with temporal consistency assessment via a simulation experiment. Let us consider controlled non-stationarity, a synthetic multivariate time series generator is employed to produce three explanatory variables, denoted by x_1, x_2, x_3 respectively, and a binary label y taking value 0 or 1 to indicate stable versus unstable regimes respectively. The stream is divided into successive windows of equal length. Stable windows are characterized by smooth oscillatory dynamics with mild modulation in amplitude, frequency and noise. In contrast, unstable windows give rise to distributional changes, including abrupt mean shifts, gradual mean drifts, and increased noise with interaction effects.

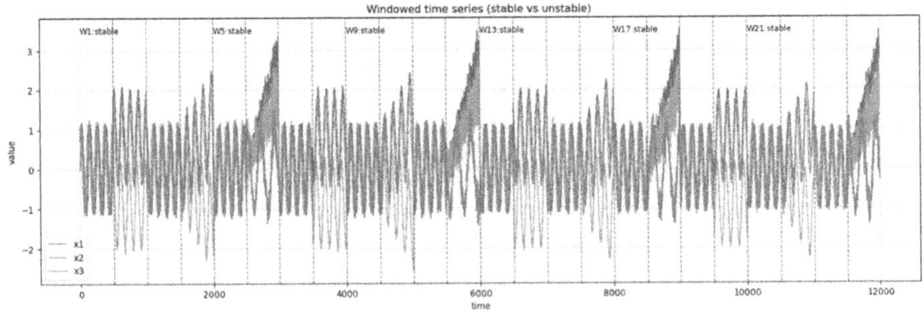

Fig. 2. Simulated time series data with stable and unstable regimes.

Figure 2 depicts exemplary simulated time series with these three types of drift. Thus, we split the sequence into twenty four segments of equal length. Indeed, six quasi-periodic segments are repeated four times.

For the first, the third and the fifth segments, we consider the following three time series: $x_1(t) = \sin(0.05t) + \varepsilon_1(t)$; $x_2(t) = \cos(0.05t) + \varepsilon_2(t)$; $x_3(t) = \sin\left(0.05t + \frac{\pi}{4}\right) + \varepsilon_3(t)$ where $\varepsilon_i(t) \sim \mathcal{N}(0,\ 1)$. Then, in the second segment, we shift each variable by a constant (mean shift) of $c_1 = 2, c_2 = -2$ and $c_3 = 1.5$. Then, for the fourth segment, incremental drift is introduced. For the sixth segment, the generation mechanism changes, and the noise is particularly bigger: $x_1(t) = 0.01\,t + \eta_1(t)$; $x_2(t) = 0.8\,x_1(t) + \eta_2(t)$; $x_3(t) = \cos(0.03\,t) + \eta_3(t)$, where $\eta_i(t) \sim \mathcal{N}(0,\ 0.4^2), i = 1, 2, 3$.

The distribution generation process was then repeated every second segment for the stable class and every sixth segment for the unstable class with parameter t adapted to the place of segments in the data stream.

The temporal protocol we employ is of a batch-style nature. A predictive model is trained on initial prefix of the stream in order to include all potential forms of instability. This training set consisted of six first segments of the time series. The trained model is subjected to an evaluation process that utilizes a sequence of non-overlapping test blocks, with each test block comprising a pair of consecutive segments (one stable and one unstable) that are of equal size. This configuration emulates deployment monitoring, whereby a model that has been trained on historical data is evaluated as new batches are received over time.

Subsequent to this procedure, the test data yielded by the process comprised a total of nine test windows, each of which was subdivided into two segments.

3.2 Predictive Modeling and Explanation Generation

In accordance with the evaluation protocol described in the preceding subsection, the predictive models were subjected to independent assessment on each test window, employing the area under the ROC curve as the quality metric. Each test window corresponds to newly arriving data that was not used during training at the given time step. Table 1 summarizes the metric values across successive evaluation windows.

As expected, given the controlled simulation setup, the predictive performance remains consistently high across all test windows. Both models yield AUC close to 1 with the lowest value being 0.93 for the neural network in the time window $9-10$. It is important to note that this behavior is intentional. The primary objective of the conducted experiments is not to optimize the predictive accuracy. Instead, the focus is on the isolation and analysis of the temporal behavior of explanations under stable predictive performance. Consequently, observed variations in explanatory signals cannot be attributed to deteriorating model quality.

For each designated testing period, explanations were computed in the form of SHAP feature attributions, which were applied to all test observations. The local attributions were subsequently aggregated to form time-indexed explanatory signals, which were used as inputs to the proposed temporal consistency analysis. Specifically, for each feature, the distribution of Shapley values within a test window was summarized into a single representative value, yielding a sequence of explanation values evolving over time.

Table 1. AUC results for XGBoost (XGB) and neural network (NN) models evaluated over different time windows.

Model	7 – 8	9 – 10	11 – 12	13 – 14	15 – 16	17 – 18	19 – 20	21 – 22	23 – 24
XGB	1.0	0.95	0.98	1.0	0.96	0.99	1.0	0.95	0.99
NN	1.0	0.93	0.98	1.0	0.97	0.98	1.0	0.97	0.99

3.3 Temporal Consistency Monitoring

In order to obtain a scalar explanation signal suitable for temporal consistency assessment, the SHAP attributions calculated according to [11] are aggregated across observations in the block via median for each feature j

$$F_t^{(j)} = \text{median}_{i=1,\ldots,m_t}\left(\phi_t^{(i,j)}\right),$$

where $\phi_t^{(i,j)}$ denotes the SHAP attribution for observation i in block t and m_t is the number of observations in that block. The resulting sequence $\{F_t^{(j)}\}$ forms a temporal explanatory signal, for which the temporal consistency index is computed $\text{TCI}(\{F_t^{(j)}\})$ independently. In addition to the calculation of the overall index, the per-step inconsistency contributions are reported to localize the time points at which the explanation stream deviates most strongly from its expected temporal behavior.

4 Experimental Results

4.1 SHAP-Based Explanation Streams

The SHAP-based results for feature x1 are presented in Fig. 3, including: (i) boxplots of SHAP attribution distributions across successive test windows, (ii) the corresponding aggregated explanatory signal $F_t^{(1)}$ obtained via the median, and (iii) the per-step inconsistency contributions derived from the proposed temporal consistency index. Additional plots containing results for neural network models are available at [15].

The analysis is conducted separately for the stable and unstable classes. This enables a comparative investigation of explanation dynamics under different data-generating regimes. For the stable class, the SHAP attribution distributions and the resulting aggregated explanatory signal demonstrate notable stability over time, with only minor deviations observed in the final test windows. These deviations are reflected by elevations in the per-step inconsistency contribution. Such elevations indicate localized deviations from the expected temporal behavior. This behavior is consistent with the fact that the stable class is generated from an approximately stationary distribution.

In contrast, the explanatory signal demonstrates notable temporal variation for the unstable class, characterized by observations drawn from multiple distributions that exhibit recurrence over time. This variation results in significantly elevated per-step inconsistency contributions, which manifest in a periodic pattern synchronized with the recurrent distributional changes. In particular, windows corresponding to distributional transitions (e.g., $11-12$, $17-18$, and $23-24$) are consistently identified as major contributors to explanation inconsistency. It is worth noting that even when the explanatory signal returns to a regime similar to earlier windows, elevated per-step inconsistency may persist due to the temporal dependence embedded in the consistency computation.

This finding underscores the ability of the proposed index to not only capture instantaneous changes but also their relative impact in relation to recent historical patterns. The findings indicate that the framework facilitates the quantification and localization of temporal instability in explanation streams. The method does not intend to explain the causal origin of such instabilities; rather, it aims to identify their occurrence and magnitude for subsequent analysis.

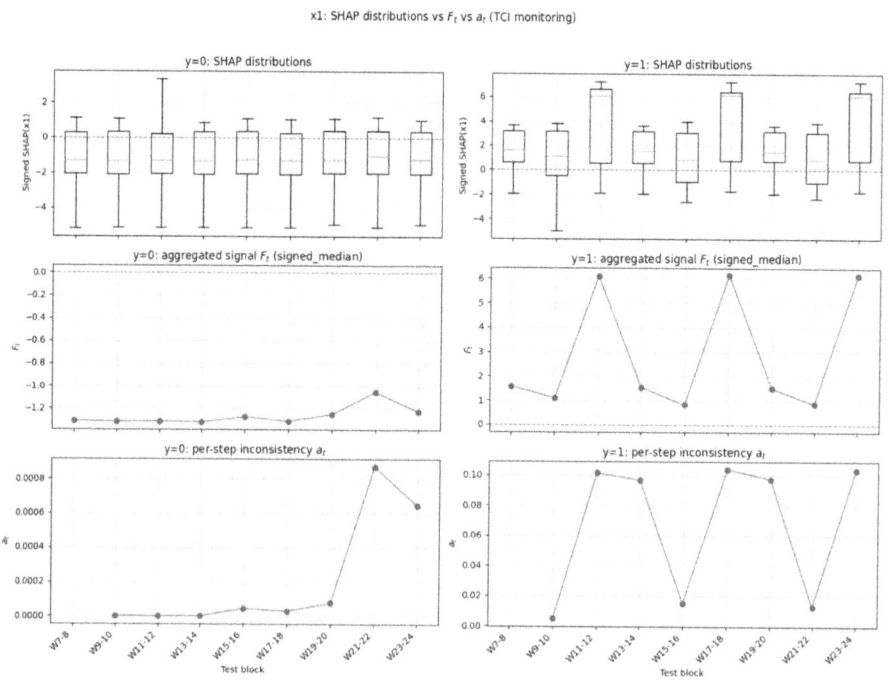

Fig. 3. Boxplots and medians of aggregated SHAP attributions for feature x1 over time steps, and per-step inconsistency, regarding stable (left plots) and unstable (right plots) classes generated using the XGBoost model.

4.2 Fuzzy Linguistic Summary-Based Explanation Streams

To further assess the proposed framework, experiments were conducted using FLS as an alternative form of explanation. We briefly recall that a fuzzy linguistic summary takes the form

$$S : Q\ R_1 \star \ldots \star R_k\ x \text{ are } P_1 \diamond \ldots \diamond P_l, \tag{1}$$

where $\star, \diamond \in \{\text{AND, OR}\}$, Q is a linguistic quantifier, $R_1, \ldots, R_k$ are qualifiers and $P_1, \ldots, P_l$ are summaries.

In this setting, explanatory streams were formulated using the product of the degree of truth and the degree of support associated with each summary. The derived summaries were based on feature values extracted from the test data and their corresponding SHAP attributions for the unstable class. The fuzzy membership functions for each feature were defined as triangular fuzzy numbers constructed based on data-driven quartiles. We considered the empirical first quartile, median, and third quartile. The terms corresponding to the first and third quartile were modeled as left- and right-shoulder membership functions which decrease or increase linearly from median accordingly. An example for feature x1 is showcased in Fig. 4.

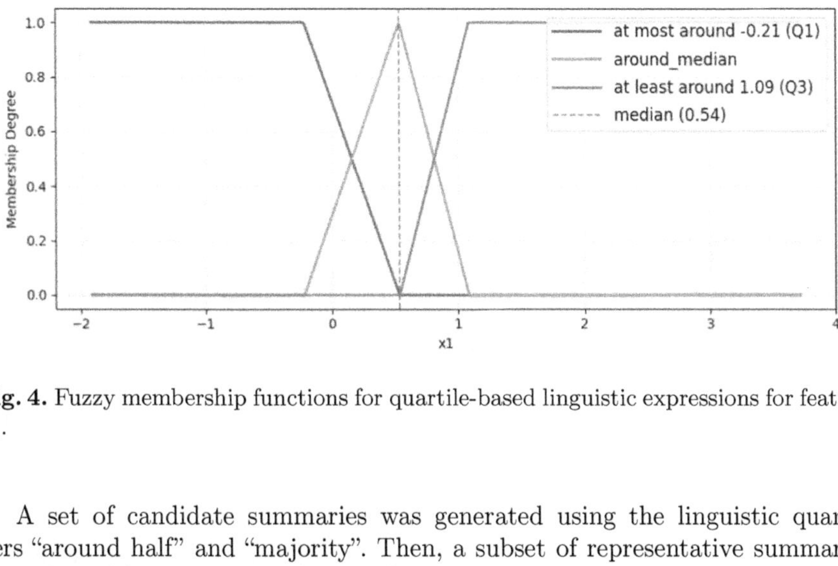

Fig. 4. Fuzzy membership functions for quartile-based linguistic expressions for feature x_1.

A set of candidate summaries was generated using the linguistic quantifiers "around half" and "majority". Then, a subset of representative summaries was selected based on their degree of support and temporal relevance. For each selected summary, TCI, the mean degree of truth, and the mean degree of support are reported in Table 2. As observed, the characteristics of the XGBoost model and neural network-based summaries are similar. The most noticeable difference between the TCI for the two can be observed for the $S16$ summary, with a value of 0.58 for XGBoost and 0.46 for the neural network.

Figures 5 and 6 illustrate the explanatory signals and per-step inconsistency contributions for the three summaries with the highest TCI generated using the XGBoost model. A comparison of SHAP-based signals and FLS-based explanatory streams reveals that the latter exhibit more intricate temporal behavior,

Table 2. Fuzzy linguistic summaries with quality measures. Quantifiers are color-coded ("majority": blue, "around half": orange); contribution polarity is indicated by color ("positive": green, "negative": red). Contributions were calculated for two alternative models (XGBoost and NN) for comparative purposes. TCI: temporal consistency index, DoT: degree of truth, DoS: degree of support.

id	Linguistic summary	Model	TCI	DoT	DoS
S2	For majority of obs. with x_1 at least around Q_3 and x_2 at least around Q_3, x_1 has a positive contribution to unstable class prediction.	XGB	0.44	0.33	0.15
		NN	0.44	0.33	0.15
S1	For around half of obs. with x_1 at least around Q_3 and x_3 at least around Q_3, x_3 has a positive contribution to unstable class prediction.	XGB	0.52	0.64	0.22
		NN	0.47	0.53	0.22
S16	For majority of obs. with x_1 at least around Q_3 and x_3 at least around Q_3, x_3 has a positive contribution to unstable class prediction.	XGB	0.58	0.24	0.22
		NN	0.46	0.36	0.22
S18	For around half of obs. with x_1 at most around Q_1 and x_2 around median, x_1 has a negative contribution to unstable class prediction.	XGB	0.95	0.82	0.08
		NN	0.98	1.00	0.10
S14	For around half of obs. with x_1 at most around Q_1 and x_2 around median, x_1 has a negative contribution to unstable class prediction.	XGB	0.95	0.69	0.10
		NN	0.98	1.00	0.10
S3	For around half of obs. with x_1 at most around Q_1 and x_2 at least around Q_3, x_2 has a negative contribution to unstable class prediction.	XGB	0.97	1.00	0.12
		NN	0.96	1.00	0.10

indicative of interactions between multiple features. While the recurring structure of the simulated data remains visible, the explanatory signals no longer align directly with single-feature distributional changes.

It is worth noting that among the selected summaries, summary $S3$ most closely follows the expected temporal structure induced by the data-generation process. In contrast, the remaining summaries display more irregular behavior. Nevertheless, the proposed framework remains capable of identifying periods of elevated inconsistency, thereby demonstrating its applicability to higher-level, relational explanations. In this illustrative example, the specific choice of the predictive model is not central. Any standard supervised classifier can be used, as the proposed consistency assessment operates on explanation streams independently of the underlying model.

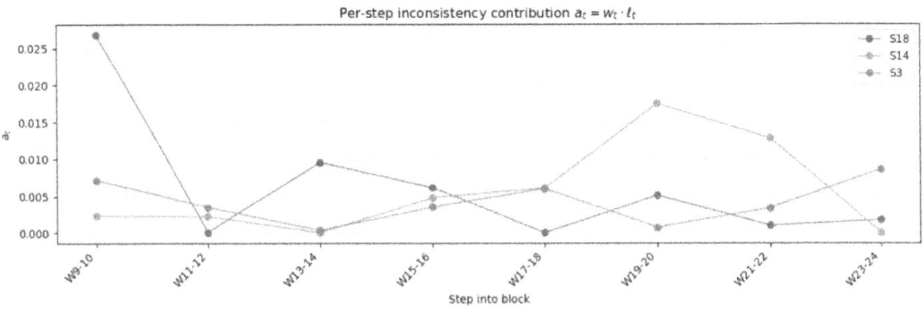

Fig. 5. Explanatory signal calculated as the product of the Degree of Truth (DoT) and Degree of Support (DoS) over time for three selected fuzzy linguistic summaries generated using the XGBoost model.

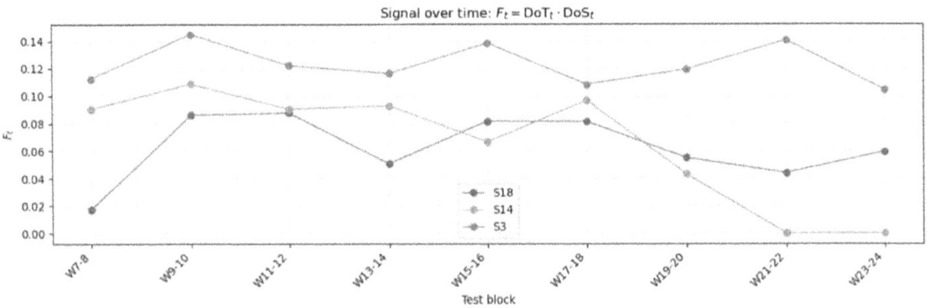

Fig. 6. Per-step inconsistency calculated on explanatory signal calculated as the product of the Degree of Truth (DoT) and Degree of Support (DoS) for three selected fuzzy linguistic summaries generated using the XGBoost model.

Whilst we have focused on feature-based explanations obtained via SHAP in this paper, it should be noted that the proposed framework is equally applicable to other explanation paradigms. In particular, fuzzy rule-based explanations produced by the GUAJE framework [16] yield time-indexed explanatory quantities such as rule activation or support, which can be treated as explanatory signals and assessed using the same temporal consistency index. A systematic comparison between SHAP-based, fuzzy linguistic summary-based, and GUAJE-based explanation streams as additional symbolic explanatory processes is reserved for future research.

5 Conclusions and Future Work

The primary contributions of this work are threefold. Firstly, a temporal consistency index for explanatory signals is introduced. This index aims to quantify deviations from expected temporal behavior in a model-agnostic and explanation-agnostic manner. The proposed index operates directly on explanation streams, thus negating the need for an underlying predictive model or explanation method. This enables a unified assessment of explanation reliability over time. Secondly, we have seen that temporal consistency constitutes an additional and complementary dimension for model evaluation, revealing differences between explanations that are not captured by predictive performance alone. By employing controlled temporal scenarios, we demonstrate that explanations corresponding to different features, rules, or models can exhibit markedly different consistency profiles under non-stationary data distributions. Thirdly, the practical relevance of the proposed index is illustrated using alternative fuzzy information granules, namely fuzzy linguistic summaries. It is demonstrated how explanation consistency can inform model selection and deployment decisions by exposing trade-offs between predictive accuracy, model adaptivity, and explanation reliability in evolving environments.

Future work will extend the current pipeline to additional model classes, incorporating fuzzy rule-based predictors implemented within the GUAJE framework, probabilistic models, neural networks and logistic regression.

Acknowledgement. The project "ExplainMe: Explainable Artificial Intelligence for Monitoring Acoustic Features extracted from Speech" (FENG.02.02-IP.05-0302/23) is carried out within the First Team programme of the Foundation for Polish Science co-financed by the European Union under the European Funds for Smart Economy 2021–2027 (FENG). Jose M. Alonso-Moral recognizes the support of the Galician Ministry of Education, Science, Universities and Professional Training (CiTIUS 2024–2027 ED431G-2023/04 grant) and the European Union (European Regional Development Fund - ERDF), the Spanish Ministry of Science, Innovation and Universities (MCIN/AEI/10.13039/501100011033/) through MAIXAI4TRUST PID2024-157680NB-I00 project, and the European Union's Horizon Europe research and innovation programme under Grant Agreement No. 101134894 (SOSfood project).

References

1. Ali, S., et al.: Explainable artificial intelligence (XAI): what we know and what is left to attain trustworthy artificial intelligence. Inf. Fusion (2023). https://doi.org/10.1016/j.inffus.2023.101805
2. Basseville, M., Nikiforov, I.: Detection of Abrupt Change Theory and Application, vol. 15 (1993)
3. Breiman, L.: Statistical modeling: the two cultures. Stat. Sci. **16**(3), 199–231 (2001). https://doi.org/10.1214/ss/1009213726
4. Casalino, G., Castellano, G., Kaczmarek-Majer, K., Schicchi, D., Taibi, D., Zaza, G.: Evolving fuzzy classification for human-centered explainable learning analytics in virtual environments. Evol. Syst. (2025)
5. Chen, T., Guestrin, C.: XGBoost: a scalable tree boosting system. In: Proceedings of the 22nd ACM SIGKDD International Conference on Knowledge Discovery and Data Mining, KDD 2016, pp. 785–794. ACM (2016). https://doi.org/10.1145/2939672.2939785
6. Doshi-Velez, F., Kim, B.: Towards a rigorous science of interpretable machine learning (2017). https://arxiv.org/abs/1702.08608

7. Gama, J., Žliobaitė, I., Bifet, A., Pechenizkiy, M., Bouchachia, H.: A survey on concept drift adaptation. ACM Comput. Surv. (CSUR) **46** (2014). https://doi.org/10.1145/2523813
8. Guidotti, R., Monreale, A., Ruggieri, S., Turini, F., Pedreschi, D., Giannotti, F.: A survey of methods for explaining black box models (2018). https://arxiv.org/abs/1802.01933
9. Kaczmarek-Majer, K.: Explaining neural networks in natural language. In: Watson, P., Farahani, H., Bezdan, T. (eds.) Introduction to Intricate Artificial Psychology with Python (2026)
10. Lipton, Z.C.: The mythos of model interpretability (2017). https://arxiv.org/abs/1606.03490
11. Lundberg, S.M., et al.: Explainable ai for trees: from local explanations to global understanding (2019). https://arxiv.org/abs/1905.04610
12. Mariotti, E., Alonso-Moral, J.M., Gatt, A.: Measuring model understandability by means of shapley additive explanations. In: IEEE International Conference on Fuzzy Systems (FUZZ-IEEE), pp. 1–8. (2022). https://doi.org/10.1109/FUZZ-IEEE55066.2022.9882773
13. Miś, K., Kaczmarek-Majer, K., Baczyński, M.: Fuzzy linguistic summaries and the double negation property. TechRxiv (2025)
14. Molnar, C., Casalicchio, G., Bischl, B.: Interpretable machine learning – a brief history, state-of-the-art and challenges. In: Koprinska, I., et al. (eds.) ECML PKDD 2020. CCIS, vol. 1323, pp. 417–431. Springer, Cham (2020). https://doi.org/10.1007/978-3-030-65965-3_28
15. Ostrowski, M.: The TCI repository (2025). https://github.com/Zylaz/StabilityMetric
16. Pancho, D., Alonso, J., Magdalena, L.: Quest for interpretability-accuracy trade-off supported by fingrams into the fuzzy modeling tool guaje. International Journal of Computational Intelligence Systems **6**, 46–60 (2013). https://doi.org/10.1080/18756891.2013.818189
17. Pedregosa, F., et al.: Édouard Duchesnay: scikit-learn: machine learning in python (2018). https://arxiv.org/abs/1201.0490
18. Ribeiro, M.T., Singh, S., Guestrin, C.: Why should i trust you?: Explaining the predictions of any classifier (2016). https://arxiv.org/abs/1602.04938
19. Rojat, T., Puget, R., Filliat, D., Ser, J.D., Gelin, R., Díaz-Rodríguez, N.: Explainable artificial intelligence (XAI) on timeseries data: a survey (2021). https://arxiv.org/abs/2104.00950
20. Rudin, C., et al.: Position: amazing things come from having many good models. In: Proceedings of the 41st International Conference on Machine Learning (ICML). JMLR.org (2024)
21. Sundararajan, M., Taly, A., Yan, Q.: Axiomatic attribution for deep networks (2017). https://arxiv.org/abs/1703.01365
22. Widmer, G., Kubat, M.: Learning in the presence of concept drift and hidden contexts. Mach. Learn. **23**(11), (1994). https://doi.org/10.1007/BF00116900
23. Zadeh, L.: Fuzzy sets. Inf. Control **8**(3), 338–353 (1965). https://doi.org/10.1016/S0019-9958(65)90241-X

A Possibilistic K-Modes Approach for Incremental Object Integration

Asma Ammar[1(✉)], Zied Elouedi[1], and Pawan Lingras[2]

[1] LARODEC, Institut Supérieur de Gestion de Tunis, Université de Tunis, 41 Avenue de la Liberté, 2000 Le Bardo, Tunisie
asmaammarbr@gmail.com, zied.elouedi@gmx.fr

[2] Department of Mathematics and Computing Science, Saint Marys University, Halifax, Canada
pawan@cs.smu.ca

Abstract. Clustering data in uncertain contexts is increasingly essential for addressing real-world challenges. This paper develops a novel incremental clustering approach, termed Incremental Possibilistic K-Modes with possibilistic membership degrees (IncPKM), designed to handle the arrival of new objects over time within a possibilistic framework. The proposed method utilizes possibility theory to manage uncertainty, allowing objects to belong to multiple clusters with varying degrees of possibility rather than fixed assignments. Unlike standard methods, IncPKM performs re-clustering as new data becomes available without re-initializing the entire process from scratch, significantly reducing computational overhead. Experimental evaluations using categorical datasets from the UCI Machine Learning Repository demonstrate that IncPKM maintains high accuracy while being more efficient than both the standard k-modes and nonincremental possibilistic k-modes methods.

Keywords: Incremental clustering · K-modes method · Possibility theory · Incorporating objects

1 Introduction

Incremental clustering is a significant technique in data analysis, as it enables the dynamic updating of cluster structures when new data becomes available, without the need to restart the entire process. Over time, new instances, attributes, or even entirely new clusters can be added seamlessly. It is particularly useful in real-world applications where datasets evolve continuously, such as streaming data or temporal databases. Several studies have highlighted its efficiency. We can mention, the work proposed in [20] where authors discuss general schemes for incremental clustering algorithms and develop a specific optimization-based method for partitional clustering. Another study was presented in [21], offering a comprehensive survey of recent incremental clustering trends. The authors examined developments in incremental clustering, highlighting emerging methodologies and applications within the field. Thus, incremental clustering offers a practical solution for handling evolving datasets in diverse domains.

B. Vantaggi et al. (Eds.): IPMU 2026, CCIS 3019, pp. 520–533, 2026.
https://doi.org/10.1007/978-3-032-28994-0_37

On the other hand, in real-world applications, various forms of uncertainty may arise when describing datasets or when assigning objects to clusters based on their dissimilarities (e.g., measurement noise, missing or incomplete information, overlapping or ambiguous classes, outliers, etc.). Accounting for these uncertainties can enhance clustering performance and support more effective decision-making. Incremental clustering under uncertainty has also been widely studied using for example belief function theory [5,6], possibility theory [8–10] [22,23] and fuzzy sets theory [24]. In [10], the authors proposed an uncertain approach based on the k-modes algorithm and the rough set theory that adds clusters over times.

In this paper, we propose a novel incremental clustering approach that addresses the uncertainty associated with assigning objects to multiple clusters. The proposed algorithm applies the k-modes method to cluster objects characterized by categorical attribute values, while employing possibility theory to compute possibilistic membership degrees through a possibility distribution. Our method allows the integration of new instances over time without the need to recluster existing objects from scratch, relying instead on the previously obtained cluster distributions. This incremental possibilistic framework is particularly useful for dynamic environments where data evolves continuously. By maintaining previously obtained partitions, our algorithm reduces computational cost while preserving clustering accuracy. It provides deeper understanding of the relation between object and cluster by using membership degrees instead of fixed assignments. Such flexibility makes the method suitable for applications in domains like pattern recognition, data mining, and decision support systems. Overall, the proposed approach offers a practical solution for handling categorical data under uncertainty and by adding new objects over time.

The rest of the paper is organized as follows: Sect. 2 and Sect. 3 provide, respectively, an overview of the possibility theory and the k-modes method and its extension. Section 4 focuses on our incremental possibilistic k-modes with possibilistic membership degrees by explaining its main parameters and algorithm. Section 5 details experimental results using real-world databases. Section 6 concludes this paper. Section 7 outlines future work.

2 Possibility Theory

Possibility theory [14] is an uncertainty framework designed to address imperfect knowledge. Initially introduced by Zadeh, it was subsequently refined and extended by several researchers, mainly Dubois and Prade [1–3]. This theory has been successfully applied across a variety of studies and research works. In the following subsections, we present its main concept.

2.1 Possibility Distribution

Within possibility theory, a central concept is the possibility distribution denoted by π, established on the basis of the universe of discourse $\Omega = \{\omega_1, \omega_2, ..., \omega_n\}$ where ω_i is an event or a state.

A possibility distribution is a function that assigns to each element of the universe of discourse Ω a value within the interval L=[0,1], with L presents the possibilistic scale. L can be defined in a qualitative context, where only order is relevant, or in a quantitative context, where it is represented by values in [0,1].

It is also important to highlight the extreme cases of knowledge in possibility theory, namely *complete knowledge* and *total ignorance*, which are defined by $\exists\omega_0,\ \pi(\omega_0) = 1$ and $\pi(\omega) = 0$ otherwise, and $\forall\omega \in \Omega,\ \pi(\omega) = 1$.

Moreover, a possibility distribution is normalized when $\max_i\{\pi(\omega_i)\} = 1$.

2.2 Possibilistic Clustering

Possibilistic clustering extends fuzzy clustering methods by addressing the limitations of probabilistic membership assignments.

Unlike Fuzzy C-Means (FCM) introduced in [15] and [16], which requires membership values to sum to one in each clusters, possibilistic clustering allows each data point to have independent degrees of belonging. This reduces the impact of noise and outliers. In fact, in FCM, outliers must still receive a degree of membership even when they are far from the cluster center. In contrast, in possibilistic clustering, points that are far from any cluster center—such as outliers—can receive very low membership degrees, or even degrees equal to zero.

The most widely known algorithm in this family is Possibilistic C-Means (PCM) proposed in [17], which introduces a possibilistic membership function that removes the constraints of probabilistic clustering. Hybrid models such as Possibilistic Fuzzy C-Means (PFCM) in [18] combine the strengths of both fuzzy and possibilistic approaches. Another improvement of the FCM is the Possibilistic Clustering Algorithm (PCA) proposed in [19] which improved robustness in noisy data environments.

Thus, possibilistic clustering provides a flexible framework for data partitioning, especially in applications where uncertainty and imprecision are significant. In this context, we propose a new algorithm that takes advantage of possibility theory to handle uncertainty and applies the k-modes method to cluster objects using possibilistic membership degrees.

Our proposed algorithm, closely related to the Possibilistic C-Means (PCM) [17], handles uncertainty through possibility theory and does not rely on the normalization constraint requiring membership degrees to sum to one for each object. This property overcomes the limitation observed in FCM-based methods. However, unlike PCM, our new algorithm is specifically designed to process categorical data and to incrementally incorporate new objects over time—capabilities that PCM does not provide.

Before presenting our contribution, the following section provides an overview of the k-modes clustering method and its extension.

3 K-Modes Method and Its Extension

In the following subsections, both the standard k-modes method and its modified variant based on possibility theory are presented.

3.1 The K-Modes Method

The standard k-modes algorithm (SKM) [4,11,12] was designed to efficiently process large categorical datasets. It relies on the simple matching dissimilarity measure and a frequency-based function as its key parameters.

Assume that we have two categorical objects $X_1=(x_{11}, x_{12}, ..., x_{1m})$ and $Y_1=(y_{11}, y_{12}, ..., y_{1m})$ with x_{1t} and y_{1t} the attributes of respectively the objects X_1 and Y_1. The simple matching dissimilarity measure d $(0 \leq d \leq m)$ is obtained using Equation (1):

$$d(X_1, Y_1) = \sum_{t=1}^{m} \delta(x_{1t}, y_{1t}). \tag{1}$$

Note that $\delta(x_{1t}, y_{1t}) = 0$ if $x_{1t} = y_{1t}$ and $\delta(x_{1t}, y_{1t}) = 1$ otherwise.

For the update of the modes, we count the frequency of each categorical value relative to each cluster and each attribute. Then, we choose the one with the highest frequency. Finally, we update the cluster mode.

The SKM algorithm is presented as follows:

Algorithm 1. SKM Algorithm

Begin
1: Select randomly the k initial modes, one mode for each cluster.
2: Computing the dissimilarity measure using Equation (1).
3: Allocate each object to the cluster with the lowest dissimilarity
4: Update the cluster modes using the frequency-based function.
5: Repeat Step 3 and 4 until all object assignments are stable.
End

SKM algorithm is a hard clustering technique in which each object is assigned to exactly one cluster. Nevertheless, in practice, an object may exhibit similarities with multiple clusters simultaneously.

To address the issue of non-uniqueness in cluster modes and to manage uncertainty regarding the assignment of objects to multiple clusters, an enhanced variant of the k-modes algorithm incorporating possibilistic membership is introduced. The details of this approach are presented in the following subsection.

3.2 The K-Modes Method with Possibilistic Membership

The k-modes method with possibilistic membership (KM-PM) [7] is an extension of the SKM algorithm that addresses uncertainty in object assignment across multiple clusters by incorporating possibilistic membership degrees.

The objective function of the KM-PM method is closely related to that of the fuzzy k-modes, as both employ the same dissimilarity measure d and a membership degree ω to capture the uncertainty associated with assigning an object to different clusters.

For fuzzy k-modes, the objective function is:

$\sum_{j=1}^{k}\sum_{i=1}^{n}\omega_{ij}^{\alpha}d(X_i,Q_j)$, where:
d is the simple matching measure, $\alpha > 1$, $0 \leq \omega_{ij} \leq 1$ and $\sum_{j=1}^{k}\omega_{ij} = 1$

For KM-PM, the objective function is:

$\sum_{j=1}^{k}\sum_{i=1}^{n}\omega_{ij}d(X_i,Q_j)$, where:
$\max_j \omega_{ij} = 1$ for all i, $0 \leq \omega_{ij} \leq 1$, d is the simple matching measure, and ω_{ij} is the possibilistic membership degree.

The main parameters of the KM-PM are:

The Simple Matching Dissimilarity Measure: enables the computation of dissimilarity between objects and cluster modes. It operates by comparing each attribute value of an object with the corresponding attribute value of the mode, as defined in Eq. (1).

The Possibilistic Membership Degree: $\omega_{ij} \in [0,1]$ is determined as follows. First, the dissimilarity values between each object and the cluster modes are computed using Eq. (1). These dissimilarity values (dis) are then transformed into similarity degrees (sim) by applying the formula:

$$sim = m - dis \tag{2}$$

where m denotes the total number of attributes. The resulting similarity value is subsequently divided by m to normalize it, thereby yielding ω_{ij} within the interval [0,1]. This normalized value represents the degree of belongingness of object i to cluster j.

Two extreme cases can be highlighted:

- $\omega_{ij} = 1$: the object i is identical to the mode of cluster j.
- $\omega_{ij} = 0$: the object i shares no similarity with the mode of cluster j.

Note that if $\omega_{ij} > \omega_{i(j+1)}$ (respectively $\omega_{ij} < \omega_{i(j+1)})$) it means that the object i belongs to the cluster j more (respectively less) than to the cluster j+1.

Updating cluster which incorporates the possibilistic membership degrees ω of each object across different clusters. Accordingly, the update of cluster modes is driven by these membership degrees.

The following steps are followed to update the modes: First, we evaluate the dissimilarities between the modes and the objects, and then we assign the weight ω_{ij} corresponding to object i and cluster j. Next, for each value v of attribute t, we compute the sum of the degrees ω_{ijtv} associated with object i within cluster j. Finally, the value v that yields the highest total becomes the new value of the mode. Thus, the update of cluster modes is formally expressed by the following Equation (3)

$$\forall j \in k,\ t \in m,\ Mode_{jt} = \max_{v} \sum_{i=1}^{n} \omega_{ijtv}. \tag{3}$$

with

$$\forall i,\ \max_{j}(\omega_{ij}) = 1. \tag{4}$$

4 Incremental Possibilistic K-Modes with Possibilistic Membership Degrees

The Incremental Possibilistic K-Modes with possibilistic membership degrees (IncPKM) is a novel approach that integrates the strengths of SKM and KM-PM to effectively manage categorical datasets within an uncertain framework. It also addresses incremental learning by allowing new objects to be incorporated over time without the need to recluster the entire partition from the beginning.

In our IncPKM, data points that lie far from all cluster centers, particularly outliers, are assigned very low membership degrees, and in some cases a membership of zero. This mechanism effectively reduces the sensitivity to noise and outliers typically observed in conventional fuzzy clustering methods. Thus, Our algorithm, like the k-modes method, handles purely categorical datasets. It cannot be applied to numerical datasets. However, it differs from the standard k-modes approach by using precomputed similarities to derive the possibilistic membership degrees of each object with respect to all clusters. In this way, our approach takes into account all similarities between objects and clusters, ensuring a more comprehensive clustering process. Moreover, The primary advantage of IncPKM lies in its incremental nature, which enables efficient adaptation to evolving datasets.

In our algorithm, objects that achieve a membership degree equal to 1 for a given cluster may still obtain very low (but not necessarily zero) degrees for other clusters, depending on their similarity profile. Consequently, highly typical objects tend to be strongly associated with a single cluster, although their typicities with respect to other clusters do not vanish completely. Therefore, while our approach does not enforce the strict core-level disjointness required in the Dubois–Prade characterization of possibilistic partitions, it does exhibit a practical form of central separation. In contrast, the coverage condition at the support level is naturally satisfied, since all objects retain at least one nonzero possibilistic degree across the set of clusters. Moreover, in our approach, the possibilistic degrees represent uncertain values, in the same sense as in the PCM framework. As a consequence, an object may simultaneously obtain nonzero degrees for several clusters when the data exhibit overlapping structures.

The main parameters of IncPKM are described as follows.

4.1 Main Parameters

The proposed algorithm, IncPKM, represents an improved adaptation of the KM-PM algorithm. Although the two approaches share certain parameter similarities, IncPKM is specifically designed to manage incremental objects.

Thus, the IncPKM employs the simple matching dissimilarity measure to calculate the dissimilarities between clusters and objects, as specified in Eq. (1). It then computes the possibilistic membership degrees using Eq. (2). Finally, the cluster modes are updated according to Eq. (3). However, the IncPKM differs from the KM-PM by handling incremental objects over time.

Our proposal also accepts as input a categorical dataset along with the specified number of clusters to be formed (k). As output, it assigns the objects to k clusters, incorporating possibilistic membership degrees to reflect the uncertainty of cluster association.

Our novel incremental approach uses these parameters to cluster objects into several groups using possibilistic membership degrees. It then adds objects over time based on the computed partitions.

The proposed algorithm computes the membership degrees not only for the initial dataset but also for newly added objects over time, subsequently updating the clusters accordingly.

An illustration of our new proposal is presented in Fig. 1.

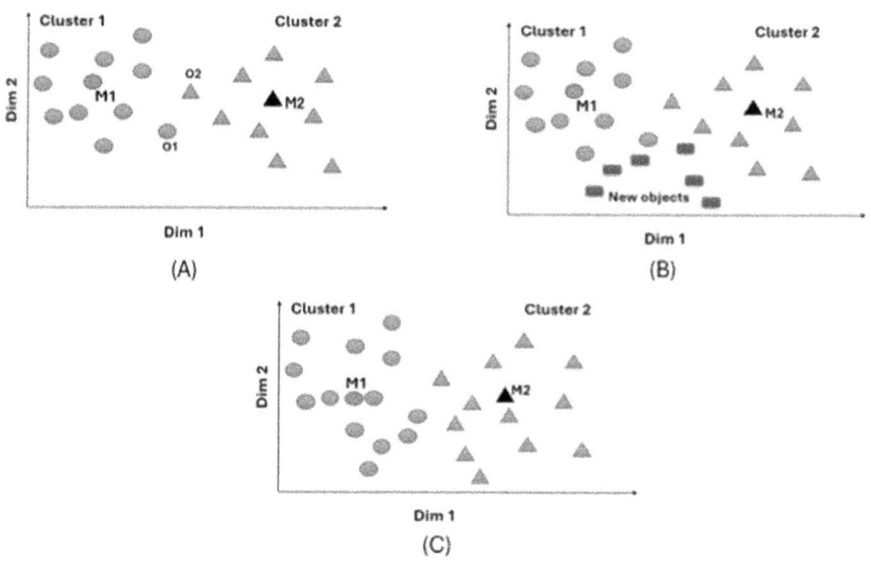

Fig. 1. Illustration of incremental Possibilistic K-Modes with Possibilistic Membership Degrees.

Figure 1 (A) presents the initial clustering results before adding new objects. The IncPKM algorithm partitions the dataset into two clusters and computes the possibilistic membership degree for each object. We can observe that some objects share similarities with both clusters, such as objects $O1$ and $O2$. It is clear that they are close to both clusters C_1 (cluster 1) and C_2 (cluster 2), and their possibilistic membership degrees are as follows:

- For $O1$: $\omega_{11} = 0.4$ (for C_1) and $\omega_{12} = 0.25$ (for C_2).
- For $O2$: $\omega_{21} = 0.39$ (for C_1) and $\omega_{22} = 0.45$ (for C_2).

Figure 1 (B) shows how data points arrive over time and how clusters evolve incrementally.

Finally, Fig. 1 (C) illustrates the final partition after updating the clusters without reclustering the initial objects from the beginning. The modes M1 and M2 are updated, and the possibilistic membership degrees are recomputed for each object.

4.2 Algorithm

The IncPKM algorithm can be outlined as follows:

Algorithm 2. IncPKM Algorithm

Begin
1: Select randomly the k initial modes, one mode for each cluster.
2: Computing the dissimilarity measure using Equation (1).
3: Allocate each object to all clusters based on possibilistic membership degrees Equation (2)
4: Update the cluster modes using Equation (3).
5: Re-evaluate the similarity between objects and modes. Reallocate objects to clusters using possibilistic membership degrees, then update the modes.
6: Repeat Step 5 until all object assignments are stable.
7: When a new object is added, compute its possibilistic membership degrees to the k clusters using Equation (2).
8: Update the cluster modes accordingly.
End

5 Experiments

5.1 The Framework

To evaluate the effectiveness of the proposed method and ensure reliable results, we conducted eight experimental runs on various categorical real-world datasets obtained from the UCI Machine Learning Repository [13]. The datasets employed are summarized in Table 1, where the columns #Instances, #Attributes, and #Classes respectively indicate the number of instances, attributes, and clusters to be formed.

Table 1. Description of the used datasets

Databases	#Instances	#Attributes	#Classes	Notations
Shuttle Landing Control	15	6	2	SLC
Balloons	20	4	2	Bal
Post-Operative Patient	90	8	3	POP
Congressional Voting Records	435	16	2	CVR
Balance Scale	625	4	3	BS
Tic-Tac-Toe Endgame	958	9	2	TE
Solar-Flare	1389	10	3	SF
Car Evaluation	1728	6	4	CE

To incorporate new objects over time, we utilize datasets from the UCI Machine Learning Repository. These datasets are divided into two parts: the first part is employed to construct the initial distribution, while the second part is reserved for the incoming objects. In other words, the new objects that arrive progressively are derived from the second portion of the dataset and integrated as new objects.

5.2 Evaluation Criteria

To evaluate our algorithm, we used three evaluation criteria namely the accuracy, the number of iterations, and the execution time.

The accuracy AC is defined by Eq. (5):

$$AC = \frac{\sum_{l=1}^{k} a_l}{n}, \tag{5}$$

where n denotes the total number of objects in the training set, and a_l represents the number of objects correctly classified within cluster l.

In our evaluation, the accuracy was computed by assigning each object to the cluster for which it obtained the highest possibility degree (i.e., a crisp assignment derived from the possibilistic memberships). We then compared these crisp cluster labels with the true classes of the datasets. This choice is standard when labelled datasets are available, since accuracy provides a direct and interpretable measure of the agreement between the produced clustering and the true class structure. Our goal here was to evaluate how well the algorithm recovers the known classes, which naturally relies on crisp comparisons.

The second evaluation criterion is the iteration number (IN). It refers to the number of iterations required by the main program to perform the clustering task.

The last criterion is the execution time (ET) corresponds to the total time needed to cluster all objects.

In our case, The ET and IN for IncPKM represent the time and number of iterations required for initial clustering plus incremental updates without restarting the clustering process from the beginning. However, the ET (respectively, the IN) associated with SKM and KM-PM reflects both the duration (the number of iterations) required for the initial clustering and the second clustering of newly introduced objects. Unlike IncPKM, this second clustering does not utilize the partition obtained from the initial clustering but recluster objects from the beginning.

5.3 Results

In this section, we present the results obtained by testing the three algorithms (i.e. the IncPKM, the standard k-modes SKM, and the KM-PM algorithm) on eight datasets taken from UCI Machine Learning Repository [13].

In our case, our primary objective was to evaluate the ability of the algorithm to recover the true class structure of the labeled datasets, which naturally relies on crisp comparisons. We also aimed to demonstrate the performance gain achieved when adding objects over time without re clustering from the beginning. For these reasons, accuracy was chosen as the evaluation metric.

The following results presented in Table 2 and Table 3 demonstrate the performance of our algorithm compared to existing methods i.e. the SKM and the KM-PM.

Table 2. The accuracy of the proposed method vs. SKM and KM-PM

datasets	*SLC*	*Bal*	*POP*	*CVR*	*BS*	*TE*	*SF*	*CE*
SKM								
AC	0.61	0.52	0.684	0.825	0.785	0.513	0.87	0.795
KM-PM								
AC	0.63	0.65	0.74	0.79	0.82	0.59	0.91	0.87
IncPKM								
AC	0.63	0.65	0.74	0.79	0.82	0.59	0.91	0.87

From Table 2, it is clear that our incremental method achieves more effective and accurate results than the standard approach, namely SKM, particularly for the Solar Flare (SF) dataset, where IncPKM reaches an accuracy of 0.91.

Furthermore, the results of IncPKM are the same to those of KM-PM, which is expected since both methods rely on the same parameters and the same clustering process.

Indeed, after clustering the newly added objects, the final accuracy of IncPKM converges to the same accuracy as that obtained by KM-PM. The results produced by the incremental possibilistic k-modes are consistent with those of the corresponding batch algorithm (KM-PM) trained on the full dataset. After processing all incoming objects, the incremental procedure converges to cluster modes and possibility degrees that closely match those obtained by the non-incremental possibilistic k-modes. This demonstrates that our incremental strategy provides a reliable approximation of the batch solution while preserving the ability to update the clustering structure as new data arrive.

Table 3. The number of iterations and the execution time of the proposed method vs. SKM and KM-PM

datasets	*SLC*	*Bal*	*POP*	*CVR*	*BS*	*TE*	*SF*	*CE*
SKM								
IN	13	14	20	21	22	22	24	21
ET/second	22.721	25.861	31.818	55.552	69.039	232.829	4149.094	5705.923
KM-PM								
IN	6	6	14	9	4	16	20	20
ET/second	18.53	21.79	26.81	47.96	51.60	109.23	162.60	296.36
IncPKM								
IN	5	5	9	7	3	11	14	14
ET/second	11.8	13.4	17.54	30.37	34.55	65.41	89.18	206.73

Looking at Table 3, we observe that the IncPKM provides better results than both the SKM and KM-PM. For example, in the case of SKM, IN for the SLC dataset is 13. This value represents the sum of two numbers: the first indicates the iterations required to cluster the initial part of the dataset, while the second corresponds to the iterations needed to cluster both the initial and the remaining parts. As noted earlier, each dataset is divided into two subsets: the first is used to perform the initial partition, and the second is used to incrementally add new objects over time.

It is clear from Table 3 that the IN required by IncPKM to cluster both the initial partition and the objects added over time is lower than the IN required by either SKM or KM-PM. These values can be explained by the fact that SKM and KM-PM require a greater number of iterations to recluster both the old and newly added objects from the beginning. Note that, the same computation is performed for the KM-PM iteration number.

It is also evident that the ET of our incremental algorithm is lower than that of both SKM and KM-PM. This improvement is due to the ability of IncPKM to update the final partitions by incrementally adding new objects over time, without the need to recluster all objects from the beginning. In contrast, SKM and KM-PM cannot take advantage of the initial clusters and must recluster both the newly added and the previously clustered objects from scratch.

To summarize, the IncPKM algorithm has demonstrated its performance compared to both SKM and KM-PM methods by achieving high accuracy and reducing the number of iterations as well as the execution time.

6 Conclusion

This paper introduced IncPKM, a new possibilistic method for incremental clustering that progressively incorporates new objects based on initial partitions. By defining possibilistic membership degrees, the algorithm captures complex relationships and similarities between objects and all clusters, providing a richer data representation under uncertainty. Evaluations on various real-world datasets from the UCI Machine Learning Repository consistently demonstrate that our approach offers significant performance gains. Specifically, IncPKM achieves high accuracy—converging with the results of its non-incremental counterpart—while substantially reducing both the number of iterations and the total execution time by avoiding redundant computations.

7 Future Work

The performance gains and structural flexibility demonstrated by IncPKM suggest several promising avenues for future research. Given that our approach successfully manages the integration of new categorical objects without re-initializing the clustering process, a natural progression would be to adapt this framework for high-velocity data streams [25–27]. In such environments, where data arrive continuously, incorporating a "sliding window" or a "forgetting factor" could enable the model to adapt to concept drift, where the underlying distribution of the categorical attributes shifts over time.

Additionally, while this paper focuses on the incremental addition of objects, we could investigate a hybrid decremental approach. This would allow for the seamless removal of outdated or irrelevant instances from the cluster distributions, which is particularly useful for maintaining the relevance of temporal databases. Finally, applying this possibilistic framework to large-scale distributed systems could further enhance scalability. By parallelizing the computation of possibilistic membership degrees across multiple nodes, the algorithm could process massive datasets while preserving the nuanced uncertainty management that defines our current contribution.

References

1. Dubois, D., Prade, H.: Possibility Theory: An Approach to Computerized Processing of Uncertainty. Plenium Press, New York (1988)
2. Dubois, D., Prade, H.: Possibility theory and data fusion in poorly informed environments. Control. Eng. Pract. **25**, 811–823 (1994)

3. Dubois, D., Prade, H.: Possibility theory: qualitative and quantitative aspects. In: Smets, P. (ed.) Quantified Representation of Uncertainty and Imprecision. HDRUMS, vol. 1, pp. 169–226. Springer, Dordrecht (1998). https://doi.org/10.1007/978-94-017-1735-9_6
4. Huang, Z.: Extensions to the k-means algorithm for clustering large datasets with categorical values. Data Min. Knowl. Disc. **2**, 283–304 (1998)
5. Denoeux, T., Su, Z.-G.: BPEC: belief-peaks evidential clustering. IEEE Trans. Fuzzy Syst. **27**(2), 111–123 (2019)
6. Bahri, M., Elouedi, Z.: Clustering data stream under a belief function framework. In: Proceedings of AICCSA, pp. 1–8 (2016)
7. Ammar, A., Elouedi, Z., Lingras, P.: K-modes clustering using possibilistic membership. In: Greco, S., Bouchon-Meunier, B., Coletti, G., Fedrizzi, M., Matarazzo, B., Yager, R.R. (eds.) IPMU 2012. CCIS, vol. 299, pp. 596–605. Springer, Heidelberg (2012). https://doi.org/10.1007/978-3-642-31718-7_61
8. Ammar, A., Elouedi, Z., Lingras, P.: Decremental possibilistic k-modes. In: Proceedings of SCAI, pp. 15–24 (2013)
9. Ammar, A., Elouedi, Z., Lingras, P.: Incremental possibilistic k-modes. In: Proceedings of RSFDGrC, pp. 293–303 (2013)
10. Ammar, A., Elouedi, Z., Lingras, P.: Incremental rough possibilistic k-modes. In: Proceedings of MIWAI, pp. 13–24 (2013)
11. Huang, Z., Ng, M.K.: A fuzzy k-modes algorithm for clustering categorical data. IEEE Trans. Fuzzy Syst. **7**, 446–452 (1999)
12. Huang, Z., Ng, M.K.: A note on k-modes clustering. J. Classif. **20**, 257–261 (2003)
13. Murphy, M.P., Aha, D.W.: UCI repository databases (1996). https://archive.ics.uci.edu/ml/datasets.html
14. Zadeh, L.A.: Fuzzy sets as a basis for a theory of possibility. Fuzzy Sets Syst. **1**, 3–28 (1978)
15. Bezdek, J.C.: Numerical taxonomy with fuzzy sets. J. Math. Biol. (1974)
16. Bezdek, J.C.: Pattern Recognition with Fuzzy Objective Function Algorithms. AAPR, Springer, Boston, MA (1981). https://doi.org/10.1007/978-1-4757-0450-1
17. Krishnapuram, R., Keller, J.M.: A possibilistic approach to clustering. IEEE Trans. Fuzzy Syst. (1993)
18. Pal, N.R., Pal, K., Keller, J.M., Bezdek, J.C.: Possibilistic fuzzy c-means clustering algorithm. IEEE Trans. Fuzzy Syst. (2005)
19. Yang, M.S., Wu, K.L.: On a class of fuzzy clustering algorithms. Pattern Recogn. (2006)
20. M. Bagirov, A., Karmitsa, N., Taheri, S.: Incremental clustering algorithms. In: Partitional Clustering via Nonsmooth Optimization. USL, pp. 185–200. Springer, Cham (2020). https://doi.org/10.1007/978-3-030-37826-4_7
21. Chopade, N., Sheetlani, J.: Recent trends in incremental clustering: a review. IOSR J. Comput. Eng. 19–24 (2017)
22. Mouchaweh, M.S., Lughofer, E.: Incremental possibilistic approach for online clustering and classification. Int. J. Approximate Reasoning **53**(2), 164–184 (2012)
23. Ammar, A., Elouedi, Z., Lingras, P.: Incremental possibilistic k-modes. In: International Workshop on Rough Sets, Fuzzy Sets, Data Mining, and Granular Computing, vol. 8170, pp. 293–303 (2013)
24. Jaworski, M., Pietruczuk, L., Duda, P.: On resources optimization in fuzzy clustering of data streams. In: Rutkowski, L., Korytkowski, M., Scherer, R., Tadeusiewicz, R., Zadeh, L.A., Zurada, J.M. (eds.) ICAISC 2012. LNCS (LNAI), vol. 7268,

pp. 92–99. Springer, Heidelberg (2012). https://doi.org/10.1007/978-3-642-29350-4_11

25. Babcock, B., Babu, S., Datar, M., Motwani, R., Widom, J.: Models and issues in data stream systems. In: Proceedings of the Twenty-First ACM SIGMOD-SIGACT-SIGART Symposium on Principles of Database systems, pp. 1–1. (2002)
26. Gama, J., Žliobaitė, I., Bifet, A., Pechenizkiy, M., Bouchachia, A.: A survey on concept drift adaptation. ACM Comput. Surv. (CSUR) **46**(4), 1–37 (2014)
27. Aggarwal, C.C.: Data Streams: Models and Algorithms. Springer, Cham (2007). https://doi.org/10.1007/978-0-387-47534-9

Cautious Self-learning via Labelwise Uncertainty Quantification

Vitor Martin Bordini(✉), Sébastien Destercke, and Benjamin Quost

Université de Technologie de Compiègne, UMR CNRS 7253 Heudiasyc, 60200 Compiègne, France
{vitor.martin-bordini,benjamin.quost}@hds.utc.fr, sebatien.destercke@cnrs.fr

Abstract. Self-learning is a widely used semi-supervised learning strategy that leverages model predictions to label unlabeled data. However, conventional approaches often ignore the uncertainty inherent in these predictions, leading to confirmation bias and overconfident models. In this work, we propose a cautious self-learning framework that integrates label-wise uncertainty quantification through credal sets. By distinguishing between aleatoric and epistemic uncertainty, our method adjusts pseudo-labels to reflect both the inherent ambiguity of the data and the model's limited knowledge. We employ a variance-based decomposition and a label-wise Beta distribution estimation to construct credal sets that mitigate class imbalance and reduce overconfidence during iterative training. Experiments across six benchmark datasets demonstrate that our approach consistently improves classification accuracy compared to hard and soft pseudo-labeling strategies, achieving superior performance. These results highlight the importance of uncertainty-aware self-learning and show that cautious pseudo-labeling can enhance robustness and generalization in semi-supervised learning.

Keywords: Self-learning · Credal sets · Uncertainty quantification · Uncertain labels · Pairwise prediction

1 Introduction

Nowadays, Artificial Intelligence (AI) tools are accessible on a wide range of devices, from laptops to cell phones. The rise of this technology has been made possible by the availability of huge amounts of data, the amount and quality of which largely determine the performances of an AI model. Many works have investigated how the choice of data can bias a model, particularly in fields such as fairness [10].

Although collecting large amounts of data to train models has become easy in many cases, the acquisition of "expert knowledge"—such as, e.g., *labels* in supervised classification—remains mostly complicated, due to a variety of reasons: ethical concerns, the availability of experts, mistakes, etc. This is notably

B. Vantaggi et al. (Eds.): IPMU 2026, CCIS 3019, pp. 534–547, 2026.
https://doi.org/10.1007/978-3-032-28994-0_38

the case in fields such as medical imaging [9,12] and natural language processing [17]. Thus, a number of works have investigated reducing the dependence to such expert knowledge: for instance, semi-supervised classification approaches [20] have been developed to make use of both labeled and unlabeled data.

In this paper, we focus on self-learning: this strategy automatically labels the unlabeled data at hand by using the model predictions as pseudo-labels. The drawback of classical self-learning algorithms such as FixMatch [18] is that they do not take into consideration the inherent uncertainty of pseudo-labels. As noted in [8], this can induce a strong confirmation bias during the training procedure [13]. A possible answer consists in quantifying the uncertainty of pseudo-labels and integrate it in the self-training iterations, so that the model is, so to say, "aware" of its own competence.

It is not only important to quantify the uncertainty but also identify its source. Aleatoric Uncertainty (AU) reflects the stochastic nature of the data-generating process, and therefore cannot be reduced. Epistemic Uncertainty (EU), on the other hand, arises from a lack of knowledge—due to scarce data or to an ill-known data-generating process. In theory, with the acquisition of additional information, EU should reduce, and possibly vanish should "infinite" data (or a very large amount thereof) be available [5]. In this case, a precise prediction could be made in the form of a single probability distribution, modeling AU solely. In the work mentioned above, the total uncertainty (TU) is defined as the sum of both: $TU = AU + EU$. An illustrative example is given in Fig. 1. The leftmost image pictures a cat that arguably looks like a dog; we expect similar images to belong to either of these two categories, hence the image is associated with a high AU. The righmost image, on the other hand, is blurry, which would ideally call for acquiring another one with a better quality. The image thus has a high EU.

A well-established way to quantify uncertainty is through Shannon Entropy H_S [2,11,21]. The core idea here is that H_S can be seen as an appropriate measure of TU. From information theory, H_S can be decomposed as the sum of the Mutual Information I and the conditional entropy H_C, which yields to measures for EU and AU, respectively. However, all those approaches aim to quantify it at a *global* level. In certain cases, such as medical imaging, the consequences of making incorrect predictions can differ between classes. This issue is addressed in [16] by introducing a label-wise quantification. We describe in this work a self-learning strategy which leverages label-wise uncertainty quantification (UQ).

This paper is organized as follows. Section 2 formally presents the semi-supervised setting and the classical self-learning approach. In Sect. 3, we discuss how to quantify uncertainty and its relation to the problem. Our approach is proposed in Sect. 4. Empirical results are reported in Sect. 5. Finally, a brief conclusion is presented in Sect. 6.

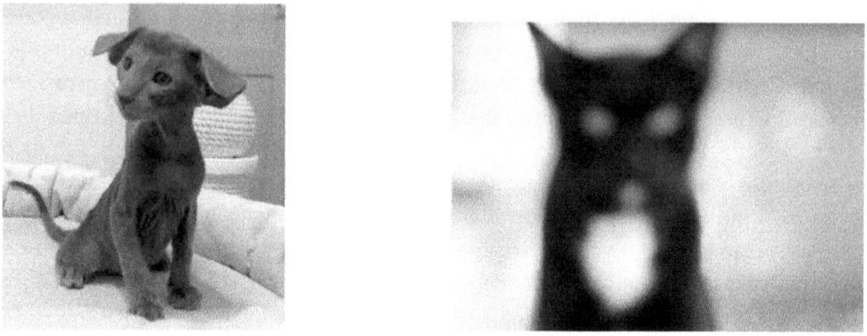

(a) Aleatoric Uncertainty (b) Epistemic Uncertainty

Fig. 1. Example to differentiate Aleatoric and Epistemic Uncertainty. The leftmost image contains high *AU* as it is hard to differentiate if it is a cat or a dog whereas the rightmost image contains high *EU* because the image is too blurry to differentiate the classes.

2 Reminders

2.1 Classical Self-learning

The semi-supervised classification problem can be described as follows: we consider an input (feature) space denoted by $\mathcal{X}$, and an output space consisting of a finite set of classes $\mathcal{Y} = \{y^1, y^2, ..., y^\lambda\}$, where λ represents the total number of classes. A labeled dataset $\mathcal{D}_L$ is constructed by sampling from the joint distribution $P(X, Y)$ defined on $\mathcal{X} \times \mathcal{Y}$, i.e. $\mathcal{D}_L = \{z_1 = (x_1, p_1), z_2 = (x_2, p_2), ..., z_n = (x_n, p_n)\}$ where p_j is a degenerate distribution on $\mathcal{Y}$ having value 1 for the true label, that is $p_j^i := P(Y = y^i|X = x_j) = 1$ if y^i is the true label of x_j. Since n is small, we would like to integrate in this problem unlabeled samples from a dataset $\mathcal{D}_U = \{x_{n+1}, ..., x_{n+m}\}$. Thus, we have at our disposal a dataset $\mathcal{D} = \mathcal{D}_L \cup \mathcal{D}_U$ composed from labeled and unlabeled samples.

The samples in $\mathcal{D}$ are assumed to be independent and identically distributed (i.i.d.). For any input $x \in \mathcal{X}$, we can estimate the class probabilities $\hat{p}_x^1, \ldots, \hat{p}_x^\lambda$. We will use p_j^i when referring to the probability for an observed instance x_j, and p_x for the probability of a given generic instance x.

Denoting by $P(\mathcal{Y})$ the space of probabilities over $\mathcal{Y}$, training a model on $\mathcal{D}_L$ is classically solved by finding the optimal parameter θ^* of a classifier $h_\theta : \mathcal{X} :\rightarrow P(\mathcal{Y})$ that minimizes the theoretical risk R_t:

$$R_t = \mathbb{E}_{P(X,Y)}[\mathcal{L}(h_\theta)] = \int_{\mathcal{X}\times\mathcal{Y}} \mathcal{L}(p_x, h_\theta(x))dP(x, y), \tag{1}$$

where $\mathcal{L} : P(\mathcal{Y}) \times P(\mathcal{Y}) \rightarrow \mathbb{R}$ is a loss function. However, in practice, we cannot calculate R_t because $P(X, Y)$ is unknown. Thus, we estimate it by using the empirical risk R_e:

$$\theta^* = \arg\min_\theta R_e(p, h_\theta) = \arg\min_\theta \sum_{(x,p)\in\mathcal{D}_T} \mathcal{L}(p_x, h_\theta(x)), \tag{2}$$

where $\mathcal{D}_T$ is the training set which initially contains all labeled samples and later on some self-labeled ones.

As mentioned in Sect. 1, we will integrate $\mathcal{D}_U$ in the training process through a self-learning scheme [18]: the procedure (see Algorithm 1) can be summarized as follows. First, the model is trained on labeled training data $\mathcal{D}_L$. Subsequently, we predict the pseudo-labels $\hat{p}$ for the instances $x \in \mathcal{D}_U$, and we select a subset $\mathcal{D}_S$ of these latter—generally those for which the highest predicted probability exceeds a predefined threshold δ, i.e. $\mathcal{D}_S = \{(x_j, \hat{p}_j)$ such that $\max_i \hat{p}_j^i \geq \delta, x_j \in \mathcal{D}_U\}$. The model is retrained on the set $\mathcal{D}_L \cup \mathcal{D}_S$, which yields to (hopefully) better predictions on $\mathcal{D}_U \setminus \mathcal{D}_S$. The process continues until all samples on $\mathcal{D}_U$ are assigned a pseudo-label where the model has a confidence of at least δ.

Pairwise Strategy. In this paper, we consider a pairwise strategy to train the model and obtain the prediction $\hat{p}$. We use the one-versus-all decomposition, in which λ binary classifiers $h^1, h^2, ..., h^\lambda$ are trained: each ones separates a class y^i from its complement $\neg y^i$ (see Fig. 2 for an illustration). Note that those binary problems are typically imbalanced, as the "negative" class $\neg y^i$ generally contains more examples than y^i, which complicates classifier optimization [6]. The probability estimates h^i given by the pairwise classifiers are normalized, i.e. we compute $\hat{p}_x^i = h^i(x)/\sum_\ell h^\ell(x)$, which gives us the vector of probability estimates $\hat{p}$.

Fig. 2. One-versus-all credal learning.

2.2 Self-learning with Uncertainty

Since pseudo-labels can eventually outnumber actual labels, erroneous pseudo-labels can induce a confirmation bias. Also, probabilistic labels, while partially regularizing this bias, are well-known to be ill-adapted when one has to represent both variability and lack of knowledge.

As mentioned in [8], a way to represent the pseudo-labeling uncertainty consists in using credal sets, i.e. non-empty convex sets K of probability distributions. For instance, [8] proposes to use for a class $y^{\hat{\imath}} = \arg\max_i \hat{p}$:

$$K_\pi^\gamma = \{p \in P(\mathcal{Y}) | p^{\hat{\imath}} \geq 1 - \gamma\}, \tag{3}$$

where γ is the degree of imprecision. While this approach may give good results, the credal set defined by Eq. (3) always contains a degenerate distribution, i.e., the one concentrating all probability on y^i, showing limited expressiveness. To overcome this issue, [15] and [1] proposed to consider a credal set:

$$K_v = \{p \in P(\mathcal{Y}) | \forall i = 1, \ldots, \lambda, \underline{p}^i \leq p^i \leq \overline{p}^i\}, \tag{4}$$

which is determined by a set of lower and upper bounds $\underline{p}^i$ and $\overline{p}^i$ over singletons obtained by applying Venn Predictors, a calibration method. Yet in [15], the calibration requires to split some samples from $\mathcal{D}_L$ to form a calibration set $\mathcal{D}_C$ that cannot be used for training: this approach might be inefficient in a context where the number of labeled data is already really scarce, which is to be expected in a self-learning setting.

Algorithm 1. Self-learning algorithm

Require: Labeled set $\mathcal{D}_L = \{(x_1, p_1), ..., (x_n, p_n)\}$, Unlabeled set $\mathcal{D}_U = \{x_{n+1}, ..., x_{n+m}\}$, Threshold δ;
1: Initialize model h;
2: Fit model h on $\mathcal{D}_L$;
3: **while** $\mathcal{D}_U$ is not empty **do**
4: For each $x_j \in \mathcal{D}_U$, $\hat{p}_j = h(x_j)$;
5: Build set $\mathcal{D}_S = \{(x_j, \hat{p}_j) \in \mathcal{D}_U | \exists i$ such that $\max_i \hat{p}_j^i \geq \delta\}$;
6: $\forall \hat{p} \in \mathcal{D}_S, \max_i \hat{p}^i \leftarrow 1$;
7: $\forall \hat{p} \in \mathcal{D}_S, \forall y^i \in \mathcal{Y}, \hat{p}^i \leftarrow 0$ if $i \neq \arg\max_i \hat{p}^i$;
8: $\mathcal{D}_L \leftarrow \mathcal{D}_S \cup \mathcal{D}_L$;
9: Fit model h on $\mathcal{D}_L$;
10: $\mathcal{D}_U \leftarrow \mathcal{D}_U \setminus \mathcal{D}_S$;
11: **end while**

2.3 Learning from Credal Sets

When considering credal sets as uncertainty representation, the loss function $\mathcal{L}$ is no longer well-defined, and it needs to be adapted in order to learn a model. The main strategy is arguably the optimistic one [7,8,19], i.e. given a credal set K_x, a current prediction $\hat{p}_x$ and a loss function $\mathcal{L}$, we define the optimistic loss as

$$\mathcal{L}_{min}(K_x, \hat{p}_x) = \mathcal{L}(\tilde{p}_x, \hat{p}_x) \text{ with } \tilde{p} = \arg\min_{\mathrm{p} \in K_x} \mathcal{L}(\mathrm{p}, \hat{p}). \tag{5}$$

Figure 3 illustrates two different scenarios that might occur with an optimistic approach: if the model prediction agrees with the credal set (i.e. $\hat{p}_x \in K_x$), then $\tilde{p}_x = \hat{p}_x$ as we want our loss to be minimized for this situation[1] (no correction

[1] Standard losses such as cross-entropy or Kullback-Leibler divergence satisfy this.

is done on the pseudo-label), but if $\hat{p} \notin K$, then $\tilde{p}_x \neq \hat{p}_x$ and $\mathcal{L}_{min} > 0$. Thus, in this case, the pseudo-label $\tilde{p}_x$ is a correction of the prediction $\hat{p}_x$ with respect to our credal set K_x. Using the Kullback-Leibler divergence for any instance x_j, Eq. (5) becomes

$$\tilde{p} = \arg\min_{\mathbb{p} \in K} \sum_{i=1}^{\lambda} \mathbb{p}^i \log \frac{\mathbb{p}^i}{\hat{p}^i} \tag{6a}$$

$$\text{s.t.} \quad \mathbb{p}^i \leq \overline{p}^i_j, \quad \mathbb{p}^i \geq \underline{p}^i_j, \quad \sum_{i=1}^{\lambda} \mathbb{p}^i = 1. \tag{6b}$$

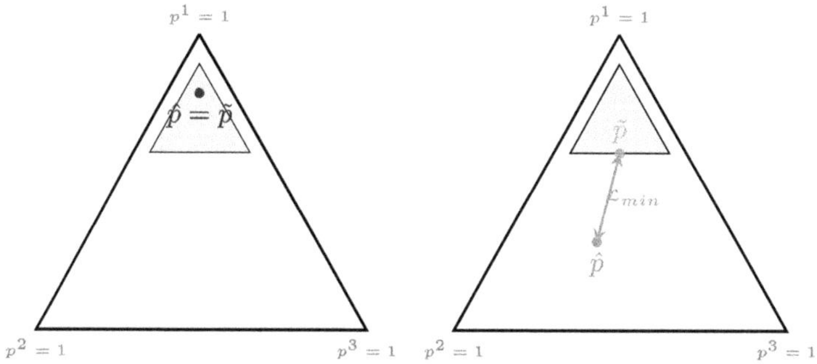

Fig. 3. Different situations for a optimistic approach.

3 Uncertainty Quantification

To avoid having to use calibration data, and also to have uncertainty quantification that is tailored to each label, we implement in this paper the label-wise approach for uncertainty quantification proposed by Sale *et al.* [16] in a self-learning context using a pairwise strategy. Let $\mathcal{P}^i_x$ be a random variable that designates the event $A = P^i_x$. We only have one observation of A as the model only predicts one probability distribution per instance x. However, under the assumption that close neighbors share similar behaviors, which is a common assumption for semi-supervised algorithms [20], we propose to use the probabilities of the $k-1$ nearest neighbors as other observations of the event A to compute AU and EU.

Formally, let $\mathcal{P}^i_{[1]}, ..., \mathcal{P}^i_{[k]}$ be a sequence of variables i.i.d. that follow the same distribution as $\mathcal{P}^i_x$ and designate the probability of event A for a point x and its $k-1$ closest neighbors in order of distance. Let Δ be a second-order distribution such that the marginal distribution Δ^i is distributed according to

$\mathcal{P}^i$, i.e. $\mathcal{P}^i \sim \Delta^i$. We desire to compute EU and AU having at our disposal only the observations $\hat{p}^i_{[1]}, ..., \hat{p}^i_{[k]}$. Sale *et al.* define the uncertainty as:

$$AU(\Delta) = \sum_{i=1}^{\lambda} \mathbb{E}(\mathcal{P}^i(1-\mathcal{P}^i)), \quad EU(\Delta) = \sum_{i=1}^{\lambda} \mathrm{Var}(\mathcal{P}^i). \tag{7}$$

Beta Distribution. In the label-wise case considered in this paper, we use a random variable $\mathcal{P}^i$ for each label: a convenient choice for the marginal second-order distribution Δ^i is the Beta distribution, i.e. $\mathcal{P}^i \sim \mathcal{B}(\alpha^i, \beta^i)$, the parameters α^i, β^i of which can be estimated for instance via moment estimation [4]:

$$\hat{\alpha}^i = \widehat{m}^i_1 \frac{\widehat{m}^i_1 - \widehat{m}^i_2}{\widehat{m}^i_2 - (\widehat{m}^i_1)^2}, \quad \hat{\beta}^i = \hat{\alpha}^i \frac{1-\widehat{m}^i_1}{\widehat{m}^i_1}, \tag{8}$$

where $\widehat{m}^i_1 = {}^1\!/_k \sum_{j=1}^{k} \hat{p}^i_{[j]}$ and $\widehat{m}^i_2 = {}^1\!/_k \sum_{j=1}^{k} (\hat{p}^i_{[j]})^2$ are respectively the first-order and second-order empirical (raw) moments, computed using the predictions made for the instance and its $k-1$ nearest neighbors.

Example 1. In a three-class problem $\mathcal{Y} = \{y^1, y^2, y^3\}$, consider the classifier trained to separate class y^i from $\neg y^i$. For instance x_j and its 4 nearest neighbors, it outputs the following probabilities: $[0.25, 0.56, 0.65, 0.78, 0.82]$. We desire to compute the estimators $\hat{\alpha}^i_j$ and $\hat{\beta}^i_j$. We calculate $\widehat{m}^i_1 \simeq 0.612$ and $\widehat{m}^i_2 \simeq 0.416$; the moment estimates for α^i_j and β^i_j are therefore

$$\hat{\alpha}^i_j \simeq 0.612 \left(\frac{0.612 - 0.416}{0.416 - 0.612^2}\right) \simeq 2.904, \quad \hat{\beta}^i_j \simeq 3.21 \left(\frac{1-0.612}{0.612}\right) \simeq 2.041.$$

4 Our Approach

As explained in Sect. 2, we aim at mitigating the impact of erroneous pseudo-labels by taking into account their uncertainty, leveraging the quantification model in [16] to do so. Our procedure can be summarized as follows. For all unlabeled instances in the training set, we compute the probabilistic outputs $\hat{p}$ using our λ classifiers. For each instance $x_j \in \mathcal{D}_U$, we compute the estimates $\hat{\alpha}^i_j$ and $\hat{\beta}^i_j$ so as to model the second-order uncertainty on $\hat{p}^i_j$ for all $y^i \in \mathcal{Y}$, and deduce epistemic and aleatoric uncertainty estimates as

$$\widehat{EU}^i_j = \widehat{m}^i_2 - (\widehat{m}^i_1)^2, \quad \widehat{AU}^i_j = \widehat{m}^i_1 - \widehat{m}^i_2. \tag{9}$$

Finally, we propose to obtain probability intervals for a sample x_j and class y^i as the interval summation:

$$[\underline{p}^i_j, \overline{p}^i_j] := (1 - \widehat{EU}^i_j) p^{*i}_j + \widehat{EU}^i_j [0, 1], \tag{10}$$

where

$$p^{*i}_j = (1 - \widehat{AU}^i_j)\hat{p}^i_j + \widehat{AU}^i_j \frac{1}{\lambda}.$$

The whole procedure is presented in Algorithm 2. In a nutshell, if the class of an instance is hard to predict due to a high *AU*, then the model output will be shifted towards the uniform distribution to avoid overconfidence. If, in addition, the model knowledge about the data is low (due to *EU* being high), then we discount the obtained probability, since the model prediction is not reliable. On the other hand, if *AU* is low, the model remains confident about its own prediction. Similarly, a low *EU* means there is no need for providing a large interval since the model prediction can safely be trusted.

Example 2. Following Example 1, we would like to estimate *AU* and *EU* given $\hat{\alpha}^i_j = 3.21$ and $\hat{\beta}^i_j = 2.07$ by applying Eq. (9). That yields to $\widehat{EU}^i_j = 0.04$ and $\widehat{AU}^i_j = 0.19$. A slight shift towards uniformity gives $p^{*i}_j = (1-0.19)0.25 + \frac{0.19}{3} = 0.27$. We then obtain the lower and upper bounds as respectively $\underline{p}^i_j = (1-0.04)0.26 = 0.25$ and $\overline{p}^i_j = (1-0.04)0.26 + 0.04 = 0.29$.

Algorithm 2. Credal labeling strategy

Require: Labeled set $\mathcal{D}_L = \{(x_1, p_1), ..., (x_n, p_n)\}$, Unlabeled set $\mathcal{D}_U = \{(x_{n+1}), ..., (x_{n+m})\}$, Percentage u of samples, number of neighbors k;

for i from 1 to λ **do**
  Initialize model h^i;
  Build set $\mathcal{D}^i_L = \{(x_1, p^i_1), ..., (x_n, p^i_n)\}$;
  Fit the model h^i on $\mathcal{D}^i_L$;
end for
while $\mathcal{D}_U$ is not empty **do**
  for $x_j \in \mathcal{D}_U$ **do**
    $\hat{p}_j = h(x_j)$;
    for i from 1 to λ **do**
      Find $\hat{p}^i_{[1]}, ..., \hat{p}^i_{[k]}$;
      Compute $\hat{\alpha}^i_j, \hat{\beta}^i_j$ via Equations (8);
      Calculate $\widehat{AU}^i_j, \widehat{EU}^i_j$ via Equations (9);
      Build $K^i_{UQ}(x_j)$ from Equation (10);
    end for
  end for
  Solve problem (6) to obtain $\tilde{p}_j$ for all $K^i_{UQ}(x_j)$;
  Build ordered set $\mathcal{D}'_U = \{(x_{(j)}, \tilde{p}_{(j)}) \in \mathcal{D}_U$ such that $\max_i \tilde{p}^i_{(o)} \geq \max_i \tilde{p}^i_{(\ell)}, o \leq \ell\}$;
  Select the first $u\%$ of $\mathcal{D}'_U$ to form the set $\mathcal{D}'_S$.
  $\mathcal{D}_L \leftarrow \mathcal{D}_L \cup \mathcal{D}'_S$;
  $\mathcal{D}_U \leftarrow \mathcal{D}_U \setminus \mathcal{D}'_S$;
  for i from 1 to λ **do**
    Build set $\mathcal{D}^i_L = \{(x_{(j)}, \tilde{p}^i_{(j)}) | x_j \in \mathcal{D}_L\}$;
    Fit model h^i on $\mathcal{D}^i_L$;
  end for
end while

5 Experiments

In order to test our approach, we trained a logistic regressor with a L_1 regularization with coefficient 0.001 through a variety of datasets (see details in Table 1) found either on the scikit-learn package (Digits and Breast Cancer), the UCIML repository (Student, Ecoli and Glass) or HuggingFace (Poem). The model was implemented from scratch using a Python 3.8 environment with the CVXPY (v 1.3), NumPy (v1.23) and scikit-learn (v1.3) libraries in a Intel $I7-6700$HQ 2.60GHz CPU so we can handle better soft labels. The sentences of the poem dataset were transformed into vectors using the HuggingFace's sentence-transformers (v2.2) library (with all-MiniLM-L6-v2 architecture). Training time was 35 minutes for Student dataset, 9 minutes for Digits dataset and less than 2 minutes for the rest. The number of the closest neighbors are 25. We split the data into 80% for training and 20% for test using 5 different seeds. 5% of the training samples are kept as labeled. Instead of manually selecting a threshold for each dataset, the $\mathcal{D}_U$ is sorted with respect to the highest probability and the first $u\%$ ($u = 5$) of the samples are taken. We compare three different strategies, all of them applied in a pairwise fashion:

- Hard labels: In this strategy we consider the labels as degenerated probability distributions. This is the FixMatch algorithm without data augmentation as it is not well defined for tabular data.
- Soft labels: In this case the pseudo-labels are probability distributions, not necessarily degenerated, i.e. the model predictions without any modification.
- Credal sets: Our approach explained in Sect. 4.

In order to make sure that the strategies are actually improving the overall accuracy of the model, we also computed two baselines: one using only labeled instances and another using all training instances. It is expected that the model starts with the same accuracy as the only-labeled baseline and increases the performance which makes it closer to the fully supervised baseline.

Table 1. Datasets descriptions

data set	# training instances	# test instances	Number of features	# classes
Breast Cancer	409	114	30	2
Digits	1437	360	64	10
Ecoli	261	66	5	5
Glass	153	43	9	5
Poem	360	90	11	7
Student	3539	885	36	3

The accuracy of the last iteration for each strategy is presented on Table 2. Those results suggest that our strategy is indeed capable of enhancing the model

Table 2. Accuracy of the last iteration using the three strategies. Note that our method has a better accuracy than the other methods.

	only labeled	fully supervised	hard labels	soft labels	credal sets
Breast Cancer	80.53 ± 5.1	95.79 ± 2.18	80.53 ± 4.49	80.53 ± 4.49	$\mathbf{81.05 \pm 3.75}$
Digits	82.56 ± 3.03	96.56 ± 0.48	84.61 ± 2.82	84.44 ± 2.62	$\mathbf{84.83 \pm 1.49}$
Ecoli	64.41 ± 7.58	77.35 ± 1.99	63.82 ± 7.65	63.53 ± 7.97	$\mathbf{64.71 \pm 8.11}$
Glass	35.81 ± 10.97	60.93 ± 5.96	36.74 ± 11.99	37.21 ± 9.3	$\mathbf{40.0 \pm 10.34}$
Poem	88.89 ± 3.51	98.22 ± 0.89	88.22 ± 5.38	88.67 ± 5.32	$\mathbf{89.33 \pm 5.99}$
Student	68.88 ± 1.32	76.18 ± 1.47	68.97 ± 2.07	69.42 ± 1.96	$\mathbf{71.25 \pm 1.85}$

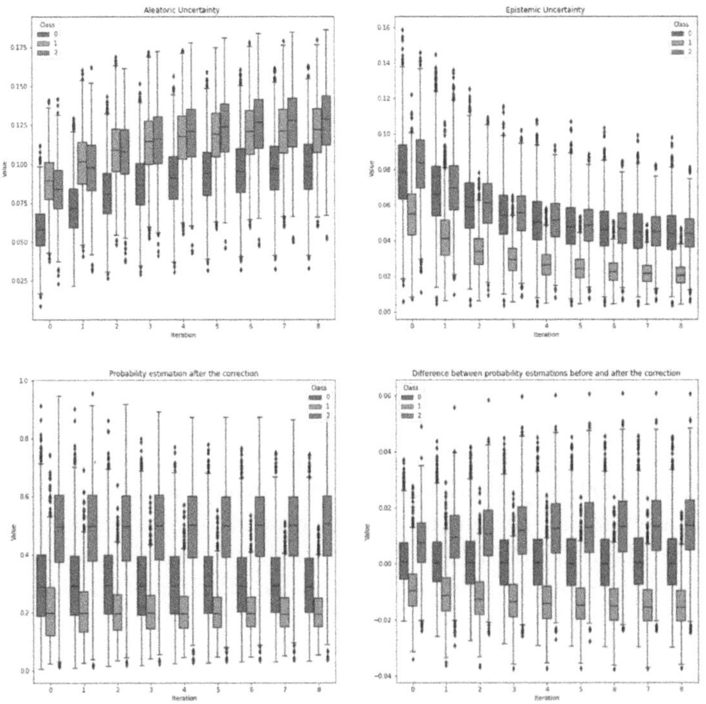

Fig. 4. *AU* and *EU* estimations as well as the difference before the credal set correction ($\hat{p}$) and after ($\tilde{p}$) for the Student dataset per class and iteration.

accuracy better than the others since we are able to get the best accuracy in all benchmarks studied. Additionally, we present the curves of each dataset on Fig. 6. The behavior for most datasets is as we expected: the accuracy gradually increases from each iteration. For some datasets, such as Ecoli and Poem, this is not true: the accuracy fluctuates. This indicates the noisy nature of a self-learning setting: the pseudo-labels are not always helpful and sometimes are even able to bias the model towards wrong predictions.

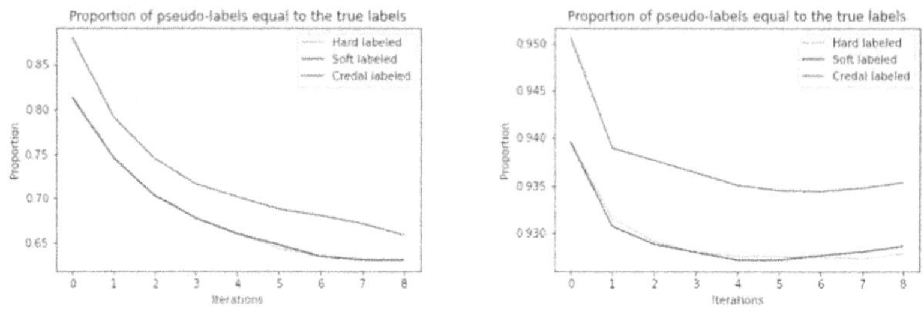

(a) Glass (b) Student

Fig. 5. Accuracy of the pseudo-labels. Note that our method is capable of creating more correct pseudo-labels, thus learning better on the next iterations. Another important point here is that the accuracy falls after each iteration due to the noisy nature of pseudo-labels.

A possible reason for the improved performance of our strategy is the number of reliable pseudo-labels added in each iteration, i.e. the proportion of pseudo-labels whose highest probability estimated ($\arg\max_i \hat{p}_x^i$) is in the same class as the true label ($\arg\max_i \hat{p}_x^i = \arg\max_i p_x^i$). This is observed on Fig. 5, where it is displayed, in the lth iteration, the average accuracy between the selected pseudo-labels (through iterations 1 to l) and the true labels. It is also noteworthy that this proportion tend to decrease, which is another indicator of why pseudo-labels are not always reliable.

Another interesting to point is to check is the effect of AU and EU estimations in each iteration for each class. Figure 4 illustrates the values of AU, EU and $\tilde{p}$ for the Student dataset for each class and iteration as well as the difference between the predictions before the credal set correction ($\hat{p}$) and after ($\tilde{p}$). The values of $\tilde{p}$ are most of the time far from 1, which indicates non-degenerateness. Furthermore, the range of $AU$and EU are similar for all classes: the maximum is at 0.18 and the quartiles are most of the time in the interval $[0.02, 0.1]$. That means the credal set has a size between $[0.04, 0.2]$ and since AU is not high, p^* is closer to the model estimation $\hat{p}$. Thus, the fact that AU and EU are not very high explains why the difference between $\hat{p}$ and the probability after the correction, $\tilde{p}$, oscillates between 0.06 and -0.04. However, although the difference seems negligible, it is sufficient to alter the model's behavior: in the case where those corrections do not occur (soft label strategy), the predictions after the first iteration are different. This is noticeable on the accuracy increase of the credal strategy with respect to the soft strategy.

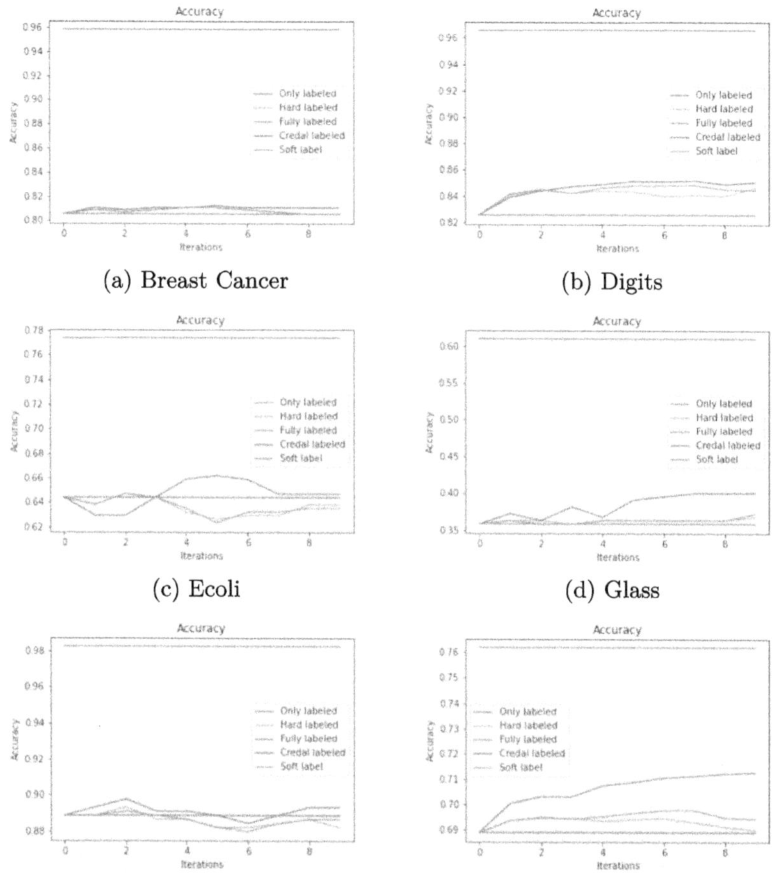

(a) Breast Cancer (b) Digits

(c) Ecoli (d) Glass

(e) Poem (f) Student

Fig. 6. Results for logistic regression using the three strategies. Note that our method has a better accuracy than the other methods. The overall behavior is expected (accuracy going up in each iteration) but the unreliability of pseudo-labels may make the behavior noisy, such as in the Ecoli and Poem datasets.

6 Conclusion

In this paper, we address the problem of self-training from data where the uncertainty in the labeling process may lead to biases in the model. We propose an approach where the pseudo-labels are credal, i.e. they correspond to sets of probability distributions. Using such credal sets makes it possible to model both aleatoric uncertainty, resulting from the classes being mixed; and epistemic uncertainty, resulting from a lack of knowledge. We implement our procedure in a one-versus-all decomposition scheme, where λ binary classifiers are trained (each separates a class from all others).

Our results demonstrate empirically how the classical approach (hard labels) for a self-learning problem can potentially bias the model, which reduces the overall model performance. This bias may be the result of overconfident predictions and the lack of uncertainty quantification in a setting where this latter is clearly present.

We stress that this paper is limited to a label-wise strategy. As a perspective for the future, it is possible to make a similar approach using a direct multi-class algorithm. In this case, the Beta distribution must be changed into a Dirichlet distribution, and the uncertainty quantification approach should be changed accordingly, e.g. using Shannon Entropy-based measures [3] [11].

Another perspective is to change the number of labeled data. Self-learning strategies are heavily biased depending on the labeled data available. Thus, by including more labeled data, the pseudo-labels should be more reliable, but the accuracy increase should be lower as there is less information to learn from unlabeled data. On the other hand, having few labeled data makes the uncertainty higher, thus we expect our approach to stand out in this case. All those hypotheses, however, must be confirmed through experiments.

On the more theoretical side, it would be interesting to connect our approach, and more generally credal self-supervised appraoches, to the framework of reciprocal learning proposed by Rodemann *et al.* [14], for instance by checking that our framework satisfy the sufficient conditions of [14] to guarantee convergence.

References

1. Bordini, V.M., Destercke, S., Quost, B.: Self-learning from pairwise credal labels. In: 27th European Conference on Artificial Intelligence, Including 13th Conference on Prestigious Applications of Intelligent Systems (ECAI-PAIS 2024) (2024)
2. Depeweg, S.: Modeling epistemic and aleatoric uncertainty with Bayesian neural networks and latent variables. Ph.D. thesis, Technische Universität München (2019)
3. Depeweg, S., Hernandez-Lobato, J.M., Doshi-Velez, F., Udluft, S.: Decomposition of uncertainty in Bayesian deep learning for efficient and risk-sensitive learning. In: International Conference on Machine Learning, pp. 1184–1193. PMLR (2018)
4. Gnanadesikan, R., Pinkham, R., Hughes, L.P.: Maximum likelihood estimation of the parameters of the beta distribution from smallest order statistics. Technometrics **9**(4), 607–620 (1967)
5. Hüllermeier, E., Waegeman, W.: Aleatoric and epistemic uncertainty in machine learning: an introduction to concepts and methods. Mach. Learn. **110**(3), 457–506 (2021)
6. Kaur, H., Pannu, H.S., Malhi, A.K.: A systematic review on imbalanced data challenges in machine learning: applications and solutions. ACM Comput. Surv. (CSUR) **52**(4), 1–36 (2019)
7. Lienen, J., Demir, C., Hullermeier, E.: Conformal credal self-supervised learning. In: Conformal and Probabilistic Prediction with Applications, pp. 214–233. PMLR (2023)
8. Lienen, J., Hüllermeier, E.: Credal self-supervised learning. Adv. Neural. Inf. Process. Syst. **34**, 14370–14382 (2021)

9. Liu, X., et al.: A comparison of deep learning performance against health-care professionals in detecting diseases from medical imaging: a systematic review and meta-analysis. Lancet Digit. Health **1**(6), e271–e297 (2019)
10. Miceli, M., Posada, J., Yang, T.: Studying up machine learning data: Why talk about bias when we mean power? Proc. ACM Hum.-Comput. Inter. **6**(GROUP), 1–14 (2022)
11. Mobiny, A., Yuan, P., Moulik, S.K., Garg, N., Wu, C.C., Van Nguyen, H.: Dropconnect is effective in modeling uncertainty of Bayesian deep networks. Sci. Rep. **11**(1), 5458 (2021)
12. Nguyen, P., Chapman, D., Menon, S., Morris, M., Yesha, Y.: Active semi-supervised expectation maximization learning for lung cancer detection from computerized tomography (CT) images with minimally label training data. In: Medical Imaging 2020: Computer-Aided Diagnosis, vol. 11314, pp. 553–564. SPIE (2020)
13. Papernot, N., McDaniel, P.: Deep k-nearest neighbors: towards confident, interpretable and robust deep learning. arXiv preprint arXiv:1803.04765 (2018)
14. Rodemann, J., Jansen, C., Schollmeyer, G.: Reciprocal learning. Adv. Neural. Inf. Process. Syst. **37**, 1686–1724 (2024)
15. Rodriguez, C., Bordini, V.M., Destercke, S., Quost, B.: Self learning using venn-abers predictors. In: Conformal and Probabilistic Prediction with Applications, pp. 234–250. PMLR (2023)
16. Sale, Y., Hofman, P., Löhr, T., Wimmer, L., Nagler, T., Hüllermeier, E.: Label-wise aleatoric and epistemic uncertainty quantification. arXiv preprint arXiv:2406.02354 (2024)
17. Sarhan, I., Spruit, M.: Can we survive without labelled data in NLP? Transfer learning for open information extraction. Appl. Sci. **10**(17), 5758 (2020)
18. Sohn, K., et al.: Fixmatch: simplifying semi-supervised learning with consistency and confidence (2020). https://doi.org/10.48550/ARXIV.2001.07685, https://arxiv.org/abs/2001.07685
19. Soullard, Y., Destercke, S., Thouvenin, I.: Co-training with Credal models. In: Schwenker, F., Abbas, H.M., El Gayar, N., Trentin, E. (eds.) ANNPR 2016. LNCS (LNAI), vol. 9896, pp. 92–104. Springer, Cham (2016). https://doi.org/10.1007/978-3-319-46182-3_8
20. Van Engelen, J.E., Hoos, H.H.: A survey on semi-supervised learning. Mach. Learn. **109**(2), 373–440 (2020)
21. Wimmer, L., Sale, Y., Hofman, P., Bischl, B., Hüllermeier, E.: Quantifying aleatoric and epistemic uncertainty in machine learning: Are conditional entropy and mutual information appropriate measures? In: Uncertainty in Artificial Intelligence, pp. 2282–2292. PMLR (2023)

Author Index

B. Vantaggi et al. (Eds.): IPMU 2026, CCIS 3019, pp. 549–550, 2026.
https://doi.org/10.1007/978-3-032-28994-0

www.ingramcontent.com/pod-product-compliance
Ingram Content Group UK Ltd.
Pitfield, Milton Keynes, MK11 3LW, UK
UKHW022111180926
475695UK00002B/101
* 9 7 8 3 0 3 2 2 8 9 9 3 3 *